CAVEAT CIVIS

CAN YOU TRUST THE POLICE?

CAVEAT CIVIS

CAN YOU TRUST THE POLICE?

Herbert G Kinnell

PUBLISHER

Scotia Publishing
325 Kenilworth Road
Basingstoke
RG23 8JW

Published by: Scotia Publishing

First published in 2014

ISBN: 978-0-9572548-2-4

Printed by:
Kingsclere Design and Print Ltd
7 Orchard Business Park,
Kingsclere,
Newbury, RG20 4SY.

To Phil and Sanne

Acknowledgement

The author is indebted to Anne Phillips for her indefatigable secretarial assistance in getting this work into print.

<u>CONTENTS</u>

FOREWORD

Quis custodiet ipsos custodies (who polices the police)?

Are British cops trustworthy? Not if they're anything like J. Edgar Hoover, for many years America's top policeman. A closet homosexual, transvestite and paedophile, he persecuted gays, blacks and communists, yet was in league with organised crime and blackmailed presidents (he served eight). He hacked phones to obtain scandal on enemies and allies alike, feeding the dirt to the notorious Hedda Hopper. He vindictively pursued personal vendettas using his FBI agents. He may have tape recorded Eleanor Roosevelt's alleged lesbian affair, his covert files including 883 senators, 722 congressmen, 12 Supreme Court judges and hundreds of the famous, such as Marilyn Monroe and Martin Luther King. His secret counter intelligence programme (Cointelpro) smeared civil rights groups, falsely imprisoning and eliminating opponents. The ultimate evil hypocrite, Hoover was, more than anyone else, responsible for the Mafia's stranglehold on America, actively undermining the Kefauver Committee's probe in 1950-51. An addicted gambler, he would bet on fixed races with tips from his underworld associates[1]. Hoover assembled the largest collection of porn in history, partly to satisfy his own voyeuristic tendencies, partly to use as blackmail – it included blue movies by Sinatra and Joan Crawford, and nude photos of male stars such as Elvis, Tony Curtis, Burt Lancaster and Charlton Heston[2].

This book tries to describe the dark side of Great Britain's police service, and suggests that the citizen should always be wary of taking police officers on trust. It explains why the public are losing trust in the police. Rudeness, corruption, drunkenness, brutality, deceitfulness, political pawnship, etc. are well-known to be chronic if not endemic problems since the early days of thieftakers, watchmen and bobbies. The great new ogres, managerialism and the Robocop culture, are proving the death knell of Dixon of Dock Green. We hear a lot about oppressive foreign police forces, but is there an adverse 'police mentality' which informs police everywhere? Are the police in fact too often the enemies rather than the defenders of the public?

Potted observations on the police

Ancient Rome had no police force. Nor did the British Empire (except in Australia, where the police were corrupt and brutal). The soldiery doubled up as policemen in the two largest empires in history. So much for the opinion that the police are a necessary evil: they are certainly not indispensable.

Under Elizabeth I it was incumbent on citizens to help the police. It was the most 'popular' (i.e. of the people) police force in the world, the principle still holding sway in America, of police accountable to the community, with local election of law-enforcers[3]. The 1964 Police Act saw the 123 forces in England and Wales reduced to 47: the proposal for only 12 regional forces would centralise and delocalise power to control law enforcement.

The Government has a duty to protect the people from abuses of police power.

'The greatest threat to the reputation of the police service is criminals in uniform like Dizaei.' Nick Hardwick, IPCC Chairman, 2010.

'The British police used to be the most respected in the world. Today they are increasingly despised by the public both for their inability to fight crime and their fixation with fashionable, politically correct dogma ... faith in the criminal justice system has never been lower.'[4]

'Are juries expected to convict defendants on the word of officers who may themselves be criminals?'[5]

'The general public has little respect for the police.'[6] Anyone who trusts the police should watch Martin Scorsese's movie 'The Departed'. 'Trust in the police is now lower than in doctors, teachers, judges or the NHS'[7].

'Only police rival judges in the freedom from public accountability which they enjoy.'[8]

'We spend more on the police than any other country in Europe but still have a very high crime rate.'[9]

An independent watchdog (the Police Complaints Commission for Scotland) ruled (2010) that more than a third of the public's grievances are not handled reasonably[10].

'The police are at least as self-serving, self-protective and ineffective as any other part of the state apparatus'[11].

The public want the police to prevent crime, the police want to increase their arrest quotas.

Three-quarters of the British public believed (2007) that the country was more dangerous than five years before, despite Government claims that the chance of being a crime victim was at its lowest for a quarter of a century. Nearly half have felt threatened in the street, with not enough bobbies on the beat[12].

When Johannesburg's 'The Sunday Independent' ran a probe into nepotism and corruption in the South African Police's Crime Intelligence Unit (the former Special Branch), it claimed there was a 'Zulu Nostra'. The editor said, after receiving an injunction banning the story's publication: 'The police wanted us to promise that we would submit to them in advance for their approval any article which we might want to write about them'. Are foreign police services more corrupt or obscurantist than Britain's? Theresa May said (in her 2011 speech to the Police Federation) that UK officers are the best in the world. There was total silence from her audience of officers[13].

'If all the police in Britain were abducted by aliens, would anyone notice?'[14]

'... the entire political class, police and all, are rotten to the core'[15].

A great irony of modern policing is that while top officers are now better educated, indeed degreed (in sociology, psychology, criminology, etc), they seem to be much more distant from the communities they are supposed to serve.

'Senior policemen have become one of the strongest pro-crime lobbies in Britain'[16].

The cast of author Tom Sharpe's comic bestsellers, such as Porterhouse Blue and Blott On The Landscape, included a sadistic policeman. Sharpe said: 'It is a vital civil act in any society to make fun of the police. When you can't, you've already landed in a dictatorial state'.

Victims and witnesses of crime are less trustful of the justice system after dealings with police .

The police is the last great unreformed public service. (David Cameron)[17].

The police are part of the problem –not the solution[18]. They try to get rid of crimes, not detect or solve them[19].

The Plain English Society has coined a phrase for police jargon – ploddledygook – because they have had so many complaints about it. Thus ACPO's Sir Hugh Orde said of the 2011 Tottenham riots: 'What we saw was almost non-existent pre-intelligence, this was spontaneous rather than organised', while Acting Commissioner Tim Godwin is quoted as saying: 'The reality is that when you are confronted with a series of situations that are operational you have to make a decision and that guidance is purely that, guidance. We were borough-based policing responding to criminality that had public order assets to respond and support if it degenerated where there was confrontation with the officers'.

Police, by taking an oath to the Crown, are state appointees whose first allegiance is therefore not to the public.

Respected Met Commissioner Sir Robert Mark called his CID 'the most routinely corrupt organisation in London'[20].

'The police have made themselves an island' – Keith Peat, former City of London policeman.

'The police are still ... an agreeable reflection of our criminal classes – basically the lower orders decked out in a nice uniform'[21].

'Whenever you give anyone a uniform and any kind of power they will always, always, always abuse it'[22].

'... the police ... still regard us almost as serfs with limited rights'[23].

George Orwell doubted the decency of the police[24].

'Most of us were brought up to respect the police and to believe they are motivated by everything that is good and decent. But that belief system is finished now'[25].

It is hard to overstate the importance of serving police officers fabricating evidence against a cabinet minister[26].

'Sentimental praise for our supposedly wonderful police is misplaced. They've gone badly wrong, and won't be reformed until we all admit it'[27].

'One by one ... the institutions we used to think worthy of our trust and respect are being comprehensively discredited. Politicians (expenses), bankers (greed), civil service (incompetence), police (just about everything) ....'[28].

'... this country's police are just another nationalised industry, infused with political correctness and run mainly for the benefit of the employees'[29].

'The pursuit of motorists by the police has now replaced property prices as a hot dinner party conversation'[30].

'The supreme blunder of modern policing was its determination to punish the otherwise law-abiding'[31].

'The Police Are Never Wrong and Must be Believed'. (Stephen Hayes on Hillsborough).

Backbench Tory MP Mark Pritchard said during a Westminster debate, 'lazy and incompetent police officers should be forced to undergo fitness tests'. His blistering attack on the rank-and-file included the accusation that some officers are ill-disciplined and willing to 'lie'. 'The police, like the BBC, are one of the last great unreformed national institutions'. Reference: Slack, J. http://www.dailymail.co.uk/news-article-1320983.

CHAPTER I

THE ARROGANT POLICEMAN

CHAPTER CONTENTS

CHAPTER I

THE ARROGANT POLICEMAN

'The arrogance of power' is not an empty phrase – all institutions which are powerful tend to employ practitioners who treat the laity with contempt. Thus doctors, judges and politicians are notoriously arrogant, and the police are no exception (e.g. all tend to cover up uncomfortable facts).

'Are you the owner of this vehicle, sir?'

Arrogant Top Cops

'Style over substance dictated his approach to Britain's top police job, and in the end Labourite <u>Sir Ian Blair's</u> vanity proved to be his downfall'[32]. His abuse of public funds for self-aggrandisement (£300,000 for refurbishing his offices) and his ignorance for 24 hours that his officers had killed the innocent de Menezes, were among a catalogue of failings, which included 'Vote Labour' slogans on police cars and lobbying for the Government's terror and ID card plans. He was accused by an employment tribunal chairman of having 'hung his officers out to dry' to prove his anti-racist credentials. In 2006 he had to apologise not only for making a crass comment about the Soham murders, but also for secretly recording phone conversations with the Attorney General and others. Blair had a 'golden circle' of white officers, claimed Commander Shabir Hussain, so that ironically Blair himself had the embarrassment of being accused of being a racist. The row over £3 million of Met contracts for his old friend, Andy Miller, was the final straw which clinched the demise of his career. Andy Hayman, his assistant commissioner at the Met, says, '... he did become aloof, there was a degree of arrogance ... he didn't listen very well, he didn't take advice'[33]. Blair's self-righteousness led him to claim bizarrely that the police killers of Jean Charles de Menezes should each have been awarded the George Medal[34]. He used public funds (£10,000) for an image makeover – a portrait. This was dubbed the 'vanity contract'[35]. He told a journalist that he had been shot at in the 1975 Balcombe Street siege, but this was disputed by other officers. He tried to distance himself from the suggestion he was some sort of hero[36].

Met chief Sir Paul Stephenson promised not to be a celebrity cop (like Sir Ian Blair?): yet he took it upon himself to sanction MP Damian Green's arrest in the Commons[37]. Blair's predecessor Sir John (now Lord) Stevens stopped the Paris rush-hour traffic so he could be followed by cameras through the Alma tunnel for his Diana inquiry. Stevens appeared on Question Time and wrote a newspaper column[38].

The Police Complaints Commissioner for Scotland has accused the Northern Constabulary of 'institutional arrogance' over its handling of the 1997 case of Kevin McLeod, to whose family Chief Constable Ian Latimer was told to apologise. The Commissioner's report criticised the fact that the family had to use the FOIA to be allowed to see the report on the way the family's complaints had been handled[39]. The PCCS was to probe why the Constabulary allegedly ignored a Crown instruction to treat the unexplained death as murder (police asserted it was accidental)[40].

Controversial North Yorkshire Chief Constable Della Cannings tried to have a building at police HQ named after herself, spent £28,400 on a shower-room at her office, as well as £500,000 on Land Rovers and Volvo V-70s for senior officers. She disrupted a police authority meeting with her distinctive mobile cockerel ring tone. She told her officers to avoid jury service at all costs[41].

The Chief Constable of South Wales told Police Review: 'There are additional pressures now that I am chief constable. I used to be able to walk around my supermarket, but now someone else will do my shopping'. His pomposity is perhaps only overshadowed by the infamous 'Mad Mullah of the Traffic Taliban', who seemed to regard himself as a sort of police superstar[42].

Strathclyde's Chief Constable Steve House praised his officers for their success in combating gangland violence, only hours after yet another shooting on his turf[43].

Swaggering jailed Scotland Yard Commander Ali Dizaei tried to hang on to his Armani designer gear in prison. He barked at jail staff: 'Don't you know who I am?'.

Families of the 7/7 bomb victims have attacked the 'arrogance' of MI5 officers, after a coroner pinpointed serious bungling in their investigation[44].

Rapist police inspector Adam Carruthers, renowned for his arrogance, refused to participate in sex offender programmes in jail or to admit his guilt or show any remorse[45].

Senior police personnel barred the rank-and-file from having a cup of tea with paramedics at an ambulance base because the water boilers might be risky, as well as banning the playing of radios on police premises because the new fee was unaffordable. This despite elite officers travelling around in top-of-the-range BMWs bought by the taxpayer[46].

An anonymous senior officer in the South East of England has remarked on the 'aloof attitude' of some senior personnel[47].

Arrogance Presenting as Classism, Sexism and Racism

Classism

Victorian classism was obvious when high-ranking soldiers had to take junior police jobs that had been kept open for them[48].

One of the first applicants to join the new Women's Police Service in the early 20th Century noted that, re the other recruits, 'Most are ladies or middleclass women, all are a better class than the average policeman'[49]. Most policemen regarded their female colleagues as inferior, even though many women police were actually superior in social class.

Surrey WPC Alison Wheeler, a former opera singer, was 'arrogant and disruptive during training', and had trouble accepting criticism, an industrial tribunal heard. She did not respect superiors, 'rolling her eyes' while being reprimanded[50].

Cambridgeshire Chief Constable Julie Spence says: 'We are not here just to catch crooks' – only a third of the police's job is 'dealing with crime', with two-thirds covering emergencies and social services[51]. Spence has also declared that speeding is the ASB* of Middle England, in fact the 'worst kind' of ASB is being committed by the middle class. But singling out middle class speeders is surely taking a political stance[52].

Chief Constable Julie Spence

A cameraman and TV producer were said to have been prevented by Met police (from the Diplomatic Protection Squad) from filming at Lord Levy's London home. This prompted a furious complaint to the Met, as Levy was not a member of the Government. But he was a tennis partner of PM Tony Blair[53]. Do social connections influence policing?

---

* Antisocial Behaviour

CAVEAT CIVIS

The Met has banned white middle-class students from applying for their prestigious internship schemes[54].

Sexism

A century ago only a few chief constables would accept that women were of any value in the force[55]. The first uniformed policewomen were unpaid volunteers.

In the 1970s and 1980s the sexist police approach to rape was successfully challenged by the women's movement's rape crisis centres. A 1982 Roger Graef TV documentary showed Thames Valley Police harassing a rape victim[56]. In the 1980s officers were taught that 60% of all rape claims were false[57].

Lothian and Borders anti-terror police chief Superintendent Keith Chamberlain was probed in 2008 over sexism claims by Chief Inspector Allison Strachan – both were based at Corstorphine in Edinburgh. In 2002 she triggered a scandal by leaving her PC partner for her boss, Chief Superintendent Douglas Watson, who in turn left his wife (he was leading a £1 million review of the force). They set up home in the Borders and adopted twins. Chamberlain left his wife and children for a probationer[58]. Musical chairs is not unknown in the police service.

A report by HMIC and the Crown Prosecution Service said there is still a culture among police where the victim assessment is too 'subjective' and 'vulnerable to stereotyping'. A third of rape inquiries in London are 'written off', and the number of offences initially recorded as rape but not proceeded with is rising[59].

Former Strathclyde officer Anne Ramsay has lifted the lid on the police's 'gang culture' in her book 'Girl in Blue', saying she was treated like a piece of meat[60].

For many years WPCs were paid 10% less than males, had to remain single and primarily given women and children to deal with. Until after WWII a male officer's fiancée had to be vetted before the marriage could be authorised. Wives were not allowed to take paid work till WWII. Even in 1946 a chief constable had to be told not to prevent four policemen's wives working as teachers[61].

A Strathclyde sergeant allegedly told a trainee WPC at the Scottish Police College to 'lose the make-up', while she claimed an inspector asked her if she had 'brought her crayons to work', and that she was referred to as 'Little Miss PC'. She tabled sex and age discrimination against the Scottish Police Services Authority , as well as Strathclyde Police[62]. In 2011 27% of Scottish police were women[63].

Sexism was unashamedly institutional in the early Met, much more deeply embedded than racism, e.g. women had to leave on marriage, they were excluded from specialist units such as the CID and doghandling (one had to be able to throw one's dog over a hedge), not to mention enjoying lower rates of pay[64]. It is claimed women still fail to access specialist police squads (e.g. firearms and mounted) because the fitness tests (especially the upper body strength test) are biased towards men. Many women can pass the 'bleep test' (a timed run between two points) but don't have the upper body strength of men[65].

DCI <u>Colin Hallinan</u> of North Yorkshire CID insisted he didn't want women in the CID, because they were a liability. Women in the force were being held back from supervisory jobs and they were taking much more sick leave than men (some even contemplated suicide). Studies in the US and Australia as well as the UK (e.g. a 1995 study partly funded by the Home Office) show that policewomen's health can be seriously affected by frustrated career progression (e.g. by PTSD). Harrogate's Chief Constable <u>David Burke</u> failed to tell North Yorkshire Police Authority about two disturbing inquiries into the management of Harrogate CID – there was excessive drinking, bullying and sexism. Hallinan was suspended for 18 months for witness intimidation, and was fined for five offences of abusive and oppressive conduct[66].

Chief Constable
David Burke

The British Association for Women in Policing (BAWP) was founded in 1987, is partly funded by the Home Office and is affiliated to the International Association of Women Police and the European Network of Policewomen[67]. Is this sexist?

Over 40% of women police officers in England and Wales were seriously disillusioned with the service and thinking of resigning, this LSE finding being consistent across all ranks. Over three-quarters were pessimistic about the way the force as a whole was going. One officer with 22 years service said that morale was the lowest she had every known[68].

17 officers out of 21 Lothian and Borders staff (both sexes) under investigation for a 'sexual and racist' email scandal were suspended or transferred as part of disciplinary proceedings[69].

Dundonian Jean Thomson may have been Scotland's first WPC, in 1918: she was called a 'police sister', but the sexist Chief Constable was not at all pleased about the appointment, and wouldn't grant her the power of arrest[70].

<u>Racism</u>

The National Black Police Association claims the Met is institutionally racist. Its president, Commander <u>Ali Dizaei</u>, was stripped of his warrant card in 2008 just six months after his promotion. The Association also backed Assistant Commissioner <u>Tarique Ghaffur</u>, who had been placed on enforced 'gardening leave' after the launch of his racism claim against Met Chief Blair[71].

A white Met policeman vowed to 'bring down all the lazy blacks …', an employment tribunal was told . White and ethnic staff were always in separate groups at Belgravia[72].

The UK's first black officer, Norwell Roberts, had his car scratched, his notebooks ripped up, and told to his face he wasn't welcome[73].

See 'The Racist Policeman' (Chapter XXIII) for a fuller analysis.

Other Examples of Arrogance

Bernard Hogan-Howe, former head of Merseyside Police and now Met Commissioner, has attacked officers who ignore some victims by 'screening out' some offences: 40% of crime victims have their cases dealt with over the phone. 'It's wrong for the police ... to be arrogant and say we don't attend a certain kind of incident.' He is one of eight chief constables who have promised to send officers to every victim[74]. Time will tell.

Karen Matthews, who arranged for her own daughter to be kidnapped and terrorised, was described by a police officer, in a histrionic flourish in front of cameras, as 'pure evil'[75].

Two Brighton cops parked in a Tesco Express disabled bay while buying their Tesco lunch[76].

Before the issue of the Queen's Golden Jubilee Medal there was huge pressure from the police to be included in the award, though even severely (and recently) wounded ex-servicemen are still disallowed – an instance of the police trumping even the armed forces[77].

Lothian and Borders Police have been accused of treating adult partygoers like children over guidance issued on excessive drinking and personal safety, but they deny being killjoys[78].

The Met's 'Cannabis Warning' dates from 2001 and involves no punishment or record, and was never even approved by Parliament[79].

North Yorkshire traffic cop David Burlingham, who beat a speeding fine by using a legal loophole, played a part in a drive to encourage bikers to slow down. Because the speed warning signs in his case had a black border they were illegal, he argued successfully. He avoided another speeding fine because more than six months had elapsed since the alleged offence, yet his force insisted he was still entitled to talk about road safety[80].

An official police statement insisted that motorists must not be distracted by anything ... even 'gorgeous people'[81].

A policeman tried to arrest Winston Churchill on his return to Downing Street for having excessively bright sidelights[82].

Commander Brian Paddick has been said to suffer from an excess of assurance – he always assumes he is right, maintaining a lofty silence if he is contradicted[83].

After seven years as Princess Diana's bodyguard Met Inspector Ken Wharfe sold his story in a tell-all book 'Diana: Closely Guarded Secret (her marriage disaster and subsequent search for love)'. Despite upsetting the princes with his exposé, he had the effrontery to accuse Paul Burrell of betrayal[84].

Police double standards in the ever-intensifying campaign to ensnare motorists (e.g. patrol cars have been pictured parked half on the pavement) has been condemned as 'appalling and hypocritical' by no less than the assistant chief constable of Avon and Somerset Steve Mortimore[85].

According to one ex-cop whistleblower traffic police (hated by other cops because they would prosecute their own) are arrogant and rude[86].

CHAPTER II

THE BIG-BROTHER POLICEMAN

CONTENTS

CHAPTER II

THE BIG-BROTHER POLICEMAN

In pursuance of its objectives, which may be at odds with those of its citizenry, the State authorises its police to spy on the public, with scant regard for civil rights. The police want to know what the public are up to, but when the citizenry quiz the police they get short shrift. The Office of the Surveillance Commissioner advises that 'Big Brother' tactics must be necessary and proportionate.

Blue anti-establishment comedian Frank Randle was harassed by Lancashire (Blackpool) Police saying his shows (featuring Roy Castle) were obscene – his heyday was in the fifties[87]. Police Scotland had to apologise for an insulting message being directed from its official Twitter account at Tory commentator Toby Young, who was debating rape threats with a Labour MP on BBC's Newsnight[88].

Since the Serious Organised Crime and Police Act people have been increasingly required to prove their innocence, the claim of wrongful arrest having disappeared from the law. This has seriously changed the relationship between public and police[89].

Les Gray, chairman of the Scottish Police Federation, wants all Old Firm football matches (Rangers and Celtic) banned. Paul Coleshill, a member of Glasgow Police Board, agrees[90].

The transformation of the British Transport Police (BTP) into a de facto reserve riot squad has taken place in a surreptitious, even sinister, manner, and till the 1980s the BTP – poorly led and supervised and ill-equippped – was a bit of a joke, but now their 'serials' (public order units) are trained to participate in major operations with no relevance to transport. Such a deployment of a non-Home Office force, partly funded from the private sector is unprecedented. The BTP featured prominently during the G20 riots, attracting a number of misconduct complaints. There is a revolving door between the Met and the BTP, though unfortunately when it mattered their radios were found to be incompatible.

POWERS

When 50 people, many of them pensioners, some in wheelchairs, met in a Tesco car park with a view to holding a march to expose the situation at Stafford Hospital – because they couldn't get anywhere with their local MP – the police told them they needed permission[91].

Police have called for the creation of a new crime of 'course of conduct' offence, which would enable them to prosecute low-level spouse-abusers. Chief Constable Brian Moore also suggests serial abusers be forced to register with police. He wants vulnerable women to be given a 'right to know' about repeat offenders and the use of conditional cautioning to be extended. The Refuge charity, however, says the focus should be on getting the basics right[92].

When the FOI became law in 2004, Ian Redhead, Deputy Chief Constable of Hampshire Police and the lead for ACPO on the issue, said 'it must be recognised that certain information should not be disclosed in the public interest'[93]. ACPO is presently (2010) exempt from the FOIA, but the Coalition Government has vowed to remove this exemption to 're-establish the relationship between people and Government'[94].

The obsessive over-use of criminal law to deal with essentially civil matters is one sign of a police state: since 1997 Labour manufactured thousands of trivial new criminal 'offences', e.g. police can now give a criminal record to a fishmonger for using an unapproved technique for weighing herring (but not cod or salmon!)[95]. A Liverpool mother was arrested and held in a cell for 24 hours for sending her son a birthday card – he was one of three taken away by a family court, despite agreeing she was 'an excellent mother' (a group called Child Snatching by the State has been set up by 200 mothers and meets in Stafford)[96].

The police are now able to seize cars from driveways and garages – including owners of motor homes, classic cars and motorbikes, only insured for summer use. Lending a car could be a nightmare under this 'continuous insurance enforcement'[97].

North Ayrshire trading standards bosses have asked police to help confiscate bootleg cigarettes from under-16s. This is the first time a Scottish council has adopted this approach[98].

An amateur photographer was chased by police after they spotted him photographing things on the seafront[99]. Sir Christopher Rose, Chief Surveillance Commissioner, has reprimanded police forces for using anti-terrorism powers to snoop on members of the public[100].

The European Arrest Warrant (introduced in 2001) is now routinely used for crimes that are non-crimes in some jurisdictions, as well as for relatively minor offences[101].

All children under 16 are being curfewed in the centre of Bangor by North Wales Police, in order to reduce antisocial behaviour, despite being widely criticised (e.g. by the Children's Commissioner for Wales, Big Brother Watch, People of Bangor Community Group) as 'heavy-handed', 'draconian' and 'simply madness'. Membership of youth groups will be compromised by the threat of fines or imprisonment[102]. Professionals such as police have been ordered to subject children to a questionnaire called the Common Assessment Framework (CAF) if they consider them 'at risk' (parental consent isn't needed if the child is over 12), i.e. any child not achieving five Government 'outcomes' (being healthy, staying safe, 'enjoying life', 'making a positive contribution', 'achieving economic wellbeing'). The CAF includes questions about sex, family life, religion, secret fears, weight, changes to their body, and 'sleeping arrangements' at home. The weight question could lead to a discussion about why the children shouldn't eat chips[103].

Following a seminal 2012 case in the High Court by a teenager, police will have to destroy images of innocent people instead of keeping them till the mugshot victim is 100[104].

Police are using antiterrorist laws to remove phones from innocent travellers and holidaymakers without having to show reasonable suspicion. They can then download and store their personal data. Up to 60,000 people are 'stopped and examined' annually as they enter Britain[105].

Stop & Search

A landmark 2008 ruling means Scottish police can be stopped from pursuing petty criminals into private homes[106]. The number of random stop and searches is rising across Scotland, with almost 0.5 million searches in 2011-12, eclipsing the Met's 428,000 searches in the same period. There is no robust evidence of a deterrent effect[107].

Barry George – cleared of Jill Dando's murder – has been stopped and searched by police for 'acting suspiciously' in a London street at 11am[108]. Angry neighbours of Tony Blair's townhouse were interrogated by armed police outside their homes: a Diplomatic Protection Group officer pointed his Heckler & Koch at a retired GP, demanding to know what she was doing and where she was going. Residents of leafy Connaught Square said that the police appeared to be gun-happy[109].

The police were given the right to stop anyone in the street and demand ID by the 2008 Immigration and Citizenship Act – refusal can mean arrest and a possible prison sentence. This power was previously restricted to times of war, and applies to anyone who has ever left the country (only those who have never left the country are exempt). Churchill rescinded the law in 1952 because it caused much resentment against the police by people asked to produce their documents. Liberty says it's sneaking in compulsory identity cards by stealth[110].

An 80-year-old and his daughter were stopped and their car searched in 2005: they were threatened with arrest by City of London Police if they failed to answer questions. It transpired that their car had been secretly 'flagged' on the police computer because it had been spotted near a demonstration against the arms trade[111].

A Briton is interrogated by police every 20 seconds, though 90% aren't even arrested, let alone charged. Police are said to be making unjustified stops to give the figures 'racial balance'[112]. Comedian Mark Thomas won £1,200 from the Met after being stopped and searched: because of his 'over-confident attitude' he was arrested and detained, officers believing he might be carrying weapons. The Met admitted false imprisonment and illegal questioning[113].

The Equality and Human Rights Commission warned that police can be sued for using stop and search powers against ethnic minorities 'disproportionately'. There is little evidence such action targeting blacks reduces crime[114].

Some areas designated by Section 44 of the 2000 Terrorism Act are not revealed to the public: police can stop and search in these without giving reasonable grounds for suspicion. A student was prevented from photographing Tower Bridge at sunset, and a mother was banned from taking a snapshot of her baby in the pool[115].

Forces in Birmingham, Manchester and Glasgow have reportedly set up 'gang-member' databases to facilitate stop-and-search, but these are sometimes based on 'weak evidence' which is often also out-of-date, and the databases are unregulated. 90% of those on the Greater Manchester database are said to be young blacks[116].

Scottish Police Authority officials and politicians are said to be worried by the huge recent increase in the number of stop and searches (e.g. in Police Scotland's Edinburgh Division there were 4,706 in April - June, 2012, compared with 8,259 in the same period, 2013). Is the new single force too influenced by aggressive 'Strathclyde-style' policing[117]?

CAVEAT CIVIS

A 15-year-old was charged by police and prosecuted for holding a placard saying Scientology was a cult[118].

Another 15-year-old, in school uniform, was held as a terror suspect for taking pictures of a railway station during a geography field trip, while a Tory MP was stopped picturing a neglected cycle path which was the subject of complaints: police insisted on a search despite him showing his Commons pass. A freelance photographer was searched after snapping the Houses of Parliament. A renowned photographer couldn't evade a squad of seven cops, who drew up in three cars and a riot van, when he pointed his camera at Wren's Christ Church. Section 44 was ruled unlawful in July, 2010 (the Home Secretary decreed it could no longer be used against members of the public[119]), but the police vowed to continue to use it meantime: the European judges said it was a breach of the right to privacy, as there aren't sufficient legal safeguards against abuse, and it can lead to racial discrimination[120]. An 82-year-old long-term Labour Party member and peace campaigner was removed from the 2005 Labour conference for protesting against the Iraq war; he was later stopped by police from re-entering the conference under the Terrorism Act.

Police used to challenge miners (Bevan Boys) because they were not in uniform, thinking they were 'conscies' (conscientious objectors) during WWII.

Former Cabinet Minister David Mellor has revealed how his boat on the Thames was boarded by a policeman who interrogated him about where the craft was registered, etc. – the officer disclosed Mellor was being stopped under the Prevention of Terrorism Act. The policeman seemed bemused when the former Home Office Minister said he found it insulting for the police to so blatantly abuse their powers. Former First Sea Lord Alan West tells how his car was stopped and searched while he was actually the serving Security Minister[121].

Suspects can be photographed, fingerprinted and DNA sampled, as well as fined, in new supermarket cells, under a review of the Police and Criminal Evidence Act. Critics say it will encourage police to issue more fines than prosecute offenders[122].

The Brixton riots were triggered by the SWAMP plainclothes operation, which used the controversial stop-and-search tactics criticised by Scarman.

In 2006-2007 police performed 1.87m 'stops' on the streets, up by a third on the previous year: the paperwork was consuming about 1¼ million hours of patrol time. Stops and searches in the same year were at their highest for seven years[123].

Without obtaining parental consent (they are not obliged to) 10 boys at a village school were strip-searched by Derbyshire Police over claims drugs might be concealed in underwear. All the police performing the body searches were male. Parents said the (quite legal) police action could undermine trust[124].

Fans Against Criminalisation claim Scottish police are becoming more heavy-handed since the 2012 Offensive Behaviour at Football legislation. Criminal lawyer Paul Kavanagh claims a large number of fans are being illegally made to give their contact details to police while going to and from matches. People have allegedly been refused taxi licences and officers' credibility questioned in court[125].

E.I.O.

Home Secretary Theresa May rubber-stamped the introduction of the European Investigation Order: EU police can order British police to transfer details (after investigation) of any UK citizen. No justification is needed[126]. Over 1,000 Britons were shipped abroad in 2009 under the European Arrest Warrant, against which there is no appeal. An arrested person can be put into custody for months or years[127]. The E.I.O. allows foreign police to investigate crimes <u>directly</u> on UK soil. British police can't argue that an extradition request is disproportionate (in one case a carpenter who removed doors he wasn't paid for was pursued round Europe; in another, Poland wanted the suspect in the theft of a pudding extradited)[128].

Raids

It has been claimed the pre-emptive G8 arrests (June, 2013) were an abuse of anti-terrorist powers and shame democratic Britain[129].

The 2009 Scottish licensing laws gave greater powers to the police[130].

Police were given Big Brother powers during the 2012 London Olympics to raid homes and businesses as well as removing posters promoting rivals to official sponsors. This has been compared to the crackdown on free speech marring the 2008 Beijing Olympics[131]. The police now have powers to enter 'land or premises', 'to remove, destroy, conceal or erase any infringing article' that resembles corporate Olympics logos (a 2006 Act allows this heavy-handed policing in an attempt to deal with 'ambush marketing')[132]. Scotland Yard secretly studied Chinese-style surveillance tactics in preparation for the 2012 Olympics (e.g. installation of miniature microphones, with conversations transmitted to a police control room). The study was prepared by <u>Tarique Ghaffur</u>, forced to step down after a dispute with Met commissioner <u>Sir Ian Blair</u>[133].

When a Christian couple asked Wyre Borough Council if they could display their religious literature alongside gay rights leaflets, the council set the police on them with the intention of 'challenging attitudes, educating and raising awareness of the implications of homophobic behaviour'. Even more outrageous than an elected body using the police to browbeat those of whose opinions it disapproves, is the ready compliance of the police, who are obviously more enthusiastic about fighting opinions than criminals[134].

Former Commons Speaker Michael Martin says police broke the law by raiding Damian Green's Westminster office. The police did not have a warrant and did not explain, as they are required to do, that the Sergeant-at-Arms was not obliged to consent[135].

In 2012 Met raids on top Sun journalists, officers allegedly went through children's bedrooms, while in one case a seriously-ill relative's mattress was searched, so she had to be moved; in another the search, it was claimed by the arrestee, lasted 13 hours and left his daughters and wife feeling violated. According to The Sun's associate editor, floorboards were ripped up and intimate letters and possessions rifled through[136].

Though the 'Barras' – Glasgow's famous open market – can be traced back to the 18th Century, in the 1920s Glasgow police were evicting and harassing the traders. 'The polis jist widnae let them settle. They couldnae ply their trade frae their cairts. It was an awfy shame,' said the 'Queen of the Barras', Maggie McIver[137].

Photography

A woman who wore a 'B ... to Tony Blair' T-shirt was arrested, and a tourist photographing a policeman in Whitehall met the same fate[138].

A father was banned by Strathclyde Police from photographing his own four-year-old daughter in Glasgow's Braehead Shopping Centre. Though they deny this they refuse to say why they were called[139].

Retired chief superintendent Chris Stevenson, who led the Soham murder investigation, says efforts to protect children by screening millions of adults have gone too far. He revealed how he himself was told to stop taking photos of his nine-year-old grandson playing football[140].

Under section 44 of the 2000 Terrorism Act, photographers are being searched by police and forced to delete pictures of government buildings, tourist landmarks like St. Paul's and even high-street shops and trains. They are asked to give their height and ethnicity. Between 2000 and 2009 about 180,000 UK citizens have been to some extent harassed under section 44. There are over 100 designated special zones in London alone where the order obtains, as well as every train station in Britain. But the exact locations of the special zones are kept secret, so one doesn't know one is breaking the law by taking a photo till after the event[141]. Austin Mitchell, MP for Grimsby, tabled an Early Day Motion condemning police action against lawful photography in public places. The police have even (illegally) asked members of the public to delete photos from their cameras[142]. Officers may be misusing their stop and search powers, as they only arrested a tiny proportion of the over one million people stopped in 2008. One person in 19 is stopped and searched in parts of London[143].

Ironically Edinburgh Police are issuing minature 'body cameras' to shopkeepers so they can secretly film members of the public committing hate crime, even though this sort of surveillance could make staff targets (see Surveillance, page 32)[144].

Investigation

People who complain about the police find the latter investigate themselves, and if one complains about the investigation – they can refuse if the complainant goes 'over time' or the complaint is invalid, because of the many exemptions the police enjoy from the FOIA – it is the police who are asked to investigate their own investigation. The IPCC rely on the very police against whom one is complaining[145].

Greater Manchester Police were accused of criminalising free speech when they confiscated a satirical football magazine, threatening people with arrest for owning a copy. The fanzine was using a spoof KKK logo to make fun of Liverpool and 'racist language' striker Luis Suarez[146].

Met commissioner <u>Bernard Hogan-Howe</u> has campaigned for powers 'to eliminate innocent people from an investigation', which would reverse the 'innocent till proved guilty' tradition. This mirrors the Home Office's 2012 plans for mass state surveillance (of e/G mail, Facebook, Royal Mail postcards, etc.) accessible by police[147].

A month after Debra Burt told a friend on Facebook she'd like to 'egg' the PM at the 2013 Canterbury enthronement (as a protest at benefit cuts), two plainclothes police turned up at her home. They had scoured the internet to track her down to check her threat status[148].

Hampshire Constabulary <u>Sergeant Paul Beale</u> visited the New Milton Advertiser because Tory Councillor Goff Beck was described as 'controversial' and revealed as making bigoted remarks to a gay colleague, as well as having received a reprimand for bullying a female colleague. The police complained that Mr. Beck's 'credibility as a person of good standing was being undermined'[149].

Incarceration

A 67-year-old was arrested at dawn, held in a police cell for six hours, and had his fingerprints and DNA taken, for using a single swear-word in front of a council official. He had been arguing about slippery stairs after campaigning for three years for safety improvements[150].

Parents suspected, maybe on malicious evidence, of harming their children are shocked to find themselves treated like dangerous criminals by the police, who arrive at the home six or eight strong: social workers seem able to enlist the unquestioning support of the constabulary (who may hold the parents in custody for up to 36 hours)[151]. Another case showing how amazingly compliant the police are with the instructions of social workers is that of immigrant parents whose six children were seized in 2010. The parents were arrested again, charged with conspiring to abduct them, despite their not knowing the children's whereabouts. The wife was forcibly stripped naked before a male officer, and held with her husband in an unheated cell without blankets. They were sectioned in a mental hospital but released after five doctors found nothing wrong with them. 28 police searched their flat in a cordoned off street, and they were arrested twice more[152].

Peace campaigner Maya Evans was convicted for reading out the names of soldiers killed in Iraq at the Cenotaph[153].

People are being arrested without being charged – employers assume guilt until innocence is proved. Police seem to be arresting merely to interview[154].

<u>Surveillance</u>

<u>Sir Andrew Leggatt</u> intimated (2002) he did not have the resources to monitor the Big Brother activities of the 1,000 or so organisations empowered to spy on ordinary citizens (see also The Parapoliceman Chapter)[155].

Journalist Jon Ronson, while investigating the background to the double murder and suicide of one Christopher Foster, was tailed by police while driving round the murder village, and told by them he looked too scruffy to be a journalist[156].

Sussex Police's Operation Crackdown encourages motorists to spy on each other and report online, so that accused drivers can't find out who is responsible. As a result thousands of drivers have received 'letters of advice' and many have had sanctions imposed[157].

Every police station is to get a drug testing device for drivers, even though it is not yet illegal to drive with drugs in one's system[158].

Police are being trained, presumably by anonymous psychologists in the Procter group, to classify the personalities or 'social styles' they encounter among the public: the Lorraine

Kelly ('amiable'), the Jeremy Paxman ('analytical'), the Lenny Henry ('expressive'), and the Madonna (the 'driver'). The idea, supposed to improve 'communication', is ironic in that the police have refused to cooperate with research to assess personality in police recruits[159].

A Canterbury Neighbourhood Watch team was disbanded after half its members refused to answer police questions about their race, sexual orientation, finances (including mortgage defaults) and religion. The Herne Bay police stopped giving them crime reports, and a Superintendent <u>Joanna Young</u> reportedly said they would have to do it their (the police's) way or not at all.

Harold Wilson ordered police surveillance on the Church of Scientology in 1975, and one police report sent to Scottish Office ministers noted: 'The organisation is mafia-like ...'. This from a service which condones Freemasonry[160].

Scottish football fans may be having their human rights traduced by new anti-sectarian police powers, e.g. some have been subjected to surveillance orders and questioning at airports when returning from holidays. Suspicions of police harassment are supported by the fact that many cases eventually brought against fans are either dropped or found not proven, e.g. one fan's application for a taxi licence was opposed by police on the strength of a Football Banning Order application which didn't result in a ban. Fans are being filmed as they watch games, and are being criminalised for partisanship rather than bigotry. A three-month sentence on an 18-year-old for sectarian remarks was reduced to a community order on appeal[161].

The Met and MI5 apparently mounted a surveillance operation against Sadiq Khan, a Muslim MP and government whip, though Scotland Yard refused to comment on whether it was involved[162].

Thames Valley and MOD Police have been 'spying' on peace campaigners, just as environmental protesters have been placed under surveillance in recent years – Chief Constable <u>Sara Thornton</u> has apologised for posting officers outside Reading's International Solidarity Centre, where the town's mayor was speaking and a film documentary about nuclear weapons was screened. The officers were recording details of attendees, saying they had been sent to 'watch out for certain people'. There were accusations that police were involved in surreptitious filming using time-mounted cameras[163].

Labour's RIPA (Regulation of Investigatory Powers Act, 2000) means police surveillance operations must be authorised, and this requires 10 forms to be completed, taking up to 13½ hours:

Sara Thornton

      Proactive Assessment and Tasking Proforma
      Application for Direct Surveillance
      Authorisation for Direct Surveillance
      Observation Point Location
      Request for Technical Assistance
      Risk Assessment

Proactive Assessment and Tasking Proforma
Review of Directed Surveillance
Closing Report
Cancelling Directed Surveillance[164]

It would be of interest to groups such as lawyers or doctors whether these rules were observed in the case of the professional described in Appendix II, and whether the surveillance using audio and visual apparatus contravened Article 8 of the Human Rights Act (1998).

Fingerprints/scanners

Police in England and Wales are being issued with mobile fingerprint scanners to apply to suspects in the street. But Liberty said it could encourage random searches[165].

Scottish police interrogated 68,500 school age children in 2009, some below the criminal responsibility age[166] (this has since been raised to 10). Scottish children as young as five are having their fingerprints taken at school, and police say they may access the data if they suspect a child[167].

The UK's National Police Improvement Agency, which is spearheading Project Midas (issuing mobile fingerprint scanners for street use), insisted that Scotland would adopt the technology, but in fact Scottish forces have scrapped the plan[168].

Mobile fingerprinting devices are now (2011) used by 28 forces[169].

Undercover

Police forces use undercover quality inspectors to check service standards such as opening hours and cleanliness at police stations, and waiting times to see an officer. 'Mystery shoppers' are used at the Met, Dorset, Cleveland, Humberside and Thames Valley[170].

School pupils in Lancashire are being offered phone top-up vouchers if they report fellow pupils to the police (e.g. for scrawling graffiti), though some say it could lead to bullying and retaliation.

The intensity of probes into suspected lesbians in the postwar WRAF meant that the police would spy on subjects from rooms they had commandeered[171].

The Met's 2011 attempt to uncover journalistic sources in the hacking inquiry was presaged by the secret three-year Operation Virid, costing hundreds of thousands, conducted by Thames Valley Police. The latter operated from a private Pangbourne office in their probe into Reading-based INS News Services. Clandestine court orders enabled the police to seize phone records without INS being told. The investigation only surfaced when an officer was dismissed. INS claimed the force's warrants were illegal and the force settled INS legal costs out of court, just before Chief Constable Peter Neyroud was due to appear in the High Court[172].

One distasteful duty of the 19th Century policeman was to monitor the conduct of war widows and wives of services personnel who were abroad on duty: they received a separation allowance. If the police found the women cohabiting illicitly they had their money withdrawn[173]. Yet the public complained that despite escalating crime rates they never saw a policeman: the new police seemed to spend their time instead enforcing red tape!

Peaceful vegetarians and violent jihadists are being lumped together by ACPO, in terms of the various undercover units dealing with them being amalgamated: the National Public Order Intelligence Unit, the National Domestic Extremism Team, the National Extremism Tactical Coordination Unit, as well as the National Community Tension Team – all being subsumed under the Met's Counter Terrorism Command. Dissent is viewed by Big Brother police as 'terrorism'[174]. ACPO, which is run as a private company, is keeping secret intelligence files and photos of almost 1,900 'domestic extremists', via its National Coordinator for Domestic Extremism (NCDE), which has a staff of 100 (about 70 are police). The unit is headed (2010) by Assistant Chief Constable Anton Setchell[175]. ACPO confirmed in 2007 that it had been advising the Home Office re undercover officers being sent into hostelries to catch bar staff serving drinks[176]. Undercover police (of both sexes) have been used as pseudo-patients to entrap a doctor prescribing diet pills quite legally (see Appendix II).

Ex-cop Derek Webb, in his new role as a PI*, put hacking case lawyers Mark Lewis and Charlotte Harris under surveillance to see if they were having an affair.

The growing number of civilian 'busybodies' ('Jacqui Smith's irregulars') able to destroy people's careers with their police powers may have been given only five days' training: by the summer of 2012 there were 2,617 licensed snoopers under the Community Safety Accreditation Scheme (80% of forces don't keep track of them). Private security guards can now hand out penalties for causing 'harassment, alarm and distress', which can come up in enhanced CRB checks. This shadow police force involves 154 organisations, 34 of which can issue a Penalty Notice for the use of 'public' electronic communications to cause annoyance'[177].

In 2011 almost 1,000 entirely innocent people were placed under surveillance wrongly, using anti-terror powers. Thus two innocent members of the public were arrested and told they were serious criminals. The commonest mistake made by police is to add the wrong digit to a phone number or address. There were 42 blunders by police and other law enforcement agencies asking for interception warrants, and the same number of errors by MI5, MI6 and GCHQ. We are being 'turned into a nation of suspects rather than citizens'[178].

Police and the Home Office are making four requests daily to Google for information on Britons, putting free expression at risk[179].

In commenting on the undercover filming which exposed abuses in a geriatric care home (Panorama 23.4.12) the police comment was that they didn't advise undercover filming!

Aircraft

In 2010 police chiefs announced they were axing 28,000 officers and could no longer respond to all 999 calls, yet were buying a fleet of spy-in-the-sky aircraft. Cambridgeshire Police have hired a special plane (at a cost of £1,500) to prosecute a health and safety motorist accused of driving while using a mobile phone. He had annoyed them by pleading 'not guilty' and was able to prove he was using a hands-free kit[180].

---

* PI = Private Investigator

Merseyside Police is one of three forces using drones (miniature remote-controlled helicopters) to locate suspects and monitor protests, motorists, flytippers and agricultural thieves, but has been forced to ground the drones following an alleged breach of an Air Navigation Order[181]. The surveillance data gleaned may be sold to private firms[182]. Kent Police is leading a group of Government agencies that plans to 'revolutionise policing' by launching a fleet of unmanned spy planes. They will help monitor protest marches, antisocial driving, thefts from cash machines, and waste management[183]. Kent Police are looking at the use of small high-flying planes that would be invisible to the naked eye[184].

The Surveillance Studies Network (2010) concluded that aerial police drones are 'more pervasive than CCTV'[185]. ACPO and its English equivalent have formed the Unmanned Aerial Systems Steering Group to discuss spy planes monitoring everyday scenes: Strathclyde Police have trialled one in rural Argyll.

Cheshire Police have been using a helicopter with powerful video technology to alert patrol cars to road misbehaviour such as speeding, mobile phone use, wrong overtaking[186].

CCTV/Asset Cameras

Though Britain has more CCTV than any other nation, only an estimated 3% of crimes are solved by them.

Over 400 new 'super-intelligent' CCTV cameras are to be installed in Glasgow to make the 'flagship' city 'smarter and safer'[187].

Police are telling alcohol outlets in Islington and Richmond they won't support their licensing applications unless they train Big Brother CCTV cameras on their customers and promise to hand over any footage. Essex and Northamptonshire are also going down this road[188].

Police and MI5 have been given access to a network of infrared cameras that can track millions of car journeys. The 'green' cameras were installed by the Highways Agency to calculate journey times, but they have been hijacked by the police. CCTV, mobile cameras and helicopters can now all read number plates[189]. 'Supertrap' high-tech cameras are very hard to spot – they don't flash and can cover all motorway lanes at once[190]. Most CCTV cameras, supposedly set up to combat crime, are not sited in appropriate positions, being used to monitor motorists in bus lanes. CCTV undermines civil liberties while giving only a slight advantage in public safety[191]. Only one crime was solved in 2008 by every 1,000 CCTV cameras in London. It is claimed police do not bother to examine the tapes[192]. The use by councils of CCTV cameras as a 'cheap alternative to policing' fails to reduce crime: many are not turned on to save money[193].

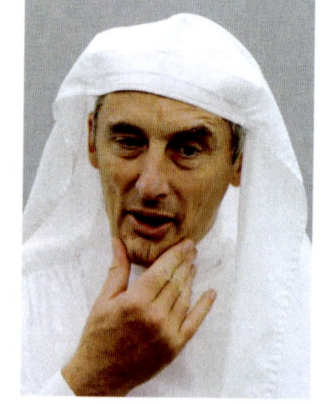

Controversial Chief Constable <u>Richard Brunstrom</u> said cameras hidden in cats-eyes could be used to detect speeding motorists[194].

Richard Brunstrom

In 2005 ACPO's speed camera liaison officer <u>Ian Bell</u> claimed Britain's roads needed up to 1,000 extra cameras, a 16% increase[195].

Bedfordshire Police have introduced 'command vans' with cameras all round the vehicle rather than just at the rear. They will catch motorbikes, which don't have front number plates[196]. The first Asset camera to detect multiple traffic offences at the same time was revealed in 2010. It checks tax, insurance and whether the driver is tailgating or wearing a seat belt[197].

Volunteers are being recruited in Soham to man street cameras to spy on their neighbours – the civilians will share a new CCTV monitoring suite with officers in a police station[198].

West Midlands Chief Constable <u>Chris Sims</u> had to apologise for siting cameras and a number-plate recognition system in Moslem areas[199].

Digital speed cameras were being introduced in 2007 which could picture drivers smoking or eating. A Scottish motorist was fined for blowing his nose at the wheel. The number of parking fines had quadrupled in the previous five years[200].

A police CCTV Smart car, with a 15ft periscope, can hide behind walls and flout normal rules like parking on double yellow lines. In 2010 there were 54 across Britain catching nearly 200,000 motorists in 2009[201]. The Met has been involved in joint operations with debt collectors using unmarked vans fitted with automatic numberplate recognition cameras. The legality of such police activities – they caught nearly 250 drivers in just one London borough – is problematic, as the technology was supposed to track terrorists. Police have hugely increased its use since 2007. When the bailiffs detect a parking debt culprit they alert police at a nearby road block: the latter pass the drivers onto another bailiffs team which collects the payments[202].

Tayside Police were the first Scottish force (in 2008) to use body-attached CCTV cameras[203].

Speed cameras which communicate with each other by satellite have been secretly tested on British roads – they can follow drivers for miles (speedspike – they combine number plate recognition with global positioning satellites[204]). ANPR (Automatic Number Plate Recognition) – linked to over 10,000 CCTV cameras in England and Wales – allows police to secretly photograph up to 14m motorists daily, keeping the details (often including the faces of front-seat occupants) for years. The images are held at Hendon without drivers' knowledge or permission. 'Liberty' was planning (2010) to take a High Court action against ACPO, whose ANPR user group defends the practice, which has 'no legislative basis'[205]. Liberty says the police action 'shows a contempt for Parliament, personal privacy and the law'. The UK CCTV network is increasing steadily, recording everyone about 70 times daily, according to police, but the figure may be as high as 300 in central London. ANPR is being used as a tool of mass surveillance. Transport Scotland have spent over £260,000 on ANPR, but have promised not to give the data to the police[206].

Edinburgh police have been accused of 'sneaky' tactics when they 'upgraded' red-light traffic cameras into speed cameras without warning drivers, as they should. Lothian Police say they don't need to advertise the altered cameras, but motoring groups say the change is unfair and pointless[207].

Many speed cameras may have increased accident rates, and only a minority of councils have agreed to publish full data on each speed camera in their area[208].

HR group Privacy International ranks the UK as the most camera-monitored European country (Scotland is only a little better). Control orders (not yet used in Scotland) can block travel or communications and impose house arrest. The defendant appeals, but evidence can be presented by the complainant to the High Court in secret, withholding it from the defendant and/or their lawyer. A man stopped by Strathclyde Police in Glasgow while testing a new iPhone app was suspected of terrorism-related activity: the police later had to apologise. Section 44 (Terrorism Act 2000) – ruled illegal by Europe – was replaced in March 2011 by Theresa May with section 47A. RIPA gives councils access to phone and internet records, as well as permission to conduct surveillance in people's homes as well as workplaces[209].

Strathclyde Police were fitting miniature video cameras to the jackets of officers in parts of Glasgow and East Dunbartonshire[210]. The same is happening to certain parapolice (e.g. traffic wardens).

Following (stalking)

The ultimate in Big Brother policing must surely be Essex police following and filming convicted Basildon burglars round the clock (the 'bother a burglar' initiative was code-named Bright Shadow)[211]. Yet two years before, it had been revealed that it took one officer over 13 hours filling in forms to obtain permission to tail a suspected burglar[212].

Trojan

'The top ranks of the Metropolitan police now think it is their job to enforce political orthodoxy rather than fight crime' – the Orwellian Big Brother state has arrived[213]. The EU hopes to infect every British computer with a police spy virus (Trojan), the justification being to crack down on organised crime[214]. Since 2009 police can hack into personal computers without a warrant (the euphemism is 'remote searching'). The Brussels edict allows European police forces to ask British police to hack home PCs, and pass on information[215]. Anti-terror police apparently searched private e-mails on Damian Green's seized computer, using the name of the director of Liberty (Shami Chakrabarti), who had nothing to do with the investigation and who labelled it McCarthyite[216].

Mobile Phones/e-mail

Under 'Deep Racket Inspections' police and MI5 can bug internet phone calls and every e-mail sent in Britain[217]. The various MI5 threat gradings ('highly likely', 'severe', 'imminent', etc) may be intended to desensitise the population against more authoritarian measures to 'protect' our security[218].

Mobile phone firms charge the police £8.7 million a year to access suspects' data. Police can see phone records without having to apply to the courts, using Section 22 of the draconian Regulation of Investigatory Powers Act (RIPA). Section 22 powers were exercised more than half a million times. The Home Office pays £8 million to firms just for data storage[219].

It was reported in 2007 that the McCanns believed they were being bugged by British police, e.g. Portuguese police seemed to have inside information when interviewing them[220].

Home Secretary Theresa May has refused the McCanns access into a 2010 review of the case because of its 'sensitivity'.

MI5 reportedly tapped the phones of King Edward VIII and his brother the Duke of York during the 1936 Abdication Crisis. PM Stanley Baldwin had called in Sir Vernon Kell, head of MI5[221]. MI5 was to be allowed to hack anyone's phone calls, texts and e-mails[222] by new (2012) legislation, but a severe civil rights concerns backlash has made this unlikely.

The Met are still (2012) storing <u>indefinitely</u> the phone data of innocent people, with 16 special downloading units now being sited in police stations across London, employing 300 officers – they can copy a phone's memory in minutes (before they had to be sent to a forensic lab). The recent Sam Hallam miscarriage of justice showed how flawed the Met's handling of private data can be (the police concealed phone evidence that could have saved Hallam seven years in jail. Privacy International warns that arrestees are likely to have their phones checked out. 'Big Brother Watch' has asked the Information Commissioner if the Met has broken UK law[223].

Foreign police will be able to access British e-mails, internet use and text messages. This revelation follows <u>Hogan-Howe</u>'s backing of the 'snoopers charter', reminiscent of <u>Ian Blair</u>'s wanting suspects locked up for 90 days[224].

In 2012 Scottish forces made around 57,000 requests to snoop on personal email and phone records, there being a rising trend in requests[225].

Databases

US computer scientists have found how to de-anonymise supposedly anonymous datasets[226]. Police are able to access the NHS medical records database because it is in the 'public interest'[227].

An editorial in 'Photographers UK' claims police have set up a database of photographers. <u>Andy Trotter</u>, Chief Constable of the British Transport Police, admitted police had misused the Terrorism Act 2000[228].

Passenger information obtained from travel agents is being used secretly by police to assign 'red flags' to innocent travellers (e.g. ordering a vegetarian meal, asking for an over-wing seat, travelling with a foreign-born spouse, buying a one-way ticket, making a last-minute reservation, not showing up for a flight in the past, a history of travelling to risk countries). Though thousands of passengers highlighted by the 'terrorist detector' database have been arrested, none has been a terrorist. Financial records and analysis of 'known associates' is checked before people are cleared for travel (47,000 in 2009)[229]. 'Under the guise of anti-terrorism the sinister apparatus of the Orwellian Big Brother state is being erected to monitor the behaviour of every citizen'[230].

A civil liberties group claims people are shying away from participating in protests because of 'intimidating' police tactics, e.g. by filming activists to make them feel uncomfortable. The police typically refuse to release information they have gained about protesters, e.g. as recorded during the 2005 G8 Gleneagles summit. Tayside Police has said it is entitled to hold images of 'non-convicted persons' on their Scottish Intelligence Database, to which about 60,000 names are added annually (their details include phone numbers and bank account details)[231].

Even police officers coming into contact with killer Jon Venables have no inkling that they are dealing with a dangerous person (his new name is on the computer without his criminal history!)[232].

Members of the public now have to worry about approaching the police in case they are put on a secret database along with suspects: this mingling means victims and suspects may be mixed up. As many as six million apparently innocent citizens, including victims, are on the new police national database[233]. (Even victims' ethnicity is recorded, together with their date of birth)[234]. West Midlands Police had amassed (by 2010) 1.1 million records of people dialling the police, Lancashire 600,000, North Wales 303,000, etc. Anti-terror laws were applied to over 100,000 people in 2009 without a single arrest for terrorism. Data-hoarding risks alienating the public: members of the latter are not there to be protected but rather are all potential wrongdoers, a mark of undemocratic states[235]. It is a sine qua non of dictatorships to hold secret police files on their peoples. The 2011 Police National Database will contain the names of a quarter of the population, including victims! The National Policing Improvement Agency, which runs it, is being closed[236].

Police cautions that are decades out of date are still appearing on databases, affecting job applications.

Scottish prison chiefs have started a huge photo database of all visitors to jail inmates – they could be barred if they refuse to be photographed (children will be exempt)[237].

It appears the police supplied information to the Consultancy Association's employment blacklist (the secretive Association is funded by the UK's 39 major construction firms), which ensures 3,200 whistleblowers or union member victims are not given jobs. The Association previously called itself the 'Economic League'[238].

DNA

Damian Green says DNA is the public's secret enemy, with (2010) more than 5.6 million citizens on the UK database, the largest in the world. Each chief constable can remove records at his or her discretion, but there is a 'postcode lottery', with a much greater chance of reclaiming DNA in Yorkshire than London, but none in Nottinghamshire. 'Exceptional circumstances' can be interpreted in different ways by different police chiefs. In Scotland only the DNA of those charged is normally kept, and then only rarely for three years. The database contains excessive numbers and putting everyone on it may prove counterproductive. One person wrote: 'All it's done is annoy me. I'm now actively anti-police.' The Tories have launched a petition: 'Return my DNA.' They recommend a targeted rather than a blunderbuss database[239]. The DNA of a quarter of the British people is now on the police database.

Before the 2001 Criminal Justice and Police Bill, police were supposed to destroy samples if a suspect was not prosecuted or was acquitted. In 2000 convicted murderer Michael Weir was freed after the Court of Appeal's ruling that DNA evidence used to convict him should have been erased. Also the Inland Revenue can now pass to police details of an individual's affairs for any criminal investigation (previously it was only for murder and treason)[240].

Over half a million names on the police DNA database in 2007 were false or fallacious (e.g. misspelt): thousands give false names or alternative spellings of their names to police. Innocent people's names may be given maliciously to police by suspects. The police were anxious to include litter-droppers, fare dodgers and dog-owners who don't clean up after their dogs[241].

A baby has had its DNA recorded by police on the national database (which by 2009 contained 600,000 samples from innocent people): the oldest on the database was over 90[242]. 1.1 million children are on the UK DNA database – it is claimed police are arresting innocent children simply to get DNA samples. West Yorkshire Police took a seven-month-old baby's DNA at the request of West Midlands, being one of 47 children under 10 that had been recorded by 2007, but the Birmingham force refused to say why they've put the baby on the national database. One 13-year-old boy, falsely accused of writing graffiti, had a six-month battle to have his database entry removed. Devon and Cornwall Police are storing the DNA of 14,383 children aged 10 to 17 who were arrested between 2007-2010, even if they weren't charged[243]. The record stays on a person's file until they reach 100 years of age[244]. A BBC personality made 40 false rape allegations against her former boyfriend, whose name stays on the Police National Computer, to the detriment of his employment prospects[245].

The Met said (2009) that it had received requests from 231 people to have their DNA removed, under the 'exceptional cases procedure', but only 31 were granted[246]. 7% of citizens are on the database (in the US it is 0.5% and the second highest is Austria with 1%). Police in England and Wales uniquely store the DNA of everyone over the age of 10 who is arrested, but this has been ruled illegal by Strasbourg judges[247].

For every innocent person removed from the DNA database, a further 253 have been added. The police have taken the DNA of 100,000 innocent people since the Government was told the practice is illegal. Chief constables say they are instructed to remove the innocent in 'exceptional circumstances' – this instruction has remained in place despite the 2008 ruling by the European Court of Human Rights[248]. ACPO secretly told chief constables in 2009 to continue with the unlawful 'Big Brother' policy of storing innocent people's DNA samples indefinitely, so that officers could still trawl the innocent for matches to crimes[249].

Police are arresting innocent people so as to maximise the number of DNA samples for their database. The Human Genetics Commission says the Big Brother tactic is creating a public 'spiral of suspicion'[250]. Police claim that the DNA of those released without charge crops up at as many later crime scenes as that of people who were convicted[251]. It was reported (January 2011) that police will be allowed to hold millions of DNA samples from unconvicted suspects[252].

'Familial DNA searches' by police are being ordered weekly for people with no immediate connection to any crime. A partial match could mean police targeting an innocent person in a background investigation or surveillance exercise. The first conviction was of a Surrey man in 2004, using this familial approach, constraints on whose use have not been made public[253]. If the police can do familial searches it is surely justified to include such when analysing police behaviour (see 'The Familial Flaw Policeman' chapter). Would research into the familial criminal background of police recruits be worthwhile – we know criminality runs in families?

10% of crime scenes are inadvertently contaminated by police DNA[254].

Anyone can now be arrested in the UK for the slightest offence and be forced to become part of New Labour's Big Brother DNA database. Young boys (one just seven) were questioned by police for trying to knock chestnuts out of trees on public ground. A grandmother's neighbour accused her of not returning a ball kicked into her garden, so she was arrested, fingerprinted and her DNA taken: the police let her go without even a caution, but only after they went through every room in her house, even her daughter's drawers.

The UK's DNA database is 50 times bigger than the French, and can now be accessed by any European country, the problem being 'false positives' (there are large numbers of innocents on the bank) who can be extradited falsely (under the Prum Agreement)[255].

Police Scotland in 2013 was storing the DNA of one in 13 adults, many (6,787) quite innocent, more than double the number held in 2002. The police can keep a suspect on record even if found not guilty. Children as young as eight are on the database[256].

Nearly 165,000 innocent people are thought to have been added to the police DNA database in the three years to 2011 (i.e. one in six profiles). Most worrying, most of 51 UK forces were unable/unwilling to say how many of the database profiles belonged to the innocent. Less than 2% seem to have been deleted[257].

A 70-year-old man who swore at someone had his DNA taken[258].

CRB

The Independent Safeguarding Authority (ISA) and the Contact Point database (which contains records on all 11 million children in England), according to Richard Thomas, Britain's first Information Commissioner, contain masses of information potentially irrelevant to protecting vulnerable people, and are a 'step too far' for freedom. The flawed CRB supplies intelligence to the ISA[259]. Errors by the CRB doubled in the year to March 2009[260].

The case of a child fined £15 in 1984 for stealing a 99p packet of meat and another child theft of £25 which took place also in the early 1980s, were still being stored on police computers (in Humberside and West Midlands respectively) in 2009. A third, held by Staffordshire Police, related to a child cautioned for a minor assault. All showed up in CRB checks when the individuals applied for jobs. A 24-year-old was turned down for nursing because of a conditional discharge she got for theft as a 16-year-old, and an 18-year-old medical student had his place at Imperial College withdrawn because of a spent burglary conviction. When an Information Tribunal ordered that records should be deleted, five chief constables challenged the ruling in the Court of Appeal[261]. A 22-year-old woman who wants to be a teacher has been blacklisted because her theft of a pencil at the age of 9 shows up on CRB checks, even though, being underage, she was not charged, merely given 'words of advice'[262].

Parents whose children invite friends to sleepovers may face criminal record checks, and babysitting teenagers may have to pay £64 to go on a database. Hosts to exchange students and au pairs will be vetted[263].

By November 2008 over 12,200 innocent people had been branded criminals (paedophiles, thugs, etc) by bungling police, the incorrect records being disclosed to various groups by the CRB. The mistakes were often made by staff entering wrong information into the Police National Computer[264].

Seven innocent people are daily falsely branded criminals because of botched records checks. During 2008-9 the CRB, a branch of the Home Office, paid over £290,000 in 'apology payments'. Over 12,000 disputed cases were upheld over the previous five years. In many cases police release details that have been recorded inaccurately. A job applicant may be rejected without being aware that the employer's rejection was based on a CRB vetting error. An IT teacher was wrongly branded three times by the CRB as a forger and thug, while a young mother who was falsely labelled a violent heroin addict was told by the CRB it was up to her to prove her innocence[265].

Access (Illegal)

CRB police files are being sold to over 50 recruitment agencies and investigators checking prospective employees' backgrounds that having nothing to do with the vulnerable. The Police Act 1997 says checks should be confined to children and vulnerable adults. Almost anyone's criminal record can be obtained because there are no proper checks. An enhanced CRB check will include spent offences, which may adversely affect employment prospects[266].

Lothian and Borders WPC Anna Wong, who trawled the top-secret Scottish Intelligence Database to spy on dozens of Chinese people she knew, was fined £1,000 and discharged from the force[267]. A police inquiry was under way in 2009 after more than 300 officers and staff accessed confidential files on Liverpool captain Steven Gerrard following his 2008 arrest[268] (see also Criminal Policeman chapter).

The University of East Anglia has made the sending of an FOI request a police matter after being besieged with requests from climate change sceptics. Norfolk Police were investigating an alleged email theft alongside the National Domestic Extremism Unit. One of those targeted said he had been questioned by police about his political beliefs; the police seemed to be looking for a conspiracy. In another case the detective demanded to know the person's internet service provider, as well as his political affiliations, climate change views and climate science qualifications. A Parliamentary Select Committee found the University had a 'reprehensible' culture of withholding information: Detective Superintendent Julian Gregory was leading the investigation into the FOI requesters[269].

FBI officers arrived unannounced at the Welsh home of the seriously-ill British mother of a young American intelligence officer being investigated for leaks of classified Afghan war documents: their questioning left the stroke sufferer 'severely distressed'. They were accompanied by a D.S. Alison Thomas from Powys Police[270].

Leaks

In respect of the arrest of Neil and Christine Hamilton, on suspicion of rape, the police leaked details and the 'secret' location of the police station where they were charged: the Met even sent a PR officer to Barkingside Police Station to deal with the media inquiries, so commonplace has become the leaking of details of 'celebrity' arrests. Yet the police arrested MP Damian Green to find the source of leaks[271]!

A crime-fighting Cumbernauld councillor warned residents about a businessman publicly branded a drug dealer by police, by posting a letter written by Strathclyde Police Chief Willie Roe. The councillor had to attend a Glasgow police station to be questioned under caution[272].

See also 'The Criminal Policeman', Ch. IV.

CHAPTER III

THE BOGUS POLICEMAN

Criminal impersonators of police, e.g. in 'distraction' burglaries, are considered an increasing problem – it is an offence under section 90 of the Police Act 1996. Bogus armed cops raided NatWest in Glasgow, yards from Strathclyde Police HQ, in the autumn of 2011[273].

19-year-old Anthony Sachs patrolled Manchester streets at night wearing an earpiece and carrying handcuffs. The bogus vigilante 'arrested' a 13-year-old for having tobacco, handcuffed him and drove him home. He handcuffed a 16-year-old but let him go after he shouted[274].

Conman Stuart Howatson was jailed in 2010 for 20 months for posing as a Met officer, using kit bought on eBay and even deceiving his wife, who believed he worked at Scotland Yard. He even pretended the head of the Met, Sir John Stevens, would be coming to his wedding, and claimed to be a dog handler, an armed officer, a royal protection officer, a senior officer on sabbatical. He gave a talk in uniform about the police, showing schoolchildren police batons. He conned friends into thinking he would buy their Spanish home, so that he could have free holidays there – he used fake bank statements showing his salary paid by the Met. His computers contained child porn images[275].

A 19-year-old Edinburgh learner driver drove around in an imitation police car (with a siren and blue flashing lights) and wearing a police-style jacket. He had taken his father's car without permission. He was given a ban, a fine and community service[276]. Drug trafficker Sean Lynch drove his American police car and a powerful police motorbike around the affluent Surrey stockbroker belt[277].

In 2009 Aberdeen stripper Stuart Kennedy, 26, denied a charge of impersonating a police officer and using a blue light in his car while trying to pull over two other cars on separate occasions[278]. But the case was dropped, after calling five times at Aberdeen Sheriff Court. His stripper act was billed as Sergeant Eros. He had also been accused of possessing two batons and a fake CS spray[279]. Kennedy was eventually fined and given community service for impersonating a policeman and having the uniform and equipment without good reason[280]. He was found not guilty of indecency (2012) when Appeal Court judges ruled his fake truncheon was not an offensive weapon[281]. Male teacher Benedict Garrett, who moonlighted as a stripper and starred in porno movies, also dressed up as a policeman[282].

Father-of-four Anthony James, 30, was almost jailed for posing as a traffic cop in his Peugeot, which he fitted with blue lights and a siren to stop other motorists, whom he lectured about their 'poor driving'. A van driver with an obsession for police cars, he was given a community service order[283].

A young mother was car-jacked in Bolton by a man posing as a police officer, who drove off with her baby. The car was soon involved in a hit-and-run, and a man arrested[284].

A joke 7ft-tall scarecrow, placed at a Norfolk roadside to promote a festival and road safety, and dressed as a policeman with a fake speed gun, was 'arrested' because a WPC felt it was 'inappropriate'. She removed it in her patrol car as she considered it a hazard. As a result its maker reported it stolen (the police had given the go-ahead to display it)[285].

Respected Scottish charity worker (Red Cross volunteer) Ian Scott, 58, pretended to be a policeman (using flashing blue lights, a siren and fluorescent jacket) to terrorise a female driver because he thought she was driving too slowly. He tailgated her and forced her to pull over. He was fined, given community service and banned from driving[286].

A bankrupt 6ft 4in Walter Mitty, self-styled 'Commander' Michael Newitt, 41, pretended to belong to the Counter Terrorism Unit of the Met and even managed to trick real policemen. He conned a sergeant at Leicestershire's Hinckley police station into supplying him with a new pocket book. He got a drink driver prosecuted after stopping him using a siren and strobe lights on his Volvo. Police confiscated handcuffs, a baton, air pistols, thunder flashes, police radio handsets and shredded identity documents. He had completely deceived his wife. He was given two years[287].

Glasgow accountant Andrew Ramsay vanished in 2006 after he was apparently handcuffed and driven away by two men posing as police officers. His skull was found in the Clyde in 2007[288].

Two impostors stole cash from at least three Glasgow OAPs after tricking their way into homes using fake police IDs[289]. Armed raider Philip Bradley, 40, gained access to a Cash Generator shop in Airdrie by using fake police ID. He was jailed for 5 years 3 months[290]. Two thieves posed as police to steal £1,300 from a Fife man in his nineties[291]. Four thieves dressed as policemen to smash down a door in a fake police raid in 2008 as a cover for an aggravated burglary. There had been a burglary at Greenwich Police Station in 2006 when uniforms were stolen[292]. Two bogus plainclothes policemen stopped, searched and robbed a 16-year-old in the centre of Edinburgh[293].

Big Brother 'housemate' Mario (real name Shaun Astbury) bragged to an impressionable teenager that he was a Scotland Yard detective before luring her into bed. He was actually a postman[294].

Struggling Scottish businessman Ian Lowrie was arrested for wearing an item of police uniform without a satisfactory explanation. He was dressed as a chief inspector (wearing appropriate epaulettes) on a former police motorbike in an attempt to help his security escort business[295].

One of Jeremy Beadle's favourite disguises to con victims was that of a policeman[296].

Conman part-time soldier, Maurice Mennie, 29, claimed he was a military policeman in order to sell bogus medals and uniforms on eBay[297].

The Old Bailey heard (2007) of a bogus police gang who ordered a manager to open his Tonbridge, Kent, Securities depot, resulting in a multi-million robbery. As he drove to work he was stopped by what appeared to be a police car. The gang were not only dressed like police but wore theatrical prosthetics. The stolen £53 million represented Britain's biggest ever bank robbery The fake police tricked the manager's wife into coming with them by pretending her husband had been in a car crash[298].

Two bogus policemen driving an unmarked car demanded a spot fine after accusing a motorist of using his mobile while driving in Stirlingshire[299]. Three fake policemen pulled over sober motorists in Bearsden and Lennoxtown near Glasgow in 2010 and made them perform sobriety tests, count backwards and recite the alphabet[300]. Phoney traffic cop Robert Connolly, an electrician, converted his old Vauxhall Corsa into an unmarked police car, which he used to stop a woman in a Volvo. He had fitted blue lights and a siren, but the latter alerted real patrol police, who arrested him. He was given a 12-month community order and community service[301].

Friends Victor Gray and Lee MacInnes, who posed as Edinburgh police to impress girls, were given community orders. They stopped a 19-year-old and took the names of her and her passengers. When caught by police they had an electric siren, blue lights, radios and a microphone. MacInnes had dressed as an officer[302].

A small group of part-time anarchists called Space Hijackers, who dressed in boiler suits, hoods and the occasional riot helmet, have been charged with impersonating police. Critics say the CPS, in a misjudged attempt to justify police tactics, used a charge normally reserved for conmen to make 11 of the group of students and young professionals face a four day trial at huge taxpayers' expense. None of the defendants' witnesses believed they were police[303].

Two gangland enforcers, Matthew Parr and Adam Woolf, pretended to be policemen to enable them to kidnap and torture a victim who owed a large sum to an underworld boss. They told him he was being arrested for smuggling and shot him repeatedly with a Taser. They were jailed for five years at Lincoln Crown Court[304].

Two Essex burglars high on drugs dressed up as cops to invade homes and attack the occupants with a hammer. They knocked at doors in Chelmsford calling out: 'It's the police. Open up'[305].

Three men posing as police in 1960 stole a lorry loaded with gin from the London Docks. They kidnapped the driver[306].

The Met quietly bought up the entire wardrobe of 'The Bill' to stop criminals acquiring uniforms that would enable them to impersonate officers. The show was the longest running (27 years) TV crime series. Authentic clothing can be bought by anyone on the internet. In 2009 over 100 stolen uniforms were seized in Greater Manchester – they had Met badges sewn on. They were used by two impostors pretending to be drug squad officers targeting dealers. The year before, Stephen Downing wore a police issue jacket with a Derbyshire constabulary armed response vehicle badge bought on the internet, to give the impression of being a policeman: he was given the maximum £1,000 fine[307].

A Lanarkshire householder was robbed of his £20,000 life savings after three bogus cops conned him into allowing them into his home. They wore high-vis jackets and said they were probing a robbery[308]. Serial burglar Martin Maloney (he confessed to nearly 600 break-ins) committed over 100 'distraction' burglaries when released on bail: posing as a policeman he entered pensioners' homes and stole their money. He would flash what seemed to be a police warrant card[309]. A gang of bogus cops beat up two Britons outside their home near Benidorm. The four men held police badges and used guns[310].

THE BOGUS POLICEMAN

A bogus 'Midlothian Policeman' tried to deceive an Edinburgh legal firm into donating to a 'police magazine' which benefits local children[311]. A bogus cop tried to con Perth and Kinross residents by asking for cash payments for fake ads in a police magazine[312].

Princess Margaret was allowed a blue police lamp on her Rolls-Royce[313].

An elderly Stirling woman was defrauded of over £10,000 when bogus police told her to move cash out of her bank account[314]. A bogus Dumfries and Galloway cop conned an 85-year-old woman out of £40,000[315].

Hitman Raymond Anderson and his brother pretended to be coppers (with uniforms and fake search warrants) to gain entry to victims' houses in at least 12 raids across Scotland. A Dumbartonshire plainclothes PC, John Watters, was suspected as being an accomplice, but it was decided to drop charges against him. 'The top brass were acutely aware of the damage it could do to the force's reputation if the full details emerged'. Thus a car found at the Stirlingshire robbery of a former CBI Scotland chairman was registered to Watters' wife – Watters' explanation was that he was having an affair, and his alibi was never checked. Another robbery could only have been accomplished by information from Watters about the whereabouts of a safe key. The best man at Watters' wedding was a gangster smuggling guns into Scotland. Watters was charged at Stirling in 1996 with assault and robbery after ID parade evidence, but the case was dropped even though police traced calls between him and Raymond Anderson. Watters resigned before he was due to face five charges of discreditable conduct. The gang illegally monitored a police radio. Though informants had pointed to Watters he was never put under surveillance (because of his police connections?). Robert Anderson, whose hitman brother is serving 30 years for murder and who has convictions for burglary, gun crime and police assault, used fake police IDs and warrants to access old folks' homes. He locked them in a room and stripped their house of valuables. In the nineties the Anderson gang wore police uniforms. On occasion Anderson used the name of a real cop to accuse householders of selling illegal passports. Anderson was given six years in 2013[316].

A gang of bogus cops struck more than 40 times in the Strathclyde, Grampian and Central Scotland regions. A 77-year-old victim was phoned by a man claiming to be a policeman saying her debit card had been found in the possession of an arrestee: a 'bank worker' then called to confirm the situation. Another 'police officer' then told her to transfer all her funds to a 'secure police holding account'[317]. Two bogus Lanarkshire cops persuaded two old folks to hand over thousands of pounds (one was an 81-year-old who gave them a four-figure sum to be sent to be 'security marked')[318].

A fake dog warden in a hi-viz jacket has been issuing £50 on-the-spot fines in Ramsgate, Kent. He has targeted people letting their dogs off the lead[319].

Glasgow forensic scientist Professor Allan Jameson was sacked by Lothian and Borders Police (he was in charge of their lab) over an incident that led to a criminal conviction. He placed a woman motorist in a state of fear and alarm, having (allegedly) waved her to the roadside and lectured her on her driving (he showed her his police-issue ID). He was fined £300 at Airdrie Sheriff Court, and allowed to return to work for the force with a warning. He then left to set up his one-man Forensic Institute, giving advice on a private basis challenging convictions based on DNA, e.g. he gave crucial testimony in the Omagh bombing trial which saw the case collapse. There is growing concern, according to the Forensic Science Service, about how easy it is for people to set themselves up as experts[320].

CAVEAT CIVIS

Engineer <u>Anthony Mitchell</u>, a Sussex Police Special Constable, became a member of a 12-strong gang of bogus British cops, the 'Black Shods', who travelled abroad to shooting competitions using fake ID cards. Mitchell, a quartermaster, reactivated guns for the underworld (one was used for a Brixton murder, another shot at Manchester Police), under the cover of his legitimate business supplying firearms to collectors and gun clubs. He was linked to 130 guns seized from crime scenes, his specialty being 'Big Mac' American submachine guns with devastating fire power.

East European and South American criminals are pretending to be policemen to fleece tourists in Britain, some using fake warrant cards[321].

'<u>DCI Jane Seymour</u> of the Serious Fraud Office' told a couple on the phone that someone had bought expensive goods using the wife's debit card, and that all their cards had been compromised. Using specialist technology the 'cop' managed to record their pin numbers, but was 'solicitous, reassuring and practical', and arranged for a police 'courier' to uplift their cards. £7,000 was purloined from the couple's funds, mostly via Euston Station ATMs. 'DCI Seymour' had an accomplice posing as an emergency services operator[322].

Fitness instructor <u>Kelvin Swann</u>, 49, was accused of pretending to be a policeman and accusing two women of offences. He would pull them over while driving or stop them as pedestrians in St. Andrews, Fife[323]. A woman driver was stopped on a back road near Cupar in Fife by a man not in uniform who pretended to be a policeman. He asked her questions but could not furnish a warrant card. His unmarked BMW's lights were flashing. He agreed to follow the driver to Cupar police station but disappeared. In court in Cupar he denied two charges under the Police (Scotland) Act 1967[324].

During the 2011 London street riots blogger 'Inspector Winter' became the talk of the police social media – he spoke of long shifts, fatigue and fear as he tried to recapture the streets. With over 3,000 Twitter fans he told of a dawn raid to deal with a looter. He even mimicked phrases in 'The Sweeney' TV series. His use of police uniforms, warrant cards and a fake identity was alleged – he was unmasked as serial conman <u>Ellis Ward</u>, in prison for credit card fraud. A number of forces are investigating him for impersonating an officer, being attached to SOCA and a member of the Royal Military Police: he fooled three women, including a special constable whose career was destroyed. Ward carried police paraphernalia – handcuffs, pocket books, witness statement forms, warrant cards, stop and search forms. The BBC and The Daily Telegraph even contacted him for interviews about his harrowing tour of duty. He may also have conned his way into police stations so he could steal documents. His blog scrapline was 'In the Job – Live for the Job'. He spent two-and-a-half years on the run, being pursued by way of Operation Pamplona. He even joined in a police internet discussion forum till he was rumbled[325].

A 16-year-old dressed up as a cop and joyrode a patrol car at 140mph around two counties, following a burglary at the Chieveley Thames Valley Police traffic section station, unprotected by alarms or CCTV. A stab-proof vest, handcuffs, speed gun, radio and breathalyser were stolen by his friend[326].

In 2005 a fake Lothian and Borders cop, teenager <u>Scott Murray</u>, terrorised an elderly couple and child during a long late-night car chase: he cornered them on a farm road near Perth. Murray was jailed for four months[327].

49

Bogus Liverpool cop <u>Derek McMaster</u> romanced two vulnerable women with marriage proposals before raiding their bank accounts. He would appear in a full police uniform with handcuffs and white shirt[328].

Three thugs posing as police officers knocked on a door and entered a house in east London to steal a pedigree puppy, a laptop and mobile phones, after battering the dog owner and attacking two other women[329].

Fife fitness instructor <u>Kelvin Swann</u>, who escaped a jail term in 2009 for a brutal attack on his girlfriend, was given 18 months probation and a community sentence for pretending to be a policeman, accosting women and accusing them of criminal offences[330].

Eight armed robbers disguised as police held up a plane at Brussels Airport in February, 2013, escaping with a huge haul of diamonds (over £30m worth)[331].

A bogus policeman tried to carjack a young mother whom he and an accomplice stopped using flashing blue lights, while she drove on the A90 between Peterhead and Aberdeen[332].

Walter Mitty one-legged bogus Stirlingshire cop <u>David Barclay</u> wore a police-style uniform when he took a woman neighbour on a high-speed car chase – he pretended to be chasing a stolen car, turning on flashing lights, giving the impression he worked for Central Scotland Police. He was fined £1,000[333].

CHAPTER IV

THE CRIMINAL POLICEMAN

CONTENTS

CHAPTER IV

THE CRIMINAL POLICEMAN

It is a great irony that the upholders of the law are themselves so prone to endemic law breaking: it was not before time that in 1998 ACPO set up a Presidential Task Force on Corruption. 'By its nature you do not know how much corruption is there. But it is always there. We just do not know how much is beneath the water'[334]. A member of the Flying Squad has said of villains and the Squad: 'We think like each other'. The Boston Strangler always wanted to be a cop.

Introduction

At a time when Redcoats were used to back up the 19th Century Glasgow Police, they had to be called when a mob stormed a Glasgow factory. The mob was led by ex-policeman Richard Campbell, who was whipped through the town and transported for life[335].

When women police first came on British streets they met with extreme hostility from the male police, apparently because the men didn't want the women to see the wholesale bribery that went on[336].

Are known criminal officers just the tip of the iceberg? Almost certainly, for two principal reasons: only a minority of general public criminals are caught, and with the well-known double standards, police committing the same offences are much less liable to be prosecuted than the public. Officers are likelier to be dismissed minus pension for making a racist or sexist remark ('thought crime') than for a criminal conviction.

742 police officers across Britain were arrested between 2006 and 2008 for crimes such as murder, child and spousal abuse, sex offences (including voyeurism) and drug possession, with the Met having the largest number of arrests (total 304, 123 of these for violence). A City of London officer was arrested for murder, but the charge was dropped. In the two year period 127 West Midlands police (including six sergeants and two inspectors) were arrested (for offences including paedophilia, rape and genital exposure, though assault was the commonest): 61 were convicted. Badger baiting featured in the Northumbrian catalogue of offences. Some convicted police are still serving, e.g. one in Cleveland after a conviction for urinating in public[337].

Liberal Democrat Chris Huhne uncovered (2009) using FOIA police criminality figures which showed that almost 1% of officers have been convicted, with more than 1,000 still serving despite their convictions. The latter include a Sussex sergeant twice convicted of assault and dismissed, only to be reinstated by the Home Office, as well as a Warwickshire officer dismissed for road traffic offences but reinstated (though later coming under investigation for perverting the course of justice). The following were not dismissed: a West Midlands officer convicted of kerb crawling, a North Wales officer who contravened the Benefit Act, five officers (Surrey, Grampian and Kent) convicted for perverting the course of justice, a Leicestershire officer convicted of supplying unclassified DVDs, an Essex officer convicted of robbery, three Cambridgeshire officers convicted of assault, a North Wales officer convicted of forgery. Home Office guidelines debar applicants with such offences from joining the force, but not if they are convicted while serving[338]. More than 40 Scots police were convicted in almost two years from 2009 of crimes which included firearms, drugs, assault, breach of peace, driving and perverting the course of justice offences.

Between 2011-13 hundreds of children, some as young as 12, have been illegally held overnight in Scotish police cells[339].

After Sir Robert Mark became Met Commissioner in 1972 he declared his CID was 'the most routinely corrupt organisation in London'. Mark admitted his aim was to create 'a good police force that catches more crooks than it employs'. The setting up of a criminal investigation unit (A10) led to 450 officers leaving because of, or in the expectation of, disciplinary action[340]. In 1997 the heads of Britain's two top police organisations, the National Crime Squad (NCS) and the National Criminal Intelligence Service, announced a major corruption probe which led to some of their officers being suspended. The London initiative in 1998 led to 57 suspensions and then 35 charges, and almost half of the 43 forces of England and Wales had officers facing corruption/dishonesty allegations: over 100 officers were suspended or charged. Some C1B3 officers were putting their colleagues' lives at risk by revealing their identities to criminals being monitored. C1B3's methods included entrapment and inducements to superinformants, and was criticised for failing in its duty of disclosure to the defence in court actions (this tactic had been responsible for many miscarriages in previous decades). In 2001 it was reported that the NCS had to expel 61 detectives. The dubious practice of getting into bed with career criminals has been highlighted by notorious cases like that of Delroy Denton, recruited by the Met to inform on his fellow Jamaicans – he raped and murdered a young woman in Brixton in 1995. In another example DS Tony Lundy retained a major drug dealer as an informant[341].

Police corruption is pervasive, persistent and affects all ranks: The Police Research Series (Paper 110) rightly asserts that corruption is not explicable in terms of a few 'bad apples', though its 'bullet point' on the causes of corruption fails to mention the 'elephant in the room', that people with criminal tendencies might be attracted to the force. This overlooked cause of corruption is supported by the universal prevalence of corrupt police practices in all societies and throughout the history of police forces. It is thought there can be self-selection for corruption: detectives may be amenable to criminal suggestion by other corrupt officers.

A secret Scotland Yard report revealed (2007) that Met police were taking drugs (especially cocaine, cannabis), associating with criminals and misusing their warrant cards. There have also been a rising number of complaints about racial discrimination. The findings of the Strategic Intelligence Assessment were released on the Met's website by mistake. The outside business interests of police are not recorded on a central register, but debt and financial irregularity issues are identified. Alcoholic (as well as drug) abuse remains a "significant threat to public confidence".

In April 2006 it was revealed 74 Met officers had a criminal record, but despite drink-driving, criminal damage, assault, etc., they were cleared to carry on working. The true number of "serving criminals" is probably higher, because the figure of 74 is only for the years 2000-2005 (another 100 officers left the force following conviction during these years). Even in the case of recalcitrant policemen it is rare for successful prosecution to be brought against a force member. In the same period 33 civilian members of staff received a conviction, with another 38 being forced to quit. PC John Kelly served in the force for four years after lying about his burglary, assault and car crime convictions. (In August 2006 the IPCC was investigating at least 76 complaints against the Met).

In 2007 Greater Manchester topped the criminal cops league with 89 convicted officers. Second was Hampshire with 35, including a chief inspector (criminal damage), a Dorset sergeant (kerb crawling) and a constable (animal cruelty). Devon and Cornwall had a sergeant without a firearms certificate and a PC who assaulted a fellow officer. Importuning in Lancashire, sending inappropriate texts in Northumbria, as well as a burglary, were offences committed by just a few of hundreds of England and Wales officers[342].

More than 940 convicted officers and PCSOs were continuing in their jobs in 2012. Assault, burglary, dangerous driving, drugs, perverting justice, etc. seem to contradict 'proven integrity' guidelines. The culprits include two detective chief inspectors and a chief inspector, all working for the Met. There may be a larger bit of the iceberg, as many forces are unable to furnish details of convictions prior to employment by the police[343].

As many as 10% of prisoners are former service personnel (the official figure is only a third of this)[344], and it is arguable that soldiers and the police share some personality characteristics.

Fewer than a third of law-breaking Scottish cops are sacked, and 156 serving officers have criminal records (e.g. five Strathclyde officers had convictions for hooliganism)[345].

Lying in Court

The first TV documentary filmed inside a British courtroom featured top criminal defence solicitor George More. He claims the police 'often alter statements and concoct evidence to suit the charges. A lot of police make up charges. If they do have some evidence, they will gild the lily. They add little pieces in their notebooks. We should be frank about it'[346]. Ludovic Kennedy showed how British police fabricate evidence, with judges almost automatically believing them and mistrusting juries accordingly. MP Matthew Parris was astounded to learn that, among his many lawyer friends, none doubted that the Met sometimes fabricates evidence. He says it is widely believed the police take short-cuts and may be gratuitously offensive.

IPCC figures show public complaints over 'irregularity in relation to evidence/perjury' have almost doubled in the four years 2004-8, while the number of 'corrupt practice' complaints has almost tripled over the same period[347]. Downing Street conducted a whispering campaign during the cash-for-honours scandal against senior Met officers handling the case[348].

Bent cop Jeff McDermid, who tried to force a confession with threats of violence, was spared incarceration because the Inverness sheriff said it would be too expensive to put him in jail. The ex-soldier had lied in court under oath, as well as to the Northern Constabulary's professional standards and conduct committee[349].

Banffshire sergeant Ewan McHardy was found guilty of attempting to pervert the course of justice, five years after tampering with his urine sample to beat a drink driving rap (he had been suspended on full pay for all that time)[350].

Human rights experts have branded confessions made to Scottish police illegal. Scotland is one of a few European countries where suspects can't insist on legal advice while being questioned[351]. This is now being changed belatedly, so that there may be a large number of appeals for convictions recorded after the introduction of human rights legislation.

Two Lanarkshire community police officers, <u>Neil Jones</u> and <u>Andrew MacRobert</u>, were found guilty and fined for fabricating breach of the peace charges against a law student and his friend. The two cops resigned before they were dismissed[352].

Central Scotland PC <u>Douglas Pishington</u> was charged with trying to pervert the course of justice and suspended from duty in 2010[353].

Merseyside DCs <u>Gary Turner</u> and <u>Austin Heath</u> were dismissed after allowing a heroin addict thief to visit his girlfriend from prison and drink alcohol so as to get him to confess to crimes he hadn't committed. The long-serving officers were planning to appeal (2007)[354].

According to former police chief and drugs tsar <u>Keith Hellawell</u>: "The CID in the early sixties was a heavy drinking world where the detectives acted above and beyond the law - beating confessions, fabricating evidence, doing anything at all that would help them gain the required result ... these irresponsible actions were fuelled by a strong belief among officers that the end justified the means". Hellawell knew what was going on, but admits failing to blow the whistle: he and colleagues would concoct the names of people they had "interviewed" and places they had "visited". Many criminals were quite ready to admit crimes they had not committed, just to win police favours. Policemen posed as other professionals like doctors, lawyers, priests and probation officers to obtain confessions. Hellawell cites a murder case which the officers managed to convince a coroner was a suicide (though the victim had been strangled, bludgeoned, stabbed several times and then gassed).

Special Branch officers involved in the Stockwell de Menezes killing allegedly participated in a cover-up in which the police log was falsified, exonerating them of any wrong doing, "... a deliberate and obvious attempt to smear the firearms officers".

The widow of British police shooting victim Harry Stanby vowed to take the case to the European Court. Chief Inspector <u>Neil Sharman</u> and PC <u>Kevin Fagan</u> faced possible charges of murder, gross negligence, manslaughter, perjury and conspiracy to pervert the course of justice after Surrey Police's reopening of the case, but will not be charged, the CPS saying there was insufficient evidence.

The Butler Report was commissioned in 1997 to examine decisions by the CPS not to prosecute any police officer following deaths in custody. The review was also triggered by a High Court finding that four West Midlands long-serving officers had lied to the judge when they denied torturing a suspect with plastic bags to persuade him to sign a pre-prepared 'confession'[355].

Greater Manchester Police Inspector <u>Mohammed Razaq</u> was arrested (2011) on suspicion of conspiracy to pervert the course of justice and misconduct in a public office[356].

The forensic technique using ESDA (electrostatic detection apparatus) has helped expose police malpractice where written evidence has been altered[357]. With police corruption acknowledged to be 'pervasive, continuing and not bounded by rank', it is noteworthy that police agencies <u>can</u> be reformed. However such reform tends not to last[358]. Police of course do not have a monopoly on corruption, e.g. other officials in positions of authority are to be found in the immigration service, where the alleged scandal of 'bribes for visas' has surfaced[359].

Further instances of police prevarication can be found in 'The Unjust Policeman' chapter.

Traffic Offences

Strathclyde PC <u>Blair Pettigrew</u>, who was allegedly caught speeding (at twice the limit) and who faced dangerous driving charges, claims his force's speed guns were faulty. For his defence he demanded officer notebook pages, speed gun calibrations and details of other drivers caught at the same place. Pettigrew belongs to the elite Football Coordination Unit for Scotland[360].

Police cars have been ticketed parking illegally near New Scotland Yard[361].

A Strathclyde Police traffic warden faced a second probe after he was caught issuing tickets while his vehicle was parked illegally[362].

Met Police Detective Inspector <u>Paul Cheeseman</u> was being investigated by the Director of Professional Standards (DPS) for allegedly trying to avoid a speed camera fine by claiming he was on duty at the time (he is said to have had his daughter in the car). Cheeseman is said to have asked a senior officer to cancel the ticket by saying he was working; misuse of a police vehicle is also alleged. The DPS was also probing Detective Sergeant <u>Neil Allen</u> over claims of fiddling overtime claims and fuel receipts[363].

Strathclyde PC <u>Salvador Glasse-Davies</u> was banned for drink-driving his BMW – the only activity listed on his Facebook page was 'drinking'[364].

Traffic policeman <u>Mark Milton</u>, caught driving an unmarked patrol car at 159 mph, 131 mph and 84 mph (in a 30 mph zone), underwent three trials before his conviction for dangerous driving was overturned, because of his "unusual driving skills". The verdict was greeted with outrage by the RAC and the Royal Society for the Prevention of Accidents.

PC <u>Mark Cuthbertson</u>, who dodged a speeding fine by claiming a Frenchman was at the wheel of his vehicle, was jailed for nine months, for attempting to pervert the course of justice. He denied his guilt repeatedly and exploited loopholes in the system long enough to retire with a maximum pension.

Greater Manchester PC <u>Tariq Mahmood</u> left a woman injured in a hit-and-run smash while he was uninsured. He tried to cover up by spraying his car a different colour and begging his sister and girlfriend to say they were behind the wheel (they refused).

In a year when Derbyshire police handed out 50,000 speeding tickets, 59 of its speeding officers escaped punishment, despite none displaying flashing lights. Nationwide, of 45,741 officers who triggered a speed trap, just 934(2%) were given a penalty ticket or taken to court.

A Police Scotland van displaying an out-of-date tax disc was spotted near Livingston FC's stadium, while a tabloid has claimed Glasgow police were casually contravening parking laws (e.g. regularly stopping on double yellows to buy fast food): an apology was forthcoming from Deputy Chief Constable Campbell Corrigan, saying 'I am ashamed of the conduct of those involved'[365].

Two Lothian and Borders PCs parked their patrol van in an Edinburgh 'loading only' bay so they could buy sausages in a butcher's[366].

Police forces have been known to set up illegal road blocks when dealing with warehouse partygoers in fields.

Greater Manchester PC <u>Daniel Adams</u> fled from colleagues to avoid being breathalysed (a helicopter was unable to keep track of him). The fastest UK police rugby player, he escaped from a pub through a graveyard, but was caught at home five hours later. Convicted of obstructing police he faced the sack[367].

The superintendent who forged and lied on a marathon application form was only fined 10 days' pay[368].

PC <u>Robert Kennedy</u> faced trial after denying (at Inverness Sheriff Court) taking a Northern Constabulary HQ police car without permission, speeding, driving without insurance and driving dangerously[369].

Nottingham PC <u>Jonathan Partridge</u>, soon to have nine points on his licence, fixed false number plates to his motorbike to avoid being caught speeding, as well as using the police computer to facilitate the ruse[370].

Theft

Dumfries and Galloway detective <u>Euan Milligan</u> pled guilty to stealing a cigarette lighter from a police station in 2009. Charges of assaulting two women, using threatening behaviour and forging with intent to defraud were dropped[371].

Policeman <u>Peter Cokell</u>, who has resigned as a PC from the Avon and Somerset force, was charged with shoplifting in a mall where he was on duty[372]. He was seen on CCTV secreting computer games inside his stab vest. He had received a commendation from his commander the year before[373]. He was ordered to complete 70 hours unpaid work and contribute to the costs of the case[374].

Paul Page

Former Royal Protection PC <u>Paul Page</u> faced up to a decade in jail for an investment scam, gambling the cash he persuaded friends and colleagues to invest out of their life savings. He told how Palace officers traded in hardcore porn and steroids, slept on duty or posed for pictures on the Queen's throne. His 'Currency Club' involved police spread-betting on foreign exchange markets, and he set up a bogus property company. He pretended his house and car had been burgled[375]. Police cars were used to escort cash from Page's business, and use of the Palace car park was freely given out. Another Royal Protection Officer, <u>Neil Watson</u>, was being investigated re his moonlighting with several businesses. Another irregular pyramid scheme – the Hearts Club – was run by another policeman until he was moved to Windsor Castle. When Page was found guilty the Met ruled out any further investigation into the Palace police culture[376].

Special Branch DI <u>Amanda McKelvie</u> was arrested and charged with the theft of an M&S leather jacket, but has escaped prosecution, being 'dealt with by an alternative to prosecution', so that no conviction was recorded[377].

Kent PC <u>David Evans</u> resigned from the force after being arrested for allegedly confiscating counterfeit merchandise from car boot stalls and selling them on the black market. He was accused of producing police warrant cards and a forged instrument 'authorising' him to seize thousands of pounds worth of goods, which included copied and pirated DVDs[378].

Nottinghamshire Chief Inspector Kim Molloy appeared in court in 2010 accused of shoplifting makeup from Tesco. She was part of an offender management programme but was suspended. She had been responsible for many special police leaving the force[379]. She was cleared[380].

Over 300 Scotland Yard detectives (almost one in 11 of all detectives) are suspected of abusing their Amex corporate credit cards. Items bought without permission include fishing rods, suits and women's clothing. Some officers seem to have filled in blank restaurant receipts to account for cash withdrawals from cashpoints[381]. In 2009 Scotland Yard awarded an amnesty to over 1,000 Met employees who had misused their corporate credit cards[382]. The 1183 Met employees who broke rules governing the use of American Express charge cards are being given merely 'training and guidance'. Jenny Jones of the Met Police Authority asks: 'What other rules do they break?' Legal action was expected against two officers who owe £1,100 and £82,000, with 50 such cases being referred to the IPCC[383]. The IPCC has had three convictions in 2009-10 of Met officers who fraudulently abused their corporate American Express cards, with six others charged, and the investigation is ongoing.

Gambling addict PC <u>John Fleet</u> was jailed for a year for stealing two winning betting slips from a dead man. Fleet tried to persuade the dead man's sister to drop her complaint about someone collecting her brother's winnings, and he filled in a false log on the Devon and Cornwall police computer. His sentences (for theft and perverting the course of justice) were allowed to run concurrently[384].

Leicestershire PC <u>Aquil Egbewo</u> was jailed for eight months in 2009 for assisting his wife cheat the benefits system over a six year period – he let her claim for the both of them and their child be processed on the pretence that he was unemployed. He denied benefit form signatures were his until expert graphologists proved he was lying[385].

E. Kilbride officer <u>Robert Chestnutt</u> claimed £21,000 in benefits (between 2000 and 2006), despite having a force pension and his wife earning (he had left the police in 1991 because of involvement in a dishonesty scandal)[386].

Sussex Chief Inspector <u>Sharon Rowe</u> and Detective Chief Inspector <u>Jim Torbet</u> were suspended in 2008 over claims they stole bottles of wine. They were bailed pending further inquiries[387]. Rowe was later convicted of shoplifting from an M&S store.

Three Met officers were arrested in 2009 for allegedly inflating their expenses claims while investigating the July 7 bombings. Others sentenced for similar offences were former DS John Gallagher, an alcoholic who received eight months suspended for two years, and former DS Richard de Cadenet, who was given 10 months[388].

Long-serving PC Shawn Pennicott's career was in ruins after he was convicted of a Tesco Clubcard scam (involving scanning a bonus voucher many times, adding up thousands of points: he conned the machine into giving him the points by inserting blank paper). He was convicted of eight charges of going equipped to cheat, given community service and fined.

During WWII police were involved in burgling during the blackouts.

Two DCs were sacked from Cheshire Constabulary, and a third officer reduced in rank, for stealing seized money (they were members of an undercover anti-burglary squad). They remain anonymous. The charges included massaging detection figures.

Central Scotland policeman Gordon Bond sold stolen goods on ebay, pretending he bought the items at a market. He attempted suicide after his first police interview.

Married PC Andrew Reid tried to cover up for his married lover when she was caught shoplifting. He admitted perverting the course of justice by letting her off with a caution after she filled in a form giving false details.

Northumbria policeman Jason Singh ran his own smash-and grab gang to fund his alcohol and cocaine habit. His superiors planted a bug in his car and overheard him plotting crimes, e.g. targeting of ATM machines. He was jailed for six years.

Ex-Met policeman John Morgan, who funded a lavish lifestyle by conning an elderly woman out of nearly £280,000, was jailed for four years (he met the victim, whose home he sold, while still a PC: he was given power of attorney).

Northamptonshire PC Neil Bull allegedly shoplifted a drink and lube from Boots, as well as protein powder and drink bottles on two other occasions. He was to be tried at Northampton Crown Court[389].

It was reported that five Merseyside Gun Crime (Matrix) Unit officers had been dismissed for selling off household goods they had stolen in a raid[390]. Later it was revealed that altogether eight sergeants had been dismissed from Manchester Police's Gun Crime Unit for selling seized items on e-bay[391]. Another three Merseyside officers from a specialist gun crime unit were suspended and bailed, accused of theft from raided homes. Goods from raids were allegedly appearing for sale on e-Bay[392].

A senior Strathclyde officer was charged with stealing £20 of meat from a Perthshire supermarket. Strathclyde Police refused to reveal whether the anonymous officer was suspended[393].

Bruce Brown, a key player in the 1972 Barclays Bank robbery in Wembley, was close to a top policeman – when officers came to arrest him, a sack of cash disappeared from Brown's attic, allegedly stolen by them[394].

When the sister of Daily Mail columnist Tom Utley lost her wallet at Embankment station and retrieved it from the local police station, over £40 cash was missing (it had obviously been handed in by someone, presumably by a member of the public)[395].

A 65-year-old Kent man, a former RAF military cop, was jailed for benefit fraud (£68,000)[396].

Former police officer David Foley received a custodial sentence for his part in the theft of £100,000 from the Dream Foundation charity (which benefited dying children with holidays, etc.)[397]. Trusted Met detective sergeant Louise Ord stole over £35,000 from a police children's charity (Child Victims of Crime) to finance a lavish lifestyle – she diverted charity income into her account instead of paying for holidays for abused children. Ord was jailed for nine months, but ordered to pay only £1 compensation[398].

Hertfordshire DS Charles Moore was jailed for 27 months for stealing £58,000 seized from crooks. He was to face his own proceeds of crime hearing in 2012[399].

Police worker Stephen Bowers and his wife made thousands selling stolen Met property (mobiles, iPods, Sat Navs, Sky HD boxes). The pair admitted theft and handling[400].

A Dedicated Source Unit (DSU) was created to fight bent detectives who would pit informants (sources) against each other, misuse the information gleaned, and pinch some of the reward money[401].

Ex-cop Ian Harrison, 70, now an anti-benefit fraud DWP officer, was fiddling benefits himself in Blackpool (he claimed Disability Living Allowance for a bad back but was filmed out and about with no obvious walking difficulty)[402].

Kent Superintendent Rachel Adams, after being accused of shoplifting in Asda (she was arrested at home hours later), stepped down as vice-chairman of the Medway Community Safety Partnership and was suspended from duty as her commander's job in charge of a population of 263,000. Essex PCSO <u>Shane Alborough</u> was found guilty of stealing from a Tesco store and given 200 hours unpaid work with £600 costs[403].

Fraud squad Detective Inspector <u>Ian Smith</u> stole £12,000 (he was heavily in debt) after being appointed treasurer of the South Shields Police Club. Having a diploma in business and book-keeping he manipulated the records for two years to cover his tracks[404].

Senior Cleveland Police crime investigator <u>Stephen Beattie</u> was arrested on suspicion of perverting the course of justice and theft, in relation to claims he 'undermined' scores of cases: an internal review identified 120 suspicious cases[405].

Cleveland policemen <u>Gary Thompson</u> and <u>Anthony Lamb</u> were jailed for a £10 m. cigarette smuggling racket. The criminal proceeds were laundered by setting up a fake company[406].

Rogue Ayrshire cop <u>Gordon Gilmour</u> pounded the beat in Larys during the day but became a burglar at night (e.g. a bowling club, a hairdressing salon: three other similar charges were dropped). He also had a drink problem[407].

An anonymous MI5 agent, decorated while a senior provincial police officer for dangerous undercover work as well as winning the Queen's Police Medal for bravery infiltrating gangs of drugs pushers and armed robbers, was caught shoplifting perfume. In 2005 another MI5 agent lost a laptop with Northern Ireland secrets at Paddington Station. In 2000 a further secret policeman left a briefcase full of secrets on a train[408].

When former fraud squad DI <u>Ian Smith</u> became treasurer of South Shields Police Club he started to embezzle, Newcastle upon Tyne Crown Court was told[409].

Three veteran members of the Flying Squad (DI <u>Frederick May</u>, DC <u>David Howell</u>, <u>Eamon Harris</u>) were jailed for seven years each in 2001 for stealing £200,000 recovered from a robbery. An informant released from jail to help them had planned to double-cross them.

Burglaring cops in Greater Manchester Police would carry a jemmy and a nail punch (for breaking car windows), sewn into special pockets in their jackets[410].

Glasgow PC <u>Nadim Ahmed</u> was charged with an insurance scam, accused of stealing jewellery from his home and wasting police time in reporting the 'theft', when he had allegedly pawned them. He was also charged with trying to defraud Direct Line insurance of £11,500[411].

Corruption

'Corruptio optimi pessima' (the corruption of the best is the worst of all).

'Falsus in uno, falsus in omnibus' (false in one, false in all).

The police are seen by the public as the most corrupt service sector. In 2003 the Home Office estimated that up to 2,000 officers and civilian staff were "potentially corrupt".

In what could prove the biggest Met corruption inquiry since the eighties, three police whistleblowers allege that a ruthless London organised crime boss involved in 'extreme violence', prostitution, money laundering, fraud and witness/informant/juror intimidation used a Yard 'sleeper' network of five bent former and serving officers to enable him to avoid justice for 30 years. Following a Sunday Times libel victory against David Hunt the claims (in a 54-page legal letter to Sir Bernard Hogan-Howe) have been released. The three complainants say they are suing the Met for failing to act on intelligence that Hunt had taken out a contract on them, their probe into his affairs having been stymied by corrupt colleagues. The trio were also subjected to a £2 million 'misdirected' inquiry lasting almost three years into baseless corruption allegations against themselves. The allegations are dynamite because they are being made by police officers.

'Criminal in uniform' Met police boss Ali Dizaei was jailed for four years for trying to frame website designer Waad al Baghdadi in a row over money[412]. Surveillance suggested Dizaei had associated with at least four major criminals. He was monitored by the multi-million-pound undercover Operation Helios, which showed he was in association with a fraudster and several major crooks suspected of money laundering. There was a suggestion that he took money from a man on bail, apparently for help with a drink-driving charge. Unauthorised links with foreign embassies (e.g. the Iranian), even brokering the sale of a foreign London embassy, were alleged. He sometimes drove a Liberian Embassy car with diplomatic plates. He had the effrontery to advise a Russian millionairess how to cover up a hit-and-run killing[413]. He was the subject of dozens of corruption allegations while at the Met, and is the most senior Scotland Yard officer to be jailed since the 1970s. Yard chiefs had been warned by SOCA about his conduct[414]. 'There was much about Dizaei that reminded Mr. Al Baghdadi [who brought Dizaei down with his persistence] of the corrupt police chiefs in Tehran where the policeman was born.' Al Baghdadi claimed he was offered large bribes to drop the case, subjected to physical provocation, as well as a clumsy attempt by beautiful girls to lure him into a honey trap. He was wrongly blamed for a stabbing, part of a general campaign of intimidation because he crossed the police 'Godfather'[415]. Dizaei was friendly with a suspect Iranian under surveillance by the Serious Organised Crime Agency for being a 'fence'[416], and had a corrupt relationship with bogus race lawyer Shahrokh Mireskanderi. West Midlands Police 'totally vindicated' this tabloid story[417]. When Dizaei was charged in 2009 with misconduct in public office and perverting the course of justice, using drugs and prostitutes and spying for Iran, it was only 14 months after the Met Police Authority promoted him to Commander. In 1999 Dizaei had faced similar charges of corruption, using drugs and prostitutes and spying for Iran[418]. He was cleared of the same kinds of allegations in 2003, as well as a charge of lying about vandalism to his car, which he dealt with in his 2007 book 'Not One of Us'. The latter caused further ill-feeling against him amongst colleagues[419]. When he won his 2011 appeal against his convictions, he was reinstated as a Met commander, but faced a retrial for misconduct and trying to pervert the course of justice. He is suing the police authority and 'a number of senior individuals'[420]. Earlier in his career Dizaei's Iranian employee Ace Bakhtyari, an illegal immigrant who lived in his employer's house, was invited to meet Scotland Yard chiefs such as Tarique Ghaffur, as well as John Reid, Keith Vaz and other ministers. Dizaei took him to the House of Commons twice. Crooked lawyer Mureskandari's lavish Christmas party was attend by senior policemen. In Dizaei's memoirs he claims he was the victim of a vendetta during a £2.2 million corruption inquiry into his conduct and his supporters were harassed in an attempt to discredit him. He could have been stopped from publishing "Not One of Us" under the police disciplinary code. He was also accused of threatening a former girlfriend. He received £60,000 compensation, with all charges dropped, in return for dropping his racial discrimination claim. Sir Ian Blair oversaw the illegal phone tapping of thousands of calls made by Dizaei. The corruption case against Dizaei costing £7 million collapsed when he was cleared of wrongdoing. This was the first case where the police reasons for justifying interception have been found unlawful. In

2012 <u>Dizaei</u> was granted permission to sue his force for racism while on bail (and wearing a tag), pending an appeal against his <u>second</u> conviction for trying to frame the innocent man. He was to call former Yard chiefs Blair and Stephenson as witnesses (his hearing was to last up to 40 days)[421].

IPCC chairman Nick Hardwick says we are becoming complacent about corruption …. 'There are no forces that are free of corruption and you should be most worried about the forces that tell you they are free of corruption.' Technological advances have aggravated corruption, e.g. Met PC <u>Mark Bohannan</u>, with 25 years' service, was convicted of using the police computer system to liaise with criminal associates. Criminals in prison are being bribed (e.g. with conjugal visits) to admit to unsolved crimes. Tory plans to increase political accountability of chief constables will increase the risk of corruption[422].

Historic police scandals include the Turf Fraud scandal (1877) – <u>Chief Inspectors</u> <u>John Meiklejohn</u> and <u>Nathanial Druscovich</u> were in the pay of two crooks who stole fortunes[423]. The mother of gambling entrepreneur John Aspinall, as Lady Osborne (she ditched her doctor husband for a baronet), paid off corrupt policemen. In the 1950s her son also had to pay off Scotland Yard officers to take the heat off his peripatetic venues. Bent police demanded bribes from Soho sex shops in the sixties[424]. Bribes to police ensured there was no action taken against Brighton's gay clubs in the fifties, when homosexuality was still illegal. In the 60s two 'scrap metal merchant' members of the Richardson gang (Eddie and Charlie) covered up crimes by paying police bribes (up to the level of Commander at New Scotland Yard). Corrupt Scotland Yard detectives have been recorded demanding thousands to sabotage a drugs trial, but the force has failed to find enough evidence for their prosecution.

Former Greater Manchester Police DC <u>Stephen Hayes</u> described Glaswegians as 'vermin' in his book 'The Biggest Gang in Britain'. Scots in Manchester were beaten up and framed by crooked cops in a bid to cleanse them from the city. Officers blamed their own thefts on their Scottish scapegoats[425]. Hayes has reported police colleagues in the Greater Manchester Police were into womanising, excessive 'free' drinking at susceptible pubs, voyeurism and thieving. Officer 'Mr. Fix-its' knew who was dealing with stolen property, the best drinking and peeping venues, etc. Shoplifters' purloined items didn't find their way back to the victim stores, or only cheap replicas of same. Burglars caught red-handed would be locked in cupboards till the police pilferers had their pick of 'stolen' items. Police stealing from cars would be let off if caught by a fellow officer. Parking ticket scams were also prevalent when police issued car fines, as well as bribes for traffic officers to be let off speeding fines. Free curries were always available at restaurants involved with illegal immigrants, while cheap jewellery, free butchers' meat, etc. were available on a similar basis. In the days when businesses left their keys in the custody of their local police station, it is said bent coppers would use the keys to steal property at night, then return them to the station pigeonholes[426].

In the summer of 2009 the IPCC was conducting the most significant investigation into Met corruption since the seventies, with six officers suspended from the Enfield borough crime squad, based at Edmonton, North London. Nigerian immigrant David Nwankwo alleged torture by slapping, kicking and waterboarding, and the planting of cannabis in his home. The cannabis charge was dropped because the defence queried the character of the police witnesses, who were the subject of a corruption investigation (a female civilian worker at Edmonton had been jailed for stealing seized items from police stores). The six officers were reportedly caught discussing the Nwankwo arrest by covert surveillance[427].

Nottingham was reported in 2006 as Britain's most crime-ridden city, when, too, 'corruption within Nottinghamshire Police was rife' (e.g. in that year former PC <u>Charles Fletcher</u> was jailed for leaking data to criminal suspects, including details of the Nottingham jeweller murder)[428].

<u>Lord Brian Mackenzie</u>, a former chief superintendent of Durham Constabulary and president of the Police Superintendents' Association of England and Wales, as well as a special adviser on policing to the Home Secretary, was made an OBE in 1998 for services to the police. Labour expelled him in 2013 for offering to do business with lobbyists in exchange for cash. He could arrange parties for paying clients in the Lords and could subvert rules that peers should declare financial interests[429].

Criminals are infiltrating police forces by using Facebook and other social networking websites, such as Bebo, on the back of recruitment drives. In 2008 15 Strathclyde officers and staff members were reported to the fiscal on corruption charges[430].

Dozens of police officers in four north of England forces (Northumbria, Cleveland, Durham and Cumbria) were investigated in 2008, after being reported by their colleagues on the Confidential Reporting Integrity Line and elsewhere. Corruption allegations were included (along with racism, etc.) – one case involved money going missing from the 'found property' department[431].

The blonde lover of Christopher Hague, one of Britain's most wanted gunmen, admits she gave him £2,000 with which he claims to have bribed detectives[432].

A tribunal heard that a black Met liaison officer concealed a six-year relationship with a murder suspect from her bosses, who eventually suspected she had only joined the force to further criminals' interests[433].

The Street Betting Act of 1906 led to bribe-taking by officers: it prohibited bet-taking in the street, but some bookies 'arranged' that police would turn a blind eye to runners. Police also tipped off bookies about impending arrests, with stooges to be arrested in place of runners. A policeman named <u>Goddard</u> was a central figure in the distribution of bribes within Great Marlborough Street Police Station in the early 20th Century. Dismissed from the force, Goddard was found guilty of corruptly receiving money from a restaurateur and night-club proprietor. The fact that senior officers failed to detect what he was up to suggests the 'rotten apple' theory promulgated in police histories can't be sustained. Thus in 1929 two sergeants and two constables at Great Marlborough Street Police Station were dismissed (accepting free meals, associating with brothel owners, etc.), and in 1931 an inspector and 26 constables were sacked from the same station for accepting money, while at least one other inspector and 23 PCs were moved to other divisions[434].

In 1853 detective <u>Jesse Jeapes</u>, who had a long exemplary record, was accused by his sergeant of selling stolen watches. Though cleared and moved elsewhere, the rumours of his corruption continued, and he was sacked in 1855. PC <u>Charles King</u> was also often allowed to work in plainclothes, but didn't cover his criminal tracks as well as Jeapes. As a result of his corruption, the Met Commissioner forbade constables to work in mufti … King was found guilty of running a pickpocket gang and sentenced to transportation the following year[435].

West Midlands PC <u>Osman Iqbal</u> was charged with corruption (running a London brothel, money laundering and drug deals): there were five counts of misconduct in a public office. There were nine others in the gang[436].

Former Met policeman <u>Neil Putnam</u> is a self-confessed corrupt cop and alcoholic spouse batterer. In 2000 he was jailed for several years on 16 counts of corruption. He informed on heavy-drinking corrupt colleagues called 'the Groovy Gang'. Putnam says he was corrupted by a fellow South East regional crime squad officer in 1991, who had stolen cannabis. When a bent detective learned about a drugs delivery, the police would seize it, keep a large portion and then sell it to the snitch, sharing the proceeds. He claims DS <u>John Davidson</u>, his boss at notoriously corrupt East Dulwich police station, was in the pay of Clifford Norris, father of Lawrence murder suspect David (Davidson investigated the murder). Davidson, nicknamed Obnoxious Jock, was arrested in 1999 for corruption (theft and dealing drugs), and another five officers were jailed in 2000 on Putnam's evidence[437]. Putnam says he had protection from senior officers across the force who have not been convicted of any offence.

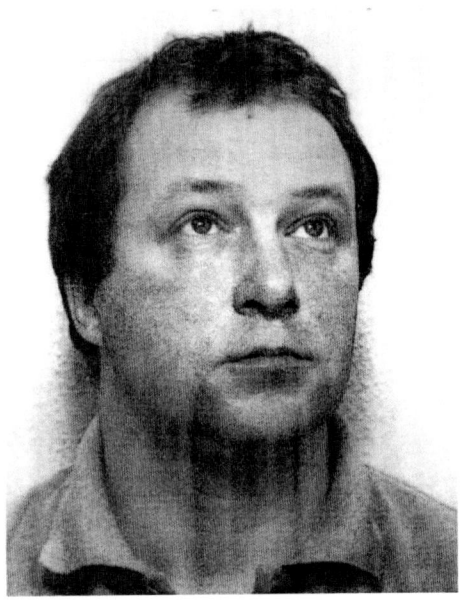

Neil Putnam

Putnam's allegations were never revealed to the Lawrence family solicitors. Davidson was found by the Macpherson Inquiry to have threatened important witnesses, the report concluding that "(the) attitude of Davidson and other officers is to be deplored". D.C. Putnam told a newspaper in 2000 that senior police protected junior officers from being investigated by CIB3, the Met's anti-corruption unit. Putnam, who, like Davidson, had been involved in stealing drugs and accepting bribes for nearly 10 years, decided to turn Queen's Evidence: he claims senior ranking officers "have still not been uncovered". Putnam revealed on Panorama[438] the extent of corruption at the prestigious South East Regional Crime Squad in East Dulwich, lasting nearly a decade. Corrupt officers included DC <u>Bob Clark</u> – he blatantly flouted regulations over the use of informants, e.g. having an affair with drug dealer Eve Fleckney – and Sergeant <u>Chris Drury</u>, who had an alcohol and drug problem. In 1996 the squad raided a house by mistake, thinking it belonged to a known dealer. They stole money they found and planted cannabis to blackmail the innocent occupants. <u>John Yates</u> of the Yard led Operation Russia, being the first to employ a detective as a 'supergrass' – six East Dulwich detectives were jailed for a total of 46 years for corruption[439]. (See Yates entry in the 'The Murdoch Policeman' chapter).

18th and early 19th Century thief-takers often set up innocent men for robberies and burglaries, collecting 'blood-money' rewards once the stooges were executed, e.g. the <u>Stephen McDaniel</u> gang in the 1750s, preceded by a Mr. <u>Wild</u> earlier in the century (the latter was eventually hanged in 1725). The miscreant thief-takers were to be found in both Bow

Street and the new Police Offices. George Vaughan was one of four London officers charged with organising offences such as counterfeiting in 1816[440].

In the 20th Century respected Lancashire police sergeant Salim Razaq, a 'mob boss in police uniform', led a double life as head of a ruthless crime family operating drug and money laundering rackets. Fellow officers thought he was a 'copper's cop'. He stored submachine guns in his home. Police overheard him talking about a key witness in a kidnap case 'being taken care of'. Razaq, known as 'The Enforcer', was simultaneously being promoted while a rising star in a Preston drugs gang. He admitted in Liverpool Crown Court misconduct in a public office, perverting the course of justice (to which his mother also admitted), possession of firearms and ammunition and money laundering[441].

'The Times' was sued by a Met detective accused of taking bribes from Russian exiles. It had been suggested he had accepted £20,000 in return for selling them confidential Justice Department information about attempts to return them to Russia to face criminal charges[442].

A London prostitute claimed that DS Graham Golder had been taking money off her for years, but he was eventually acquitted at trial. His station, Stoke Newington, had a particularly unfortunate history: 'the deaths in custody, the verballing, the planting, the fitting-up (e.g. 'noble cause' corruption, where evidence is fabricated where the police know they are dealing with a real villain), the excessive use of violence, the racial abuse, the theft of dead men's property, the profiting from drug dealing, the skimming of money, the dozens of serious complaints, the hampered complaints investigations, the hundreds of thousands of pounds in compensatory payouts ...' . One woman who died in 1991 in the station's domestic violence unit was stabbed to death by her husband when officers left them unsupervised[443]. Shiji Lapite, kept in a neck hold in a police van in 1994, was the fifth black person to die while in the charge of Stoke Newington police - there was no disciplinary action against officers. One officer, Leblond, about to be charged with expense fiddling, took an overdose, went on long-term sick leave and eventually left the police. The police make an odd distinction between the kind of self-interested corruption of such officers and the "noble cause" corruption of fitting-up people who are believed, for example, to be involved with drugs. Gerry Carroll, a sergeant accused of planting drugs, committed suicide with a police handgun in court toilets. The Hackney Community Defence Association advises people against making complaints to the police, suggesting civil actions are more likely to obtain results. When victims of the police receive substantial civil action settlements, the police invariably admit no wrongdoing. Police officers under investigation frequently exercise their right to silence, and are rarely willing to speak against colleagues.

Met PC Geoff Whitehead was accused of gambling at work, making foul-mouthed remarks about a female officer, selling counterfeit videos, CDs and cigarettes, and kicking sleeping homeless people[444].

Another Met PC, Leonard Fadahunsi, probably of Nigerian origin, who worked in Tower Hamlets for a decade, was suspended in 2013, accused of lying to obtain a British passport (he is said to have pretended to be a British citizen). He was then remanded in custody by Thames Magistrates Court to face trial[445].

Jersey's deputy police chief Lenny Harper, heading an investigation (2008) into child abuse and a possible murder, made influential enemies in the Channel Islands when he began a campaign against 'corrupt officers' in his force[446].

CAVEAT CIVIS

The 2005 AMEX scandal involved Met officers buying stolen personal goods worth perhaps £1 million. By early 2010 six had been charged and three convicted, with investigations continuing. American experience suggests the risk of a greater degree of political accountability by the police – as instanced by the Tories' elected Commissioners – is even more corruption. Popular media-savvy officers would be harder to get rid of. Also, serious criminals could run for office, as the new Commissioners will not be vetted. The IPCC has no power to compel officers to speak with them during investigations[447].

Superintendent Ray Mallon's ('Robocop') controversial Middlesbrough zero tolerance experiment was a failure. While crime decreased, this largely involved improper procedures which could themselves have been unlawful. Policing in Teesside was brought into disrepute[448]. Britain's longest-running and most expensive police corruption probe (Operation Lancet), centring on Mallon, into 60 Cleveland policemen, collapsed after costing £6 million, and has led to demands for a public inquiry into the investigation itself. The Cleveland Chief Constable is now being investigated because of alleged dirty tricks against Mallon: Barry Shaw, who instigated the inquiry, was accused of using MI5 in a campaign against Mallon. Most of the evidence for the 393 criminal allegations - supplying drugs for confessions to assaulting suspects, etc. - came from criminals.

At least 10 officers were suspected of a 'Plebgate' plot to discredit cabinet minister Andrew Mitchell. As well as the Met, West Mercia, West Midlands and Warwickshire may have been involved. A relative of one officer was also arrested[449]. An anonymous male PC in the Met's Diplomatic Protection Group was arrested on suspicion of misconduct in a public office, in connection with 'Plebgate'. The arrest prompted claims of a wider cover-up[450].

Nick Herbert, former police and criminal justice minister, demanded in the wake of the Mitchell 'Plebgate', urgent reforms to the police service to restore public trust. He attacked the 'cancer' of corruption among a minority of officers. 'Corruption may not be endemic, neither is it an aberration'[451].

A Met policeman (thought to be a superintendent) who claims there was a Plebgate conspiracy to 'stitch up' Cabinet Minister Andrew Mitchell has hired a lawyer for his own protection. A police colleague (whose name is known to the press) 'orchestrated' the plot, the whistleblower claims he was told by a superior officer. The new account has been described by the head of Operation Alice as 'serious and highly pertinent' to his inquiry. The whistleblower says the toxic 'plebs' word was added to the original police log. The Met has been desperately trying to trace the whistleblower, demanding Mitchell's lawyers reveal his identity[452].

The biggest problem with using criminal informants is that doing deals with them may encourage corruption (some would say guarantee corruption).

Scottish Crime and Drug Enforcement Agency director general Graeme Pearson told the 2007 Scottish Police Federation conference that Columbia, Italy and some states in the former Yugoslavia and Russia have seen police corruption flourishing, and he expects Scottish gang bosses to likewise target MSPs and police. He reminded his audience that Capone virtually bought the Chicago police force.

When London private eye Daniel Morgan was found in 1987 with an axe buried in his head, police were implicated (the victim's business partner was friendly with them), but no one was ever charged. His brother believes he was murdered to prevent him whistleblowing on police corruption, and says Daniel could not believe how many police officers were bent.[453]. Despite compelling evidence the CPS declined to prosecute anyone. The failure to solve his murder, despite five police investigations, compounded that of the Police Complaints Authority to investigate properly. Police corruption was a major factor in the demise of the first probe. 'The police were silent, evasive, dishonest, arrogant, nonchalant, patronising and insolent'[454].

Bernie Silvers, who arranged the murder of seven prostitutes and earned the reputation of being London's biggest corruptor of police, was defended by Sir Michael Havers, who later became Attorney General. Two of Silvers' character witnesses were Scotland Yard Commanders.

Some of the detectives working in the Brinks Mat robbery squad were promoted into sensitive positions within the force. Inquiries into corruption within the investigation were mostly inconclusive (one senior policeman facing disciplinary charges was allowed to retire abroad through sickness). Scotland Yard is still tarnished with the unanswered questions connected to the gold - at least two unsolved murders, the unexplained suicide of an alcoholic CID man, possible Freemason cover-ups.

Met robbery squad DC Martin Morgan was caught moonlighting for a crook – tracking down a business partner who had robbed him. Morgan and DC Declan Costello were arrested in a sting operation. Morgan admitted conspiring to falsely imprison, while Costello pled guilty to conspiracy to cause actual bodily harm. Morgan used the police computer and a search warrant falsely[455].

The 1920s' nightclub queen of London, Kate Meyrick, kept being fined or imprisoned for bending the rules, so she decided to bribe a Sergeant Goddard, the CID man in charge of nightclub prosecutions. A veteran of 234 raids, he was eventually uncovered by an anonymous tip-off. A later source of police corruption was the restriction on pornography, which engendered much bribery.

The offices of the "Milton Keynes Citizen" were raided by officers from Thames Valley and Hertfordshire in 2007 in an investigation into police corruption and the leaking of sensitive police information. Two police officers and a journalist were among five arrests.

Claims of police corruption over the Mick Jagger drug raid surfaced in official papers released in 2004. The singer alleged that D.S. Robin Constable went straight to a box supposedly containing cannabis, whispering that he could go free for £1,000. But the Director of Public Prosecutions took no action against the policeman because of "insufficient evidence".

At least one officer investigating an 18-year-old student's murder was on the payroll of notorious gangster Clifford Norris, resulting in the investigation being deliberately botched. The "Norris factor" emerges at key points in Sir William Macpherson's 1999 report into the murder of Stephen Lawrence.

In Joel Miller's 2003 assessment of UK police corruption for the Home Office, intelligence (from PSUs - professional standards units) over a one year period from some forces showed about ½ - 1% of police staff were potentially (though not necessarily) corrupt. Individual corruption is documented by the leaking of police information. Internally-networked corruption is less common, and not much in evidence outside London. Miller records an instance of internally-networked corruption within the South East Regional Crime Squad in the early 1990s: a particular team within SERCS at Dulwich called themselves the "Groovy Gang" and were organised around D.C. <u>Bob Clark</u>, who was romantically involved with their female informant. The drug dealing informant would pass on information about rival dealers, so that they could be taken out by her police co-conspirators, who would gain kudos and steal her rivals' cash during raids. On one occasion a cannabis dealer escaped arrest by offering cash and drugs. The team members were being protected by more senior officers turning a blind eye. Corruption is "pervasive", continuing and independent of rank, and is not merely attributable to a few "bad apples". Widespread corruption has been found in New York, Chicago and L.A., as well as New South Wales and Queensland.

Greater Manchester Police DCI <u>Ken Seddon</u> – once head-hunted to root out corruption in Australia – admitted using false instruments to acquire loans to purchase phantom vehicles[456].

Corruption is not limited to just police officers: it also involves those in support roles. 10% of those implicated by intelligence are support staff, both for corruption, and for unethical behaviour in general. This is a finding that is not evident in traditional images of police corruption. Special Constables are also involved. Corruption and other unethical activity involved both detectives and uniformed officers (the latter perhaps less commonly associated with traditional images of corruption). The ranks of officer involved mainly ranged between constable level and inspector level, though there were some examples of higher-ranking officers implicated in corruption or other unethical behaviour. A piece of research by Caless (1999), based at Kent County Constabulary, examined 120 cases of corruption identified by a range of anonymous forces and came to similar conclusions: they included substantial numbers of officers with both detective and uniform backgrounds; over half were constables, about a quarter were sergeants or inspectors, and less than one in 20 were higher ranks (ranging from chief inspectors to chief superintendents). But it should not be assumed that the higher ranks are less often corrupt or unethical. A significant finding of this research is the existence of two broadly distinct organisational forms of corruption: "individual corruption" (by far the most common) and activity which involves more than one member of police staff, operating together, - "<u>internally networked corruption</u>", which appears, overall, to be less common. Special Constables, detectives and uniformed officers preponderate: higher ranks may be just as criminal, though their absolute numbers are naturally smaller, reflecting their proportion of total staff. Small forces and rural areas are just as prone to corruption.

As superiors' attention naturally goes to officers who are not performing well, they neglect the corrupt officers who are often good performers (cf. bogus doctors who are usually excellent performers). Three key features underlying corruption are poor security awareness, a performance-driven culture and protection by police colleagues.

Corruption investigations are especially difficult for several reasons, e.g. they differ in important ways from other, more conventional, types of police investigations. As one investigator noted: '*I've investigated every type of crime there is ... but this is unique.*'

One of the key challenges to corruption investigations, noted by PSU staff in forces with more experience, is the difficulty of using standard criminal investigative techniques against police officers, who are very often aware of such methods, and so in a good position to evade detection. In conjunction with their legal defence teams, they are particularly good at exploiting disclosure rules.

Internal investigations risk being compromised because suspicions can circulate within a force if details become known by staff outside of PSUs, or if investigating personnel are recognised. Such risks of compromise are likely to be greater for smaller forces where there are fewer people, who are better known to one another.

Some PSU staff feel there are particular difficulties in achieving convictions of police staff, at least with respect to police officers, e.g. juries are reluctant to convict officers, there being sympathy for the "Dirty Harry" variety of officer, and some officers evade investigation by claiming ill-health.

The kingpin of the corrupt WWII Folkestone police force - six constables and a sergeant were sacked, the Chief Constable had to resign, and at least another six policemen were probably involved - was P.C. Derek Morgan, who had been burgling houses since 1935. He left the police to set up a furniture removal firm which provided a cover for his criminal colleagues still in the force burgling vacated houses. Other wartime police got into more minor crime, such as the theft of fish.

Three Met officers colluded in arresting a young student at the 2010 protests[457].

Corrupt Greater Manchester cop Phil Berry was jailed for four years after admitting conspiracy to commit misconduct in a public office. Berry, while working as an undercover drugs squad officer, received from a gangster a £20,000 BMW and Premier League match tickets in return for a list of rival drug dealers in Bolton[458].

Sussex PC Darren Graysonmark helped his drug-dealing partner launder money[459].

A young mother was arrested for smoking cocaine by an officer from the notorious Stoke Newington station; she alleges he was a 'bent copper' and framed her for selling crack, so that she ended up in Holloway. The officer committed suicide[460].

Some 19th Century officers became involved with organised gangs who stole expensive dogs[461].

Some agencies are averse to accepting anonymous reports of corruption, and there are prominent examples of police being openly antagonistic towards members of the public alleging corruption[462].

PI Jonathan Rees has confessed he paid police for information and spied on senior officers who were targeting his agency over 'suspected links to a corrupt circle of south London police'[463].

Scotland Yard's 'Supercops' – five hard-drinking Flying Squad gang members who ripped off villains – were behind bars in 2003 after the UK's biggest –ever corruption probe. They stole £200,000 from a £1.4m robbery, raided a Royal Mint bullion van and packed £70,000 in coins into their car boots, filched £14,000 from a box under a criminal's bed, skimmed money off amounts seized by other police, making up the deficit with forged notes, planted evidence from a 'first aid kit' containing balaclavas, guns, etc. One of them parked his stolen Mercedes in police station yards. CIB3 set up a sting (Operation Ethiopic) which trapped <u>Kevin Garner</u>, who was ex-Army and had passed out of Hendon with the highest-ever exam results: he decided to whistleblow and take medical retirement. In 2001 DI <u>Fred May</u>, DS <u>Eamon Harris</u> and DC <u>David Howell</u> were found guilty of conspiracy to steal and trying to pervert the course of justice. Garner and <u>Terry 'Meathead' McGuinness</u> – who once sparred with Frank Bruno – got seven years after pleading guilty to 19 crimes (stealing cash and drugs, handling stolen goods and perverting the course of justice)[464].

Gordon Goody, probably the mastermind of the Great Train Robbery, says there was no evidence to link him to it, but the police produced 'incriminating' shoes he hadn't worn during the heist[465].

<u>Ronnie Howard</u>'s book 'Ronnie's Looking For Trouble' is an account of his time as an undercover West Midlands copper. He has been a gun-runner, contract killer, drug smuggler, football hooligan and thief. He claims corruption was rife throughout the force – he describes 'doing a screw' (planting drugs) and skimming informants' payouts (e.g. a lot of his fellow officers would take half)[466]. A colleague even suggested framing the band UB40 to make themselves more high-profile.

In 2002 the Met exposed a corruption ring in the force involving two civilian staff passing information about secret operations as well as officers' details to Yardie gangsters, with whom they were thought to be having relationships[467].

Bent Pakistani Muslim Met PC <u>Zeeshaan Chaudry</u>, regarded as a role model for young people, offered fake driving licences and passports and drugs seized from dealers. He was even willing to plant terrorist devices on gangsters' rivals, then arrest them, and he could get police badges made in Pakistan[468].

Brian Paddick says when he joined the Met some of his colleagues were corrupt, violent, bigoted drunks.

PC <u>Mark Bohannan</u>, jailed with his wife for corruption, became her drug pusher's 'Man Inside the Met' – she received free cocaine for six years in return for secret information he passed to the dealer. Bohannan carried out 475 illegal checks via police databases for the drugs baron. He was jailed for three years[469].

Tun Lee, a former SOCA intelligence officer, claims the agency is riddled with corruption and bureaucracy (he has informed the IPCC), e.g. a probe into a crime boss was dropped when a new officer (with alleged links to the suspect) took over the case, while a claim of serious sexual misconduct from a female SOCA employee was covered up. In a training exercise a 'blacked up' white actor played the suspect, and recruits were abused while being selected. A major case collapsed because of non-disclosure. Targeting several top criminals was dropped because it was 'too difficult'. A suspected Notts 'Mr. Big' may have got off the hook because of contacts inside SOCA (the businessman allegedly used his police contacts to run a drug dealing ring). Surveillance is run 'by committee', allowing criminals to escape because of their tardiness. Lee says he was assaulted in a SOCA selection course, and on a surveillance course instructors swore profusely (this was part of a 'scalping' policy toward candidates they wanted to fail). Another accusation is of 'industrial tourism' – flying out on a drugs pursuit and having a holiday driving back. The NPIA* denied Lee's allegations in respect of the training course[470].

During the 1970s an anti-corruption inquiry saw over 70 officers from the Obscene Publications Squads investigated.

Met detectives had 1,400 credit cards confiscated in 2008, after a corruption inquiry found almost £2m unaccounted for[471].

A haulage firm boss was suing (2002) Humberside Police for £5 million because he claimed he was forced to flee Britain after a botched sting left him bankrupt and homeless. Each time he was asked to smuggle drugs by dealers he refused, but instead of helping him the CID asked him to work as an informant. 20 writs against officers accuse them of corruption, entrapment and abuse of power[472].

The University of Sussex is launching an MA in Corruption Studies[473].

Bob Quick, the former head of the Met's anti-corruption unit, admitted to Leveson that he pressured The Guardian to halt its probe into possible corruption in the Stephen Lawrence inquiry. The two journalists involved left the paper to publish their material about police corruption in their book 'Untouchables'[474].

One of three senior Cayman Island officers, ordered to take indefinite leave by the Governor after a corruption investigation, was 'love rat' former Strathclyde officer married Stuart Kernohan, the Police Commissioner (i.e. he was in charge of the force). He had been acting chief constable of Merseyside just before taking up the Caymans appointment. The suspensions were 'to facilitate inquiries' by police in the UK. While a Strathclyde officer he had become involved in a love triangle with a murder witness. There was fallout from a corruption probe into deputy police commissioner Anthony Ennis and the layman Net News editor (they were cleared), which may have compromised Kernohan and another two suspended officers, deputy commissioner Rudi Dixon and Superintendent John Jones[475].

Ali Dizaei was released (2012) from prison just two weeks into his three-year sentence for corruption. He was expected to be formally sacked after a police hearing[476].

Strathclyde Chief Constable Stephen House told the Leveson Inquiry that he had 'no doubt' there are corrupt officers in his force. His force had instigated 45 probes into information leaks in the previous five years, mostly about celebrities[477].

Officer 'A' tells of the corrupt and criminal Western Australia police force, running the full gamut from stealing and disclosing confidential data to perjury, drug trafficking, etc: the force wasn't getting to grips with the problem, corrupt officers still being employed while Officer 'A' was there. Former WAPOL officers confirmed illegal behaviour of all sorts (assaults, sexual/racial bullying, intimidation, etc.): their reports are to be found in the Perth press[478].

Some nightclubs have a register for cops to facilitate their queue-jumping.

---

* NPIA = National Policing Improvement Agency

Officers with power to authorise surveillance applications may give blank pre-signed authorities to trusted detectives, even though this, of course, is illegal. One who did this regularly briefs the Cabinet.

Senior officers turn a blind eye to corruption below them in case exposure reflects badly on them.

A gay officer who stole seized drugs from his force's evidence stores was allowed to resign quietly, as was a sex pest officer who was known to have been arrested in a kerb-crawling sting but was still allowed to join the force[479].

A senior Flying Squad officer has claimed of his officers and the villains: 'We think like each other'. They referred to the anti-corruption unit, A-10, as 'The Gestapo'.

London villain Rusty Humphreys always said he didn't corrupt the police – they corrupted him! Top detective Virgo expected a monthly backhander of £2,000 (worth much more now).

It has been alleged under privilege by lawyer Mike Schwarz at a parliamentary committee he had evidence that detectives from the Met's Proceeds of Corruption Unit took bribes of up to £20,000 for information about a fraudulent Nigerian population – a few senior officers who controlled anti-corruption inquiries were accused of leaking data for cash to PIs[480].

Met PCSO George McNaught, awarded the commendation of the High Sheriff of London, was jailed for six months for issuing hundreds of fake fixed penalty notices to people whose names and addresses he found on lost property items[481].

A detective and three former PCs were arrested (May, 2012) for bribing Met colleagues[482]. A global corruption survey found 8% of UK interviewees claim to have bribed a police officer[483].

Scottish drug criminal Eddie Lyons spoke to Strathclyde PC John Cameron so frequently that his nickname was The Special Constable. Many think he was a registered police informant[484].

Met CID officers and PIs allegedly hacked Government minister Lord Malloch-Brown, Cressida Dick and a senior female civil servant. It is claimed the police were members of SCD6, the anti-corruption unit being probed over bribery[485]. A serving officer and three ex-officers-turned-PIs were arrested about illegal payments.

Though Cleveland's chief constable Sean Price was dismissed (October, 2012) for gross misconduct, he retains his full pension (up to £128,000). His sacking means the allegation that he abused his force credit card and covered up the arrest of his wife, DCI Heather Eastwood, for being drunk and disorderly, did not proceed. He could still be prosecuted for corrupt procurement. He was described as a shameful liar by the IPCC. The last chief constable to be sacked (Stanley Parr of the Lancashire force) had been perverting the course of justice in cases involving his Masonic cronies[486].

Private detective agency RISC Management was being investigated for allegedly bribing Met officers to obtain inside information for wealthy clients. A list of their paid confidential sources, uncovered among computer files, was being kept secure in Gibraltar by Risk Solutions, a management company. Anti-corruption detectives will demand the list through the courts if it is not surrendered. Two RISC executives allegedly bribed SCD6 (an anti-money-laundering unit) officers (e.g. constable John MacDonald) for information. The executives were former Met detectives Keith Hunter and Cliff Knuckey: MacDonald has been arrested and placed on restricted duties[487].

Corruption allegations have been added to the mental instability and adultery claims against Michael Todd, the late Chief Constable of Greater Manchester. He may have been engineering extortionate 'redundancy' payments or promotions for colleagues who helped cover up his philanderings. An inquiry had cleared him of financial malfeasance, but it has now been revealed some aspects of the inquiry were not disclosed in the inquiry report, e.g. a computer containing explicit sexual videos of Todd and his lover, most of whom apparently didn't know they had been filmed[488].

Moves against police corruption were to be announced by Home Secretary Theresa May in 2013[489].

About 800 Met officers have been found guilty of crimes or misconduct in four years (17 quit over sex attacks, 43 accused of corruption – 37 were proved – 18 quit over drink driving). In the same period 111 West Midlands officers resigned while under investigation[490].

The corruption revealed in the 2002 Home Office paper 'Police corruption in England and Wales: An assessment of Current Evidence', is 'still likely to be simply the tip of the iceberg…'. Examples include police thieving during raids, and using their power to obtain money or sexual favours. 'Information compromise' has largely replaced the 'traditional' type of corruption, i.e. groups of detectives in specialist squads involving dishonesty with informants, now largely confined to the Met[491].

A Strathclyde cop's estranged wife shopped him to his superiors, leading to a corruption probe (Operation Asteroid), with, allegedly, cash and drugs found in officers' lockers. Belongings seized by the Glasgow crime task force could not be traced when their owners claimed them. It was one of the biggest internal probes ever in the force's history[492].

Veteran Met DC Martin Morgan was jailed for seven years, his friend DC Declan Costello for 30 months, for forming an unholy alliance to kidnap and torture a criminal's partner. They were trapped in a sting by the Met's anti-corruption unit. The judge said: 'The poachers and gamekeepers became indistinguishable[493].

In another Flying Squad case former DC Kevin Garner became a supergrass for six years against former colleagues. Ostracised and segregated in prison, he caused the collapse of a major corruption trial against four colleagues because he could no longer cope with the stress. 16 of the 50 officers at the Squad's Rigg Approach offices were suspended, but a few suspensions were lifted (three were convicted, three dismissed or resigned, six retired)[494].

Tory MP Geoffrey Dickens' explosive 50-page dossier highlighting paedophiles in high places referred to the notorious Elm Guest House, as well as police corruption. The copy he gave to the Home Office in 1984 seems to have vanished, and his family destroyed their copy on his death[495].

Disgraced former Met commander <u>Ali Dizaei</u> lost his 2013 appeal against his conviction for framing an innocent man for assault in a row over money[496].

When Nigerian James Ibori was sentenced to 13 years in London for corruption, the solicitor (Mike Schwartz) for another arrestee alleged the Proceeds of Corruption Unit had itself been corrupted: 'cash £5000 for information' had been found itemised in a ledger, but detectives may have accepted bribes of up to £20,000 from PIs[*]. Ibori had defrauded the Nigerian state of over £150m.

Ex-cop <u>Stephen Hayes</u> says fabrication of evidence happened every day at various levels of the Greater Manchester force[497].

Former Hampshire WPC <u>Rebecca Swanston</u> was charged with giving criminals confidential information to undermine her force's investigations. She was also accused of not reporting a case of possession of Schedule I drugs (and the culprit's confession to assault with a weapon). She was sacked after a 2012 misconduct hearing. She had been arrested with another WPC who soon resigned[498].

SOCA's submission to Leveson pinpoints police corruption and perverting the course of justice. Investigating officers obtained The Blagger's Manual, which outlined the best way for the police to access private details from HMRC, banks, utilities and the NHS. SOCA took six years to act on its dossier[499].

Over 4,000 officers have committed criminal offences in the last five years, being sacked, forced to resign or otherwise disciplined (gun-running, drug pushing, sex crimes, domestic violence, fraud, drink-driving and shoplifting were some of the offences). Criminality is getting worse in the police[500].

Spousal Abuse

PC <u>George Park</u> was accused of chronic domestic abuse (e.g. cutting up his partner's clothes, throwing her to the ground, pummelling and stabbing his spouse). He and his mother were also accused of trying to pervert the course of justice by instructing two children to give false information to police. Park was remanded in custody because of allegedly breaching bail.

'Hero' Northumbria PC <u>David Rathband</u>, blinded by fugitive gunman Raoul Moat, was later arrested by his own force on suspicion of spousal assault, while suing the force for 'abandoning' him.

DC <u>Warren Wattie</u> was convicted at Aberdeen Sheriff Court of two throttling attacks on his wife.

Somerset police traffic officer and marksman <u>Terry Hatton</u> assaulted his wife because there was no bread to make toast: he used a police manoeuvre to grab her arms. He was given a year's conditional discharge, which meant he could keep his job[501].

---

[*] PIs = Private Investigators.

Breach of Peace

Detective Sergeant <u>Scott Douglas</u> was accused of assaulting a man in a bar in Ayr in 2009, but found not guilty. However, he <u>was</u> fined for committing breach of the peace at the pub[502].

Special Lothian and Borders policeman <u>John Neilands</u> was arrested after he and a group of friends allegedly caused mayhem when refused an after-hours session at a pub. Pub staff claim he demanded access by flashing his warrant card.

Acting DCI <u>Neil Thompson</u>, head of Scotland Yard's elite Paedophile Unit, was arrested in 2005 for being drunk and disorderly in a Soho street after refusing to pay a £60 fixed penalty. Thompson denied the charge but was "medically certified sick" shortly after the incident.

An anonymous Strathclyde policeman has been charged with sectarian breach of the peace and suspended from duty. This was in connection with YouTube footage of Rangers fans trashing toilets at Celtic Park, mocking the death of a former Celtic legend and chanting: 'If you hate Strathclyde Police, clap your hands'[503].

Assault

Kent Detective Sergeant <u>Ollie Tingley</u> was jailed for 90 days for threatening a man with an eight-inch blade during a raid. The head of his area's robbery squad, he and DC <u>Luke Barlow</u> (given 300 hours' community service) were found guilty of common assault, with beating of their victim, an arthritis sufferer[504].

In 1964 the Flying Squad's <u>Harold Challenor</u>'s arrest record was second to none, but defendants claimed to have been beaten. He was caught stitching up a member of the National Council for Civil Liberties by planting drugs. In 1989 the West Midlands Crime Squad was disbanded for misconduct (e.g. a manslaughter conviction was overturned after detectives handcuffed the victim to a chair and put a plastic bag over his head to elicit a confession).

Three policemen from Reading's drug-related violence team Operation Falcon were sacked in 2007, and one had to quit following allegations of assault and criminal damage. The breaches of the discipline code related to use of force, abuse of authority and dishonesty. Thames Valley Police refused to name the officers.

Inspector <u>Mahmood Sabri</u>, of the RAF Auxiliary Police in Egypt, had his own office in the vast British Moascar army base. His senior officers made themselves scarce when their enforcer (Sabri) was questioning Egyptians suspected of theft or terrorism.

PC <u>Peter Lightfoot</u> served seven months of a three-year sentence for beating up an arrestee – he was caught on video.

In 2008 the car of Jonathan Billingshurst, who had no history of violence, was attacked in North London by the Met's Police Detective Crime Squad with baseball bats. The officers pretended the assault was intelligence-led. The Enfield crime squad has been involved in 43 questionable incidents, with 16 officers being questioned.

West Yorkshire traffic cop PC <u>Keith Empsall</u>, with 24 years on the force, jailed for two months after being filmed punching and kicking an arrestee, was released pending the outcome of his appeal[505].

An anonymous West Yorkshire officer was to face a misconduct hearing after an alleged assault on an Asian which triggered rioting in Leeds in 2001, the Police Complaints Authority (PCA) announced[506].

Controversial Met policeman <u>Brian Paddick</u> claimed on an anarchist website that some of his colleagues were 'criminal thugs' who usually 'get away with it'. Writing under his pen name 'Brian the Commander' he was responding to claims of police brutality during the 2002 Millwall football riot. He said: 'I would not like to say what size of minority are criminal thugs masquerading as police officers'[507].

Greater Manchester riot police who attacked a group of peaceful football fans at a pub after a match were condemned by an internal inquiry and labelled 'despicable' by police bosses, but will not be prosecuted because their superiors don't know their names. The PCA (Police Complaints Authority) ruled the supporters had been criminally assaulted, and nearly £100,000 was paid in compensation[508].

Complaints

Complaints against Scottish officers hit record levels in 2007 in most forces but only 1% led to any disciplinary action (only 39 of 3,005 complaints were actioned - 16 were criminal, of which there were two convictions, while the other 23 were given warnings).Complaints against Scottish police again reached record levels in 2008, up by a quarter (from 6,840 to 8,558 cases), an average of one for every three officers. 10 police personnel were convicted of criminal offences, and six subjected to misconduct proceedings for corrupt practice (out of 575 misconduct proceedings 102 related to neglect of duty)[509]. In Scotland police themselves investigate complaints against them (there is no equivalent of the English IPCC), just like the Royal Military Police.

Chief Superintendent <u>Jeanette Joyce</u>, Strathclyde's most senior woman officer and the policewoman tasked with rooting out corruption in Scotland's biggest force, was the subject of a 42-page complaint by colleague Detective Inspector Mike Lockhart. She heads the Complaints and Discipline Unit, which in 2006 reprimanded 20 officers - a further eight resigned in the face of evidence against them. Lockhart planned to sue her as well as Strathclyde's Chief Constable <u>Willie Rae</u> (he claims bullying and victimisation).Joyce gave a damning report into the way the police handled Dunblane killer Thomas Hamilton's gun licence application.

In 1998-99 the Police Complaints Authority investigated more than 4,100 complaints against policemen. In 2005 an official complaint was logged about 20% of police officers (a record of 40,385 allegations - a rise of 16% in a year - were mostly not upheld), with many facing more than one allegation. A further 2,000 civilian staff and community support officers were reported to the IPCC.

Sexual Offences

Lothian and Borders police were asked by Dumfries and Galloway to investigate rapist serving officer <u>Adam Carruthers</u>, amid accusations that senior cops had failed to properly investigate allegations of up to 20 rapes committed by him[510]: Freemason links were a possible reason.

Met DS <u>Nyles Mullin</u> was dismissed for gross misconduct for harassing his ex-girlfriend, a WPC, with abusive texts after she dumped him. He falsely blamed a female colleague (whom he also wrongly claimed to be his lover) for using his phone[511].

Ex-Met police sergeant <u>John Staddon</u>, 76, was jailed for 15 months 43 years after carrying out a "terrifying" sexual assault on his sister-in-law in her home. This is thought to be the longest ever period between offence and conviction. The victim kept it secret through fear of not being believed.

Adam Carruthers

Central Scotland cop <u>Stephen Cooperwhite</u> was convicted of raping a WPC and another female victim (who was pregnant), using physical force on them including punching. He also beat up the seven-year-old son of one of his victims. He was arrested as he completed training at Tulliallan. During his trial he tried to humiliate his victims again by calling them lying 'bunny boilers'[512]. <u>Cooperwhite</u> was jailed for six years.

See also The Lustful Policeman Chapter.

Computer Misuse/Leaks

North Yorkshire Police's Deputy Chief Constable <u>Adam Briggs</u> was investigated for possibly using a police computer to view inappropriate material (28 of the force's officers have been disciplined for computer misuse)[513].

A Reading police community support officer was detained in 2008 by detectives probing an armed robbery in the town – her boyfriend had been held on suspicion. The PCSO – whose name wasn't released – is suspected of aiding the robbery by monitoring her police radio[514]. Reading DC <u>Karen Brown</u> was charged with breaking the Data Protection Act, but she was not suspended by Thames Valley Police[515].

North London (Brent) WPC <u>Keiley Patton</u> appeared in court (2008) accused of burglary and misconduct in public office – passing on confidential information from the police computer and warning a thief of information obtained via her police radio. Other allegations were of obtaining Class C drugs and obtaining car insurance by misrepresentation[516]. She was only jailed for seven months.

WPC <u>Anna Wong</u> was suspended by Lothian and Borders Police in 2009, being faced with 54 charges of illegally accessing personal data using the police computer[517].

Corrupt ex-officer DC <u>John Jones</u> betrayed his colleagues by helping a murder suspect and drug dealer, using information from the police computer[518].

Lanarkshire WPC <u>Jennifer Farries</u> used her force's computer system to view crime reports on her ex-boyfriend, father and brother, as well as other named individuals. She pleaded not guilty and was not suspended[519]. 23 of 26 of the charges were dropped when she made a deal with the prosecutor. Medical reports were ordered on her[520].

Central Scotland PC <u>Gary Chapman</u> was found guilty of perverting the course of justice and multiple charges of illegally accessing files. He had helped a teenager escape a vandalism charge by coaching him what to say to police[521].

A Met antiterrorist (SO15) officer was dismissed after he bugged a promotions exam room (in Kensington police HQ) to give him an advantage over rivals[522].

West Sussex WPC <u>Grania Hale</u> was jailed for 14 months after tipping off a friend about a drugs raid on their house in Haywards Heath. In 2010 she admitted misconduct in public office[523].

E. Kilbride PC <u>Thomas Firth</u> used secret police computer records in a vendetta against a neighbour. He was fined after admitting recklessly disclosing information[524].

Three Northern Constabulary officers contravened the Police (Scotland) Act 1967, while a Lothian and Borders constable was convicted of breaching the Data Protection Act.

PC Gerard McCartney appeared at Elgin Sheriff Court (2007) accused of leaking details of a freed child sex pervert.

Scots PC <u>Paul Dailey</u> admitted using the computer at Kinross police station without consent. He unlawfully accessed the Tayside Police Integrity System, the Police National Computer, the Scottish Criminal Records Office and the DVLA system. Dailey disclosed data to a businessman. His estranged wife claims he secretly ran up huge debts, lied about unpaid bills, and, she suspected, was having an affair with a neighbour[525].

Former Tayside WPC <u>Karen Howie</u> was jailed for 27 months for alerting criminal suspects. She claimed she was blackmailed by her co-accused, who had photographed her snorting mephedrone, threatening to tell her colleagues. She admitted perverting the course of justice and breaching the Data Protection Act. The sheriff accepted that she was suffering from depression[526].

Murderous underworld drugs boss Colin Gunn paid Nottinghamshire Police DC <u>Charles Fletcher</u> and PC <u>Philip Parr</u> to access high-profile cases on the Police National Computer for him (e.g. the Marian Bates murder in 2003 and the revenge murders of the Stirlands)[527]. In a period of just six months alone, the Notts force had to reject six applications to join from persons with links to organised crime: they had been groomed to infiltrate and provide intelligence to crime bosses[528]. Fletcher may have been placed in the force by Gunn as a 'clean skin'. In 2000 a corrupt senior police officer – later jailed for cocaine offences – tried to register Gunn as a major informant. The big question is how many other officers were corrupted by Gunn. Officers were offered double time to patrol Gunn's Bestwood estate, but there were no takers, so the police 'allowed' Gunn to 'police' the estate, like the Met had the Krays[529]. Because 'bent' officers were suspected of working with the deadly Nottinghamshire

Gunn gangsters, Operation Utah (2003) was conducted with the utmost secrecy – 20 undercover 'untouchable' officers were involved. Crooked cops were tipping off the Gunns when a raid was imminent[530].

Married Chief Constable <u>Terry Grange</u> of Dyfed Powys Police stood down after a probe was launched by the IPCC into alleged financial irregularities and illegal accessing of a police computer – it is claimed he sent inappropriate messages to a woman from his work computer. He was ACPO's spokesman on child protection and sex offenders[531].

Greater Manchester Police PC <u>Philip Berry</u>, an intelligence officer with their drugs unit, was jailed for four years for selling secret details of informants to a pusher for cash, football tickets and a BMW. While the dealer got six years, Berry was released because he had served half his sentence while in custody[532].

William Hosie

Bent Tayside PC <u>William Hosie</u> faced a long prison spell for giving a drug-dealer friend tip-offs about police operations for more than a year. Hosie admitted perverting the course of justice and failing to pass on information to colleagues. The pusher had Hosie's number in his mobile phone under the name 'Don Beech', a corrupt detective in 'The Bill'[533].

Ayrshire police sergeant Allan Jackson was charged with illegally obtaining personal data – he allegedly told two constables to check Saltcoats police station records as to whether an individual had a firearms certificate. The information is said to have gone to a sergeant and chief inspector at Kilmarnock[534].

Lothian and Borders Chief Inspector Allison Strachan was charged (2012) with accessing information on police computers without authority (including the force's Fettes headquarters)[535].

A SOCA report revealed how rogue PIs and corrupt cops conspired to access police computers and delete evidence in trials, as well as other illegal machinations[536].

Ex-SAS soldier and bent Strathclyde cop <u>Jeff Jones</u> hacked the Scottish Intelligence Database at Clydebank police station to identify the whereabouts of the supergrass who had been instrumental in the jailing of his lover's brother for a gangland murder. He faced seven charges of illegally accessing the databases[537]. Jones was also charged with demanding money with menaces[538]. He was being probed by the Strathclyde's Professional Standards Unit over allegations he tried to collect a debt for a murderer serving life[539].

Strathclyde Police investigated 369 complaints of criminality against its officers in 2010 (218 cases were of leaking sensitive information) – in 2000 there were only about 20 such allegations. Three officers were sacked in that year (and one civilian), but details about these weren't revealed. The police refused to identify 27 gangs trying to infiltrate their ranks.

A change in police culture over recent years is said to have made it easier to corrupt officers[540].

More than 300 police officers and staff were caught in 2011 misusing the police database, but the low level of sanctions meant that 263 got away with it. One who made 658 checks on neighbours and family just got a warning[541].

Met DCI April Casburn, a counter-terrorism officer, denied ever asking the News of the World for money. She admitted ringing the NOW (speaking to journalist Tim Wood) but denies misconduct in public office[542]. She was jailed for eight months. Casburn was found guilty of corruption (asking for money for information), having tried to undermine her colleagues' inquiry. She was the first to be convicted under Elveden[543].

Met PC Paul Flatley was to be prosecuted for allegedly conspiring to commit misconduct in a public office (i.e. receiving £4,000 in cheques and over £2,000 in cash in exchange for leaking information)[544].

Surrey PC Alan Tierney admitted two counts of misconduct in public office – he told The Sun about Rolling Stone Ronnie Wood's arrest for beating up his girlfriend and about (former England captain) John Terry's mother for shoplifting. A second anonymous cop also pleaded guilty to misconduct[545].

Officers (e.g. Detective Ryan Coleman-Farrow) of the Met's specialised rape (Sapphire) unit would intimidate victims into withdrawing claims so targets could be met. Three very senior officers were involved, two of whom were promoted, with one retired. This was revealed by the ninth IPCC inquiry. As a result of the scandal Kirk Reid, 'the night stalker', wasn't caught and went on to attack 100 more victims[546].

Wiltshire Chief Superintendent Andy Rowell was arrested under Operation Elveden on suspicion of misconduct in a public office (he was the most senior officer arrested by February, 2013, a fortnight after the jailing of DCI April Casburn)[547].

Nepotism/Abuse of Position

In 2010 Grahame Maxwell of North Yorkshire Police was the first chief constable in 35 years to face a disciplinary hearing, over allegations of nepotism during a recruitment drive which attracted 350,000 calls. He allegedly gave assistance to one of his relatives as well as a relative of his deputy Chief Constable Adam Briggs, who faces a lesser charge for his part (misconduct rather than Maxwell's gross misconduct) – see also Computer Misuse, p78. Two civilian police staff

Grahame Maxwell

81

have already been dismissed for gross misconduct (trying to get round the recruitment process for their own gain). A PC has been given a final written warning[548], as has Maxwell (2011) after admitting serious misconduct. Maxwell was accused of trying to 'discredit' his nepotism misconduct investigation (by challenging some senior police figures, and the IPCC's investigators' abilities). Briggs was given 'management advice' and allowed to retire on full pension[549]. 34 years before, Stanley Parr, Chief Constable of Lancashire, had been dismissed after facing 26 charges[550].

In a separate IPCC investigation the Chief Constable of Cleveland allegedly helped the daughter of Police Authority chairman David McLuckie get a job[551]. It seems a policeman whistleblower had contacted HM Inspectorate of Constabulary about the awarding of business contracts (see also next section).

Some officers were social guests of Jimmy Savile at his Leeds home, just as another Broadmoor 'trusty' and sexual deviant, Gordon Rowe, entertained police at his home (see Appendix I). Did the two know each other[552]?

The former chief of the secretive Consulting Association claimed police helped blacklist 3,000 construction workers over 15 years by providing personal details from databases. The IPCC was investigating[553].

Fraud

Nigerian Oluwagbemiga Oshin tricked his way into the Met despite a string of convictions for dishonesty and assault, simply changing his first name. He was jailed for nine months[554].

PC Michael Matts was jailed for a year for lying to his employers that he had cancer, then establishing a bogus bicycle business while on sick leave. He even convinced his policewoman fiancée to bring forward their wedding because of his 'illness'. He produced forged instruments to falsely support his positive financial status[555].

Ex-policeman Paul Johnston became a fugitive gangster. After the failure of one business his Wing Guard firm landed a lucrative contact at the prestigious Glasgow Harbour development[556].

Derek Bonnard, Cleveland Police's Deputy Chief Constable, was dismissed after being found guilty of misusing his corporate credit card and obstructing a bullying inquiry involving his boss, Sean Price[557]. Chief Constable Price and Bonnard had been arrested, as was Caroline Llewellyn, a former solicitor to the Cleveland Police Authority, all on suspicion of misconduct in a public office, fraud by abuse of position and corrupt practice. Mr. Price, who earned around £200,000 a year, including a £50,000 'retention' package, left his wife to move in with D.C.I. Heather Eastwood, 14 years his junior, while Ms. Llewellyn took a voluntary redundancy payment of over £213,000.

Ex-policeman Jim McCormick was arrested in 2010 on suspicion of fraud, with claims that his company ATSC's 'bomb detector', sold to the Government for use in war zones, didn't work[558].

Disgraced ex-cop <u>Robert Chestnutt</u> was freed after serving just one day of a seven-month prison sentence for benefit fraud. He boasted 'he was given special favours because he used to be in the police'[559].

Bigamist conman <u>Roderick Sangster</u> was once a Church of Scotland minister and policeman (with the Met and Grampian forces). He skipped bail, went on the run, but then gave himself up in the south of England. One of his faux pas was forging a partner's signature to obtain a £10,000 loan[560].

WPC <u>Rachel White</u> illegally banked over £13,000 in benefits while working on her beat[561].

One of the BNP leader Nick Griffin's bodyguards was an ex-detective convicted of fraud[562].

Former Humberside PC <u>Stephen Spelloay</u>, a cocaine addict, was jailed for eight-and-a-half years for fraud[563].

Leicestershire Police's acting deputy chief constable <u>Gordon Fraser</u> was investigated (2010) about his involvement with overseas property deals which might lead to allegations of fraudulent misconduct. Two West Midland officers were also being probed after their suspension[564].

Greater Manchester WPC <u>Laura Nagulapalli</u>, a former model and air stewardess, was made to quit the force after being convicted of mortgage fraud. Now living in Australia, she denies being one of philandering Chief Constable <u>Michael Todd</u>'s conquests (he was found frozen to death on Mount Snowdon)[565]. She had become the face of a major police recruitment drive.

At the Newmarket Races in the 1920s mounted police had money tucked into their boots to overlook the antics of various fraudsters, while bookies were giving tips to the beat men. However, bookmaker bribing was much worse in working class districts away from the races, thanks to the 1906 Street Betting Act. At Xmas the superintendent at Hammersmith's 'F' Division welcomed bookies and publicans bearing gifts. The Turf Fraud Scandal of 1877 (Madame de Goncourt case) had involved four top London detectives being tried for a swindle involving fraudulent racing tips. One Inspector <u>John Meiklejohn</u> had been taking bribes from bookies for years. Chief Inspector <u>Nathaniel Druscovich</u> had also been in the pay of Harry Benson and William Kurr, who stole fortunes. The Detective Branch as a result was absorbed into the CID[566].

A Sussex Police constable was jailed for money laundering[567,568].

Merseyside Detective Chief Inspector <u>Anthony Doyle</u>, former deputy head of the Drug Squad who featured in the TV series 'Mersey Blues', was found guilty of aiding his mistress to claim benefit by pretending they lived apart[569].

Chief Superintendent <u>Jim Trotman</u> was cleared in court (2011) of charges of arson, insurance fraud and perverting the course of justice, though he faced an internal probe. He had been arrested a year before in uniform in front of colleagues, having been tipped to become a chief constable[570].

Greater Manchester Police PC <u>Fawad Ahmed</u> used his knowledge as a former RBS cashier to swindle the bank out of almost £½m: 42 fake accounts were opened by an accomplice. He also tried to bribe NatWest staff. He was jailed for four-and-a-half years[571].

Trainee Met PC <u>Mohammed Butt</u>, 45, was recruited by his double-alias wife to defraud three insurance companies by pretending she was deceased. He was jailed for 18 months. His wife ran an Islington off-licence while maintaining two identities for years[572].

Trainee WPC <u>Emma Rayfield</u> and her boyfriend were members of a £4 million car ringing gang: false identities were created for stolen BMWs, Porsches and Ferraris. They bribed a DVLA official to issue false documents.

Top unnamed police trainers at the European Police College in Bramshill (Hants) have been found guilty (by the EU's anti-fraud agency Olaf) of defrauding taxpayers of tens of thousands of pounds, yet no criminal prosecutions have been brought for the fraudulent expenses claims, use of official cars for private purposes, personal bills paid, homes equipped with furniture, abuse of mobile phones[573].

48-year-old ex-Lothian and Borders cop <u>Colin Burgoyne</u> of Edinburgh admitted defrauding benefits in 2006 and 2007. He was given community service instead of a custodial sentence because he promised to repay the £16,938 within a month[574].

Met PC <u>Steve Trendell</u> was given a six-month suspended sentence and 250 hours community work in 2006 for moonlighting as a bathroom and boiler fitter while on sick leave. He admitted two counts of obtaining money by deception[575].

High-flying Met WPC <u>Davinder Gill</u> – on the Home Office's High Potential Scheme – lied that she had been mugged and her handbag containing her mobile phone and Barclaycard taken. In fact, she had left it in a bar during a drinking session. The fake account got her a better model of phone from her insurance company. A jury convicted her of obtaining property by deception (she pled guilty to two charges in 2005 and 2006, and one in 2004, of attempting to obtain by deception)[576].

<u>Roberta Vaughan-Owen</u>, who once worked for North Wales Police, was accused with her sister of insurance, benefit and tax fraud[577].

South Yorkshire policeman <u>Nigel Cranswick</u> was jailed for over ten years for a £330m unprecedented VAT fraud. He and his fellow conspirators faked paperwork to invent bogus sales of mobile phones. He had set up a company while still an officer to generate the paper trail[578].

Tayside WPC <u>Linzi Sherry</u>, who defrauded £6,000 from an insurance company for crashing her car in 2007, escaped a custodial sentence. After the crash she had driven the car to her father's farm, where she hid it for two months before making her claim (she insured it just following the crash with the help of her boyfriend PC <u>Mark McLuckie</u>, who provided the dodgy insurance document). She had repeatedly driven the car without insurance. The pair of fraudsters resigned in disgrace[579].

The Met Police Sikh Association was probed by the IPCC over alleged financial irregularities affecting its social fund. The Association receives £50,000 annually from the Met Police Authority[580].

Despite suspected Met detectives' credit card fraud being flagged up by an auditor in 2004, £2m of expenses were still not accounted for in 2007[581].

Former Surrey WPC <u>Vanessa Turner</u> falsely received over £45,000 in benefits from the UK while living in Australia – she said she was a single mother living in Croydon. The judge called it a 'deliberate, systematic fraud', ordering 160 hours unpaid work and costs of over £2,000[582].

Two Cleveland PCs, <u>Gary Thompson</u> (a Gulf War vet) and <u>Anthony Lamb</u>, were jailed (2012) for illegally importing 60 million cigarettes in a £10 million smuggling racket, laundering their ill-gotten gains through a fake fish tank company[583].

Disgraced North Yorkshire traffic officer <u>Rachel Hewitt</u> was jailed for 18 months after extracting cash donations from colleagues by pretending her daughter had terminal leukaemia. She was also given time off and preferential shifts at work: her bosses didn't bother to check the tissue of lies about tumours, doctors' appointments, etc. They should have demanded the usual proof of illness. The money was used to assist Hewitt's daughters' showjumping careers[584].

PCSO <u>George McNaught</u>, the first 'Blunkett Bobby' to be awarded a commendation of the High Sheriff of London, for pinning down an armed suspect, was jailed for six months for issuing hundreds of false fixed penalty notices. A canister of CS gas which went missing from a police locker room was found at his home[585].

Two ex-cops running a property company were facing jail for swindling clients: former police inspector with British Transport Police, <u>Aime O'Grady</u>, and her husband <u>Eugene</u>, for 12 years a Special Constable in London. They forged documents (including a standing order), stole cheques, and she adopted disguises (wigs, glasses, etc.) to fool the tenants she fleeced. They were found guilty of obtaining property by deception and perverting the course of justice. She was also convicted of theft[586].

Drugs

West Yorkshire Police drugs agency detective <u>Nicholas McFadden</u> and his chief accomplice, his brother Simon, stole over £1m. of seized drugs and sold them back to the streets. His mistress, fellow police officer <u>Tanya Strangeway</u>, was given some of the loot: she admitted money laundering. McFadden, a member of the Organised Crime Group, was jailed for 23 years[587].

Leading barrister Victoria Edmonds-Shakell, who had represented police officers in disciplinary proceedings, was charged in 2009 with supplying crack cocaine and heroin to her husband[588].

Three women police staff, a WPC and a PC were arrested (2009) as part of an investigation into a cocaine dealing ring at a Slough police station[589]. Charges against three of the arrestees were dropped, but PC <u>Matthew Kille</u> and C.P.S.O <u>Lisa Slavin</u>, both of the Thames Valley force, were charged with misconduct and possessing cocaine with intent to supply[590].

Strathclyde Police recruit <u>Patricia Lovis</u> was arrested after a drugs raid on her home – officers allegedly found cannabis plants being grown.

After a serial criminal accused WPC Annett Stone of taking cocaine and amphetamines with him over an 18-month period, she sneaked him into police HQ, boasting she was untouchable because she was an officer. Avon and Somerset Police confirmed she was under investigation in 2008[591].

Former Glasgow PC Michael Norden left the force after being caught with drugs in 2003, becoming boss of a nine men gang which supplied Renfrewshire, Ayrshire and Lanarkshire from its amphetamine factory. Norden was injured by a car driven at him by a rival gangster. He was sentenced in 2008 to eight years, but by 2013 was in an open prison[592].

Six Lothian and Borders Drugs Unit officers were suspended on gardening leave in 2008: DI Garry Inglis and five unnamed uniformed officers. Inglis had been thrown out of the elite Drug Enforcement Agency after a 2001 drink driving conviction.[593].

Two Hendon trainee police were arrested in 2008 for supplying Class A drugs[594].

Lothian and Borders PC Christopher McGinn was charged (in 2008) with drugs offences (cocaine) and perverting the course of justice. His appearance at Haddington Sheriff Court was in private. He was jailed for two years, but is being allowed by his Police Board to keep his pension[595,596].

Gay PC Darren Grayford was given 18 months for laundering drug money for his boyfriend. Met WPC Kayley Newman was sacked after she spent a night with her boyfriend though knowing he was on the run. The suspected burglar went on to commit criminal offences because she failed to reveal his whereabouts. She admitted conspiracy over illegal communications exchanged while he was in prison[597].

Northumbria Police PC Paul Thompson, arrested by undercover colleagues, was charged with drug offences – a conspiracy to flood the North East with cocaine[598].

Ross Kemp has interviewed (Sky, 7.3.11) a Juarez (Mexico) drugs cartel member who claimed dealers are sent to London, where they open markets and bribe Met drugs officers.

Ex-Commander Brian Paddick's former lover Renolleau claimed they regularly smoked cannabis together. Paddick should have informed his superiors that Renolleau was at the time on bail for alleged fraud.

In 2009 a Sussex policeman was placed on bail accused of cocaine possession and money laundering[599].

Former Met drugs squad detective Michael Daly, central to the largest-ever single seizure of cocaine in the UK and Ireland, was jailed for 22 years, to run consecutively with the eight years he was already serving. He had been dismissed from the Met for drink-driving, becoming the partner of the killer of a policeman[600]. Daly's brother Joe was jailed in Ireland in 2008 over the Lucky Day plot[601].

Hero West Midlands sergeant Andrew Smith, who rescued a man from a burning building in 2001, was suspended after being arrested on suspicion of selling drugs in a gay club[602].

Former Met Detective Sergeant Sid Fillerg was re-arrested in 2008 in connection with the 1987 axe murder of PI Danny Morgan (he had been arrested in 1989 but released without charge). Met Commissioner Sir Ian Blair has admitted the first probe was 'compromised'. Morgan's family claim he had found evidence of a drugs network involving corrupt Met officers. Another Met officer was arrested in 2008 suspected of leaking information about the new investigation[603].

Met PC <u>David Price</u> was suspended after he admitted growing cannabis with his girlfriend at their Somerset home, having been filmed by a neighbour drying the plants[604].

333 Scottish cops have criminal records – one Lothian and Borders chief inspector with a drug conviction is still serving. Offences include vandalism and perverting the course of justice, with probably half being committed while serving. It is likely the numbers constitute the tip of the iceberg[605].

Strathclyde Police officers <u>Andrew Duncan</u> and <u>Laura Hilson</u> were charged with dealing heroin while on duty but were not suspended despite facing up to five years. They were also accused of perverting the course of justice by charging an addict with possession without revealing they were the source of the drug, neglect of duty and creating false reports[606].

24 Tayside drug squad officers were to be questioned as part of an investigation into criminality in the force[607].

Strathclyde's PC <u>Dean Burnett</u> was accused of stealing cash, drugs (cocaine, heroin, amphetamines, cannabis, Viagra and ecstasy) and sex toys linked to 98 cases while working at Glasgow's high security Govan police station, as well as dealing drugs, including heroin and diazepam[608]. He even acquired a sub machine gun with which he was going to confront senior management at his station, but he changed his mind (despite severe mental problems, including suicidal ideation, he was put in control of seized weapons). Appearing in private at Glasgow Sheriff Court he was bailed – why was his case heard in private? Special treatment for upholders of the law (he is a law graduate)? He was jailed for 45 months.

Ayrshire Inspector <u>Gordon McLanaghan</u>, who was caught with a load of alcohol stolen from Ayr's police HQ, was suspended for at least two years on full pay. But medical reports got the charges dropped. One law for the public and one for the police?

Met PC <u>Ross Callaghan</u>, who was awarded twice for bravery, was facing dismissal over the possession of a tiny quantity of cannabis. He was caught in a police 'sting' under exactly the same 1971 Act that his boss <u>Brian Paddick</u> admitted breaching. People wondered how he could preside over his junior's misfortune without being labelled a hypocrite[609].

DC <u>Austen Warnes</u> was moved from a national crime squad to a local station because of his superiors' suspicions. He went on to help frame a young mother (for drugs offences) involved in a custody dispute, and was jailed for four years[610].

By the middle of 2001 61 officers seconded to the National Crime Squad (set up in 1998) had been returned to their own forces in disgrace, e.g. after allegations of drug dealing[611].

Recruitment Profiling

In three-quarters of Scottish forces would-be officers are now being vetted by internet websites rather than the traditional interview at their home without warning[612]. This dumbing down of the vetting process is now also being used to screen medical students, who can use intermediaries to appear more competent.

Children between 24 and 30 months are being tested to determine their tendencies to crime, drug abuse and mental illness when they are older, yet police are resistant to their potential recruits being subjected to such profiling[613].

Hundreds of servicemen are being arrested across Britain every week, e.g. in Kent alone four daily on average over a three-month period in 2010[614]. This author suspects a minority of soldiers and policemen share a tendency to criminality.

A CID lecture to new recruits asserts that 'the difference between the psychological profile of a good detective and the psychological profile of a successful criminal is paper thin'. This is interesting, as there seems to be resistance on the part of the rank-and-file police to profiling research. This author believes the statement to be true, but we desperately need evidence[615].

Kidnapping

Special constable Raza Ahmed was probed (2008) over the alleged abduction of a teenage theft suspect while off-duty in Glasgow (she was based at Partick police office). Ahmed apparently wanted to eventually join the police full-time[616].

Documents about the disappearance of a child in 1957 reportedly named members of an alleged paedophile ring which included Scottish police officers (as well as members of the Crown Office and former Scottish Office).

Double Standards

Hampshire Constabulary, whose officers have been convicted of benefit fraud, possessing cannabis plants, discharging a firearm, affray, actual bodily harm, drink and disorderly conduct, possession of an offensive weapon, criminal damage, theft and common assault, may be operating a two-tier system in regard to employees' criminal convictions. Unlike lawbreaking members of the public, police officers are protected by the Police and Misconduct Regulations. It seems police civilian staff are being sacked for minor infringements while police officers convicted of more serious offences are allowed to keep their jobs[617].

Police are accelerating the processing of asylum seekers by bypassing official channels (in police parlance the 'Ways and Means Ad' means they bend but don't break the law). They have to make 'favour' phone calls because government departments don't work together and have incompatible computer systems. As a result the growing asylum crisis is being obscured. Interpol has described the British vetting system as 'flawed'[618].

Trespass

East Sussex PCSOs in 2009 started walking into Hove homes with open doors during a burglary crackdown, startling homeowners. One female PCSO climbed through a living room window and lectured a woman in her kitchen about crime prevention: the woman was 'totally shocked'. Critics say the officers may have committed trespass. (More burglary-prevention beat policing is what the public want, not police acting as well-meaning burglars themselves.) 2007 figures show that each officer solves one crime every six years, on average[619].

Other

Rogue Scottish ex-cop <u>Paul Johnston</u>, a leading figure in Scotland's security firm wars, fled to Spain with his millions as he faced a ban from running such firms[620].

A would-be terrorist who used to police London streets and who went to train in Pakistan was arrested (along with two others) when he returned[621].

A 28-year-old Scottish policeman has been charged with vandalising the toilets in Celtic Park at the last Old Firm SPL game (2012)[622].

CHAPTER V

THE CRUEL POLICEMAN

CHAPTER CONTENTS

CHAPTER V

THE CRUEL POLICEMAN

The Cruel Policeman

The front page of the short-lived *The London Policeman* newspaper, 21 September 1833. The image shows two constables of the New Metropolitan Police taking a tray of sweets from a young street-seller and ignoring youths throwing stones just around the corner. The constables also seem oblivious to the various missiles, including a cat, being thrown at them[623].

In Victorian Birmingham sergeants and inspectors of the New Police (who at first were distinct from the nightwatchmen) would brow-beat their constables, 'as if they were slaves' – the New Police were generally a militarised force. Incidents of bullying are recorded in the Victorian Met barracks, e.g. an unpopular colleague was tied to a bench and held under the station pump, while a philandering Irish constable was drenched with a bucket of whitewash[624].

This author believes that one trait which a minority of police and soldiers share is gratuitous cruelty, as can be seen in repressive regimes around the world, but also on occasion in democratic societies. Psychological cruelty is common in the playground, and seems to be commoner than physical cruelty in UK police forces.

A very old lady with a loving family was admitted to hospital with an eye infection. When her relatives took her home police turned up saying they had abducted her: the hospital had made her the subject of a DOLS (Deprivation of Liberty Safeguard) order[625].

Dyslexic Essex PC Owen Brooking was expecting £500,000 compensation for being forced out of his job, after a 2008 tribunal hearing. He had been labelled 'thick', 'lazy' and 'stupid'. The university graduate was told by senior officers that he lacked grit for failing to get round his problem. One of his supervisors, PC Dawn Phillips, told colleagues he was only good for taking fingerprints[626].

The informant who finally toppled Britain's most corrupt officer has told how he refused to be bullied by Ali Dizaei's mafia-style browbeating[627].

Former Strathclyde chief inspector Gordon Cummings claims he was harassed and bullied by senior officers, who repeatedly blocked his promotion over a 30-year period. His wife wrote: 'Strathclyde Police still relies on the suppression of complaints by subtle and sometimes overt threats towards its officers'. Two senior officers were accused of discreditable conduct, suppression of complaints and neglect of duty. Cummings' complaints included corrupt and immoral practices, e.g. cronyism and nepotism[628].

When a mother reported her two sons missing to a Strathclyde police station, the duty officers treated her with contempt and apathy, no one taking her fears seriously. Knowing her children were dead, police left her in a waiting room with drunks, and her sister not allowed to be with her when she was told the tragic news. It took five years and a report from another force (Central Scotland) for her to receive an apology from Strathclyde[629]. Officers failed to visit the boys' home even though it was only yards from the police station. The report was logged in the wrong place. The mother is set to sue over the police's 'lack of respect' and competence[630].

After Police Federation Chairperson Jan Berry's valedictory address severely criticising Home Secretary Jacqui Smith, Berry's son asked her: 'Mum, why did you bully the Home Secretary?'[631].

When a driver speeding to get his wife to the doctor in case she miscarried was stopped by police, they impounded the car, leaving the couple stranded at the side of the road[632].

The parents of a severely mentally disabled 15-year-old girl claim Hampshire Police treated her more like a suspect than a victim when she said she had been raped by a fellow pupil. A tribunal has awarded the family £85,000 over the school's failure to protect her, but the force refused to comment[633]. The BBC broadcast a hard-hitting documentary in 1982 showing detectives ridiculing and bullying an upset rape victim[634].

A Leicestershire patrol car officer drove past a woman being dragged down the road by her hair, because it was near the end of his shift[635].

The IPCC reported that there had been a 23% increase in complaints about Thames Valley officers, the main complaint being rudeness[636]. 50% of complaints about police are about rudeness (in 2009-10 complaints rose to a record 58,400 – these also include neglect of duty). David Gilbertson, former HM Assistant Inspector of Constabulary, says police are rude because they are trained to be[637]! Gilbertson's exposé of the police service, due in the autumn of 2011, was published in 2012.

Retired policeman Jim Hodgkinson advises smacking children as chastisement[638].

Thames Valley Police gave a mother of two a caution for 'cruelty' for leaving her 14-year-old son in charge of his three-year-old brother for half an hour. Because the caution was flagged up under CRB checks, she was suspended from her job, and claims she is now unemployable[639].

Detective Inspector Gilbert Houalla of Thames Valley Police was told to 'mind his language' after complaints from a senior female officer that he shouted and swore at her at High Wycombe police station[640].

When the Church of Scotland was heavily involved in socially engineering Tinker (traveller) children, there were always two policemen available to facilitate the separation process. One Perthshire woman threw herself in front of the police as they and a church minister wrenched away her three children: she later drowned herself in the River Tummel[641].

In 1911 a 17-year-old who out of hunger stole two eggs was sentenced at West Ham Police Court to two months hard labour[642].

An 18-year-old with Down's syndrome from Lanarkshire was charged with a racist assault – the family were put 'through hell' for seven months before the charge was dropped[643].

An elderly couple (the husband had cancer) were arrested by West Midlands Police on suspicion of the manslaughter of their severely mentally ill recluse daughter, who died of inanition at their home. They had repeatedly tried to get help for her, several psychiatrists visited and she was hospitalised, but it was to no avail. Sandwell Mental Health NHS Trust refused to comment[644].

Treatment of an alleged rape victim by Northern Constabulary at Wick Police Station has been described as 'degrading, obscene and shameful': she had to strip naked as people walked past an open door. She says: 'Being raped was the worst thing that ever happened to me ... until the police got involved'. Two officers sent to the rape scene took over three hours to arrive, and police refused to allow her mother to comfort her while she made her statement. After enduring the forensic medical she wanted to go home to sleep but they wouldn't let her. When she was brought back to the station to make a further statement she was accused of concocting the story – a fortnight later police handcuffed her on her own doorstep, warning her she could be charged with wasting police time[645].

Two Greater Manchester cops – PC Jason Harvey and Sergeant Andrew Kennedy – were jailed for inflicting 'deliberate cruelty' on a young woman in their custody[646].

In 1952 five times as many homosexual 'offences' were proceeded with by the police as in 1938[647].

A YouTube video clip allegedly shows two Central Scotland Police officers speaking to a disabled female teenager in a derogatory manner in a tenement close[648].

Undercover cop <u>Mark Kennedy</u> says he felt embarrassed to be a police officer after he was beaten up by fellow officers at the Yorkshire power station (he was dragged to the ground and punched, kicked and stamped on). He feels guilty about infiltrating people who have a social conscience[649].

Two Police Scotland officers – <u>Robert Ovenstone</u> and <u>Stuart Kelman</u> – have been suspended after admitting behaving to female teenagers (and a young boy) in a threatening manner. The girls, from a residential home in Easter Ross, were handcuffed and made to walk through manure in their socks in the dark. The PCs were initially facing charges of abduction[650].

An anonymous custody sergeant at Peckham police station called a 16st Portuguese man a 'fat Greek' but wasn't disciplined[651].

A frail 84-year-old dementia sufferer was placed in handcuffs by Greater Manchester PC <u>Alan Twentyman</u>, because the latter was afraid for his own safety[652].

In North Wales the 'Traffic Taliban' Tasered a sheep blocking the A55[653].

Norfolk PC Graham Cogman, a Christian, says he has been persecuted since he objected to wearing ribbons to celebrate a gay event. He accused a small number of officers of abusing the police's internal investigations procedures to intimidate him. He was taking the force to an employment tribunal[654].

Grampian Police banned balaclavas in Stonehaven, seizing one from an innocent schoolboy protecting his head from the cold. The reason ostensibly was that wearers could be mistaken for terrorists or thugs[655].

Suzanne Dow, a graduate who, terrorised by her evil neighbours, begged the police for help, committed suicide when none came. One officer, fed up with her pleas, emailed a colleague: 'You just can't win with some people can you?'[656].

In the 1960s and 1970s every CID officer in Manchester had an electric shock machine, jokingly called an 'aide-memoire'[657].

Over 9,000 mental patients were held in police cells in England and Wales in 2012[658].

A campaigning SNP councillor, deputy leader of Glasgow City Council, was handcuffed after collapsing in a police station with angina. Billy McAllister has complained in the past of failure to curb Glasgow crime clans and claims he is the victim of a vendetta because of personal animosity against him. When he was taken to hospital two uniformed officers stood outside his ward for four hours[659].

Cruelty by Proxy

The Scottish Police College at Tulliallan is secretly training foreign police accused of human rights abuses (for a record £400,00 in 2011): China – police criticised by UN for involvement in torture – United Arab Emirates (police suppressing political dissidents), Saudi Arabia – torture and discrimination against women. Chinese police in Tibet used lethal force against unarmed civilians in 2008: their role is to obey Party decrees, not uphold the law. Clients also include wartorn Sri Lanka, where there have been multiple atrocity accusations[660].

THE CRUEL POLICEMAN

CHAPTER VI

THE ECCENTRIC POLICEMAN

CHAPTER CONTENTS

CHAPTER VI

THE ECCENTRIC POLICEMAN

Mystical/Religious Eccentrics

Unsurprisingly, our boys in blue are not immune to superstition and charlatanry.

Devon and Cornwall Constabulary had two spare officers with time to tell BBC filmmakers on Dartmoor that the locals had reported UFOs (a new episode of 'Sherlock' involved filming in darkness)[661].

In 2008 South Wales Police reported one of their helicopters was nearly struck by an aircraft 'flying saucer-shaped' in the skies near Cardiff[662].

A Scottish massage therapist, whose special 'lingam' manipulation includes the genitalia, offers stressed-out policemen a 'full tantric experience' at a discount (at least two officers have taken up the offer, she says). The therapist claims on the internet: 'I am now massage therapist for Lothian and Borders Police and a member of the Lothian and Borders Police Federation'. She believes she is entitled to do this because she has joined forces with Staff Discounts UK, which arranges cut-price deals with businesses for police workers and their families[663].

Bizarrely Kent Police called their attempt to cut crime on Hallowe'en 'Operation Pagan' – the Pagan Federation forced a name change, branding the naming 'grossly irresponsible'[664].

Dyfed Powis Police spent over £20,000 on a murder investigation when psychics claimed to have contacted the ghost of the alleged victim (who had, in fact, committed suicide). The cops went on a wild goosechase looking for a horse, a lion and someone called Fox[665]. South Wales Police raised their helmets and caps as a mark of respect for a sacred bull[666]. UK police forces won't admit they use psychics to help them solve crimes, but blind clairvoyant Sharon Neill says the Met approached her several times to help them solve murders[667].

While some foreign police forces, particularly in Africa, use witchcraft in their detection techniques, UK police personnel are no strangers to such outmoded beliefs. For 20 years a psychic named Nella Jones helped the Met snare serious offenders, including murderers. 'Nella gave invaluable assistance on a number of murders', says DCI Arnie Cooke[668]. The Pagan Police Association helps officers who cast spells, attend rituals, etc., to make their beliefs compatible with their police work. They have been given special permission for the eight pagan holidays of the year (summer solstice, Hallowe'en, fertility dates, etc). There are probably over 500 pagan PCs in Britain. PC Andy Hill of Staffordshire Police is a witch and the founder of the website Pagan Police Group UK – he hopes to be allowed to put his spells online. He claims to have cast spells to facilitate his promotion prospects. Another leading light in the movement is PC Andy Pardy of Hertfordshire Police, where Superintendent Simon Hawkins says the force has recently appointed two pagan chaplains. There is reportedly a 50-strong coven in the Met[669]. The Police Pagan Association has been endorsed by the Home Office and the National Policing Improvement Agency[670].

Self-styled UK experts on Satanism include policemen, who explain to social workers how to detect key 'indicators', e.g. talk of blood-drinking, animal mutilation, masks[671].

A shrine to a dead police dog was established in Nottingham in 2009[672].

Ghostly apparitions at 17th Century Bramshill House, a residential police training college for senior officers, have baffled the best police minds in the country[673].

A Wiltshire Police sergeant has reported sighting three tall aliens dressed in white overalls inspecting a new crop circle, but the force would not name the officer[674].

An FOI request to Police Scotland revealed officers belong to some offbeat religions such as The Church of the Latter Day Dude (Dudeism being 'an ancient philosophy that preaches non-preachiness' and 'practises as little as possible', Jedis and jedi Knights, 'Never Take a Knife To A Gunn Fight', wicca paganism and spiritualism[675].

Former North Wales Chief Constable <u>Richard Brunstrom</u> was dubbed the Mad Mullah of the Traffic Taliban for his strong opinions on speeding motorists, e.g. he used a photo of a decapitated biker for a road safety campaign without the family's permission. He also submitted to a 50,000 volt Taser discharge for an article he had written, and tested his Colwyn Bay headquarters' security by breaking in (the real reason why he 'broke into' his own police HQ was later said to be that his access pass didn't work, i.e. it <u>wasn't</u> to test security). Also, secret papers revealing his reaction when the news leaked out were somehow destroyed[676]. He called for the number of speed cameras to be trebled, ordering his officers to 'hide behind road signs and walls' (his North Wales force even hid in their own horsebox to catch drivers). He claimed Ecstasy is safer than aspirin. He had to apologise for referring to 'queers' in public toilets, and spent thousands investigating 'anti-Welsh' remarks by TV personality Anne Robinson. A Welsh Druid, he defied CPS advice by probing claims that Tony Blair shouted an anti-Welsh comment after a poor Labour showing in Wales[677]. He predicted in 2008 that all drugs would be legalised within a decade - in 2008 he argued for the decriminalisation of heroin[678]. He once proposed putting a syringe and needle vending machine for heroin addicts outside Colwyn Bay police station. A PhD in zoology, his name as an honorary druid being Prifgophyn (spider), he has directed traffic in Brighton wearing a gorilla mask.[679] His force was to be the first in Britain to replace helmets with baseball caps (black T-shirts and combat trousers to be introduced at the same time), despite pubs in Rhyl not admitting people in baseball caps after 9pm (a ban backed by Brunstrom)[680]. American SWAT-style headgear was issued to the 1,600 officers of North Wales Police, who also use body armour[681]. In 2006 he launched a points-scoring scheme for his men – 10 points for an arrest, one for a stop-and-search, etc: poor scorers would be sent on improvement courses. If police time is wasted points would be deducted. He had been forced to drop a similar scheme for traffic officers (they would be disciplined for not scoring at least 200 monthly). Scoring can lead to abuse and enable police evidence to be attacked[682].

A Christian police group has benefited from a £10,000 Home Office grant to encourage people to pray crooks are caught[683]. The Christian Police Association, which has 2,000 members, says in one area burglaries fell by 30% when churches prayed. One can 'adopt a cop' by praying for officers, teams, places, issues[684]. Inspector <u>Roger Bartlett</u> is 'convinced' that faith work has had a positive effect on policing in Barnstaple, Devon[685]. An official C of E exorcist, as part of the 'the hidden ministry of the church', the inspector casts demons out of police stations[686].

Officers throughout the country have been handing out Scientology propaganda booklets, which describe all drugs as 'poison'. Scientology is being used by the police to promote its anti-drugs campaign in schools. One booklet the Met hands out says L. Ron Hubbard created the best detoxification procedure. In 2007 there was a City of London Police inquiry into about 20 officers accepting cinema and charity dinner tickets with personal appearances by Tom Cruise: their Chief Superintendent Kevin Hurley has praised Scientologists as 'a force for good – raising the spiritual wealth of society'[687]. Chief Superintendent Ken Stewart, also of the City of London Police, appeared in a promotional Scientology video filmed outside Bishopsgate police station. London Scientologists may be using letters of praise from the police to secure a discount on their rates. In 1984 High Court judge Mr. Justice Latey said that the Church was 'corrupt, sinister and dangerous'[688], and for many years American Scientologists were banned from Britain by the Home Office.

Nottinghamshire Chief Constable Steve Green asked his officers to wear green ribbons – to 'symbolise belief in Muslims as people of peace' – after the London July bombings.

Car-crazy Eccentrics

Chief Constable and road policing spokesman Mick Giamrasi insists the idea of traffic cops 'playing snooker' with people's cars is an urban myth. The idea is that police treat the motorways as a snooker table, with innocent motorists being stopped because of the colours of their cars. When, say, 15 reds have been 'polled', they go for the other colours sequentially, aiming for the highest 'break'. They can play 'snooker' by intercepting other police stopping motorists, which may lead to reckless driving.

Essex Police chiefs staged a mock car chase for the Channel 5 series Police Interceptors. An attractive TV presenter pretending to steal a Lamborghini sports was pursued by four officers in two fast patrol cars breaking the speed limit and flashing their blue lights[689].

Police in Richmond have been taking valuable items from cars left unlocked to teach careless owners a lesson, but they could be breaking the law (they leave notes about where the 'stolen' items have been taken, i.e. Twickenham police station)[690].

Three male Staffordshire officers were reprimanded (2009) for allowing four teenage girls to pose for sexy pictures (published on Facebook) at their station, wearing police caps, helmets and fluorescent jackets, and draped over squad cars[691].

Police cars with sirens blaring and blue lights flashing raced into the playground of a West Sussex school after an alien spacecraft crash-landed there (a stunt funded by the Government's 'Everybody Writes' scheme). The scene was taped off and real officers were in attendance, yet pupils were 'traumatised' by a teacher's 'abduction'[692].

Grampian Police launched an investigation into claims that a patrol car was used to give partying colleagues a lift home; allegedly with a flashing blue light. The four officers involved were unnamed[693].

North Yorkshire Chief Constable Della Cannings sent a Xmas card showing her crashing a sleigh into a tree and being arrested outside her police HQ (the investigating officer asked if she or Santa was driving). The card could be regarded as distasteful because of the force's unenviable RTA death record (in the four summer months of 2006 14 people died, and between 2004 and 2006 an average of three motorists a month have died in the county, with 50 seriously injured[694]).

ACPO's 2010 annual conference involved Britain's senior police chiefs being driven in an executive coach for half a mile instead of their walking. The coach was escorted by two mounted officers and a marked patrol car containing gun-toting officers. £500,000 of public money was spent on the three-day jolly (ACPO is funded with £10 million from the taxpayer)[695].

Lincolnshire Police are using a tractor to combat rural crime (Operation Fusion): it has a blue light and police livery, and will be used to encourage farmers to 'tag' their machines for easier owner identification (over 2,000 tractors were stolen in 2009)[696].

Thames Valley Chief Constable Sara Thornton has condemned some of her officers over emails encouraging police to cash in with overtime during a terror probe[697]. Two Thames Valley Police patrol cars and a MoT van chased a disabled man in a wheelchair for nearly a mile in Reading. Other police on foot and bicycles joined the pursuit. He had been shouting abuse at two beat cops – it took six to catch him[698].

The Central Motorway Police Group says sneezing while driving could lead to prosecution for dangerous driving[699].

Lincolnshire PCs Robert Topliss and Adrian Wootton were caught on the camera in their unmarked car making foul-mouthed, abusive remarks about members of the public, their bosses, etc. They would talk about their desire for sex with a girl they had passed, and how they could get promoted. The comments surfaced when a motorist caught on the same tape appealed the loss of his licence: the prosecutor failed in his attempt to have the video played in court without sound[700].

ACPO's traffic boss, Northamptonshire Deputy Chief Constable Suzette Davenport, wants to place new drivers on probation by granting them only graduated licences, subjecting them to extra rules such as a limit on the number of passengers they can carry[701].

Offbeat Fellow Law Enforcers

In Newcastle-under-Lyme circus performers (e.g. fire-eaters and stilt walkers) have patrolled with police to try to prevent alcohol-fuelled violence, while in Greater Manchester police distributed bubble-blowing pens (Operation Sherry) with the same idea. Lancashire Police have handed out lollipops to Blackpool drinkers, and these have been upgraded to 'goody bags', also containing a bottle of water, a drug awareness pack, biscuits and an anti-drink-spiking cap[702].

Strathclyde Police spent thousands in 2009 to hire Pix Angels models to take photos of Christmas revellers (and then download them onto social websites like Facebook and Bebo), to stop drink driving. Police had to accompany the 'angels' round the pubs. The new Commander for Glasgow city centre, Chief Superintendent Bernard Higgins, masterminded the scheme[703].

Chief Superintendent Colin Terry was condemned for participating in a carnival dressed as Osama Bin Laden, despite having helped build a police force in Afghanistan.

Devon and Cornwall Police have called his actions 'misguided' and referred him to the IPCC. He was moved from the Afghan job in 2008 because he was a 'security risk'[704].

Actors have been helping police role-play as a way to increase their understanding of sex trafficking. It is the brainchild of the Scottish Crime and Drug Enforcement Agency[705].

Ex-cop Bob Johnstone claims police investigating the notorious Bible John murders had witness Jean McLachlan hypnotised by a Glasgow hospital psychiatrist to help her remember clues[706].

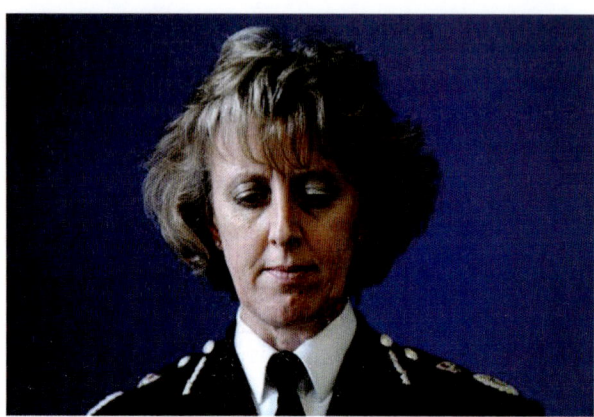

Sue Sim

TV survival expert Ray Mears was asked for help by Northumbria police in hunting Raoul Moat, along with two psychologists[707]. Acting Northumbria Chief Constable Sue Sim held a meeting during the Moat hunt to dampen local fears. She began by performing a health and safety demo, pointing out the emergency exits, her delivery being in the style of a trolley dolly[708]. She criticised sexist jokes about her hair and make-up as she led the Raoul Moat manhunt[709].

ACPO has told forces to ask criminals for advice on combating crime – they will join Independent Advisory Groups as 'critical friends', some of whom can access police intelligence after signing the Official Secrets Act[710].

In Warwickshire police are allowing Boy Scouts to earn their community challenge badges by pulling over speeding drivers and lecturing them on how important road safety is[711].

Lancashire officers have been sent to M & S to learn good manners[712].

Children as young as four were told by Cumbria Police to draw pictures of drug dealers, junkies and crime scenes for a competition (a seven-year-old's bank raid picture won)[713].

Other

Humberside police sergeant Alfie Moore was allowed to bring his 2009 show 'The Laughter Police' to the Edinburgh Fringe, with tales of junkies (he spends much of his time running around after junkies – he collects heroin prescriptions, Special Brew for alcoholics, Nicorette for smokers), yet award-winning blogger DC Richard Horton's Night-Jack website was closed down, with his Lancashire Police bosses giving him a written warning[714].

Four Thames Valley officers caught on video using a riot shield as a sledge while on duty have been reprimanded – the clip appeared on YouTube[715].

One of Britain's most popular police magazines, Police, published monthly by the Police Federation of England and Wales, has been criticised for featuring an ad for an internet company selling medieval-style leg irons, neck collars, wall-anchored handcuffs and prison suits[716].

Royal police guards allegedly acted as 'ball boys' while Prince Andrew practised his golf strokes, instead of guarding him[717].

Northern Constabulary police adviser Dr. Paul Monaghan was suspended, accused of sending possibly defamatory emails about police bosses using a pseudonym[718].

Facebook friends of Michael Adebolajo, implicated in the Woolwich soldier's murder (2013), included two serving police officers[719].

Dr. Harold Shipman was furious because a senior officer at Ashton-under-Lyme police station labelled him a boring mass murderer[720].

Police 'weapons' to reduce street violence include Manchester police doling out lollipops to stop people shouting in the street. Young people in two Derbyshire towns are being given free cinema tickets to replace a pub crawl: PCSOs will hand them out at strategic points. £2.50 taxi vouchers are also being offered by police to get people home quickly, as well as flip-flops to stop drunk women in high heels falling over in Torbay[721].

David Mulhern, Scottish Police Services Agency chief, was in 2009 taking legal action against his bosses to halt disciplinary action against him. He had broken the law by having blue flashing lights on his civilian car, and his wife had poached a key SPSA employee for her business. Grampian Chief Constable Colin McKerracher accused Mulhern of talking 'absolute nonsense' about plans to close Aberdeen's forensic lab[722].

Royal guard John Hayter, a PC for 33 years, faced a police investigation over an internet remark about G20 victim Ian Tomlinson: 'I see my lot have murdered someone again. Oh well, s... happens.' This was only 10 days after the death. Hayter has a history of sneering at his high-profile job on the net[723].

A 2009 Northamptonshire Police initiative has officers shouting through megaphones: 'This is the police, shut your windows and lock your doors, don't let burglars in.' They enter unlocked homes, waken the residents and talk to them about security[724]. Two female PCSOs invaded 11 homes in Hove in just one day because residents left their homes wide open to thieves. The Taxpayers' Alliance commented: 'Breaking in is invasive, unnecessary and terrifying for victims'[725]. One housewife was surprised in her kitchen.

Frontline WPCs were about to be given bulletproof bras in 2009 (like the German Bundespolizei). The first policewomen in uniform had been suffragettes, and being ladies, weren't paid.

North Yorkshire Police have released an e-fit image of Dick Turpin hundreds of years after he was hanged[726].

Avon and Somerset Police are handing tiny jingling silver bells to shoppers to attach to wallets, phones, etc., to serve as a warning to pickpockets[727].

Mail on Sunday columnist Peter Hitchens gave his award for 'idiotic constabulary pronouncement of the week' to DS Andy Brennan, who announced that a welfare fraudster was 'pure evil'[728].

Two senior officers – Chief Superintendent Heather Valentine and Chief Inspector Mick Wood, head of training and head of driver training respectively – were marooned overnight at the Met's Hendon training centre because of a snowstorm. Next day their boss's 'swagger stick' was found broken on his office chair with a cheeky note with an image of The Saint saying 'Don't be a naughty boy'. All involved in the resulting inquiry were told not to talk in public. Hendon has been plagued by scandals over the years (in 1998 five instructors were dismissed after being caught in the rooms of female probationers). Wood and Valentine have been moved to other jobs in London[729].

The late Greater Manchester Chief Constable Mike Todd claimed children involved with gun crime should be treated as victims[730].

While Met Chief Sir Ian Blair attacked the middle classes for thinking they are 'too clever' to become police officers, another Met Police Commissioner, Sir Robert Mark, also used the Richard Dimbleby lecture to launch (1973) an unprecedented attack on lawyers (crooked solicitors are more harmful than their clients)[731]. Sir Ian Blair and two other senior officers threatened legal action against the IPCC over its de Menezes report[732].

Officers in dozens of forces are making compensation claims that their TETRA radars are making them ill. One family claims their police relative's cancer was caused by the 17.6 hertz frequency[733].

Essex policeman Andy Bliss has told his officers to bicycle 15,000 miles monthly in order to beat crime[734].

South Yorkshire's Chief Constable Meredydd Hughes, ACPO's roads chief, campaigned for more speed cameras and harsher sentences for motorists: he was disqualified for speeding at 90 mph. Terry Grange, Chief Constable of Dyfed-Powys, resigned amid allegations of computer misuse and sending a woman inappropriate emails. Maria Wallis, Devon and Cornwall police chief, was forced out because of weak management, e.g. taking officers off the beat to attend diversity courses. The Warwickshire force under Keith Bristow has strong links to Stonewall, runs a 'Rainbow Employee Network', issues 'Equality Duty Awards' as

Terry Grange

well as leaflets telling officers how to deal with minorities (e.g. Somalis and travellers)[735].

Red and yellow cards were given by City of London Police to football fans during the 2010 World Cup if they misbehaved: a yellow card if thrown out of the pub, with a red card for intransigence that could lead to jail or a fine[736].

Three Scotland Yard firearms officers who gave evidence to the inquest into the shooting of barrister Mark Saunders may have inserted song lyrics (including those of George Michael, Duran Duran and Chris de Burgh) in their evidence. Fellow cops were said to have 'rolled with laughter' at the alleged prank[737].

Gay PC Neil Bloomfield told a tribunal that Hampshire Police's dress policy discriminated against him for wearing a gold earring – female officers are allowed to wear earrings[738].

According to LibDem MP Norman Baker, the police operation to investigate Dr. Kelly's death began about nine hours before the weapons expert was reported missing[739].

Sir Ian Blair had to apologise to the parents of Holly Wills and Jessica Chapman for the way he described their deaths ('Almost nobody' could understand why the Soham murders became 'the biggest story in Britain', he said, accusing the media of 'institutional racism' for reporting the case in depth)[740].

An unnamed Norfolk officer slipped a supermarket security tag into his sergeant's jacket pocket, so that he had his bags searched every time he visited Tesco. The culprit was punished with extra duties[741].

Surrey Chief Constable Denis O'Connor, whose driver got off with a warning for a speeding offence, has insisted the driver should be prosecuted (O'Connor was asleep in the back of the car)[742].

Fife Constabulary Chief Inspector Robin Lumsden, who is obsessed by Nazis, was caught boasting about his BMW's Hitler number plate, six years after telling his superiors he had disposed of the N5DAP plate (mimicking the initials of the Nationalsozialistische Deutsche Arbeiterpartei). Lumsden trades Nazi memorabilia on eBay using the number and writes books on the subject[743].

Tayside Chief Constable John Vine stunned senior lawyer guests at a Perth Bar Association dinner by making a tasteless and offensive joke about suicide bombers. The police chief is a former ACPO president and was in charge at the 2005 G8 summit at Gleneagles[744].

John Vine

West Midlands officers have been warned – on pain of disciplinary action – that wearing the chin strap on their helmets (like Dixon of Dock Green) was 'inappropriate'. The strap must be tucked inside the helmet[745].

A tubby Met policeman ensured his equipment included a Twix bar, tucked into his stab vest.

Ian Oliver

Grampian Police introduced blanket drug testing in the late 1990s for all its officers under controversial Chief Constable Ian Oliver, who has proposed all MPs should have their urine checked too[746].

Oxfordshire Chief Inspector Andy Boyd pays from his own funds to buy birthday cakes for offenders in order to cut crime. He tells them: 'On your birthday we wish you well, we would hate to see you in a cell. Time to change your ways, go straight, if you don't you know your fate'[747].

Met officer Superintendent Leroy Logan says children turn to crime because their parents are afraid to smack them[748].

In 2007 the Chief Constables of Essex (Roger Baker) and Cambridgeshire (Julie Spence) refused to pass on the Home Secretary's seasonal goodwill message to their officers (they were miffed about Jacqui Smith's position on their pay dispute)[749].

Leicestershire officers were ridiculed for patrolling on children's BMX bikes, flaunting the force logo to try to bond with hoodies[750]. Surrey Police constables and PCSOs were ordered to dress up as Ernie the Engagement Elephant (each costume cost over £500) to teach crime prevention to children, while the force was cutting £28m from its budget[751].

Police auction off (on the internet) items that come their way, e.g. South Yorkshire Police had a black 32b bra for sale, while Plymouth Constabulary had a No 37 cast-iron Plympton house number[752].

William Fraser, erstwhile Chief Constable of Invernessshire, appealed to Whitehall for help in protecting the Loch Ness Monster. Fraser warned of a hunting party intent on capturing the monster dead or alive and opined: 'That there is some strange creature in Loch Ness seems now beyond doubt, but that the police have any power to protect it is very doubtful'[753].

The first policeman on the scene of Eddie Cochran's fatal car crash, David Harman, retrieved Cochran's undamaged guitar, on which the rumour has it that he learned to play. Harman became Dave Dee, of Dave Dee, Dozy, Beaky, Mick and Titch (the band had a score of top 10 hits in the mid-1960s)[754].

Former Met Commander Ali Dizaei was investigated over claims he gave advice to a wealthy heiress about possible police failings in a hit-and-run death incident[755].

Sir Ronnie Flanagan recommended police hand over their 'business cards' when they stop a suspect, so that they may be held to account later[756].

Dorset Police spent thousands on two helicopters and a host of detectives to stage a mock police investigation for a school project, a creative writing exercise. The hoax frightened many children and parents[757].

Strathclyde Police have fuelled the hysteria against Buckfast tonic wine by their claim that the drink was linked to over 5,000 crimes[758].

Dumfries and Galloway Chief Constable Patrick Shearer says children must be targeted before birth to stop them becoming criminals (he was 2010's ACPO chairman)[759].

Essex Police's Operation Bright Shadow meant uniformed police following six known criminals around Basildon, walking into shops with them and following their cars, filming them surreptitiously[760].

Former Met chief Lord Ian Blair claims that rebelling is 'triumphantly admirable'. Conflict is 'an essential part of natural and human progress'[761].

A loose cannon Met police sergeant founded his John Syme League, which led to the formation of the Metropolitan Police Union. His threats to the Home Secretary and a former superior got him six months in jail[762].

Midlands Police borrowed a 168mph Lotus to 'patrol' motorways, offering 'the opportunity to engage with the police and reinforce the life-saving message of road safety'[763].

Met PC Alistair Hunter was alleged to have hung up on emergency callers if he didn't like their attitude (he was suspected of swearing at a caller). The details of the abortive calls were apparently changed , perhaps to make them less traceable. The case was referred to the IPCC[764].

In 2010 Cambridgeshire Police planned to spend almost £3,000 on 'Shewees' (plastic funnels to enable WPCs to use male urinals). Shewees were turned down as an investment by TV's Dragons' Den[765].

Greater Manchester Police's Twitter 'stunt' – they posted details of all incidents reported in 24 hours, to show how much 'social work' they do – was exploited by pranksters displaying spoof incidents. It made the public think: if police could find time to post over 1,000 incidents, they can't be all that busy[766]. Greater Manchester Police are now giving preferential treatment to those minorities with vulnerable 'alternative sub-culture identities' such as punks, goths, emos and metallers. Officers are to be given special sensitivity training in responding to their complaints. Assistant Chief Constable Garry Shewan says: 'The launch of this new strand of recordable hate crime is a major breakthrough'. The police are trying to change the law to give more severe sentences to those who abuse those with unusual dress sense or unusual tastes[767].

A medical trial tested the effect of magnets on menopausal symptoms in 35 Dorset policewomen, who had the devices (called Ladycare) attached to their underwear. The research was apparently not a proper controlled trial, and was released to the media by its author, a Harley Street doctor, without being published[768].

The sub-Commandant of the Women's Police Service during WWI was <u>Mary S. ('Robert') Allen</u>, a former militant suffragette. She was a trailblazer in the use of the hunger strike[769].

WPCs are demanding baggier trousers, and the National Police Uniform Working Group may also be advising a change of colour from black to blue[770].

Hampshire Police scrambled a helicopter and armed officers to hunt for a tiger reported on a golf course – it was a soft toy tiger[771].

Tayside Police's bizarre 2011 training course uses videos of Susan Boyle and Christina Aguilera as well as stories about witches, images of bullying and a transsexual and homosexual kissing[772].

About half of UK forces have issued lifestyle guidelines for their officers, advising how to shop (do it on a full stomach), visit the toilet, keep fit (by 'cleaning or housework'), make a sandwich (keep them in fridge overnight), eat sitting down, use herbs and spices to cut down on salt, fluff up pillows, etc. Durham Constabulary urges its policemen not to leave their wives to do the chores, and to ensure their mattress is comfortable. The waste of resources on such control freakery has been criticised[773].

Strathclyde's Chief Constable <u>Steve House</u> said the smoking ban and cheap alcohol may explain the rising murder rate in the West of Scotland[774].

Notts PC <u>Nick Hubbard</u> says crime has fallen on his beat because former criminals receive so much money from benefits.

Surrey Police's aviation squad have been touring village halls with a rocket launcher to warn the public of the dangers of terrorism. Residents are to dial 999 if they spot anyone lurking with a missile launcher[775].

North Lincolnshire Police's Flying High Project hopes to turn antisocial youths into pigeon fanciers[776].

Sussex Chief Superintendent <u>Graham Bartlett</u> wants his Brighton and Hove patch to treat rather than punish addicts, but Home Office Minister Nick Herbert forbids even a discussion of drug decriminalisation[777].

In 2007 the Met mounted a summer campaign against street crime called 'Operation Tiffanie'[778]. Is there a police guidebook for such operational names, or is it left to the individual police team leader?

The ultra-liberal Met Commissioner Sir <u>Ian Blair</u> has revealed how he nearly became an actor, e.g. he directed plays at Oxford University: he wore long hair and a beard in those days[779].

Thames Valley Police were widely criticised for recruiting two 16-year-old PCSOs. Hampshire PCSOs are being taught alongside under-16s to skateboard to make them seem 'cool' to youngsters[780]. Hampshire Police took part in skateboarding workshops as a crime-fighting initiative[781]. Yet police have breathalysed a man using a child's scooter attached to a strimmer engine, and another using a skateboard[782].

Ian Pointon, chairman of the Police Federation in Kent, wants officers to show their tattoos to the public to 'break the ice'. He thinks tattoos should no longer be stigmatised[783].

Hampshire Police handed out a cult picture card game to children to make themselves seem more 'cool and approachable'. The cards come with a top tip (such as 'Always eat breakfast', which actually can make children fat by making them hungry sooner!) and a note about the policeman's favourite bit of policing. There are 48 of the 'cop swap' cards to collect (prizes may be given for a full set)[784].

A 2007 Strathclyde Police 'Staying Safe' leaflet advises Scotsmen against talking to or even looking at lone women on the streets at night[785].

The Met's Positive Citizen photo-card scheme bribes children to behave with offers of cheap fast-food, as well as clothes and computer games[786].

Greater Manchester Chief Constable Peter Fahy says his force should be 'more like Argos' in his defence of the closure of police stations[787].

Met officers were being sent out in 2007 to identify every PSE (Public Sex Environment), describe it and interview its users. Results would then be used to instigate the 'multi-agency management of PSEs'[788].

Chief Constable Peter Fahy

As with other state institutions the upper echelons of the police keep coming up with new 'management-speak', such as the Met's 'C3i' project – a mechanism to 'communicate' with the people of London! C3i is 'one of the biggest changes … the Met has undertaken in the last 175 years'. Another gem is the PACT (Positive Action Central Team) whose aim to recruit more BME* and women will be achieved by a 'five-strand action plan, delivered across a series of pan-London and individual borough events and initiatives …'[789].

The Met established (2003) a Crime Academy at Hendon, with courses for DC and DS ranks, and plans for a formal degree qualification for detectives.

After nail bomber David Copeland's attack on the 'gay' Admiral Duncan pub in Soho, the Met set up a mobile station staffed only by gay officers[790].

---

* BME = Black, Minority, Ethnic

Durham Police have bought 10,000 sweets (with admonitions to be quiet written on them) to hand out to noisy university students[791]. The same force released a picture of an armed robber's backside to help trace him. Their unique appeal asked: 'Do you know this bum?'[793]

According to Gloucestershire Police burglaries plunged when street lights were switched off – they believe darkness deters criminals. This counter-intuitive proposal reinforces the reluctance of forces to come out at night, especially on beat patrol.[792]

Sir Ian Blair (now retired) demanded that the law on assisted dying be altered because it is 'incoherent and unsafe' – he is a member of the Commission on Assisted Dying, financed by an activist who is said to suffer from Alzheimer's[794].

Lothian and Borders Police sent brightly coloured Xmas cards to petty criminals on the run to remind them of their outstanding arrest warrants[795].

While Vaughan Williams was looking out over the Channel composing 'The Lark Ascending' in 1914, he was served with a caution from a local policeman (a Boy Scout thought he looked like a spy!)[796].

Two Stornoway patrol officers in uniform stole the show at a pub when they played an impromptu gig on guitar and drums[797].

The Met's 'head of diversity' has asked officers to enter a politically correct 'gender equality' poetry competition, to coincide with International Women's Day. Scotland Yard refuses to reveal the salary of the Director of the Diversity and Citizen Focus Directorate, which has 36 staff dealing with faith, race, age, disability, gender[798].

The Rev. Mark Sharpe says his rural Worcestershire parishioners subjected him and his family to harassment, slashing his tyres, smearing animal excrement over his car, putting broken glass on his driveway, poisoning his dog, severing his phone lines, stealing his heating oil, tampering with his post, sending threatening letters and making abusive phone calls. A churchwarden told him to get rid of his beard. Sharpe claimed constructive dismissal. He had previously taken the MoD to an industrial tribunal alleging sexual harassment and discrimination – as chaplain on two Royal Navy ships he says he was subjected to a stream of violent porn. He won compensation of an estimated £50,000. Before all this Sharpe had been a policeman for 12 years[799].

Notorious police killer Magdi Elgizouli, a chronic schizophrenic with a hatred of police, was being released (2012) deliberately into an area with few police on the streets, to protect his mental health: the Met agreed to this[800].

Essex PC Jonathan Martin has mocked on Facebook celebrity Falklands veteran Simon Weston's facial disfigurement, and describes his own job as 'rosser, filth, pig, bacon, plod', adding, 'I have to deal with human bacteria all day. Thus I loathe and despise humankind'. He has also joked about the Michael Barrymore pool death[801].

Three members of the elite firearms unit of Manchester Police appear to be fooling around on an internet image: one is pointing a shotgun at another's backside. PC Jan Terry was shot dead accidentally in 2008 by a similar gun: there were no criminal charges over the shooting, but the three have been sacked from the unit (including it seems, an instructor who took the photo). Terry belonged to the same force[802].

A 36-officer squad to guard the Olympic torch on its 70-day journey was oversubscribed by 664 applications. The lucky candidates were given psychological counselling to prepare them for being away from home, with end-of-jaunt training to help them 're-integrate' into the Met[803].

In a recent insider exposé of the Surrey CID Officer 'A' admits to schoolboy pranks, eg. removing car wheels of a colleague who welded his locker shut[804].

In Barnet cops have twittered a photo of a dog dressed as an officer[805].

The £2m Madeleine McCann police review will spend more taxpayers money looking into about 100 psychic sightings previously overlooked[806].

South Wales Chief Constable Barbara Wilding said teenage criminals need to be urgently placed in the care of the Church. She wants substantial funding for her project[807].

Commander Brian Paddick, at one point the UK's highest ranking gay officer, has admitted anarchy appeals to him[808].

Sergeant David Hamilton, secretary of the Tayside branch of the Scottish Police Federation, has suggested 999 calls should cost 50p[809].

The Straw 'Bear' Festival in Whittlesey, Cambridgeshire, has a straw-covered 'bear' collecting for charity while accompanied by dancers and musicians, then ceremonially burnt. An overzealous policeman put a stop to him in 1909 because the 'bear' was begging. The festival was restarted in 1980[810].

Ex-Strathclyde cop David Wilson, who lives on benefits and a small police pension, pretended to be a millionaire aristocrat (he was a 'knight' with an OBE) in an ad for a young 'gorgeous' girl to join him on a luxury cruise to his £250,000 cave house on Santorini. He lied that his wife left him – she died of heart disease – and that he had cancer and epilepsy[811].

Humberside Chief Constable David Westwood hired comic poet Ian McMillan to help officers cut violent crime. He will improve how they talk to the public and help them express their thoughts in verse.

North Wales Chief Constable Brunstrom's force had their worst-ever burglary detection rate in 2003, whereas it had exceeded the three million speeding ticket target set by the 'Mad Mullah', whose anti-speeding obsession so outraged motoring organisations. In fact, his traffic cops have had to admit hundreds of minibus drivers had been wrongly convicted (they had been fining and pointing drivers of eight-seaters exceeding 50mph, when they are allowed to do up to 60mph: it is buses with nine seats or more which have a 50mph limit). Brunstrom made his officers carry stress balls and sun cream, and believed heroin is harmless[812].

When Met Police Commissioner Hogan-Howe suggested millions of professionals, especially intensive care nurses and teachers, should be drug tested at work, he didn't make any mention of his own officers, though it should be mandatory for 'all occupations'[813].

THE ECCENTRIC POLICEMAN

Chief Constable Peter Fahy of Greater Manchester Police has said all officers should have a university degree, dubbing the old-fashioned 'university of life' approach 'bull ...'. Fahy was also ACPO's spokesman on workforce development[814].

The Met has been using pedometers to check if officers are walking.

200 officers at Heathrow were banned from wearing Union flag badges in support of two forces' charities, but many have refused to obey the edict[815].

Essex Police warned parents not to buy their children toy weapons for Christmas, in case they get shot. The same force scrambled a helicopter and armed officers when a plastic pistol was spotted on a car's backseat. It had been left by two young brothers. A 14-year-old from Berkshire was taken to court for squirting a water pistol at an off-duty policewoman: held for eight hours before being charged, he was exonerated when magistrates threw out the case[816].

The Met has distributed posters around London urging the public to see the world from a thief's viewpoint. They say: 'Thieves see your possessions differently, take care when they're on show'[817].

ACPO's 93-page bicycle guide warned officers not to arrest suspects 'while engaged with the cycle', and eat and drink so they don't go hungry. The 'Police Cycle Training Doctrine' reminds them to 'rear scan' (look over their shoulder) to see what is behind them. 'Deployment into a junction' advises how to turn left or right at a junction. The manual, which was to be mandatory, was never issued[818].

In a highly unusual tactic Durham Police have changed Burnhope street names (named after local criminals, the Wrights) to emphasise that an organised criminal group cannot act with impunity[819].

Avon and Somerset PC Doug Crossan has reported his 13-year-old son for fraud over a £3,700 iPad bill[820].

Police officers are bringing supplies of weapons and drugs into schools to 'educate' the pupils (e.g. in the street names of illegal drugs and handing round cannabis for them to sniff). This approach seems to be based on the prevailing whims of the transient policy makers rather than on evidence of its efficacy. It could even be counter-productive (certainly Just Say No campaigns are a waste of time)[821].

To encourage diversity and integration South Yorkshire Police sent three Sheffield WPCs dressed in burqas into the city centre, putting themselves 'in the shoes' of members of the female Muslim community. But critics say the burqa is a symbol of the oppression of women – that police should be catching criminals instead and that the exercise shows the police are having a nervous breakdown[822].

Thames Valley Police chief inspector Andy Boyd decided to deliver birthday cakes and cards to serial offenders to let them know they were under surveillance[823].

Police Scotland has banned officers from putting pictures of themselves in their blues on internet sites such as Uniform Dating, as such postings bring the force into 'disrepute'. Uniform Dating was established by former Met detective Geoff Hyams in 2004. Ambulance and Fire Service chiefs allow their staff to appear on such sites in uniform[824].

CHAPTER VII

THE FAMILIAL FLAW POLICEMAN

Criminality runs in families, so one way of screening recruits to reduce the chance of selecting potential wrongdoers would be to do CRB (or even DNA) checks on the families of recruits. After all, the police are very keen to put the rest of the population on their databases. Police are strong advocates of familial DNA testing, which narrows down suspects using forensic material from relatives, and have protested strongly against a Government decision to destroy six million DNA samples[825].

Marxist <u>Clare Solomon</u>, the main organiser of the 2010 student protests, was expelled from the ultra-left Socialist Workers' Party because of her extremism (she is president of the University of London Union, and a contributor to the revolutionary website Counterfire). Her father is a policeman[826].

Hampshire father <u>Andy Copland</u> shot dead his four-year-old daughter and seriously wounded her mother before committing suicide. A grown-up daughter (from another liaison) is a policewoman[827].

Policeman's son <u>Aman Kassaye</u> was convicted of stealing £40m in jewels during Britain's biggest gems hold-up[828].

The Muslim fanatic who burned poppies at a Remembrance Day protest was labelled 'crazy' by his father, a former Royal Navy policeman[829].

<u>Billy Blundell</u>, a violent East End gangster in the 1970s, was a policeman's son from Essex.

The father of <u>Steve Wright</u>, the Ipswich prostitute serial killer, was a military cop.

Child killer (April Jones) <u>Mark Bridger</u>'s father was a police officer with an outstanding career in the City of London Police[830].

Chief Superintendent <u>Alison Rose</u>, who runs an art business, supplied paintings (presumably for gain) to her own West Yorkshire Police, and despite being under investigation her policeman husband refused to comment. The force refused to release details of its purchasing policy[831].

Counter-terrorism Met detectives <u>Daren Pooley</u>, <u>Nevill Caldecourt</u> and <u>Peter Allbut</u> were charged over an alleged £100,000 rental expenses fiddle in Leeds. Three family members were also charged with the fraud[832].

A boy of ten with ADHD and special needs was arrested and locked up by police after squabbling with a classmate. Durham Police 'were told about … his condition and clearly took no notice'. The boy's father is said to be a police officer.

West Midlands policewoman <u>Melda Wilks</u> was accused of helping her son after he allegedly knifed to death a Hollyoaks TV actress, by allowing crucial forensic evidence linked to the murder to be removed[833,834].

Former Scottish policeman <u>Edmund Ross</u> – jailed for four years in 1997 for attempting to pervert the course of justice – has denied covering up his son's alleged involvement in an Orkney racist murder by shooting[835]. He blamed a Masonic plot for his son Michael's conviction, with Northern Constabulary police chiefs being involved. D.C. <u>Bob Petrie</u>, who was part of the original murder inquiry, was the Grand Master of the Kirkwall Kilwinning Masonic Lodge[836].

Norfolk police inspector <u>Norman Cox</u> was sacked after £75,000 was found buried in his back garden during a money laundering investigation. He was not charged with any crime and is still entitled to receive his police pension. His twin brother and nephew were jailed for seven years for their involvement in an illegal immigration racket.

In 2000 The Sunday Times obtained tapes revealing corrupt Scotland Yard detectives demanding thousands of pounds (£50,000) to sabotage a drugs trial by exposing the informant's name. The bribe request was made to a Turkish businessman (a former policeman), whose son <u>Erkin Guney</u> was jailed for 14 years but who may have been set up.

<u>Laura Foley</u>, the security guard sister of a Met WPC based in Deptford, tried to steal a TV during the 2011 London riots. Their mother works for the Met as a 999 operator[837].

A policeman's nurse wife caught selling fake designer clothes on eBay was given community service instead of jail[838].

The struggling businessman brother of policeman <u>Steven Richards</u> was shot dead by two policemen when he fired crossbow bolts at surrounding homes, one theory being that it was a 'suicide by police'. He had been arrested on suspicion of drink driving: he was being evicted and had split from his wife[839].

When the mentally ill daughter of a Scots policeman was arrested on suspicion of murdering her two children, it transpired that her ex-husband had warned Sussex Police weeks before about her disturbed behaviour. The children were found in her car boot[840].

The Halifax personal financial counsellor wife of PC Barrie Keown, of Lothian and Borders Police, embezzled £25,000 of a pensioner's money[841].

A female Met CID officer has (2012) two brothers in prison: she never visits them because of the red tape requiring special permission to visit[842].

Paedophile <u>Martin Cusick</u> is one of triplets (he has a twin brother and a sister) who joined the police on the same day[843].

In 2008 <u>Craig Flowers</u>, Lanarkshire policeman son of Norrie Flowers (once an inspector with Strathclyde Police, now head of the Scottish Police Federation), was questioned over several alleged offences, including handling cocaine[844] in Glasgow, Lanarkshire and Loch Lomond[845]. He was jailed[846].

The son of would-be Greater Manchester Police Commissioner <u>Roy Warren</u> was a benefit fraudster[847].

Deborah Cregan, the stepmother of the one-eyed suspect accused of the murder of two Manchester WPCs, was a retired officer on the same force. She slammed her door on journalists investigating the story[848].

A bedridden ex-policeman, who had been given an award for saving people from a blaze, was killed by residential arson (committed by his wife and adopted son)[849].

Martin Olej, the son of retired police inspector <u>Stephen Olej</u>, was found guilty of an OAP's arson murder[850].

Graham Chapman, the gay member of Monty Python, who destroyed his life and career with drink and with sexual experimentation, was the son of a policeman[851].

Corrupt Yorkshire Police drugs squad detective <u>Nicholas McFadden</u>, who resold over £1m of seized drugs back to the streets, was jailed for 23 years. His accomplices included a WPC colleague and his brother Simon[852].

There has been a recent family slaughter incident in Brazil which adds to the anecdotal evidence for the familial flaw theory: a 13-year-old shot dead his policeman father, his mother (who had served in the military police for 16 years) as well as his aunt and grandmother and, soon after, himself[853].

Callous bookkeeper Margaret Ann Kelly, who stole £350,000 from her trusting employer while he was attending two separate family funerals, was jailed for almost three years. She was in a relationship with a Lothian & Borders policeman for some time[854].

CHAPTER VIII

THE FICTIONAL AND MEDIA POLICEMAN

Shakespeare's romantic comedy 'Much Ado About Nothing' has Inspector Clouseau's predecessor, the accident-prone constable Dogberry, who thinks he's cleverer than Colombo. All his policemen are the bungling ancestors of the <u>Keystone Kops</u> and <u>Police Academy</u> students[855].

Charles Dickens presented a favourable image of the new police detectives: he was an admirer of a contemporary Inspector Field, who is often assumed to be the model for Inspector Bucket in '<u>Bleak House</u>'. But even police apologist Dickens eventually told friends he had lost faith in police detectives, and newspapers started talking about their greed motive – shades of the 18th Century blood-money scandals. Journalist William Russell used the pseudonym 'Waters' for his fictional detective series in 'Chambers Journal', published as the popular '<u>Recollections of a Detective Police-Officer</u>'. '<u>Tom Fox: Or, the Revelations of a Detective</u>' was another mock memoir extolling the detective's virtues as superior to those of 'the common peeler'. Police detective Jack Hawkshaw, a central character in Tom Taylor's '<u>The Ticket-of-Leave Man</u>', was an honest master of false identities. There was likewise a favourable depiction of Sergeant Cuff in Wilkie Collins' '<u>The Moonstone</u>', the first English detective novel[856]. Coppers were mocked and labelled as brutes and swindlers in the crowded British music halls until the end of the 19th Century[857].

Edwardian writer H. H Munro's novel '<u>When William Came</u>' prophesised a police state after a German invasion. In modern Britain police have become oppressive and perverse in their dealings with the innocent, but with an often pathetic approach to the guilty. Thus 'police bail' is a sort of traumatic punishment without trial[858].

Modern police TV 'docu-soaps' show police playing to the camera, as if they are not just Big Brother, but <u>on</u> Big Brother! The late-night shows – StreetCrime UK, Brit Cops – Zero Tolerance, Frontline Crime 999, Cops With Cameras, Police Interceptors, CCTV Cities, Night Cops, Nightwatch, etc - reveal a brutalised, uncivilised British public with police officers becoming brutish and decivilised to match, swearing and shouting, menacing innocent revellers, throwing their weight about: uniformed bullying as mass entertainment. Members of the public stopped and found to be doing nothing illegal end up being filmed anyway. Police officers seem on these shows to routinely handcuff non-resisting suspects, which is an assault. Minor traffic violators are humiliated by sarcastic dressing-downs. On 'Nightwatch' an officer irrelevantly mocked a suspect's false teeth, while on digital TV one police squad boasted to camera how they managed, with the help of a helicopter, to catch a suspect, who was cycling slowly across fields – just before a rival squad arrived. 'Cop voyeurism' is not doing the police service any favours[859].

The vigilante movie '<u>The Outlaw</u>' has corrupt police being bribed to turn a blind eye to paedophilia.

Actor Philip Glenister, star of BBC1's hit police drama <u>Ashes to Ashes</u>, has been told by disillusioned real detectives: 'We wish we could nick villains the same way you do'. Politically incorrect DCI Gene Hunt's old-school style gets fulsome praise from police and public, but not politicians[860]: He uses abusive language such as 'fairy boy', 'bender', 'spastic' and 'Paki', yet this neanderthal Clint Eastwood type of detective was a pin-up. <u>'Life on Mars'</u> Manchester cop Hunt was named in 2008 as the UK's favourite TV hero, with at

least one police station with a picture of DCI Hunt behind the counter. The show's lack of political correctness and rough language have helped make it a great success. Camel-coated Hunt will rough up a villain if it gets a confession. 'Life on Mars' won an International Emmy for best drama series. One Daily Express reader suggested police use 'Life on Mars' instead of 'The Bill' as training aids, accusing the Police Federation of 'blaming everyone and their dog' for the ills of present-day poor-quality policing. However, all references to Gene Hunt were banned by a Surrey deputy chief constable in his county's stations, including news articles[861].

American filmmakers have been much more explicit about the dark side of the police than the British. Thus all is explained by the title in the American <u>'Psycho Cop'</u> movie series. <u>'The Killer Inside Me'</u> features a psychotic sheriff whose father is a doctor. <u>'Blue Velvet'</u> is now a cult classic of the 'mad cop' genre. Films such as <u>'Bad Lieutenant'</u> suggest it is the people meant to protect who should be feared the most. <u>'Brooklyn's Finest'</u> elaborates the theme that there are only shades of gray in the police, no longer the simplistic black and white of many old police movies[862]. In the black and white classic <u>'Where the Sidewalk Ends'</u> New York cop Dana Andrews beats a suspect to death and tries to frame a local gangster. In the early black-and-white movie <u>'Johnny Come Lately'</u> the town's corrupt police force are controlled by local gangsters. A myriad of cop film thrillers (e.g. <u>'Dark Blue'</u>) show variations on the corruption theme. <u>CSI</u> – the most-watched TV series in the world – is characterised by fast, high-tech detection and finality of outcomes, unlike the real world[863]. In the truth-based Hollywood cop thriller <u>'Till Death Us Do Part'</u> spouse-abusing L.A. policeman Treat Williams has been kicked off the force for arranging an abortion. He plots with his mistress to murder her husband for the insurance. Veronica Hamel plays Kitty Dodds in the movie <u>"Conviction - The Kitty Dodds Story"</u>, based on a true story: to protect her children, a maniacal cop's wife had to kill him, but she was convicted of murder because his police colleagues covered up his severe psychiatric problems.

UK scriptwriters don't tend to portray police in such a negative light. In the 1980s' UK, with the crime rate rising, clear-up rates falling, and a series of miscarriage of justice cases, the public began to question whether the police were in fact as impartial as portrayed in TV dramas and documentaries[864]. The amiable, avuncular PC George Dixon was created for the movie <u>'The Blue Lamp'</u> (1950), to be continued in <u>'Dixon of Dock Green'</u>, the popular 1955-1976 TV series, and <u>Z Cars</u> can similarly be viewed as a PR exercise for the

English police. Dixon was resurrected in a BBC radio series in 2005, such was his lasting appeal, quite a different character from the police 'maverick' of modern TV and film, such as the tough, cynical rule-breakers of <u>The Sweeney</u>, etc., who usually apprehend their quarry after wielding fist or gun. 'The Times' thought 'The Blue Lamp''s depiction of London's police as unduly rosy[865]. '<u>The Offence</u>' (1973), despite Sean Connery's fine character study of a policeman cracking up, was a flop[866]. David Peace's '<u>Red Riding</u>' quartet of novels deals with police corruption in the context of the Ripper hunt[867] (see page 122).

The persisting 'classist' division between rank-and-file officers and their superiors (increasingly Hendon-trained) is shown in a 'Police Review' poem of 1936:

> 'Now they're shouting for recruits
> To wear regulation boots,
> To patrol the dirty streets on town beats
> So that the Hendon 'nobs' can get the 'cushy' jobs.
> And snore till ten in the morning.'

Emsley, C. 'The Great British Bobby', p222

A BBC four-part TV drama, G.F. Newman's '<u>Law and Order</u>' of the late 1970s, outraged the police as well as the Prison Officers' Association with its anatomising of the rotten core of policing and the criminal justice system[868].

Thriller writer Ian Rankin says crime fiction is ideal for sociological analysis: cops have access to every layer of society.

Marge (of '<u>The Simpsons</u>') is cynical about the police: 'The law is powerless [to help you]'. The police attitude is: 'We can help if you're dying'. The Springfield Police Force is portrayed as perennially inept.

Jimmy McGovern's BBC1 drama '<u>Accused</u>' portrayed the British Army in Afghanistan as a brutish, corrupt and dysfunctional institution (the police service has much in common with the Forces). Bullying and alcohol are rife on the front line, cover-ups are normal. The story concerns two offenders who are excused prison if they go to Afghanistan: one is picked on by a psychotic corporal, who throws excrement over him.

Billy Murray played a dodgy DS in '<u>The Bill</u>', while Todd Carty played a racist PC in the same series who murdered a colleague[869]. ITV axed '<u>The Bill</u>', Britain's longest-running police drama series, in 2010. Watched at its peak by 10 million, viewing numbers had plummeted to under four million. Jeff Stewart, who played PC Reg Hollis in 'The Bill' from 1984 to 2008, slashed his wrists on the set when he was fired. Reg Hollis was the only surviving original character, and Jeff was the highest-paid cast member[870].

Macho detectives were infamous for roughing up suspects to extract confessions: their superiors would often turn a blind eye. But researchers have found that 'good cops' like Tom Barnaby (<u>Midsomer Murders</u>) are more effective in eliciting admissions of guilt[871] in real life.

In 1948 the Chief Constable of Gloucestershire announced that the radio serial "<u>Dick Barton, Special Agent</u>" was "crime propaganda" and demanded it be banned. The "Police Chronicle" supported this move.

The BBC has <u>Eastenders</u> detectives being bribed and talking to outsiders about the case in their 'Who killed Archie Mitchell' storyline.

119

'Blitz' (2011) is a 'barmy cop' thriller – a South London version of Dirty Harry. There has been serial killing of officers, but because of the film's absurdities, e.g. a vigilante cop murder conspiracy, one doesn't sympathise with the psychotic, alcoholic hero's (played by Jason Statham) Michael Winner-type law-and-order stance. Heavy-handed detective Jason, on the verge of being sacked from the force, is put in charge of the investigation.

P.C. George Dixon had a clenched fist tattoo on the crown of his head which would be revealed when he briefly raised his helmet. Inspector Morse had 'I LOVE MUMMY' on the knuckles of his hands, which he usually covered up with driving gloves. Enid Blyton's PC Plod sports a butterfly tattoo on his neck, with 'Big' and 'Ears' on his knuckles[872].

No police series is now complete without a prominent gay storyline[873]. Nicholas de Jongh's play 'Plague Over England' includes a scene of a tutorial for young policemen in how to seduce men in lavatories in 'honey traps'. Scottish actor James McAvoy, after making his name in family hits, plays baddie Bruce Robertson in the film version of 'Trainspotting' and author Irvine Welsh's black comedy 'Filth' – a depraved Edinburgh cop who is a racist, transvestite philanderer into autoerotic strangling and bestiality. Bruce plots against his colleagues. The film was to start shooting in Glasgow[874], and shows Scots indulging their love of deep-fried food. Welsh claims the film has been banned in India[875]. The 1998 novel 'Filth' had been considered 'unfilmable' by critics, but Welsh considers the 2013 adaptation an 'almost perfect cinematic realisation of my book'[876].

Ex-doctor (real-life) Jed Mercurio (of medical drama 'Cardiac Arrest' fame) has scripted a new five-part BBC2 series 'Line of Duty' about police corruption, hitherto largely avoided by police dramas. It stars Scots stars Martin Compston and Adrian Dunbar, as well as Neil Morrissey[877].

Cop fictional plots reflect crime fashions, e.g. putting young thugs on the straight and narrow (Dixon), Z Cars race to burglaries, the Sweeney to security vans being held up, then drugs, followed by terrorists, people-trafficking and now serial killing.

In one episode of the new 2011 comedy TV series of 'Rab Nesbitt' an armed response unit swarmed round Rab's flat like the Keystone cops, having mistaken a table leg for a gun.

Because of Inspector Lestrade (Sherlock Holmes) fictional police are idiots for the next 50 years. In Enid Blyton's Mystery series Theophilus Goon is the idiot policeman.

The title of a 2008 ITV series based on police killer Harry Roberts, 'He Kills Coppers', is taken from a yob football chant 'Harry Roberts is our friend … He Kills Coppers', of the late 1960s. The £3m series is based on Jake Arnott's best-selling novel.

In the Scottish BBC TV soap 'River City' a bent cop does a deal with a loan shark who has murdered a Shieldwich detective. There is little chance of the gangster being caught as he is paying crooked DI Whiteside (played by Michael Nardone), who heads the investigation. Shane Doyle, another shady officer (in Emmerdale), is a heavy boozer in league with a crime family, ending up dead after he attempts a rape.

In 2007 the BBC cancelled a politically sensitive drama it was making about the de Menezes shooting. In 1987 the BBC had banned four episodes of 'Miami Vice' because the police show contained 'gratuitous violence'[878], yet ITV happily screened the US TV series 'Dexter', a police forensic specialist whose nocturnal vigilante campaign against Miami criminals has him dismembering his screaming victims using knives and power tools.

CAVEAT CIVIS

When Thames Valley Police appointed a new Acting Chief Constable, Sara Thornton, who doesn't much admire detective dramas, the 'Lewis' series was banned from filming at St. Aldate's police station in the middle of Oxford – Morse's old HQ – even though it has a plaque commemorating the collaboration between the force and the detective.

In the movie 'Murder by Decree' Sherlock Holmes (Christopher Plummer) and his sidekick Dr. Watson (James Mason) find in their hunt for Jack the Ripper Freemasonry at the heart of the Metropolitan Police: the Police Commissioner Sir Charles Warren is party to the conspiracy. Fact or fiction? (See The Masonic Policeman chapter).

Sir David Jason's slapstick sitcom 'The Royal Bodyguard' was a bit of a disaster[879].

A 2012 'Coronation Street' plot has twisted, pathologically jealous WPC Kirsty, a control freak, assaulting her fiancé Tyrone[880].

In 'Magnum Force' Clint Eastwood's Dirty Harry hunts for the vigilantes who are executing San Francisco's killers – they turn out to be his fellow officers. In the old Clint Eastwood cop thriller 'The Enforcer' the criminals managed to get their hands on a police Taser, which they used to kidnap a state governor.

'The Sweeney's' Dennis Waterman gave young men the idea of joining the force, suggesting the reckless, macho image is what attracts some recruits[881] (See The Mentally Ill Policeman chapter). In 'The Professionals' William Bodie is a ruthless ex-mercenary, while Ray Doyle is a hot-tempered police detective. The violent series was to be a rival to The Sweeney. Actor Martin Shaw claimed his character Doyle was little more than a violent puppet[882].

Movie actor Herbert Lom played Charles Dreyfus, the crazed boss of bumbling Inspector Clouseau, in the Pink Panther films. Dreyfus became more and more demented by Clouseau's incompetence[883].

The late Michael Todd, Greater Manchester Chief Constable (see also The Mentally Ill Policeman chapter), admitted fans of TV cop dramas (like The Bill and Inspector Morse) might do a better job than some of his officers, whom he labelled 'incompetent and lazy'. Todd revealed his disbelief when monitoring officers interviewed burglars: suspects weren't asked basic questions (e.g. other crimes in which they were involved) or offered 'escape clauses'. Officers failed to plan an interview around witness statements and forensic evidence and other standard questioning techniques. Some rank-and-file officers were said to be 'alarmed' by Todd's comments, despite several forces reportedly failing to react promptly to 999 calls[884].

'Taggart', the now defunct longest-running detective series, is classified in France in the film noir genre because of its dark story lines[885], featuring an unkempt cop with a bad temper. 'Wallander' has been said to be a Swedish version of 'Taggart'.

'The Blue Lamp' (BAFTA 1951 for best British film, screenplay by ex-cop Thomas Bennett Clark) was, until the late sixties shown to every UK police recruit. The 'Dixon of Dock Green' TV series ran for 430 episodes (until 1976). Most present-day junior ranks are antipathetic to Dixonesque community policing, especially foot patrols (and especially solo sergeants who used to shadow their constables on foot), though avuncular actor Jack Warner (who played Dixon) had six real cops from Paddington Green as pall-bearers at his funeral.

In the light of Met research showing the public gain more information from 'The Bill' about the police than from any other source, historian Andrew Roberts says the scriptwriters shouldn't make Sun Hill police station such a hot bed of iniquity: 'nowadays the criminals in 'The Bill' are likely to be the police officers themselves – psychopaths, drug addicts, multiple male rape'. Thus Superintendent Tom Chandler commits suicide, Sergeant Craig Gilmore's boyfriend contracts HIV, WPC Cass Richman is kidnapped and murdered by a serial killer staking out the station, Polly Page is being tried for murder, Debbie McAllister is into lesbianism, PC Des Taviner has petrol-bombed five other Sun Hill cops to death and then probably suicided. Interestingly, the better-looking the officer on the show the nastier they are, which goes against the usual theatrical grain. Some fans have The Bill's theme tune as their mobile phone's ring-tone[886].

Tough Chicago officer Jimmy Malone in 'The Untouchables' was played by Sir Sean Connery, the only role for which he won an Oscar. Connery based Malone on 6ft 2in Edinburgh Sergeant George Gray, who ruled with an iron fist (literally) in the Fountainbridge area of Edinburgh, where the star grew up[887].

The original 'buddy cops' genre 'Starsky & Hutch' –high speed car chases, cool dialogue, funky music – led to Bodie and Doyle ('The Professionals') and New York cops 'Cagney and Lacey'.

To help counter adverse media stories about PCSOs the Home Office paid £800,000 for two series (shown on ITV) of counterblasting propaganda, 'Beat: Life on the Street' (2006 and 2008). Though it looked like a documentary the series was devised by government advertisers.

The humorous side of Scottish policing is delineated in the 'Harry the Polis' series of six books by former Strathclyde officer Harry Morris.

The hit US cop show 'The Wire' comes from the pens of anti-detective novelist George Pelecanos and others called in by crime reporter David Simon, whose book 'Homicide, A Year on the Killing Streets' was similarly based on reality. British novelist David Pearce's equally dark writings lead to Channel 4's brutal drama trilogy about violent, corrupt police in a northern England force in the seventies and eighties, the gritty Red Riding. The first of the three films focuses on torture of suspects and attempts to discredit the Assistant Chief Constable of Manchester, engaged to probe mistakes in the Yorkshire Ripper hunt.

CHAPTER IX

THE FINANCIAL POLICEMAN

CHAPTER CONTENTS

CHAPTER IX

THE FINANCIAL POLICEMAN

Policing Today

The modern police force has no time
To waste on things like solving crime,
The job now of the boys in blue
Is to increase their revenue.

Jenny Grove, Kew, Surrey

A cash nexus means vested interest, which means bias, the antithesis of justice. Not all policemen are greedy, but many are. The question is, can their acquisitiveness overshadow, and interfere with, their core function of protecting the public? This chapter proffers the answer.

Chief Constable Meredydd Hughes of South Yorkshire has warned cuts will mean more crime[888]: such financial threats by police can be political propaganda. (see 'The Political Policeman' chapter)

ACPO 'PLC'

ACPO is offering expenses only to actors in a film about terrorism aimed at civil servants. Actors' union Equity has reported ACPO to HMRC, who enforce wage laws, for asking the actors to work for nothing[889].

In 2003 ACPO complained to the Home Secretary of an increased strain on their resources[890]. Run as a private business, ACPO has spent millions of Home Office money meant for counter-terrorism work on luxury flats for senior officers (MI5 takes out mortgages on expensive central London properties to house its spies): the spending on flats in the Westminster area may be about £1.6 million a year. Assistant Commissioner John Yates, formerly head of ACPO's Terrorism & Allied Matters (TAM) committee, sanctioned this.[His career is further considered in 'The Murdoch Policeman' chapter]. ACPO refuses to disclose the number of flats, who occupies them or how many are empty most of the time. ACPO's money-making activities include selling Police National Computer information for up to £70 (it pays only 60p to access the details), and selling 'police approved' logos to firms marketing anti-theft devices. They even have a senior officer banned from driving running a private firm for training speed-camera operators[891].

ACPO approves of forces selling footage of police road traffic action to series such as 'Police, Camera, Action!' and 'Road Wars', even taking a 10 percentage. (Derbyshire Constabulary netted nearly £32,000 in six months, while Thames Valley Police refuses to reveal what it charges, as do the Met, Hampshire and other forces.[892])

ACPO (dubbed Police Chiefs PLC) decreed in 2009 that speeding drivers were to be sent on retraining courses rather than given the usual penalties and fines, with ACPO running the only database recording which motorists are eligible for 'retraining' on the Speed

Awareness Schemes: ACPO's new company (Road Safety Support) will earn millions. RSS makes millions supplying advice and expert witnesses to help prosecute drivers[893]. RSS also trades with about 30 camera partnerships, receiving part of their Government grant[894]. ACPO (established in 1997 as a twice-yearly dining club!) earns £32m advising police forces and the Government, and employs retired senior police officers on fat salaries (e.g. former Hampshire Deputy Chief Constable Jean Redhead on £50,000). It also oversees anti-terrorism procedures, but because it is a private company it is not accessible by FOIA, is not subject to public scrutiny, with its decisions being mostly taken in secret. ACPO could be breaking the law by increasing police powers beyond those approved by Parliament: it actually campaigns for increased police powers. It may be keeping large amounts of cash from public funds in its bank accounts[895].

ACPOS has recommended more expensive 0845 numbers for its Scottish forces: Grampian, Fife and Dumfries and Galloway have 0845 numbers. The public can be charged up to 30p a minute from a mobile[896]. ACPO Scotland costs over £5m annually[897].

ACPO CPI Ltd's monopoly on accrediting companies who want their staff (warden, security, etc) to have para-police powers, is worth up to £600 per firm and £132 per employee. 'State-sanctioned vigilantism' is how critics describe the Community Safety Accreditation Scheme[898].

Two Scottish forces were planning to privatise their custody suites, which might see other sections of policing privatised (Rehance took over prisoner transport in Scotland in 2004)[899].

The Met's commercial partnership manager says his job is to make money for the force, selling special services – special units have been established (e.g. the City of London Police's Insurance Fraud Enforcement Department, funded by the A.B.I.) that are entirely paid for by private commissions from banks, car firms, insurers, credit card companies, etc. A 2005 Court of Appeal judgment warned that the practice risked compromising impartiality. In 2002 banks funded the Dedicated Cheque and Plastic Crime Unit (since 2004 it is funded by the banking industry's Financial Fraud Action UK). The Vehicle Fraud Unit is paid for by the car financing trade body but is run by ACPO[900]. Like all monopoly services, policing has the potential to generate an increasing fortune.

The Compensation Bandwagon

The Police Federation in England and Wales puts members (who don't have to pay) in touch with personal injury lawyers, who admit their aim is to 'maximise compensation' for police officers, who are receiving £20m annually (£42m in the two years 2011-13, over 8,000 cops claiming £67 million in four years). Thus Norfolk WPC Kelly Jones is suing a burgled petrol station owner when she tripped over a kerb (she made 11 allegations, including his not doing a risk assessment before calling the police)[901].

Police today have a tendency to sue for compensation at the drop of a hat, and to use golden cheerios in the form of medical retirements to get rid of difficult, incompetent or criminal officers. In 2000 only 8% of retirements were for ill-health: this is now over 60%. The Police Federation provide free specialist legal services for officers at industrial tribunals and those claiming for damage (e.g. loss of sex drive)[902].

North Yorkshire Chief Constable <u>Grahame Maxwell</u>, guilty of gross misconduct, was dropped from his job with a £247,000 payout[903].

Cleveland Constabulary armed response officer <u>Nadeem Saddique</u>, arrested by his colleagues during a domestic dispute, won £10,000 compensation from his force. The arrest was found to be 'disproportionate' and a serious error of judgment (the arresting officers didn't consult the alleged victim)[904].

Met WPCs <u>Julie Facey</u> and <u>Paula Church</u> were suing their force for £1m each for sexual discrimination and sexual harassment by three colleagues. PC Church said PC <u>Jason Bell</u> kissed her against her will, and when she refused his sexual propositioning, he threatened to kill her if she went out with anyone, defaced her car and bombarded her with texts[905].

Former WPC <u>Tracey Ormsby</u> is suing Strathclyde Police for £1.5 million after she was hit in the chest with a pineapple at a Glasgow protest in 2001 (no protective gear had been issued).[906]. She was awarded just £3,000, the judge branding her a liar who pretended to medical experts she was suffering from post-traumatic stress disorder. She was accused of trying to blackmail her married lover, DC <u>Alastair Brown</u>, to be a witness for her in court – otherwise she would show his wife compromising photos. He revealed she would stalk him and his wife, 'terrorising' him whenever he tried to end the affair[907].

Police officers have taken to the compensation culture like ducks to water. <u>Sir Ian Blair</u> was so fixated with the fashionable agendas of inequality that he laid himself open to litigants with their claims of discrimination. His PC approach helped to create the present climate of permanent grievance. Assistant Met Commissioner <u>Tarique Ghaffur</u> is a classic instance – in return for dropping his lawsuit he received £300,000, a lump sum pension payment of £522,000 and a pension of £85,000 a year (he was allowed to retire early)[908]. He claimed proper procedures were not followed by <u>Blair</u> when a firm was paid £105,000 to review the work of his Olympic security planning team. Ghaffur was offered counselling and therapy for his stress (he sued the Met for £1 million for racism), but those he accused were not entitled to help from the Met's occupational health staff[909]. He reportedly rejected a larger sum to settle his case, because he would have had to declare Sir Ian was not a racist[910]. With <u>Blair</u>'s own

Tarique Ghaffur

£1m pay-off, it emerged the taxpayer had to fund two Scotland Yard chiefs for a year[911]. Another senior Asian officer claiming racism was Commander Shabir Hussain, who demanded £750,000, saying Sir Ian favoured for promotion his 'golden circle' of white officers[912].

Asian detective DS Gurpal Virdi, who won over £300,000 from the Met, received another race case payout in 2008, with Scotland Yard issuing a public apology to him. The Met had wrongly accused him of sending racist communications to others as well as himself. He had another outstanding claim over disability.

Two would-be policemen have sued Strathclyde Police for sex discrimination because being colour blind meant they were rejected[913].

Hampshire WPC Kerry Ann Taylor won nearly £5,000 from her force for making her clean up a cannabis factory without providing thick gloves (she cut her thumb while groggy from cannabis fumes). The county's chief constable Andy Marsh ran up £145,000 costs taking her to the Court of Appeal to try and overturn the 2005 ruling[914].

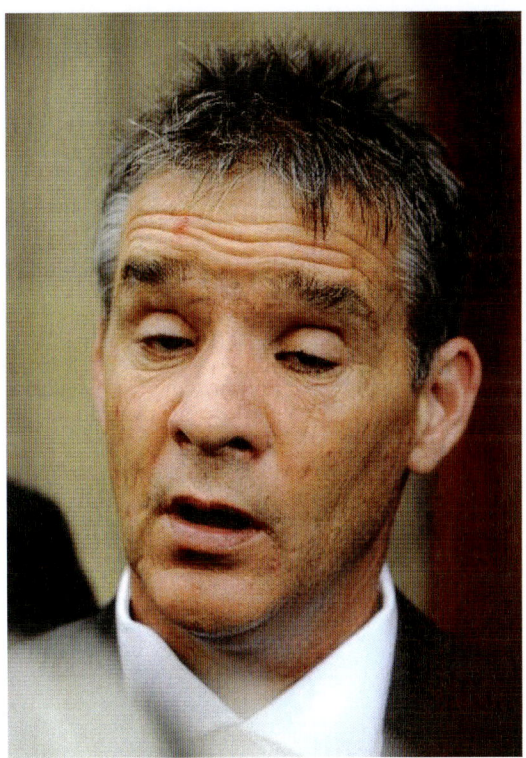

David Rathband

P.C. David Rathband, wounded by Raoul Moat, was suing Northumbria Police for up to £1m, arguing that uniformed police weren't warned of Moat's threat to target them[915]. Northumbria Chief Constable Sue Sim told David Rathband to sue the force[916]. He committed suicide by hanging.

Dog handler WPC Janice Flynn, of Lothian and Borders Police, is suing her force as a result of being injured by an Alsatian[917]. Large sums are paid to police dog handlers bitten by their animals, with dozens of bitten members of the public also receiving payouts[918].

A Sussex Police WPC has been off work for over five years with stress, having won £575,000 at an industrial tribunal – she was subjected to sexual discrimination by her 13 male colleagues[919].

Greater Manchester Inspector Diane Bamber, who claimed to have been humiliated by failing the traditional endurance test known as the 'shield run', stands to win her sex and age discrimination case against her force. This opens the door to thousands of other female officers to claim payouts[920].

Scots ex-policeman <u>Morton Wylie</u>, who claimed a drug to relieve Parkinsonian tremor turned him into a gambling addict, lost his £100,000 damages claim at the Court of Session in Edinburgh.

Devon PC <u>Anthony Cross</u> tried to claim compensation after breaking his wrist in arresting a suspect (who was arrested for GBH but never charged). However, the officer was accused of lying about how the injury happened and charged with fraud and attempting to pervert the course of justice[921].

Devon and Cornwall WPC <u>Lesley Hart</u>, while off work with long-term stress, took part in the BBC's fitness and agility test 'Total Wipeout' in Argentina – competitors negotiate an extreme obstacle course. She had previously been on long term sick leave for a shoulder injury. She is now suing the force, claiming she was not offered enough help to return to work[922].

PC <u>Richard Seymour</u> is suing a Surrey burglary victim for £10,000 because he said he had torn his Achilles tendon when he fell into a drain. PC <u>Fiona Clark</u> sued (for £400,000) for hurting her back lifting boxes, while DI <u>Brian Baker</u> won £7,000 because cannabis fumes exposure caused him to snore, which affected his marriage. PC <u>John Franklin</u>, injured by handcuffs on a safety course, won £108,000, with PC <u>Lesley O'Shea</u> suing for £200,000 for slipping on a banana. PC <u>George Smillie</u> recived an estimated £10,000 after he damaged his knee playing football on a training course. Hertfordshire Police paid £550,000 to a civilian staff member who broke an elbow falling on ice in a car park. Sussex Police Inspector <u>Chris Poole</u> won £10,000 from a landowner after being attacked by a herd of cows spooked by the policeman's dog.[923].

Black Transport Police officer <u>Peter Vince-Lindsay</u> brought 14 allegations of discrimination against the force, but he was rebuked by a judge for his 'unjustified' claims, in particular that he wasn't supported quickly enough when struck by snowballs[924].

Hero Fife Constabulary PC <u>Colin Bissett</u> was suing the Scottish Police Services Authority for £300,000 after he was forced to retire early because of a police driver training accident, which ruined his sex life[925].

Dumbartonshire WPC <u>Maureen McInnes</u> was suing Strathclyde Police for axing her after 20 years because of her physical disability[926].

Lothian and Borders acting deputy chief constable <u>Ian Dickinson</u> raised employment tribunal actions against the Central Scotland and Dumfries and Galloway forces, on racial discrimination grounds. He claimed there was an anti-English bias when he applied for jobs. For over four years he lived in East Lothian while his family remained in Hull, so that he often had to make the 500-mile round trip home (once at least when he was on call)[927].

Homosexual Hampshire Constabulary Special Branch PC <u>Neil Bloomfield</u> told an industrial tribunal that by being refused permission to wear a gold ear stud he was being singled out because of his orientation. The force's personnel director was, he claimed, wearing large gold earrings (breaching the dress code policy) when she admonished him for wearing a stud. Other heterosexual officers were wearing such jewellery, he said[928].

Met officer <u>Fiona Rowntree</u> won £135,236 at the High Court following her medical discharge in 2001 – she had been depressed while working on child abuse cases[929].

CAVEAT CIVIS

Wiltshire police civilian worker Susan Leffers was set to receive £10,000 for her sexual harassment complaint against Deputy Chief Constable David Ainsworth. This would prevent the allegation being made public[930].

Three women planned to sue the Met for the emotional distress to which they were subjected by undercover cop Mark Kennedy, whom they say 'duped' them into sex. Kennedy says he had to bed them to retain his credibility. He himself is planning a compensation claim for £100,000 against the force for its failure to support him, causing him, too, emotional distress[931, 942].

Police chief Alison Halford of the Merseyside force was awarded £25,000 because her phone was tapped 'illegally' during a probe into her apparent dereliction of duty; she supposedly frolicked in her undies at a millionaire's pool party just when it was feared the IRA was about to launch an attack[932].

WPC Alison Wheeler, a former opera singer, was sacked for 'cowardice', after she allegedly refused to help (e.g. use her CS spray) when a colleague was being beaten by thugs outside Walton police station in Surrey. She went on to claim £350,000 for unfair dismissal[933].

The Colin Stagg honeytrap (in the investigation of the Rachel Nickell murder) was a classic police blunder, though it was more a blunder by the expert psychologist/profiler Paul Britton, a former policeman. Detective Inspector Keith Pedder's detailing an undercover WPC to explore Stagg's sexual fantasies was a disaster for all concerned (the WPC received a large sum to compensate for her trauma)[934].

In 2001 a Cumbrian constable received compensation of £15,000 for being posted to a station he didn't like. In the North of England armed officers claimed damages for witnessing a shooting – any onerous task in the line of duty is seen as an opportunity to cash in[935].

Police paid over £0.5 million in compensation in 2008 for botched raids[936].

'Canoe man' John Darwin threatened to sue police if they didn't return £100 they confiscated from him on his arrest[937].

David Mulhern, former Deputy Chief Constable with Central Scotland Police, became head of the Scottish Police Services Authority but left with a £90,000 compensation package after only two years, following allegations of misconduct and mismanagement[938].

Scottish civilian police staff have threatened to work to rule because the power politics of the new Scottish Police Authority are putting their futures in jeopardy. The redundancy bill for staff may reach £60m[939].

Lothian and Borders WPC Louise McGarva won compensation because her training left her with a fear of sirens[941].

Cambridgeshire WPC Stephanie McLachlan, forced to resign for disobeying an order, was awarded £50,000 compensation, having claimed sexual discrimination[943].

Staffordshire Police paid out over £20,000 to a police worker in compensation for tripping over a carpet and £26,000 to an officer bitten by a dog. Staff claims totalled £167,000 in three years, but came to £565,000 when civilian claims (e.g. wrongly smashing down a front door - £21,000 – and leaking private data - £71,000) were added[944].

Met WPC Eileen Waters was awarded £270,000 in an out-of-court settlement of her rape claim. The CPS decided not to bring charges, and her tribunal claim failed. She said she was raped by another officer in a London police hostel, but wasn't examined or interviewed for another three months. The Met argued that because she and the alleged assailant were Crown servants there was no legal obligation to protect them from workplace harassment. Another Met policewoman, Sarah Locker, won a package worth up to £1m : she complained of bullying, sexual and racial harassment. Martin Long, a sergeant at Hillsborough, was given a £330,000 payout after nine years, claiming PTSD, while Dee Mazurkiewiez received a large amount for sexual harassment (male Thames Valley colleagues nicknamed her 'massive cleavage') – she was off with stress for thee years[945, 940].

Strathclyde sergeant William Brown failed in a £100,000 compensation bid after falling on damaged stairs marked with warnings[946].

Met PCSO Rachida Sobhi was suing the Met for failing to make her a WPC, despite being sacked. She had a historic theft record and a recent fixed penalty for dropping a cigarette butt[947].

The Consultancy Gravy Train

Sir Ian Blair, forced to quit in 2008, was planning (2009) to capitalise on his notoriety by becoming an expensive adviser to Middle East countries, telling them how to run their forces (see also John Yates in Murdoch Policeman chapter). Blair resigned with a £1 million pension and settlement package[948].

Former Thames Valley traffic cop Chris Howell was making a fortune from Drive Tech's awareness courses[949].

The National Policing Improvement Agency quango, which spent £70 million on management consultants, advertised over 340 jobs paying up to £88,597 (more than thrice a PC's salary)[950]. The quango is now to be closed down: was it worthwhile?

Former Met Commissioner Lord Stevens made £1,000 daily for being in charge of the Diana inquiry (double his Met salary for a part-time post). He was known by former Yard colleagues as 'Captain Beaujolais' because he loved fine wines. He made a fortune in the private sector since resigning in 2005. His security/forensic company Axiom International stood to gain from a lucrative multi-million deal to train over 100 Libyan police officers[951] for Gaddafi, while they were on an 18-month course at Huddersfield. Stevens received £30,000 a year as chairman of Quest, which led the probe into soccer transfer 'bungs'. He is also a director of BAA, a business consultancy, Travelex and LGC! He wouldn't reveal his emoluments from these directorships. Scotland Yard wouldn't explain why it took nearly a year to give details of his Diana payments under the FOIA[952].

The Home Office spent £17,000 flying <u>Sir Ronnie Flanagan</u> to the UK to chair nine meetings (police chief appointment panels)[953].

The Met's acting commissioner <u>Tim Godwin</u> was retiring on a £160,000 pension to take up a consultancy with Accenture, which earns tens of millions from police contracts. He was vacating a job worth £243,000 annually, so it is presumably worth his while. Another senior Met officer, <u>Ian McPherson</u>, was also leaving to work for consultancy rival KPMG in Canada. Accenture has undertaken contracts replacing police with civilians, as well as reviewing HR, transport, overtime and forensics: it also supplies IT services. Godwin will be working in the company's 'police centre of excellence'[954].

Police eager for compensation are making frivolous claims (totalling over £12m in five years) for slips, bruises and other minor problems (e.g. £17,500 for 'deafness' caused by a computer, £550,000 for breaking an elbow in an icy car park).

Hundreds of police officers are being allowed to retire on a lucrative pension and then return to work for their force in a civilian capacity – in one force on the same day they retired. Some beneficiaries of the 'revolving blue door' can earn more than their former police salary by acting as consultants. Over half the 106 Surrey officers who retired between 2005-2008 returned in a civilian role. A detective may come back as a civilian investigator.

ACPO bosses have signed lucrative contracts with companies run by former colleagues (retired senior police being paid up to £1,100 daily as consultants), e.g. former Cumbria assistant chief constable <u>Graham Sunderland</u> became a consultant to ACPO just a month after quitting the force in 2009 to set up his company, Epic (G9). Over £800,000 was paid to 10 consultants.

<u>Andrena Quinn</u>, head of the new Scottish Police Authority, spent £800,000 on 'behavioural management training' (almost £429,000 was received by Hollin Consulting to reduce the time spent 'looking for keys' among the initiatives developed by staff). Hollin's relationship with her covered two previous jobs, and she had received personal coaching from them. Taxpayers Scotland says: 'Public bodies try to arrange expensive perfection in their working practices' while cutting services to their customers[955].

Dorset Chief Constable <u>Martin Baker</u> quit on a £90,000 pension, five days before becoming a director of two consultancies offering services to the new crime commissioners. 'One Team Policing' was started by former assistant chief constable <u>Mike Glanville</u> and former chief superintendent <u>Gill Downell</u>, who lives with Dorset Police's HR director. The company offers tips on 'cost reduction', 'strategic leadership' and 'working with the media'[956].

Extravagance

Oxfordshire Police took to the skies to follow a family who might have purloined twigs from a nature reserve. An Essex Police helicopter searched for someone who may have tampered with a fruit machine[957]. Hertfordshire Police dispatched a helicopter costing £1,000 to help catch a shoplifter[958].

Police spent £2,500 on a five-star hotel (Brighton's De Vere Grand) instead of meeting in their own free venue[959].

West Mercia Police spent £3m on a new gatehouse and driveway shortly after axing nearly 300 jobs to save money[960].

With the Strathclyde force over £34 million in the red, its new Chief Constable Stephen House, who earns £234,0000 annually, claimed almost £6,000 for carpets and curtains[961].

Greater Manchester constables are being issued with expensive Blackberry mobile phones for sending messages to the public[962].

Cash-strapped police have been spending over £26 million annually on hire cars (e.g. for undercover operations): £70,000 daily for five years[963].

Police forces are paying more than £800,000 a year so that officers can listen to music at their desks, in canteens, in prison, etc. Some forces have only recently started paying for royalties[964], which should have been paid before.

Stephen House

New police recruits had to shower in the dark at Tullialan training college because the latter is so short of money, according to the Scottish Police Federation[965].

Worldwide jaunts by police are costing taxpayers a small fortune. Australia is a popular destination: Cambridgeshire Chief Constable Julie Spence's trip to a women's policing conference cost £5,000, while Nottinghamshire Police spent over £7,000 sending Chief Constable Steve Finnigan to Sydney (as well as India and the US). A Devon and Cornwall's officers' India trip cost £1,403 for a 'top management programme', while Greater Manchester's assistant chief constable Ian Seabridge's visit to a US gun crime conference cost £1,593. Lothian and Borders sent their deputy Chief Constable Tom Halpin on a £9,491 US sojourn. Three officers from South Yorkshire drew up a 'memorandum of understanding' with Pakistan police in Lahore at a cost of £2,930, with the same force funding a chief superintendent's visit to a US crystal meth conference for the sum of £6,149[966].

Scotland Yard, too, has amassed a huge (£12.9m) bill in three years by allowing its officers to jet around the world in first and business class (e.g. 5,014 to many destinations ahead of royal and political visits or holidays). 501 officers checked out all John Prescott's 'pointless junket' destinations, including Barbados and Jamaica. The flights are being booked by individual police personnel or by large departments, e.g. the Specialist Crime Directorate[967]. In 2007 the Yard agreed to send anti-corruption officers (to be known as 'The Sunshine Squad') to the Caymans: for 21 months the 'mother of all jollies' meant sometimes 12 officers at a time pursuing their inquiries in the wealthiest country in the Caribbean. The farce involved a judge being wrongly arrested and awarded £1 million compensation from the Met, who had to pick up the bill for £4 million[968].

Forces across Britain spent £3 million on tea and biscuits in 2008. Top 'refreshment' force was Lothian and Borders Police which spent £383,000, with Hampshire Constabulary in second place[969].

Controversial Chief Superintendent Anne McGuire had an en-suite bathroom installed in her recently extended office at Strathclyde Police's 'A' Division in Glasgow. Earlier in 2009 she was being investigated for allegedly bullying male police (up to 25 complained about her 'robot' style of management[970]).

In 2008 Essex Police used 73,000 pens, some of them costing £5 each[971].

Met Deputy Commissioner Tim Godwin spent £91 on return rail travel (to a 2010 chief constables conference), while the same day Assistant Commissioner John Yates claimed £148 for the same journey, and Assistant Commissioner Ian McPherson's claim was £399.99[972].

34 police forces have squandered over £1.5 million on promotional gifts like cycle helmets, pencils, fridge magnets, stress balls and beer mats. Such publicity spending is irrelevant where the public can't chose their police force[973].

The National Disabled Police Association closed down in 2010 because funds dried up. The Gay Police Association has advertised for a treasurer, strategic coordinator, events manager, community adviser and PR officer, but has trouble filling the roles. Vice-chairman Vic Codling combines the roles of training as well as national coordinator, while another officer is staff association officer and projects manager. These duties can interfere with actual police work. Such groups may meet on official premises and in work time, and are funded by the Home Office. The National Trans Police Association wants applications for its Springboard programme for 'female identifying' officers, paid for by the Women and Work Sector Pathways Initiative from Skills For Justice[974]. Hundreds of thousands have been spent on fringe police groups (gays, transsexuals, Sikhs, Christians, disabled, black): the issue came to notice in 2006 when Merseyside Police organised a transgender conference despite only one recorded attack on a transsexual in a year[975].

Police spent over £6.5 million in 2008 on tracking and bugging mobile phones (these were fees to the phone firms). The true total probably exceeds £10 million (11 forces, including the Met, said they were unable to produce figures)[976].

Greater Manchester Police employed (2008) a 'diversity director' at £67,000 annually[977]. A team of officers from the same force examining the Met's handling of the Plebgate affair was led by deputy chief constable Ian Hopkins, who has been warned over hospitality he received four times from Manchester City FC, which he failed to declare timeously. The Chief Constable's advice stopped short of formal disciplinary procedures[978].

Kent Constabulary's purchase of expensive unmanned drones to 'revolutionise policing' (i.e. spy on the population) gives the lie to the continual bleating of chief constables about the 'lack of resources' which justifies their failures. In fact the police have never been better funded, with their total budget increased by 60% since 1997 to £11 billion in 2010 (the number of officers has risen by 14,000 in that period). Compared to 80,000 officers in 1959 there are now (2010) more than 140,000[979].

A six-month-old police station was repainted for a royal visit at a cost of £9,000[980].

In 2010 a dozen British police picked up 'vital' security tips for 2012 with a £120,000 trip to the Winter Olympics in Vancouver. They were dubbed the 'skiing squad' by envious officers. Significantly British Transport Police, with a key role in 2012, did not send any officers to Vancouver[981].

A 2007 report claimed billions meant for policing over the previous decade had been diverted into Home Office bureaucracy rather than fighting crime (since 1997 spending on the justice system increased by 5% on average annually – the total police budget in 2007 was £12 billion, yet violent crime doubled over the decade)[982].

Manchester Police had a spare police car with blue lights blazing to escort Wayne Rooney to hospital for a check on his sprained ankle[983].

Leicester Police decided to initiate the prosecution of a teenager over a 53p fraud, which cost taxpayers £1,200 despite the 'culprit' pleading guilty and being given a conditional discharge[984].

Four senior policemen (ACPO president Sir Hugh Orde, Greater Manchester's Chief Constable Peter Fahy, Sussex Chief Constable Martin Richards and Dorset's Martin Baker) were rescued by the Royal Navy from Spain ahead of stranded tourists because they 'had to get back to their desks'[985].

English forces are replacing smart shirts and ties with casual polo tops, ostensibly to reduce costs[986].

When Greater Manchester Police posted over 1,000 incidents on Twitter, Taxpayers' Alliance commented: 'Resources could be better deployed ...'[987].

Greater Manchester Chief Constable and ACPO spokesman Peter Fahy was accused of being 'utterly irresponsible' for saying spending cuts could put vulnerable children at risk, and has admitted 'some of our headquarters operations had got too big'. He also says police numbers have been kept artificially high[988].

30 police officers, an arsenal of guns and a lion expert were sent to catch two dangerous dogs in a house in Blackburn. The huge operation lasting 30 hours is estimated to have cost £30,000[989].

IT company Capgermini wined and dined senior Met staff (including officers) on seven occasions in the 11 months before being awarded a £193 million extension to an existing contract. As well as dinners the largesse included networking parties, and a police sailing regatta (Sir Paul Stephenson stayed overnight on a yacht supplied by Capgermini). Assistant Commissioner Ian McPherson resigned on the day the Met published its register of corporate gifts (he topped the freebies list of current officers), but he said there was no link[990].

The Inspectorate of Constabulary says forces can save over £1 billion annually (>12% of their budgets) by working more efficiently. Reducing stop and search paperwork alone will save over 800,000 hours of police time a year[991].

Cambridgeshire Police's replacement of panda cars with electric vehicles was a fiasco – they didn't go fast enough, and the batteries went flat after 30 minutes[992].

Cheshire Police's 'Brief The Chief' project asks the public how they can save money; they used a special exhibition vehicle, but the public branded the exercise as a waste of time and money[993].

There are 80,000 back and middle office police non-officer staff in England and Wales.

Baroness Doocey, a member of the Met Police Authority, has asked why police bosses have chauffeur-driven limos. She could also well ask why the police always have to have top-of-the-range BMWs, Range Rovers, etc[994]. Scottish police top brass have spent well over £1m on 109 luxury cars (Audi A6 Sports, Jaguars, Range Rovers, BMWs, etc.) for themselves (Grampian spends the most)[995], while the new Police Scotland warns of 3,000 job losses – ACPO refused to comment[996].

Cumbria Police spent £10,880 on funding a three-word 'brand' for the force ('Safer, Stronger Cumbria'). The TaxPayers' Alliance comments that this is '… a waste of money that will do nothing to make Cumbria safer or stronger. If they want to build trust, they should be working to convince the public that they aren't distracted by this kind of presentational nonsense'[997].

Repairs to a new Gloucestershire Constabulary sports car rammed by criminals it was trying to catch, cost £20,000 (the crooks got away)[998].

A youth with a rucksack was seen running from a steam railway line in Leighton Buzzard. Chased by a police helicopter, he was caught and 'given advice'. The same force followed teenagers on a moped on park land. They were apprehended, given a warning and letters sent to their parents[999].

Cambridgeshire's Chief Constable said she couldn't afford to respond to 999 calls, while frittering away taxpayers' money on an internet blog[1000].

The new Scottish Crime Campus in Gartcosh, Lanarkshire, is costing £65 million, its design based on the FBI's J Edgar Hoover Building in Washington D.C[1001].

Armed Leicestershire Police and a helicopter were mustered to a hospital where a man was reported to be carrying a gun – it was a pistol-shaped belt buckle[1002].

David Gilbertson, former Met Assistant Commissioner, says policing became a 'business' after Tony Blair, e.g. Sir Ian Blair secured the use of a £1 million riverside penthouse. John Stevens (now Baron Stevens) had a flat in Marylebone, while Peter Neyroud had an apartment in Dolphin Square when he became chief executive of a Home Office quango. These flats were bought out of police funds.

The Met amassed a bill of almost £0.5m for protecting Tony Blair at the Iraq War inquiry. He still has two armed officers at his London townhouse[1003].

Cash-strapped Greater Manchester Police has spent £101,000 on two bits of art for its new Newton Heath HQ[1004].

The NPIA increased its personnel, in the year from 2010, from 1,489 to 1,538: it spent £100,000 on taxis, £1,800 on a beehive, £2,500 on an expensive restaurant. 150 staff with credit cards racked up average annual bills of £20,000[1005]. Yet it is being phased out.

Police forces have hired expensive top PR firms to make them look better[1006].

Forces are squandering millions (at least £4.8m in 2011) on full-time union staff, with annual increases – enough to pay for 200 beat officers. Most money goes to Police Federation officials[1007].

Despite cutting thousands of jobs West Yorkshire Police has spent nearly £300,000 on luxury cars ('for their personal and professional use') for seven senior officers[1008].

The eight Scottish forces saddled their replacement, Police Scotland, with over £5m in interest payments on a debt in excess of £100m. The true debt level may be higher, as two forces were unable to provide figures[1009].

Police spend more per head on takeaways for prisoners than is spent on food for patients and frontline troops[1011].

Incentives for chief constables have included stamp duty and private school fees, cars for spouses, satellite TV, relocation packages and 'lifestyle coaching'[1012].

Fines

Police are accused of using fines as a quick way of 'resolving' cases (including shoplifting and drug possession) that would take too long to investigate properly. On-the-spot fines are being used excessively for minor offences and issued by pseudo-police officers and others on incentive bonuses to issue as many as possible. These changes in law enforcement were initiated by the Police Reform Act (2002). 'Accredited persons' can include bouncers and other jobsworths, some of whom, like the police, have criminal convictions. The main criterion used by the police for accreditation is a Security Industry Authority licence, which, however, overlooks assault and battery convictions over five years old[1013].

Over 24,000 Dorset drivers had £1.5m in fines refunded because a speed camera had been operated illegally for a decade[1014].

Until 2007 camera partnerships operated by police were allowed to keep a proportion of fines. Thames Valley Police had the greatest number in England[1015].

Mersey Tunnel Police Chief Inspector Anthony Tierney told his officers to drastically reverse the downward trend in motoring fines. Motoring groups think the tickets are just a money-making measure[1016].

The war on motorists continues, with a 50% increase in fines for minor infringements such as driving with a defective light[1017]. A 'headlights' clampdown by Lancashire Police resulted in 20 middle-aged motorists being fined for misuse of headlights (flashing warnings to other motorists) in just one week. The Association of British Drivers say police are using 'the wrong process for the wrong reason', while the AA thinks it is a moral and legal minefield[1018].

Overtime

Some officers policing the miners' strikes of the 1980s boasted of the substantial overtime payments they enjoyed while deployed in the colliery districts[1019].

Scotland Yard's former anti-terror chief, Assistant Commissioner John Yates, used air miles from official trips abroad to defray the costs of up to hundreds of his family's flights, breaking the Met's rules. In 2009 he flew to two 'overseas business meetings' at a total cost of over £6,500. He may have to pay outstanding tax over the matter[1020]. (See also Yates entry in 'The Murdoch Policeman' chapter)

The 2010 police overtime bill of £500 million gives an incentive to clockwatch and manipulate shifts[1021] (speed camera patrols were once very popular with overtimers).

There has been a 90% increase in police overtime in a decade despite a record rise in police numbers[1022]. If lengthy notice is not given of a change of shift overtime kicks in[1023]. In 2009 Labour ministers wanted to cut police overtime payments by £70 million and ban beat officers from driving top-of-the-range cars. Over ten years average overtime payouts spiralled from £1,500 to nearly £3,000 per officer[1024]. Some officers are almost doubling their salaries with overtime[1025]. A PC doubled his salary to over £100,000 in 2008 with overtime; four sergeants also earned six-figure sums. The number of civilian staff virtually doubled in three years[1026]. Overtime payments in 2007 were equivalent to almost £3,000 for every officer in the UK – more than 12 times the amount the Home Secretary would save in the later pay row[1027]. More than £1m annually is being paid in overtime by Strathclyde Police for policing football matches[1028]. Scots police forces earned £34 million in overtime in 2010, with high earners accumulating £20,000 each on top of their salaries[1029].

Police overtime cost nearly £500 million in 2008, the average per officer having risen from £1,400 (1998) to £2,300 in that year. In 2008 each of the Met's officers collected an extra £4,558. New regulations mean officers regularly spend an entire shift on one arrest (they must consult the CPS on every case, then spend up to two hours filling in the 'pre-charge advice' forms[1030]).

Between 2002 and 2007 there was an increase of almost 50% in overtime costs, with many officers doing more hours in overtime than their regular quota. Officers who claimed more hours than they worked by not 'clocking off' received no punishment. Four hours' overtime can be claimed for just taking a phone call when off-duty. One in six England and Wales forces don't have formal policies on when overtime can be claimed[1031].

In 2009 Herts Constabulary launched Britain's first private policing scheme in Royston, allowing businesses to buy extra patrols of uniformed officers – a two-man team costs £50,000 a year[1032].

It was announced (March, 2011) that to save £2m, all police stations in Sussex were to close their front desks. Over the decade to 2011 police overtime payments – part of the service's 'Spanish practices' or, more politely, 'culture' – averaged a million pounds daily. In the same decade, police spending rose by 90%, while the number of officers increased by only 13%. Policing the Royal Wedding was to cost as much as £20m, thanks to double time on the bank holiday designated by the PM[1033].

100 police operating in a speed camera hotspot earned £500,000 a year in overtime from the Essex Safety Camera Partnership. 'Greedy speedcamera partnerships are squandering money to run their businesses', says the Safe Speed campaign group: 'an outrageous job creation scheme'[1034].

42 sergeants and 130 constables have been doubling their salaries by claiming overtime for the Specialist Protection Unit even when they are at home. They are the only Met officers who are paid for being on call[1035].

Police sergeants are being paid considerable amounts of overtime for manning the Met's call centres because of a staff shortage (almost 1,000 civilian staff left in 2010): apparently staff have to ask leave to go to the toilet. The police are much more expensive than civilians[1036].

Moonlighting

A Police Review magazine survey showed 4,300 officers have second jobs such as lingerie seller, hypnotist, TV extra, chauffeur, horse dentist, cake maker, shoe seller, butler, bus driver and sports coach, but most second jobs are involved in property lettings[1037]. Do moonlighters have higher sickness/absenteeism rates? This author could draw no conclusions from the inadequate responses of police forces to his FOIA requests.

A century ago many Met Police moonlighted by taking other jobs, so nothing new there. Are police using sickness to cover up moonlighting? Certainly both are on the rise, but research is needed to establish a causal connection. Some policemen have been found guilty of "medical absenteeism" (e.g. covering up moonlighting). Secret filming by police chiefs has exposed a succession of cases where police have been caught moonlighting while off sick.

In 2010 forces reported an average 36.9% increase in paid outside work since 2005, yet it is believed many moonlight without disclosing it, a disciplinary offence. Very senior officers also have outside financial interests, including three Met commanders[1038].

Former Met Police commissioner Lord Stevens' private detective agency Quest was involved in providing information on women involved in the Max Mosley scandal[1039].

Police in 2008 were taking second jobs in record numbers, having set up a website to advertise their moonlighting businesses (bobbyjob.co.uk)[1040], which include property letting, divers, party organisers, beauty therapists, models, nurses, football referees, body piercers, overseas property developers, artists, disc jockeys, photographers, hang-gliding instructor, piper, P.I. , dance teacher, but the most popular were plumbers, plasterers and mechanics. Northamptonshire Police's moonlighting officers include a pilot, Avon rep, ice-cream man, artists, cleaner, plumber and paramedic[1041]. 'Critics ... demand police spend more time catching criminals and less time lining their pockets'[1042].

Some moonlighting officers work as cabbies or barpersons illegitimately – they wouldn't get permission because of a potential conflict of interest: a function of the police is to license pubs and taxis[1043].

In 2011 3,000 Met officers had second jobs, including 48 film extras, hypnotherapists and antiques dealers, compared with just 444 making the same declaration in 2005 (i.e. 10% of the force in 2011 compared with 1.5% in 2005). There were 30 masseurs in the force. One WPC moonlights as a nurse[1044]. 10% of Humberside officers moonlight to boost their income[1045]. Moonlighting jobs include taking in ironing, running gambling websites and training greyhounds. Sussex Police have 107 different jobs[1046].

Belvoir, one of Britain's largest letting agencies, says its franchisees include policemen (the top performers can turn over £700,000 annually)[1047].

In one North Wales force support staff each takes 20 days off annually without permission.

Assistant Chief Constable of Avon and Somerset Ingrid Lee, who led an inquiry into her force's dealings with Savile, was being investigated about her business relationship with serving and retired officers of West Yorkshire Police. The Avon and Somerset force declined to reveal whether any of her business associates were members of the Savile Friday Morning Club[1048].

A 2010 survey revealed a third of London firefighters held down second jobs[1049].

Married Strathclyde PC Suckbir Mann was suspended after being caught working as a gay escort (as 'Master Rajj') – he commissioned photos of himself only wearing a turban for a new gay sex website. 16 months after the revelation he remained suspended on full pay[1050].

About 10% of officers have income from non-police jobs (e.g. worm breeder, off-licence owner, commodore in a yacht club, ski guide, Ann Summers organiser, drone operator, jewellery salesman), with the registers of police business interests detailing 8,669 secondary occupations. The CIC has found widespread moonlighting that could interfere with police duties, with managerial monitoring virtually non-existent[1051].

Off-duty cops from 21 forces are being paid thousands to teach others to use Tasers – they hire themselves out as private contractors, draining police budgets. This would seem 'a highly unusual interpretation of the rules about allowing a business interest'. The lucrative training work is being fuelled by the wide distribution of Tasers, which take up to 18 hours initially and six extra hours annually[1052].

A Met register of second jobs for 2012 included 26 hypnotists. The Chief Inspector of Constabulary has uncovered extensive evidence of moonlighting that could be incompatible with police work. A Sussex cop has an interest in a gambling website[1053].

In Rio de Janeiro moonlighting policemen are hired by shopkeepers to hunt down and kill children who steal and non-paying customers[1054]!

Pay & Bonuses

The police are much the most expensive part of the criminal justice system[1055]. The Winsor review of the 33-year-old police pay and conditions structure has angered officers by suggesting an overhaul of shift and overtime payments. Winsor proposes five-year service commissions instead of the existing 'jobs for life' culture[1056]. The Winsor review confirmed (2011) that federated officers (less senior ranks) cannot be made redundant[1057]. In the 12 years to 2007 police pay rose at twice the rate of inflation – more than the average in both public and private sectors[1058]. 'The Mail on Sunday' journalist Peter Hitchens claims the Police Federation never complains about the political correctness imposed on its members, yet makes a huge song and dance about pay, about which they obviously care more[1059].

Scotland's most senior officer, Stephen House of Strathclyde, was paid a bonus in 2009 for his first six months in post. Bonuses are awarded on the basis of 'self-evaluation' by chief constables (the 'gravy beat' at the top of policing)[1060, 1061]. Scottish Police were to share (2010) £10m in bonuses despite forces planning to cut staff to save cash[1062]. Attempts by 'The Times' to ascertain the bonuses paid to police chiefs were blocked by individual forces, with almost 40 forces breaching the FOIA: they wouldn't disclose 'personal information'. Cooperation from the police authorities, initially excellent, dried up when ACPO intervened[1063]. Chief constables can collect up to 15% of salary in bonuses every year. The Police Federation says bonuses facilitate a 'target-driven culture'[1064]. Bonuses rose 6% in three years, beginning in 2002 and were given to officers for performing their normal duties, e.g. 136 senior Met officers shared £567,000 in 2009, a 70% rise in two years[1065].

'Plastic' PCs cost £12,000 for each crime they solve (most of the offences are traffic violations). They are not allowed to carry handcuffs, make an arrest, conduct interviews, deal with serious crime or patrol after dark[1066]. PCSOs are now (2013) paid more than police recruits[1067].

Scottish officers will earn abut £0.25m more during their careers than their English counterparts[1068].

A police recruitment drive was swamped when 20,000 people called in one day for just 60 posts[1069].

Thousands of ill police officers are on 'restricted duties', receiving full pay for as little as one hour's work a day – 2,000 in London alone. If extrapolated nationwide perhaps 10,000 officers get full salary for part time work. This is in addition to 1.2 million sick days taken annually in England and Wales, with each officer taking an average of 9.3 days off sick. Many of the 'restrictive' duties could be done by much cheaper civilian staff. Former Home Secretary David Blunkett reported that a third of all officers retire early on health grounds. In 2003 a Greater Manchester policeman on long-term sick leave with a bad back clandestinely became a parachute instructor. Another 'bad back' officer PC Andrew Hesketh launched a damages claim against his force, only to resign when it turned out he had pretended to have slipped on a wet floor at Bury police station. Two traffic cops from the same force, Sergeant Geoffrey Roberts and PC Howard Jones, were ordered to repay £5,000 they had made as private safety consultants while off sick[1070].

ASK ME
THE TIME: £1
DIRECTIONS: £2
REPORT A
CRIME: £10
MAKE AN
ARREST: £50

The cash-strapped South Yorkshire force's cutback meant (2009) a recruitment freeze: yet they were paying officers bonuses for 'competence-related' achievements (amounting to £18 million in the previous five years). The Chief Constable, Meredydd Hughes, says (his bonus would be £21,600 to top up his £144,510 salary): 'Every police force in the country does these schemes'[1071].

Some PCs are earning more than their senior officers, (e.g. one Met officer earned more than £100,000 p.a.), which has raised the question of their ability to do their job effectively[1072].

In 2009 a tribunal ruled that police are entitled to payments for being 'on call' during their leisure time, when they must not drink alcohol and stay close to their station: officers (especially the CID) had been battling for four years to achieve this[1073].

Retired Met assistant commissioner Ian Johnston was (2009) Britain's highest-paid officer on £260,000 annually as Chief Constable of the British Transport Police. Deputy Assistant Commissioner Alf Hitchcock left the Met with a pension at the age of 44 to join a Home Office quango, the National Policing Improvement Agency, as Deputy Chief Constable on an estimated salary of £120,000 (the 'gravy beat')[1074].

One Daily Express reader wrote in: 'Did citizens realise that when they paid the police precept – lumped in with their council tax payment – that a proportion of that money would go into paying their bonuses and, therefore, not directly to combat crime and keeping our communities safe. I would lump this scandal into the same bag as the MPs' expenses fiasco and the phenomenal bonuses available in the banking industry'[1075].

Though the Strathclyde force was battling a £35 million cash deficit in 2009, it paid senior officers almost £100,000 a year in bonuses, e.g. Assistant Chief Constable John Neilson picked up a tax-free £10,000 bonus for meeting targets he set himself[1076].

Police involved in royal protection overseas are traditionally among the top earners. 38 Met officers earned six-figure salaries in 2008, including former Commissioner Sir Paul Stephenson with a salary of £253,622[1077], though this has also been quoted as £280,489[1078]. Rank-and-file SO1 police bodyguards earn on average £70,000 a year. One protection constable earned almost £100,000 (overtime was worth more than his basic salary)[1079].

Officers can put themselves forward for a bonus. Two PCs and a sergeant received £455 between them for attending a fatal accident[1080].

Scottish officers were paid over £14 million in bonuses in 2008 (£875 on average per head, though some officers got nothing while others got thousands). Most of the payments to rank-and-file are CRTPs (Competence-Related Threshold Payments) or SPPs (Special Priority Payments). Only Strathclyde among the Scottish forces confirmed it had shared £46,500 among chief officers and superintendents, but the force refused to say who got what[1081].

Chief constables are receiving secret incentives such as private school fees, cars for spouses, stamp duty, satellite TV, relocation packages, home security, lifestyle coaching. Recipients include Norfolk's Chief Constable Ian McPherson, Yorkshire's Sir Norman Bettison, Roger Baker of Essex and Sean Price of the small Cleveland force (his reward package exceeded those of far larger forces[1082]). Despite their sizeable 'off-book' payments Price and Bettison have lashed the Government for skimping on police pay. They and eight other chief constables wrote a letter condemning the then Home Secretary[1083].

Police forces are paying £500 bonuses to lure experienced officers from other forces. Provincial forces like Essex are now responding in kind to the Met's recruitment bonus scheme (Essex had lost 194 police to the Met in three years)[1084].

Some police chiefs are being 'rewarded for failure' with merit bonuses, despite their forces performing poorly (cf. the banks!). Thus three chief officers of Lincolnshire shared a £40,000 bonus in 2007, yet it was rated one of the six worst forces in England and Wales[1085]. Top-ranking Greater Manchester officers claimed over £323,000 between 2007-10 in bonuses despite the force being ranked bottom (or near) in national league tables[1086]. It has been asked, in respect of the Home Office's suggestion of introducing performance-related pay for the police, how this idea squares with some forces having clear-up rates as low as 20%[1087].

Stephen Kershaw, director of Police Reform and Resources, claims £50 million of anti-terror funds could be in jeopardy if police wages are not controlled. There are six applications for every constable's job[1088]. One of the first things Mrs. Thatcher did was to improve police pay, so that a rookie cop was paid more than a primary school teacher[1089].

Publicising nonsense 'plots' (e.g. the 'Pope plot' and the Muslim street cleaners in 2010) strengthens the police's hand when it comes to increasing their budgets. It can be argued that the police merely 'manage' crime now, which keeps budgets sky-high, rather than trying to stop it altogether[1090]. Compare greedy doctors, who historically were lampooned for welcoming disease and pestilence.

The salary of Sir Hugh Orde, President of ACPO, who told frontline officers they must share the pain of wage and job cuts, has risen by more than £27,000 – his pay-and-pension package amounted to over £210,000 in 2010, an increase of 14% over 2009 (e.g. the pay rise alone would have paid for a dedicated town centre beat officer in Cannock, who has been axed)[1091].

Police and Crime Commissioners (PCCs) have been accused of hypocrisy for upping their and their staffs' salaries (e.g. some are on over £100,000) while discharging thousands of front-line officers. They were supposed to save cash and improve transparency and accountability. Cumbria's PCC Richard Rhodes reported four of his staff to the police for revealing his costly limo trips – three were arrested and one bailed. PM David Cameron ordered a probe after MPs were incensed by this 'outrage against democracy'[1092].

CAVEAT CIVIS

The Police Federation was considering a mass march and rally in London in the run-up to the royal wedding, in protest at prospective pay cuts. The Winsor report proves that the police are relatively well-paid[1093]. Controversial bonuses of up to £5,000 for just doing the job are to be axed (but not in Scotland: police are exempt from the Scottish Government's ban on bonuses[1094]). 'Special priority payments', costing about £90m annually, for demanding working conditions (e.g. for being dog handlers![1095]). 'Competency related threshold payments' amount to another £90m ('grab-a-grand'). These two payments are received by 100,000 officers (over two-thirds of all officers). The Met recently described pay and benefits as 'better than ever' and 'special deals' may 'pleasantly surprise' experienced officers[1096]. The biggest ever police rally (January 2008) was about pay – more than a sixth of officers paid to police the streets of Britain were in Central London. The BNP mayoral candidate Richard Barnbrook was seen at the front of the march. The approximately 25,000 on parade all wore baseball caps[1097] (shades of a certain former Welsh chief constable!).

Assistant Chief Constable of Central Scotland Police, <u>John Mauger</u>, was paid £50,000 to stay home while complaints against him were investigated[1098].

Secret lucrative multi-million-pound redundancy payments to 12 senior MI6 officers have reportedly antagonised over 200 rank-and-file officers also qualifying for payments that are, however, reduced. The 12 were called 'The Dirty Dozen'[1099].

West Midlands officers who have, they claim, been forcibly retired, are being asked to return as special constables for no wages.

The hunt for 'supercop' to head up the new National Crime Agency is in jeopardy, because the salary of £140,000 is considered too low.

Despite in 2008 the police securing 'the best multi-year settlement in the public sector'[1100], Home Secretary Theresa May met jeers and stony silence when she addressed police union members in 2011: they were furious at proposed pay and overtime pay cuts. A disfigured and blinded PC asked her in a video played to the conference: 'Do you think I'm paid too much?'[1101]

West Yorkshire's Chief Constable <u>Sir Norman Bettison</u> says his annual pay of £213,000 is much too high. He blames Patrick Sheehy's 1992 review, which recommends public sector pay mirrors the private[1102]. A few years ago hardly any police chiefs were earning six-figure salaries, but now extravagance is the norm[1103].

Despite threats of redundancies of rank-and-file officers, police chiefs have created a new £100,000 'Deputy Chief Constable' job, to be shared by several south-west English forces[1104].

In 2007 police used YouTube in their latest pay protest, posting video footage of a hero cop being ambushed by a maniacal knifeman, to illustrate the daily dangers they face[1105].

Greater Manchester Police's southern division offered cash 'bribes' to stop their officers taking sickies, greatly improving the force's sickness rate. It was the brainchild of Chief Superintendent <u>Alan Cooper</u>.

When Deputy Commissioner Paul Stephenson waived his performance bonus, he effectively forced Sir Ian Blair to do likewise with his £25,000 bonus – Blair reportedly sent his deputy a private handwritten letter which suggested disloyalty. Sir Ian's office was given a £300,000 refurbishment when he became Commissioner[1106].

The Met was still (September, 2011) paying John Yates his £185,000 salary, saying he was on leave and had undertaken a handover period. By remaining an employee for two further months he was entitled to his full £123,000 a year pension[1107].

In 2008 a judge cleared the way for English police to challenge the Home Office decision to limit that year's pay award to 1.9%[1108].

Performance-related pay has destroyed teamwork – now, instead of officers protecting one another, it's every man for himself[1109].

The wage bill for Scottish police has, despite an increase in officer numbers of only 160, increased by £40 million in the three years from 2008. Support staff are being replaced by officers on twice the pay, to keep numbers up[1110].

Generous salaries and perks have pushed most police into the top 20% of all earners: the average officer earns (2012) over £40,000 annually, over £45,000 in London (almost half of all the Met have incomes in the UK's top 10%)[1111].

The Police Arbitration Tribunal (PAT) was threatening to break the Chancellor's pay cap at the start of 2012. The Police Federation had been lobbying MPs to support the PAT finding[1112].

Sir Ian Blair wanted a £25,000 performance bonus while the de Menezes criminal case was ongoing, despite his salary of £228,000[1113].

Since 2008 Scottish police have received nearly £24m, in bonuses for putting up with 'unpleasant' things like bad smells, attending road accidents and clearing snow[1114].

UK police are incentivised to criminalise the public rather than prevent crime (e.g. police chiefs can get up to £15,000 in 'performance' bonuses p.a., depending on how many people their officers fine, caution or charge[1115]). Even specialist units can be drafted in to collect fines, e.g. Strathclyde armed officers were told to 'get out there and start ticketing'[1116].

Scotland's new single force has six assistant chief constables earning up to £106,000[1117]. Seven of Scotland's eight chief constables have missed out on top jobs in the new single force, as lower ranks have leapfrogged up the hierarchy. But the taxpayers could be paying some of their six figure salaries for another five years because of contractual obligations[1118].

Taxpayers will pay for the six-figure salaries of two former chief constables even though they haven't achieved new posts (only one of eight chief constables has secured a senior post in the new single force)[1119].

New Essex Chief Constable Stephen Kavanagh earns £17,500 more than his predecessor despite the force having to find £42 million annually in savings (he will earn £192,000)[1120].

Pensions

The police was one of the first working-class jobs to be made pensionable[1121].

Taxpayers are spending £2 million daily to plug a massive gap in police pensions: in 2006 the bail-out was only a quarter of current subsidies. Longer-living officers may now draw index-linked pensions for longer than they have actively served[1122].

Over 50% of police in some forces retire on medical grounds (unlike ordinary police pensions, medical pensions are index-linked), so that £1 in every £7 of crime-fighting budgets is spent on pension payouts. A medical pension can almost double the normal pension.

Shamed Scottish drugs cop Christopher McGinn, caught selling cocaine in a pub toilet, has been allowed to retain his pension. Police who commit offences in the US lose their pensions. McGinn also keeps his salary for the period he was under suspension[1123].

Bob Quick

Anti-terror Met chief 49-year-old Bob Quick quit in 2009 after losing the confidence of the Home Secretary when he almost endangered an operation to smash an Al Qaeda spectacular, yet will receive a pension fortune (of more than £114,000 a year) despite his major blunder. Quick in 2008 authorised the raid on Damian Green's Commons office without a warrant[1124].

Three of the UK's former top policemen (Sir Hugh Orde, Sir Ronnie Flanagan and Sir Ian Johnston) cashed in (2009) on public sector retirement deals worth more than £3 million each ('millionaire cops'). Their pensions are based on two thirds of their final salary, and they are entitled to tax-free lump sums up to three times their final year's salary[1125].

Ian Burnside, a chief superintendent with Lothian and Borders Police, went to court to prevent his divorcing wife getting any more of his £765,000 pension[1126].

Top Strathclyde officers Detective Superintendents George Lambie and Robert McCann were rejected for a controversial scheme to obtain pension benefits while still working. It lets officers 'retire' with pensions after 30 years' service, then rejoin at their previous pay level.

Chief Superintendent <u>David Christie</u> was given a tax-free £150,000 pension lump sum after 30 years service, yet stayed on earning his full salary.[The scheme exempts the beneficiaries from needing to make any further pension contributions[1127]].

David Christie

It was revealed (2009) that it is costing the taxpayer almost half a billion pounds annually to bail out the police pension fund. Police pensions are paid from two sources –council tax and general taxation[1128]. More than £1 billion of taxpayers' funds have been added to police pension schemes between 2006-9 (there was a 60% increase in 2009 over 2008, which was double 2007)[1129].

Police forces in Northern Ireland, City of London, Lancashire, Merseyside, Leicestershire and Lincolnshire are paying more pensions than salaries, and this trend may spread to other forces[1130].

A corrupt Sunderland cop who resigned was allowed to remain anonymous and keep his pension[1131].

Of 70 officers killed between 2000-2007, about a third were driving to their police station or from work and the injury benefits system covers this at present. This is because in the past police were required to commute in uniform. Officers forced to leave work because of injury on duty receive a 'gratuity' of four times salary[1132].

The Police Federation launched legal action (2008) to force the Government to give new enhanced pension payouts to retired cops. Changes had removed the right of retiring female police to receive larger pensions than men because they live longer[1133].

<u>Sir Ian Blair</u> was paid £580,000 in his final eight months as Met Chief, with a likely pensions pot of around £3.5 million[1134]. He received a lump sum of £672,000 and a pension of £126,000 annually, because an inquiry into alleged corruption (he awarded £3m of Met contracts to a close friend) wasn't formally completed before he took early retirement (leaving the Police Authority without a penalty)[1135]. The loophole which enables officers to resign under duress (facing disciplinary action) and keep their pensions, has been used well over 1,800 times in a decade. In two years since 2011 an unprecedented number of senior police have been sacked[1136].

Some of the UK's largest police forces have more retired officers (getting their pension) than there are active officers – officers can often retire before they reach 50 (after 30 years' service). The scheme – the most expensive per head in the public sector – has 140,000 retirees, costing £2 billion (for 2008). Two senior British Transport Police on six-figure salaries are also claiming pensions from their previous Scotland Yard jobs. Police authorities claim they are addressing the problem of 'spurious' early retirements[1137]. Forcing 2,000 top officers with 30 years service to retire early will cost up to £200m[1138].

'Rank-and-file officers are disgusted that their bosses are becoming millionaires'[1139].

Essex Police were trying (2010) to claw back the pension of corrupt D.I. Robert Sloan, jailed for helping a dangerous criminal avoid prosecution. He had been secretly recorded giving advice on how to demolish a prosecution charge of handling stolen cars. The Police Federation was expected to oppose any bid to forfeit the pension[1140].

When 38-year-old D.C. Steve Pennington was jailed for drink driving he resigned before being sacked so that he wouldn't miss out on his medical pension (which will cost at least £½ million), thanks to his Chief Constable Barry Shaw, of Cleveland Police, against Home Office guidelines. Though too drunk to stand he asked colleagues to give him a lift and forget the matter. Shaw had already admitted a "monumental misjudgement".

The chief constable of the British Transport Police, Andrew Trotter, reportedly enjoys a salary of about £150,000 a year as well as a £70,000 pension, because he had spent over 30 years in the police: a 'double dipper'. Police can apparently retire as young as 50, then being rehired almost immediately in the same posts, receiving a monthly salary plus pension[1141].

Sex-change Strathclyde WPC Abigail Austin (who was once paratrooper Ian Hamilton) threatened to quit because she was only entitled to a WPC's pension[1142]. A male PC who changed his sex, becoming Linda Grant, won a pension starting at age 60 (instead of 65), and was awarded £20,000 costs[1143].

Police chief John Yeates was allowed to return to his old job the day after retiring as director of the Scottish Police College in Fife, with a £300,000 pension payout. The 'new' civilian job had not been advertised, and no candidates were up for interview. He kept his luxury police home on the campus. Though the move involved one of Scotland's most important police jobs there was no official announcement[1144].

One-seventh of funds spent on police goes to pensions, soaring to £2.5billion in 2009-10. Only the judiciary among public-sector workers have more generous pensions (i.e. as a proportion of pay) than police[1145].

50-year-old police retirees with generous pension payouts are being quickly re-employed as civilian workers at up to £55,000 p.a. In Scotland the 'double-dip' practice may be costing as much as £10m p.a. Unbelievably, two forces purported not to know how many civilian staff were ex-officers[1146].

Some Scottish police will be paid off when the forces merge (2013) but still get golden goodbyes of 15 months salary and a £10,000 cheque. Under threat are forensics and control room workers. The merger will cost £60m[1147].

Disgraced Cleveland Chief Constable Sean Price was labelled a liar and a bully and found guilty of gross misconduct, but kept his leaving payout of about £300,000, despite the IPCC saying he had failed 'the police service as a whole and the public of Cleveland'[1148].

Quangos

The National Policing Improvement Agency costs £474m[1149]. It was supposed to be abolished in 2011, but was still funtioning in August, 2012. ACPO may also be facing the axe.

Vic Emery, Chairman of the Scottish Police Authority, has drawn up plans to make 1,400 staff redundant, yet helped his business partner get a job at the quango without it being advertised[1150].

Sick Leave

Burgeoning sickness rates of the police service are allied to widespread abuse of the medical pension system. 70% of Merseyside police take early "sick retirement", which is often viewed as covering up in serious allegation cases.

The equivalent of the whole (3,673-strong) Kent Constabulary are off sick every day in England (10% of Kent officers are off every year on long-term sick leave of more than four weeks)[1151].

The 2008 wage bill for police on 'restrictive or recuperative duties' (which may mean the 8,276 officers working as little as an hour daily) was £248m for England and Wales. Such officers are paid their full salary[1152].

It has been claimed there has been a cover-up in relation to police medical absenteeism (CID = Cops in Deckchairs) - it may cost £250 million annually. In the West Midlands an average of 2½ working weeks are taken off sick annually. At one stage in Sussex 50% of early retirements were sickness retirements. In South Wales an Inspector Thomas was demoted (to constable rank) because he pretended to have flu, while a Sergeant Hayter sold double glazing while off sick. PC Matt Rooney, 50, claims he was forced to quit Strathclyde Police on medical grounds when there was nothing wrong with him: he won £50,000, as well as a legal victory in his fight to get his job back. He has commendations for bravery, and believes he is the target of a long-standing campaign by senior officers to get him out of the force because of his outspokenness.

'He has just uttered one
'Ello when he
discovered it was time
to go off sick...'

Greater Manchester Police are paying (2012) 512 officers up to £2m annually to do sedentary jobs or stay home on account of stress and backache, both notoriously difficult to diagnose (half are on 'medically restricted' duties, i.e. over 6% of the force's complement). £800,000 a year goes to 266 officers who are on <u>full</u> 'medically restricted duties'[1153].

Over half the Met's complement are overweight, with 1% morbidly obese and over a fifth obese. In 2011 Sussex PCSOs took an average of 11.5 days each off sick, compared with seven for regular officers. 30% of absences are due to orthopaedic (neck, back, knee and foot) problems[1154].

An MoD policeman in his thirties was hit by a tennis ball during firearms training, taking at least three days off sick. A female MoD officer fractured a rib climbing through a window to help a locked-out colleague. One policeman injured his back when he stepped backwards, forgetting he was working 3 feet up in the air[1155].

Met PC <u>Andrew Quinn</u> pocketed £300,000 sick pay (for stress) during a decade off work (he never actually started work). He had injured his back during training[1156].

Police and firemen are among the worst sicknote offenders, e.g. they are absent from the workplace for longer periods[1157].

In 2001 the Met was offering free psychiatric help to its officers who are off sick for over four weeks. Long term sick leave means mental illness in at least 30% of cases. WPC <u>Angela Moore</u> was awarded £250,000 for depression and PTSD after an accident on duty: she developed driving phobia[1158].

Strikes

There were police strikes in Hull and Manchester in the 1850s, and in the Met in the 1870s and 1880s. In 1872 100 were suspended and ringleaders jailed. Sir Robert Peel had considered his men to be unskilled labour, and they were paid accordingly[1159]. In an 1890 strike the police held meetings in a working-men's club, the premises of the Social Democratic Federation, Britain's first Marxist party[1160]:39 officers were sacked.

In 1918 a <u>PC Thiel</u> was fired for union activities, resulting in his union (Lloyd George did not recognise it) immediately suspending their no-strike agreements and demanding improved pay and Thiel's reinstatement. 10,000 of the Met's 19,000 officers went on strike: flying pickets did the rounds of police stations all over London. Guardsmen had to replace the striking Downing Street police guards, but soldiers refused to clear striking police from Whitehall streets. The police got their demands, including pensions for widows and reinstatement of all police union activists (by 1919 the union had 55,000 members and, now affiliated to the TUC, organised large demos throughout London)[1161].

Humberside Police have five people working full-time for unions, the annual salaries totalling almost £155,000. One, <u>Steve Garmston</u>, left the beat after more than twenty years[1162].

In August 2008, the police's proposed industrial action involved a work to rule[1163]. Pay talks collapsed despite the Home Office offering 2.325% (the Police Federation wanted 3.5%)[1164].

Militant public sector unions were threatening to bring out PCSOs (among others) on strike[1165] in 2011.

The Scottish Police Federation's 2008 vote for the right to take industrial action was unprecedented, even though Scottish police received the full 2.5% rise awarded by the Police Arbitration Tribunal in 2008[1166]. When Jacqui Smith refused to backdate the 2.5% pay rise the Police Federation called on her to resign and over 20,000 police marched on London[1167].

Firemen's threat to strike on Bonfire Night 2010 was branded as 'reckless' and 'cynical' and could cost lives[1168]. Similarly the police's threat to strike can be seen as dangerous: under a 1919 law they agreed not to strike, but only if their pay was acceptable! A 2007 vote by the Police Federation's constable section showed 77% supported rethinking the laws against striking (striking officers face up to two years in jail)[1169].

'I think they're working to rule...'

The Met had to man their three 999 call centres, when the handlers went on strike, by taking officers off patrol[1170]. Notts Police support staff (including PCSOs) went on strike because of compulsory redundancies[1171].

In October 2011 English forces were planning to 'work to rule' over pay and spending cuts. Plans to withdraw out of hours cover were being made by the Police Federation[1172].

In 2007 PCSOs, who do have the right to strike, got a better pay deal than regular officers, who can't strike and whose Police Federation believed the government was using PCSOs as policing on the cheap[1173].

Suspensions with Pay

A 2007 survey of Britain's 52 police forces revealed 276 officers (including a superintendent) were suspended but still receiving full pay. Investigations into suspended officers can take years, the average (2007) being 10 months. It took seven years to fire two officers at the heart of a fraud scandal in London. The Police Service of Northern Ireland has (2007) the most officers suspended[1174].

A Strathclyde officer, who has not been named, was on suspension with full pay for 4½ years (by February, 2009). As recently as 2008 there were 40 Scottish officers serving suspensions[1175].

Lothian and Borders Special Branch officer <u>Greg Anderson</u>, suspended in October 2008 and convicted of 'neglect of duty' (relating to seized drugs in March, 2011), was still receiving full salary in April, 2012. Chief Constable <u>David Strang</u> refused to entertain a press inquiry (from the Daily Record) about the matter. Anderson was given a cabbie's licence even though suspended officers aren't supposed to work, and Strang didn't object, as he could have in the light of Anderson's criminal conviction. The force had spent £615,641 in five years on 28 suspended officers. Anderson finally resigned after a press campaign. It meant he bypassed a disciplinary hearing[1176].

In 2008 more than 260 suspended officers (on 'gardening leave') cost £7.8m. Police take up to three weeks sick leave a year, costing at least £4m weekly. The average length of suspension is said to be 10 months, but by spring 2008 an RUC officer had been off work for seven years and five months. A Hampshire PC returned to work in 2008 after being suspended in 2001 – it was over two years before he was charged and 16 months before he was cleared in court. He was tried again on new charges seven months later. Though again cleared he remained suspended. After another two years a misconduct investigation found there was no case to answer. In Sussex DCI <u>Peter Salkeld</u> was paid during his two year suspension until he was jailed for three years (he abused his work credit card and a police widows' grant)[1177].

Taxpayers are facing a large bill for <u>Ali Dizaei</u>'s legal aid for his 2012 retrial: he claims he has been left in debt from previous legal cases. He has compared his imprisonment to that of Mandela and Gandhi[1178].

An inspector has been taken off frontline policing to cover the suspended civilian manager of the Strathclyde Police Recreation Association, who has been paid full salary while suspended for a year – by 2008 there had been no contact from the police about the suspension[1179].

Seven of Scotland's eight forces (Northern Constabulary declined to provide figures) have spent over £5.3m in five years on 170 suspended officers, including an assistant chief constable (<u>John Mauger</u>) still earning his £150,000 salary (accused of being a bully and liar) after two years, a Special Branch officer who spent 3½ years on full pay (drugs were found in his house), more than a year <u>after</u> he was convicted of neglect of duty, as well as a chief inspector (<u>Allison Strachan</u>) convicted of trawling police databases illegally: she was suspended for 22 months[1180], then fined £400 in 2012.[1181]

Ali Dizaei

Even after being convicted and suspended on full pay the Met still subsidised <u>Ali Dizaei</u>'s trip to Iran, where he is known as 'General Dizaei'[1182].

Waste

All public institutions are wasteful, some more than others. Here are just a few examples of police waste.

A number plate recognition post was manned by <u>eight</u> police officers, yet on one day in Basingstoke in 2007 just five officers were available for a population of 150,000. Many officers have reported finding two-thirds of their colleagues missing when they came on duty[1183]. There are about 100 officers less per 100,000 population in the UK compared with the European average.

A Lancashire police station is closing a month after the completion of a £200,000 facelift, which included disabled access[1184]. The Met spent £68,000 moving Scotland Yard's revolving sign 15 yards, even though they are selling the building[1185].

Police had to pay out £2.3 million in 2005 to people who had been wrongly arrested, with many settlements including a 'no publicity' clause. Claims for unlawful detention are the fifth commonest complaint, after allegations of assault, failure of duty, rudeness and harassment. The Met had to pay out over £70,000 to a large group of antimonarchists arrested in 2002 during the Golden Jubilee Celebrations[1186].

North Yorkshire Chief Constable <u>Della Cannings</u> installed an ensuite shower in her office, costing taxpayers £30,000. It may mean financial regulations governing police forces have been ignored. A senior North Yorks officer called it 'a dreadful waste of money'. The force has been criticised for almost doubling the council tax police precept in three years, and spent £0.5m on Volvo V70s for senior officers[1187].

13 forces around the country have spent over £20,000 on 'flat-pack cops' (life-size cardboard cut-outs). Several forces have had them stolen[1188].

Officers in the eight Scottish forces cost taxpayers £43,000 over three years by filling their cars with the wrong fuel (repairing vehicles can cost more than £5,000)[1189].

Despite facing extensive budget cuts West Midlands Police spent £100,000 on black shirts[1190].

Police chiefs have spent £2.4m on digital notepads (Personal Data Assistants) despite complaints they make the job more difficult. Only two Scottish forces have used their £1,000-a-time Taser guns in five years, with two dozen having to be replaced or repaired in four years[1191].

The police mount expensive advertising campaigns, at public expense, banging their own drum[1192].

CAVEAT CIVIS

Six policemen broke into a home at dawn, discovering only enough cannabis to merit a warning. Vast amounts of police time and money are spent on dealing with illegal drugs[1193].

Nottinghamshire Police have produced a 7,000 word, 22-page manual on how to write emails and use the internet[1194]. One force has banned their officers from charging their private mobile phones and other gadgets at work.

Jersey's authorities say its child-abuse inquiry was a huge waste of time because the police got it wrong. Thus dozens of statements named abusers, but the witnesses were unreliable. No children died at 'Colditz' care home, police say[1195]. The thing that triggered the £4.5m probe was probably a bit of coconut, not a child's skull[1196].

Regarding the probe into Assistant Chief Constable John Mauger (on £104,000 p.a. for three years' 'gardening leave'), Forth Valley Divison of Police Scotland has revealed £0.5m has been set aside to take the case forward[1197].

Medway Police were criticised as 'absurd' after they made PCSOs pick up rubbish – councils already employ people to do this in an area (Lordswood in Chatham) where car crime has rocketed and where there were plenty of burglaries. Blundering Cambridge Police set up a speed trap in a traffic jam[1198].

South Yorkshire Police sent two officers on an expensive trip to South Korea to retrieve images from a mobile phone, It was part of a probe costing £80,000 into the death of a drunk Pole in Barnsley[1199].

British police are being sent on 'forensic hypnosis' courses (costing thousands) led by an American celebrity therapist[1200].

Warwickshire Police, who told the public to arrest criminals themselves, set up a racism hotline in eight languages, but it was axed after two years because no one rang it[1201].

Sussex Police, criticised in 2007 for spending £102,000 on translators, has now issued picture cards to help them communicate with eastern European immigrants . West Yorkshire police are taking Urdu lessons at a cost of £1,400[1203]. Scots police have spent over £2m on translators in the three years from 2008, and the figure is rising. The languages involved include Tagalog, Pasto and Amharic[1204]. UK forces are spending over £75,000 daily on translators for migrants, and thus spending is growing fast as immigration increases. The Met tops the league with £29.3m in three years. Some police interpreters are earning £100,000 a year, with some using a stacking 'scam' to overcharge the police, i.e. understating travel time so that they can book as many jobs as possible.[1205]

The huge cost of speed cameras has arguably been largely wasted: Department of Transport figures show only 3% as the proportion of accidents caused by drivers exceeding the speed limit[1206].

Norfolk Police have been accused of wasting £35,000 on a new logo almost identical to the existing one, being issued in order to be more 'people-friendly'. The force has been criticised for plans to cut the number of stations with 999 response teams from 35 to six. In 2008 the force announced it had stopped fully investigating crimes it believed were unlikely to be solved[1207].

A 17-page form has to filled in by police asking permission to move a CCTV camera, while permission to tail a burglar takes more than half a day to complete the relevant forms. Police must log extensive details on every child they encounter, even if they are not at risk[1208].

A tabloid survey in 2007 revealed a PCSO solves on average just one crime every six years, while a PCSO team has issued just 15 fines for a cost of almost £10 million[1209].

A police blunder caused an expensive court case over three dead goldfish (possibly due to bleach poisoning) to collapse. Police had forgotten (or couldn't afford) to send fish tank water for analysis[1210].

Scotland Yard lost £30m when it re-invested in a failing Icelandic bank (Landsbank) shortly after withdrawing the cash on its financial expert's advice[1211].

ACPO in Scotland has rubbished claims that money is being wasted on eight HQs, the Government wanting to drastically reduce this number[1212]. Scottish police have wasted over £2m over five years due to blunders requiring compensation[1213]. Edinburgh police were given 276 parking fines in 2009[1214].

The Yard's Operation Gestalt – a probe into 20 serving and retired Customs and Excise officials, involving over £1 billion in evaded tax – has been dropped after costing £5m[1215].

When one tyre on a police vehicle needs changed the other three plus the boot tyre are changed routinely: there are about 35,000 police vehicles in the UK, and at least a fifth of them suffer a flat each year[1216].

Kent Police, which is laying off 500 officers, sent two officers to hunt for lost shopping trolleys[1217].

A report by Sir Denis O'Connor, HM Chief Inspector of Constabulary, found police were so inefficient that £1 billion could be cut from Government funding without cutting services. The report also found only a ninth of officers and PCSOs are visibly available to the public[1218].

Police moved out of a property they owned to rented premises. The old police headquarters was put up for sale as an empty property, but was soon occupied by squatters[1219].

CAVEAT CIVIS

Eight Greater Manchester Police vehicles and 20 officers descended on a quiet residential street to arrest one loitering 'hoodie' when an alert came in from a Neighbourhood Watch member[1220].

An £80,000 unmanned Greater Manchester Police surveillance balloon turned out to be a white elephant because of the British weather[1221].

Former Thames Valley Chief Constable Peter Neyroud has called for fewer meetings attended by top officers, after it was revealed (in the Police Review) that senior officers spend 100 days a year in meetings[1222].

Bungling police chiefs from several forces (including Cambridgeshire) wasted almost £½m in testing dodgy electric squad cars (they are too slow, and the batteries go flat after 30 minutes). They also squandered money on waterless eco-toilets which were abandoned after problems with cleaning and blockages[1223].

Neither Northumbria's Police Federation branch, nor the force itself, would help financially the PC blinded by killer Moat (e.g. with hospital parking charges)[1224]. He committed suicide. Yet Northumbria Police spent £1.7m on 'corporate communications'.

In 2011 the Home Secretary and the Met's boss responded to pressure from No. 10 to pour further resources into the Madeleine McCann hunt – Metropolitan Police Authority member Jenny Jones branded a new investigation a 'ludicrous' waste of money. Much of the funding given by the public may have been wasted or diverted by previous inappropriate probes[1225]. The Yard boasted (spring 2012) that they would solve the mystery: DCI Andy Redwood has 36 detectives and civilians for the job (Operation Grange)[1226]. The Met's review of the McCann case is set to reach £2m in its first year (working on the case are four DCIs, five DS, and 19 detective constables)[1227].

Police forces are giving the names of at least 30,000 members of the public monthly (without their consent) to marketing companies, to gauge the response to inquiries, e.g. 999 calls. Thus over £700,000 was paid in 2010 to two firms (Bostock Marketing Group and Swift Research of Leeds): Surrey Police alone spent £108,000 on opinion surveys[1228].

Strathclyde Police have been accused of wasting police time when 10 officers turned out at a friendly football game between Rangers and Celtic: there were only 50 spectators[1229].

The Met is spending thousands on theatre tickets (for top West End shows) for 210 offenders and problem school pupils. It is hoped such 'diversionary activities' will prevent trouble in Enfield[1230].

Police are spending millions on bottled and cooler water, to supply their offices and meetings[1231]. A £1m. scheme to give Blackberry phones to over 3,000 South Yorkshire officers needs further finance after they quickly became 'out of date': the buttons were too small and required long passwords[1232].

New four-wheel-drive estate cars for firearms officers were found to be too small for them, so the gas-guzzlers were passed on to the rank-and-file. A new fleet of customised fast-pursuit vehicles were found to be uncontrollable at speed unless a quarter ton of sand was placed in the boot[1233].

THE FINANCIAL POLICEMAN

West Midlands Police have spent almost £4m on private security guards to protect its own stations – some even perform front-desk duties[1234].

The Met is willing to spend time probing the theft of a packet of chewing gum from the Foreign Office, also £10 which had gone missing. Other thefts from the F.O. which warranted police help included that of grapes, hair straighteners and a jar of Vaseline[1235].

Police officers are being brought back from holiday to give evidence in court, e.g. one was returned from a career break in Australia to give testimony for just 23 minutes. Some fly home to find they aren't needed after all. Strathclyde Police flew home two PCs from Hong Kong and back again. Lothian and Borders also regularly fly officers back[1236].

Scottish police have been diverted to accompany rangers protecting birdlife (in fact only five rare birds)[1237].

When celebrity Jemima Khan asked the Met to help find her lost Bengal cat, two WPCs turned up to investigate in under 24 hours. There was no suggestion that the disappearance was suspicious. This is the same force that refuses to send officers to burglaries if the suspect has fled. Ms. Khan's neighbours report that despite thugs, thieves, vandals and even a gunman terrorising them, there was little interest from the constabulary[1238].

The 2006 police raid on the late peace protester Brian Haw in Parliament Square cost the taxpayer over £111,000[1239].

Two Fathers4Justice campaigners were acquitted after a trial costing an estimated £0.5m over three years. They had tried to handcuff themselves to Margaret Hodge as a citizen's arrest. The legal costs were inflated by a heavy police presence throughout the hearing (to prevent further protests)[1240].

Hampshire Police sent two constables to persuade an eight-year-old to go to sleep at 3am[1241].

There are no official figures of how many cops leave for police jobs abroad.

Lothian and Borders Police spent thousands sending cards to burglars and sex offenders asking them to give themselves up[1242].

Merseyside's 'Snorkelling Squad' was sent to Grand Cayman Island to solve a Caribbean gangland murder spree – the same island where the Met's 'Sunshine Squad', on a similar mission, attracted an outcry in 2009. The squad included Chief Constable Jon Murphy, Detective Chief Superintendent Brian McNeill, ACPO officials and former head of the force's crime operation unit, and Detective Chief Superintendent Tony Doherty, head of the Matrix and organised crime squad. They were reportedly sight-seeing and sunbathing. 16 other officers were to spend six weeks on the island[1243].

The Royal Family charges the taxpayer for the keep of their armed SO14 protection officers. The Palace refused to comment on policemen being charged for accommodation, when the Royals don't contribute anything to SO14 costs. Officers spent £318,000 in four months, including the cost of accompanying Prince William and Kate during French skiing trips. Rent is also paid by the police to the Queen for Balmoral estate cottages for SO14[1244].

Even while Kate Middleton was not yet engaged to Prince William, when as a member of the public she was not entitled to formal police protection, she was given an escort of six officers[1245]. At least eight Met officers were diverted from other duties so that Prince Harry and his girlfriend could leave a nightclub at 4 am in peace[1246].

The Home Office in 2010 spent, of all government departments, the most on 'spin', at £73 million, and the most on temporary staff (£161 million, which could put 33,000 constables on the streets). The Ministry of Justice was the biggest spender on taxis (£3.4 million)[1247].

The NPIA's head has admitted wasteful spending (on lingerie, beehives, lavish hospitality, karaoke equipment, etc)[1248]. A senior NPIA official has received a pay-off of £500,000 – the quango's mantra is 'to boost police efficiency', yet has wasted £6 million on government credit cards[1249].

Police officers working in the Police Federation are being given time off official duties to campaign against spending cuts – the cost involved could put 300 extra officers on the street: 623 officers and civilian staff were allowed to work part-time on union duties at taxpayers' expense in 2010/11, with a further 99 staff allowed to work full-time on employment relations. In 2010 police forces and the Home Office spent £7,290,331 on wages for union officials[1250].

Lothian and Borders Police spent £120,000 on a new logo – to show they are the police. It will cost even more to brand cars, uniforms, etc[1251].

A Tayside Police 'tweet on the beat' trial , hailed as a revolution in Scottish policing, has only one officer still using the site. Some officers feel they could be at risk of posting something compromising to the force, with obvious career implications[1252].

Staffordshire Police paid £480,00 to management consultants to tell them how to save money – don't make so many arrests[1253].

Fife Constabulary has banned their officers from wearing American-style sunglasses, chewing gum, consuming food in their cars, musical ringtones on mobile phones. Pullovers must only be worn in police offices, sleeves mustn't be rolled up, and there are restrictions on hair dyes. The 24-page 'Dress and Personal Appearance Standard Operating Procedures guide' has been described as a 'waste of money'[1254].

Eight Lothian and Borders Police chiefs had a 'jolly' stay at a luxury 4-star country club, the Dalmahoy Hotel, to discuss cutting costs. They also reportedly hired a conference centre there despite having appropriate facilities at force headquarters in Edinburgh, and despite the force being cash-strapped. The officers included Chief Constable <u>David Strang</u>, Deputy Chief Constable <u>Steve Allen</u>, Assistant Chief Constables <u>Iain Livingstone</u> and <u>Bill Skelly</u>, and were joined by 'Director of Resources'

Chief Constable David Strang (left)

Peter Thicket and Susan Mitchell, in charge of the 'transforming the service' drive to reduce costs[1255].

When Lothian and Borders Police put officers' packed lunch provision out to tender the schedule of stipulations ran to over 45 pages (10,000 words)[1256].

According to former Met officer John Kenny the old eight-hour shift pattern was less wasteful of resources than the new complex shift patterns which have taken over: these try to synchronise the deployment of manpower with expected demands. In theory this is more efficient but may prove counter-productive,. Cynics may suspect this 'complicating tendency' of ACPO and the Home Office may be an attempt to confuse the public, so that it is much more difficult under the new system to assess efficiency, e.g. by comparing like with like[1257].

The Met has spent over a quarter of million pounds in two years calling directory enquiries and the speaking clock[1258].

To comply with the Protection Services Standard police must fill in forms with 1,099 questions[1259].

Hants Police Authority bought a new HQ in Chandlers Ford in 2008, but have now changed their mind: they are now taking over a new HQ in Winchester[1260].

Own car park crashes have cost Scottish cops over £250,000 to repair 764 prangs in three years. A Scottish officer settled out of court for a large but undisclosed sum for injuries received when his advanced driver training car careered off the road[1261].

Scottish forces are paying at least £¼ m annually to criminal grasses without having to account for the money[1262].

Councils have spent over £0.5 billion on CCTV cameras over four years[1263].

Devon Police scrambled an expensive helicopter to chase a group of 'doggers' (three men and a woman were caught, but another woman escaped), yet reportedly other forces make life easier for gay doggers[1264]!

Wigan Football Club won a £300,000 court case against Grater Manchester Police over the cost of policing matches. ACPO's Andy Holt says he thinks clubs should pay more[1265].

Tayside Police have paid out at least £5,500 after 25 (perhaps more) blunders – filling up with the wrong fuel – in five years[1266].

Careless officers in Cumbria and Northumbria have pranged their cars in police car parks hundreds of times in three years, costing £97,000. The Cumbrian force refused to give details of collisions[1267].

Cleveland Chief Constable Sean Price, on a salary of £208,000, spent £55,0000 on his force credit card (including £7,000 on restaurants and £1,000 on flowers)[1268].

South Yorkshire Police's intention (2012) to replace regular officers on the streets with PCSOs has been criticised by the latter's creator; they claim 80% of what patrol officers do is not related to crime at all. Blunkett says they should help police, not replace them[1269].

CAVEAT CIVIS

The Department for International Development managed to spend £5m on foreign police investigations, e.g. DCs Peter Clark and John McDonald went to Nigeria as witnesses in trials of money launderers[1270].

Strathclyde's Chief Superintendent <u>Bill Fitzpatrick</u>, the central figure in claims that an ex-colleague's elderly relative was given expensive 12-day special protection, is to quit the force on full pension. The request had been made by former Assistant Chief Constable <u>John Neilson</u>, who received the Queen's Police Medal in 2009. The controversial patrols only came to light when Sergeant Martin Porter complained (to an employment tribunal) about how he suffered stress when he criticised the way the operation was conducted[1271].

In <u>Surrey</u> 200 officers were replaced by 1,300 civilian staff[1272].

Devon and Cornwall Sergeant <u>Mark Ruston</u> withdrew from the trial of his alleged attacker at Exeter Crown Court when he found it would clash with his Olympic duties guarding the torch, despite his claiming it was the worst violence he had seen in 14 years. The Recorder, who had therefore to register a not guilty of assault verdict, was not too impressed by the officer's attitude[1273].

<u>Sussex Police</u> were due (summer 2012) to sack 500 officers and 550 staff but had just appointed five press officers. Staff are being appointed to teach cops how to tweet. What really matters to police: spin[1274]!

Up to at least 176 police officers are working as union representatives full time for the Police Federation, costing taxpayers nearly £6m annually (e.g. Devon and Cornwall has 10 union officers, the Met 19)[1275].

The Police Federation want to be allowed to keep fit during work time, if there are to be compulsory fitness tests[1276].

According to new regulator Tom Winsor police are spending too much time at their desks doing 'two-fingered typing' rather than fighting crime. He has watched officers standing in a queue for up to four hours to book a suspect[1277].

Scotland's new police service has cancelled its new logo, which was illegal as it wasn't checked with the Lord Lyon: £100,000 of taxpayers' money was wasted, and going ahead without the approval of the heraldic authority would incur fines[1278].

Scotland's police have been accused of waste for squandering around £50,000 on commemorative dinners, dances, badges, coins, whisky glasses, even a variety show, all in memory of the dissolving forces[1279].

West Midlands officers were given taxpayer-funded hypnotherapy and aversive therapy to help them stop smoking[1280].

As in the NHS, PFI initiatives have infiltrated the police, e.g. in 'superstations' like the one authorised by Kent Police Authority at Medway. Bureaucratic red tape means officers aren't allowed to change light bulbs – they have to order toilet rolls, site rubbish bins, etc. by filling in private contractors' forms or calling an emergency hotline[1281].

<u>Lancashire Police</u> handed out cards to householders to put in their windows to warn off carol singers[1282].

Sussex Police, criticised in 2008 for spending £100,000 on Indian head masseurs for stressed staff, has hired a style guru to boost officers' self-confidence. Superintendent June Rhodes said similar practices were common among other forces[1283].

Andrena Quinn, head of the Scottish Police Authority and interim CE of the new Scottish Police Authority, ran up an £800,000 bill for 'behavioural management training' with private consultants[1284].

Scotland's new police authority may change its mind over a move to a new headquarters in Stirling because of a potential procurement blunder. It may cost taxpayers over £100,000[1285].

Cops are wasting time and taxpayers' money (estimated at over £1m. annually) recording small gifts offered while they are on duty, even when not required to do so[1286].

Warwickshire Police's party for travellers at their HQ spent thousands of taxpayers' money on a Roma band, a 'graffiti project', art workshops and dancing[1287].

Norfolk Police spent £255,000 on a new website because it makes them 'more visible'[1288].

The Met has signed deals with over 300 companies worth £3.5 billion, including a £1 billion IT contract , £4.6m on surveys of what people think about it, and £600,000 for 'conflict management services'. A London Assembly Police and Crime Committee spokesperson says: 'Police officers tell me they see waste all the time at the Met ... it costs £100 just to put a whiteboard up. There is waste at every level of the organisation'. The Met plans to sell its New Scotland Yard headquarters. It leased five electric cars for £64,000[1289].

The Scottish Prison Service pays the full-time salary of a Strathclyde police sergeant to place disgraced security firm G4S under surveillance, to ensure it is doing its job properly. The SPS has spent over £0.25 m. to watch G4S and its rival Reliance[1290].

Police officers are increasingly working in backroom jobs, while part-time civilian volunteers (special constables) are helping to fill the frontline vacuum more and more[1291].

Tayside Police has given every community cop a £300 smartphone, so they can tweet on the beat to appear 'more human'. All but one of the Scottish forces use Facebook[1292].

Sussex Police had to pay millions extra to private security firm Reliance Secure Task Management for six years running because they locked up more suspects than their PFI contract allowed. This type of arrangement may be a major factor in the rapidly increasing use of cautions[1293].

Nearly 200 officers are working full-time for their union the Police Federation[1294].

Over £60,000 has been spent by Scottish forces in five years repairing police vehicles damaged after the wrong type of fuel was used[1295] (see also page 152).

Hertfordshire Police were accused of wasting money after dispatching a helicopter to catch a shoplifter who had stolen meat from Tesco[1296].

The Met has been accused of an 'unjustifiable' waste of money – in 2002 it was employing 64 race relations advisers ('diversity trainers') while seriously short of front-line officers[1297].

Grampian Police's 'Operation Wellside', which teaches adults how to cross the road, has been criticised for wasting police time[1298].

Scottish police spent around £3m in 2008 on an army of PR operatives[1299].

The unpopular 'police precept' rose by about £1.5 billion in the decade since 1997, though only £800m went on recruiting more officers, who spent less than 20% of their hours on the beat[1300].

The cost of Police Scotland's computer revamp has almost quadrupled to £45 million[1301].

Instead of bulk-buying equipment, the police waste millions because forces cannot agree on standardising uniforms, boots, etc[1302].

Thousands of hours that Scottish officers could have spent patrolling have been lost because they are being shunted around the country (eg. Strathclyde's Licence and Violence Reduction Unit taking four hours out of a ten-hour shift to and from the east coast), in order to 'share best practice'[1303].

Resources

The public have no say in what is the best use of police resources.

At least 12 of the 43 English and Welsh forces were reducing their full-time complement of officers at the start of 2010, despite Government assurances that police resources were ring-fenced. Unpaid volunteers (Special Constables) will fill many of the gaps[1304]: Bracknell Forest police's 'Operation Labrador' asks dogwalkers to be their unpaid 'eyes and ears'.

When a stolen car's whereabouts were told to the police, they said they didn't have the resources to investigate the case (they would charge £125, however, for someone to go and pick up the car)[1305]. When a burglary victim asked police to apprehend the thief who had stolen his computer (he had traced him), they said it would be too expensive[1306].

Strathclyde DC John Sharkey told a court he was banned from quizzing a drug suspect because the force couldn't afford the overtime[1307].

By 2009 the hunt for Madeleine McCann had cost a British police force £745,000[1308]. The new (2011) Met review will cost even more, to little effect, according to critics: the latest figure is £2m.

Strathclyde Police were facing a budget black hole in 2010 of up to £35m[1309]. This budget slide was upped to nearly £60m in the red early in 2010[1310].

A teenage girl who managed to escape a serious sex attack was told by Dorset Police they couldn't justify doing a DNA test, because she hadn't actually been raped, and resources were short[1311].

Volunteer Special Constables are for the first time to help investigate serious crimes in Hampshire. The use of amateurs has been criticised at a time when detection rates are the lowest for decades[1312]. Derbyshire Police are sending out untrained civilians with mobiles and reflective jackets to patrol their own streets, with less powers than CPSOs. The latter have been under scrutiny when it transpired that dozens were involved in drug-dealing, assault and fraud, bigamy and racism: one was deported as an illegal immigrant[1313].

The Government's 'red tape tsar' Jan Berry says officers spend just 13% of their day on patrol. Police have been told to patrol alone to save resources. A 2009 White Paper advised cutting the helicopter fleet, adopting a standard national uniform and patrol car, as well as cutting office staff[1314].

A Cambridgeshire shopkeeper had to drive a suspect shoplifter to the police station because, despite four 999 calls, he was told repeatedly that police were too busy to respond[1315].

Many of Scotland's police stations are not fit for purpose – 11 need urgent attention, with 35 in poor physical condition. An expert report says Strathclyde Police 'lacked a strategic approach', and criticised the force's proposed new £50m capital projects, which would mean ending up with a large deficit[1316].

The Norwich city centre police station closes early for the evening. A banker was kicked to death 200 yards away one evening when he went to help a homeless Lithuanian, who had been attacked by a mob[1317].

ACPO's 2008 eco-driving guidelines to make traffic cops save money – turn off the air conditioning, turn off the engine when stationary, share vehicles, stop excessive braking, revving or acceleration, leaving behind inessential equipment, use video conferencing – have not gone down well with drivers, especially as ACPO is even threatening checks to see the code is being observed[1318].

To save money on expensive barristers, serious criminal cases are being downgraded or charges dropped, and cautions are rising fast[1319]: dumbing down justice.

Police are failing to check thousands suspected of accessing paedophile websites because of lack of resources. The Child Exploitation and Online Protection Centre (CEOP) says the huge volume of data (about 400 intelligence reports monthly, each capable of producing hundreds of names) severely stretches its manpower[1320].

Many of Britain's police forces are failing to check crucial CCTV tapes because they are 'too busy'. The Met told a burglarised trader that they didn't have time to watch a tape from a camera in front of his premises, while a woman who had a handbag stolen was told by a Met officer: 'It's not our job to check the CCTV cameras'. But detectives won't know if there's something incriminating on camera until they view the footage, and victims are not even allowed to check the latter (one council said this would be illegal). Humberside Police have a 'screening policy': commercial burglaries and assault are not routinely investigated unless they meet certain PC criteria (racist, homophobic, etc)[1321].

When a teenager was mugged in London for his phone, he told the officers in a police car, but they said they couldn't do anything because they were short staffed and it was Hallowe'en[1322].

Because of staff shortages the police are now allowed to recruit foreign nationals. In 2006 440 police were controversially taken off the beat to tackle the illegal immigration shambles[1323].

Derbyshire Police assigned only one detective to investigate a violent robbery which led to murder, because up to 40 officers were busy probing some stolen chickens in Operation Function. The IPCC said six unnamed officers were disciplined over the matter[1324].

After receiving a tip-off about a robbery that would take place in a Cheshire village, all that police did was to leave an unmanned patrol car near a jeweller's shop, which was duly robbed[1325].

The Lancashire Chief Constable has announced he can't afford to pay his 427 PCSOs from 2011, and lack of resources may mean thousands more face the axe around the country[1326].

Strathclyde Chief Constable <u>Steve House</u> says his cash-strapped force wouldn't pay for policing Olympic football matches[1327]. Police Scotland under him is discontinuing paying the insurance for mountain rescue teams, who claim this will seriously risk public safety.

Devon and Cornwall Police have been banned from charging their mobiles and plugging in kettles to save money. At one station they reportedly had to wear coats and gloves at their desks[1328].

Leicestershire Constabulary is selling furniture, computers, cameras and patrol cars on eBay[1329], as well as 'bling' (e.g. jewellery) bought by villains: the force will get a percentage, though most will go to the Home Office[1330].

Up to £1.3m flowed into the coffers of West Midlands Police in two years as payment for tipping off recovery firms about accidents and abandoned cars[1331]. Forces are making millions by 'selling' accident details to breakdown firms (one force alone made £1.3m in just one year). Their 'administration fee' is up to £25 per vehicle, and ACPO says they are doing nothing wrong[1332]. Greater Manchester Police 'referred' 32,855 cars in 2009, but refused to say how much they had made. It is likely more than three-quarters of forces are making the charge. In one year West Midlands Police made an estimated £622,275 from contractors' tip-off payments for car crashes[1333].

Avon and Somerset police have been told to catch the bus, walk or cycle to save money[1334] and North Yorkshire Police were told to pay for their own boots, while senior police drove around in expensive cars[1335]. Her Majesty's Inspectorate of Constabulary found North Yorkshire Police – the force handling the search for missing chef Claudia Lawrence – 'lacks specialist skills and resources'. HMIC also found Cumbria, Lincolnshire, City of London, Cheshire and Wiltshire forces below standard[1336].

Kent Chief Constable Mike Fuller warned the Home Office he needed increased resources to cope with an immigrant crimewave which had contributed to a rise in violent crime of over a third in five years[1337].

PCSOs may be replaced by unpaid Special Constables, members of the public who would be given powers of arrest and council tax rebates – a suggestion from ACPO. Norfolk Constabulary is considering a loyalty card scheme for Specials[1338].

Befordshire Police is thinking of closing police stations and replacing them with Skype[1339].

The Met are trying to sell an office block (Curtis Green Building) inside the Whitehall secure zone – it overlooks the MOD and Downing Street. It could be sold to Russians[1340].

For 'minor crimes', witnesses and victims wanting to report these will have to pay to phone the 101 police hotline[1341].

Merseyside Police faced a bill of millions in 2010 for policing the LibDem conference because they didn't ask for funds[1342].

Married West Midlands Police director of finance and resources Derek Smith, a member of ACPO, has quit over an expenses claim for an unapproved hotel stay with a blonde female colleague. His advice led to hundreds of job losses in his force. In 2011 a £40,000 BMW series car (normally used by undercover police) was stolen from outside his home – it was filled with sirens, police radio and special covert blue lights, raising questions as to why a civilian staff member had such a vehicle for his 'personal use'[1343].

Police in training are simulating car chases by <u>pushing</u> their vehicles to save money. North Yorkshire villagers are paying for petrol for a patrol car borrowed from a garage[1344].

West Yorkshire Police told a theft victim to track down the culprit himself 'because we are short of resources'. The year before, a passing policeman in Hull refused to help chase a thief, telling the victim to ring 999[1345].

Officers given expensive smartphones (costing £80 million) spend <u>more</u> time in the station (e.g. two hours more per shift), instead of their efficiency improving[1346].

The 1996 Police Act allows forces to provide 'special' police services to 'any person' who can pay for the service.

Strathclyde is to gobble up Edinburgh's 130-year-old mounted police force to save resources, but Edinburghers think their officers will be less effective as a result[1347].

'Team' rather than 'beat' policing was pioneered by a Scottish force – Grampian. One team subsumed ten traditional beats and comprised a sergeant, four PCs and a radio car: English cities such as Liverpool soon jumped on the 'cost-saving' bandwagon[1348].

Lothian and Borders Police charged £400,000 for policing Zara Phillips's Edinburgh wedding (2011)[1349].

Two months after an IT businessman was almost killed by three burglars with crowbars, a Met officer told him the DNA samples from his fingernails had been returned because the force couldn't afford to pay for the analysis: the police would be sending them again when funds might be available[1350].

Gay Chief Inspector <u>David Lyle</u> has been seconded to look after his gay colleagues, at the taxpayers' expense – the first Scottish coordinator of the Gay Police Association (GPA). This, while a Scottish force are employing civilian staff for murder and rape investigations. The GPA refuse to say how many members they have in Scotland. Lyle, the first openly gay

Scottish officer, 'came out' while he was married and took part in Gaydar's online 'Sex Factor' competition to find the world's sexiest gay[1351].

Strathclyde Police are changing the logo on vehicles, stationery, etc. (from 'Working Together – Building Safer Communities' to 'Keeping People Safe'), despite their facing the axe in 2013, and even long-serving officers are being asked to sign pledges to keep people safe[1352].

The Met is predicted to spend £40m on phone hacking but only £36m on child abuse: there are just 27 officers to track paedophiles, with 150 (possibly to rise to 200) devoted to hacking[1353].

Officers from just one Scottish force – Lothian and Borders – have made 3,000 calls in three years to find out the time, despite being told they must have a working watch at all times. £8,800 was also spent calling directory enquiries[1354].

'Crimewatch' presenter Nick Ross says he couldn't sell the programme to the police: even after the BBC1 controller commissioned a three-month run: only three chief constables would participate in the first transmission[1355].

West Yorkshire Police have axed police sunbeds in social clubs and gyms to save electricity. West Midlands Police are substituting microwaves for 122 ovens in its police stations to save money[1356].

The public will be diverted to supermarkets, libraries , etc. as 264 police counters are closed by chief constables[1357].

The Police Federation says forces don't have the resources to monitor the internet[1358].

Grampian Chief Inspector <u>Tom Forrester</u>, involved in an RTA while using a blue light to dodge traffic when there was no emergency, has been paid over £175,000 while on gardening leave. His pension will not be affected[1359].

The cost of police dealing with an incident of serious violence rose by almost 60% in the four years to 2009 (up from £5,890 to £9,376). A similar increase has been found with fraud[1360].

Scottish police have spent £13m. over three years on doctors, e.g. casualty surgeons are earning up to £200,000 annually on top of their normal salaries for responding to incidents. Fife Constabulary's doctor earned over £210,000 in 2012[1361].

When this author asked (under FOIA) various English forces: (1) How common in police remunerations is the 'retention' package? and (2) Do officers with secondary jobs in your force have higher sickness or absenteeism rates?, the request for information was refused, on the ground of lack of resources.

Over four years the Met gave £26,500 sponsorship to Muslims involved in the annual Global Peace and Unity. One speaker at the event said suicide bombings were justified by Salman Rushdie getting a knighthood. The Met also employed Tunisian Mohamed Ali Harratt as a terrorism adviser though he was wanted by Interpol because of alleged terror links[1362].

Huge police resources go into fighting drink-driving, one of the lesser causes of road accidents (see The Harmful Policeman chapter for the police as a cause of road accidents). Drink-driving may be behind considerably fewer than one-sixth of the total number of UK road deaths. Certainly only 6% of the 230,000 casualties of all severities in 2008 'occurred when someone was driving while over the legal alcohol limit'[1363]. This should be compared with the 3% figure for speeding as a cause of serious RTAs.

Other money-earners (including criminal)

The Police Federation has been accused of scaremongering when they warn cuts will mean 'Xmas for criminals'[1364]. Derek Barnett, president of the Police Superintendents Association, warned (2010) cuts could cause riots in the streets[1365].

Rapist ex-cop Adam Carruthers has been given up to £100,000 Legal Aid to sue Dumfries and Galloway Council for the pension contributions to his pension they had reclaimed. This is in addition to £110,000 he has already been given for his trial, and to fund civil actions while in prison[1366].

Police in the Victorian period are said to have 'acquired' watches from drunks on their way home from the pub, so 'if you want to know the time – ask a policeman'[1367].

Lost cash handed into police stations in Scotland often goes missing. An undercover tabloid survey found Strathclyde, Northern Constabulary and Lothian & Borders said they did not have wallets handed in by reporters, but they were soon found when the press offices were contacted (one had to make up the wallet's contents from petty cash!)[1368].

Deputy Assistant Commissioner John McDowell, the Met's national coordinator of terrorist investigations, was questioned in 2009 about a possible misuse of his American Express corporate credit card (the IPCC was handling 33 Met Amex cards, including McDowell's). DS Richard De Cadenet, who served under McDowell, was sentenced to 10 months in 2008 for misappropriating £70,000 on his card, and McDowell's former boss, Andy Hayman, resigned in 2007 after disclosures about his expenses. Met sergeant John Gallagher was given a suspended sentence for card misuse[1369].

Fraudulent royal protection officer Paul Page and his wife reportedly spent money on an extravagant lifestyle to give them a 'veneer of credibility'[1370]. Some royal protection officers were into property and investment schemes, others were moonlighting. They would sit on the throne and use police cars to escort cash from Page's business, allowing friends to use the Palace car park. An anti-corruption team knew about Page's misdemeanours but amazingly let him carry on with his £3m property scam. After a jury found him guilty of fraudulent trading – he controlled six firms – the Met ruled out any further probe into the culture at the Palace[1371]. The spread-betting syndicate (the Currency Club) run by the Palace's SO14 (the scheme collapsed with many police losing substantially) had security cameras reversed to conceal the men receiving envelopes full of money. 130 officers across the country were involved[1372]. One royal protection officer says another would sell Dutch porn to colleagues while on duty: others were playing poker for money, and senior officers turned a blind eye, claimed Page[1373].

Durham Constabulary PCs <u>Maurice Allen</u> and <u>Damien Cobain</u> admitted selling guns handed in for disposal[1374].

Damien Cobain

Maurice Allen

Chinese immigrants set up a cannabis farm in a Dornoch cottage rented to them by PC <u>Neil Bremmar</u> – the plants were worth over £300,000[1375].

<u>Sir Ian Blair</u>'s close friend Andy Miller carried out work for Surrey Police when Sir Ian was Chief Constable there (1998-2000). The Met also gave Mr. Miller lucrative contracts (over £3 million) during Sir Ian's time as Met Commissioner, yet the latter was cleared of favouritism by Sir <u>Ronnie Flanagan</u>, appointed to head the Home Office probe into the matter[1376].

<u>Norman Brennan</u> retired from British Transport Police after being disciplined for 'misconduct' related to his media and campaigning activities. He often referred to his status as a police officer to give extra credibility to his pronouncements. His 'Victims of Crime Trust' was to be dissolved voluntarily in 2010 after the Charity Commission's finding that hundreds of thousands of pounds of donations were unaccounted for – Brennan was accused of 'mismanagement'. The charity failed to file accounts for more than four years. Less than 3% of donations was spent on 'direct charitable purposes' over the decade following its founding in 1994[1377].

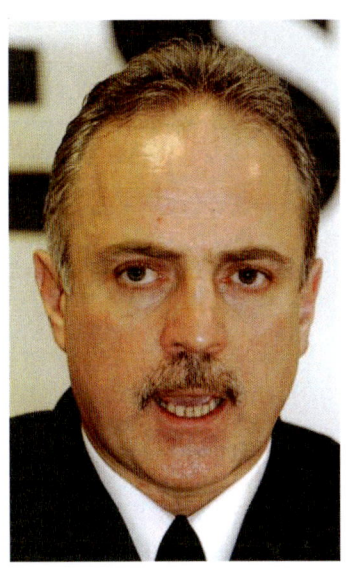

Norman Brennan

Northumbria PC <u>Mick Butter</u>, responsible for monitoring pubs and clubs across Sunderland, was made to resign after being caught disclosing confidential information – and taking free meals and hotel accommodation. As club and pub staff were reluctant to give evidence, the 50-year-old officer got off with a criminal caution after admitting misconduct in a public office[1378].

Former police inspector <u>John Meggison</u> was being probed (2007) over claims he sold his old uniform for £175 on eBay. He was believed to hold a top civilian job with Essex Police[1379]. Black warrant card wallets, which can be used by criminals to masquerade as officers, were being advertised (2007) for only £9.99 on the auction website[1380].

Inspector <u>Jillian Kerr</u> was accused of using her official pass to avoid feeding an Edinburgh parking meter. Traffic wardens had complained to Lothian and Borders Police because her mini didn't look like a normal unmarked police car. When questioned she denied knowing what a reporter was talking about, and a force spokesman refused to reveal her identity. PC <u>Andrew Higgins</u> was accused of using a disabled badge to park outside his work station[1381].

It is alleged WPC <u>Victoria Thorne</u>, who had been with Northumbria Police for seven years, had a secret life as a £100-an-hour escort, one of The Notorious Girls, an organised prostitution ring of 70 women. 'Kelly' appeared on the agency website in provocative underwear poses[1382]. Thorne was jailed for 15 months in 2009.

The luxury car-hire business run by his wife from the home of Britain's top anti-terror policeman, Assistant Commissioner <u>Bob Quick</u>, was operating without the correct licence, and drivers had not had CRB checks (Quick's own Jensen Interceptor was among the chauffeur-driven cars available). He had to withdraw an accusation that the Tories had 'corruptly' planted the limousine business story to undermine his Damian Green raid[1383].

A key aide to Scottish Police Service Authority boss <u>David Mulhern</u> quit her job to manage his millionaire wife's tearoom in Glasgow. The SPSA, with an £80 million annual budget, has been accused by senior police chiefs of interference (the head of the SCDEA – 'Scotland's FBI' – claimed Mulhern's SPSA drowned his organisation in red tape, and the Deputy Chief Constable of Strathclyde Police blames the SPSA for his decision to resign). Mulhern reportedly broke the law in 2008 by keeping emergency lights on in his BMW[1384].

A retired Tayside policeman won a Land Tribunals for Scotland arbitration decision allowing him to buy his traditional police house. Senior officers fear they may be unable to police rural areas if this paves the way for a mass sell-off of the houses[1385].

Anti-terrorist <u>DS Richard de Cadenet</u> was jailed after diverting £73,000, using his force's American Express credit card to treat his mistress, pay for a football club box, clothes, etc. Other officers bought holidays and Rolex watches[1386].

London PC <u>Amerdeep Singh Johal</u> was jailed (2008) for six years for trying to blackmail and extort money from sex and other offenders[1387].

Interim Met chief <u>Sir Paul Stephenson</u>, who took over when <u>Sir Ian Blair</u> stepped down over the £3m of Met contracts given to the latter's friend Miller's consultancy Impact Plus, was quizzed by auditors in 2008. Stephenson's colleagues say he failed to question his boss (being <u>his</u> deputy) about the friendship[1388].

Sir <u>Ronnie Flanagan</u>, who headed the inquiry into the Miller affair, was to take the unprecedented step of issuing Sir <u>Ian Blair</u> with a 'regulation nine' notice, placing him under formal investigation[1389]. Miller's company, Impact Plus, advised Sir Ian on his leadership style, communications strategy and the main messages that should be emphasised[1390]. In 2010

Sir <u>Ronnie</u> had £17,000 spent by the Home Office on flights from his Abu Dhabi home to chair nine meetings and was paid £1,000 a month for leading the police chiefs' panel[1391].

27 of the UK's 52 police forces use 0845 numbers which charge 40p a minute to call one's local station, the public being encouraged to use them for 'non-emergencies'. Forces that refused to disclose their 0845 earnings included Avon and Somerset, but five forces made a total of £33,000 in a year[1392].

Police don't bother checking stolen bikes' security tags – they are auctioned for police charities[1393]. Police sell on retrieved stolen property, often without informing the owner, and there may be no attempt to return the latter's item(s)[1394]. British Transport Police sergeant <u>Mike Burnett</u> was sacked for selling a police helmet on eBay[1395].

In 2009 an inquiry was being suggested into how criminal and DVLA information was obtained by PIs, who then sold them to journalists[1396].

Police chiefs have threatened to remove officers from Scotland's football stadia unless SPL Clubs can pay £5m[1397].

Surrey Police are charging potential recruits up to £1,000 for training <u>before</u> being offered a job[1398].

Former Cambridgeshire Chief Constable <u>Ms Julie Spence</u> claims that speeding by even a few mph is a 'middle-class hypocrisy'. Writer Frederick Forsyth calls this 'uniformed pretentiousness'[1399].

Police guarding the House of Commons earn more than the MPs (one got £72,000 in 2009), some earning more than double the basic £31,176 of a typical beat man[1400].

<u>John Yates</u>, the Met's Assistant Commissioner, was reprimanded by the Commissioner after complaints about him using air miles from his official trips to buy his family cut-price flights. Yates and his wife of 25 years split in 2009, and he is now in a relationship with an Australian ex-Yard Press officer[1401]. (See also 'The Murdoch Policeman' chapter).

In 2010 almost 9,500 police were receiving full salaries (over £285 million) for secretarial work, an increase of 20% over four years, with another 2,000 on long-term sick leave, i.e. at any time 10% of police are on such leave or limited duties[1402].

Police retire at about 50 on two-thirds pay. If they are ill like anyone in any normal job, why do they get full pay[1403]?

Civilians are being used to assist with murder inquiries, e.g. the private firm Police Associates Register conducts door-to-door and CCTV investigations. This outsourcing of core police functions may impair trust (e.g. corrupt officers might get jobs with the private firms)[1404].

Tony Blair's police protection squad was probed to see why they apparently bought a rocket launcher on expenses. The IPCC also queried whether a protection officer broke rules by accompanying Blair to the Middle East (the officer's partner had worked for Israeli security), and probed a senior colleague who approved the officer's trips to Israel and Gaza. In the first four months of 2010 police joined Blair on holidays and over 21 international trips[1405]: his bodyguards' expenses claims included £30 ladies' shorts (for a male officer) and a £1.19 packet of Percy Pigs (a type of sweet)[1406].

ACPO has suggested axing all Special Priority Payments and bonuses because money is tight, as well as offering payments for taking several years off[1407].

The National Policing Improvement Agency – set up in 2007 to get better value from the £9 billion policing budget – faced claims it ordered over 200 automatic assault rifles it didn't need at a cost exceeding £400,000, just to use up its budget. It allegedly hadn't put the gun order out to competitive tendering, as it should have under E.U. law. Its 2009 chief executive, Peter Neyroud, admitted the NPIA spent £71m on consultants in a year, some earning £2,000-£3,000 a day. The NPIA also paid £23,000 a year for Neyroud to use a flat in Westminster: he also had a flat at Bramshill House, Hampshire but, according to a former policeman who worked there, the training centre had a culture of heavy drinking (he also claimed he had seen a deputy chief constable and a colleague 'skinny-dipping' in the lake on the 269-acre estate[1408]). The NPIA paid off 156 staff in 2010-11 at a cost of £6.1m, yet increased its permanent headcount by 49[1409]. The NPIA has splashed out taxpayers' money on credit cards, lavish hospitality (£6.5 million in four years) at their Hampshire Bramshill headquarters: designer lingerie, visits to castles, a beehive, rhododendrons, National Theatre tickets, karaoke items, restaurants and bars, five star hotels, airsprung beds, sports kit, payment to a golf company. Ministers experienced 'blocking tactics' by top civil servants when they tried to probe how many police have been abusing the procurement cards for personal purchases. Ironically the NPIA is responsible for making efficiency improvements to forces' spending[1410].

Barry Phillips

With no previous experience, family members of police officers have been given lucrative contracts to type witness statements, e.g. a company registered at the home of former Flying Squad chief Barry Phillips was paid £1.7 million over five years for transcription services, while another run by two police wives has been paid £1.8 million by the Met. The Met refused to say whether the firms got the contracts from the units where the officers were working, or whether competitive tendering or word of mouth was involved[1411].

D.C. Jim Kerr, cleared in court of assaulting a passenger on a train, was being probed by his Central Scotland Police bosses, but is to sue British Transport Police[1412].

A century ago a Newcastle police inspector warned that a policeman is 'subject to temptations that the ordinary man in the street cannot know of'. His sergeant added: 'You can have no conception. It is hard to be honest when your pocket is empty'[1413].

Police are allowed to keep 25% of any assets taken in raids on prostitutes' premises. A Luton woman who worked from home had her door broken down and £700 taken from her purse, as well as her computer, phone, driving licence and passport, with no receipt given: her neighbours are supporting her in court[1414].

Northumbria Police took delivery of a £50,000 sculpture (the glass and steel structure looks like a ball bearing in a hula hoop) at their new Wallsend HQ on the same day staff were told 450 jobs were to go. The sculpture is named 'Total Policing'[1415].

Commander Paddick's investigation of Met expenses led to two arrests and one high-profile resignation (almost £2m on American Express cards were unaccounted for)[1416].

Police forces have had their counter-terrorism funding cut by millions after a secret audit found they were diverting the cash to other things, e.g. City of London Police were getting £3.7m for a 'ring of steel' that no longer exists, with senior officers being given luxury apartments. Part-time PCSOs were being recruited with the money. When first asked about the funding cut City of London Police refused to discuss it[1417].

Beat police spend more time off work than on duty (up to 20 days were annually at home) catching criminals, according to a 2010 HMIC report. When police are most needed (e.g. Friday nights) they are least available. Just 3.5% of the total complement of officers are on average available for emergency response, and in one force it was as low as 1.2%. There are legal provisions in place that prevent forces making officers redundant[1418].

Kent Police are paying over £9 million a year of taxpayers' cash to 350 staff already receiving generous pensions[1419].

A Northumbria Police deputy chief constable left the force with a £300,000 lump sum plus pension, only to then take up a £100,000 a year post as Acting Chief Officer on Jersey[1420]. Lothian and Borders Superintendent Carol McLean retired on a £35K pension and a £195K lump sum, the next day starting the same job with a £15,000 pay rise, as civilian head of criminal justice at the Scottish Police Services Authority[1421].

ACPO was scheduled to spend £½m of taxpayers' cash on a champagne gala for its annual conference (2010), having made almost £400,000 'surplus' from similar events in the two previous years. ACPO is thinking of replacing 28,000 beat officers with civilians. Individual forces will cover hundreds of pounds for their officers' travel, etc[1422].

The absenteeism rate among Scottish police is 4.3%, about 20% higher than the private sector[1432]. Is it related to moonlighting? The authorities ay they cannot answer this question..

Under the Police Act (1996) forces made £17 million in 2009 by hiring their officers to shopping centres, supermarkets and motorway service stations. 28 of the 48 UK forces were into 'rent-a-cop'. Other venues paying for, e.g., PCSO policing, were schools, universities, airports, hospitals and even a drag-racing circuit[1424]. Top Merseyside officers, including the Chief Constable, were hired out, according to him, to Grand Cayman Island: 16 other officers were to continue their investigation, again paid for by a foreign power[1425]. Richard Branson's Virgin Media secretly bought the help of Met officers to probe a multi-million fraud involving illegal set-top boxes. The 2008 arrangement guaranteed the Met Police Authority a quarter slice of any compensation Virgin secured. A Liberty spokesperson commented that it is tantamount to hired guns for the rich. Branson also offers cheap holidays to Met officers. The discounted holidays are regularly advertised in the Met's internal magazine: their new boss Boris Johnson says he knew nothing of this[1426].

THE FINANCIAL POLICEMAN

A 2010 report by King's College's Centre for Crime and Justice Studies found police using dishonest methods to boost their pay ('Spanish practices', such as claiming for taking a call just following a shift, or ensuring arrests are made outside working hours). Though over the previous decade the number of officers rose by more than 15,000 to over 142,000, with an extra 16,000 PCSOs as well - the largest UK police service ever – this did not result in the expected decline in overtime[1427]. Police budgets increased 50% in a decade, with no obvious effect on already-falling crime rates. Also, as the British Crime Survey reveals, crime fell in 1998 at the same time as police numbers were falling – rates carried on falling while police numbers started going up, i.e. no correlation exists. In 2010 only eight minutes out of every hour is on the beat, <u>less</u> than in 2004/5[1428]. Increasing abortion rates seem to be genuinely linked to falling crime rates, rather than police numbers.

A known thief conned scores of police officers – he says at least 300 from the Met, Bristol and Kent, some high-ranking – in a Madoff-style pyramid investment scheme. They even visited his luxury farm for parties round his pool, but if they had done a CRB check they would have detected his 1985 and 1986 convictions. The FSA closed down his KF Concept firm in 2004, leaving 8,500 victims in the care of a trustee[1429].

Greater Manchester officers have spent up to 80 minutes completing a holiday request form: it can take 20 minutes just to find a form on the force's computer[1430].

Jailbird Jonathan Rhys, who worked for News of the World's Andy Coulson and was boss of PI firm Southern Investigations, bribed serving and retired officers to get stories, according to 'Panorama', which obtained secret police transcripts of talks with Southern Investigations[1431].

Brian Paddick claimed that <u>Sir Ian Blair</u>'s force had become intoxicated with power, a 'diamond' group of senior officers seeing themselves as 'untouchable', leading, e.g., to expenses scandals[1432]. City financiers are being asked to volunteer to help Met fraudbusters[1433].

McDonalds is helping fund a team of police and civilian street marshals to patrol Leeds city centre at night[1434].

Sussex Police say they recover over 1,000 stolen vehicles annually, collecting up to £195,000 in recovery fees from victims[1435]. Strathclyde traffic officer <u>Stephen Greenhorn</u> is the owner of 911 Recovery, who seize cars for the force: he admits he's handed over, while in uniform, two cars to his own truck drivers. His Strathclyde bosses deny there is a conflict of interest. The AA, who have the lucrative towing contract, use 911[1436]. A police letter given to motorists who've had their car stolen tells them they have to pay £105 for it to be 'forensicated' (checked for clues). There are no similar fees for any other police service (£100 for storage has to be paid as well)[1437]. Retired Scottish police inspector Jim Michael had to hire a truck to collect his grandson's stolen motorcycle, which had been found by police near where it was stolen within hours. He had to pay a fee of £150, of which the police get a cut. He says it's wrong for a victim of crime to be charged to recover their property: when he was in charge of a pound at Midlothian there was no fee for recovering vehicles[1438].

Met PCs <u>Ross Anders</u> and <u>Damon Goodman</u>, who lived together and planned a 'civil wedding', tried to sell a valuable memento (the Order of Service) from the tenth thanksgiving service for Princess Diana on eBay. Despite taking an oath of allegiance to the Queen, the Met thought the appropriate punishment was 'words of advice'[1439].

Hertfordshire Police are demanding that TV programme company Endemol pay for their investigation into alleged racism on set. The police won't provide security in future unless the bill is settled[1440].

Essex Police have asked Epping residents if they can park their private cars free on private driveways all day, arguing it could help deter burglars. It would save officers paying parking charges[1441].

Generous benefactors are supplying Britain's police chiefs with tickets to the Cup Final, Wimbledon, Royal Ascot, the opera, health spas, Twickenham[1442].

Less than half of forces in England and Wales give staff clear guidance on acceptance of gifts[1443].

Shamed Durham cop Maurice Allen, who sold amnestied firearms for personal profit, was backed by the Police Federation in his successful attempt to regain the reduction in his pension ordered by the Police Authority. An accomplice, Damian Cobain, also had his pension forfeiture reduced. The two received suspended jail sentences in 2010. A farmer had told police he had 'bought it [his stolen shotgun] from the police'[1444].

Compensation claims have been refused by some police authorities after they downgraded the 2011 riots to 'violent disorder' incidents[1445].

In a large number of US cities the local councils have given in to police and firemen who have demanded huge pay rises and pensions, meaning other essential services being severely cut or scrapped. Some cities are bankrupt as a result.

Scottish and English forces are involved in an unseemly wrangle over a provisional bill from north of the Border for the policing of the Olympic and Commonwealth games, following a dispute over payment for the help given to English forces to quell the 2011 riots[1446].

Special Branch officer Greg Anderson has been suspended (over cocaine claims) on full pay for 42 months (by April, 2012), longer than any current Scots officer. In three years Scottish forces have spent £2.5m on wages for 65 suspended officers. His name was highlighted in the context of cocaine-dealing colleague Chris McGinn. One Scots officer was suspended on full pay for almost four years before retiring[1447].

'Driving Awareness' courses are a nice little earner for police at £90 per session[1448].

At least 14 Scots officers have been caught making unauthorised journeys in force patrol cars and misusing letter headed notepaper[1449].

The Police Federation said the choice of civilian Tom Winsor as Chief Inspector of Constabulary 'beggared belief'. Winsor's two reports proposed a fundamental shake-up of policing, particularly raising retirement age, scrapping various allowances, and giving chief constables power to make officers redundant: great resentment was caused[1450].

Police drafted in from outside for the Olympics will receive a 'hardship allowance' of £30 nightly if their accommodation has no en suite facilities, with 10,000 officers enjoying a £50 allowance for each night away from home[1451].

Scottish forces are accepting largesse from private companies for cars and staff. Stagecoach has funded a travel liaison officer in Fife, while Grampian Police now have a wildlife liaison officer, thanks to the Maersk oil company. GlaxoSmithKline have given £10,000 for a car. Auto Service and McEwans, the Perth department store, have bought cars for Tayside Police. Other sponsors include William Hill, while councils, airports, etc. 'buy in' officers for their premises. Are conflicts of interest liable to be creeping in[1452]?

Crooked ex-cop <u>Paul Johnston</u>'s rogue Guardian Security firm went bust owing £1m, but by phoenixing continued trading while he was on the run in Spain[1453].

The Met fought the BBC for six years to retain the commercial rights to the blue police box used at street corners by the Met until the 1960s. The Patent Office eventually ruled that the BBC's claim for the Tardis (in 2002 the image had been used by them for 26 years) took precedence. The force has retained the rights to the blue station lamp[1454].

It emerged in 2003 that the Met and other forces would only respond to burglar alarms if the owner had paid their registration fee[1455].

Crime prevention officers often got kickbacks in the Greater Manchester area from security firms. Cops were swanning around with big houses, yachts, Rolls Royces[1456].

CHAPTER X
THE HARMFUL POLICEMAN

CHAPTER CONTENTS

CHAPTER X

THE HARMFUL POLICEMAN

In 2010 there were 33,859 complaints against police[1457]. These almost doubled in an earlier three year period (2004-2007), with over 4,000 claiming they had been assaulted. There were 29,000 complaints in the year to March 2007, i.e. one complaint for every five officers: about a quarter were for failure of duty and 15% for alleged assault.

The Violent Policeman

In 1867 the Birmingham Daily Gazette campaigned about 'the terrible and cruel punishment inflicted upon lads by irate and passionate policemen' in the poorer working-class districts. The police in the East End resembled an army of occupation, according to some, especially during industrial conflict when blacklegs had to be protected[1458].

Wiltshire Police custody sergeant burly Mark Andrews, who was dismissed in 2010 following his treatment of a female suspended drink driver (he threw her on the floor, along which he dragged her), had been investigated about another incident in 2008, when a man was allegedly punched and kicked by Andrews, but the IPCC allowed him to continue working. The two officers accused of lying to help Andrews have been named: PC Mark McIntyre and Acting Sergeant Kate Smith, who were to receive 'words of advice'. The recent victim said: 'Who do you trust after that?'[1459]. The Police Appeals Tribunal ordered that Andrews, sacked following an internal inquiry – his six-month jail term for assault was quashed on appeal – must be reinstated[1460].

CCTV cameras captured (2005) a policeman (PC Mulhall) delivering five blows to a young epileptic black woman before she was dragged away with her trousers around her legs, the images echoing those of the notorious beating of black motorist Rodney King by LAPD officers in 1991.

Met officers involved in the 2004 Parliament Square bloodying of scores of hunt supporters were referred to the CPS for possible charges (the three who faced trial were acquitted), but the IPCC report refused to endorse claims of police brutality. However the IPCC chairman (who received an initial 425 complaints) said: "The images of injured hunt supporters cast a shadow across the reputation of the Metropolitan Police Service'. The Met have been accused of instigating 'tit-for-tat' revenge prosecutions against official complainers (about police brutality at the demo). The IPCC says it has to pass on complainants' details to the police. A farmer who is Master of a Hampshire hunt claimed a policeman at the Parliament Square protest hit him with a truncheon, leaving him with a deep head wound. The crowd had pushed him forward, and CCTV footage apparently captured a PC Jenkins deliberately hitting him on the head. Met officers will hit peaceful Countryside Alliance demonstrators over the head with truncheons, but simply look on when looters rage through Clapham[1461].

PC Andrew Shovelar, who had won awards for bravery, would beat his partner if she disobeyed his cruel and bizarre 'ground rules' (e.g. she mustn't talk to him for 30 minutes on his return from work). He would allegedly call her 'retard' or 'spastic' and the c-word, lock her in the house, kick or try to strangle her. If he was off work she had to drive around in the car all day while he stayed alone at home.

CAVEAT CIVIS

Hero policeman <u>Chester Smith</u> was charged with spraying a football boss with CS gas before framing him for fighting and resisting arrest. Smith also allegedly tried to wriggle out of a speeding charge.

A victim of rapist police inspector <u>Adam Scott Carruthers</u>, jailed in 2001 for 12 years, has pleaded with the parole board to keep him in jail because of his dangerousness.

Assistant Chief Constable of Essex <u>Peter Lowton</u>, one of Britain's most senior officers (he worked on the Jill Dando case and was in charge of 650 officers), was arrested at home for allegedly assaulting his partner. His responsibilities included terrorism, organised crime and critical incidents.

Scotland Yard detective <u>Paul Turpin</u> broke his teenage lodger's leg with a spade to get him out of his property in Hertfordshire, a court was told in 2007.

PCs <u>Beverley Coombes</u> and <u>Catriona McFaydyn</u> were investigated after being caught on CCTV using 'excessive force' to arrest a pregnant woman, who subsequently lost her unborn baby. One WPC allegedly told the woman: 'If you weren't pregnant … I would be wrapping a truncheon around your head'.

Black Salford WPC <u>Carla Street</u> 'beat up a blonde' who caught her PC lover's eye at an Asda store.

A woman claimed at Nottingham Crown Court she was raped in a police cell by custody sergeant <u>Paul Banfield</u>, who denied this and another rape charge and indecently assaulting a third woman at Parkside police station, Cambridge. However he admitted indecently assaulting two other women in a police environment.

The Met paid out about £4,000 in an out-of-court settlement to a teenager who was dumped in a rubbish bin by a plain-clothes officer. The latter's identity was not released and he escaped criminal charges, just given a written warning[1462]: another classic example of double standards.

A disabled man has told how he was dragged by police from his wheelchair twice during the 2010 student riots[1463]. The IPCC has ruled that the Met used excessive force in dragging Jody McIntyre from his chair (December 2010). The incident should have been recorded as an assault but it was allowed to over-run the six-month term, so that no officer could be charged (unlike rioters, who have been charged within days!)[1464]. Double standards again?

An Aberdeen Royal Infirmary anaesthetist – she set up a field hospital for the injured in the 2010 Westminster student riots – has warned of a repeat of the Hillsborough disaster if police persist with kettling. She said people couldn't move their feet or hands for hours, with some having respiratory problems and symptoms of severe crushing[1465].

Strathclyde constables <u>Thomas Clark</u> and <u>Andrew Glover</u> allegedly assaulted innocent Glasgow (Milngavie) householders whom they should have been helping – one had had his home and car vandalised. Clark tried to cover up the victims being forced to the ground and handcuffed by filing a false report, and was jailed for three months for his 'abject treachery'. Glover was convicted and fined[1466], but they were cleared of assaulting the innocent men by the Appeal Court in Edinburgh in July, 2011[1467].

Strathclyde PC John Wardrop, a key player in an anti-domestic violence operation, threatened to kill his own estranged wife – he bombarded her with menacing and obscene calls. Despite 25 years' service and several awards, he was convicted and fined for aggravated breach of the peace, but was appealing[1468].

Jealous Strathclyde ex-policeman Shazhad Rafia assaulted his ex-mistress, whom he was stalking, after he saw a man picking her up – the latter was beaten up too. Rafia also told a man who was threatening suicide to 'go ahead and do it'[1469].

Mark Jones

In 2010 the CPS decided that four of the Met's Territorial Support Group's PCs (Nigel Cowley, John Donohue, Roderick James-Bowen and Mark Jones) should be charged with causing actual bodily harm to Babar Ahmad in 2003[1470]. He was badly bruised, but they were cleared.

Off-duty Berwick police sergeant Neil Mutch was charged (2010) with assaulting a schoolgirl and using threatening behaviour[1471]. Met PC Karl Bartlett, 6ft 3in, was found guilty of inflicting 'disgraceful gratuitous violence' on a 14-year-old in a car pulled over for using a mobile. The teenager was thrown against the car, headbutted and his feet were stamped on[1472]. Bartlett was given a three-month suspended sentence and ordered to pay £400 compensation to the boy. The ex-soldier was guilty of a 'momentary abuse of power'[1473].

West Yorkshire PC Keith Empsall was warned he should expect a prison sentence after being caught on a student's camera beating up another student in the street who was drunk. The film showed the officer giving three punches and a kick before handcuffing the arrestee and dragging him to a patrol car by his hair. The video shocked millions who saw it on TV[1474].

In G20 CCTV pictures a burly unnamed Territorial Support Group sergeant was seen raising his baton before striking a woman on the legs, causing her to collapse on the ground[1475]. Sergeant Delroy Smellie was cleared by a judge of assault, claiming self-defence[1476]. At the G20 demo there were 296 complaints about police behaviour, 83 investigations, but not one prosecution[1477].

Detective Constable Damien McIntyre was arrested and suspended from Staines Police charged with assaulting a colleague and making threats to kill[1478].

Lanarkshire PC Scott Miller appeared from custody at Glasgow Sheriff Court charged with assaulting his partner[1479].

A dawn raid by the Met on former No 10 aide Ruth Turner has been described as an example of police heavy-handedness. Former chief of staff Jonathan Powell's wife has attacked the police for 'Gestapo tactics' in relation to the cash-for-peerages inquiry[1480].

British police have targeted all ages with 50,000 volt, skin-piercing Taser guns (from 12 to a demented 89-year-old), including a commuter in a diabetic coma on a bus (despite the latter wearing a special diabetic tag around his neck) – he was the first UK citizen to receive compensation (for being Tasered by West Yorkshire Police). Tasers were fired (between 2004 to 2009) 1,765 times (officers call it 'sparking up'). 334 people in the US died in seven years after being Tasered, according to Amnesty International. In 2010 the police were investigating introducing an even more powerful rifle version. 'Drive-stun' involves repeating the 50,000 volt shock. Northumbria is the top of the Taser use league. Children and small adults are at increased risk of heart attacks. Police in England and Wales fired (or threatened to) Tasers against at least 142 under-18s in 2008-2009[1481]. Cornwall PC James Thompson, who Tasered a drunk at a party, was suspended from using the gun until he underwent retraining[1482]. Greater Manchester Police blasted a man having an epileptic seizure with a 50,000 volt Taser[1483].

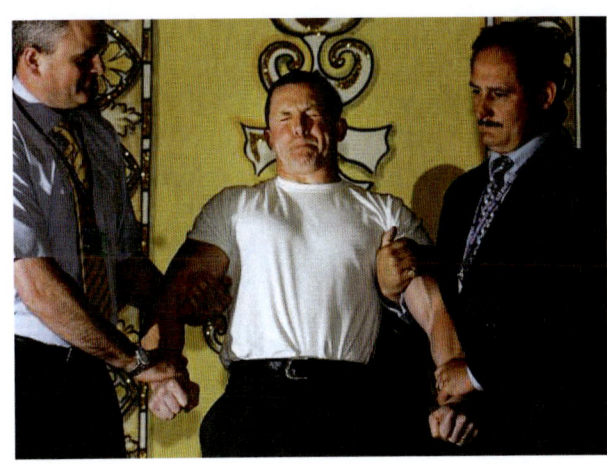

A Kent policeman shows the pain of being stunned with a Taser electric stun device during a demonstration at a Police Federation Conference

When firearms police tried to storm the carriage of the Docklands Light Railway train, where a knifeman was holding several hostages, one of the latter was Tasered by mistake[1484]. The 'Super Taser' police who shot Moat had been given only ten minutes' training[1485]. An innocent sufferer from Guillain-Barré syndrome was Tasered in the groin by Avon and Somerset Police, who wrongly thought he had been driving without insurance[1486].

Strathclyde PC George Park, who worked at Glasgow Sheriff Court, was jailed for 18 months for several vicious spousal attacks (punching and trying to slash her head), but walked free because of time served. A social inquiry report described him as 'potentially dangerous'[1487]. The serial wife-beater was eventually sacked over two years after being imprisoned, thus earning £90,000 while inside. He had gone sick, which delayed his sacking – he failed to attend two disciplinary hearings.

Six armed Cambridgeshire police terrified an elderly couple clutching their zimmer frames – there had been a wrong tip-off about a loaded shotgun[1488].

OAP and grandfather Robert Whatley won over £20,000 damages from Gwent Police (despite their refusing to admit liability) because they smashed his Range Rover's windows after stopping him for a seatbelt offence. The two police were filmed by their own patrol car's camera. The incident was watched by over 30 million people on Facebook. The victim was recovering from a stroke. It is again of interest that the officers' identities were concealed, and they are back on duty[1489].

Former Strathclyde PC <u>Ian Martin White</u> threatened to kill his neighbours and headbutted the arresting policeman. White was also convicted of smashing their windows. He verbally abused a neighbour and breached his bail conditions but wasn't punished – the victims claim they have not had any support from the police or courts, so they are having to move house. The force refused to comment on the reasons for White's resignation[1490].

At first Greater Manchester Special Constable <u>Peter Lightfoot's</u> victim, a frontline soldier, was convicted of assaulting 20-stone Lightfoot, but, thanks to CCTV evidence revealed by a tabloid, the policeman was later found guilty of perjury five times in the case, and causing ABH (grinding the lance-corporal's face into the ground and banging his head and cracking him over the head with a police helmet). Though incarcerated for 20 hours the victim was not given access to a solicitor, despite having 14 injuries. It emerged that despite a complaint about Lightfoot to the Professional Standards Branch – that he had been seen kicking someone in 2007 – he was never prosecuted[1491]. On this occasion he was jailed for three years.

Dumfries & Galloway Police officer <u>Neil Cawthorne</u> faced a disciplinary hearing after being fined £600 for assault (he repeatedly struck a suspect on the head during an interview at Newton Stewart police station)[1492].

Strathclyde PC <u>Ross Cartner</u>'s career was in the balance when he was found guilty of assault while off duty[1493].

Two Tayside officers, PC <u>George Stewart</u> and WPC <u>Shirley Tindal</u>, failed to have the assault charges against them thrown out at Dundee Sheriff Court. The trial of the accused, who denied the charges (Stewart is alleged to have cuffed the female complainant in a crucifix position during a 'bizarre' attack), was continued in 2012[1494]. <u>Stewart</u> was convicted of assault and ordered to pay his victim, a bail hostel worker, £1,000 – he had wrapped sticky tape around her face, 'an act of some brutality', 'unprofessional' and 'juvenile' according to the sheriff. He had left the woman hysterical. It was the end of his 15-year career. <u>Tindal</u> was cleared, but the sheriff said she had 'not told the truth'[1495].

Two Caithness Police officers (one was <u>John Waters</u>) gave a hiding to a cheeky boy in Thurso in 1957, leading to the scandal of the 'Thurso boy': a government inquiry was critical of police behaviour. There were other assault cases in Wrexham, London and Birmingham. Being a bully or hooligan was no longer an excuse for aggressive police behaviour, the courts were deciding[1496]. When Gunter Podola, suspected of shooting a policeman, was beaten up (1957) in Chelsea Police Station, the Met Commissioner paid £300 to settle proceedings against one of his constables. Sir Robert Mark tells of a senior post-war Manchester detective who asked suspects: 'Will you talk or be tamed?'. A refusenik would have his head held in a toilet bowl and repeatedly flushed. There was also electric torture by battery chargers to encourage confessions[1497].

During the Chinese premier's visit to London the Met were accused of brutal policing in Bishopsgate, e.g. wrenching placards from peaceful protesters.

When a lodger claimed her Chinese landlord had stopped her removing her belongings, three police officers forced their way into his house, twisted his arms behind his back, put him in a neck lock, punched his face and struck it with keys, as well as kicking him in the back and racially abusing him. He had to walk home from the police station in his bare feet. A jury found the police had fabricated their note-book entries and lied on oath. He was initially awarded £220,000 damages. None of the officers was disciplined[1498].

A 14-year-old girl in foster care, having been previously assaulted in different foster care, was arrested under s.46 of the Children Act at her mother's home and charged with police assault. She should only have been thus forcibly removed from her parental home if she was in danger, but she wasn't. The girl says one of the four officers kept banging her head on the floor. She was put in a cell[1499].

Ayrshire PC Peter Cullen was charged by colleagues (and kept in cells overnight) with inflicting serious injury on a man in custody at Saltcoats Police Office. The officer was bailed, but Strathclyde Police said he was still on duty awaiting trial as well as an internal disciplinary hearing[1500].

Off-duty Met PC Raul Raines – a firearms licensing officer – refused to help a pensioner who had collapsed (she later died), after he had a road-rage row with her 72-year-old husband, whom he grabbed, leaving him 'scared witless'. Raines wouldn't even call an ambulance (the pensioner had just had heart surgery). A disciplinary hearing found him guilty of 'discreditable conduct' but he only received a written warning[1501].

Somerset PC Terry Hatton was sacked (2012) for misconduct after admitting spousal assault (his reason: there was no bread in the house for toast)[1502].

A Bolton policeman in riot gear was caught by cameras seemingly punching a 63-year-old anti-fascist at an English Defence League clash in 2010. The 63-year-old was charged with using threatening behaviour, but the charge was dropped. The IPCC said the CPS is to decide whether to proceed against the officer[1503].

Strathclyde firearms instructor Steven Campbell, convicted of assault – he had been accused of raping his former partner – and sacked, has appealed his sacking[1504].

The conviction of rookie Ayrshire PC Ross Cartner for assault on a night out was overturned on appeal[1505].

Tayside PC Douglas Fisher (an ex-TA soldier) was accused of repeatedly assaulting a man with his baton while on duty in Dundee[1506].

Crazed former Dumfries and Galloway sergeant John Kelly tried to decapitate his teacher ex-wife after drugging her, running her car off the road and throttling her. She was permanently disfigured. He was trying to simulate an RTA, leaving her to burn to death: his wife fled her home just before he was released from prison[1507]. He was jailed in 2006, his sentence cut to 10 years on appeal. His parole appeal was turned down in 2011.

Despite two Tayside Police drugs squad officers being charged with assault (one accused of a number of attacks and suspended, another with one accusation not suspended), their identities were not revealed. A probe uncovered 'matters of concern'[1508].

Durham custody sergeant Stephen Harvey was found guilty of common assault and fined: pensioner David Healer, who was peppered, then tortured, was to take a civil action against Teeside Police[1509].

Tayside PC Douglas Fisher was found not guilty of battering a nightclub bouncer with his baton[1510].

A sheriff has been criticised for merely admonishing West Lothian community police officer David Purves for terrorising his wife and daughter by breaking into their home with a hammer after she locked him out[1511].

Harm from vehicles

Compensation claims against police drivers involved in RTAs had in 2002 soared by almost 30% in a year – more than 7,000 people sued after crashes with police vehicles (deaths had risen from nine in 1997 to 30 in the first nine months of 2000). Victims of crashes involving police vehicles (about 50 a day) were paid compensation of about £3.5 million in 2006. Deaths from accidents with police cars have risen more than fivefold since 1997 (from 9 to 48 annually). Between one and 11 police pursuits out of every 1,000 now lead to a death. The IPCC has found police drivers are taking unnecessary risks in high-speed chases.

Two Greater Manchester traffic officers pulled over a sports car and, suspecting drink driving (it was allegedly being driven erratically), drove it off but soon crashed the £30,000 vehicle[1512].

Royalty Protection officers Sergeants Paul Waldron and Graham Daly, both specialist drivers, were involved in a good weather crash on the private Balmoral estate. Their 4x4 Range Rover flipped onto its roof – no other vehicles were in the vicinity[1513].

PC Timothy Dunning (Thames Valley Police) was acquitted at Reading Crown Court (February 2007) of a single charge of dangerous driving (he still had a trial for drink-driving to come). He already had a speeding conviction and had been disciplined for using alcohol on duty. Though he admitted failing to stop for the police, accused by officers of speeding, and giving a false name and being obstructive, he faced no charges on these counts: would such consideration be afforded to a member of the public?

An officer was excused a speeding fine in South Yorkshire (2006) because he said he was on an emergency call (yet he picked up a Chinese takeaway on the way).

A senior Manchester policeman was taken off frontline duties (2004) after being cleared of drink-driving on a technicality caused by the charging officer. A Merseyside officer was fined in 2004 for driving while talking on her mobile. An officer was jailed (2006) for killing a woman while drink-driving in Berkshire.

Lancashire Constabulary PC Stephen Burgess avoided a speeding conviction under the little-known s.87 of the Road Traffic Regulation Act (1984), that allows marked emergency vehicles to speed even if there is no emergency. Another instance of double standards? In 2003 the North Wales Chief Constable was prosecuting his own officers for speeding where there was no emergency (at least 11 were convicted)[1514].

A police car in Elgin called to a break-in struck a young man in the street early in the morning – two men were due to appear in court[1515].

Detective Sergeant <u>Ian Lennox</u> admitted speeding in Perthshire after being spotted by his colleagues[1516].

Two people died and four were seriously injured when a car crashed in Haringey after a chase by a marked police car in 2007.

Police helicopter pilot <u>Ian Kingston</u> was charged with dangerous driving in his BMW after allegedly speeding at over 100mph through a 40mph limit.

A man and woman were injured, one seriously, in a road accident. The man was hit by a passing South Yorkshire police vehicle while he was being questioned at the roadside by West Yorkshire police. A drunk teenager was killed as he crossed the M23, being struck by at least five vehicles, including a police car[1517].

84% of drivers trapped by cameras are fined, but only 0.5% of officers. Police high-flyer Sergeant <u>Desmond Russell</u> killed a TV executive by jumping a red light at twice the speed limit, but escaped jail when he was cleared of dangerous driving. Double standards again?

Three traffic officers crashed their unmarked Skoda into a central reservation on the A33 near Southampton. A Police Scotland van on a 999 call in Dumfermline crashed into a car, injuring two pensioners[1518].

A woman who suffered horrific injuries after being struck on a pedestrian crossing by a police car on a 999 call (the 'emergency' was a boy shoplifting lemonade), was awarded over £3 million.

A South Wales police driver drove over a man's foot, which needed a cast for a shattered bone, but the victim was given an £80 fixed penalty ticket which said he had run into the police car causing a dent. The officer allegedly said: 'Sorry, but I've got to do this to cover myself'.

South Manchester WPC <u>Jayne Marsh</u> crashed her car while off-duty and almost three times over the drink-drive limit.

A woman was killed when a speeding police van driven by WPC <u>Janet Wynne Jones</u> ploughed into her – the 'emergency' was a row over a bus fare, and the police vehicle traversed two sets of red lights.

As head of roads policing for ACPO <u>Chief Constable Meredydd Hughes</u> led the crusade against speeders (including hidden speed cameras), but was accused of driving

Chief Constable
Meredydd Hughes

183

at 90mph in a 60mph zone. He was allegedly caught speeding for the third time (in South Yorkshire, South Wales and lastly North Wales, where one of Brunstrom's cameras caught him)[1519]. <u>Hughes</u> stood down from his ACPO roads portfolio following his driving ban[1520]. He was fined £500 when one of his officers was caught speeding: they couldn't determine who was at the wheel of the police car – on average seven times a year South Yorkshire police drivers who have broken the law can't be identified[1521].

John Lennon's mother Judy was killed in 1958 by a car driven an off-duty policeman without a licence.

A police Volkswagen van designed for eight was seen driving through Tower Hamlets with 14 officers in it.

<u>PC Ross Buirds</u> was charged with causing the death of a fellow Met PC when his BMW crashed – he was off-duty.

A coroner ruled at an inquest (2007) into the death of a police motorcyclist that the Honda machine posed a serious threat to the lives of riders.

It is claimed Central Scotland traffic cop PC <u>Jacob Marshall</u> collided with another car on the M9. Allegedly speeding at 120mph to 'attend an emergency' he faced a dangerous driving trial[1522].

Matthew Binley

More than 150 policemen had drink-driving convictions in 2006, but the figure must be higher, as five forces didn't take part in the study. Inspector <u>Paul Gee</u> of Durham Police was clocked driving at 118 mph through an accident blackspot near Falkirk, while the head of a police driving school. Seven police forces admitted in 2006 that their worst speeding offenders were their own officers. In 2005 Avon and Somerset Police refused to prosecute any of the 760 of its patrol drivers caught speeding.

Two Strathclyde police officers were carpeted for illegal parking at a sandwich shop, ignoring other illegally parked vehicles[1523].

Former PC <u>Matthew Binley</u> and his mother (wife of a Tory MP) admitted conspiracy to pervert the course of justice: she lied about being behind the wheel when in fact her son had crashed their car while drunk (he admitted drink driving).

Binley, who tried to flee from officers at one point, resigned from Northamptonshire Police in 2010 after years of allegations which included assault and one of a sexual nature[1524].

Former Scottish police sergeant Ewan McHardy (a 'top traffic cop') diluted his urine in an attempt to dodge a drink-driving charge, having failed to provide a breath test twice by saying he had a cold and asthma. He was found guilty of perverting the course of justice and fined £6,000[1525].

Surrey Chief Superintendent Guy Darby was carpeted in 2008 for using his phone while driving, as well as being probed for entering the London Marathon using a dishonest subterfuge[1526].

Rookie policewoman Stacey Pyke was killed when she fell asleep at the wheel of her car as she drove home from her first night shift. A Grampian WPC was seriously injured in a car crash on her way to work[1527].

The RAC has pinpointed a number of areas where collision rates have risen 'markedly' since cameras arrived[1528].

Blunders by Scottish police have cost over £2 million in a five year period, e.g. a Glasgow mother's sternum was crushed after she was hit by a police van (police vehicle accidents prompted most claims - reversing into parked cars, lampposts, etc.)[1529].

Strathclyde PC Stewart Denham faced charges of dangerous driving and driving at excessive speed when he crashed into another car in 2010: his colleague was injured. The police car was marked and had its blue lights on[1530]. He was convicted of dangerous driving after writing off his £50,000 marked BMW when he crashed into the other moving vehicle at 100mph: the conviction was only achieved after 27 court dates[1531]. He is appealing the sentence.

During a police chase of a stolen ice cream van the latter crashed into an unmarked police vehicle. The van was stopped in Surrey, and the culprit apprehended[1532].

Strathclyde PC David Sherrington crashed his patrol car into a BMW after driving through a red light, but was given an absolute discharge despite pleading guilty to careless driving[1533]. Do magistrates have a pro-police bias?

West Yorkshire police driver Sergeant Neil Greenwood collided with a car on the wrong side of the road, because he overtook a line of cars (using his flashing lights) - he was late for an 'essential' training course. He was found guilty of failing to comply with white lines, and careless driving[1534].

Because of its annual £200,000 car accident bill, South Yorkshire Police have fitted parking sensors (at up to £500 a time) because its officers are so bad at reversing. The impacts often happen at police stations, meaning two vehicles are damaged. Adrian Shurmer, a former police driving instructor, is certain driving standards have fallen[1535].

Four Central Scotland Police officers on a driving course, as well as a teenage driver, were injured in a head-on crash in Perthshire[1536].

Notts Superintendent Helen Chamberlain was recorded doing 79mph in a 50mph limit, but claimed her force's speed gun was inaccurate. Sergeant Craig Jones, of North

Wales Police, was fined £500 with £1,000 costs, for driving at 98mph in a 50mph limit while transporting a prisoner – an organised crime officer, he claimed the limit was unenforceable because the signs were unlit. PC <u>Matthew Stott</u> was allowed to keep his licence despite admitting speeding at 100mph on his way to work[1537].

Suffolk special sergeant <u>Mykal Trim</u> stood trial for dangerous driving for blocking a road with his patrol car to stop a drink-drive suspect, whose Mitsubishi crashed into the police car. Trim's colleague, special police inspector Paul Booker, had internal injuries and a broken back and pelvis[1538].

A father of two drowned in Fife in 2010 after crashing a stolen van into docks following a Central Scotland Police chase by two police vehicles[1539].

Two Strathclyde police on a 999 call were hurt when their patrol car crashed into a taxi. The police declined to comment on the 999 call[1540].

A police car's crash near Basildon in July 2011 meant a taxi driver and two policemen had to be treated in hospital (one officer was critical)[1541].

A South African driver rammed a Kent police car after a two-mile chase because he thought bogus cops were trying to carjack him, as happens in his home country[1542].

Stirlingshire PC <u>Jacob Marshall</u> was facing trial accused of driving at excessive speed and hitting another car while on duty on the M9[1543].

Strathclyde traffic cops had to drive at 140mph to catch a race car fan[1544].

In 2007 a Met police driver was filmed flouting the new law banning hand-held phones in cars. His superiors said there may be 'operational' reasons for such flouting, but critics say this means police can always be exempted, setting the worst possible example[1545].

A policeman who raced at up to 60mph to collect a Chinese meal was cleared of speeding: P.C. <u>Stephen Akrill</u> said he had an operational excuse (though he had ordered the meal 20 minutes in advance). He had <u>not</u> been called to an accident and, anyway, he wasn't taking the shortest route and wasn't flashing lights[1546].

In 2005 PC <u>Mark Milton</u> was cleared of speeding, despite driving an unmarked patrol car at 159mph on the M54: road safety groups were outraged[1547]. In April 2010 a BMW police car, with its blue lights on but not answering an emergency, crashed into another car on the M8, causing major disruption[1548].

A Strathclyde police van collided with a taxi in Glasgow while rushing to attend the Royal Wedding Facebook fracas. Two officers suffered minor injuries but the taxi driver was seriously injured[1549].

Scottish police crashed their cars nearly five times a day in 2010, with nearly 10% occurring in their own car parks. Most cases are considered by a Police Vehicle Collision Board[1550]. Scottish ambulances were involved in an accident almost daily in 2009[1551] (1,244 crashes in the three years to 2011[1552]). In two years since 2010, Durham Constabulary's patrol cars were involved in 120 accidents, the costliest in its own HQ's car park (nearly all the crashes involved officers reversing into bollards, lampposts, etc.)[1553]. Scottish ambulance crews have amassed a £70,000 repair bill after crashing 128 times in about a year[1554].

Paramedics and police seem to have something in common here. Police car crashes cost English forces nearly £22,000 daily (writing off nearly 500 of their vehicles at a cost of £2.6m in 2008-9), and there has been an (almost) 100% increase in police car-related road deaths[1555]. Cheshire and Staffs forces have notched up 238 crashes in their own car parks, costing an estimated £116,000 in 2½ years[1556].

A 79-year-old pedestrian who was struck by a West Midlands patrol car in Birmingham, was hospitalised. The case was referred to the IPCC[1557].

When a motorist's high-performance Lancer Evolution was driven to the police pound by uninsured traffic officers – he had narrowly failed a breath test – they crashed it, making it a write-off[1558].

Lothian and Borders community policeman Roderick MacLeod crashed his car into a tree after a dinner party, pretending it had been taken by joyriders, adhering to the lie for four months. He admitted careless driving, attempting to pervert the course of justice, and making a false insurance claim[1559].

A South Yorkshire officer was excused a speeding fine in 2006, arguing he was on an emergency call – he picked up a takeaway on the way. A senior Manchester policeman was cleared of drink-driving in 2004 because the charging officer did not follow correct procedure – yet he was transferred from frontline duties, while a Merseyside officer was fined for driving while using her mobile phone in the same year[1560].

Two Northumbria Police motorcyclists were caught speeding through a Scottish accident blackspot near Jedburgh. They were not prosecuted (although Lothian and Borders Police initially served an intention to prosecute notice) because they were supposedly on 'training exercises'. Yet interestingly the Scottish force weren't warned that such practices were to occur on their patch[1561].

A West Midlands Volvo police car answering an emergency collided with a BMW at a junction in Huddersfield, injuring seven people, including two babies. The incident was referred to the IPCC[1562].

Central Scotland PC Jacob Marshall clipped another vehicle while he drove to an oil spill at 140mph. His partner PC Barry Manson told the court that police are driving on the M9 at speeds of up to 150mph every day. Marshall denied dangerous driving in court[1563].

PC Craig Atkinson was facing trial (2012) at Kilmarnock Sheriff Court charged with dangerous driving and speeding in Ayrshire in 2011, causing a crash with another vehicle – four people were injured[1564].

Fife Police have been allowed to investigate a head-on car crash involving Norma Graham, their own chief constable: it is apparently claimed she was on the wrong side of the road. Scotland's Campaign against Irresponsible Driving said the crash should be investigated by a completely independent group[1565]. She announced her retirement at the age of 49. She failed to appear at Kirkcaldy Sheriff Court for a second time re causing the crash. A sheriff refused to accept her defence evidence and found her guilty of careless driving. She has retired on a full pension[1566]. She was awarded the Queen's Police Medal in 2008[1567], being Scotland's first female chief constable[1568].

THE HARMFUL POLICEMAN

A 22-year-old Scottish rugby player lost his legs when he was struck by a <u>Strathclyde Police</u> van while it was flashing its blue lights[1569].

A <u>Cambridgeshire</u> traffic cop was the second to be caught by retractable bollards – his patrol car airbag went off when he hit one. When he staggered from the car, having been 'smacked in the face', a mocking crowd of dozens of bystanders clapped[1570]. Two <u>Greater Manchester</u> firearms officers crashed their £30,000 BMW into bollards, on their way to an incident, watched by laughing bystanders[1571].

A police car was a write-off after crashing into a van on the A8 in Renfrewshire (on 26.1.12). No one was seriously injured: two officers were taken to hospital[1572].

While off duty, <u>Tayside</u> PC <u>Scott Kerr</u>, accused of 'showing off' in his high-powered Audi when he struck two Dundee pedestrians, was found guilty of careless driving, despite his denial. He was fined and given penalty points, but escaped a ban[1573].

Ex-forces personnel have twice the death rate from car accidents compared with civilians.

The Police Federation is threatening that police drivers could refuse to chase fugitives in the light of the case of a traffic officer taken to court over a fast pursuit chase. A jury cleared <u>Hampshire</u> PC James Holden prosecuted for dangerous driving (he pursued a burglar through several red lights and the wrong way along a dual carriageway). They want officers not to have to show the same 'duty of care' as a member of the public[1574], and to be exempt from dangerous driving legislation when attending 999 emergencies[1575].

Two <u>Essex</u> police officers were hospitalised after crashing their car into a traffic island – it burst into flames. No other vehicles were involved[1576].

A <u>Tayside Police</u> car collided with a stolen car driven by a teenager[1577].

Stirlingshire PC <u>Jacob Marshall</u> was accused of driving dangerously at excessive speed, hitting another vehicle, while on duty on the M9 in 2010[1578].

<u>Essex</u> PC <u>Tracy Watts</u> was banned for three years (but avoided jail with a suspended sentence) for, drunk on Vodka, crashing her sports car while four times over the limit[1579].

A youngster died when he crashed his moped while being chased by police[1580].

In 2011-12 45 Staffordshire officers crashed into the <u>backs</u> of cars in their own car parks. In past years an officer would be banned from driving for a week, now there is no sanction[1581].

The Procurator Fiscal has appealed against a sheriff's decision to clear Grampian Chief Inspector <u>Tom Forrester</u> of serious traffic offences, particularly that of encouraging PC <u>Ashley Forbes</u> to drive dangerously as they were late for a flight. Forbes was found guilty of lesser charges of careless driving and failing to stop. The unmarked police car caused another two cars to collide[1582].

A stolen car was chased by police across two counties at 100mph, crashing into a Toyota whose young driver has been left crippled[1583].

A hit-and-run driver escaping from police killed a 12-year-old boy at a level crossing in Bradford[1584].

While Lothian and Borders PC Hamaad Khalid may have been using his mobile when he killed a father-of-three in a hit-and run- encounter, neither the officer, nor another driver who hit the victim, were breath-tested by attending officers. When the victim's widow asked questions she says a senior officer fobbed her off with the comment, 'You've been watching too much CSI', and the force refused to comment to the media[1585].

Ex-west Yorkshire WPC Leona Mudd sued a 13-year-old girl she knocked down and injured in an RTA, saying she (the officer) suffered PTSD as a result. The child had to have two operations on a broken ankle[1586].

Stirlingshire PC Jacob Marshall was to go on trial accused of hitting another car while on duty on the M9 while driving at 120mph[1587].

Two Grampian officers who crashed their police vehicle head-on with another car had to be hospitalised, as did the other driver[1588].

Two Essex patrol constables were hospitalised after their car collided with a traffic island and burst into flames: no other vehicles were involved[1589].

A marked Tayside Police vehicle crashed into a stolen car driven by a 19-year-old in Perthshire[1590].

A 12-year-old schoolgirl was hospitalised with a fracture after being hit by a police car while getting off a bus in Glasgow[1591].

Norfolk Chief Constable Ken Williams, the UK's top traffic cop (i.e. chairman of ACPO's traffic committee) was to be prosecuted for driving without due care and attention, after he was in a head-on collision. He was awarded the Queen's Police Medal in 1992[1592].

After a man was allegedly knocked down by an unmarked Met police car and assaulted outside his home by at least five officers, his leg and wrist were broken, and they taunted him when he asked for medical help. He was charged with the attempted assault on an officer, and bound over for £100, but an investigation was ordered when it was realised a neighbour had filmed the incident[1593].

Paul McCartney's ex-wife lost a leg after being struck by a police motorcycle in London[1594].

Tayside PC Gary Johnston allegedly struck a father and daughter with his car in Dundee, but he denied the charge of careless driving[1595], which was thrown out at Dundee Sheriff Court after a three day trial[1596].

A legal firm used a horrific Strathclyde Police RTA to publicise their helping the guilty (non-police) driver to keep his licence by claiming the police were largely to blame[1597].

A probe by the PIRC (Police Investigations and Review Commissioner) into Police Scotland Tayside Division failings, which prevented a hit-and-run in Angus that nearly killed a woman. The police had been warned twice by the perpetrators, another about his driving under the influence of drugs, but they failed to perform intelligence checks which could have led to the driver being stopped and arrested before the accident, and were using an old intelligence system with out-of-date information. The mother said: 'They couldn't get me out of the police station quickly enough'[1598].

Harm from Guns

Police are involved in more than 50 firearm operations every day (an increase of 70% in six years).

In a decade British police have shot dead 30 and injured 30 more. One man holding a table leg was shot in the head from behind. The two responsible Met officers, Sharman and Fagan, testified that he was facing them, but they refused to be interviewed by Panorama for its programme 'When Cops Kill' (15.10.06). When their suspension was lifted by Commissioner Stevens and the IPCC decided to take no disciplinary action, this led to the victim's family declaring: 'Police can just do what they want and get away with it'.

On the few occasions British police use firearms, they tend to shoot the wrong person, e.g. in the Stephen Waldorf case (1983). Hostage Gail Kinchin and her unborn baby were fatally shot accidentally by West Midlands police dealing with a siege in 1980, and mother-of-six Cherry Grace was paralysed when she was shot in bed (triggering the 1985 Brixton Riots). Businessman Nicholas Gaubert, whose parents are doctors, was shot twice by Leeds police (2007) with a stun gun while he was in a diabetic coma, fearing he was a suicide bomber (despite his wearing a warning bracelet). Stun guns have killed at least 220 in the U.S.

Mentally ill martial arts enthusiast and arsonist Anne Sanderson was shot dead by police in Sevenoaks, Kent, after waving an imitation gun at an officer. Mental patient Keith Larkins was shot dead by police near Heathrow after firing blanks from a replica gun.

A police marksman accidentally shot and seriously injured a colleague during a 'firearms awareness' training exercise in Kidlington (Thames Valley Police HQ). He had to have a life-saving operation, while two Sussex officers were suspended after one was injured at a Gatwick firing range[1599]. Met Diplomatic Protection Group officer Des Stout accidentally shot himself in the leg – it is believed he hadn't put on the gun's safety catch during a practice session[1600]. Churchill's bodyguard, ex-policeman Walter Thompson, shot himself accidentally in both legs with his service revolver.

Innocent Abdul Kahar Kalam was shot by police when they raided his home in June 2006.

Three senior police officers who helped plan the East Sussex raid that led to a naked, unarmed suspect being shot dead in his bedroom, faced a total of 15 disciplinary charges (one of the inspectors also faced four charges of falsehood).

'Mad mullah of the traffic Taliban' Richard Brunstrom, once North Wales's 'ever-more-peculiar' Chief Constable, subjected himself to a Taser's 50,000 volts ahead of his force's plan to issue 'a substantial number' of the guns to rurally-based officers.

Scottish police have shot more animals than criminals. In 2003 a depressed woman was gunned down by police in Scotland's first attempted 'suicide by cop' (she survived)[1601]. Two Aberdeen public schoolboys went out to shoot a spoof James Bond film, but police, thinking they were criminals, pointed guns at them (there were about 20 firearms officers). The boys were spread-eagled on the ground[1602].

One of the firearms officers who shot barrister Mark Saunders swore during his evidence at Westminster Coroner's Court[1603].

Top royal protection officer Chief Superintendent Ian Boyes was suspended in 2010 when he accidentally fired a shot inside Holyroodhouse. He had been awarded the Member of the Royal Victorian Order in 2005. PC Michael Slade fired two shots by mistake on the royal train as the Queen slept nearby in 2000. It was revealed in 2009 that a protection officer at Buckingham Palace was allowed access to guns despite suffering side-effects from steroids, in which the police were running a racket (on one occasion he put a gun in his mouth, telling his girlfriend he was going to commit suicide). Royal protection officer Paul Page, a gambling addict, is said to have threatened a friend who had talked to police: he would 'take revenge'[1604].

Police officers need a huge boost to their firepower (e.g. the C9 Minimi machine gun) to combat terrorism, claimed the Met's John Yates[1605], who has since stepped down.

Tasers have been fired 279 times in three years by police in Durham, Cumbria and Northumbria, i.e. 11 times the total for the whole of Scotland in the same period (only firearms officers are allowed to fire them in Scotland)[1606].

A six officer squad Tasered a confused dementia patient at his home before manhandling him to the floor with a view to his transfer to hospital. His wife has criticised the behaviour of the police (as well as the doctors), and is considering making a formal complaint[1607].

An 83-year-old man with psychiatric problems was Tasered by West Midlands Police after he walked out of a care home with a knife. The 2011 incident was only revealed two years later after a FOI request[1608].

Shotgun licences were being granted in 2010 by Lothian and Borders Police to young teenagers[1609].

Police have asked for Tasers which can fire two shots without the need to reload. An officer who shot a blind retired architect carrying a white stick was not subjected to disciplinary action[1610].

Police with sidearms have begun to appear at Paddington Station[1611].

A 27-year-old Cumbrian bodybuilder died from a heart attack an hour after he had been stunned four times in a minute by Taser, as well as sprayed with pepper and held down, handcuffed and put in leg restraints. Drugs may have largely contributed to his death. If the Tasering was at least partially responsible it is thought he would have been the first UK person (by 2013) to have died in this way[1612].

Three people are shot daily by police armed with Tasers (50,000-volt), yet the Police Federation wants to arm every officer by increasing the number of stun guns to 36,000. Greater Manchester are the biggest users, with almost twice as many firing as the Met[1613].

A gun has been found in a plastic bag in the Kirkwall (Orkney) garden of ex-police sergeant John Miller, a close associate of Eddie Ross, whose son is serving at least 25 years for shooting dead an Indian waiter (the murder weapon was never found)[1614].

In the four years since 2004 Tasers were used almost 2,700 times by police in England and Wales[1615]. Police have been told by its manufacturer Taser International not to fire the Taser at a suspect's chest in case it triggers a heart attack. Tasers are used seven times daily (2009)[1616].

Sexual Harassment

Policewoman Senel Ismail, falsely accused of having a series of affairs with male recruits – a tradition known as 'Operation Rainbow' – was awarded a five-figure out-of-court settlement which involved a gagging clause. After graduating from Hendon, she was allegedly pestered for sex by a police sergeant and an inspector in Kent. The case would have been 'hugely embarrassing' to the Met had an employment tribunal gone ahead.

Police Scotland were probing two cops caught on tape ridiculing a gay woman helping them solve a crime. One hadn't replaced his phone properly, so that after her call one officer sang 'she has a lesbian lover' to a Phil Collins tune, while his colleague seemed to refer to her partner's mental health[1617].

Devon and Cornwall PC Nestor Costa, who was commended for risking his life to prevent an explosion, faced the sack over claims that he put inflammatory riders and obscene comments on another policeman's Facebook profile.

A police firearms officer, the only female armed officer among 18 men serving at Gatwick Airport, who suffered taunts about her breasts, was hounded out of her job, but won her claim for sex discrimination.

Hundreds (perhaps thousands) of Britons accused of paedophilia by the police in Operation Ore were actually credit card fraud victims.

Lesbian Greenock cop Heather Atkinson, a Special Constable, terrorised her former partner for a year because the victim had taken up with a new girlfriend[1618].

Miscellaneous

PC James Hardy, of Chesterfield, was given a suspended sentence and community service for passing details of suspects to a thug planning 'vigilante justice'.

A Brighton teenager was awarded £42,500 after he was bitten by a police dog while allegedly involved in a brawl. A four-year-old girl was savaged by a police dog in a park while the German Shepherd was in the care of an unnamed off-duty Essex policeman[1619]. Police forces have paid out £770,000 compensation to victims of police dog bites in three years[1620].

CAVEAT CIVIS

A solicitor suffering from breast cancer was suing Scotland Yard claiming she was unfairly dismissed because of her condition.

Strathclyde Police were ordered to apologise to a teenage boy for holding him in custody for more than two days, flouting child detention laws.

As a result of the police's anti-paedophile Operation Ore there have been more than 30 suspects' suicides.

Chief Superintendent Anne McGuire was probed by her own Strathclyde force over claims she worked her staff too hard.

The treatment of the late Labour MP Fiona Jones by Nottinghamshire police in their investigation into alleged irregularities in the funding of her political campaign, left a lot to be desired. Notts told Derbyshire police they had destroyed their file on her at her insistence, but she denied this. As a result of Derbyshire's report some Notts police were given mild internal admonition ('advice'), and four were charged with disciplinary offences (including neglect of duty and 'falsehood and prevarication'), but these were eventually withdrawn in 2003. Her civil case against Notts Police was thrown out by a judge in 2005, shortly before her death.

In 2001 Inspector Ali Dizaei, once tipped to be the first ethnic chief constable, was suspended, accused of spying, fiddling his expenses, corruption, using prostitutes and steroids, and being a drug addict. In 2003 he was offered a huge financial settlement or reinstatement after being acquitted twice at the Old Bailey; £7 million of taxpayers' money and thousands of hours of police time were wasted on charges too trivial to sustain a dismissal case. In 2011 his conviction was overturned, so that he could be re-tried for various alleged criminal offences. (See also 'The Criminal Policeman' – Corruption p62).

In 2007, when kerb crawling in Scotland became illegal for the first time, Edinburgh police stopped over 400 men cruising in Leith's red light district. But critics say the women will be driven further underground or online. Scotpep (an Edinburgh-based prostitute support group) says the new law will make prostitution more dangerous – girls will jump into cars too quickly because of fears of being stopped by police, who may visit drivers at home[1621]. Likewise Ipswich prostitutes claim that police had made their situation more dangerous in the period leading up to the murders, by targeting them and forcing them into isolated areas (three ASBOs had recently been imposed on prostitutes)[1622].

During Operation Ribble (code for the honours probe) retired headmaster Des Smith was dragged from bed in a dawn raid by police and thrown in a cell along with violent criminals – he spent eight hours there. The ordeal led him to consider suicide.

When a Ugandan arrived at Heathrow with her mother in a wheelchair, her passport was confiscated and she was arrested by four policemen, who refused to assist the invalid relative. When she was released after 36 hours, their passports were withheld, meaning luggage couldn't be reclaimed, nor could she get employment[1623].

A Lancashire PC won £5,000 compensation after three of his colleagues arrested him over a parking row, following a complaint from his neighbour, retired superintendent Anthony Green. The PC was handcuffed and put in a Morecambe police cell for 10 hours before his release on bail[1624].

THE HARMFUL POLICEMAN

A Perthshire man smacked his 11-year-old son twice on the leg for throwing a tantrum (trashing a room and shouting and swearing at his mother). Teachers told police, who arrested and charged him. He was convicted of assault after being banned from living with his family for two months. The police action and court case have caused the family far greater distress than the smack[1625].

White racist Met PC <u>Geoff Whitehead</u> allegedly said another officer was a 'f..... lesbian' and a 'f..... dyke', gambled at work, sold counterfeit cigarettes and cassettes, and often kicked sleeping homeless people to move them on[1626].

Ex-WPC Anne Ramsay, who wrote a warts-and-all account of her 14 years with Strathclyde Police, tells of officers who 'lived for getting stuck in with their truncheons', would delight in arresting fans of the team they didn't support. There were cover-ups when senior officers' names were found on receipts after raids on sex saunas. She even got a barrage of sexist remarks when she had to dress up as a prostitute for crime reconstruction[1627].

Blonde divorcee Detective Superintendent <u>Ellie Baker</u> – head of West Midlands Crime Support Unit (43 departments such as the fraud and drugs squads) – helped Helen Mirren research her Jane Tennison role. Colleagues made false allegations against her, e.g. promising junior officers promotion in return for sex. Friends say she was the victim of a witch hunt, though she was suspended over claims she conned a pensioner into giving her money and jewellery. She returned the gifts, but the police reportedly spent about £1 million on the non-criminal inquiry[1628].

<u>Kevin Hamilton</u>, former head of Cheshire Police CID, received a restraining order for harassing neighbours after being blamed for suicides in his street. The Detective Chief Superintendent had to resign as senior investigator for the IPCC. He spat 23 times on cars, being caught in Operation Sustain with the use of CCTV and DNA evidence[1629].

PCs <u>Byron Emerson-Thomas</u> and <u>Aled Bartlett</u> came to blows in the parade room at Cardiff's Fairwater police station over who should drive their patrol van first since it had been fitted with a new radio: Bartlett refused to hand over the keys at the end of his shift and needed eight stitches after his colleague punched him[1630].

The black PASGT (Personnel Armour System for Group Troops) 'coal scuttle' helmet worn by police hunting killer Moat is based on WW2 German helmets, which can look alarming to the public[1631].

Speed cameras may have caused almost 28,000 road crashes. While almost a third of drivers have seen 'erratic behaviour' by motorists trying to avoid the flash, almost a half found cameras distracting and four-fifths look at their speedometer. Cameras have made the roads more dangerous by replacing effective policies[1632].

TV presenter Chris Tarrant's ex-wife claimed she was 'terrified' when confronted by 'aggressive and angry' PC <u>Peter Groves</u> in a row over a parking ticket, so that she drove off, resulting in her being pursued with blue lights and siren and wrestled to the ground[1633].

Police in Kennington, S. London, have been told to limit the use of sirens because of a flood of complaints: they are allegedly 'far worse than the fire brigade or ambulance service'[1634].

The Police Federation wants the police to have the power to order dangerous people to be injected with a sedative, claiming this would help them deal with 'Excited Delirium Syndrome' and reduce deaths in custody. However, Inquest says the proposals are dangerous[1635].

Four Devon and Cornwall PCs were probed (2010) for allegedly trying to break into a car to retrieve a lost mobile phone[1636].

A damning report has decided police were too concerned with a rapist's complaints about infringement of his rights by the monitoring officers: Anthony Rice raped and murdered while on licence[1637]. A suspected paedophile United Reformed Church vicar was released to assault hundreds of children across the country, most of them occurring after Hampshire Police had been warned about his activities: they failed to seize his computers and released him on bail[1638].

A man with an IQ of 69 is thought to have triggered the Forest Gate raid in which a man was shot by police but no terrorists found. 250 officers had descended on the address in Operation Volga[1639].

One militant suffragette has described how police would tip her out of her wheelchair, pinion her arms behind her, move her into a 'hooligan crowd', or disable the wheels[1640].

Some policemen have always been much rougher than is necessary, e.g. in the interwar period a Liverpool City policeman called Birtles was remembered by his colleagues as rather too enthusiastic in a fight. An ex-army Bedfordshire PC, who joined the force in 1932, was proud of being 'rough and ready' and would be chosen by his Dunstable sergeant to deal with known troublemakers on Saturday nights (he would bash them round the head rather than take them to court)[1641].

Some officers used WW2 regulations to harass a social superior or someone they didn't like: one admitted being vindictive in prosecuting a peer in Claridges for keeping his light on. Much resentment against the police was engendered in normally law-abiding families by their pursuit of deserters and conscription-avoiders.

A gay Ugandan asylum seeker was awarded £100,000 by the Home Office after it admitted breaking the law, endangering his life by deporting him while his case was pending: their removal officers allegedly dragged him by handcuffs and struck him in the shoulder and groin[1642].

When Swindon scrapped its fixed speed cameras the number of convicted speeding motorists dropped by over 40%[1643]. Yet Gwent's Chief Constable Mark Giannesi predicts the number of fatal crashes will soar if cameras are turned off[1644].

Royal protection officers are being issued with Tasers after the attack on Charles and the Duchess in 2010; members of the Diplomatic Protection Squad will also be similarly armed[1645].

In the de Menezes case the Met was fined at the Old Bailey for failing to protect the public under health and safety legislation[1646].

Up to 12 Essex police officers were probed when their inappropriate comments appeared on Facebook: wanting to beat up rioting students, describing a paedophile who exposed himself as 'a dirty scum pervert', commenting on an American cop who floored a suspect by shoving him in the neck: 'How cool is the copper!' 'I have to deal with human bacteria all day, every day. Thus I loathe and despise human kind'. One officer volunteered he was 'off to Southend tonight with his band of merry men to dish out some justice'. The officers apparently didn't think their comments could be read by the public; a number have been given 'words of advice'[1647].

Scottish cop <u>Martin Folan</u>, accused of brutality against five prisoners (one had to have a testicle removed) in New Zealand, was cleared by a jury in 2011[1648].

Glasgow Special Constable <u>Jamie Dodman</u> was charged with having a knife at Prestwick Airport. He was released on bail[1649].

The Met decided to fight the High Court ruling that 'kettling' a group of G20 protesters was unlawful. Two judges condemned officers for using batons and riot shields to clear a road[1650]. 'Circling', as employed in the 1984 miners' strike, was the forerunner of kettling, which has now been endorsed by the Court of Appeal, overturning the High Court ruling that officers used unjustified force[1651].

The landlord of murdered landscape architect Jo Yeates was to sue Avon and Somerset Police for false arrest[1652].

Tattooed MOD PC <u>Stuart Niven</u>, a diehard Manchester City fan, was pictured holding a burning Manchester United flag, calculated to enrage opposition fans[1653].

Oppressive Ugandan dictator Museveni uses the police, trained by British police, to shoot at peaceful demonstrators[1654].

Nottinghamshire PC <u>Mark Johnson</u> was given a conditional discharge and a £2,500 fine in 2010 for leaving two Alsatians to die in his baking car the year before[1655].

North Tyneside Police ran a league table in which they won points, not for helping people but for collaring them (three points for an arrest, one for a summons or penalty notice). The cops reportedly used the results to bully each other. Criminals in the know could use the practice to claim wrongful arrest[1656].

After N. Wales Chief Constable <u>Richard Brunstrom</u> became a guinea-pig to illustrate the effectiveness of the 50,000 volt

Mark Johnson

Taser, he warned the public if they disobeyed Taser-armed officers, 'You will not enjoy the consequences of disobedience'[1657].

An estimated 5.2 million of homeowners don't report crimes in case the police crime maps showing rising statistics put off buyers and renters. Nearly a quarter of landlords and sellers say they wouldn't report a crime[1658].

In the hacking scandal the most serious reputational damage will almost certainly prove to have been sustained by the police. Some, including successive Home Secretaries, have believed for decades that the police culture is rotten. An MI6 official has revealed how shocked he was 'by systemic and malicious police leaks about an important case in which the Secret Intelligence Service was involved'[1659].

In the 1991 Orkney child abuse scandal, police and social workers grabbed nine youngsters from their beds, convinced that the children had been abused by paedophile devil-worshippers. (Lord Clyde's inquiry, which cost £6 million, lambasted the overzealous social workers: police were also involved in the 'therapy sessions' the children underwent, and were heavily criticised by the inquiry – their thinking had been 'coloured by undefined suspicions')[1660].

Lothian and Borders Police say eight people were injured by police horses in two years, with only three hurt by horses in Strathclyde. Six Strathclyde officers have been hurt while using their bicycles, but only three Lothian and Borders and one Central Scotland officer[1661].

Tayside Police were told by a sheriff to review their practices after treating a Forfar family 'like criminals' when their teenager died of SUDEP (Sudden Unexpected Death In Epilepsy). Officers threw them out of their home because it was being treated as a 'crime scene'[1662].

A 19-year-old Glasgow medical records clerk regrets going to Strathclyde Police to report being mugged in the Kelvinhall underground on her way to work – she suffered a chipped cheekbone – as she was charged with wasting police time[1663].

The IPCC has ruled that in the Met's raid on the home of reggae star Smiley Culture, in which he died from a stab wound, there were aspects of the operation which 'were not satisfactory'[1664]. Strathclyde Police used a battering ram to enter a Paisley home at 7am because of a noise complaint: the student occupier, who was lapdancing in a thong, was charged with breach of the peace, as well as giving a false name and swearing at officers[1665].

In 1961 police broke up a demonstration over the murder of Patrice Lumumba (ex-PM of the Congo): several people were trampled. In 1985 the Brixton riots were triggered by an accidental shot during a police raid. Violence broke out a week later in Tottenham when a woman suffered a heart attack during a police raid on her home, and several people were injured by shooting[1666].

When an 85-year-old former army officer's house caught fire he was arrested for trying to rescue his possessions, which went up in smoke while he watched from a police van (firemen were on strike). The fire could have been extinguished if the police had allowed the owner to tell the army firemen that there was a swimming pool in the rear. He said the Dyfed-

Powys Police had harassed him before this by stopping his car several times and revoking his gun licence. He was suing the force for wrongful arrest, false imprisonment and assault[1667].

When Tasers were used at the Dale Farm evictions (2011) this was the first time they had been used on activists, marking a worrying escalation of their deployment[1668].

Surrey PCSO 46-year-old Kim Biochat falsely claimed to be a victim of a hate campaign by a fellow PCSO – handwritten poison pen letters were sent to senior officers. Biochat had become obsessed with the idea that her female colleague was trying to be more popular than her. Biochat left threatening notes in her own car and locker. Detectives spent thousands on the case, including £1,665 on expert handwriting analysis (which showed Biochat had written the letters)[1669].

Paul Brown, a former police bodyguard of Princess Diana, was claimed to have terrorised a young mother by bombarding her with more than 130 abusive text messages in a week. Sussex Police issued him with a warning notice under the Harassment Act.

Two sex workers, who were apparently victims of stalking and committed suicide by carbon monoxide, left letters of complaint about their treatment by the police. DC Ryan Coleman-Farrow of the Sapphire Unit, which specialised in sexual crimes, allegedly discontinued cases without authorisation[1670].

A mother has told of her 'hell' at being arrested by Greater Manchester Police after gatecrashers invaded her daughter's party. The company director's conviction and conditional discharge for obstructing an officer was overturned, and she is now pursuing a complaint against two officers (the arresting and the custody officer). She claims the police were aggressive and over-reacted, and she was denied access to a solicitor. Defence CCTV evidence had been destroyed by the prosecution[1671].

Police are testing a 'laser dazzler' that can 'blind' rioters and other suspects[1672].

Northern Constabulary accused a 22-year-old woman of concocting rape claims – she was arrested, accused of wasting police time and forced to strip in a cell with the door open.

In six years Strathclyde Police have recorded 39 CS gas injuries to their officers[1673].

Mail columnist Littlejohn says it is bloody-mindedness which makes the police close motorways in both directions whenever there's even a minor accident. 'They don't consider it any of their business to keep the traffic flowing. The general public can go to hell as far as they are concerned'.

Pub landlady Karen Murphy was cleared after a six year fight of illegally downloading Premier League footage using a Greek decoder. It is claimed the police should never have prosecuted her.

WPC Linda McBride pleaded not guilty to being in charge of a police dog that was out of control: it attacked a man in Falkirk[1674].

A 16-year-old epileptic, autistic special school pupil wouldn't leave Acton swimming pool (2008), so Met Police restrained him with two sets of handcuffs, as well as leg restraints, and he was bundled soaking into a police van cage section: he apparently was not allowed a carer to accompany him. He seemed to have been so obsessed with the pool water he couldn't bear to leave it. A judge awarded him £30,000 for post-traumatic stress, aggravation of epilepsy, etc. Commissioner Hogan-Howe not only refused to apologise but is to appeal the judgment at public cost[1675].

A black teenager who killed an innocent bystander in the 2011 Tottenham riots planned to become a policeman[1676].

Bernard Hogan-Howe has been asked to explain the 'disproportionate', 'bully-boy' tactics used by his officers against The Sun's political journalists: though not charged with any offence 'they are being treated worse than terrorist suspects'. Two senior Met officers running the probe, Sue Akers and Cressida Dick, previously received adverse press comment (in the Climbié and de Menezes cases respectively), so there may be personal motivations at work here. Are the police embarrassed by some of their past dealings with News International?[1677]

Thames Valley Police warned the Met that Dizaei would play the race card to further his ambitions. Even the IPCC pressured the Met to discipline him, to no avail. His Ph.D. thesis attacked the 'racist' Met[1678].

After 19 months John Mauger, Assistant Chief Constable of Central Scotland Police, remained suspended (February 2012) on full pay. A leaked report alleges he lied about having high-security clearance, refused to wear regulation uniform, acted in an oppressive manner towards colleagues, and publicly criticised his chief constable, losing his force £650,000 funding, etc. The inquiry consumed over 5,500 hours of police time. Mauger refused to comment on the report[1679].

Bernard Hogan-Howe has announced that more officers are being trained to support baton round teams, so that plastic bullets can be deployed more spontaneously[1680].

Lincolnshire traffic officer Sergeant Craig Dunderdale was banned for 16 months for drinking and driving – he had been a road safety campaigner, and involved in a crackdown on speeding bikers[1681].

When a drunken Kuwaiti government official was Tasered because he wouldn't stop urinating outside Tony Blair's London townhouse, he had to be taken to hospital. He was charged with assaulting an officer. He doesn't understand English[1682].

Northern Constabulary PC Robert Ovenstone has been charged with abducting two 15-year-olds from a children's home, handcuffing them and making them stand shoeless in manure, then making them walk down a track in the dark wearing socks but no shoes. He is also accused, along with PC Stuart Kelman, to have behaved towards the girls in a threatening or abusive manner, as well as threatening to strike a boy at the home with a baton[1683]. Ovenstone was given community service, quitting the force, while Kelman was fined[1684].

Former Met PC Abdul Rahman is suing the force over his resignation, accused – he says wrongly – of attending a Pakistani terrorist training camp. He claims racial and religious discrimination[1685]. The Met applied to have the Rahman case heard in secret.

Black Birmingham father of two <u>Kingsley Burrell Brown</u> died in hospital in 2011 shortly after being in police custody, having alleged he had been beaten up by police. A year later there were no answers and no funeral[1686]. (See also Custody Blunders, p228).

Met PC <u>Philip Juhasz</u> was sacked for drunkenly abusing a Pakistani restaurant manager while off-duty. He said 'Do you know who I am? I'm a police officer'. He was also accused of saying: 'Go back to your f…. country', but a charge of racism was not upheld (Juhasz had been at first convicted of a racially aggravated public order offence)[1687].

A frail dementia patient was handcuffed because Greater Manchester PC <u>Alan Twentyman</u> felt his own safety was at risk. DCI <u>Koran Sellers</u> justified the use of the restraint, but Chief Constable Sir Peter Fahy admitted a policeman should never have been present[1688].

A six-strong <u>Lincolnshire Police</u> team Tasered a terrified unarmed dementia patient, tying his arms and legs together and bundling him into a police van. Two months later he was still receiving hospital psychiatric treatment[1689].

17 Staffordshire Police vehicles, as well as the military, closed the M6 over a bus passenger smoking a fake cigarette. One passenger feared she would be shot after being disembarked from the coach at gunpoint, <u>three hours</u> after it was realised there was no immediate threat. Innocent passengers were allegedly ordered to keep their arms by their sides and walk towards armed officers. One female passenger was frisked and ordered to sit in a police 'contamination zone' on the motorway. The people were scrutinising the passengers with binoculars. The force denied it over-reacted.

The Police Federation want 36,000 Tasers, to supply every officer on street duty[1690], in the light of an increase in single patrolling[1691]. They also want to be armed for the first time with assault rifles used on the battlefield[1692].

A 78-year-old grandmother was Tasered by <u>Lincolnshire Police</u> after she stabbed her Alzheimer's husband while in a deranged state. Since when have police Tasers replaced tranquillising medication from doctors[1693]?

A recurrent theme of this chapter is obviously that, in case after case of confirmed assault, the officer is cleared, sooner or later. The justice system does not seem to appreciate the corroding effect on public trust: a two-tier system is not what the public expect or deserve.

Promising Surrey batsman Tom Maynard, 23, was killed by a Tube train while being chased by police who suspected drink driving: having abandoned his car he was crossing the railway on foot[1694].

Over 4,000 people claimed in 2007 to have been assaulted by police (there were 29,000 complaints in the year 2006-2007, i.e. one complaint for every five officers, with four-fifths being against male officers[1695]).

Half of Scotland's eight forces have announced a crackdown on officers wearing tattoos after crime victims reported being alarmed by 'thuggish-looking cops'. Tattoos will have to be concealed. Tattooists say demand for tattoos from police and potential recruits is high[1696].

CAVEAT CIVIS

In a public lecture in the US in 2010 DI <u>Colin Welsh</u> – lead Met child abuse investigator – spoke disparagingly about prosecution SBS (shaken baby syndrome) cases (there are about 250 in the UK annually), which had failed mainly because of expert defence witnesses who question the infallibility of the 'triad' diagnosis which held sway for many years. The triad can happen naturally. Welsh described how doubting doctors could be excluded from trials, by questioning their qualifications, employment history, research papers and reporting them to their regulatory bodies. Top neonatal Oxford neuropathologist Dr. Waney Squier's practice has been referred by Welsh to the Human Tissue Authority, and she had been reported to the GMC by the National Policing Improvement Agency, with negative results – she says she and the SBS sceptics are being witchhunted so police can improve their conviction rates by excluding them from court[1697].

A policeman won compensation (the public isn't allowed to know the amount) from his Tayside bosses, after testifying against them led them to target him. PC Jim Shaw helped a fellow policeman win £15,000 for being bullied by his police superiors for opposing solo patrols.

A groom who argued with the DJ compering at his wedding was threatened with a Taser, handcuffed and put in cells, by 15 Warwickshire police with a dog and helicopter, ruining the wedding. He was freed without charge after 10 hours[1698].

An Edinburgh football fan suffered life-threatening injuries after falling through a roof as he was chased by Lothian and Borders Police[1699].

West Mercia Police had to apologise when campaigners took exception to their 'Safe Night Out' posters they said implied rape victims were to blame if they were drunk. Another poster said men 'could' be breaking the law if a person hasn't given consent for sex or touching: anti-rape campaigners said there is no 'could-be' about it[1700].

West Midlands PC <u>Lee Rimell</u> was arrested after Facebook was forced to reveal his identity as a 'troll' who hounded a mother with abusive and vile messages, such as that she was a prostitute, child abuser and drug dealer. Rimell allegedly used a fake account with the name Cuthbert Bollingsworth Smyth, as well as hacking into his victim's email account. He was not suspended[1701].

In an effort to 'raise awareness among children about the dangers of weapons' the Met have been handing out Heckler & Koch MP5 submachine guns to children, who may be photographed by friends and family. The weapon is used by the SAS, the Police Service of Northern Ireland and the Met's Specialist Firearm Command. The initiative has been criticised as glamourising guns[1702].

A temporary chief constable of Cumbria was suspended after complaints from two of his most senior officers about his 'heavy-handed management style'. He is chair of the charity 'Bullying UK', and has campaigned against inappropriate behaviour on social media – he is a frequent user of social websites[1703].

Former Met detective Bernard Cambi has claimed that Surrey Police would dump difficult cases in a tray labelled 'too difficult', and that there was a bullying culture in the Epsom and Esher stations. He was giving evidence in favour of <u>Alison Wheeler</u>, sacked for 'cowardice and incompetence' (she was suing for £350,000 for her 'victimisation'). She allegedly stood by as a PC colleague was beaten up outside Walton police station in 2007. It was expected, Cambi said, that colleagues would inform on each other[1704].

A farm worker lost his job after his car was seized and crushed by Tayside Police in a case of mistaken identity – they wrongly thought he was a drink driver[1705].

When victims of domestic abuse report the matter to the police their children may be removed and forcibly adopted so they don't have to witness the partner's violence[1706].

Strathclyde Police broke down a Peebles great-grandmother's door because they thought she was growing cannabis: in fact the plants were parsnips and parsley[1707].

The Met employed 25 officers in the arrest of Damian Green for highlighting the immigration shambles[1708].

Website Policeoracle.com, which offers advice about becoming an officer, displays news from police forces, and carries ads for a mortgagee firm sanctioned by the Police Federation, also sells 12 types of knives like those used by criminals. The site is run by ex-cops for cops[1709].

Seasoned political journalist Simon Jenkins was stopped by 'a loud-mouthed, rifle-toting officer in an unmarked car for allegedly 'driving dangerously' round Hyde Park Corner' '[1710].

Cheshire Police have tested windows and doors surreptitiously at night – if unlocked they knock the occupiers up for a security lecture'. 'Operation Golden' aims to reduce burglary rates, but the police admit some residents will not be happy about being wakened[1711].

Jobsworth council workers backed by West Lothian police officers demolished a Guy Fawkes bonfire with a tractor and digger. The site had been used for bonfires for over three decades[1712].

Frances Andrade committed suicide after the ordeal of her rape trial – she had been told by police not to have counselling (Greater Manchester Police accused Surrey Police of being responsible for this advice). Psychologists (probably) told the police counselling might trigger 'false memory syndrome'[1713].

The front door of a pensioner couple was smashed in by drugs police because their moss phlox plants mimicked the smell of cannabis[1714].

Neil Richardson, Scotland's second-highest ranking cop in Scotland's new (2012) single force (Police Scotland), was accused of misconduct in relation to a police pipe band bullying row which he was investigating (Chief Superintendent Anne McGuire was accused with other police chiefs of harassment and bullying). A cover-up was alleged[1715].

Thames Valley WPC Rachel Garrett claimed her male superiors (Gaz Chiarella and Roy Atwell) victimised and bullied her, e.g. by cancelling her wedding leave without informing her and being ordered to perform a duty she wasn't trained for. She was 'overscrutinised'. She was suing her Chief Constable for disability (she was asthmatic) and sexual discrimination. She had previously recorded various complaints relating to body armour for female officers and on-call allocations. Tribunals awarded her two payments for hurt feelings[1716].

It has been claimed civilian staff at the Scottish Police College at Tulliallan were subjected to 'systematic bullying', with complaints being ignored[1717].

Despite a 10-month inquiry by Grampian Police into alleged 'Sweeney-style' tactics by Tayside Police drugs squad, they will face an internal force probe over working methods, but not criminal charges[1718].

Greater Manchester PC Stephen Hudson was seen on CCTV manhandling a teenager because he refused to empty his pockets: the six-footer forced the 4ft 8in boy against the station counter, making him scream out in pain. The officer said he was using an authorised restraint technique ('pain compliance'). A judge gave him a suspended jail sentence, saying he had inflicted 'deliberate degradation and humiliation', commenting that the laughter of three other observing officers (including a sergeant) was 'bullying of the worst form'[1719].

A former head of the SAS's counter-terrorist team was suing the Met after being arrested in a 'hard stop' (armed police force a car to halt) on suspicion of leaking intelligence reports to a journalist. With his career in ruins as a result of the police action, the allegations were eventually dropped. A senior cop said the probe was a 'scandalous waste of time and money'[1720].

Former Met PCSO Jahangir Alom was arrested over an alleged plot to carry out a major terrorist attack[1721].

Sussex Chief Constable Martin Richards has been reported to the IPCC over claims of 'undue influence' in an alleged sex attack inquiry[1722].

Tayside PC Douglas Fisher, a TA soldier, was to stand trial accused of repeatedly batoning a man while on duty[1723].

'We live in a vindictive punishment culture in which so-called 'public servants' [like police] have no higher purpose than to persecute those who pay their wages'[1724].

Wiltshire Police sergeant Mark Andrews, who dragged a woman across the station floor (she was left partially blind), was sacked, but was now set to get his job back[1725].

Detective Superintendent Michael Orr claims he was victimised by three senior officers over his alleged 'bungling' of the Kevin 'Gerbil' Carroll case. He thinks he has been made the scapegoat for the Carroll probe fiasco by Strathclyde's Deputy Chief Constable Ruaraidh Nicolson, former Deputy Chief Neil Richardson and former Assistant Chief Constable George Hamilton[1726].

Durham custody sergeant Stephen Harvey was fined £50 for common assault[1727].

Nine Met Enfield cops were found guilty of discreditable conduct in relation to brutal behaviour in the Edmonton district (torture, e.g. pushing a suspect's head into a bucket of water, the mishandling of seized goods, e.g. a Mercedes car, the use of baseball bats, smashing a bible over a suspect's head, etc.). A disciplinary hearing had been abandoned by the IPCC[1728], the inquiry having taken four years. Only one officer received a written warning in respect of torture.

A pensioner father claims Strathclyde Police mounted a harassment campaign against him for not revealing the whereabouts of his wife and schizophrenic son, on the run in Spain because she didn't agree with the compulsory treatment order applied to her son. The father says he doesn't know where they are[1729].

Met Commissioner Hogan-Howe said an officer who lied in an email pretending to be a member of the public who'd witnessed Chief Whip Mitchell's outburst (he didn't) didn't affect the original police account[1730].

Children who listen to police drug lectures at school are more likely later to try banned substances – the officers seemed to reduce their fear of experimenting with drugs[1731].

Former Met Commissioner Sir John Stevens admits he got hate mail from his own officers[1732].

Strathclyde Police's head of HR, Margaret Mowat, was suspended, being described as a bully and control freak, a 'Hyacinth Bucket' character[1733].

Three giggling pranksters off-duty Sussex cops sabotaged the CCTV camera of a householder who had been burgled for the first and only time. No action was taken against the trio – Sergeant Dominic O'Brien, PC Gerard McKenna and PC Ellen McArthur[1734].

Esther Rantzen has said Commander Peter Spindler's focus on celebrities in Operation Yewtree could deter abused children speaking out[1735].

Record numbers of police were being disciplined for rudeness towards the public: in 2002 the most officers were sacked or disciplined (41 in a year) since records began in 1985. People claiming they have been wronged by the police are wanting damages more and more (in 2001 forces received 16,000 compensation claims, up 33% in a year)[1736].

'If riot police don't find trouble in front of them, then they go looking for it – indeed, cause it'[1737].

Veteran BBC broadcaster Stuart Hall, who denies charges of historic sex assaults, has questioned the police's 'clear pursuit of celebrities'[1738].

The Personnel Committee of West Midlands Police, the UK's second largest force, has revealed that its officers have become more accident-prone, with injuries due to accidents nearly double those due to assaults. As a result the force's 'seasonal danger' campaign warns officers to watch out for sudden downpours in spring, bright sunshine in summer, leaves in autumn and even icy roads in winter[1739].

Police Federation chairman John Tully admitted that the Plebgate 'police' log 'could be a fake', saying 'it is nothing like a police log'[1740]. A Sunday Times leader suggests the import of the Mitchell (Plebgate) affair is, for the police, very grave indeed: 'It is hard to overstate the importance of serving police officers fabricating evidence against a cabinet minister'[1741].

A Greater Manchester PC was arrested after claims he attacked two women in a kebab shop. He was suspended but given anonymity[1742].

The National Police Improvement Agency (NPIA) has implied newsagents are involved in drugs, having taken an ad out showing the sign in front of a newsagent's saying 'Sweets, Mags, Drugs*'. The idea was to recruit Special Constables – the ad said: 'As a Special Constable you will discover sides to your community you never knew existed'. The Advertising Standards Authority upheld a complaint from the National Federation of Retail Newsagents who said the ad was offensive and misleading[1743].

Chief Constable Stuart Hyde was suspended (2012) by Cumbria Police Authority for alleged 'serious misconduct', and the matter referred to the IPCC, having received in the same year the Queen's Police Medal.

The Chief Constable of South Yorkshire Police, David Crompton, has apologised for 'inappropriate and insensitive' remarks – he accused the Hillsborough families' victims of lying about the disaster[1744].

Lawyers for the monk makers of Buckfast tonic wine were planning to sue Strathclyde Police after the latter asked selected shopkeepers to 'tag' the wine bottles with a label identifying the shop of purchase. The police are claimed to be unfairly stigmatising the brand, because other bottles of alcohol aren't thus branded[1745].

An unnamed WPC who was guarding No 10 on the night of the Plebgate affair was arrested over alleged leaks to the Press. She may have been the female officer who helped write the 'fabricated' police log which claimed Mitchell called officers 'f…….. plebs'. She was the fourth arrest in Operation Alice[1746].

Nottinghamshire Police have banned a glazier from repairing police station windows because he has been caught speeding. This apparently is in line with national policy[1747].

Chainstore Lidl had its licence in a Glasgow supermarket suspended for selling alcohol to a Strathclyde Police 'test purchaser', but this was overturned at the Court of Session[1748].

A retired Parkinsonian businessman was stopped from driving because Tayside Police thought he was drunk: he was stopped 14 times in a few months after 40 years of accident-free driving[1749].

Four Thames Valley Police officers were disciplined over an alleged harassment campaign whose target was PC Alexander Ash's former girlfriend, who claimed she was stopped over 70 times by his police colleagues. She ended the relationship when she found out he was seeing someone else. Police reports on the forensic science graduate, she said, prevented her getting jobs (including that of Special Constable), her car was seized more than six times, and she was cleared of careless driving charges twice. Ash and another police officer were fined and reprimanded, with two others given mild disciplinary action for 'irregular procedcure' and incivility. The victim's father accused the police of having a 'gang mentality'. The police eventually apologised[1750].

The IPCC has informed 3,213 blacklisted workers (e.g. an engineer repeatedly victimised for whistleblowing safety hazards such as asbestos) that it is 'likely that all special [police] branches were involved in providing information that kept people workless'. Campaigners were told for five years (the practice had been going on for decades) that they were talking nonsense, but they now believe there is incontrovertible evidence of a conspiracy between police and the industry: the Consulting Association's (CA) blacklist, funded by 40 constructions firms, was discovered (2009) by an Information Commissioner's office raid. However, the officer recently put in charge of the police's inquiry (Operation Herne), DI Steve Craddock, insists the IPCC is wrong – the IPCC is standing firm, especially in the light of confirmation of a meeting between the CA blacklisters and undercover cops in November 2008. The officers were from the national extremism tactical coordination unit. Tellingly some of the blacklisted workers have been offered compensation by eight major companies[1751].

Avon and Somerset constabulary had to apologise to a British landlord wrongly suspected of murder, compensating him with £50,000 for loss of rent and damage to his properties. The force delayed clearing him of suspicion for two months[1752].

CHAPTER XI

THE HISTORICAL POLICEMAN

The 16th Century English policeman was known as the harman beck (literally the 'magistrate's beak'). The first uniformed police were nicknamed 'Jenny Darbies' (from gendarme) and banned from talking to each other or even the public[1753].

In the 17th Century, starting in 1618, vagrant children were rounded up in London by the police, to be sent to Virginia to work in the tobacco fields. Constables were to 'walk the streets' and forthwith apprehend all such vagrant children, both boys and girls, as they shall find in the streets and in the markets or wandering in the night, and commit them to Bridewell' (the prison near Blackfriars Bridge). The children were shackled for transportation. The poet John Donne, the Dean of St. Paul's, blessed the enterprise, yet of 300 exiled children only 12 had survived by 1624[1754]. During the 17th Century rampage of 'Witchfinder General' Matthew Hopkins in Essex and East Anglia, two of the Essex Chief Constable's cattle died while passing the house of a suspected witch (Elizabeth Clarke), and soon after his newborn son died. The old woman was hanged[1755]. England's first police force, the Bow Street Runners, consisted of only eight men (called Red Breasts because of their scarlet waistcoats), but their founder, the scoundrelly 18th Century lawyer and writer Henry Fielding, also organised a horse patrol, mostly ex-soldiers, to hunt for highwaymen[1756].

The Thames River Police were the world's first uniformed police force (1798), antedating the second, viz the Glasgow force, in 1800 (forming the template for forces in cities like New York, Dublin and Melbourne). But the English force was also a Scottish first – its founder's book 'Police and the Metropolis' was the inspiration. Philanthropist tobacco baron Patrick Colquhoun was also Glasgow's Lord Provost. Corrupt river workers were so incensed at the new police efficiency they threatened to burn down the new police station. He also founded the world's first Chamber of Commerce. His 'The Commerce and Policing of the River Thames' was very influential and the River Police were incorporated into the Met in the 19th Century[1757].

Jonathan Wild, the archetypal crooked cop, was a self-appointed 18th Century 'thief-taker' from the West Midlands. He made out that he had been responsible there for hanging 60 criminals. By the 1720s he was not only in charge of the policing of London – the Privy Council asked his advice about highway robbery – but also of London's criminal fraternity: the thief-taker masterminded thefts and then sold the booty back to his victims (this reminds one of Edinburgh's crooked Deacon Brodie, played brilliantly in the movie by Billy Connolly). Wild's downfall came when he arranged for a rival thief, Jack Sheppard, to be hanged. The death was blamed on Wild, and he was jailed. In John Gay's 'The Beggar's Opera' the main character, Peachum, a crooked thief-taker, is based on Wild. Daniel Defoe famously recorded the non-fictional story of the criminal rivals[1758].

In the Victorian period city police were housed in 'barracks', despite persistent concerns about military traits being fostered in the force.

According to the first and joint Met Commissioners, the most important duty of the police, as enunciated in the 'Nine Principles', is the prevention of crime (the 'General Instructions' of 1829). Modern police seem to have forgotten this.

THE HISTORICAL POLICEMAN

In the first few months of the establishment of Peelers in 1829 many recruits resigned and many were sacked, their replacements experiencing much the same: some hated the discipline, others the violence.

Sir John Moore, the hero general of the Peninsular War, trailblazed in 1803 a new system of discipline and a new relationship between officers and men. Two decades after Moore's death Colonel Charles Rowan (who had served with Moore) adopted organisational protocols, e.g. insisting that commanding officers should be judged by the paucity of crimes in their regiments, not the punishments they dispensed. The Rowan principles remain at the heart of the police service code of conduct, another sign of the military origins of police thinking[1759].

Many Victorian Scottish Highlanders who took jobs (like watchmen) in the cities couldn't speak English. Victorian police stations left much to be desired in terms of their squalor and appalling sanitation, e.g. there was a typhus outbreak in one station and the water supply had to be cut off to Wandsworth[1760].

A century ago 33 of the 44 county chief constables in England were ex-army, while three were naval officers. In Wales, half the 12 chief constables were former army officers. Modern police seem to want to paramilitarise the police with state-of-the-art weaponry. (See the Harmful Policeman Chapter – Firearms).

Charles Dickens and Wilkie Collins tried their best to popularise the New Police, but the old concern about the very idea of a policeman continued, particularly the plainclothes officer who is unidentifiable (Napoleon's police minister Joseph Fouché was a contemporary bogeyman who inflamed the public's fear of the undercover man)[1761].

The rule that women had to leave the Met if they married was not repealed until 1946, and women police had to wear woollen stockings until 1954, and were allowed to carry a regulation handbag from 1968. They couldn't be dog handlers or mounties till the seventies, when, too, they first achieved pay parity with men (1974). The uncomfortable Stanley uniform for WPCs remained unchanged until 1931. The early women constables were labelled 'plonks' by their male counterparts[1762]. Prospective wives were vetted for respectability and sobriety[1763].

One of the multiple incarnations of the infamous Danish conman Jorgen Jorgenson was a policeman (he was alternatively a convict, gambler, pirate, traitor, alcoholic, tramp!). He informed on fellow convicts in Tasmania and became a 'bush constable'[1764].

Victorian bobbies carried smelling salts routinely to revive swooners.

In Victorian times men released early from prison ('ticket-of-leave men') protested they were subject to police harassment which made it extremely difficult to go straight[1765].

The Victorian policeman opened the houses of murder victims to the public, who were charged for the privilege. Murder corpses were also routinely left in situ for the public and then the juries to view (the former, again, had to pay)[1766]. ACPO's money-making proclivities are nothing new.

In the mid-19th Century Boards of Police Commissions were responsible not only for Edinburgh's police force but also public health, lighting, drainage, cleaning: two policemen acted as sanitary inspectors[1767]. In some urban forces the police also doubled as firefighters[1768].

In the 1970s the Flying Squad's independence under Sir Robert Mark was ended, with divisional detectives now being commanded by the uniformed branch. Now overtime payments meant the detectives had to stop working after a certain number of hours – previously 'The Squad' worked extra hours for nothing. Now, too, if they arranged to meet informants in off-duty hours, they might be suspected of corruption[1769].

Two Home Office agents in the 1840s forced a teenage boy (Edward Jones), who had been stalking Queen Victoria, onto a ship bound for New Zealand. When the captain refused they had to bribe another captain to take 'the Boy Jones' to Brazil. He returned, but was abducted again by Scotland Yard's secret police and kept prisoner on a naval ship for five years[1770].

In 1936 Scotland Yard announced that female undercover officers would start road patrols, striking gongs if drivers exceeded 30mph[1771].

In the second half of the 19th Century Met DCI George Clarke, who was known to everyone as 'the Chieftain', appeared in the dock accused of participating in a bookies' scam (punters were invited to place bets on behalf of a supposed racing 'expert' whom the bookies wouldn't touch!). Three Met detectives and a solicitor were arrested, and they were joined by Clarke, denounced by the fraudsters' leader. Though acquitted, Clarke was ordered into retirement by the Home Secretary, and historians have argued he may have been guilty all along[1772].

Corrupt connections between offenders and the early constables and watchmen was a perennial problem since the start of the Met[1773]. The Met's anti-corruption squad was popularly known as 'Rubber Heels'. The 'Trial of the Detectives' (1877) led to a government inquiry into corruption in the detective branch[1774].

Are police primarily political enforcers or peacekeepers? That the police instinctively try to infiltrate spies into social reforming groups (see the recent furore about undercover cops and eco-protesters) is seen in the Coldbath Fields riot (1833), where there was very little sympathy for an officer who was killed - a jury found his killing was 'justifiable homicide'. Police spies were introduced into the National Union of Working Classes, leading to a select committee inquiry. London police were ordered into the 1910 South Wales coal dispute by Churchill[1775]. A large police force helped infantry and cavalry deal with antisemitic riots in 1911[1776].

The case of fugitive spouse murderer Daniel Good in 1840 highlighted the Met's ineptitude, so that the Bow Street Runners – disbanded in 1839 – had to be reinstated[1777].

The infamous Victorian armed robber Charles Peace was so confident about police incompetence that he lived above a police station, while a notorious forger's hideout was 200 yards from a Met detective's home[1778].

One charge used by Edwardian police to incarcerate suffragettes was conspiracy. Suffragette Grace Roe had never done anything militant but was arrested on a conspiracy charge, force-fed and drugged in prison for several weeks in 1914[1779].

CHAPTER XII

THE INCOMPETENT POLICEMAN

CHAPTER CONTENTS

CHAPTER XII

THE INCOMPETENT POLICEMAN

'We are inclined to excuse police incompetence, allowing them to be the judges of their own performance'[1780]. 'There remains a culture of insitutionalised incompetence at Scotland Yard, where poor performance seems to be rewarded with promotion'[1781].

Sins of Commission

Miscellaneous

Derbyshire Constabulary sent an innocent boy of six a letter encouraging him to confess to being a career criminal so he could make a 'fresh start'. He could be spared jail by confessing and getting treatment for his drugs addiction. Somehow the police had wrongly entered his details on a repeat offenders database[1782].

A huge police crackdown on Glasgow's red light district forced sex workers onto the net, with its relative 'safety' for the hookers, who are now much less visible[1783], but some as a result moved to more dangerous areas.

A policeman's mother agreed to help tackle a criminal family if the Staffordshire force protected her anonymity, but blundering cops blew her cover by leaving her name on paperwork given to her nuisance neighbours. She was awarded £99,000 against the force for being abused and hounded, and has cost taxpayers (for safe houses, protection, etc) perhaps £785,000 in two years[1784].

Derbyshire Deputy Chief Constable Alan Goodwin attacked motorists for a lack of respect for victims of fatal accidents: they should be prepared to sit in jams as a mark of respect for the dead[1785]. Furious motorists accused motorway police (this time Avon and Somerset) of total over-reaction, closing 27 miles for a one-vehicle crash that wasn't blocking the road (the vehicle had ploughed into a field)[1786].

The year-long Special Course at the Bramshill National Police College is for constables promoted to acting sergeant. The 'graduates' – impressionable candidates indoctrinated to tow the managerial line and be rewarded with fast track promotion – do little actual operational police work. When they reach ACPO rank, they follow Home Office guidelines. Most police failures in the last quarter of a century stem from the 'Special Course' policy, according to officers within the CID[1787]. For 'Special Course' read 'managerialism'.

Instead of the Met stopping Muslim cleric Anjem Choudary's hate-filled internet speeches, they helped his family go into hiding after the Woolwich atrocity[1788].

When coloured Jay Abatan was killed outside a pub – the inquest was held 11 years later – Sussex Police bungled the inquiry, and officers were disciplined[1789].

A Dundee couple arrested (and detained for five days) while walking their dog, were wrongly accused of participating in a blackmail plot. The couple found a bag placed by the police to catch an alleged extortionist. The husband was handcuffed and was refused bail at Dundee Sheriff Court[1790].Though all charges were dropped (Tayside police were accused of 'burying bad news' by announcing their faux pas on the day Gordon Brown became PM), the couple were planning to sue the force, whose elite group's sting went so badly wrong[1791].

A woman stalked for more than two decades – the stalker had held her at gunpoint and smashed her right knee – plans to sue Fife Police after being arrested for wasting their time (they had secretly installed CCTV outside her home). She said: 'You think the police will want to help you and then they turn it around and blame it on you, making it look like you're mad or something'. She had been remanded in custody for a week[1792].

Police may have known about Michael Adebolajo's extreme beliefs as early as 2003, when he joined the to-be-banned Al-Muhajiroun. He was involved in the murder of soldier Lee Rigby in 2013[1793].

When Derek Bird went on the rampage paramedics were held back by police, so that members of the public had to help victims.

When Pamela Stephenson dressed up as a sexy WPC, to gatecrash, along with Fergie and Diana, Prince Andrew's stag night, they were apprehended by police after pretending to 'arrest' another of their friends outside Buckingham Palace gates. Only when Diana shared some crisps with the police did they finally recognise her[1794].

The Met's four-year £7m anti-terror investigation of Ali Dizaei (Operation Helios) was later condemned as 'seriously flawed', and mishandled from 'start to finish', by the IPCC. In a 2004 report the latter 'deplored' the Met's decision to make a back-door deal with Dizaei[1795].

David Strang, till recently Chief Constable of Lothian & Borders Police, triggered furore when in 2010 he called for thousands of criminals to be excused jail. The soft-touch cop is now Scotland's chief inspector of prisons[1796].

Six uniformed Met officers left their marked van illegally parked on double yellow lines and blocking a taxi rank, while they queued in a sandwich shop. The van was there for at least 15 minutes, whereas despite the shop's business parking permit they sometimes are allowed less than a minute to unload. Officers are supposed to obey traffic regulations[1797].

Police pulled over a driver whom they wrongly thought was uninsured: she had just changed policies, but the traffic officers still impounded her car. The Met arrested not only a gardener for a minor traffic offence, because he mentioned he was leaving the country, but his boss as well. The latter drove his car away when told it was seized, but was pursued as if he were a terrorist[1798].

In the 'salt poisoning' Joshua Williams case the police investigation swung wildly from sheer incompetence to MI5-style surveillance (one policewoman wouldn't search the family garden because she was wearing high heels)[1799].

Cheshire Police were advising jewellers in 2006 – there had been eight armed raids on local jewellers in a year – to put tape measures on doors so that, if robbed, staff can tell the heights of robbers. Other advice was to keep a notepad handy to write down descriptions, and a mobile phone to take robbers' pictures[1800].

The police investigating the 'theft' of Diana's personal items have been severely criticised for 'grossly misleading' Prince Charles and Prince William over the case, presenting unproven allegations as fact[1801].

In the Stephen Lawrence case a local racist group was known about, but a botched police enquiry led to charges being dropped[1802].

Lancashire Police have given both of a pair of identical twins ASBOs because they couldn't tell which one was causing trouble[1803].

Kent Police's scheme to stick yellow tickets on cars (if they contain valuable items or if the cars are insecure) has been called an 'advert to thieves'[1804].

A decade after the 'devil worship' fiascos in the Orkneys, Rochdale and Nottingham, the urban myth raised its ugly head again in 2003, triggered probably by a police officer's interview with a mentally disturbed woman. Murdo Fraser, Northern Constabulary's Chief Inspector of the Western Isles, claimed his force had sufficient evidence to charge people. The Crown Counsel disagreed, and the charges were dropped[1805].

Tests on the laser gun LTI:20.20 Ultralyte show that thousands of motorists may have been wrongly fined because of the way it and similar machines work and are handled by police officers. The quality of speeding evidence presented by the police – and accepted by magistrates – has been described by many of the accused as 'abysmal', there being a serious bias against motorists who opt to go to court to prove their innocence. The gun was designed as a piece of surveying equipment, not to measure traffic speeds. In some American states police are not allowed to use the LTI. Anyway, only about 3% of accidents are caused by excessive speed[1806].

Despite 688 crimes, a burglar was given another chance, education and a rent-free home. Amazingly Essex Police hailed the 'innovative' approach taken here was a 'success', despite the culprit concerned having re-offended, and they are to continue with the programme. The nonsense approach had been trialled by Hertfordshire Police[1807], whose latest (2012) avant-garde idea is to apply the dubious lie detector to paedophiles.

Rank and file Sussex officers were furious when their bosses handed them guidelines showing them how to dress properly – the leaflets included photos of 'perfect cop' and 'shabby cop'[1808].

Two Kent policemen were called to rescue a driver trapped in his security van, but they soon became trapped inside with him[1809].

Rob Shorthouse, Strathclyde's £85,000-a-year head of communications, has apologised for asking hundreds of retired officers to contact a dead officer for information. This error has been attributed to the increasing civilianising and depersonalisation of police culture[1810].

Ian Oliver, former Chief Constable of Central and Grampian, quit the latter in 1998 after he was criticised about how a young boy's murder by a paedophile was investigated, and over allegations about his personal life. He has condemned the new Police Scotland[1811].

Gloucester Police burst into the home of a man and his three-year-old son after they thought his tomato plants were cannabis[1812].

Many officers have been lost to the beat by absorption into the Crime Management Unit, the Crime and Disorder Partnership, a Prolific and Other Priority Offender Unit, the Asset Recovery Unit, the Joint UK Immigration Service, etc[1813].

Bedfordshire Constabulary gave out 49 shotgun and other firearms licences to under 18s (one to a 10-year-old) in 2009[1814]. A holder of six licences (three shotgun and three section one weapons) committed triple murder/suicide on New Year's Day, 2012, despite a warning to Durham Constabulary years earlier. Some forces grant or renew gun licences based on phone calls or postal questionnaires[1815]. Gun licences are being issued to underage children, e.g. 13 under-10s in three years, a Gloucestershire seven-year-old given a shotgun licence, while eight-year-olds were issued with licences in Cumbria and West Mercia[1816]. Reportedly killer cabbie Michael Atherton was given a gun licence despite a history of violence – ironically the son and brother of two of the victims introduced him to guns[1817]. A rich gun enthusiast, who used to fantasise about a killing spree when he had a nervous breakdown, was able to renew his licence because police failed to check his mental state (his doctor was never told by police he had the guns)[1818].

During the Moat saga Northumbria Police curiously told the public he was mainly a threat to police. They also seemed to believe his boast that he had kidnapped two men (the 'kidnapped' men were later charged with conspiracy to commit murder)[1819].

Criminals are being given stolen bicycles by Suffolk Police to help them go straight[1820].

Six street cleaners wrongly arrested over a supposed plot to kill the Pope could sue the Met for unlawful detention[1821].

PC Angela Cornes was promoted to sergeant even though she had repeatedly failed to help Banaz Mahmod when the latter's life was at risk. The Met disciplinary hearing collapsed after the key witness refused to testify, but she didn't even receive a written warning: another four Met officers and two West Midlands detectives did receive one, while another Met constable received words of advice, re how Ms Mahmod's allegation of historical sexual abuse had been investigated[1822].

It has been claimed that the police's use of criminal profiling has proved useless (and sometimes worse than useless, as in the positive profiling of Colin Stagg in the Rachel Nickell case)[1823].

Armed Met police Tasered an innocent person when they tried to target a knifeman on a train[1824].

Residential 20mph speed limits may not result in any appreciable improvement in road safety, according to the Department for Transport, e.g. when the limit was lowered in Portsmouth at a cost of £500,000 the number of people killed or seriously injured on the roads went up[1825]. Before 2004, many local authority/police partnerships installed speed cameras regardless of the number of accidents: money was raised from drivers where safety was not being compromised[1826].

Humberside Police planned to replace police specialising in rape and child sex abuse cases with civilians to cut costs. But the force's senior detectives criticised the 'dangerous' plan. Likewise half the complement of constables in Hull's Public Protection Unit are being replaced by civilian investigators known as IO5s[1827].

The widow of the barrister shot dead by police was 'devastated' when told police had lost his last message for her – it was in a box considered a key piece of evidence[1828].

Police have miscounted the number of violent crimes on our streets – up to 15,000 serious assaults were apparently counted as lesser crimes. Police are solving fewer than half of recorded violent crimes[1829].

When senior officers realised they could use section 5 to maximise only lucrative targets (e.g. by arresting drunks – Drunk and Disorderly arrests didn't count towards targets), suddenly there would be no inebriation arrests. Urinating behind a bush, climbing a tree, dancing in flowerbeds – all became s.5, often against the officers' better judgment. But s.5 could seriously affect a person's future (it meant being arrested)[1830].

Sussex Police sent out thousands of flyers urging residents to visit its website for tips on cleaning up their neighbourhood. Unfortunately the leaflets directed the public to a porn site, which includes stripping policemen in its repertoire[1831].

Norwich drug cops burst into a family home and handcuffed the occupant in front of his terrified children, but they had got the wrong house[1832]. Likewise, the Yard's plan to arrest Damian Green in a dawn raid at his home was abortive because they got the wrong house – they had been spying on a separate address[1833]. A Cricklewood brain tumour patient's home was smashed in, including internal doors – causing thousands of pounds of damage – but police had got the wrong address: an officer arrived with a bunch of flowers[1834]. Lothian and Borders Police drugs cops ignored a neighbour's warning that they were battering down the wrong door, that of a widow whose husband had been a special constable: six officers crashed in during the early-morning raid[1835]. Cambridgeshire Police raided a female colleague's new home because the heat it was emitting made it look like a cannabis factory[1836]. Despite the protests of a widow in the remote Scottish Highlands that her window plants were tomato plants, Northern Constabulary officers insisted on sending samples for analysis, removing her two dogs, keeping her son under guard in a bedroom and handcuffing her nephew. The police didn't apologise[1837]. Armed police raided Eastenders star Steve McFadden's home in search of guns, after hoax calls: no guns were found[1838].

Two Greater Manchester Police constables fell asleep in the afternoon in their patrol van outside a jewellery shop, in one of Manchester's busiest shopping areas[1839]. Two Edinburgh traffic officers were allegedly caught sleeping on duty, in a YouTube clip[1840].

Jobsworth South Wales traffic cops slapped 52 parking tickets in a quiet Cardiff street while the cars' owners were in bed. The residents as a result put their cars fully on the street, effectively blocking it (they had parked on the pavement to ease traffic flow). The police quashed the tickets[1841].

A businessman who rushed 420 miles home from holiday because Dorset Police wrongly told him his shop had been burgled, picked up a speeding fine[1842].

West Yorkshire Police have been caught storing DNA along with the residue of a takeaway in a police fridge, leaving samples to defrost[1843].

Sir Paul Stephenson was in attendance when a burglary ring home was entered by force – the occupant had been arrested hours earlier[1844].

A Nottinghamshire motorist who got two speeding fines when his car was parked, successfully contested them and won an apology from Notts Police[1845].

Sir Paul Stephenson

Eight Strathclyde officers had to pay hundreds of pounds after their illegally parked cars were towed from outside the Stewart Street station in the centre of Glasgow[1846].

Ex-Strathclyde acting inspector Gerry Gallacher has criticised his force's hands-off approach to organised crime gangs in north-east Glasgow in the 1980s. The criminals complained about tough policing, so Gallacher and others were transferred out of the areas where they were successfully disrupting the growth of the crime empires (complaints of corruption by the criminals – e.g. planting drugs and framing on a gun charge – were unfounded). Gallacher tells of a Rangers-supporting DI who announced in a briefing meeting that there had been 'a lot of Catholics locked up at the weekend' (the Catholic Gallacher didn't know the DI was a bigot). He declined an offer to join the Masons – the Vatican had ruled against it – and believes others were promoted thanks to their membership of that body[1847].

Rodger Patrick, a retired D.C.I. with West Midlands Police, claims forces are using various 'gaming' tricks to give the illusion of lower crime rates, reflecting well on their performance. HMIC tends to underestimate the extent of 'cuffing', 'stitching', 'skewing' and 'nodding'. Senior officers are either directly managing 'gaming', or turning a blind eye to it[1848].

An Indie band, The Thirst, was held by armed Staffordshire police at gunpoint after a CCTV operator thought he had seen a gun, while a police helicopter hovered above. The band were held overnight and forced to give DNA samples. The police have apologised[1849].

The Met has apologised for labelling six innocent film actors as wanted football hooligans (the actors were from 'The Firm', a film about hooliganship in the 80s)[1850].

Complaints about police being rude and late have increased by 10% in a year[1851].

The Hillsborough disaster began when Chief Inspector Duckenfield ordered a 16-foot-wide gate in the stadium's outer perimeter to be opened, to allow last-minute fans quick entry and avoid crowd trouble outside the ground. These fans were encouraged to access the ground quickly, even though there was no room left. The resulting Leppings Lane enclosure crush killed fans at the front of the terrace[1852].

Detective Inspector David Smith was in 2003 facing charges of misconduct in relation to his bungled Shipman investigation – he made a series of fundamental errors. He then compounded the felony by lying to his superiors and to the Dame Janet Smith inquiry. The detective kept no proper record of his investigation[1853].

Suffolk Police issued a computer image e-fit of a wanted robber, but he was unidentifiable, as his face was almost completely obscured[1854].

Nearly 25,000 Dorset motorists are to have £1.5m fines refunded – and their points revoked – when a speed camera was found to be operating illegally for a decade[1855].

A crashed driver was in a coma and fighting for life (2008) after police allegedly took five hours to find him (a PCSO couldn't find the wreckage)[1856].

An identity thief stole Catherine Machala Bennett's identity and was charged under the false name by police, so giving a criminal record to the genuine person[1857].

The trial of two men accused of beating unconscious Les McKeown, former Bay City Roller, collapsed after police destroyed vital evidence. (All stored items not marked as trial exhibits are got rid off after a year.[1858]) Efforts to use improved DNA techniques to re-open the Lesley Molseed case (mentally handicapped Stefan Kiszko spent 16 years wrongly in prison) were hampered by the victim's clothing having been destroyed by police[1859]. The Met destroyed the CCTV evidence of the death of their Commissioner Sir Paul Stephenson's daughter's fiancé, so the case had to be dropped[1860]. The case against a Scottish drugs trial fugitive collapsed because the ecstasy he was charged with dealing had been mistakenly destroyed.

In April 2009 police released most of 12 Pakistani students arrested in connection with what Gordon Brown called 'a very big terror plot', no evidence of any kind having been produced. Yet the students have still been smeared as "a threat to 'national security'."[1861]

South Wales Police apologised for giving a widow her estranged husband's suicide rope[1862].

Because items seized as part of the Scottish five-year Operation Kia probe into supposed loyalist terrorists went missing, Tayside Police were being sued in 2007 by a cleared suspect (there were 17 cleared in an exercise that cost £4m). His pictures of the Queen and Diana, a painting of William of Orange, two memento Rangers footballs, two clocks and £620 cash were never returned. Princess Diana's picture was destroyed on instruction by Dundee's Procurator Fiscal[1863].

CAVEAT CIVIS

In 2008 Rizwaaen Sabir and a colleague were arrested by Nottinghamshire Police at Nottingham University for downloading part of an Al Qaeda Training Manual and emailing it to other staff. The case dragged on for three years and was about to go to trial when the police decided to apologise and pay compensation. The material could be bought in bookshops: the student was using it for his degree preparation[1864].

The National Policing Improvement Agency have criticised the behaviour of Greater Manchester Police who fought Rangers fans in Manchester in 2008. One officer claimed there was a 'a lack of coordination and mix of skills, experience, vehicles and equipment[1865]'.

Greater Manchester Police finally (2002) apologised to Shipman's victims' relatives and admitted their investigation had been flawed, allowing him to continue his murderous spree[1866].

Hailey Giblin has told how the police bungled the probe into Huntley's molesting of her, which left him free to commit the Soham murders. After the Soham trial the Buchard Inquiry found the Humberside police case file on Huntley was 'inaccurate in almost every respect'[1867].

West Yorkshire Police kept the wrong man locked up for four days (the two had the same name and date of birth). They moved him hundreds of miles to Dundee. There was another recent mistaken identity case in Dundee: a grandfather and his wife spent five days in custody after armed police mistakenly arrested them in a Dundee car park during a blackmail stake-out[1868].

HMIC has criticised Cumbria Police's management of 'crucial incidents and major crime' as 'poor' in a 2006 report, revealing that the force had no 'major investigations team' or even a murder investigation policy[1869]. Yet Cumbria's police-run website for young schoolchildren included a link to footage of a boy stabbing a burglar in the chest with a samurai sword. The 'Bill The Burglar' site teaches youngsters as young as five about crime prevention[1870].

Cressida Dick

Operation Trident (tackling black gun crime) headed by Cressida Dick used rap group Roll Deep in an anti-firearms video despite their having written lyrics glamourising shootings. Despite songs like 'Wickedest Ting' ('One phone call we send for the hitman. People due ... Drive-by shooting ... bang bang bang. Sounds of the gunning from my hand') and 'They Should Know' ('I got a semi-automatic spraying machine. And I'm erratic…'). Commander Dick says 'Roll Deep are highly credible'[1871].

Golfer Colin Montgomerie evaded a driving ban with the help of a lawyer nicknamed 'Mr. Loophole', who argued that the use of a speed gun near Carlisle had not been to ACPO guidelines (this was the third time the lawyer had got his client off a speeding charge)[1872].

In a 2010 report by the Chief Inspector of Prisons, the Chief Inspector of Probation and the Chief Inspector of Constabulary were criticised for concentrating on 'catching and convicting' gang members rather than protecting them from harm[1873].

Swindon, the first town to switch off all its speed cameras, saw a decrease in crashes. Contrary to what police say, drivers are safer when allowed to use their own judgment[1874].

A worried father was arrested by police in a dawn raid after he told neighbours a man cleared of abusing his two daughters was living nearby. The father was charged with breach of the peace after delivering 35 letters to locals, the letters producing new evidence against a man who now faces 18 abuse charges. He told police more than five years before of other possible child victims, but officers refused to go and see the families concerned.

The hunt for Milly Dowler's killer was conducted by incompetent Surrey officers – Chief Constable Mark Rowley has said sorry to her parents for missing significant leads[1875].

The national crime-mapping website has a reportedly 10% error rate, but how do we know the other 90% is correct[1876]?

MPs demanded an independent inquiry into a 'bungled' fraud investigation by Norfolk Police and NHS Counter Fraud Investigations, including a high-profile raid by 50 officers (none were fraud specialists) on Cawston Park Hospital, which cost £2m and lasted three years. The case was thrown out of Ipswich Crown Court in 2009, when, too, the business went into administration. The judge told the hospital's proprietor: 'You leave vindicated, with your good name intact …'[1877].

Though West Yorkshire Police charged a man with harassing his ex-wife for sending her only two letters, the trial collapsed on the first day: the judge told him, 'We're sorry for wasting your time'[1878].

Colin Stagg seemed to fit the profile of Rachel Nickell's murderer provided by Paul Britton, a clinical psychologist and ex-policeman, and this greatly influenced the police, particularly DI Keith Pedder, in charge of the investigation. But the ex-policeman was wrong. The CPS lawyers should have realised that offender profiling had never been used as the main plank of the prosecution's case in British law[1879].

West Midlands Police took a coachload of 19 Asian Muslim thugs from Dudley on a daytrip to Blackpool to prevent them becoming involved in antisocial behaviour. On arrival some chanted racial abuse, which resulted in a young father being kicked senseless in front of his children and pregnant girlfriend. Chief Superintendent Mark Robinson, of Sandwell police, defended the decision to bus the thugs out of town[1880].

Six Essex cops called to a disturbance got stuck in a lift because their combined weight caused it to break down. They were too late to make arrests, and were eventually rescued by the Fire Service[1881]. Almost half of police recruits are overweight or obese[1882].

Police ignored a member of the public's calls for help in regard to hooded louts desecrating a war memorial, but when she tried to act on her own she was hassled by police[1883].

Lancashire Police re-arrested one of Britain's most wanted paedophiles after letting him go by mistake[1884].

Police, fire and the ambulance service all use different radio systems, none of which may work underground[1885].

The Chief Constable of Suffolk, Alastair McWhirter, said police are suffering physical symptoms from doing too much paperwork – they sound like R.S.I[1886].

A grandmother driving to collect her dying mother for a hospital appointment was wrongly arrested on suspicion of stealing petrol. While she was in a cell her car was stolen. She said 'I cannot trust the police any more. I didn't feel that way before, but all they did was pass the buck'[1887].

An Australian multi-millionaire says he is to receive a £372,000 payout for wrongful arrest by the Serious Fraud Office (over alleged BAE corruption) – he was awarded it from Government central funds. He spent six days in Pentonville[1888].

Hertfordshire Chief Constable Frank Whiteley, an ACPO spokesman, has suggested Neighbourhood Watch members could do police jobs such as street patrols, checking car tax discs, spying in secret groups on criminals[1889].

Thousands of criminal suspects could lodge human rights compensation claims because police broke the law over bail rules. Time spent on bail should always have counted towards the 96 hours maximum suspects can be held in custody (under the Police and Criminal Evidence Act)[1890].

Lord Chief Justice Lord Judge says a third of police fines are given to violent or professional criminals when they should have been brought to court. Police are being issued with ticketing machines to issue Penalty Notices for Disorder to drunks, vandals and shoplifters instead of taking them to court[1891]. Police fixed penalty fines are only stored locally, not counting as a criminal conviction. In 2010-2011 there were over 28,000 tickets for harassment, nearly 36,000 for drunkenness, 37,000 for theft, 15,000 for cannabis possession[1892]. An £80 fixed penalty was the only punishment issued by West Midlands Police to a teenager whose false rape allegation led to an innocent man being beaten up and another imprisoned[1893]. Despite 50 members of the public suffering a sexual or violent attack daily by an offender spared jail in favour of community punishment, the police have been giving cautions to rioting arsonists, burglars and knife possessors (three-quarters of 2011 rioters already had criminal convictions). This is another example of the rapid growth in the 'cautions culture' in the police service[1894]. 4,500 serial offenders (with 15 or more convictions) were given cautions by police in 2011[1895].

Britain's top forger, Scot 'Hologram Tam', and five of his multi-million pound Glasgow gang were eventually jailed in 2007, their first conviction in 1998 having been overturned on appeal because of flawed police procedure (search warrants had the wrong date on them)[1896]. The Scottish Parliament tightened the law on warrant procedures in 1999 after a series of blunders let drug dealers go free – procurators fiscal were put in charge thereafter of all requests for search or arrest warrants. This was just a week after an Ayrshire case of a heroin dealer was dropped because the arrest warrant was wrongly named, while in 1998 police who had seized a large amount of cannabis, a gun and ammunition had to drop the charge because their warrant was for the wrong address. Yet in a 2007 Glasgow case a gang of cocaine dealers walked free because Strathclyde drug squad officers had wrongly addressed a warrant (it was for another innocent address in the same street): the police continued to search and seize drugs worth £150,000 despite knowing the warrant was incorrect[1897].

Hampshire Constabulary, desperate for recruits, turned to applicants who had had rejection letters[1898]. Lancashire Police hired more PCSOs in 2006 than PCs for the first time (212 versus 166)[1899]. Over 6,000 officers had left their forces in recent years, it was reported in 2007[1900].

Elite police (including riot squad and fast response drivers) across England and Wales were doing call centre work instead of the work they're trained for in 2007. Even the Met's CO19 firearms officers were manning 999 phones[1901].

The IPCC admitted wrongly telling journalists that shooting victim Mark Duggan fired at officers before he was killed[1902] prior to the 2011 riots. The officer present at the Mark Duggan shooting whose bullet lodged in a colleague's radio suggests faulty marksmanship[1903].

A Scotsman bought a motorbike from a Lothian and Borders police auction, then had it seized because police said it was stolen[1904].

Lothian and Borders Police not only gave a speeding ticket to an ambulance delivering a transplant organ to hospital, but sent traffic officers more than 100 miles to Newcastle to check with the driver's bosses that he was indeed carrying the organ[1905].

Essex Police are shutting almost half their stations, and reducing the 24 hour cover in the rest, with a view to possibly using Twitter and Facebook, as well as the telephone[1906]. Greater

Manchester Police are dismantling all their round-the-clock public access stations except one[1907]. Lancashire Police will no longer attend non-home burglaries – a telephone investigation is all that is offered and it might be two days before details are taken in a 'telephone appointment'[1908].

There are three grades of 999 calls: Grade One (threat to life or limb), Grade Two (includes Grade One not attended immediately – supposed to be attended within an hour), Grade Three (includes Grade Two where there was delay because there were no officers available). This downgrading allowed one force to claim a 95% success rate in Grade One and Two responses.

Target-driven CPS lawyers – desperate to only process winnable cases – are asking police to collect excessive amounts of evidence for minor cases ('investigating every drunk to the level of a terrorist'): the CPS are not accountable for the amount of police time they tie up: one officer recounts how they demanded 15 statements from 15 witnesses, three times each – a case has to be 'watertight'. The CPS also downgrades crimes (e.g. 'threat to kill' to 'breach of the peace') to help ensure a conviction[1909].

Greater Manchester Police have been accused of being 'panicked' into arresting, charging and holding without benefit of bail the nurse accused of the insulin serial killing of the Stepping Hill Hospital patients[1910]: criminal charges had to be dropped.

As Met Commissioner in 2002 <u>Sir Ian Blair</u> suggested dropping the crown from the Met's insignia for non-Christian officers. In 2005 he altered the Met's logo from 'Working for a Safer London' to 'Working Together for a Safer London' and allowed police Range Rovers with 'Vote Labour' slogans transport Tony Blair during an election campaign. He was criticised for failing to stop publication of Ali Dizaei's controversial book and he personally tried to portray de Menezes as a more credible suspect than he was[1911].

Female firearms officers' guns are too big for them to handle safely, so they risk shooting themselves or others, and they are often given uniforms that don't fit properly, with boots designed for men[1912].

Former policeman Iain Gordon has sympathised with a cancer sufferer who was searched by police looking for drugs – he agrees police nowadays seem incapable of maintaining a happy medium. 'They seem to go from zero policing to gang policing ...'. Rookie constables are apparently advised on their first week on the job: 'Trust no one, believe nothing and check everything'[1913].

A businessman has called Stornoway police 'crazy' for destroying his lost passport – it was out of his possession for only an hour when it was handed in.

Police arrested over 63,000 homeless people in 2007, up 27% in five years: they keep re-arresting the same people[1914]. A homeless Bristol man was arrested for begging, having previously been cautioned: the court case over 60p cost taxpayers £1,500[1915].

Six officers from West Yorkshire Police, alerted by thermal imaging from their helicopter, smashed down a neighbour's gate to gain access to a garage suspected of 'hothousing' cannabis. If the occupant hadn't returned home police would have used their battering ram (they had broken the lock on a neighbour's gate)[1916]. In fact, a heater was simply keeping guinea pigs warm[1917]. A police helicopter's infra-red camera detected what the operators felt was a cannabis property but officers found it was the house of PCSO Zally Huseyin. Cambridgeshire Police compounded the felony by alleging the mistake was due to shoddy insulation[1918]. Greater Manchester Police apologised to a dinner lady for smashing into her property at 6.30am, wrongly thinking she was running a drugs den. The same force raided a house after reports of a figure holding a gun in the sitting room: it was a cardboard cut-out of Lara Croft[1919]. Football boss Harry Redknapp won his case alleging an unlawful raid on his home by City of London Police. His wife was alone at home. They were awarded damages[1920]. Seven Strathclyde officers from its Pro-active Crime Team smashed into a retired teacher's flat in a bungled dawn drugs raid. The lead cop wouldn't believe they had got the wrong address. Though the victim has demanded an apology, none has been forthcoming[1921]. Nottingham Police raided an innocent man's home after a stolen iPhone GPS sent them to the wrong address[1922]. Met officers acting on behalf of Portuguese police hunting for Madeleine McCann raided the London home at 2am of an innocent woman in her 70s, as well as another house with a similar address. This came at the same time that Portugal's Policia Judiciaria revealed they were pursuing leads from clairvoyants[1923].

A 2011 PCCS (Police Complaints Commissioner for Scotland) found an increase in complaints against the Northern and Fife Constabularies. The commonest complaint (one third of complaints) was of 'irregular procedure' (duty performed in an improper manner), the second was rudeness (16%)[1924].

Hundreds of police ('evidential review officers') have to check the 3Rs of their more junior colleagues – arithmetic, spelling, etc: the Met employs as many as 500, mostly sergeants (sometimes called 'case director sergeants'). The Millgarth police station in Leeds had a banner warning of 'theives', West Midlands couldn't spell 'Merseyside', Essex Police misspelt 'calender' in leaflets for thousands of children, while an Old Bailey judge wasn't very pleased that the police charge sheet misspelt 'grievous' four times[1925].

During the Pope's visit police and stewards at first refused to let MP Anne Widdecombe leave Hyde Park to get the train to Birmingham where she was commenting on Cardinal Newman's beatification. At Birmingham pilgrims were forced by police to walk two uncomfortable miles to access the ceremony, and then another two miles to get out of the park once the Pope had left[1926].

In 2009 37,000 cautions were given for ABH (Actual Bodily Harm), which previously would have been punished by community order or custody[1927].

In Edmonton, Ontario, it takes police about an hour to process a criminal, while in Edmonton, North London, it takes on average over ten hours[1928].

Lothian and Borders Police may scrap front counter services in some areas and reduce services in others: policing reduction by stealth[1929].

Brodie Clark, the senior UK Borders Agency official in dispute with HS Theresa May, said he only relaxed passport controls on the advice of the police, who demanded it 'to avoid public disorder'[1930]. German police helped Hitler to power using this argument.

The mother of tragic model Sahar Daftary, who died in a fall, has revealed that when police officers returned with two black sacks she thought they would contain Sahar's possessions: instead there was a random collection of clothes and shoes that weren't her daughter's. Their callous joking that the clothes must be 'Manchester sizes' was typical, she says, of a police investigation that betrayed the girl. The family claim they weren't interviewed till a fortnight after the death[1931].

The Met hierarchy was furious at the claims of a report (by The Guardian newspaper and the LSE) that the summer 2011 riots were partly due (after poverty) to their stop-and-search tactics. Almost 75% of the study's respondents said they had been stopped in the previous year, and many said the riots were 'payback'[1932]. During the riots police had to use their own mobiles, as the official radio system (the high-tech digital Airwave) collapsed. Some forces had no idea how many officers were on duty, and some were left 'directionless'. Officers were, as a result of the communication dysfunction, always a half hour behind the rioters. There were severe equipment shortages, e.g. police had to be transported in school buses[1933].

In the Jill Dando case the police scored an own goal by taking a coat to be photographed at a studio used to process recently discharged guns before it had been forensically examined[1934].

Cambridgeshire Police have been ridiculed for sending householders an email giving crime prevention tips which contained blunders (wrong words, nonsense phraseology)[1935]. In 1994 the Met's Flying Squad head, John O'Connor, said: 'Cannabis is a decriminalised drug'[1936]. The police admit their advice to Home Secretary David Blunkett to downgrade cannabis in 2004 was wrong[1937]. Scotland Yard defends the policy of just giving warnings to cannabis users – despite the 'softly softly' approach contributing to a huge increase in cannabis use – because it 'reduces tension' between users and police[1938].

At the time (1993) of the Stephen Lawrence murder police had no written instructions on how to deal with exhibits[1939].

The mother of Mark Blanco, murdered in Whitechapel in 2006, claims DI Mark Dunne, in charge of the initial police investigation, botched it, even suggesting her son had committed suicide like his brother (Dunne has since been promoted to Deputy Chief Inspector of Homicide Command). She details the following: (1) The crime scene was not secured; and was declared 'non-suspicious' just a few hours after the 'accident'; (2) no forensics of the victim's clothing were performed; (3) the three prime suspects were described as 'unfairly maligned' by police, and their mobile phone records went unchecked (one wasn't interviewed properly because he was 'difficult to catch up with'); (4) when one of the suspects confessed to murder he was not taken seriously, and the confession wasn't reported by the police to the coroner, who dismissed Dunne's suicide conclusion and ordered a second investigation[1940].

In 2002 top police chief Rick Naylor was mugged in Sheffield, which he had called the safest British city (it was Home Secretary's David Blunkett's constituency). He was punched and his laptop demanded[1941].

Thousands of speeding convictions may be questioned after Strathclyde Police admitted their Falcon device may record speeds from nearby cars which are going faster. The issue arose during the trial of PC Blair Pettigrew, accused of driving over twice the speed limit[1942].

THE INCOMPETENT POLICEMAN

Merseyside DCs <u>Gary Turner</u> and <u>Austin Heath</u> have been sacked (but retain their pensions) after they allowed a criminal to exit prison so he would confess to crimes he had not committed, encouraging him with strong drink[1943].

One in eight DNA records is thought to be inaccurate: 550,000 false, misspelt, etc. names. Many criminals are using other people's names if they are caught[1944].

A BBC reporter was wrestled to the ground by six Staffordshire policemen who thought (wrongly) that he was a terrorist with a bomb (he is Pakistani). The force said it was pleased the way its officers responded[1945].

In 2008 <u>Sir Ian Blair</u> was criticised by DPP Sir Ken Macdonald for suggesting charging celebrities like Kate Moss and Peaches Geldof apparently snorting drugs on camera – Blair had 'completely misunderstood the law'. Thus the law requires prosecutors to prove a substance is either a class A or class B drug, but this cannot be done if the only evidence is film[1946].

The Met spent 18 months probing a DNA sample in the 'spy in the bag' death, only to find it belonged to a police forensics officer[1947].

A West Sussex police car parked on double yellow lines in Crawley was clamped by a member of the public[1948].

A Nottinghamshire PC and WPC smashed a car's window to save a dog overheating in the sunshine, but it was a cuddly toy. Compensation was paid[1949].

A North London borough had 24-hour police cover till 2010, when the local station was closed for 'efficiency' reasons. When the Safer Neighbourhood Team is not on duty (at night) the only service available is a mobile response team. A 2011 policy change means that nearly all applicants for full-time Met posts have to serve as unpaid (uniformed) Specials for at least 18 months, meaning their training will be deficient[1950].

An unnamed Surrey officer sent, by mistake, a Twitter message (pre-written for a police app) that a plane had crashed in the centre of Camberley. Why would such a serious incident be pre-loaded into computers[1951]?

A study by the LSE and The Guardian of 130 officers in the thick of the 2011 riots found not only were they not deployed in the worst areas but they had no access to the Met's radio channel.

The £1.7m scheme to make huge savings by giving police smartphones made only £600,000 in savings – officers using the new devices actually spent <u>more</u> time in the station. The handling of the Mobile Information Programme by the NPIA (and H.O.) has been criticised by the Public Accounts Committee: the scheme was halted in 2010[1952].

The police who raided the Krays on a grass's information botched an identity parade, so they had to be released the next day. The Krays had informants inside the Met; so they could keep one step ahead[1953].

When Hampshire Police opened up a field so that travellers, who were blocking a road, could turn their caravans around, the trespassers took over the field. The council says the police shouldn't have allowed access. The police having supervised a breach of the law did nothing to resolve the situation[1954].

Two British detectives sent in 1990 to help bring Julie Ward's killers in Africa to justice ended up using the chief suspect as their guide. Chief Constable Stoddart of Durham says the two officers had 'undertaken what is at best a poor investigation, at worst hopelessly flawed'. In 2008 a secret report claims that British officials obstructed the victim's father's campaign for justice[1955].

A female thug who broke a student's nose was merely given a police caution, but a journalist is taking up the victim's case[1956].

A Nottingham police officer advised a farmer to dig a deep trench to stop doggers getting onto his land, but the PC forgot about this when he returned to the scene, causing £2,000 damage to his patrol car[1957].

Tayside Chief Inspector Conrad Trickett has urged his officers not to arrest suspected criminals because of an expected strike by court solicitors, resulting in the accusation of giving offenders an 'easy ride' (Strathclyde Police issued similar instructions). Tayside Police have apologised to Fife Police for wrongly saying the latter was responsible for an illegally parked Volvo squad car[1958].

Police told whistleblower Dr. Linda Reynolds that there was no foundation to her Shipman allegations.

The re-conviction rate of offenders from the Intensive Surveillance and Supervision Programme is 90%, yet it is the flagship community scheme[1959].

A joke witness statement by a West Midlands police dog was mistakenly submitted to the courts[1960].

The National Crime Recording Standard was introduced to 'record crime in a more victim-focussed way', i.e. once a crime report is generated at the call centre, it is hard to get it to go away, even though there has been no crime[1961].

At police stations in England and Wales 17-year-olds are treated as adults, so that they are (illegally) deprived of the support (e.g. relatives being present during questioning) to which children are entitled (one committed suicide after a drunk and disorderly arrest)[1962].

A Scottish serial paedophile with convictions for following a boy home (two years in jail), abducting a boy from a swimming pool (40 months), indecency towards boys aged 11 to 13 (1 year for breaching probation), watching teenagers using a skate park, was given a mobile phone by police to keep him safe. But he used the phone to contact three potential victims, breaching a SOPO (Sexual Offences Prevention Order)[1963].

A Lancashire officer accidentally locked himself and three colleagues in a cage with a violent person, while another was inadvertently locked in a car backseat by his colleagues (the doors had child locks) as a suspect jogged by. Two female police sergeants exchanged stories about their sex lives in their patrol car, not realising their giggling conversation was being broadcast to every police car in north London[1964].

The Government is to stop police issuing large numbers of unconditional cautions for serious crimes like rape, murder threats, wounding, weapon possession, supplying Class A drugs and perverting the course of justice. Police seem to be misusing cautions to improve detection rates[1965].

Over 200,000 members of the public a year have been using the Scottish police stations whose front desks are to close, the busiest being Craigmillar (Edinburgh), presently open for 17 hours daily seven days a week. The six rural stations and their houses on Lewis are all being sold off, so now policing will only be accessible in the capital Stornoway. The closures were announced without a proper public consultation which suggests the natural authoritarian tendencies of the Scottish police are alive and well: the Stephen House unfulfilled promise that no one would notice the changes on a day-to-day basis was not a surprise to many. Police Scotland is also planning to axe seven of its ten regional emergency control rooms[1966].

Police have apparently threatened to pass badgers cull protestors' data to opposed farmers' lobbying group NFU[1967].

Custody Blunders

A group of Cambridgeshire custody officers have been caught on CCTV joking as they watched a man smashing his head against a cell wall: 'We are overdue a death in custody'[1968].

Of 2,500 people taken into custody under section 136 by Sussex Police, only 800 were taken to a mental health unit (they were held in cells under the section, but should have been transferred without delay)[1969].

The woman dragged across Swindon police station before being thrown into a cell by Sergeant Mark Andrews – he has been cleared on appeal of assaulting her – says he should never again be put in charge of a custody suite. She claims there is 'one rule for the police and another for members of the public'. Wiltshire's Assistant Chief Constable had branded the sergeant a disgrace to the force after his conviction – he was suspended until his internal conduct hearing[1970].

A police officer who now lives in Spain has kept his Cambridgeshire custody inspector job[1971] (serving firemen have also lived abroad).

A dying prisoner's calls for help went unanswered at Dundee's police HQ because the custody officer was surfing the net and the buzzer system was switched off: Stuart Lewis was responsible for 16 prisoners[1972].

A Dunbarton teenager was found dead in his cell at the town's police station after being arrested for a minor offence[1973].

A man dying from a brain haemorrhage was locked in a cell for 25 hours because he looked drunk. Officers falsified his incarceration records[1974].

A probe was launched into the death of a 34-year-old arrestee in a cell at Grampian Police's HQ in Aberdeen[1975]. The Butler Report was commissioned to address, in particular, the failure of the CPS to prosecute deaths in police custody[1976].

North Wales Police had to rescue a member of the public from their Rhyl station after they locked him in by mistake[1977].

The barrister dragged away in handcuffs while defending a client at the High Court received £100,000 and an apology from the Met. He fell into a diabetic coma in his police cell because the police confiscated his insulin. He had been arrested when he was the one who was attacked. The Met's apology ads appeared in the Law Society Gazette, Barrister Online and the Daily Cause List[1978].

A Met Police bungle allowed Babyshambles popstar Pete Doherty to walk free even though he had breached bail: though in custody he wasn't brought to court within 24 hours of his arrest[1979].

A diabetic teenager who collapsed unconscious was arrested and taken to Lyndhurst police station instead of hospital[1980].

Three Dorset police allowed a drunk to die of hypothermia in their cells[1981].

A man left in a coma in a Sussex police cell – custody officers were not told of a possible head injury when he was being manhandled to the ground by several officers arresting him for being drunk and disorderly and resisting arrest – needs full-time care for the rest of his life. The custody sergeant's care was described by the IPCC as 'perfunctory … and possibly negligent', but he escaped discipline when he was transferred to a civilian job within the force. Two Reliance custody assistants were also said to have a 'perfunctory' approach but could not be disciplined: one was accepted as a trainee officer with Sussex Police. The CPS decided on no prosecutions[1982].

Sins of Omission

Miscellaneous

Police in some parts of the country investigate just 10% of offences of theft from a car. In 2009 the Met screened out 75% of criminal damage and vandalism, two thirds of

burglaries, 22,000 sexual or violent offences, 4,200 of harassment, 802 GBH offences, nine rapes and a murder[1983].

The average burglar now (2012) has 12 offences to his name, the highest number ever recorded, yet half of them are given community orders or fines rather than prison[1984].

Police fail to investigate a third of crimes reported to them (including burglaries, drug trafficking, sexual (and violent) assaults), i.e. well over a million crimes in England and Wales annually. New Scotland Yard drops almost half of all investigations after an initial screening – in Warwickshire over half are not probed[1985].

A 2008 British Crime Survey found only 3% of crimes led to a conviction[1986]. We imprison far fewer criminals for every crime committed than any other western country, which helps explain why we have more crime[1987].

In 2001 an unnamed Lancashire PC with 18 years' service became the first officer in Britain to be dismissed for under-performing under a 1999 Act, after two warnings to improve[1988].

More than 100 lawyers have resigned from the IPCC because of a 'culture of incompetence'. The IPCC had been welcomed by lawyers at its birth in 2004, but they now criticise its favouritism (for the police). One glaring example of incompetence is that of Christine Hirst – her son was stabbed to death in 2000 – who was still awaiting the resolution of her complaint (that police had failed to protect him even though the killer had made repeated threats) nearly eight years later[1989].

The number of members of the public in Scotland unhappy at how police handle complaints rose by a fifth (in the year to 2010), the Police Complaints Commissioner for Scotland reports[1990].

When an all-day rave blocked a main road in Oxford, Cressida Dick decided to withdraw her officers rather than disperse the crowd, to avoid hurt and damage and 'a lot of very bad publicity'[1991].

The 2005 Politeia report into the recruitment, leadership and morale of Britain's 43 forces, says that recruits are low quality, leadership is poor and there is a structure of divided authority. 'Both training and employment lack direction, and even a sense of fundamental purpose, with confusion about what the police are employed to do and how well they do it'. Training has been compromised by a lack of clear standards and sometimes qualified staff, and the drive to attract graduates has failed[1992]. A leaked 2006 Downing Street report 'Policy Review: Crime, Justice and Cohesion' attacked police for failing to improve their performance, despite large budget increases. It says, 'There is still little chance that a crime will be detected and result in a caution or conviction'[1993].

The family of an 84-year-old pensioner, whom police say died in 1998 by choking on her false teeth, has fought for the truth for four years – a pathologist says she suffered facial blows, her purse with thousands of pounds was missing, and an independent inquiry revealed a catalogue of police errors. Officers dismissed the family as 'unsavoury agitators'. The Crown Office has now pronounced the death as suspicious, e.g. a drug addict who lived near the old lady gave £2,000 (the amount missing from her purse) to a relative for 'safekeeping' just after her death[1994].

CAVEAT CIVIS

Almost a quarter of drinking outlets sold alcohol to children between 2004-2006, yet increased powers given to police to tackle the problem are not working. Often the laws are not being enforced at all[1995].

Since the advent of Police Scotland murder detectives are travelling around the country to investigate violent deaths, but critics claim they will waste crucial time getting to incidents (the first 48 hours may be the most critical), and officers may not have the requisite local knowledge[1996].

West Midlands Police has been criticised (2010) for telling officers not to fight crime at the end of shifts, to try to cut overtime bills. The force was also criticised in 2007 for spending £40,000 on hypnotism to help staff stop smoking[1997].

Thugs have run riot for six years in an East Sussex town because security cameras have been rendered useless by the glare from powerful street lights. 'The police have known about this problem for years but they've never done anything about it', said one resident[1998].

Early in 2010 Gordon Brown promised to name and shame forces which were not getting officers out on the beat – the target being that 80% of officers' time should be spent on patrol[1999]. Only one in 58 officers is out on patrol, despite an increase in police numbers. In an eight-hour shift only a little over an hour is spent on patrol. There are 2,400 out of a total complement (2007) of 143,000 officers on patrol at any time[2000]. In 2006 the cost of police paperwork had risen by 24% in one year to £625 million[2001].

Scottish forces have admitted they cannot monitor the most serious sex offenders, e.g. in some parts of Scotland there is just one officer to track 100 such criminals. There may be at any one time between 150 and 300 on the run[2002].

Barrister John Cooper has expressed grave concerns about the Deepcut police investigation – Surrey Police has apologised for the mistakes its officers made. In particular, the civilian police could have investigated the Army deaths, but there was an assumption of suicide in all cases[2003].

Norfolk Constabulary let off two vandals (caught on CCTV)

// OH LOOK, THE FIRST POLICEMAN OF SPRING \\

smashing parked cars because they were jobless foreigners and it would cost too much to take them to court. The force has also been criticised for letting suspected rapists and thieves go free in 2006 because they failed to enforce arrest warrants (1,692 alleged felons were at large)[2004].

D.I. <u>David Smith</u>, who carried out the first Shipman probe, committed many blunders, including a failure to take notes during interviews with GP Dr. Reynolds and an undertaker who had also voiced suspicions, to check Shipman's criminal record (he falsified documents and had a drug abuse conviction), to compare the number of Shipman death certificates with other doctors', and to order postmortems on three Shipman patients who died in the first week of the investigation in 1998. Smith 'never understood the issues, never had a plan of action ...'[2005].

There have been several child porn allegations against Soham family liaison detective <u>Brian Stevens</u> that appear to have been ignored: prosecutors offered no evidence against him on charges of indecently assaulting two schoolgirls (aged 13 and 14) and distributing and possessing child porn (this was provided by a third schoolgirl but was also ignored). Child porn was found on his laptop and he agreed he had posed in Net chatrooms posing as a girl and sending pictures to strangers. Stevens was exonerated after a catalogue of blunders by police and prosecutors: a source at West Midlands Police said detectives were furious that the vital evidence was not used[2006].

Catastrophic failings by Oxfordshire Police (and social services) allowed a paedophile ring (of men from places like Leeds, Bradford, London and Slough) to sexually torture girls for eight years – abusers would queue up in corridors of Oxford hotels and bedsits[2007].

In 2003 the Police Complaints Authority found that the Avon and Somerset Police investigation into the curious death of judge Andrew Chubb was 'far from thorough'. The police admitted their probe 'was not of the standard we would expect or require'[2008]. When his body – he died in a fireball – was released for cremation, it had not had a forensic PM, no blood samples were taken, nor were his lungs examined, nor witnesses traced[2009].

The Met Commissioner was officially notified in 2007 he would be criticised by the IPCC – one of 20 senior police to be rebuked over the handling of the de Menezes shooting. Sir <u>Ian Blair</u>'s senior officers' failure to brief him fully shows he was 'not in control of his organisation'[2010].

According to an ITV 'Tonight' programme (4.5.07) police are not following up CCTV or other evidence in relation to credit card fraud (e.g. addresses where stolen goods are to be delivered). The police have also been <u>over</u>-zealous, e.g. one Simon Bunce was accused of downloading child porn (Operation Ore) and held for nine hours, his computers being confiscated. His card had been cloned, but it was six months before charges were dropped. In the TK Maxx scandal the police showed indifference.

Scotland Yard missed several chances to intercept four terrorists months before the bungled suicide bomb attacks of 21/7 (the leader was seen by officers at least four times before the bombings, and was on bail for suspected extremism)[2011].

Northamptonshire Police were called by a farmer to a traveller's camp, to which they had trailed thieves. Five officers turned up in marked cars but wouldn't enter the site 'for health and safety reasons'. When the farmer offered to search the thieves' van, he was told he would be arrested[2012].

The violent crime detection rate in England and Wales slumped by a third in the decade from 1997, while offences and police numbers soared, according to a 2008 Tory analysis of Home Office figures[2013].

Police will have to reopen 700 cases where a bogus Cheshire forensics expert gave evidence or supplied reports. He conned police and courts for three decades[2014]. Conman Trevor James 'Jim' Bates, a TV repair man who pretended to be an expert computer analyst, trained hundreds of officers and was an expert witness in scores of trials (including child porn and that of a senior Met officer, DC Brian Stevens)[2015].

The risk of being killed in a traffic accident has increased by a third since the introduction of speed cameras. This may be because the police are failing to put enough traffic officers on the road[2016].

West Midlands Police spent £100,000 on a failed attempt to find protective headgear that will fit over turbans. Former West Midlands Superintendent John Mellor said the scheme was 'health and safety gone mad'[2017].

Met chief Sir Paul Stephenson has admitted beat patrols have been neglected, with officers left behind desks, in cars or doing 'social work'. An HMIC report found 90% of the public thought it should be the responsibility of the police to tackle thugs[2018] rather than paperwork.

Avon and Somerset Police were lambasted by child protection groups for failing to alert the public about a 'dangerous' paedophile who had been on the run for four months (he was charged with 26 serious sex counts). The police claimed they were following national guidelines which say they mustn't alert the public till they have exhausted all lines of enquiry[2019]. It emerged in late 2010 that none of Scotland's 28 on-the-run sex offenders are on a police website (the CEOP, i.e. Child Exploitation and Online Protection) designed to alert the public[2020]. In 2007 the police had lost track of 322 sex offenders[2021]. In 2008 bungling police had lost track of 337 sex offenders, but unbelievably forces refused to name them or issue photos, maintaining revealing these facts would hinder attempts to trace them[2022]. Perhaps as many as 400 registered sex offenders were missing in 2009 (the Met had most – 124 dangerous offenders missing)[2023]. A Blackburn mother whose daughter is being pimped by Asians has given car registration numbers and dozens of names from the girl's mobile phone to the police, but nothing has been done. Affected parents are meeting lawyers to discuss possible action against the police. Hundreds of families have gone for advice to CROP (Coalition for the Removal of Pimping), which is based in Leeds. Despite 'Operation Engage', the mothers rather than the police are leading the fight against pimping[2024]. When a Shrewsbury mother reported to police that a paedophile was grooming her daughter they said they were powerless to help, so she set up her own sting to catch him red-handed, resulting in him being prosecuted and ordered to sign the sex offenders' register[2025].

Police were failing (2006) to track down thousands of dangerous bail jumpers (3,273 rapists, thieves and violent offenders), the worst area being London[2026].

Greater Manchester Police have been criticised for refusing to pursue two joyriders in case the culprits fell off the vehicles and claimed compensation. Greater Manchester was voted in 2006 the UK's 'champion' offender by the Campaign Against Political Correctness[2027].

Leading barrister Michael Mansfield suggested (2010) Jill Dando detectives were not making serious enquiries (his client Barry George was cleared at a second trial), e.g. the possible Serbian assassin lead[2028].

A major drugs probe (Operation Perdition) became chaotic when Tayside Police left a top-secret folder in a suspect's home. The expensive operation was scrapped, with the detective involved being given 'corrective advice'[2029].

Kent Police were unaware a pensioner had been murdered until undertakers found a knife in his back. D.C. Linda Robb said it was because he was lying on his back[2030].

Men assaulted by their partners (over 40% of domestic violence victims are male) are often ignored by police: only rarely will they take the man's side[2031].

A 999 operator with South Wales Police was sacked and one from Gwent disciplined after a young mother was murdered because officers took too long to get to her (she had called twice but her calls were wrongly routed). The victim was stabbed 22 times[2032].

A 2010 survey of 'Sunday Post' readers found two-thirds believe police have 'given up' on the streets and don't take anti-social behaviour seriously[2033]. Police fail to pursue half of calls about antisocial behaviour, which some officers don't see as 'real police work'[2034]. Leicestershire Police's head of criminal justice, Superintendent Steve Harrod, declared (2009) that 'low-level' hooliganism is no longer, since a change in the law in 1998, the police's responsibility. Officers, he said, could now only hand out reprimands and 'final warnings' (unless the offences are 'serious')[2035]. The Chief Inspector of Constabulary has found the way police databases log information about harassment, verbal abuse and vandalism is 'inadequate'. At least half of police forces find it 'very difficult' to identify repeat victims of antisocial behaviour. In almost a quarter of ASB incidents officers didn't turn up[2036]. There are 26 incidents of ASB every minute[2037].

Police in England till recently refused to evict squatters even when they had broken in and changed the locks, claiming it is a civil matter (even though damage to the property is a criminal offence). One Barking man's furniture was thrown into the street while he was out walking his dogs, but the police would do nothing[2038].

An Edinburgh chip shop broke gambling laws for over a year under the noses of Lothian and Borders Police round the corner from Gayfield Police Station, who were supposed to be tackling gambling under Operation Cobra. Officers were regular customers but failed to notice the illegal fruit machine[2039].

Acting Chief Superintendent Martin Walker was ordered to appear at Hove Crown Court after 'blundering incompetence caused a Crawley petrol bombing trial to collapse'. Vital CCTV evidence seized by Sussex Police had been mislaid for two years[2040].

Ian Brady had pictures in his cell of victim Keith Bennett's grave, but the police wouldn't pursue it. Greater Manchester Police were severely criticised for the way they conducted the Moors hunt for the children's bodies[2041].

Merseyside Police faced a huge bill (2010) for policing the Lib Dem conference because they failed to ask for funds, thinking the Lib Dems wouldn't get into power[2042].

Two Greater Manchester policemen couldn't find a missing householder's body in his cellar because it was too dark and the door was difficult to open, so they launched a missing person appeal[2043].

The sentence of an Edinburgh teacher for child porn had to be delayed because Lothian and Borders Police refused to view his 4,000 indecent images a second time[2044].

When a tabloid told the West Midlands Police about an alert for escaped sex offender John Cronin, the bungling officers denied he was missing, despite a memo having been sent to them a few weeks before. This was the second time cops had lost him[2045].

Avon and Somerset Police advised a man who had his motorbike stolen that they could only chase the thieves if the latter were wearing crash helmets[2046].

A young criminal can be arrested 50 times before anything is done to punish him or her[2047].

Poor communication between the police and other arms of the justice system mean half of all dangerous criminals leave jail without any risk assessment or monitoring, e.g. a city financier was stabbed to death at his Chelsea home by recently released Damien Hanson – an order banning him from parts of London was not enforced by the Met[2048].

When a schoolteacher was assaulted at a carnival by a thug, she asked two Wiltshire officers standing nearby to arrest him, but they refused to help. Soon after she alerted other policemen, but they too refused. When her friend remonstrated about their lack of action, one officer threatened to arrest him instead. She was told if she wanted to pursue the case she should go to the police station the next day, but it was closed[2049].

When a Swindon housewife, burgled eight times and targeted by thugs, locked two officers inside her home because police were failing to tackle crime, eight other police arrived to throw her in the cells and charge her with obstructing police (the officers were unaware she had left the front door unlocked)[2050]. The Advisory Service for Squatters' website advertises the services of a Hungarian handyman who says he has opened over 100 properties for squatters. The ASS provide workshops on how to occupy homes, which they 'market', yet the police do nothing[2051]. When a Harley Street neurologist and his pregnant wife were shut out of their home by squatters, the police said they could do nothing unless he could prove they had broken into the property[2052]. Police in England are notoriously loathe to evict squatters who have committed illegal entry but now have no excuse since the proposed law to criminalise squatting has materialised. When Met Police were called to a house occupied by squatters with a fake tenancy agreement, they apparently didn't bother to check its validity further when they couldn't contact the bogus landlady: they refused to give her supposed mobile number to the real owner[2053].

A Hertfordshire pensioner who reported burglars ransacking a neighbour's house while in his pyjamas was told by the 999 operator that police needed 'proof' of a break-in before responding. No officers attended the Harpenden incident, and the next day the neighbour's jewellery was seen to be missing[2054]. Greater Manchester Police apologised for taking a week to respond to a 999 call from a family attacked in their home by intruders[2055].

Though Dorset Police arrived in time to apprehend a burglar, responding to a householder's 999 call, they not only failed to arrest him but gave him a lift home in their patrol car. The police only took the householder's statement when she went to the station and demanded action. A member of the Dorset police authority says this isn't the first case of its kind. Dorset Police refused to discuss the case with the press[2056].

Met police were condemned by Tory MP David Davies for failing to make even one arrest after radical Muslim protesters called for the Pope's execution. He compared this with the swift arrest of a Welsh Christian who used Bible quotations in an anti-gay campaign[2057].

When Islamic cleric Abu Hamza was convicted of incitement to murder, it emerged he had been under investigation by the Met for years (he had been allowed to spread his terrorist poison for a decade, despite a huge amount of evidence of his nefarious links).

Bournemouth Police told shopkeepers not to report thefts of goods worth less than £75 (but were warned not to infringe shoplifters' human rights). When a couple performed a citizen's arrest on a gang of car vandals near Holyhead police station, the duty sergeant refused to come out and deal with the criminals on his doorstep[2058]. High Street chain stores have in a decade launched 600,000 private legal actions against shoplifters, because police no longer pursue many shoplifters – a warning or, in the case of persistent offenders, a small fixed penalty fine, is all that is on offer from the police[2059].

When abusive husband Stuart Horgan seriously wounded his wife and killed his two daughters, Thames Valley Police took an hour to enter the murder house. The inquest criticised them for the inexplicable delay and found their plans for responding to armed incidents 'too prescriptive'[2060].

In 2007 the UK was named the EU's crime capital, with the most burglaries and the largest number of assaults[2061].

The 116 PCSOs in Cumbria, who cost £3m to employ, gave out just one fixed-penalty notice between them in the whole of 2009, while Northumberland's 435 PCSOs averaged just two-and-a-half fines each in 2009-10[2062].

Veronica Packman went missing in 1985, but Dorset Police wrongly closed her missing person's file, and when, in 1986, a woman purporting to be Veronica reported to a police station, police failed to verify her identity. Though her murderer has been convicted her body was never found[2063].

Police are getting no information about extremism from within the Muslim community[2064].

11 of 30 English forces don't record the nationalities of killers or victims, and others have information gaps. About half of forces won't say, even though about 20% of killers in England and Wales are foreign[2065]. The criminal records of tens of thousands of foreign offenders are not being checked even when they're arrested in the UK - police are asking for the criminal histories (in their country of origin) in only one in seven EU nationals, so that annually about 30,000 foreign offenders are appearing in UK courts without the benefit of background information. Amazingly, police may be ignorant of the fact that they can request the records[2066]. A Czech killer allowed into Britain carried out sex attacks, but police were unaware of his presence. Many foreign EU nationals don't undergo background checks even

after they are arrested here[2067]. The police are allowed to see the records of any arrestees from Europe. Thus a Lithuanian child rapist beat and raped a woman after arriving in Britain.

Lady Stern's review of how the justice system deals with rape uncovered 'shocking police failures' during the investigation stage, e.g. in the case of John Warboys, who may have committed over 100 offences, and Kirk Reid, suspected of 71 offences. She called for the sharing of police intelligence across London, and for the setting up of specialist rape units[2068]. Some forces are 'no-criming' up to 40% of rape allegations which should have been included in crime statistics. Police interest in rape claims can 'wane' after 24 hours, while some officers treat the victim as 'a liar' from the start. In Northumbria 172 out of 382 rape reports never reached official Home Office records. In 2007 HMIC said the way forces record and investigate rape should be improved[2069]. In Scotland only 3% of 'rape' cases reported to police reach conviction (rape convictions in the 1970s stood at over 30%)[2070]. Nearly 60% of those <u>charged</u> with rape are convicted – the problem is so few are charged: only 6% of rapes lead to a conviction in England and Wales[2071]. More police have achieved fewer convictions. HMIC report that police failures are a key reason why few rapists ever appear in court. Police don't properly investigate the background of rape suspects, forensic examinations of victims are inconsistent, and inter-force detection rates vary from 22% to 93%[2072]. Avon and Somerset Police let off over 600 sex offenders (including 11 rapists) with a caution between 2005-2010[2073]. A girl of five was raped repeatedly by a registered sex offender as police (as well as social workers) failed to warn the child's mother that he was a known paedophile. At least one Scots child becomes a sexual predator's victim every six hours, but there may be far more, as police don't keep records distinguishing between child and adult victims[2074]. Scottish police forces are being given the go-ahead to ignore underage sex[2075]. Over 10% of alleged rapes are being classed by police as 'no crime' and some 'incorrectly' removed from crime statistics[2076]. When a new 'elite' rape unit was established in West Lothian the percentage of cases solved slumped[2077].

Up to 600,000 Scots criminals can challenge their convictions because they were questioned without being provided with a lawyer[2078].

Less than 10% of chief constables have experience leading a major crime investigation[2079].

Between 1997 and 2005 speeding convictions rose from 700,000 to almost two million, yet there was a significant decline in prosecutions of more dangerous drivers who are harder to catch (e.g. drink-drivers or those who ignore traffic signs). With the highest number of roadside cameras in Europe the UK is falling in the safety league[2080]. The number of convictions for careless driving dropped from 125,000 in 1985 to 28,000 in 2006[2081].

The question has been asked whether it was the police who decided not to prosecute Venables (one of the James Bulger killers), when he allegedly re-offended (affray and possession of cocaine in 2008)[2082].

According to the 2010 report of Chief Inspector of Constabulary Denis O'Connor, in some parts of the country only one in 16 officers is available for patrol, meeting the public or taking phone calls from crime victims[2083].

Despite 15 burglaries in a month in houses clustering around police HQ near Lincoln, no arrests had been made by summer 2010[2084].

One tabloid's columnist covering the Raoul Moat story said that Northumbria Police acted like a bunch of Keystone Cops, having to call in 15 other forces[2085]. Thus they failed to instal surveillance in the home of Moat's close friend even though they knew Moat went there the day after murdering Chris Brown – they could have caught him if they had, because he returned there[2086].

In 2003 original police reports showed violence increasing by 22%, but after statistical 'adjustments' the figure was just 2%. In Northumbria violent crime was up 118%, but was this simply because of technical changes in police reporting[2087]?

Greater Manchester's Chief Constable Peter Fahy has warned that police aren't trained to deal with mentally ill offenders, despite the NHS letting many out onto the streets and the police being asked to make assessments about the risk of them offending[2088].

The police have been hopeless in enforcing the foxhunt ban, showing chief police officers can to an extent choose which laws to enforce (other examples are drugs and rape, as well as selling alcohol to underage customers and sexual behaviour in underage teenagers)[2089].

In the tragic case of Fiona Pilkington and her children Leicestershire Police apparently failed to 'link' 33 serious incident complaints made by her over 10 years. A friend of Fiona has said: 'Some of us contacted the police … but our pleas fell on deaf ears'. The Assistant Deputy Coroner for Rutland and North Leicestershire has criticised the police for their failure to recognise Fiona's vulnerability[2090]. By late 2010 the family blamed for driving Fiona and her daughter to their deaths were reportedly still terrorising the neighbourhood, despite police vowing to clamp down on ASB[2091]. A fatal house blaze occurred an hour after the family concerned had again called Derbyshire Police about the louts terrorising them[2092].

There have been hundreds of complaints to the Noise Abatement Society complaining that victims have to try mediation before ASBOs will be issued. This means sitting face-to-face with the perpetrators. The police usually won't themselves trigger an ASBO application. Despite the rise in complaints police figures show a drop in the number of ASBOs issued[2093]. In 2009, 10,415 complaints about antisocial behaviour were made to police, but not a single ASBO was imposed during that time[2094].

Killer policeman Garry Weddell's lawyer brother allegedly failed to notify police about his brother's behaviour on a number of occasions. Though the brother stood surety, he has been excused having to pay for his brother jumping bail[2095]. [See Familial Flaw Policeman chapter].

We no longer seem to have a police emergency service but plenty of officers available for routine investigating. With the introduction of a graded response to calls from the public, officers were given an excuse for not dealing with incidents immediately, but the new system has caused huge backlogs[2096]. When a pub landlord held burglars whom he'd caught red-handed, the police took 50 minutes to arrive, even though the call was graded for immediate response[2097].

A victim of identity fraud had to change his name and move home to avoid bailiffs, but Greater Manchester Police said they couldn't help because no crime had been committed under British law. Yet such fraud is the fastest growing crime in Britain (80,000 people affected in 2006)[2098].

Almost 50% of hospital casualties from Scotland's RTAs don't tell the police, who may also be rating casualties less seriously now than in the past (bicyclists are most likely not to have a serious injury recorded by the police)[2099].

The Serious Fraud Office has had its credibility repeatedly damaged by expensive, failed prosecutions, e.g. one of the biggest Ponzi frauds, a price-fixing drug company case (embarrassing numerical mistakes were made in its budget accounts), and the BAE Systems fiasco[2100].

ACPO guidance states that suspects on motorbikes mustn't be chased because of the risk to the offenders, so that the welfare and rights of an offender is considered more important than the duty of arrest[2101]. It seems that the failure of thieves to wear crash helmets obviates pursuit, and this risk assessment consideration now applies to quad bikes as well – South Yorkshire Police refused to apprehend a gang who had stolen a boat[2102].

Police in London student demos failed to order masked demonstrators to unmask[2103].

The days of a police station in Four Marks in Hampshire is a dim memory, so that the village – which shares a beat officer with three other villages – now has to have unpaid volunteers wearing Street Watch vests showing the Hampshire Police logo. Antisocial behaviour had been getting seriously out of hand as the police presence had withdrawn[2104].

Only 13% of police time is dedicated to investigating crime, according to a 2010 HMIC review entitled, 'Where Are The Police?'[2105].

Crime-fighting officers are supported by a shoestring budget, compared with the huge amount spent on support staff[2106].

Police in England and Wales issued 129,000 cautions to under-16 tearaways in just two years[2107]. 73,000 burglars were assigned cautions between 1998 and 2008 (20% of the total)[2108]. Police are now allowing tens of thousands of criminals, especially young offenders, to escape with cautions (6% in 1971, leaping to 20% in 2006)[2109]. Tens of thousands of criminals reoffend within days of being given a caution: in 2011 police handed out 235,000 cautions[2110]. Robberies are at their highest level for a decade, knife offences are up 10% in a year, with violent crime up 11% according to the British Crime Survey[2111] – yet police records report a 4% <u>fall</u> in crime[2112]. Many English forces let thugs with knives off with just a caution (on average more than a third of those caught: in Wiltshire only 15% are charged, i.e. there is a postcode lottery)[2113]. A Bolton man found a knife near a fatal stabbing, but when he called Greater Manchester Police he was told: 'We haven't got time to pick it up – can you just throw it away?'.

Lothian and Borders Police have had to issue 11 promises to the public in an attempt to improve their performance[2114].

The Hebridean island of Tiree, though packed with summer visitors, was left without police cover when the local officer went on holiday, despite assurances from Strathclyde Police top brass[2115].

Just one person is imprisoned for every 96 crimes (of the 9.5m UK crimes per annum), according to 2010 Ministry of Justice figures[2116].

19 Lothian and Borders Police said sorry to the family of a missing man whose body they missed lying in a hedge at his Edinburgh home. The dead man's son is a detective inspector with the force[2117].

Chief Inspector of Constabulary Denis O'Connor, who called for police to 'reclaim our streets', has admitted he was forced to move house because of yobs. He declares that a 'strategic error' was made in the seventies that downgraded the importance of street patrols[2118].

Celtic star Georgios Samaras got off a phoning-while-driving offence because arresting police failed to check the mobile's call register to determine the time of the last call[2119].

Police have failed to properly monitor seven terror suspects who ought to have been under strict control orders (they were living under curfews but have disappeared)[2120].

The Yorkshire Ripper's investigation was a fiasco, Sutcliffe being brought in for questioning at least nine times. He matched the photofits, and had been arrested in a red-light district in 1969 carrying a hammer. One detective's report suggesting he was the Ripper was lost[2121].

Greater Manchester beat WPC <u>Annie Bennett</u> chased criminals for nine months without realising she had been pregnant. She was in a brawl a fortnight before her emergency caesarean[2122].

The IPCC called the bungling of the hunt for serial sex attacker 'The Doorstep Stalker' a 'shameful chapter in the history of the Metropolitan Police': three unnamed officers – a superintendent and two inspectors – faced misconduct hearings in 2010[2123]. A rapist questioned by Derbyshire Police about a sex attack struck again just an hour later[2124].

Fingerprint evidence is far from a definite method of convicting offenders, new research from Southampton University claims, but the head of fingerprint training at the Central Police Training and Development Authority disagreed[2125]. Only a tiny percentage of crimes are ever detected by fingerprint evidence alone[2126]. US police detectives have manipulated and fabricated fingerprints to frame many people.

The ASA (Advertising Standards Agency) has ruled that the Home Office claim that 'You can now expect your neighbourhood police to spend 80% of their time on the beat ...' to be misleading (most of the time is spent in meetings, with only 14% on patrol)[2127].

The parents of a teenage cyclist killed by a careless driver had six complaints upheld by the Scottish Police Complaints Commissioner over the police handling of the death: he ordered an apology almost seven years later. The officers had been accused of lying and falsifying evidence to avoid the driver being prosecuted[2128]. Lincolnshire Police among others were criticised for allowing a hit-and-run driver (who had killed a father and son) to flee to Pakistan[2129].

Britain's 43 forces have almost as many civilian staff now as 'real' police, with Surrey and Northants already having a minority of officers[2130].

In the decade to 2010, the Home Office reveals, the number of police warnings issued for car defects such as bald tyres had fallen by two-thirds[2131].

In 2009 the Scottish Government was ready to hire a civilian with no experience of fighting crime to run the Scottish Police Services Authority, to replace the controversial David Mulhern, who had left with a £90,000 payout after allegations of mismanagement and misconduct. The SPSA controls IT, forensics (including fingerprinting), police training and procurement, as well as the SCDEA (Scottish Crime and Drug Enforcement Agency)[2132].

The Police Federation has rejected calls (e.g. from Lord Young) for the service to be exempted from health and safety laws – in May 2010 three Glasgow University students had to jump into the Clyde to save a drowning woman while police stayed on the riverbank awaiting the arrival of the Fire and Rescue service[2133].

A stowaway who entered Britain by hanging onto a private jet was allowed to walk free after police just gave him a caution because they ruled there was 'no immigration issue'[2134].

Newbury MP Richard Benyon has claimed that the police and CPS allow hundreds of local criminals to escape the court system. Thus a nursery school worker possessing child porn was merely given a caution and placed on the Sex Offenders Register, without appearing in court[2135].

An investigation of the criminal justice system in Lanarkshire exposed administrative chaos, e.g. crime victims given the wrong information, a culture of 'churring' (cases being continually delayed): in one case Strathclyde officers failed to submit paperwork until 16 months after the offence[2136].

A property developer with children had to take steps to have a drug dealer, known to the police and dealing next door to him, jailed for six years. The police had failed to answer his desperate pleas to help protect his family. The vigilante citizen compares his experience unfavourably with the zero tolerance approach of the police in France[2137].

In the Derrick Bird case Cumbria Constabulary was fiercely criticised on the local newspapers' website for its tardiness in running him to ground[2138]. Three officers started to tail him just minutes into his rampage. Emergency paramedics were not allowed by police through their cordon to attend the injured[2139]. A wealthy Cumbrian gun enthusiast who imagined killing people when he had a mental breakdown has revealed police let him keep his weapons. Antidepressants made him prone to terrible rages[2140].

Strathclyde Police chiefs were told to probe gangster Eddie Lyons's property empire five years before his huge mortgage fraud led to his conviction (in 2003 he was also exposed for running a Glasgow community centre with police backing)[2141].

HMIC (Her Majesty's Inspectorate of Constabulary) revealed in 2007 that there may be only one in 40 officers free to answer 999 calls, with only one in 58 out on patrol at any time[2142].

It's a criminal offence to make obscene phone calls, yet when Jonathan Ross and Brand did just that, there was not a word from the Met[2143].

With 'micro-policing' Greater Manchester Police are being instructed to stand in the middle of crime hotspots – to see if it scares criminals off[2144].

Strathclyde Police took five years to apprehend a convicted killer who failed to turn up for his trial. They couldn't trace him though he was living openly only 15 miles from his old address[2145].

Police recruits used to have to be at least 5ft 10ins tall, but there is now no minimum height requirement[2146].

Glasgow cabbies have warned that a woman will be killed unless police clamp down on rogue taxis[2147].

Met chief <u>Sir Paul Stephenson</u> indicated to Prince Charles that he was prepared to resign because of the police failure to protect Charles from the mob[2148].

Former Met chief <u>Sir Ian Blair</u>'s inquiry into allegations of his force's misconduct in respect of Daniel Morgan's murder in 1987, was savaged by the Met Police Authority. There were four previous failed police investigations of police involvement. The dead man was a PI, and his business partner may have illegally hired off-duty police officers[2149].

Terrified staff at a Scottish kebab shop, targeted by racists, threatened to call in the Turkish government because they claimed Lothian and Borders Police weren't doing enough to stop the physical and mental abuse[2150].

The Criminal Justice Act (2003) gave the courts power to order a no-jury trial where there was a real chance of jury tampering, which implies that the police may not be up to protecting jurors[2151].

People would be more assured if, instead of police notice boards announcing: 'Warning, thieves operate in this area', 'Police operate in this area' could be substituted[2152].

An English police force has set up a hotline for anyone who feels the need for a police escort after withdrawing money from a cashpoint[2153].

Between 2006 and 2008 the number of shoplifters given on-the-spot fines by police more than doubled – the offender doesn't get a criminal record and a third of the fines are never paid. Even a violent offender was cautioned by Sussex Police for GBH[2154]. The British Retail Consortium has called for more police action against organised shoplifting gangs and the targeting of offenders who cross police boundaries[2155].

Victims of £2.4m Lib Dem donor Michael Brown say police allowed him to jump bail and flee abroad[2156].

Lawyer Tom Winsor, who was reviewing police conditions, has said three Rs skills needed for entry to the service have fallen 'significantly' since the 1930s. Two senior officers reportedly said standards were lowered to assist BEM recruits. Criminal barristers sometimes refer to the 'barely literate' quality of police evidence[2157].

Commander Peter Loughborough

Commander <u>Peter Loughborough</u>, a.k.a. Earl Grey, 7th Earl of Rosslyn, was awarded a Queen's Police Medal for 'services to policing', yet allowed the student mob to terrorise Prince Charles and Camilla a year later (despite being in charge of 400 officers). He was recommended to the Met by his cousin Lord Strathaven, a detective in London's Paddington. Loughborough was in charge of royal security during the Aaron Barschak and Fathers 4 Justice scandals, and is thought to be the only policeman member of his gentleman's club, White's in St. James's (Barschak was allowed to kiss Prince William on both cheeks)[2158].

Police mistakes led to the chance to charge Baby P's mother with assaulting him being missed several weeks before his death[2159]. Met Police closed their case on Baby P the day before his death.

Essex Police failed to collect CCTV footage of a smash-and-grab raid for nine days because an officer was on holiday[2160]. 40% of complaints about Scots officers are left unanswered beyond a 40-day deadline, said a 2014 report by the Police Investigations and Review Commissioner.

None of the over 101,000 people stopped and searched in 2009 was later arrested for a terrorist offence[2161].

The 1990 poll-tax rally spiralled into a proper riot as the Met failed to contain anarchists involved in widescale vandalism, the day ending with 330 arrested and 110 injured[2162]. So much for the 'unprecedented' Tottenham riots of 2011(over 3,000 were arrested).

Northumbria Police have boasted that people in Sunderland will feel safer by 2023, but have been criticised for not doing enough about crime now[2163].

The family of a three-year-old victim of a paedophile won a negligence lawsuit against South Wales Police over a series of blunders[2164].

Lancashire Police were forced to cancel £126,900 of speeding fines after their camera monitoring unit was found to be shambolic[2165].

Derbyshire Police forgot they had left hundreds of bottles of urine near a public footpath, after finding them hoarded in a house[2166].

Police sergeant <u>Alex Forbes</u> was investigated by his own Northern Constabulary because he allegedly failed to lodge vital reports in time, allowing criminals to escape prosecution[2167].

The father of the man found dead in Michael Barrymore's pool accused blundering police of letting the killer escape justice. An independent report revealed two vital pieces of evidence – a door handle and thermometer – were not recovered by police, and blood stains on the victim's clothing were not properly examined. Barrymore's aide was allowed to contaminate the death scene. Essex Police gave the father a formal apology[2168].

As 'dogging' has become more prevalent around the country, police have adopted an increasingly lower profile: Surrey Police have even spent £124 on tea and biscuits to 'build trust' with the A31's dogging 'community', and produced a 'hate crimes' manual to protect vulnerable doggers, many of whom are gay. One Puttenham dogger know as 'Bob the Builder' wore only a hard hat, but the police only spoke to him without arresting him[2169].

Two boys suspected of torturing two others, then throwing one into a ravine, had been questioned by South Yorkshire Police hours before over another attack[2170]. The police deny failings after the first attack – the boys failed to appear for interview but it is alleged police took no follow-up actions[2171].

Grampian's Chief Constable <u>Ian Oliver</u> resigned over a botched murder probe[2172].

British police initially missed the fact that the 2010 airplane bomb from Yemen was an explosive[2173].

All charges against three suspects of running a cannabis farm had to be dropped after Grampian Police took DNA samples from two of the men without a warrant[2174]. Grampian is Scotland's cannabis capital, with 197 police raids, beating Strathclyde with only 117 busted sites[2175].

Hundreds of serial offenders are being issued with as many as nine or 10 police cautions in a year instead of being taken to court[2176].Cautions overtook convictions as punishment for violent crimes for the first time in 2008 (the number of cautions for assault had more than trebled to over 118,000 in five years, with a near-doubling of the most serious violent attacks)[2177]. Ten sex offenders daily are let off with a caution[2178]. Home Office figures (2009) reveal 111 rapists (including 66 child incidents) have been let off with a caution. The Met's Sir Paul Stephenson has condemned the 'uncontrollable increase in cautions'[2179]. Three masked men in balaclavas and gloves were caught on a church roof by South Yorkshire Police – rolled up lead was found nearby but they only received a caution because of 'insufficient evidence': they may have just been admiring the view from the roof, said the police, even though most of the roof's lead had been stripped (there had been monthly thefts of lead for 10 months)[2180]. Police are now <u>cautioning</u> offenders for GBH, while in less than two years on-the-spot fines for shoplifting were used twice as frequently[2181]. Only one in every 135 crimes ends with the offender being sent to prison[2182]. Police are letting thousands of violent and repeat offenders off with cautions, which is 'demeaning' to the victims of violence. This includes those conspiring to murder and joyriders who kill[2183].

Attempts to modernise police uniforms (e.g. baseball caps instead of helmets) have been unsuccessful. The Met Commissioner has called on 'scruffy' officers to 'smarten up'[2184].

Scottish firearms cops were banned from the London Olympics because they were less well trained than their English colleagues (all English forces have achieved a National Police Improvement Agency firearms certificate, but Strathclyde has the only Scottish one)[2185].

The Met were not trained to deal with <u>failed</u> suicide bombings at the time of the Stockwell shooting[2186].

When a 999 caller reported a burglary he was told by Cambridgeshire Constabulary to investigate the crime himself, as they were too busy[2187].

Though Romanian squatters had smashed a window in Tottenham to gain access, two PCSOs took no action when they visited the property[2188].

The Serious Organised Crime Agency is badly flawed, e.g. its drug seizure success rate has been poor[2189].

Leicestershire's Chief Constable Matt Baggathas admitted 40% of crime victims are not visited by an officer, because of a 'fog of over-supervision and administration'[2190].

Thames Valley policemen are being tested on whether they can ride a bicycle by taking a test <u>online</u> and marking it themselves by self-assessment[2191].

A crooked builder who fleeced hundreds of householders was finally pursued only after he defrauded banks[2192].

49 out of 85 rookie cops at the Scottish Police College failed basic fitness tests[2193].Trained officers are now resisting annual fitness tests[2194]. Almost half of recruits to an unarmed force were found to be obese or overweight, but ACPO says there is 'no evidence' fitness testing would justify the cost: only specialist squads like dog and firearms sections are to be tested. ACPO is also worried too many officers would fail regular weight checks[2195].

Only 13 police officers (out of 43,000) were sacked for being incompetent in the decade to 2008 (under the 'incapability procedure')[2196]. This is comparable to the teaching profession, which has been much criticised for failing to get rid of deadwood.

A disabled man was wrongly arrested for fraud by Lothian and Borders Police and driven 110 miles from Northumberland to court in Edinburgh before police found they had the wrong man. He was then left to make his own way home[2197].

A child abuse victim who helped bring to justice two paedophile brothers first told Leicestershire Police about them 15 years before, but that investigation was botched (e.g. a WPC confronted him about his story <u>in front of</u> the perpetrators, so he ran out of the room)[2198].

Official histories of the police often miss out continuities between the old and new Victorian police: violence between the police and the working class, incompetence (officers never there when you needed them), corruption[2199].

Former Shadow Home Secretary David Davis has revealed <u>Bob Quick</u>, former Chief Constable of Surrey, and then head of special operations at the Yard, didn't know a basic piece of law about charging terrorist suspects (viz the threshold test). In the arrest of Damian Green, Quick was not enforcing the law, he was inventing law[2200].

It has been opined that most senior policemen would never rise above the rank of sergeant-major in the army.

Strathclyde PC <u>Aksoi Ozer</u> was interrogated over his faulty translation of a secret taped confession of four Turkish men accused of murdering a young vice girl, which led to the charges being dropped. Two experts rubbished the supposed self-incrimination of the tape[2201].

South Wales Police officers were so slow responding to 999 calls from the frantic parents of a toddler that a paedophile was able to carry on abusing the three-year-old, whom he kidnapped. The IPCC Wales commissioner found at least three officers, including a senior inspector and a superintendent, should face a misconduct panel[2202].

Leicestershire Constabulary detective Nina Hobson's undercover exposé of the force included officers who, while on duty at night, would watch porn DVDs instead of going out on patrol, as well as a culture of laziness, e.g. ignoring calls, and an officer driving past a woman being dragged by her hair down the street, because the officer was near the end of his shift. She also claims performance-related pay has destroyed the teamwork essential for efficiency[2203].

Locals asked about Britain's biggest drugs raid – on a Rastafarian 'temple' in South London taken over by Yardies – why it had taken the Met so long: the Church had become a no-go area for decent people over a period of years. The venue was called the Church of the Holy Smoke[2204].

The IPCC was investigating the Thames Valley police response to a 'domestic incident' – they left after 30 minutes. The mentally ill son of the household allegedly blinded and tried to rape his nurse mother just 90 minutes after the police's departure[2205].

A pensioner who dragged himself to safety after being attacked by a gang in London, was let down by police who decided he was not a crime victim (he had two broken arms and five broken ribs) – the police have since launched a murder hunt. It was a Met inspector who had decided the man was not a victim of crime[2206].

Despite persistent rumours that murderer William Henry Burry – hanged in Dundee prison in 1889 – should have been their suspect, no one from the Met travelled north to investigate, possibly because the Met didn't want to appear stupid (they couldn't solve five (Ripper) murders on their own patch, whereas the Scottish Police solved one)[2207].

The Met was criticised in 2009 when 5,000 protesting Tamils brought Central London to a standstill – they stormed through a cordon round Westminster (the law limits protesters to 50)[2208].

A book reviewer reported his car stolen, but Met police would only issue a crime reference number, not investigate its disappearance.

Police have been told not to serve arrest warrants at prayer times during Ramadan[2209].

The father of missing Claudia Lawrence wanted an independent inquiry into the police handling of the case, claiming that they were 'uncivil, rude, abrupt and dismissive' to people offering information. After 14 months (by May 2010) North Yorkshire Police, with 30 allocated detectives and a spend of £600,000, had found no clues: their continual harping on about her 'complex and mysterious' social life may have given rise to unwarranted innuendo[2210]. Scottish police have DNA profiles for only 7% of long-term missing people, making matching the long-term missing to unidentified bodies extremely problematic[2211]. Four months after a couple's graduate son, Christian Vetten, was reported to police as missing in West Africa, British police had failed to contact Interpol. There had been no official search (the Foreign Office had also ignored the case)[2212].

George Galloway has asked why no one has been arrested for making repeated threats against the life of a Scottish football manager, involving suspect packages and bullets sent by post[2213].

Suspected killers of Deepcut soldiers were not properly investigated by Surrey detectives, said the Devon and Cornwall force[2214].

An anonymous police chief has exposed how he was told to take a holiday, but when he tried he was told there were already too many officers on leave[2215].

Alerted by a missing woman's family, West Yorkshire Police visited her home but didn't search the garage, where her murdered body was secreted in a suitcase[2216].

When a man tried to report his vandalised car in person at his local police station, Humberside Police told him he had to phone it in. When a member of the public called a West Midlands police station to report his girlfriend's car being vandalised, he was told to phone the AA[2217]. In another Humberside case a shopkeeper chasing two thieves stopped a marked patrol car, but the police driver wouldn't give chase, instead telling him to call the police! He did, but the officers assigned to the crime missed the call because they were celebrating at a party[2218]. Two Leicestershire officers coming to the end of their shift ignored reports of a woman being beaten up by a man[2219].

The Home Office crime website has been shown to be flawed, so that police have been forced to write to residents to explain how crimes from a 'wider geographic area' may have been mistakenly attributed to their streets[2220]. Thus Portsmouth's Surrey Street was said to have been the scene of 136 crimes in a month, when in fact there were two[2221].

HMIC Denis O'Connor has criticised police tactics in the G20 protests as 'inadequate', out-of-date and needing overhaul. The Met said it would review officer training[2222].

Police chiefs struggled to hear radio messages about the de Menezes shooting, the Met control room was so noisy[2223].

When child actor Daniel Roche's parents complained to Scotland Yard about a Facebook stalker (the internet provider had failed to act), they said there was nothing they could do, referring them to eVictims charity. The bogus pager even tried to arrange a meeting with a girl[2224].

A former senior police officer was very critical of the South Yorkshire Police because of their refusal to accept a missing person report until 24 hours had elapsed: groomed girls often turned up within the time limit, but were seldom properly interviewed[2225].

A leading barrister has criticised police for failing cyclists: excuses of not seeing cyclists 'seem to be too readily accepted by the police and the CPS, so there isn't a prosecution when there should be'[2226].

Tayside Police turned to Twitter to keep them in touch with the public. Their website 'My Police' was supposed to give people a chance to comment on the force[2227].

Cardboard models of policemen were scrapped by Essex Police after they failed to reduce crime levels[2228].

Like doctors' decline in clinical competence because of an over-reliance on technology, so police forces can't get nearly enough detectives because of a growing reliance on forensic science[2229].

Are official crime figures apparently going down because they no longer include the vast amount of antisocial behaviour, as revealed by the new police website[2230]?

Special Constables take the same oath of allegiance to the Crown as regular officers, whereas PCSOs are not sworn officers: the latter are increasingly being asked to perform tasks for which they have neither the legal powers nor the appropriate training[2231].

Computer buff Martin Gilbertson says he warned West Yorkshire police about two of the July 7 bombers, but they deny his warnings were received, even though he also made these publicly. The police have called him an egocentric liar.

A mother punched to the floor in her home by a thug was exasperated when Warwickshire police told her not to call them because it might make matters worse: she should try to sort it out on her own (she had been told at first that an officer would attend)[2232].

Jersey Police declared (re the children's home inquiry) a crucial bone fragment couldn't be dated because of its low collagen content, due to a 'lime-rich environment'. In fact, Oxford scientists say the opposite is true[2233].

When a 37-year-old man complained to the police that a crazed female stalker was making his life hell with threatening phone calls and vile sex slurs, they treated the matter as a joke[2234]. In a BBC Panorama programme on stalking (24.1.11) a victim says the police wouldn't believe her, believing the stalker instead. A conclusion of the programme was that police fail to interpret a pattern of incidents properly, as so often happens with repeat ASB against the same victim. With getting on for 150,000 stalking incidents in the UK in 2010, police only recorded 53,000[2235].

West Yorkshire Inspector Andy Sullivan has banned his men from tackling thugs in a children's playground after dark because it is too dangerous[2236].

Strathclyde WPC <u>Patricia Lovis</u> claimed she was unaware her boyfriend was growing cannabis in her spare room, though the stench of cannabis was obvious standing out in the street[2237].

Apart from police cells, building and fleet management, IT training and control-room operators have all been privatised, as well as, in some forces, securing crime scenes, door-to-door inquiries and fingerprinting[2238]. Seven English and Welsh forces may have 'dumbed down' police surgeon work in 2006 by outsourcing the work of almost 100 GPs to a private firm, Veritas Management, which places more emphasis on nurses. Veritas doctors will be expected to work over much wider areas than before[2239]. A Lancashire father, who dialled 999 after his son was beaten up by thugs on the way home from school, was told he should have rung a non-emergency number instead. As the incident was not a matter of life and death it was not an emergency. Tracy Young, who recently left the force after becoming 'completely disillusioned', says calls are now mainly taken by cheaper staff, but they don't have the knowledge to deal with things properly[2240].

Women's groups are critical of the lack of police action against brothels with sex-trafficked victims (ACPO says there are 342 brothels in the West Midlands)[2241].

Over half of Britain's 6,000 speed cameras are switched off at any one time and in some areas only 10% can catch offenders, a veritable postcode lottery[2242].

Police could have arrested one of the 2007 London bombers months previously if they had followed up a lead (the officer who should have followed it up went on leave). At the incident firefighters were hostile to paramedics and wouldn't enter the tunnel to go down the track[2243]. A Northants man died after Fire and Rescue personnel refused to rescue him from a frozen lake (they were not trained in water rescues)[2244]. The police are similarly hamstrung by Health and Safety. A jewellery shopkeeper says Hampshire Police refused to investigate a rooftop robbery because it would mean their climbing a ladder to get evidence, and health and safety rules precluded the 15 foot climb (the burglars had left muddy footprints)[2245]. In 2005 police called to deal with vandalism at a Rochdale church refused to inspect the damage because they didn't have specialist 'ladder training'. The police have taken on board the health and safety mantra that they shouldn't put themselves in any danger to protect the public: <u>their</u> wellbeing now comes first[2246].

Eastern European immigrants are operating a car insurance scam which involves retaining return ferry boarding cards. This allows them to drive in Britain illegally: if stopped by police the latter often feel it is too much trouble to check with foreign authorities and insurers[2247].

Police have admitted their initial "confidential" and "discreet" investigation into Dr. Harold Shipman was flawed.

Jeffrey Archer's breaking of prison rules has uncovered the fact that 99% of infringements are normally ignored.

Peter Smyth, chair of the Met Police Federation, said that operations against demonstrators have been allowed to degenerate into pitched battles because of the ambiguity of orders coming down the police chain of command[2248].

A recent straw poll of front-line officers found few were aware of section 127 of the Mental Health Act relating to vulnerable adults (which applies to, e.g., the adult learning disabled who are being abused). Abuse of <u>children</u> is an arrestable offence, but not that of vulnerable adults, who therefore fall through the net (e.g. in Buckinghamshire's Longcare scandal – see Appendix I)[2249].

A blind, disabled Glenrothes householder is afraid to park outside his house because of vandalism (e.g. tyres deflated and paint thrown over his car), as he can expect no protection from Fife Police, who told him they could only act if his tyres were slashed. Pouring paint is not an offence because it can be removed![2250]

When Dawn Watson was raped by a stranger at 16, police accused her of making it up, especially as she was not a virgin. DNA evidence led to her attacker admitting the assault 30 years later[2251]. When a mother of five reported East European men had raped her, ethnic tension led to street violence, but South Yorkshire Police just gave her a fixed penalty fine – she admitted she had lied – instead of facing jail for perverting the course of justice[2252].

Devon and Cornwall Chief Constable <u>Stephen Otter</u> has been offered crime prevention advice, as he had items, including his police-issue Airwave radio, stolen from his police car parked outside his home[2253].

The 2010 British Crime Survey (based on interviews with the public) revealed a 14% increase in burglaries, contradicting police figures which showed a 7% <u>fall</u> in burglaries[2254].

Fewer than 10% of uniformed officers in some forces are available on the frontline at any one time, with more officers on duty at quiet times and less at times of maximum need (e.g. Fridays after midnight)[2255]. HMIC's 2011 report found that a third of police force employees never perform any type of 'frontline' policing[2256]. A member of the public in the West Midlands wrote to a tabloid in 2008 that the last time he saw a police officer on foot was 10 years before[2257]. A judge attacked the absence of police in Wellingborough town centre the night a man was stabbed to death on his 21st birthday[2258].

Night rapist killer and burglar Delroy Grant was allowed to claim over 1,000 elderly victims because the Met compared his DNA with that of another man with the same name[2259]. In 2011 (24.3.11) the Met gave a public apology for missing the chance to apprehend Grant.

In the Levi Bellfield case, police received 92 allegations of indecent and other assaults, as well as obscene phone calls, yet he was allowed to roam free. Due to failure to record information at the beginning of the Milly Dowler case, Bellfield, the main suspect, may never be charged with her murder: he has been given life for killing with a hammer. He lived yards from the spot Milly was last seen. For months police thought Milly's father was a suspect: his house, car and phone were bugged[2260]. Likewise three doctors gave police clear warnings about the signs of abuse on Baby P before his horrific death. A police probe launched in 2006 saw his mother arrested, but nothing came of it, a DC telling her there would be 'no further action'[2261]. The Yard has been accused of ignoring warnings about Baby P's mother's evil boyfriend[2262].

Police say they can't give stalkers' victims information as to when the stalker can leave mental hospital, or when he (or she) is due to be released, unless the victim presses charges. But some victims are afraid to go to court, so feeling even more unsafe because the police won't help[2263]. 120,000 people are stalked annually, but many victims won't tell the police. Just 53,000 are recorded as crimes, with only one in 50 ending up in the offender being jailed. Two-thirds of female victims are dissatisfied with the police response[2264].

Less than 1% of hoaxers making bogus 999 calls are prosecuted[2265].

When there was a wreck off Lyme Regis, the coastguard says the police allowed people to ransack the cargo. There were violence and physical threats on the beach[2266].

Re the Finsbury mosque and Abu Hamza – police were told by the Muslim community for years he was causing concern, but no action resulted.

In 2007 it was revealed the number of armed police was falling while gun crime was escalating; the drop was greatest in the areas with the biggest increase in offences[2267].

In the Longcare scandal Thames Valley Police twice failed to properly investigate claims of sexual abuse, ill-treatment, neglect and assault against Gordon Rowe, proprietor of two homes (for vulnerable adults) near Slough. Questions were asked about Rowe's close relationship with some policemen (a police friend's helmet was found at his home during the third inquiry, Operation Skip). The third inquiry was not to be made general knowledge to other Slough police officers, some of whom were frequent social visitors to Stoke Place (one of the homes). Rowe lent his police friends minibuses for fishing trips. Residents were providing free labour to two unnamed officers. One friendly policeman was used by Rowe to 'warn' two residents about their behaviour. They were both given 'admonishments'[2268]. (See Appendix I)

The report of the investigation into John Mauger, Assistant Chief Constable of Central Scotland Police, was delayed for a third time: by May 2011 he had been on gardening leave for 10 months[2269].

The Ministry of Justice has refused to rule out giving Jon Venables a fourth identity. It will hinge on police assessment of the threat to him. A new ID costs £¼m.

A Muslim 'terrorist sympathiser' was paid by police to teach them how to combat terrorism (he had attended an extremists' training camp). He had been under MI5 surveillance because of his links to the 7/7 leader. The Met sent about 20 officers to his Muslim Youth Skills consultancy for training (ACPO also sent a member of staff on his course). The Met says they don't do background checks on organisations with which they are involved[2270].

Psychologists have identified key personality traits in childhood linked to later antisocial behaviour, but police won't cooperate with such research in their own recruitment programmes[2271]. Northumbria Police's denial of liability in the case of rapist policeman Stephen Mitchell (they allowed him to become an officer despite a previous sexual offence) is more problematic since the Lister v. Hesley Hall Ltd judgment (2001) helped tilt the balance in favour of claimants[2272].

After the 7/7 bus bomb in Tavistock Square, the nearby British Transport Police HQ went into 'lockdown', so that officers were unable to leave their building[2273]. Vandals have wrecked a special British Transport Police train campaigning against vandalism[2274].

THE INCOMPETENT POLICEMAN

Sir Paul Stephenson has been criticised by the Police Federation for saying health and safety regulations should not hamper officers in performing their duty. Police at present operate under the Police (Health and Safety) Act[2275].

A young woman student has told how she put her life at risk to interrupt a violent street robbery in Bristol (three hooded thugs were throttling the female victim), while two Avon and Somerset police officers sat in their patrol car a short distance (25 yards) away. The student waved and shouted to no avail, having to dial 999. The officers got out of their car, but then got back in again[2276].

When customers found their Barclays branch in Leigh-on-Sea was unlocked and unstaffed, Essex Police eventually responded by two PCSOs arriving by bus (a police car passed the bank but didn't stop) 35 minutes later, despite 999 having been called[2277].

When a serial burglar, a heroin addict, phoned Lancashire Police to arrest him after he broke into a football club, he was told officers were too busy to attend. So he went on to smash up a nearby Conservative Club[2278]. Non-domestic premises now merit only a telephone investigation when burgled.

Two Devon and Cornwall PCSOs hid in a room and called for real officers to rescue them from an angry 13-year-old[2279].

Police solve just over a quarter of the crimes they probe (and they only probe two-thirds of reported crimes), with 18 England and Wales forces showing falls in detection rates[2280]. Police officers detect an average of 11 crimes a year, PCSOs one every six years[2281]. 400 Lancashire PCSOs, paid over £19m over three years, gave out just 19 penalty notices between them (for litter dropping, cycling on the pavement, etc.). Notts paid £7m to 265 PCSOs in a year during which only six crimes were detected[2282].

When teenager Ahmet Osman was wounded by gunshot in 1988 by a psychotic teacher, judges found police knew about the latter's obsession but failed to warn or protect the victim. Such a warning is now called an Osman warning: numbers have increased dramatically in recent years.

Surrey Police apologised for mistakes in the hunt for Milly Dowler's killer, e.g. Rachel Cowles' family reported her attempted abduction immediately to the police, who took no action. After three years a letter to police from Mrs. Cowles pointed to a connection, but ironically the charge of abduction against the murderer was not pursued. Would the incident being aired in court have embarrassed the police?[2283]. Journalist Donal MacIntyre says he and his wife received an apology from Surrey Police in relation to the latter's failure in dealing with a revenge attack they had suffered[2284]. An anonymous Surrey CID officer has written an exposé of the force ('The Crime Factory', 2012).

Over 50 senior officers working for SOCA (Serious Organised Crime Agency) are sharing a £5m golden goodbye so that cheaper, less experienced officers can be employed, even though the quango hasn't managed to topple the UK's biggest criminals[2285].

The Home Office admitted that MAPPA (Multi Agency Public Protection Arrangements) had lost track of 211 sex offenders and at least 109 dangerous criminals[2286].

Durham Police were criticised for allowing a rave to carry on at a house whose owner was away. The neighbours reported more than 200 people were trashing the property[2287].

A Hampshire father who phoned 999 to report that his son had been knocked unconscious by a drunk, was told to write to his MP rather than bother the police, who were too busy to investigate[2288].

Strathclyde WPC Michele Selby couldn't be bothered to arrest a convicted thief even though he was committing burglary (she confiscated his tools), because she wanted to deliver some letters[2289]. She was jailed for a year, her explanation being contradicted by a fellow WPC on duty with her at the time of the offence[2290]. She was released after six days pending an appeal[2291]. Her jail sentence was quashed after 12 days, to be replaced by probation and community service orders[2292]. Such fast-track justice is never an option for members of the public, cynics might observe.

Newly hired 16-year-old Thames Valley PCSOs can't deal with a cinema disturbance if an 18 film is being shown: in law they are children. PCSOs are not allowed to tackle serious crimes or violent thugs, nor confiscate alcohol from violent drunks[2293]. Some PCSOs have fought with each other, urinated in the street, and shopped while on duty[2294]. A former editor of 'Police Review' saw two PCSOs chatting to each other walk past an incident where a suspect was being wrestled on the ground by a restaurant manageress[2295]. In Essex PCSOs can't even help children across the road because they lack training (they used to perform the task for many years without training)[2296]. South Wales Police seized about £300,000 worth of cannabis but lost some of it to thieves because two PCSOs apparently didn't guard the store properly (e.g. just had the front of the building under surveillance)[2297]. PCSOs were labelled worthless after a YouTube video clip in the spring of 2008 showed how impotent they were in dealing with ASB in the form of drunken yobs[2298]. Cheshire Police has banned officers from cycling in case they fall off, unless they have passed a proficiency test. PCSOs are lecturing in schools about cycling but aren't allowed to cycle themselves[2299]. Two PCSOs were told by a known paranoid schizophrenic that his daughter had been cloned and his mother had a grave under her car, but they didn't record the incident because they thought he was joking: he had 20 convictions. He murdered a stranger the following day[2300]. Brian Paddick recounts how PCSOs had to be rescued from a London shopping centre when they were besieged by local youths who knew they had no power[2301]. The acronym 'Chimps', used to describe PCSOs by 'proper' officers, stands for: 'Completely hopeless in most policing situations'[2302].

A prisoner who went AWOL from Castle Huntly near Dundee went home, but it was five months before police turned up to arrest him[2303].

When millionaire Richard Green – the world's leading authority on Sherlock Holmes – was found garotted on his bed (after trying to stop an auction of Conan Doyle's papers), police failed to conduct a forensic examination, and the CID didn't bother attending[2304].

The Met missed bringing Ronnie Biggs to justice (after being told by a tabloid he was in Brazil) because they failed to consult the local police chief[2305].

One reason for the delay in Sir Ian Blair being told about de Menezes was that his personal team was too top-heavy: at least two assistant commissioners, several deputy assistant commissioners, commanders and lots of superintendents[2306].

Greater Manchester PCs <u>Mark Derbyshire</u> and <u>Damian Harrison</u> were disciplined for forgetting to report a dead body in the street[2307].

When Lancashire Police handed over to the county responsibility for erecting road signs, they said their officers, though trained to use ladders themselves, were not trained to teach others to climb the 4ft ladders[2308].

Cheshire's Chief Constable <u>Peter Fahy</u> has held forth about the evils of drink, but one resident in his patch complained: 'I live about 10 doors down from the police station and have stopped bothering to report gangs of drunken youths at the end of my road to the police because nothing gets done'[2309].

Small value theft is now being ignored by police, e.g. a supermarket security guard didn't report two separate thefts of packets of steak from the cold cabinet (it was captured on CCTV), because police wouldn't come out if the theft is worth less than £100[2310].

Convict George Roberts remained a fugitive living for long periods at his mother's, despite being arrested twice (in London and Pontefract) . He even worked for the MOD and HM Customs, and registered with the Inland Revenue[2311].

Only one knife thug in ten is jailed[2312].

Tabloid reporters monitored areas affected by horrific crime, finding virtually no police on patrol, yet three-quarters of Britons fear there are too few police on the streets (an Ipsos MORI survey showed)[2313].

When a bicycle was stolen from No. 42 in a street, the police attended days later at <u>No. 34</u>, asking where No. 42 was[2314].

When two Lewisham bus passengers refused to stop smoking crack, the driver pulled up at one of Europe's biggest police stations (housing the CID, special constables, the Criminal Justice Unit and the Serious Crime Directorate). He was told to phone 999 as they were too busy to investigate. Later two officers on horseback were sent out but could not find the culprits[2315].

Sussex Police took a DNA sample in 2002 from a serial sex attacker nicknamed the 'Thursday Rapist', but forgot to send the swab for analysis for four years. Consequently he was free to carry out sex attacks on females (one as young as 12), as well as two burglaries, over the next six years[2316].

<u>Steve Green</u>, Chief Constable of the Notts force, had to step down after losing the confidence of his Notts Police Authority bosses (e.g. he said his force couldn't cope with crime)[2317].

Hampshire Constabulary spent three weeks and thousands of pounds searching for a missing woman, finally finding her body at her home, which they had searched incompletely[2318].

Devon and Cornwall Constabulary have instructed officers not to hold out a hand to drowning swimmers, nor to throw a lifebelt if they may be pulled into the water. Two Dorset officers carrying life-saving equipment were ordered not to board a lifeboat to give assistance to a suspected heart attack victim, because they weren't trained in sea survival. Vandals daubed graffiti over two days in a Bristol building: police decided it was unsafe to enter. A village in Gloucestershire has had police foot patrols withdrawn because its lanes have no pavements[2319].

When a former barrister retrieved her handbag from a mugger, she was amazed to be told by the Met that no crime had been committed as she had got the bag back[2320]. The police later backtracked, saying the incident constituted <u>attempted</u> theft, but this was also wrong.

The Met missed a series of chances to intercept four terrorists (including gang leader Muktar Ibrahim) months before the bungled suicide bomb attacks on July 21[2321]. The Met has shown a worrying tolerance of attempts by Islamists to establish Sharia law in the UK[2322]. In 2006 it was revealed some police forces still did not record antisemitic incidents, despite an ACPO directive[2323].

The boss of a private Scottish ambulance company accused police of refusing, after initially agreeing, to provide an escort for a dying German patient rushing to catch a plane back to his homeland. Police told the ambulance to extinguish its blue lights – they had stopped it because of its 'unusual markings'[2324].

Former Met Assistant Commissioner David Gilbertson reports that Tottenham riot constables spoke of a ' 'lack of leadership, confused command and control, and the mind-numbing inefficiency of their bosses.' 'There was no strategy, no plans, no nothing' ', said a Territorial Support Group officer[2325]. The official inquiry (by the Riots, Communities and Victims panel) into the 2011 riots found that the police had abandoned the streets, allowing the spread of contagion by giving the impression of surrender[2326]. One 16-year-old Hackney resident said, of the 2011 Tottenham riots, 'People did what they did because they could. The police just stood there and watched so we thought 'why not?' '[2327]. The most senior officer in Haringey, Detective Chief Superintendent <u>Sandra Looby</u>, jetted off on holiday to Florida despite warnings that Mark Duggan's shooting could trigger violence[2328]. An MP claims about the Tottenham riots that there was a failure of police intelligence[2329]. Police in Croydon ran out of handcuffs[2330]. The IPCC has admitted neither it nor the Met formally told Mark Duggan's family of his death. The IPCC also apologised for earlier rejecting the family's complaint[2331] but eventually cleared the 11 CO19 officers concerned of any criminality[2332]. Detective Superintendent <u>Singh</u>, who led the Gold Group during the 2011 London riots, said, in relation to Duggan's death, 'Our hands are tied' – he implied it was the IPCC's job to deal with it. Yet community leaders warned several times about the police's failure to contact the bereaved family, pleading that 'tensions were rising', but these concerns went unheeded[2333]. A similar inexplicable failure at the end of the year by Manchester Police to contact the bereaved parents of a murdered Indian student, was ironic in that it was a policeman of the same ethnicity as this victim who failed Duggan's family. A bystander at the Tottenham riots has told how a policeman told him they had been ordered to withdraw because protection of life was more important than the protection of property[2334]. The Met failed to appreciate how big their task was in dealing with the 2011 Tottenham riots, so that they lost control of the streets, according to the Home Affairs Select Committee, while a joint Guardian/LSE report claimed that anti-police sentiment was a significant factor[2335].

Almost half the UK population are so afraid of burglars that they keep a weapon near their beds[2336].

Burglary and assault rates in Britain are the highest in the EU, according to the European Crime and Safety Survey[2337].

Some forces don't seem to want to enforce the laws on child seats in cars (e.g. the Greater Manchester and the two Yorkshire forces)[2338]. Less than half the UK forces have enforced the 20mph speed limits near schools and in built-up areas[2339].

When a laptop belonging to an American who had been a security adviser to the FBI was stolen, the Met told him he had little chance of recovering it: he gave them technical advice which enabled them to retrieve the computer[2340].

A 75-year-old man who punched a youth after suffering years of antisocial behaviour, despite complaints to the police, was convicted of assault[2341].

Peter Chapman, who killed a 17-year-old girl after grooming her on Facebook, was one of 60 dangerous sex offenders monitored by just one untrained Merseyside WPC. One blunder occurred when police downgraded his dangerousness without a proper assessment: his status remained the same despite Chapman failing to comply with his registration terms. The police monitoring unit was unmanned at various times[2342].

Despite strong evidence, Lothian and Borders Police refused to treat the killing of a Chinese man by a 16-year-old thug as a racist crime. The police eventually admitted 'significant failings', but the family, backed by Scottish Labour's shadow cabinet secretary for justice, are demanding an investigation into the police actions[2343]. Lothian and Borders Police will also no longer attend accidents where only vehicles are damaged (meaning drink-drivers could get off), and will advise some 'lower level' crime victims to make an appointment to see an officer, instead of sending one to investigate[2344].

A senior Greater Manchester Police officer has admitted that their target response time for non-violent thefts and burglaries is four hours[2345].

A 14-year-old was stabbed to death in Enfield only hundreds of yards from a police station on the verge of closure[2346].

When a householder rang his local police station in the Scottish Borders to report youths smashing up a phone box, he was told: 'Send us an email'[2347].

The victim of an eBay scam phoned Peckham police station because it was the closest to where she sent the cheque, but as she lived in Strathclyde they told her to phone there. But they told her to phone the Met, who directed her to a police website. Days later she was asked to go to her local station in Giffnock, but there they told her to complain to eBay. Then the Home Office suggested she contact ACPO, but they were unavailable[2348].

It took months for Scottish police to detect that £120,000 had been stolen from Hamilton police station by a civilian worker – the seized money had been left in a holdall. The thief spent a quarter, burying the rest in his garden[2349].

In 2007 only one in 13 police were on the beat in Scotland at any one time.

In many urban areas as few as three officers are on patrol at night, and even where there is a combined population of up to 200,000 only 10 officers can be summoned in an emergency[2350].

By 2007 someone was being attacked every 12 seconds on UK streets (violence was up by 5% over the previous year)[2351]. In the same year it was claimed police were struggling to keep the lid on a significant rise in muggings since Street Crime Initiative funds were used up, and it has become clear that an apparent fall in serious violence was largely due to a change in the rules on how police record threats to kill[2352]. In 2007 there were 290 muggings every day in Britain, with fatal shootings, vandalism and drug offences all up, so that every member of the public stood a 25% chance of being a crime victim. Yet the Government insisted communities were safer than ever[2353]. A 2012 report by HMIC reveals that burglaries, rape and muggings (up to a quarter of all crimes) are being ignored by police, who wrongly record that there hasn't been a crime. ASB is often mislabelled as 'nuisance'. The true ASB incident number could be double the official 3.6m estimate[2354]. When a member of Daily Mail columnist Tom Utley's family was mugged (the fifth mugging of the family), they decided there was no point reporting it, for nothing had come of them telling police about the previous four, except a police offer of 'victim counselling'[2355]. Police will no longer be able to ignore ASB if three separate complaints have been reported, or if five people from five different homes in the same area complain about the same issue. If police still won't respond, they can be disciplined by a 'crime commissioner' – a 'community trigger' system[2356].

Gloucester Police have been accused of incompetence in respect of the Wests: there were missing children and nannies, a prior violent rape, a report to police from the mother of a missing girl last seen at 25 Cromwell Street – Rose West answered the door wearing the girl's slippers[2357].

The full police files on gay serial killers Roy Hall and Michael Kitto were found in an Edinburgh attic by a News of the World reporter. Hall escaped through North Berwick's police station toilet window because officers didn't check their car boot, which contained a body (it was only found when Lothian and Borders CID arrived)[2358].

Nearly 15,000 police officers never made an arrest in 2010, e.g. over 1,000 of 2,076 Derbyshire officers made no arrests[2359].

Claims of slavery at a Bedfordshire camp run by Irish traveller gangmasters were made by 28 men since 2008, but the police didn't make a raid until the autumn of 2011. Some victims were kept in horseboxes and kennels. They were partially starved and their heads shaved[2360].

Strathclyde's Chief Constable has called for a review of the Scottish Police Services Authority's forensic service because of a large backlog in processing samples[2361]. The Scottish police service has 'a significant intelligence gap on human trafficking'[2362].

Forces are closing over a third of stations and cutting their public access hours, giving the message to criminals that policing is in retreat, according to the Police Federation[2363].

Wiltshire Police gave a geriatric jewel thief four days to get away (he stole £25,000 of gold chains from a shop)[2364]. Lanarkshire Police hunting a sex attacker waited three days before appealing for witnesses, despite being immediately alerted by a tabloid newspaper[2365].

In the Stephen Lawrence case the police were concerned more about whether the victims were gang members rather than who the perpetrators were, e.g. they never found the murder weapon. The investigating Met officers lacked leadership from the senior officer <u>Stephen Groves</u>. No policeman was ever disciplined (e.g. for throwing away the suspects' names, senior officers refusing to accept the use of the 'Nigger' word was racist, and no one trying to stem Stephen's blood loss)[2366]. Stephen Lawrence's parents were awarded £320,000 for the police blunders which nearly allowed the killers to get away with it[2367].

It has been claimed <u>Bernard Hogan-Howe</u>, by accepting the Silkin proposals hook, line and sinker, insulted the integrity of his Met officers and played the game of the Home Office, which is trying to control what the media are told[2368].

Lord Watson MSP, who introduced the Scottish ban on fox hunting, has urged police to enforce the law, as it appears as many foxes are being killed by hounds as before his legislation[2369].

Almost eight suspects daily walk free from courts because police (or prosecutors) botch the paperwork or don't turn up at court, costing the taxpayer £72,000 monthly.

Record numbers of drivers (171,000) have been fined for using mobiles while driving, indicating that the police crackdown over almost a decade is failing[2370].

When Indian student Anuj Bidue was murdered in Salford (at Xmas 2011), Greater Manchester Police didn't bother to inform his family, who learned about it on Facebook. The force had to apologise[2371].

The father of John Kilbride, a Moors murder victim, penetrated a police roadblock with a knife, threatening to kill Myra Hindley[2372].

Police are failing to address the hidden problem of elderly domestic violence, despite half of the 96,000 adults referred to adult safeguarding services in 2010 being geriatric[2373].

NAPO (National Association of Probation Officers) has warned that the police (as well as others) are failing stalking victims: only 2% of over 53,000 stalkers are jailed, even though some 'high risk' offenders who flout repeated restraining orders go on to murder their victims[2374].

Many of the people – 1,000 daily – who go missing never turn up. When 19-year-old Luke Durbin disappeared from his home in Woodbridge the police told his mother she was wasting their time, when she in fact knew he could have been murdered. She says the police let her down: only after 4½ years did the Suffolk and Norfolk Police mount a proper search. 140,000 under-18s go missing in Britain every year.

When Scottish people were scammed by rogue firm Cost Reduction Services, police initially turned away victims who lost money. After the press stepped in the police launched a fraud probe into the get-rich-quick scheme, and detectives have now contacted the UK Government's Companies Investigation Branch. One victim, who lost £15,000, said that at first he was 'basically' told by an officer to get lost, because it was a 'civil matter'[2375].

Ex-army officer Tim Collins has criticised the leadership quality of top police officers: 'We have got some top social workers running police forces', which are crippled by a 'do nothing' culture, with far too many crimes being 'brushed under the carpet' by police reluctant to investigate them[2376].

Sex trafficking of young foreign women in Scotland uses their superstitious susceptibilities (witchcraft) to control them: the victims, who have experienced widespread police corruption in their own countries (foreign police are involved in rape and trafficking) say there is a culture of ignorance and disbelief among Scottish police.

Violent prisoner Andrew Farndon was transported through Suffolk by taxi without a police escort – he escaped[2377]. Category A prisoner John Anslow, charged with murder, went on the run for the third time: Staffordshire Police had not provided an escort but organised a £10,000 reward for his capture.

Over 10% of murders are committed by 'bail bandits' – more than 350 killings in five years, with nearly 90 rapes a year[2378].

The trouble with the Home Office's new crime statistics is that the official police website doesn't allow the public to put the figures in context[2379].

A mother who was a rape victim after her drink was spiked was disbelieved by Suffolk Police, who eventually had to apologise after she complained to the IPCC. Key witnesses were not interviewed, nor were the suspect's house or car searched. The case against the suspect collapsed because of the police's failure to collect forensic evidence. Because of her experience she developed psychiatric illness and lost her business[2380].

A suspect in a double murder who handed himself in at Lewisham Police Station was told to wait in a queue by the desk officer. He was eventually arrested after agreeing to wait[2381].

When the gangsters were jailed who ruled the European 'burglary capital' – the Bestwood Estate in Nottingham – crime reportedly rose, because 'they deterred crime more effectively than the police'[2382].

Dorset Police wanted unpaid civilian volunteers to monitor CCTV cameras, as they didn't think it was worth their own officers doing the work (the force doesn't bother to monitor their 26 cameras, by their own admission). The Police Federation disagrees[2383].

The Met refused a written request from a LibDem parliamentary candidate to investigate the payments (at taxpayers' expense) by disgraced MP Derek Conway to his full-time student son (£50,000 was involved)[2384].

In 2008 crime victims faced a 72-hour wait to see an officer, with even 999 callers not seeing anyone for three hours (according to the Policing Reform Green Paper), the brainchild of Sir Ronnie Flanagan, (whose study found police 'criminalising' children who play hopscotch or build snowmen)[2385].

The final processions of fallen servicemen in Canada have police outriders, but the latter are denied these in Britain by, e.g. Thames Valley Police, who have defended their anti-ceremonial duty stance. The MoD won't comment[2386].

A householder who captured a burglar in his home was assured by Lincolnshire Police they would be right round, but three hours later no help had arrived, so the miscreant had to be released when his gang besieged the house[2387].

'Civilian assistant investigators' were being trialled by Central Scotland Police in 2008 (they would have a few weeks' training and £22,000 a year).

In the search for missing nine-year-old Shannon Matthews police were tipped to search the flat where she was eventually found, by at least two people. Not a single officer seems to have interviewed the stepfather's uncle, the culprit. The charity Missing People passed on concerns to the police, who didn't act on them – the uncle had been involved before in kidnapping children[2388]. There were several pointers to Mick Donovan as being the young girl's kidnapper: (1) he had had his children taken away by social services and so was known to police; (2) a neighbour of Donovan reported him to a missing persons helpline – the neighbour was told West Yorkshire Police would be informed; (3) a young father contacted Crimestoppers about Donovan's suspicious behaviour; (4) a female neighbour was questioned about Donovan two years before[2389].

Lincolnshire Police (e.g. in the person of PC Daniel Gilmore) and Notts Police (in the person of PC Mark Stacy) couldn't find the body of a driver in his crashed car, reported by 999 calls, in fact couldn't find the crash site[2390].

A girl who starved to death was visited by police four months before (her five siblings were emaciated at the time of her death), but there was no follow-up.

Notts Police apologised for telling a family whose home was being ransacked by eight robbers wielding axes: 'Call back in half an hour, we're busy'. They arrived in three hours[2391].

A Reading pub landlady was arrested in front of her family and customers for not appearing in court, but she never received the summons, which had gone to an old address. She was jailed for two days, and the magistrate had to apologise[2392].

Home Office guidelines said (2008) that three hours was a good response time for police for emergencies. Police sergeants spend almost half their time behind their desks[2393].

The Scottish Government and HM Chief Inspector of Constabulary called for better policing of fraud, which increased in Scotland by 16% between 2006-7[2394].

The Met's CCTV expert DCI Mike Neville has described the technology as 'an utter fiasco'. No one watches the films. Only 3% of London muggings have been solved with the help of CCTV. A Home Office study of 14 systems found only one had cut crime (in a car park). 80% of footage is of such poor quality it is virtually worthless, and there are over 400 incompatible formats. 90% of systems operate illegally (largely due to data storage issues)[2395]. CCTV gives authorities an excuse to reduce police patrols, so militating against fighting crime. Street robbery and violence have risen as cameras have proliferated.

Kent Police have told residents of Sevenoaks that they were unable to tackle revellers in the dark, and if they didn't have prior intelligence of a rave, they couldn't raise the manpower quickly enough to deal with it. Also if the police intervened at night, the hippies might have accidents on the way home. So the taxpayers' lives had to be blighted[2396].

Astonished Rangers fans had their hotel bookings cancelled a week before the 2008 Cup Final on police advice – the Manchester Police told guesthouses they wouldn't respond to outbreaks of trouble at B&Bs[2397].

When John Yates was ACPO spokesman on rape, he said detectives aren't always as professional with rape as with other serious crimes; there should be a rape team in every force, so that the 6% conviction rate could be improved (there is a postcode lottery: in some areas there are five times more convictions)[2398].

Trevor James 'Jim' Bates, a TV repair man who claimed falsely to have an engineering degree, joined the police database of qualified witnesses. He was used in dozens of serious cases (child porn, a senior Met officer, rape, etc.). Bates attacked police involved in Operation Ore, and defended DC Brian Stevens, the Soham liaison officer jailed for faking an alibi to escape porn charges, as well as Gurpal Virdi, accused of sending racist letters to himself. Bates' history included a spell in a Leicester mental hospital where he was treated with LSD (Lysergic acid diethylamide). The police hadn't checked his background or qualifications. A much more prolific bogus expert was Gene Morrison, given five years (2007) for pretending to be a forensic psychologist, and in 2005 lip-reading expert Jessica Rees falsely claimed to have an Oxford degree[2399].

The body of 28-year-old Vinny Derrick was not found for over eight years by Greater Manchester Police, despite it being near the spot under the M60 flyover where he was last seen[2400].

Former Scotland Yard Detective Chief Superintendent Kevin Hurley has accused the Met of 'warped priorities and tactical incompetence', and he talks about 'the rot within the top ranks of the Met'[2401].

Police arrested two robbers in a stolen car with hammers and balaclavas, but they were released to carjack, kidnap and torture a former aide to the Queen Mother a fortnight later: he was made to tour cashpoints to withdraw money for the gang[2402].

When Tory MP Andrew Selous reported his stolen briefcase to a police station it was full of police playing billiards – they didn't seem too concerned about looking for his briefcase.

Though a quarter of women suffer domestic violence during their lifetime, only 16% of incidents are reported to police.

Nearly 700 registered sex offenders have been on the run for over a year (one for nearly 10 years), with nearly 850 at large in 2012, i.e. those going AWOL had more than doubled in two years. More than 2% of all the registered are missing[2403].

Northumbria Police PC David Rathband's twin brother has formally complained about the force's care of their officer before his suicide[2404].

Wiltshire Police are reported to be using night-vision goggles (to help detect allotment vandals). 'Darkness is no longer the criminal's friend', said one PC, yet police generally are loathe to come out in the dark (even suggesting dousing of street lights will reduce criminality!)[2405].

When Sunday Times journalist Daisy Waugh had her mobile phone stolen she had to phone the police twice, when she was sent on a series of redials and diversions, ending up with an extension where a recorded voice advised the line was defunct[2406].

For decades the police have failed to enforce the law against transgressions of the 1967 Abortion Act (and its 1990 amendments): abortion on demand has been the order of the day, as seen recently in some British clinics operating with pre-signed medical permission documents.

Only the Met appears to keep statistics on attacks by teenagers on their parents – it is one of the least recorded crimes[2407].

The brother of a murdered woman has attacked police for refusing to support victims' families. ACPOS wouldn't support his main contention that there should be a central point of contact with police throughout a criminal investigation. He says he didn't see a liaison officer for months: when he did the officer merely collated information, not offering support. It took ages to get answers to simple questions. Assistant Chief Constable Ruaraidh Nicolson said the case comparison proposal would be too difficult to implement[2408].

A tribunal report criticised Kent Police for failure to charge GP Dr. Navin Zala over a patient's 2007 complaint: she alleged the doctor touched her breasts inappropriately. Soon after, two other women came forward with historic allegations. The GMC says it contacted the police in 2007 about the complaint, and continued its inquiries after police dropped the case[2409].

It is estimated up to 100,000 girls and women have been circumcised illegally because, campaigners say, police are reluctant to interfere for fear of being labelled racist: none of the UK's 43 police forces has secured a conviction, which can lead to a 14-year sentence[2410]. For three decades female circumcision has been illegal, with specialist units set up in hospitals to deal with it[2411].

The IPCC has no automatic power to investigate 'outsourced' (privatised) police personnel: private firms have been invited to assume some of the responsibilities of Surrey and West Midlands forces, and South Wales, Lancashire and Cleveland have already outsourced frontline jobs. G4S – the world's largest security firm – wants to extend from its prison and immigration roles to policing. Another nail in the coffin of police accountability[2412]?

Scottish police take twice as long as other UK forces to perform checks on would-be childcare workers[2413].

Lancashire Police no longer attend 'non-residential dwelling' burglaries, as a cricket club chairman found out when he reported a break-in at his pavilion. He was offered a telephone appointment two days later to give details – as a result he branded his local police 'call centre cops'[2414].

Street robberies rose by 8% in 2011, with a 15% rise in 'personal acquisitive crime' (the largest annual increase in a decade), according to the Crime Survey for England and Wales (2012). Crime in public correlates with police availability[2415].

In Manchester 7,000 defendants have been cautioned 10 times by police, therefore avoiding prosecution. Surely the police in such cases are perverting the course of justice[2416]?

Probationer beat officers ('probies') are often being supervised by other recent recruits (three quarters of beat police are probationers)[2417].

When a CID officer's mother tried to interest the Woking Police in a drug dealer across the street from where she was helping him move into a new home, they said they were too busy! If a cop can't rouse the cops, what chance has the general public[2418]?

The Assistant Chief Constable of Greater Manchester Police, <u>Steve Heywood</u>, was heavily criticised for playing down the obvious racist element in the Heywood (Rochdale) street grooming case – the nine-strong all-Asian gang abused only white girls. Heywood said: 'I have no indication racism played any part', but a spokesman for the Muslim youth support group, the Ramadhan Foundation, retorted: 'It's absolute rubbish to suggest race isn't an issue'. Detective Chief Superintendent <u>Mary Doyle</u>, like Heywood, emphasised that 'getting hung up on race and ethnicity issues' detracted from what was simply child abuse. The police had to apologise to a victim they had arrested who reported the Pakistani gang in 2008, when she was 15 (her underwear provided forensic evidence) – they only started their probe in late 2010, leaving as many as 47 vulnerable girls, known to social services, to be given alcohol, cigarettes, gifts, food and money. One drink victim had to have sex with 20 men in one night. The failure of the police to crack down on the problem may have contributed to the February 2012 riot in Heywood where takeaways where abuse occurred were attacked – bricks were thrown at police and windows smashed. A Daily Mail leader suggested it was likely that 'the police were and still are unwilling to acknowledge the racial link out of what sounds like political correctness'[2419]. Police could have neutralised the Rochdale sex grooming network in 2008 (it took a further four years to being some perpetrators to justice)[2420].

<u>Lothian and Borders Police</u> have been criticised by a tabloid for failing to trace, and take action against, a man who has threatened on the internet to violently rape a woman who says she was raped by a footballer and another man (there have been 13 arrests for similar threatening 'trolling' in the case of the woman raped by a Sheffield United and Wales player). The culprit works for the Government's Student Loans Company in Glasgow, being traced quite quickly by the newspaper[2421].

The number of appeals when police fail to record a complaint increased in five years (2006-2011) from 902 to 1,435[2422].

Dorset Police told a vicar it would take months of surveillance to catch lead thieves targeting his church – he caught one in five hours[2423].

Convicted paedophile Kevin Rooney, despite being monitored by MAPPA (Multi Agency Public Protection Arrangements), which includes police, was free to rob, rape and murder an OAP in her home. He had been placed in a B&B whose owners weren't advised of his past[2424].

<u>Met Police</u> called by a St. Georges Hospital patient to his bedside because staff refused to give him a drink of water, did not intervene when doctors told them he was behaving irrationally because of a brain tumour – he died of dehydration the next day[2425].

<u>Lancashire Police</u> want <u>staff</u> to patrol the Royal Blackburn Hospital to stop attacks on patients[2426].

A 2012 Civitas report says there is unequivocal evidence that slightly better policing (a mere 1% increase in the detection rate) would prevent 26,000 burglaries, 85,000 thefts, 2,500 robberies and 1,800 frauds annually[2427].

Not only did police miss several chances to catch Delroy Grant, serial night stalker (of old people), but they say they are too busy to interview him in prison to listen to his admission to hundreds of other crimes[2428].

When DS <u>Willie Robertson</u> produced a missing person's rings from his pocket sometime into the probe by Grampian Police Superintendent Alan Smith, there was an intensive re-examination of every officer's role at the victim's house in the first few days of the inquiry. Smith said he was 'surprised, confused and concerned' by the re-appearance of the rings. Even though the victim was still missing the rings and other personal effects, which might show the husband murdered her, they were returned to him[2429].

The Serious Fraud Office didn't carry out even one raid in the financial year to 2012, despite conducting 47 raids the previous year and despite a rise in financial crime. The agency had to apologise and admit mishandling information in the Iceland Kaupthing bank case[2430].

When a publican was viciously attacked, leaving him with several injuries (including one probably inoperable), Northumberland Police gave the violent thug a caution, and wouldn't reveal the attacker's identity without a £75 admin fee – the victim needs this information to take court action. In 2011 739 cases of GBH were given simple cautions[2431].

Some 500 Scots police officers are devoting all or part of their time replacing axed support staff (firearms inspectors, control room operators, custody personnel, etc.), for which roles they are under-qualified[2432].

<u>Cumbria Police</u> allegedly ignored warnings for three years about a Carlisle shopkeeper who ran an underage brothel[2433].

The clear-up rate of violence by Ulster paramilitaries, eg. in Derry, is only 4%[2434].

A Sunday tabloid reported in 2003 that when the public approach the police they find 'bureaucracy, suspicion and an offhand attitude'. The same tabloid reported that when a parent tried to get <u>Bedfordshire Police</u> to arrest thugs he identified as having stolen his son's bicycle at knifepoint, he was told the cells were full. A promise to get back to him was never kept. A Reading resident reported that when he told the police of drugs being peddled in a car park they told him there were another 20 'shopping' sites – they would do nothing because it was only soft drugs[2435].

Members of the public reporting a crime by phone are quite often exasperated to find the distant call centre refuses to put them through to the local station.

'I am a police officer trying to find an alternative career because of the lack of interest, bad management and total disregard for officers' welfare and morale. This is in addition to the massive charade to fool the public. While off-duty I have experienced the inability of the police to provide an adequate service'[2436].

<u>Avon and Somerset Police</u> were accused of taking too long to respond to reports that the vice-president of a W.I. was missing – she and a doctor friend had died in a mudslide. Police were also criticised for failing to secure her house, despite a friend's request the day before it was burgled[2437].

Police Scotland has been allowed to start without a unified IT system (it has eight mutually incompatible systems). This makes tracking dangerous criminals more difficult[2438].

A district judge has condemned <u>South Yorkshire Police</u> for handing out on-the-spot fines to violent French youths because they couldn't speak English. The judge felt the police took the lazy option[2439].

<u>Avon and Somerset Police</u> refused to charge a Polish scrap metal thief who, caught red-handed, admitted the offence but maintained he was ignorant of the law. The police say they would have had to prove mens rea[2440].

Police told whistleblower Dr. Linda Reynolds that there was no substance to her allegations against Shipman.

HM Inspectorate of Constabulary has criticised Essex Chief Constable <u>Roger Baker</u> for sending his officers out to take statements from <u>all</u> reported crime victims[2441] (other forces are selective as to which incidents to attend).

In the case of the murdered schoolgirl Tia Sharp, 100 Met Police missed finding her body in her grandmother's house at least three times, despite the use of sniffer dogs. Also the prime suspect, the grandmother's partner, was allowed to go missing and remain free for several hours. Former senior detectives have criticised the police for taking eight days to find the body, secreted in the attic[2442].

Serial prostitute killer Stephen Griffiths knew murdered sex worker Rebecca Hale well, but police did not follow this up[2443].

Police manpower allocated to monitoring paedophiles is subject to a postcode lottery[2444].

Tens of thousands (perhaps 30,000) of women and girls have been subjected to FGM (female gender mutilation), yet there has been not one prosecution, so hundreds of historic cases are now (2013) being probed. The UK has the largest number of vulnerable women in Europe. This is just one of many laws which the police choose not to enforce: others include selling alcohol to children, under-age sex, abuse of arrest warrants, credit card and whiplash injury fraud, seatbelts for children in back seats, abortion since 1967, gay dogging/cottaging, extreme internet porn, pursuit of bail jumpers, honour killings, violent deaths of blacks in London, possession of cannabis[2445,2446]. New laws on car child seats were often not enforced, with some forces dismissing them as impractical[2447].

A Kirkcaldy man tried to report a drug dealer near a police station but had twice to come back later because it was closed (a fifth of Scottish stations have closed or reduced hours in six years from 2007)[2448].

40% of victims of crime are never visited by police, while detection rates for violent crime are at their lowest ever, under 50%[2449]. Police are hugely under-recording violent offences to manipulate their crime-fighting statistics: the Chief Inspector of Constabulary found an estimated 5,000 violent offences a year are not treated as crimes by officers[2450]. Many forces don't record crimes where children under 10 are thought to be responsible. The crimes include rape, shoplifting, assault, robbery, vandalism, burglary and arson[2451].

Scotland Yard's officers are no longer allowed to change a tyre, because of health and safety considerations. They may have to wait for hours for private firms like VT Critical Services (they have a decade's contract from the Met') [2452].

Savile could have been stopped as early as 1964 by police[2453].

Most UK crimes are now dealt with by penalty notices, so don't get counted in official statistics: even police assault and resisting arrest violently are sometimes excluded[2454].

Over 5,300 officers in England and Wales are on restricted backroom duties, usually on full pay, because of 'malaise' or 'fatigue'. In one force 500 specialist police (e.g. firearms, dog handling) failed a fitness test[2455].

A North Wales 14-year-old schoolgirl was raped after police missed three chances of apprehending her attacker David Edgerton (a previous rape, an attempted rape and an assault on a girl of 10)[2456].

The Met has quietly dropped their probe two years after the most serious breach of royal security in years, i.e. Prince Charles and Camilla being besieged by a mob in London's West End[2457].

Princess Eugenie had her BMW stolen when she and her protection officer left the keys in the ignition[2458].

Retired DCI Peter Jay forgot to bring handcuffs when he and his two officers arrested Dennis Nilsen[2459].

Though retired Met deputy assistant commissioner Sue Akers received 'words of advice' about her involvement in the Victoria Climbié abuse case, and was criticised over her evidence to Leveson (she also called a colleague a serial killer as a joke), she was awarded a CBE. She was also accused of heavy-handedness in the Met's three 'media crime' inquiries (Weeting, Tuleta and Elveden)[2460].

It took 45 visits by Fife police before they applied for a closure order in the case of a 20-year-old woman's extreme antisocial behaviour (she couldn't control the behaviour of visitors). This author experienced a similar case in Hampshire where a 17-year-old and her visitors ran amok, but police bent over backwards not to apply for a court order[2461].

Ignoring the evidence

John O'Connor, ex-chief of the Flying Squad and once tipped to head the Met, says the Jill Dando police ignored evidence that a professional assassin might be involved, accusing them of 'shoehorning' evidence to build the case against Barry George[2462].

The Audit Commission said (2006) police were ignoring callers reporting a crime. They were routinely not answering the phone, not returning calls, not making promised follow-up visits. Just under half of forces give only a poor or fair service with regard to non-999 calls. Forces have not matched their staffing to the volume of calls[2463].

When consultant psychiatrist and powerboat world champion Dr. Ian Falkouski went to the police at Poole complaining of anonymous hate phone calls, the officers were hardly able to hide their indifference. He again failed to be taken seriously by Limehouse police. Yet when the doctor was falsely accused of rape by his stalker, the police took his accuser seriously, with a devastating effect on the doctor's life[2464].

One deliberate car crash gang has been linked to 400 staged accidents, but the police refused to investigate unless the insurers paid them[2465].

80 Met police were unable to find a murdered 12-year-old's body in Croydon, despite it lying only a few feet from her bedroom in her grandmother's house, which was searched four times. There was a very obvious stench. Officers were reprimanded[2466].

Stephen Lawrence's mother has told how police bungled the murder hunt and treated her with contempt: 'Even the dogs in the street knew who'd killed our son. But the police just didn't give a damn'[2467]. Within 48 hours anonymous letters to the police gave them the names of four out of five of the suspects, but a policeman screwed them up and threw them away.

Leicestershire officers were caught by an undercover camera refusing to believe rape allegations (as well as ogling porno and making sexist comments)[2468].

Police often don't turn up for youth court hearings. In one case the officer supposed to present CCTV evidence doesn't turn up, hasn't obtained the evidence or sent a report/comment. The judge ... practically shouts: 'That is discourteous to the court, he has wasted all of our time and not to bother to send someone else is not acceptable. I'm getting fed up of this – it is happening all the time'[2469].

When an intruder broke into a primary school (St. Stephens in Canterbury) and threatened staff, police failed to respond to four calls – in fact they never turned up at all[2470].

The police, though receiving 1,200 calls daily from women saying they've been physically abused, have traditionally never been keen to intervene in 'domestics', with many women turned away. (One officer told a victim to go home, stop nagging and make sure she got a good dinner ready for her partner coming home)[2471].

A TV news item reported that architect Robert Anderson had filmed youths attacking him at his Warrington home, and had handed the tape to the police, but they took no action – the crime had already happened, it was explained[2472].

Brian Paddick announced after the July 2005 bombings 'Islam and terrorism do not go together'[2473].

Though Strathclyde Police found (2006) a teacher's computer was linked to a child porn exchange website he was allowed to carry on downloading depraved images for six years, as no action seems to have been taken[2474].

For three years a badly beaten victim waited for his attacker, who had been arrested, to face justice, but the culprit was freed by a judge because Lincolnshire Police had forgotten about the case, even though the accused tried to remind them (his solicitor wrote to the force four times but got no reply)[2475].

A burgled Warwickshire homeowner called 999 to be told that burglary was no longer considered a serious offence; and he should deliver the thieves' hacksaw to a police station himself. It had taken him three attempts to get through to Stratford police station to report the crime[2476].

Police are refusing to attend burglaries if the burglar has fled, civilian 'scenes of crime' staff being sent instead (the 'sole response' approach). The chairman of the Police Federation said (2007) the number of officers available to respond instantly was falling, as so many were chasing elective government targets, yet the police is supposedly an emergency service. Only one crime in 39 leads to a conviction, a Home Office study has found[2477].

When staff at a Lanarkshire branch of the Bank of Scotland forgot to lock up when they went for lunch, a customer assumed the police would attend when she set off an alarm, but they failed to respond, even after she set off a second alarm[2478].

When the chief executive of East Sussex NHS Trust had her precious dog stolen from her Sevenoaks garden, and was then tormented by threatening texts, she claims she was told by Kent police, 'It's just a dog'. She even had to demand a crime reference number[2479].

North Yorkshire Police refused to enforce a new law on child car seats because they decided they didn't have the legal right to measure children at the roadside, or demand birth dates. South Yorkshire and Greater Manchester Police likewise refused to impose fines[2480].

Bradford police failed to act when a young dialysis patient was brutally attacked by thugs: his mother tracked down crucial CCTV footage and handed it over to police. She said: 'The police have lost all credibility in my eyes'[2481]. An anonymous senior policeman claimed that officers were put at risk in the 2001 Bradford race riots by being sent into action ill-equipped (e.g. batons and shields too short) and because police chiefs ignored warnings that violence was highly likely[2482].

When in 2007 hordes of scavengers on Branscombe beach grabbed masses of shipwrecked goods, Devon and Cornwall Police said the treasure hunters were doing nothing illegal, but Maritime and Coastguard Agency officials were furious that police had not restricted beach access till much of the booty was gone[2483].

Police are still refusing to enter mosques even when a terrorist suspect is inside[2484].

An investigation by Consumer Focus, a statutory rights body, found (2010) victims of crime who report incidents to the police are often dissatisfied (three out of 10), with their concerns being given a 'low priority', even serious cases like assaults on children. The commonest problem was having to wait days for a response[2485].

Manchester schoolteacher Linda Walker was given six months for firing an airgun at the feet of yobs after police ignored at least 15 complaints about a long (two year) campaign of abuse and vandalism (the police computer for obscure reasons is unable to group repeated reports of harassment at the same address). Another abused individual was allotted a beat policeman but the latter didn't log complaint e-mails and was transferred without telling the complainant: after about 50 reported incidents the police said they had no record. A formal complaint about the beat cop was never pursued: 'Trying to get help was worse than the harassment itself'[2486].

Under Surrey Police's 'multiple cautions' a burglar got off with a caution, despite admitting 113 offences (cautions enable crimes to be recorded as 'solved' even though they aren't[2487]).

Police were apparently indifferent to the whole 'DVD bootleg thing', despite Triad gangs from China being involved in their mass pirating in 2003.

Gloucestershire Police refused to recover a stolen van from a travellers' camp because the criminals there made it dangerous, according to the vehicle's owner[2488].

A former Grampian WPC was shocked to be told by her own force to investigate a robbery at her home herself. The police wouldn't even call the stolen mobile phone in case it would infringe the thief's human rights[2489].

Humberside Police have told shopkeepers not to report thefts of under £20, instead noting details in a log book[2490].

Northumbria Police ignored a warning from Durham Prison that dangerous Raoul Moat was on the loose[2491].

In 90 minutes one London O.A.P.'s Connect card was used to clear £2,000 out of her account at a store, three supermarkets and a bank, but the crime management unit of Wandsworth police wrote: 'We have reviewed the crime but so far there is not enough evidence to continue with further inquiries and the case will now be closed'. This despite the thief being caught on cameras in Sainsbury's, Next and Barclays[2492].

A Liverpool gun crime campaigner says: 'I have seen these teenage gunmen march down my own street, but the police just don't want to know'. The police know who the gang members are, and where they live[2493].

When two toddler brothers were found stabbed to death in their Manchester home in 2008 – their mother was sectioned as a result – it was revealed police had gone to the house following concerned phone calls hours earlier, but apparently did nothing[2494].

In October 2010 the Home Secretary promised that members of the public who have been repeatedly ignored by police when complaining about antisocial behaviour will be given new powers to demand action – ASB will be treated as criminal. Victims will be able to name and shame officers who don't act[2495].

A Humberside PC refused the plea for help of a shopkeeper chasing two young thieves and told him: 'Ring the police'. He dialled 999, was assured police were on their way, but nobody came because they were attending a retirement party. When he went to the local (Hessle) police station there were shouts and cheers from inside the building, and they knew nothing about his call[2496]. In another incident involving the same police station (Peeler House), a motorist called in to report his vandalised car, only to be told he must ring in instead[2497].

When a couple phoned 999 shortly after confronting Cumbria killer Derrick Bird, offering an Ordnance Survey map reference for Bird's precise whereabouts, the police operator turned them down, and failed to warn them to leave the area because Bird was very dangerous[2498].

Schizophrenic sex offender Robert Napper was identified as a threat to women in the mid-1980s, but the Met ignored a tip-off from his mother linking her son to Rachel Nickell's killing. The police persisted in making mistakes until nearly 100 women had been assaulted[2499]. When a paranoid schizophrenic turned up at West Midland Police's Steelhouse Lane station in Birmingham's city centre asking for help she was turned away. The mother stabbed her three-year-old to death later that day, then trying to dissolve the body in acid[2500].

When a parked car was hit in Leighton Buzzard 500 yards from the police station, neighbours phoned police but were told officers wouldn't attend until the owner reported the smash[2501].

Greater Manchester Police told a vicar's wife, shot at by youths as she walked her dog in the park, to use another park. Having heard nothing from the police the next day she tried to get through to them on the phone for an hour, with no success. Only the next day did an officer appear, but the culprits hadn't been caught[2502].

A Norfolk pensioner who fought a nine-year battle against yobbish behaviour turned down a Home Office monetary 'Taking a Stand' award because police had let him down so badly[2503].

Victims of credit and debit card fraud were told in 2007 not to bother reporting the crime to police. Police teams specialising in card fraud were being disbanded, despite there being 700,000 cases in 2006 (about this time the world's biggest card scam was ongoing, with 45.7m card numbers being stolen from the computer systems of TJX)[2504].

Five years before the Soham murders Hailey Gibling says she was abused by Huntley, but Humberside Police wouldn't believe her: if they had, the murders may never have happened, as, if he had been placed on the Sex Offenders Register, he wouldn't have got his school job. There were two failed police investigations of the Gibling case. Huntley has now admitted he abused Mrs. Gibling[2505].

Just one police officer in 40 is free to answer 999 calls, the rest being tied up on 'special duties'. Police chiefs won't let them be redirected to emergency calls (one unnamed force had 800 officers officially on duty for a shift with only 20 being available for 'response duties'). Is this dereliction of duty? Patrol cars spend almost half their time driving around with no attempt to target crime hotspots. 999 calls are downgraded if no police are available, with one sergeant advising his constables to ignore incidents that don't affect performance targets. Merseyside Police found as many as 500 calls monthly could be incorrectly graded. These facts were contained in a 2007 Inspectorate of Constabulary report[2506].

In 2009 Sharon Hodgkinson was hailed in the Press as the 'Superwoman of Suburbia' – she was a resident of Bolton's most notorious Johnson Fold estate – but she has had to give up her fight against the thugs after a threat that she and her children would be shot dead. What action did the police take? 'They never even returned my call'[2507].

Lazy Central Scotland PC Matthew Turner faced jail for letting criminals go free in Falkirk – he binned information on over 14 crimes, giving colleagues a string of excuses[2508].

It was claimed in an ITV 'Tonight' programme on bullying that police are ignoring Internet bullying (e.g. on Facebook).

A Glasgow mother whose two sons were murdered was ignored when she begged police to hunt for them (she had received a terrifying call from their father). Strathclyde

Police denied she was told she had to wait for 24 hours, and insist proper procedure was followed[2509].

After four 999 calls over two hours, a Wisbech shopkeeper bundled the suspect into his van and drove to the police station to hand him over – they had been too busy and he could let him go if he liked[2510]!

Police Federation chairman Paul McKeever branded as a 'national disgrace' the fact that police don't take burglaries seriously[2511].

Scottish landowners are angry that police are not taking enough action against rogue travellers who are trespassing[2512].

Leicestershire Police repeatedly ignored single mother Fiona Pilkington's pleas for help after suffering years of abuse by local vandals, a court heard during a hearing into the killing of her disabled daughter and her suicide[2513]. Police classed her as an 'over-reactor', and have applied to the High Court for a compensation claim by Fiona's mother to be thrown out[2514]. The Equality and Human Rights Commission has blamed police for failing to deal with victimisation of the disabled: 1.9m disabled were crime victims in 2010, but the police only recorded 1,567 cases[2515]. South Yorkshire's chief constable, Meredydd Hughes, said that could never happen there. In fact, two Doncaster sisters had bricks through their windows, threatened daily, etc. Despite 41 visits from Hughes's officers, the harassing family were allowed to carry on, despite all having ASBOs. Hughes commented (wrongly): 'Look, nobody's been murdered. Nobody's been assaulted. Nobody's been robbed.' She also maintained the ASBOs were working[2516]!

A screaming rape victim was abandoned to her fate by blundering London PC Matthew Harris, who interrupted the attack, questioned the rapist but didn't speak to the victim. A neighbour had alerted the police[2517].

The police have been ignoring the rantings of even the most firebrand Muslim preachers, so, e.g., incendiary cleric Abu Qatada was allowed to spread his ravings undisturbed[2518].

ACPO guidelines are urging police chiefs to turn a blind eye to some forms of public indecency, such as 'dogging' and 'cottaging'[2519], perhaps because so many of those involved are gay – police are not supposed to be homophobic any longer. Before WWII police prosecuted an average of 300 gays annually: this rose to 1,500 postwar, over 1,000 of whom would be jailed. One gay man says following his arrest for cottaging he was made to strip and bend over at the police station – one officer commented, 'You could lose your truncheon up there'.

A neighbour of an innocent young Hackney father, who was murdered because he asked drug thugs to be quiet, says: 'The police were called many times, but often they didn't bother coming out. I haven't seen them since the beginning of the year'. He was speaking in October[2520]. When a young mother was robbed with violence outside her home it took seven months for the police to get her statement ready for her to sign – a detective made an appointment to see her but never turned up. In the decade to 2007 Labour increased the number of police by 5% while the number of offences increased by 186%[2521]. Senior Northampton judge Richard Bray has warned of a rise in vigilante crimes caused by poor police response times. He says: 'Nobody bothers to phone the police any more …. It is because the police do not actually come round so people go out themselves and deal with it'[2522]. 'Gang culture has taken over the urban areas – and why? It's because there's no police presence to counter the threat. Instead all we've got are poorly trained PCSOs … We can afford to spend … on the 2012 Olympics but seemingly can't keep our streets safe for young people … No one bothers to report minor crimes because the police don't bother to attend such incidents'[2523].

The Met has apologised for blunders that left sexual predator Kirk Reid free to claim at least 20 more victims (he is suspected of hundreds of attacks). Though a prime suspect in 2004 (his name had been flagged up to a specialist Met sex crimes team), inexplicably officers failed to arrest and question him, causing a four year delay. He had come to police attention 12 times (by end of 2004), but was never visited or asked for a DNA sample. His half-brother Roger is a Met PC[2524]. The specialist Met detectives lost victim statements, bungled forensic tests and subjected an innocent man to repeated arrest[2525]. Police failed to arrest Reid, despite having his numberplate and descriptions of a man resembling him. The judge in Reid's case said: 'For many years these women were neglected by individual police officers and by collective police attitudes'[2526]. The IPCC has conducted an inquiry into why he was allowed to slip through the police net[2527]. When a teenage passenger claimed she had been drugged and molested by London taxi driver John Warboys, suspected of being Britain's most prolific sexual predator, the Met refused to believe her and set him free to carry on offending[2528]. Another victim's semen-stained trousers were not sent by officers for DNA analysis in late 2007 – if they had been, Warboys' national database entry would have matched[2529]. Nottingham Police smashed a Facebook paedophile ring but took almost four months to arrest a pregnant mother-of-eight suspect[2530]. Police took over a year to track down a drug courier bail-jumper <u>at his home</u>[2531]. Another Met (female) officer in the CID had two brothers in prison (2012)*.

DC <u>Angela Sullivan</u>, part of the Surrey Police team which failed in 2007 to arrest Jimmy Savile for his assaults on vulnerable girls at Duncroft residential school, is working on a fresh Savile probe (Operation Outreach)[2532].

A Kidlington householder who tried to report a burglary at Thames Valley Police headquarters (Kidlington police station was shut) was turned away – because 14 officers were playing poker. Given a non-emergency phone number, an operator told him a PC would be in touch, but a week later he had still heard nothing. Gambling is legally permitted at the headquarters[2533].

In 2007 Wiltshire Police were planning to close counter services in two-thirds of its stations, despite violent crime rising by 25% in the year to 2006[2534].

Journalist Graham Duffill, who belongs to a Met Police recreational club, found police did nothing when he was beaten up by a neighbour in once salubrious Barnes Village. Despite several calls over four days the assailant remained immune. Duffill also reports how a friend's student relative was beaten up with his housemates in Eastbourne by a knife gang who lived nearby – the police were phoned but hadn't done anything[2535].

Since 2007 the banks have been responsible for card fraud investigations, details of which they are supposed to pass on to police organisations such as the City of London specialist bank fraud unit. Local police will only now act if the card is stolen. But even then

---

* Personal communication

anecdotal evidence suggests the police don't bother to utilise CCTV evidence[2536]. South Yorkshire Police halted a probe into a credit card scam due to 'lack of evidence', despite the victim giving the police the paper trail to the culprit[2537].

Cambridgeshire's Chief Constable <u>Julie Spence</u> – whose force has cash to run a police dog blog – says police can't attend every 999 call, <u>and most people don't expect them to!</u> In her Peterborough patch a man reported an attacker coming to get him. The police refused to attend, and the man was badly beaten. When the victim called 999 again because the man had returned, and was assaulting him again, the police attended eight minutes later, <u>after</u> the second beating[2538]. <u>Julie Spence</u> apologised to two nurses who, despite three calls to police, had to wait four hours for help after a gang of intruders threatened to rape them[2539].

Daily Express feature writer Simon Edge says he and his partner made at least 40 calls to complain about a two-year campaign of vandalism against their house. Police denied knowledge of their case, seemingly because of the way police record incident phone calls. If one suffers a series of low-level incidents that don't individually constitute full crimes the police refuse to give a crime number, which enables all calls to be filed under one heading. Thus the police's bureaucratic rules for recording phone calls mean they are unable to recognise the problem exists: one gets a unique CAD number every time one calls[2540].

The son of the 'British Fritzl' warned police about the horrors endured by his sisters (made pregnant 19 times) 11 years before any action was taken. Police believe the girls could have been raped thousands of times[2541].

Amateur video footage posted on a YouTube site showed police officers 'running away' from demonstrators in London[2542]. (2011)

Lothian and Borders traffic cops who found a missing nurse tied up in her freezing car boot, left her there for nearly half an hour suffering from hypothermia and dehydration: she had been in the boot for 11 days[2543].

Thousands (4,256) of criminals – including rapists, violent offenders, paedophiles and burglars – were being let off by police in just one year[2544].

When Hampshire Police supposedly investigated 92 deaths at Gosport War Memorial Hospital, a newspaper revealed some of the relatives had not been interviewed. The NMC* failed to probe nurses who were involved, which compounded the felony[2545].

In 2008 Met Assistant Commissioner John Yates said police fail to take rape cases seriously[2546]. ACPO has called for cases of consensual under-16 sex cases to be no longer automatically referred to them[2547].

When a businessman was charged with kicking a pigeon to death, the case, costing thousands, was thrown out as the police had lost the bird's body[2548].

When a university graduate was knifed to death in South London (March 2008) a witness rushed to the local police station but found it was closed at weekends. A student was stabbed to death on the steps of journalist Richard Littlejohn's local police station, which closed but had officers working inside. A Burnley father called the police non-emergency

---

* Nursing & Midwifery Council

number by mistake when he went to help his son being attacked by a gang in a public park in broad daylight – officers reached the scene too late, though there was a police station half a mile away[2549]. When drunken thugs crashed a car into a house, the householder and neighbours held them till police arrived 70 minutes later. Not only were the police called five times, but police driving past the scene wouldn't stop[2550].

Just one complaint in 60 about illegal foxhunting is fully investigated by police. When foxes are killed the hunters usually convince the police that they were accidental deaths[2551].

When young men threatened a female landowner who told them they were trespassing, she called Sussex Police, but they merely rebuked her for her folly in resisting the louts. They ignored her assurance that she could identify the offenders[2552].

Some police forces (e.g. Dyfed-Powys) are letting off 60% of serious offenders with a caution. Issuing a caution to a drunk carries the same 'target weight' as prosecuting a sex attacker. Out-of-court 'disposables' are now, for the first time in modern history, over half of all offences[2553].

Animal handler Sergeant Ian Craven was banned from keeping dogs for three years, after leaving two dogs to die in his car from hyperthermia[2554].

A report from the Constabulary Inspectorate and the CPS Inspectorate revealed that UK police don't bother checking the criminal records of foreign rapists and other criminals[2555].

Only two of the 43 forces in England and Wales have teams dedicated to finding criminals on the run (83,500 jumped bail in 2010, with only 32,000 actually prosecuted)[2556].

When burglars raided the South Oxon home of one of the UK's richest men for the second time in six weeks, he was dismayed that the CCTV images of the raiders were not publicised by the police until the day of the second robbery, allowing them to strike again – there have been several burglaries in the immediate area[2557].

A man suffered a weekend theft from his car in Abingdon police station car park. Thames Valley Police said they weren't prepared to check the CCTV because the private firm running the cameras would charge an out-of-hours call-out fee[2558].

Police minister Nick Herbert claims there is no simple link between crime levels and police numbers. H.M. Chief Inspector of Constabulary found police were so inefficient that forces could shave £1 billion from government funding without cutting services[2559].

The Greater Manchester force, which achieved the lowest rating in a police efficiency report in October 2010, provided a schedule via tweeting of the calls it receives daily – huge numbers are irrelevant and a waste of police time. But the fact that police wasted resources on preparing this schedule, just before cuts were to be announced, has been described as a shameful political exercise designed to derail police funding cuts[2560].

That there has been a police failure in dealing with football sectarianism is evidenced in the six-point plan the clubs agreed to deal with the violence; one is the greater enforcement of existing legislation to tackle the drink-fuelled Catholic/Protestant clashes[2561]. The police claim they can't stop football's hate songs, because there are too many fans to arrest[2562].

CAVEAT CIVIS

Brian Paddick says the Met's failure to stop the 2010 student riot was due to its Public Order Branch losing its most effective officers (Mick Messenger and Jo Kaye) when Ian Blair took over. Blair replaced the experienced Assistant Commissioner in charge of the Branch with controversial Tarique Ghaffur, who had little experience in the public order area. Blair also abolished the elite Special Branch, which was supposedly expert in intelligence gathering: its inadequacy was obvious in its failure to monitor crucial internet 'chatter'. There was also a failure to deploy Forward Intelligence Teams[2563].

Police can't be sacked or made redundant, being servants of the Crown, but they can be forcibly retired after 30 years' service if cuts are needed, which means the loss of the most experienced officers[2564].

Sir Ronnie Flanagan says many forces tend to 'overrecord and underdeliver'[2565].

As he left Crimewatch after 23 years, presenter Nick Ross criticised the 'tick-box mentality' and 'restrictive practices' of modern police forces, saying the latter work 'mainly for lawyers and the courts, rather than for the public'[2566].

Bailiffs charging for 'phantom visits' is a criminal offence under s. 2 of the Fraud Act, but it is alleged the police turn a blind eye, e.g. when an instance was reported to West Yorkshire Police they said they couldn't act because it was a 'a civil matter'. As with foxhunting, squatters who break into property (in England), etc., the constabulary feel they have discretion as to which laws to enforce[2567]. After sections 63-67 of the Criminal Justice and Immigration Act of 2009 tried to ban the most extreme forms of pornography, in particular images which depict life-threatening acts like sexual strangling, it soon became clear police were disinclined to investigate cases[2568].

While numbers of reported incidents of gay and transgender hate crime rise dramatically throughout Britain (e.g. over 170% in Oxford in 2010, in London's West End 21%), police forces are closing down specialist LGBT liaison officer posts. The figures must be the tip of the iceberg, as three quarters of victims fail to report the crimes[2569].

Only half of assaults and robberies in Scotland are reported to police, with one in eight victims of violent crime taking the law into their own hands[2570].

Police numbers in England and Wales fell more in 2010 than since records began in the 1970s. It is claimed Humberside have fewer officers than at any time since 1974[2571].

When WWII double agent Eddie Chapman ('Agent Zigzag') phoned English police in 1944 saying he was a British spy and needed help, he was told to go to bed.

The deaths of 13 young blacks in a fire in New Cross in 1981 were mishandled by the Met, who seemed to show an 'Establishment lack of interest'. The inquest was puzzlingly held three months after the fire, long before the police had finished their probe, so that, to the families' chagrin, open verdicts were recorded[2572].

When TV presenter Nabila Ramdani was targeted by online racist abusers, the Met (Paddington Green) responded to her concerns with disdain and silence (she names DS Steve Worthington in this regard: he, she claims, did not consider calling a woman a whore would constitute a criminal offence, and, anyway, it would 'take weeks' and 'mounds of bureaucracy' to probe the matter, and the offenders might be able to absolve themselves)[2573].

275

Text messages that could have cleared a wealthy businessman accused of rape before the ordeal of a court case were withheld from the CPS for four months by Thames Valley Police[2574].

A policeman's wife suffered 17 years of beatings by him because senior Greater Manchester officers closed ranks to protect PC Frank Chamberlain, an alcoholic who beat her throughout her four pregnancies (she suffered fractures). The wife was never asked by police how she received her injuries, and she developed a psychiatric illness. Chamberlain was jailed for 3½ years. The force refused to probe other officers over cover-up allegations involving perverting the course of justice: not surprising, as police are loathe to investigate other police[2575].

A quarter of police forces were unable to provide figures for 'honour' killings. One 'honour' victim recounted to police her father's attempt to murder her, but the officer did not understand or believe what she was being told. The girl identified her future murderers[2576].

A paedophile on the Sex Offenders Register who is running a website offering parenting advice claims Northamptonshire Police say that's OK, but they refuse to discuss individual cases[2577].

Scottish police forces are letting off travellers who are parking illegally and plaguing communities: only one group was charged with trespass in five years[2578].

The family of Moors murder victim Keith Bennett have criticised Greater Manchester Police for not diligently hunting for his body – they allegedly delayed acting on a letter that killer Ian Brady may have written revealing the burial site[2579].

Victims of the Rochdale child sex ring run by an Asian gang may sue in the light of Greater Manchester Police (and councils) missing 127 warnings from healthcare staff: the IPCC is probing the force's role. Strathclyde Police ignored signs that a paedophile was still a high risk, so failed to warn the neighbours of a four-year-old boy, who was raped as a result (police didn't check if there were children near his flat)[2580].

Police recorded nearly one million violent crimes in 2007 but either failed to detect or deal with them properly[2581].

When underage girls leave home to live with older boyfriends police usually refuse to intervene unless the girl herself complains, so making a mockery of the legal age of consent. Like fox hunting, etc. the police seem to reserve the right as to which laws to enforce[2582].

A Polish scrap metal thief caught red-handed escaped justice because he told cops he didn't know it was a crime. The firm concerned had suffered a spate of thefts[2583].

In the Camden Ripper (Anthony Robinson) case, despite a woman's body being clearly butchered, the suspect was only charged with criminal damage to a door[2584].

Strathclyde fraud police returned a mortgage fraud suspect's personal belongings over two years after raiding his home[2585].

The IPCC has reported an increase in the number of appeals to them from members of the public dissatisfied with the way their complaint was handled by the police, and the proportion of appeals upheld has also increased considerably. Most complaints are about failure to do the job or being rude, with 20% of police workers having an allegation against them. 10% (over 6,000) were of assault (80 of sexual assault). In 2011 there were 1,374 cases where police decided not to even register a complaint: in most of these the IPCC decided the police were wrong and should re-examine the case[2586]. The number of complaints against Scottish police increased by 13% in 2011, with 40% of allegations relating to incompetence, while 15% were due to rudeness[2587]. The IPCC overturned nearly two-thirds of appeals against police rulings that complaints (of rudeness, laziness or failing in their duty) are unfounded[2588].

Police repeatedly failed to bring paedophile Jimmy Savile to book in at least six sex inquiries, including: in the late 60s underage sex in the Top of the Pops changing rooms, in 1971 a 15-year-old Top of the Pops 'groupy' committed suicide (she named Savile in her diary, which reportedly was never returned by the police), abuse of patients at Stoke Mandeville Hospital, in 2007 an indecent assault at an Approved School for Girls, in 2008 Sussex Police received a complaint about a historic assault. There was even one instance of an allegation that Savile had paid off the police[2589]. A lawyer for some of Savile's victims has suggested seven police forces should face investigation: they had complaints which they didn't pursue (e.g. Surrey, Sussex and Jersey)[2590]. Surrey Police failed to interview the first Savile whistleblower, a headmistress of a school for disturbed girls.

An internal Met staff audit (2012) has revealed the crisis in morale: two-thirds of officers wouldn't be confident of giving a good service if they were members of the public. Just over a quarter trusted their chiefs 'to lead with integrity', and less than a fifth believed their senior managers' decisions were in the best interest of the communities they served[2591].

Since 2001 170 Scottish officers have sprayed others or themselves accidentally with CS, mostly involving Scotland's smallest force, Dumfries and Galloway (100 incidents in five years)[2592].

South Wales Police had four complaints against them upheld by the IPCC, including that of taking 'too long' to arrest a husband after his first violent attack on his wife (he later shot her). 24 different cops dealt with the 'domestic', but they didn't communicate with each other sufficiently[2593].

A sniffer dog was stolen from under his handlers' noses at Lancashire Police headquarters[2594].

Police are 'dumbing down' penalties for thuggery involving the victim's loss of consciousness, e.g. a £50 fine or a warning letter (police 'formal adult warnings' have risen 12% - warnings are not legally regarded as convictions). This diversion of criminals from prosecution is being made without publicity or debate[2595].

A careless Tayside policeman sparked an alert by losing his CS gas spray on duty[2596].

Surrey Police were unwilling to believe the Russian Mafia were involved in the death of a Russian whistleblower, who had been hired to investigate a serious tax fraud by a businessman. The latter's lawyers claim the police 'brushed off' their attempts to reveal the victim's role as an informant against Russian organised crime, fraud and corruption[2597].

Though there has been a record rise in police officer numbers detection rates have fallen – it may be more are replacing back-room staff lost in cuts[2598].

Figures from the IPCC showing the number of complaints not recorded by police and so referred to the IPCC are shown below.

Year (1 April to 31 March)	Total number of appeals received	Of which the number of non recording appeals received
2011/12	6476	1435
2010/11	6307	1252
2009/10	5584	1259
2008/09	4634	1009
2007/08	4141	1070
2006/07	3347	902
2005/06	2457	Not available
2004/05	1033	Not available

Table showing number of appeals to the IPCC

When a policewoman's husband saw a man breaking into his car he made a citizen's arrest and extracted a confession, till Durham Police arrived. Though they saw the damage to the car, they said there was 'insufficient evidence' to prosecute the would-be thief[2599].

Surrey Police arrested an 11-year-old pupil at his village school threatening him with handcuffing if he didn't agree to accompany them. They thought his bag of sherbet was amphetamine (they weren't allowed to taste it). The boy was incarcerated and his home searched with a warrant[2600].

Thames Valley Chief Constable Peter Neyroud said 'despised' role-playing tests for promotion-seeking officers were putting many off advancing their careers – he had too many acting sergeants and inspectors who couldn't be confirmed in their jobs because they can't pass the exam (it has a high failure rate)[2601].

A court case of racism had to be dropped because the main witness, PC Geoffrey Warburton, failed to attend. He was at motorbike races, having told colleagues he was looking after a sick relative. Warburton was not suspended while a probe into his conduct was ongoing[2602].

A Mid-Wales sheltered housing complex warden who apprehended a burglar had to wait two hours for police help, while in North Yorkshire a neighbour who rang 999 to report a burglary in progress was promised an immediate response, but found no one came. A disabled spinster returned home to find it had been ransacked despite a neighbour's call – police took 2½ hours to respond. Derbyshire Police took five days to respond to a 999 call (a gang stole a van loaded with £10,000 worth of goods), and three days to respond when a father and his young daughter were assaulted in the street[2603].

Operation Capital, costing £1m, has left Edinburgh crime victims waiting days for help, wth only one detective dealing with CID enquiries, and one probationer coping with over 20 call outs. A dead officer was left on a work rota. Morale plunged to an all-time low, as patrol cars raced around trying to replace beat cops[2604].

The number of police on the streets, compared with now, can be gauged by the origin of the term of 'beat' officer: a 'beat' was the distance one cop could call another by beating his truncheon on a metal lamppost. One chief superintendent says when he joined in 1974 he had 2,300 officers, putting out many more officers on the front line than today with a complement of 3,800. The ratio of backroom to frontline staff (compiling statistics, intelligence packages, best value, schedules of 'restorative justice' initiative, research and training projects, etc.) is often 5:1. Foot patrols attract the lowest pay and status, resulting in detected crime falling from 40 to 24 per cent in two decades[2605].

Alan Goldsmith, deputy chief constable of Lincolnshire, admitted the push to stop illegal immigrants working in the food industry had been abandoned[2606].

A retired chief inspector has damned the Avon and Somerset force he once served after he was told he would have to wait a week for an officer to investigate a theft from his greenhouse. His local police station was closed, his call being transferred to Taunton, 25 miles away. Now a district councillor he said: 'I am angry and sad at what the police service of which I used to be proud has come to'[2607].

Thousands of motorists without insurance or road tax were escaping prosecution because of a police obsession with catching speeders. The RAC Foundation said it seemed revenue is taking over from safety[2608].

In a landmark case two North Yorkshire police officers had their speeding convictions quashed because speed camera signs are illegal if surrounded by a black border. The Assistant Chief Constable of Cleveland (where the offences occurred) was not amused by his follow policemen's actions: 'To say we are disappointed with this is an understatement'[2609].

Surrey Police was one of the first forces to announce it was no longer going to respond urgently to car crimes, as a resident in the village of Warlingham found: he reported louts smashing up a car outside his house. Another neighbour phoned 999 about the 'ongoing crime' but was also brushed off. In 2002 the Met was considering 'downgrading' things like neighbour disputes and burglaries. While car crime is downgraded clampdowns on speeding attract more resources: investigation of car crime depletes budgets, speeding brings money in[2610].

When a West Yorkshire householder caught a burglar red-handed, though the latter was arrested, the police soon decided to drop the case because of 'insufficient evidence to press charges'. Two years and 15 court dates later, he finally got his man with a private prosecution[2611].

A major Met operation ('Operation Cotton') costing £25m collapsed when a judge branded it 'massively illegal' (police laundered money back to their suspects – 'state-created crime'). The suspects were laundering drug money[2612].

Two Surrey officers became stranded on top of a disused Guildford cinema while checking for squatters, so they had to ring 999 to be rescued[2613].

In 2002 the Met announced they would only take action in hit-and-run cases where there is major damage to property or vehicles or the victim is seriously injured. Such cases of 'selective policing' including the overlooking of cannabis abuse in Lambeth so that officers could attend to more serious crime. The Met said they would not proceed if they don't have the registration of the culprit vehicle, or witnesses won't agree to attend court. A woman victim was knocked down and the offending car ran over her legs, its number was taken and there were plenty of willing witnesses, but the Met refused to pursue action: her MP wrote a letter of complaint to the Met's Commissioner[2614].

Hogan-Howe admitted to a select committee that he hadn't seen the Mitchell police log or the CCTV evidence[2615].

Met WPC Karen Jones, the officer at the centre of the Anna Climbié murder case, was labelled 'supremely incompetent' for not visiting the crime scene where the child was tortured, in case she caught scabies. Seven other cops were also facing disciplinary proceedings in relation to the case[2616].

The Great Train Robbers could have been caught much earlier if police hadn't made serious errors (e.g. a local police chief asked for dog teams but was ignored)[2617].

Tony Clarke, a police officer who retired in 1998, says the lowering of the entrance qualifications and the introduction of proportional ethnic representation throughout a force (a failed American idea) has led to poorer quality cops in the last quarter of a century[2618].

A newcomer to a pit village in County Durham was terrorised by thugs: 23 windows were smashed in under a month, her car was wrecked, excreta and fireworks pushed through her letter box. 'Die Bitch' was painted on her door. In four years she reported over 180 crimes but received no help from the police, her MP or Tony Blair. The police made it clear they thought she had brought many of the problems on herself[2619].

The Police Inspectorate has revealed an alarming deterioration in discipline, e.g. sergeants can't get constables to obey orders, because the latter won't expose themselves to situations they perceive as dangerous and the former fear they will be accused of bullying if they try to force constables to comply. Many officers seem to prefer safe, pointless bureaucracy[2620].

An obsession with paperwork among police (among others) lets criminals who go on the run stay at liberty. In three-quarters of police areas officers don't enforce warrants unless they are given paper copies, which are not legally required. In some police stations custody sergeants refuse to accept on-the-runs unless they see an unnecessary paper warrant[2621].

DPP Keir Starmer says Savile could have faced trial on three occasions if police had been more thorough. Savile threatened two female officers with his legal team – they interviewed him under caution in 2009. He was eventually given 'words of advice' by a senior officer after a 2007-9 probe into four allegations by Surrey and Sussex Police[2622].

Police filed a crime report after a peacock damaged a car by pecking at one of the rubber seals[2623].

In Bournemouth it took nine policemen to arrest a speeding cyclist and put him in a police van, though he hadn't actually broken any law[2624].

Essex Chief Constable Roger Baker said in 2008 that beat officers will disappear within 15 years[2625].

The Unsolved

Police are failing to investigate about 850,000 crimes annually because they think they're 'unsolvable', with up to 90% of some offence categories being 'screened out'. Thus Hampshire Police's 'triage process' screens out 'low-level' crime. There are wide variations between forces. Most thefts are never probed[2626].

It has been asserted that Surrey Police have the worst record in Britain for solving cases, a success rate of under 21%. Overall, it has been suggested no more than 25% of crime is ever solved.

18 police officers investigated smashed windows at shamed RBS banker Sir Fred Goodwin's Edinburgh home: though the vandals were a group called Bank Bosses Are Criminals, the crime remains unsolved[2627].

Since 'statutory charging' was introduced in 2006, large numbers of cases have been dropped by police, e.g. in 2008 out of 550,000 arrests 160,000 were dropped, never getting to court[2628].

In 2008 almost half a million violent criminals escaped justice, with over half of violent crimes unsolved – the worst detection rate since records began in 1975 (when 81% of violent crimes were solved). Officers spend their time solving minor offences for which quick fines can be charged, while eschewing taking time-consuming real criminals to court[2629].

Despite reinvestigation the 2000 fatal stabbing of waiter Surjit Singh remained unsolved in June, 2013. The bungled handling of the case by police (and prosecutors) led to two critical inquiries (one found evidence of 'institutional racism' on the part of the authorities, the other identified widespread failings). The Lord Advocate admitted the victim's family had been failed[2630].

Burgled commercial firms were sent fingerprinting kits by Lincolnshire Police and told: 'Carry out DIY checks on your workers'. Scenes-of-crime officers were axed by the force and volunteers asked to help walk police dogs[2631].

'The rise of technology has coincided with a decline in traditional policing methods [and a rise in] bureaucratic roles [for officers][2632]'. This development has mirrored the decline in the solving of crimes.

Serious crimes in Scotland may go unsolved because the Scottish Police Services Authority had not (by August 2010) adopted DNA Boost, which helps unscramble DNA from other contaminating fluids at the crime scene. It is thought the number of provable cases can be improved by 15% with the system: Scottish forces have 860 unsolved attempted murders going back ten years[2633]. 'Operation Advance' (started in 2004) uses advances in genetic fingerprinting to re-examine thousands of unsolved sex crimes committed in the previous 18 years, but some police forces do not take kindly to the re-opening of cold cases[2634].

In Norfolk crimes which don't meet 'solvability' criteria are transferred to local Safer Neighbourhood Teams, who visit victims[2635].

900 sex crimes committed between 1973-1995 in the Humberside area remain unsolved. When a 45-year-old Humberside woman was raped at the age of 16, the police said she was lying: DNA evidence led to the perpetrator's conviction and imprisonment 29 years later[2636].

Police failed to investigate more than 1.5m reported crimes in 2008. 'Screening out' as unsolvable means about a third of all offences are dismissed within hours. Thus nationally about three-quarters of theft and handling offences are screened out, with 70% of criminal damage, 15% for violent offences[2637]. Police are solving only a quarter of the most serious crimes, with 3.1m offenders able to defeat justice in 2009[2638], [2639]. Police are failing to deal with almost 40% of crimes, e.g. the Met in 2008 found at least half of crimes not worth pursuing. On average only 27% of crimes are solved[2640].

Of 97,531 crimes committed in the Met's jurisdiction in 2002, the Yard claims to have cleared up less than one seventh. The truth is much worse, for the Met counts as a cleared-up crime anything where the suspect appears in court (as well as a caution accepted by the suspect). The true figure for unsolved London crimes is estimated at over 90%[2641].

Crucial DNA samples from serious unsolved crimes were left in a fridge at Kennington police station for four years. The fridge was over-filled, so that samples fell out when the door was opened[2642].

Greater Manchester Deputy Chief Constable Simon Byrne has revealed officers might ignore half of all crimes because they are 'unsolvable'. Yet his force sent three officers to admonish two boys for playing street football, warning they could get ASBOs[2643].

Police forces shelve half of all crimes unless evidence is readily available. Crimes other than 'serious' are screened using a 'solvability matrix' – the opposite of 'zero tolerance'. The Met screens out about a third of burglaries. ACPO has advised forces not to disclose their screening methods[2644].

The Met has the worst English and Welsh clear-up rates for murder, burglary and robbery, having solved just a fifth of crimes in 2007, less than half the 48% rate of the top force, North Wales. Many forces admit that clear-up rates are decreasing[2645].

Shoddy investigative work into the Lockerbie bombing by Scottish police has been alleged, now that the key piece of material evidence (fragments of bomb timer) used by prosecutors to implicate Libya is thought to be a probable fake. In the Lockerbie case there was evidence unidentified US agents had visited the site early on, and Scottish police may not have been able to control certain intelligence agencies contributing to the gathering of much of the evidence: working for different countries could have meant conflicts of interest not consistent with the search for the truth[2646].

UK detectives are struggling with an increasing backlog of over 1,100 unsolved murders, but the true total is likely to be much higher. The situation will get much worse with the phasing out of the Forensic Science Service[2647].

THE INCOMPETENT POLICEMAN

CHAPTER XIII

THE INSECURE POLICEMAN

It is a great irony that the police service is one of the more insecure public institutions.

Computers leak like sieves. Their use is supposed to have increased crime detection, but it is arguable that as police technology has advanced the crime clear-up rates have fallen dramatically.

Suffolk's Assistant Chief Constable Paul Marshall launched a high-profile anti-burglary campaign in 2011, which included a touring bus with the slogan 'Close It, Lock it, Check it.' on its side. At the same time a burglar entered Bury St. Edmunds police station through a back window that had been left open by mistake. Lancashire Police only found the lead had been stolen from the roof of their Great Harwood police station when water poured in during a rainstorm[2648]. Suffolk Police tried to establish how a mentally ill burglar – discovered by a cleaner – broke into Felixstowe Police station while all the officers were out on patrol[2649].

Security firm P & B Security, launched by the sons of Lewis 'Scooby' Rodden (jailed for a security protection racket), landed a lucrative contract to guard the new Glasgow £10m HQ of crime agency Clyde Gateway. One of the sons admitted that at one point his father was a 'consultant' to P & B. The firm's Security Industry Association licences were suspended in 2011[2650].

Rookie Strathclyde PC David Johnstone was seen talking on his private mobile just after leaving a secret briefing about a gangland murder. He resigned before three disciplinary charges against him could be heard. These revelations surfaced weeks after Deputy Chief Constable Neil Richardson had warned that 27 gangs were trying to infiltrate their people as recruits into the ranks. Three other Strathclyde officers and a civilian have been sacked for leaking information to gangsters. Of 369 cases, 218 concerned passing sensitive information about suspects, informants and investigations[2651].

Over 190 computers, laptops and data sticks containing top secret data were lost or stolen at the MOD in 2010[2652], despite police guards. A lost mobile phone containing top secret information – thought to belong to a Faslane MOD policeman – has been described as a major security breach[2653]. The MOD also loses large amounts of deadly arms, fuel and uniforms[2654].

The trial of Tayside WPC Margaret Law, accused of tipping off a drug dealer about a surveillance operation, collapsed in 2010; she was cleared of attempting to pervert the course of justice. The case cost at least £100,000 - a charge referring to a fake raid put out on the police radio was dropped before the trial[2655]. Dundee police worker Heather Fairfield illegally inspected 653 private police computer records (between 2001 and 2010) and passed the information to her son as well as others. She pleaded guilty to breaching the Data Protection Act[2656]. Another WPC from the same force Karen Howie pled guilty to leaking sensitive police computer information on a counterfeit suspect: she had at first denied the charge. Her 18-year police career ended in resignation[2657]. Poor password security by Tayside Police enabled foul-mouthed hackers to deface their website with 'online graffiti'[2658]. A Fife police sergeant and a detective were among dozens of Tayside Police disciplined for illegally accessing confidential databases: there were 22 internal probes in two years. Most culprits received formal warnings (one was fired)[2659].

MSP Tommy and Gail Sheridan were demanding (2011) a full inquiry into how CCTV footage of their police interviews was leaked to the BBC[2660].

A confidential child abuse video was left at a bus station by a blundering Strathclyde policeman. The tapes described a father's assault on his three-year-old son. Senior officers admitted the force was at serious fault'[2661].

Overnight thieves stole uniforms from a police station in Uddingston, Lanarkshire[2662].

Royal chauffeur Brian Sirjusingh – at the centre of a security scandal after taking a £1,000 bribe to give a guided tour of the Queen's cars to two undercover News of the World reporters – has landed a £30,000-a-year post as a uniformed Met custody officer. He claims to have been a Royal Logistics Corps soldier. His girlfriend had been able to access his Palace flat without security challenge. The reporters were introduced to Sirjusingh by a vice girl, and they were shown the secret security codenames used for the cars by police protection officers[2663]. A Palace guard – a member of the Met's elite Specialist Operations Unit – smuggled in a female convict: as she was a first-time visitor, the guard should have alerted his colleagues. The male guard was not suspended[2664].

A Lothian and Borders police computer bought at a car boot sale contained training details of over 200 officers, official letter templates, memos, crime scene photos (including of headless crash victims) and training manuals: none of the data was secured by passwords. The month before a dogwalker had found amnesty weapons, crucial court evidence and parts of police uniforms in a skip outside a Lothian and Borders police station at Peebles[2665].

Critics of the 2008 ACPO guideline advising police to use convicted criminals as key advisers on major operations, warn that the 'advisers' could tip off criminal associates or pass on pre-operational information. The ACPO document stresses that criminal records 'should not prevent an applicant from being appointed'[2666]. Hertfordshire Police has hired 12 serial burglars to give their officers crime-prevention advice, as part of their Choices and Consequences project. The criminals, who have to undergo drug rehab and a curfew, are being called 'security consultants' and will be spared prison terms[2667].

Scotland Yard has exposed a corruption ring within Stoke Newington, North London, which was passing on to Yardie gangsters details of secret operatives as well as names and addresses of officers.

Lothian and Borders Police investigated 26 (22 officers, four civilians) of its staff for internet and database misuse: 17 were handed either verbal or written warnings[2668].

Surrey Police sergeant and self-styled TV pet detective Colin Butcher resigned after his force began probing complaints that he passed personal information about a woman to her estranged lover. Butcher runs Complete Investigations Ltd (which specialises in marital infidelity) and The Pet Detectives agency[2669].

Top-secret entry codes to 73 London police stations were stolen from a civilian contractor's car: the Met's most senior operational commander was awakened at 1am, as the theft meant terrorists had access to 80% of the capital's stations[2670].

Thousands of items of police equipment – worth well over £700,000 – have been lost or stolen in England and Wales: three dogs (one a sniffer), 27 motor vehicles, 50 computers, 104 radio handsets, 149 satellite navigation systems, 189 mobile phones, 109 batons, 187 pairs of handcuffs, 113 torches, 141 police caps and helmets, two metal replicas of officers (lost by Durham Constabulary), a cardboard replica (from Suffolk Constabulary), a mannequin (Essex Police), an ornamental urn (Warwickshire Police), a truck (Staffordshire), 305 cones (Derbyshire), uniforms worth £6,000 (Norfolk), three flat screen TVs (Cheshire), seven laptops (Devon and Cornwall), two marked South Wales Police cars. In three years to 2010 Greater Manchester Police had £90,000 worth of gear stolen: handcuffs, uniforms, body armour, sirens, dozens of bicycles[2671]. In some instances of theft the offenders were officers or police staff[2672]. In the three years from 2008 Kent Police have had £50,000 worth of property stolen (including a police car and three pairs of handcuffs)[2673].

Robert Wright, a convicted drugs trafficker, acted as a security 'consultant' to the Sheffield Police's CCTV Liaison Unit.

Two bungling Dumfries officers found a knife on a suspect thief but let him go without checking that he was on bail and had a violent past (he was a convicted rapist and robber). Hours later he sexually assaulted a woman on waste ground[2674].

In 2006 police downgraded 999 calls, including burglaries, to non-emergencies, so that specialist squads, which absorbed beat officers, could concentrate on targets[2675].

A burglar at Logica CMG in South-East London stole (2006) the bank account details and insurance numbers of over 15,000 Scotland Yard officers, apparently including Sir Ian Blair: three missing laptops had the details of pay and pensions for civilians as well, and have not been recovered[2676].

In 2007 Scottish police were to be banned from using slang dialect (such as 'barneys', 'shooting the craw', 'jakeys') on their walkie talkies, as the national police radio system got started. Countless errors, including fatal ones, have resulted from inappropriate communications[2677].

Because they have given up regular foot patrols, the Met didn't spot the London car bombs, oozing fumes and smelling of petrol, as they sat on London streets[2678].

A myopic Met policeman who didn't have his glasses failed to spot a forged invitation letter which helped pro-hunt protestors invade the Commons. Eight of them having been waved through by him, five reached the Chamber itself, in what has been described as the biggest security scandal for centuries. A suspicious JP tried to raise the alarm twice but nearby police ignored him[2679].

Joshua Karney, one of the UK's most wanted paedophiles, was still on the run in 2008 because Barnsley police let him go with a fixed penalty for being drunk. Only later did 'routine procedure' reveal he was dangerous and on bail: he had given a false name, but fingerprints proved his identity[2680].

Travellers set up camp on a site in Bishop's Cleese, Gloucestershire, earmarked for a new £20m police station. The chairman of the council said: 'I'm a bit surprised the police weren't more conscious of security in terms of preventing access'[2681].

West Midlands Police spent nearly £4 million on private security guards based in Surrey to protect its own stations (the security budget having risen 25% in three years). The TaxPayers' Alliance says it is a waste of public money[2682]. Yet the force lost a crime prevention banner, a £40,000 liveried Range Rover, dozens of sat-navs, mobiles, patrol bikes, seized drugs, blue lights, toilet rolls. A £20,000 liveried Shogun was stolen by an anonymous officer, who was prosecuted and sacked. Cash went missing from a police gym. Computers, CS spray, breathalysers, warrant cards, handcuffs, helmets, batons, vests – there is little that hasn't been stolen[2683].

The Police National Computer for England, Scotland and Wales is not linked up with the Northern Ireland Police Service databases, the crime computer black hole having to be filled in by Google during a swoop on terrorist Johnny 'Mad Dog' Adair. Hundreds of Ulster criminals could be operating invisibly in Scotland[2684].

Armed police guarding Gordon Brown's Fife home forgot to check what Google's street view cameras had online (surfers could zoom in on Brown's gate, entry phone and CCTV cameras)[2685].

Leicestershire Police gave clearance (2010) to an ink bomb package to continue its journey to the U.S. , having failed to detect it contained explosives. Officers also disbanded the cordon around East Midlands Airport's freight distribution centre, until news arrived of the Dubai bomb, leading to the cartridge being re-examined[2686].

'I'm embarrassed', said Sir <u>Paul Stephenson</u> about the 2010 Millbank Tower invasion. There were just 225 officers to deal with 50,000 student activists, and at the height of the trouble there were just 20 police to deal with the Tower. There were even internet warnings of a potential riot, with direct action, and it took three hours to send in reinforcements. David Cameron said angrily that the police should have done more to protect his party's base[2687]. The Met has been accused of 'blundering ineptitude' re their preparations for mass G20 protests, e.g. at a security meeting officers joked about bankers' red braces and Porsches[2688].

A female member of the public was sent a police machine gun by domestic courier by mistake: it should have gone to Dorset firearms officers. Dorset Police are to continue using the supplier[2689].

<u>Peter Vaughan</u>, Chief Constable of South Wales, has said security considerations prevent him going shopping on his own[2690].

A Muslim adviser to the Met was wanted by Interpol accused of terrorist offences, but Britain refused to extradite him (he co-founded the Tunisian Islamic Front)[2691].

Senior Surrey Police officers investigating their own Deepcut inquiry prejudiced it by briefing the Army on what they found (at one meeting Major General John Kerce was present, even though he was in charge when two of the deaths occurred)[2692].

A terror raid on Pakistani students had to be brought forward when Met Assistant Commissioner <u>Bob Quick</u> committed an unforgivable security breach by inadvertently showing secret papers to the media[2693].

Boy racers in Gloucestershire have posted details of what they claim are unmarked Cheltenham police cars (fitted with speed cameras) on Facebook[2694].

More and more communities are hiring private security to offset the decline in the police's ability to do the job (e.g. in Highgate, North London). The trouble is private security firms often hire people who are insufficiently vetted[2695].

A Ghanaian woman abducted a toddler from Walworth police station, though she had been arrested for alleged immigration offences[2696].

A Met firearms expert was removed from operational duties after leaving her gun in a shop toilet[2697].

Police recruits are now being vetted by checks on social websites, instead of by the old-fashioned home visits, which could, unlike the Facebook checks, unearth drug dealer partners, etc[2698].

Official police photos of dead bodies have found their way into the hands of touts[2699].

A FOIA by 'The Sunday Post' in Scotland has found over 100 items of police property go missing annually on average, including in one year police car number plates, a hostage negotiator licence, motorbikes, log books, a £20,000 radio, speed guns, illuminated police signs, satnavs. The front gate of a station (stolen from Northern Constabulary in 2005), a public payphone (from inside a Lothian and Borders station) in 2004 and a PVC police anti-thief warning banner have disappeared, as well as all the more usual paraphernalia. The Taxpayers Alliance comments: 'It is tragically ironic that the police are unable to crack down on crime even on their own premises'[2700]. The door bell from the front counter of Livingstone police station in West Lothian was stolen, as well as three police hats, a high-vis jacket, a waistcoat and the keys for a police vehicle. A cell key was stolen from Jedburgh police station[2701]. High-security Cathcart Police Office in Glasgow has experienced a series of thefts of money and jewellery from officers' lockers: there is a policy not to have CCTV in locker rooms. In 2009 goods valued at £21,446 were stolen from Strathclyde police stations, including welcome mats, charity box, camcorder, mountain bike and pedal cycle, spectacles, motorcycle, police jacket, sugar and theatre ticket. Lothian and Borders lost an emergency outside telephone, while a Fife Constabulary staff member stole £605[2702]. A thief walked in behind a policeman (who used his swipe card) and stole four Immigration Service laptops full of secret information from the West End Central station near London's Oxford Street, supposedly one of the most secure police stations in Britain. The thief returned them because they were of no use to him[2703].

The G20 officer quizzed over a newsvendor's death should have been retired, the subject of a serious disciplinary charge, but was able to return to the same force through a vetting mistake, which has been branded 'appalling' and a 'huge embarrassment' to Scotland Yard[2704].

TV crime troubleshooter Donal Macintyre was attacked, with his wife, for being a prosecution witness: despite his high profile the police were unable to protect him. Thus his attacker was only brought to justice when his complaint to Surrey Constabulary led to a second team of investigators being put on the case[2705].

Isle of Mull police had to let a drink driver go after they locked themselves out of their station[2706].

A senior civilian counter-terrorist officer at the South West Regional Intelligence Unit and Avon and Somerset Police HQ lost his briefcase on a train – it contained Serious Organised Crime Agency documents about terrorism[2707].

Princess Beatrice's BMW was stolen when she left the keys in it while she bought a sandwich. Her police bodyguard faced disciplinary action as a result[2708]. A woman stole and crashed a £40,000 police car in Swansea when officers left the keys in the ignition[2709].

'Well that's reassuring, Mavis – our street doesn't get a mention'

Online crime maps, showing the pattern of crime levels in neighbourhoods, are compiled by police but can in fact aid local criminals, aggravating crime hotspots and increasing public fear of crime. Some forces such as West Yorkshire give the location of each offence (except burglaries) monthly. Detection rates are not included on the maps[2710].

A Strathclyde police officer, part of Operation York targeting drug dealers in Paisley and Johnstone, lost his notebook containing operations, suspects' names, etc[2711].

Dyfed Powys Police hired Dr. Marcos Hourmann as a police surgeon though he had been convicted of manslaughter. They had left vetting to an outside agency[2712].

A British jihadist in Pakistan may have worked as a PCSO in Greater Manchester Police, with access to police databases that could be useful to terrorists planning attacks[2713].

Northumbria WPC <u>Lucy Bevan</u> trawled through the national computer to identify potential boyfriends and snoop on their relatives (she accessed secret files 151 times in one month)[2714]. High-profile police officers are reported among 850,000 elite Stratfor internet account holders whose personal and other details have been hacked. Amazingly this prestigious site didn't encrypt the accounts[2715].

Two Hampshire Police patrol cars were clamped while on security duty for the Queen, with their crews inside, though the clamping firm denies this (their clamper was arrested)[2716].

Conman Andrew Waldron – jailed for a £500m fraud – managed to get jobs with Gloucestershire Police (2002), the UK Border Agency (where he was head of an investigation unit) and the Home Office (2005-2009), because no one (including the police) checked his credentials properly[2717].

In 2011 the Houses of Parliament were in the grip of a stolen property crimewave: in the first six months there were twice as many thefts as in the whole of 2010. Items taken included laptops, PC computers, iPads, satnavs, cash, keys, flowers, shoes, rugs, whisky, beer casks, golf clubs, jewellery, tax discs, a knife, a medal, a coat and an orchid. This is despite armed police guards from the Met's SO17[2718]. Amazingly the Westminster police didn't check the intruder entering the Commons Select Committee meeting grilling Murdoch on 19th July 2011: the large blancmange pie could have been something deadly. When thieves ransacked Ed Miliband's Westminster office (2012) questions were once again asked about police efficiency: an independent review of security ordered by the Speaker criticised security as 'inadequate'[2719]. Intruders tried to break into the Labour leader's Commons office <u>three</u> times in the first three months of 2012[2720].

Between 2005 and 2011 400 officers and staff have been disciplined or dismissed for computer misuse. In 2010 PC <u>Mark Bohannan</u>, a field intelligence officer with the Met's Territorial Support Group, was convicted of passing information to his cocaine-taking wife and her dealer, being rewarded with money and drugs: he was jailed for three years. Met PC <u>Robert Nicholson</u> was dismissed after starting an affair with a 14-year-old girl, whose records he had accessed. Police have run checks on neighbours before buying a house, as well as on prospective partners of their relatives[2721]. Over 200 Met police officers and support staff have been identified illegally accessing the Police National Computer over a decade, with half of the offences occurring in the three years from 2008. 400 police have been disciplined for such offences across Britain. Senior officers believe such abuse occurs 'frequently'[2722]. In the three years to 2010 almost 1,250 cases of police misusing databases came to light: only about 25% led to officers and support staff receiving criminal convictions (the worst force for the latter was Kent). A Notts sergeant was jailed for 12 months for accessing police systems illegally[2723]. Ex-Strathclyde PC <u>James Addie</u> was charged with hacking into the Scottish Intelligence Database files at Johnstone police station of some of Scotland's biggest gangsters, while another officer has been accused of security breaches relating to Scotland's most wanted man[2724]. Eight Essex police (three officers, five staff) have been sacked for illegally accessing the Police National Computer – one PC and one PCSO are facing criminal charges, while another PCSO has been cautioned. All eight passed information to people outside the force. The abuses were apparently 'routine' – in 2011, the year before, three Essex officers resigned and several other staff disciplined for computer abuse[2725]. Senior Tories, including Lord Howard and David Davies, have accused <u>Hogan-Howe</u>'s Met of subverting legal process by running a 'disgusting and improper' campaign of 'leaking and spinning' against cabinet minister Andrew Mitchell. Keith Vaz (Labour chair of the Home

Affairs Committee) said the leak showed Scotland Yard should not be allowed to investigate the case[2726].

Seized goods worth thousands go missing from police stations' secure stores, some being key pieces of evidence against criminals[2727]. Scottish public bodies have lost hundreds of items storing personal details of staff and the public (e.g. in 2009 Strathclyde Police lost an unencrypted tape with staff personal details and a USB stick with investigation details)[2728]. Warwickshire Police have had £113,000 (seized from criminals) stolen from a 'secure storage area' in their former HQ in Leek Wootton[2729].

On 20.6.11 the Serious Organised Crime Agency (SOCA) had to take its website off-line after hackers invaded it (a 'distributed denial of service' attack)[2730]. Computers used by the whole Met were compromised in June, 2011. Hackers were, only days before, suspected of shutting down the Spanish police's website[2731]. The IPCC may have been targeted by computer hackers stealing information for unscrupulous P.I.s, e.g. several of the key findings of the de Menezes inquiry were leaked before the official report was published[2732].

Greater Manchester Chief Constable Mike Todd, now deceased, had his uniform, police baton and document-containing briefcase stolen from the boot of a car parked outside his city flat[2733].

Greater Manchester Police PC Carl Waldron, working on the new intelligence base report recommended by Bichard, was suspended after he told the internet of his top-secret work shadowing serious criminals. On a sleazy website he dropped his uniform trousers and waggled his truncheon. The divorcé posed stripping his uniform to full-frontal[2734].

Lewisham WPC Hayley Cloud was paid by a car-ringing and drug-smuggling crime syndicate to access police records, leading to her being jailed for two years[2735].

In 2006 police detective Charles Fletcher was jailed for seven years for passing on sensitive information . Grampian PC Gerard McCartney was charged with revealing secret details of a paedophile to a member of the public. He denied breaching the Data Protection Act[2737].

An unnamed Greater Manchester DC was suspended after a memory stick containing the details of nearly 2,500 informants was stolen from his home in Oldham. There was also information about previous police operations, targets for arrest and officer details. It is believed the stick, which should not have been taken home, was not encrypted, again contrary to procedure. The IPCC and Home Office are involved in the case[2738].

Between January and May 2011 40 thefts from police were reported compared to 19 during 2010 and 15 in 2009[2739].

Crime author Ian Rankin has revealed a senior Lothian and Borders police chief helped him infiltrate the Tulliallan police college so that he could research his 1992 book Resurrection Men: the officer is thought to have been the chief constable Sir William Sutherland[2740].

Up to six illegal immigrants may be working at the Met[2741].

CAVEAT CIVIS

Were reporters tipped off by police when Harry Rednapp was arrested over tax charges? He was found not guilty after five years (an initial City of London probe – Operation Apprentice – cost £1m, the subsequent Met investigation up to £8m)[2742].

Strathclyde Police parked their marked patrol car full of firearms for 20 minutes on a disabled bay outside a Paisley supermarket, while they shopped[2743]. A Strathclyde officer was suspected of stealing £100,000 drugs and cash from Scotland's most secure police station, Govan in Glasgow, where terrorist suspects are questioned[2744].

In 2009 Deputy Chief Constable of Avon and Somerset, Rob Beckley, insisted on using his own non-encrypted personal computer when he joined the force in 2007, so that when it was taken from his car the thief could access anti-terrorism details, private information about police officers, as well as data on criminal probes, suspects, undercover operations, etc[2745].

Lancashire Police admitted (2008) that thieves had plundered £50,000 of their equipment from their stations and vehicles, as well as a roadside speed camera worth £24,000 in 2003[2746].

Despite an intruder accessing the northern runway at Heathrow just before a visit by the Queen (he was spotted by the public, not police patrols), the Met said they were 'happy' with security. A fortnight before, Greenpeace activists had managed to enter a plane at Terminal 1[2747].

When hackers Team Poison claimed to have eavesdropped on the Yard's counter-terrorism branch via their 'outdated' secure communication system, the Met insisted its systems had not been breached. The recordings were posted on YouTube[2748].

In 2008 £700,000 of property was stolen from police premises, including a Lancashire Police headquarters sniffer dog and a Northumbria Constabulary spaniel under special training, as well as two metal replicas of officers[2749].

Up to five armed officers are thought to have been at the Plough pub when PM Cameron's party left his little daughter there. The elite VIPSOI specialist protection officers were led by Chief Superintendent Bob Salt[2750]. The police guards are not being disciplined[2751]. In 2007 No 10's prime ministerial offices were invaded by a drug addict and his girlfriend, unchallenged by police guards[2752].

Convicted sex offender and 'con merchant' Harbinder Singh Rama was allowed by the Queen's police guards to stand close to her on the royal barge in the 2012 Jubilee[2753].

The security at the Leveson inquiry was so lax that a freelance filmmaker walked straight in to accuse Tony Blair of being a war criminal[2754].

Scotland Yard – in charge of security at the Olympics – lost the keys to Wembley Stadium. It would cost tens of thousands to replace the laser keys. 13,000 officers were guarding the Games[2755], yet undercover police smuggled a fake bomb into the Games site[2756].

There is a secret list of supposed radicals, including Al Qaeda, said to be working in British police forces. Many alleged jihadists have not been dismissed because, it is said, police don't have the 'legal power' to get rid of them. Forces such as the Met (thought to have eight infiltrators) have to rely on unreliable overseas agencies to vet foreign applicants. A policeman is understood to have been removed from his post because of concerns about his conduct after a major anti-terrorist operation[2757].

Met Royal Protection security officers at the infamous Prince Harry party in LA, where nude photos of the royal were taken surreptitiously and passed around the world, have been accused of being 'asleep at the wheel'. A witness claimed some police officers were so busy enjoying the party they were distracted from preventing pictures being taken of him[2758].

The attempt to privatise the NHS is being mirrored in the 2012 proposal to privatise the police, with essential functions handed over to security firms (who have proved less than efficient at guarding prisoners)[2759].

In a three year period Leicestershire Police had 29 items stolen from stations and patrol cars, including roof lead, helmets, handcuffs, £3,000 cash and confiscated drugs[2760].

Inadequate police checks (e.g. on the Police National Computer) are making border controls porous (only 600 entrants a year are checked against Interpol's database of stolen passports, while France and Switzerland check millions)[2761].

The Home Office has for years fallen victim to audacious heists, e.g. in 2001 it lost nine laptops, with another nine stolen in the prison service, while in the same year the Lord Chancellor's department lost almost £160,000 worth of equipment stolen, including a CCTV camera and security light. The Home Office refuses to reveal whether their own staff or external contractors were responsible for the pilfering epidemic. The MOD lost more than any other department (e.g. of 1,933 items stolen over five years, 1,173 belonged to staff charged with protecting national security)[2762].

Sussex Police swooped on a businessman's home while he was out, wrongly seized his Mercedes car on suspicion that it was involved in an accident (his car was nowhere near the accident location at the time). The car was stolen from an unlocked police car park (the CCTV covering the car park contained no film). His insurance and the police both refused to compensate him – with £100,000 legal costs his final bill reached £172,000[2763].

A gang burgled Linwood police station in Renfrewshire, stealing a computer, batons and handcuffs. Vandals also covered nearby Johnstone's police office with graffiti[2764].

CHAPTER XIV

THE LETHAL POLICEMAN

CHAPTER CONTENTS

CHAPTER XIV

THE LETHAL POLICEMAN

It can be argued that doctors kill more people than they save. Can the same be said of policemen? Under Article 2 of the Human Rights Act police have a statutory duty to preserve life.

It was announced in late 2010 that paramilitary police machine-gun squads were being established across Britain, with marksmen in all squads. MI5 and the SAS will have an input, but the development risks creating the infrastructure of a police state, changing the image of the British bobby forever[2765].

There have been 1,433 deaths following police 'contact' since 1990 (i.e. RTAs, shootings, custody deaths, etc.), but <u>no</u> convictions for manslaughter (e.g. not one conviction out of 250 deaths).

Occasionally there are reports of hero cops who <u>save</u> lives, e.g. in Edinburgh where an officer saved neighbours from a blaze which killed a man. Interestingly, the policeman's name was not released[2766]. Two women in East Lothian were also rescued from their burning homes by police. (STV Local News 9.4.13). Again, a G8 protester almost leapt to his death from an occupied five storey building but was saved from plunging by specialist officers. He was bleeding heavily from a head wound[2767]. These were the only cases the author could find in his research.

Police Chases/RTAs

Between 2004-2009 more than 150 died in police-related car accidents (79 during police pursuits) in England and Wales. In 2005-6, 48 people died in police–related accidents[2768].The IPCC estimates that between one and 11 of every 1,000 pursuits lead to a death. Most police chases are triggered by traffic offences, with some false alarms[2769]. Around 30 people are killed annually as a direct result of police chases, but by 2009 the toll had risen to 40 in a year. The IPCC says officers take 'unnecessary risks' chasing vehicles which could be caught later[2770]. IPCC chairman Nick Hardwick claims there is a lack of motivation among forces to assess the risks when pursuing offenders[2771]. In 2009 MPs (and safety campaigners) were forced to agree with a Daily Express crusade that there were too many police chase deaths[2772].

Traffic PC <u>Sean Schofield</u> killed a motorist in Lancashire while learning how to track speeding drivers (he was doing over 100mph on a road with a 60mph limit)[2773]: the force was criticised for allowing speed training on country roads (a police car killed a pensioner[2774]). Lancashire Police also chased a stolen car which crashed in Cumbria, leaving a teenage occupant fighting for his life[2775]. Another teenager was fatally injured in a crash in 2011 with a marked police van in Manchester. The incident was referred to the IPCC[2776]. In 2010 a teenage cyclist was killed by a speeding car being pursued by a police patrolman in Salford[2777]. Another three men were killed in a car (wrongly thought to be stolen) being pursued by Greater Manchester Police. A teenager was killed and another critically injured after they accepted a lift from a driver who was then chased by Greater Manchester Police. In six years 27 have died in accidents involving Greater Manchester Police vehicles – the worst record in the UK after the Met[2778].

The General Motors 'stolen vehicle slowdown' microchip may put an end to high-speed car chases (the engines of all new cars would be fitted with it)[2779].

Two friends were killed in Bradford in 2009 when their car was in collision with a stolen Mercedes, which West Yorkshire police had just started chasing 75 seconds before[2780].

Some police drivers mislead senior officers by claiming they were not in a pursuit when inspectors later find they were. A man was killed in a car which crashed near Chesterfield while being chased by Derbyshire Police in 2008[2781].

Kent PCSO Brian Johnson was jailed for two years for causing the death by dangerous driving of a schoolgirl during an adventure holiday. Johnson persisted in trying to cross a flooded river and she was drowned[2782].

A psychotic (schizophrenic) driver killed an innocent Reading couple while he was being pursued by police. Matthew Kalliher had jumped a red light in the belief he could make it change colour[2783].

Traffic PC John Dougal was not using his siren or blue lights when his patrol car, reaching speeds of over 90mph in a 30mph zone, killed a schoolgirl at night. He resigned from Northumbria Police after his conviction for causing death by dangerous driving (he was jailed for three years). An IPCC spokesman said he had taken 'totally unnecessary and unacceptable risks'. He was a qualified advanced driver[2784].

10,000 lives could have been saved if speed cameras had not replaced traffic police on motorways[2785].

A schoolboy was killed when he crashed in his father's Mercedes (which he had stolen) in a high-speed police chase, while in 2008 eight officers were taken off driving duties: a biker was killed after a 50 mile chase by a convoy of police cars and the force aircraft. Later the same year two suspect drug dealers' car hit a wall in Oldham while fleeing a patrol: an innocent passenger died with them.

A teenager died and another was critically injured when a stolen car being followed by police careered into a railway bridge in Rugby, Warwickshire[2786].

A pensioner was killed in 2009 by a marked police car answering an emergency call[2787].

A woman's arm and leg were fractured after police driver Alasdair Sharp crashed his police custody van into her in Holyrood Park, Edinburgh – she then suffered a stroke. The officer admitted careless driving[2788].

Not all police crashes end in fatalities. A couple were arrested at Balmedie (Aberdeenshire) when their car crashed into a police Range Rover while they were being chased by another police vehicle[2789].

Essex police chiefs were criticised in 2009 for staging a fake car chase for a 'cops and robbers' Channel 5 show. The 'thief' was pursued by four officers in two 150mph patrol cars, sometimes breaking the speed limit and using their blue lights. It was all filmed from an expensive helicopter[2790].

A driver who killed a teenage girl (Jessica Harrison) during a Staffordshire police chase (they had tried to caution him for not wearing a seat belt) was jailed for eight years in 2010 (he had a string of driving convictions[2791]).

Special constable James Denton was jailed for three years for causing the death of a young mother in Portsmouth by dangerous driving. He had been using his mobile phone. The beat officer also worked as a scenes of crime investigator[2792].

Two Algerians were killed in Luton late at night by an out-of-control marked police car which had collided with another car. The police said their car had been showing lights and siren, but some witnesses dispute this. The two officers in the car were unharmed[2793].

The driver of a minibus died after crashing into an M74 barrier during a high-speed police chase in 2010[2794].

A boy run over by an unmarked police car was then struck by other cars[2795].

A 20-year-old man was killed by a train as he tried to escape from police endeavouring to stop a car they believed was uninsured[2796].

A grandmother and mother of three taking a stroll with her husband in Bromley in 2008 was killed by a police car: Met PC Malcolm Searles was jailed for 6½ years for the killing during a 104mph 'joyride' in the town: he raced his patrol car around residential streets to 'show off'. Searles was delivering a birthday card with siren and lights blazing[2797]. But the IPCC refused to comment on reports that the driver was newly-qualified and had gone for a takeaway or was delivering a birthday card. Does this sort of obscurantism on the part of the IPCC encourage the public to consider it biased in favour of the police? The 'black box' recovered from the patrol car disclosed the terrifying speeds and route it had taken.

It was claimed PCSO Helen Murray caused a crash that killed her son and his best friend[2798].

17 officers in England and Wales have been killed (2003-2008) while driving home from night shifts, so West Midlands Police are giving them a free taxi home[2799].

Former Somerset and Avon police inspector Keith Bridges crashed his car in France while drunk, killing his wife, stepdaughter and two passengers, but walked free with a two-year suspended sentence for

PC Malcolm Searles

'homicide involontaire' from a court in Bergerac. When in the force he was part of a special unit which provided drivers for dignitaries[2800].

PC Thomas Hart

A bride-to-be was killed when a police van driven by Cleveland PC Thomas Hart ploughed into her car: he denied causing death by careless driving[2801].

Former policeman Graeme Lamb was arrested on suspicion of causing his wife's death by dangerous driving (a lorry ran her over in Gateshead). He was later charged with manslaughter[2802].

Sussex Police driver Stewart Chalmers skidded on ice and killed a young pedestrian. The force investigated their own officer and he is now back at work[2803]. Lincolnshire police inspector Paul Stubbs, whose careless driving killed a father-of-two, also kept his job[2804].

Grampian PC Mark Davey was killed aged 28 when his patrol car crashed into a tree in 1995[2805].

A motorcyclist was killed when a Dorset Police speed camera van made him brake and skid. The IPCC had to decide whether the accident came into the category of 'death following police contact'[2806].

A teenage girl was killed in North Staffs by a car being pursued by police with sirens and blue light over the matter of a seat belt not being worn[2807].

Grampian Chief Inspector Tom Forrester was cleared of inciting a junior officer to drive dangerously, causing two other vehicles to have an accident. The police driver was given an absolute discharge for careless driving[2808].

Numbers of road deaths are at their lowest level for 85 years despite more and more speed cameras being switched off[2809].

A 21-year-old man died in 2007 after jumping into the icy River Ayr to escape from police.

A policeman was jailed for killing a woman while drink-driving in Berkshire[2810].

A drink-driver crashed into a police patrol car near the Forth and Clyde canal in Dunbartonshire. There were no injuries[2811].

A child and a man were knocked down in Dundee by a marked Tayside Police car, which wasn't responding to an emergency[2812].

Lothian and Borders Police declined to name a policeman charged with drink-driving after allegedly crashing into several vehicles, while attempting to flee from fellow cops. He has not been suspended. Another Edinburgh PC – Hamaad Khalid – was charged with traffic offences while off-duty (a father of three died after being knocked down), but the case was dropped. An outside force (Central Scotland Police) is to probe how Lothian and Borders handled the crash, e.g. Khalid drove off but was not breath-tested when he returned to the scene. The dead man's widow is suing Khalid[2813].

Despite North Wales Police abandoning a car chase (the driver was a drunk burglar), the errant car hit an oncoming 4x4, being literally torn in two by the impact. Miraculously no one was seriously hurt[2814].

A 52-year-old pedestrian was killed by a Tyneside police car on 7.1.12, a Saturday night: the two officers in the car suffered minor injuries. The incident was referred to the IPCC[2815].

A police car was destroyed in a horrific smash with a van in Renfrewshire on the A8 in late January, 2012: two officers had to be taken to hospital[2816].

An unmarked West Midlands Police car killed a Chinese student on a pedestrian crossing while responding to a call about a stolen car[2817].

The football fan who fell through a garage roof while being chased by police died two days later[2818].

Scots PC David Brown was accused of killing a cab driver by dangerous driving, having admitted causing death by careless driving. He had crossed a red light on a 999 call. He was cleared but the victim's family was 'deeply shocked and disappointed'[2819].

A study by the LSE and The Guardian of the 2011 summer riots which questioned 130 police talked of a 'war against the police'. Inefficient deployment (e.g. too weak in the worst areas) and incompatibility of police radio channels were just two factors found that explained the initial policing fiasco. One young person died after being chased by police and crashing his moped[2820].

PC Christian Parker, the Met driver of a crashed patrol car (it hit a tree), died shortly after he was responding to a 999 call. His female colleague was in a serious condition in hospital[2821].

In 2003 a Merseyside Police 4x4 ploughed into 85-year-old Clara Laurenson after colliding with a car as it negotiated a junction at St. Helens, where officers were later ordered not to rush any more to catch criminals red-handed, replacing the 10-minute target for 999 calls[2822].

North Yorkshire PC Andrew Branagh died when his patrol car, on the way to an accident, crashed into a tree[2823].

A 13-year-old London girl was killed by a police patrol car shunting her vehicle into traffic lights while chasing an uninsured car – three family members were injured[2824].

In Newcastle-upon-Tyne a teenager was killed by a squad car doing 100 mph catapulting her into the air; the car, according to some witnesses, showed no headlights or flashing lights and its sirens weren't activated[2825].

Dorset Special Constable <u>Collette Carpenter</u>, trained to fine drivers for using mobile phones, killed a biker while using her phone at the wheel. She escaped prosecution even though she lied to police about receiving a call while driving[2826]. She later admitted using the phone throughout her entire journey[2827]. Would a member of the public have been prosecutred in these circumstances?

A West Yorkshire Police van rolled forward while unattended, killing a pensioner[2828].

PSNI WPC <u>Philippa Reynolds</u> died in an RTA, with two other officers in their unmarked car suffering minor injuries. The police had turned into the path of a speeding suspected stolen 4x4[2829].

Shootings with Firearms

The HMIC report on the Tottenham riots warns that police may shoot arsonists in future: some say such provocative bravado may be counter-productive, inflaming instead of dampening unrest (this is what usually happens in the US)[2830].

33 people have been shot dead in 15 years since 1995, (22 people were also injured by shooting in a six year period), but in only two of the shootings were marksmen identified[2831] by the IPCC – another nail in the IPCC's coffin in terms of their partiality. Neither the Metropolitan Police, ACPO nor the Home Office will reveal the percentage of police who are armed, but former Flying Squad commander John O'Connor estimates it at 10%. Brian Paddick thinks the old-fashioned bobby is being transformed into a high street storm-trooper. A review of Operation Kratos means that when confronted with a suicide bomber the police can shoot without shouting a warning[2832]. Use of firearms by the British police has reached a record high level, prompting fears that police are being armed "by stealth".

Police are calling for permission to use dumdum bullets – banned for use in war since 1899 – as they cause almost instant death. They were used to kill de Menezes. What was the Met's motive in taking the unprecedented step of offering the de Menezes family an immediate ex-gratia payment[2833]? In 2006 anti-terrorist police shot <u>Mohammed Abdul Kahar</u> in the shoulder using normal bullets, and he survived (he was innocent of bomb-making). In 2008 a Guildford man, mental patient David Sycamore, was killed by Surrey Police because they wrongly thought he was pointing a gun at them[2834]. The Met's 3,000 firearms officers are adopting hollow point 'unsurvivable' ammunition for standard use: the bullet destroys vital organs by expanding inside the body[2835].

Some Met officers are thought to have attended terror training camps in Pakistan – in one force an officer has reportedly circulated videos of beheadings and bombings in Baghdad. One would-be terrorist was about to try to become a cleaner with the Met, but was jailed for nine years[2836].

Depressed pensioner <u>Mervyn Tussler</u> was shot dead at his warden-assisted retirement home after refusing to surrender to police. He may have been brandishing a firearm[2837]. The pensioner, a collector of antique guns and a gun club member, had apparently been told by social services his wife would be taken permanently into care, leaving him devastated[2838].

A man seriously wounded by police marksmen at Carfin Station in Lanarkshire was only carrying a piece of wood, though he had phoned police to tell them he was armed[2839].

An unidentified Greater Manchester Police police officer shot colleague PC Ian Terry dead in a training session that went wrong in 2008 – the victim, who wasn't wearing a protective vest, had brandished an unloaded weapon, playing the role of a suspect. The killer officer claimed he wasn't told the role-playing exercise had been altered to a 'shoot scenario'[2840], and wasn't prosecuted, the CPS ruling that there was insufficient evidence, to the fury of the widow[2841]. Terry was shot dead by a single shotgun blast in a disused warehouse – locals had not been told the police were using it for firearms training. The last training death shooting was that of Special Constable Arthur Guest in 1941 by his instructor. At least three more officers have been killed by accident[2842]. In 2007 a police worker was accidentally shot in the chest at the Thames Valley Police HQ during a 'firearms awareness' training session by PC David Micklethwaite (the revolver was a powerful Magnum). PC Samuel Lock was killed inadvertently in 1950 while cleaning a pistol at a police station.

An inquiry has found there was no legal justification for the shooting dead of black criminal Azelle Rodney (he was shot six times), despite the IPCC finding no charges should be brought against any police officer. His mother has demanded unreserved apologies from both the police and the IPCC (BBC1 News 5.7.13).

Barrister Mark Saunders, shot dead by police in 2008, was a former T.A. soldier and had over 200 rounds of ammunition, though his shotgun was empty, with the safety catch on, when the weapon was found beside his body[2843]. Despite being categorised by police as being in a 'special population group' (i.e. vulnerable person), seven officers fired at him, out of 59 firearms officers armed with 100 weapons (including Heckler and Koch MPS carbines, 9mm Glock 17 pistols, G3 assault rifles, shotguns, CS gas, baton rounds and tasers). The police had repeatedly reassured Saunders that no one would shoot him[2844]. He begged to see his wife, but wasn't allowed, and had been taking antidepressants[2845]. The coroner concerned in the case has called for a return to 'common sense' policing, and criticised the firearms jargon which involves at least six protocols in over 300 pages of instruction: Met Police (97 pages), ACPO (90 pages, 32 pages and 46 pages), Home Office (18 pages), National Policing Improvement Agency (22 pages)[2846]. The coroner also wrote to the Commissioner saying he should note the jury's verdict that police didn't properly consider the victim's vulnerability (e.g. they refused to let his best friend or wife through the cordon). The police had allowed Saunders to renew his firearms licence only months before. Commander Superintendent Michael Wise was kept in the dark about key developments, e.g. the fact that bronze commander Inspector Nick Bennett delegated some of his duties to another officer[2847]. Saunders' mother said of the anonymous police marksman who shot her son (one of several who allegedly inserted popular song titles in their evidence): 'Was it all such a game … If this man can approach the inquest with such an attitude it makes you wonder about how he approaches shooting his gun to kill a man'[2848].

Detective Superintendent Brian Craddock retired on health grounds shortly before a report into his handling of the police killing of Scots father Harry Stanley in Hackney, the latter's family accusing Craddock of a whitewash. The victim was returning home with a chair leg in a plastic bag; when he was challenged from behind by two firearms officers , who had been misinformed about an Irishman with a gun in a bag. As he turned round he was shot dead. A second inquest jury overturned an earlier open verdict and decided the shooting was unlawful[2849]. The police tried to make out Stanley had a 'death wish' because of a history of cancer (he had recovered), and that the shooter acted in self-defence. The widow says rather than investigating why they killed her husband they were trying to find some dirt on him - they wanted the family tree, and took names and addresses of those who had come to pay their respects. The identities of the killer cops have not been revealed[2850]. See further attempts to smear the innocent in Appendix IV.

Surveillance officers felt de Menezes wasn't about to detonate a bomb, was not armed nor acting suspiciously. They wanted to detain him, but were ordered to hand over control to the firearms section[2851]. Three witnesses to the de Menezes shooting contradict the two killer officers' claim that they yelled an 'armed police' warning[2852].

Despite gunning down an innocent man at point-blank range, officers are allowed to write up their notes <u>together</u>. Such collusion is not allowed to civilian witnesses, as acknowledged by the IPCC. Yet the IPCC claims that if they banned conferring, officers might refuse to give any account at all. This 'right to confer' of the police dates from the 1950s[2853] and is contained in ACPO's Manual of Guidance on the Police Use of Firearms. Met Deputy Assistant Commissioner Cressida Dick (later promoted) led the chase from her Scotland Yard control room, whence she gave the order to 'stop' him. She has admitted there was 'miscommunication' during the operation[2854]. De Menezes was at first thought by Met commanders to be suicide bomber Hussain Osman, but one log, made 20 minutes before the shooting, noted he had been ruled out as the suspect. Yet Cressida Dick confirmed: 'It is him'[2855].

Police marksmen are taught not to shoot at limbs but to aim at the torso.

Scotland Yard's secret elite CO19 firearms police unit is 550 strong. A sergeant with the unit says they're a necessary evil[2856]. Could this comment apply to the police in general?

Friends of Guildford Cathedral victim <u>David Gamose</u> claim he did not fire at police, that his gun was a replica[2857].

Unarmed father-of-two <u>Anthony Grainger</u> was shot dead in 2012 in a parked car by Greater Manchester Police a few weeks after being wrongly suspected of stealing a memory stick containing the names of nearly 1,100 police informants. Even after being cleared, he was subjected to six weeks of covert surveillance (Operation Shire), being described to the firearms team as highly dangerous. The stick was the second one to go missing in 10 months. 14 months after the incident the IPCC probe had still not reached a conclusion[2858].

A Rastafarian brandishing a novelty cigarette lighter shaped like a gun was shot dead by police and in 2001 a Liverpool schizophrenic holding a sword was also despatched by a firearms unit. In 1998 a naked, unarmed man was shot dead by officers in his own home[2859].

Between 1991 and 2001 police in England and Wales shot no fewer than 41 people who turned out not to be carrying a firearm. Not one of the officers has been convicted of any criminal offence; the vast majority were not even prosecuted. In the fatal St. Leonards raid, where police suspected a drugs dealer named Tosh was in possession of cocaine and a firearm - they were wrong on all counts - the subsequent Kent Police inquiry showed that three officers knew this and lied to get authorisation for the raid.

THE LETHAL POLICEMAN

Paul Whitehouse

The Gangmasters Licensing Authority (GLA) quango has been accused of exploiting the publicity engendered by its false claims that it had uncovered child Romanian slaves in Worcestershire, to save itself from budget cuts. A GLA policy officer whistleblower revealed the 'sham'. The GLA's chairman Paul Whitehouse has been accused before of misleading the public: he was Sussex Chief Constable when naked and unarmed James Ashley was shot dead without warning (while naked in bed) in his Hastings home in 1998 during a police raid. Whitehouse asserted Ashley was wanted for attempted murder, but former Hampshire Chief Constable Sir John Hoddimott accused him of lying. Whitehouse resigned, with a reported £1 million pay-off[2860].

For the royal 2011 wedding over 550 members of the Met's CO19 specialist firearms unit were told to 'shoot to kill' in a secret briefing[2861]. A 2011 HMIC review of riot tactics proposed the use of lethal force against arsonists in future[2862].

Four Lincolnshire Police marksmen shot dead a stray cow in a Grantham car park[2863].

Two senior SAS officers who train police firearms officers say the latter are trigger-happy and too concerned with their personal image – looking 'gung ho'. There is no assessment of psychological or physical fitness, no profiling. The soldiers describe a series of alarming incidents at Hereford, but they couldn't fail policemen they thought unsuited to the job. Many security firms in Iraq wouldn't employ former firearms officers. The SAS say firearms units were small 'cliques' with professional standards below those of the military[2864].

The Tottenham area erupted in riots (August 2011) after a Met CO19 Unit marksman shot dead a local man, about whom a man who knew him said: 'I know the police were harassing him ... following him. If you're from Broadwater Farm, police are on you every day, you're not allowed to come off the estate. If you come off the estate they follow you'[2865]. The family of Mark Duggan are to sue the Met if he was given no chance to surrender before their shooting him dead[2866]. In November 2011 two officers were being investigated re the gun reportedly found in the possession of Mark Duggan, whose shooting dead by police triggered riots. The gun was a converted replica Bruni pistol. It was discovered wrapped in a sock on the other side of a 14ft fence: witnesses say they saw the police throw it there[2867].

North Wales Police authorised the use of firearms on almost 1,000 occasions between 2001 and 2005. Welsh MPs noted that the rural north of Wales saw a much greater deployment of armed officers than the cities of South Wales[2868]. Likewise, officers of the Civil Nuclear Constabulary, who patrol with machine-guns the Caithness site (Dounreay) of the former power plant, have been accused of harassing holiday makers and locals[2869].

In 2011 baton rounds were pre-authorised for the first time for a planned protest march on the British mainland. 17 people (including eight children) had been killed in N. Ireland with rubber or plastic bullets[2870].

Because of the background to the 2012 Peterlee double murder/suicide by gunshot, Durham Constabulary referred the case to the IPCC. The killer's family had informed the Durham Police three years before of his self-harming intentions. Durham Police had returned triple killer Michael Atherton's six guns when he denied he would shoot himself. They apparently did not interview his partner (which happens in Canada), though they knew he had a history of domestic violence between 2005 and 2007[2871]. His three shotgun licences and three more specialist section one licences (which have tighter controls for firearms such as semi-automatic rifles, pump-action shotguns) were continued till the New Year tragedy[2872].

In 1987 the PCC decided not to act against Inspector <u>Douglas Lovelock</u>, who shot and crippled <u>Cherry Grace</u> – the incident triggered the Brixton riot of 1985.

Ex-con <u>Michael Fitzpatrick</u>, who had committed three armed robberies, was shot dead by Sussex Police in 2011 when they went to arrest him. He allegedly told a friend he knew the police were out to kill him. The police said he 'pulled out a handgun'[2873].

Most police shooting victims are posthumously recognised as no real threat to the public. Deborah Coles of "Inquest' said: "These deaths are not subjected to scrutiny by a public inquiry, and so the lessons are not learned and police feel they can act with impunity". Coroner Dr. Stephen Chan sparked outrage when he instructed a jury that they could not decide a Scots grandfather had been unlawfully killed by police marksmen in 1999.

A 31-year-old man with a psychiatric history who went on a knife rampage died after being shot by a Bedfordshire Police Taser outside his mother's home[2874].

Criminal <u>Anthony Grainger</u> was shot dead through a car windscreen in an ambush of a gang of robbers in the Cheshire village of Culcheth (Grainger's £6m drugs trial had collapsed when a juror contacted a defendant on a social network). He had been linked to a police corruption plot (attempting to bribe a drugs squad policeman with a BMW car, etc. to pass on secret information)[2875]. By April 2012 no officer had been interviewed by the IPCC over <u>Mark Duggan</u>'s death, and the 31 firearms officers involved in the fatal shooting of <u>Grainger</u> (he was weaponless) refused to be interviewed. The family say 'the cover-up starts on day one'. Grainger had been arrested in August, 2011, on suspicion of stealing very sensitive information from a policeman's car[2876]. The police had no real reason to surmise that Grainger or his two companions were armed before he was killed by a single bullet from a police machine gun: the officer may face a murder charge (he remains anonymous)[2877].

Scot <u>Ian Henderson</u> was a colonial policeman showered with honours by the British government for crushing the Mau Mau uprising in Kenya (1952-1960), using brutal dirty tricks which have been condemned since on human rights grounds. He then became 'head of security' in the British Protectorate of Bahrain, remaining there long after it became an independent autocracy. He and his staff would be accused of torture and murder of opponents of the ruling Sunni al-Khalifa family over the next few decades: they had an appalling record on human rights. The Met reluctantly began an investigation into Henderson's 'crimes' but it came to nothing (he was known as the 'Butcher of Bahrain', but he had used electrode torture before in Kenya as a member of Special Branch). Police from Britain helped to suppress Mau Mau. Henderson was awarded the King's Police and Fire Services Medal[2878].

Several police trainees have been shot dead and have died of CS Gas inhalation (one canister struck an officer fatally in the chest)[2879].

A report by Birmingham City University criminologists on 'family annihilation' between 1980 and 2012 included policemen and soldiers among the 59 male culprits. It argued the increasing incidence of the crime was due to 'masculinity in crisis'[2880].

Inadvertent killings

Gloucestershire traffic cop David Driver left an unconscious man to die by the roadside and then lied in his notebook to cover up his fatal inaction. He pleaded guilty to perverting the course of justice[2881].

When a 41-year-old father-of-two with a package of heroin was ordered by an Ayrshire policeman to spit it out he tried to swallow it, choking to death[2882].

Off-duty Aberdeenshire WPC Diane Taylor believed a murder accused that there was no one in a burning car, in which his wife died[2883].

Police held back would-be rescuers as three people were burned alive in a house fire near Doncaster, saying they had to wait till firemen arrived. South Yorkshire Police refused to say when exactly the Fire Service did arrive[2884].

Vulnerable David Askew was unlawfully killed after being subjected to years of vandalism and mockery by feral youths. Greater Manchester Police visited him regularly, but, despite his learning difficulties and physical frailty, they thought he was part of the problem – his mother had called the police 88 times. No one was prosecuted over his death. The IPCC pointed out the force's 'systematic failures', especially neglecting to link the calls made as constituting evidence of a true hate crime[2885].

'Boy racer' Jason Brain, who had multiple driving convictions, killed seven (including himself) when he smashed into an oncoming car – he had been reported to police a week before driving a motorbike dangerously, but nothing seems to have been done, despite Gloucestershire Police's claim that they take all reports of illegal motoring extremely seriously. When the husband of the witness who had reported Brain with no result followed up with another visit to the police station, he was told police had done nothing because there seemed to be a vendetta against Jason: people were always reporting him. Brain drove without a licence, insurance or MOT[2886].

Ex-cop James McCormick's fake explosive/dead body detector, based on a useless plastic gold ball finder (Gopher), fooled the world for a decade. Police and other forces as well as Britain's Home Office hadn't tested it before buying it. A false sense of security given by the device may have led to innumerable deaths[2887].

When a Blackburn man tried to save his son from a gang he was stabbed to death – he had phoned police on a special line given him after a previous attack but couldn't get through. When he rang a non-emergency number (to which it might take police five days to respond), he was told to stop shouting. The IPCC has launched a probe into Lancashire Police's handling of the calls[2888],[2889].

The IPCC criticised police in the case of violent schizophrenic Nicola Edgington, who beheaded a stranger in the street, having made several calls to the police warning she was very dangerous. Though they took her to a hospital secure unit she was allowed to leave because the police didn't check their computer, which would have told them she was a matricide[2890].

South Yorkshire Police prevented neighbours from rescuing children from a burning house: a three-year-old and its parents died. The officers weren't reprimanded, rather they were commended[2891].

When the hunt was on for the savage killer and sexual mutilator of trusting women victims, Neville Heath, the police instructed newspapers not to print his picture. His next victim, Doreen Marshall, would probably have recognised him – instead, she fatally accepted his invitation to dinner (her mother had shown her an article about him in the Daily Mail)[2892].

Shooting with Tasers

Tasers were fired by UK police in 2011 at least 1,081 times (compared with 744 in 2010).

Amnesty International claims 334 people died between 2001 and 2008 after being struck by Tasers in the US, where the X-Rep (used in the Moat stand-off) was responsible[2893]. One theory of the Moat suicide is that the Taser triggered the fatal reaction[2894]. Moat's family believe the police fired the fatal shot[2895]. Rothbury villagers have accused police of putting them in danger by allowing 'business as usual' while Moat was on the loose[2896].

Strathclyde Police were issued with Tasers for the first time, in 2010, to non-firearms officers (who had used them 29 times since 2005)[2897].

Bodybuilding taxi driver, 27-year-old Dale Burns from Barrow in Cumbria, died after being Tasered three times at his home. He had been smashing up his property[2898]. The Chief Constable of Cumbria has admitted he knew the Moat Taser hadn't been authorised in the UK, and that he didn't know what its effect might be[2899].

The death of a Tasered Widnes man may have been due to his stabbing himself[2900], but it was the third Taser-linked death in a week.

Met Chief Bernard Hogan-Howe wants the use of Tasers to mushroom, with every car in his force carrying a 50,000 volt stun gun. In seven years of Taser use in the UK (since 2004) there were three deaths. At least two members of the Met Police Authority thought it a very bad idea (one said: 'it would do irreparable damage to the reputation of our unarmed police service'). Ethnic minorities are more likely to be Tasered[2901].

Within a week in 2011 three people (including Dale Burns – see above) died in incidents involving police use of stun guns or pepper spray: 53-year-old father-of-two Philip Hulmes, who had threatened suicide, died half an hour after being Tasered, and 25-year-old Jacob Michael died after being pepper sprayed. The charity 'Inquest's Helen Shaw says: 'For too long there has been a pattern of cases where inquest juries have found overwhelming evidence of unlawful and excessive use of force or gross neglect, yet the police do not seem to have learnt the lessons from these previous deaths … it is imperative that the police are reminded that they cannot act with impunity'[2902].

A Stoke-on-Trent motorist died several months after being Tasered (and then allegedly injured by police carrying batons). He had been arrested for alleged motoring offences. The IPCC was probing 'police use of force'[2903].

A suspected car thief was apparently not sufficiently incapacitated by being Tasered up to four times, so was shot in the stomach, leg and hand with dum-dum bullets in south east London (2012). In 2007 Brian Loan was the first UK man to die after being blasted by Taser (he had apparently been in good health)[2904]. Witnesses claim Met marksmen Tasered a black university graduate after shooting him four times with live bullets: he was recovering in a secure psychiatric ward at Bethlem Royal[2905].

Jordan Begley died after being shot by Taser by Manchester Police called to a neighbours dispute. He had a heart condition. The force fires Tsasers more than any other force[2906].

Though police Taser policy prohibits using one where there is flammable liquid, a Plymouth man died after being turned into a human fireball when an officer Tasered him. He was holding a fuel canister in one hand and a naked flame in the other[2907].

Police want to be armed with cutting edge assault rifles as used by the British Army – it would be the first time they shared the same type of weapons[2908].

A man holding a can of flammable liquid suffered life-threatening injuries after being Tasered by a Plymouth policeman. He was set on fire[2909].

Negligence Killings/Manslaughter With Police Involvement

15 major forces decided to take no further action (NFA) against almost 3,000 domestic violence arrestees, soon after the latter had been questioned about similar offences: they went on to commit murder, rape and assault (30 other forces couldn't provide figures, so the problem may be three times as great). Abused women have to call the police on average three times before action is taken[2910].

An intoxicated man was run down and killed on the M57 because Merseyside police regulations prevented two policemen helping him – they didn't have the 'right training' or 'equipment' (strobe lights and high-visibility vests). When they radioed for help the operator got the location wrong, and the call was wrongly given low priority, so the victim was hit by two cars before police arrived[2911].

Derbyshire Police admit they arrested the ex-partner of Rachael Slack – he had a history of mental illness – after his threats to kill her. Released, he stabbed to death Rachael, her son and himself a few days later[2912].

When PC Richard Allen started making advances to a Polish girl whose complaint against her abusive partner he was investigating, the partner threw her to her death out of the window[2913].

The parents of murdered black teenager Stephen Lawrence received £320,000 for police bungles which caused further distress, and a six-figure sum was paid to the family of Victoria Climbie, murdered while she was in the case files of child protection detectives. The family of de Menezes got over £100,000 from the Met in an out-of-court settlement[2914].

A violent schizophrenic, with a long history of convictions, stabbed to death a man on a bus who had asked him to stop throwing chips. The killer should not have been out and about: he had been released from a London jail despite Merseyside Police having a warrant out for his arrest for burglary[2915].

When police arrived in response to a terrified woman to deal with a shooting, they sat in a lay-by discussing how they could ensure their own safety[2916].

A pregnant mother who killed herself and her three children turned Suffolk Police away from her home just hours earlier – they were probing claims that the children's father had been stabbed, but did not insist on entry[2917].

A pensioner who was stabbed and beaten to death by her mentally ill husband told Sussex Police a few days before that she feared for her safety after he was discharged from a mental hospital[2918].

Suffolk Police (and others) were accused of disastrous failures that ended in a baby's murder by his violent father, who had a prison record. Police had been called twice to incidents[2919]. The man convicted of the Suffolk prostitute murders was stopped by police part way through his killing spree[2920]. Suffolk Police stopped 'Suffolk Strangler' Steve Wright twice during his murder spree but released him to murder three more women[2921].

Cheshire Police were called twice to incidents involving a Muslim teenager and her family, and she had made an impassioned plea to be saved from her abusive parents a few months before she died, in what is thought to have been an 'honour killing'[2922].

Essex Police were told by Jeanette Goodwin five times about her dread of a jealous ex before she was stabbed (2011) and the same force took 'inadequate action' over the former partner of Christine Chambers, who was shot along with their daughter at their Braintree home[2923].

A man found dead in a harbour in 1997 may have been in a fight with an off-duty Northern Constabulary officer – the force was criticised by another force's chief constable for 'inexplicable' blunders in their inquiry. A PM (postmortem) found the victim's injuries were consistent with a kicking[2924].

11 witnesses claimed they saw members of the Met's Special Patrol Group striking Blair Peach, who was knocked unconscious during an anti-National Front protest in Southall in 1979 (he died the next day). A previously secret police report concluded that a police officer was likely to have struck the fatal blow. Six retired officers involved have all been unable or unwilling to identify the assailant: officers lied and obstructed the inquiry. The report has had hundreds of pages blanked to protect identities, despite Sir Paul Stephenson advocating transparency! The case took 20 years to resolve. The death has been likened to the Ian Tomlinson case. One pathologist thought Peach had been struck by a lead-weighted rubber cosh or a hosepipe filled with lead shot – such weapons were carried by police in 1979[2925]. After the riot a police raid on the SPG's offices found a horde of unauthorised weapons (e.g. illegal truncheons and knives): one officer was trying to dispose of a metal cosh, while another turned out to be a Nazi supporter[2926].

It has been suggested that in large crowds of police a 'group mentality' takes over, so that they go looking for trouble.

A Cleveland Police PC was convicted of killing his wife (he stabbed her 96 times) because of diminished responsibility: <u>Graham Jones</u> went free after five years[2927].

In 2010, 18 years after <u>Rachel Nickell</u>'s murder, the Met apologised publicly to her former partner and son for bungling the probe into her murder. The IPCC said she and her daughter could have been saved if police had acted on tip-offs that Robert Napper was a serial rapist: in 1992 he ignored a letter to attend a police station, but no action was taken. He was also eliminated from the 'Green Chain' rape inquiry on the ground that he was too tall. He was jailed for weapons offences. Despite his previous conviction and being found loitering near a park, again no action was

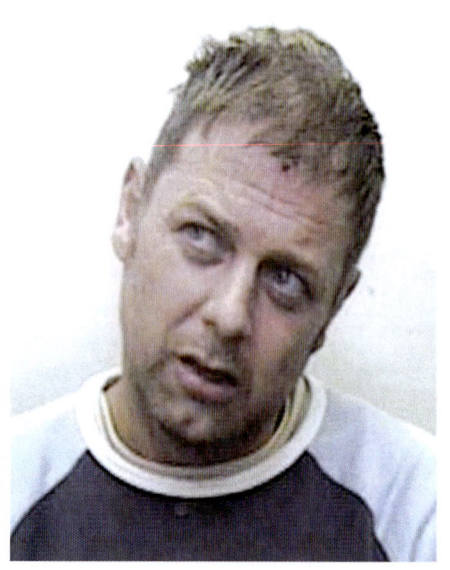

Graham Jones

taken[2928]. Only when he murdered <u>another</u> woman (and her daughter) was he arrested (and convicted in 1994), and his DNA linked to the Rachel killing in 2004. The undercover policewoman at the centre of the bungled 'honey trap' investigation received £150,000 for 'stress'[2929]. Scotland Yard was facing a huge compensation claim in 2009 for its failure to prevent Rachel Nickell's murder: her child's father instructed a leading London law firm. London Police missed a series of opportunities to arrest the mentally ill murderer before his disastrous catalogue of up to 86 sex assaults was ended.[2930] In 2008 Commander <u>Simon Foy</u>, head of the Met's homicide squad, admitted that the murder was preventable if the police had not made six crucial blunders: (1) the call from Napper's mother about Napper's confession re the Green Chain rapes was never followed up, (2) Napper's identification as killer by a neighbour never followed up, (3) failure of Napper to respond to police letter (after a third witness had named him as a suspect) never followed up, (4) Napper wrongly considered too tall to be Green Chain rapist, (5) finding of a Mauser pistol with Napper's fingerprints never followed up, (6) Napper spotted climbing over a Green Chain walk fence but allowed to go[2931]. Colin Stagg, wrongly accused of the murder after the infamous honey-trap operation, received an apology and £706,000 compensation. Stagg remained a pariah for a decade because police remained convinced, falsely, that he was the killer[2932]. The IPCC was scathing about the fiasco, pinpointing the wrong decisions in the 1990s. The police have refused to compensate Rachel Nickell's son (or to pay his legal costs). No disciplinary action was ever taken against the officers involved. This is a recurrent theme throughout this book.

Police blunders allowed violent serial rapist and paedophile Peter Chapman to kidnap, rape and murder a 17-year-old. Before he killed her he had served seven years for what he did to two prostitutes, and he should have been reporting to the police, but they failed to monitor him. He was wanted for arson and driving his car illegally 26 times – if he had been pulled up, the teenager wouldn't have died. His unlicensed, uninsured car was driving through police cameras[2933].

CAVEAT CIVIS

Matt Baggott, Chief Constable of Leicestershire Police at the time Fiona Pilkington made 33 calls for help, refused to apologise for his force's failures that led her to kill her disabled child and herself. Her complaints about the thugs had been dismissed by his police as 'over-reacting'. An inquest jury blamed the police and council – the latter too refused to apologise. Fiona Pilkington's family eventually won a five-figure sum from Leicestershire Police in an out-of-court settlement[2934]. Baggott became Chief Constable of Northern Ireland, where he was attacked by a member of the Northern Ireland Policing Board for not offering his personal apology, given that he was responsible[2935]. Home Secretary Alan Johnson also attacked the police who told the tragic mother to 'ignore' the thugs, and that they were 'too busy'[2936].

Tony Martin, jailed for shooting dead a burglar, says the police are just as much to blame for his death – they had done nothing about his home being repeatedly raided[2937].

Ten Lincolnshire Police officers failed to help an accident victim lying in 18 inches of water: they wouldn't climb down a 15ft bank, instead standing around drinking tea. They did not know the father-of-six was dead[2938].

The killer of Harry Potter actor Rob Knox could have been removed from the streets months before the stabbing, but though he was a suspect for an attempted knifepoint robbery police took no action: the Yard disciplined two officers in this regard. Only after the actor's death was the incident thoroughly investigated[2939].

Two French students were butchered in London by two killers who stabbed them 244 times. One killer was free on licence following failures by, among others, the police – he was not returned to jail despite a relentless crime rampage. The victims' fathers intend to sue the authorities[2940].

A mother of three was stabbed to death six hours after warning Suffolk Police in a 999 call that she might be attacked – she was allegedly told that officers would be with her within an hour[2941].

Lynn McMillan was suing Strathclyde Police claiming that they failed to protect her from a violent ex (who sent her 100 threatening texts and phone messages) before he was killed by her new partner, who stabbed him 21 times. Senior officers have admitted failures led to the death[2942].

When a teenager battered and left a schoolgirl for dead, South Yorkshire Police let him off with a 'final warning', to replicate the attack, this time fatal, on a young woman. The survivor says the police told her it was his word against hers, even though her body was covered in bruises, stamp marks and a damaged eye[2943].

The IPCC said West Midlands Police 'failed a vulnerable woman' by not sending an officer in response to her call: a half hour later she was stabbed to death in front of her daughter, who also called police to beg for help: 'A man's trying to kill my mummy' – a few minutes later officers found her mother lying dead[2944]. West Midlands WPC Melda Wilks was in court with her son (charged with murdering his girlfriend), accused of assisting him by washing his clothes[2945].

A terrified abused wife, stabbed to death by her husband, had told Greater Manchester Police he was going to kill her. He told her during one beating: 'One day I will kill you …

One day you will die', and during another beating: 'This is your final hour'. Police arrested him, then released him on condition he stay away from her. He was arrested again soon after, but not prosecuted[2946].

In 2008 only two UK forces refused to operate fixed speed cameras, and both recorded significant falls in road deaths; police slashed deaths by 40% without them. The anti-fixed camera campaign group Safe Speed says because of cameras 'the relationship between the police and the public is now at an all-time low'[2947].

A young London mother found dying with her hand chopped off had twice called police about spousal molestation, but no action was taken. Her husband was arrested on suspicion of her murder, but then released on bail[2948].

A Briton murdered his girlfriend in Germany but the information did not reach British police, and he went on to murder a girlfriend in England. His family are angry about 'a serious catalogue of errors' by Essex Police, e.g. officers talked to him while her body lay feet away but took no action when he told them she had gone away. They later saw him in the victim's car in a remote area, probably looking for a place to hide the body[2949].

A pregnant mother and her toddler were knifed to death by a mentally-ill ex-boyfriend a few days after he was released from custody without charge by Derbyshire Police – the victim had gone to them because of his threats to kill her[2950].

A woman who suffered from mental problems called 999 twice as she was battered to death in 2006 by an alcoholic neighbour, her body later found in her burnt-out flat. The victim's second call was logged as a 'duplicated incident' and then closed. Likewise eight of the reports Fiona Pilkington made to police in 2004 were marked 'incident closed'. Leicester Police were too busy to attend: the Home Secretary said the police had an unacceptable mindset, also attacking their failure to deal with antisocial behaviour[2951]. A father of four was killed by a brick after asking a gang of drunken yobs outside his home to 'calm down'. The family had been tormented by youths for months, constantly phoning police for help[2952].

Wiltshire Police failed to protect a pregnant woman from her violent Portuguese ex-boyfriend, despite the latter being a well-known risk to her. The police first declined to arrest him because they couldn't find an interpreter (he spoke good English). Then when she called police saying he had turned up in a pub making threats against her, they didn't respond because they were rescuing a dog, while a WPC refused to attend on 'health and safety' grounds[2953].

The family of a 22-year-old murdered by a gang of youths – he had been stabbed seven months earlier by, they think, the same gang – says he had phoned the Met every day for five weeks but police never even took a statement[2954].

The IPCC has found Greater Manchester Police perpetrated a series of blunders in the run-up to the arson murders of a couple (their daughter suffered severe burns). PC Lee Naylor, who had been dealing with the family, failed to visit them after the first arson attack[2955]. Greater Manchester Police have been condemned by the IPCC for 'total failure' to help a young mother stabbed 82 times by an ex-boyfriend, despite repeated calls for help (five times in the week before the murder)[2956]. A baby died of neglect in Manchester at just over a year old, though police had been called to deal with the alcoholic mother when he was three weeks old, and again six months later. A few weeks before his death relatives again alerted police[2957].

A mother and son shot dead in 2003 by her estranged chartered accountant husband might have been saved if Thames Valley officers had followed 'standards of basic policing'. Police failed to interview the Berkshire man despite his waging a year-long vendetta of death threats and vandalism against his wife and children. An independent report found Thames Valley had no domestic violence policy, failed to notice warning signs, and once the killing had started, took over six hours to enter the house containing the bodies. In 2002 the husband had made threats to kill, but these were not investigated. The West Berkshire Safer Communities Partnership report also criticised the police's record-keeping and follow up[2958].

A young mother murdered by her psychotic ex-boyfriend had begged Warwickshire Police for help after he broke her window and threatened to cut her throat, but two investigating officers did not take her seriously, not even recording the incident as a crime[2959].

A neighbour of tragic Fiona Pilkington said she alerted police many times about the campaign of abuse, but police said they were too busy to help. She called the police inaction a 'disgrace': 'They couldn't even be bothered to turn up in the street'[2960].

Gwent Police as well as South Wales Police were criticised for failing to act urgently when Joanna Michael was stabbed 22 times by her ex-boyfriend after he found her in bed with someone else. She bled to death by the time her 999 call produced a response. One 999 operator was sacked and another disciplined[2961].

20% of children killed at home are already known by Met Police to be at risk of domestic abuse, e.g. a baby died after his mother was stabbed to death, a report into 54 London child deaths found[2962]. One of two women who died in a suspected suicide pact in Putney (the Met received a letter from one of them warning of the impending suicides) had made a formal complaint about the Yard re how they had dealt with harassment allegations she had made against a man[2963,2964] who had stalked her. The case was referred to the IPCC. Five Met officers were under investigation by the Yard's Directorate of Professional Standards after a series of blunders meant a young Muslim woman was murdered by her own family. She had warned police five times in the two months before her death (even writing a letter naming henchmen being sent to kill her), but police dismissed them, e.g. a female officer said she thought the victim had concocted the story to get her boyfriend's attention. On one occasion WPC <u>Angela Cornes</u> dismissed her call as a New Year's Eve drunk – she had been forced to drink a bottle of brandy by her father. Cornes even considered charging the young woman with criminal damage because she had broken a window to escape[2965].

A rapist freed early from jail murdered his disabled fiancée despite supposedly being under police supervision. Because the murder went undetected he raped and stabbed his dead fiancée's carer to death when she arrived for a routine visit. Hampshire police said they had considered him a low or medium risk[2966].

Gordon Stalker, killed by multiple stab wounds, had told the police that paranoid schizophrenic Stephen Dunn, subject to a restraining order, had warned him: ' You are a witch – you've stolen my soul – I'll see you burn'[2967].

The victims of a murder/suicide were well enough known to police (and social services) for the latter to have warned the mother her children would be removed if she didn't separate from the 'violent and possessive' father of the two murdered children. The Iraqi Kurd presumed perpetrator was in trouble with the police (e.g. for shoplifting). The victim's ex-husband said: 'I don't understand why the police didn't help her and the children'[2968].

A 2009 incident that didn't, but might have, led to a fatality, was that of an Edinburgh takeaway besieged by racist thugs yelling they 'wanted blood'. After ten 999 calls over 90 minutes, the owner was told by the police operator: 'I am aware of your situation. Don't call again'. Lothian and Borders Police were criticised by the Police Complaints Commissioner for Scotland[2969].

Despite 88 complaints by learning disabled adult David Askew's family, he was 'abused to death' by thugs, the police not recording (a) the incidents as hate crimes, or (b) as a series of, rather than separate, incidents[2970].

A mother-of-three was killed by a mentally ill stalker hours after she pleaded with Suffolk Police for help. She was told detectives would visit her the next morning. The IPCC said an officer should have been sent at the earliest. The murderer throttled his victim, then shot her with a bolt gun: he was also armed with an axe[2971]. A woman was murdered by her partner in front of her teenage son as two Northants PCs (<u>Ron Frater</u>, a black officer, and another) in their village ignored calls to attend. They said they were involved in combating prostitution in Northampton, and this had to take precedence, but in fact they recorded nothing about this in their notebooks. Frater had been house-hunting the previous night in the village, and allegedly returned to do the same at the time of the call. The two officers were given final written warnings for 'gross misconduct', and their behaviour labelled by the IPCC as 'deeply disturbing'[2972].

Reggae star Smiley Culture died in his kitchen during a police raid on his Surrey home. He was on bail for supplying cocaine. His song 'Police Officer' made it into the 1984 charts[2973]. A 37-year-old suspected drug dealer died during a drugs raid on his Perth home by Tayside Police[2974].

Though police had been called a couple of times previously to the home of a divorcé, their actions did not stop him murdering his two children[2975].

When an 'abusive monster' Leicester father was thought to have killed his partner and their two children before committing suicide, it transpired there had been previous police involvement: the police refused to give details but confirmed they had contacted the IPCC[2976]. The infamous Fiona Pilkington case also involved Leicestershire Police.

Dr. Aisha Gill, a senor lecturer in criminology at Roehampton University, claims that, in relation to violence against women, there is a 'historical lack of action by the police along with their maltreatment of women when responding to 'honour' crimes'. Dr. Gill has spoken to many women who have vowed never to use the criminal justice system to combat violence they might experience[2977].

An innocent Lincolnshire couple were gunned down by hitmen after a catalogue of errors by seven Nottinghamshire police officers, e.g. the first Lincolnshire officer contacted (after 999 calls from the victims were relayed) was at an airport going on holiday, while the second message from Notts was faxed to a closed incident room. Notts Police also failed to give the victims witness protection[2978]. The same force failed repeatedly (11 times) to answer young mother Casey Brittle's pleas for help: she was beaten to death by her ex-boyfriend, who was well-known to police for his violent tendencies. Six officers have been disciplined and four reprimanded[2979].

A man was left floating face down in a two-feet deep Hampshire lake for almost an hour as police, firemen and paramedics awaited a specialist water rescue crew[2980].

Murder victim Angela Hoyt reported Home Office crime adviser Martin Collett to Hertfordshire Police for harassment a few days before she was strangled. The IPCC was investigating (2011). Collett's body was found not far from the murder scene[2981].

The IPCC was investigating whether the plight of a 38 year-old mother and her baby daughter was taken seriously over a two-year period. They were murdered by the baby's father, despite the victim trying to get police help the previous week (she sent them 100 of his threatening texts). The father of the surviving child claims the police ignored him when he begged them to enter the house[2982].

According to the IPCC three investigations by different forces over several years – Bedfordshire, Cambridgeshire and Lancashire – were 'flawed' in relation to mentally vulnerable Michael Gilbert, who was assaulted, abducted, enslaved, robbed and eventually beheaded. His body was dumped in pieces in a lake in Bedfordshire in 2009.

Two Greater Manchester PCSOs watched a 10-year-old drown (after he had saved his sister) because they weren't trained to save him. Their identities were kept secret, and their senior officer said their inaction was appropriate. Officers are no longer trained in swimming or lifesaving. In fact officers are trained not to enter the water, in the interest of their own safety[2983]. The force has also banned all its officers (including PCSOs) from riding bikes in case they fall off.

A toddler died from 75 injuries inflicted by his 19-year-old carer: police had 'lost' details of a previous allegation that she had assaulted a sibling[2984].

In 2006 Canning Town resident Peter Woodhams was shot and killed outside his home for challenging a gang indulging in antisocial behaviour. Eight months earlier he had been stabbed in the neck in similar circumstances: despite five calls he made to the police about the incident he wasn't even called to make a statement[2985]. Every rule of procedure was contravened: there were no forensics, no photos. The Newham Police ignored anonymous calls identifying the perpetrators and didn't bother collecting blood-stained clothing from the victim's partner, who phoned them every day for five weeks following the knife attack – her statement was never taken. A neighbour handed in the fatal spent bullet case but police lost it. The original investigating officers, DC Adam Scott and DS Darren Case, were found guilty of gross neglect and resigned, only to be reinstated by Tarique Gaffur, who downgraded their punishments. The Newham Borough commander, Chief Superintendent Michael Johnson, got an office job at Scotland Yard and was then put in charge of the Territorial Support Group. The Met set Yardie Delroy Denton free in Britain, despite his ruthless criminal background – he boasted of having killed seven women – because he was an informer. He went on to rape and murder a young Brixton mother in 1995, despite raping a schoolgirl the year before[2986].

Strathclyde Police admitted not properly monitoring a sex maniac who raped and murdered a 10-year-old and her mother in Ayrshire – no formal risk assessment was carried out on him, his deviant sexually violent behaviour going unheeded. His record in Cumnock police station had no trace of his offender profile or even a warning note of his riskiness. A newspaper leader asserted: 'Police are too frightened to do their job'[2987].

Greater Manchester Police didn't take murder victim Clare Wood's complaints about her ex-partner seriously: they took three months to charge him with domestic violence, even though he repeatedly broke bail conditions. He strangled and burned her before hanging himself. He had used fake identities on the internet looking for partners, threatening them, and kidnapping one at knifepoint[2988]. Garry Shewan, Assistant Chief Constable of Greater Manchester Police, and ACPO's lead officer on the subject of stalking, admitted that victims have been failed by the police. Just over half of victims report to the police, and of these over 75% wait until they have suffered at least 100 alarming incidents[2989].

Merseyside Police failed to monitor rapist Peter Chapman, leading to the negligence killing of Ashleigh Hall. Another such case was that of two Northamptonshire officers who, though in the vicinity of a violent assault on Louise Webster by Martin Ashby which led to her death, refused to attend and drove away. They said they were busy on another incident. Though the IPCC's ruling was of gross misconduct the officers kept their jobs, receiving final written warnings: discipline is a matter for secret panels nearly always. The police investigate themselves. There is no overarching GMC-like body looking at misconduct hearings[2990].

A murdered 41-year-old and her daughter had repeatedly warned Coventry Police that an alcoholic illegal immigrant, who had been deported three times, planned to kill her. They warned police he was a madman (e.g. he had assaulted a female stranger, calling her a prostitute). He had described how he would kill her – throw her off a bridge – and he did. In 2011 the IPCC were probing the police handling of the case[2991].

Christopher Foster shot his wife and daughter dead and committed suicide in 2008, but West Mercia Police knew he had presented a danger for two years, e.g. he had a firearms licence which could have been revoked. Police officers used to drop into his business for a coffee, turning a blind eye to a traffic offence, and they knew he had threatened to kill his accountant and perhaps other business associates. The murderer's brother says he has lost faith in the police because of their incompetence and insensitivity[2992]. West Mercia Constabulary allowed rapists and a paedophile (almost 100 sex offenders altogether) to go free between 2002 and 2007[2993].

A father has criticised Fife Police for refusing to give his desperately ill epileptic daughter a lift to hospital – she was foaming at the mouth, and the roads were congested[2994].

PC Shah revealed (2007) how her colleagues failed to complete basic risk assessment paperwork in the case of the Harvey Nichols stalking case. Six months before the victim was murdered she had called police to report her ex-boyfriend had threatened to kill her[2995].

When a filicidal Hampshire killer's ex-wife complained to the police about his dangerous behaviour she says they weren't interested: it happens all the time with rowing divorced parents, they said[2996].

Three people were killed when their car crashed on an oil spillage road about which the police had been informed several hours before[2997].

The police claimed that human rights legislation meant they couldn't stop convicted woman-beater Barry Stone murdering his former girlfriend[2998].

Met DS <u>Darren Case</u> and DC <u>Adrian Suett</u> were sacked for gross dereliction of duty, but allowed to keep their pensions. They had made 'appalling' mistakes over a knife attack on a hero father later shot dead by a hoody. His partner, after the throat slashing, had rung police every day for five months, with no result. The two dismissed officers failed to interview a witness properly, did not call for a scenes of crime officer, didn't photograph the scene or make proper records in their notebooks. They failed to name five suspects[2999]. Journalist Janet Street-Porter recounts the case of a 15-year-old immigrant girl whom she says was badly let down by the Met. She had been repeatedly threatened by a stalker but nothing happened after her family told the police several times how a crazed student had harassed and assaulted her. Officers said they were powerless to protect her[3000].

A violent alcoholic wife-beater nearly killed his wife, but when police attended, alerted by neighbours, they arrested the wife instead because he told them she was drunk. He later murdered her within weeks[3001].

The widow of Garry Newlove – kicked to death by drunken thugs outside his home – accused police of failing to deal with a string of incidents prior to the assault. She says: 'Garry saved somebody from a beating but the police came after the event – so there was no policing'.

Negligent Essex Police let down a domestic violence victim five times before she was stabbed to death by her ex-lover, who had been convicted of attacking her. The police, an official report said, had failed to 'provide an essential emergency response to a high-risk victim'[3002].

A convicted child sex offender was dumped unsupervised at an Edinburgh B&B very close to a children's nursery. Though being monitored by MAPPA the guest house owner was told nothing of his past – the offender two days later murdered an elderly woman in a nearby sheltered housing complex. MAPPA guidelines state that the Chief Constable could have disclosed past offences[3003].

A member of the Met's Flying Squad shot dead a raider in a Woolwich wages snatch in 2002[3004].

The jury which cleared cop <u>Simon Harwood</u> of Ian Tomlinson's G20 manslaughter was not told about the 10 previous claims of violence and brutality which have riddled his career: while in the Territorial Support Group he allegedly kneed a handcuffed man in the kidneys, racially abused a teenage girl and twisted an AA patrolman's handcuffs[3005]. <u>Harwood</u> has said the newspaper vendor could have been shot for obstructing police[3006]. The Met has apologised to the Tomlinson family and compensated them with substantial damages and costs. The Met branded Harwood's actions as 'excessive and unlawful' and confessed to 'significant failings' in letting him rejoin the police despite his misconduct history[3007].

Despite police in Coventry being called 27 times to the home of tortured to death four-year-old Daniel Pelka, many of the occasions fuelled by alcohol and involving knives, no action was taken[3008].

A known psychiatric patient who made threats to kill his former lover and their son, was released by Derbyshire Police to stab them to death five days later[3009].

Custody Deaths

19th Century juries had concerns about police behaviour. Thus when a 32-year-old Thames waterman died the day after being held overnight in cells at Shadwell High Street, the jury returned a verdict in 1833 of 'wilful murder by a policeman of K Division of the Metropolitan Police'[3010]. Over 40 years more than 1,000 people have died in police custody, e.g. young black schizophrenic Ricky Bishop died in custody before he entered the police station[3011].

The body of Christopher Alder, who died in 1998 in Hull Police custody, was mixed up with the body of a 77-year-old female Nigerian. The custody officer, an ex-paratrooper, was cleared of manslaughter but found guilty of misconduct in public office: several officers were later disciplined. The IPCC ruled that there had been a most serious neglect of duty, but was itself accused of unwitting racism.

Over a recent eight year period about a quarter of the (over) 400 people who died in contact with police (including Article 2 deaths in custody) were mentally challenged. A 2012 Panorama programme instanced the cases of black schizophrenic Sean Rigg (no police arrived despite four calls, then he was found dead, the family being assured wrongly that CCTV had recorded everything) and Roger Sylvester. No officer has ever been convicted in such cases. The IPCC has been accused of failing to conduct a fair and independent investigation into the death in custody of Sean Rigg. The IPCC had, even after four months, refused to interview the officers involved. It seems the police's lawyer removed key passages from the police report for the IPCC's perusal, but the coroner found the truth. The family say they have been denied access to information: '... our eyes have been opened to the injustice and discrimination suffered by many families at the hands of the police'. The family tried to force the IPCC to treat the officers as suspects. Out of 20 custody death victims, of 15 families who responded to a Panorama survey, 14 were very dissatisfied with the IPCC (poor professionalism, too slow, etc.). Eight of nine senior IPCC investigators were ex-cops (in Rigg's case), constituting a sort of Old Boys Club. (The biggest test ever for the IPCC will be the Hillsborough review). The police had refused to attend on one occasion after the deceased's carers at his mental illness hostel required help to get him to a place of safety[3012]. His death in custody (from a heart attack) has become a 'cause infame', taking four years for the IPCC to report that 'unsuitable force' had been used to restrain him, as well as an 'absence of care' being exercised. The Maudsley's Mental Health Care Team told the victim's hostel to call the police instead of coming out to give him treatment. When the police said Sean was faking unconsciousness, yet it was months before the IPCC interviewed the officers concerned. The IPCC was said by the family to be 'completely useless', having missed vital evidence. It took six 999 calls from the hostel over three hours before police attended. Rigg's solicitor says the police lied under oath: they say the 40-year-old musician had only been manhandled for seconds, but it was actually eight minutes. They claimed he was sitting upright, while Rigg was actually hunched up in the footwell of the police van. Half of deaths in custody are of the mentally ill[3013].

An IPCC report showed how neglect led to the death of black war hero Christopher Alder at the feet of four laughing officers – he choked on his own blood on the police cell floor. Humberside Police have allowed three to retire on health grounds, with packages worth up to £0.5 million, even though they refused to cooperate with the IPCC. Racist remarks had been made, and hospital medical staff had refused to treat him. The 400 page IPCC review pointed to 'systematic failures' within the police. The Alder family are suing Humberside Police[3014].

Four West Midlands officers were arrested on suspicion of the manslaughter in custody of Kingsley Burrell (he died three days after his arrest). The four, due to be interviewed by the IPCC, walked out before the session started[3015].

Black suspects feature disproportionately among custody deaths (e.g. 1997-1999, 43% versus 8% of white deaths). Of 19 deaths of custody blacks (1990-1996) nine were to do with the behaviour of the officers involved. Of seven black deaths, only one led to a criminal investigation[3016]. Black prisoner Colin Roach apparently shot himself in jail (1983), while Shizi Lapite was kept in a neckhold in a police van (1994) – the fifth black person to die while in the care of Stoke Newington officers, against whom no disciplinary action was taken. Aseta Sims died in 1971, Michael Ferreira in 1978, and Tunay Hassan in 1987. A sixth, Vandana Patel, was killed by her husband (1991) after officers had left the couple alone.

A mentally-ill father of three died in police custody after officers deliberately ran him down, then denying him medical help till it was too late to save his life, Leicester Crown Court heard in 2006 - ten policemen were on trial.

Though mentally ill James Herbert, 25, was on drugs, he was taken into police custody despite pleas from his mother to have him taken to hospital under a s.136 Place of Safety Order. He was stripped naked and his ankles and wrists handcuffed. He died on the cell floor in a coma (the IPCC has ordered a new investigation). In 2011-12 there were over 9,000 sectioned patients[3017].

Tayside custody PC John Sergeant lied about a heroin addict who died in custody, and admitted falsifying records over the death[3018].

Forces have been warned about the use of Emergency Restraint Belts (ERBs) after the death in custody of schizophrenic Thomas Orchard in an Exeter police station. An ERB was used around his head (they are designed for limbs only), but ACPO say they knew nothing about how common the ERB's use is, and, anyway, they wouldn't have sanctioned its use. The family have not been allowed to see the station's CCTV footage, their relative's antemortem coma being unexplained. The IPCC wrote to every chief constable to find how often the ERB was used around the country (of ten forces who replied eight had ERBs)[3019]. Norfolk Police have admitted using the ERB as a 'spit hood' 83 times, but there seems to be little monitoring[3020].

Murder Arrests

Cheshire PC Martin Forshaw was arrested on suspicion of murdering his WPC fiancée, who had apparently suffered fatal head injuries when their BMW crashed into a tree, but the car was barely damaged[3021]. He had decided to cancel their wedding because he still fancied his ex, by whom he had a child. His fiancée had just finished her probationary period with Greater Manchester Police, while he was self-defence instructor to Cheshire Constabulary. Forshaw had been to an ex-partner on late night visits[3022]. He was jailed for life[3023].

PC <u>Des Campbell</u>, formerly based at Cranleigh Police Station (Surrey) in the nineties, pleaded not guilty (2010) to pushing his Australian wife off a cliff in Sydney in 2005. He had taken her to the Royal National Park beauty spot, even though she didn't like camping. He had obtained a very substantial sum of money from her[3024]. He had quit Surrey Police after facing an investigation into an allegation of indecent assault. The 'sexual predator' was also said to have conned a WPC out of thousands of pounds while still in the UK. At the time of his wife's funeral, which he didn't attend, he was staying in a five-star hotel with one of a string of girlfriends. He described his murder victim wife as 'pig ugly but filthy rich' – he stood to make over £200,000 from her death (she had changed her will in his favour: he married her in secret because of her family's opposition)[3025]. Campbell was jailed for 24 years.

Ex-cop <u>John George</u> stabbed and strangled an 82-year-old woman in her home, while former police inspector <u>Howard Wilson</u> shot two police officers dead and paralysed a third after a bank raid. The two Scots have set up an online computer firm, Nethisto Interactive (George had been investigated for computer scams while in Edinburgh's Saughton prison). Wilson had carried out a series of robberies with violence on OAPs[3026].

In 1950 Glasgow PC <u>James Robertson</u>, a small-time thief, ran over the mother of his child – they had been having an argument. He logged a false report of the incident[3027].

Gay mass murderer <u>Dennis Nilsen</u> was a former soldier and policeman (for 11 months a Met beat cop)[3028].

Inspector <u>Garry Weddell</u> strangled his wife at home and tried to fake her suicide by hanging her body in the garage. Her forged 'suicide' note was detected by a forensic linguistics expert. Released on bail, Weddell went on to commit a homicide/suicide[3029].

Police inspector <u>Garry Weddell</u> was released while awaiting trial on the charge of strangling his wife. While on bail he was not banned from handling guns, even stealing a gun from Luton Shooting Club, where he had shooting lessons weeks before gunning down his mother-in-law[3030].

ANC activist Ruch First was murdered by letter bomb in 1982. The man who organised the killing was policeman <u>Craig Williamson</u>. Ruch has a Public Heritage plaque in Camden.

City of London policeman <u>Adam Lowe</u> has been charged with the murder of a barrister's clerk in the Alibi bar in the Square Mile.

Jealous wife <u>Sally Challen</u>, an office manager for the Police Federation, has been charged with bludgeoning her husband to death[3031].

In 2001 Kent PC <u>Karl Bluestone</u> used a hammer to murder his wife and two of their children (a three-year-old and an 18-month-old), having warned her on their anniversary: 'No divorce – the only way out is death'[3032].

A Spanish graphologist has named Chief Inspector Frederick Abberline – the Met detective who led the hunt for Jack the Ripper – as the serial killer. Jose Luis Abad compared the Chief Inspector's writing with that in the Ripper's supposed diary[3033].

<u>Peter Foster</u>, thought to be a former DI made redundant recently from Surrey Police, was arrested in connection with the murder of DC Heather Cooper, based at Guildford. Foster's house is opposite a police station, and he may have been in an elite unit dealing with violent crimes[3034]. Foster, her former partner, has denied stabbing her to death[3035].

Karl Bluestone

Leicestershire Police Inspector <u>Tobias (Toby) Day</u> was found dead at his Melton Mowbray home along with his wife (a former Met officer like her husband) and youngest child – his two eldest children were taken injured to hospital. He suspected his wife of adultery. Day had been sacked the week before, for misconduct, including misusing police systems and dishonesty, but this fact had not been released to the press. The day before the murder/suicide Day had been told by his force that reporters had found out about his dismissal. The IPCC were alerted and were investigating[3036]. Neighbours claimed 'perfect neighbour' Day forced his wife to watch as he tried to kill their children before murdering her and committing suicide[3037].

<u>John Christie</u> served four years as a Special Constable at Harrow Road police station. Timothy Evans' last words: 'It was Christie that did it'. The police believed a former cop first. <u>Christie</u> was a serial killer (of six women) at the infamous 10 Rillington Place[3038].

Hampshire Police Sergeant <u>Tina Nash</u> was remanded in custody for trying to kill her lesbian lover, colleague Sergeant Sara Glen. Reporting restrictions at Aldershot magistrates court were not lifted[3039].

The Boston Strangler always wanted to be a cop.

Former police detective <u>Ivan Esack</u> (he left the Kent force in January, 2010) was arrested after his estranged wife was stabbed to death in her celebrity hairdressing salon in front of staff. On his football agency website he describes himself as 'a person that people can trust'[3040].

CHAPTER XV

THE LUSTFUL POLICEMAN

CHAPTER CONTENTS

CHAPTER XV

THE LUSTFUL POLICEMAN

Preamble

The historical policeman was often portrayed chasing after female cooks and servant girls. Strathclyde Police dealt with 127 sex crime allegations against officers in the five years to 2009[3041], but this may be the tip of the iceberg. The Met has denied it protects officers against sexual misconduct allegations, even though only 1% of complaints by members of the public were proven (four out of 311 complaints) between 2000 and 2009. When allegations included those by fellow officers, 43 of 492 allegations were substantiated. Women Against Rape said the figures show there should be impartial independent investigation of such cases (this reminds one of claims that the Army should not be allowed to police itself)[3042]. A 2005 Home Office study found sexism was rife among officers[3043].

Police have a 16% chance of divorce, below nurses, chefs and secretaries (20%), but well above dentists, optometrists and clergymen (2-7%)[3044].

Marital Problems

Lots of police officers do have extramarital relationships, says Royston Martis, deputy editor of Police Review[3045].

WPC <u>Maxine Barham</u>, who had been in the Army, has become a model. She has revealed how common she found sexual misbehaviour is in the force: '… everyone is at it, in patrol cars, at the station … I did it with one senior PC in a police van on duty'. Shortly after joining the force she caught four officers in flagrante delicto in her hotel room at a force swimming competition. She herself had another session in a shower at her East London police station in Havering. At a Christmas do a WPC gave a PC oral sex under the table while her husband sat a short distance away. She knew of patrol car PCs who would give drunken girls a lift home so they could have sex with them[3046].

Former CID detective <u>Paul Young</u> sued his Somerset ex-lover for custody of their springer spaniel but lost the case[3047].

(a)   Womanising

<u>Nick Long</u>, an £85,000-a-year IPCC commissioner who led the investigation into how police dealt with Raoul Moat's shooting spree, left his wife of 39 years in 2010 for a junior Asian colleague, a married lawyer and fellow commissioner[3048].

Married police driver <u>Timothy Reid</u> had a two-month affair with a witness, having sex sessions when he was on call. He divulged to her the names of criminals he had arrested, and used the police national database to glean information about her ex-partner. He was dismissed from Cheshire Police, lost his pension and received a suspended sentence[3049].

A former North Yorkshire policeman, said to have been romantically involved with missing Claudia Lawrence, has been urged to come forward[3050].

Strathclyde's married 'Inspector Undies' Tom Halbert got his nickname because of a lingerie fetish, but more seriously he was investigated for exchanging confidential information for sex (a rapist's mother says he would help overturn her son's conviction, and she believed his colleagues were involved in a cover-up. She claims he would turn up for sex while on duty). He would tell his wife he was playing golf or working late and sent hundreds of late-night x-rated texts when his wife was asleep[3051]. Strathclyde Police Inspector Samantha McClusky was being probed in 2009 over a fracas with a female rookie cop trained by her sergeant husband at the Jackton training complex in Lanarkshire. The inspector reportedly confronted her over phone video footage circulating among the trainees, which allegedly showed the sergeant outside the Social nightclub in Glasgow[3052].

Cheating Cumbrian PC Stephen Cassells had his wife arrested for drink-driving (she was banned for 18 months) after a fracas at his love nest. He restrained her on the ground and told his mistress to call the police[3053].

Tayside Police gave a lucrative job to Inspector Caroline Lindsay after her husband Gordon Scobbie was made deputy chief constable of the force. They had both walked out on their marriages when employed by Strathclyde Police[3054]. A former Fife Special Constable told a court how married police Sergeant Douglas McCarroll had stalked her and pushed her 'over the edge': he became 'strange' after she rejected his advances[3055]. Tayside's Western Division Chief Superintendent Iain Bell left his wife of 25 years to set up home with fellow Tayside Police officer Leigh-Ann Gregge, with whom he reportedly admitted committing adultery. His wife wanted a £600,000 divorce payout[3056].

Assistant Met Commissioner Tarique Ghaffur's wife obtained an injunction barring her husband's family from her home. She divorced him on the grounds of adultery, but nothing came of her formal complaint to Greater Manchester Police about his affair (she thinks because he was Asian). His mistress was WPC Doreen Mellor, who had accompanied him on a 'policing tour' of India. He eventually married an Asian for his second marriage[3057]. Married Met Superintendent Simon Ovens was caught on a live video link kissing and cuddling an unknown pretty woman after he forgot to turn off the screen[3058].

Cheating British Transport policeman Christopher Parkins divided his time between his wife and mistress. He concealed from both the fact he was on long term sick leave, pretending to be a firearms officer working for Scotland Yard, and that a hitman was after him. The mistress sought help from a domestic violence unit, and he admitted harassment[3059].

The wife of Chief Superintendent Ian Burnside won a £500,000 divorce settlement after he moved in with her best friend. He was (2007) on secondment to H.M. Chief Inspector of Constabulary[3060].

Michael Reid, the 'Bonking Bishop of Brentwood', had affairs with three women connected with his Essex church, including his choirmistress. He founded the Peniel Church in 1976. He lost his claim for unfair dismissal. He is a former police officer[3061].

Probable suicide Chief Constable <u>Mike Todd</u> had a secret stash of porn and a sex toy hidden in a suitcase in his office (the suitcase also contained female undies and high heels, a vibrator and basque which <u>didn't</u> belong to his wife). His conquests included a married police superintendent, his personal assistant, an investigative journalist and a married poet. In particular, before his tragic death he was sure his affair with the married chief executive of Manchester Chamber of Commerce was about to be exposed[3062]. The report by Sir Paul

Chief Constable Mike Todd

Scott-Lee, Chief Constable of West Midlands, found Todd's affairs had 'adversely impacted' upon the reputation of the force and left him vulnerable to blackmail[3063]. Because Todd was regarded as 'inspirational' a blind eye was turned to his cheating on his wife (he was linked to 38 women in six years). A Met source said there were 'concerns among some that he was exploiting people under his command. In many other walks of life this kind of behaviour would have been seen as predatory, but for some reason everyone in policing was prepared to put up with it'. Two weeks before his death he sent 'inappropriate' texts to a senior civil servant he had met at a conference – he apologised when she rejected him. Some of the policewomen linked to him were later promoted, which is damaging to the force. His womanising seems to have been admired by some rank and file. One of the lothario's conquests (she denied this) was said to be PC <u>Laura Nagulapalli</u>, who had a criminal past. A former model and air hostess, she was living with a married police inspector when she was arrested over an insurance fraud[3064]. Another of Todd's amours in the force was promoted ahead of more qualified candidates. Yet another liaison was with a new recruit[3065].

Married Hampshire PC <u>Gary Bayldon</u> faced jail in 2008 after admitting having sex regularly, while on duty, with a woman he first met on a 999 call, and propositioning a female arrestee. He had also been accused of having sex in his patrol car, kissing a woman witness and giving another money to buy underwear before asking her to perform an act on him in some woods. When <u>Bayldon</u> appeared at Kingston Crown Court accused of lewd acts with several women while on duty, he denied nine misconduct counts between 1998 to 2007[3066].

In 2005 two Guildford PCs were jailed for 15 months for having sex with a woman they met while on a 999 call[3067].

Married Devon and Cornwall PC <u>Darren Burdaky</u> was suspended over a secret liaison with a serial shoplifter he was supposed to be reforming – she claims he stalked her after she tried to break off the affair (he threatened her with prison). Burdaky was subject to another complaint of witness intimidation. He allegedly prevented his lover from being arrested several times: he was served with a harassment warning[3068].

Assistant Met Commissioner <u>John Yates</u> split from his wife in 2009, and in 2010 was expecting a child by a former Yard press officer[3069], whom he married shortly before taking up his Middle East post – Bahrain's strict Islamic laws prohibits unmarried couples living together[3070] (see also The Murdoch Policeman chapter).

Sussex D.C.I <u>Martyn Underhill</u> was suspended (2009) for allegedly having sex with a colleague while on duty. He was praised for catching the Sarah Payne paedophile killer[3071].

Two Essex WPCs who claim they were sexually harassed (including stalked) by three male colleagues launched a £2m action. One was asked to perform a sex act on a PC as he drove a patrol car; he also masturbated sitting next to her while on patrol. One WPC claims PC <u>Jason Bell</u> asked her about her underwear and threatened to kill her if she went out with anyone, daubed messages on her car and flooded her with text messages. The women claim the Met tried to cover up their complaints, and at the start of 2009 were signed off work sick[3072].

A Salford PC allegedly beamed to his colleagues a photo of him juxtaposing his genitals to the face of a sleeping WPC. Another man at Manchester's Press Club, where the group of police were drinking, dropped his trousers and struck lewd poses. If the WPC makes a criminal complaint a gross indecency charge could result[3073].

Married DI <u>Simon Ashwin</u>, attached to the Yard's elite Directorate of Professional Standards, was sent home from an undercover Caribbean investigation over an affair with a blonde divorcee who threw him fully-clothed into a pool. The Met's 'Sunshine Squad' ran up a bill of millions during the bungled inquiry into Caymans police corruption. Ashwin lied to the blonde he was divorced. She claims he was repeatedly very drunk when she turned up for rendez-vous. Other policemen, too, she says, were getting drunk every night. A judge in the case was awarded £1m compensation for being unlawfully arrested by British policemen. The blonde said of Ashwin: 'He was supposed to be exposing crooked policemen and instead he was the most deceptive one of all'[3074].

Married Lancs PC <u>Mark Buckley</u> was jailed for a year, having failed to investigate a burglary because he was with a call girl. He showered gifts on two female crooks, tipping off all three women with information from confidential computer records. He sent 'personal and sexual' letters to the girl crooks in jail[3075].

Married Grampian Inspector <u>Keith Farquharson</u>, convicted of sending an x-rated poem ('Gasping For It') to a WPC (he was demoted to constable as a result), was subjected to fresh allegations from women in the administrative unit to which he had been shunted. He was suspended in 2009 pending further investigations. He was allegedly one of three senior Grampian policemen having affairs with the same traffic warden[3076]. Aberdeenshire special constable <u>Graeme Duguid</u> resigned when he was accused of taking indecent photos of a woman he handcuffed to a bed, while he was on duty. He was cleared after a trial at Aberdeen Sheriff Court[3077].

Married Buckinghamshire superintendent <u>Gilbert Houalla</u> had a relationship with a female officer, thought to be a Detective Inspector, but she claimed he shouted and swore at her. Chief Constable <u>Sara Thornton</u> recently ended a liaison with Houalla, whom she took to two State banquets at Windsor Castle[3078]. Ms. Thornton, a vicar's daughter, was awarded the CBE for services to policing: she also holds the Queen's Police Medal[3079].

Police protection officer <u>Paul Rice</u>, Shadow Chancellor Alan Johnson's bodyguard, admitted to affairs with Johnson's PA as well as his wife[3080]. Rice was sacked for discreditable conduct without notice in 2011 after a misconduct hearing in private. Rice was a carefully vetted special operations constable[3081].

In 2011 Chief Superintendent <u>Jim Trotman</u> was cleared by a jury of charges of arson, fraud and perverting the course of justice. Outside court he hugged his mistress[3082]. An Oxford (Boar's Hill) swinger's club was mentioned in the case: its members had heard rumours Trotman had got his mistress pregnant[3083].

Lothian and Borders Chief Superintendent <u>Mark Williams</u> separated from his wife after he was caught having an affair with a civilian member of staff at his force's Fettes HQ[3084].

Wiltshire Deputy Chief Constable <u>David Ainsworth</u> was being investigated by South Wales Police over 24 allegations (mostly from women) that he made bawdy and personal remarks to colleagues. He was known as 'The Brain' because of his sharp intelligence[3085]. He committed suicide: separated from his wife, his girlfriend found him hanged in his garage[3086]. A female police civilian worker is to receive a £10,000 out-of-court settlement, for sexual harassment and 'damage to feelings', against <u>Ainsworth</u>: she is one of two dozen officers and staff who lodged complaints against him[3087].

Married Kent P.C. <u>Daniel Capel</u> was sent to probe a dispute between a model and her boyfriend, but ended up trying to go to bed with her, sending her a string of sexy texts and naked phone pictures and telling her he could get her boyfriend put in prison. Capel was arrested for sending indecent pictures and inappropriate behaviour, forced to resign, but will retain his pension[3088].

Married Cumbria PC <u>Mark Fisher</u> (nicknamed Fish the Flirt by colleagues), who worked in the force's public protection unit, was jailed for four years for abusing his position to set up affairs with vulnerable women – he used the police computer to obtain information about three women. He was found guilty of five counts of misconduct in a public office[3089].

<u>Sir Hugh Orde</u>'s wife left him after his affair with Met officer <u>Denise Weston</u> (who once worked undercover in the PSNI) – they had a child – became public knowledge. His travel expenses were much higher than any other chief constable – he travelled regularly to marathons in which his mistress also participated. His force refused to provide details of his expenses. He missed an important memorial service for murdered officers to visit one such marathon alongside his mistress[3090]. The Assistant Commissioner of the Met <u>Andy Hayman</u> quit after a probe into foreign trips with police sergeant Heidi Tubby and the sending of 400 electronic communications to a woman member of the IPCC during the de Menezes inquiry (see also The Murdoch Policeman chapter).

Married North Yorkshire PC <u>Matthew David Fisher</u> targeted five women for sexual favours, using the force computer to locate three of them. He had sex with one in his police van while on duty. He had admitted two charges of misconduct in public office, and faced another four[3091]. He made 52 attempts to contact a female member of the public he had met in a supermarket – they had sexual contact in his police van at a bus station. He was found guilty of abusing two women he was supposed to be helping. Twice married, over four years he coaxed sexual favours from women by bombarding them with calls, and would offer drunk women lifts[3092].

Married Gwent firearms officer <u>Shaun Jenkins</u> drove a married woman to his home in his patrol car, telling his colleague to wait in the car while the pair spent 40 minutes in the bedroom. He was in uniform and left his loaded gun on the dressing table. Gwent Police gave him an official warning, but the husband told the PCC, which ordered a gross misconduct hearing. He was dismissed but was appealing[3093].

Married Greater Manchester PC <u>Troy Van-Eda</u> 'used his uniform' to bed five women while on duty. One he had pulled over for not wearing her seat belt, and this led to a six-year affair which ended when she found out about his other mistresses and she reported him. On one occasion they had slept together at a police station. Another woman claimed they were engaged. Van-Eda was sacked for gross misconduct[3094], but says he wants his job back because he's done nothing wrong[3095].

Suicide PC <u>David Rathband</u>'s cheating on his wife led her to seek a divorce when she found out (his paramour was a 7/7 survivor)[3096].

Married Chief Constable of Dyfed-Powys <u>Terry Grange</u> used his police credit card to fund hotel trysts and alcohol with his lover at times he was supposed to be in official meetings (she even accompanied him to some of these instead of his wife). He sent over 100 'sexually explicit' emails from his force computer to the mistress, whose complaint of 68 liaisons when the affair ended meant his resignation as Chief Constable, but the CPS ruled out criminal action against him and he received a full pension. Grange was ACPO's spokesman on sex offenders and child protection and was highly thought of in senior police circles[3097].

South Yorkshire Assistant Chief Constable <u>Stephen Chamberlain</u> scandalised his colleagues by his affair with blond inspector <u>Helen Chapman</u>, wife of one of his sergeants. He was also accused of assaulting his ex-wife, who married and divorced him twice because of his infidelity: her rape allegation was 'glossed over' by his officers. It was also claimed he used his police handcuffs to lock his cohabitee's arms behind her back during coitus[3098].

<u>Brian Paddick</u> has revealed that his first gay encounter was with another officer, and that he had had affairs with women police (one black WPC propositioned him). He claims he was in a homophobic organisation. A Christian, he became engaged to three women, then married a beautician, from whom he concealed his orientation for most of their marriage[3099]. According to a colleague, he once said 'policing is God's work'. His childless marriage lasted five years. Friends think he has used his gayness (he is a 'scene gay', not shy about being seen out and about in gay spots) to help him advance in the Met, but he was warned not to visit the gay Shadow Lounge club[3100].

When Officer 'A' and his partner separated, a colleague was getting a divorce, followed by a third DC, while a fourth officer had been thrown out by his pregnant wife. 'A's partner alleged he had bugged their home[3101]. Another DC's estranged wife invited him back only to accuse him of rape, leading to his imprisonment (she later confessed she had lied).

Married Met diplomatic protection squad PC <u>Ricci Giff</u> went on trysts with a secret mistress when he should have been on duty. Colleagues found pictures of her on his mobile posing in nothing but his gunbelt, complete with Glock pistol and Taser, after she committed suicide. They exchanged obscene text messages. He was sentenced to nine months[3102].

(b)   Wayward partner/mistress

Ex-Aberdeenshire cop Colin Begg's wife was ordered to pay £10,500 compensation for selling fake designer clothes on eBay[3103] (see also The Familial Flaw Policeman chapter).

Strathclyde constable Raymond Thomson was quizzed by his superiors after his wife embezzled over £90,000 from her employer[3104], for which she was jailed for two years[3105]. A former policeman has told how sex-scandal Edinburgh GP Dr. Ewan Crawford had a five-year affair with his wife, which ended the policeman's marriage[3106]. The policeman's complaint to the GMC led to the doctor's downfall[3107].

A single mother who had a one-night stand with Met PC Matthew Tarrant falsely accused him of rape after he shunned her advances. She was jailed for two years[3108].

A cop's ex-wife dated rapist Iorworth Hoare. Her daughter says her mother's marriage to the policeman was 'miserable'[3109].

The husband of murdered Met Special Constable Nisha Patel-Nasri was arrested for alleged drugs offences[3110]. The husband of murdered policewoman Sharon Beshenivsky banned her parents attending the Home Secretary's unveiling of a memorial to her[3111].

Hertfordshire police sergeant's widow Jennifer Bibby, Neighbourhood Watch coordinator and regular churchgoer, was caught on CCTV vandalising neighbours' cars with eggs and flour[3112].

Police were called when Central Scotland's Chief Inspector Donald McMillan – he is head of road policing – and his wife, a civilian worker in the force, had a Christmas Day row. The procurator fiscal decided they would not face charges[3113].

Strathclyde WPC Kelly O'Brien, battered by her brutal boyfriend PC Barry Quinn, whom she met at police training college, lost her job after a 12-hour disciplinary hearing. Quinn admitted assaulting her as well as a female toddler, and is battling to keep his job[3114].

Married Tayside WPC Paula Wales 'snogged' a wanted criminal in his bedroom – she was separated from DCI Iain Wales (also of the Tayside force). She denied at Dundee Sheriff Court (2012) wilfully neglecting her duty[3115] and was cleared even though she had accessed the wanted man's police files[3116].

Ex-policeman Andy Norman left his wife to run off with athlete and Olympic medalist Fatima Whitbread, whom he married in 1997 (he had met her in his capacity as sports promoter) – they separated in 2005 after he had an affair. Reputedly Norman was quite a bully and he was implicated in a sports writer's suicide (the latter had been critical of Norman in print)[3117].

Former Northampton WPC Susan Rae lost her bizarre High Court attempt to prevent her husband divorcing her (the rare 'defended divorce') because of her unreasonable behaviour (she has a psychology degree). Thus she took the fuse out of the washing machine to stop him ruining her clothes, and threw away ham he'd bought because it wasn't organic. She dismantled the TV aerial to ensure their sons did more homework, and filled wardrobes with charity shop clothes. A family party she organised got out of hand. Her husband has moved in with another woman[3118].

Heterosexual Assault/Harassment

Ayrshire PC Gavin Hamzah appeared in court in private in 2010 on charges relating to sex attacks on four women[3119]. Lothian and Borders PC and Kirk elder Steven Kellock admitted sexually assaulting a teenage girl during a church outing. Placed on the Sex Offenders Register he told police, 'I am not a bad man'[3120], receiving a Community Payback Order instead of jail.

Married Grangemouth PC <u>Christopher Robb</u> sent lascivious texts to a 19-year-old after she had given him a statement in the course of a vandalism probe. Suspended for over a year, Robb faced losing his job[3121].

Married South Wales traffic cop <u>Jamie Slater</u> offered to let female motorists off in exchange for sex, and had sex with prostitutes in his police car while on duty. He harassed the motorists who refused his rendez-vous[3122]. North Wales trainee detective <u>Timothy Jones</u> forced a female heroin addict to give him oral sex and then sexually attacked her in his police station, a court heard. He was also charged with raping another woman who had called for help[3123].

WPC <u>Barbara Lynford</u>, the only woman in an 18-strong firearms team at Gatwick Airport, won damages of £575,000 for sexist harassment from her colleagues – they humiliated her with comments about her anatomy, calling her a 'whoopsy', 'lipstick' and a 'daisy'. The squad allegedly watched porn on duty, slept on the job, radioed sightings of girls to each other, and spent more time in the canteen than on patrol[3124].

Sex pest former Special Constable <u>Patrick MacKinnon</u> became an outcast over sexual assaults on two women on the Hebridean island of Canna, where he had been raised. A heavy drinker and possessor of unlicensed firearms, he was found hanged in 2010. He was on the sex offenders' register[3125].

Lothian and Borders police sergeant <u>Kevin Storey</u> was charged with two counts of rape and two attempted rapes, involving a number of women[3126].

Married sex-pest Dumfries and Galloway PC <u>Brian Wilson</u> admitted making indecent remarks to five female colleagues (the former Marine offered sex in the back of a police van). He resigned and was given community service[3127]. Rapist police inspector <u>Adam Carruthers</u> tried to get a job at Tesco after his release from prison. He had raped two women while in uniform, with 38 other women claiming he had raped, attacked or harassed them during his 20 years with the Dumfries and Galloway force. He had tried before to get a job with access to women[3128]. Pervert policeman and ex-soldier <u>Dean Stewart</u> sought legal advice from Carruthers as he fought for his pension. Stewart was convicted, in the longest trial of its kind in Scottish legal history, on three charges, including one of abducting and sexually assaulting a woman in his patrol car, and one involving a 15-year-old schoolgirl[3129]. He was jailed for five years. One victim committed suicide, according to friends, because she hadn't been taken seriously. He was only brought to justice after Lothian and Borders police were brought in[3130]. He has been accused of using Masonic links to cover up his crimes (he was jailed for 12 years)[3131]: see The Masonic Policeman chapter.

A Northumberland Police detective was arrested in 2009 over claims he sexually assaulted women prisoners (he is thought to have been questioned about 20). He is accused of offering freedom for sex[3132]. Many of his victims have been refused compensation by the Criminal Injuries Compensation Authority because they have criminal records[3133]. He was jailed for life in 2010.

While serving as a police officer, <u>Khalid Anwar</u>, from Edinburgh, allegedly raped and assaulted a woman, having illegally accessed information about her on the police database, as well as using his uniform to inquire about her door-to-door. He denies the charges[3134]. Anwar was found guilty (2013) of raping a woman he met on a dating website, as well as leaving her in a state of fear and alarm. He had been accused of sending her a text: 'I hope you f........ electrocute yourself and die', as well as threatening to publicise naked pictures of the victim. He was remanded in custody pending sentencing[3135].

Married father-of-two Devon and Cornwall PCSO <u>Peter Bunyan</u> was jailed for seven years for misconduct in public office – sexual affairs while on uniformed patrol. He illegally accessed data on prospective lovers (he slept with one up to ten times while on duty) using the Criminal Information System. He turned his radio down while having sex and encouraged a mentally ill woman to email explicit picures of herself to his police station[3136].

Married South Yorkshire Police officer <u>Lee Wilcox</u> was imprisoned for nine months after having intercourse with a vulnerable woman he met on duty[3137].

Ex-lawyer Lothian and Borders superintendent <u>Iain Livingstone</u> (the youngest in Scotland) was suspended after allegations of sexual assault from colleague WPC Wendy Paterson. Though drink was allegedly involved, prosecutors decided not to proceed[3138].

A Lothian and Borders Police sergeant <u>Paul Greig</u> was suspended after being charged with two counts of rape which predated his joining the force[3139]. Sex pest Lothian and Borders PC <u>Andrew Burt</u> was granted a full pension despite indecently assaulting three women (including a mother and daughter) while under the influence.. He would have lost his pension if he had been dismissed, but his superiors dragged out his conduct investigation so that he could retire on a lucrative payout – the force refused to discuss Burt's bonanza. One victim said, 'The police always look after their own'. Burt slapped and groped women's breasts and between their legs[3140].

Two unnamed Central Scotland PCs were accused in 2009 of drunken sexual misbehaviour at a colleague's wedding reception in Forest Hills Hotel in Aberfoyle: a 31-year-old WPC allegedly performed a sex act under a table on a 33-year-old male officer. They had both arrived at the wedding already drunk, and continued their naughty behaviour after being observed. The WPC may have been moved to another station, while the male has been off sick. Police bosses are keen to handle the affair within the force, as, if any of the other horrified police made an official public indecency complaint, it could end up in court, with an officer being put on the sex offenders' register[3141].

Kent Police's Detective Superintendent <u>Murphy</u> was arrested by Dutch police after a claim that a woman in a hotel bar had been groped during an exchange trip to Holland. He was released without charge but his employers notified (the alleged victim claims he followed her into the ladies' toilet[3142]).

Married Detective Sergeant <u>Adrian Ramdat</u> allegedly twice assaulted Inspector Amanda Lowe (once breaking her ankle), with whom he was having an affair. Both were with City of London Police. Ramdat was jealous of her previous liaison with a high-ranking officer, calling her a 'slag' and 'disgusting'. He said he was used to being nasty to people[3143].

Strathclyde Police sergeant <u>Steven Campbell</u> was accused in 2010 of raping and attempting to murder a woman (on several occasions), as well as indecently assaulting her with a sex toy and taking indecent photos. There were also two firearms charges. Despite the seriousness of the charges, he was not suspended[3144]. Strathclyde PC Dean Stewart, jailed for five years for several sex attacks (e.g. while in uniform on a 28-year-old woman and two teenage girls), failed (2007) to overturn his conviction[3145]. Another Strathclyde PC, Barry Quinn, admitted battering his WPC girlfriend Kelly O'Brien and a toddler. They were both forced to resign[3146]. Married Strathclyde PC Graham Smith was cleared of raping a married solicitor when he answered her emergency call in Glasgow's West End. He apparently admitted having sex but claimed it was consensual. Allegedly he asked the woman's husband and his police partner to leave before the sexual encounter, and even more incredibly he was offered a sexual favour in return for ending the investigation. He was facing an internal inquiry, a report having gone to the deputy chief constable[3147]. Strathclyde PC Craig Horne was on trial in Glasgow in 2009 accused of indecently assaulting three police cadets. One charge involved him exposing himself, another said he lifted a girl up by her bottom. He also allegedly stroked the leg of a cadet[3148].

Married Bristol PC Kenny Lewis denied three counts of rape and one of misconduct in public office; while admitting five other misconduct offences, all sexual, while on duty. A court heard (2009) how he handcuffed and raped a lap dancer in her home. He also had sex, jurors were told, with a female arrestee whom he drove to a beauty spot in his police car (he tracked her down later using the police computer). He would use his contact with women as witnesses, victims or perpetrators as an excuse for stalking them, often under the pretence of further inquiries[3149].

Married Fife police sergeant Douglas McCarroll, accused of harassing volunteer Special Constable Nicola McIntosh, a mother-of-three who is separated from her husband, walked free from court, despite his stalking behaviour over 14 months (he kept texting her, she said, and banged on her door and windows, through which he would peer). He was still suspended by Fife Constabulary in March, 2011[3150]. Newly-wed Fife PC William Crawford was sacked after his superiors decided he raped a woman while his wife slept in the next room: he denied the incident, and there was insufficient evidence to bring a prosecution. He won an appeal to be reinstated but his chief constable challenged it, and so the case was to be heard again. Crawford was also charged with 12 offences (eight assaults, two breach of peace, assault with intent to rape and attempting to pervert the course of justice) between 1984 and 1998, but they were thrown out. The rape 'victim' claimed investigating officers knew her and breached confidentiality[3151].

Lancashire Police's Stuart Fillingham was suspended over allegations of 'inappropriate behaviour' with a female colleague at the force's HQ. In 2010, another senior IT specialist in the same force, Peter Van Parys, was convicted of exposing himself to neighbours. Police found video material showing he had secretly filmed women in a bath[3152].

PC Gopal Dehar raped a woman on their first date, Birmingham Crown Court heard in 2006 - he had been introduced by another constable who had dealt with a burglary she had reported.

Surrey's Deputy Chief Constable Ian Beckett avoided a sexual harassment allegation disciplinary hearing by retiring[3153].

In 2004 Northern Constabulary traffic cop Bob Kennedy, a father of three, was banned for 18 months and fined £800 for dangerous driving (at 121 mph) – he trained advanced drivers and police recruits. He was reinstated but sacked again over sexual harassment of WPCs, including making sexual gestures at one of them (as well as making inappropriate remarks)[3154].

Met PCSO Debra Plucknett claimed constructive dismissal, in that when she complained she was being sexually harassed by fellow officer Clive McDonald, Sergeant Stewart Cook stopped her leaving the room by ramming a chair against the door. She said McDonald sent her a text: 'Make love to me', repeatedly asking her out on a date[3155]. Met PC Ben Staff admitted assault, harassment and obstructing a police officer (he tried to stop himself being arrested). He was conducting three affairs at the same time, and was involved in a fracas when they ambushed him. He escaped a jail and community sentence[3156].

Thames Valley Police Sergeant Mark Downing spanked a female officer over his knee while telling her she was a 'naughty girl'. On another occasion he slapped her on the bottom, and allegedly sexually assaulted another woman. Colleagues had stopped inviting him to social occasions because of disinhibited sexual behaviour, like putting a hand up a woman's top[3157].

US military policewoman Lynndie England was one of a group of soldiers who mistreated Iraqis in Abu Ghraib in 2004: rape, other forms of sexual abuse, urolagnia[3158]. Though this is an American case it perhaps illustrates that not only can women participate in the foulest offences, but that one should never assume that ex-military personnel will necessarily make ideal police officers (see Mentally Ill Policeman chapter, p353).

Charges of rape against Strathclyde sergeant Steven Campbell (by his cop partner) were dropped after he was sacked, but the victim of the rape (and attempted murder) was to ask for a judicial review to re-indict him[3159].

Greater Manchester Police Sergeant Peter Jee, a father of two, was jailed for two years after he sexually molested a psychiatric female patient of 46 who had called 999 (he made her perform a sex act)[3160].

Reading British Transport Police PCSO Samuel Freeland received six-and-a-half years after a six-day trial for raping a teenager after doping her drink[3161].

Avon and Somerset PC Phil Headley, who won an award for fighting sexism, was sacked for sexually harassing a riot squad WPC about her sex life. The WPC was on sick leave because of the stress[3162].

In 1998 Sir Ian Blair, as Chief Constable of Surrey, had to suspend his Deputy Chief Constable Ian Beckett before the latter was acquitted at trial of indecently assaulting a female staff member at force HQ.

Homosexual Problems

Huddersfield PC Mark Carter – a former Mr. Gay UK – was charged (2010) with male rape and other sexual offences, as well as offences in respect of body-building drugs[3163].

Married South Wales PC Haydn Evans lived a double life as a gay sex predator, using the police computer to check on his lovers' health records, etc (he had picked up six men in cruising haunts[3164]).

Two of novelist E. M Forster's most significant relationships were with policemen, despite homosexuality being illegal. One, <u>Bob Buckingham</u>, was 'the love of his life', according to Forster's private papers[3165].

Gay BBC presenter Kristian Digby, 32, was found dead in his flat in 2010. Sources close to him suggested his ex-partner, a former policeman, found the body at 7.45 am[3166].

Two gay Hampshire policemen – Special Constable <u>Steven Ponder</u> and his partner dog handler PC <u>Ivan Sigston</u> (an ex-soldier) – have had a baby boy after the former's married sister acted as surrogate[3167]. Sigston was still 'wed' to a male banker, while Ponder was 'married' to a male cleaner: they were witnesses at each other's 'weddings'. The cleaner is sure Ponder and Sigston were having an affair behind their 'husbands' backs, but Ponder accused <u>him</u> of adultery in divorce papers[3168]. In 2008 over 90 police officers were on Brighton's Gay Pride march. In 2007 the Hampshire force's controversial ban on wearing uniform at the march was lifted, and in 2009 the County's new chief constable was planning to take part[3169]. Gay Hampshire PC <u>Neil Bloomfield</u> claimed he was banned from wearing an earring because he was homosexual, and wanted compensation for hurt feelings. The force admitted Detective Sergeant <u>Andy Lupton</u> had called him 'a f***ing faggot'[3170].

Strathclyde PC <u>Suckbir Mann</u> was still suspended in 2008 on full pay two years after being exposed as a gay prostitute. He had sold £100-an-hour three-in-a-bed sex, under the pseudonym Master Rajj[3171]. A year later he had still not been sacked, being on 'sick leave'. He used to pose in crotchless leather trousers and a studded cap in an advert online[3172].

West Midlands Police's chief of their special branch, <u>James Horton</u>, used an official police Twitter account to send messages to gay men, but was allowed to resign prior to disciplinary proceedings, enabling him to retain his pension[3173].

A former SAS soldier allegedly strangled his gay ex-British policeman lover <u>John Bradshaw</u> at their home in France. The ex-soldier made a full confession[3174].

Gay West Yorkshire PC Mark Carter wept when he was cleared of raping a man and sexually assaulting another three men[3175].

Ex-Met detective <u>Dan Neal</u>, who served on the Operation Yewtree Savile inquiry, was censored by Big Brother as he boasted of gay sex with a married celebrity, who is furious about the claim.

A police training centre was revealed to be keeping Gay Times (which has carried police recruitment advertising for years) under wraps. The magazine describes the police position of avoiding the magazine's "potential for offence" as a return to "Victorian attitudes".

Lesbian Problems

Lesbian Dumfries and Galloway WPC Tracey West – branded a freak by Sergeant <u>Michael Service</u> – won £10,000 damages at an employment tribunal. She had been subjected to a 'relentless series of homophobic conduct'[3176].

Lesbian Greenock WPC <u>Heather Atkinson</u> was found guilty of waging a campaign of intimidation and terror against her former lover, who had started seeing a mutual friend, an ex-WPC. Atkinson chased them at high speed for 13 miles, and another time assaulted the new partner[3177].

In the early days of women's policing it seems they may have been attractive to aggressive lesbians looking for partners[3178].

Lesbian Hertfordshire WPCs Lisa Curchun and Nicola Stewart were thrown out of a Harpenden pub – the landlady claimed they were groping each other. They reported the landlady to colleagues and she was charged with conduct likely to cause distress, but she was cleared by St Albans magistrates[3179].

Lesbian police sergeant Samantha Hale lied about a car crash to cover up her sexuality, but was cleared of perverting the course of justice[3180].

Gay Military Police captain Karen Tait was sent home from Afghanistan for 'sexual misconduct', i.e. conducting herself like a 'lovestruck teenager' with colleague Sergeant Caroline Graham, an employment tribunal heard. The 'inappropriate relationship' allegedly undermined operations[3181].

Cardiff police sergeant Melanie Ernest was found guilty of harassing her female law tutor, being given a two-year Prohibitive Activity Order and ordered to pay costs. She bombarded the object of her sexual obsession with calls, emails, gifts, flowers. Police fitted the lecturer's home with a panic alarm after the policewoman threatened to kill her and commit suicide. Ernest pestered her at her law school office. The victim had to move home, and change her phone numbers and car[3182].

Lesbian PCSO Sylvia Cooper was cleared of sexually assaulting five colleagues (it was claimed officers were so uncomfortable they would change their shifts to avoid contact with her). She was recommended for a Women in Policing Award during her service[3183].

Novelist Patricia Cornwell's lesbian affair with Caroline Nicholl, former chief superintendent with Thames Valley Police, ended in bitter acrimony, with the writer alleging the policewoman was a threat to her[3184].

Paedophilia

Scotland Yard's Paedophile Unit has arrested police officers[3185], and perverts among 184 paedophiles arrested in the world's biggest internet child abuse investigation by CEOP included police officers[3186]. Police consultant Joseph McCabe was sacked by Scotland Yard after his arrest on child porn charges, accused of possessing 13,358 images[3187]. Senior officers have allegedly assaulted boys in care homes, eg the Peter Righton ring in London being investigated by Operation Fairbank. (Ref: The Daily Mail 27.6.13, p20).

50 police officers suspected of downloading child porn were targeted by a 2002 crackdown on paedophilia (Operation Ore), the biggest yet in Britain. PC Robert Smith, a Met control room worker, admitted three charges of making indecent photos of children. Scotland Yard detectives were 'shocked to their boots' to find paedophiles in the Met[3188]. Met Police sergeant Anthony King had 25,000 hardcore child porn images yet was given the 'appalling sentence' of only 15 months[3189].

Strathclyde Police Sergeant <u>Tom Murray</u> committed suicide (by inhaling the fumes from his petrol lawnmower) a week after being charged with sex attacks on three young girls – the three-year paedophile probe was one of Scotland's longest sex-crime investigations. There had been many complaints over the years, but nothing was done. One victim who went to the police claimed there had been a huge cover-up over the years[3190].

A judge branded former Hampshire cop <u>Gordon Hunter</u> a 'disgrace to the uniform' for abusing two boys, jailing him for seven years. Some of the offences took place in his marital bed, and included attempted buggery[3191]. Hampshire PC <u>Michael Keogh</u> denied sexually abusing a child for two years before raping her when she was 16, Portsmouth Crown Court heard (2009). He plied her with alcohol before abusing her. She told the court Keogh was indulging in a string of affairs, including with a WPC[3192].

Essex PC <u>Russell West</u>, a self-acknowledged internet predator, told a 13-year-old: 'You're going to have my babies'. He used a false name to register with the online chat service. He was jailed for 30 months[3193]. Married Essex PCSO <u>David Harrison</u> sent sex texts to a 13-year-old girl he had been detailed to help through a bullying ordeal[3194].

Hero Norfolk PC <u>James Clifford</u> was charged (2010) with child porn offences and having sex while on duty[3195].

West Midlands D.I. <u>Glen Boulton</u>, who investigates paedophilia, was suspended (2010) after being charged with child sex offences (girls) decades before. A Government adviser on child protection, he was also on a local 'safeguarding children' board, and contributed to a Ministry of Justice document which helps young witnesses[3196].

Married South Yorkshire Police Federation treasurer PC <u>Andrew Burton</u>, responsible for monitoring sex offenders, 'groomed' and met a 13-year-old girl by sending her 750 text messages. His wife is also a PC, and he became depressed when she admitted cheating on him with another officer[3197].

In 2009 former marine and Strathclyde policeman <u>John McFadden</u> denied performing satanic sex abuse on a child, as well as using lewd, indecent and libidinous behavior towards three other youngsters in a town near Glasgow[3198]. McFadden told a victim demons would kill him and his parents and drag them to hell unless he carried out vile sex acts. He dressed in a black cloak and used a crucifix, skull and crossbones, onyx ring and devil mask. He was found guilty of child sex abuse[3199]. Strathclyde Police officer <u>Iain Duncan</u> was selected to join his force's child protection unit. The trouble was he was a paedophile who had downloaded images on all five levels of COPINE (Combating Paedophile Information Networks in Europe) – level 5 involves children and bestiality or sadism. He had images of babies and toddlers being abused: they were so depraved the judge at his trial banned the website's name being revealed. He was jailed. Married with a baby, he admitted to distributing as well as possessing banned images, swapping pictures with 25 fellow perverts by email[3200]. Refused bail from Barlinnie Prison, he was charged under section 52 of the Civic Government Scotland Act 1982[3201].

A paramedic has claimed the Cullen Inquiry into the Dunblane massacre was seriously flawed. Central Scotland Police, who should never have been chosen to investigate the background, she says, because they were implicated, repeatedly renewed Hamilton's gun licence despite chronic warnings. He had friends in the police, and Cullen read none of the preparatory material which has been locked away for a century. Sandra Uttly, who was involved in the aftermath of the killings, believes Hamilton was a major porn provider to a ring which included police, who in turn protected him from allegations. The dossier comprising 106 documents held in the National Archive reveal why over 20 complaints did not lead to court action. One report revealed a senior prosecutor returned pictures of children – seized as evidence before the tragedy – to Hamilton. Others link the gunman to the Freemasons, in which some police officers are heavily involved[3202] (see 'The Masonic Policeman' – next chapter).

Humberside Police Chief Superintendent <u>Alec Alexander</u> was given 10 years for paedophile activities – for some time he had been 'protected by his position and a wall of silence within the police force'[3203]. Having caught many paedophiles during a 30-year career, he was himself a child molester who raped his own daughter during a decade of abuse, starting on her seventh birthday. She appeared among 60,000 images of children on his home computer. A trained hostage negotiator, he had disowned his daughter because she was pregnant when she married[3204].

PC <u>Colin Murray</u> was sacked by Tayside Police after his conviction for exposing himself to a young girl. He paid hundreds to a US website for a sick paedophile collection of computer images and videos of torture, rape and animal abuse on children from the age of three. He was given a year plus a two-year licence period, and placed on the sex offenders' register for 10 years[3205].

Married Dffed-Powys PC <u>Geoffrey Harries</u> was stabbed to death by a drunken neighbour. Harries was facing child porn charges[3206]. A police cover-up was alleged in a Panorama programme (03.12.00) about the Welsh priest paedophile case. He had resigned after 2,000 child porn images were found on his computer[3207].

Scottish ex-cop <u>Alexander McBride</u> was accused (2009) by two sisters, whom he had child-minded several decades previously, of sexually abusing them in a car and a Glasgow house[3208]. When one sister told a priest at confession, she was thrown out of the confessional. Strathclyde PC <u>Richard Gill</u>, one of the Anderton community policing team, was arrested accused of taking indecent pictures of a child: he was taken home to change out of his uniform[3209].

PC <u>Kristian Abbott</u> was jailed at a Manchester court in 2009 for confronting a 15-year-old girl runaway in his patrol car with a sex act. He was cleared of inviting another girl to strip in his marked car soon after returning from honeymoon[3210].

Intelligence that could have led to the arrest on child porn charges of two policemen who played key roles in the Soham murders case, was known to the British police for a year (23 of the 30 officers on the list of UK-based subscribers had not been arrested by Sept. 19, 2002).

The global internet paedophile ring run by two gays in Lincolnshire, revealed in May, 2011, had two police subscribers (they have reportedly been dismissed from the service).

Grampian police sergeant <u>Neil Shand</u> was charged with taking and possessing an indecent image of a child. He was arrested by his own force and appeared behind closed doors at Banff Sheriff Court[3211] (does this constitute special treatment?).

MOD constable <u>Troy Tubbritt</u>, who guarded AWE at Aldermaston in Berkshire, was jailed for two years after being caught twice downloading child porn (over 5,000 images and pictures of girls 5-15 years)[3212].

A young Northants mother has told how police refused to believe she was raped by P.C. <u>Daniel Listman</u> after she accepted a lift home in his patrol car. He was dismissed from the force but never charged with the 2001 attack. He then went on a nine-year campaign of sex attacks on 13 victims (including children) of both sexes[3213]. This horrific sequel might never have happened if Listman had not been given special treatment.

Black Bethnal Green custody PC <u>Robert Nicholson</u> was sacked after stalking a vulnerable 14-year-old girl with text messages: he had met her on duty. He used police databases to check the girl's background – she lived in a care home. He was charged with two counts of sexual activity with a minor, but was cleared by a jury[3214].

Former Wiltshire policeman <u>Thomas Stevens</u> killed himself in a churchyard just before he was due to go on trial for child sex offences (both sexes) dating back to the 1970s[3215].

Police sergeant <u>Paul Greig</u>, suspended by the Lothian and Borders force, was found guilty in 2011 of raping two young sisters (six and eight) in 1975 while he was their babysitter. He had threatened the girls their father would be jailed and they would be sent to a home if they told anyone[3216].

26-year-old Sussex sergeant <u>Philip Savidge</u> was charged with possessing 54,000 indecent images of children (including babies) and with 42 offences of making and distributing them: 1,681 of the images were alleged to be 'prohibited and extreme'. Savidge was a volunteer with a Scout group, though none of the scouts were involved in the charges. He has quit the force[3217], being jailed for 27 months.

Met police sergeant <u>Darren Dearling</u> was facing jail after admitting downloading over 4,000 child porn pictures. He lives with his mother in Surrey. Some images were rated at the second worst depravity level, featuring child rape[3218].

PC <u>Nick Oliver</u>, a traffic officer in Portsmouth, resigned after being caught with child porn[3219].

In 2003 the investigation into child sex charges against Cambridgeshire's DC <u>Brian Stevens</u> collapsed (his colleague PC <u>Tony Goodridge</u> pleaded guilty to possessing child porn in the same year). The police's incompetence in the case included their so-called computer expert making crucial errors in assessing Stevens' computer: the police had also waited nine weeks before searching for the telephone records that are needed to establish who has

Brian Stevens

downloaded what: the evidence by then had gone[3220]. Cambridgeshire Police sergeant <u>Dominic Liversedge</u>, 27, had a 14-year-old girl's initials tattooed on his wrist because he 'fell in love' with her. He befriended her family when he took a lead role in an amateur drama group. His texting the girl progressed to kissing and touching her intimately. The tattoo included the phrase 'best buddies till the very end'. He pleaded guilty to sexual activity with a child under 16 and was jailed for a year[3221].

Tayside Police family protection unit officer, DC <u>Iain Ledger</u>, a divorcé, was suspended (2011) after describing on the social network site '4D interactive' performing paedophile acts. Though placed on the sex offenders' register his superiors refused to reveal whether he was still on full pay (why would they prevaricate unless he was?). The court described his expressed fantasies as 'obscene, disgusting and almost depraved'[3222]. <u>Ledger</u>, who made 11 obscene calls to other men on a chatline about paedophile sex, was put on probation and the sex offenders' register for three years. Tayside Police say he was still suspended by end January, 2012[3223].

Special Constable <u>Andrew Barber</u> from Ipswich was found guilty in 2012 at Norwich Crown Court of rape and sexual activity with a child. Barber kept a victim's bra and knickers as trophies, so obsessed was he with girls' underwear[3224].

Merseyside community cop <u>Simon Terns</u>, in his forties, denied grooming a 13-year-old girl, letting her climb on top of him in a bedroom. He called her 'babes' and offered her a 'good rubdown'. He 'sextexted' her: 'If you're a naughty little devil it could be sex sex sex sex'[3225].

Known Jersey paedophile <u>Roger Holland</u>, 42, had an indecent assault conviction regarding a learning disabled girl in the back of a St. Helier police van, and was jailed for two years for assaulting two underage girls (and five others). Yet he was elected to the island's Honorary Police in 1992, re-elected in 1995, and only suspended in 1999[3226].

Thames Valley Police officer <u>Mohammed Younas</u> who raped a young girl, at times every other day, for eight years, was jailed for 18 years[3227].

Former policeman <u>Peter Kirk</u>, 78, from Surrey, was jailed for 14 years for repeatedly raping a girl and sexually assaulting another child[3228].

Strathclyde Special PC <u>James Murnin</u> was arrested by fellow officers for swapping paedophile images online (via Windows Live Messenger). His email address was found on an English sex offender's computer[3229]. <u>Murnin</u> was sentenced to seven months for accessing child porn, some of which was level 5, the worst[3230].

Military policeman <u>Anthony Ellis</u> was dismissed and jailed for two years for downloading child porn[3231].

Transgender Officers

The National Trans Police Association speaks for transgender, androgyne, intersex and cross-dressing officers and wants the police service to become the employer of choice for their members[3232]. The NTPA has about 50 members, some having surgery, some just cross-dressing: all want taxpayer funding. They say police are now institutionally P.C.[3233].

'Before you turn on the charm, Philip, that's Nigel my new bodyguard'

PC <u>Adam Smith</u> has become PC Alexandra Smith, sharing female locker rooms and facilities. She was due in 2010 to have a private sex change operation in Thailand. She is allowed to frisk women on the street. Her close friend <u>Chloe Davis</u>, a transsexual previously known as Clive, is a diversity officer in the same North Wales force. Alexandra – 'Lexie' – will receive sick pay while recuperating[3234].

Sex swap soldier <u>Ian Hamilton</u> (previously a captain in the Parachute Regiment) joined Strathclyde Police in 2009 (she is now <u>Abigail Austin)</u>. After a row about pension rights she won an undisclosed compensation payout from the Army for sexual discrimination after being refused permission to wear a woman's uniform. There was a 2008 Channel 4 documentary about her entitled 'Sex Change Soldier'[3235]. She is Scotland's first transgender cop. She had her operation in Thailand, while still in the Army.

Former sailor <u>Steve Quinn</u> was to become Met WPC Stephanie Quinn after finishing training[3236].

The UK's first transgender officer (2001) was Sergeant <u>Chris Lamb</u> who, after 26 years in the force, became Sergeant <u>Nicola Lamb</u>[3237].

Former Grampian and British Transport policeman <u>Carol Mapley</u> (formerly David) was selected as Scotland's first 'sexswap' council election candidate (for Dumfries and Galloway). She says she was hounded out of the Transport Police . She reverted to masculinity in 2001 after spending 14 years as a woman (her 'transitioning' being in 1987), but changed again to femininity in 2007. Having served 18 years as both man and woman as an RAF reservist, she is now a trainee social worker. She wants to be an MSP and serves as

Labour's transgender officer for the whole of the UK. She is a Quaker and lives with her female partner[3238].

Pornography (adult)

Police officers in the Gatwick Airport firearms unit were reported to have watched porn while supposedly on duty[3239].

Royal protection officer Paul Page claims colleagues traded Dutch porn in Buckingham Palace (officers also ran poker games for money)[3240].

439 officers and support staff have been disciplined (sacked or warned) for looking at internet porn and social networking sites; the figure could be much higher because some forces refused to disclose details. A Lancashire inspector was given a written warning, as was another Lancashire officer, while another inspector on the force was caught looking at 'porn images via the internet'. South Yorkshire was the worst force – 53 culprits, including an officer who posted an 'unauthorised video on a commercial internet website', and a sergeant warned over the inappropriate use of an email. On average more members of staff than officers in every force have been punished. In Cheshire 51, including two inspectors, were warned[3241].

Fed-up Cheshire PC James Eardley quit the force to feature in porn movies, first appearing in a live internet sex show[3242]. Likewise saucy Met WPC Kat Morsia has quit the force to take up pole dancing with exotic dance group The Fetish Crew. She was a lap dancer before joining the police[3243].

Six cops were sacked and 16 civilian staff were either sacked or resigned for watching online porn at work. More than 600 police and 50 staff have been disciplined. Widespread net abuse included sending and receiving offensive emails[3244].

Leicestershire officers were caught, on the 2005 Dispatches exposé by WPC Nina Hobson, gloating at porn and making sexist remarks to female colleagues (porn on an officer's mobile phone featured a woman and a horse). Porno posters were displayed at a police station[3245].

Other Lascivious Behaviour

West Midlands Police have posted on the net a 'revised uniform, equipment and appearance policy' which bans officers from wearing revealing underwear of inappropriate colours, in case the VPL (visible panty line) reveals itself. Baseball caps can only be worn in certain units, whereas Essex Police officers can wear baseball caps, hoodies and trainers freely when on the beat[3246]. There are even rumours of spot checks to ensure the underwear code is being observed, with male officers being told they mustn't show their boxer shorts when on duty[3247].

Pervert MOD PC Andrew Ryan was jailed for five months and put on the Sex Offenders Register, for voyeurism: he had filmed naked women and girls in changing rooms[3248].

Serious injury specialist lawyers are to sue Northumbria Police for damages for victims of rapist cop Stephen Mitchell[3249]. Former soldier Mitchell attacked up to 30 women in a five year terror reign at Pilgrim Street in Newcastle. Mitchell, a divorcé originally from Glasgow, was arrested (2010) accused of raping or sexually assaulting 19 women over eight years, involving 43 offences (seven of rape, 17 of indecent assault and 19 of misconduct in a public office)[3250]. His victims were allegedly vulnerable young women (drug addicts/petty criminals)[3251]. While in the army he allegedly tried to rape two male soldiers and sexually assault a third. Military police took no action, and details of the accusations (he had stood trial in Edinburgh on one, but there were suspicions of witness intimidation, and the case was dropped) were not recorded on the police database. References from his military days were never sought by his future police employers. At one stage he hacked into the national computer to check on his ex-wife and her new partner, but he was only given a small fine. He moonlighted running a massage business. He was allowed to rejoin the force in 2008 after being sacked in 2007 for 'consensual' sex with one of his victims. He would tell his victims he was untouchable. His nickname was 'Pervey Steve'[3252]. Northumbria Police has at last started to pay compensation to his victims[3253].

Talking with servant girls and female cooks was a particular concern of the mid-19th Century Police Commissioners about their new police constables, as it was a regular subject for lampoons in the media[3254].

Lustful Met PC Tom Cranfield, who protected the Pope when he visited the UK, arranged sex sessions in his patrol car with a stranger he contacted on a dating website. While on duty he took pictures of himself in uniform in a police station W.C., and put them on the net, even suggesting the Pope had blessed his sex acts. He also branded PCSOs 'stupid'. He sent one woman a string of overt emails and topless pictures of himself, arranging to meet her in a marked car[3255].

Former Special Constable Jane Dearie was one of rapist Dumfries and Galloway inspector Adam Carruthers' 38 victims[3256].

Sex pest Strathclyde cop Gavin Hannah was given 200 hours community service for groping two women officers after a Xmas night out. (His case was heard in private.) He resigned from the force[3257].

In 2010 Northumbria Chief Constable Sue Sim was told a police colleague had sexually assaulted a WPC in her bedroom in the late 1980s at the Aykley Heads training centre in Durham. The letter was forwarded to be dealt with by Durham Police[3258].

Strathclyde Police employee David Kennedy, 49, arrested for allegedly flashing at two women and a young girl on three occasions, was allowed back to work while on bail[3259].

Strathclyde PC John Wardrop, fined for bombarding his estranged wife with abusive texts, had his conviction for breach of the peace overturned on a technicality: his wife was alone when she received the messages – breach of the peace cannot be committed in private[3260].

Senior British Transport Police officer <u>Masood Khan</u> had a 'quickie' sex session in an interview room at Gatwick Airport with a woman he met on an internet singles site. His pseudonym was 'Michael K. Plod'[3261].

Masood Khan

An irate reader of 'The People' in 2007 wrote, re the Cheshire PC who <u>joined</u> doggers: 'I bet this is just the tip of the iceberg in terms of police behaving badly while working. Gone are the days when the public respected the bobby on the beat. Some police think they are above the law they are employed to enforce'. Abigail Kirk, Bournemouth[3262].

34-year-old PC <u>Joe Pierce</u> resigned after being caught romping in public on his police car bonnet with two vice girls. Pictures of the encounter appeared on a notorious sex website with the caption: 'Police, Camera, Action'[3263].

Because Lancashire D.S. <u>John Cragg</u>, a rape victim support officer, had an affair with an alleged victim and frequent sex with the mother of an eight-year-old rape victim at her home, two court cases collapsed[3264].

Gwent armed cop <u>Shaun Jenkins</u>, who had sex at his home with a married woman while on duty, was sacked but then reinstated after the Police Appeals Panel ruled he could reach his gun, his trousers staying around his ankles (his colleague waited for 40 minutes outside in an armed response vehicle). The IPCC has condemned the decision, as it will 'undermine public confidence in the credibility of the police discipline system'[3265].

Three Scottish police officers faced serious sex-related charges in seperate cases in the same court on the same date.

In November 1961 four Met officers were suspended because of allegations against them by two men in respect of the activities of a camera club[3266].

Eight women are suing the Met, saying they were duped into long-term relationships with undercover officers. Thus <u>Mark Kennedy</u> is said in legal papers (he is being divorced from the mother of his two children) to have had relationships with <u>three</u> women. Two officers fathered two children but didn't partake in their rearing, so the children know nothing about their fathers' activities (one officer had been named as <u>Bob Lambert</u>, who has admitted tricking a second woman into a long-term relationship). One of the officers monitored his mistress and their child by reading confidential police reports[3267].

Central Scotland PC <u>Douglas Dishington</u> (nickname PC Dishy), was told to resign following claims he cuckolded a husband to whose domestic disturbance he was called, to 'give a fright' to the householder's stepdaughter. The PC was also accused of giving his own young son lifts in his police car, and giving a false alibi for the stepdaughter[3268].

An officer took sexual advantage of a widow whom he had to tell about her husband's death[3269].

CAVEAT CIVIS

Lothian and Borders acting sergeant <u>Adrian Merron</u>, a former RUC officer who had been involved in a youth crime crackdown near Dalkeith, was charged with public indecency in Edinburgh streets and obtaining classified information from the police computer. He was suspended from duty in 2008 for 'wilful neglect of duty'[3270].

Glasgow cop <u>Martin Cusick</u> appeared in court under the Sexual Offences Act after going on the run to Canada[3271].

Married Peeping Tom Essex cop <u>David Smith</u> drilled a hole in the wall of his station so that he could ogle women in their changing rooms. Concealed cameras caught him in a sting with a decoy officer. Smith, who was given a three-month suspended sentence, is now an HGV driver[3272].

Strathclyde mounted WPC <u>Alison Whyte</u> was transferred from her horseback unit for having an affair with a friend's husband[3273].

On one occasion <u>Dizaei</u> accused two constables of damaging his car, but it transpired one of his many mistresses was responsible. He once threatened to murder the mother of one of his mistresses 'like a dog'. He was returned to jail in February, 2012, for framing an innocent web-designer[3274].

Merseyside Police Chief Constable <u>Mark Brew</u>, in charge of over 100 officers, on the force's Matrix anti-gun and gang disruption teams, was sacked when four allegations were upheld against him. He ordered a constable on duty to drive him 200 miles home from a conference (instead of his taking a train). Married Brew also left a junior in charge of a conference to visit a married lover's home. He used his work mobiles to view porn and sent smutty texts to two other women, thought to be cops[3275].

Tayside Police's Chief Constable <u>Justine Curran</u> sent smutty texts ('He must have a big willy') to her PA, speculating on the size of a senior cop's manhood (he was having an affair with a civilian worker in the force). The matter came to light when the PA was charged with an insurance scam. Curran was previously assistant chief constable at Greater Manchester Police – her marriage having broken up she moved north and started dating senior cop Gordon Meldrum. But the joint police board gave her a vote of confidence[3276].

'Spank Nights', run by a Bristol-based fetish clothing designer, encourages wife-swapping in 'anything goes' dungeons, attracting senior policemen and judges (among others)[3277].

'You think I should also claim for whiplash injuries? But I feel fine.'

Some senior officers warned that billeting hundreds of police in a Dorset holiday camp during the Olympics could lead to 'drunkenness, debauchery and unwanted pregnancies'. One said: 'I foresee lots of drunk cops ... criminal damage ... public disorder ... assaults, illicit sex, divorce ... I predict ... the caravan site having to call police'. Police being accommodated in the camp will attend a course in 'integrity and professional standards', and will be given an allowance of £80 daily[3278].

Northants Inspector <u>Daemon Johnson</u> was sacked for posting a photo of his genitalia on Facebook[3279].

Former acting assistant chief constable of Grampian <u>Ian Paterson</u> resigned as charity boss of The Aberdeen Council of Voluntary Organisation after being charged with an indecent assault and another offence under section 3 of the Sexual Offences (Scotland) Act 2009. Paterson worked with the force for over 40 years. It hasn't been made public why Paterson appeared in court <u>in private</u>[3280].

Scottish PC Gary Cryans was cleared of indecently assaulting three female colleagues after a week-long trial at Glasgow Sheriff Court[3281].

Scots police officer <u>Stephen Cooperwhite</u> was to stand trial in 2013 charged with raping a Paisley woman in Benbecula (as well as three other assaults on her in Paisley and Benbecula) and another in Stirlingshire[3282].

Paedophile Cyril Smith told Rochdale Police he had spanked boys saying: 'This will kill my mother'. Police investigated him from 1974 to 1979. The police files about the case vanished[3283].

West Midlands Police officers sexually harassed a vulnerable survivor and blackmailed others with criminal charges if they didn't change statements[3284].

Disgraced Central Scotland PC <u>Gordon Isdale</u> used police databases to stalk a transsexual woman he met on duty. He used a fake name to court her. The lothario cop also pursued at least six other women[3285].

A scorned mistress started an airport punch-up when she saw her boyfriend, West Midlands PC <u>Mark Davies</u>, had had a secret holiday with colleague WPC <u>Elaine Turner</u>. The mistress and PC Davies have three children[3286].

British Transport Police PCSO <u>Samuel Freeland</u> from Reading spiked a teenager's drink before raping her. He had been awarded a Certificate of Commendation[3287].

Former Strathclyde special constable <u>James Murnin</u> was jailed for seven months, his email address found on a sex offender's computer in England: he was part of a porn image network[3288].

Married South Yorkshire Police detective <u>David Turner</u> was back in uniform and behind a desk after being found having a tryst with a woman in his unmarked police car while on duty. His suspicious wife had a PI keep an eye on him[3289].

The CPS was to investigate evidence that <u>Brian Stevens</u>, the Soham officer sensationally cleared of child porn charges, as well as charges of indecently assaulting two teenage girls, was given his crucial alibi (shortly before his trial) by a former lover who worked for the CPS. She had worked behind the bar at Huntingdon police station and allegedly had a string of policemen friends while she was married[3290].

One of the two officers involved in the Jessica Chapman and Holly Wells murder inquiry was PC Antony Goodridge, who faced 14 charges of possessing an indecent photo and one of possession with a view to distributing it[3291].

Dorset PC Steven Rigler was placed on trial accused of making a girl perform a sex act on him as he drove her home in his patrol car. He tried to clear himself by writing himself a blackmail letter[3292].

Central Scotland PC Craig Rankin was shown mooning on TV while travelling with the Tartan Army to Belgium. He was warned and fined[3293].

Nottinghamshire PC Tony White, awarded the Queen's Gallantry Medal for catching serial killer Donald Neilson (the Black Panther), faced prison for indecently assaulting four teenage girls at a cadet corps he set up: he ordered 'recruits' to call him 'sir' or 'captain'[3294].

With the collapse of his third marriage South Yorkshire Assistant Chief Constable Steve Chamberlain set up home with Inspector Helen Chapman, who is estranged from her police sergeant husband, working with her at the same station[3295].

The 'sexual antics' of Avon and Somerset Chief Superintendent Graham Cowley (e.g. a WPC allegedly had her hand down his trousers) and other officers (including five female) scandalised dignitaries at a charity dinner, making the force a 'laughing stock' (e.g. two officers groped each other on the dance floor, and a WPC danced around 'with her skirt over her head'). It was even claimed two officers had sex in the street outside the venue. There were even complaints against officers attending to receive awards for absent retiree officers[3296].

Inspector Sandford Vann pretended to his mistress, a Met civilian worker, he was splitting from his wife, so she started preparing for their wedding. He forged a divorce document to convince her. He was given a nine-month suspended sentence[3297].

Dumfries and Galloway inspector Adam Carruthers was charged with rapes and sexual assaults on three women, several of them using his police-issue baton. One alleged victim said he used a peeled banana[3298].

Married South Yorkshire traffic cop John Wetherall was having affairs behind his wife's back using his patrol car. He was caught by his vehicle's video surveillance system.

Stephen House, Chief Constable of Police Scotland, says men who are drunken wife-beaters should be banned from drinking alcohol. Asked about the number of police officers who are themselves wife-beaters, he said it involved only a tiny percentage of officers but revealed that he knows of responding officers who form relationships with the victims they have gone to protect[3299]. Edinburgh DI Gordon Cowe was arrested twice in two days accused of attacking his wife in their Edinburgh home (on the second occasion he was held in custody)[3300].

Instructors at the Greater Manchester Police training school would seduce new recruits[3301].

CHAPTER XVI

THE MASONIC POLICEMAN

A former editor of 'Police Review', Brian Hilliard, says if you wanted to become a member of the Met's Flying Squad in the fifties you had to be a Mason. He says: 'I don't think I've spoken to a CID officer of the period who wasn't a Mason'[3302]. Freemasonry is especially prevalent in the City of London Police[3303].

A Freemasons' lodge within Buckingham Palace was launched in 2008, with male servants and royal protection squad police as members. Plans for 'The Royal Household Lodge' had been blocked by senior officials earlier in the year, so the name was changed to Mulberry Lodge. The Lodge has policemen as Grand Master and Secretary[3304].

It has been alleged that the Jack the Ripper murders were perpetrated according to Masonic ritual: the subsequent 'police cover-up' was led by the Met's Commissioner and Assistant Commissioner, both Freemasons. The Ripper murders involved an official cover-up of immense proportions that "confirmed that Freemasonry really was the unseen power behind the throne and government alike". Commissioner <u>Warren</u> impeded the investigation at every turn. The Scotland Yard Home Office Ripper files remained secret for 90 years. Divisional police surgeon <u>Dr. Bagster Phillips</u>, a Mason, is the person most likely to have removed the Masonic symbol from the scene of one of the Ripper victims. He certainly tried to conceal vital testimony about the nature of the injuries he found.

There have been allegations of charges against criminal Masons by police Masons; of unfair promotions for Masons, non-Masons hounded out of the service; of blackmail and violence; of discipline eroded by a system in which a Chief Constable or Commander can be made to kneel in submission before one of his own constables, and of robbery and even murder planned between police and criminals at Lodge meetings.

In 1877 every member of the Detective Department at Scotland Yard, up to and including the second-in-command, was in the pay of a gang of vicious swindlers (e.g. one William Kurr). In 1977 Scotland Yard detectives were again in the dock on serious corruption charges (the criminals belonged to the same Lodges as the cops). New recruits often failed to work at their exams, because Mason relatives and friends assured them Mason membership would ensure their advancement. David Thomas, of high standing in the police, has asserted that though only a small percentage of police are Masons, they are mostly of high rank, so their influence on the service is disproportionate, even incalculable. In the Met Freemasonry is strongest in the CID.

Police inspector <u>Adam Carruthers</u>, jailed for 12 years for raping two women, may have used Masonic links to cover up his crimes. 31 women in Dumfries & Galloway have come forward to accuse him of sexual assaults. His sexual conduct brought warnings from his bosses, dating back 16 years, but he was still promoted. The first inquiry collapsed in 1998. When there were complaints he was simply moved (See also Name Index, p642).

When the total police complement in England and Wales was 135,000 it was estimated some 22,000 (or one in six) were Freemasons. This compares with one in 30 of the English population. There are 9,000 lodges in the UK, and in some there are police and active criminals in the same lodge. Thus in 1979 armed robber Leonard John Gibson (given 10 years in 1981 for a silver bullion heist) became Worshipful Master of the Waterways Lodge, when there were eight policemen members, including senior detective John Brian McNeill. Gibson was well known to Scotland Yard – he was pictured in their 'Handbook of Violent Thieves'. The ruling Grand Lodge decided at first that such robbers could stay: it took them nine years to conclude the mix of police and criminals was toxic. There is even a one-off single-profession lodge (Manor of St. James), consisting only of police: normally against Masonic rules, yet it was 'consecrated' in Freemasons Hall. One policeman coined the phrase 'A firm in a firm' to describe the situation, with Masonic loyalty being stronger than loyalty to the police.

Non-Mason Brian Hilliard has revealed that Masons have tried to interrupt the conviction process of other Masons accused of criminality. Granada TV reported on Masonic corruption in the cases of DS John Symonds (imprisoned for soliciting a bribe to 'fit someone up') and Superintendent William 'Bill' Moodie, in charge of an Obscene Publications squad and a member of a Surrey lodge (he got 12 years in 1977, having made illegally £40,000 annually). Moodie and other corrupt officers entertained porn merchants at Masonic functions, e.g. porn king Ron 'The Dustman' Daley. One villain, Phil Cuthbert, involved in high-profile robberies like the 1978 City of London Daily Mirror heist, was taped revealing £80,000 bribes in 1982 to bent Masonic detectives. Symonds was guaranteed immunity, though he felt he had to flee abroad after receiving death threats (another top Masonic cop in their Connaught Rooms made a menacing throat-slitting gesture towards him) for listing corrupt colleagues (Moodie, Mason Ken Drury, and others). He revealed how you had a better chance of promotion in the CID if you were a Mason, agreed to be corrupt or to condone corruption. Moodie was in 1969 put in charge of the three major inquiries into corruption in the 1970s while he was extorting 'protection money' from Soho pornographers.

'The Times' published articles on the matter in 1969, as did 'Private Eye' and 'The Observer'. Met officer Alan Holmes was pressurised to betray a crooked police commander with possible links to notorious Kenneth Noye – his conversations were secretly recorded: he committed suicide. Met Commissioner Sir Kenneth Newman tried to address the situation in his guideline booklet 'Principles of Policing'.

Freemason Alf Parrish, the Chief Constable of Derbyshire, was appointed by a committee comprising Masons, but resigned in 1985 over £30,000 expenses. Masons were the county's 'secret government'.

Islington Chief Inspector Brian Woollard, once a fraud squad high-flier, became a 'persona non grata' overnight when a corruption probe began into holidays, gifts, bribes by building companies. A housing official and two of Woollard's fraud squad bosses were Masons, as was the assistant Director of Public Prosecutions involved in the case. Woollard's career was wrecked by the Masonic influences, especially at Wembley, whence he was transferred: he would have to complain about his treatment to officers he was complaining about. He was dismissed the service in 1988 for 'going AWOL', but he claimed to have medical justification for his absence.

A Watlington publican alleged Masonic police harassment, especially from Inspector Ron Duncan, of the St. Mary's Lodge in Thame, over the renewal of his licence. All the opponents of the renewal (head of the town ratepayers association, councillors, etc) were Masons, and seven officers attended court to have the pub closed, making the landlord bankrupt. He claimed the police from Thame would come and sit in the pub car park three or four times a night, which must have intimidated some customers[3305].

The chief player in the horrific Longcare scandal, Gordon Rowe, seems to have been a Freemason, allegedly having told staff he had a good relationship with the Slough police, whose three investigations were inconclusive (the Slough Lodge is very well-attended)[3306]. A witness in the Longcare scandal had to be taken to Windsor police station for interview because of Gordon Rowe's Freemason friends at Slough police station[3307] (see Appendix I). Masonic influence, too, allegedly facilitated the Dunblane massacre (see previous chapter, 'The Lustful Policeman').

Eddy Ross, disgraced ex-policeman father of Orkney racist killer Michael Ross, blamed a Masonic plot for his son's conviction, with Northern Constabulary police chiefs being involved. D.C. Bob Petrie, who was part of the original murder inquiry, was the Grand Master of the Kirkwall Kilwinning Masonic Lodge[3308].

When the Home Office tried to establish a voluntary register of Masonic policemen in 1999, only 37% responded, and of these only 1.1% said they were Masons, but the true figure was estimated as 10 times higher. The Home Affairs Select Committee found Freemasonry may have contributed to serious miscarriages of justice in the 1970s by the West Midlands Serious Crime Squad.

"The insidious effect of Freemasonry among the police has to be experienced to be believed" - David Thomas, a former head of Monmouthshire CID (1969).

Leading Police Federation officers have established their own national Masonic lodge led by Met officer John Tully: the 'Sine Favore' lodge is derived from the Federation's motto 'Without Fear, Without Favour'. A 1998 Parliamentary inquiry (home affairs select committee) has warned of public fears that 'Freemasonry can have an unhealthy influence on the criminal justice system' (the inquiry examined Masons' roles in the abandonment of a probe into N. Ireland's shoot-to-kill policy and the malpractice riddling the West Midlands Serious Crime Squad). Martin Short's 'Inside the Brotherhood' argued that the large numbers of Masons in the police force perverts justice[3309]. The Federation refused to say whether any of its officials had revealed Masonic links[3310].

It has been alleged a 19th Century conspiracy of police and criminals led to the dissolution of the Met's original Detective Department: every member was being bribed by a gang of swindlers, and Chief Detective Inspector Nathaniel Druscovitch, who was put in charge of the investigation into the Department, was himself a bent Mason. It is said Operation Countryman in the 1970s ('Countryman' had also referred to crooked Masonic Inspector John Meiklejohn a century earlier) resulted from a Masonic City of London commissioner turning a blind eye to corruption.

In 2001 the United Grand Lodge of England tried to improve the image of Freemasonry by hiring the PR agency MPA.

As with the police service, Freemasonry may also have a disproportionate influence in the prison service, whence there has been an 'unacceptably low' response to Masons to declare themselves voluntarily: it is believed there are 'large numbers' of the undeclared in Northern Ireland, London, Manchester and Durham prisons. Thus in a Southern English prison four posts were available for senior officers, but all went to Masons (there were 16 applicants), and Leyhill jail in Buckinghamshire printed the 'Book of Ritual' for the Kirklees Lodge in Yorkshire (the 188 page book bore the logo 'Printed at HMP Leyhill')[3311].

Despite failing the Strategic Command Course several times – only one attempt is allowed – one can become a senior officer if one's face fits (e.g. in the right Masonic Lodge). Trainee detectives are supposed to undergo monthly assessments, but can be let loose on the community without any assessments at all[3312].

CHAPTER XVII

THE MENTALLY ILL POLICEMAN

CHAPTER CONTENTS

CHAPTER XVII

THE MENTALLY ILL POLICEMAN

Are police officers at a higher than average risk of mental illness? The author has not found it possible to trace academic studies, but the raised sickness absence rates and prevalence of alcohol problems are perhaps pointers. Met Police psychiatrist Dr. Derek Summerfield says he witnessed a 'culture of entitlement', with officers faking mental illness to claim gold-plated pensions. In 2003, almost half of all health retirements were on mental grounds. Up to 180 police monthly report having stress-related problems[3313].

Alcohol Problems

Of 2,800 constables serving in 1830 only 562 remained four years later, four-fifths having been dismissed because of drunkenness. In the Victorian era alcoholism was no barrier to progress in the force, e.g. one William Ashe joined the Leeds Police, then switching to Middlesbrough in 1866. Despite like many of his colleagues being disciplined for being drunk and unfit for duty, he was promoted to sergeant[3314]. Even before the establishment of the New Police, their predecessors the Watchmen patrols were often accused of drunkenness. A Victorian music hall ditty confirms alcohol and policing were close companions:

'If you want to get a drink, ask a P'liceman!
He will manage it, I think, will a P'liceman!
If the pubs are shut or not
He'll produce a flowing pot
He can open all the lot, can a P'liceman!'

'In my experience, most coppers can drink most journalists under the table', says famous hack and author Richard Littlejohn[3315].

Lothian and Borders inspector Jillian Kerr was disciplined for falling asleep in a taxi after a boozy Christmas night out: the driver having to take her to a police station because he couldn't rouse her. In 2007 she had been investigated over claims she avoided feeding a parking meter by saying she was on official business – she displayed a police notice on her private car[3316].

Drunken Strathclyde PCs Graeme Key and Adam Kelly clashed with bouncers when the latter refused them admission to Glasgow's Bamboo Club because they were too drunk. One cop tried to use his warrant card to obtain admission, and one of the stewards was allegedly punched[3317].

Drunken Grampian PC Kenneth Burnett hurled foul abuse at other police and football ground stewards. He was only fined £750, despite also saying other officers 'were lying'[3318].

An incident at Bedford's Wellington Arms pub involved two plainclothes officers arriving with blue lights flashing so they could join friends for a drink[3319].

CAVEAT CIVIS

The Met has adopted a zero-tolerance approach to drinking on duty, using 'mobile substance abuse testing units' with the authority to breathalyse suspect officers. Only undercover detectives visiting pubs will be exempt[3320].

Former Met WPC Fiona Daniels, suing for sexual harassment, described a macho culture of drinking and lewd comments[3321].

Drunken Tayside PC Graeme Hobbs called his station to report himself for running riot. He was arrested by colleagues in the centre of Carnoustie and spent a night in the cells at his own station[3322].

Trusted senior property officer Jack Cook at Worcester police station stole nearly £3,000 of cash seized from criminals, to dissipate on drink[3323].

Fife police sergeant Andrew Sneddon allegedly collapsed drunk after the Scottish Cup Final, with worried fans dialling 999. He was also reportedly found drunk in Glasgow the previous year after the League Cup Final. But despite this, he was still being considered for a promotion to inspector. Also in 2007 another Fife policeman, PC Colin Nicoll, was found slumped drunk in his car after an international; he was three times the limit[3324].

Disciplinary action was taken against five Sussex officers for drunken behaviour after a session at their social club: one vomited in an office, another was caught urinating against the station wall, while a third is accused of exposing himself while walking through the police canteen[3325].

Met PC Geoff Jackson stole a riot-squad vehicle from his Paddington Green station after a drinking session. Driving at excessive speed he crashed into a central reservation, then went to sleep in the back of the van. He was jailed for 90 days after admitting driving without insurance or consent and without due care[3326].

Met Police lawyer Veronica Morley and her daughter were killed in a speeding car crash – she was driving three times over the limit, as well as having a high blood sedative level[3327].

Lothian and Borders PC David White crashed while almost three times over the limit. He was forced to resign after being found staggering from his wrecked car at a roundabout[3328]. WPC Sarah Brand, also from that force, tried to run down while drunk her love rat husband and his nurse lover, whose car she vandalised. It was alleged she struggled violently with her WPC colleagues as they tried to arrest her[3329].

Kent Police inspector Dione Mayfield lied to colleagues to evade a drink-drive charge – she was nearly three times over the limit when she hit the car of a mother doing the morning school run. She pretended a non-existent person was driving, so has been sacked[3330].

Former Warwickshire WPC Hayley Scoter received six months jail after lying about a drink-driving offence. She crashed into a lamp-post while three times over the limit, failing to stop after the accident. She was fined, banned and sacked. She was reinstated after telling an appeal judge that someone else was driving, but the friend admitted she asked him to take the blame[3331].

As late as the 1930s many brewers and pubs would leave bottles of beer outside their premises for the night-time beat man[3332].

Former Tayside traffic cop <u>Gordon McKay</u> evaded a dangerous driving charge despite doing 118mph while over the limit. He was banned and fined only, because he was an advanced driver[3333].

Strathclyde probationary PC <u>Neil Rennie</u>, who had a drink problem, faced losing his job after refusing to take a drink-drive breath test[3334].

France's tough riot police, the CRS, threatened strike action over a ban on drinking alcohol on duty. They have been pictured smoking and drinking while policing a demonstration[3335].

Police officer <u>Tom Lloyd</u> resigned 'amid claims that he got drunk and sexually harassed a woman at a police conference': he had taken a holiday during the most serious murder case his force had ever investigated[3336].

Dumfries and Galloway PC <u>Robin Linton</u> admitted drink-driving on duty, for which he was fined and banned[3337].

<u>Sir Ian Blair</u>, while head of the Met, was named on an internet blog as being 'the worse for wear' with alcohol at public events, his accuser being Brian Coleman, Tory deputy chairman of the London Assembly[3338]. The Daily Mail reported increasing concern among senior officers about his drinking (2006-7): one raised the issue with the chief executive of the Met Police Authority. New Scotland Yard's Blair's predecessor <u>Sir John Stevens</u> was nicknamed Captain Beaujolais because of <u>his</u> fondness for fine wine[3339].

Met Police firearms officer PC <u>Gary Withers</u> was discovered in a tent outside St. Paul's Cathedral after a drunken night out by City of London Police officers, who were considering whether disciplinary action was appropriate. Withers, ex-Army, had been asked to leave the Savoy Hotel, where he had been drinking[3340].

Strathclyde PC <u>Douglas Reid</u>, 48, told Central Scotland officers he had 'had a bucketful' when they caught him drink driving (his car was badly damaged in the resulting crash). He swore at them. He was banned and fined, and his job was in doubt[3341].

The King's Centre for Military Health Research says two-thirds of male sailors, airmen and soldiers drink to dangerous levels (those returning from abroad are almost 25% <u>more</u> likely to have drink problems than those who stayed at home)[3342]. Does the other 'macho' service, the police, have the same problem?

In 1962 three City of London PCs were 'required to resign' for drinking on duty[3343].

Strathclyde cop <u>John Reid</u> was so drunk when caught driving a force sports bus the wrong way down a one-way he couldn't remember being caught and locked in cells. As well as an alcohol problem he had severe debt problems[3344].

Cumbria PC <u>Ivan Allonby</u> was banned from driving and fined for drink-driving a police van.

Shetland PC <u>Jonathan Mustara</u> admitted to drink-driving on his way to work at a police station in Lerwick. He was fined and faced a disciplinary inquiry[3345].

Surrey Police has, disturbingly, phased out its Occupational Health Department. Officer 'A' tried to hang himself. He says he knows many officers with mental breakdowns. A colleague in Surrey committed suicide, another was a failed suicide[3346]. Officer 'A' – a member of a police family – crashed drunk through a plate glass window – he'd been cuckolded by a friend, the girl saying she was fed up with his long hours as a smelly undercover junkie. He says he has witnessed colleagues getting away with crashing their cars while inebriated.

Every major 'cop shop' used to have a subsidised bar, and fist fights between senior detectives were not unknown. Alcohol is a major problem in the police so that, even if the bars have gone, detective induction still includes a 'How to drink sensibly' talk[3347].

A PC emptied a glass of urine over a prisoner and later danced on a table partly undressed while drunk. Another cop who was thrown out of the police bar at closing, broke into a pub to carry on drinking – he was arrested as a burglar but pleaded alcoholism requiring treatment. He wasn't dismissed[3348].

Northumbria PC <u>Christine Thomas</u> was banned for 16 months for drink driving in County Durham. She was said to have turned to alcohol because of a marital dispute re custody of her daughter. She faced dismissal after 28 years in the force[3349].

When Sir Paul Condon took over as Met chief he turned the Tank – a cheap windowless bar on the ground floor of New Scotland Yard, where 'key strategy meetings' were held – into a gym[3350].

Essex WPC <u>Tracy Watts</u> was given a three-year ban and suspended sentence after crashing her sports car while four times over the limit[3351].

Met PC <u>Philip Juhasz</u> was sacked for drunkenly abusing a Pakistani shopkeeper at King's Cross station[3352].

Fife Sergeant <u>Thomas McGinn</u> was to stand trial accused of being in charge of a car while more than twice the drink-drive limit. He denied the charge, saying he had no intention of driving the vehicle, but was found guilty[3353].

Hertfordshire Acting Superintendent <u>Elizabeth Byron</u> was head of her force's traffic unit, with responsibility for drink driving, before being caught more than three times over the limit. She received a temporary driving ban[3354].

When Welsh ex-cop <u>Andrew Rees</u> was stopped for drink-driving he said it must have been the alcohol in a cake he'd eaten that put him over the limit[3355].

Former operations head of the National Crime Squad and resident expert on ITV's Watching the Detectives show was convicted of drink driving[3356].

Suicide

Sussex Detective Chief Inspector <u>Jim Torbet</u> hanged himself after allegedly being caught shoplifting wine along with Chief Inspector <u>Sharon Rowe</u>, district commander at

Worthing. Torbet had been part of the force's Professional Standards Unit. Married Wiltshire Police PC <u>Phillip Salsbury</u> threw himself in front of a train as his mistress confronted his wife, who some time previously had received an anonymous letter exposing the affair. However, her husband had managed to persuade her there was nothing in it[3357].

Sussex Police communications manager <u>Mike Taylor</u> jumped off a Beachy Head cliff after telling his wife that his new boss was 'screwing with his head'[3358].

In 1911 <u>D.I. Chantler</u>, 37, an unmarried man who had been on the force for 16 years, was found shot dead in the cells at Hastings Town Hall. He was holding a revolver which was evidence in a murder he was investigating[3359].

Met PC <u>David Pilling</u>, renowned for combating drug dealers over 13 years on a beat around Covent Garden and Holborn, was found dead in his flat from a huge heroin overdose (there were also traces of cocaine and ecstasy in his system)[3360].

South Yorkshire PC <u>Anthony Mulhall</u>, who was filmed repeatedly striking a black woman, died on the same mountain range as <u>Mike Todd</u> earlier in 2008. The police refused to comment on the circumstances. His police officer wife Letitia reported him missing[3361].

Ex-policeman <u>Peter Boatman</u> whose 'Pro-Tect Systems' supplied unapproved <u>X-12</u> Tasers to the Moat police – his licence was withdrawn as a result – committed suicide: police refused to say how he died[3362].

Wiltshire firearms officer Sergeant <u>Richard Fuller</u>, once commended for bravery and approaching retirement, apparently committed suicide at home in 2005 – he was a bodyguard to the Duchess of Cornwall, in charge of security at Ray Mill House, her six-bedroom country home. In 2006 he was cleared of using unnecessary force in an arrest, after which he took an anger management course. He had just finished building an extension to his thatched cottage. Married with three children[3363], his wife had left him because of his violent temper, it was claimed. It was the third time she had walked out. He kept a collection of licensed guns at home[3364].

Peter Boatman (L) with the Taser electric stun device, demonstrating the weapon at a Police Federation Conference.

Suicide <u>Mike Todd</u>, who left notes for his family, was tipped to head the Met (he had an honours degree in politics). He reportedly had suffered from manic depression for several years. He is thought to have sent a 'threatening' text to his blonde lover shortly before his death[3365].

Dorset inspector <u>Neil Munro</u> fell off a ferry in 2008[3366]. This followed a 'humiliating' four-hour disciplinary hearing into claims his paperwork was faulty. He broke down in tears. The inspector's marriage also had problems, and in 2005 he had started seeing a psychologist because of bouts of depression. He had expressed suicidal thoughts to her, and talked to another officer about a missing person who spoke of drowning himself by jumping off a ferry[3367].

British police lieutenant <u>Tom Darling</u>, while serving in Malaya, killed himself by shooting himself in the head during a game of Russian Roulette[3368].

Police believe crazed Met inspector <u>Garry Weddell</u> was planning a bloody rampage after killing his mother-in-law while on bail for his wife's murder (he had faked her suicide). He had twice breached bail conditions[3369].

Truro-based PC <u>David Stone</u>, a separated father of three, was found hanged at his home in Cornwall. Crime was not suspected[3370].

Hampshire Police sergeant <u>Hugh Moroney</u> hanged himself when he was forced to exchange his beat for a desk job. He was estranged from his wife[3371].

Devon and Cornwall Chief Inspector <u>Graham Bird</u> hanged himself in his garage after learning that his wife had been having an affair with fellow officer Inspector <u>Peter Willingham.</u> He couldn't stand the idea of other officers discussing his cuckolding. He had been using a police computer log to track her movements[3372].

Norfolk PC <u>Mike Gard</u> was found dead after apparently committing suicide with his own licensed shotgun near Norwich[3373].

Met uniformed sergeant <u>Gerry Carroll</u> committed suicide with a police-issue handgun (shooting himself through the brain) in the toilets of the custody suite at Barkingside magistrates' court. There had been complaints he had planted drugs on people, but at his inquest no outstanding allegations against him were revealed: his suicide was blamed on tinnitus.

West Yorkshire PC <u>Kevin Ellis</u> was found dead in woods hours after being arrested in connection with criminal offences. The force refused to formally name him or give the reason for his arrest. There were no suspicious circumstances[3374].

Met beat PC <u>John Johnson</u> killed himself by jumping from Battersea Bridge. He had served 29 years and was twice named community constable of the year. He told his GP he was upset about being moved from his regular beat, and he had taken cocaine before he died. The coroner recorded an open verdict because 'there are doubts as to his ability to formulate the intention of suicide'[3375].

Though medically retired, Met PC <u>Keith Gray</u>'s death from an overdose of painkillers was recorded by the coroner as accidental, his marriage having broken down. He had made three previous attempts[3376].

Wiltshire Deputy Chief Constable <u>David Ainsworth</u>, under investigation by South Wales Police for making sexual remarks to colleagues (there were up to 24 allegations, mostly from women), was found hanged at home (there were no suspicious circumstances).

He had been separated for several years and worked for the Forensic Science Service in Birmingham, being known as 'The Brain'[3377]. He had accused the force of making him a 'pariah'[3378].

Adam Rickwood had a burning ambition to become a police officer, but committed suicide in a young offenders' institution at the age of 14[3379].

Met dog handler Sergeant Ian Craven was treated in hospital after an apparent suicide bid (slashing his wrists/throwing himself from a moving vehicle), following the deaths of two police dogs in his car. It is thought Craven had been disciplined over the loss of another dog at the Met's dog training centre in 2004[3380].

Former Met policeman Paul Charles drove his car off a cliff at an Isle of Wight beauty-spot in an apparent suicide pact with his estranged wife. Suicide notes were found at both their homes (she had made previous suicide attempts)[3381].

Leicestershire Inspector Adrian Rowlson was found dead in 2007 a fortnight before he was due to be sentenced for severely beating a policewoman.

Northumbria traffic PC David Rathband, blinded by gunman Raoul Moat, was detained by colleagues on suspicion of a domestic assault: his wife subsequently left. In February 2012 he twittered his intention to suicide ('RIP PC Rathband')[3382], which he fulfilled.

Cleveland Police Detective Chief Superintendent Stewart Swinson was found dead having apparently leapt from a railway viaduct (the death was not suspicious). The father-of-two took part in the initial Operation Sacristy probe (it lead to the arrest of the force's Chief Constable Sean Price, his deputy and a force solicitor) – the investigation had to be taken over by an outside team[3383].

Royal Military Policewoman Anne-Marie Ellement hanged herself in her Wiltshire barracks. A lance corporal friend says she told her that work colleagues were 'making her life hell' and 'belittling' her[3384]. Lance-corporal Ellement claimed to have been raped by two Military Police colleagues, but no charges were brought: she hanged herself at Bulford Camp, where there was bullying and harassment[3385].

Officer 'A' was alcoholic and suicidal. He reveals another Surrey DC committed suicide by walking into the sea, while another hanged himself in his parlour. 'A's father told him about a DC, a passenger in a light plane, who deliberately fell to his death. A chief inspector cut his wrists when his wife's false accusation of domestic violence meant he was sacked. In fact 'A' says he personally knew six officer suicides. A 1993 PTSD (Post Traumatic Stress Disorder) police study claimed the rate for that disorder is 15%. There are no figures for UK police suicides[3386]: a cover-up because of the stigma?

An unnamed Met firearms officer walked into North Woolwich police station and committed suicide by gunshot. He worked at the Aviation Security Command at London City Airport[3387].

Peter Foster, the policeman jailed for murdering his officer partner Heather Cooper, hanged himself in his cell[3388].

Strathclyde firearms officer PC <u>Rod Gellatly</u> committed suicide at a Glasgow police station[3389].

Special Branch DI <u>Bill Lloyd</u> was found hanged in his Camberley home's garage shortly before he was due to guard PM Blair. He had remarried a year before after the break-up of his first marriage[3390].

Pregnant Special WPC <u>Tammy Paterson</u>, 24, hanged herself in her police uniform days before she was to abort her lover's child. Married with a daughter, she dreamed of becoming a regular officer[3391].

Wiltshire Police inspector <u>Bill Darling</u> and his female partner were found shot dead[3392].

West Midland detective <u>Teresa Fraser</u> was excused prosecution on a charge of taking speeding points for her husband, Leicestershire's assistant chief constable who committed suicide by stepping in front of a train. He had been probed about an alleged Florida timeshare fraud[3393].

A Met Protection Squad cop was found with a fatal gunshot. There were no suspicious circumstances[3394].

In 2012 2,550 service personnel (11,000 since 2007) were treated for mental conditions: since 2003 there have been 123 suspected or confirmed suicides[3395].

Psychosis

Former Shropshire police inspector <u>Anthony Hall</u> claimed, as Henry VIII's direct descendant, to be the true British King, not George V. He hoped to be the first policeman to become King, and the first policeman to cut off the King's head, or shoot him like a dog. The authorities and George were so worried – Hall made a series of raving speeches in 1931 to large crowds – that they tried, but failed, to get doctors to section him. He was repeatedly arrested for use of 'scandalous language' after speeches in Birmingham's Bull Ring[3396].

Essex probationer policewoman <u>Alison Cotter</u>, a former Army PE instructor, was accused of a drunken assault on several people in her local pub. A police surgeon reported that she appeared to be under the influence of drugs or 'in the early stages of mania...'. The failure of a key witness to appear at her trial resulted in all charges being thrown out[3397].

Married Ayrshire police inspector <u>Tom Halbert</u> ('Inspector Undies') admitted sending threats to a rookie WPC because she wouldn't reciprocate his continued advances after a nine-month affair while he was off sick with 'mental health difficulties'. A high-profile member of his violence reduction unit, he was interviewed on TV shows. He was excused from attending court after psychiatric reports. He had threatened the WPC with Regulation 13, which concerns the dismissal of new recruits[3398] (see also Lustful Policeman chapter).

<u>Janey Antoniou</u>, a molecular biologist and geneticist, was also a mental health trainer with the police. She is delusional and experiences auditory hallucinations[3399].

Psychopathy

Psychopathic traits in Met personnel were well recognized in the 19th Century: a large proportion of recruits resigned or were dismissed in days, weeks or months. They went

AWOL, got drunk, went with prostitutes, tipped off friends about police actions and abused their superiors. In 1834 the Police Commissioners admitted to a parliamentary select committee that drunkenness was the cause of most dismissals[3400].

Stephen Hayes, a sergeant in the Greater Manchester Police, describes himself and his colleagues as 'a crowd of psychopaths'. Hayes admits his own father, a military man, was a psychopath and he himself inherited the trait[3401].

Retired Met inspector Graham Walters seized his police sergeant wife around the throat until she lost consciousness. He had flown into a rage and smashed her laptop onto a coffee table, over her approaches to her previous husband. He locked himself in their garage and refused to deal with constables, only a fellow inspector (there were shotguns stored in the property). The inspector was charged with assault by beating[3402]. (See also The Harmful Policeman chapter).

Drugs

It is feared as many as 1,000 Scots officers – 6% of the total force – use drugs regularly[3403]. Strathclyde was in 2008 carrying out compulsory drugs and alcohol testing on all new recruits, with random tests for their first two years. The Scottish Police Federation has stopped plans to impose the tests on all 7,000 officers. The idea was to cure the 'boozing coppers' culture as portrayed in 'The Sweeney' and 'Ashes to Ashes'[3404]. ACPOS in 2009 promised to randomly test all officers up to rank of chief constable for illegal drugs, but most Police Scotland divisions don't test post-recruitment. Only Tayside Police found two officers had taken illicit drugs – both resigned[3405].

Slough PC Matthew Kille and CPSO Lisa Slavin, caught skiving from work to indulge in cocaine-fuelled orgies, were given suspended one-year sentences[3406].

One male officer has stated: 'Smoking cannabis is a sub-culture. I know of six to ten individuals [in the police], and suspect a lot more smoke'[3407].

Met PC Paul Smith stole and smoked confiscated cannabis to relieve the stress of being a policeman. He was caught red-handed by surveillance cameras set up by his colleagues to check for the missing drugs[3408].

The Met introduced random drug testing for officers in 2006. A leaked report had revealed at least 60 officers were on cocaine (in eight months four officers tested positive and resigned)[3409].

Fife Constabulary PC Graham Drummond was suspended in 2006 over claims he was taking cocaine on duty. His stepfather is also a Fife officer. 158 Scots officers have convictions (assault, attempt to pervert justice, drink-driving, etc.): Fife was the only force which refused to give the information (about drug-taking) under FOIA[3410].

A phone hotline has been set up in Scotland (Tayside) because police officers addicted to drugs are too scared to seek help. By midsummer 2009 Tayside Police had their first officer testing positively for cannabis[3411].

Ex-Met detective <u>Ray Wilding</u>, who presented Crimewatch, was accused by his girlfriend of having steroid-induced mood swings and being pathologically jealous of her old boyfriends[3412].

Met PC <u>Ross Callaghan</u> was dismissed by a disciplinary board after smoking cannabis, despite having two bravery awards. Ironically his conviction for possession came while working in Commander Paddick's 'softly-softly' zone[3413].

Met PC <u>Charles Challis</u>, who famously arrested Tony Blair's son Euan for being drunk and incapable, was fined for possession of cocaine[3414].

Stress

During the summer of 2008 the equivalent of 1,000 police a day were calling in sick with stress, depression, etc. Suffolk Police's sick leave costs spiralled from about £80,000 in 2003 to over £750,000 in 2007. Half of officers were absent three weeks a year. Average sick leave was 13.5 days (average in public sector was nine days; the private sector average was seven days)[3415].

420 Scots officers are off sick on an average day – the true figure is probably higher. Former Strathclyde PC <u>Matt Rooney</u> won £½m after being forced out because he was off sick with stress. Of Strathclyde's 81,716 sick days (2008), 11,712 were due to stress[3416]. Sick days among Scottish police, at 10.5 a year, compare with the UK average for all workers of 8.4 days[3417]. Strathclyde Police were opening 'peace rooms' for stressed-out officers, to 'restore their karma'[3418]. Scotland's officers have taken over 300 years worth of days off in just under two years (2008-9), with stress blamed for the increasing amount of sick time[3419].

The Archbishop of Canterbury's daughter <u>Katharine Welby</u> has described her recurrent bouts of severe depression. Her father has spoken of concerns about his own mental state, <u>his</u> father having been alcoholic. Katharine is a former police officer[3420].

Scotland Yard's 'Shrinking Clouds' scheme involved watching a DVD and being given an 'anti-stress card', which advised officers to eat fruit and veg and take deep breaths. 'Breaking the state' means 'stepping away from difficult situations'. Previous schemes included 'Triggers' for firearms personnel and 'The Camel's Back', to prevent managerial stress.[3421].

Hindu Met WPC <u>Hina Parekh</u> took 848 sick days in six years for stress related to alleged racist abuse and bullying. She had joined the force in 2004 as a PCSO[3422].

The police equivalent of the MOD's Headley Court is Flint House (Oxfordshire), which is a retreat for officers with mental and physical problems: 10-15% of the residents will be suffering from stress, PTSD, etc. In 2008 in England and Wales 225,000 sick days were taken due to stress and related conditions. Most forces once had welfare departments, but no longer[3423].

Police dog handler PC <u>Mark Johnson</u> was too stressed to appear in court after his two Alsatians died in his car during a heatwave. He had won third place in the national police dog trials in 2007[3424]. He finally appeared in court after failing to turn up twice. His address was concealed by court order to avoid revenge attacks.

Sussex Police have employed masseuse companies to provide anti-stress Indian head massage for its call centre workers. Chief Constable <u>Martin Richards</u> defended the scheme[3425].

In a Scottish case of severe flooding the police dealing with the victims were so distressed they asked for counselling. Then their counsellors became so upset themselves that they too needed counselling[3426].

Stressed cops cost the taxpayer at least £32 million in 2009 (the cost does not include that of covering their absence[3427]).

In 2008 the cost of anxiety and depression in police forces was almost a million a week. 50% of cases are said to be related to home problems (relationships, money, etc.) rather than work-related. Strathclyde's sick days lost (28,563 in 2008) trumped even the Met's (26,098). The Met spent £500,000 on 15 occupational health counsellors[3428].

A five-hour 'emotional survival' training course is compulsory for all frontline police in Hertfordshire, dog handlers and control room staff. The meditation sessions are based on the teachings of US policeman Dr. Kevin Gilmartin, who is now a psychological guru. Herts Police has sent 1,000 officers on the training because many were 'cynical and negative'. The amount spent on the courses is not being released[3429].

In England and Wales officers averaged two sick days a year (2006) because of stress; the sick pay involved would put 1,200 extra police on the streets in a year. In Lancashire stress was responsible for almost 25% of all police absences. The true figure must be higher, as many officers are reluctant to admit psychological problems[3430].

Rules making it harder to take medical retirement mean officers struggling with long-term stress[3431].

Churchill's wartime bodyguard, seconded policeman <u>Walter Thompson</u>, wrote voluminously, but only makes the slightest mention of his (Thompson's) mental breakdown.

Former Lothian and Borders WPC <u>Louise McGarva</u> is suing her force for £500,000 for post-traumatic stress disorder following a 2007 training exercise (a fake riot), leaving her afraid of police cars and sirens. She alleges the trainers were negligent. The force revealed she had a history of psychological injury, needing stress counselling after a 2004 child death inquiry[3432].

A 2012 report on Army morale concluded that Iraq reservists had suffered 'elevated rates of mental disorders' compared with regular soldiers. Could this apply to the less well-trained members of police forces? Nearly 500 military personnel a month ask for mental treatment. Research is needed into the mental illness rates of PCSOs compared with regular officers[3433].

Thousands of police were to get regular stress checks, a Home Office working group agreed, to help cut sick leave, absenteeism and early retirement. Vulnerable staff would as a result of the psychological testing be able to get help from occupational psychologists. Interestingly the police still resist such testing for vulnerability in new recruits[3434].

In 2012 one in seven Lothian and Borders officers was off sick for 10 or more days in a row. A force spokesperson put it down to stress[3435].

Record numbers of Scots police officers are taking days off sick with stress (an increase of 37% in only four years)[3436].

Met DC Andrea Brown, on psychiatric sick leave for 18 months, flew to the Caribbean when she was supposed to be meeting police chiefs, who said she hadn't been granted leave. She claimed her boss had falsely boasted of having sex with her[3437].

Self-Harm

Police officers have been described who shoot themselves and create emergencies to gain attention, relieve stress, etc[3438].

Though undercover cop Mark Kennedy has admitted to self-harming, his official psychologist found nothing untoward in his mental state. There wasn't one prosecution from his many years of infiltration[3439]. The Chief Inspector of Constabulary says undercover police can't be banned from having sex with their targets[3440], as Kennedy did.

Bizarre Behaviour

Met PC Gordon Warren has been fighting for compensation for 26 years after being forced out of his job for refusing to join in the police 'canteen culture', which resulted in him being diagnosed by his inspector, and the police doctor, Dr. Bott, as being mentally unstable and paranoid, but independent medical referees gave him a clean bill of mental health. Though the High Court ruled in his favour in 1988 he was still fighting for compensation over two decades later [3441].

Labour MP Kate Hoey attracted this comment from London mayoral candidate ex-police commander Brian Paddick: 'Hoey is bonkers – she and Boris make a perfect couple'[3442].

Retired Lancashire chief inspector Malcolm Herbert allegedly waged a poison-pen campaign on the Isle of Skye which broke up a marriage. He was convicted of a breach of the peace in 2008 after a year-long investigation into his bizarre behaviour. He was often seen about town in Struan dressed in jodhpurs and riding boots (he has a riding school), and it is claimed he sent similar letters to a teenage stable girl. In 2006 an x-rated business card offering sex was passed around his victim's local pub. At one point he was charged with making inappropriate sexual gestures and remarks to underage girls, but this was later reduced to conducting himself in a disorderly manner[3443].

A former policeman who became right-hand man to end-of-the-world cult leader 'Messiah' admitted he himself was 'really evil'.

'Gay slayer' Colin Ireland adopted for himself a sort of informal neighbourhood patrolling function, reporting to police anything he deemed untoward[3444].

Two 'light boxes' to treat SAD (seasonal affective disorder) have been installed in New Scotland Yard for police sufferers[3445].

Officer 'A' says he and a colleague used to speed on superbikes on public roads[3446].

In the case of the firearms officer who allegedly inserted song titles in his sworn evidence, the IPCC found that the song titles were 'everyday, colloquial words and phrases that had legitimate and relevant meaning to the inquest'. But the same policeman later (2011) admitted boasting that he <u>had</u> inserted the titles, saying the boast was a joke caused by stress: he was facing a misconduct hearing as a result.

An unnamed ex-cop who posed as DC <u>Nick Burton</u> (a serving officer) in a five-year internet vendetta against Essex Police, admitted harassment but was only given a caution[3447].

Other Psychological Difficulties

Gloucester chief inspector <u>Phillip Haynes</u> claims failure by his boss to recognise his dyslexia, which makes him struggle at job interviews, prejudiced his promotion[3448].

Employees who quit their jobs and then change their minds (e.g. because a mental illness has cleared up) are entitled to return to work. West Mercia WPC <u>Sarah Jane Hinsley</u> left when she felt she couldn't cope. After treatment for depression she wanted her job back but the force refused. An employment tribunal found against her, but an appeal tribunal overturned this decision[3449].

A solicitor for Northumbria Police has revealed that some officers on sick leave develop such a hatred for the employer that they cannot return to work, as it would be too stressful. The matter was highlighted by an employment tribunal brought by WPC <u>Alison Doyle</u> against Northumbria, claiming compensation for disability discrimination: in 2001 a doctor confirmed her permanently disabled, but this assessment was overturned by the High Court in 2005[3450].

Assistant Chief Constable <u>John Mauger</u>, of Central Scotland Police, was put on gardening leave in 2010 over several allegations, including insubordination and inefficiency. Grampian Police Chief Constable <u>Ian Oliver</u> had to resign in 1998 over a bungled murder hunt[3451].

Strathclyde WPC <u>Anne Ramsay</u>, who wrote about racism, sexism, bullying and religious sectarianism in 'Girl in Blue', was left with post-traumatic stress, and summarises her 14 years in the force: 'I have no faith in the police any more'[3452].

Peel's decision to establish the Met in 1829 was because the decrepit, useless constables and watchmen were too incompetent to confront new levels of crime. But the case of watchman <u>Francis Haley</u> shows that the new broom may not have swept all that clean: he became a 'new policeman' despite being a known Irish alcoholic, and had to be brought before Bow Street Magistrates' Court for being drunkenly riotous and assaulting a gentleman! When arrested by the Bow Street Patrol he swore at them before informing them that he had just been appointed to the New Police. Again, in 1842 new Birmingham constable <u>George Bakewell</u> wrote in his pamphlet 'Observations on the Construction of the New Police Force' of the inefficiencies of the new police, yet while he seems to have been dismissed for being drunk and disorderly, Birmingham Police gave him a good conduct reference[3453].

When Moat died, the moment was hailed by crazed-sounding whoops by police at the scene[3454].

Mental Problems in the Military: Analogous?

Though mental problems in the military (20% of British front-line troops have mental problems[3455]) are not directly analogous with those in the police, it is worth noting that, historically, policemen were often ex-Army or navy, so that one might expect that alcohol, aggressivity, PTSD, for instance, might be found in both types of national service. NAPO (the National Association of Probation Officers) estimates there may be 8,500 ex-servicemen in prison out of a total of 92,000, with the vast majority ex-army , mostly infantry (the MOD disagree, saying only 3% are ex-military). One expert found (2006) only 2% armed-service personnel suffer from PTSD, with alcohol the main problem, followed by depression[3456]. In the 19th Century the prevalence of sailors among the inmates of lunatic asylums was seven times what would be expected. Reservists in Iraq suffered 'elevated rates of mental disorders' compared with regular troops[3457]. 500 troops a month are seeking psychiatric help after serving in Iraq and Afghanistan[3458].

In about 1900 the 'Police Review' noted 'with distaste' that of England's 44 chief constables, 33 were former army officers, three were naval officers, only three having risen through the ranks: in Wales six of 12 were former army officers and two from the ranks[3459].

It is believed that even SAS soldiers are much more likely than average to have been in care as children[3460]. Children in care have an increased risk of mental illness as adults, and ex-soldiers often apply to become policemen. Ex-US naval-man-turned-cop Christopher Dorner, sacked by LAPD for lying about a colleague, went on a killing spree to avenge himself by murdering officers and their families (he murdered one policeman and injured two others) . The African-American wrote a rambling paranoid manifesto on Facebook, but psychiatrists said he didn't seem psychotic[3461].

Soaring numbers of the military are self-harming: the UK has one of the highest under-25 self-harm rates in Europe. There is a disproportionate rise in self-harm in the Navy. More service personnel, it was revealed in 2007, had committed suicide in the previous 20 years than died in military action. In 2006 Defence Secretary Liam Fox revealed three of the four Deepcut deaths soldiers had a history of self-harming[3462]. A senior NCO has revealed how Deepcut Army training instructors (corporals and sergeants) beat and sexually harassed Royal Logistic corps rookies in the 1990s. Between March and November 2002 more than 45 soldiers went AWOL. 43% of Army personnel believe that discrimination, harassment and bullying are an endemic problem in the Army[3463].

Alcoholic former ex-soldier and Perthshire policeman Brian Coutts was spared jail after admitting his fourth drink-driving offence (whereas a forester admitting his third offence was given four months in the same court complex)[3464]. Surely double standards.

A British soldier allegedly shot dead an 8-year-old Iraqi girl as she played in the street, while soldiers were handing out sweets to children[3465]. Over 300 sailors in the Royal Navy have been accused of sexual misconduct over a five-year period (including 13 rapes, 63 sex attacks and a string of paedophile incidents)[3466].

Young combat troops are more than 50% more likely to commit violent crimes after serving compared with non-combat soldiers, who are three times more prone to violent acts compared to non-service personnel (21% as against 6%)[3467]. More than 20% of serving troops and veteran troops under 30 commit violent crime (cf. with less than 7% of the general male population). It is notable that serving in Afghanistan/Iraq was not a <u>direct</u> cause of violent offending. There <u>was</u> a link between combat and alcohol abuse, anger and PTSD[3468].

The National Police Improvement Agency has confirmed to the author (February 2010) that the national recruit assessment centre does not involve personality profiling using psychometric tests. All soldiers are to be psychometrically screened before <u>exit</u> from the force[3469]. As research has shown an association between personality type and prejudice, the NPIA tried to get such a study off the ground, using the well-known scale 16PF to measure personality traits, but the police refused to approve it. All frontline soldiers are 'to get psycho-screening in a bid to cut combat stress' (a study by Kings College, London, found 20% of Britain's armed forced have symptoms of common mental disorders, with 13% alcoholic)[3470]. Almost 10% of British soldiers have had treatment for psychiatric conditions (some 2,510 in 2010 alone)[3471].

Unlike the police, being a BNP member is allowed in the armed forces[3472]. Two-thirds of ex-soldiers imprisoned in the UK have committed sexual, violent or drugs crimes, an MOD report showed. Soldiers are twice as likely as other prisoners to be jailed for sex offences. Prevalence studies throw up different figures. Military veterans are the largest single occupational group in prison in England and Wales (the official figure is 3.5% of prisoners)[3473], but according to 2012 research by campaign group No Offence 10% of prisoners are former soldiers. At least 8,500 former service personnel are in custody (nearly 10% of prisoners), but a pilot study at Dartmoor found almost 17% of inmates had been forces members. Ex-forces personnel have twice the car accident death rate of civilians.

Lesbian Lance Bombardier <u>Kerry Fletcher</u>, who was awarded almost £200,000 for being sexually harassed by a male sergeant, hopes to join the police[3474].

Five US soldiers have supposedly formed a 'death squad' to target innocent civilians for sport. They are also said to have dismembered the bodies of civilians, keeping bones, skulls or fingers as trophies, and photographing them. Drug use was reportedly widespread among the US infantry[3475]. A major investigation into the prestigious US Naval Academy revealed a rampant drug culture. As well as 'spice' (synthetic cannabis), cocaine, mephedrone, methadone, mescaline and magic mushrooms were being abused by the midshipmen[3476]. There has been a sharp rise in sexual violence in the US military (260,000 assaults in a year, or over 70 daily compared with just 19,000 two years earlier). The Pentagon report says 6% of military women had unwanted sexual contact in 2012[3477]. By 1944 large numbers of women in Normandy made formal complaints about rapes and thefts by US soldiers, coming to fear their 'liberators', whom they called 'bandits in uniform'[3478].The number of Scottish soldiers taking illegal drugs (cocaine, ecstasy, ketamine, 'speed', valium, cannabis) soared in 2012[3479].

There have been graphic allegations of British soldiers of both sexes abusing and sexually humiliating Iraqi civilian detainees in camps. They are accused of piling prisoners in heaps and giving them electric shocks. Though the MOD were investigating 33 cases, there are rumours there were hundreds[3480].

Almost £1m has been paid in compensation in 2012 to men in the military who have been sexually assaulted (seven out of eight rape cases are male, reveals the MOD)[3481]. [Blacking the genitalia ('blackballing') of unpopular fellow soldiers is not unknown among schoolboy army cadets].

Baha Mousa's death by a violent and cowardly beating at the hands of members of the Queens Lancashire Regiment had 'cast a dark shadow' over the army, said General Sir Peter Wall, head of the Army. Some interrogation techniques, though banned since 1972, had become 'standard operating procedure' in sections of the Army (no reference to the ban was made in training manuals). The brutality of the soldiers was compounded by their conspiracy of silence[3482]. The killing of Mousa and seven other Iraqi prisoners of the British was 'just the tip of the iceberg', according to Mousa's family solicitor. He said there were thousands of allegations of mistreatment by British troops, possibly implicating every battle group as well as the special interrogation team. Female soldiers are claimed to have offered detainees sex in exchange for information[3483].

Ian Pointon, of Kent Police Federation, says tattoos can be an icebreaker for frontline cops, some of whom have been recruited from the Armed Forces (many of the latter have tattoos)[3484].

CHAPTER XVIII

THE MURDOCH POLICEMAN

CONTENTS

CHAPTER XVIII

THE MURDOCH POLICEMAN

The Murdoch Policeman

Murdoch's Sky TV features a regular US documentary series 'Power, Privilege and Justice', in which veteran author and broadcaster Dominick Dunne tells how are the mighty fallen in America. That title could encompass the Murdoch scandal in Britain. The forced exit of the Met commissioner and his deputy at the same time (July, 2011) was unprecedented.

Nearly all the unacceptable foibles of the police described in this book are to be found in the News International (N.I.) saga: greed, adultery, corruption, collusion, cover-up, political bias, incompetence, etc. Who knows – the judicial inquiry might even find Freemasonry part of the toxic mix (this author's inquiry to the residing judge whether this came within his remit about this went unanswered - twice)? This scandal is the worst the Met has experienced since the early 70s.

Alastair Campbell has criticised the hacking inquiry police: there must be reasons behind their vigorous approach in the cash-for-honours scandal under Blair, compared with their 'lacklustre' performance in the initial hacking probe[3485]. Hundreds of pounds were paid by the News Of The World to the policeman who discovered that Denholm Elliott's daughter was down and out (she was soon after found dead). There is a long history of the NOW and the police getting into bed together. A solicitor suing the News Of The World says he was told by Met DS (now detective inspector) Mark Maberly that 6,000 phones may have been hacked. The Met deny this – he was, he says, being accused by the police of lying, and has demanded the Met give up documents that could establish the exact number[3486]. The IPCC says that if Surrey Police had probed the News of the World's actions in the 2002 Milly Dowler hacking case (nothing was done), hacking would have been stopped in its tracks: '… senior officers … appear to have been afflicted by a form of collective amnesia …'[3487].

Ironically the PCC (Press Complaints Commission) found the whistleblowing Guardian at fault over the hacking scandal. But then the PCC would perhaps say that – there are editors and a former police chief on its board[3488]!

The police hacking probe (Operation Elveden) is to look at 'why did the first police investigation fail so abysmally?', in particular the matter of payments to police. The Times (a News International paper) will continue to employ Andy Hayman, who led the Met's original probe into the NOW phone hacking. He was Assistant Commissioner for Specialist Operations when he investigated Glenn Mulcaire in 2006-7[3489], whose huge legal fees were paid (till July, 2011) by News International.

It is alleged Andy Coulson 'condoned' secret payments to police when he was the NOW editor: emails seen by the BBC indicated he authorised cash payments which would be routed through family or girlfriends. Officers may have sold lists of phone numbers (e.g. of 7/7 victims or families of dead victims)[3490].

Army officer Ian Hurst says the Met tried to sweep his computer hacking case under the carpet[3491].

The Murdoch Policemen

<u>Yates</u>*

Assistant Commissioner <u>John Yates</u> jumped before he was pushed by his Police Authority, which was about to suspend him. He was probed by the IPCC: he denies favouritism – getting the daughter of his friend Neil Wallis a job in the Met, as well as vouching for that friend to get an extremely controversial Met PR position, according to the Met's chief PR official Dick Fidorcio. Neil Wallis was the chief executive of the News of the World (NOW) and wrote speeches for Yates (as well as Commissioner <u>Stephenson</u>). Yates was friendly enough with Wallis for 12 years to know the latter's favourite tipple – they used to meet to watch sports matches. Wallis, while on the PR contract for Yates and Stephenson, was paid over £25,000 by News of the World for crime stories he got from the Yard[3492]. Wallis ('The Wolfman') was not only providing 'crime exclusives' during 2009 – 10 for the News of the World while working for the Met, but also other newspapers[3493]. Yates lied to Parliament when he said (2009) that all hacking victims had been contacted, and in 2011 the chairman of the Home Affairs Select Committee told him: 'Your evidence is not convincing. Do not regard this as the end of the matter': he was recalled to face another grilling days after resigning. He had admitted his 2009 judgment – not to reopen the hacking inquiry – was 'pretty crap' (his examination of bags of files was cursory, lasting only six or eight hours). Yates has 'form' here: his other high profile abortive 'investigations' were the collapsed Burrell theft trial and the cash-for-honours fiasco. David Mellor said: 'If it had been left to the police it would all have been shovelled under the carpet'.

John Yates

Yates denies an affair with Rebekah Brooks, formerly Murdoch's most senior UK editor, a rumour which has circulated in police and media circles (he had already left his wife for another woman). Along with his boss he tried to persuade 'The Guardian' it was on the wrong track about hacking, its coverage 'exaggerated and unwarranted'. He didn't tell anyone about Wallis (regarded as a 'monster' by some colleagues) being hired by the Met. He didn't declare his meetings with journalists because he regarded them as 'private' (Stephenson tried to justify such meetings). When a claim was made that No. 10 tried to wreck the cash-for-peerages investigation and that Yates was the source of this claim, the Met refused (and still refuses) to comment. MP Chris Bryant says Yates must have been 'fibbing' to Commissioner Stephenson about there being nothing in 'The

---

* See page 450 of The Secretive Policeman chapter.

Guardian' story. The Commons Home Affairs Select Committee has said there was certainly no 'real will' on the Met's part to overcome News International's (N.I.'s) failure to cooperate. Yates, the son of doctors, held an inquiry into Met corruption which led to six officers being sent down[3494]. He admitted he had come under heavy pressure from No. 10 in relation to the cash-for-honours scandal – Tony Blair's aides said he could resign as PM if he was embarrassed by the probe[3495]. Prescott's first judicial review of NOW hacking was refused because Yates blocked it[3496].

Yates' epitaph will be as the man who, whether by incompetence or malice, downplayed the industrial scale of hacking. Certainly the late Sean Hoare, the first whistleblowing NOW reporter to highlight the problem, was convinced that hacking was endemic.

A former senior Downing Street aide has accused Yates of indulging in 'histrionic gestures' during the 'loans for peerages' probe, orchestrating a 'fiasco' that nearly paralysed No. 10, after the Met allegedly made a series of leaks. The police, said Jonathan Powell, had dug themselves in too deep to be able to retreat with dignity[3497].

Yates was appointed at the end of 2011 to take charge of reform of the controversial Bahrain police force, used to violently suppress the populace[3498]. Bahrain's riot police used live bullets against protesters in 2011, and hundreds were tortured, so Yates will have his work cut out. The King was invited to the Queen's Jubilee banquet at Windsor Castle: he has direct control of the Bahrain police[3499]. It was Yates's failure to interview the Queen over the Burrell affair which torpedoed his inquiry[3500].

Cabinet Minister Francis Maude accused Britain's leading counter-terrorism policeman of scaremongering in a row over cuts[3501].

Hayman

Andy ('Asbo') Hayman was described by the Home Affairs Select Committee (20.7.11) as 'complacent', having 'seriously undermined confidence in the police', and about the same time ex-Met officer David Gilbertson said police 'blogs' and chatrooms were buzzing with criticisms of senior officers in general and Hayman in particular (the publication of Gilbertson's exposé of the police was mysteriously delayed – it was due out 1.9.11 but arrived in 2012). Hayman 'lost his rag' with the Select Committee when asked if he had taken bribes, yet he accepted hospitality (dinners) from N.I. while investigating the latter for criminality. The Committee deplored the fact that he took a job with N.I. less than two years after he was responsible for investigating its employees. They reported (20.7.11) that he (and others) bungled the initial hacking investigation. Hayman insisted his men had interviewed every suspect and 'left no stone unturned'. This wasn't true, according to the committee[3502]. He had become too

Andy Hayman

close to the Murdoch empire, e.g. dining with the NOW's editor Coulson while in the middle of the 2006 inquiry into the hacking of Prince William, as well as his lunching with NOW personnel in November 2005 and April 2007 (two months after the jailing of NOW reporter Goodman and P.I. Mulcaire). He met journalists at Soho House (a private club) instead of at the Yard, wining and dining them using his expenses account: he refused to be interviewed by C4's Dispatches about his conduct. His spending had sparked a secret probe by Gwent Police, whose findings have never been made public. His credit card bills came to more than the rest of the Met's management board put together – they triggered the inquiry that led to his resignation in 2007.

Only some of the hospitality Hayman shared with the press was declared in his official register[3503]. His conduct had been 'unprofessional and inappropriate'. So paranoid was Hayman he reportedly told Paddick to install a sophisticated alarm system at his home in case rogue journalists tried to plant drugs. His social contacts eventually led to him becoming a columnist for 'The Times', ostensibly the most morally innocent of Murdoch's UK papers. So the 'revolving door' has police working as journalists, journalists for the police (half of the Met's Press Department had been NOW journalists).

Hayman was photographed leaving a pub with Mrs. Nikki Redmond, an IPCC worker with whom he allegedly exchanged 400 out-of-hours texts and phone calls inappropriately[3504] while he was responsible for anti-corruption, professional standards and discipline[3505]. Hayman's foreign trips with Sergeant Heidi Tubby also came under scrutiny in 2007, as did his American Express card payments for hotels and drink ('inordinate amounts' of drink). He spent considerably more than his superiors, e.g. his boss Sir Ian Blair. He used his force credit card to buy champagne for a female journalist at Chelsea's Oriel wine bar, and enjoyed dinners with journalists like NOW's Lucy Panton, the wife of a Met detective[3506]. Two counterterrorism officers, a DC and a DS, were arrested in the same year on suspicion of stealing £70,000 using their Amex cards. ACPO's president Ken Jones ordered his chief constables to conduct audits of all their cardholders. When the force's top anti-terrorism officer resigned in December 2007, no-one from Government, the Home Office, Scotland Yard or ACPO was available to comment on an important TV channel.

As anti-terror police chief Hayman was found to have misled the public over the de Menezes shooting: the IPCC found he gave the impression – two years after the shooting – that de Menezes was one of the bombers, when by then it was quite clear he wasn't. Though cleared of misconduct over Stockwell he was given 'words of advice' over misleading the public and Sir Ian Blair afterwards[3507]. The IPCC report revealed that Hayman deliberately withheld the information from Sir Ian Blair that the wrong man had been shot[3508].

Hayman was known for his 'Essex wideboy' vocabulary, and went from Chief Constable of Norfolk to head of anti-terrorism, though he had no experience of such policing. Re the Forest Gate shooting inquiry the IPCC upheld only two of 150 complaints, yet Hayman had to make a public apology (ironically he was awarded a CBE a few days later). Married Nikki Redmond, the IPCC employee sent 400 texts and calls by him while the IPCC was preparing its de Menezes report, was given the job of press officer for ACPO's terrorism unit, headed by Hayman, who presided over a £1m ACPO office refurbishment. Pictures of Redmond and Hayman together surfaced after sharing a drink in pubs near Liverpool Street station, while he was supposed to be supervising a major terror alert. At one stage IPCC sources suggested it might consider disciplinary action against him[3509].

Hayman didn't tell Prescott he was a hacking victim, even though he was working with the politician (the police had opposed the first judicial inquiry).

Met detectives wanted to mount a corruption probe in 2000 into police being bribed by journalists: despite a 'huge volume of intelligence' being accumulated, Hayman blocked it for being 'too risky' – he was in charge of professional standards, yet later was probed about police leaks to journalists.

Stephenson

Paul Stephenson resigned as Commissioner (July, 2011) when it was revealed that he and his wife had received hospitality worth a considerable sum at Champneys, which had Murdoch connections. Champneys' managing director Stephen Purdew was a friend of Rebekah Brooks, and his son did work experience in MP Keith Vaz's office. Purdew is godfather to another of the Vaz children and Vaz happens to be chairman of the Home Affairs Committee investigating the scandal.

The Met arrest of Brooks two days before her Westminster appearance seemed suspicious to some. Thus it could be construed as a warning to her not to divulge matters damaging to the police. Only the previous week police had said explicitly they didn't need to speak to her (she had been offering to help for six months). MP Adrian Sanders suggested the arrest was to take the spotlight off the police.

Stephenson had 18 dinners with Murdoch top brass (e.g. with Wallis, later arrested) during his force's botched investigation into the Murdoch machinations. The Champneys sojourn had not been inserted in the police register by March, 2011 – it should have been. Wallis (deputy editor of the News of the World) wrote speeches for Stephenson, and 10 of the Met's 69 PR staff had previously worked for N.I. With three score of its own press officers why did the Met also need the help of Wallis? Stephenson confirmed that, on the advice of his lieutenant John Yates, he had (in December 2009) pressurised The Guardian to drop the hacking story.

Stephenson and John Yates are thought to have received up to £0.5m between them after signing gagging orders barring them from suing the Met or telling how the latter had treated them. The Audit Commission has ordered a review of how the pay-offs were agreed. A member of the Met Police Authority says it is wrong for any public organisation to be so secretive: at first officials tried to cover up the 'termination payments'[3510].

Stephenson told Leveson he didn't consider phone hacking 'a priority' in 2009. He dismissed a well-researched newspaper report that hacking at NOW went beyond one rogue reporter as just 'noise' – he admitted he hadn't even read the story. He says the behaviour (leaking stories to the press) of some senior colleagues was 'corrosive' – the dysfunctionality was prevalent at the most senior level[3511].

Other Murdoch cops

Most of the police who will be shown to be compromised are probably more junior than the above: they will be identified when the (smoking gun) emails are examined during the Leveson judicial inquiry. We already know that a royal protection squad officer (thanks to an email N.I. found in 2007) sold diary and phone details of several royals for a reported £1,000, and that Coulson and Goodman were arrested (July, 2011) for allegedly bribing cops.

In 2003 a junior Devon and Cornwall Police officer was exposed as having provided information from the national computer to a number of P.I.s (one of whom in 2000 commissioned the officer to search for Gordon Brown's and apparently MP Martin Salter's intimate details), but a judge blocked prosecution of the network of private detectives. Another P.I. suspected of bribing police is Jonathan Rees, who had a relationship with NOW's Alex Marunchak (then Dublin editor), who was an interpreter for the Met while working for the NOW (he interpreted for at least seven suspects). Peter Clarke, who headed 12 detectives on the original hacking inquiry that reported to Hayman, admitted it wasn't exhaustive. Thus of about 4,000 victims only 170 had been contacted by July 2011. Steve Roberts, head of the anti-corruption squad, has revealed that journalists often wanted to take him out to lunch, but changed their mind when he said he would be accompanied by his PR officer.

The Met announced at least 30 inquiries are ongoing into the hacking scandal. The diary of former Met Commissioner Lord Stevens – he may have wined and dined News International executives – has been traced[3512].

John Prescott's phone was tapped by private detectives working for Murdoch's News Group Newspapers: it is claimed the police knew but didn't tell him. In fact News Group PIs allegedly hacked into 'thousands of mobile phones[3513]. The police knew of many victims, it is claimed, but again didn't tell them.

Met PC Paul Flatley was jailed for two years for selling stories to the News of the World. He was paid about £8,000 for dozens of stories including Prince William's engagement and Paul Gascoigne's mental health sectioning[3514].

In 2009 Scotland Yard detectives faced questioning by the Commons Home Affairs Committee as to whether police were paid by journalists for confidential information about celebrities[3515]. There was anger in July 2009 over Scotland Yard's refusal to re-open their 2007 investigation (the newspaper's royal editor and a private detective had been jailed for illegal surveillance with regard to Royal Household phone calls). Liberal Democrat MP Chris Huhne says the review by John Yates was suspiciously quick in what the latter described as a complex case. 'Where there is a potential neglect of duty by a police force, surely another police force or the IPCC should look into the matter. Instead, we merely have assurances from the same department that conducted the original investigation that it did so well and thoroughly'. Brian Paddick, former Deputy Assistant Commissioner of the Met, said: 'John Yates is in charge of the department that did the initial investigation, so not only have we the police investigating themselves, but the department that investigated it investigating themselves[3516].

By November 2011, police revealed the possible number of NOW phone hacking victims was 5,795[3517].

Sir Ian Blair faced allegations by Ali Dizaei in 2006 that he organised the targeting of the private phone calls of ethnic policemen (especially during Operation Helios).

The Met-Murdoch Interface

Just as Freemasonic collusion can on occasion explain why police inquiries get nowhere, so secret Met-Murdoch connections can explain the experiences of celebrities like actress Leslie Ash, who met a brick wall when she tried to find out from the police who had hacked her. She says: 'If you can't trust the police, whom can you trust? They're corrupt'.

The de Menezes family were likewise bewildered as to why the police didn't approach them with the hacking information earlier: they fear the police are again trying to cover up their own wrongdoing. That the police's obscurantist instinct is still alive and well, despite the hacking scandal, is shown by the High Court ruling , only obtained in the summer of 2011, by Hugh Grant and Jemima Khan, forcing the Met to hand over information about their alleged hacking by a P.I. (Glenn Mulcaire) working for NOW.

Again, there was the puzzle of why N.I. put under surveillance Crimewatch presenter Jacqui Hames, a WPC with the National Crime Faculty, and her husband, Detective Chief Superintendent Dave Cook, head of the West London murder squad, who was investigating the axe murder of P.I. Daniel Morgan (he had been probing what corrupt Met officers and South London criminals were getting up to). Mulcaire had obtained Jacqui's warrant card and payslip numbers, which must have been sold to him by her colleagues. N.I. refuses to answer who instigated Mulcaire's snooping, so Ms. Hames is set to sue N.I. for answers, while her ex-husband is likewise about to sue for harassment. Surrey Police knew about the hacking of Millie Dowler's phone almost a decade before her parents found out, their lawyer claims: if true, why did it take nine years for this to be revealed?

The incestuous ties perhaps began when the Met helped Murdoch move from Fleet Street to Wapping and protected his newspapers there from strikes. Tentacles develop because, according to ex-Commander John O'Connor, cops notoriously cow-tow to politicians, because of their careers. Add to this politicians' subservience to too powerful media moguls, and we have a perfect potential storm for corruption.

Some ex-Met cops set up themselves as 'stringers', who provide a conduit for information to be supplied illegally by officers directly to the press. 305 journalists working for 31 newspapers and magazines were found to be using just one criminal P.I. hacker. NOW journalist Paul McMullen had a pot of £3.1m with which to pay police. A favourite drop-off spot for bribes to cops was McDonalds, round the corner from Wapping[3518].

The Home Affairs Select Committee criticised Dick Fedorcio, the Met's communications chief, for apparently showing 'no due diligence' in vetting Neil Wallis, the ex-NOW executive hired by Scotland Yard in 2009. Ex-Flying Squad officer Dick Kirby says: 'The reputation of Scotland Yard is in tatters'. The IPCC's Deborah Glass says public confidence has been rocked, and Thames Valley Deputy Chief Constable Sue Akers – brought in by the Met to conduct the police inquiry – says: 'Public confidence in the police is seriously at risk'. But again, is her appointment one more example of the police investigating themselves? The Home Office has instructed the Chief Inspector of Constabulary to act as an independent arbiter, but he is himself an ex-Met assistant commissioner. At least 30 inquiries are planned or under way, as well as one by the Serious Fraud Office, into alleged hush payments signed off by James Murdoch. Dick Fedorcio, the Met's PR chief, let NOW crime editor Lucy Panton file a story about corrupt Ali Dizaei on his own computer in his Scotland Yard office, using his personal email[3519]. Fedorcio's resigning from the Met just before disciplinary action is 'highly damaging to public confidence' – the IPCC's deputy chairwoman Deborah Glass also ruled that the Met's decision to give ex NOW boss Neil Wallis a £1,000-a-day job was not a result of corruption[3520].

Ex-P.I. Sean Hoare's post-mortem could not determine his cause of death: his testimony would have been invaluable for the inquiry offered by No. 10. As it is, he claimed that (1) Coulson asked him (and others) to hack into phones, and (2) NOW reporters used bought police technology to locate people using their mobiles. Interestingly the Met interviewed Hoare under caution, but the outcome of this interview is unclear.

There seems to be a consensus that the IPCC (Independent Press Complaints Commission) is seriously flawed – not surprising there are conflicts of interest when there were editors and an ex-Met boss on it along with Wallis.

If insult could be added to injury in this extensive imbroglio, it happened at the grilling of the Murdochs by the Culture and Media Select Committee: police security (five officers in the Commons room) failed to stop a man attacking the 80-year-old Rupert Murdoch. The result could have been tragic if the attacker had really been dangerous. But the Met even tried to spin this severe embarrassment: it wasn't a security failure because it was a 'public hearing'!

Former managing editor of the NOW, Stuart Kuttner, was arrested on suspicion of corrupting police with bribes and phone hacking[3521].

Former Met Commissioner Lord Stevens wrote a regular column for the 'News of the World', while in 2005 Sir Ian Blair's son Joshua had work experience on 'The Sun'. The teenage sons of two ex-Met commissioners were given work experience at The Sun[3522]. Even former Director of Public Prosecutions Lord MacDonald is advising the NOW over the hacking scandal[3523]. Lord Ian Blair seems to have authorised over lunch with her the borrowing of a police horse by Rebekah Brooks ('Horsegate').

A Surrey policeman was referred to the IPCC in 2011 on suspicion of leaking information to the News of the World about Millie Dowler in 2002, when he was taken off the case[3524] (he had been sent to Surrey Police headquarters in Guildford to collect documents)[3525].

A Met detective constable investigating phone hacking (on Operation Weeting) has been arrested for allegedly leaking details of the inquiry to 'The Guardian'[3526]. Instead of the Met using the normal route to seek evidence about leaking, i.e. the Police and Criminal Evidence Act, to force The Guardian to surrender documents about the Millie Dowler story which would reveal the paper's source, the police decided to use the 1989 Official Secrets Act. But are the police the best arbiters of what is in the public interest? This use of the law was almost unprecedented, and was authorised by Detective Superintendent Mark Mitchell, though it may conflict with article 10 (freedom of speech) of human rights legislation. The Met made a humiliating U-turn over its bid to force The Guardian to disclose its sources about the hacking scandal: the Old Bailey application for a production order was cancelled after widespread outrage in newspapers and other media. This was the new Commissioner's first faux pas[3527]. The only previous similar attempt collapsed in 2000 due to a public outcry: a former military intelligence officer and Tony Geraghty, author of 'The Irish War', had their homes raided by MOD police in the early am. Also in 2000 an attempt to obtain Guardian and Observer documents relating to David Shayler failed[3528]. Former Labour minister Tom Watson, who has campaigned on phone hacking, has strongly condemned the police move against The Guardian: 'It is an outrageous abuse and completely unacceptable, that having failed to investigate serious wrongdoing at the News of the World for more than a decade, the police should now be trying to move against The Guardian'[3529].

Clive Goodman's letter (written in 2007) was available to police, who ensured its full contents were not revealed[3530]. Two versions of the letter were provided to the Culture Media and Sport Select Committee of the Commons – in the Harbottle & Lewis version the names of the journalists he exposed had been redacted <u>at the Met's request</u>[3531].

As chief executive at News International, Rebekah Brooks has confirmed the 'rogue reporter' defence in the phone hacking case. She has admitted her paper paid police officers for information, which is illegal[3532]. She had told MPs in 2003 that The Sun – the paper she once edited – had paid police for tips[3533], but News International refused to comment on her statement that payments had been made to police officers[3534].

Brian Paddick was seeking (2011) a judicial review of the police investigation into the phone-hacking scandal[3535]. He and Lord Prescott won the right to a judicial review (2011) into how the Met handled the News of the World phone hacking inquiry[3536].

Paul McMullan has been named as a (former) journalist who paid police for tips[3537]. Alex Marunchak – the News of the World's Dublin editor – is the most senior NOW official linked to illegality (bribing police officers) in the hacking scandal[3538]. Mirror reporter Wensley Clarkson has also confirmed police were paid bribes.

Met anti-corruption officer <u>Steve Roberts</u> was warned off investigating police leaks to the press (for payments) in 2003. Police knew about their men being bribed in <u>2000</u> but nothing was done[3539]. Roberts was advised if he went after the press but couldn't prove charges, they would retaliate strongly. (The 'cover' used by corrupt officers was to register journalists as bogus police informants, so 'legitimising' the payments)[3540]. Labour MP Chris Bryant has highlighted the close relationship between police and the Murdoch press, with senior officers being wined and dined by NOW executives. He says, 'We know that the NOW paid police officers for information', and that there was a 'very dirty smell' surrounding the police handling of the original inquiry[3541].

News International passed a dossier to the Met listing possibly illegal payments to detectives by the News of the World. The BBC claimed that Andy Coulson approved the payments while he was editor[3542].

Met PC <u>Jeremy Young</u> and <u>Scott Gelsthorpe</u> were jailed for hacking computers and tapping phones of celebrities and the rich via their PI agency – Young ran the agency while on sick leave from the Met with 'depression' (his doctors gave him 1,600 days off in five years). The two pretended to be Scotland Yard detectives[3543].

The News of the World got stories quickest, it is claimed, because it was closer to the police than other tabloids (along with its sister papers, The Sun and The Times, all in the News International stable). Because of the huge political influence of N.I., Scotland Yard didn't want to alienate Murdoch's journalists. There was a culture of omerta among the press and the Brown government, and, it can be argued, among the police elite, e.g. the IPCC refused to speak to the C4 'Dispatches' programme (4.10.10) which exposed the phone hacking scandal, while, regarding the culprit journalist Mulcaire, police were very reluctant to cooperate with anyone, particularly celebrities who wanted to know if they were on Mulcaire's hacking list. News of the World boss Rebekah Brooks wouldn't appear before the Culture Committee. The Met interviews new witnesses in the scandal <u>under caution</u>, so that they can be arrested if the police are close to the truth. Was the police proximity to Murdoch the reason for the paucity of the original investigation? Why did the police appear to limit the inquiry to royals, neglecting the masses of other famous people, none of whom were warned

(Brian Paddick was one of their own kept in the dark). Of 6,000 victims the Met only released details of a small proportion.

Ex-MI5-trained policeman Derek Webb, now a PI (his business is called Silent Shadow), snooped on scores (over 150) of celebrities for the NOW, including Princes William and Harry (raising questions about the competence of their police guards). Webb was hired in 2010 to stalk Mark Lewis, a hacking victims lawyer, to find compromising personal things to discredit him from opposing the NOW[3544].

The first 'Sun' journalist to be arrested by the Met's Elveden team investigating bribes to police was Jamie Pyatt[3545].

Cheshire Police were investigating allegations about breaches of the Data Protection Act by Alec Owens, a former Special Branch officer. Detectives removed from his home a memory stick relating to his work for the Office of the Information Commissioner (OIC), from which he resigned in 2006. It is alleged he furnished The Independent with information he obtained during his work on Operation Motorman (2003), which probed the use of PIs by the media. It is unusual for the police rather than the OIC itself to conduct the investigation. Owens was due to appear at the Leveson Inquiry: he says the police want to know what he is going to divulge at the Inquiry[3546].

Surrey Police were so convinced that Milly Dowler's father had killed her they were blind to other suspects: they mounted an anti-terrorist-style operation against him[3547]. Her parents insist they were told by a police officer that Milly's voicemails had been erased, but Surrey Police have declined to comment. At the end of 2011 it was becoming increasingly likely (but not certain) that police were to blame for deleting (inadvertently) Milly's voicemail messages[3548]. Surrey Police were aware of a caller purporting to be Sally Dowler seeking information in 2002, but haven't explained why they didn't investigate that deception in 2002[3549].

Re the PI hackers allegedly employed by News of the World journalists, the police apparently chose not to inform everyone who had their mobile phones hacked or pursue other journalists suspected of similar hacking[3550].

The Society of Editors says tighter controls on how the police and press interact could lead to officers closing ranks. Filkin's guidelines suggest reporters use tactics like 'flirting' and plying officers with alcohol[3551].

A retired 52-year-old Met officer was arrested (January, 2012) but not named by the IPCC, who then gave him up to Thames Valley Police. He was suspected of leaking information to a journalist[3552]. A 39-year-old Met cop was arrested and bailed on 11.2.12 in connection with the hacking inquiry: being a police officer, as usual anonymity was maintained.

The News of the World (NOW) hired several police officers. 13 police officers had been arrested by 28.1.12 during the Elveden hacking operation into bribe-taking[3553].

NOW chief crime reporter Neville Thurlbeck has revealed that, as a registered confidential source for police for nearly a decade, (his codename was 'George') he not only exchanged information with officers but sometimes paid them[3554].

Former Mirror crime reporter Jeff Edwards revealed (Newsnight BBC2. 27.2.12) that, when he worked for the News of the World (1980-85) in the same capacity, he was switched from the crime desk because he wouldn't bribe police for stories (there were leaks even up to the level of chief constable). Deputy chief commissioner Sue Akers told Leveson the 'tradecraft' at 'The Sun' was the bribing of a wide variety of public officials, including police and health. Akers (Head of Elveden) has accused 'The Sun' of organising a 'culture of illegal payments to police', with some receiving 'retainers'. 'Tradecraft' involved hiding cash emoluments by paying them to a friend or relative of the source[3555].

John Prescott says the Met concealed large-scale hacking by NOW, which 'supported and assisted an organisation guilty of criminal behaviour and prioritised this over the rights of thousands of potential victims'[3556].

A police horse was loaned to Rebekah Brooks in 2008 by the Met. It was returned to the police in a 'poor' condition[3557]. A senior Met officer may have given Brooks inside information about the failed hacking investigation. It is not known whether the suspected transaction involved a payment of money[3558].

Sir Denis O'Connor, the Chief Inspector of Constabulary, has blamed Home Secretary Alan Johnson for being unwilling to examine phone hacking, so O'Connor dropped it[3559].

Brian Paddick has criticised Deputy Assistant Commissioner Peter Clarke's excuse for not pursuing the first hacking inquiry, i.e. it would divert resources from the more life-threatening terrorist fight.

Alleged payments for information included money to a female prison officer[3560].

Former Parliamentary standards commissioner Elizabeth Filkin told Leveson that the Met's rank and file were astounded by senior officers 'filling their boots' (e.g. with free tickets to sporting events), with lavish gifts from the press, and suspected that deals were being made to cover up embarrassing stories about their seniors[3561]. Lord Stevens (Commissioner 2000-2005), the 'Copper's Copper', whose autobiography was entitled 'Not for the fainthearted', admitted to Leveson that he was paid up to £7,000 a time for writing articles for the News of the World: he now regrets writing them[3562].

Former NOW executive editor Neil Wallis says he advised Lord Stevens and Sir Paul Stephenson on how to get the Commissioner's job, boasting he was 'well connected' within the Yard. Three senior Met figures – Yates, Stephenson and Fedorcio – have quit over their links to Wallis[3563].

Former Met Police Commander Ray Adams headed a secretive unit at a company controlled by Rupert Murdoch, and has been accused in a Panorama programme of being involved in an alleged plot to destroy Sky's biggest rival (ITV-owned ON digital). A 1987 corruption probe examined allegations that Adams and other officers had been involved improperly with criminal informants (e.g. killer Kenneth Noye): the DPP cleared Adams, as did the Macpherson Inquiry (1998), though the latter noted there were 'strange features' to his evidence[3564].

Detective Chief Superintendent Philip Williams, who led the probe into the 2006 hacking allegations, was asked to review the files found in the possession of P.I. Glenn

Mulcaire, but convinced his superiors there was no further evidence. Two colleagues, DI Mark Maberly and Detective Chief Superintendent Keith Surtees, were also charged with examining the files. CPS chief Keir Starmer had a meal with Rebekah Brooks just a few days after his decision (2009) not to reopen the case[3565].

The police blogger 'Night Jack', who was unmasked by hackers at The Times in 2009, is to sue News International for damages[3566].

Tory MP John Whittingdale – chair of the Commons Culture Committee which probed 'NOW'* editor Andy Coulson – said the Met has 'very serious questions' to answer about 'thoroughness and attitudes of the Met Police at the time'[3567].

Unlike the Sun journalists arrested in the hacking inquiry, who were all named, the Met officer also arrested (thought to be a Territorial Policing Command officer) remained anonymous – one law for the police once again[3568].

A 52-year-old female officer was arrested (December, 2011) for accepting a News of the World bribe[3569]. Surrey PC Alan Tierney, a member of the Elveden team, was given 10 months for leaking stories about John Terry (and his shoplifting mother) and Ronnie Wood. The judge commented that it was 'a disgraceful way for a police officer to act'[3570].

Half of the Met's press department are former NOW journalists (2012).

MP George Galloway was forced by the Met to go to the High Court to get them to reveal their material about him being hacked.

A Murdoch chauffeur (Paul Maley) told the government in 2011 that he had been detailed to pay off police officers with cash packages (more than a dozen times). He claimed his lawyers had a black book with the names of corrupt cops, kept locked in a secret place; and that he had been subject to intimidation to prevent him revealing the names (phone warning, damage to his car, animal excrement through his Surrey letter box). Maley's being charged at Guildford Crown Court with impersonating a police officer was another attempt to discredit him: the judge acquitted him (the police allegedly withheld evidence which could have exonerated him)[3571].

The IPCC is to probe whether Craig Denholm, Deputy Chief Constable of Surrey, knew that Milly Dowler's phone had been hacked by the News of the World. His successor – DS Maria Woodhall – was also referred to the watchdog[3572].

As part of Operation Elveden Met DCI April Casburn was charged with misconduct in public office for allegedly leaking information to the NOW[3573]. She was convicted and jailed.

Yet over 500 contacts were logged between a Guardian journalist and DC Peter Cripps, but the Met claimed no action can be taken against him as he has retired. One law for the tabloids, another for the qualities[3574]? Recently retired Frank Armstrong, holder of the Queen's Medal and Assistant Commissioner for the City of London Police, was arrested by nine officers on suspicion of misconduct in public office. Again he had spoken to journalists[3575].

---

* News of the World

Experienced crime correspondents have received threatening phone calls from anti-corruption officers demanding the source(s) of their information, the Met even trying to force a Guardian journalist to reveal her sources with the Official Secrets Act. Yard officers talk of a reign of terror under black Deputy Assistant Commissioner <u>Pat Gallan</u>, who heads the Professional Standards Unit[3576].

Police, says Leveson, conducted themselves with 'integrity' at all times during the first phone hacking probe – Operation Caryatid, when Royals thought their voicemails were hacked by the News of the World in 2005. Leveson has demanded a draconian restriction of the public's right to know what the police are up to, e.g. the public and the press would be banned from knowing if a crime suspect has been arrested. He did not find any extensive evidence of police corruption[3577].

CHAPTER XIX

THE PARAPOLICEMAN: DUMBED-DOWN POLICEMAN?

Outsourcing of services now occurs throughout British society, from government departments to banks to councils to courts, so it is not surprising law and order functions are being increasingly shunted out of direct police control. In September 2011 there was an expansion of civilians with fining powers: street wardens and traffic marshals, housing officers, etc. The police are paid for accrediting the 'parapolice', though some forces don't use the scheme[3578].

In 2002 Labour backtracked on its controversial plans to let non-police/non-tax agencies (councils and quangos) monitor phone and e-mail records[3579], and town halls are to be banned from training hidden cameras on law-abiding members of the public and using undercover agents to spy on them over 'bin crimes' and school catchment area rules, but they will still be able to use Big Brother surveillance to monitor underage sales of alcohol and cigarettes[3580]. Thousands of council jobsworths were being trained in 2007 to place smokers under surveillance[3581].

In return for helping Warwickshire Police man speed traps and advising motorists on the dangers of speeding, Boy Scouts are presented with a 'community challenge badge'. The Scouts can give a verbal or written warning[3582].

It is claimed Edinburgh Council has been fining drivers illegally for 12 years, having made a fatal error in the wording of the fines. When parking was decriminalised the phrase 'initial charge' should have been removed from a new Traffic Regulation Order (TRO)[3583].

2010 guidance to chief constables from ACPO tells them to target 100,000 private security guards and 50,000 door supervisors with their Home Office's Community Safety Accreditation Scheme (CSAS), which empowers authorised civilians to stop people, take their photo, ask for name and address. 'Jacqui Smith's Irregulars' included car park attendants, dog and park wardens, housing officers and hospital security staff. They can issue fines for littering, dog fouling, cycling on footpaths, throwing fireworks, railway trespassing, begging, as well as force under-18s to surrender alcohol, and stop vehicles for testing. ACPO CPI Ltd has a lucrative monopoly of approving companies whose staff want the police-style powers[3584]: its charge of £600 per firm creates an obvious conflict of interest. ACPO says the Police Reform Act 2002 gives chief constables the right to employ civilians to operate speed cameras, but others disagree[3585].

A Scarborough charity's housing officials decided to cut down crab apple trees because the apples posed a safety risk and blocked light, despite the protests of the occupants of the charity's houses[3586].

One can shoot squirrels but not sell them. Trainee hairdressers are not allowed scissors in the classroom. One cannot import Polish potatoes into Britain or fish in the River Esk without authorisation, or stage more than 12 events annually at a church hall (or similar venue) without a full alcohol licence, own a donkey or pony without a passport with the animal's picture, or smoke on an open railway platform or a covered bus stop, It is a crime to 'disturb a pack of eggs when directed not to by an authorised officer', as well as not reporting a grey squirrel in one's own back garden[3587]. An Army veteran was banned from mowing his local cemetery lawn (where his mother was buried), because it was 'too dangerous'. A pub had to tear down St. George's Cross bunting because it could 'distract cyclists or drivers'[3588].

Anti-crime stickers, put up to deter opportunistic criminals, were banned as a fire hazard by an Essex council, even though the local fire station said the stickers were not dangerous[3589].

You can be fined for dropping bread while feeding the ducks in Sandwell (West Midlands), where 24 street wardens are accredited by police: one 70-year-old woman faced a fine of £2,500 for refusing to pay a penalty notice for dropping cigarette ash at a bus stop[3590]. Litter police hounded the owner of a car from which they saw an apple core being thrown in Wolverhampton. She denies the offence, saying it must have been a friend who was sitting in the car while she shopped. After 11 months the case may end up costing the taxpayer £5,000, as she insists on a jury trial[3591]. A Derbyshire pipesmoker was fined £50 by a council warden for dropping a match which was burning his finger[3592].

A council warden threatened a man and his elderly mother with an £80 fine for feeding the birds in a Leicester park. When the birds ate the bread, the jobsworth demanded the mother's name and address. The warden ignored drunks urinating on the grass and supping from cans, telling the birdfeeders that it was his job to 'educate transgressors'. There was no sign banning feeding the birds[3593]. A young mother feeding ducks with her little boy was fined £75 for 'spreading litter' by a council warden – there were no signs banning bird feeding[3594].

A Dorset shopkeeper was banned by her council from selling 'racist' golliwogs at a vintage market on her Enid Blyton-themed stall. The justification is that the rag dolls (replaced in the Noddy books by goblins) might trigger 'public order problems'[3595]. A schools inspector claims she was intimidated in her home by a Braintree council jobsworth after he traced her for 'fly-tipping' old newspapers in a supermarket recycling bin[3596].

A Devon householder was accused of littering for sweeping leaves from a roadside tree into the gutter – the council workman reduced her to tears, saying she was fly-tipping and refused to remove the leaves into his litter truck[3597].

Bristol council jobsworths ordered a picnic family on Clifton Downs to remove their 'semi-permanent structure' (a windbreak) or face a fine (£500 if it went to court). A group of five-year-olds in Sunderland were soaked when a park attendant demanded teachers take down a mini-marquee for 'health and safety' reasons[3598].

Council 'bin police' all over the country are punishing hundreds of households with fines larger than those given to shoplifters (up to £110 compared with £80). Local authorities in 2009 also issued 25,000 statutory notices threatening fines for recycling breaches. Newcastle-under-Lyme demands rubbish is sorted into nine bins. A Canterbury resident was fined £700 plus court costs for putting waste into blue sacks rather than grey bins. The power Labour gave councils makes many of them overbearing[3599].

A Cardiff animal lover who save some doomed goldfish from the University Hospital of Wales, where he was a volunteer, was threatened with interview under caution, arrest, prosecution and a £1,000 fine. Officials said he should have spent a month applying for a licence, to comply with the Welfare of Animals (Transport) Order 2006, yet this was an emergency[3600].

A teacher was angrily confronted by security guards while photographing near the 2012 Olympic site (none apparently showed ID), and his ID and cameras were demanded even though he was on a public path[3601].

Neighbourhood Watch members have been asked to substitute for police in various capacities – checking car tax discs, patrolling crime-ridden estates, spying on criminals. The suggestion has been included in a memo from ACPO to chief constables[3602].

Assistant Chief Constable Andy Holt has called for football referees to wear microphones to curb players' foul language. Sir Alex Ferguson has mocked Superintendent Mark Payne for saying foul-mouthed striker Wayne Rooney should be arrested[3603].

London traffic wardens are being replaced by enforcers with computers and smart surveillance apparatus that can spot an offence miles away[3604].

In the spring of 2011 30,000 census 'police' began calling at a third of Britain's homes. A visit from these non-compliance staff could result in prosecutions for failure to complete forms[3605].

Scottish Reliance prison transfer officer Stephen McGrath, sacked following convictions for drink driving and groping a woman in a pub, was found with a large amount of stolen currency[3606].

A Glasgow teenager was threatened with a fine by two Council enforcement officers when a gust of wind blew a biscuit out of his hand. Though the Council dropped the charge they insisted intent to drop the 'litter' did not need to be proved[3607].

A mother who dropped a piece of sausage while feeding her young daughter was fined £75 by two officers from her Cumbria 'environment crime unit' (pigeons ate the evidence)[3608]. South Lanarkshire Council is to fine children £50 for dropping litter[3609].

A two-year-old Walsall boy was threatened with an Asbo for laughing too loudly at TV's Thomas The Tank Engine and being a 'noise nuisance'. His accusers were West Midlands housing officials. He can't yet read, but was asked in a letter to be 'mindful' of his neighbours[3610].

Council snoopers monitored the contents of the bins of over 30,000 families in 2010: they divided the contents into 13 categories of waste (as well as 52 sub-categories). Sometimes specific streets are targeted to supply data on certain types of people. Thus parts of Scunthorpe are described as being in 'Municipal Dependency' – watching a lot of TV, having low aspirations, while the nearby people are classified as living in 'Suburban Comfort'. Coventry, Reading, Birmingham and many other authorities have increased spending on 'waste audits' to analyse which sort of people throw out more rubbish[3611]. Councils' 'waste audits' allow officials and private contractors to rummage through bins to determine the wealth and race of families, using 'social profiling' techniques (categorising them, e.g., as 'wealthy achievers', 'hard-pressed', etc).

THE PARAPOLICEMAN: DUMBED-DOWN POLICEMAN?

David Jones, the creator of the children's cartoon character Fireman Sam, was detained at Gatwick Airport because he commented about a Muslim passenger passing through security ahead of him with her face covered by a hijab. A policeman was present while a security officer tried to make him apologise to satisfy their PC agenda (a Muslim security officer had taken offence). All passengers must show their faces at passport control. Jones is claiming unlawful arrest and detention[3612].

Surrey and West Midlands Police are advertising for private firms to take over beat policing, detaining suspects and investigating crimes, on behalf of all forces in England and Wales (arrest will not be part of the remit). But such privatisation means the police may be less accountable (with no access by the public to the IPCC), and may compromise safety and cost of services (e.g. PFI in the NHS)[3613].

Traffic wardens are being issued with surveillance cameras that work in the dark hidden in their badges –they are not obliged to tell drivers they are being recorded[3614]. Policing by camera is now widespread in London[3615].

Hampshire Police have recruited 12 students at Portsmouth University to patrol the campus in high-vis jackets.

21 new traffic offences (2011) are now enforceable by councils.

Rail ticket police are landing rail passengers with large fines and criminal prosecutions over innocent mistakes. Inflexible inspectors hand out instant justice without using discretion. A sentence of three months in jail is no longer a 'last resort' – now 'strict liability rules' are applied, e.g., passengers who forgot their ticket but can prove purchase still face sanctions[3616].

Bath's head traffic warden and five of his staff have been disciplined by police for illegal parking[3617].

An East End street trader was convicted at Thames Magistrates Court of eight offences under the Weights and Measures Act, including selling bowls of loose chillies for £1 without stating the exact quantity[3618].

PC Konk the Clown was detained by humourless 'security' personnel at an airport: they confiscated his plastic handcuffs[3619].

The drawbacks of PCSOs, so prevalent on the streets of England and Wales (Scotland refused to have 'dumbed-down' officers), are described elsewhere in this book (see The Imcompetent Policeman chapter). Suffice it to mention a few more here. They have never been independently evaluated, despite there being (outside London) typically four PCSOs to every officer, with the Met having up to eight per officer. In over 20 London boroughs they are deployed in vehicles, sometimes in plainclothes, and some are manning police stations. Their role is even being extended to drugs and terrorism, despite background checks not always being performed (one Met PCSO was merely suspended when it was found he was an illegal immigrant). In several areas of Kent they didn't give out a single fixed penalty ticket in a whole year – the few tickets that were issued cost £650,000 each (10 were for bicycle maintenance offences). Though comprising only a fifth of the (non-police) workforce, they attract over half of all gross misconduct cases (especially computer misuse):

one even made a false allegation of crime. They have lowered the status of constables by the suggestion that patrolling is a low-skill activity[3620].

West Lothian Council leads an 'emissions partnership' which employs 'emissions officers' to fine motorists who let their car engines idle. They can issue verbal and written warnings. The partnership has been accused of being 'like the Stasi'[3621].

Using antiterrorist RIPSA powers, Scotland is planning a compulsory state guardian for every child, recording devices in GP surgeries, with midwives being told to spy on patients, as well as a national database of personal details. Councils can intercept emails and stalk suspects (East Renfrewshire has installed covert CCTV at a primary school and a bowling club). RIPSA encourages cracking nuts with sledgehammers[3622].

CHAPTER XX

THE PC POLICEMAN

CONTENTS

CHAPTER XX

THE PC POLICEMAN

Douglas Murray, Director of the Centre for Social Cohesion, says: 'The police as a force have been wrecked for more than a decade. They are the victims of politically correct nonsense and have ended up having an institutional nervous breakdown'[3623]. Sir Ian Blair's tenure at the Met is widely viewed by rank and file officers as a failure of political correctness[3624].

Jan Berry, the government's 'anti-red-tape tsar', says almost a third of the cost of every policing process is wasted in bureaucracy[3625].

An anonymous South-East of England police inspector says (2011) data collected by police are 'no longer a reflection of performance, but an exercise in deceit of the public'. Thus a vast array of crimes are reclassified by minimising 'crime managers', using subterfuges such as 'badger damage', 'frost damage', 'lost' (instead of stolen). Instead of deterring crime, police chiefs are engaged in social engineering. The whistleblower's police phone directory lists at least 32 'diversity' officers, all with desk-bound jobs. Practical safety instruction for police consists of one day – much more time is given to diversity awareness, with having to explain weekly to supervisors what the officer has done to promote cultural diversity objectives. Now encouraged to wear Gay Pride badges, police can't wear war medals any longer because Irish and Muslims might take offence. St. George's flag has been banned by English forces. Police have to doff their boots when entering a Muslim house. Form-filling includes a Display Screen Risk Assessment (14 pages) detailing working environment risks, even though all furniture is centrally supplied, already approved. The treatment of drunk and disorderly people can be through the courts (under section 5 of the Public Order Act) or by putting them in the cells, or sent home: the month's crime statistics will determine which option is followed (if crime rates are too high managers will order no arrests under section 5). When Home Secretary Theresa May 'abolished' the requirement, as part of officers' annual appraisal, to describe three objectives for raising public confidence, this carried on with a new title of 'public satisfaction' objectives[3626].

In the UK much of what is considered 'hate crime' – bigotry, racism, xenophobia, homophobia, etc. – would in the US be acceptable under First Amendment principles[3627].

Race

A grandfather who asked Strathclyde Police to keep an eye on his house while he was on holiday, in case Lithuanian squatters tried to occupy it, was warned he could be arrested for racism[3628].

Where once we had the Police Federation, the Superintendents Association and ACPO, now we also have the Black and Asian Police Association, a Muslim Police Association, the Lesbian and Gay Police Association and the National Trans Police Association: just the way to lose the support and confidence of the public[3629].

A 77-year-old Hampshire grandmother was threatened with arrest for inciting religious hatred by putting a humorous sign on her gate: 'Our dogs are fed on Jehovah's

Witnesses'. Kent Police have a Homophobic and Transphobic Reporting Line, a Hate Crime Action Group, a Minority Ethnic Action Group and a Fairness Action Group. These are all subsumed under the Diversity and Fairness Strategy Board, part of a new Citizen Focus Performance Gold Group, chaired by a deputy chief constable. This nonsense is replicated across the country. In 2008 Basil Brush upset the Southern England Romany Gipsy & Irish Traveller Network – Dame Rosie Fortune tries to sell him pegs, lucky heather and a palm reading. Thus Northants Police had to assess a video of the glove puppet to determine if he was racist[3630]. 'The zealous over-use of the criminal law for essentially civil matters is a classic indicator of a police state'[3631].

'Multi-point entry' is the latest wheeze to encourage non-white police applicants, i.e. transferring from another occupation into the police into a rank above constable[3632]. In 2007 ACPO asked for the right to institute positive discrimination, i.e. promoting female and BME candidates ahead of white male recruits, irrespective of merit[3633].

A pub singer was arrested for racism when he sang a regular number in his repertoire, the classic chart hit 'Kung Fu Fighting'[3634].

It would be much safer to relocate the Notting Hill Carnival to nearby Hyde Park, but neither the Met nor the Mayor have been willing to agree because of the dictates of political correctness[3635].

Thames Valley Police asked a vicar his ethnic background before they would send out an officer to investigate a burglary at his church: he wouldn't be given a crime number if he refused to answer such questions, which were part of 'best practice' – from April 2008 victim ethnicity was a legal requirement[3636].

The Met demoted a mascot called Steve (officers dressed up as PCSO Steve to popularise the police service to schoolchildren), because he was 'too white, blond and male' – Sir Ian Blair ordered three new 'ethnically diverse' mascots at a cost of £15,000[3637].

Anti-terrorism officers carrying out spot checks at key sites following the 2007 outrage were told not to target people based on age or ethnicity, even though all the suspects in the failed attacks were young Asian or Middle-Eastern adults. Police bosses were criticised for not using racial profiling, being more concerned with upsetting minorities than protecting the country[3638].

Gloucestershire Police employed undercover officers to eat in Indian restaurants in the hope they would hear racist language (Operation Napkin). Because author Lynette Burrows expressed mild disapproval of gay adoption on BBC Radio Five Live she was questioned by police[3639].

Branded as a racist by Asian Met officer DS Shabnam Chaudri – because he had made some clumsy remarks during a lecture – DS Tom Hassell survived a six-year witch-hunt, allegedly badly handled by Sir Ian Blair. Hassell's 30-year police career was rubbished by PC bosses. Though his immediate bosses had immediately dismissed the complaints, he was eventually vindicated, but he is furious that the allegations were given credence while his defence was largely ignored[3640].

The initiative of Sussex and Herefordshire Constabularies to arrest shopkeepers for the 'hate crime' of selling golliwogs (likely to incite a breach of the peace) has been followed by Staffordshire: a golly mascot was confiscated from the radiator of a Land Rover[3641]. The car's owner, a restaurant manager and collector of golliwogs, finds it strange that police can remove bits from your vehicle without contacting you[3642]. A shopkeeper took her golliwogs off display when Cheshire Police told her a woman had complained they were offensive[3643]. The case against a grandmother accused of racial harassment for putting a golliwog in her house window, was dramatically dropped by the police[3644].

The son of a friend of journalist Richard Littlejohn was rejected as a recruit by Surrey Police because he wasn't of the right gender or a BME. An ad for an 'Awareness Event' in Guildford concludes forcefully: 'If you cannot promote dignity, respect and equality, don't apply'[3645].

A 71-year-old priest who wrote about his Christian views in his parish newsletter was interviewed by the Met on suspicion of inciting racial hatred (in his local borough there had been five murders, 33 rapes, thousands of burglaries in the previous year). He wasn't charged[3646].

The Black Police Association reportedly stopped 50 black officers giving DNA samples to help identify the rapist Night Stalker, because of political correctness, though Chief Inspector Leroy Logan, who chaired the BPA, denied this. The BPA complained that the procedure should also have applied to white officers[3647].

Tayside Police and the Met investigated 'Sun' journalist and former editor Kelvin MacKenzie for anti-Scots racism because he called Scots scroungers on the BBC's Question Time[3648].

A controversial 2004 C4 programme, Edge of the City, which claimed white schoolgirls were being groomed by Bradford Asian men, was pulled just hours before it was due to be broadcast because of police pressure[3649].

West Ham was subjected to an FA and Met investigation in 2007 over a video of supporters singing racist songs (e.g. 'I would rather be a Paki than a Jew', referring to Tottenham's large Jewish fanbase[3650]).

The Met's ban on officers wearing Union Flag badges to support UK troops raised enough controversy for Sir Paul Stephenson to lift the ban. Frontline police had called the ban 'completely crass'. Officers at Heathrow had already been told to take down a Union Flag erected on Armed Forces Day because it wasn't an 'approved ensign'[3651].

A black Liverpool woman was arrested for calling her neighbour a leprechaun, charged with racially aggravated harassment[3652].

West Yorkshire Police are paying officers to learn Urdu[3653].

An anonymous Lancashire officer who displayed a small Union Flag in his patrol van was reported by two Asian cops and reprimanded. The Commission for Racial Equality doesn't support flag bans as this is contrary to the right to freedom of expression[3654].

Because of a huge rise in thieving when travellers arrived in London, a specialist police squad was set up to tackle them, yet the Met has told its staff to 'celebrate' the contribution of Roma to 'London's culture and diversity'[3655].

Met PC Ray McQuarrie filed a complaint for racial discrimination when an MP called him a 'scuffer' (Scottish for 'chav').

When Liverpool City Council decided to remove a street's display of St. George's flags, their truck was accompanied by police in an unmarked van. The pretext was health and safety[3656].

Sussex Police arrested a man who protested to his council about the 'do as you likey' attitude of travellers flouting planning laws ('likey' rhyming with 'pikey')[3657].

Avon and Somerset WPCs (as well as the Assistant Chief Constable) were issued with Muslim-style headscarves to improve race relations[3658].

In 2009 police forces around the country were told by ACPO to recruit gypsies, so they have been inviting young travellers to their training colleges. ACPO's 'Local Employment Targets For Under-Represented Groups' declares that forces must reflect the communities they serve. Tory MP Philip Davies says forces are now becoming institutionally PC[3659].

In 2010 the Met told a couple whose home had been taken over by squatters that they were being 'racist' for questioning the squatters' right to live in Britain on benefits[3660].

The height restriction for entry to the police was abandoned in 1999 to avoid discrimination against, e.g., the Chinese[3661].

The West Midlands Police have pledged to increase recruitment of minority officers, but were accused of reverse discrimination against whites. In 2006, Gloucestershire Police were ordered to compensate white who had lost out. Avon and Somerset's chief constable Colin Port had to offer the chance to reapply to all excluded potential recruits[3662].

A Diversity Health Check report from the Met found a 'white backlash' from officers angry at the time 'wasted' on diversity. Many believe the promotional prospects of white heterosexual males are being compromised. Another report – from the Independent Commission on Mental Health and Policing – found racist attitudes towards mentally ill ethnic minority people[3663].

Religion

The Met's 300-page 'diversity handbook' advises officers how to arrest a witch (don't touch her spells book or ceremonial dagger, the athame, and don't interrupt a pagan ceremony). Wiccan terms (e.g. 'wickening') and religious dates are included, as is advice about atheists and various obscure religions[3664].

The Home Office has given 15 times more funding to a Muslim police support group than to its Christian equivalent[3665].

A 62-page Faith and Culture Resource booklet – produced by Kent Police to 'break down barriers' – includes such gems as substituting 'personal name' for 'Christian name', 'family name' for 'surname' and 'mixed parentage' (for 'mixed cultural heritage') instead of 'mixed race'. One should also avoid putting cups of tea on the floor in case it offends cleanliness sensitivities[3666]! In 2010 Edinburgh Police banned phrases such as 'old biddies' for pensioners and 'batting for the other side' for gays[3667].

THE PC POLICEMAN

In 2009 Hertfordshire Police had a 'champion of faith', Superintendent <u>Simon Hawkins</u>, and in Staffordshire PC <u>Andy Hill</u> has founded the Pagan Police Group UK.

35 Strathclyde policemen were detailed in 2011 to infiltrate the crowd at the next Old Firm match to arrest anyone singing sectarian songs[3668]. Strathclyde Police won't list sectarian songs they class as illegal, but are making sectarian hate crime a priority over other types of crime by allotting officers just to this activity[3669]. They have issued a list of banned songs to the Old Firm (thought to include The Famine Song, The Billy Boys and others glorifying the UDA and IRA). But critics say singing sectarian songs isn't necessarily breaking the law, with lyrics about political history rather than religion. However, Rangers fans have been prosecuted for singing The Famine Song, which a High Court judge has described as racist[3670].

A senior BNP member was arrested by South Wales Police after The Observer passed them a video of him burning the Koran in his garden[3671].

Two London Underground workers were found not guilty of biting the heads off black jelly babies in a 'racially intimidating manner' in 2006. The investigation lasted two years, the trial eight days, costing £250,000[3672].

A Bedfordshire PC resigned because he gave a Muslim colleague a Xmas gift of alcohol and bacon as a joke: his superiors were not amused[3673].

PC officers in Bath (Avon and Somerset) wanted to ban hog roasts because they could offend Jews, Muslims, vegetarians and the homeless: they could even start a riot as the proposed stall would be sited near Big Issue sellers, and animal rights campaigners would also be likely to protest[3674].

West Midlands Police were criticised by broadcasting watchdogs for complaining about the whistleblowing C4 filmmakers who exposed racist Islamic preachers in British mosques (the police had made a formal complaint to Ofcom)[3675].

ACPO has suggested rubber bootees should be worn by sniffer dogs to respect Muslim sensitivities, but many Muslims think the idea is not necessary and is an example of PC[3676].

Police seem to take anti-Muslim activity more seriously than anti-Christian behaviour. On one occasion Muslim protesters held up placards outside Westminster Cathedral declaring 'Islam will conquer Rome' and 'Jesus is the slave of Allah', but the police did nothing[3677]. Yet two Christians handing out Bible extracts in a Muslim area were told by PCSOs they were committing a hate crime[3678].

The apparent anti-Christian bias of the police contrasts with statistics showing nearly 70% of British people say they're Christian, with three believers for every non-believer[3679].

A briefing memo 'Entering Muslim Households' from Avon and Somerset Police advises that such premises should be treated as if they are mosques. Officers are not to practice 'rapid entry' or dawn raids, and to take their shoes off. There is no specific guidance like this for other faiths[3680].

A Muslim demonstrator dressed as a suicide bomber was pictured in 2006 standing beside a London police vehicle protecting Muslims demonstrating over the Danish cartoons (of the prophet with a bomb fuse on his head)[3681].

British Transport Police attracted ridicule when they dropped the word 'Christmas' from a national publicity poster to avoid upsetting other faiths and unbelievers. ('Holiday' was substituted)[3682].

Norfolk Police have been issuing a compass to all jailed Muslims, so they can face Mecca during prayers (a hand-held compass or compass painted on cell ceiling)[3683].

Strathclyde Police have threatened to crack down on football fans singing the Hokey Cokey because it is sectarian, being a parody of the Mass[3684].

Bedfordshire Police order their officers to doff their shoes when entering a Muslim home, even if making an arrest. They must avert their gaze from families present and never use police dogs, because they are 'unclean'[3685].

Northamptonshire Police have enlisted the help of an imam to 'interact' with local Muslims and investigate crimes[3686].

Sexuality

The British Association for Women in Policing suspect some forces are not doing enough to ensure gender equality[3687].

The Police (Health and Safety) Act of 1997 introduced risk assessment into policing, often with perverse or comic effects. Street preacher Dale Macalpine, wrongly arrested by three uniformed officers for saying to a gay PCSO being gay is a sin, won £7,000 as well as his legal costs from Cumbria Police (he was held for seven hours and charged with an offence under Section 5 of the Public Order Act 1986, viz uttering 'threatening, abusive or insulting' words). The police apologised to him, and he said he hoped 'the police will in future do their duty defending freedom of speech'. Another public preacher, Anthony Rollins, was handcuffed and arrested for condemning homosexuality, being awarded £4,250 damages by a court against West Midlands Police[3688], whose Neighbourhood Watch survey asked homeowners if they were bisexual or gay[3689].

Teachers and social workers in Scotland no longer (since 2010) have to report underage sex to police, to avoid embarrassing the children[3690].

'Doggers' and 'cottagers' indulging in casual outdoor sex (illegal under the Sexual Offences Act 2003) must be protected by police under new 'hate crime' ACPO (Scotland) guidance. Officers are urged to arrest anyone suspected of attacking sex participants, even though outdoor sex is unlawful. One unnamed Kent officer said: '… people who break the law have more rights than the normal man or woman on the street'. ACPO says verbal abuse by passers-by can give doggers post-traumatic stress[3691].

Jan Berry, former chairman of the Police Federation, has admitted she was probably promoted too fast, out of political expediency[3692] (i.e. because of her gender).

A Christian campaigner, arrested by South Wales Police for handing out leaflets opposing homosexuality, had the charges dropped in court, but was planning to sue for wrongful arrest, false imprisonment, malicious prosecution and breach of human rights[3693].

An inspector with Lothian and Borders Police was made Scottish coordinator for the Gay Police Association in 2006 (nearly all of the estimated 1,600 gay or bisexual officers keep their sexuality secret). Stonewall's 'Diversity Champions Programme' promotes a Good Practice Forum for workplace equality, and Lothian and Borders have joined the Programme[3694]. The force has had itself listed among the 20 most 'gay-friendly' institutions in Britain – it flew a rainbow flag over its HQ[3695].

Suffolk Police paid £400 for polo shirts and Gay Police Association pin badges for gay liaison officers. Beer mats to raise awareness of domestic violence cost Northumbria Police £3,200[3696]. Cumbria Constabulary commissioned a range of maternity wear for expectant policewomen, who had complained about unflattering XL-sized trousers and blouses[3697].

Kent Police have warned its officers about using terms such as 'afternoon' and 'my dear' in case they cause offence. They should also take their shoes off when visiting someone's house, and not put an arm round anyone[3698].

When a 67-year-old wrote a letter to Norwich Council objecting to a planned gay march, calling them 'sodomites' who spread sexual diseases, two police officers visited her home to warn her she had committed a 'hate crime'. Likewise, police knocked on the door of two devout Christian pensioners who wanted to distribute Christian leaflets beside gay rights literature[3699].

Wolverhampton Tory councillor Jonathan Yardley was questioned by police for two hours for making a gentle quip publicly about the status of the trans-gendered: did he harbour 'malign thoughts' about trans-gendered people? Once one could only be investigated for one's deeds, now the police have taken on board thought crimes, to tackle racists, homophobes, etc. Tory MP Damian Green was arrested for simply speaking out about immigration. Police seem to have made no objections to becoming Orwellian gauleiters[3700].

The Chief Constable of Suffolk ran up a rainbow flag above Bury St. Edmunds police station to celebrate Gay and Lesbian History Month.

Police are now banned from imposing height limits because they discriminate against women, and equality duty 'may involve treating some people better than others'[3701].

The State in the UK now expects police to deal with certain views about extramarital sex: people have been harassed by police for saying one's sexual orientation can be changed[3702].

Two Cheshire policemen turned up at a 10-year-old's home because he supposedly called a school friend 'gay' in an email. They said it was a very serious offence[3703].

'Homophobia' has led to writer Lynette Burrows and Sir Iqbal Sacranie, former head of the Muslim Council, being interviewed by the Met over harmless remarks they made on the radio. Sacranie said Islam considers homosexuality a sin[3704]. Campaigner Lynette

Burrows received a call from a senior police officer warning her that her remarks on Radio 4 about gay men adopting children were homophobic.

Former 'One Man And His Dog' TV host Robin Page was awarded £2,000 by Gloucestershire Police after a five-year battle to clear himself. He was arrested for a 'hate crime' when he joked at a pro-hunting rally: 'If you are a black, vegetarian, Muslim, asylum seeking, one-legged lesbian lorry driver, I want the same rights as you'. He was put on a Homophobic Incidents Register, and a sergeant allegedly wrote about Page's impending trip to Kenya: 'Let's hope he gets eaten by a crocodile'[3705].

Tayside Police's new 'diversity awareness' handbook warns officers to say 'staffing' instead of 'manning' the phone, which is sexist. 'Ethnic minority' becomes 'visible minority' or 'minority ethnic', 'migrant' replaces 'immigrant', 'lady' must not be used on its own (only with 'gentleman'), 'girl' applies only to under-17s. The police guide is titled: 'It's all PC'[3706].

Police ordered a new publican to remove an 'offensive' message from his blackboard, under section 5 of the Public Order Act: 'Faggots and mince not on the menu', referring to the previous gay tenants of the pub. The Taxpayers Alliance thinks such investigations are a waste of police time[3707].

In 2006 the Home Office encouraged police to host gay-friendly information workshops in venues such as nightclubs to enhance reporting of homophobic hate crimes. The guidance emphasises that school pupils taunting each other as acting 'gay' should be reported to police. But such criminalisation of children is controversial[3708].

In the 1940s and 1950s lesbians in the police could set up home together in police accommodation: section houses were often divided into rooms shared between two women. The police were much less liberal in the 1920s about male homosexuality, which was illegal. Thus a Carlisle man arrested on a fraud charge was found to be carrying another man's love letters to him: they had met through an ad in 'The Link', which published coded gay ads – the police charged the editor with conspiring to corrupt public morals[3709]. Staffordshire Constabulary boasts not about how many crimes it solves but how many gays it employs[3710]. How times change.

In response to a complaint, English police in the fifties would obtain a search warrant to raid shops selling saucy seaside postcards and seize offending stock, under the 1857 Obscene Publications Act[3711] (its modern equivalent – the 1959 Obscene Publications Act – is becoming increasingly irrelevant[3712], thanks, among other things, to the internet).

Retired North Wales Police detective sergeant John Atkinson was arrested for calling lesbian acting superintendent Michele Williams a 'dyke' – she took offence, despite having worked with him for many years. He complained he was handcuffed, stripped and refused access to a toilet. Lesbian WPC Sarah Fellows had overheard the remark and complained[3713]. The police then tried to interview him without his clothes, which were eventually returned to him soaked in urine. He was taken to court by what had been his own force, but cleared. The same force spent 96 hours and £4,000 investigating anti-Welsh comments by TV host Anne Robinson.

When Lord Montagu of Beaulieu reported a stolen camera to the local police while some Boy Scouts were camping on his estate, he was arrested, and instead of the police probing the theft, he was charged with offences against one of the boys. He was acquitted, but his witch-hunt had started. In 1954 he was arrested at 7am: with two others he was charged with 'conspiracy to incite certain male persons to commit serious offences with male persons'. This charge hadn't been used since Oscar Wilde, so that the police were seen to be publicly pursuing a purge of society homosexuals. Ironically the trial led to the decriminalisation of homosexuality[3714].

Chief Constable <u>Richard Brunstrom</u> escaped in 2005 without even a reprimand after referring to 'queers' at a staff meeting, though he apologised.

A Lancashire couple questioned by police in their home after they complained that their council was promoting gay rights but refusing to distribute Christian literature, were given an apology and compensation of £10,000. Stephen Green was arrested and charged for handing out Christian literature at a gay rally.

When customers complained to a pub landlady about two lesbians kissing and heavily petting in the bar, she excluded them but ended in court accused of a public order offence ('homophobic behaviour') – they were off-duty police officers who live together. One, <u>Nicola Stewart</u>, was a Hertfordshire drugs squad officer, her girlfriend a Bedfordshire officer.

It took four policemen to investigate an 11-year-old who was accused of calling a 10-year-old school friend "gay" in an e-mail: two at his school and two at his home (the latter told his mother, a magistrate, they were investigating a "very serious" homophobic crime). His angry father says he has constantly contacted the police about break-ins at his business, but never gets a suitable response.

A Hampshire hotelier, landlord of the Penny Farthing in Lyndhurst, received a police visit over a sign which read: 'Poofters welcome here!'[3715].

A senior nurse was punched in the face in front of two police officers, but the CPS wasn't interested, yet when her policeman husband described a senior officer as a lesbian, he was arrested, stripped and dragged through the courts[3716].

West Midlands Police upbraided a Wolverhampton councillor for joking about transsexuals. The 1986 Public Order Act allows this. All police are now trained to assume political correctness is right[3717].

A crime-fighting councillor was interrogated by West Midlands Police for two hours for making a humorous quip about transsexuals[3718].

Children who engage in 'transphobic' behaviour (bullying transgender people) will be probed by police, even though there have been virtually no incidents[3719].

A Strathclyde Police chaplain (a retired Church of Scotland minister) claims he was forced out of his unpaid job because he opposed gay marriage, being told he had contravened the force's 'equality and diversity' policy.

500 police officers and staff in the high crime area of Humberside were taken off duty for an awareness course on sex changes costing thousands. The force was criticised in 2004 by the Bichard Inquiry into the Wells and Chapman murders for deleting sex claims against Ian Huntley which might have prevented him getting a job at their school[3720].

A Christian Norfolk policeman was forced to quit after 15 years' service because he responded to a 'politically correct' campaign (by email and poster promoting things like Gay History Month) by quoting 'homophobic' Biblical texts. He said the service has a 'bias against faith'[3721].

The Met advertised in 2009 for gay, lesbian, bisexual and transgender police to join SO14 to guard the Royal Family, as these minorities are underrepresented in the Royalty Protection Branch[3722].

When the 2008 criminal Justice and Immigration Act was being framed, several peers were worried that the new offence of 'incitement to hatred on grounds of sexual orientation' could be misused to prosecute free speech. They had noticed an increasing tendency of police to threaten individuals for speaking out against homosexuality[3723].

In 2009 the Met replaced the Union Flag outside Limehouse police station in East London with the striped 'rainbow flag', the gay rights banner, to celebrate a LGBT history month, though this was to breach police rules. Similarly under Brunstrom in North Wales, the gay flag was flown outside police HQ[3724].

It was claimed Scottish police are the most modern in Europe when it comes to employing transsexuals (by 2009 the total was seven)[3725].

An officer was reprimanded for exclaiming 'Bugger it' while discarding a report he was writing – a gay colleague overheard him and made a complaint. Hampshire PC Angela Smith was appointed a liaison officer to Fabuliss, which supports transvestites, as well as its splinter group Fabwags, for transvestites' wives and girlfriends[3726].

Jargon

All institutions and professions develop their own jargon as a kind of protective cloak, even armour, against the laity (doctors, lawyers, the clergy, etc. all try to confuse the ordinary person).

The new (2013) Police Scotland code of ethics contains 25 pledges which are mandatory for all staff. Critics say it is full of 'gobbledegook', with no mention of prevention, detection or solving crime. Criminals must be treated in a 'humane and dignified manner'[3727].

A new piece of meaningless PC police jargon (ploddledygook) is 'delivering citizen focused policing'[3728]. Waves of political correctness have washed over the police force in recent years, as they have every other institution of the state, replacing previous simplistic forms of management jargon with new much more impenetrable and verbose descriptive 'speak'. Thus Norfolk Police renamed their Control Room 'Citizen Focus Demand', while Suffolk Police now have a Director of Knowledge Architecture and a Head of Citizen Focus. Other superfluous 'nonsense' designations are Director of Criminal Justice Charge and Head of Protective Services. A Humberside Police press release says burglaries are caused by 'insecurities'[3729].

The codes of practice laid down in the Police and Criminal Evidence Act (1984) are the origin of most police red tape paperwork[3730].

The CIC, Sir Denis O'Connor, has criticised 'telephone directory' police manuals (often with no summaries), and says a moratorium on publishing new guidance should be made permanent. Thus ACPO guidance on the use of limb restraints runs to 16 pages. The tidal wave of guidelines means expensive specialists are employed to help meet them, taking resources from the front line. O'Connor recommends the target-related-doctrine must be replaced with erstwhile professional discretion: the 1829 police handbook contained 52 pages, compared with the current 6,497[3731] (this huge volume increase affects every handbook one can think of, from the Inland Revenue's manual to the US-derived psychiatric classification DSM handbook).

In relation to 'Problem Oriented Partnerships' awards, Avon and Somerset Police have given this advice to officers: 'Following the problem solving mythology as a supportive framework to work the problem through: Understand where the drivers and demand originated; Articulate your aim as SMART and understood the impact you intended; Ensure research and analysis was coherent and the findings informed your direction (responses)'[3732].

Greater Manchester Police blew £100,000 on Storytime sessions (labelled Operation Jackanory by detectives forced to participate) for 200 top officers – bonding events supposed to improve performance by getting them to recount stories about their jobs. The stories (only 'positive' ones) were then pasted on a storyboard to form a 'business strategy'. Everyone made things up, as they couldn't talk about things like rape or murder. Consultants Storytellers Ltd were hired by Chief Constable Peter Fahy to enlighten him (give him a 'vision') of the force's future through sessions at the Manchester Piccadilly hotel[3733].

The Met's ban on its officers describing louts as 'yobs' (because it is 'alienating') was supported by Sir Ian Blair. Greater Manchester Police have stopped calling their Rochdale sub-divisions 'townships' because of the apartheid connotation: the same force will admonish you if you describe someone as 'fat' (they are 'of heavy build' instead). Cornwall Police told a witness not to say 'gypsy skirt'. Officers are being sent on language training courses (to avoid, e.g., 'accident blackspot' and 'manhole cover')[3734]. PC police chiefs have banned 'nitty-gritty', so the Home Office's John Denham wasn't conforming when he used the phrase in a speech. 'Egg and spoon' rhymes with 'coon', so being 'a good egg' is suspect. Met PC David Nixon said male officers were regularly cautioned for using the term 'WPC' instead of just PC. 'Pikey' is out, and one officer with a Spanish background found 'Spanish practices' offensive[3735].

In 2000 Greater Manchester Police issued a politically correct list of phrases which were taboo, e.g. 'deaf and dumb' had to become 'deaf without speech', 'wheelchair bound' must become 'wheelchair users', 'foreman' must become 'supervisor'[3736].

The Met's most senior female officer Lynne Owens has helped design a 'friendly' approach to policing violent demos, e.g. explanatory glossy brochures are now to be handed out so that protesters can understand why helmeted police shout and use 'kettling'[3737].

Tayside Police have replaced the phrase 'manning the phones' with 'staffing the phones', to comply with their new diversity awareness guide. But the public may prefer their police to be crook-catchers rather than PC – a worthy subject for one of the many police surveys of public opinion[3738].

An ACPO paper on policing being submitted to civil servants contained this sentence: 'The promise of reform which the Green Paper heralds holds much for the public and Service alike; local policing, customised to local need, with authentic answerability, strengthened accountabilities at force level through reforms to police authorities and HMIC, performance management ... so as to better equip our service to meet the amorphous challenges of managing cross force harms, risks and opportunities'[3739].

Warwickshire Police have banned the use of phrases like 'Evenin' All' (because 'evening' has different meanings in different cultures), 'businessmen', 'housewife' and 'child' (children are, instead, 'young persons'). 'Boy' and 'girl' may also give offence, so use 'young people'. The instructions form part of nationwide guidelines for police and fire services as to what language staff should use, e.g. don't say 'frequented', as this has a criminal connotation – say 'often' instead[3740].

Met Police must not say 'straight', rather 'heterosexual'[3741].

Disablism

Met deputy assistant commissioner Steve Roberts has admitted his force is recruiting unsuitable officers (e.g. dyslexics, physically disabled, those with incompatible religious beliefs) in its attempt to be PC. Thus Muslim PC Alexander Omar Basha was excused guard duty at the Israeli embassy on 'moral grounds', while a female Muslim recruit refused to shake the hand of Sir Ian Blair; a Seventh Day Adventist and an orthodox Jew wanted their Sabbaths off[3742].

ACPOS consulted 75 groups to produce a 140-page 'diversity handbook', which has admonitions like 'Don't lean on a disabled person's wheelchair', don't use the phrase 'blind as a bat', and don't ask a disfigured person what happened to them. The booklet cost nearly £5,000.

Health & Safety

Before a police officer tries to save a life he must consider 238 possible hazards ... to stop him suing his own bosses, he is trained to see hypothetical risks to himself as far more important than the actual safety of the public he is supposed to be serving[3743]. The RA1 (emergency services risk-assessment form) means officers must check the list of hazards before any operation that is spontaneous but requires the intervention of a senior officer. Then RA2 ('risk activities'), RA3 (levels of risk) and RA4 (recommendations) are completed by the senior officer. Every department in the force now has a risk assessment adviser, and there is a whole department just processing RA1s. In 2003 Commissioner Sir John Stevens and his predecessor Lord Condon were prosecuted for breaching health and safety rules (officers in pursuit fell through roofs), but they were acquitted[3744].

Senior detectives from SOCA (Serious Organised Crime Agency) have been sent on 'treasure hunts' round London landmarks, to enhance their investigative skills. One 'team-bonding' exercise involved detectives approaching uniformed officers to find the answers to trivia questions posed by their bosses (e.g. Jane Attwood, SOCA's deputy director for prevention and alerts, owns a gastro pub which holds popular quiz nights)[3745].

One car criminal's 15 rooftop protests cost £500,000, because police had to stand by and ensure he didn't fall off[3746].

In one force electric kettles are banned for health and safety reasons, while their large Arnold batons have been withdrawn by their diversity department because they made ethnic minority teenagers feel uncomfortable. PCSOs aren't allowed to work after dark[3747].

An Essex school is having to pay almost £2,000 annually for police officers to help children cross the road, because it has been decided PCSOs (who do it without charge) don't have the necessary training[3748].

Hundreds of police from four forces were sent on a three-day training exercise in 2010 to prepare for a massive earthquake, costing almost £1m[3749].

Health and safety guidelines stopped PC Robert Bolt saving a drowning man by entering the water right away, because he had to first fetch a canoe, as his training decreed[3750]. Likewise PC Tony Jones was ordered not to assist a man in a lake who seemed to have drowned[3751]. The public may be bemused by police being under the control of firemen when there isn't a fire. Two young men returning from a night out jumped into a freezing canal (losing their wallets, cameras and phones) to save a drowning man (he lived), against the advice they had received when they dialled 999 (i.e. 'Don't enter the water')[3752].

ACPO produced a 93-page pamphlet on bicycle safety, so that, e.g., Northamptonshire Police ruled officers must complete 10 hours training before being allowed on a machine. It advises wearing padded shorts, avoiding kerbs at corners, and how to balance while braking[3753]. New regional police guides to riding a bike have replaced the discredited ACPO guidelines (scrapped in 2009). Lothian and Borders says hand signals should be maintained for three seconds, using the technique from the film Gregory's Girl – saying 'one elephant, two elephants, three elephants'. The West Midlands force tells one how to cycle downhill – adopt a neutral pedal position – and has a seven-point guide on 'Getting off the cycle', which includes using brakes to stop the machine, encourages the use of lip balm and sun cream and warns that 'dogs don't like cyclists and may even pursue you'. They also advise eye protectors as essential defence against swarms of insects. Essex officers must have been on an advanced course before they are allowed to pursue suspects. Even then they have to perform a 'dynamic risk assessment', including assessing the weather and checking whether the suspects' human rights might be breached (e.g. endangering their safety), as well as taking account of nine other factors – permission to ride without a helmet can only be given when a supervisor has carried out a risk assessment (Gwent insists even undercover officers wear a helmet: they must also not go 'off road', and one element of its 11 point 'operating procedure' is dismounting at least hourly and walking about for at least five minutes). West Midlands' guide shows how one should wear 'defined cycle underwear with a padded crotch'[3754]. Officers on bicycle patrol are also being handed hundreds of pages of advice about what they should eat (flapjacks and Jaffa Cake are recommended) and wear, how to revive their flagging energy levels, how to deal with chapped lips and sore behinds, airborne insects, etc. The 21-page Met booklet is used by other forces[3755].

To combat climate change Cambridgeshire Police chose to replace its panda fleet with an electric car which was not fast enough to chase villains, and whose battery would go flat in half an hour (recharge took six hours)[3756].

During the 7/7 London bombings, victims died in agony because the emergency services were ordered to stay out of the tunnel in case there was a second device (there wasn't). Police officers are now trained to view hypothetical risks to themselves as trumping the actual safety of the public they are supposed to serve[3757].

The Met have set up a team of officers to visit firms whose employees have committed mobile phone offences and demand to know their 'risk management strategy'. If the firm doesn't give the right answers it can be charged under health and safety regulations.

A Gloucestershire PCSO was removed from her rural beat because her superiors decided the narrow country lanes didn't conform to health and safety legislation. Another PCSO can't use the bus to get to work, because of health and safety guidelines[3758].

Devon and Cornwall Police have offered free nicotine gum and patches to incarcerated suspects banned from smoking on all force property. The same force told an amateur drama group staging a pirate pantomime that their fake arms (e.g. plastic cutlasses and a toy spear) had to be kept in a secure case in a locked room with restricted access. The actors had to notify the fire brigade and observe adequate security arrangements. A named person had to accompany the plastic arsenal when it was being moved[3759].

A 64-year-old veteran swimmer refused a pool attendant's order not to dive in the pool, as he'd done for 20 years, because of new health and safety regulations. Two police officers appeared at the poolside and ordered him to leave the complex. He did so but was later arrested at home. The retired civil servant, never in trouble before, was found guilty of a public order offence.

Under-18s in East London were banned in 2009 from buying eggs and flour in the run-up to Hallowe'en, with shopkeepers asking for ID from egg-purchasers and refusing to sell to the under-aged. Police in Somerset, Norwich and Warrington have encouraged similar bans. Police were advising residents not to open their doors and handing out 'no trick or treat' posters, with various go-away messages. Some forces patrol schools with the message that Hallowe'en tricks may lead to jail or at least a criminal record. 'The police prefer blanket bans to hands-on law enforcement'. Great Yarmouth Police took 56 teenagers to Alton Towers to stop them 'trick or treating' their neighbours[3760].

Under new guidelines from the HSE (they became subject to its rulings in 1998) police 'may choose not to put themselves at unreasonable risk'. Health and safety guidelines have been accepted by ACPO and the Police Federation[3761].

Human Rights

A 17-year-old in Southampton was allowed by police to clamber around a roof for six hours throwing missiles at people and cars; they even supplied him with burger and chips. Eventually his mother persuaded him to come down[3762]. When a suspected thief was trapped on a Gloucester roof the police acceded to his demand for a bucket of KFC and a bottle of Pepsi, instead of forcing him down. They admitted later they had misinterpreted the terms of the Human Rights Act[3763].

Lothian and Borders Police sent letters to serial burglars in Edinburgh pleading with them to stop (these super-housebreakers are responsible for about half of all break-ins in the city)[3764]. They have also ordered all their officers to cover up tattoos (even though not offensive) while on duty, but the Scottish Police Federation say the bans could be challenged under Human Rights legislation[3765].

Hampshire Police found a £20,000 stolen caravan but told the owners they couldn't have it back because it was occupied by a gypsy family – evicting them would breach their human rights. Officers asserted they had 'no lawful powers' to retrieve the vehicle: the owners would have to take civil proceedings[3766].

Greater Manchester Police no longer make suspects wear 'oppressive' boiler suits while testing their clothing – they are now driven home to change instead[3767].

Devon and Cornwall Police have launched an Antisocial Behaviour Diversion Scheme as a new 'punishment' for 'minor' offenders: the two-and-a-half hour sessions replace fines or community penalties. Offenders will watch DVDs and discuss their crimes[3768].

North Yorkshire Police let off with a caution a 6ft 2in intruder who attacked and terrorised at 3am a farmer and his partner: eight police vehicles had arrived at the scene but there was no police arrest (the farmer had made a citizen's arrest). The police said there could be no burglary charge as there was no evidence of intent. This 'soft policing' was justified by the fact it was the man's first offence, he was in the Army, and he was too drunk to remember what he did. The victims said he <u>wasn't</u> intoxicated[3769].

2008 ACPO dog handling guidelines suggested police should take animal-fearful criminals' feelings into account before unleashing dogs on them, and reminding them that some criminals may be allergic to dog hair. ACPO has advised in its dog training manual, which has a detailed HR (Human Rights) police statement, that police animals should be muzzled. Police dogs in <u>Richard Brunstrom</u>'s North Wales Force were taught to head-butt suspects instead of biting them[3770].

Cambridgeshire Chief Constable <u>Julie Spence</u> demanded that her officers be nice and mannerly with unruly yobs, accusing police of being 'classist' because they treat the classes differently[3771].

Suffolk Police warned householders in 2007 that three prolific burglars were about to be set free, but refused to name them or release their ages or photos, to preserve the villains' human rights[3772]. Police banned a shop owner's photo of a jewel thief, which was to warn other traders, because it would breach the thief's human rights. In fact the HR (Human Rights) Act applies only to public bodies, not individuals[3773].

In 2004 the Met changed the phrase 'gang rape' to 'group rape' to avoid stigmatising the rapists[3774].

Details of a crime is recorded by officers in the small green 56-page EAB notebook (Evidence in Action) which starts with the advice: 'Plan For Human Rights'. 17 police officials process 131 pieces of paper to deal with one small offence[3775].

A Met card to be kept behind the warrant badge advises that police are now expected to endure verbal abuse, and that suspects shouldn't be handcuffed 'just' because they might be dangerous[3776].

A police officer who arrested a masked teenager suspected of threatening to stab a headmaster faced disciplinary action when the suspect complained he had banged his head during the struggle.

A crime buster who made a video of crack dealers outside his home has been banned from filming by police and warned he is breaching their civil liberties.

The mother and stepfather of a 13-year-old girl were threatened with court action about her truancy, but when they try to get her out of bed she threatens her mother with the police. When she was marched back home by her parents at midnight because she was out gallivanting, she called the police, who said she was within her rights to object[3777].

Police have been told to consider the feelings of criminals' families before naming and shaming them. The privacy of offenders trumps public protection[3778].

Although a burglary victim could identify a suspected burglar from a large port-wine stain on his face, the police discounted this, covering it up in an identity parade, in case it infringed his human rights. His description was broadened so that the statutory eleven comparison individuals could be provided[3779].

In 2009 Devon and Cornwall Constabulary introduced a 'customer satisfaction' survey, using a hotel-style questionnaire, for prisoners, e.g. they were asked how 'safe' they felt on the custody suite and how 'fairly' they were treated[3780].

A rape victim's boyfriend who posted CCTV images of the suspect on Facebook was warned by Manchester Police to shut the site down in case it 'victimised' the culprit, despite their taking seriously a name suggested by a contributor. The boyfriend was furious that the attacker's rights were to be prioritised[3781].

Red Tape

Red tape (e.g. 'stop and account' forms) consumes about 50% of police time, according to former Suffolk chief constable Alastair McWhirter Officers must record the ethnic background of anyone they speak to while on the beat[3782].

Every officer in England and Wales has been issued with a 2,600 page rule book. In one burglary probe 30 officers were needed to take the case to court[3783].

Police manuals give detailed instructions as to how to perform the simplest tasks, e.g. use of handcuffs and CS spray, or how to deal with 'high risk' cricket matches. Police should take drunks home to stop them coming to harm. In 2009 police quangos added more than 2,615 extra pages of guidance to existing manuals (the 93-page guide to bike riding was withdrawn after a public outcry)[3784].

The police are one of five authorities which separately inspect anyone who needs an alcohol licence, e.g. to serve a few glasses of wine on a yacht charter. The licence requires a £190 application fee, an £180 annual fee, a one-day course, as well as the submission of 10 copies of a 40-page form[3785].

It takes over 1,000 procedures and 70 CPS and police forms before a domestic burglary can be prosecuted[3786].

One force uses a 28-page booklet to record a missing person – another has a 16-page booklet. Road accident reports range from a 44-page booklet to an eight-page A4 pack. Punishing a child involved in a school playground scuffle carries as much weight as arresting a killer or rapist. A Cheshire man was cautioned for being in possession of an egg with intent to throw. 19.3% of an officer's time is spent on paperwork[3787].

If a policeman wants to observe a suspect through a window a 16-page form seeking permission must be filled in first, while one document signed by a senior officer is enough to authorise the shooting of someone. Also, arrested suspects' details must be entered in between four and eight databases. Investigation of a crime only starts when it has been assessed by four different officers. Nine officers will be supervising a student officer investigating a burglary. In one force area the arresting officer in a shoplifting case must transfer the case to a specialised team. With major crime investigations forces must prove they are up to standard by answering 1,099 questions. Because internal communications are sent to every officer, officers have to waste time (up to 45 minutes daily) wading through the irrelevant e-mails. Performance and target culture still reigns supreme at local force level[3788].

A 2008 Policing Green Paper announced a new 'bureaucracy champion' who would make a 'bonfire of forms' by creating a new layer of officialdom[3789]!

Lancashire PC Tony Cobban refused to sit on a mountain bike for a PR photo because his force had banned officers from riding without the correct licence: the photo was to commemorate a gift of several bikes to the force by Halfords[3790].

Other

Cambridgeshire's Chief Constable Julie Spence says speeding is 'middle-class antisocial behaviour, probably among the worst kind of antisocial behaviour ...'[3791].

Kent Police has introduced a new neighbourhood initiative: two villages have been invited to bimonthly meetings with local officers online[3792].

Inspector Mark Scoular says he was horrified at the state of Met policing when he returned after a break of five years: most new officers 'just do not know the job' because PC themes such as diversity awareness had replaced practical training[3793].

In 1936 Portsmouth's Chief Constable, a Mr. Davies, banned fruit machines and other mechanical gambling aids from pubs and clubs[3794]. In the same year Portsmouth pub landlords voted to ignore a police warning forbidding games (such as darts) on Sunday[3795].

Peter Fahy, Chief Constable of Greater Manchester, banned designer stubble in his force. It is just as well he is allowing beards and moustaches, as these have been de rigeur for officers in the Victorian and Edwardian eras respectively. Sir Robert Peacock – the longest serving head of Manchester City Police (1898-1926) – had a pointy moustache[3796].

Notts Police Chief Constable Julia Hodson says officers must re-learn discretion instead of adhering to 'rigid' guidelines[3797].

The expansion of 'hate' legislation by Labour encouraged authoritarian-minded police to look not at people's actions but at their words, with 'thought criminals' arrested and even convicted.

Dr. John Coxhead, a Derbyshire sergeant and liaison officer with gypsies for a decade, says preoccupation with diversity training often replaces work application and is often a waste of resources. Tackling discrimination does not depend on what people learn in a classroom once a year[3798].

Manchester officers are to be trained to say 'no' politely. The politeness drive will encourage nodding, introducing oneself by name and appropriate body language. Cops will be urged to say to crime victims 'I understand' and 'I can help you'. Shouldn't politeness come naturally[3799]?

The police are so neurotic about political correctness, e.g. Islamophobia, that they have transmuted into political gauleiters. In 2004 Channel 4 postponed their documentary 'Edge of the City' (about Bradford Asians targeting white girls for prostitution and drug abuse) because of pressure from Colin Gramphorn, West Yorkshire's Chief Constable[3800].

A householder plagued by gangs was told by a PC officer that the gang outside his home was there for 'tribal reasons – if they went elsewhere, they might get beaten up by a bigger and more dangerous gang'. He was also told on another occasion the police were trying to find jobs for problem youths, and it was also suggested he should have a formal meeting with the thugs on neutral territory, as though their nuisance – creating rights were equivalent to residents'[3801].

When a villager from Yorkshire complained to police his village was a no-go zone run by 'hoodie scum' (after his girlfriend's car was blockaded and she was attacked with traffic cones), Superintendent Keith Lumby told him: 'You can't go branding youths 'hoodie scum' – that doesn't give ... the right impression'[3802].

The softly-softly approach by the police to travellers is evidenced by ACPO's statements that opposition to illegal gypsy camps is often 'unfounded' and based on 'ignorance and prejudice'. Instead of being evicted, the gypsies should be asked if they need welfare help, and be given a 'conduct code'. In one force there was a £2,000 police party for travellers at Woodcote House (headquarters of Warwickshire police), with a graffiti board, bouncy castle, face-painting and cricket lessons[3803].

Advertising Christmas specials with jokes is now against the law, a South Wales shopkeeper found when he continued his decade-long practice of lacing his ads with jokes from the internet. Three police turned up at his shop to warn him the flyers were potentially inflammatory or offensive, and must be withdrawn from circulation[3804].

Health and safety rules protect individual officers rather than the public. Thus Kent Police cited health and safety for failing to break up an illegal rave. Police at the 2004 killings at Highmoor Cross near Henley were criticised for trying 'to eliminate risk rather than manage it'[3805].

With crime and disorder rampant the police now believe they should as a priority harass people because of the lawful views they hold. The 'victim culture' police agenda assumes the victim's absolute innocence[3806].

When two Merseyside policemen (including a DCI) appeared in court (to testify against two Christian hoteliers accused of insulting a Muslim guest), they were backed by a six-strong team from the force's specialist hate crime unit, but the case was thrown out. The police had used wording like 'bigotry' and 'intolerance' to justify the prosecution. Does this sort of case bring the police into disrepute[3807]?

Manchester officers were sent on special courses to improve their manners. They were to be taught not to swear, speak sarcastically or 'act overbearingly' and how to stand at a door (the wrong stance could be considered 'rude')[3808].

South Wales Police have ordered an Asian shopkeeper to stop adding jokes to his adverts, or else face arrest for a public order offence[3809].

A Strathclyde Police chaplain (a retired Church of Scotland minister) claims he was forced out of his unpaid job because he opposed gay marriage, being told he had contravened the force's 'equality and diversity' policy.

CHAPTER XXI

THE PERVERSE POLICEMAN

CONTENTS

CHAPTER XXI

THE PERVERSE POLICEMAN

Targeting the Law-abiding

The target culture means the theft of a milk bottle is as important as murder[3810]. 'Too often, police and prosecutors pursue victims rather than culprits, yet they refuse to admit that their priorities are woefully wrong'[3811].

The police are alienating their natural supporters by pursuing otherwise law-abiding citizens with fines, incarceration, suspended sentences or community service for trivial offences. The Police Federation has intimated pressure to meet the 'Offenders Brought to Justice' target has meant the criminalisation of Middle England. Police are motivated to obtain a detection, even when it isn't in the public interest[3812].

The perverse policeman targets the law-abiding instead of the law-breaker, incredibly sometimes one of their own[1*]. This is ironic and counterintuitive: one naturally assumes the police service will channel their scarce resources to combat the truly criminal. Journalist Andrew Brown quotes (in 'Watching the Detectives', 1985) one officer criticising the Criminal Justice Bill: 'It's given us all sorts of niggling powers: just enough to annoy the public. We can arrest someone for littering now, [but] it's taken away almost all the powers we need to catch criminals.' How often do the police go off on a tangent? Is it possible that most of their time and energy is taken up with trivia, and that the examples in this chapter are only the tip of the iceberg?

A grandmother against whom a hate campaign was waged by teenagers, causing her to make a citizen's arrest, led to her being charged by police instead, following a nonsense counter-allegation by one of the youths. She was found not guilty in eight minutes, her lawyer criticising the Crown for bringing the case[3813].

Three neighbours who were driving a young vandal to the police station – he had thrown a brick through a window – were intercepted and arrested for kidnap by the very police they had summoned. They were cleared after nine months of court battles[3814].

A retired military police officer erected an electrified wire around the inside of his garden fence in Cornwall because he was being plagued by vandals, but a policeman soon visited his house and warned him the yobs could sue him for negligence if they hurt themselves while trespassing[3815].

In Slough uniformed officers confiscated sparklers from young children even though they were being supervised, while in Bromley someone reported a neighbour for letting off

---

* Thus in March 2013 Frank Armstrong, a decorated and distinguished former Assistant Commissioner of the City of London Police, was arrested for passing information to the Press (no money was paid). He organised personal protection for Tony Blair when he was PM. PC Roderick Lund was locked up by three of his own force after being handcuffed for refusing to move his car following a complaint by his neighbour, retired police superintendent Anthony Green, that he couldn't access his driveway. PC Lund was awarded £5,000 in an out-of-court settlement after lodging in court his case for unlawful arrest, false imprisonment and using unreasonable force. Ref: Disley, J. 'Parking row PC wins £5K pay-out'. Daily Express. 28.10.10, p4.

fireworks after 11.00pm. The accused says it was well before this, yet he was visited a few days later by a sergeant and constable. At the police station he was arrested, and after being photographed, fingerprinted and his DNA taken, he was locked up and interviewed under caution. But he was never shown any hard evidence against him. He chose to go to court rather than a fixed penalty. The government has set up a hotline for neighbours to report each other for burning the 'wrong' kind of material on Bonfire Night[3816].

Kent Police handcuffed and charged an 85-year-old woman who allegedly made abusive comments close to a mosque, and two young Bristol men were arrested, accused of hate crime on social media, yet the UK's most high profile hate preacher, Anjem Choudary, is allowed to spew out his incendiary comments, like the white soldier murdered in London should 'burn in hell'[3817].

A worried father was arrested by Fife Police in a dawn raid after he told neighbours a paedophile was living nearby, and charged with breach of the peace. The police had refused to alert people in the area, and families are disgusted at the way Fife Police handled the situation. One father said: 'These people aren't fit to wear a police uniform. We should have been alerted immediately'. A year earlier Fife Police were accused of failing to act against a paedophile childminder (who committed suicide), despite official complaints over several years[3818].

Thanks to a 19-year-old's devotion to his town's war memorial, the British Legion collected a prize for Norfolk's most improved memorial, and he won a Young People's Role Model of the Year award. He was congratulated by the Queen, but when he improved the irrigation to the flora around the monument he was accused of failing to obtain permission and causing criminal damage. The police initially referred the case to the CPS, but dropped it when it was reported in the press[3819]. A gardener was charged by Easter Ross Police with vandalism after restoring a local eyesore: a neighbour had complained[3820].

When a father intervened in a fight between children by putting one of the yobs in his car, driving him to the main group and making them all apologise to each other, then returning him to his friends, the adult was charged with kidnap after being arrested by up to 10 officers in three cars. After a £20,000 series of court cases (two magistrates and three Crown Courts) the Crown accepted a reduced plea of common assault. The judge criticised the action of the police and CPS: 'To put a handle of kidnap on this is ridiculous'[3821].

A Renfrewshire father and his young son were feeding birds at a shopping centre in Erskine, when Strathclyde Police turned up to warn him he faced court action for littering (even though the birds had eaten all the bread)[3822].

A beggar sitting outside a bank with an orange toy gun was handcuffed and led to a police van by three police officers, including Constable Greg McKenzie, who had arrived in an unmarked car. A weapons expert confirmed the gun was a child's toy: the arrestee had found it on waste ground[3823].

Journalist Petronella Wyatt received a visit from a policeman who threatened 'further action' if her 6"-tall dog kept barking[3824].

When a Birmingham pensioner trying to stop travellers trespassing in a conservation area was turned away by West Midlands police, the latter, he says, refused to give him their inspector's name and the gypsies soon moved into the historic site. The travellers were threatening to return and 'sort him out', but he says the police did not act on this[3825].

A restaurant manager who stopped yobs after they broke into his premises called Sussex Police, who then arrested him because the culprits had accused him of assault (he only pushed a couple of them). The police say he should have observed from a safe distance[3826].

A mother was arrested for refusing to return a cricket ball to neighbours' children after it had damaged her car. She was photographed, had her DNA and prints taken, and the police seized the £3.99 ball as evidence[3827].

A former soldier confronted a gang with a knife after being tormented by them for five years. The police threatened the victim with prison, and it emerged that the ringleader had been treated by them to a dream meeting with his football heroes[3828].

When a passer-by helped a crying five-year-old down from a tree at his school (whose health and safety policy banned teachers from rescuing him even after an hour), the school reported her to the police and she was given a verbal warning by a Wiltshire PCSO for 'antisocial behaviour'[3829].

A couple have been fined £80 by Hampshire Police for 'criminal damage' after painting their garden fence: a neighbour complained that paint flecks had splashed on her side[3830].

Mary Kerswell discovered her medical records contained inaccuracies about her. She arranged to pick up a copy and paid the requisite fee. When she tried to collect them, receptionists refused to hand them over, so she refused to leave without them. The police were called and handcuffed her, but have apologised[3831].

When a British family returned from holiday to find squatters had taken over their North London home, the police wouldn't help at first, even though the back and front doors had been forced and the owners could prove it was their house. The police did help remove the squatters when a tabloid intervened[3832]. Police adopted a neutral stance in the face of organised squatter gangs who forged tenancy contracts[3833]. Now squatting is fortunately illegal in England.

Children at village hall discos in Lincolnshire are being breathalysed by Humberside police to try to cut antisocial behaviour[3834].

A 10-year-old was told by Kent Police she could be arrested for playing hopscotch, which constituted criminal damage. Her father said the incident had impaired her confidence to play outside. Government-funded Play England, which promotes outdoor play, says they've received a wave of complaints about over-the-top police behaviour[3835].

A retired couple who stood up to an abusive 'neighbour from hell' spent a day in police cells and were advised to plead guilty to disorderly behaviour (repeated complaints to police had allegedly come to nothing). Their community garden was being fouled by the neighbour's three dogs[3836].

Crimebuster Darren Gibbett, who videoed crack dealers outside his North London estate home, was banned by police from filming in case he breached their civil liberties. A subject he filmed assaulted him, but the police said the person had every right to retrieve the film: if Gibbett persisted filming he would be liable to arrest and prosecution.

A youth smashed the window of a shop in Bridlington, and threatened to firebomb it. The owner and his son were charged with kidnap for locking the 12-year-old thug in his car, and he lost his business. After a six-month ordeal the judge ordered the jury to clear them. They had taken the boy home initially because Bridlington Police Station was usually unmanned. There have been a series of fiascos where the public who tried to stop crime have been arrested.

Gloucestershire police arrested a boy whose football bounced off a parked car when it was blown by a gust of wind. The 15-year-old was kept in cells for an hour before being released on bail, and his father expressed outrage at the 'heavy-handed' treatment. It took three Greater Manchester Police officers to warn two young (11 and 12) brothers that their harmless kickabout was illegal, and could attract ASBOs under the Highways Act 1980[3837]. Though Blackpool has problems with violence (more than twice the national average), binge drinking (over 2,000 hospital admissions annually) and sex attacks, police launched a campaign (2006) in the South Shore area against children playing football in the street. Stirlingshire Police threatened brothers aged five and nine with ASBOs for playing football outside their home[3838]. When a police constable dialled 999 to complain about the two-year-old next door kicking a ball against his fence, three of his uniformed West Yorkshire colleagues turned up to question the toddler's parents for 15 minutes. A housewife was arrested, fingerprinted and DNA-sampled for allegedly stealing her neighbour's football (it was never found, the police even going through her drawers). When a schoolboy accidentally kicked his ball through a pane in a neighbour's greenhouse, he was tracked down by two officers, a patrol car and the Thames Valley Police helicopter with a thermal imaging facility. The police recorded the incident 'for future reference' – this would come up later in an enhanced CRB check, possibly affecting employability. The police also said the 15-year-old could face an ASBO if his 'behaviour does not improve'[3839].

Hampshire Detective Superintendent John Fox's career was ruined when, while off-duty, he tried to stop two juveniles behaving antisocially: they accused him of assault. Though the Crown Court threw out the charge the damage was done.

A 66-year-old grandmother spent a night in a Bournemouth police cell after standing up to three abusive teenagers who invaded her garden armed with staves. She was alleged to have assaulted them while drunk (she denies this). Likewise a 63-year-old and his disabled wife were tormented in their home by a gang of snowball-wielding youths: his wife had her glasses broken. The police wouldn't help, so he clouted one who had sworn at him. He was arrested.

Three 12-year-old children were arrested for playing in a tree – then photographed, interviewed and locked up. Their **reprimand** (the juvenile equivalent of a **caution**) remains on file for five years. The two girls and a boy had never been in trouble before.

A 15-year-old Burnley boy was arrested and thrown in a police cell for throwing a snowball at a car. He was prosecuted under a little-used 19th Century law in 2006, and fined £100.

A Christian carer for the elderly who painted a public message of forgiveness on the boarded-up house of a difficult family she helped get evicted, was issued by police with an

£80 notice for vandalism (<u>she</u> had had her home and car vandalised and defaced). The community was said to be furious with Dorset Police for punishing innocent people: the police confirmed no youths responsible for the criminal damage to her property were arrested. Two Avon and Somerset policemen, acting on a tip-off, lined up six young children in their quiet Burnham-on-sea cul-de-sac (the main culprit was a five-year-old who had been given coloured chalks by his mother). Though the children were hopscotch marking the police told them off for drawing 'graffiti'. Their parents were told not to let their children play in the street, and one mother was advised one of the children was not dressed warmly enough[3840]. A 10-year-old girl guide was fingerprinted, threatened with an ASBO and fined £40 by Lancashire Police for marking a wall with crayon[3841]. Six Gloucestershire officers were sent in a riot van to deal with a 15-year-old who wrote on a wall with a Twix chocolate bar. The charge of criminal damage was dropped only on the day of the trial[3842].

A 14-year-old Cambridgeshire girl was arrested, put in a cell, DNA tested and appeared in court five times. She had agreed to accept a police reprimand for jokingly 'pinging' a fellow pupil's bra, but the family were then informed by a <u>PC Sturgeon</u> that she wouldn't simply have to admit to common assault, but accept her action was 'of a sexual nature'. The girl's faith in the police is shattered. When the cars of her father and neighbours were vandalised some time before, the police 'didn't even bother to visit'.

After a two-mile chase a hairdresser cornered one of three vandals who smashed her front window, but she was horrified when the Lincolnshire Police let him go. The police promised to keep her informed, but eventually her husband had to go to the police station to be told the outcome.

Troubled by yobs repeatedly trashing their farm with no help from the Lakeland police, a couple played a practical joke on two suspicious youths (the man pretending to chase his fiancée with an axe). The couple received a caution, which meant the girl couldn't resume her job at Barclays[3843].

A few days before a Home Office appeal for a return of active citizenship, Lord Phillips of Sudbury was given a ticking off by police for apprehending a cyclist riding a bicycle on the pavement[3844].

A Renfrewshire pensioner ended up in a police cell for trying to stop a vandal smashing up his car; he was charged with assault by the police[3845].

Terminal cancer patient farmer Tracy St. Clair Pearce dialled 999 after travellers (who were trespassing on her land) threatened to kill her – she claims she was challenged by men wielding a knife and chainsaw, bombarding her with missiles and exposing themselves. It took Essex Police 35 minutes to arrive: they gave her a three-hour interrogation. Two days later armed police arrived at night to remove two shotguns, and her licence was confiscated thereafter. No action was taken against the gypsies[3846].

When a councillor and former mayor, now a 62-year-old postman, ticked off a 13-year-old who had walked all over his prized flower bed (his wife works in a garden centre), grabbing him by the collar, the boy apologised and went off to school. His friends, however, told their headmaster, who complained to the police. <u>Six weeks later</u> the police took a statement from the councillor and he had to appear in court, where he was cleared, the magistrate questioning why the case had ever reached court[3847].

CAVEAT CIVIS

A Wiltshire policeman ordered a Swindon eight-year-old to destroy his toy gun (or he would be arrested), because it was an 'imitation firearm', and his sister to stop riding her toy car on the pavement. The boy was afraid the police would take him away. When two relatives remonstrated they were told to shut up[3848].

A judge criticised Greater Manchester Police for hauling into court (without CPS approval) a 12-year-old boy who threw a cocktail sausage at a neighbour who had been verbally aggressive to him. The terrified boy was locked in a cell. The case was dropped after costing the taxpayer thousands of pounds[3849]. Two Essex constables ordered a 13-year-old boy out of bed around midnight because he'd thrown an apple at another boy in school, five days before. The 'culprit' was made to sign a 'neighbourhood resolution form'[3850].

Two 21-year-old girls who flashed their breasts at a CCTV camera on the beach at West Worthing (no one else was around) were arrested for outraging public decency. The police dropped the charge before the case went to court[3851].

A 16-year-old was dragged through Swindon Youth Court at a cost of £5,000 for causing a penny's worth of criminal damage to a plastic bag – he was given six hours community service – yet a 14-year-old in Hampshire Constabulary's patch who shot a girl in the eye with an air rifle escaped being punished because he was 'too young' to know what he was doing[3852].

A CPSO's garden was regularly vandalised by drunken youths, but when he forcibly restrained one till the police arrived he ended up in court charged with assault (the judge threw it out). The endless police mantra 'don't take the law into your own hands' assumes they are always at hand. They are notoriously often not available quickly enough, and, just as worryingly, they may not be anxious to sort out any problems[3853].

As a 40-year-old walked past a Channel 4 presenter as she reported live from Oxford, he pinched her bottom. Thames Valley Police tracked him down and gave him a caution for breaching public order[3854].

Strathclyde Police impounded spare ribs for forensic examination after a thug dropped them from a Glasgow high-rise onto a police car, whereas the same force ignored appeals for a full inquiry into lethal items thrown from the same tower block[3855].

Northumbria Police handcuffed and arrested a teenager for barking at two Labradors on the ground: his behaviour may have caused 'alarm, harassment or distress'. He was fined by magistrates, but the case, which may have cost the taxpayer £8,000, was thrown out on appeal[3856].

Staffordshire WPC Gibbs stopped her panda car to upbraid three boys riding a go-kart for not having a tax disc or insurance. Days later their parents received a police letter accusing their sons of antisocial behaviour. The same force's Sergeant Peter Davies threatened to prosecute villagers for giving away bottles of sherry on tombola stalls without a licence[3857].

When an ex-paratrooper and college lecturer saw his young daughter being threatened by a gang of hooligans, he grabbed hold of one and tried to make a citizen's arrest. Instead of pursuing the thugs North Shields Police arrested him, handcuffing and holding him in a police station before being released without charge[3858].

A London householder who took pictures of hoodies as evidence of their antisocial behaviour claims he was told by a PCSO he was breaking the law after the teenagers called the police[3859].

As a Highland sports fan was returning from training with his shinty stick (caman), Lothian and Borders Police warned it was an offensive weapon and told him not to be seen with it in public again[3860].

A financial adviser was given a caution by Sussex Police (having his fingerprints and DNA taken) for squirting his neighbour with a garden hose during a gardening dispute[3861].

A man with a heart condition refused an on-the-spot fine from a Greater Manchester PCSO for dropping an apple core, so was held in a cell for 18 hours, and had his DNA and fingerprints taken (he denied the charge). He says five policemen were sent to arrest him, but police deny this[3862]. Referring to the case a 2008 tabloid leader said: 'No wonder the British public's respect for the thin blue line is at an all-time low'[3863].

When in Bolton tearaways started arsonising wheelie bins, the police and council, instead of taking on the miscreants, introduced more draconian regulations for householders on disposing of their rubbish[3864].

Two police officers and an official from Natural England ordered two pensioners cockling on Norfolk mudflats to stop, warning them against doing it again, as they were breaking an ancient law which banned beach cockling 'within the distance a spear can be thrown by a man on a horse'. Two Sheffield PCSOs gave a caution to the owner of a fancy dress shop because he'd dressed up a dummy as Colonel Gaddafi, calling it 'inappropriate' and liable to create 'community tension' – no one had complained about it. A Kent householder took to task cricketers whose balls kept landing in her garden. She was arrested by two of the cricketers, who were off-duty police, and detained in the pavilion till a police car arrived to take her to a Maidstone cell. After being held for six hours she received a fixed penalty notice for public disorder and verbal abuse[3865].

When a West Sussex resident made a citizen's arrest – 10-year-old youths were throwing stones and threatening his wife – he was arrested on suspicion of kidnapping, the youths being treated as shocked witnesses. It took months before the CPS withdrew the threat of a trial and jail sentence. The family were then again intimidated, but found the police would do nothing[3866].

A Wiltshire pensioner was charged with possessing an offensive weapon for chasing off yobs who were stoning his home. The gang had laid siege to his house for over two hours, police not having turned up. When they did arrive they arrested him, allowing the youths to escape. The 65-year-old's windows had been smashed five times in six months[3867].

A British woman who tended a war memorial was convicted of assault, criminal damage and a public order offence, after challenging youths she believed were vandalising it (there had been months of vandalism). She grabbed one's shirt collar, and threw a bike into the road. None of the youths were prosecuted. The trial cost £100,000, and was described by the defence lawyer as 'PC gone mad'[3868].

An ex-Royal Navy amputee and councillor, who went to the aid of a mother and baby being harassed by youths in the middle of the night, was himself arrested and locked up. Kent Police had noticed a truncheon in his back pocket (he didn't use it)[3869].

A 73-year-old law-abiding pensioner was arrested for shouting at a gang of youths who were throwing rocks at ducks. Falsely accused by the louts of assaulting one of them, a policeman arrested the pensioner at home, telling him to remove his shoelaces before being taken to the Nottinghamshire Police station, where he was locked up for the first time in his life – he has diabetes and heart disease. He had made several complaints about antisocial behaviour, but he found himself arrested instead[3870]. Former Chelsea footballer Dennis Wise was questioned by police after he chased a 13-year-old whom he claims was one of a gang throwing missiles at his pregnant wife and children. The boy's mother claims the star attacked her son, who wasn't injured[3871]. When celebrity Chris Tarrant threw a small dining implement at a fan pestering him in a restaurant, he was arrested at his hotel in the early morning by flak-jacketed police and thrown into cells[3872].

A community hero, a café proprietor, was warned by South Yorkshire Police he faced up to 10 years in jail for possessing a firearm with intent. He had fired two shotgun blasts in an unsuccessful attempt to disperse 15 drunken youths who were damaging plants in the park where had had his café and was volunteer keeper. He was given a suspended prison sentence and community service and has lost his café: he says he had no help with the repeated antisocial behaviour from the police[3873].

The Met arrested a 12-year-old boy, holding him for four hours and having his DNA and prints taken, for flicking a piece of paper at a classmate (which was classed as GBH). He appeared in court several times over three months before the case was dropped. His eight-year-old brother was given a reprimand for his graffiti[3874].

When a Portsmouth businessman made a litter lout pick up the leaflets he had torn up (he grabbed the 12-year-old by the coat after receiving a barrage of verbal abuse), the police – whom he had called – held him for eight hours on suspicion of common assault. He was not charged but is fighting to get his photo, DNA, etc. taken off the database[3875].

A 12-year-old schoolboy had a scuffle with another boy: months later two South Yorkshire Police officers arrested him at dawn in his bedroom. At a Sheffield police station his DNA and prints were taken before he was released on bail. His father wanted to wake the child himself, but he was also threatened with arrest[3876].

A 50-year-old whose grandfather was killed in the trenches and father was a WWII pilot, faced arrest for tackling louts she blamed for vandalising a war memorial garden[3877].

Two neighbours were handcuffed and incarcerated by Lancashire Police for making a citizen's arrest of two louts planning to assault another teenager. The case, thrown out by magistrates, cost thousands[3878].

As with some of the historic sex allegations against celebrities, police have increasingly arrested people merely to interview, rather than charge them. The trouble is employers assume guilt until proved innocent[3879].

Gloucestershire Police arrested a householder who slapped one of a gang who had been throwing snowballs at his front door. When his wife ventured out her glasses were broken: the police took all day to arrive. They advised victims to stay indoors. The householder was put in a cell for several hours and given a caution[3880].

Two teenage girls in cowgirl outfits – they had been at a Cowboys and Indians party – were arrested and spent several hours in police cells because one of them had a toy gun with which they had allegedly threatened other motorists. The armed police were in four jeeps, there were two dog vans and helicopters, and the girls were cautioned for possession of an imitation firearm[3881].

A PCSO visited an 11-year-old's home when her school complained about a Facebook group she established that criticised her headmistress for failing to deal with a difficult pupil[3882].

A 48-year-old college lecturer was taken to court after standing up to bullies who had punched her nine-year-old son in the street and swore at her. Police charged her with breach of the peace[3883].

Motoring

When a have-a-go hero, a grandfather, confronted a car-jacker (who had a knife) with his spirit level, the police in Birmingham sprayed him with CS gas and arrested him as well as the knifeman. He spent five hours in the cells[3884].

Over half of car owners report being stopped by traffic patrols over an alleged road offence[3885]. A driver travelling in her newly bought Volkswagen Polo with her two sons (one with cerebral palsy, one a toddler) who was stopped and given a ticket for having an uninsured vehicle, claimed she was left stranded when Lothian and Borders Police impounded the car. They withdrew the fine the next day, because their database hadn't been updated by the Motor Insurance Bereau. The young mother had to borrow money to retrieve her property[3886].

A woman whose car was stolen and burned out lambasted the thieves on Facebook, but police gave her a ticking off for being offensive to the thieves[3887].

When hundreds of drunken ravers illegally occupied Lord Cardigan's land in Savernake Forest, the police helped them park their cars, as if sheer numbers gave them a licence to vandalise with impunity. Wiltshire Police said: 'We decided to negotiate with rather than evict the participants'. Lord Cardigan was greeted with abuse and threats, one of the ravers telling him to 'sod off and die'[3888].

A 61-year-old composer was arrested by four Met officers and held for questioning for six hours for leaving a Sainsbury's car park without paying a £5 parking ticket[3889].

When a motorist was fined for playing his car radio too loudly, the policeman concerned only heard the noise when the driver wound down his window to ask directions: a judge quashed the fine[3890].

Wiltshire Police pulled over a motorbike enthusiast's hearse, which was a bike with a sidecar, taxed as a car (so that helmets didn't need to be worn). The funeral procession hadn't been speeding but they had to after the police left to get to the crematorium on time. The police photographed the hearse[3891].

CAVEAT CIVIS

Traffic police are traditionally the bane of the middle classes. As the number of road cops has fallen so have road fatalities.

Police in Victorian London were preoccupied with traffic, with men being taken off night duty to deal with daytime traffic. In the 20th Century traffic policing before WWII began to bring police into conflict with the respectable middle class, and from the 1950s the growth in car ownership increased such confrontations[3892]. Bernard Hogan-Howe says motorists caught twice using a mobile phone while driving should be banned, and young drivers caught only once should have to retake their test[3893].

A retired engineer found himself with a criminal record for having a Swiss Army-style knife in his glove compartment, which Devon and Cornwall Police searched after he had passed a breath test. The knife was confiscated[3894].

A window cleaner was cautioned by police when he was caught driving while wearing a Bin Laden mask. They could seize his car if he was spotted wearing the terrorist's caricature again in the next year. His warning notice was for driving in 'a careless and antisocial way'[3895].

Ayrshire Police booked a pensioner poppy seller as she unloaded charity cans into her shop, because she was illegally parked for two minutes. She said: 'They made me stand like a criminal and ran all these checks (on brakes, tyres, etc.)'[3896].

A photographer was given a ticket for using his mobile while driving – he says he was stationary and there were no calls on the phone at the time stipulated in the summons. He wanted to fight the case, but was told at the police station that the bench would always believe the word of two police officers. The way the law is worded, you are considered guilty if you are just seen in possession of a mobile. The presumption of innocence is now the presumption of guilt. Another person in the same situation decided to go to court, but the magistrates, though they found him a 'very credible' witness and were impressed by his evidence, said they had to believe instead the word of a WPC (so-called 'protected privilege'). One Midlands officer was taken to task repeatedly for not meeting his fixed-penalty quota, and journalist Richard Littejohn attests that many officers tell him they despair at the way they have to target law-abiding middle-class motorists over trivial offences[3897].

Cheshire Police sent up a plane to prove their case against a lecturer accused of using a mobile phone while driving[3898].

Strathclyde Police stopped a senior civil servant three times in five days suspected of drink-driving, following tip-offs from the public. Working on behalf of crime victims he fears a vendetta against him (his breath tests were all negative) – he represents the Crown Office and might criticise chief constables[3899].

A Bedfordshire pensioner drove after a handbag thief, but because her car grazed a lamppost in the chase she ended up in court (the thief escaped)[3900].

A bin lorry driver was given a £30 ticket by a Northants PC for obstruction – his lorry was just doing its job in a narrow street. The officer called for backup and four police cars arrived[3901].

West Yorkshire Police are 'stealing' cars if they find them 'unsecure' – owners have to pay £150 to get them back[3902].

Meredydd Hughes, head of road policing for ACPO, demanded stricter drink driving laws, so that less than a pint could mean a loss of licence, even though there is no conclusive evidence as to whether casualties are reduced by lower limits. He described the 2006 Xmas campaign as the 'most productive' ever, with 91,658 motorists facing 'disqualification, a fine or imprisonment'.

A law-abiding couple returned to their car after shopping, but police thought it had been stolen and used in a major crime (it wasn't). When their innocence had been established they protested to the officers surrounding it, but they were told: 'I should keep quiet because you can still be arrested'.

West Yorkshire Police issued an innocent 11-year-old with a summons for driving offences, but when the error was pointed out to them, they still insisted on a court case. Bradford magistrates dismissed the case out of hand.

A woman driver was nearly run off the road by another driver three times, but the police told the victim, who gave them the other motorist's registration number: 'You must understand that we need more than one witness to the offence before we can do anything about it'. This doesn't apparently apply to 'illegal' berrypicking.

A road rage victim took a photo of a passenger in the other car she says attacked her. Yet police ticked her off: 'You brought this on yourself – people round here don't like being photographed'. A year later the police had not interviewed or arrested anyone, though they had the other car's registration and insurance details.

A salesman became the first driver (2007) to get licence points for eating a sandwich at the wheel, thanks to Cheshire Police.

A lorry driver accused of warning other motorists about a speed trap was cleared after a two-year legal battle, because the police couldn't prove any speeding motorists had slowed down. The Court of Appeal's Administrative Court refused the DPP's request to appeal to the Law Lords.

A taxi driver was incarcerated in a high-security jail for leaving his fog lights on and refusing to pay the police fine (he was handcuffed in court).

A Lancashire driving instructor, Tahir Mahmood, splashed a police officer by driving through a puddle he hadn't noticed. He was prosecuted at an estimated cost to the taxpayer of £20,000, but the case was thrown out. A taxi driver who speeded to a police station because a woman passenger in his cab was being assaulted was given a speeding fine.

Nine Nottinghamshire police with a riot van swooped on a group of parents, collecting their wheelchair-bound children from their special school, to hand them £30 on-the-spot fines. The police said they were dealing with 'inconsiderate parking'[3903].

A Staffordshire shopfitting company has a yard where scrap metal merchants come and go at all hours. Because police saw travellers loading up, they informed the firm's director that it wasn't enough for his company to be licensed and insured, it was his duty to ensure anyone taking materials from him has a waste transfer certificate[3904].

The details of people cleared of minor offences such as failing to wear a seatbelt may remain on the new DNA database: police, backed by the CPS, also want fingerprints and footwear imprints to be stored[3905].

An 81-year-old former mayor, barely able to walk, was charged with assaulting two burly Kent policemen. The OBE holder's car was stopped but he refused to get out, so they dragged him out[3906].

A millionairess was charged with dangerous driving even though she was escaping from two men at night: she drove from side to side at a very low speed to throw one off her bonnet (he was unhurt). When she dialled 999 she was arrested, but the men were not charged. The case was thrown out of court[3907].

Northumbria Police spent 13 months and £10,000 pursuing a female motorist for holding an apple at the wheel of her car (she eventually received a £60 fine)[3908].

Celebrity socialite Tara Palmer-Tomkinson, normally asked for her autograph by police, was stopped by Essex traffic police, who insisted she accompanied them to the police station (she was arrested) because they didn't have a breathalyser in their car. They tested her seven times because the results were all negative. One policeman allegedly was aggressive, sneering that she was just a rich girl in a BMW. She had to hitchhike home because they said she was unfit to drive[3909].

A disabled woman, asleep in her car, was fined because the disabled parking disc was not the right way up. A bishop's secretary was prosecuted for riding a London bus with an Oyster card 80p short of the full fare, while a father who displayed a pirate flag on his property because that was the theme of his daughter's party, was threatened with prosecution for contravening the Town & Country (Control of Advertisements) Regulations 1992. Lancashire Police lost a four-year battle with a driver whom they had arrested for allegedly playing a CD too loudly in his car.

A composer who refused to pay £5 for a lost parking ticket at a supermarket was later arrested by four officers at his home, fingerprinted, DNA taken, and held in custody for six hours[3910].

A Somerset shopkeeper took to warning motorists visiting her shop if PCSOs were ticketing cars outside so they could avoid a penalty – she says a new parking crackdown was ruining her business, and a parish council meeting passed a vote of no confidence in the police because enforcement of the new parking rules had caused a slump in trade. The shopkeeper claims she was warned by police she faced arrest if she interfered with the PCSOs by warning people[3911].

Police chiefs stepped up anti-motorist moves in 2008 by using a quota-based approach (one force demanded five speeders a month, with 24 motoring arrests), issuing extra tickets, reducing the room for officers' discretion. Thus Norfolk was fixing performance targets for traffic offences. The danger is alienating the motoring classes[3912].

While <u>Richard Brunstrom</u> was in charge North Wales Police gave out 4,200 speeding tickets monthly, yet solved only 41 out of 693 car crimes and 6% of burglaries[3913].

A motorist was fined by police for sounding his horn when a pedestrian stepped in front of his car, as this constituted 'excessive' use of the instrument[3914].

A motorist unfastened his seatbelt, as he sat in a stationary queue of traffic on the A12, his engine switched off and his handbrake on. He was given a fixed penalty notice by Sussex Police for not wearing his belt. Another motorist was convicted of obstruction in Grimsby for warning oncoming drivers of a speed trap on the A46, despite, by so doing, helping them to be safer drivers and obey the law[3915].

Police zealously prosecute motorists driving at 80mph instead of 70mph on motorways in clear conditions in open countryside[3916].

Sussex Police ordered cars to be removed from a street – East Harting villagers found mis-spelt police leaflets on their cars to this effect, even though many don't have garages – so that two patrol cars could escort a supersize mobile home to an illegal travellers' site. Workmen were also told to remove their trucks. The gypsies had moved in on a holiday weekend[3917]. Recalcitrant residents' cars would be towed away at their own expense[3918].

A young driver was given a fixed-penalty fine for looking at a pretty girl walking along (technically driving without due care and attention). The traffic cop showed him a high-quality image of himself taken by the car's camera. Allegedly one of the two officers had also been distracted by the girl. Another case of 'public servants' sent out to persecute those who pay their wages? The official police statement insists that motorists must not be distracted by anything … even 'gorgeous people'[3919].

A member of the public received a torrent of abuse from Avon and Somerset PC <u>Aqil Farooq</u> when he complained about Farooq's police van reversing the wrong way up a one-way. When the man tried to photograph the officer, the latter knocked his camera to the ground. Wrongfully arrested, he was accused of 'assaulting an officer with a camera, resisting arrest and being drunk and disorderly'[3920].

A two-year-old girl's name and details are being held on file by Wiltshire Constabulary after being accused of hitting a car with a stick. Children's rights campaigners condemned the police decision to treat the girl as a 'suspect'[3921].

Merseyside Police pulled over a driver going home from work and fined him £30 for playing music too loudly on his car radio[3922].

Record numbers of the middle-aged are being 'criminalised' by police chasing targets, e.g. a speeding motorist is now given the same weight as a rapist. A first conviction or caution increased by 50% between 2001 and 2009. Harriet Sargeant's report in 2009 found incidents which once would have been ignored are now treated as crimes[3923].

When a pregnant woman phoned Staffordshire Police to report nearly being run down by a speeding driver, a policewoman who visited her at her half-decorated home referred her to social services for being a potentially unfit mother, resulting in the council alerting her midwife[3924].

A North Wales police car with sirens and blue lights was rushing to a fatal accident, but turned round to give a motorcyclist a fixed penalty notice for a non-regulation number plate (it was 80mm too short)[3925].

A driver was pulled over by Mersey Tunnel police and quizzed for half an hour for laughing at the wheel. They told him that laughing while driving can be an offence[3926].

Dorchester traffic police ordered an 86-year-old driver to remove a two-inch chrome boxer dog mascot from his car bonnet, which he has had since 1960 on various cars, or he would be fined and given penalty points. The police said the dog was 'dangerous to pedestrians'[3927].

Chris Tarrant's ex-wife was wrestled to the ground by Surrey PC Peter Groves, who had chased her over a parking ticket she refused to pay. She described him as a 'psycho' who was out of control – he forced her Saab to stop in a country lane[3928].

A coach driver was given an ASBO for driving his bus through Holyrood Park (Edinburgh), which is still the Queen's property so that commercial vehicles are banned under archaic law[3929].

Only 3% of car accidents are caused by speeding drivers, yet the nearly 7,000 speed cameras can't detect 'careless or reckless' drivers who are responsible for three times as many accidents[3930].

Strathclyde community cop Stuart Gray fined a motorist £50 for blowing his nose with the handbrake on (he was also given three points)[3931].

A passer-by was arrested by Avon and Somerset PC Aqil Farooq and a WPC colleague after he photographed them reversing up a one-way street the wrong way and parking at a fish-and-chip shop. They falsely charged him with 'assaulting' an officer with his camera (in fact the PC, who shouted '…. off, this is police business' knocked the camera to the ground), resisting arrest and being drunk and disorderly[3932].

When a motorist attended his Newcastle-upon-Tyne DVLA office to renew his tax disc he was arrested and incarcerated for three hours because his MOT certificate was the wrong shade of green: staff wrongly thought it was fake and called the police. Though it was genuine the motorist's details will remain on the DNA database for six years[3933].

Religion

West Midlands Police were ordered to pay over £4,000 for arresting a Christian anti-gay campaigner who said gays will go to hell: he was handcuffed and put in the cells for several hours. A judge condemned the police[3934].

An elderly evangelical Christian holding a placard was attacked by a mob of gay campaigners, yet he was the one arrested, prosecuted and convicted for a public order offence.

Cumbrian Police arrested a street preacher who had told a gay PCSO homosexuality was a sin: he was locked up for seven hours and had his fingerprints, a palm print, a retinal scan and a DNA swab taken. He was released on bail after being charged under the Public Order Act 1986[3935]. Campaigners say section 5 of the Public Order Act is being used over-zealously by police to arrest critics of Scientology, gay rights opponents, street preachers, students making jokes, etc[3936]. Similarly, terrorist legislation's section 7 may be overused against journalists.

A Muslim leader urged police to investigate extremism in mosques after 'preachers of hate' were caught by an undercover filmmaker, but West Midlands Police prevaricated: they were 'considering the footage'. Channel 4 called the West Midlands Police's later complaint (that the Channel misled viewers by quoting extremists out of context) 'perverse'. Ofcom ruled that 'Undercover Mosque' was legitimate[3937].

A grandmother was ordered to remove a 30-year-old sign making fun of Jehovah's Witnesses, because it could incite 'hate crime'. Protection only became law in 2006 for Witnesses.

A Christian campaigner was arrested by South Wales Police for peacefully handing out leaflets at a gay rally, because they contained anti-homosexual quotations from the Bible. He refused to accept a caution. South Wales Police have a special unit dedicated to dealing with anti-gays. His arrest has been represented by C of E evangelicals as 'an onslaught on freedom of speech'.

A Catholic Celtic footballer who blessed himself during a match was cautioned by Glasgow police. The Crown Office pursued the case and the goalkeeper will now have a criminal record.

A former soldier was jailed for 70 days by Carlisle magistrates for burning a Koran in retaliation for the burning of a poppy and the abuse of returning servicemen[3938].

Following the police wartime witch-hunt of spiritualist Helen Duncan (despite Churchill and George VI being among her clients), the head of another spiritualist church was warned by the police that <u>she</u> could also face prosecution. Following Duncan's release from prison another of her séances was the subject of a police raid in 1956: she was dead within three months[3939].

Lancashire Constabulary threatened a Christian Blackpool shopkeeper for displaying Bible passages on his TV screen – two officers questioned him for nearly an hour. A complaint against the police was being formulated[3940]. Lancashire Police have apologised to him over the DVDs, and admitted they had misinterpreted the Public Order Act, but refused to admit he was threatened with arrest. He claims the police subjected him to an 'aggressive inquisition' for almost an hour[3941].

When a Muslim guest in a private B&B complained to police about the Christian hoteliers' comments about aspects of Islam, the couple were arrested under the Public Order Act (designed to deal with serious civil disturbance)[3942].

A Baptist church minister may sue Police Scotland after being detained (dragged, he claims, from Perth High Street) for preaching 'too loudly' in the centre of Perth: one officer told him he was 'in breach of the peace', though he wasn't using amplification, while another said the noise level wasn't the issue, it was the content of the sermon, but the police wouldn't clarify[3943].

Burglars/Thieves

When a son rushed to his widowed mother's house to confront a burglar who was terrifying her, he was arrested along with the thief because the latter said he had been assaulted. The injured son was taken to hospital, where the police remained even in the XR room, and then put in jail for a night[3944].

The home of a disabled farmer who aimed a shot at a fox was stormed by 16 armed Essex Police officers after he inadvertently struck two burglars, not realising he had hit anyone. His firearms licence was revoked[3945].

When celebrity Mylene Klass spotted teenagers peering through her kitchen window after midnight, she grabbed a knife and banged the window. Though they made off, she was later visited by police who warned her that to wield an 'offensive weapon' is illegal, even in your own home[3946].

When Devon and Cornwall Police entered (some say trespassed) people's homes surreptitiously as an 'anti-crime initiative', they collected any valuable items and left them in 'swag bags' for the owner to find[3947]. A Met WPC, to highlight the dangers of burglary (Operation Popping), walked into a lone woman's front room while she watched TV[3948].

Former traffic warden and store detective Wendy Challis-Jones, who had won two bravery awards, caught a bicycle thief in York after a chase, but was arrested by police accused of assaulting the hoodie. She was fingerprinted, and had her mugshot and DNA taken. The arresting officer is said to have told her aggressively: 'You stop there. Don't move'.

Jam-making Gloucestershire pensioner Ian Blayney, 67, was tracked down by police and accused of theft over a rowan berry-picking incident in Cheshire alongside a canal (his car had been caught on CCTV). The hunt had taken the police three months.

When Dr. Otto Chan's computers were stolen by North London burglars police didn't send anyone, though there are three police stations nearby, so he put up a reward poster himself, but he was nearly arrested because police said he had breached the Theft Act by promising 'no questions asked', and he could be prosecuted for trying to buy stolen goods! The Met now refuses to send officers to burglaries unless these are ongoing.

A former Halifax Tory councillor went to investigate a break-in at his wife's shop but was arrested, handcuffed and put in a cell. Because he was carrying an axe for defence he ended up with a caution and his weapon confiscated.

In the case of 'salt poisoning' mother Marianne Williams – she was cleared – Wiltshire Police broke into her home to look for 'evidence' while she was with her dying baby in hospital.

An Essex businessman marched an employee thief through the town with a 'Thief' placard round his neck, to Witham police station. The employer was charged with false imprisonment, and though the case collapsed, he had to pay £13,000 compensation and legal costs for 'humiliating' his employee[3949].

THE PERVERSE POLICEMAN

A homeowner was arrested by Greater Manchester Police on suspicion of causing GBH with intent after a burglar plunged from his balcony, suffering head injuries[3950]. Brave grandfather Peter Flanagan stabbed an armed burglar (a convicted criminal) to death in self-defence, but instead of being hailed a hero Greater Manchester Police treated him as a murder suspect for a harrowing month, being held in custody for three days[3951].

A father of two was hauled off from his bed to a cell at 3am, being left there for 11 hours (officers were too busy to deal with him), wrongly suspected of stealing a TV[3952].

When a father and son apprehended an illegal immigrant burgling their scrap metal business – it had been repeatedly burglarised – they were arrested and dragged through the courts by Leicestershire Police, despite the father being married to a police officer. The police had refused to go on the roof to arrest a Romanian career criminal, for health and safety reasons. While in custody the father, accused of attempted murder, suffered a heart attack and was planning to sue the force[3953].

Instead of waiting to find if there are suspicious circumstances, police now arrest the householder immediately if an armed intruder is killed during a burglary: guilty till proved innocent[3954]. When a hard-working Asian shopkeeper was attacked by a career criminal who stabbed him several times, the thug was accidentally killed by his own weapon. The police arrested the shopkeeper, who had to wait 12 days before he was told he wouldn't be charged by Lancashire Police with murder[3955]. Herefordshire Police arrested a 'hero homeowner' who shot in the leg a suspected burglar who broke into his home while he watched TV. Locals were furious that the police had arrested him for attempted murder[3956]. A terrified Glasgow teenager who shot with an airgun a drug addict would-be burglar – the latter had thrown a missile at the teenager's stepfather – was jailed for a year**[3957]**.

Yorkshire Police arrested a York woman who had caught a bicycle thief. They put her in a cell for 10 hours, where she cried her eyes out. She said the arresting officer had a 'frightening, aggressive voice'[3958].

When a Norfolk farmer complained about a theft of machinery he got no response from the police, but three squad cars turned up following a complaint that he had left mud on a local road. A brewery boss who detained a cat burglar expected thanks from Gloucester Police, who, however, locked him up instead[3959].

A regular DIY B&Q superstore customer was arrested and dragged out in handcuffs, fingerprinted and interviewed under caution at North Shields police station. He had been accused (wrongly) of stealing a sink plug (it was his own he had brought in for comparison)[3960].

In 2002 10,184 burglars were incarcerated compared with a record 15,509 motorists (only 2,200 of whom had committed serious offences). The number of jailed drivers (up by 400% in a decade) had not improved road safety in the 10 years. The easy motorist target greatly improves imprisonment statistics, and provides much filthy lucre[3961].

When a Cornish shopkeeper hit back at shoplifters when he was physically attacked he was taken to court charged with assault – he pleaded guilty to avoid a prison sentence. The thieves got fixed penalties[3962].

An Asian shopkeeper drove a 15-year-old shoplifter back to the latter's home, but less than 48 hours later he was arrested by Lancashire police at his door at 4am. He was interviewed in a cell and DNA and fingerprints taken. CPS lawyers advised the case should be dropped, but a senior officer appealed that decision and the shopkeeper was put through a nightmare for 10 months before a judge decided not to proceed. The case cost the taxpayer nearly £50,000[3963].

A Mr. Ali was forced to change his name and move house because his identity was stolen and debts were piled up in his name, but Greater Manchester Police told him no crime had been committed. When bailiffs arrived he called the police, but they said if he didn't pay up they would help the bailiffs[3964].

The best friend of a hair salon manager offered to do the books for her, but proceeded to carry out a three-year £125,000 loans fraud against HSBC using her friend's identity. The salon stylist was arrested at home by 13 detectives and put in a police cell – her husband was also arrested – and both had nervous breakdowns[3965].

Millionaire business man Munir Hussain fought back against a career burglar who had subjected his family to a knifepoint ordeal, beating him with a cricket bat. The householder received a two-and-a-half year jail term, while the real criminal walked free[3966].

A Skelmersdale shopkeeper Tony Singh was arrested (2008) after fatally stabbing his violent mugger with the latter's own knife, while a Devon pensioner – secretary of a village-in-bloom committee – was arrested for assault after cuffing a teenager with a bundle of church minutes: he had been kicking a football through flower-beds, calling her names and threatening her. Magistrates gave her an absolute discharge, but she now has a record which prevents her visiting relatives in Australia and the US[3967].

When a repeatedly burgled Leicester householder told police he again had intruders, they told him it would taken them two days to respond. He captured one of the culprits, but was arrested, charged with kidnapping and held in a cell for 36 hours. He was given a suspended 12-month sentence, as well as 200 hours community service[3968].

A young farmer saved his mother from being run down by burglars – their farm had been plagued by thieving intruders – by firing buckshot (meant for rabbits) at their van, but he was arrested and bailed by North Yorkshire Police, with the threat of being charged with attempted murder (the culprits were unharmed)[3969].

A burglary victim was in Bournemouth police custody for allegedly attacking an intruder whom he caught cycling away with a bag. The victim's arrest was on suspicion of wounding with intent[3970].

Race

South Yorkshire Police were called to a house in Rotherham where a father was trying to rescue his daughter, who had been drugged by an abusive Asian gang. Instead of arresting the abusers, the father and daughter were charged with 'racial harassment'[3971].

A man suspected (wrongly) of uttering racial abuse during a traffic dispute seven months earlier, was ordered off a Heathrow flight by four armed police, who drove him away in a police van with barred windows. He was held for six hours and then released without charge. Scotland Yard has refused to apologise for their disproportionate policing[3972].

THE PERVERSE POLICEMAN

When Cambridgeshire Police's <u>Julie Spence</u> took the middle class to task for speeding, (a) why did she single out the middle class, and (b) why did she not answer the charge that speed cameras <u>increase</u> road deaths and are, in fact, a money-making scam? She certainly wasn't adhering to the spirit of her force's 'Integrated Equality Scheme', which means she should be valuing all groups without favour. In 2007 she drew a lot of flak when she pinpointed the large number of drink-drivers from Eastern Europe: she was accused of fostering racism[3973].

In 1935 14 women were fined at Great Yarmouth Police Court for telling fortunes at kiosks, the piers and the pleasure beach[3974].

<u>Richard Brunstrom</u>'s force was accused of having twisted priorities, solving 6% of burglaries while issuing 4,200 speeding tickets in the same month (Brunstrom was a hardline speed camera enthusiast) and spending £4,000 investigating Weakest Link presenter Anne Robinson's anti-Welsh remarks – four senior officers were detailed to investigate the remarks (the BBC director general was interviewed), but this information had to be extracted under FOIA. The Chief Constable advocated the legalisation of drugs. In 1999 Tony Blair is said to have offended against political correctness by referring to the 'f...... Welsh'. Seven years later detectives from North Wales travelled to London to investigate. Brunstrom ignored CPS advice to drop the inquiry.

A Somerset pub landlady was investigated by police in 2006 for inciting racial hatred: her St. Georges Day celebration allowed children to throw homemade arrows at the dragon on a Welsh flag. Two officers questioned Angie Sayer for two hours. In the same year the CPS had to drop public order charges against a student who called a police horse 'gay'.

When a sales manager sent his council an e-mail complaining about plans to site a recycling skip behind his house, he included a quotation from Pastor Niemoller about the Nazis. A policeman turned up at his home early in the morning to warn him he could be charged with harassment.

In 2006 Herefordshire police arrested a Bromyard shopkeeper for selling golliwogs (they confiscated three), and West Sussex police said they were treating as 'a priority' a complaint about golliwogs being displayed in a Worthing store. Two officers arrived at a shop in Wrightingon in Lancashire and confiscated two golliwog-style rag dolls because they suspected 'racism'. The owner was told to remove the remaining gollies from sale. Eventually the police allowed the dolls back on sale.

A 14-year-old schoolgirl was arrested in 2006 because she didn't want to be educated in a class that couldn't speak English (they spoke Urdu). She was body-searched, her fingerprints taken and her shoelaces removed. After interview she was locked in a cell for over five hours. A tabloid newspaper has called for the arresting officer to be sacked from the Greater Manchester force. The school's community policeman allegedly said the matter wouldn't be left to rest. The school (in the Salford area) is the same one where a ten-year-old was prosecuted earlier in 2006 for calling fellow pupil a 'Paki' and 'Bin Laden'.

Warwickshire Police threatened the villagers of Meriden with arrest for trying to protect a piece of greenbelt land from a group of wealthy gypsies intent on building a permanent mobile home park. The police removed the protesters' signs: the residents have been told <u>they</u> are the ones breaking the law for erecting 'Help Save Meriden's Green Belt' signs without planning permission[3975].

When an Aberdonian as a joke painted a garden gnome black as a gift to a pal who had become engaged to a black girl, the pal managed to get the police to pursue the matter in court – he was fined £200[3976].

Essex Police sent three officers at midnight to arrest a taxi driver for, in a minor altercation, calling an aggressor a 'Scotch ....'[3977].

When a celebrity portrait photographer offered to help a Muslim woman with her shopping she was kicked, but she was charged by the Met with a 'racially aggravated assault' – she claims she was 'a statistic to help the police meet a target'[3978].

Basil Brush was being investigated by Northants Police for racism (his show featured a gipsy selling heather and pegs)[3979].

Tory MP Tim Loughton, a former government minister, endured a six-month race probe ordeal at the hands of the police, after describing a voter (who claims a Romany Gipsy background) as unkempt. He was asked if he had mental problems. The investigation was suddenly dropped by the CPS after possibly costing up to £100,000.

Animals and Plants

As a gesture of goodwill a retired bank manager trimmed a communal beech hedge for almost three decades, but new neighbours called the police because he didn't ask their permission. The police agreed to attend and warned the householder he might be committing an offence: they also warned the complainant not to discuss it with the press, according to him[3980].

A retired military policeman, who quite legally culls grey squirrels by shooting, pretended to have drowned one in sympathy with a window cleaner, who was given a criminal record and £1,547 costs after being prosecuted by the RSPCA. The retiree was arrested at the request of the RSPCA, handcuffed and held in a cell for nine hours, then interrogated for an hour by the RSPCA, a cop in attendance. Northumbria Police said the RSPCA was 'leading this investigation'. Similarly Carlisle Police held a man for six hours while the RSPCA removed his 90 ponies: he hanged himself. The police now seem to regard themselves as the charity's enforcement wing, even though its officials are all ordinary members of the public[3981].

A householder was arrested by Ayrshire Police for moving two tiny mussels, contravening the Wildlife and Countryside Act[3982].

An auctioneer who tried to sell an antique chest of drawers containing 100-year-old birds' eggs was arrested and charged, under wildlife protection laws, by Northumbria Police. His prints and DNA were taken at a police station. The tip-off came from the RSPB which had seen the auction catalogue. An NHS executive who used to own the cabinet was interviewed twice by police[3983].

People fined for allowing their dogs to foul the footpath are going to be forced by police to provide DNA.

When an elderly farmer scared off a dog that was worrying his lambs, by firing a warning shot from his shotgun, six police cars arrived with dozens of officers, five them armed. He was armlocked, handcuffed, and locked in a cell. He claims an officer swore at him. Despite being photographed and fingerprinted he was released without charge.

Tayside Police warned builders they could face police action if they killed protected lizards on a site[3984]. Lancashire Police are mounting a 24-hour guard over the rare lady's slipper orchid at a secret location on a golf course[3985].

When a boxer dog in the back of a couple's car was mistaken by a fellow motorist for a body, Clackmannanshire Police turned up at their door and checked out if anyone living with them was missing[3986].

12 policemen, along with vets and eight trading standards officers, set up a roadblock and cut their way into a field to slaughter a pet cow that had once lived on a farm where a BSE calf from another herd had been found[3987].

An animal lover displaying a banner outside a race meeting saying hundreds of horses are raced to death in Britain, was told to dismantle it because it might cause 'alarm, distress or harassment'[3988].

When a puppy's owner retrieved the animal from quarantine kennels prematurely, up to eight Lothian and Borders Police in four patrols swooped on his home, cordoning off the street, to recapture the pet[3989].

Acting on a tip-off the Met raided the Belgravia home of Jose Mourinho, Chelsea's manager, because his Yorkshire terrier hadn't completed all the health checks demanded by the pet passport scheme[3990].

Northumbria Police arrested a man for growling at two Labradors, under Section 5 of the Public Order Act, but this Act doesn't apply to the feelings of animals. The man was incarcerated for five hours: the case cost £8,000[3991].

Three Tyne & Wear officers arrested a bird egg collector for collecting eggs 35 years earlier when he was a schoolboy. They confiscated his book of bird records, telling him it could be used in evidence against him. He was given a caution. A waitress was given 'suitable advice' after a thorough investigation by South Wales Police when a customer called her 'smelly'[3992].

After Jeremy Clarkson appeared on the BBC's 'Countryfile' he was reported by police wildlife officer Josh Marshall for allegedly interfering with barn owls, approaching which requires a licence. The BBC denied a contravention of the law. Ironically PC Marshall seemed to himself cause offence when he appeared on the programme the previous week[3993].

Social Workers

A learning disabled eight-year-old assaulted his older sister but told the police his respectable father had done it. Though he retracted his story on video the English police adhered to his earlier version and arrested the father, who was never charged. Social workers became so threatening that the family escaped to Ireland where they had roots. They settled there happily but the social workers tracked them down, thanks to the grandmother being arrested (by 10 officers), handcuffed, held in a cell and told by police to reveal the family's whereabouts or she would be charged with perverting the course of justice. At no time were court orders obtained[3994].

The home of an NHS nurse and part-time dog breeder was raided by two RSPCA officials and five policemen, complaining she had too many dogs in the house. The RSPCA told Leeds social workers the home was untidy, which led to the nurse's son being taken into care. When a Coventry couple took their newborn son to hospital with a fractured arm, social workers were called and the mother arrested, handcuffed and held by police for nine hours: although not charged, the couple were placed on police bail. A London couple had their six children seized by social workers on what seems to be flimsy hearsay. When the next baby was born to the couple, three social workers and five policemen entered the hospital ward and wrenched the baby from the breastfeeding mother at 3 am[3995].

A Cheshire mother who was facing trial for the criminal offence of sending a birthday card to one of her children (she had permission from another judge), was stopped on the outskirts of Widnes (where her adopted children lived) by an unmarked police car, arrested, handcuffed, held in a cell for a day and her car seized. The police alleged she was in breach of a court order forbidding entry to the town, but they eventually accepted she didn't intend to enter the town. She was given a £150 bill for their impounding her car. She has been arrested several times (even though a court agreed she had been an excellent mother), once when she merely exchanged a friendly wave with one of her children in the street[3996].

A police officer was on the panel which had to decide whether an eight-year-old from Newcastle-upon-Tyne should be taken into care because he was too fat.

When jockey and trainer Vicky Haigh fled to Eire to prevent her unborn baby being seized by Notts social workers, the baby's father was threatened with arrest for 'perverting the course of justice' – he refused to tell UK CID officers where she was (he didn't know!). The CID tried to insist on searching his house without a warrant[3997].

A young mother, a care assistant, put her four-year-old back in the car for a few minutes because she was throwing a tantrum in a shop. The next day a Bedfordshire policeman turned up at her home to tell her she had treated her child inappropriately. A bystander had given the police her car registration[3998].

A mother of three had her children snatched from her by 14 Hampshire police officers in a dawn raid when social workers wrongly diagnosed Munchausen's by proxy. A judge described the raid as 'utterly disproportionate' and 'itself abusive of the children involved'. The Constabulary recognised their officers' actions had been 'perceived to be heavy handed' and 'had a significant long-term effect on the family'[3999].

Trivial Crime

Police arrest 40 pensioners daily on average in Britain, criminalising them for trivial offences (e.g. a 71-year-old rollerblader, a 73-year-old reprimanding youths throwing bricks at ducks – he was thrown into a police cell – a 72-year-old pensioner involved in a dispute about neighbours' rubbish gassed with CS and becoming comatose, a great-grandfather accused of stealing a bathroom plug the B&Q store didn't stock (he was fingerprinted and DNA taken). The true numbers of 'grey crime' may be much higher. Selling a goldfish earned a shopkeeper a fine and electronic tag. A 70-year-old was arrested for criminal damage for cutting conifers back too vigorously. Around 90% of the arrests involve men.

Many forces have their own targets, so are tempted to go for 'easy collar' arrests of more vulnerable members of the public to boost their figures[4000].

Householder Richard Jeffrey was ordered from his home so police could examine his car. His windscreen washer bottle was empty so he was given three penalty points and a £60 fine[4001].

A busload of Yorkshire schoolchildren were driven to the local police station after refusing to pay 5p for a ticket they thought should be 3p[4002]. This would be 'kidnap' if a member of the public did it!

A young woman who helped herself to food from Tesco rubbish bins was arrested at her home and taken in handcuffs on suspicion of theft by finding (carrying a maximum seven year prison sentence). The police said if she didn't open her door they would use a battering ram. Police say they found two cannabis cigarettes in her flat, and this has resulted in an extra charge of possessing. This police action has serious implications for 'fregans', who salvage food discarded by supermarkets to ensure it isn't wasted[4003].

Farmer and former TV presenter ('One Man and His Dog') Robin Page has told how he was arrested by 'thought police' from Staffordshire, who travelled 200 miles to his Cambridge farm, whereas after six burglaries and break-ins on his farm no policeman was prepared to travel four miles from Cambridge to take a statement (Britain is the most burgled nation in Europe, with twice the average rate). He had been accused in a newspaper report about Frampton Country Fair of bombarding visitors with pro-hunting propaganda which could have been construed as showing 'criminal intent'. The Gloucestershire officer wanted to interview him under caution with a view to prosecution; he refused without a lawyer being present, so he was put in the cells (arrests and detention are apparently becoming normal in British police stations, for administrative convenience). Page claims the officer lied that he had been given a warning about a caution interview. The police couldn't tell him what he was supposed to have said: they asked <u>him</u>. He got the impression the police disliked traditional country folk like him, and while he was dealing with the Gloucestershire Constabulary a Frampton farm (in their patch) was burgled for the second time in a short period. The farmer caught the burglars, but the police never arrived (apparently turning up at the wrong farm): the culprits eventually were not charged, just cautioned. About the same time five officers from the station concerned staked out a local hostelry (where a skittles competition was being held) and breathalysed a man who hadn't had a drink for years. Page relates another incident in Dover, when he tried to photograph threatening behaviour of anti-hunt protesters – his audience were being abused as they arrived, e.g. with stink bombs – a Kent police inspector said he would be arrested for provocation! And he claims police just sat in their car and watched while a Hertfordshire man received a fractured skull from a baseball bat as he watched the Vale of Aylesbury hunt.

60-year-old Patricia Gibson replaced a wooden post in her fence which builders had dislodged, but her neighbours (the local police Chief Inspector <u>John Martin</u> and his wife) called the police and accused her of causing a two-inch gap in their driveway. Mrs. Gibson was arrested, interviewed at the police station and had her photograph, fingerprints and a DNA swab taken before she was released on bail.

Two 14-year-old girls playing hopscotch in the street were told to stop by police because chalking the grids was a 'low-level crime'. The girls had to scrub the pavement to prevent their actions 'developing into more serious matters'. When residents in Halesowen had previously been warned not to play ball games in the street, police had advised them that games like hopscotch were OK.

When a 13-year-old schoolboy threw a pink marshmallow at another it was classed by a Devon and Cornwall sergeant and PC as 'common assault' – they removed the 'culprit' from school. The force refused to say whether a CPS file was being prepared, or whether charges were to be brought. The force has the lowest % coverage by uniforms of any force in England and Wales, yet they have manpower to conduct perverse policing.

A pensioner was threatened with a £50,000 fine or prison if he returned windblown sand back to the beach. When an amusement arcade owner refused to obey a council order to remove a prize flower display, three policemen and two police cars arrived with council staff and a lorry.

A 64-year-old woman was charged with theft for picking wild mushrooms in an ancient woodland, and put in a police cell. The taxpayer's bill could reach £100,000.

A wheelchair-bound crime victim (she suffered eight burglaries) faced jail for holding two policemen hostage for an hour to highlight her area's crime rate. She was put in a police cell for seven hours.

North Yorkshire Police threatened to fine fish and chips customers £50 for queuing outside a seaside café. Again they are keen to enforce petty rules while far more important problems are ignored.

A 40-year-old father of two was arrested, handcuffed and led away in his pyjamas for refusing to return a ball kicked into his garden in Lancashire. Warwickshire Police arrested a householder for refusing to return a ball which smashed into his greenhouse.

A family who tried to sell Princess Margaret's 1954 N.I. card on e-Bay were arrested and charged with handling stolen goods. They assumed once they explained how they came into possession of the card innocently the police would drop the matter, but no such luck.

Police spent six months investigating a 12-year-old boy who threw a slice of cucumber at an allergic black schoolmate, who had to be admitted to hospital. They issued a caution for assault occasioning actual bodily harm. This means his DNA, fingerprints and photograph will be added to the national database.

A killjoy Humberside policeman fined a young father £80 for spraying his four-year-old son with silly string, which was confiscated. Humberside Police – shamed by the Home Office in 2006 as the joint worst performing force – confirmed the police action was quite correct.

When Thames Valley Police found that a health-care assistant had left her children unsupervised at home for half an hour they gave her a formal caution, recorded at the CRB as being 'for committing an act of cruelty on a child or young person'. She was suspended from her job for 18 months, and the caution prevented her reinstatement, which could leave her unemployable[4004].

When a King's College Cambridge student appeared on BBC2's University Challenge with a red Mohican haircut and second-hand RAF jacket and medals, Cambridgeshire Police knocked on his door to warn him it is a criminal offence to impersonate an RAF officer (they had been alerted by a viewer)[4005].

An elderly Lincolnshire parish councillor and his deputy cut the wire to an alarm which had been going off at a deserted cottage for two months. This led to nine court appearances costing perhaps £40,000 and eventually police cautions. The police service declined to comment[4006].

For 20 minutes two Dorset policemen watched three young girls picking daffodils in a public park, then warned their parents they could be arrested for criminal damage. This left the children in tears and too afraid to return to the park[4007].

County Durham Police have threatened to arrest children for throwing snowballs at people or cars[4008].

It took 100 Strathclyde police, nine sheriff officers and a council crew in balaclavas to evict a Glasgow family – who had been in their home for 35 years – because they were resisting a compulsory purchase order[4009].

Kent Police arrested a man in his garden on Guy Fawkes night: he was accused of discharging fireworks after 11pm. He was held in custody for several hours, photographed, fingerprinted and DNA sampled. He refused to pay the fixed penalty so was fined with costs in court (a total of £810)[4010]. He still protested his innocence, leading to the quashing of his conviction on appeal, after 10 months and a small fortune in court fees[4011].

"In recent years the police have moved from instinctively protecting taxpaying property owners, first to a position of studied neutrality and now to actively siding with aggressors ...". A woman and her elderly mother, who were arrested by four Cumbria officers, then jailed, for the crime of feeding the birds in their back garden, are suing the police for damages. The Chief Constable of Avon and Somerset launched a manhunt to find who drew a Hitler moustache on a Pitcombe councillor's poster: again, four officers were dispatched on door-to-door inquiries. Some police seem to relish pursuing the most trivial matter on the weakest evidence[4012].

Gloucester Police used a helicopter, eight officers, two dog units and three patrol cars, to arrest two people who took 47p worth of scrap from a rubbish tip[4013].

A woman in a state of advanced pregnancy was among passengers threatened with arrest by British Transport Police after walking from one of scores of trains stranded by vandalised signals[4014].

Two officers arrested a man for using his laptop in the street – he was to be charged with using another person's Wi-Fi broadband connection[4015].

Lothian and Borders Police stopped the car of five comedy actresses in fancy dress doing a PR stunt for an Edinburgh fringe show. They were ordered out of their car and warned their green water pistols were 'threatening weapons' and they could be mistaken for terrorists: they feared spending a night in the cells. The police gave them 'words of advice', saying they could have charged the girls with breach of the peace[4016].

In 2007 two Met policemen and two Hackney council officials seized two sets of imperial scales from a market stall run by one of the original five Metric Martyrs (whose criminal convictions for selling in imperial measure were upheld in 2002)[4017].

A male stripogram was charged with impersonating a policeman after real Grampian officers thought he was real. 'Stripper' was emblazoned on his stage uniform[4018].

Though a very minor schoolboy incident (one boy threw his friend's bike dustcap in a ditch as a prank) was dealt with by 'community resolution' (a written apology and replacement of the cap), it counts as a 'solved crime' for the force's statistics. The police had arrived within minutes and frogmarched the culprit home[4019].

A magician was quizzed by West Midlands Police for bending a fork in a bar[4020].

A crime victim claims he has been banned by Grampian Police from selling his car as it is 'evidence in a criminal investigation' (no one has been charged)[4021].

According to the 2008 Flanagan report officers have to meet targets by arresting even the most minor offenders (one officer charged someone who had built a snowman on a path with a public order offence, and a child was prosecuted for chalking the pavement). Up to 70% of information is entered into police computers more than once, again to help achieve targets (falsely)[4022].

When a 12-year-old schoolgirl painted a single finger with nail polish in Boots to see how it looked, police were called because she couldn't pay the £6.29 for the Revlon item: she was held in an office for an hour before three officers arrived, and was only freed when her parents arrived to pay the cost of the polish. The police said they could forcibly restrain the girl because she was over 10[4023].

A headmaster risked being banned from teaching because of the criminal record he received for fishing with an out-of-date licence he had forgotten to renew with Kent Police[4024].

The Police Federation has revealed police had to stop probing a paedophile ring so they could pursue targets for less serious offences, while a senior detective and traffic officer were diverted to enforce seat-belt regulations in a specially-equipped car, instead of tracking known criminals[4025].

Scottish Police have labelled dozens of young children (one as young as two) as criminals[4026].

The neighbour of a senior police officer was arrested for 'criminal damage' – a tiny crack in a driveway. The case was, unbelievably, referred to the IPCC. The lady in question was photographed, fingerprinted and DNA taken[4027].

London Mayor Boris Johnson was being investigated by the Met's art and antiques unit in 2008, five years after admitting he took a souvenir from Baghdad (a cigar case from the home of Tariq Aziz), shortly after Saddam's fall[4028].

A sportsman who on principle refused to pay £3 to a rafting company was arrested by North Wales Police, his fingerprints, photo and DNA taken, and he was locked up. This was at the time when <u>Richard Brunstrom</u> was Chief Constable. The canoeist was arrested under Section 11 of the Fraud Act 2006[4029].

Two treasure hunters were arrested by a Nottinghamshire helicopter, four patrol cars and eight officers on foot – the hunters were using metal detectors in a field (the site was protected)[4030].

A Cheshire Police patrol car was diverted from attending a fatal crash to order a scarecrow's owner to dismantle it – it was dressed as a traffic officer for a competition. The owner was warned if he didn't he could be accused of impersonating a policeman[4031].

In 2008 a 76-year-old was led away to jail in handcuffs by Norfolk Police for not paying his council tax[4032].

A Kent police canteen cleaner was sacked and given a caution because he was filmed putting three spoons of coffee from a jar into his cup[4033].

Essex Police sent a helicopter to chase two boys who had nicked some plastic goalposts, with a dog team in pursuit on the ground[4034].

When a Bristol student chalked a slogan on the pavement four police arrested him – he was locked in a cell for two hours, his picture and DNA taken[4035].

When a Christian pensioner wrote to her council to object to a gay pride march, she received a visit from two police officers who told her she may have committed a hate crime. Her letter was 'an intention of hate', referring to homosexuals as 'sodomites' who spread sexual diseases as well as being responsible for the 'downfall of every empire'. Stonewall criticised the police's action, and the Christian Institute were investigating whether the police had breached the grandmother's rights to free speech and religious liberty[4036].

An elderly Blackpool widow was arrested and charged with assault for prodding a thug who was throwing stones at her window. He bruised her wrists but said this was in self-defence[4037].

Police Scotland decided, with all its problems with drugs and violent offending, to mount a licensing sting operation (Operation Cabinet) in Glasgow to catch a short-staffed bar owner at an early-morning pub who gave out only one roll and sausage (instead of two) to two undercover officers who were each having a beer. The senior officers who sanctioned the sting refused to explain why they thought it should be given priority[4038]. The High Court is being asked by the sheriff court to rule on a Bill of Suspension lodged by the defendant. This petitions the Court to dismiss the charges and award expenses to the barman defendant, who lost his job because the pub lost its breakfast licence.

Health and Safety

Not only did a retired police officer going on a walking holiday have his Swiss army knife confiscated at the airport, but he was also prosecuted: a judge acquitted him after he had suffered months of anguish.

Police readily attended an Essex primary school to ensure a ban by the headmistress on parents entering the playground (citing health and safety) went smoothly.

When a lost purse was handed into police it contained white tablets and a bank card which didn't belong to its elderly owner, a Sunday school teacher and former magistrate. The tablets were tested for drugs, the police apparently saying they were positive for cocaine. When the devout Christian and former nursery school head, who had been praised by the Queen, insisted they were sweeteners, a second test proved negative.

Torquay (Devon) police since 2006 have insisted (in pursuance of their zero tolerance policy) that a kebab shop has to hire a bouncer – which is financially crippling.

Essex Police have set up roadblocks to catch employees smoking in company cars. 'Sniffer' council wardens and uniformed officers will check inside vehicles for smoke. Firms allowing smoking in their mobile 'workplaces' can be fined £2,500[4039].

A sandwich seller who passed food to pupils through the school gates was asked to move on by Greater Manchester Police: the school had banned pupils from leaving the grounds at lunchtime without permission (some didn't like the school food)[4040].

Bizarre advice from the Department of Health said businesses should call the police if people refuse to extinguish cigarettes[4041].

Police are demanding 'risk assessments' from old soldiers and their families before a Remembrance Day parade is allowed[4042].

A student put his foot in a tube station lift door to keep it ajar for his friend. He was arrested by three BT Police and handed to three Met policemen, who handcuffed him, printed him, took his DNA and shoelaces and put in a cell. He was told he had not actually committed a criminal offence, but he could go home if he accepted a caution, which would afford the three cops a 'sanction detection'. Likewise children are being criminalised for building snowmen by the side of the road[4043].

The headmaster of a West Sussex school announced that PCSOs would enforce a safety test permit which would be needed before pupils would be allowed to ride their scooters to school. When parents declared the idea 'ridiculous' Sussex Police said its officers would only offer safety advice, despite their officers issuing permits at the initial session[4044].

An 86-year-old Gloucestershire cheesemaker,who has supplied an ancient cheese rolling event for a quarter of a century, had a 'heavy-handed' visit from three police officers who advised her to stop providing the 12 inch cheese, as she could be personally liable for any injuries sustained by participants[4045].

Firearms

Ex-policeman John Bacon says he and colleagues would list the officers they wouldn't want to turn up at an incident with a firearm, as they would cause them greater harm than the criminals. He suspects this is still true[4046].

Dorset Police raided a gift shop to seize 30 pocket calculators shaped like guns. They also seized 10 toy shotguns. They said the toys might breach the Violent Crime Reduction Act 2006. Police on occasion charge members of the public with wasting police time: what about when the police themselves waste police time? As usual, it seems there is one law for the constabulary[4047].

THE PERVERSE POLICEMAN

Four South Yorkshire patrol cars and two armed officers surrounded the car of a war games enthusiast who had a rare deactivated weapon in his possession. He was taken to a police station and charged with possessing an imitation firearm in a public place. After five court appearances he was allowed to keep the 1934 sub-machine gun[4048].

A member of a historical re-enactment society left his imitation gun visible in his car in readiness for a display the next day. Because he refused to let police destroy his props he was charged – he was given a year's conditional discharge for possessing an imitation firearm in a public place[4049].

A 12-year-old North Tyneside primary schoolboy was arrested on suspicion of possessing an imitation firearm[4050].

An American vicar working in England was jailed for keeping a tiny antique gun (a .22 derringer) hidden in his vicarage after suffering a burglary[4051].

A Scot who inherited a 125-year-old Belgian revolver from his hero grandfather as a boy, narrowly escaped a five-year sentence after being arrested by Lothian and Borders Police. He had played Cowboys and Indians with the gun[4052].

A white English historical arms collector is sure the police were monitoring his phone calls (police arriving at his house could only have known he had left a gun barrel out of its locked cabinet from a phone call to him to this effect from his wife). There have been a number of cases of licensed shotgun owners being harassed by police, e.g. confiscating guns if a husband tells his wife where he keeps the gun cabinet key[4053].

When Shropshire Police responded to a 'man wielding a gun' alert found the 'gun' was a sex toy tucked into the man's belt, they arrested him anyway[4054].

When a businessman frogmarched an assailant to a London police station – the thug had shot his son in the head – he was arrested by four police and incarcerated for seven hours, being told he was being held for assault with a deadly weapon (his car keys were 'mistaken' for a knife). The father said the police did nothing about the youths wandering around shooting people with an airgun[4055].

A man who pointed a toy light-up battery gun at a baby to make it laugh was arrested by Sussex Police who scrambled eight patrol cars and an armed unit to charge him with possessing an imitation firearm in a public place[4056]. A fancy dress party involving cowboy outfits with fake six-guns attracted a posse of armed Leicestershire Police with four cars and a helicopter[4057].

Over half of arrests for possessing firearms, and a third of arrests for possession of firearms with intent, result in no charges being brought[4058].

Three gamekeepers were hunted by North Yorkshire Police and dragged through the courts for tackling suspected poachers. They were charged with affray, and one with possessing a firearm with intent to cause a fear of violence. The suspects were not charged, but a jury found the keepers not guilty[4059].

Lothian and Borders Police charged a 'Braveheart' (William Wallace) impersonator with firearms offences after seizing his replica weapons (flintlock pistol and short muskets)

440

which can't be converted to firing guns. A film stuntsman who had been doing his act for 19 years, he can now no longer work in schools. Police have told him he will need a licence even if he has his guns returned. He would often have police and their horses stand beside him for tourists to take pictures[4060].

Five officers in unmarked cars, two with submachine guns, raided a house from which the householder had posted a picture of a toy mortar tube on Facebook (the police arrived <u>seven weeks</u> after the posting)[4061].

Other

It took two PCSOs, two regular officers and a police van to confront an 84-year-old war hero for cycling three yards through a pedestrianised shopping precinct. Their attitude was so aggressive the pensioner's bank manager called the police[4062]!

The bins of Gloucester households were left unemptied if the lids weren't fully closed. To deal with the residents' anger the council asked police to patrol during collections[4063].

A hungry nightshift worker who helped himself to a few of his colleague's biscuits was arrested by Newcastle Police for theft (his defence: he thought the company had bought the biscuits for staff). He was given a conditional discharge, but had to pay costs[4064].

Cambridgeshire Police were due (2010) to give heroin addicts free needles, and a manual about the most effective drug dose and the best veins to inject ('Harm Reduction Kits'), with the DH (Department of Health) backing the scheme[4065].

The police broke down journalist Janet Street-Porter's front door looking for cannabis (in vain), and removed items from her flat, but they didn't have a search warrant. Nine months later she was raided again, this time with a warrant, and the police claimed to have found a (tiny) amount of cannabis, which she denies was there. She pleaded guilty to avoid publicity, and was phobic about policemen for about five years.

A devoted son who took his terminally ill mother to a Swiss suicide clinic was arrested and questioned by police. Four detectives and two uniformed officers raided their house and removed documents and a computer.

When famous wartime test pilot Alex Hemshaw brought central Birmingham to a standstill by flying upside down over City Hall, the Chief Constable told him he had to make a statement to the police, but he refused (the Lord Mayor had arrogantly ordered him to give a city centre display).

An 83-year-old retired army captain was 'thrown in the back of a police van' for trying to save family treasures from his home, which was burning down: he was forced to watch his heirlooms going up in flames. He was arrested because he refused to stay out of the burning building, but he is suing Dyfed-Powis police for wrongful arrest. His wife was, he says, locked in the back of another police car: neighbours were also threatened with arrest if they tried to enter the house.

A West Midlands PCSO wrote a letter threatening sanctions against three little girls (aged three, four and seven), because of their 'intimidating' behaviour when playing out of doors[4066].

When a librarian with no convictions called Sussex Police because she had been threatened by a woman with a string of convictions, they arrested her instead, hooding her with a 'spit hood', taping her legs together and bundling her into a van in front of jeering onlookers. WPC Katrina Saunders was one of the officers who subjected the victim, rather than the perpetrator, to the degrading treatment. A court threw out the case against the victim, who was planning to sue the police[4067].

When Cherie Blair gently tapped a young prankster on his back with her right hand, six police officers were sent to investigate the incident at a sporting event (officials from Child Protection in Sport had referred the matter to Strathclyde Police).

Radio 2 DJ Jeremy Vine was forced by Cambridgeshire police to apologise after broadcasting a fake news story that Ian Huntley had been killed, even though the BBC had only a handful of complaints and it was clearly labelled as fictional.

Tesco staff called police because a driver wanted to pay for £95 worth of petrol in pound coins[4068].

Thames Valley Police confiscated (2011) the traditional starting pistol used in a historic Oxfordshire village fun run, saying it could be turned into a lethal weapon. They had sanctioned its use in 2000[4069].

When a muppet was delivered to a Scot's next-door-neighbour because he was out, he called Strathclyde Police, who, bizarrely, called on the neighbour to demand the return of the toy[4070].

When players and about 50 Old Firm fans turned up for a friendly game they were stunned that a dozen or so uniformed Strathclyde police had turned up with two vehicles[4071].

Vast numbers of homes are invaded and trashed by squatters, yet this until recently was a 'civil matter' to the police in England and Wales (not in Scotland). Yet the 'theft' of a kitten receives a conviction[4072].

Wigan Police have seized a plaque that honoured a Dunkirk survivor, who had just died, from a cross in a memorial garden. The friend who placed it there may be accused of criminal damage[4073].

An 11-year-old girl has been told by South Yorkshire Police (as represented by PC Alan Dickens) she cannot visit her sister's grave if she wears her school uniform: she visits it almost daily on her way home from school. PC Dickens told her mother that her daughter's uniformed presence in the Barnsley cemetery would give the school a bad reputation[4074].

Devon Police warned a 68-year-old farmer he would be arrested if he tried to force out travellers who had invaded his farm, but his landlord (the Dartmoor National Park Authority) has given him an enforcement notice. This means he must evict the invaders or face fines of up to £20,000[4075].

A member of the public seen on YouTube throwing a 19-year-old off a train because the latter didn't have a valid ticket and refused to get off at the conductor's request, was charged with assault by British Transport Police[4076].

Warwickshire Police raided a shopkeeper's village home when a drug dog mistook the odour of the legal evergreen creeper, moss phlox, for that of cannabis[4077].

When a son took his 104-year-old mother out of her care home in Somerset for Xmas lunch at his home, two policemen turned up demanding she be returned because there had been 'no prior warning' to care staff. The police insisted the son's action was contrary to his mother's Court of Protection order: he denied this, but was forced to return the old lady[4078].

When a father told police he had accidentally downloaded child porn he was banned from being alone with this young daughter until there had been a lengthy investigation (he thought it was a music site). He feels guilty till proved innocent. Humberside Police say there is a queue, so the inquiry could take a year[4079].

Dorset Police Tasered and gassed two stag night friends of a bridegroom, whom they made don a rude costume and tarred and feathered. The pair were then handcuffed, arrested and sentenced to wear tags. Their convictions were overturned when a judge saw CCTV of what happened[4080].

A Parkinson's patient who is a sports fan claims he was arrested at the Olympics by Surrey Police for not smiling enough, and taken to Reigate Police Station. He says officers asked him about his attitude and why he didn't appear to be enjoying the men's cycling road race. He was released after two hours of questioning. His medical condition makes smiling difficult[4081].

When a Reading trainee male nurse performed a citizen's arrest on a prowler he was arrested on suspicion of assault[4082].

A Manchester United fan was arrested and handcuffed at work for taking the Club's ball during a pitch invasion: he was spotted on CCTV[4083].

When a farmer forced travellers off his land with a digger – they had cut his gate padlock – Sussex Police threatened him with arrest[4084].

An honest student who handed in a mobile phone he had found was arrested by Merseyside Police for 'theft by finding'. He had phoned a friend of the owner to say he would leave it at the nearest police station. He was held for four hours and had his DNA taken[4085].

A young father who gave a dressing down during a 15 minute drive to an 11-year-old gang leader who was terrorising his sister, was given a year's supervision order plus community service, after being arrested and charged with kidnapping by Greater Manchester Police[4086].

A wealthy businessman was arrested by Sussex Police in front of his family over an email deemed 'offensive' to gypsies, though he hadn't written it. He was fingerprinted, his DNA taken – it is being held indefinitely despite his acquittal – and his computers seized[4087].

A mother who was overheard in a supermarket threatening to smack her children when they got home if they kept misbehaving, was secretly followed home by an off-duty policeman, who reported the incident – which is being kept on record – to Hampshire Police's child protection team. <u>Six weeks later</u> two officers arrived at her home[4088]. A Greater Manchester youth worker who slapped his 13-year-old daughter for 'terrorising' a neighbour was hauled off to the police station and locked in a cell. By agreeing to a caution he now acquired a criminal record for the first time (a s.39 offence of common assault on a minor)[4089]. Four police officers and a specialist child support officer arrested a father on suspicion of assault for smacking his seven-year-old son for wandering off[4090].

After a pensioner wrote to Norwich City Council objecting to its allowing a gay pride march, two policemen turned up at her home to question her about the 'hate incident' and lecture her about the 'effect words can have on other people'[4091].

A father whose house had been pelted with apples by youths tried to make a citizen's arrest, but he was arrested by Hertfordshire Police at his home and charged with common assault (he says before the police heard his side of the story). The case against him was dropped[4092].

Met Police helped close down a fast-food shop in 2009 for the crime of opening too near a Leytonstone school[4093].

A Cheshire man was cautioned for being 'in possession of an egg with intent to throw', while a West Midlands woman was arrested for criminal damage to a barrier when her foot slipped on her accelerator pedal, and a Cheshire pensioner who cut back a neighbour's conifers was also arrested for criminal damage. Two Manchester children were arrested for possession of a plastic toy pistol[4094].

Stephen Cragg is a criminal barrister who says the police often use disproportionate force and too many officers when they make an arrest. Complaining to the IPCC gives one only an 11% chance of a complaint being upheld. A senior cop told journalist Jenni Russell that if you give the police power they'll find a way to use it[4095].

A father was 'heartbroken' to find himself charged with assault for tackling thugs to stop his five-year-old son being mugged[4096].

A father of three confronted a drug dealer in the latter's home after finding his family had been supplied with heroin by the dealer, whose bags of heroin he flushed down the WC. The father was given two months in jail for invading the dealer's home[4097].

An 84-year-old grandfather, the former leader of Gwent County Council, faced an assault charge over claims by youths (who had been terrorising him for months) that he hit one of them with his walking stick. He had tried to persuade Gwent's Chief Constable that he and his wife had been made virtual prisoners in their flat, with their car severely vandalised. Their garage was jammed shut, they were verbally abused, etc. but the police arrested the husband anyway[4098].

When the eye of one of two schoolboys indulging in horseplay was hurt, the other was charged with GBH with intent – he was fingerprinted, etc.

Ayrshire PC <u>Stuart Gray</u> gave a £60 ticket to the driver of a stationary vehicle who blew his nose for 'not being in control of his vehicle', but the magistrate threw the case out. PC Gray, known as PC Shiny Buttons for his zealous approach, once gave a fixed penalty for littering to a person who dropped a £10 note accidentally[4099]. Strathclyde Police also gave a driver a £60 fine for blowing his nose while his van was at a standstill in traffic – again he was 'not in control of the vehicle'[4100].

A man attending a Surrey theme park whose paracetamol was mistaken for cocaine was arrested, handcuffed, ordered to strip, locked in a cell for seven hours and interrogated by Surrey CID officers[4101].

Two coachloads of carol singers – 90 members of an All-Women's Choir – were flagged down by motorcycle police, who signalled the coaches to follow them. When with flashing lights and screaming sirens they arrived at a football ground the ladies realised the police thought they were Chesterfield supporters on their way to a game, instead of them being given an escort to their Xmas concert[4102].

Lothian and Borders Police sent 18 officers to seize garden gnomes in dawn raids, suspecting they were stolen: one brother and sister were handcuffed as police searched their homes, despite claiming the garden items belonged to them (she says police even rummaged through her underwear drawer). The family were interrogated at Dalkeith police station[4103].

Ten Essex Police officers arrested and incarcerated (for five hours) a driver whom they thought had stolen the car he was driving – he hadn't. He was handcuffed, stripped and DNA and fingerprints taken before the cops realised they had made a mistake. They even breathalysed him in the street[4104].

A man punched by a Met officer (he claims it was Territorial Support Group Officer James Hendrick) was charged with assault himself – he was to sue for malicious prosecution and false imprisonment. The police failed to hand over to his solicitor a doctor's report and pictures of his injuries[4105].

Uniformed constables were to be posted at Christmas discos in two Scottish schools with breathalysers and 'dip strips' to check whether pupils have been drinking[4106].

A 55-year-old Clackmannanshire father of three said: 'It's unbelievable that I'm getting in trouble with the law for protecting an old woman'. An estate agent showing a pensioner round a drug den block of flats had reported him to police (who detained and grilled him at the local police station), because he warned the lady of the drinking and burglary in the flats[4107].

A Glasgow man was charged with feeding a sausage roll to a police horse, while a whole neighbourhood police team has been sacked after the officers were caught playing cards and cleaning golf clubs while on duty supposedly patrolling the streets[4108].

A Bournemouth preacher convicted for 'harassment' after being assaulted by pro-gay hecklers had been displaying a placard saying 'Stop Homosexuality'. He was pelted with mud but police arrested <u>him</u> and he was fined £300[4109].

The parents of two siblings were arrested, handcuffed and locked up over a nappy burn. The children were taken away for eight months[4110].

445

A Lincolnshire farmer was threatened with arrest when, having called police to evict ravers on his land, he tried to evict them himself because they refused to intervene (this was apparently because there were only 70 trespassers, not the statutory 100). The police deliberately overlooked the criminal damage the ravers were causing, the farmer claimed . Essex Police arrested a landowner corporate financier when he tried to stop a ravers' party in one of his barns (they had broken through a padlocked gate) by unplugging an electric lead. The barn had already been broken into by revellers in the same month[4112].

Gwent Police placed GP Dr. John Diggle under surveillance for weeks, photographing his house round the clock from across the street. A neighbour had complained the GP's son had thrown an egg at his car: the neighbour was a former cop. The GP received police compensation of £50,000[4113].

When a Tory candidate threatened vandals, rather than pursue the vandals themselves, the police's first reaction was to prosecute him[4114].

A farmer who shot at a vehicle being driven straight at his mother by a thief was arrested and held on suspicion of attempted murder. The farmer says: 'It [the experience] has completely changed my view of the police. They have acted like bullies who have turned someone who was very supportive into someone who wants nothing more to do with them'[4115].

Until the change in the English law on squatters (making squatting a criminal offence) police often didn't treat forced entry and vandalism as enough evidence of illegal occupation. In one case a Romanian gang changed the locks and installed their own furniture, but the Met accused the owner of racism when he questioned the squatters' right to live in Britain on benefits[4116].

When an ex-serviceman collared a stone-throwing youth, the police 'hotline' left him on hold. Then when officers arrested him on suspicion of kidnap and charged him with assault the CPS went along with this travesty of justice[4117].

Almost 70% of Britons want to see PCSOs scrapped: in 2007 the hiring of 16-year-olds was banned. A Manchester man spent 18 hours in a police cell after he was stopped by a PCSO for dropping an apple core[4118].

After a mother confronted a group of playground bullies at her daughter's Tyne and Wear school, she was arrested at home, handcuffed and incarcerated for over five hours: ten cops in three police cars and a van were required, even though a statement by one of the bullies that she had been hit by the mother had been withdrawn. The police soon dropped the case[4119].

A 20-officer unit led by Inspector Nevin Hunter of Devon and Cornwall Police was touring Britain with special powers to seize black market caviar from top restaurants. The unit is under the control of Defra's Animal Health division[4120].

The Met are moving on street ice cream vendors (as well as burger and hot-dog vans) in Harlow in case they 'cause a nuisance' or make children fat. Customers are told brusquely to go home[4121].

Devon and Cornwall Police arrested a gardener on his way to a job, charging him with having offensive weapons (he carried axes, a scythe and knives for clearing undergrowth). When he was cleared, the judge ordered prosecutors to give him a public apology[4122].

A grieving mother who watched her son die of an asthma attack was arrested by South Yorkshire Police for his manslaughter 'because the coroner had raised concerns' (but he had already issued a death certificate with the cause as asthma). The police arrived at her home 12 days after the death with dogs and riot vans. She was held in custody for eight hours[4123].

Gloucestershire Constabulary smashed down a pensioner's front door when she failed to answer the phone, then charged her £100 for repairing it. She had been out at the shops before discovering officers in her home[4124].

Warwickshire Police threatened a woman, who had taken her mother from a care home to live with her, with smashing in her door with a battering ram if the old lady was not handed over and forced back to the home she didn't like. The daughter called it a 'gestapo' raid[4125].

In 2009 Cambridgeshire police concentrated on street football as a priority target, while Moray Council in Scotland was actually recruiting a £20,000 a year 'Street Football Coordinator' to encourage street football[4126].

A bagpipe busker was arrested and his instrument seized by Dorset Police because he was causing shop staff 'distress'[4127].

A father of two was smashed in the face by bottle-wielding vandals, so that he nearly lost an eye before his house sustained a barrage of bottles. He had been awakened by his wife as they besieged the house. He chased them away, but when the police belatedly arrived they arrested him, though he was bleeding heavily, on suspicion of assault[4128].

Met Police charged a filmmaker with stealing electricity worth 0.003p (he had turned on the supply momentarily in order to turn off an alarm which would bother neighbours). He was held in a cell for six hours[4129].

An Ayr man charged with 'having sex with a bicycle' was given three years probation and placed on the Sex Offenders' Register[4130].

A Berkshire company director who challenged a gang of young thugs attacking his stepson outside his home – he allegedly stabbed one – was arrested on suspicion of attempted murder. His wife claims her life was threatened. His Jaguar car had been repeatedly vandalised[4131].

When Stephen Lawrence's family refused to release to the Met their 'Blue Book', which contained details of supporters coming to their home from all over the country, they were bizarrely accused of interfering with the police investigation into Stephen's murder[4132].

MSP Margo MacDonald said of Police Scotland's crackdown on Edinburgh saunas: 'Stephen House has taken a developed policy that has had the acquiescence of civic society and destroyed it'[4133].

THE PERVERSE POLICEMAN

A Del Boy impersonator was ordered by Sussex Police to deflate a sex doll he was driving around Bognor Regis as a stunt recreating an 'Only Fools and Horses' episode. He was threatened with arrest under the Public Order Act[4134].

CHAPTER XXII

THE POLITICAL POLICEMAN

CONTENTS

CHAPTER XXII

THE POLITICAL POLICEMAN

Introduction

Former Home Secretary Kenneth Baker: 'The police must be above politics in our country'[4135]. It can be difficult to determine whether it is politics or managerialism (itself originally a political imposition, but since growing exponentially) which has been responsible for at least 15 major structural changes to the service (e.g. justified by Asset Management Plans) in recent times, the gradual withdrawal of service, often by stealth, the outsourcing of even core functions to less accountable private agencies, superspecialisation (throwing up a myriad of specialisms such as POLSA – Police Search Adviser), etc. Several decades ago the London Borough of Newham had five custody suites, soon to be reduced from two to one. Officers are increasingly patrolling only in vehicles from 'warehouse-style' buildings situated well away from residential areas. Who is deciding these huge changes? Certainly not the public.

Scottish forces used to be accountable to local police boards, which included politicians. Now in a centralising move the watchdog Scottish Police Authority (SPA) has replaced these, its members being appointed by the Scottish Government[4136]. The Chief Constable of Scotland's single force is battling with Vic Emery, head of the Scottish Police Authority, over who is to control civilian staff and who will control force finances and other services. The two have consulted lawyers to resolve the power struggle[4137]. Within weeks of the inauguration of Police Scotland, the watchdog SPA was in disarray, as a 'crisis of leadership' developed with the loss of three senior staff (the chief executive, the finance director and the strategy planning and performance director)[4138].

In Greece POASY, the powerful police union, has threatened to arrest members of the troika (the EU, the IMF and the European Central Bank)[4139].

The traditional story of policing suggests a picture of the pristine bobby as more or less a citizen in uniform, having his primary relationship with the local community. But now coppers are instruments of the state, with central control by politicians and high-flying graduate policing professionals[4140]. An anonymous officer said in 2008: 'Politics currently control the police'[4141]. ACPO president Ken Jones has called for a written constitution for the constabulary to deal with the complaint that the police are being used by the government for political purposes[4142].

UK police are torn between their national and local functions, whereas other countries (e.g. France and Italy) separate them.

Three Scottish police officers are being sent to Malawi to train that country's forces to deal with public disorder (during the 2011 riots there 20 were shot dead)[4143].

Ships' captains were blacklisted if they refused to command Victorian 'coffin ships' (overinsured so they were more profitable if they sank), and refusenik seamen were jailed. Police were used to escort ships with recalcitrant crews until they were too far from land for the sailors to swim ashore[4144]. The old, locally accountable system was essentially to police local byelaws passed by councils who were also responsible for ensuring their enforcement. The Met, which comes low on the efficiency table, ironically thinks it is best qualified to run the more efficient forces. The nationalisation denied to Sir Robert Peel is coming to pass, and state police is the essential precursor to a police state. A Scottish history professor and leading military expert at Oxford University has suggested an independent Scotland could militarise Police Scotland so it could join the EGF (European Genarmerie Force) alongside five other countries[4145].

The Special Patrol Group (SPG), which morphed into the Territorial Support Group (TSG), was widely reported to have started to operate as a paramilitary unit[4146]. The early Victorian militaristic police are on the way back.

Role-play exams for promotion-seeking officers have been described as 'absurd', putting some off climbing the ladder. Chief Constable Peter Neyroud said: 'I have so many officers in acting sergeant and acting inspector posts that it is like having a cast of thespians. They cannot be confirmed in their jobs because they have not passed the Home Office exam. To insist on a test that is no indicator of the competence of an officer is the politics of the madhouse'. The 'Objective Structured Performance Related Examination' was brought in by the Tories in 1991[4147], presumably on the advice of nameless and unaccountable psychologists.

The first Met Commissioner, Sir Richard Mayne, wrote: 'The primary object of an efficient police is the prevention of crime, the next that of detection and punishment of offenders'[4148]. Now there is little pretence at prevention, detection is falling and punishment increasingly dumbed-down.

Applications for consideration as elected police commissioners include TV presenters, glamour models, ex-cops and ex-army personnel[4149].

Theresa May's move to allow foreign senior cops to become chief constables was described by one of the latter, now retired, as 'a smack in the face for police leadership'[4150].

George V threatened the blackmailing mistress of his father (Edward VII), Daisy Warwick, with committal by police to Holloway Prison: she backed down.

Civilian managers ('organisation men') enjoy the rank and emoluments of chief inspectors: female managers like to be addressed as 'Ma'am'[4151].

'Too many policy chiefs see their constabularies as the shock troops of New Labour, promoting Marxist orthodoxies rather than fighting crime'[4152].

State's Enforcers

It is not well understood that forces such as the MOD Police (and others) are not accountable to Parliament yet carry arms (and may use them), institute covert surveillance, and wear uniforms identical to Home Office forces instead of those more appropriate to elite security guards. An amalgamation in 2004 of the MOD Guard Service (a civilian body) and the MOD Policing Agency, the MOD Police (the Ministry of Defence Police and Guarding Agency) are allowed by 'Concordats' to operate heavily armed patrols beyond military sites (over 75% of their 2,500 officers are armed). As MOD Police may not be as well-trained as regular firearms officers, concerns have been raised as to whether junior MOD officers would have the necessary judgment as to when to use their weapons. Thus Wiltshire Constabulary depends on MOD Police for over 30 military bases, but this arrangement has never been scrutinised.

Europol's officers have diplomatic immunity. The EIO (European Investigation Order) does not allow a crime's 'proportionality' to be considered. Designs backed by Interpol have been made for a European police car, which could one day patrol British streets[4153]. Ferenc Banfi, a former Hungarian communist and now director of the EU's Bramshill police academy in Hampshire, has predicted there will be an EU FBI-style, cross-border force within a decade. However, the Home Office says no such force is being planned in Britain – this contradicts Banfi's statement that British intelligence experts are leading talks[4154]. The European Gendarmerie Force (EGF) is the first police organisation to come under direct EU control and is composed of 800 paramilitaries from several countries (not the UK).

Superintendent Steve Pearl, head of the domestic extremism police squad, was forced to resign just days before anarchists invaded the Tory Party headquarters – the unit's commander, the National Coordinator for Domestic Extremism, also retired. This may have been partly responsible for the disastrous handling of the activists, and the major reorganisation of NETCU (National Extremism Tactical Coordination Unit) – it was to be merged with the National Public Order Intelligence Unit and the Confidential Intelligence Unit – may well have contributed[4155]. The Met wouldn't or couldn't put anyone up to discuss the Millbank riot on Channel 4 (11.11.10).

Sir Ian Blair proposed in 2005 that the police should be allowed to bypass the courts by seizing vehicles and driving licences without going before a judge: he describes this iconoclastic suggestion as 'modernisation'[4156]. In the past chief constables tended to interpret legislation so as to maintain the political status quo. Thus, as virtual civil servants they were never apolitical, e.g. police acting as strike-breakers in the Tonypandy riots in 1910. They interpreted the law during the 1984 miners' strike as giving police the right to prevent lawful movement around the country.

An MSP called for an independent probe into 'harassment and victimisation' of Celtic fans by Strathclyde Police – the Green Brigade say police formed a kettling cordon for

Sir Ian Blair

no good reason. A leading QC compared the actions of about 200 cops with a police state[4157].

Protests

Liberal commentators have described the Victorian Met patrolling the poor districts of the East End as similar to an army of occupation. Police were invoked to protect blackleg labour. The most important operation for the Met acting as a sort of national riot squad was the sending of 90 police officers to Birmingham in 1839 to deal with Chartist demonstrations. But at one stage the police had to be rescued from the Bull Ring by the Army[4158]. In 1910 police charged Sutton Workhouse inmates with drawn truncheons when rioters demanded tea with bread and butter instead of porridge for supper[4159]. In 1912 the Government ordered the police to raid the HQ of the suffragettes, who were arrested[4160]. The same year hungry families were turned away from food depots, threatening them with starvation[4161]. The Met clashed with anarchists, socialists, Jews and Irish while protecting blackshirts in Cable Street, East London, in 1936[4162].

It has been claimed Aberdeenshire Police (Police Scotland) have acted as a private police force for Donald Trump, who is accused of bullying landowners. His proposed but largely abortive developments have the SNP government's backing[4163]. Grampian Police were to be asked by MSPs to respond to charges that they exceeded their powers while dealing with opponents of the controversial US tycoon[4164].

Manpower shortages led to the first Special Patrol Group in London in 1965. This was a mobile unit designed to support the constabulary in areas with, say, a high crime rate, but by 10 years later it was more or less an anti-riot squad[4165]. In 2006 Tony Blair ordered police to step up operations against animal rights extremists, and 2007 saw Britain's biggest ever crackdown by 700 police. One of the raids was on a re-homing animal welfare centre which had nothing to do with animal rights[4166].

In 1907 mounted police dispersed 800 suffragettes outside the Commons and in 1910 there was a battle outside Parliament between 400 suffragettes and 600 police on 'Black Friday'[4167], when officers beat, brutalised and sexually assaulted suffragettes. There was a cover-up over the assaults.

In 1960 over 500 police officers battled with rent protesters marching on St. Pancras Town Hall[4168]. Chief Constable Sir Norman Bettison of West Yorkshire asked for emergency powers in 2010 to ban the English Defence League from marching through a Bradford Muslim neighbourhood[4169]

A century ago Argyll County Police sergeant Norman Morrison was 'sacked', reinstated, and won a fight against a decision to retire him on ill-health, yet he was the principal founder of the Scottish Police Federation. He and two colleagues, Constables Campbell and Ross, were 'compulsorily' retired – Morrison campaigned for improvement in pay and conditions (e.g. a weekly rest day), being ordered to withdraw from the National Union of Police and prison officers[4170].

Paul McKeever, chairman of the Police Federation, has said officers patrolling anti-cut demonstrations would have 'a lot of sympathy' with the protesters[4171].

More than 600 innocent delegates, peace activists, visitors and Blair opponents were detained by Sussex Police at the 2006 Labour Party conference in Brighton under the

Terrorism Act (introduced to deal with violent fanatics) as part of 'Operation Otter': none were suspected of violent intent. The detainees had to fill in a form giving name, address, age and ethnicity, and these data were stored. One 80-year-old was stopped, searched and questioned for wearing a politically incorrect (i.e. anti-Blair) T-shirt (a woman also claimed she was prevented from entering a shopping centre for wearing similar apparel). Operation Otter cost an estimated £3 million, involving 1,300 officers using 'section 44' powers.

250 officers were used to arrest two men (2006) believed (wrongly) to be in possession of a chemical bomb, while Sir <u>Ian Blair</u> used 78 officers (at a cost of £7,200) in the middle of the night to disperse a cardboard display protesting against the Iraq War in Parliament Square. The police action against the pacifists was described as a 'huge over-reaction'. <u>Sir Ian</u> was forced to admit that he misled the Metropolitan Police Authority about the cost of removing anti-war hoardings from outside Parliament: it did <u>not</u> cost only £7,200, rather over £27,000. In 2005 14 officers were deployed to arrest pacifist Maya Evans, who had read out the names of British soldiers who had died in Iraq.

Police were widely criticised over the arrest of 25 peaceful pollution protesters at Nottingham East Midlands Airport in 2006. A teenager and a 21-year-old student were held in solitary confinement for 36 hours, not even allowed a phone call. Their money, keys and mobiles were confiscated. The student's computer – which had essential coursework on it – was seized from her flat. Police broke down the door of a 17-year-old's mother's house and a college lecturer's computer was seized from his home, even though it was his daughter who was at the protest.

A male nurse named Agency Nurse of the Year for 2006 was searched by police for shouting 'boo' at Tony Blair. They also took his date of birth and contact number.

The police ban demonstrations outside Westminster while Parliament is sitting, which defeats the object of protest. The Peterloo Massacre by drunk yeoman constables – sent in by the Deputy Constable to suppress peaceful protesters led by the radical orator Henry Hunt, who preached universal suffrage – killed 15, and left 650 injured. Many more women reformers in the crowd were cut by sabres – they were particularly hated by the authorities.

Over £5m was spent in 10 months policing the 2007 anti-nuclear protests at the Scottish Faslane submarine base: there were over 900 arrests[4172].

A carnival team of 17 dressed as Ali Baba and the 40 Thieves and wearing burkhas – meant as a send-up of Prince Charles's plan for a mosque near Newquay – were sent home by Devon and Cornwall Police accused of racism[4173].

Dorset Police officers who used work computers to sign up to an online petition to protest against Labour plans for road tolls could be disciplined[4174].

In 1961 the Met's Commissioner <u>Sir Joseph Simpson</u> banned a ban-the-bomb demo due to take place in Trafalgar Square[4175]. Devon & Cornwall Police used special dispersal orders to move crowds off Polzeath Bay beach in 2007. It is claimed they incarcerated one boy in a cell because he refused to move off the beach at curfew[4176].

20 Strathclyde Police swooped at dawn on a North Lanarkshire primary school to end a parents' protest[4177]. Fife Constabulary were (2002) investigating allegations that Strathclyde officers were heavy-handed with protesters at the closure of a Glasgow swimming pool[4178].

When Prince Charles married Camilla at Windsor Register Office, police forcibly removed people who were protesting quietly about her suitability as a future queen consort[4179].

Work and Pensions Secretary Iain Duncan Smith asked the police to get tough on anti-capitalist protestors who claimed young people were being forced to work for nothing and were invading shops to sabotage the welfare-to-work scheme[4180].

Met Commander Christine Jones was heavily criticised for condoning disrespectful demos at Mrs. Thatcher's funeral, and for suggesting protesters contact police if they want to stage a demo[4181].

Strikes

During the 1984-5 miners' strike some police behaved poorly, and some boasted about the overtime the strike was bringing them. The police's behaviour suggested they were becoming the enforcers of an oppressive authoritarian state, with ordinary policing continuing as a backdrop. In 1984 they charged striking miners at the 'Battle of Orgreave' in South Yorkshire[4182]. During the strike police from all over UK used to stop men who were lawfully travelling to pickets. The arrested were warned about civil actions[4183]. The 'A', 'E' and 'D' Divisions of the Met were involved in hand-to-hand fighting at Coldbath Fields with union members of the NUWC, who had been demonstrating peacefully. During the strike there was no question but that the police were 'Maggie's Boys'[4184]. In the aftermath of the strike Fife Constabulary secretly demanded a legal crackdown on union rights, i.e. enhance public disorder policing powers (e.g. making mass picketing illegal), upgrading the sanctions allowed by the Conspiracy and Protection of Property Act, 1875. This revelation obtained under the FOIA has prompted calls (e.g. from the NUM) for an inquiry into police behaviour, which led to the criminalisation of 500 protesting miners, with resulting heavy fines and dismissal. The 1985 Fife report recognised the policing methods made the public so angry they had badly damaged trust in the police (see also The Trustless Policeman chapter)[4185].

In 2010 Scots police chiefs were at loggerheads with unions over plans to give more protection to workers who deal with the public: USDAW blasted police opposition – they think a new law unnecessary, and don't want the Emergency Workers Act (which covers police, fire and ambulance personnel only) extended in any way[4186].

In 1911 striking Welsh miners in Clydach Vale threw stones at police and colliery officials, besieging them in a hotel[4187]. In the same year London police were sent to Hull to fight thousands of striking workers[4188], and armed police (over 1,600 special constables) were brought in to try to break the London dock strike. Birkenhead was a flashpoint, and a demo on St. George's Plateau on August 13 (Bloody Sunday) was violently suppressed: 'As policemen were aiming cruel blows upon the heads of men, women and children ... dozens lay bleeding and unconscious, citizens were to be seen lying helpless on the ground', reported an eyewitness. The police ensured that film of the protests had the scenes of their attacks on the crowd edited out[4189].

During the miners' and other strikes the police were always there first, thanks to routine phone-tapping, which chief constables always denied. Though in 1985 guidelines were issued by Strasbourg as to when phones could be tapped, there was no right to know if one's phone had been tapped, and, if considered to be in the public interest, it could be kept secret (e.g. in N. Ireland). For decades before this even terrorists in the USA had the right to know they were under surveillance.

According to Anthony Wedgewood Benn, Arthur Scargill was physically attacked on a platform by a "working miner". According to the press it was in fact a retired policeman who launched the assault.

There were violent confrontations between police and strikers at Grunwick (1978) and Wapping (the mid-eighties)[4190], and during the Winter of Discontent there was fighting between police and bakery workers outside a Berkshire factory[4191].

When in 2008 the lorry drivers were on strike the Labour Government ensured there were plenty of police available to hold up the truckers and give them warnings[4192].

An anonymous former senior officer, who worked in Glasgow and Lothian and Borders, has told how he was 'so appalled' by the actions of colleagues during the miners' strike that he refused to take part in policing it. He says police would throw coins at miners and taunt them: they had a 'gang mentality' and admitted they enjoyed a 'good battle', relishing their soubriquet of 'Maggie's boot boys'. They would, he said, just throw miners in a van without proper evidence[4193]. South Yorkshire Police refused an interview with BBC News re Orgreave (1980's miners' strike) revelations[4194].

Immigrants

Lancashire Police forcibly rounded up over 1,300 Chinese ex-merchant seamen who were settled with their families in Liverpool. Their repatriation happened during the early years of WWII[4195].

Greater Manchester Chief Constable and ACPO spokesman Peter Fahy has been criticised as 'utterly irresponsible' and 'inflammatory' after saying government cuts could put children at risk, even appearing to attack ministers by commenting 'Whitehall doesn't get it'. The Daily Mail commented that Fahy 'should concentrate on the 90% of police officers who aren't available to protect the public at any one time, rather than the 10% who are … his job as a privileged and well-paid public servant is to implement policy, not participate in agitprop politics'. Fahy, when ACPO's diversity spokesperson, said the 'migrant crimewave' is a myth, but when his report was made public it said: ' EU accession migrants are continuing to present challenges across a range of police activity'. Fahy admits 'We've kept that number [of police officers] artificially high'[4196]. In fact figures extracted from 19 British forces in 2011 under FOIA show arrests of foreigners had almost doubled in three years: the largest rises were in forces managing rural areas (e.g. in four years Cambridgeshire saw a 17,689% rise, Durham a 62.9% rise). The total in 2010 was 91,234 foreign nationals, compared with 51,899 in 2008, but the true number is likely to be much higher, as 33 forces technically broke the law by not providing figures[4197].

The Met's Bob Quick has been cited as an example of an 'ultra-politicised' police chief, whose arrest of Damian Green was a blatant breach of the right to free speech (on immigration)[4198]. In 2006 ACPO opposed Home Secretary John Reid's plan to transfer hundreds of officers to shore up his failing Immigration Service. The police chiefs said they wouldn't provide the officers[4199].

Centralisation

ACPOS were backing a single Scottish force, after previous attempts at unification met fierce opposition. Such central control was naturally favoured by the managerial elite of the service. But centralisation would make the north-east of Scotland more vulnerable to crime[4200].

The SNP Scottish Government has declared that two founding principles of Police Scotland are (1) protecting the public from 'Westminster cuts' and (2) 'enhancing national governance', rather than upholding the law and catching criminals. Critics have now called Scotland a 'police state'[4201].

The argument that it will save money is unconvincing, as this didn't happen in England, according to the Scottish Police Federation[4202].

David Copperfield, former Staffordshire PC Stuart Davidson, who has decamped to Canada, says British policing is now a job creation scheme for bureaucrats, and that only 50% of people in the Greater Manchester Police area think the police are doing an 'excellent or good' job. He says with less money and far fewer police they do a better job in Edmonton than GMP. In Canada a superintendent would take a close interest in, say, burglaries, but never in the UK, where they are not hands-on. In Canada there are no hordes of crime auditors, crime management units, policing pledge compliance teams, etc[4204]. The Tories are committed to return to 1950s-style policing by introducing Canadian-style directly-elected police commissioners to run forces across Britain.

There has been a crescendo of disapproval over the election of police chiefs proposal, e.g. from ACPO, worried about political interference risks, and the Association of Police Authorities says 'turmoil may be unleashed'[4205].

SOCA replaced (2006) the NCS (National Crime Squad, founded 1998), and was replaced itself (2013) by the National Crime Agency (NCA). Though the NCA has a much wider remit (e.g. child protection, cybercrime and border policing) it is not being allowed more funds (the changes to all its logos will be costly). Critics say it is merely a rebranding exercise[4206]. NCA is controlled directly by the Government, yet its head can issue orders to chief constables, who are therefore no longer independent of government. The NCA's officers are civil servants who can be given a sworn constable's powers of arrest, etc, and have to obey their superiors who may issue politically biased orders. Robert Peel would turn in his grave[4207].

Terrorism

Politician David Davies has revealed that when Bob Quick, past Chief Constable of Surrey, became head of Special Operations at the Yard, he was ignorant of a fundamental piece of law about charging terrorist suspects, and in arresting Damian Green he was not enforcing the law, he was inventing new law[4208].

Labour was accused (2010) of keeping the nation in a permanent 'state of emergency' to justify authoritarian anti-terror laws[4209].

The Met used stop and search powers to escort three pensioners from Heathrow after the five officers present decided the 'Stop Airport Expansion' logo on their T-shirts was 'inflammatory'. They would be arrested if they returned within 24 hours – the pensioners were headed for a march in the village of Sipson. One of the pensioners – a retired emeritus reader in psychology – said the police's manner was 'overbearing and arrogant'[4210].

Britain is at risk of 'coming close to a police state', the Archbishop of York warned after the arrest of terrorist suspects in Birmingham[4211].

Pensioner Walter Wolfgang, a staunch Labourite whose family were victims of the Nazis, was manhandled from the 2005 Labour Party Conference by burly stewards (a constituency party chairman who protested about his ejection was also manhandled). When he tried to re-enter the Brighton venue he was arrested under anti-terror laws. The conference was described as more like a national socialist rally – there were cheerleaders to encourage applause and yellow-garbed stewards to stifle dissent[4212]. During the conference Sussex Police detained 600 innocent people, with forms completed detailing name, address, age and ethnicity. The misuse of anti-terrorism laws (no detainee was arrested or charged) has even been seen stopping cyclists running red lights in London[4213].

Sir Ian Blair warned in 2007 – to justify to the Commons Home Affairs Select Committee an increase of the 28-day limit (for holding without charge) to 50-90 days – that Britain faced an 'epidemic' of terrorist plots. These, he said, were becoming more numerous, ambitious and sophisticated. Blair also wanted children at risk of joining criminal gangs to be taken into care, even though children's homes have a terrible record of allowing young children to get into crime[4214]. It was claimed Tony Blair 'politicised' police chiefs with regard to new anti-terror laws. It was said MPs received phone calls, e-mails and letters from chief constables, at the behest of ACPO[4215]. Since leaving the Met under a cloud Blair has been campaigning for a change in the law on assisted dying.

Politics have severely emasculated the antiterrorist capacity of the Police Service of Northern Ireland, now being riddled with political correctness. During the Troubles, possibly a third of IRA volunteers were Special Branch informants, but MI5 is not an adequate substitute for Special Branch, not having the local knowledge they need any more[4216].

The chairman of Enfield's (North London) park society was informed by the Met he had breached S. 44 of the Terrorism Act, because he had filmed police driving their car erratically across the park[4217].

A 12-year-old's Facebook protest led to his being threatened with arrest by anti-terror police. He was hauled from his class in Oxfordshire, just because he wanted to save youth centres from the axe[4218].

A white trainee accountant made a jokey threat on Twitter to blow up Robin Hood Airport. As a result a week later he was being quizzed by Doncaster Police as a potential terrorist, though he was eventually merely prosecuted for making a nuisance call. He lost his appeal against his fine and sentence, and he was sacked from his job. The 'Spartacus Campaign' to support him soon took off, and at one point it was the most popular subject on

Twitter worldwide: 15,000 people made their own tongue-in-cheek threats to bomb the airport[4219].

When police arrived to arrest Lana Vandenberghe, the secretary who leaked information about the shooting of de Menezes, they smashed down her door, but she was never charged or prosecuted.

An example of the police's obsession with the weapon rather than the person who might use it is that of the accountant who was seen holding a cricket ball by a policewoman. She revealed to him it was a 'very hard object' and ticked him off for possessing a 'potentially lethal weapon': he should not be carrying it in public.

A Birmingham man, a one-legged NHS worker, who bought materials on eBay to make fireworks for a family party, had his home smashed into by West Midlands Police three months later, because they thought he was a terrorist. The police refused to say who had provided the information[4220].

The Terrorism Act is a gift to the officious 'perverse' policeman, e.g. a woman was arrested under it for walking on a cyclist-only path[4221].

Under the 2000 Terrorism Act a Dundonian was arrested by two squad cars for walking along a cycle path: she was put in the cells. In London a cricketer was challenged to explain why he was carrying a bat, while an 11-year-old was stopped and told to empty her pockets. Police bosses have been rewarded with up to £19,000 in performance bonuses, so they have a vested interest, not in preventing crime, but in criminalising as many of the public as possible. In the nineties police could only arrest people for something serious, now one can be arrested for anything[4222]. Amnesty International has condemned the use of section 7 of the Act to intimidate a journalist (David Miranda) at Heathrow Airport – he was working on a whistleblower story. The Home Secretary said it was the police, not the Home Office, who decided to use the power (which should only have been used to question the suspect if section 40(1) allowed it). Miranda claims the police threatened him with prison[4223].

A Hartlepool lorry driver was charged with arson for holding a bonfire on Bonfire Night. 14 police officers had raided his fireworks party on the village green, incarcerating the hapless organizer and taking his fingerprints and DNA[4224].

Social Work

The home of a dog-breeder and his wife (a vice-chairman of her local Tory Party) was invaded by two RSPCA officials and 18 policemen, who had been tipped erroneously that the couple had guns. Their child was taken into care, and the wife had a miscarriage in a police cell. The child was told her parents were dead, and for three years they tried to have her returned via 74 court hearings. The child was adopted. The 1989 Children Act allows such Kaffkaesque tragedies: social engineering by the social services routinely involves the police service[4225].

The police seem exceedingly compliant in supporting the seizure of children by social workers, being prepared to act with unnecessary aggression against defenceless mothers, according to Telegraph journalist Christopher Booker, and Sir Paul Stephenson himself said in late 2010 that 'providing cover for social workers, etc.' had taken the police 'away from their core responsibilities'[4226].

The police seem to be willing to assist the extreme measures to which the family protection system will go to hide its activities from responsible scrutiny by the media and Parliament. A mother who, seven months pregnant, wanted to protest to her MP about the conduct of her case, was arrested and held in police cells intermittently over 2½ days (at one point she was dragged by police from her hospital bed after midnight to spend another spell in a dirty cell)[4227].

Unit Beat Policing

The Chief Constable of Lancashire Eric St. Johnston reorganised policing in Kirby (celebrated in 'Z Cars'), with a central foot patrol and the surrounding areas patrolled by cars only: 'Unit Beat Policing'. This development in the1930s was the start of the slide down the slippery slope to our present situation, when the ambulant officer is almost extinct. By 1968 60% of the population of England and Wales were subjected to this new style of policing[4228].

In 2007 the Sunday Express was running a 'Police Crusade' to get readers to support moving police back into their communities[4229].

Strathclyde's Chief Constable Steve House promised to introduce 'old-style policing with a hard edge', with the number of police on patrol daily to rise from 500 to 2,600, who will operate in 194 beats. He also wanted to force out officers after 30 years' service[4230].

The number of new police trainees at Scotland's Police College in 2010 was cut by 90% - now down to 19 compared with 197 in 2009. As officers can't be made redundant, 'middle' and 'back office' civilian workers will be replaced by trained officers, who will be lost to the front line[4231]. The Home Office is to replace the discredited four-year-old SOCA (Serious Organised Crime Agency) with a National Crime Squad.

Now that there are substantially more (196,000) police and they're comparatively well paid, the paradox is that we never actually see them[4232]. Regular foot patrolling ('bobbies on the beat') was stopped by the Home Office's Police Advisory Board in 1966 (without consulting the public), since when foot patrols are only occasionally used for special occasions (e.g. after a series of three rapes in Glasgow city centre in 2010), or in circumscribed areas in some city centres[4233].

Just 10% of police time is spent on patrol, and at any one time only 3.5% of officers (in one force only 1.2%) are available for emergency response[4234]. To make up the deficit the Home Office wants the public to patrol with police, as well as introducing part-time reservists to protect villages. There will also be 'virtual' beat meetings on social websites[4235]. Labour's law and order election strategy (2010), which claimed that neighbourhood police spend 80% of their time 'on the beat', was heavily criticised by the Advertising Standards Authority[4236], as this figure included time spent in meetings.

The new managerialised and psychologised policing doesn't recognise the crucial importance of beat patrols, rather is all about response times, targets, 'measurable performances', etc., mirroring the MBA mantras of the best business universities. Police 'effectiveness' is converted into its bottom-line cost[4237]. The hidden and unaccountable puppeteers of such practices may be the modern equivalent of industrial psychologists.

The big new idea that policing should be run as a business explains the closure of 600 police stations in a decade with another 40 under threat in 2007. Closure means more police have to spend more time travelling to work, with less time on the beat[4238]. The police are trying to <u>detect</u> crime as their main aim, but public want, firstly, crime to be prevented, secondly, community policing, thirdly, foot patrols. Peel said (one of his Nine Principles) it is the <u>absence</u> of crime, not dealing with it, that is the true test of police efficiency. It was once a matter of pride to report after a shift that nothing had happened[4239]. Not any more: we are now trying to close the door after the horse has bolted.

Journalist Peter Oborne counted, in one afternoon in 2004, 50 uniformed police around Whitehall, but none in the central West End[4240].

A Dutch scheme where districts take control of officers is being considered as a way of cutting crime[4241].

<u>Bernard Hogan-Howe</u> has claimed families are safer in their homes than they have been for a generation, but Victim Support insists burglary remains a very real threat[4242].

Cadder

The Supreme Court's Cadder ruling (vicious Peter Cadder won an appeal against his conviction for stabbing because police interviewed him without a lawyer) means many Scottish prisoners have a new ground for appealing convictions. Police will now have to provide more space for legal consultations[4243].

Corroboration has long been essential to any convictions in Scotland, unlike the rest of the UK, and this may contribute to the country's poor rape conviction rates[4244]. The European Court of Human Rights in one of its rulings implied that the confessions extracted by Scots police – innocent of legal advice – are illegal. If there is no lawyer present at interrogation, the breach of rights means a fair trial cannot be guaranteed. Thousands of Scots may be affected. Vulnerable young Scottish people are also being interviewed without help from an adult[4245].

Criminals who confess early in their prosecution could get their jail time cut, and some Tory MPs think Justice Secretary Kenneth Clarke is trying to soften the criminal law[4246]. He was trying (2012) to give the government the power to make court hearings secret.

When the Tottenham riots were in full swing the Met's emergency response – codename Operation Withern and circulated to senior officers – recommended holding all riot-related arrestees in custody, and asking the courts to refuse bail after they were charged[4247].

DS <u>Mark Kearney</u>, who controversially recorded an MP's prison cell conversations, claims he was recruited to a propaganda operation by <u>Sir Charles Pollard</u>, former Thames Valley Chief Constable, to influence a Royal Commission into Criminal Justice's outcome. He was to leak cases to the press which showed suspects escaping prosecution by exercising their right to silence. Kearney was facing separate criminal charges in 2008 of leaking information to newspapers[4248] (see also The Murdoch Policeman chapter).

Drugs

Despite recent research suggesting cannabis may have a psychotogenic effect, most of the 162,610 cases of cannabis possession in England and Wales (2009) merely receive a feeble 'Cannabis Warning', which has no legal status and is not recorded nationally. It is recommended by ACPO as the first option, being tantamount to the virtual decriminalisation of the drug. Here we have the police interpreting the law to suit their convenience in regard to a Schedule II (later III) drug. They are known to be much more draconian in relation to Schedule III diet pills, because the latter are not politically correct[4249]. In 2007 ACPO guidelines overturned a government undertaking – that under-18s would still face the full might of the law – by advising that children smoking cannabis should no longer be automatically arrested[4250].

The new Met Commissioner, hardliner <u>Bernard Hogan-Howe</u>, broke ranks in 2007 with his ACPO colleagues by advocating a U-turn on the relaxation of the law on cannabis[4251]. Chief Constable <u>Tim Hollis</u> of Humberside Police has proposed decriminalising the personal use of drugs like cannabis. Hollis is chairman of ACPO's drugs committee. He also called for a review of the current drug classification system, and wants alcohol and nicotine to be included in attempts to tackle illegal drugs[4252]. Sussex Chief Superintendent <u>Graham Bartlett</u> wants Brighton and Hove to treat rather than punish drug users, but Nick Herbert, his political master, forbade even discussion of decriminalisation[4253]. In 2004 ACPO had added its voice to the move to weaken the law against cannabis[4254].

Politically-inspired Police Stings

It has long been claimed by Keith Richards that the Rolling Stones were targeted by drugs police in 1967 because the Establishment feared their influence on the nation's youth: Richards says it was David Sniderman, a police informant and drug dealer, who set them up – he was a guest at the Stones party. Jagger and Richards were jailed for possession but later acquitted on appeal. Sniderman later said he was recruited by British and American intelligence as part of a plot to discredit the band[4255].

This author suspects a similar government conspiracy (involving the MHPRA and 'Big Pharma') to discredit amphetamine-based diet pills by using an English police force and the GMC to have the only doctor ever struck off for prescribing them quite legitimately. This alleged 'sting' was combined with (illegal) moves, which were overturned by the diet industry at the European Court, to have the pills banned[4256]. The Department of Health was forced to make the CAS (centrally-acting appetite suppressants) legal again: see Appendix II.

Red Tape

Seven million hours are estimated spent on bureaucracy annually by English officers, with 52.5% the proportion of each shift spent on red tape. 3,600 new criminal offences were brought in by Labour[4257], greatly swelling the red tape burden.

Despite the Home Secretary announcing the end of the targets of the National Policing Pledge in the summer of 2010, many chief constables are so addicted to box-ticking that they are still forcing their people to abide by the red-tape pledge: they simply reissue it as a pledge of their own region, no matter what Theresa May says. They have the power to do this[4258]. Their hubris in relation to their political master was shown by the way they treated her at their 2011 Police Federation conference.

Humberside Police have told shopkeepers to phone police only if thieves steal more than £20[4259].

Greater Manchester Police and Met officers have complained about excessive bureaucracy (e.g. it takes 80 minutes to complete the paperwork to ask for time off)[4260].

The NPIA quango (costing £500m in 2010) has been said to have grown too big[4261], and is now supposedly (2011) being abolished.

Surrey Police are just one force accused of empire-building, e.g. civilian and officer numbers increased in nine years by 1,215 (the question being: who generates more red tape, staff or police?)[4262].

For every £1 spent on preventing crime, £80 is spent on treating it. The public is getting more police, but less policing. Tayside Police have counted 1,150 different red tape forms. In 2004-5 the Met spent over £100m on 'non-incident-related paperwork'[4263].

Burglary tends to be well-reported, so that an increase would indicate a genuine rise, whereas domestic violence and hate crime are traditionally under-reported, so that recording more of the latter doesn't necessarily mean an increase[4264].

The Scottish Police Complaints Commissioner is to be renamed the Police Investigations and Review Commissioner: why the urge to change the names of quangos? Unnecessary name changes always incur unnecessary costs. At an estimated cost of £0.5 billion Ian Blair changed the Met's logo, inserting 'together' and making it easier for myopic people to read[4265].

The police service 'has become an inflexible bureaucratic nationalised industry, too often putting its employees before the public'[4266]. Policing has become a risk-averse occupation, its leaders promulgating 'Policing Pledges' and 'Charters' while they ignore their subordinates' steady disengagement from the public.

Police/Politician Interface

Ex-cabinet minister Andrew Mitchell complained to the IPCC of the Met's 'dishonest and illicit' campaign to destroy him, including their leaking to the press the suggestion that the IPCC inquiry would dismiss his claims. He was also demanding an apology from the Home Secretary for briefing the cabinet against him[4267].

Met Assistant Commissioner Bob Quick accused the Tories of 'corruption' and 'spiteful' behaviour that put his family 'at risk'. They (including David Cameron) tried to 'intimidate' him into dropping a probe into the Damian Green Whitehall leaks[4268].

Tony Blair called in Special Branch to try to stop a former tax inspector writing him angry letters. Scotland Yard drew up a secret surveillance report on the 'irritant'[4269].

PM Alec Douglas-Home ordered a secret investigation into rumours that Lord Boothby was involved with criminals, so sent Home Secretary Henry Brooke to question the Lord. Brooke then asked the Met Commissioner, Sir Joseph Simpson, who lied that there was 'no ongoing investigation of any organised criminals'. Then the truth hit the Mirror's front page about the police investigation of an alleged homosexual peer-racketeer relationship. The high-level cover-up (Labour didn't want their closet skeleton Driberg exposed either) grew into a huge scandal[4270].

When Sir Ian Blair appeared on his first morning as Commissioner to back Tory demands for householders' increased rights against burglars, No. 10 was furious – Sir Ian had changed his mind by 11am. In 2005 he backed Labour's plan for ID cards a few weeks before polling day.

The controversial left-wing campaigning 'charitable' organisation Common Purpose (CP), which receives millions of pounds of taxpayers' money, has police links, e.g. with Sir Paul Scott-Lee, ex-chief constable of West Midlands Police, which sent 27 officers on a Common Purpose leadership training course. A CP 'graduate' is the Met's Cressida Dick. Lord Ian Blair was also a strong supporter of CP, while Met Deputy Assistant Commissioner David Gilbertson also attended CP training sessions. CP's modus operandi has been described as a 'modern version of a freemason's handshake'.

Assistant Commissioner Tarique Ghaffur alleged, with a dossier of at least 30 accusations of political in-fighting at the top of the Home Office and the Met, that Moira Wallace (the H.O.'s (Home Office) director of police and counter-terrorism) had conspired with Sir Ian Blair to strip him (Ghaffur) of his responsibilities, e.g. to replace him as head of Olympics Security . The slide towards central control of the police was evidenced by the idea floated by Tony Blair in 2002 that 10 selected chief constables should report regularly to 10 government ministers on crime in their patches. Again, during the 2000 'fuel crisis' the Cabinet Office told all regional Home Office officials (who control regional 'directors of crime') that the media were portraying an ineffective police service. Regional directors were to instruct chief constables to make far more arrests, police should occupy fuel depots, drive tankers and deal more firmly with protestors. Home Office staff should be infiltrated into fuel depots and public gatherings to spy on police actions[4272].

Police bureaucracy tsar Jan Berry, a former Police Federation chair, has criticised some senior policemen for being too obsessed with getting their forces high up in 'league tables' of performance instead of responding to what the public want: officers were not being given discretion in handling minor crime because it adversely affected clear-up-rates[4273]. Berry has been quoted as saying that politicians were bringing the force to its knees.

Jan Berry

One recent decision crucial to the politicisation of the police was that to put chief constables on fixed-term contracts instead of tenure, so that they are now too fearful to speak out in case their contract isn't renewed. In 2001 David Blunkett started to micromanage all aspects of police operations, with chief constables identified and publicly humiliated, and forces receiving no extra funds unless they agree to implement H.O. pet projects, e.g. the introduction of PCSOs (which Scottish police refused to have). Large areas of inner cities are no longer policed effectively, e.g. for fear of appearing racist higher levels of crime (e.g. black-on-black murders) are tolerated. Political 'cowardice' on the part of the police leads to a lack of even-handedness and ineffectiveness in dealing with terrorist bombings[4274].

In 2010 Norfolk Chief Constable Phil Gormley ordered his officers to improve performance, not chase targets[4275].

Michael Todd, the chief constable who was found dead in the Welsh mountains, had a first-class honours degree in politics[4276].

Scottish justice secretary Kenny MacAskill, in a 2010 secret letter to police boards, ordered that all future senior appointments must be discussed with the SNP government, with no new contract to exceed three years. The latter will of course greatly reduce the political independence of the service[4277].

Brian Paddick

Former Met policeman Brian Paddick seemed to be interested in running again in 2012 against mayor Boris Johnson, and was seen dining with bisexual Carina Trimingham, the new partner of politician Chris Huhne, with perhaps the idea of mopping up the gay and lesbian vote[4278].

Tony Blair was flown in Gaddafi's jets on two occasions to hold secret meetings with the dictator. He was accompanied by British policemen (four on one of the visits)[4279].

In 2009 Met chief Sir Paul Stephenson reversed a ban on police wearing Union Flag badges to support UK troops: hundreds of officers had threatened to defy the order[4280].

The Met's decision to arrest Damian Green was 'disproportionate' and 'difficult to understand or justify', said a committee of MPs[4281].

'Criminal offence has been redefined as the giving of offence. Bad ideas are ... considered worse than bad deeds'[4282]. Again, no one has consulted the public about this crucial change in philosophy.

There is a rota of 20 Met police guarding one of Tony Blair's homes (e.g. six have been filmed outside the premises at one time, some armed), at a cost of £6m annually[4283]. The bodyguard police claim £25,000 in expenses alone (e.g. for staying in five-star hotels).

The new doctrine of 'restorative justice' (e.g. as advocated by prisons minister Crispin Blunt) means, instead of punishment, resolution by dialogue and 'therapy', which cruelly insists victims set out how they feel, the last thing they need: anyway, criminals lack the essential empathy needed to make the dialogue work[4284].

Gaffe-prone Sir Ian Blair was made a peer. Brian Paddick reportedly wrote on a website in favour of anarchy[4285]: he has a degree in politics.

The Scottish Police Services Authority was ready in 2009 to hire a civilian with no police experience as its head, and the Scottish Government was in agreement. The SPSA spent well over £900,000 in its first year on training, PR, etc. and its spending on consultants in six months in 2009 was double that in its first year[4286].

Former New York prosecutor Jessica de Grazia says elected police commissioners on US lines can predispose to corruption and damage faith in the justice system (de Grazia, who produced a critical government-commissioned report into the Serious Fraud Office in 2008, was in charge of 400 lawyers, fraud investigators and prosecutors)[4287]. ACPO says the Coalition government's plan to give the public more influence over policing is 'perverse' and dangerous. ACPO insists it has a duty to participate in discussions over the future of the police[4288]. Labour and Tories wanted a unified force, while the Lib Dems opposed it. Would a single police chief be undemocratic?[4289] The chief constables of Northern, Grampian and Dumfries and Galloway are worried about a 'central belt bias' against rural areas, with loss of officers and stations, less emphasis on road safety clampdowns, etc[4290].

The Met is the most politicised police force in England. In Jersey, where police and politicians often socialise together, there is a parallel system of Honorary Police – only they can charge suspects. The 12 Chief Honorary Constables have seats in the States Assembly: custody sergeants have to put their prosecution cases to these volunteers, who can decide not to prosecute. Politicians have repeatedly blocked attempts to deal with Jersey's many unlicensed guns, with some firearms' licences being granted despite applicants having criminal convictions[4291].

The row over plans to abolish CHCs (Community Health Councils) called into question the government's commitment to genuine democratic scrutiny of the NHS, and the same is about to happen with the police. For many years the London police have been accountable to the community through a network of about 40 Police and Community Consultative Groups. The PCCGs are run by lay volunteers and their meetings open to all: local police commanders can be questioned. In 2000 control over London's police shifted from the Home Office to the Metropolitan Police Authority, which is now taking control of the PCCGs, because they "do not appear to be representative of the community". Thus the MPA can veto a PCCG's democratically elected chairman. The chairman of the Westminster PCCG says the MPA handles the matter in a "Stalinist" manner. "It is real Big Brother stuff. They want control". A leaked letter showed Home Secretary Charles Clarke offered money to police forces that volunteered to be merged. ACPO refused to submit plans for the proposed merger[4292].

War veterans comprise 10% of those appearing in criminal courts, so it is perhaps ironic that politicians clamour for antisocial youths to be sent to army cadet centres, e.g. Tory MP Philip Davies said this would 'sort them out'[4293]. The Home Office's desperate suggestion that army colonels could be drafted in to run the police belies the fact that the forces' senior management is just as bad as that of the police[4294]. Of course, this had already been tried in the 19th and early 20th Centuries, and ACPO will resist revisiting this scenario[4295]. Acting Met head Tim Godwin clashed with David Cameron over the latter's suggestion the army could be used to quell the 2011 riots: he had also implicitly criticised Cameron when he said politicians 'who weren't there' shouldn't make judgments about the Met's response to the violence[4296].

Despite the main message of research since the 1960s into the mission of the police that there is much more to policing than crime-fighting, the managerialism that has infiltrated and come to dominate other public services like the NHS eventually hijacked the police service. The 'core business' of crime-fighting was now the be-all and end-all, so 'success' (efficiency and effectiveness) was measured only by arrest, clear-up and crime rates: previous police functions such as dealing with antisocial behaviour was nowhere to be seen. In 2010 police across England and Wales recorded 200,000 antisocial incidents[4297].

The government wanted to give film producer Michael Winner an OBE for supporting the police.

Celebrities and politicians are being sounded out to become police commissioners (there will be 41 elected police and crime commissioners outside London). Senior police officers can also apply. Elected commissioners on American lines could damage the legal system: major scandals in New York included recording serious crimes as minor offences and failure of the elected commissioner to properly investigate allegations. Also in the US prosecutors can start investigations, whereas the UK is completely dependent on the police[4298].

There are now more lawyers than police officers in Britain[4299].

Scottish police voted by a large majority (78% of delegates at a Scottish Police Federation conference) against a single national force, whereas the Association of Scottish Police Superintendents were all in favour[4300].The chief constables of Grampian, Dumfries and Galloway and Northern Constabulary wrote an 'open' letter to newspapers criticising the merger as a 'step too far', but Graeme Pearson, ex-deputy chief constable and a former director of the Scottish Crime and Drug Enforcement Agency (he was bidding to become a Labour MSP), slammed their action, saying they 'shouldn't be involved in politics'[4301]. Pearson has also criticised the methadone treatment programme and its cost, risking this issue becoming a political football.

The Scottish Police Authority will interfere with previously sacrosanct 'operational independence' by challenging police commanders' decisions to spend large sums on prolonged probes. The Association of Scottish Police Superintendents is not very happy with this[4302].

Police raided the BBC's London offices with regard to a programme on Northern Ireland.

In 1986 former British cops were being recruited by South Africa's apartheid regime to help suppress township riots[4303].

When PM Cameron asked the Met to hunt for Madeleine McCann in 2011, critics said it created a dangerous political influence precedent, not to mention a likely waste of resources[4304]. The Met was able to release a 30-strong squad for the purpose (but didn't have the resources to properly probe the hacking scandal and widespread bribery of police).

Norfolk police swooped on a clothing stall at an agricultural show and fined a trader for displaying a 'Bollocks to Blair' T-shirt (it was legal to sell them). An anonymous 'denunciation' – such as was found in Franco's Spain – had precipitated the police action. The policeman concerned made clear he was carrying out the wishes of an anonymous complainant.

PC Richard Eccles, secretary of North Wales Police Federation, was disciplined for encouraging fellow officers to sign an online petition against the government's road toll plans.

A few months after retiring, Lord Stevens, Britain's most senior police officer, wrote a book profiting from rubbishing a Government minister (Blunkett). It is worrying when a policeman divulges information gleaned in the course of his duties.

Police bravery awards were given out by the Police Federation at No. 10 (7.7.11), sponsored by 'The Sun'. This is one sign of the link between the 'three Ps': police, press, politicians[4305].

The Labour government's detection culture led police to cherry-pick jobs: if a box can be ticked, that job will be done, others neglected. Officers have a monthly detections quota, competing with each other for the most detections in a month. It has become a sport[4306]. Prevention of crime is now the least of the police's priorities.

Lord Stevens

Michael Craik, Northumbria's police chief, echoed another chief constable in proposing that the legal drinking age should be raised to 21[4307].

Just as a parliamentary committee can be used to browbeat their own officials (e.g. Elizabeth Filkin), so Assistant Commissioner Yates, because of his probe into government honours corruption (large Labour donors were almost 7,000 times likelier to receive a peerage than non-donors), was pressurised by the House of Commons Public Administration Committee, disrupting an ongoing police investigation. Government ministers publicly tried to smear Yates, though many stayed anonymous: one senior minister suggested Yates, who was compared with Kenneth Starr (who probed Clinton's finances), was part of a 'politically motivated conspiracy'[4308] (see also The Murdoch Policeman chapter).

Scotland's justice secretary decided to merge his eight forces in the biggest shake-up for 35 years[4309]. Critics of the new single Scottish police force warn the new Chief Constable of Scotland will be too vulnerable to government pressure, with meeting arbitrary targets becoming more important than doing what is most appropriate for public safety[4310].

Senior Met officers ridiculed the PM's decision to appoint an American 'supercop' to advise on gang warfare: London's mayor joined them in an outspoken attack on his call for 'zero tolerance' policing (which originally referred to police corruption in the US). ACPO's chief, Sir Hugh Orde, says tough US tactics aren't possible in the UK because of Human Rights legislation. Orde also dismissed politicians' claims that Ministers had ordered the tougher approach that stopped the violence[4311]. The British have sent their police all over the Commonwealth for many years, but won't allow the Met to appoint a foreigner as Commissioner[4312]. This exclusion policy was under review in 2013.

When John Prescott escaped a probe into claims he broke the law by having sex with his mistress at work (policemen have been convicted of having sex while on duty), there were suspicions that Met Commissioner Sir Ian Blair vetoed an investigation because of his close ties with Tony Blair[4313].

Ian Hanson, chairman of the Police Federation, says Cameron should hang his head in shame: it was an absolute disgrace that he had criticised police tactics[4314].

Home Secretary Jacqui Smith became a little too close to some senior police officers in relation to the plans for 42-day detention, e.g. appearing to resist MPs' scrutiny[4315].

Coalition ministers plotted to stop Sir Hugh Orde becoming Met Commissioner by urging rival chief constables to apply even after the closing date for applications[4316]. His uniform was specially made for him (at his request) by the Met's in-house tailors. It resembles the Met Commissioner's usual uniform, but doesn't belong to any force and has no legal basis; especially the hat, on which he wears an ACPO badge. He should have worn his Irish uniform, which is green[4317].

The CPS allowed Essex Police to procrastinate over MP Chris Huhne's driving case. Would this have happened if he had not been a senior politician[4318]?

Sir Ian Blair, 'a most political policeman' – 'Blair by name, Blair by nature' – has been described as a politician first and a policeman second. He accused the media of bias by giving more coverage to white than to black victims of crime, therefore being

Sir Hugh Orde

institutionally racist[4319]. A week after 7/7 he told the media that the bombers were unknown to police and what the death toll would be – he was wrong on both counts[4320].

Forces are judged by their figures for detection targets, not how well their community policing is going[4321].

Her Majesty's C.I.C., Sir Ronnie Flanagan, was described as well-nigh 'certifiable' for proposing a cut in police numbers[4322].

When Richard Brunstrom advocated in his 2007 'Drugs Policy' report the legalising of drugs, ACPO described his attitude as 'a counsel of despair'[4323]. ACPO has criticised some Home Office performance scores: police are judged to be doing less well if whites are happier with their local force than the BEM population is[4324].

In 2007 Tony Blair refused a formal probe into details of sensitive police operations being leaked to the media (e.g. at the time of anti-terror arrests in Birmingham in January that year – the leaks appeared to derive from police sources), despite a warning given by Peter Clarke, the Met's counter-terrorism chief[4325]. The latter, when in charge of the hacking inquiry, concentrated his resources on terrorism because that was more dangerous than hacking – or at least that's how he justified the hacking demotion to Leveson.

Ken Jones, ACPO's president in 2007, proposed that terror suspects should be locked up indefinitely – he was backed by the Met[4326].

Despite the PC Yvonne Fletcher shooting, the English police were detailed in documents found in Tripoli after Gaddafi's fall as having been especially keen to become involved with his regime[4327]. Several senior English police officers visited Libya in 2007: chief superintendents Bob Rose (head of Hampshire Police operations), Walters (head of the Met's Royalty, Protection and Protocol squad) and superintendent Stuart Twigg, international policing adviser, met with senior Libyan police[4328]. British police leapt into action to protect Saif Gaddafi from an apparent assassination plot – the Met's Special Branch rushed to his London home and put him on their 'at-risk' register[4329]. Compare Yates in Bahrain (see The Murdoch Policeman chapter): too close to dictatorship for comfort?

One Met policeman, according to the IPCC report into the de Menezes episode, said he had been told the IPCC was excluded from the inquiry not just by Sir Ian Blair, but also on the authority of Tony Blair. If true this would imply No 10 was compounding the Met's felony, i.e. not performing its duty of immediate referral of a shooting to the IPCC[4330].

PM Tony Blair was accused of abusing his position by ensuring his local Durham police force received extra cash[4331]. Local police forces in the UK are not accountable, unlike in the US.

ACPO has been said to have morphed into a branch of the Home Office[4332].

A stallholder at a Norfolk country fair was fined £80 on the spot by a policeman who told him someone had complained T-shirts he was selling had the logo 'b......s to Blair'. The trader, who couldn't leave his stall, would have been arrested and taken to a police station if he didn't pay up, under the Public Order (Riot) Act[4333].

Sir Ian Blair faced calls to quit in 2007 after allegedly informing Cabinet ministers – prior to the findings of the criminal investigation into cash-for-peerages – that Tony Blair would be exonerated. Inquiry head John Yates was pursuing claims that No. 10 had deleted e-mails about honours from its computers. Sir Ian owed his job to the PM and was apparently protected over de Menezes and the Attorney General phone calls by No. 10[4334].

The late Peter Wright was involved, as deputy chief constable of Merseyside, in the Toxteth riots, and helped police the miners' strike, but was most notorious for his stewardship as South Yorkshire's chief constable when the Hillsborough disaster occurred[4335]. In that disaster saga the Sunday am meeting between South Yorkshire Police and Mrs. Thatcher seems to have been pivotal: it marked the start of the 'scurrilous' reports that fans were partly responsible[4336].

Scotland's First Minister threatened to order police not to man polling stations if PM Cameron tried to force an early referendum on Scottish independence, but Tory Lord Forsyth says Salmond doesn't have the power to do this[4337].

The proposed single police authority for Scotland was, according to Alison McInnes, Lib Dem MSP, not about improving efficiency and local accountability so much as political control. The new authority members will be directly appointed by ministers, who must approve the choice of the one chief constable for Scotland, henceforth to be made by the authority. The Government will 'determine strategic police priorities' and direct the new authority as to how to manage matters relevant to the 'the policing of Scotland'[4338].

New Labour introduced the concept of 'criming' – everything has to be 'crimed' as detected or undetected, in accordance with very complicated Home Office Counting Rules. 'Undetected' crimes are bad news for officers, so these get attributed to dead villains ('scrotes') or 'reclassified' (e.g. a burglary as a trespass), which the Home Office deletes from their ken. 'Criming' linked offences as separate incidents gets several detections for the price of one. Every division and force is given a class-A drugs target – in Surrey the target was 50 per annum[4339].

Prison officers have accused the police of slowing the execution of warrants for immediate custody offenders because the jails are full[4340].

84 police were injured during the Brixton riots (1981), when youths from the black and white communities rose up against the police after a black youth was stopped and searched[4341].

Strathclyde Police have demanded new powers of entering and searching without a warrant, even though the power, available to police in England and Wales, can lead to lengthier trials and leave senior officers open to censure[4342].

British American Tobacco helps fund the pro-smoking lobbying campaign group Common Sense Alliance, run by Peter Sheridan, former Assistant Chief Constable in Northern Ireland, and Roy Ramm, a former Met commander, who tried to claim they were acting in a personal capacity when they warned that plain cigarette packs would encourage smuggling and facilitate terrorism[4343].

A Warwickshire spokesman at the 2012 Police Federation conference told Theresa May: '… we no longer trust you in the police service … end of story.': the Home Secretary had to speak in front of the protest slogan 'Cutting Police by 20% Is Criminal'. The police accused her of 'diva-like' behaviour because she demanded her own podium without this backdrop. About 30,000 officers marched through London, some calling for the right to strike. The Home Secretary announced the police were to be given greater powers to prosecute 'lower level offences', replacing prosecutors[4344].

Even though Parliament hadn't yet debated whether a new quango, to be called the National Crime Agency, was a wise move, the Government was hiring the top managers. The NCA's director (who will answer to the Home Secretary) will be able to control chief constables – such a national police force was anathema to Sir Robert Peel (SOCA flopped because it didn't have this crucial power). The NCA will be controlled by the Government, aggravating the Big Brother tendencies of the police[4345].

Hampshire Police offered (2010) £41,600 for a 'diversity manager'.

Cover-up

It has been commented that today's police 'service' is all about reassuring 'stakeholders' (i.e. the public) and addressing the public's fear of crime with massaged statistics and soothing statements[4346]. The Police Management Training Directorate has stated that the job of chief police officers is to manage large organisations, not to mess about chasing criminals all day[4347].

In 2006 Sir Ian Blair announced that burglary in London is becoming so rare that the residents of council estates are leaving their front doors open. Yet one Haringey resident said: 'I have been burgled three times and the police were very uninterested every time. I meet up with my ... girlfriends ... each week ... and one afternoon we discovered that three of us had been burgled that week'[4348].

One former police officer, who expressed disgust at the Met's decision not to prosecute police who had abused corporate credit cards, said: '... the general public has little respect for the police. The main problem is that senior officers are far too politically minded'[4349].

Fewer police are sent out at night – when more criminals are about – possibly because there are also fewer members of the public to see them on patrol[4350].

Scottish police chiefs accused (2011) the Scottish Government of misleading the public over cuts to forces[4351].

Bristol's Stapleton Road is a lawless hotbed of murder, rape, drugs, robbery, shooting, knifings, etc., yet is a paradise of law and order according to the Home Office's crime map[4352].

There has been a 30% increase in the number of traffic lights, parallel to the rise in speed cameras, between 2000 and 2008, but the decisions about their use (e.g. bus priority) are taken secretly behind closed doors[4353].

The police's punishment of motorists is efficient and certain, that of other lawbreakers much less competent.

In one force officers were told to reclassify almost 2,000 drunk and disorderly arrests as Section 5: any who refused were disciplined. But when a new 'crime manager' arrived he condemned the new practice as illegal as well as unethical, as people of previously good character were being criminalised to increase sanctioned detections[4354].

Former undercover cop <u>Mark Kennedy</u>, who used a £7,000 modified Casio G Shock watch to record the eco-activists' meetings, has claimed that the police are 'at war with the CPS'. The CPS 'misled the courts', there being <u>eight</u> inquiries so far into undercover policing (to June, 2011)[4355].

The Police Federation has opposed the Policy Exchange's suggestion that officers increase their visibility to the public by wearing uniform to and from work[4356].

Apparently the Met urged the Attorney-General to seek an injunction against the BBC revealing material that had already appeared in The Guardian regarding the 'cash for honours' scandal. This pressure may have been because the police believed the allegations could prejudice a future prosecution. But no charges had been brought, so it may be that the police were excessively jumpy about offending top politicians. The Attorney-General tried unsuccessfully to cover up the whole business, which would have again suited Scotland Yard[4357].

As a West Midlands chief constable failed to be challenged over corruption in his force by the Police Authority, the question is whether the situation would improve if there had been an elected commissioner[4358].

A serving Met officer, a member of the Diplomatic Protection Group, played a key role in the downfall of Chief Whip Andrew Mitchell, yet he was <u>not</u> a witness despite sending two e-mails to his MP which seemed to corroborate the official police account (the officer did not reveal himself as a policeman). CCTV footage gainsays the police log and the e-mails, and there is the question of who leaked the story to The Sun and The Daily Telegraph. How did the officer know about the official Police Federation account of the incident? An officer was arrested seemingly in connection with the case[4359].

The 1984-85 striking miners have campaigned for 500 of their number to have their criminal records (which got them sacked and made them unemployable) erased. They insist the Thatcher government colluded with the police and the courts to crush the NUM and the strike. To June, 1984, the police posted to the Bilston Glen colliery were local, but then other forces without local loyalties were drafted in. Police snatch squads seemed to be targeting union officials. Alex Bennett, an NUM official from Monktonhall Colliery, was convicted of breach of the peace on the evidence of two cops he says he had never seen before and lied that he willfully forced his way through police lines. He was blacklisted and sacked, but later won an unfair dismissal claim. He insists there should be an inquiry into alleged victimisation: 'We were treated like hardened criminals'. South Yorkshire Police are scheduled to be probed over the 'Battle of Orgreave', and two MPs have asked for a new Bilston Glen investigation, arguing it may uncover evidence of a police cover-up (like that of Hillsborough)[4360].

The Police Federation expressed 'great regret' at the arrest of a member of the Diplomatic Protection Group on suspicion of misconduct in public office (in relation to the demise of Chief Whip Mitchell)[4361].

In the 1985 Battle of the Beanfield 1,300 police trapped hippies in a Wiltshire field to stop them staging a free festival at Stonehenge: the bloody confrontation saw 16 hippies hospitalised and over 500 arrested. One traveller claimed: 'There was no justice for the travellers and no legal motivation for what they (the police) did. They behaved like animals – they were the outlaws'[4362].

Most candidates for election as police commissioners were politicians[4363].

In the 'Battle of Cable Street' (a Jewish area) 83 were arrested before Oswald Mosley was persuaded to end his march. The police were accused of being antisemitic when they turned on protesters.

Murdered Ulster lawyer Pat Finucane's widow has criticised Sir Desmond de Silva's probe into his death (it revealed the RUC proposed Finucane as a UDA target, MI5 supplied the weapons and both the police and Army misled ministers). She called it a whitewash for suggesting there was 'no overarching state conspiracy'. It is 'a confidence trick dressed up as independent scrutiny'[4364].

A recent tabloid leader had the following question for the Scottish police: 'Are the Scottish police really too afraid of the [Data Protection] Act to protect the public [from sex offenders including paedophiles]?' This was in response to the revelation that the police were refusing to reveal the identities of 16 Scottish sex offenders on the run for fear of breaching their human rights[4365].

To protect the profits of Olympic sponsors the State gave the police criminal powers to enter 'land or premises' and to 'remove, destroy, conceal or erase any infringing article', such as protected logos like 'Games', 'Gold', 'Summer' and a picture of the London skyline[4366].

When beat officers were taken to police industrial disputes like the miners' strike, they were never properly replaced – neighbourhood policing teams were an inadequate substitute[4367].

Ian Blair boasted that he refused to enforce Tory anti-trespassing laws when he was a senior Thames Valley cop. He has been described as 'terminally arrogant'[4368].

By spring 2012 the Met's 'Operation Grange', a further attempt to find Madeleine McCann, had cost taxpayers £2m. in a year[4369]. The saga continues in 2014.

Putting the Scottish Police Services Authority (SPSA) in charge of the Scottish Crime and Drug Enforcement Agency (SCDEA) in 2007 was claimed by some senior policemen to have undermined the latter's ability to confront organised crime[4370].

The police are among public institutions which benefit from taxpayer-funded PR (in 2012 there were over 500 press officers available for the civil service, NHS, etc.)[4371].

Ex-Met Commissioner Lord Blair was criticised for urging the public to boycott the elections for police and crime commissioners, saying the new large police areas are too big for one person to manage properly[4372].

Bouncers have been given official police kits to act as scenes-of-crime investigators: more evidence of the dumbing-down of policing[4373]? There are now cannabis-sniffing kits given out by police to householders to shop their neighbours.

The MOD's 'private' armed police force of 3,500 are now carrying out stop and search on thousands of tourists and other suspects who match 'certain profiles or behaviours'. Their uniforms are virtually indistinguishable from other police forces, but are not under Home Office control[4374].

Senior officers were furious in 2003 when an American was put in charge of the Home Office's Police Standards Unit, whose function is to monitor and advise forces[4375].

During a State visit to Britain in 1999 by the Chinese president police seized placards from demonstrators. To avoid court action the Met admitted they were wrong[4376].

Police Federation leaders have voiced concern at DPP Kenneth MacDonald's record of defending terrorists, as well as the QC's conviction for possessing drugs[4377].

The outgoing chief constable of Avon and Somerset failed in getting a High Court injunction to stop the new Police and Crime Commissioner from replacing him ('inducing his retirement').

A senior Cabinet minister was quoted (August 2011) as saying: 'The police are the worst led in my lifetime. The leadership are politically correct jobsworths who spend their time worrying about their salaries, pension and uniforms'[4378].

'They [the police] have become the uniformed wing of New Labour, not preventing crime or seeing that it is punished – but mediating neutrally between 'victim' and 'offender' and spying out political incorrectness, in their own ranks and beyond'[4379].

BNP leader Nick Griffin was arrested in 2004 for exercising his right to free speech by predicting that Britain would suffer a terror attack by British-born Muslims quite soon – the July 7, 2005, bombings were perpetrated only a few days after the Griffin case came to court[4380].

During the 1926 general strike teenage miners were imprisoned for sedition[4381].

An environmental activist said she was offered money (tens of thousands) to act as a spy for Strathclyde Police, who also tried to bribe another member of protest group Plane Stupid, a Glasgow School of Art student[4382].

Tariq Ghaffur has accused former Met Commissioner Sir Ian Blair of not only putting his force 'in the pocket of New Labour' but of manipulating the cash-for-honours inquiry into alleged Labour corruption so as to win influence in the Home Office[4383].

In 2007 39,000 people were cautioned for 'actual bodily harm' (ABH carries a penalty of up to five years in jail)[4384].

Labour was accused of 'politicising' the police over its plan to use the Met's then leading anti-terrorism officer, Bob Quick, to persuade MPs of the need to extend detention (from 28 to 42 days) without charge. Gaffe-prone Met Commissioner Ian Blair likewise had to admit misleading MPs by overstating the gravity of the UK's terror threat (he doubled the number of plots actually disrupted)[4385].

The 'McLibel' trial, the longest civil trial in British history, was allegedly triggered by a 1986 libellous leaflet attacking McDonald's, co-written by undercover Met officer <u>Bob Lambert</u>, who used the alias Bob Robinson, now lecturing in terrorism studies at St. Andrews University. He had affairs with four women while undercover, having a child by one[4386].

Met Commissioner <u>Bernard Hogan-Howe</u> has admitted victims instead of police should decide whether officers investigate a crime, i.e. that 'screening out' should be phased out[4203].

CHAPTER XXIII

THE RACIST POLICEMAN

CONTENTS

CHAPTER XXIII

THE RACIST POLICEMAN

Racism

The 1999 (Sir William) Macpherson report labelled the Met as 'institutionally racist'[4387]. A decade later the Home Affairs Select Committee claimed the police were still institutionally racist: most forces (including Sussex) had not implemented the Macpherson recommendations. Over half of ethnic minority individuals, when asked to consider the Stephen Lawrence investigation, believed there would be similar failings in 2009[4388]. Macpherson had criticised the Met for not managing to get anyone convicted of the Lawrence stabbing[4389]. He found there had been a failure of leadership by senior Scotland Yard officers, and that Met policemen had been incompetent[4390]. The main witness to the Stephen Lawrence murder told the police the five assailants had shouted racial abuse, but the police treated it as an ordinary fight and him as a hostile rather than a vital witness and victim (he only escaped by running off). 'At the scene the police treated me like a liar; like a suspect instead of a victim, because I was black and they couldn't believe that white boys would attack us for nothing. They tried ... at the police station, to get me to say that the attackers didn't call us 'nigger' '[4391]. The inquiry found that the Lawrence family were treated in a much less sympathetic manner by the police than might have been the case if they had been white. In the 1993 inquiry for two weeks the police investigated the <u>victim</u> instead of his murder (he had no priors). While the killers eradicated evidence, the Lawrence family were probed (see Appendix IV).

The judgment that the Met was 'institutionally racist' is supported by the very small (<2%) increase in ethnic representation among the various ranks (constable: an increase of 1.5%, sergeant: 1.6%, inspector: 1.3%, chief constable: 1.9%) in the decade after 1992. At the close of the 1970s there were just over 100 ethnics in a Met force of around 25,000: by the end of 1983 the number of blacks and Asians had nearly doubled; but the Policy Studies Institute found a bleak picture of racism among the white majority, with even the higher ranks being oblivious to the distress their banter caused[4392].

If the police are racist, it is not for lack of BME (Black Minority Ethnic) force organisations:
Metropolitan Police Muslim Contact Unit
Catholic Police Guild of England & Wales
Christian Police Association
National Trans Police Association
Jewish Police Association
Metropolitan Police Emerald Society (Irish Staff Association)
Chinese & S.E. Asian Staff Association
Metropolitan Police Sikh Association
Association of Muslim Police
National Black Police Association
National Black Crown Prosecution Association
Metropolitan Police Hindu Association

The various police gender pressure groups should also mean there is no sexism in the service:

British Association of Police Women
Association of Senior Women Officers of the Metropolitan Police
ACPO Women's Forum
National Trans-Gender Police Association
Gay Police Association

Gloucestershire Police have banned the police slang word 'Polac' (accident involving police car) because of its racial connotation[4393].

'Operation Trident' targets black-on-black murder and violent crime. Black people who are charged are more than twice as likely as whites to have their cases dismissed[4394].

A century ago, the police were accused of racism in connexion with their hounding of George Cedalji, whose case was taken up by Sir Arthur Conan Doyle. Until it was repealed, a curfew law applied to alien seamen in Liverpool, who had to report to police: this varied around the country[4395].

Peterborough, which has one of the biggest British Polish communities, was the venue in 2010 for training exercises in how to deal with rioting Eastern European immigrant workers and football hooligans. Operation Iceni was branded 'a breeding ground for racism'[4396].

A marcher at a demo against a BNP bookshop, which had allegedly provoked a number of racist murders (including Stephen Lawrence) in Welling, claims that the march was violently attacked by the police, with many innocent protesters injured[4397].

'Coconutgate' (white inside, brown outside) involved four police from the specialist hate crime unit and one civilian staff member. Ethnic people's activist and ordained minister Shirley Brown was found not guilty by a Bristol council investigation, but convicted at Bristol Magistrates' Court. To the police 'there was no difference between the real bigots and racists and someone who made an unfortunate mistake in the heat of the moment'[4398]. Derbyshire Police among others regard the use of 'choc ice' or 'coconut' as racist.[4399].

Met Superintendent Raj Kohli, brother of Scots TV stars Sanjeev and Hardeep Kohli, has claimed Glasgow City Council waged a racist vendetta against the family's business because it is run by their Asian father. But a housing boss says this is nonsense: the running of Kohli properties, let to students, leaves a lot to be desired (e.g. two tenants suffered carbon monoxide poisoning)[4400].

Though 20% of offences are perpetrated by non-British individuals in some parts of England, only two Scottish forces (Fife and Grampian) record offenders' nationality. Foreigners in England and Wales are twice as likely as indigenous Britons to be charged with or found guilty of a killing[4401].

According to the NPIA (National Policing Improvement Agency), 'stakeholders' (such as the police) refused to cooperate with a proposed research study which would examine the association between personality type and prejudice (racist, sexist), as well as dishonest tendencies[4402].

Whereas chief constables were once all white, ex-servicemen, usually right wing and socially unrepresentative, England and Wales now (2012) has four female and one black.

While off-duty, six Met PCs sent racist messages to each other, but they inadvertently sent them to other officers, who complained to the IPCC[4403].

Ali Dizaei authorised a PhD thesis on 'racial discrimination within the police', yet he was unsympathetic to ethnic minorities, making fun of 'Pakis', singing derogatory songs, and even slagging off his own nation: 'Iranians arc bloody stupid'. The 'corruption cop' uscd his police badge to get free night club champagne[4404].

Bedfordshire Constabulary's letter of objection to a proposed traveller site was considered by Bedford Council to 'breach the Race Relations Act'[4405].

Some parts of the police service – firearms, robbery and anti-terrorism squads – are for whites only[4406].

Dean and Dean, the law firm at the centre of the Met's race wars (Ghaffur, Dizaei, the NBPA, etc.) was closed down by the Solicitors' Regulation Authority following mis-accounting by Dizaei's close friend, the Iranian 'mail-order solicitor' Mireskandari, whom Dizaei advised about how to fight the Met's prosecution of him[4407].

Strathclyde WPC Anne Ramsay's exposé of the police culture in her book 'Girl in Blue', tells how she was (wrongly) called a 'Tim' (Irish Catholic) because the name on her warrant card was Bernadette. Another recruit, an Asian, was referred to as 'the Paki'[4408]. She reveals how she was expected to fit into a world where racism was rife[4409].

Staffordshire police were accused of racism when 30 of them arrested a Brixton band (The Thirst) at gunpoint, using a helicopter and dogs: they were wrongly thought to have a gun in their car[4410]. The force had to apologise.

Former Scotland Yard detective Neil Sankey is trying to prove, on behalf of the 'Birthers' protest group, that Barak Obama falsified his birth origin to make him eligible to become President. Sankey denies he is a racist conspiracy theorist[4411].

DC Richard Taylor denied in court a charge of racially abusing a bouncer in Aberdeen[4412].

One Greater Manchester PC has boasted that he would like to bury 'Pakis' under a train track. Many BME officers say they are refused promotion or blocked from specialist posts because they do not belong to networks which decide such matters. Of 266 of the most senior police only eight are BME. BME officers are five times more likely to be investigated by their force than white colleagues[4413].

PC Javid Iqbal is suing Bedfordshire Police, claiming he was forced out of his job by officers who called him a 'f...ing Paki', made fun of his beard and launched a 'smear and witch-hunt' against him, with a string of complaints about his performance. In another employment tribunal case (in London) an 'apartheid culture' was said to be in vogue at Belgravia police station, with separate vans for white and black staff[4414].

Merseyside Police PC Steve Bettley was dismissed because he had 'knowingly' been a BNP member, though he claimed he was enrolled by someone else without his knowledge.

A police spokeswoman said that the party's views are not compatible with the values and duties of the Police Service[4415].

A claim by the equality tsar Trevor Phillips that the police are no longer racist has angered board members, concerned that he is allegedly covering up the problem (several have resigned). The CRE (Commission for Racial Equality) was under investigation in 2009 for extravagance and £30,000 worth of missing personal computers[4416].

Kent Police were facing undercover racism tests to see if they treat black and white crime victims the same, while in Durham a team of 24 volunteers were to make fake 999 calls[4417].

The police still refuse to enter mosques even when a terrorist suspect is inside[4418].

In 2007 Stephen Otter, Chief Constable of Cornwall and Devon, surrendered to pressure from a local racial equality group, so that his detectives had to pull out of an ITV Manhunt appeal aimed at apprehending an Afghan wanted for serial sexual assault[4419].

Referring to the Dizaei case in 2007, a Tory London's police authority member suggested that 'sheer bloody anarchy' reigns in the Met[4420].

A Muslim leader accused 'overcautious' police of failing to tackle Asians forcing young white girls into prostitution, for fear of being branded racist[4421].

After a harmless playground tiff, an 18-year-old Down's lad was questioned and charged by Lanarkshire Police with a racist assault. It took seven months for the Procurator Fiscal to drop the charge, without an apology for the hell the family had been put through[4422].

From 2009 police have had to collect data on antisemitic incidents[4423].

A vicar is in despair because the police will do nothing about his church being under siege from vandals, yet a single phone call from the local mosque will bring an immediate response, often from senior officers[4424].

Wiltshire Police ordered a football fan to remove an England St. George flag from his car – because it might be perceived as racist[4425].

Two Christian preachers were banned from handing out leaflets in a 'Muslim area' (Birmingham's Alum Rock district) by a West Midlands officer, or face arrest for committing a 'hate crime'. The Muslim PCSO, Naeem Naguthnay, allegedly quizzed the ministers about the Iraq War and told them they could be attacked. He is claimed to have said: 'This is a Muslim neighbourhood and you are not supposed to be here'[4426].

95% of Muslim police are in junior ranks[4427].

Tayside Police have had to apologise for using an ''unclean' Alsatian pup in an advertising campaign – it offended Muslims, even though it was a trainee police dog[4428].

Tafazal Mohammod – described as a suspected terrorist sympathiser (an 'individual of interest', according to MI5) – has worked for the Met running training courses via his company 'Muslim Youth Skills', about 'engaging' Muslim youths. Mohammod attended a training camp with the July 7 ringleader (for whom he gave a job reference), and charges

Scotland Yard £115 per head for its courses. The Yard has a deliberate policy of not vetting such self-styled 'experts'![4429]

ACPO says the idea of a migrant crime wave is a sinister myth invented by the media to create dissension, yet about an eighth of the prison population – almost 10,000 inmates – are foreigners. The Met reports half of all organised London gangs are BMEs, while 10% of all crime in Britain is carried out by Eastern Europeans[4430]. Cambridgeshire's Chief Constable has warned of a 'huge surge' in organised crime caused by the migrant influx[4431].

Norwell Roberts

In 1972 black PC Norwell Roberts was being used by the Met's PR machine to advertise their equality credentials (the Commissioner praised him fulsomely in the press), at precisely the same time that he was being abused by many of his colleagues, including senior officers. In post-war Britain, though hospitals and transport welcomed Commonwealth immigrants as workers, the police, in spite of their vacancies, resisted[4432].

In 2006 Ali Dizaei and Tarique Ghaffur opposed profiling of airplane passengers, but were accused by the Police Federation of helping terrorism by their 'blissful ignorance'[4433]. But the Federation won't countenance personality profiling of their own rank-and-file recruits.

The Scarman report (into the 'swamp' policing of the 1976 Notting Hill Carnival riot and the 1981 Brixton riots) rejected claims of institutionalised racism in the police.

The BBC, in its documentary 'The Secret Police', exposed racist cops at a training centre. Chester PC Steven Salkeld boasted he would 'give [Asians] grief'. Eight officers were shown to be very right-wing[4434].

MP George Galloway says police at Hampden's League Cup final stood back and allowed sectarian and racist abuse[4435].

When 14 blacks died in an arson attack in Deptford in 1981 the police were accused of lack of response, even cover-up, and there was silence in the press. The indifference of the authorities led to marches.

The Metropolitan Police apologised to a black activist after publishing a long-awaited report that found officers had harassed him and his family for years, but removed the report from the Internet only hours after its publication.

Police officers for whom English was a second language achieved top marks in 2007's promotion exam OSPRE Part II (Objective Structured Performance-Related Examination), whereas colleagues born in Britain didn't do so well[4436].

White middle-class students have been banned by the Met from applying for prized internships[4437]. Reverse racism?

When black Bristol councillor Shirley Brown called a fellow Asian councillor a 'coconut', she apologised immediately, but the Tory 'victim' would not relent. Two inquiries and a major police probe (four officers from the specialist hate crime unit) led to Brown's conviction as a racist, the irony being she had been a lifelong antiracist campaigner. The case cost taxpayers thousands, and the police did nothing when she was subjected to persistent racist abuse[4438].

ACPO recommended (2008) that all police should be taught the Koran and Sharia law, in a secret 40-page document[4439].

Cardiff's Chief Constable James Wilson campaigned in the interwar years against miscegenation, arguing that half-caste children resulted from inherited degeneracy: the whole race had become 'leavened'. This 'defender of the white race' was knighted in 1946, yet he has a half-Jamaican descendant through his bête-noire, mixed marriage[4440].

Four months after a former policewoman and social worker told a group of eight drunken noisy Kent university students to go home, she was arrested in her nightgown and charged with using racially aggravated threatening words or behaviour. When the Lib Dem councillor appeared in court she denied the charge[4441].

West Midlands Police refused to provide any evidence to support allegations that C4's 'Undercover Mosque' was racialist. The Assistant Chief Constable Anil Patani wrote an illiterate letter to C4 that his force's priority 'has been to investigate the documentary and it's (sic) making with as much rigour as the extremism the programme sought to portray'. One observer comments that this 'perfectly captures the police's pig-headed, irresponsible and sloppy handling of the whole affair'. Patani has a record of extreme sensitivity to minority groups' demands. 'Dispatches' also highlighted how Islamic extremism can become criminal, e.g. Abu Hamza lectured young Muslims on how to bring down a plane at Heathrow and young men with baseball bats took over Luton mosque, but the police did nothing[4442].

British Transport Police in Scotland are to be taught sectarian songs so they can deal with bigotry on trains[4443].

The zealousness with which Scottish police tackle fashionable 'hate' crime is demonstrated by the case of a thug who racially abused a Monklands Hospital doctor in Airdrie: for telling Dr. Richard Stevenson 'F... off back to England', he was jailed for six months[4444].

'If the police had done their job, I would have spent the last 18 years grieving for my son rather than fighting to bring his killers to justice' – Stephen Lawrence's mother (2012). The officers arriving at the murder scene knew no first aid, nor did they apply it[4445]. Richard Stone, expert witness to the Macpherson inquiry, says there hasn't been much change in police attitudes since the inquiry[4446].

Brian Paddick says when he started in the police in 1976 racism was quite overt, but he saw nothing wrong with it. Only three of the 117 top Met officers are BEM. It remains to be seen how racism in the Met is dealt with now that governance of the police by the pro-equality Metropolitan Police Authority has been replaced by the Mayor[4447].

Teacher Stuart Lawrence, brother of racially murdered Stephen, has called for an independent inquiry after the Met rejected his racial harassment claims: he alleged he had been stopped and/or searched on 25 occasions, many times in his car (he has always had a clean licence)[4448].

Strathclyde Police have ordered two amateur Old Firm teams to play behind closed doors and out of town (allegedly the police also wanted an 8am kick-off). The Blantyre Celtic and Rangers don't want the fans segregated as the police demanded: football, they argue, facilitates social cohesion[4449].

Daily Mail (formerly Sun editor) journalist Kelvin Mackenzie suggests, in the light of reports that 19 Met officers are only being 'investigated' for racism, that Commissioner Hogan-Howe starts treating people equally[4450].

It has been claimed the Met failed to investigate properly the 2010 death by fire of a bus driver because he was black. A secret police report says the investigating officers blundered, e.g. they said he had committed suicide, and took a year to take a crucial witness statement. The victim was a police informant. DS Christopher Kirk was part of the probe, and admitted an omission by his officers[4451].

Dr. Richard Stone, one of the Macpherson inquiry team, says (2012) he still considers the Met is institutionally racist[4452].

Bevan Powell, head of the Black Police Association, says the Met can't be trusted to deal with racism on its own, so there should be government intervention in the form of an organisation like the Stephen Lawrence steering group. In the previous five years only two out of 2,270 officers accused of racism lost their jobs, and even these two were allowed to resign rather than be dismissed, so they could retain their pensions[4453].

A black fireman claims he was arrested and Tasered while trying to help police, because he was black. He was cleared of obstructing police by magistrates[4454].

City of London Police were facing (2012) an employment tribunal brought by an ex-trainee officer, Anthony Joseph, who claims he was forced to resign by 'insidious bigotry'. Allegedly senior ranks let racist remarks go unchallenged, e.g. that black people have a 'predisposition towards crime'. Just 5.8% of City of London officers are BEM, compared with 9.6% of the Met[4455].

Complaints of racism against police have more than doubled in 10 years. Unsurprisingly police, who adjudicate on the complaints against themselves, find most are without foundation. Fewer than 1 in 40 accused face official punishment. Most racist incidents are probably not reported, so the figures suggest the service is in denial[4456].

The Met has banned its IT staff from using the words 'blacklist' and 'whitelist'[4457].

A Civitas report says police fail to probe crimes committed by ethnic minorities (e.g. 'honour crimes') because they are afraid of being branded racist[4458].

Four Thames Valley antiterrorism cops visited an eight-year-old Muslim's home after she told classmates her uncle wanted to get a bomb. Hundreds of young Muslims have been targeted under 'Prevent and Channel' projects, costing £77m so far – they aim to prevent al Qaeda recruitment[4459].

Police treat multi-ethnic communities (eg Sikhs, Somalian Moslems, Roman Catholic Congolese) not as one neighbourhood but as discrete groups: cops used to identify with communities by living with them.

Stop and Search

Thousands of illegal immigrants who should be deported are routinely set free because police fear the racism charge if they check a suspect's nationality (enhanced checks triple the number of illegals identified)[4460]. Yet an international report by the Open Society Justice Initiative reveals police in England and Wales use racial profiling more than any other force when stopping citizens without evidence they have committed a crime (use of Section 60 has risen over 300% between 2005 and 2009)[4461]. Most forces in Scotland refuse to record criminals' nationality, and though courts will soon have to do so, police will not be forced to do likewise[4462].

Only 13% of stop and searches lead to an arrest. Section 44 of the 2000 Terrorism Act and Section 60 of the 1994 Criminal Justice and Public Order Act dispense with the need for an officer to have reasonable grounds for suspicion. Very rarely are people told they needn't answer questions other than provide their personal details, at the time of the stop[4463].

Police are stopping whites to avoid appearing anti-Asian. Lord Carlile, independent reviewer of anti-terror laws, says police are using the power for non-terrorism purposes. Searches in 2008 trebled to over 124,000[4464]. Carlile has warned against police using an anti-terror law to stop pictures of the police being taken (it only covers a photo likely to be of use to a terrorist)[4465].

Some police officers would invent evidence to secure a 'sus' conviction, according to Brian Paddick. In 1978 a young black man in the dock at Highbury Corner pled guilty to 'sus'. Paddick's colleague explained that the 'guilty' man had done nothing, but was given the choice of 'sus' or a burglary rap ('sus' needed no corroborative evidence)[4466].

The Runnymede Trust, a race relations think tank, claimed in 2009 that police forces discriminate deliberately against ethnic minorities: they 'are more racist than a decade ago' (e.g. much more likely to stop and search)[4467].

A black driver with no criminal record and a clean licence was stopped by police ten times in a year[4468].

When MP Diane Abbott's brother's Mercedes was stolen by three armed thugs, three Met detectives interrogated black Hugh Abbott as to whether he was a criminal, rather than hunting for the gang. He was asked if he really had a Mercedes, about his financial status and whether he had been drinking[4469].

West Midlands head of training, Superintendent <u>Chris Pretty</u>, was demoted after calling a model BMW car 'black man's wheels', adding to the urban myth that BMWs are only driven by black criminals[4470].

Frank Bruno says he was stopped by police and accused of stealing his own car, without them performing even cursory checks[4471].

The Battle for Brixton (1981) was the biggest breakdown of law and order in Britain for two centuries (300 police officers were injured). The police had launched Swamp 81, which meant using their stop-and-search powers 1,000 times – one of the triggers for the disaster[4472].

Black citizens are 26 times more likely to be stopped and searched than whites, Asians 6 times[4473]. The abuse by police of stop and search powers is shown by the fact that with more than 100,000 people stopped in 2009 there was not one arrest[4474]. The 'Sus laws' led to race riots in London, Birmingham and Liverpool, and in 2010 draft Home Office police guidance would again have allowed race to be a basis for stop and search without suspicion[4475].

Drug arrest bias is worse in the UK than the US: blacks are six times more likely than whites to be arrested for drug offences (three times in US), and 11 times likelier to be imprisoned (10 times in US) for these offences[4476]. Thames Valley Police have been criticised (2010) by the Equality and Human Rights Commission for stopping and searching black people six times as often as whites, i.e. in a 'disproportionate' manner[4477].

Stop-and-search was blamed for the 1981 Brixton riots and the 1985 Handsworth riots in Birmingham, and was condemned by the Macpherson Report, but in 2007 Keith Jarrett, president of the National Black Police Association, called for an <u>increase</u> in the strategy in black communities[4478]. 'Operation Swamp' (which increased stop-and-search) arguably set Brixton ablaze in 1987, but ironically there were no policemen to be seen as looters roamed (e.g. ransacked the Windsor Castle pub on the Saturday night). It was the police who bore the brunt of criticism in the Scarman Report, even though 5,000 rioters had rampaged through Brixton. Lambeth Council has renamed the riots the 'Brixton Uprising'[4479].

Vanessa Feltz has revealed callers to her radio show include blacks stopped and searched – a 14-year-old simply walking home in the early evening, a job applicant in a suit and carrying a briefcase on the way to an interview, a woman on her way to a dinner party[4480].

Muslim leaders have claimed Scottish Asians have been targeted with stop searches by British Transport Police at Glasgow's stations and subway[4481].

Stop-and-search has doubled since the Stephen Lawrence inquiry, according to a Southampton University study – 14% of shooting killing incidents are due to legal firearms[4482].

It is claimed police use stop-and-search to intimidate, and if the person refuses to give their name, 'the intimidation will worsen, they start making threats'. Police apparently target 13-16-year-olds in particular[4483].

A black man stopped by police in August, 2011, in Beckton, East London, recorded his conversation with several officers, when he claims the racist 'N' word was used. Though one officer (PC Alex MacFarlane) was suspended, the CPS decided not to prosecute him and two colleagues. They are reconsidering this, and the case has been referred to the IPCC. The victim reportedly was throttled by another officer, and the third officer has been placed on restricted duties[4484]. Police don't take action against <u>black</u> urban men who call each other 'n.....r'[4485].

Brian Paddick's secret 2004 report warning of racism among Met officers said black citizens were being disproportionately targeted under 'stop and search', but was ignored by the top brass[4486].

Compensation

The problem with the waters of racism is that they are constantly muddied by greed. Black police van driver PC Amechi Onwugbonu gave evidence of assaultive behaviour by white <u>PC Jones</u> against three youths. Jones was cleared of racially aggravated behaviour and his white colleagues were found not guilty of cover-up. Jones was also accused of attacking a terrorist suspect, and was appearing in the dock with three other officers.

The Met had previously compensated a white officer for racial discrimination – Detective Chief Superintendent <u>Barry Norman</u>, who led the £22m corruption probe into <u>Ali Dizaei</u>[4487]. Norman received £40,000 compensation, having claimed his career suffered as a result of the <u>Dizaei</u> inquiry[4488].

Andy Ball

British Transport Police Acting Chief Superintendent <u>Andy Ball</u> has dressed up as a Ku Klux white supremacist who subjects a black officer to a mock trial at Surrey's Tadworth training college. Ball was responsible for educating the force about racial sensitivities, yet told the young black he shouldn't walk on a zebra crossing's white lines. Ball was only given 'words of advice'. An employment tribunal found the force behaved in a racist way against a black detective. Another officer, of mixed race, claimed she was the victim of racist abuse, but settled out of court, so that the officers concerned weren't disciplined[4489].

Gurpal Virdi

Sikh DS <u>Gurpal Virdi</u>, who had already won £240,000 from the Met for sacking him (they wrongly accused him of sending racist messages to himself and colleagues and he was reinstated), he claiming racial discrimination, won a further £4,500 and a public apology from the Met in 2008. Reinstated, later in that year he had another claim to be completed. He said he had been victimised, e.g. by allowances not being made for his failing vision when he took police exams. He claims he was framed by white Ealing colleagues when he threatened to expose the way they dealt with race crime. A tribunal found the Met had tried to entrap him in a taped interview and failed to interview him in an informal way as with a white policeman[4490]. He had previously given evidence on racism in the Met to the Stephen Lawrence inquiry.

The National Black Police Association announced in 2001 that sex and race discrimination cases were costing the forces over £20 million annually, but the figure would be much higher if out-of-court settlements are added. Victims of crime payouts are far lower than the jackpots paid to officers who 'milk the system'[4491].

Commander <u>Shabir Hussain</u> accused Sir Ian Blair of racism in 2008 but went on to lose a racial discrimination claim. He retired (2010) with a 'bad knee' and a pension pot worth up to £350,000, having been awarded by Met chiefs a year's temporary promotion to Deputy Assistant Commissioner on a salary £40,000 more than his commander's salary. His ill-health pension was approved by the Met Police Authority, though he reportedly has been seen walking unaided and without discomfort (a few weeks previously he was hobbling and using a walking stick at a police chiefs' dinner)[4492]. <u>Hussain</u>, the Met's head of traffic policing, had sued for £0.75m for failure to become deputy assistant commissioner (he also says he had suffered racist graffiti when promoted to sergeant[4493]).

Sikh PC policeman <u>Gurmal Singh</u>, told to remove his turban to do riot training, was awarded £12,600 compensation by an employment tribunal. He said he suffered humiliation and stress, but the tribunal rejected 13 of his 15 allegations[4494].

<u>Tarique Ghaffur</u>, the UK's most senior Asian policeman, claims a 'barrage' of death threats against him were made by serving officers. Apparently because of his £1m discrimination claim a number of senior colleagues felt it was no longer possible to work with him. On his part he decided not to formally notify the Yard of the threats because he could no longer trust the Met to protect him[4495]. His racist accusations demoralised colleagues and plunged the Met into a damaging 'race war', but he was humiliated when he had to settle out-of-court for a quarter of his claim[4496].

A Muslim chef sued the Met for religious discrimination because he was asked to cook pork products for '999 breakfasts' – the hearty fry-ups are traditional for officers going on shift[4497].

The Yard's top Muslim woman, Yasmin Rehman, has sued for 'repeated discrimination', despite being paid £60,000 a year as director of partnerships and diversity. A Sikh constable was rejected by the operational support unit of the counter terrorist branch because his turban prevented the regulation headgear being worn. When he claimed discrimination, West Midlands Police wasted £100,000 on head gear that would fit – it didn't[4498].

DC Bailey, a member of the Greater Manchester Black and Asian Police Association, was suing for discrimination (2008) because he came to work in full African dress (claiming the rules allow 'cultural dress') but was sent home. He was upset that WPCs don't have to wear ties but men do[4499].

Tooting terror suspect Babar Ahmad won £60,000 from the Met for assault by five or six arresting officers in 2003 (one was to face criminal proceedings over an unrelated incident) – at one point he was told to pray on his knees and asked, 'Where is your god now?'. His genitals were exposed and touched[4500].

Wiltshire firearms officer Amjad Farooq, removed from his job with the Diplomatic Protection Group guarding the PM on 'national security grounds', launched a compensation claim in 2008. It was the first employment tribunal held behind closed doors[4501]. His superiors had learned his children attended a mosque with alleged connections to a radical preacher[4502].

Met Police Commissioner Blair used his 'very significant influence' to pinpoint his chosen officers for promotion, to the detriment of other candidates, a race discrimination hearing was told (2008).

It is claimed Kate Middleton's bodyguard Ieuan Jones intimidated a black WPC in the Territorial Support Group with racist (and sexist) abuse, with the Met agreeing to pay compensation of £300,000 out-of-court, despite their having refused to investigate the victim's complaints. These included being given white face paint as a Xmas present. White officers called her 'groid' (for 'negroid' and 'bif' – black ignorant xxxxxx). Jones, instead of being disciplined, was promoted to D.S.[4503]

Six white members of the Met's Territorial Support Group are suing the Met for racial discrimination[4504]. West Yorkshire Sergeant Peter Richmond is suing his force for racial discrimination, claiming he missed out on promotion simply because he is white. An Asian officer was fast-tracked into a job he was applying for: an internal job description stated the force wanted an ethnic in the position[4505].

At one point Yasmin Rehman's action in 2008 against Sir Ian Blair's Met was the fifth by ethnic-minority officers or staff[4506].

Deaths and Race

Over 200 Hertfordshire police and civilian staff faced disciplinary action in 2006 for allegedly networking a video of a black man being decapitated. Recipients of the sick e-mail added comments like, 'Look what happens when you run from the police'. The offending e-mail was investigated earlier in 2006 when it was circulated by Merseyside officers[4507].

Thousands of Muslim women are terrorised by the threat of honour killings, yet very few such cases result in prosecutions because of the police racism paranoia[4508].

The Broadwater Farm riots started when black resident Cynthia Jarrett died from a heart attack when police raided her home[4509].

Recruitment

Police recruitment may not be a level playing field. One white applicant discovered all the ethnic minority applicants had had a day's training to help them, yet no white applicant had been offered this[4510]. Brian Paddick describes recruitment discrimination against high-calibre white males.

A Muslim WPC refused (2007) to shake the hand of Sir Ian Blair at a passing-out parade – because Muslim women shouldn't touch a male stranger – and also to have her photo taken with him – in case it was used for propaganda to enlist Muslim women (there are less than 20 among the Met's 35,000 officers)[4511].

Gloucestershire Police deselected over 100 white potential recruits simply because they weren't BME, though their adverts didn't admit their intention was to discriminate against whites, as part of an 'advance diversity' drive. The police later admitted their approach was illegal. Likewise Avon & Somerset Police rejected 186 white applicants[4512].

Muslim Met recruit PC Zaheer Zamir dropped his racism claim when it became known he lied about being Assistant Commissioner Tarique Gaffur's nephew, and that he may have lied about his qualifications. His claims included being the object of racist taunts at Hendon Police College[4513].

In the BBC documentary 'The Secret Policeman' a white Greater Manchester recruit damns the memory of murdered black teenager Stephen Lawrence (saying his killers should be given immunity), and threatens an Asian colleague. He describes the Macpherson Report as 'a f........ kick in the bollocks for any white man', and boasts of admiring Combat 18 and the Ku Klux. A chief constable of Greater Manchester admitted there was 'institutionalised racism' in his force. The undercover reporter was admitted to the force without being asked his views on race[4514].

Police recruitment from ethnic minorities is falling, and many ethnic minority organisations now advise non-cooperation with the police[4515]. ACPO president Ken Jones has said police recruitment should be biased in favour of non-whites. He denied ethnic quotas resulting from positive discrimination would lower standards[4516]. Race watchdogs attacked (2007) ACPO plans to consider introducing quotas for ethnic minority recruits, arguing that these could actually worsen community relations[4517].

Controversial race 'diversity' targets instituted after the 1999 Macpherson Report made it more difficult for white men (but not women) to join the police. Some forces overstepped the mark by positively discriminating[4518].

The IPCC's 2004 report on Dizaei 'deplored' the decision of senior Met officers to do a back-door deal, they being more interested in 'effective diversity recruitment' than the discipline process[4519].

The Islamisation of the British police is proceeding apace. As many as eight Met officers and staff are suspected of extremist links, Islamists being deliberately admitted to the force with the idea that they can help oppose Islamic radicalism. The erstwhile head of the Met's Muslim Contact Unit, Commander Robert Lambert, feels fighting terrorism requires partnerships with, e.g., Salafists (Sunni theocrats) – one Salafist was an officer in the Unit. Forces have abandoned the usual vetting criteria in an attempt at hiring BMEs, especially when it comes to hiring PCSOs, but this may mean compromising the security of police operations[4520]. A secret list of up to eight police and civilian staff suspected of Al Qaeda links has been drawn up: it is claimed the police have no legal power to dismiss them. It is unlikely the Met is the only infiltrated force[4521].

Police recruits who fail anti-racism tests can become serving officers. Hampshire Police gave a second chance to 252 applicants in 2007 who had narrowly failed entrance tests[4522].

NPBA and **BPA**

A Civitas report suggests that white Christians are unfairly targeted by police over hate crimes compared with ethnic and religious minorities. CPS decisions may be influenced by the National Black Crown Prosecution Association. The latter has denied this[4523].

A group of white police officers has campaigned to have the NBPA (National Black Police Association) and the BPA (Black Police Association) wound up[4524]. The NBPA was itself accused of being racist by a guest speaker at its conference – he had been invited by mistake and emphasised the NBPA's ban on full white membership. He was asked if he wanted an escort from the conference building because he had enraged some of the audience[4525].

The National Association of Muslim Police has warned that the anti-terrorism strategy encourages Islamophobia[4526].

A BBC Panorama programme claimed a sizeable number of ethnic minority officers suffer racism at work, but Asian Chief Superintendent Mak Chishty is worried about the increasing militancy of the NBPA[4527].

In 2008 the NBPA not only urged ethnics not to join the force, but announced they would boycott any recruitment drive, saying it would intensify its ethnic recruitment boycott in protest at Sir Paul Stephenson's appointment[4528]. The irony is that the NBPA is itself racist – a separatist organisation of the BME (black and minority ethnics). Nobody has been sacked for saying that Muslims can't trust the police, even though it's highly inflammatory. The Met has the Association of Muslim Police, the Christian Police Association as well as the Met Police Hindu Association: this is all divisive, not inclusive[4529].

Dizaei was expected in 2007 to accuse senior Met officers of trying to 'take out' NBPA members, in revenge for NBPA claims that they had failed to accept the Macpherson Report into the botched Stephen Lawrence investigation[4530].

By 2008 over 300 officers had contacted branches of the NBPA, e.g. there is claimed to be a persistent racist 'canteen culture', and many complaints centre on promotion. There was still only one BME borough commander out of 32[4531].

The Association of Muslim Police has accused 20 forces of refusing to cooperate with a service discrimination audit (only 23 revealed how they treated Muslim officers). The Serious Organised Crime Agency has been accused of racism for allegedly using a 'blacked-up' white actor to play an African in a training exercise[4532].

The Met Muslim policeman (PC Alexander Basha) excused guard duty at the Israeli Embassy had to be moved to a police safe house, over concerns for his safety. Basha's marriage had been 'blessed' by hate preacher Omar Bakri Mohammed, yet he was allowed to join the Diplomatic Protection Group, for which he would have been vetted by Special Branch[4533].

The British Sikh Police Association claims ACPO has no respect for its members. A Sikh PC was awarded £12,500 for racial discrimination and harassment – he was ordered to remove his sacred turban during riot training and had been the victim of an 'offensive violation of dignity'[4534].

Police officer Steven Hutt was sacked (1999) for calling a difficult suspect a 'black bastard'. He was eventually reinstated, with the Black Police Association condemning this[4535].

Cover-up

There is significant under-reporting of racial incidents: 'We are only seeing the tip of the iceberg'[4536].

Channel 4 won £100,000 from West Midlands Police for falsely accusing the channel of faking footage in 'Undercover Mosque' (the CPS was also party to the false accusation). Police told Ofcom the words of imams were heavily edited to make them more sinister, so stirring up racial hatred, undermining 'community cohesion' and 'feelings of public reassurance'. Ofcom concluded the documentary was legitimate, but West Midlands failed to take down their original pejorative website. Eventually the CPS and the police admitted their allegations were wrong. The police had argued the clerics' pronouncements were taken 'out of context', but they never explained what was the correct context for: women are 'born deficient', homosexuals are to be thrown off mountains, 10-year-old girls should be hit if they refuse to wear the hijab'[4537]. 'If the Chief Constable of the West Midlands and the head of the CPS won't resign, they should be sacked'[4538].

A senior policeman has accused top officers in the Greater Manchester force of ignoring a report from an Oldham officer which highlighted increased racial tension in the Lancs. town and the risk of violence.

In one Inner London school class (with mostly black pupils), none would phone police if their mobile was stolen[4539].

The Met's report in the 1980s into the West Midlands Serious Crime Squad was kept secret, with obviously no action taken, for serious complaints continued. Birmingham's Chief Constable disbanded the Squad in 1989 and the IPCC and West Yorkshire Police found coloured people being targeted, sometimes with torture to ensure confessions, including partial asphyxia using plastic bags. One officer said his fist was a 'truth drug'. Though the Squad was found guilty of disciplinary offences (e.g. claiming excessive overtime), not one officer was ever legally prosecuted[4540].

Individual Racists

Black Met PC Wayne Bell, who made monkey noises and ape gestures at a black suspect, was finally sacked in 2007 after a failed prosecution, a misconduct panel, two police reviews and a High Court challenge. He had called the suspect a badly-behaved chimp. Bell's white colleague PC Neil Wakeling was also disciplined for failing to report Bell[4541].

For many years Commander Ali Dizaei 'poisoned race relations within the Metropolitan Police'. He used the issue for his own ends as president of the National Black Police Association. Thus Commander Shabir Hussain launched an NBPA-supported racial claim against the Met, while at the same time Assistant Commissioner Ghaffur – rumoured to be encouraged to pursue his attack by Dizaei and the NBPA's dodgy 'legal adviser' – was about to follow suit with a lengthy indictment of the 'racist' force, when Dizaei's false assault allegation caused his campaign to unravel[4542].

Wayne Bell

Black Met WPC Joy Hendricks punched and kicked a white sergeant in 1998 over a series of insults[4543].

Strathclyde PC Christopher Halaka was arrested at a taxi rank in Perth after another Strathclyde policeman accused him of chanting IRA slogans, reporting the alleged sectarian abuse to Tayside Police[4544].

A Grampian Police 'diversity liaison' officer visited an Aberdeen kilt maker with a warning about his 'racist' T-shirts urging Scottish football fans to back 'anyone but England' in the World Cup. The officer was supposedly following up a complaint, but in fact was acting on his own initiative[4545]. Another of the store's T-shirts which could 'spark racial unrest' was one with the slogan 'Algeria, USA and Slovenia Supporters Club'[4546].

White Essex PC Phil Trus, a firearms officer, was alleged to have made a racist remark in a police station about a black man who had drowned: someone should have thrown the victim 'a rope of bananas'. The case was referred to the IPCC[4547].

Sunday Times columnist Rod Liddle has revealed how in the 1980s a House of Commons policeman told him that soon the 'chill wind of Odin' would blow the immigrant scum from the streets of Britain. Though police cannot be BNP members, ACPO says they can be members of the Revolutionary Communist Party of Great Britain (which seeks to violently overthrow the state) as well as Sinn Fein[4548]. Retired Strathclyde chief inspector Charles Reid was on an internet list of BNP activists in 2008.

Strathclyde Sergeant Gavin Ross, a training officer at the Scottish Police College at Tulliallan, was probed for allegedly abusing an Asian sergeant, using swearwords to refer to his Muslim faith[4549].

Fife PC Gregg Loudon was facing the sack in 2008 for shouting and swearing bigoted abuse and chanting sectarian songs at a Glasgow football match. He had been drinking with friends, being arrested for refusing to stop when challenged by police[4550].

A white officer promised to 'bring down all the lazy blacks, one by one'. Met policeman Asad Saeed said, in his discrimination claim, that he and his ethnic colleagues 'were treated like dogs'. Another support officer, Peter Campbell, told how white officers played 'spot the PCSO' at night[4551].

Senior Yard bureaucrat Martin Tiplady, OBE, member of ACPO, sits on the Commissioner's powerful management board and is in charge of HR at the Met. Having won accolades for his efforts to boost ethnic recruitment, he was accused by a black woman official in the Met's Strategy and Improvement Department of misconduct[4552].

Slough PC Nick Bond referred to some Romanian gypsy families as 'society's worst nightmare' and a 'a plague to their own countrymen'[4553].

Scottish anti-terror Detective Sergeant Andy Goodwin of Strathclyde Police is alleged to have made a racist remark to an English colleague after England lost a football match in 2007. In 2006 the Commission for Racial Equality in Scotland reported that anti-English sentiments had become a problem[4554].

34 years ago Tariq Ghaffur was excluded from a Manchester police station because the white desk cop couldn't believe an Asian could be a PC.

A white Berkshire man was taken to court for racially abusing three white security guards, calling them 'honky wannabe cops'. ('Honky' is slang for white person)[4555].

Sergeant Henry Beresford, of the British Transport Police, and responsible for teaching other officers to be racially sensitive, stood by while PC Mike Parker, wearing a Hitler shirt, subjected a Jewish subordinate to Nazi salutes. He also allegedly subjected the victim to anti-semitic comments and a previous black victim to a mock Ku-Klux-Klan-style trial. Beresford was only fined. Another BTP officer, DS Alison Martin, was given a formal warning after allegedly referring to an Asian caller as a 'Paki bastard'[4556].

A Middlesex Asian shopkeeper was hauled away to a police station while his family was having breakfast, accused of writing an unsigned, misspelt racist letter to London's Mayor, abusing other Asians. The police seized the family's computers and kept them for weeks – his son couldn't access his homework or his father his business accounts. The police eventually dropped charges in a case where the victim had from the outset obviously been set up by someone with a grudge[4557].

Met PC Geoff Whitehead, an employment tribunal was told, would refuse to pick up ethnic minority staff in the force van, leaving them to walk over a mile back to the station: he used his role as a driver to operate an apartheid culture[4558].

During Sir Ian Blair's tenure at Scotland Yard there was an illegal bugging operation into black and Asian officers in the Met. This raised fears of a secret police attempt to sabotage racial discrimination cases brought against the force. This was the first time the reasons put forward by the police to justify phone hacking have been found to be unlawful (at least 30 racial cases were brought while the Met was bugging the NBPA)[4559].

Drunken Met PC Philip Juhasz told a Pakistani shopkeeper to 'go back to your …. country'. He was convicted of a racially aggravated public order offence. Other officers tried to cover up the incident in court to preserve his good character. Juhasz had tried to get half-price food by boasting he was a cop. Since Macpherson only one of 120 Met police guilty of racism was dismissed. In 2012 four officers of the Police Service of Northern Ireland were suspended over sectarian and racist text messages, and referred to the IPCC. Met PC Joe Harrington was accused of assaulting and racially abusing a 15-year-old in custody at Forest Gate police station (2011): he is on restricted duties. A sergeant and two PCs from a Newham tactical squad were suspended accused of using racist language, while a call-handling PC is on restricted duties for screening out BME calls. A PC and staff officer are accused of using racist language in Islington. Two Met police officers – accused of racially stigmatising a number of PCSOs in Wandsworth – were suspended, whereas five Territorial Support Group officers accused of racist attacks on children remained on duty. An unidentified cop was accused of racially abusing a member of the public in Camden, while a black WPC was accused of using racially abusive language against both black and white police colleagues (she is on restricted duties)[4560].

Met PC Alex MacFarlane was to be prosecuted for allegedly telling a young black man 'You will always be a nigger' in the back of a police van. Hogan-Howe says there is one racial complaint against the police every day[4561].

An unnamed police officer was suspended and charged with a sectarian hate crime arising from Rangers fans vandalising toilets at Celtic Park (the clip identifying the officer appeared on YouTube)[4562].

Brian Moore, the new head of the UK Border Force, was formerly a Borough police commander in South London. In 1999 he was questioned by a senior officer over alleged involvement with a Met police holiday group whose acronym is W.O.G.S., a derogatory term for black people[4563].

DCI Mark Ling, in charge of a 2013 case of child abduction by a teacher, had been suspended in 2011, found guilty of gross misconduct and given a final warning. He had, while District Commander in Hastings, been accused of sending racist and sexually explicit text messages to colleagues, one mocking the town, another an allegedly racist joke about model Katie Price's disabled son, who is blind and autistic[4564].

Databases

The ultra-liberal Sir <u>Ian Blair</u> admitted in 2002 that most muggers are black. The Met hold black men responsible for more than half of muggings and street crime, and more than two thirds of shootings, with black women also accountable for more than their fair share of violent crime[4565]. 30% - 40% of black men were on the DNA database, compared with 10% of white and Asian men[4566].

Almost a quarter of black children (10-17) over 10 have their DNA retained on the police database, whereas less than 10% of white youths have been added. In most cases the profiles are kept when they become adults[4567].

'Racial profiling' by police in England and Wales increased during 2011, with blacks 30 times more likely than whites to be stopped and searched under section 60 – the worst international record for such discrimination. Home Office data reveal less than 0.5% of s.60 searches led to an arrest (for possession of a dangerous weapon), five times less than a decade previously – the IPCC agrees that 'blank' searches (yielding no arrest) antagonise minorities and are 'hugely intrusive'. When the new Met Commissioner, <u>Bernard Hogan-Howe</u>, took charge as chief constable of Merseyside, section 60s rose from 1,389 to 23,138 within five years[4568].

After the 2003 ITV file 'The Secret Policeman' the Commission For Racial Equality made 125 recommendations, concluding that racism is at the core of policing. Three-quarters of 360 responders in a 2008 Black Police Association survey ('Messages from the Front Line') said they had experienced racism (e.g. 'I was treated like a slave'). Racism is now more discreet, having gone underground. Two Stockwell Transport sergeants were found to have Ku Klux paraphernalia in their common room. BME recruits are twice as likely to drop out in the first six months, having to work harder than whites to prove efficiency, loyalty, etc. Of 2,755 firearms officers only 50 were BME. One black copper was 'overqualified', yet many tried to prevent his promotion: the playing field was not level. 88 BME officers have won over £1m in five years, and six of the most senior cops have taken the Met to court over race. BME are much more likely to be investigated by their own force than whites (in Strathclyde five times as often, in the Met two and a half times as often), e.g. if they complain about racism. Three-fifths of BME said in five years the prevalence of racism was the same or had got worse.

Apparently urban black men habitually call each other 'n....r', but the police don't charge them as they might a white man[4569].

The Met was to become the first public body to adopt a diversity policy of prioritising top jobs for blacks and women: if just as qualified as whites or male they will be preferred ('tokenism', as some would call it)[4570].

CHAPTER XXIV

THE SECRETIVE POLICEMAN

CONTENTS

CHAPTER XXIV

THE SECRETIVE POLICEMAN

The Cover-up Culture

This chapter will suggest institutionalised omerta is endemic not only in the Mafia but in the UK's police 'service'. A detective driven out by a false accusation says the police culture is incestuous, arrogant and more concerned with covering backs than admitting mistakes: the rules are conspiracy, collusion and face-saving. Some detectives try to maintain the 'traditional detective culture' of secretiveness and individualism[4571]. Self-serving spin and presentational exaggeration, run by the expensive PR industry, have replaced telling the public the facts. It has been suggested by newspaper editors that Leveson has encouraged public and state authorities to conceal information that should be public property[4572].

Forces across Britain are covering up the dismissal of 160 officers annually by trying them in secret hearings (in three years to 2011 477 have been sacked, 52 demoted and hundreds fined or reprimanded – all surreptitiously). Many accused are suspended (on full pay) for long periods (a Grampian officer for almost five years before his case came up). Sergeant Ewan McHardy, arrested in the north of Scotland for drink-driving, tried to cheat by watering his urine sample. He was paid £160,000 while suspended from work[4573]. 'The Times' investigation found a postcode punishment lottery (sacking or a fine for the same offence). Though the IPCC has been able to order public hearings (since 2004), only one has been held (a second was to be held in the G20 case)[4574].

Police forces have secretly removed dozens of sex offenders from the Sex Offenders' Register, citing Article 8 of the Human Rights Act and data protection[4575].

Much police misconduct is witnessed by rank-and-file officers, but little is reported – this is similar to the medical profession.

A harassment victim couple were referred to a plausible beat policeman who said to e-mail him with every incident. The victims did this, but the cop was soon transferred, yet didn't think to tell them: he wasn't logging their e-mails. With even about 50 complaints the police still said they hadn't heard of them. The police computer had no way of grouping regular reports of low-level intimidation at the same address. The victims made a formal complaint about the officer but it was never pursued. 'Trying to get help was worse than the harassment … the real nightmare was the behaviour of the police'[4576].

Because amphetamine-related crime often occurs within the closed doors of the speed culture, such crime is largely ignored by police, rarely leading to arrests or convictions[4577].

Constable Brian Carswell, who removed footage of his assault on a teenager from the latter's mobile phone, was jailed for six months, one of the charges being trying to defeat the course of justice[4578].

A series of chief constables (14 of the 43 forces in England and Wales) are using Leveson's report on Press standards as a pretext to avoid naming suspects when they are arrested or charged. ACPO is conceding that suspects should be named in 'some' circumstances[4579]. Police Scotland have also refused to reveal names of homicide victims where no one has been convicted. There were over 500 unresolved murders in the Strathclyde force area alone[4580]: this figure only surfaced because of a bureaucratic blunder, and Police Scotland has admitted it may not release the pan-Scotland figure.

'Neighbourhood Policing' (previously Safer Neighbourhoods) is actually 'Ward Policing', with a Ward comprising up to 12 or more neighbourhoods) – spin rather than substance. Only 11% of manpower is devoted to Neighbourhood Policing.

A leaked police memo (from Detective Chief Superintendent Peter Barron) reveals that serious crime across Britain is greater than official figures show. There could be 58% more GBH cases, 20% more gun crimes and 15% more knife offences than supposed. The memo emphasises there has been appreciable under-reporting of violent crime[4581].

Ex-cop Ian Woolford was excused a speeding fine issued by his old force after insisting he couldn't remember who was driving[4582].

A policeman sacked after accusing his superior Sgt Mick Haggart of stealing a skull from a crash scene won £400,000 compensation. The tribunal ruled the force's 'true motivation' for sacking him was 'for making protected disclosures' against colleagues[4583].

Britain's FBI – SOCA (Serious Organised Crime Agency) – has been criticised for being 'too secretive'. Set up in 2006, the quango's role is unclear to many, including police personnel. SOCA keeps talking about its successes, and risks alienating other police units[4584].

Not one of the non-journalist clients (e.g. lawyers, insurers, blue-chip companies) who hired rogue PIs has been publicly identified by SOCA, which sat on the information for many years. SOCA promised in 2010 that the names of 102 clients would be sent to the Information Commissioner to determine if any of the102 (there may even be another 'super-secret' five and a further list of 200) has committed data protection offences: this hasn't happened and none has been arrested or charged, unlike journalists. Sir Ian Andrews, the SOCA chairman who protected the firms' identities, has resigned after breaching SOCA's code of conduct (a former MOD mandarin, he failed to declare his interest in a private investigation firm he started with his wife)[4585]. Potentially the scale of wrongdoing of the hacking scandal could be dwarfed by that of the names concealed by SOCA for over five years (the police still won't make them public, nor are they investigating the names' relations with four private detectives jailed for obtaining information illegally)[4586]. When several young friends were injured in a car crash (one was seriously brain damaged) PIs hired by the UK's largest insurance body illegally trawled through their phone, employment and benefit records, but SOCA officers who probed the case never told the crash survivors they were victims of intrusive surveillance[4587].

Scotland's elite police – the Scottish Crime and Drug Enforcement Agency – are using FBI-style ID shields, but don't want to show them to anyone. A tabloid was refused permission to photograph the badge by Gordon Meldrum, of the SCDEA, which managed to get itself made exempt from FOI[4588].

In 1966 'Bobbies on the beat' were secretly phased out by the Home Office Police Advisory Board (under a Labour government)[4589].

'The Driver's Survival Handbook' purports to be 'The Insider Information The Police And Government Don't Want You To Have'[4590]. It was co-authored by Martin Thwaite, an ex-traffic policeman who has since been made a virtual outcast by his former colleagues because of his revelations.

Two women attacked by disgraced footballer Marlon King say that police asked them not to speak publicly about it – because it wouldn't be 'fair' on him[4591].

The evidence for the police claim that in areas covered by speed cameras the accident rate has fallen by 47% has never been released[4592]. A relative of a Lockerbie bombing victim has called a police review of the atrocity a 'stitch-up'[4593].

It's quite common for camera police to hide their cars or themselves (e.g. behind trees or gravestones), as trailblazed in the US and Australia. One ruse was to turn a marked police van into a scruffy builder's vehicle, which critics say proves revenue takes priority over safety – Derbyshire Police denied the van's transformation but the number plate was the same. Police in North Wales converted a horsebox into a 'stealth' speed camera[4594].

Though all 43 police forces in England and Wales were asked under FOI for nationalities of murderers and victims, only 25 replied[4595].

Scottish police are refusing to reveal to the Scottish Information Commissioner the names of officers investigating the mysterious death in Wick of Kevin McLeod in 1997[4596].

When the police hide things and their cases collapse, the costs awarded against the CPS can't be recovered from the police (because of Treasury rules), which means some officers are always up for chancing their arm. Thus in one high-profile case, that of the BNP, the criminal barrister concerned pointed out that if the existence of an undercover policeman was not disclosed, it could seriously damage the prosecution case (he had not been included in police transport when he was 'arrested' along with 14 BNP members).

Since 2004 police could take DNA samples from anyone over 10 who was arrested: by 2007 358,000 children were officially on the register, but in fact the number is far higher – by 2009 at least 1.5 million. The Home Office has always been reluctant to release the figures for children: no other European country criminalises such young children[4597].

Britain's chief constables were accused of hypocrisy when 10 refused to reveal if their DNA had been entered on the National Database (they were Bedfordshire, Cleveland, Essex, Gloucestershire, Humberside, Kent, Merseyside, Notts, Suffolk and the Met), even though it is a requirement for police to add their details when they join the force[4598].

In 2007 a coroner ordered an inquiry into an alleged cover-up after Britain's worst water poisoning scandal at Camelford in 1988. 'The Daily Mail' uncovered a pivotal unpublished police report which reveals the treatment plant was not supervised at the time of the toxic delivery. The Devon and Cornwall Constabulary account refers to 'a massive and instant contamination of the water supply'. Did commercial concerns – a prosecution could be politically damaging to Tory privatisation plans – ensure that the people of Camelford were first deceived and then ignored? There has never been a public inquiry. South West Water was prosecuted but only fined a tiny sum, and, strangely, there were no convictions by the police[4599].

The National Audit Office reported in 2008 that the number of children who carry knives had almost doubled in less than a decade, but the actual figure is much higher because police are not obliged to record details[4600].

The lawyer brother who stood bail for killer police inspector <u>Garry Weddell</u> was let off the £200,000 bill. The prosecutor alleged that the lawyer had failed to notify police about his dangerous brother's behaviour on a number of occasions[4601].

Prosecution witnesses may be told nothing by police about the case to which they have been called before going on the stand[4602].

It has been claimed that in a Scottish murder case – Nat Fraser was jailed for 25 years for the murder of Arlene Fraser in 1998 – police at the centre of the case had been put under tremendous pressure to change their stories. One WPC said she would be branded an informer if she told which colleague ordered her to stay silent. Another officer was 'interrogated' by serious crime squad police in a bid to break him down[4603]. Fraser's defence lawyer at his hearing accused the police of 'staggering incompetence', and maintained 'Somebody has died … there is a reek about the police'[4604].

The father of a boy who drowned as two police community support officers stood by claims he only found out his son had died four months later from a TV report on the inquest: even then no one from the police contacted him[4605]. The police at first refused to identify the support officers, but they were eventually named as <u>Andrew Furnival</u> and <u>Helene Weatherburn</u>, much to the anger of police chiefs[4606].

In 2007 thousands of police threatened covert industrial action over pay, e.g. by refusing to work on days off and calling in sick[4607].

When police finally solved the murder of Walter Humphrey after half a century, the victim's family were outraged that police refused to reveal the killer's identity in case it offended his family[4608].

Two daughters of Sion Jenkins, convicted of murdering his foster-child Billie Jo, did not give evidence at his trial because police convinced his lawyer it would prove 'disastrous' to his case, it has been claimed[4609].

Britain's most secretive private club – the Special Forces Club – has had an influx of police officers. Membership has traditionally been limited to the SAS, SBS, MI5 and MI6, but the increasing numbers of undercover anti-terrorist police are eligible, to the dismay of existing members[4610].

High-flying lawyer Martin Parkes committed suicide after he was 'fitted up by police'. The police raided his home and charged him with helping criminals, but the case was thrown out - the judge accused the police of using underhand methods and 'entrapment'. His family claim the police had a vendetta against him because he successfully defended criminals[4611].

Many criminals may be working with the vulnerable because of blunders in police background checks, the errors dating back for many years. Yet no public announcement was made. The Home Office denied a cover-up but couldn't explain why the information was kept secret. The problem revolves round the use of 'non-sanction detections': police know a crime has been committed by a suspect but no charges are brought[4612].

Police investigations of doctors are performed in great secrecy, according to solicitor Wendy Hesketh.

When July 7 bombing victim Anthony Fatayi-Williams' mother landed at Heathrow after the outrage she was met by a policeman, who said he was just ascertaining she had arrived in the UK, and the police would be in touch. In fact the police knew then that her first-born was dead, but six days on, police hadn't told her he'd been in the morgue all along, although they had known this[4613].

Scot Sandra Brown has been trying to prove her father, Alexander Gartshore, abused and killed a young Lanarkshire schoolgirl (Moira Anderson) in 1957. Fellow paedophile and disgraced church elder James Gallogley claimed Gartshore was part of a ring which included high-ranking police officers, Crown Office figures, Scottish Office workers and lawyers. Brown is sure this explains why the case has not been solved – on his deathbed Gallogley said Moira wasn't the only victim of the ring. She says the police are worried that releasing their secret dossier might jeopardise arrests[4614]. There are growing demands for the Lanarkshire Police to make public their dossier about this, the longest cold case in Scotland. Several FOIA requests have been refused by the constabulary, despite the deathbed confession of Gallogley, a friend of Fred West, in 1999. Police treated the case as simply a missing person inquiry until the Lord Advocate ordered them in 2012 to reopen it as a homicide. It is possible a local (Coatbridge) paedophile ring enabled a cover-up[4615].

For some years the Home Office refused to reveal how many police were being taken off the beat to act as jailers inside police stations[4616].

Steve Williams, chairman of the Police Federation, has revealed frontline officers are being pressured to minimise recorded crime[4617].

It is recorded that when policing the 19th Century political hustings 'Derbyshire and Birmingham officers, together with a few Nottingham men, drew their staves and used them most improperly'. But, of course, none of these officers could be identified[4618].

The National Trans Police Association is demanding a new vetting system to avoid transgender recruits having to reveal previous identities when they join, with serving members being protected if they change jobs. They want the taking of recruits' DNA to be performed 'more discreetly'[4619].

Some experts suggest that because police culture is so homophobic there is a reluctance to thoroughly investigate the deaths of sex workers[4620].

Though WWII looting was a capital offence, many policemen overlooked it, especially as they sometimes accepted bribes to do so. Reporting of such crimes was censored in case it undermined morale[4621].

How often do undercover officers become agents provocateurs, are there guidelines to control them, and should the police hierarchy (politicians by another name) be spending huge amounts on invigilating groups exercising their right to protest?[4622] Such questions have not been resolved.

Nearly 6,000 police officers were let off without fines in 2004 alone, having been caught speeding on camera[4623].

Police investigating the death of a millionaire judge in a mysterious fire allowed crucial evidence to be destroyed the day after his death. His mistress alleged the authorities tried to stop her fighting to find out the truth: "They were trying to cover up their mistakes".

The Labour government deliberately misled parliament over secret plans to privatise part of the police force, including a new detention officer empowered to carry out intimate body searches. A leaked Home Office briefing paper instructed the H.O. Minister Lord Rooker not to tell his fellow peers of plans to contract out detention officers to the private sector: "On no account read out the following paragraph ...".

A tabloid leader asks if we can expect anything but a whitewash in regard to inquiries into several killings of innocent men by police. Scotland's eight police forces spend at least £2 million a year investigating each other: but critics have demanded an independent watchdog, claiming too many inquiries end in secrecy and whitewash.

Even in 2001, Mirror journalist Gary Jacobs, who investigated corrupt police officers in 1964, was still not allowed to identify them. He was still not allowed years later[4624].

When Paisley man Antony Storrie died of a cocktail of legal high drugs, it took a lengthy independent probe before police revealed he had been arrested minutes before he died. Politicians condemned Police Scotland for keeping quiet about the death being in custody[4625].

Many police officers cover up their moonlighting in "unacceptable" jobs (e.g. taxis, pubs, fast food outlets). The HMRC has demanded[4626] from chief constables details of officers who register their extraneous jobs, but officers could still be concealing such unapproved jobs. Nowadays even corruption inquiries typically end in accusations of corruption among inquirers. The IPCC has admitted they often don't interview police officers involved in investigations – some won't come for interview unless under caution, and sometimes those who do come won't say anything. 200 officers resign annually to avoid misconduct hearings.

Official homicide figures in Victorian Britain grossly underestimated the number of murders, manslaughter and infanticides, especially within the family. Police and coroners (who would record open verdicts in cases where people had clearly been killed) showed a marked reluctance to investigate closely the sudden deaths of infants (a very high number of "accidental suffocations" were recorded). Beat constables were routinely violent.

It has been claimed police officers in the Jeremy Bamber case not only contaminated the scene but destroyed and withheld crucial evidence, though this has not been verified.

After WWII, when capital punishment was suspended, there was much anger in the police force that a police killer was to live. But then as now, their true feelings were censored: they were not allowed to write to the press or express their opinions in public.

A Scot whose sons were falsely accused of killing their brother has revealed the depth of corruption at the heart of the police probe. "The main feeling is that no one tells you anything. It's all hidden. There's probably a lot of things we should know but still don't". The family are still not allowed to see another force's report on the matter.

When great-grandmother Annie Davies was found dead at home with her purse containing £2,000 missing, police claims of an accident flew in the face of the evidence. After a four-year fight for justice the family have obtained an admission from the Crown Prosecution Officer that her death was suspicious. Officers had "smeared" Annie's family to expert witnesses by dismissing them as "unsavoury agitators" (see also Appendix IV). At least one witness contacted the Crown Office to question police impartiality: the police position remained unchanged through three inquiries and six reviews.

In the spring of 2011 PM Cameron refused calls for a public inquiry into the hacking affair. The matter was to be left to the police, despite there being an obvious conflict of interest in the police probing whether journalists bribed policemen in their own force[4627]. Then there was Leveson.

It was claimed on a Panorama programme (3.12.2000) that Welsh Police colluded with the Roman Catholic Church to cover up the case of a paedophile priest.

HMCIC for Scotland (Chief Inspector of Constabulary) has accused senior officers of failing to look into complaints properly. In 2007 only 39 of 3,005 complaints made to police (about assault, racism, corruption, rudeness, etc) led to disciplinary action. The Scottish Government refused to identify forces criticised for not following procedures[4628].

The number of burglaries as shown by the British Crime Survey (based on interviews with the public) soared by 14% in 2010 (one burglary a minute), contradicting the police's own figures which showed burglary down by 7% (yet 75% of burglaries remain unsolved)[4629]. Of 34 countries the UK was the worst for people being afraid to go out after dark[4630].

The IPCC has been strongly criticised for investigating just one of the nine forces accused of failings in the Savile scandal, and that one, West Yorkshire, referred itself to them. Surrey, the Met, Sussex, Thames Valley, Lancashire, Greater Manchester, Cheshire and North Yorkshire have all escaped scrutiny[4631]. Retired West Yorkshire inspector Mick Starkey ('Inspector 5') is to be fully investigated over claims he helped Savile evade prosecution: he 'acted on behalf' of the paedophile before he was interviewed by Surrey officers probing sex abuse allegations. One of the nine Savile 'Friday Morning club' cops had repeatedly refused to say whether he was 'Inspector 5'[4632]. Transcripts of the Surrey Police interview(s) appeared to show detectives taking a 'kid-glove' approach to his misdemeanours. Operation Newgreen (2013), conducted by West Yorkshire Police, found no evidence that Savile was shielded from arrest by his social relationship with police. But that force's credibility has been seriously questioned by its behaviour in relation to 'Plebgate'[4633].

Prisoners on the run now can't be named, so as to protect their human rights[4634], according to police. In 2011 the names of 47 dangerous criminals on the run couldn't be revealed. This was despite Dano Sonnex being left at large to murder two French students (Bonomo and Ferez) in 2009: he should have been recalled by police to prison[4635]. This is reminiscent of the pressure from "non-stigmatists" (such as Jeremy Bentham) which led to prisoners' identities in 19th Century penal institutions being concealed (they were also isolated from each other).

A man who had caused death by dangerous driving didn't realise that the police had a video of him causing the accident. He thought in the first weeks the police were trying to gain his trust, but, though they had enough evidence to prosecute him, they clearly did not want him to know that. By implying they were sympathetic they were trying to find out what he would say, to see if he would lie. If he did he would then be shown the video, forcing him to make admissions where the video contradicted his statement. Looking like a liar, a jury would be more likely to convict and invite a harsher sentence.

A Scottish TV team investigating war crimes suspect Anton Gecas were summoned to secret meetings with Scottish detectives, one of whom allegedly confided that they (the police) were told "not to get a result in the Gecas case". Evidence the police had uncovered about his alleged crimes was reportedly even stronger than the STV evidence. The journalists were warned not to use their private phones. On another occasion the suspect's war records disappeared shortly before STV were due to examine them.

Royal Military Police who investigated alleged killings of civilians by British soldiers in Iraq (led by Lieutenant-Colonel Mendonca) were said by The Sunday Times to have previously covered up criminal behaviour in their own ranks. One officer is reported to have spoken of the need to "protect the organisation".

Single mothers have been barred in Scotland from checking with police whether a new partner is a registered sex offender, it being left to the police's discretion to tip mothers off (women in England will be given the right).

The media were expelled by police from a firefighter's rally in Edinburgh in November, 2002.

DC Johnno Hills was suspended on full pay for daring to speak to a Sunday newspaper about Government constraints on policing: he condemned the Home Office for its obsession with statistics instead of supporting frontline policing.

There was allegedly a police (and press) cover-up and lack of response over the death of 14 black people in an arson attack at Deptford. The indifference of the authorities led to marches in 1981.

The case of Collette, murdered by her mentally ill former partner in 2005, could become the first to be heard in public after the IPCC decided to use new powers to lift the usual secrecy around its hearings, ordering exceptional cases to no longer be sub judice.

A mother has criticised police for waiting months before releasing CCTV showing two people who could be her teenage son Jesse James's killers.

Houdini's greatest trick may have been hiding his secret life as a Scotland Yard spy.

In the aftermath of July 7 some families were not told their dead relatives were lying in a police morgue. Marie Fatayi-Williams has written a book "For The Love of Anthony", in which she describes how she gave her missing son's details to the police again and again. But each time she called for an update she was informed there was no record of any previous call: for six days the police deliberately concealed her son's whereabouts.

When Dr. Fiona Clarke was found dead at debt-ridden James Cook University Hospital in Middlesbrough, police refused to reveal how she died, despite FOI (she committed suicide).

The FOIA had to be used to reveal that police spin doctors earn double the pay of beat constables (even junior press officers are paid £2,000 more). The Police Federation warned in 2006 that chief constables were secretly planning to axe a fifth of the force in the next five years.

It was revealed in 2006 that police are holding the DNA records of over one million innocent people - eight times more than had previously been admitted.

The report into the murders of Lin and Megan Russell by psychotic Michael Stone criticised those responsible for the tragedy, but all the names of the latter were removed on police advice.

Police data underestimate road deaths, and suggest road casualty figures are falling. In fact, if hospital figures are used, the number of deaths or serious injuries has actually risen.

When an Arab teenager ran amok in a parked holiday jet at Stanstead Airport in 2002, police kept this security breach secret until the press heard about it.

Paul Burrell made it known to the police that he had had a meeting with the Queen, but this crucial claim was not followed up, suggesting gross dereliction of duty by the police. The police kept the royal family in the dark over Burrell, failing to inform them that, after all the items he sold, there was no evidence of theft.

Superintendent Chula Rupasinha allegedly failed to pass on information about the killing of PC Sharon Beshinevsky. He has been probed over his links to a suspect, Raza ul Haq Aslam, who was convicted of taking part in the robbery which led to the constable's death.

Keith Waterhouse once said: "You can always tell a serious demo by the fact that the police play down the numbers present".

When a mother was involved in a fatal crash (children were killed) police said she had taken heroin - they had written privately to the hospital where she had been taken to obtain a blood specimen. The defence were told the specimen was left by mistake to degenerate on a windowsill, so they couldn't have access to it. The police were accused of a cover-up[4636].

Up to 90 UK police officers have been revealed as subscribers to Internet child pornography, and the police are letting many suspected paedophiles off with a warning, but they deny or refuse to discuss the issue of warnings. However, one police source revealed: "The National Crime Squad has told us not to give out figures".

In the 1991 disciplinary tribunal hearing of Alison Halford, the first ever woman deputy chief constable, it was opened and closed pending disclosure of files by the police, who appealed against the disclosure order. Halford asserted that her phone had been tapped and that she was under surveillance by her own force.

The police have the power to concertina many crimes into one or two (e.g. in the 2011 London riots multiple robberies were flagged up as a single crime, while in the case of the 2007 Comic Relief one small theft (by a child keeping cash it had collected) was magnified into 542 offences (every single sponsor – 542 – was interviewed at great cost)[4637].

The main expert witness used by the CPS to convict motorists in contested laser speed gun (LTI 20.20) cases - a former police officer, <u>Frank Garratt</u> - is also boss of the company importing the devices into Britain. One accused, Alastair Slade of London, has requested the video of his "crime" from police six times, to no avail.

When a serving policeman used "coppersblog" on the internet to reveal a police literacy scheme to help gypsies pass their driving tests, the whistleblower was tracked down, disciplined and warned about his future conduct.

Home Secretary Theresa May refused to identify certain chief constables who are failing to cut bureaucratic form-filling and target-setting[4638].

In a Channel 4 survey of children in custody (14.6.11), only half of police forces replied. 52 forces were asked under FOIA for details of weapons seized in schools, but only 27 responded[4639].

Police will be forced to reveal the numbers caught by each GATSO , as well as the pre-installation numbers caught. League tables will be published for the first time. Speed is responsible for less than 5% of accidents[4640].

The British Crime Survey showed an increase in crime in 2010/11 (especially a huge rise in burglary and theft), yet the number of crimes recorded by police fell (many victims don't report incidents)[4641].

Psychologists say they can now predict a life of crime even in toddlers, yet the police service still resists profiling of police recruits to exclude those with criminal traits[4642].

Rapist cop <u>Adam Carruthers</u> may have used his Masonic links to conceal his crimes. Thus despite complaints he was still promoted to inspector[4643]. Leveson has failed to respond to a question from this author as to whether Freemasonry is being probed in his inquiry.

Critics of the 'cash for cameras' policy say police under-report R.T.A. figures, e.g. in 2006 59/100,000 were killed or seriously injured, (down from 86 in 1996) according to police, whereas hospital admission figures have stayed broadly stable, with about 90/100,000 affected[4644].

Over two million violent attacks go uncounted every year, because, say two academics, the BCS (British Crime Survey) excludes large numbers of repeat offences, in a 'misleading' and 'truly bizarre' tactic: accurately measured, violent crime would rise by over four-fifths, burglaries by a fifth. The BCS limits arbitrarily the number of times a victim can suffer the same offence to five annually, as well as excluding all crimes against children under 16[4645]. 40% of muggings are committed by under-16s, but it took a FOIA request to extract this from England and Wales' 43 forces[4646].

Over 20,000 soldiers had committed crimes since leaving front-line duties by 2010, contradicting Government claims that fewer than 3,000 ex-soldiers are behind bars. Campaigners suggest 8% of the prison population are veterans, with another 8% doing community sentences[4647]. This author suspects the criminal propensities of the military may afford a hint as to those of the police service, which may also recruit a minority with psychopathic personalities. Almost 500 officers facing disciplinary proceedings over two years for misconduct and incompetence were allowed to resign rather than face the music, allegedly because it saves money. Thus victims of police waywardness are denied the chance to see them face justice. Over the two year period the BBC's Panorama found 1,915 officers had been found guilty of misconduct – only 382 were sacked[4648]. If police miscreants faced the justice they deserve, their incarceration rate might approach those of military veterans.

Police forces such as the Met, Dorset, Cleveland, Humberside and Thames Valley employ quality inspectors ('mystery shoppers') at £100 daily, to monitor police stations (cleanliness, time to be seen, etc)[4649].

In the case of the shooting dead of two robbers by Flying Squad officers near the HSBC at Chandler's Ford, a crucial document – the 'tactical adviser's log' – was lost by the IPCC. Only a photocopy with missing pages is available[4650].

The Met says <u>Mark Stone (Kennedy)</u> was sent all over Europe (before his three month suspension) advising governments how to deal with protesters (he infiltrated activist groups whose 'crime' was having a social conscience). After resigning he went back into the activist community. Nobody was ever convicted as a result of his undercover work costing millions. Michael Meacher says that perhaps powerful people running power stations influenced chief constables. Following the eco-warrior disaster, ACPO was not only stripped of covert policing but also all other 'operational' duties, as well as its Association of Police Authorities funding. ACPO is now reduced to giving 'guidance' and 'leadership'[4651]. HMIC was in 2011 charged with investigating ACPO's decade-long infiltration of the protest movement, as to whether operations were 'authorised in accordance with law', and 'proportionate'. The IPCC had already announced a probe into Notts Police over allegations it suppressed secret surveillance tapes (recorded by Mark Kennedy, one of up to 15 undercover officers) that could exonerate six activists police tried to prosecute. The National Public Order Intelligence Unit (NPOIU) is the largest of ACPO's domestic extremism units, and ACPO has admitted it needs better governance. Police minister Nick Herbert refused to comment on claims by MPs that Vince Cable and Caroline Lucas were listed on the domestic extremism database for simply being at peaceful protests[4652].

Strathclyde Police, Grampian Police, Tayside Police and Northern Constabulary refused quite legitimate FOIA requests for numbers of sex offenders in their areas[4653]. Scottish Police are refusing three-quarters of calls to confirm the presence of paedophiles in a locality. Some of the grounds for refusal – disclosure would not be 'relevant', the information might be passed to others, the application wasn't made correctly – have been criticised[4654]. None of Scotland's eight police forces would name sex offenders whom they know have changed their names and/or identities quite legally: an offender can keep reporting to police under his old name (in England offenders must inform police <u>before</u> they change names)[4655].

Like doctors, police are rarely willing to whistleblow on colleagues.

The Met were investigating accusations that MI6 knowingly used 'rendition' to send Gaddafi opponents to his torture chambers[4656].

In 2012 the Government planned to allow secret hearings for 'sensitive' cases, e.g. police shootings: Kenneth Clarke was spearheading the legislation[4657], which would cover up the mishandling of the London bomb atrocities. Even the monitoring 'special advocates' have expressed severe reservations[4658].

It is not widely realised – though clearly set out in the IPCC's 'How to make a complaint against the police' – that before a member of the public's complaint can proceed it has to be vetted by the force against which the complaint is being made. The complaint has to be 'recorded', but the IPCC is not allowed to do this without authorisation from the police. This is quite different from the regulators of other professionals, such as nurses, doctors or lawyers: the institutions they work for have no veto on referral to the GNC, GMC or Law Society. Why should the police be different?

No. 10 tried to conceal PM Cameron's connection with Rebekah Brooks' Met Police horse[4659].

In relation to the Mark Duggan killing the IPCC has told the coroner it may have sensitive information about the police it couldn't release to him, blocking an inquest – an alternative public inquiry would be held behind closed doors. The reason given by the IPCC is a law preventing the coroner hearing phone-tapping surveillance evidence: RIPA (2000) – under section 17 the IPCC can't even explain to families why the information is subjudice. Sections of the press are campaigning against even more draconian secrecy powers (the extension of 'closed material procedures', where cases are held in camera)[4660].

Though assaults (especially biting) on officers are on the rise in Scotland, most injuries sustained are interestingly not reported. Thus some police are not taking their own advice to report crime[4661].

The family of Azelle Rodney – shot dead by police in 2005 – still awaits a public inquiry seven years later[4662]. The police shooter ('E7') released a volley of eight shots into him, an unlawful 'pre-emptive' killing according to a retired High Court judge, who also accused the police of lack of planning, excessive force during the so-called 'hard stop' and a 'chaotic aftermath' of the incident. E7 had previously shot dead two armed robbers and received an apology for being branded a 'serial killer' from controversial senior Met officer Sue Akers[4663].

When a tabloid's journalists rang round the eight Scots forces they didn't have much luck getting through to divisional commanders (only Strathclyde's top cop spoke to them)[4664].

An EU directive will give offenders the right to know what information the police hold about them and even to have it deleted[4665].

When a snitch's CID handler was arrested for malfeasance and conspiracy to supply Schedule I drugs, the case never made the press, nor was he imprisoned – it would have been too embarrassing for his managers[4666].

31 English and Welsh forces retained for five decades 492 body parts from those (including children) who had died suspiciously, but didn't tell relatives or obtain permission, despite the cases being solved. The true number of samples retained is likely to run into thousands. Some forces are paying for new funerals[4667].

One little-known force, not under Home Office control, yet armed and partly owned by foreigners, is the Civil Nuclear Constabulary (CNC), which comes under the aegis of the Department of Energy and Climate Change. Headed by the first UK Chief Constable not to have a police background, it is funded by nuclear industry firms like the French EDF. Its officers have jurisdiction up to 5km, but can go anywhere in the UK if pursuing an investigation. Here are private companies with access to restricted databases. The regulatory CNC Authority has close links with the industry, leaving it open to accusations of toothlessness and bias. The CNC is not accountable to Parliament. The question arises as to why there should be police on military or civil sites[4668].

Eight women who claim they were seduced by undercover cops are fighting to stop their lawsuits being held in camera, saying the police who sanctioned the invasion of their privacy should not be allowed anonymity. Police lawyers are trying to move the case to an obscure tribunal (the Investigatory Powers Tribunal) where:

(1)   the claimants will not automatically get a full hearing;

(2)   the claimants cannot cross-examine witnesses;

(3)   the claimants cannot view any evidence;

(4)   there is no right of appeal.

The layman would be forgiven for assuming the Met and ACPO are trying to stack the cards in their favour) thereby compounding the felony (the women claim their right to privacy was infringed, amounting to degrading treatment). A miscarriage of justice could be the outcome[4669].

The Mafia have nothing on the British police service when it comes to omerta. Coppers are as tight-lipped a bunch as you are likely to encounter – stonewalling is built into their core nature.

ACPO/ACPOS

A bizarre two-day ban by ACPOS on speed detectors in police cars was triggered after a Scots force expressed concern that radio waves from their digital system could interfere with the detectors. ACPOS refused to name the force, but it is understood to be Strathclyde, and that force refused to comment[4670].

Attempts by 'The Times' to ascertain the bonuses chief constables enjoy (since 2006) were blocked by almost 40 forces, breaching the FOIA, and this obfuscation was compounded by a memo circulated nationally by ACPO. The Taxpayers' Alliance said the secrecy in relation to taxpayers' money is arrogant, damaging and quite unacceptable. Citing the Data Protection Act, the police chiefs not only refused to reveal the amounts, but also what the payments were for[4671].

From October 2011 ACPO, presently exempt from the FOIA, is to be subject to the same freedom of information laws as MPs and other public bodies. Police receipts and financial deals dating back to 1997 will be open to scrutiny by the public[4672].

Home Secretary Blunkett was accused of a crime "cover-up" for planning to slash the number of times police forces release details of crime rates. A spokesman for ACPO admitted that for forces which presently publish monthly it would mean they were being less open with the public.

ACPO denied (June, 2007) that Britain hosted CIA flights (extraordinary rendition), though its conclusion was based on little more than media cuttings. "Liberty" said ACPO hadn't been straight with them (a letter of reply to them took 18 months to be published, at the same time as the Marty revelations of official lies and silence). Only eight days before the ACPO announcement (amid cries of "whitewash"), a CIA-marked transport aircraft landed at the Mildenhall US base in England, to be met by armed military police.

ACPO refused to come on BBC Newsnight (20/06/07) to answer the charge that credit card fraud was being decriminalised due to a secret instruction from the H.O. not to investigate card fraud.

Hundreds of violent criminals and paedophiles may be working with the vulnerable because of blunders in police background checks (CRB checks are not being cross-referenced with the 'non-sanctions detections' database). The Home Office denied any cover-up – the problem dates back at least nine years – but could not explain why the information was kept secret. An ACPO review of the matter 'revealed no concerns around public protection in any other force' (apart from the Met).

Compared with their American counterparts, who are much more open and forthright, the Met failed to reveal the arrest of entertainer Rolf Harris, supported by ACPO's unhelpful guidelines on disclosing arrestees' names. News of the investigation was readily available on the internet[4673].

SOCA

The Serious Organised Crime Agency (SOCA) knew in 2007 that criminal P.I.s were being hired by lawyers, insurance companies, debt collectors, etc. to hack computers, according to a leaked copy of Project Riverside. SOCA's boss Trevor Pearce, has been referred to the IPCC by a hacking victim who claims that he has misled parliament by failing to give vital hard-drive evidence to Scotland Yard, despite saying he had (see also 'The Cover-up Culture', p499)[4674].

UK Police Forces Involved in Cover-up Stories

Avon and Somerset

Colin Port, Chief Constable of Avon and Somerset Police, has been accused of defying a High Court Order to return computers suspected of holding masses of child porn, which contained legally privileged or special procedure material. The police chief was served with a summons alleging contempt of court[4675].

Police are setting secret targets (e.g. 150,000 speeding motorists in 2004 for the Avon and Somerset force) for the number of drivers they plan to trap with speed cameras, suggesting the cameras are cash cows rather than safety devices. No police region would reveal their accounts to the press, but it seems certain police officials make private estimates of how many £60 notices they need to issue to make their books balance.

Avon and Somerset Police kept body parts from more than 100 murder victims for decades but didn't inform relatives – police can retain organs for 30 years.

CAVEAT CIVIS

Cambridgeshire

A secret report revealed (2005) that senior officers leading the Soham murders inquiry were inept and indecisive, but much of its 70 pages remains barred, covered by Public Interest Immunity certificates. Several bits of the sections released by Cambridgeshire Police have been edited, the names of the officers involved removed[4676].

Just after the bodies of Holly Wells and Jessica Chapman were found, the Daily Mail was sent a long letter from a Soham mother. She said she and other parents were worried about the police asking the media to withdraw from the area. They feared this was more to do with the police covering up their mistakes than protecting the parents of the murdered children, who felt safer with the press around asking questions. One of two Cambridgeshire policemen appearing in court contemporaneously - DC Brian Stevens - was the liaison officer sent to look after the Chapmans. He and PC Tony Goodridge were charged with downloading child pornography as a result of information forwarded by the FBI. The police refused to say if Stevens had been assigned as liaison officer before, during or after his being charged. Intelligence that could have led to the arrest of these two Soham "porn policemen" was known to the UK police for a year. There are apparently 30 police officers from across Britain on the American child porn list (2007).

The interview with Hailey Edwards was videoed by police regarding her claim that Soham murderer Huntley had sexually assaulted her years before - nothing was done - but police kept telling her solicitor that the video had been destroyed. She had to go to court to force police to hand over police statements to her lawyers.

Central Scotland

Scottish speed cops have been accused of hiding behind trees to ensnare drivers. Critics claim such tactics make a mockery of the official police view that they are trying to deter speeders, not catch them[4677].

Scottish forces have refused to reveal how many Tasers they have. Almost 100% of Scottish officers want to carry the devices in every police car[4678].

Four anti-shoplifting Stirling policemen lied to cover up for undercover colleague PC William Cowrie, who threw an innocent shopper against a plate glass window[4679]. Inappropriate behaviour by undercover investigators has attracted criticism[4680].

When Kevin McLeod was drowned with possible evidence of foul play, the family had to use FOIA to get a copy of Central Scotland Police's 2003 probe into the local force's management of the case[4681].

Central Scotland Police refuse to reveal details of a complaint against Assistant Chief Constable John Mauger, who is earning £100K a year while on 'gardening leave'[4682].

City of London

City of London PC Adam Lowe, who was present at a nightclub when a man was killed during a brawl, was sacked after an internal inquiry found him guilty of gross misconduct relating to honesty and integrity[4683].

The novel 'Snow Hill' is writer Mark Sanderson's attempt to reveal the police cover-up of a 1936 murder. A City of London policeman told his son of crimes (sexual assaults, drugs, blackmail and a killing) linked to a senior officer at his station, Snow Hill. There was no word in the newspapers about the murder of a young policeman; and the City of London Police Museum's records make no mention of it. The homophobic but hypocritical senior officer homosexually assaulted his men, using blackmail to ensure they remained silent. The victim died from an overdose of the drug used to sedate victims prior to assault. Snow Hill was adopted as a euphemism for gay. Around the same time in the 1930s a police commissioner sacked two constables for having a cup of tea while on the beat – he himself covered up his own crime of scalding his wife during a row, and was never punished[4684].

Cleveland

Comedian Chris McGlade was arrested and questioned by police after setting up a website which made allegations against Redcar councillors and Cleveland Police[4685]. The county's Chief Constable, Sean Price, was the first chief constable in 35 years to be sacked (for misconduct) in October 2012: one charge was that he tried to bully staff to cover up for him.

Cumbria

The whistleblowers who revealed that Richard Rhodes, Cumbria's Police and Crime Commissioner, charged £700 for two chauffeur-driven trips, were to be prosecuted[4686].

Derbyshire

Derbyshire Chief Constable David Coleman, well known for his ruthless pursuit of speeding drivers in recent years[4687], was accused of 'madness' after refusing to publish 'wanted' photos of two escaped murderers because it might breach their human rights and data protection laws. Lord Chancellor Falconer criticised Derbyshire Constabulary for suggesting the HR Act prevented the publication of the pictures. The Act in fact explicitly allows police to print 'wanted' pictures if it is in the public interest. ACPO however says the pictures should only be released if the criminal is dangerous[4688].

Devon & Cornwall

Devon and Cornwall Police Authority chief executive Graham Davey was suspended in 2009, but the reasons not released. The same force's chief constable Maria Wallis quit in 2006 accused of serious professional misconduct. Their finance director Colin Papworth was suspended in 2008[4689].

Dumfries & Galloway

Dumfries and Galloway Police asked Lothian and Borders to investigate serving police inspector Adam Carruthers, because senior local policemen failed to properly examine allegations he had raped up to 20 women. Jailed in 2001 for raping two women (three other women then came forward with accusations of sexual assaults) Carruthers may have, insiders suggest, used Masonic links to cover up his crimes. Amazingly, he was promoted even though his behaviour was known about. One of the assaults involved the use of his police truncheon[4690]. After prison he tried to lie his way into a new telesales job involving schools, claiming his career ended 'due to issues outwith my control'[4691].

Dumfries and Galloway Police refused to reveal (2012) how many officers were involved in the enhanced Lockerbie probe[4692].

Dunblane

Police HQ at Stirling Castle allowed Thomas Hamilton to keep all the guns with which he committed the Dunblane Massacre, against the advice of the village policeman, who had begged for them to be removed[4693]. It has been alleged the Cullen inquiry into the Dunblane massacre was fatally flawed because crucial evidence was not given to it. A female former paramedic claimed that police were involved in a paedophile ring that covered up Hamilton's abuses and allowed him gun licences. She says he was a major provider of pornographic material to the ring[4694]. A secret police report about the 1996 Dunblane massacre warned of Thomas Hamilton's capability of violence five years before, and called for his firearms licence to be revoked. The files from Lord Cullen's inquiry had been subject to a 100-year closure order, but Lord Advocate Colin Boyd agreed to make them public. One revelation was that there was an off-duty policeman at the school at the time of the shootings - he was never identified nor called to give evidence, though he played a part in the immediate aftermath.

Dyfed-Powys

While ACPO spokesman on child protection issues[4695], Chief Constable Terry Grange of Dyfed-Powys Police was investigated over an alleged cover-up of claims of child abuse against a judge who was his friend. He is also believed to have spent time with a mystery woman while he was supposed to be at official meetings. He also faced an inquiry by the IPCC into financial discrepancies.

Essex

Essex Police refused to reveal the cost of the police inquiry into the Chris Huhne-Vicky Pryce speeding case[4696].

Fife

The family of a dead Dundee child were still waiting for justice four years on: Tayside Police had failed to answer calls which might have saved his life. But the family were banned from seeing the report on the matter by neighbouring Fife Police - they faced a court battle if they were ever to have a chance of viewing the report.

When high-ranking probation official Vincent Barron, in charge of a Home Office database of sex offenders, was suspected of supplying child porn to a paedophile ring, his hearing before Kirkcaldy Sheriff's court in 2005 was, unusually, held in camera, prompting allegations of a cover-up: court officials and the police were reluctant to give details of the case.

A report into the murder of Scots teenager Karen Dewar by a known sex offender revealed police had not carried out two risk assessments and had failed to record information on the sex offenders' register, despite the culprit having been accused of 14 sexually related offences between the ages of 10 and 16. Fife Police were told to improve their information systems.

Gloucestershire

Gloucestershire police are keeping secret files, a "Homophobic Incidents Register" (HIR), on anyone accused of making anti-gay remarks. Former TV presenter Robin Page, who was arrested on a march by Gloucestershire Police in 2002 for 'inciting hatred' (all charges were dropped), has found he is on the secret HIR, containing files on people <u>accused</u> of making anti-gay remarks but never convicted of a criminal offence[4697].

Grampian

Frank Greig, one of Scotland's most notorious murderers (of a vicar's daughter), has been questioned over a serious sex assault in the 1970s, but Grampian Police refused to reveal the crime in which he is a suspect[4698].

Greater Manchester

The Greater Manchester PCSOs who wouldn't enter a lake near Wigan to save a drowning boy failed to attend the inquest, and had their identities protected by the police[4699], until media pressure grew too great.

The Chief Constable of Greater Manchester, <u>Mike Todd</u>, who appears to have committed suicide, threatened the BBC with a 'Hutton-style' inquiry if a police racism programme, 'The Secret Policeman', went ahead. Todd also warned that police forces could withdraw cooperation with programmes such as 'Crimewatch'[4700]. In 2003 the Commission for Racial Equality demanded from all 44 chief constables that they provide evidence that they comply with the Race Relations Act. Todd's force was at the centre of the racism storm, and HMIC warned the force that parts of its 'culture' were sexist and racist: police recruit <u>Rob Pulling</u>, wearing a Klan-style hood, was shown mouthing 'kill a Paki' and claiming Stephen Lawrence 'deserved' to die. Police sealed off part of the village of Halam for Todd's family funeral[4701]. The inquest into his death would not investigate his sexual affairs, the investigating coroner confirmed. Though his womanising was well known at Scotland Yard he was given glowing references by the Met so as to obtain the Greater Manchester Chief Constable job[4702].

Hampshire

Hampshire Police sergeant <u>Paul Beale</u> challenged the New Milton Advertiser over stories about town councillor Goff Beck – the paper's article revealed the latter had been accused of bullying a female councillor and making homophobic remarks to a gay colleague. Beale has been given 'suitable advice' for his 'perceived lack of neutrality'[4703].

Hertfordshire

Hertfordshire Police refused to provide a photo of a killer to the Welwyn Hatfield Times. The person had been banned from pubs, and the paper felt it essential to publish his picture so publicans could recognise him. The police said they would only release a picture of someone who had been given a sentence of less than three years[4704].

A campaigning bird lover battling to save rare parrots says Hertfordshire Police tried to ban photos he took of DEFRA officials destroying their nests[4705].

Humberside

A public enquiry revealed that Humberside Police had failed to share intelligence with Cambridgeshire Police about Ian Huntley's history of sex attacks on girls when he got the caretaker job at Soham Village College. The Chief Constable of Humberside, David Westwood, lost his job over it[4706]. Humberside were criticised for destroying their Ian Huntley file. Yet they kept a secret list of Irish people (including English of Irish descent) in its area, whether or not they were suspected of breaking the law: names and other details were fed into a Special Branch database[4707], no matter how trivial.

Jersey

A Jersey politician (an ex-Minister of Justice) accused of leaking a police report claimed asylum at the House of Commons because he thought he wouldn't be given a fair trial on Jersey. The report concerned the conduct of a male nurse on the island[4708]. Lenny Harper, former Strathclyde deputy divisional commander and Basingstoke detective, then deputy head of the States of Jersey Police, was accused of withholding information about the Jersey Child Abuse inquiry from the police who replaced him, as well as leaking information to the media[4709]. Harper insists the nepotistic establishment in Jersey means police, lawyers and politicians socialise together or are related. He claims to have uncovered corruption, but the response of the authorities was to suppress everything. Only Honorary Police – a system parallel to the States of Jersey Police consisting of elected lay people, e.g. businessmen, who can countermand the Jersey force – have the power to charge suspects. Thus Harper's attempts to tackle the huge number of licensed (and unlicensed) firearms were repeatedly blocked: some licences were knowingly granted to applicants with criminal convictions (he says he even found a rocket launcher in the possession of a police civilian employee). He says he found employees using police money to buy computers for private use, while some stored porn[4710]. When a 'fragment of child's skull' found at the Jersey children's home turned out to be a piece of wood or coconut, police kept this under wraps[4711].

Lenny Harper

Whistleblower DC Peter Cook claims to have uncovered a vicious paedophile ring – whose friends included senior police officers – with victims in both the Channel Islands and the UK, and that his superiors had stopped him from alerting police abuse specialists in London. 'Jersey is an oligarchy, where the elite look after each other'[4712].

Kent

In 1986 PC Ron Walker of Kent Police alleged scores of Kent detectives were routinely fabricating crime figures by persuading criminals to confess to crimes they didn't commit. There is an incentive to 'cuff' crimes (the crimes disappear up the cuffs of the officer's uniform), as the police then appear to be more effective than they really are. More than half the 43 police forces do not have auditing systems essential to prevent such abuse[4713].

Lancashire

A Rangers fan has accused Greater Manchester Police of double standards when they used CCTV camera evidence to identify 49 other fans suspected of rioting, but told him they were useless for finding the officer who allegedly assaulted him[4714].

'Night Jack' (Lancashire DC Richard Horton) was sometimes very critical of senior officers, and advised members of the public under police investigation to 'complain about every officer ... show no respect to the legal system or anybody working in it'. When he was identified after a campaign by 'The Times', he received a written warning from his superiors and rendered ineffective[4715].

An officer who served with Lancashire and Greater Manchester Police says statistics have always been recorded in a way that presents a force in a favourable light. 'It is done so as to enhance the reputations of chief constables. The truth is immaterial[4716].'

More than 50 people have been shot dead in Manchester in the nine years since 1999, yet would-be MP Martin Eakins was told by a community officer that armed crime in Wythenshawe and Sale East was 'not too bad', only hours before a robber held a gun to the MP's head during a pub raid[4717].

A grieving mother has criticised Manchester Police for waiting months before releasing CCTV footage which could pinpoint her son's killers[4718], while Merseyside Police told a mother a paedophile was grooming her seven-year-old, but refused to reveal the pervert's name or whereabouts[4719].

At least 60 Blackpool schoolgirls, nearly all white, were groomed for sex by workers, mainly Asian, at seedy takeaways. The 2003 report by Lancashire Police wasn't publicised, yet in the next few years two suspected sex trafficked girls went missing, presumed dead[4720].

70% of Merseyside Police take early sick retirement, which is often seen as a cover-up in serious allegation cases.

Leicestershire

British police employed lawyers to gag Portuguese detectives to prevent the exposure of ex-pat perverts living near the area where the McCann child disappeared. Chief Constable Ken Jones of ACPO wrote to the Portuguese prosecutor to formally request the names of the 80 local paedophiles be kept 'strictly confidential'[4721]. Leicestershire's Detective Superintendent Stuart Prior also blocked the move by flying to Portugal and threatening legal action[4722]. British police secretly listened into the Portuguese police's interrogation of Kate McCann about her daughter. A dossier of covert electronic and physical evidence, along with forensic reports, led to the McCanns being classed as suspects (local police set up surveillance teams to monitor their movements and emails 24 hours a day, body language experts apparently suggesting the mother's demeanour indicated she had something to hide, etc.). Britain's Serious and Organised Crime Agency gave guidance to Portuguese police[4723]. British (Leicestershire) police files on the Madeleine McCann hunt were to remain closed unless her abductors were caught[4724], but now (2013) seemingly a political decision at the highest level, Wikileaks has revealed a message from the UK's ambassador to Portugal to his US counterpart that British police were working with the Portuguese to build a case against the McCanns. The comments suggest British police had a far greater role in the investigation than they have given the public to understand[4725]: they were accused of trying to prevent DNA information (allegedly linked to the McCanns' hire car) from being made public[4726]. PC Martin Grime, whose sniffer dogs supposedly detected blood and human remains in the McCanns' holiday apartment, says he has been asked by UK police not to comment on the McCann case. The canine evidence helped convince the Portuguese to name the McCanns as arguidos[4727].

In 2006 the IPCC launched a probe into Leicestershire Constabulary after policewoman Nina Hobson filmed an undercover exposé of the force[4728].

The Rutland and North Leicestershire assistant deputy coroner criticised the police for apparently failing to link the 33 serious complaints (the number verified by the IPCC) made over 10 years by tragic Fiona Pilkington (neighbours' pleas also fell on deaf ears). Coroner Olivia Davison also resisted the constabulary's attempt to derail her probe by requesting a ban on the reporting of the case[4729]. Following an internal inquiry the force decided to discipline no officers over the Pilkington affair, blaming 'system failure', a common excuse in NHS scandals. One prominent columnist has commented: 'The uselessness of the police in such matters is well known to anyone who really needs them'[4730].

Lothian & Borders

Lothian and Borders Police failed to inform the public about hundreds of crimes committed in Edinburgh in a single day. Police had told reporters there was nothing of 'press interest', so that the facts had to be extracted under a FOI request[4731].

Secret payments of almost £200,000 were made by Lothian and Borders Police to supergrasses over four years – they were only revealed after a 14-month FOI battle by the Daily Record, which had already forced Strathclyde Police to admit the payment of £760,000 over a similar period. However, the Information Commissioner allowed three smaller forces (Central, Grampian and Tayside) to keep their informer spending secret: Strathclyde police were criticised for offering cash to a green group member of Plane Stupid[4732].

A police watchdog voiced fears over failings within Lothian and Borders Police, who had withheld vital information from the procurator fiscal. Officers up to Deputy Chief Constable Tom Halpin seemed to believe this acceptable[4733].

A serial sex offender known as the Da Vinci Code rapist was escorted from his Scottish jail by an entourage of MAPPA police minders, who attended to his every need. Neither Lothian and Borders Police, Midlothian Council nor the Scottish Government would comment on the VIP treatment of Robert Greens.

It has been alleged bird crime police tip off gamekeepers they are planning to visit. Former RSPB investigator says a Borders policeman told him to go to the police office in the next village because his station colleagues were too friendly with the keeper being probed[4734].

The Met: De Menezes – the attempted cover-ups

The name of the officer who killed de Menezes was kept under wraps, and the Met appointed one of their own to investigate – Roy Clarke, a retired anti-corruption officer, who said '… the official police reaction to the shooting … suggests we are led up the garden path by the authorities when it suits them'. At the inquest 49 officers giving evidence were allowed to remain anonymous (including the two shooters)[4735]. A senior officer involved in the de Menezes manhunt, Detective Chief Superintendent Jon Boutcher, said nothing went wrong with the operation[4736]. The jury, barred from returning a verdict of unlawful killing, rejected a string of claims by key police witnesses, saying they believed passengers rather than the police[4737]. A senior Met officer flew to Brazil to offer £15,000 compensation to the parents of de Menezes. This might make one suspicious that this could have been an attempt to buy their silence. In 2006 the family were barred from seeing an official report into his death. Operation Kratos, the shoot-to-kill policy that led to his death, was agreed in secret at a meeting at MI5's London headquarters in January, 2003. Special Branch detectives were alleged to have falsified a surveillance log to cover up the fact they had wrongly identified de Menezes as a suspected suicide bomber. The CPS did not dismiss the possibility that the log was changed (to read "And it was not Osman") to distance Special Branch from the shooting. One officer was forced to admit doctoring the records of how and why they came to shoot de Menezes[4738].

Sir Ian Blair tried to stop the IPCC inquiry into the de Menezes shooting, as well as immediately assuring the public that the shooting was "directly linked" to terrorism. The Met muddied the waters by allowing wrong accounts of the suspect's "suspicious" behaviour (wearing a big jacket, hurdling a turnstile, running from police, etc.) to leak out. It took a month of leaks from the IPCC before de Menezes was exonerated. The whistleblower who leaked the saga was suspended. London Underground insisted at least three of four cameras were in full working order, which appeared to contradict police assertions that "technical problems" meant no footage of the Brazilian's final moments existed: none of the five CCTV cameras on Stockwell Underground station were supposedly working, their tapes blank[4739]. It was claimed in the High Court (December, 2006) that the de Menezes killer marksmen lied to investigators to justify their actions. Sir Ian Blair's 2006 Christmas message to the force's 30,000 employees and tens of thousands of police pensioners ignores the year's many setbacks (Forest Gate, de Menezes, taping Goldsmith, Soham murders "not a big story", 'Londoners can leave their doors open', etc.). Blair refused independent investigators access to Stockwell Tube station after the de Menezes shooting, as was revealed in a letter he wrote to the Home Office on the day of the tragedy, but permanent secretary Sir John Gieve replied that it would not be "necessary or desirable" to block the independent probe - yet it was delayed anyway for three days. The fact that the CCTV tapes had been removed, but not replaced, the day before the de Menezes shooting, fuelled the conspiracy theory of a police cover-up.

The shooting was followed by weeks of misleading information from the Met, e.g. it was claimed de Menezes had emerged from a property under surveillance (his flat in the block was not under surveillance), he was wearing bulky clothing (he wasn't), he vaulted over a ticket barrier (he used a pre-paid travel card to go through it), he ran down to the platform (he actually walked to the train). Police claimed to have identified themselves before shooting (leaked documents suggest officers didn't properly identify themselves)[4740].

Brian Paddick claims he was sidelined by Ian Blair after the Stockwell shooting because he disputed the Commissioner's version of events on the day of de Menezes' death.

Blair was accused of trying to prevent Paddick appearing at the inquest[4741]. A Special Branch officer known as <u>Owen</u>, who admitted tampering with evidence (deleting text from a note), was cleared of any wrongdoing[4742]. For the inquest the Inner London South Coroner was controversially replaced by a pliable retired High Court judge who told the jury what verdict(s) they couldn't return, e.g. attributing blame to individuals[4743].

The IPCC found that de Menezes had at first been ruled out as a terrorist by surveillance officers, but was still followed and shot by another team. Another leak suggested Special Branch had tried to falsify evidence about the events leading to the killing[4744]. <u>Sir Ian Blair</u> was kept out of the loop about the blunder for 24 hours[4745].

It was claimed in the High Court (December, 2006) that the de Menezes killer marksmen lied to investigators to justify their actions. No witness confirmed their claims that they had shouted "armed police". Because de Menezes was killed SAS-style and not police-marksman-style, some questioned <u>Sir Ian Blair</u>'s assurance that it was police who were the shooter(s). The Yard declined to comment on whether members of the counter-terrorist Special Reconnaissance Regiment, seconded to the Met, were actually responsible[4746]. In 2007 <u>Blair</u> was being asked if the SAS stormed the de Menezes home: the press photographed men apparently armed with SAS weapons and wearing military clothing with SR (Special Reconnaissance) insignia, raising the question of the exact breakdown of who was involved in the bungled Tube operation. Blair confirmed an SAS man was on surveillance duty at the victim's home. The Tory leader of the London Assembly said: 'I have deep-seated concerns about the leadership of the Metropolitan Police Service'[4747].

<u>Sir Ian Blair</u> wrote to the Home Office after the shooting saying he should be able to suspend Section 17 of the Police Reform Act, which obliged him to report everything to the IPCC. Arrogantly he wrote: 'I have therefore given instructions that the shooting ... is not to be referred to the IPCC'[4748]. Allegations against <u>Blair</u> and other senior officers of misleading the public over the de Menezes affair and attempting to delay or prevent the IPCC investigation might constitute a criminal charge of 'misconduct in a public office'[4749]. Inspector <u>Glen Smyth</u>, the Met's Police Federation chairman, was gagged by fellow officers after backing <u>Blair</u> over the de Menezes shooting. Sir Ian had received an unprecedented vote of no confidence from the police's London Assembly[4750]. The IPCC have highlighted his denying independent investigators access to the Stockwell Tube scene, the witnesses and evidence for several days. The IPCC report showed large discrepancies between the accounts of eight officers and the passengers[4751]. <u>Brian Paddick</u>'s version of events seemed to contradict the official Yard account that they didn't know the Brazilian was innocent till the next day.

An anonymous detective sergeant, a counter-terrorism officer, was suing the Met for loss of overtime pay and promotions and religious discrimination, in the aftermath of the killing. Another allegation says a chief inspector was replaced with another to give more favourable evidence at the 2008 inquest, so perverting justice[4752].

The IPCC was heavily criticised for wasting taxpayers' money by breaching procedural rules in the de Menezes case: the bulk of criticism against three officers was left out of the report. However, the report was a damning indictment of the Met's failures and their effort to cover up their mistakes.

The Met: Other cover-ups

Scotland Yard reinstated (2009) its elite Celebrity Squad (officially the Special Enquiry Team) to investigate crimes affecting the royals, VIPs and showbiz figures: its watchword was discretion in 'sensitive' enquiries (i.e. cover-up). It disappeared in 2007 in a shake-up of the Met[4753].

Met DCI Clive Driscoll claimed his probe into child sex abuse in Lambeth in 1998 was hijacked by Scotland Yard as soon as politicians, including an MP, were named as suspects[4754].

Pictures of the July 7 bombings only appeared in UK papers because they'd been leaked to the US ABC TV network by the American government – UK police deemed the images unfit to be shown to the British population[4755]. The Information Commissioner ordered police to release film of the July 7 bombers after a three-year FOI attempt by the Press Association[4756].

If Sir Ian Blair had been forced to quit over the de Menezes shooting, a secret plan was drawn up to install ex-RUC boss Sir Ronnie Flanagan as acting commissioner at Scotland Yard. Blair admitted he had grossly understated to the Met Police Authority the cost of removing anti-war campaigner Brian Haw's protest hoarding - the cost was four times higher. Blair was forced to apologise to Lord Goldsmith for secretly taping a phone conversation with him.

Julie Ward's father has accused the Met, among others, of 'treachery' in helping the Kenyan authorities cover up her 1988 murder. Thus Met officers supported a 'preposterous' theory that Julie abandoned her jeep[4757].

Police will suppress the true death toll if there is a 'catastrophic' Al-Qaeda attack on Britain, according to secret Scotland Yard plans. Leaked memos suggest a serious terrorist attack will have 'political implications' that could damage the police[4758].

Coroner Dr. Stephen Chan banned a jury from finding that Scot Harry Stanley had been unlawfully killed by Met marksmen (he was carrying a table leg in a plastic bag). The widow's lawyer says there was strong evidence that would have enabled the jury to reach a certain verdict (they had to leave it open), and the Scottish Human Rights Centre said the jury's support for the widow showed they wanted to return an unlawful killing verdict. A spokesperson for Inquest said the jury had been denied the proper opportunity to decide themselves if these officers were telling the truth. There was an hour's gap in the police statements which was unaccounted for. The jury gave the nearest they could to blaming the police- an open verdict[4759].

The police dealing with the 1958 Notting Hill riots withheld vital racial information from Home Secretary Rab Butler.

The Met ignored a boy's complaint he was sexually abused by a VIP paedophile ring at the infamous Elm Guest House in Barnes, which operated between 1977 and 1983 and had alleged links to the political establishment. This was despite confirmatory evidence from a second boy, who was formally interviewed, and supports fears of an establishment cover-up[4760].

The Met reportedly refused to let DCI <u>Phil Wheeler</u>, severely criticised for negligence in the Climbié Inquiry, be interviewed by journalists (he refused to speak to Fiona Bruce of BBC TV's 'Real Story' on 29.3.04). An article on Shaken Baby Syndrome was removed from the Met's website. Police in the 'Baby P' case were accused of letting their investigation into child abuse claims 'drift'. '... when one officer was replaced by another, case notes were not passed on. No photographs were taken of the child's injuries when police visited. A specialist doctor emailed police re calling an independent review but received no reply'[4761].

Some suspect that if the American who filmed the G20 incident concerning Mr. Tomlinson had not given his material immediately to the media, we would never have known what happened. The inquiry found that the unnamed police officer concerned had his face covered by a balaclava, and he appeared to have removed his epaulettes with their identifying number[4762]. 'The police have a nasty habit of lying on these occasions. Their first response was that they hadn't touched the victim. Nothing new about that. The true facts about the death of ... de Menezes had to be extracted from them – like stubborn molars'[4763]. If the police <u>can</u> conceal their faux pas, it appears they <u>will</u>.

Shadow Home Secretary David Davis claims the Home Office knew the 'low copy number' DNA technique was flawed, possibly allowing dangerous criminals to escape justice, and it appeared the Home Office had tried to mount a cover-up. The Home Office replied that it hadn't been made public because the <u>police</u> wanted it kept secret[4764].

Around the clubs of St. James's in Victorian London a vicious paedophile ring operated, but the police did nothing because many of those involved were members of a powerful elite[4765].

Whistleblowers accused Met Police Commissioner <u>Sir Ian Blair</u> of turning a blind eye to allegations that murdered Special Constable <u>Nisha Patel-Nasri</u> was running escort agency Seventh Heaven and possibly enjoyed a corrupt association with a senior officer. She and her husband boasted of having protection high up in the Met[4766]. Three of the Met's anti-corruption unit allegedly withheld evidence in the trial of six officers charged with a racist attack: they are claimed to have blocked the release of film footage, helping the six to be acquitted. The three may face charges in the unprecedented case, which involves their unit, the Directorate of Professional Standards, as well as the IPCC[4767].

The Met's Special Demonstration Squad used 80 dead children's identities in the 1980s to investigate racist groups.

The same elite SO19 squad which shot de Menezes also killed barrister Mark Saunders. Negotiations with the victim only lasted twenty minutes but Scotland Yard wouldn't comment on negotiation procedures. Brian Paddick expressed concern as to why the police marksmen were wearing balaclavas. 'It may be that after the de Menezes shooting officers do not want to be identified publicly. It could be that senior officers are allowing marksmen to protect their identity'[4768]. Concerns were also raised about the marksmen conferring over their accounts of the incident before providing statements. The IPCC said: 'We get individual statements from civilian witnesses. It should be the same for police officers'[4769]. In America police marksmen are identified[4770]. This is allowed by ACPO's Manual of Guidance On The Police Use of Firearms. By 2008 the IPCC had called three times for conferring to end, because it generated 'concern and suspicion'[4771]. ACPO's revised guidelines stopped short of banning the practice[4772]. The family of Mark Saunders sought a declaration from Mr. Justice Underhill that there was an unlawful failure to disclose information about the investigation[4773].

A fatal shooting of alleged gang member Azelle Rodney (April 2005) by Met officers led to Government proposals to create a new category of 'secret inquests'. There was still no inquest four years later. The dead man's mother thinks the delay was because the police don't want to disclose their surveillance methods in court. The 2005 Inquiries Act gives Ministers wide powers to set the remit of an inquiry and to decide what can be made public[4774].

The boyfriend of a girl raped by Savile at the BBC was told by the police he could be arrested for making such a claim[4775]. One victim was warned she could be arrested for wasting police time.

Former Met Commissioner Lord Condon has been accused of conspiring to cover up Diana's murder. He had breached his duty to reveal evidence of a plot to kill her[4776]. Condon and Assistant Commissioner Sir David Veness (ex-Met anti-terror chief) were accused of 'ignoring' Diana's secret document, which Scotland Yard spent six years sitting on. Their failure to act led to claims of a deliberate cover-up[4777]. With regard to Diana's death the main witness statement was lost by the police. Questions the French police never satisfactorily explained in relation to her death were: (1) the scene was scrubbed clean and re-opened in a few hours, (2) the traffic police report was not included in the official report, (3) Erik Patel, the first witness, was ignored and silenced by police, even being handcuffed, bundled into a van and taken to police headquarters (he couldn't understand why the paparazzi had been arrested, because he saw none around the car). Police said Patel was lying (he was interrogated by the Brigade Criminelle). His original statement was "lost". Police put out a statement that Henri Paul was very drunk, before blood alcohol results were available. The speedometer couldn't have been stuck at 120 mph, according to the manufacturer, and police soon conceded this. Mercedes was never allowed to examine the vehicle. The car crashed at 65 mph (final estimate), but this fact was never released. Police maintained Paul's fridge contained a bottle of Martini and one of Bacardi, but failed to mention his 240 bottles of Coke. Paul's blood sample was not made available to the family. Police refused to say how Paul's body was identified. Police found illegal drugs in the car, but this was covered up. The "suicide" of paparazzi James Adamson, under observation by the French secret police, was not believed by those close to him (he had claimed to have been at the crash).

A senior Met officer who investigated Diana's death, Jeff Rees, was accused in court of liaising with spies[4778]. Diana had accused the head of the royal protection squad, Deputy Assistant Commissioner David Meynell, of bugging her car and home. Meynell appeared to give contradictory accounts of the seriousness with which he took her complaints[4779].

More than 10% of murders are committed by people on bail, but some of the biggest constabularies are unable to provide figures[4780]. Princess Diana's death could have become a murder inquiry if British police had not held back a 'murder plot' note in which she predicted she would be killed[4781]. The letter from Princess Diana's divorce lawyer Lord Mishcon was kept secret by the British police, who only made it available to French authorities some three years later. Princess Diana's sworn note stating that Prince Charles was planning an 'accident' to her car, was not disclosed by the Met to the British public or press for six years[4782]. 'International Letters Rogatory' were sent to the Home Office. Sir David Veness was plagued by royal security blunders[4783]. There were claims that a number of witnesses, including a senior policeman, lied to the inquests[4784]. With no formal inquest into her death, a 2003 YouGov opinion poll found 75% of the population believed she was murdered[4785].

The main witness statement was lost by the police. A key witness in Operation Paget claimed that British police tried to get him to change his story about the engagement ring with thinly-veiled threats. The jeweller wrote a detailed letter of protest to <u>Lord Stevens</u>, who was in charge of the police probe[4786]. <u>Stevens</u> changed one of the key conclusions of his probe into the death, fuelling fears of a cover-up. He had told Henri Paul's parents at a preliminary hearing that Henri had not been drunk, but a month later Stevens said he was three times over the limit[4787]. In 2008 <u>Stevens</u> demanded an apology for 'scurrilous allegations' that he had not investigated the death properly[4788].

An original police report into the 1979 death of anti-racism campaigner Blair Peach at a National Front demo has remained secret, suggesting a cover-up. The inquiry by Commander John Cass, of the Met's internal complaints department, is thought to have recommended the prosecution of police officers who allegedly killed Peach with a blow to the head[4789].

The CPS claims there were only <u>three</u> missed opportunities to prosecute Cyril Smith, but there were further cover-ups by London's park police and the Met, despite the catalogue of reports of him as a predator abuser of boys[4790].

The IPCC announced a 62-year-old former police constable and a Scotland Yard worker were arrested in 2009 over an alleged cover-up of possibly crucial evidence in the Stephen Lawrence murder case. The case had been referred by an internal Met review. The IPCC was investigating why the material was allegedly not disclosed to either the Kent or Macpherson Inquiries[4791].

Sadiq Khan, a high-profile Labour Muslim MP, was secretly bugged by Scotland Yard during private meetings with a constituent. There was no suspicion the MP was committing a criminal act[4792].

Details of the 1971 Lloyds Bank Baker Street raid – dubbed the 'walkie-talkie robbery' – were kept secret by police, who imposed unusual reporting restrictions. This secrecy is exploited in the 2008 movie 'The Bank Job' to suggest the vault contained compromising photos of Princess Margaret[4793].

The Metropolitan Police Authority accused Scotland Yard in 2008 of fiddling crime figures and clear-up rates, and revealed the Met's Computer Aided Despatch System is based on an airport baggage-handling system[4794].

A nest of four Al-Qaeda spies was uncovered in the Met in 2008[4795].

Met files on the anti-war movement from 1968 were still secret in 2008. Special Branch fed scaremongering stories among friendly journalists, including two at 'The Times'[4796].

Brian Paddick says matters threatening the Met's reputation were routinely raised at a senior officers' 'diamond' group meeting, as well as at 'morning prayers', when some of the 'diamonds' met the Commissioner. Paddick claims there is a group of 'untouchable' Met officers whose behaviour is 'swept under the carpet'[4797]. As previously suggested, if the police can conceal their faux pas, they <u>will</u> if it suits them, which it so often does.

Shortly after the death of Billy Tallon, the Queen Mother's eccentric, alcoholic retainer, police are said to have removed his address book[4798].

Police disciplinary hearings are not open to the public, unlike most doctors' hearings. It has been recommended they are open in serious cases only. The disciplinary tribunal which sacked disgraced police chief <u>Ali Dizaei</u> was held in secret[4799].

Senior police officers in the spring of 2002 expected an inquiry into a gay police chief – over drug allegations made by his former partner James Renolleau – to result in a whitewash. <u>Paddick</u>'s relationship with Renolleau (who was on police bail at the time) was not revealed to his Scotland Yard bosses. However, the rules state that officers needn't reveal such a liaison if the person is a close friend[4800].

Sir <u>Ian Blair</u> publicly praised his men for their 'astonishing professionalism' in the bungled Forest Gate raid (just as after the Stockwell shooting he claimed officers had 'played their socks off'). Yet the Met soon had to apologise to the Forest Gate community for the 'hurt' it had caused[4801].

Police Minister Hazel Blears said (2006) that the revelation that Sir <u>Ian Blair</u> covertly recorded a conversation with Attorney General Lord Goldsmith was 'a very serious matter'[4802].

Scotland Yard refuses requests (e.g. from 'The Times') for information about the secret SDS (Special Demonstration Squad), known as 'the Hairies' because the officers don't have to cut their hair or shave. The SDS is supposed to prevent disorder, having been set up in 1968 to deal with anti-Vietnam War protesters. In 2010 SDS officer <u>Peter Daley</u> revealed his work in the 1990s: for four years he was a Trotskyist protester six days a week – he won an out-of court settlement from the Met for PTSD[4803].

The coroner is reported to have refused the admission of the IPCC to G20 victim Tomlinson's first post-mortem. Also an inspector in the City Police at first refused to identify the officer concerned, and the Met wouldn't produce a spokesman for Newsnight[4804].

The IPCC accused the Met of stalling its inquiry into the Stockwell shooting disaster: <u>Sir Ian Blair</u> denied he had attempted a cover-up by asking that his force's hunt for bombers should take priority over any outside investigation[4805].

The police and MI5 were to be questioned in court in 2010 over whether they could have done more to prevent the July 7 bombings, but survivors were banned from asking their own questions and also denied a judicial inquiry[4806].

Senior Scotland Yard officers colluded in bringing a fallacious disciplinary case against junior detective DS Howard Shaw, who reported DI <u>Kevin Williams</u> for cheating (accessing questions on an internal database just prior to being interviewed for a promotion in the Met's e-crime unit): Williams now (2010) worked in the counter-terrorism unit, while Howard Shaw was forced out by Williams and Detective Superintendent <u>Charlie McMurdie</u>. Shaw says: 'My story shows how difficult it is to be a whistleblower in the police'[4807].

Daily Mail columnist Peter McKay questions whether the public can have much confidence in 'cosy inquiries' in which those under suspicion, e.g. <u>Sir Ian Blair</u> in respect of the Andy Miller contracts and his handling of the de Menezes aftermath, are 'investigated' by colleagues[4808].

Officers have been banned from hiding their shoulder numbers to avoid identification, in the light of the behaviour of some police at the G20[4809]. The CPS could have charged PC Simon Harwood, involved with the G20 Tomlinson death, immediately with assault – the case dragged on beyond the six-month time limit for such a charge[4810]. The failure of the CPS to charge Harwood with manslaughter was described by his family, unhappy also with the police probe, as a 'big cover-up'[4811]. He was sacked in 2012 but retained his pension.

The police were accused of a cover-up after a royal protection officer was knocked down by Prince Andrew driving his Range Rover – he failed to stop. Friends of the officer claim he has been pressurised to 'keep his mouth shut'[4812].

In the early noughties in Operation Cotton the Met had set up two undercover officers on the Costa del Sol to operate as money launderers for seven years, at a cost of millions. The accused were supposed drugs and tobacco smugglers working with corrupt politicians in Gibraltar, but at trial the judge called the prosecution's assertions 'state-created crime', and threw it out (2004). This sort of scenario enables empire-building by senior officers by pursuing questionable agendas. Undercovers are supported by their 'uncle', their debriefer, and they are routinely quizzed by the department's psychologist. The tentacles of the psychologists seem to reach every part of the police service, but they are nowhere to be seen when their advice causes trouble.

Undercover SDS officer DC Mark 'Flash' Stone lived a double life with environmental activists, drinking with them, helping them organise their activities, making love to them, etc., for seven years. He seemed to them to be vehemently anti-police. The police are facing lawsuits from some of the women he allegedly slept with[4813]. A German MP says legal action in Germany can be taken against him for 'trespassing' in people's private lives, i.e. starting sexual affairs with activists linked to G8 and G20 protests in that country[4814]. A 'Mail on Sunday' leader asked: 'Why do we even have such a body as the National Public Order Intelligence Unit, which turned Mr. [Mark] Kennedy (a.k.a. Stone) into a spook?'[4815] The undercover cop has revealed how he was savagely beaten by five colleagues at a protest – they didn't realise he was one of them! The Met's NPOIU has been pressed to reveal the extent of its covert monitoring of peaceful activists[4816]. It was Notts Police's decision to withhold secret recordings of Kennedy's dealings with protesters that caused the collapse of the climate change trial. Kennedy revealed how colleagues enjoyed expensive Volvo cars and flats, with up to 14 hours' overtime daily[4817]. DPP Keir Starmer, QC, has written (2011) to the ecoactivists infiltrated by undercover officers like Mark Kennedy, inviting them to appeal against conviction because his secret activities were not disclosed. The Met at first refused to confirm that Mark Stone was an undercover cop[4818]. Undercover detective Jim Boyling even married an environmental activist he was spying on. A.k.a. Jim Sutton when he infiltrated 'Reclaim the Streets', Boyling at first didn't tell the woman he was to marry his real occupation, and encouraged her to change her name by deed poll (to conceal their liaison from his Met seniors, but this subterfuge was unsuccessful[4819]). On returning to uniformed duties he was formally commended by a Met assistant commissioner. He was the fourth officer identified by the press (others were Lynn Watson and Mark Jacobs). Boyling affirmed under oath in court that his name was Jim Sutton (his operational name – he also had a fake occupation of cleaner), while defending himself and other environmental campaigners (Reclaim the Streets) against a charge of disorderly behaviour. This deliberate manipulation of the justice system has caused embarrassment to

Hogan-Howe's major review into the deployment of covert police. At first Scotland Yard declined to comment. Peter Black, a fellow undercover officer, claims the Boyling case is not unique – being prosecuted is part of the cover. It is alleged that not only were campaigners' discussions with their lawyer compromised by the police action (Boyling being present at confidential interviews), but that Boyling 'played a major role in initiating conduct which was then prosecuted'. There are at least eight inquiries into undercover police, including by HMIC. Boyling could face a perjury inquiry[4820].

A main factor in the £50m collapse of the Daniel Morgan pub axeman murder case was the discovery of several crates of police files that should have been revealed to the defence two years before[4821].

Keith Vaz (home affairs select committee) wrote to Sir Paul Stephenson to ask why the latter's 2010 parliamentary testimony seemed to fall short of giving 'the full facts'[4822].

In 2002 the Met submitted distorted ethnic minority recruitment figures to the Home Office (this included mixed-race, Cypriots, Irish and white Commonwealth), hoping no one would notice . A shop break-in during the 2011 London riots by 100 raiders was only classed as one crime, leading critics to say police are again massaging figures . The Met under Sir Ian Blair was accused of massaging crime figures, e.g. 'fudging' the murder rates by misrepresenting some 7/7 deaths, under-recording tens of thousands of less serious offences and issuing a huge number of cannabis warnings (logged as 'non-sanction detections')[4825].

A letter supposedly penned by Jack the Ripper has re-entered the public domain decades after disappearing from the archives of the Met. It has been alleged that some clues about the Whitechapel Murders were either forgotten about or covered up. As early as 1889 the police were spreading the rumour that Jack the Ripper had died by drowning at the end of 1888: senior officials of the police and government helped to give the rumour wide acceptance when they mentioned it in their memoirs. The secret Scotland Yard Ripper files were officially closed in 1992. 'Jack the Ripper's' letter disappeared from the archives of the Met to reappear decades later in the possession of former policeman Donald Rumbelow. Sir Charles Warren, Commissioner of the Metropolitan Police at the time of the Ripper, arrived on the scene to declare that the message on a wall ("The Juwes …") above the piece of a victim's bloody apron, was "meaningless" and ordered that it be washed away, even before it was photographed. Warren, a Freemason, was probably trying to cover something up. The battle for the release of secret Ripper documents - the Met is resisting a former CID head's attempts vigorously – has cost the taxpayer thousands. The ledgers detail the police's dealings with thousands of informants from 1888-1912. The case has even had a senior officer giving evidence anonymously from behind a screen. The Met claims release of the documents would endanger national security[4826]. Really? A century later?

Royal bodyguard Ken Wharfe apparently kept his treachery from his colleagues, friends and even his wife. He revealed he had been working on his book ("Diana : Closely Guarded Secret") for 3½ years. Wharfe severely embarrassed the Royal Family by breaking the traditional silence of royal protection officers. All police officers are required to sign the Official Secrets Act.

MP Kate Hoey, a former Home Office minister, says the Paddick scheme in Brixton was a "smoke-screen" for softer cannabis laws. A senior police officer, Deputy Assistant Commissioner Michael Fuller, head of the Met's drug directorate, asked to evaluate the controversial "softly softly" cannabis experiment, was told his report was "too negative" by

Home Office officials; the report was shelved and never made public. Indeed, members of the Metropolitan Police Authority have never been shown a copy. Police service whitewashing suspicions have been aroused by the decision not to prosecute gay Commander Paddick for allowing cannabis to be smoked at his home, while more than 5,000 people were convicted of the same offence between 1990 and 2000. The Met always claimed the Lambeth pilot was a local initiative launched by Paddick, but in fact the press found that virtually from the start it was approved by the highest echelons in the police and Home Office.

Scotland Yard knew of a threat to "nobble" the foreman of the jury in the Guinness fraud trial, but Lord Justice Henry, the trial judge, has confirmed he knew nothing of the threat to the jury during the six-month hearing in 1990.

The Met's obscurantist tendency elicited the following tabloid leader in 2009: 'It is grotesque, unbelievable and bizarre that the country's main police force and the chief law officer should be involved in manoeuvres of this kind' (i.e. a gagging order). The case was that of the BBC fighting for the right to report a story (the 'cash for honours' scandal): the Met sought an injunction rather than relying on the strict contempt of court laws. The media were not to be allowed to know what they were barred from reporting[4827]. Lord Goldsmith's High Court injunction to gag the BBC from reporting on the cash-for-honours saga was, he confirmed, requested by the police.

Scotland Yard pressed for murder charges against two teenage boys over the death of Damilola Taylor, as a result of a secret bugging operation which made them feel they were on the right track. The tapes were never disclosed in court (for "legal" reasons), and the boys were found not guilty after a trial of 11 weeks.

When three alleged Arab terrorists were arrested in 2002, on suspicion of plotting to release poison gas on the Underground, the arrests were kept under wraps, with suggestions that the Yard deliberately withheld news of them to "avoid causing panic".

Scotland Yard is reluctant to divulge whether its Crimes Against Humanity Unit is still tracking Nazi war criminals.

When two men posing as suicide bombers in London in 2006 went unchallenged by police, the latter stopped the press taking pictures.

Former Met Commissioner John Stevens' book "Not For the Faint-Hearted" recounts how as an officer he made so many arrests he was known as "Swifty Stevens". But, though this was the heyday of corruption, racism and violence in the Met, he tells nothing of these.

Scotland Yard's controversial shoot-to-kill policy for suspected suicide bombers was secretly changed in 2005, but the Met refuses to say what the new rules are. This is the third time such measures have been put in place without public debate.

When Detective Chief Superintendent Jack Slipper flew to Rio to arrest Great Train Robber Ronnie Biggs he offended the federal Brazilian police by giving them only the briefest warning of the arrest, but this was kept secret for 30 years. The incident led to the Foreign Office making the Flying Squad apologise to Chief Garcia, but the move was kept secret to prevent bad publicity.

According to the BBC's "Panorama", self-confessed corrupt policeman DC Neil Putnam alleged that his colleague in the Stephen Lawrence investigation (Operation Athena Tower), John Davidson, prevented the killers being brought to justice by taking money ("a good little earner") from the father of one of the accused. Davidson was charged with handling vulnerable witnesses. Assistant Commissioner John Yates agreed Davidson was a bent cop, but denied Putnam's assertion that he (Putnam) had told the Met about the danger Davidson represented: the Met refused to release notes of the crucial interview, and wouldn't let Panorama's Mark Daly see them. The allegation about Davidson's corruption never reached the Macpherson Inquiry. (See also Appendix IV).

Dr. Francis Tumblety was Scotland Yard's prime suspect as Jack the Ripper, but this fact remained unknown for 80 years till a letter by Special Branch head Inspector Littlechild came to light - it was written 25 years after the murders in response to a journalist. The large Scotland Yard dossier on Tumblety has gone missing. The revelation that the Yard had let him go would have proved very embarrassing.

Tom Driberg (later Lord Driberg) was chairman of the Labour Party as well as a notorious gay predator in the toilets of Soho. When young men he had tried to 'touch' reported him to Scotland Yard, the latter ran him home in a squad car (the press also turned a blind eye)[4828].

Tottenham community leaders' concerns at the lack of information about the 2011 Duggan shooting, and the intensity of local anger were not passed to the IPCC till it was too late[4829]. Senior Met officers insist that during the Tottenham riots no PCs were instructed to hold back, but front-line officers' version is different. A Met officer blogger ('Inspector Gadget') says cops wanted reassurance they wouldn't be disciplined if a rioter was seriously injured, but this wasn't forthcoming: he insists officers were ordered not to advance. The insistence of the police leadership that 'bobbies on the beat' are not the answer to crime, has been gainsaid by the effect of the saturation policing which brought the riots to an end[4830].

The Met covered up for some time the true cost of their controversial crackdown on the late anti-war protester Brian Haw. Sir Ian Blair had said to the Police Authority the bill was £7,200, but updated this privately to over £27,700. A new estimate which included opportunity costs totalled over £111,000[4831]. In 2007 it was reported (BBC1. 6.3.07) that the Met had tried to gag The Guardian in the cash-for-honours scandal.

Sunday Times journalist Rod Liddle was censured by the Press Complaints Commission for saying the great majority of London gun, knife and street crime was committed by young black males, but weeks later the Met, forced by the FOIA, released data which proved 'the majority of people held responsible for street crime, gun crime and robbery in London were young, black and male'[4832].

The Met refused to identify a 58-year-old officer whom they sacked for dismissing scores of 999 calls as non-emergencies (they included armed burglary, rape, child abuse, threatened suicide). The IPCC found 141 of his calls, over a three-month period, had 'significant performance issues', with 19 amounting to gross misconduct. It was decided there wasn't enough evidence to prosecute him but the IPCC said 'his performance beggars belief'[4833].

PC Simon Harwood, who attacked Ian Tomlinson, was to face the first public disciplinary tribunal in the Met's history (the IPCC ruled): inquest jurors say he deliberately used excessive and unreasonable force. Yet a gagging order was in force to stop the media publishing material relating to the case: it couldn't even be reported why the coroner made the ruling, publication of which is also prohibited. Police initially denied Tomlinson had contact with officers before his death[4834]. DPP Keith Starmer said a manslaughter charge against Harwood was dropped because of experts' disagreement over the cause of death of the newspaper seller[4835]. It has been suggested that the Met's tactic of 'kettling' – protestors are hemmed into a small area – may have played a role in the death[4836]. In 1870 PC John Norman killed a man with a baton-blow to the head[4837], so when Harwood struck Tomlinson, who died soon after, resulting in this affair being described as the most serious disciplinary charges ever levelled against a PC, this wasn't true[4838]. Two of Harwood's previous victims – a black female subjected to racial abuse and a road rage victim – had been paid off secretly[4839].

Simon Harwood

The mother of Troy Hurst, murdered by neighbour Albert Reid in 2000, whose entry on the National Database was 'extremely dangerous' and 'has the potential to kill', had a seven-year fight to bring the Met Police to account. On the night of the murder there were four 999 calls from the victim and his father. The Met resisted at great cost the reopening of the inquest, which may have revealed 'systemic failings' – under Article Two of the 1998 Human Rights Act the authorities must 'take reasonable steps to safeguard the lives of individuals'. Mrs. Hurst in 2003 obtained a High Court order for the reopening but the Met appealed, and in 2005 at the Court of Appeal the Met argued the inquest preceded the start of the Human Rights Act so was not subject to Article Two. However, despite Mrs. Hurst winning again, the Met managed to get the decision overturned in the House of Lords, with the help of Labour's Lord Falconer[4840].

Hackers ('Anonymous') have eavesdropped on a sensitive conference call between the Met and the FBI about hacking. Anonymous have revealed a Met officer admitted making a secret application to a court to postpone the London trial of two alleged hackers at the FBI's request (the cop admitted: 'We've cocked things up in the past, we know that'[4841]).

By the start of 2012 the Met hadn't replied to a Daily Mail FOIA request for answers to the following: how many police investigations into the Press are currently taking place, how many officers are involved, how much is it all costing? A newspaper reporter who asked a senior Met officer a legitimate question about a case received a menacing call from the anti-corruption squad, demanding to know why he was asking the question[4842].

The Met was forced in 2012 to concede that it had 'breached a legal obligation' from 2006 onwards in not warning phone hacking victims about the invasion of their privacy. The 2010 group victim claim was defended at first by the police, despite there being at least 829 'likely victims'[4843].

A witness to the 2012 Westminster bar brawl involving Scots Labour MP Eric Joyce claimed that a policeman tried to cover up the incident[4844].

The Met ordered the detective probing Lucan's whereabouts to discontinue the probe, even though Lucan was reliably sighted in Africa – the officer was denied funds by senior Met cops[4845].

The Met 'authorised the movement' of rubber bullets 22 times in two years, but refused to give details of where they were to be used in 2010-11. Senior officers wanted to use baton rounds in the 2011 riots but firearms officers couldn't be deployed in time: if they had been used, consensual policing would have been compromised[4846].

The Met delayed informing the media of the attempted murder of Russian banker German Gorbuntsov. Only a Russian newspaper blowing the gaffe revealed the international nature of the shooting, i.e. the Met apparently tried to suppress an important story, probably to prevent compromising the Olympic Games[4847]. What else is being covered up? The Met chose to downplay the shooting of Gorbuntsov – the first attempted <u>criminal</u>, rather than political, assassination in London. It was four days before his identity was confirmed, and the death was reported in Moscow first[4848].

An elite Met cop, whose name was not revealed, was carpeted for buying police badges from a BNP activist: the force refused to say whether a police email account was used[4849].

It was claimed (2012) that a report by the Met's anti-corruption unit was not revealed to the 1998 Stephen Lawrence inquiry: the documents are said to concentrate on the integrity of Commander <u>Ray Adams</u>. Though the Home Secretary offered to meet Stephen's mother, the National Black Police Association has never been granted a meeting with Mrs. May[4850]. The Met has invoked the IPCC over claims that corruption may have impeded the Stephen Lawrence inquiry. The Met was refusing to reveal if its detectives' searches had disclosed any evidence of concealing reports[4851].

The IPCC has ordered the Met to discipline an unnamed officer (for racially discriminating against Stephen Lawrence's brother), whom the Met's professional standards unit had cleared.

The IPCC's procedures have been labelled unfit for purpose when a four-year inquiry into the now-disbanded Enfield Crime Squad (the disciplinary hearings were as usual held behind closed doors) ended with no dismissals and no senior officers held to account. Six cops were reprimanded, two given written warnings and a sergeant reduced to constable. The offences included smashing up a car, threatening 'waterboarding', mishandling seized stolen property, driving an uninsured car the wrong way up a one-way and crashing it. Operation Sumaq was one of the biggest carried out by the Met's anti-corruption unit. A probe into the IPCC by the Commons Home Affairs Select Committee started in June, 2012[4852].

The Met's internal affairs unit has investigated allegations that police smeared MI6 'body in bag' spy Gareth Williams (by leaking false reports that he was a transvestite whose sex game went wrong), but decided not to discipline anyone[4853].

Robert Mark, 'The Lone Ranger from Leicester' wanted to 'make virtue fashionable', but found the Met a secretive, Masonic place, where the CID looked down on 'uniforms'.

No one was charged over the Tory Chief Whip/police confrontation, so why did the Met launch an inquiry into who leaked the story – a story clearly in the public interest[4854]?

Sir Bernard Hogan-Howe ruled out making 'false' apologies 'at this stage' over the disturbing use of dead children's identities by undercover officers[4855]. He declined to be interviewed re the leaking of the Mitchell story to the press. He is accused of making no record of what he said to reporters, which is contrary to Leveson guidelines[4856].

When two Scottish schools were closed by police because of a threatening phone call, the police refused to tell parents the nature of the threat[4857].

HM Inspectorate of Constabulary has unearthed a major problem of inaccessible intelligence while reviewing police handling of accusations against Savile. Hundreds of files on VIPs were kept so secret that police probing alleged offences couldn't see them. The reason (?excuse) for the secrecy was supposedly to prevent corrupt officers selling stories to the papers, i.e. protection of the elite took precedence over child protection. Commander Peter Spindler confirmed important people were protected by high levels of confidentiality[4858].

Many crime victims' only contact with police is now via a call centre. Officers must not now treat every report of criminal damage (almost a third of all offences) as a crime if there was 'no idea how it happened'. Unsolvable crimes will also not be investigated[4859].

Undercover Met cop Peter Francis, using the alias Pete Black, a member of the covert political spying Special Demonstration Squad (motto: By Any Means Necessary) revealed he and three colleagues were ordered to find 'dirt' against murdered Stephen Lawrence's family and discredit Stephen's close friend Duwayne Brooks, who was with him when the murder occurred. His mother said the family had always suspected police had been amassing evidence about her visitors, and feels this revelation is the worst of all that happened in the case. Francis's 'hunt for disinformation' lasted four years – he infiltrated an activist group called Youth Against Racism in Europe. Senior officers withheld his role from inquiry head Sir William Macpherson. Duwayne was arrested and charged in 1993, before the case was thrown out. The secret SDS unit, unknown to many senior officers, was established to monitor anti-Vietnam protestors and morphed into its current manifestation, the National Public Order Intelligence Unit. Met Commissioner Paul Condon handed out bottles of whisky personally to SDS members, according to Francis, yet he denies knowledge of SDS[4860].

Why do all officers leaving the Met have to sign the Official Secrets Act? Might the latter be used to gag genuine whistleblowers whose information should reach the public[4861]?

Senior Met officers knew for up to 15 years that criminal PIs had infiltrated its witness-protection programme, yet did nothing about it: the private investigators also worked for the Murdoch corporation and were heavily involved in intimidating 'supergrass' witnesses (at least one major criminal trial collapsed as a result). Details of the suppression of the revelation that the programme was being compromised were to be found in a SOCA report leaked to the press[4862].

MI5

British Intelligence failed to pass on to Ulster police crucial information about the Omagh bombers, which might have prevented the biggest atrocity of the Irish Troubles. The blame is put on Special Branch[4863], which has been criticised for destroying records[4864].

Police intelligence files, released under data protection laws, have revealed how Tony Blair called in detectives to try to silence an angry letter writer who was bombarding him with correspondence. The writer had to appeal against an order blocking the release of MI5 files signed by Jack Straw; Robin Cook signed a similar blocking order on release of any MI6 files.

A case against animal rights activists was dropped because Special Branch officers would have had to be identified.

Michael McKevitt, founder of the Real IRA, which was behind the Omagh bomb outrage, was said to be likely to serve a shorter sentence in an arrangement designed to cover up MI5's Irish role. Also two Garda officers are believed to have helped MI5 in anti-Real IRA operations.

New evidence of Liberal Democrat MP Sir Cyril Smith's paedophilia, covered up by Special Branch and MI5, has been found in a police dossier[4865].

Norfolk

Norfolk Police have been accused of trying to cover up a 999 call, which allowed burglars to escape with their loot. BT confirm the call was made. The Norfolk force has been criticised before for delays in responding to 999 calls. Tony Martin – jailed for killing a burglar at his remote farmhouse – complained police either failed to arrive or arrived late at break-ins to his property. When a police guard was assigned to him after travellers put a bounty on him, Norfolk police refused to discuss the cost of the exercise[4866]. In 2004 they took over four hours to respond to a nine-year-old girl being indecently assaulted and abducted[4867].

In the 1960s Porton Down chemical warfare doctors dropped thousands of tonnes of cadmium across the English countryside (there were over 100 experiments with the toxin between 1957 and 1964). A retired Norwich PC remembers his force was asked to place 30 monitoring devices in police houses around the city, with the purpose being kept secret. The one person who asked about the device in his garden was told it was to monitor traffic[4868].

A leaked Norfolk Constabulary memo accuses the rank-and-file officers of classifying non-crimes, such as car vandalism, as crimes, to help people claim on their insurance. The memo emphasised: 'One of the targets this year is to keep recorded crime down to 1500'[4869].

Northern Constabulary

Northern Constabulary Chief Constable Ian Latimer, forced to apologise over a bungled death probe, refused to ask another force to re-examine the case as a murder investigation[4870].

Police insist lawyer Willie McRae, an SNP activist, killed himself (by shooting), but conspiracy theorists argue a political assassination. Suspicions were raised by Northern Constabulary's refusal to hold an inquiry[4871].

In 2003 Scottish police forces were spending annually £6 million investigating each other, accusations of professional misconduct having reached an all-time high in that year. Northern Constabulary Police closed their £2.5 million inquiry into Kevin McLeod's death in 2003, claiming there had been no cover-up. This was despite his family's fury over the retirement – shortly before his misconduct hearing – of the Constabulary's Deputy Chief Constable, Keith Allen, who refused to participate in the Police Board proceedings[4872]. Critics claim too many inquiries into allegations of police blunders end in secrecy and whitewash. Central Scotland was reinvestigating the death over the way Northern Constabulary looked into the case.

When a five-year-old Moray girl went missing - her body was eventually found in a canal - Northern Constabulary kept the media and public in the dark during their investigations.

Northumbria

Northumbria Police has been accused of hiding a large percentage of crime from the public – hundreds of serious crimes like rape and armed robbery have been concealed for no good reason. Britain's fifth-biggest force released, over a two week period, just 27 out of more than 17,000 crimes and other incidents (i.e. less than 1%). The force spent £1 million annually on a Press Office (in 2010 this had risen to £1.7m), which mostly puts out releases on supposedly reducing crime figures. A journalist has noticed 'a disturbing trend in recent years for the police to release fewer crimes to the media'. Northumbria's 'corporate communications' department issues propaganda on falling crime rates to meet 'public confidence' targets; in other words 'police spin'[4873]. Thus they might release details of a stolen dog or a minor road accident but 'omit' GBH, armed robbery, rapes and burglaries[4874]. Five MPs backed an early-day motion criticising Northumbria Police, whose spin claims they have the highest public confidence figures (66%) in England and Wales. Police press releases numbered five over a three-day period: under FOI there were 4,665 incidents, including 674 crimes[4875].

When Raoul Moat was killed, Northumberland Police refused to say if he was Tasered before or after the fatal shot, and it took the IPCC to reveal there had been two Taser shots. The police demanded a news blackout about Moat's private life, and asked that already published material on the subject be removed from news websites[4876]. A Northumberland councillor tried to find out how much his constituents would have to pay towards the Moat 'Operation Bulwark' by asking its cost (under FOI). But the Northumbria force unreasonably refused to release the figures until the IPCC investigation was complete – the IPCC were not investigating anything remotely related to the costs. After lodging a complaint and giving the media the story, the councillor was eventually promised the information – he says Northumbria Police are by far the hardest to elicit information from[4877].

Northumbria Police have also been accused of downplaying the cocaine problem in North-East pubs (the drug, referred to by the police as 'dangerous chemicals'), after at first refusing to reveal the full extent of the drugs market. Despite Operation Achilles finding cocaine traces in most Northumberland pubs (it took a FOI request to establish this), an officer said drug-taking and drug-related crime was 'not a major issue' there. Martin

535

Callanan, MEP for the North East, said, 'I'd like to know why the police were reluctant to release the full figures in the first place and why they didn't say it was cocaine that was involved'[4878].

Northumbria was also asked under FOIA if any member of staff had been disciplined (in the aftermath of the Stephen Mitchell rape scandal) or if there were any recommendations made to prevent a similar scandal, but they refused to say if there had been an inquiry. Deputy Chief Constable Jim Campbell says they 'now have a very effective Counter Corruption Unit'. They had been presented in 2005 with a chance to probe Mitchell's background when his ex-wife made several allegations to them about him, but nothing happened[4879].

North Wales

The BBC's 2003 documentary 'The Secret Police' unmasked eight racist officers at a training centre in Chester: one was PC Rob Pulling of North Wales Police, who, wearing a Ku Klux Klan-style hood, said he would like to kill an Asian officer and suggested Stephen Lawrence deserved to be murdered. Cheshire PC Steven Salkeld threatened to 'pull over' Asians and 'give them grief'. Yet Home Secretary Blunkett implied these facts shouldn't have been unearthed, when he called the programme a 'covert stunt' and accused the BBC of 'attention-seeking'[4880].

Labour Lord Mackenzie of Framwellgate, an ex-policeman and adviser on police issues to the Government, received a threatening letter from North Wales Deputy Chief Constable Clive Wolfendale after Mackenzie denounced the force's investigation into Blair's alleged anti-Welsh remark as wasteful and 'trivial'. Lord Mackenzie said the Wolfendale letter was 'diabolical' and 'befitting the Stasi secret police'. The CPS had advised the North Wales force to drop the Blair inquiry but maverick Chief Constable Richard Brunstrom (see Eccentric Policeman) insisted on pursuing it. Wolfendale was criticised in 2004 for performing a 'rap' song for the inaugural meeting of the force's Black Police Association.

Nottinghamshire

HM Inspectorate of Constabulary's 2000 analysis of crime reporting practices (England and Wales) confirmed for the first time that under-recording was widespread, e.g. Nottinghamshire had been manipulating crime figures since the start of league tables. Thus an inquiry by the Bedfordshire force found over 9,000 1996 incidents recorded in alternative systems didn't appear in the Nottinghamshire's official crime statistics: a supposed fall in recorded crime of 7,700 was a fiction – the true figure may even have risen. Nottinghamshire was also the leader in massaging clear-up statistics using so-called TIC (Taken Into Consideration), or write-offs by prisoners (which might account for as much as 30% of cleared up crimes). The trouble is these may be concocted, e.g. some were found to be committed against people who had never been burgled, or the prisoner was locked up at the time of the supposed crime.

A district judge has severely criticised Notts Police for their practice of resolving 'serious offences' through reprimands. Superintendent Helen Chamberlain was caught speeding at 79mph in a 50mph zone, but was let off by the junior officer concerned[4881].

Notts PC Nick Hubbard has highlighted the case of a 10-year-old who stole from all the other patients during an overnight stay in a maternity unit – she attacked a nurse who tried to stop her. She could only be charged with 10 crimes though she had committed 21 (there were 14 victims)[4882].

Three judges strongly criticised undercover activists, especially P.C. Mark Kennedy, whom they labelled an agent provocateur. They quashed the convictions of the activists. Notts Police were found to have suppressed evidence[4883], and have escaped misconduct proceedings (failing to declare the use of undercovers to prosecute activists), though the IPCC criticised the force's 'collective failings'[4884].

Police Scotland

Police Scotland has removed 23 sex attackers from the Sex Offenders Register (to protect their human rights) without telling their victims, who might live in the same area[4885].

Police Scotland have been accused of trying to downplay the true numbers of murders in Scotland[4886]. Labour's justice spokesman Graeme Pearson was asking why the new force told a Scottish tabloid nothing worth noting had happened on one day (in July, 2013) when in fact there were almost 2,000 crimes (including 243 attempted murders, rapes, robberies, etc), this admission only being wrested from the Chief Constable as a result of a FOI request. Police Scotland apparently uses stop-and-search legislation more than any other UK force[4887].

Police Scotland's Major Incident Team refuse to reveal who asked them to investigate the source of the information in two 2012 tabloid stories about illegal bullying and other misconduct (e.g. data protection breaches) by senior officers including Deputy Chief Constable Neil Richardson[4888].

Scottish media organisations have had great difficulty in getting information about incidents from Police Scotland, e.g. the latter couldn't tell 'The Courier' if a helicopter hovering above a Scottish Defence League demo was theirs or not, and the same newspaper was only told about an attempted abduction in Fife two days after the incident. Certainly 'The Courier' is no longer able to access information about local crime as was the case with the old local forces[4889].

Almost £1.2m has been paid to informants (CHIS – covert human intelligence sources) in five years by two of the former eight forces. Police Scotland has declined to release the figures for the other six[4890].

A FOIA request has revealed there are almost three times as many serious assault victims in Scotland who turn up in hospital as are recorded by police[4891].

RUC

In 2002 Omagh bomb victims' families feared their landmark legal action against the Real IRA could be compromised after detectives from the Police Service of Northern Ireland said they would refuse to give evidence in court. Their reluctance might have been because they would probably be challenged about a damning Police Ombudsman's report (officers were accused of not acting on an anonymous tip-off and of poor judgement). Cover-ups by the RUC and Special Branch (creating false entries and notes, and baby-sitting killers) was revealed by the Police Ombudsman in 2007.

South Wales

South Wales Police denied that social networking sites had anything to do with the 17 young suicides in Bridgend in just over a year. Assistant Chief Constable David Morris called an extraordinary press conference at which he virtually blamed the media for the suicide cluster. But covering up the reporting of suicides can lead to erroneous speculation[4892].

South Wales Police were condemned by the IPCC in 2006 for blundering over the kidnap of a three-year-old abused by serial paedophile Craig Sweeney. The IPCC was also expected to condemn the MAPPA (Multi-Agency Public Protection Arrangements) team responsible for preventing Sweeney re-offending, but the IPCC said their report might be kept secret, leading to an accusation of cover-up by the child's mother[4893]. South Wales Police were condemned by the IPCC for blundering over the child's abduction. Not for the first time has the IPCC been seen as the policeman's friend.

South Yorkshire

Hillsborough

Hillsborough Special Constable Debra Martin was the first officer to admit she was pressured into taking part in a huge police cover-up (as a result she received hate mail from colleagues at work). She was forced to change the time in her account of a Liverpool fan's death to hide the fact he could have been saved. The police allowed only one of the 45 ambulances on to the pitch, using the excuse that the victims of the disaster died almost instantly. At least 12 officers are thought to have been ordered to change their statements. She was hounded by a WPC who told her: 'You're a liar. We don't even know if you were there. It's probably all in your imagination.' A retired PC whose statement was similarly doctored has released a letter proving the Government knew of the cover-up – it is contained in more than 300 boxes of secret files in the possession of South Yorkshire Police[4894]. These secret files, normally locked away for 30 years, were to be released a decade early: relatives believe a decision taken at a meeting between South Yorkshire Police and Margaret Thatcher, days after the tragedy, meant the police would not be blamed for what happened[4895]. Was there a deliberate cover-up by the Thatcher government to protect the police for Hillsborough blunders because the Tories felt indebted for the police's support in the miners' strike? Why were Liverpool, with more fans than Forest, given smaller stands? Why were the fans trying to ferry the injured (a total of 766 were injured) to ambulances outside pushed back by police? Why did police say Liverpool fans had turned up without tickets, when at least one of the injured had his ticket in his pocket? And why can't the relevant Cabinet papers be released immediately under FOIA[4896]? David Duckenfield was the officer who ordered the fatal opening of the gate at Hillsborough. Duckenfield, together with NHS Yorkshire Ambulance Trust and Sir Norman Bettison, refused to cooperate with a BBC Panorama investigation. Officers' statements were vetted before release, and this was confirmed by Labour Minister Angela Eagle in April, 2009. The notorious W. Midlands police were asked to adjudicate. The South Yorkshire's Chief Constable's offer to resign was refused. The Taylor Report blamed police organisation for the disaster. The Information Commissioner ordered the Cabinet Office to release the Hillsborough files: the Commissioner criticised the Cabinet Office for its unjustified delays in acceding to a BBC FOIA request over two years before[4897].

Though South Yorkshire Police caused the Hillsborough tragedy they smeared dead Liverpool fans and doctored evidence by 164 officers (116 of these being critical of the force). Police even took blood samples from children as well as adults, on the coroner's orders, to try to link the deaths to alcohol. <u>Peter Wright</u>, the then Chief Constable of South Yorkshire Police, was the cover-up enabler who blamed the 'drunken' fans so that his force would be exonerated: he retired a year after the Taylor Report exposed the police machinations. The police computer was accessed to see if the victims had criminal convictions. An Inspector Calvert admitted police witnesses were coached. The police even tried to discredit a medical witness to the carnage because of her perceived contrary briefing: Dr. Joan Ashton was told to shut up, and anyway was just a publicity seeker who wasn't a 'proper' doctor (she worked in public health!). PC Mark Lewis alleged he overheard Lord Chief Justice Taylor and Chief Constable (now Lord) Dear 'cooking the books' in the back of his police car (one said, 'I suppose blame should be placed against the fans') but the PCC and DPP said there wasn't enough evidence to proceed against the two top men (it was the first-ever accusation of conspiracy involving the head of the judiciary). <u>Paul Middup</u>, the then secretary of the South Yorkshire Police Federation, briefed 'The Sun' such that the paper accused fans of stealing from the dead and urinating on officers: as a result to this day Scousers won't buy 'The Sun'. <u>David Duckenfield</u>, the chief superintendent in charge at the ground lied that fans forced their way through an exit barrier, when actually he ordered it to be opened: he retired on a medical pension (severe mental illness). <u>Sir Norman Bettison</u>, the present Chief Constable of West Yorkshire, tried in 1989 (as a chief inspector) to publicise the police account using a biased video presentation and contributing to the whitewashing Wain Report. He was the 'black propaganda mastermind'. When he was appointed Merseyside Chief Constable in 1998 several police authority members resigned in protest, and after retiring in 2005 he controversially was appointed the head of the West Yorkshire force in 2007. Bettison was knighted in 2006 for 'services to policing', but was still trying to criticise fans' behaviour in the autumn of 2012. However, he soon had to make a humiliating apology to save his skin when his own police authority said it would institute an inquiry[4898].

The late Chief Constable <u>Peter Wright</u> convened a meeting which decided the police mustn't take the blame. He described the Taylor finding (the disaster was mainly due to a failure of police control) as 'harsh', hoping the coroner 'would draw different conclusions'[4899].

The Hillsborough inquiry raised questions which remained unanswered. Mrs. Thatcher was told the police report was 'defensive bordering on the deceitful', yet sanctioned the police's 'culture of impunity'. The force betrayed 'the very basis of policing' – the cover-up was unprecedented in Britain. There has been a call for the victims' death certificates to be altered from 'accidental' to 'unlawful killing'. The Police Complaints Authority ordered the force to start disciplinary proceedings against <u>Duckenfield</u> and deputy superintendent <u>Bernard Murray</u>, in charge of the control room at the ground: his officers banned paramedical services from entering the ground – their equipment could have saved 41 lives. 14 officers were awarded £1.2 million in damages (1996) for 'psychological illness', but relatives were banned from claiming for similar post-traumatic stress disorder. There have been calls for the original inquest to be quashed, as a miscarriage of justice is now known to have occurred. Among others the police ignored red light warnings about the stadium for eight years before the disaster, particularly its lack of a safety certificate[4900].

On the day of the Hillsborough disaster the police gathered in an auditorium at the ground to discuss it, but excluded all non-force personnel, including doctors and nurses[4901].

Witness statements were sent to solicitors Hammond Suddards, <u>hired by the South Yorkshire force</u> so that the statements could be systematically doctored, re-typed and returned for signing. Officers were told not to record their experience in their pocket books, rather to write their 'recollections' on separate sheets 'in their own time'. One PC was told by an inspector not to open a gate which would have relieved the pressure[4902].

A Hillsborough families' QC has told coroner Lord Justice John Golding police handheld CCTV evidence may have been tampered with, and the IPCC was interviewing all 220 living police officers suspected of doctoring their reports[4903].

Only now (2013) has it been revealed that senior South Yorkshire officers asked in 1991 for handouts from a charity fund (intended for Hillsborough victims' families) to send cops on holiday, refurbish kitchens and gyms in police stations (including redecoration of Bettison's own HQ and window blinds), buy exercise bikes and 'worthwhile gifts' for officers on sick leave, decorate police houses in Rotherham to encourage cops to 'live in places where they might not want to live!' Police wanted their own convalescent home, counselling services and an occupational health unit financed by the disaster fund. It is unclear how much of the latter went to the police[4904].

In the Moors Murders case South Yorkshire Police wouldn't reveal their dig sites and refused to be interviewed, yet they prosecuted some of their own in 2006 for failure to disclose information.

Former South Yorkshire Police sergeant <u>Richard Sainsbury</u> claims the CPS dismisses evidence a jury should see and hear[4905].

South Yorkshire Police are accused of ignoring for over a decade allegations of the sexual abuse of white girls by Pakistani gangs. Rotherham police found evidence of thousands of such crimes, according to secret documents seen by 'The Times'. Officers were criticised in 2002 by the Home Office for regarding victims as 'deviant and promiscuous' while not probing the men[4906].

Strathclyde

A 50-year-old trainee policeman being hired by Strathclyde Police was hailed as a victory for anti-ageism, but then refused to identify him or allow him to give interviews. He is TV star <u>Gilbert Martin</u>, who was thrown out of his home after keeping a love child secret from his wife[4907].

Officer Shirley McKie's career was ruined after being accused of leaving a fingerprint at a murder scene she was not meant to visit. The High Court decided the print wasn't hers, but Strathclyde police never apologised, and an investigation cleared the Scottish Criminal Records Office of responsibility for the flawed evidence. McKie says: 'If a

Shirley McKie

serving ... officer can be stripped of dignity, have a career and life destroyed because the system refuses to accept mistakes can be made, what chance does the man in the street have... there's a great big club out there where the rules are conspiracy, collusion and face saving'[4908](see also pp 588, 589).

Strathclyde PC Thomas Clark, jailed for three months for assaulting innocent men, was appealing the sentence in 2010. He allegedly tried to cover up what had happened by filing a false report which amounted to a 'concoction of exaggeration and lies'[4909].

Strathclyde PC Steven Smith went on trial in 2010 accused of lying to a fellow officer to help his gay lover avoid a theft probe, as well as using a police computer for non-policing purposes[4910].

When WPC Anne Ramsay (author of 'Girl in Blue', the exposé of sexism, bullying, etc. in Strathclyde Police) left the force, she was made to sign a paper saying she was no longer fit to be a police officer[4911].

In his most recent book* retired cop Paul Harrison claims DS Joe Beattie, who was in charge of the Bible John manhunt, thought the culprit was a fellow officer (probably undercover) given early retirement on health grounds – when Beattie's superiors heard the prime suspect was a policeman they shut down his investigation. The following prima facie evidence could suggest a high level cover-up. The first victim (Helen Puttock)'s sister insisted she saw the culprit show Helen a warrant card as they left the Barrowland dancehall (it was, she said, identitcal to Beattie's own card). The surviving sister also saw the killer when she visited Beattie's HQ at Marine police station (he said she must be mistaken). Barrowland bouncers apparently recognised his photofit – they had been involved in a fracas with him but he made them back off by flashing a warrant card. One young cop pulled in repeatedly because of his manner and short hair and resemblance to the photofit ended up an assistant chief constable[4912].

Though the number of Strathclyde serious traffic injuries recorded by police has fallen, the number of minor ones have apparently risen: police may now be reporting more serious injuries as slight. There are huge discrepancies between hospital and police statistics (almost half of the hospital injured don't tell the police[4913]).

The family of a teenage cyclist killed by a car have accused Strathclyde Police chiefs of a seven-year cover-up over his death. The parents say senior officers are protecting colleagues. Scotland's Police Complaints Commission upheld six complaints about the force's 'unreasonable' behaviour. HMIC (Her Majesty's Inspector of Constabulary) for Scotland told Strathclyde to re-interview the senior officer on duty, Jim Weir, about his version of events, but they refused[4914].

Two months after the 2010 Loch Lomond explosion there was still an information blackout; even Strathclyde Police Authority had to write to Strathclyde Police to ask how the investigation was progressing[4915].

Strathclyde Police had to be ordered to reveal the number of sex offenders living in deprived parts of Glasgow: they are 'dumped' in poor districts. This was in the wake of the murder of a schoolboy by a teenage sex offender[4916].

---

* Harrison, P. Dancing With The Devil. Vertical Editions. 2013.

Strathclyde PC <u>Mark Burnett</u> was suspended after being charged with stealing evidence worth up to £175,000. The force refused to elucidate the nature of the allegations, and again the officer appeared in private, so that the details wouldn't be disclosed[4917].

Though Glasgow paedophile <u>Martin Cusick</u>, a former police officer, vanished in 2005, it was only 2½ years later that Strathclyde Police eventually released his photo and confirmed they were hunting him. He was supposed to have been monitored by Strathclyde's MAPPA system (introduced after a young Glasgow boy was killed by a known sex offender). Politicians and children's campaigners lambasted the delay in notifying the public[4918].

When a restricted scar-faced patient went on the run while on unescorted leave from a Glasgow psychiatric hospital, Strathclyde Police wouldn't let the public know about his background[4919].

A Strathclyde WPC claims she was filmed by her firearms police sergeant partner <u>Steven Campbell</u> while he raped her, and is to ask a judicial review to overturn the decision to drop charges of rape and attempted murder (he pled guilty to assault and illegal possession of ammunition). The two were colleagues in the Special Support Unit – he has been sacked – and carried on a 13-year relationship (after their split in 2008 he entered a relationship with another female officer and is now married). A letter from Solicitor General Frank Mulholland told the victim that the Crown Office planned to destroy the video footage at the heart of the rape allegations, though the Lord Advocate has now promised the footage will be kept secure[4920].

Strathclyde former Assistant Chief Constable <u>John Neilson</u> arranged for officers to guard his wife's elderly aunt, at a cost of £25,000. The 'protection patrols' only surfaced when Sergeant Martin Porter complained about 'Operation Park Road' – because of the stressful way Porter says his complaints were handled had led him to take the force's governing body – the Strathclyde Police Authority – to an employment tribunal[4921].

Despite concerns being raised over the years about apparent links between Strathclyde officers and the Lyons gang (involved in the Glasgow drugs trade), nothing was done. Thus there were claims that <u>Detective Superintendent Michael Orr</u> put pressure on a forensic scientist to change her testimony: he and his deputy <u>Detective Inspector Callum Young</u> have already been reprimanded about their conduct in the case, particularly they way they dealt with corrupt PC <u>Derek McLeod</u> (suspected of leaking information to Lyons). Thus Young, according to the book 'Caught in the Crossfire', described the Lyons boss David an 'alright guy', as well as contradicting previous Chief Constable Willie Rae's opinion (that Lyons was a drug dealer) as 'spurious'[4922].

Strathclyde Superintendent <u>Steve Reed</u> was suspended from duty on full pay after being moved to an office role. The inquiry into the claims (not revealed) involved the force interviewing up to 40 police staff[4923].

Surrey

Allegations of sexual abuse, bullying and degrading treatment at Deepcut barracks came to light during the Surrey Police inquiry, which only became public as a result of a leak. Surrey Police were allowed to vet a report by Devon and Cornwall Constabulary into its own bungled investigation. Surrey admitted they might not allow it to be published (August, 2005). The families of the four dead soldiers had been locked in a battle for two years with

Surrey Police to find out what officers had discovered. Surrey Police took officers off frontline duty to travel throughout Britain to obtain permission from 800 witnesses to release their report to the families, who say this was a delaying tactic. Durham Chief Constable Jon Stoddart wrote a letter in his capacity as senior officer in ACPO's Homicide Working Group, suggesting the lack of a 'think murder' mindset among Surrey detectives could have compromised their investigations, which doubt the families of the Deepcut deceased had already strongly voiced. Following failed attempts to have the letter disclosed, the Information Commissioner ruled it must be made public, yet large parts of the letter still remain secret. Despite Devon and Cornwall's investigation of Surrey's probe and then the Blake Report, there has never been a public inquiry[4924]. Senior Surrey police investigating the Deepcut deaths pulled out of a meeting with ballistic and forensic experts which might have shed light on one of the deaths. The ostensible reason was that, while refusing to allow the families to have a record of what was said, they wanted their own[4925]. Parents of the dead Deepcut soldiers are reported to have started legal action to see two police reports into the deaths – the Devon and Cornwall Police report into Surrey Police's conduct were not made public. The original Surrey report had also never been shown in full to the families, and Surrey Police have been accused by lawyers for the latter of breaching the European Convention on Human Rights[4926]. Surrey Police, says the father of one of the Deepcut soldiers, lied when they said that there was no MOD involvement in their investigation[4927]. Surrey Chief Constable Denis O'Connor and his deputy Robert Quick reportedly refused to visit the family of a dead Deepcut soldier as arranged, because of media interest in the case[4928]. Ballistic expert Frank Swann's 'compelling and apparently conclusive testimony reveals alarming contradictions and failings in the official inquiries that branded them 'suicides'.' His report came amid the family's accusations of an Army cover-up. Swann believes police had barred him from performing vital tests and claimed detectives were not looking as hard as they might. The police admitted their inquiries had unearthed a number of disturbing allegations unrelated to the deaths (including male rape)[4929]. The head of Surrey CID has revealed more thorough PM examinations should have been carried out on the Deepcut "suicide" soldiers. The MOD is still refusing a public inquiry. Barrister John Cooper has expressed the families' grave concerns about the police investigation into the Deepcut "suicides". There were fresh demands (spring, 2011) for a public inquiry after the long-awaited review by Devon and Cornwall Constabulary claimed Surrey and military police probes failed to collect all relevant evidence, e.g. potential suspects were not properly investigated[4930].

Chief Superintendent Guy Darby was investigated in 2008 over claims he got a place in the London Marathon by pretending to be his son. The head of Surrey Police's strategic development, in 2006 he was given a formal warning after being caught using his mobile phone while driving[4931].

Top Surrey Police officers were accused of having 'collective amnesia' about the hacking of Milly Dowler's phone. They were unable to explain to the IPCC why, despite the police probe team's head Craig Denholm receiving documents mentioning it, nothing was done for 11 years; there was knowledge of the hacking 'at all levels' of the team[4932].

Sussex

Paul Whitehouse, the Chief Constable of Sussex, was forced to quit over his attempts to justify the police killing of a naked, unarmed man in a bungled raid.

Tayside

Tayside Police were being allowed by information watchdogs to keep secret the number of motorists caught by one of Scotland's most notorious speed cameras on the A9[4933], but this secrecy was abolished in 2011.

Tayside DI Paula-Jane Wales was suspended after being accused of withholding information which could have helped colleagues catch a suspect. She had already appeared in court charged with obtaining or disclosing data without consent[4934].

Tayside Police claim a killer who struck in 1912 is still being hunted, but have refused to reveal how the investigation is going into the murder of the Dundee spinster.

Thames Valley

Thames Valley Police refuse to reveal their Operation Mason file on the death of Dr. David Kelly[4935]. The MOD was prepared, in the case of Dr. David Kelly, to block a police investigation into a secrets leak. The evidence of Dr. David Kelly's closet confidante Mai Pederson, who doesn't believe his supposed suicide, was never given to the inquiry into his death. The then Assistant Chief Constable of Thames Valley Police, Michael Page, attested that her statement 'contained nothing of relevance'[4936]. The Hutton Inquiry did not deal with Pederson's statement, and the authorities refused an inquest. A file of police evidence submitted to the Hutton Inquiry on David Kelly's death has never been made public. It is labelled: "Not for Release. Police Information Only". Thames Valley Police were satisfied with the Hutton Inquiry's conclusions about David Kelly's death. When Assistant Chief Constable Michael Page retired in 2006, the eulogy at his farewell was given by Lord Hutton himself, but the latter was unable to give MP Norman Baker a copy[4937]. According to Baker, the police operation to investigate Dr. David Kelly's death started around nine hours before he was reported missing[4938]. Thames Valley Police detective Graham Coe says he lied about aspects of the statements he provided to the Hutton Inquiry, which critics said was a whitewash. Coe confirmed there was a 'third man' with him and DC Colin Shields at the scene, where there was 'very little blood'. Could the third man have been from MI5[4939]? Thames Valley Police have eventually revealed that David Kelly's mobile phone and watch had no fingerprints, just as his knife, pill pack and water bottle had none[4940]. Mobile phone records which could reveal David Kelly's movements before his death – his death certificate doesn't specify place of death – were ignored by police[4941]. Thames Valley Police failed to collect vital evidence provided by Dr. David Kelly's close friend Nigel Cox[4942]. The flight log of the helicopter hired by Thames Valley Police which visited the Kelly death scene for five minutes has been redacted. Why has the flight been kept secret[4943]? Dr. Kelly's widow says police stripped wallpaper from their sitting room on the night of his disappearance. DC Shields, one of the police first on the scene, did not appear at the Hutton Inquiry[4944]. Thames Valley have been accused of illegally accessing Facebook information involving David Kelly's death. They will be forced at a tribunal to explain how the private site was accessed. The force was trying to find evidence to support its refusal of a FOI request[4945].

One consequence is that police lose the opportunity to appeal for witnesses. The Home Office target of reducing the 'fear of crime' means censoring the news. Likewise, according to the Oxford Mail, the Thames Valley force, like others, releases only a tiny proportion of crimes to the media[4946].

Organisers of a cancelled Islam Fair in Reading were told by police they had "no intelligence" to justify the force's objection to the event. It is thought the original information about the organisers' motives came from Special Branch, but that local police found the information to be wrong.

Slough neighbourhood PC Nick Bond was quoted at a community forum: 'A lot of people say they feel intimidated when they see [Romas]. They don't believe in education, government or laws. They come to feed on our society because very few intend to work. When a police officer asks them, 'Why did you come to England?' they say: English laws are soft and the shops have a lot of choice and are easy to steal from.' When a newspaper contacted Bond he said: 'I've been told off. I can't speak to you'. PC Bond faced disciplinary proceedings for supposedly contravening the force's 'diversity and ethnicity' policy[4947].

Dozens of vulnerable underage girls were trafficked in the Oxford area, but Thames Valley Police refused to reveal the ethnicity of the suspected paedophile gang members. Nor would they say whether the victims came from care homes or foster care[4948]. Freed victims of child prostitution say there is a culture of ignorance and disbelief among police[4949].

Transport Police

The discovery of the body of a girl who was killed by a train was delayed for two weeks because a British Transport Police officer lied to Essex colleagues. She told detectives the victim couldn't have been in a collision because of sensor technology in every train (this doesn't exist). The IPCC substantiated four complaints about the police operation[4950].

Hero British Transport Police inspector Gavin McGowan was charged and suspended over claims he lied to escape a speeding rap, claiming he was on duty at the time, despite being in an unmarked car[4951].

Warwickshire

The name of a former policeman accused of stealing £113,000 from Warwickshire Police headquarters was kept secret by the force. ACPO says it plans to stop all forces revealing the names of arrested cops, to 'protect them from being linked to 'heinous crimes' of which they are innocent'. Yet they gave innocent Christopher Jefferies' name to the press (2010), before they had any evidence he murdered Joanna Yeates[4952].

West Mercia/West Midlands

PC George Bakewell's pamphlet 'Observations on the Construction of the New Police Force' (1842) stressed abuses and incompetence of many men in the Birmingham force, where, as elsewhere, there was a huge turnover of staff. Bakewell said he had resigned with honour in 1841, but there is evidence that he was dismissed earlier for being drunk and disorderly. Yet the Birmingham Police gave him a certificate of good conduct[4953].

West Midlands Police took nine months to inform the public that a convicted rapist, branded extremely dangerous, was on the run.

West Mercia has kept the body organs of 44 victims unknown to their families[4954].

When an MOD laptop was stolen (2008), West Midlands Police advised the theft be kept quiet, despite it containing the personal (including bank) details of 600,000 people[4955].

West Yorkshire

The IPCC criticised West Yorkshire's ex-Chief Constable <u>Sir Norman Bettison</u> for 'abusing his position' in the aftermath of Hillsborough, saying he would have faced 'gross misconduct' charges if he hadn't resigned. There were calls he should be stripped of his knighthood and honorary Fellowship from Liverpool John Moores University[4956].

West Yorkshire Police were accused of an 'Orwellian' attempt to silence a man who said he had been harassed by Lucy Tate, Britain's youngest magistrate. <u>Detective Sergeant Vanessa Gardner</u> and <u>D.C. Steve Williams</u> made him sign a statement promising not to talk to the Press about the case. They allegedly said they had been asked to 'nip the situation in the bud'. Concerns about the police behaviour were expressed by Labour MPs Denis McShane and Austin Mitchell. The alleged victim had a second police visit, when they interviewed him for an hour, taking details of his email and mobile phone[4957].

Jimmy Savile, while being questioned about sexual offences under caution by Surrey Police, boasted to them of his police contacts who would help him get round abuse claims. Thus an inner circle of police (dubbed the Friday Morning Club) met every week at his Leeds penthouse: they included a retired West Yorkshire Police inspector and a currently serving officer (there were up to nine officers in the Club)[4958]. Not only did Jimmy Savile hold regular weekly coffee morning chats with his local force, but he was invited to a VIP lunch with senior officers and to open a police gym. Despite multiple complaints against him, he was chosen in 2008 to front two crime prevention campaigns in Leeds. Another claim is that a police officer knew of him taking girls to a barge for parties. A police report exonerating officers was dismissed by victims as a 'bag of lies'[4959]. Savile was named in a 1964 intelligence file as a member of a vice ring grooming underage girls from an approved school, but the police seem to have ignored it[4960].

The police and H.S. Theresa May issued secret 'gagging orders' to cover up intelligence as to how MI5 could have prevented July 7, at the public inquest into the affair. West Yorkshire Police's gagging order sought to prevent the disclosure of files on contacts between the 7/7 gang's boss and a known Islamist extremist, and two other Home Office orders (public interest immunity certificates) banned release of minutes of a clandestine MI5 committee and details of police counterterrorism officials, as well as of 'technical operations' and summaries of MI5 terrorist inquiries. In 2010 MI5 said, with the backing of the then Home Secretary, that the inquest should not investigate its role[4961].

West Yorkshire Police conducted a secret investigation into their own officers during the Ripper inquiry. One ex-Ripper Squad detective wrote: "I have always believed that the hoaxer was a police officer". Lancashire and Wearside newspapers complained about police stonewalling.

One Bradford (West Yorkshire) policeman has told how he was stopped by his superiors when he spoke out about forced marriage in Britain (some claim it is the biggest form of slavery in the country): in nine months in 2013 there were reportedly 5,000 calls to a helpline[4962].

Wiltshire

A WPC sued her force after learning that her husband of 15 years, Sergeant <u>John Coppen</u>, was a bigamist, and that Wiltshire Police allegedly conspired to prevent her finding out the truth, shielding the sergeant from being prosecuted. An internal inquiry in 1998 recommended 'no further action'. The original police file has been destroyed. The sergeant is now married to the personal assistant to Wiltshire's Assistant Chief Constable[4963].

A judge branded two Wiltshire PCs liars as he jailed sergeant Mark Andrews for his treatment of Pamela Somerville (the sergeant was released on appeal, but dismissed from the force). The two police witnesses' evidence was questioned by the judge, so much so that he wrote to the Chief Constable expressing his concern: Wiltshire Police refused to release their names[4964].

Following an inquiry into Wiltshire's Deputy Chief Constable David Ainsworth by South Wales Deputy Chief Constable Colette Paul, a complainant was set to receive a secret package of about £10,000 for sexual harassment and 'damage to feelings'. Wiltshire Police refused to reveal the conclusions of DCC Paul's report[4965], which, however, led them to seek an out-of-court settlement, presumably to conceal the full facts. It has been claimed that the new Border Force chief – former Wiltshire Chief Constable Brian Moore - neglected accusations by 27 female staff of sexual harassment by Ainsworth, Moore's friend. He suggested to two victims they seek a direct apology from Ainsworth, then, after further complaints, just gave him 'management advice' and sent him on a diversity course[4966].

Yorkshire (see also p538)

Inspector Mark Manning, who conducted the Kieran Fallon race-fixing investigation, was accused of 'deliberately deceiving' the Chief Constable of Yorkshire Police – who authorised the surveillance of a gambler accused of organising the scam – as to how much money was thought to be involved. He was accused of falsely stating a figure of £2 million to ensure he got permission for the secret bugging[4967].

The inquiry into the Yorkshire Ripper case by senior police figure Sir Lawrence Byford was still an official secret by 2003 (apart from a brief superficial summary in the House of Commons library), so that homicide detectives are not allowed to study it to learn lessons. Even Byford didn't uncover crucial evidence about Peter Sutcliffe's sexual motives, which junior police covered up – Sutcliffe was wearing makeshift underpants which exposed his genitals, suggesting a severe sexual deviation aspect to the murders, but the detectives present when he removed his clothes did not tell senior officers. So psychiatrists concluded: 'There is no suggestion that he is a sadistic, sexual deviant'[4968]. It has been alleged in connection with the Ripper that there may have been a police cover-up relating to "Wearside Jack". A 2001 ITV film reiterated the popular suspicion that the police might be covering up for one of their own. In 2001, too, former Ripper Squad detective Dick Holland finally admitted that the West Yorkshire police had conducted a secret investigation into their own officers during the inquiry. TV investigative journalist Sheilagh Matheson says: "They (the police) don't want to know because it was an embarrassment, a dreadful cock-up. Policemen's careers were sidelined because of it; it was a public humiliation, and I don't think anybody wants to be reminded of it." Confronted with the police's unwillingness to reinvestigate, the public have looked to a string of murky coincidences that seem to point to a general rot within the force: Oldfield's role in a wrongful conviction, Holland's involvement in the framing of a man for murder (1976), the fact that Sutcliffe's solicitor also represented a Ripper Squad detective later charged with selling information (for other instances of miscarriage of justice, see 'The Unjust Policeman' chapter).

In the Hillsborough fiasco 450,000 documents had not been disclosed by police even after 23 years[4969]. At Hillsborough dozens of ambulances were refused access to the ground by police, who falsely told the paramedics that it wasn't safe to enter[4970]. Fresh inquests and a new police inquiry have been ordered into Hillsborough[4971]. The names of 1,444 retired and serving officers have been given to the IPCC for its Hillsborough probe. The IPCC is to focus on potential criminality and police misconduct. The Home Secretary is considering legislation to <u>force</u> police to give evidence, even though they were only witnesses[4972].

There is to be no probe into Savile's close relations with some senior police officers, which could help explain his avoiding persecution[4973].

Only after 11 months was the public told of criminal charges against Tayside drugs squad officers: two were charged but not brought to court (both were suspended). A further 24 officers were to make themselves available for interview. There were 446 claims of excessive force, discrimination and corruption made against Tayside Police <u>staff</u>, including 42 civilians and eight special constables[4974].

Operation Fairbank will assess whether an 'all-party' London paedophile ring consisting of ex-government ministers, Tory and Labour MPs, as well as a Liberal, abused boys in council care at a London guesthouse in the 1980s. The central issue of the probe will be whether, despite a raid in 1982 and abuse allegations in 2003, no action was taken by police, suggesting a Met cover-up[4975].

The Met has been accused of trying to 'hide its dirty laundry' after demanding that the claims its undercover officers tricked women into relationships should be heard by the Investigatory Powers Tribunal in secret (it historically has upheld only 1% of complaints)[4976].

The official police log of Plebgate was written by <u>Toby Rowland</u>, who belongs to the Diplomatic Protection Group, as does the cop who sent the fake email, <u>Keith Wallis</u>. When Deputy Chief Whip John Randall contacted Wallis to arrange a meeting the latter declined but sent <u>another</u> email telling the same story. Commissioner <u>Hogan-Howe</u> had said early in the saga: 'I am 100% behind the officers. They accurately reported what happened'[4977].

Scotland Yard worker Jairo Dos Santos made £32,000 selling the secrets of the Royal Family's bodyguards to the press but he is accused of breaching data protection laws (over their expenses): he was to be retried in 2013 because his first jury failed to reach a verdict[4978].

When Tory ex-Chief Whip Andrew Mitchell met the Federation representatives of West Midlands, West Mercia and Warwickshire, they said they were told nothing new, when in fact he had given them new and full details of what he said[4979]. Mitchell has accused rogue officers of 'a sinister smear campaign'. A head of MI6 was stopped by police from entering Downing Street to attend his own leaving party[4980].

The West Mercia Police's internal probe into Plebgate suggested lying by three officers, according to the IPCC, because the probe's main conclusion – that Inspector Ken MacKaill, DS Stuart Hinton and Sergeant Chris Jones should face misconduct hearings – was altered at the last minute to clear them. The force has declined to comment on who ordered the report to be changed. Unprecedentedly the Home Secretary and PM demanded hearings and apologies to ex-Cabinet Minister Mitchell, whose secret recording of a meeting with the officers proved they lied. West Midlands Police and crime commissioner Bob Jones called for the abolition of the IPCC – surely an overtly partisan and political stance (he also says there was only <u>one</u>, not two discrepant reports): the Police Federation, too, has turned a minor altercation into a PR disaster for them . Met Commissioner <u>Hogan Howe</u> not only pre-judged 'Plebgate' by dismissing the conspiracy theory, but then allegedly leaked a whitewash version of events and failed, even after 13 months, to achieve a satisfactory conclusion! A lawyer has claimed that officers found to have given false testimony are seldom prosecuted[4982].

Almost half of all police forces were unaware of how many children went missing in their area annually[4983].

In 2011 over 1,800 sex offenders (including 30 rapists) were given reprimands and warnings rather than being taken to court. Cautions were given to arsonists, drug dealers and death by dangerous driving. Eight forces refused to provide information to journalists[4984].

It is claimed that a Met anti-corruption command report wasn't disclosed to the 1998 Macpherson inquiry: corruption may have influenced the probe[4985].

An initially anonymous former Met officer, but later identified as PC <u>Abdul Rahman</u>, is suing the force after resigning because of an accusation that he had attended a terrorist training camp. The case will mostly be heard in secret, and a vetted 'special advocate' assigned to him in place of his lawyer[4986].

Police have been secretly storing hundreds of body parts of suspicious death victims for over 50 years long after the cases were solved. Many relatives were kept in the dark. Some parts belonged to children[4987].

A whip-wielding dominatrix and her anonymous MI5 husband agreed he <u>did</u> set up Max Mosley in the S & M scandal[4988].

The late Tory MP Sir Irvine Patrick told The Sun the fans were to blame for the Hillsborough disaster, but insisted he had been given 'wholly inaccurate' information by the police[4989].

A pictorial self-defence instruction manual (which recommended holds that might attract allegations of brutality today: placing a foot on the suspect's throat, sitting on his back or performing a 'wrist twist') was issued in 1907 to City of London police recruits, who were warned not to show the pictures to the public. The pictures were hidden in force archives for decades[4990].

Council chiefs have been forcing Southampton cabbies to record all conversations in their cabs, and police are allowed to access these[4991].

Thousands of civilian 'busybodies' (including shopping centre staff) have been licensed under the Community Safety Accreditation schemes. They can destroy people's careers (e.g. in teaching and nursing), yet have as little as five days' training. By July 2012 154 organisations have been accredited by 27 forces in England and Wales, yet only 20% of these forces keep tabs on the activities of those involved. There is a danger, it is claimed, that the accredited become a shadow police force[4992].

Norfolk Police were no longer recording criminal damage as crime, e.g. car vandalism, if there is 'no idea how it happened', there being a target set to 'keep recorded crime down to 1,500'[4993].

Internal advice to West Mercia Police officers told them to inform striking firemen that they weren't welcome at incidents, but the force refused to comment[4994].

Two policemen (one Strathclyde, one Lothian & Borders) faced internal probes after being filmed trying to stop members of the public filming them in separate incidents in Glasgow (a man's mobile knocked to the ground and smashed by an officer, who denied lashing out) and Edinburgh (officer smacking a camera out of the way)[4995].

Off-duty Detective Chief Superintendent Richard Munro, a high-flier seconded from Fife Constabulary to HMIC, was mugged (his warrant card stolen) in a street on the edge of Aberdeen's red light zone in the early hours. Grampian Police have referred a report of the incident to the Procurator Fiscal. HMIC refused to comment on Munro, though it boasts on its website: 'HMIC not only conducts and publishes its activities openly, but also expects and encourages similar appropriate openness from police forces'. In 2002 another Fife officer, Alan Meldrum, who guarded Prince William, was accused of spousal assault and stripped of his gun licence, and the year before Chief Inspector Robin Lumsden had to remove his car number plate spelling out the initials of Hitler's Nazi party[4996].

When journalist Rachel Johnson told in her column how the police were dragging their feet over her son's stolen laptop, despite its tracking software revealing the location, picture and identity of the man in possession of it, lo and behold, the police recovered it using a search warrant. An officer then phoned to 'reassure' her, but added, rather sinisterly, '... we don't want to read any more about this in The Mail on Sunday'[4997].

The police have helped 'reduce' crime by reclassifying thousands of serious crimes as minor, cautioning cases previously sent to court, recording several separate crimes in one street as one incident, recording theft as lost property, discouraging the public from reporting some crimes (e.g. ASB), inducing criminals to admit to past crimes (thus 'solving' them), charging people with little prospect of the cases proceeding (these are then recorded as 'cleared up'), switching police to easier tasks (e.g. speeding drivers) where clear-up figures look better, etc[4998].

Police rules in the past have meant up to 50% of violent attacks (e.g. brawls and pub fights) are excluded from official statistics if victims don't want to press charges. Chief Superintendent Ian Johnston, of the Police Superintendents' Association, said: 'We have always acknowledged that there is a huge under-reporting of crime' (e.g. of victims under 16 years of age)[4999].

Before Ken Wharfe left the police senior officers had heard he was collaborating with a Fleet Street journalist on a book containing revelations about Princess Diana. But when they confronted him he flatly denied it. When the book appeared, Met Commissioner Sir John Stevens was 'appalled' and demanded to know how Wharfe's superiors had allowed it[5000].

By January 2013 Cumbria's top cop Stuart Hyde had been suspended for four months while allegations about his behaviour continued to be investigated by South Wales Police. The nature of the allegations was kept under wraps[5001].

Grampian Police were forced to admit that an anonymous officer had been dismissed for rudeness, when Inspector <u>Ian Swan</u> let it slip[5002].

It took 4½ years and millions of pounds for Superintendent <u>Ray Mallon</u> to admit, at the 11th hour, 14 charges, including nine of neglect of duty, three of falsehood and prevarication, one of discreditable conduct and one of misconduct towards a member of the police force. Claims of malpractice within Middlesbrough CID (supplying drugs for confessions, tipping off suspects, ill-discipline, etc.) were the subject of Operation Lancet. Ironically, Mallon is credited with trailblazing 'zero tolerance' policing, but was said by his chief constable to be at the centre of an 'empire of evil'[5003].

The Government has expanded the number of 'get-outs' that allow the police to ignore many crimes while taking credit for solving 'unsolved' crimes. If police don't have enough evidence, they can still claim to have 'detected' the crimes. So inept forces can still present a glowing 'detection' record, e.g. the counting rules allow officers to record only 'one crime per person'. 'Violence against the person was up by 90% over a five year period, but the true figures four times that'[5004].

Police have been accused of exaggerating reductions in crime (their figures showed a 7% fall in car crime, burglary and vandalism, while the National Crime Survey's 2012 survey revealed a similar fall of 8%). The Office for National Statistics say police are under 'informal pressure' to meet targets, which may mean downgrading of some crimes so that these disappear from the figures[5005].

John Crawley, an IPCC commissioner from 2004-2008, has accused the organisation of being too slow to react and too close to police[5006]. The IPCC tried to prevent Channel 4 showing (22.4.09) the Tomlinson tape, which pinpointed the culprit U41 officer (he was left-handed).

In 2004 the Chief Constable of West Yorkshire Police persuaded Channel 4 to cancel a documentary about Asian pimps in Bradford[5007].

Around 80 officers (perhaps more) from the Met's secret Special Demonstration Squad (SDS) used stolen dead children's identities to create fake passports, starting in the 1960s. A former undercover SDS cop says it was just like the Stasi[5008].

The Met Police Authority was accused of trying to bury news that two of their controversial officers – <u>Ali Dizaei</u>, alleged to have six mistresses, and <u>Maxine de Brunner</u>, once accused of making false claims against Paul Burrell – had been given £90,000-a-year jobs as Commanders[5009].

Officers have been told they shouldn't talk about crime in case the public gets frightened. Police are the most likely of all public servants to 'talk negatively' to the public about their job[5010].

Savile emphasised his social connections with senior officers in Leeds, his hometown, and how he could call in 'favours'. Officers would visit his home, have tea and read his hate mail, which they would destroy at his request – they would examine any letter forensically as a 'favour'. The police decided not to tell the BBC he was being probed, thinking article 8 of the E.C. on Human Rights meant they didn't need to warn other organisations. Nor was information shared between forces, e.g. Surrey Police failed to inform Thames Valley (protecting his adventures at Stoke Mandeville). It took nearly a year before Surrey and Sussex forces realised they were both investigating him at the same time[5011].

Perhaps presaging the advent of 'secret arrests' (See The Unethical Policeman), the Met refused to release the name of an 83-year-old Berkshire man arrested on suspicion of historic sexual offences. Under this approach people can be taken off the streets without anyone knowing, with the police non-accountable[5012].

Conclusion

This chapter could have been divided into 'active' and 'reactive' cover-ups, the former where police go out of their way to be non-transparent, the latter where they don't instigate the concealment but act as rubber walls off which requests for information bounce. The end result is the same: infuriating obscurantism by forces who should know better. The examples quoted here may just be the tip of the iceberg – secretiveness seems to be endemic in police culture.

CHAPTER XXV

THE TRUSTLESS POLICEMAN

CONTENTS

CHAPTER XXV

THE TRUSTLESS POLICEMAN

Introduction

'The most law-abiding sections of society are losing faith [in the police] the fastest'[5013]. According to David Gilbertson, author of 'The Death of Constable George Dixon'[5014], the police service has never been held in lower esteem.

Former Met Special Branch officer Chris Hobbs says the force is so intent on preserving it reputation that it will come down heavily on anyone rocking the boat. 'It's run like a dictatorship and if you dare challenge the system, you've had it. If you take on the Met as a whistelblower, you'll never win. I was forcibly retired after making my concerns known'. It's not just the public who have lost their trust in the Met, he says, but cops themselves: 'The hierarchy don't have the trust of the troops on the ground'[5015].

There will always be people who trust authorities: this personality trait of being impressionable seems to be inherited (half of Dr. Shipman's patients still believe he was innocent!). But even trusting people reading this book will hopefully agree they can learn from the sceptics[5016]. The question 'But why should we trust the police?' has now appeared in the press, perhaps for the first time so blatantly[5017]. The more contact people have with the police, the less confidence they have in the police[5018] (as with doctors).

The police have increased their crime detection rate by inflating the number of crimes they know are easily detected. This massaging of figures suggests dishonesty[5019]. In fact, true crime detection rates are falling.

Once Royal Mail was your friend, but not any more, just like the police. 'The police forces of this country have broken their covenant with law-abiding people and now they lack friends when they need them most'[5020].

Psychologists are re-examining possible physiognomic clues to trustworthiness, e.g. people with a wider visage tend to be more devious[5021], but police are notoriously resistant to the idea of their personalities being assessed.

American gypsies call the police 'muskers'.

A senior police officer was interviewed on BBC2's 'Hard Talk' programme (12.6.12): the journalist's parting comment was, 'Some would say the police have lost the trust of the British public'.

Vic Emery, chairman of the new Scottish Police Authority, said police had lost the trust of the public in Scotland. Forces had been poorly governed for years and police chiefs tend to reject all criticism as an assault on their 'integrity'. The SPA would have to exercise stricter financial monitoring. 'Trust me, I'm a police officer' is no longer enough[5022].

Signs of Loss of Trust:

When Vanessa Feltz was in Sicily during the Tottenham riots the locals said, when they knew she was from London: 'Ah, England. Your people hate your police'.

Over the decade to 2009, 'the relationship between public and police has been badly, and unprecedentedly, corroded ..... A police force less trusted, more resented than at any time since the 19th Century'. This leads to the press pouncing with glee when the police let the side down, e.g. Assistant Commissioner Bob Quick was pilloried for displaying secret documents in public[5023].

Bob Quick reveals all

Ofsted has threatened to prosecute two policewomen who had informally exchanged babysitting duties with each other's children. Thus not even the police can be trusted to behave as responsible mothers[5024].

Journalist Nigel Burke began a 2009 tabloid article about the police: 'I am afraid of the police now. Aren't you?'[5025]. To compound the felony of mistrust, police officers are now said to have become terrified of talking to the press[5026], rendering them even more distant from the public whose trust they need.

Scottish police are no longer allowed to question suspects without their solicitor being present, suggesting they are no longer to be trusted[5027].

Many of the Trafalgar Square 2010 student fees protestors had a benign view of the police until they underwent the 'Kids' Kettle'. Resentment of the government education cuts was replaced by resentment of the police[5028].

The Attorney General declared to a parliamentary committee in 1854: 'When you get a policeman ... you look upon him as a person on whom you may ... rely ... it was not until I became a criminal judge that I saw the necessity of extreme watchfulness over them ...'. In the mid-19th Century there were accusations of constables manufacturing malicious or trivial prosecutions in order to supplement their income[5029].

Half of UK citizens feel unsafe in their own homes[5030]. Three-quarters don't know any of their local officers and two-thirds believe the police give poor value for money[5031]. Two-thirds also wouldn't object to the police being shown lack of respect[5032].

Assaults and vandalism by public

The rise in assaults on officers is arguably a symptom of increasing lack of trust[5033]. An average of three Scots police officers are being attacked daily by youths, some as young as eight (at least 5,500 youths over the five years from 2004, but because several forces don't collate this information the total is likely to be much higher)[5034].

Police services across Scotland experience hundreds of vandalism incidents every year, e.g. in 2007-10, 748 in Strathclyde (176 attacks on property, 561 on vehicles, 11 on equipment). In Fife 71 vehicles were vandalised in the same three years, while Grampian Police reported 76 incidents involving police property in 2007-9, e.g. 29 police cells were vandalised. There were 43 incidents reported by Lothian and Borders in three years, including stoning and puncturing cars and soiling of cells with blood and excrement. Tayside Police had 149 incidents in 2007-9[5035].

56 PSNI officers were injured in further Loyalist/Republican clashes (summer 2013). Scaffolding and paving stones were thrown by rioters at police[5036].

One manifestation of the racial tension which erupted at the inquest into the terrible New Cross fire was the angry black mantra: 'Police lie, 13 die'[5037].

Two Croydon girls drinking stolen wine during the 2011 riots told the BBC, 'It's about showing the police we can do what we want'. They were anti-police, not 'political' protesters – they didn't even know who was in power[5038].

A third of Scottish police officers were assaulted in 2012, a far higher proportion than the rest of the UK. The Scottish Tory Chief Whip says '... the sheer level of assaults ... shows a widespread disrespect for their work and authority'[5039].

Under-reporting of crime by public

Most violence is never reported to the police, especially by members of more reclusive communities like the Chinese (whose immigrant members may have unfortunate memories of the police in their homeland, or they may fear too close inspection of their citizenry documents).

Muggings reported to the police have dropped by 50% (from 75% to 38%) in only 15 years[5040]. Failure to report crime is the most worrying sign of loss of trust[5041].

Official Reports

The MacPherson Report even suggested trust should become a government target – there should be a 'Ministerial Priority' for 'increasing the trust of ethnic minorities in the police', 'associated with Performance Indicators'.

Police have broken their 'psychological contract' with the public to protect them from antisocial behaviour, said former Met chief Sir Paul Stephenson. This comment followed up Her Majesty's Inspectorate of Constabulary report that police had 'retreated from the streets' over three decades, and that 90% of the public felt it was the police's responsibility to tackle thugs[5042]. Keeping the peace was taking second place to hitting crime targets[5043].

The public are much more questioning and unwilling to support the police than they were ten years ago. In the spring of 2013 a Future of Britain survey of over 2,000 members of the public found only 26% trusted the police to have their interests at heart, just 7% ahead of the big supermarkets[5044].

Only a quarter of the public trust the police's ability to control crime (2006), the lowest percentage among the five countries of the OECD (the figure is 40% for Spain), yet the UK police enjoy the highest proportion of GDP. A 2008 poll found that, of 30 OECD countries, the UK had the lowest rate of trust (only 20% of people) in the Government's ability to deal with crime. Complaints against police doubled – the increase mainly from the middle-class – between 2005 and 2008.

The 1999 HMIC report, ordered because of falling confidence in the service, found that public confidence was being undermined by corruption and racism [BBC News 10.6.99].

Embarrassed West Midlands cops who set up a 'Rate Your Local Police' website to encourage feedback from the public, found it filled with bitter complaints. An officer called in to investigate a crime kept a woman waiting while he went for a takeaway[5045]. One reader wrote into the Sunday Express suggesting anti-police sentiment was behind the popular support for killer Moat[5046].

Confidence in the police has fallen in the 20 years from 70% satisfaction in 1989 to 46% in 2009[5047]. Compared with other professionals trust is now lower in the police. Under 10% of officers in England and Wales are devoted to Safer Neighbourhood Policing[5048].

The think tank Reform says Britain now has the world's most expensive justice system but ineffective in fighting criminals. It is bureaucratic, technocratic and Robocop-like, without a human face[5049].

Ten times more people are angry with the police than officially complain about them (in four years from 2004 complaints soared from 15,800 to 28,000). The Police Complaints Commission confirmed: 'People are less satisfied with the police than in the past'[5050].

Under half of Scots have confidence in the police, says the 2010 Inspectorate of Constabulary's Scottish policing performance framework report[5051].

The British Social Attitudes Survey (2010) found growing distrust of the police, and support for the way the police are managed has fallen from 77% (1983) to 62%[5052]. Three-quarters of people say they have lost faith in the police's ability to confront anti-social behaviour[5053]. Around only 40% of the public believe police can reliably deal with minor crime, a third don't have confidence in the police and around half say they don't do a good job[5054].

The £974m. NPIA (National Police Improvement Agency) presided over a massive collapse in public confidence in the police[5055].

According to a former HM Assistant Inspector of Constabulary, 'The police have never been held in lower esteem'[5056].

According to BBC research (2001) public confidence in the criminal process is low, with at least half the public losing trust because of miscarriages of justice (two-thirds feel not enough has been done to prevent miscarriages)[5057].

A 2007 IPCC report revealed that nearly half of all complaints are of rudeness and laziness (in 2006-7 there were 29,000 complaints in England and Wales, a 10% increase on the previous year, almost double since 2004). The rudest officers seem to be in Bedfordshire, with a 40% rise in a year. Tellingly for trust in the police, nine out of 10 complaints were found by forces to be 'unsubstantiated', i.e. of those investigated, which merely constituted a third of complaints[5058].

Complaints against the police have increased for seven years in a row. 40% of crime victims never get a visit from an officer, and police wrongly write-off thousands of thefts and vicious assaults as 'no crime'[5059].

Hoax calls

South Yorkshire Police received 1,500 hoax calls in 2008[5060], another sign of disrespect.

'Police baiting'

'Police baiting' was recorded in 1927 by a magistrate in London's East End, who condemned the practice as a 'form of big game hunting'[5061].

Slang synonyms for police – rozzer, fuzz, pooh-pooh, smokey, etc. – are another symptom of disgust by certain sections of the population.

Games

A students' game revealed at the 2010 London riots shows the contempt in which the 'intelligentsia' hold the police: 100 points for making an officer bleed (so that he requires hospitalisation), 50 for landing a blow, 20 for a punch, 10 for throwing a missile[5062].

Strathclyde Police were being taunted by show-off youths posing for YouTube clips of 'pigging' – climbing onto police vehicles. Operation Access was mounted to stop the 'piggers'[5063].

Causes of Loss of Trust:

Police actions/inactions

A report by Lee Rainbow, chief of the UK's National Policing Improvement Agency, as well as an expert in offender profiling, advised that the McCann family 'is a lead that should be followed', in the disappearance of their daughter[5064]. When the McCanns learned this, they could be forgiven for mistrusting police, especially when evidence against them was 'developed' by British police, helping Portuguese police to build their case against the parents, according to the UK's ambassador to Portugal[5065].

In Operation Pomeroy record examplary damages against Cleveland Police were awarded to solicitor James Watson for unlawful imprisonment and abuse of power – Chief Inspector Tony Riordan (now retired on full pension) focussed 'unhealthily' on Mr. Watson, maliciously procuring search warrants to seize 26 boxes of documents. It took the victim four years to clear his name – even though the CPS exonerated him he was still regarded by Riordan as a suspect. Police procedures were found wanting, e.g. things were never written down, while all six tapes and six back-up tapes 'failed'. There were no reasonable grounds to suspect the victim, whose wife says: 'The police wanted to ruin us' [5066].

A top-secret complaints dossier on former Tayside Chief Constable Justine Curran – she admitted her 'sex texting' was inappropriate – has gone missing from the 'executive corridor' of the North Command Area Dundee HQ. Despite the complaints from 'staff loyal to Tayside Police' she has become Humberside's chief constable[5067].

Former police cadet Robert Garside's achievement – recorded in the Guinness Book of Records – of 'running' round the world has been seriously questioned, e.g. he flew thousands of miles and gave Africa a miss[5068].

A significant breach of trust was committed by Scottish PC Matthew Turner, who was nearly given a jail sentence for being too lazy to investigate crimes: he had about 14 cases – he admitted neglect of duty[5069].

Police have been accused by lawyers and football fans of creating a 'banning order industry' that is treating fans unfairly – the civil orders bring financial incentives, criminal convictions don't. The Home Office and ACPO set a mandatory number of orders that must be issued. Some football police posts are totally funded by the banning orders[5070].

Tape recordings show police continually reassured the ill-fated barrister Mark Saunders that he was 'not going to die'[5071]. The police ensured he did.

Northumberland ex-traffic cop <u>David Rathband</u>, blinded by Raoul Moat, claimed he has been abandoned by many of his former colleagues. His firearms colleagues were exonerated of any wrongdoing in Moat's suicide[5072].

We can't always trust the police to uphold the law, e.g. the law on fox hunting is so complicated and full of loopholes that they seem to have all but given up trying to enforce it[5073].

Retired cop <u>John MacMillan</u>, who chauffeured VIPs and senior officers over a 57-year career, was banned and fined for dangerous driving, despite his insisting that he was innocent and that witnesses had misidentified the driver of his vehicle[5074].

A strange man caught in a house by the owner was let go by police without charge. Vandalised allotment owners in Wiltshire found the police equally useless – one intruder was caught and the others' descriptions given to the police, but the latter discarded a unified list of damage (they said each victim had to complain individually, but when they did, one was told the police could only pursue theft, not damage, another told there were no details logged with the crime number given, another who was given a crime number told he didn't need to report anything else). The allotment holders were called to a meeting by the police, but the arranging officer didn't attend. Because the apprehended youth hadn't been detained at the crime scene he couldn't be charged, despite being found with stolen tools. Other material evidence had been lost by the police. No fingerprints were taken because they didn't have enough staff. Descriptions of suspects couldn't be processed because they weren't accompanied by the names and addresses of the suspects! Three weeks after this, another allotment site was similarly raided[5075]!

Forth Valley Police (formerly Central Scotland) and Lothian and Borders are the Scottish forces readiest to employ police retirees on full pensions as civilian staff[5076].

The use of civilians to help with murder inquiries may erode public confidence, e.g. outsourcing may mean poor vetting and corrupt officers back on the job, as well as discouraging forces from training the police's own staff[5077].

The UK is providing police officers to Mogadishu (Somalia)[5078].

Despite its denial, the Civil Actions Unit of the Met has ordered its 35,000 officers not to arrest foul-mouthed people who swear at them, as the courts don't believe police can be caused distress by swearwords. One perpetrator has been compensated for false arrest (for swearing) by the courts. Police must also be able to justify the use of handcuffs[5079].

Kent Police have told war veterans they won't police Remembrance Day parades any more – so much for the much-vaunted 'Community Policing'. The 85 Royal British Legion branches are not amused[5080].

PACE (Police and Criminal Evidence Act – 1984) is why policing is mostly a matter of filling in forms, being based on the assumption that the police can't be trusted[5081].

Undercover cop <u>James Bannon</u> fell for a suspect's relative and risked becoming one of the heavy drinking football hooligans he was supposed to investigate[5082].

In a 2008 Cabinet Officer report ordered by No. 10, 'respect tsar' Louise Casey blamed Britain's 'walk on by' society on a loss of trust in the police: people are afraid to help victims partly because they are afraid of facing arrest[5083].

Research shows that the police call centres championed by government have been a PR disaster, damaging confidence because they alienate locals from their police[5084].

Perhaps the most important example of police <u>inaction</u> leading to mistrust is, of course, the absence of beat bobbies.

Dame Elizabeth Silkin's draconian new guidelines for press/police relations rules that all police, including whistleblowers, must keep a record of conversations with journalists and this will be 'audited', and alcohol should be eschewed. But this will enable senior cops to channel all communications via official spokespeople. The result may be an undermining of trust in the police[5085].

The Chief Constable of Tayside awarded a man a commendation for helping an injured child, but when they visited him to announce he was hand-picked for the award, they arrested him for growing cannabis in his bedroom, which they had smelled. The award was withdrawn[5086].

Three officers weekly are sacked for misconduct, so that 'respect from the public has been less forthcoming than it once was': this quote is from a tabloid leader, which also advocates personality and background checks prior to entry. Unfortunately the police won't agree to personality profiling[5087].

Police are hiring staff from private security giant G4S to assist in murder and other serious crimes by acting as 'focal points'. This, the most significant contracting out of frontline jobs, means the private staff are under no obligation to co-operate with the IPCC. This is likely to reduce further public confidence[5088].

UK police make less than half as many arrests as their US counterparts (e.g. nine in England and Wales compared with 21 in America). The public are increasingly unhappy with police responses, e.g. the proportion of people saying they do a 'good or excellent' job fell from two-thirds in 1996 to under a half in 2004-5. This study by the Institute of Public Policy Research is supported by Harriet Sergeant's Civitas report, which revealed that the middle classes have lost faith in a police service which targets the law-abiding just to meet Home Office targets: the respondents complained particularly about 'neglect of duty' and 'impoliteness', as well as treating incidents as crimes that would have before been ignored[5089].

A Humberside and North Yorkshire Police speed trap collared two speeding cops, PCs <u>Thomas Holiday</u> and <u>Paul McGuigan</u>, but they were told they could escape severe penalties after saying they were policemen. Serial speeder McGuigan challenged the charges in court but was found guilty[5090].

Claims by police that they want to deter speeders, not catch and fine them, are contradicted by scenarios such as police hiding in undergrowth to clock cars; when their equipment detects a speeder they break cover[5091].

Some forces are taking up to 30% longer (in 2012 than two years before) to respond to emergency calls. Bedfordshire changed its targets in 2011 from 10 minutes to 15, staff were warned not to complain publicly about cuts because of the risk of lowering confidence in the force[5092].

The Home Office's senior adviser on police reform has revealed officers waste an hour before they clock off (recording how many meetings they have had, whom they have spoken to and how many leaflets they have dished out – all logged in some system which is only needed because of a shortage of trust). A playground scuffle might end up requiring 50 different forms. In 2008 1.7m. crimes were not investigated because police were spending so much time filling in forms.

A Scots traffic lawyer has been flooded with work since Police Scotland's roads crackdown started in 2013. Speeding fines in Edinburgh have risen almost four times in a year, and there has been a doubling of seatbelt and mobile phone offences in the same period. A record number of drivers have been stopped and searched by Police Scotland since it started six months previously (there were 310,784 checks in this period) . With stations and control rooms being sold off, the traffic crackdown increases the suspicion that revenue raising has replaced protection of the public as a priority for Police Scotland (a blitz in Edinburgh using unmarked cars snared hundreds of drivers, while in Glasgow two officers ignored a drunken brawl to pull over a driver on his mobile phone, which is more lucrative)[5094]. Meantime police are tracking down only 25% of Scottish burglars (the proportion solved has fallen over a decade)[5095], and only one in 15 of those viewing paedophile images is arrested[5096]. One summer Saturday in 2013 the Sunday Mail, under the FOIA, discovered that Police Scotland had recorded 1,921 crimes (including two attempted murders, three thefts, four rapes, 12 sex assaults, 13 arson attacks, 16 serious assaults, 20 weapons offences and 173 drug crimes), yet didn't tell the public about them[5097]. When asked in 2010 how many unsolved murders they had on their books, the Strathclyde force said 53, but the actual number was over 500 (dating back to 1942). Then they said they had no details of the cases, after which they said for the victims' families publicity would pose a risk. The police next said releasing information could damage public confidence. Finally they asserted the families of victims would be upset[5098].

Home Secretary Theresa May told MPs (2013) that accusations of falsifying an account of a private meeting of three senior police officers with ex-Cabinet Minister Andrew Mitchell, as part of a 'wider agenda' to pressurise him to resign, struck at the heart of public trust in the police. Keith Vaz, chairman of the Home Affairs Select Committee, said he had never witnessed a 'more damning verdict' from the IPCC about a police investigation[5099].

Crime Figure Inflation

The Children's Commissioner Professor Sir Al Aynsley-Green says: 'Many kids tell me they don't trust the police. They don't have any respect for the police because they see them as the enemy. Young people are easy prey for the police to boost their crime statistics and the kids know this and resent the police for doing it'[5100].

Based on officers' testimony the Met Police Authority revealed (2008) victims of mobile phone thefts are tricked into not reporting a crime, and generally there was 'deliberate and intentional' manipulation of crime statistics. 'Classification drift' occurs when police change the definition of crimes to meet targets. Focussing on 'easy' crimes means police losing skills and inclination to tackle 'hard to solve' crimes[5101].

Scotland's new police supremo, Stephen House, admitted officers across the UK had 'fiddled' official crime figures[5102].

According to a 2010 Home Office report, Improving Public Confidence in the Police Service, talking about crime can worry people and give the police a negative image. Police forces must assert there is a low risk of crime in their area, regardless of 'recent reported incidents'. Police in England and Wales were marked (from 2009) on a public 'confidence' measure (in 2010 it was only 49%). Police were told to play down crime. Officers spend too much time criticising their jobs, and they have a lower perception of the latter than other public section workers[5103].

West Midlands Police dealing with the lethal stabbing of a 16-year-old on a Birmingham bus aroused public anger for boasting of a reduction in bus crime[5104].

Uniform changes

A North Wales Police survey of nearly 1,200 people found they didn't trust officers in the new, trendy 'more approachable' uniforms. Cops wearing baseball caps appear less professional, honest, helpful and competent[5105]. Police wearing white shirts and ties are thought more trustworthy than those wearing polo shirts[5106].

'Stormtrooper' gear

e.g. Tasers

Home Secretary Jacqui Smith's plan to issue police with 10,000 new Taser guns was overturned by the Yard because they could 'damage public confidence'. Amnesty says Tasers are linked to hundreds of deaths in North America[5107].

The Police Federation and the specialist equipment manufacturers have lobbied to transform the old-fashioned bobby beyond recognition into a kind of stormtrooper, with damaging consequences for the public's trust. (Did the Federation receive any consultancy fees from the manufacturers?) This militarisation must be eroding policing by consent, which distinguishes Britain from most of the rest of the world, where policing by force is the order of the day[5108].

Internal Strife

As well as external loss of trust, there seems to be an increase in internecine strife, particularly in the Met. One senior source said of the Ghaffur-Ian Blair confrontation: 'There has been a complete breakdown in trust'[5109].

Ali Dizaei reportedly made false claims in his book 'Not One of Us' about Inspector Ian Kibblewhite, who sued him for libel. The BBC also had to apologise to the Inspector, because extracts of the book were read out on Radio 4[5110].

Criminal Behaviour

Strathclyde Chief Constable Willie Rae said of pervert policeman Dean Stewart's actions (abducting and sexually assaulting a woman in his police car, lewd behaviour towards an underage girl, etc.): '[they were] a betrayal of the trust placed in him ... [and had damaged the] fundamental structure of confidence which society must place in the police service'. But then the myriad of malfeasant police officers in this book testifies to the same conclusion. Stewart's trial was the longest of its kind in legal history in Scotland[5111].

One of the victims of serial rapist Dumfries and Galloway Police Inspector <u>Adam Carruthers</u> said: 'When I first met him I had complete trust in the police'[5112].

Tabloid columnist Virginia Blackburn says the police have traditionally occupied the same role in British society as doctors and priests, so that she describes the behaviour of the traffic cop who won't impound their cars if women say yes to his sexual propositioning, as 'a profound breach of trust'[5113].

A young model's quarrel with her boyfriend in Kent led to a policeman being called. She says: 'I could never trust a policeman again', after PC <u>Daniel Capel</u> followed up his visit by bombarding her with explicit messages, as well as a picture of his genitals. He even stalked her at 3am with an excuse. He assured her he could get her boyfriend sent to jail[5114].

A QC in the Neil Lennon murder plot trial at the High Court in Glasgow has suggested police could be involved in sending suspicious packages to Celtic targets[5115].

Rupert Murdoch says he's known 'for decades' his journalists were paying police officers for information[5116]. 8% of the public in contact with UK police have handed over a bribe[5117].

Former Met Chief Lord Ian Blair says it is 'incomprehensible' that death trial PC <u>Simon Harwood</u>, cleared of the manslaughter of Ian Tomlinson at the G20 disturbance, was able to easily join another force after dodging accusations of an off-duty assault. This was just three days after retiring on the eve of a 2001 disciplinary hearing. He wasn't even charged alternatively with assault (he had admitted to the use of excessive force, suggesting one law for the police). The jury weren't told about the 10 previous accusations lodged against Harwood of violence and misconduct (e.g. arresting someone unlawfully for assault, racially abusing a 14-year-old girl, kneeing a handcuffed man in the kidneys)[5118].

In 2011 over 300 police and civilian staff were caught illegally accessing computer records, but of the 178 officers disciplined for misusing the database only 30 resigned or were sacked. One Lancashire officer was only given a final warning despite making 658 checks on neighbours and family. Of the backroom staff only 31 were fired or quit out of 146 caught. Those caught may be the tip of the iceberg[5119].

A Met civilian officer passed Police National Computer data to ex-cop <u>Alan King</u>. When a PI's office was searched documents revealed a network of police selling information. King was given a conditional discharge[5120].

Heavy-handed Behaviour

The BBC's Jane Peel observed: 'This isn't the first time the police have been criticised. When journalist Suzanne Moore had her ID and passport demanded because of a £1 bus fare she wrote: 'Policing depends on trust and a certain amount of goodwill from those not committing crimes. Already many different communities feel that the police are not on their side'[5121]. One occupational category which particularly distrusts the police is that of the prostitute[5122].

Of 210,013 citizens stopped and searched, only nine were charged under terrorist legislation. The police have been allowed to override civil liberties to defend our safety, but are blatantly abusing their stop and search powers: 'We do it because we can'[5123]. This is a huge cause of mistrust in the black community.

A third of the public don't have confidence in the police. 114 people in the Sneinton Dale area of Nottingham were mass-arrested on suspicion of aggravated trespass and criminal damage to a power station, i.e. before the supposed trespass even happened, far less was aggravated. 'The public no longer trust the police. The police no longer trust the public'[5124]. Roger Graef showed in his TV series on Thames Valley Police that officers, feeling a threat from the public, always react with hostility[5125].

Chief Inspector of Constabulary Denis O'Connor said (2009) police behaviour during the G20 protests risked undermining the sacrifice of officers who die protecting the public: 'It is disappointing and hugely concerning'[5126].

Public/police Standards Disparity

In 2009 one West Midlands officer had to wear a hand-mounted camera on duty to monitor his conduct following allegations of misbehaviour[5127]. With so many officers having criminal convictions one never knows if the policeman before you is trustworthy. Police getting off with offences, or being under-punished, is disastrous for their image. The figures for crimes committed by police must be a huge underestimate.

There were 1,433 deaths 'following police contact' (deaths in custody, shootings, road traffic accidents/pursuits) between 1990 and 2012, but no convictions of police officers in relation to these. We can surmise such a clear-up rate wouldn't be acceptable to police if members of the public were the prime suspects[5128].

75% of the population believe the police have failed to deal with antisocial behaviour and drunken violence, and neither listen to what people are saying about crime and rowdiness. The poll of over 500,000 adults in over 300 council areas was commissioned by the Department of Community and Local Government[5129].

A higher standard of acceptable behaviour is being demanded of members of the public than the police when faced with grave danger. Thus businessman Mumir Hussain who was jailed for GBH on a burglar who had threatened his family with knives, remains a convicted criminal even though his sentence was suspended. Different standards apply to the de Menezes police – Cressida Dick has been twice promoted since the 2005 tragedy and been awarded a Queen's police medal, no officer faced trial, and health and safety proceedings came to nothing. The argument of a life-and-death situation holds in both cases (the police nearly always remain anonymous). Another nail in the trust coffin was the Ian Tomlinson cover-up[5130].

Ian Johnston, President of the Police Superintendents' Association, says public confidence in the police has been damaged by the constant targeting of motorists with speed cameras (the police nearly always get off with inessential speeding). He also says confidence in them is low because stations are often not open, they don't answer the phone, and, having recorded an offence, the victims aren't updated: the policeman classically promises to call but never does. Or letters warning of criminal misdoings are ignored. Rudeness and incivility comprise half the complaints against police[5131].

The farce of the undercover police infiltration of eco-activists has thrown up the tabloid headline: 'A Boy's Own Fiasco That Wrecks Trust In The Police'[5132]. Likewise the shocking case of Fiona Pilkington led to another tabloid's comment: 'The public have lost faith in the authorities'[5133].

'The behaviour of officers at the Police Federation conference towards Theresa May was puerile and demeaning. Ridiculous, immature statements, such as the Government wanting 'revenge' for police opposition to Tory reforms in the Nineties, serve only to show the current character of our once-admired boys in blue. They cannot see beyond their own selfish demands'. The chairman asked the Home Secretary directly: 'Do you sleep at night?'[5134]. How rude.

The Met's former Assistant Commissioner John Yates said before his resignation that the Met could struggle to regain public confidence after the 'very damaging episode', i.e. the hacking and police bribery scandal[5135].

The sociologist Geoffrey Gorer's tabloid (The People) reader survey in 1951 surprised him, in that less than 20% of the respondents had any criticism to make of the police, and these were about individuals with character or behaviour defects rather than the police as an institution. But one man from Sidcup did say officers were too taken up with minor traffic offences and, 'Freemasonry should be barred in the Police Force'[5136].

Solution

Julia Hodson, the Notts Chief Constable, thinks she has found the perfect formula to restore public trust: CE+CI+CS+VCxC=PC, i.e. Community Engagement (CE) combined with handling Critical Incidents (CI), delivering Customer Satisfaction (CS) and dealing with Volume Crime (VC). Multiplying the total by Communication (C) equals Public Confidence (PC). Hodson's 'manor' is one of Britain's worst burglary and gun crime hot spots[5137].

The proportion of Britons who say they trust senior police officers has fallen from nearly 75% to under 50%[5138].

Strathclyde Police Acting Chief Constable Campbell Corrigan posed with a £350,000 collection of cars supposedly seized from criminals, their registrations replaced by a 'SEIZED' number plate, windscreen stickers said 'one criminal owner'. In fact they were borrowed from a car showroom. But critics say such PR stunts risk compromising public trust[5139]. Not one of the cars seized by the force was sold under proceeds of crime laws, most being handed back to their owners, despite Corrigan asserting they would be sold to fund crime-fighting: PR spin again takes precedence over the truth[5140].

According to a survey by training company Results International police come well below dentists, hotel receptionists, hairdressers and council workers in terms of customer service attitude[5141].

One sign of the decreasing trust in the police is the increasing internet 'trolling' when an officer is killed on duty (e.g. the killer may be lionised). The police ignore this culture change at their peril[5142].

Strathclyde Police's new Facebook site has been bombarded with abuse and complaints[5143].

A family looking for answers to their son's mysterious death in Wick harbour have asked witnesses to contact them rather than the Northern Constabulary, whom they say they no longer trust[5144].

333 serving Scottish police have criminal records. Offences include perverting justice, vandalism, domestic abuse and serious assault. A Lothian and Borders chief inspector was still serving despite a drug conviction. The figure may be higher, as not all data have been made public[5145]. Nearly two thirds of convicted officers (there were 44 in Scotland between 2010-13) are allowed to keep their jobs[5146].

In 2001 less than a quarter of all crimes were cleared up. The situation is actually much worse than it seems: the British Crime Survey says most offences are unreported (the public has lost trust in the police's ability to deal with them)[5147].

There were 714 reports of vandalism to Scottish police property in a two-year period, and over 3,000 working days lost over three years because of assaults on officers and staff[5148].

At the start of 2013 Ulster police officers came under gunfire, while mobs threw bricks and fireworks at police[5149].

The last phrase of a 'thieves website' on a Facebook page, Aberdeen Boyz Stig Ftp, stands for 'f... the police' – in one post they threaten to bomb Grampian Police HQ[5150].

The police's ability to predict a crime as 'unsolvable' has been called into question: 'How they can know that a crime is 'unsolvable' until they have made at least some effort to solve it is deeply puzzling'. Over half of the 93,558 London burglaries in 2008 weren't investigated, likewise with three-quarters of cases involving theft or handling stolen goods[5151].

The Committee on Standards in Public Life says police (and politicians) are now the least trusted public servants[5152].

A Kent pub landlord was arrested for trying to stop a drunken thug who smashed his windows, and had to spend £5,000 before he cleared his name. The police had charged him with causing GBH, but after six months magistrates threw the case out. The landlord, a former fireman, said: 'I don't think I can ever trust another policeman again'.

CHAPTER XXVI

THE ULSTER POLICEMAN

The highest number of complaints against British police in 2010 was against officers (three or more per officer) of the Police Service of Northern Ireland: 376[5153].

Ulster Police were told of the plan to assassinate lawyer Pat Finucane but did nothing about it, so as to protect their informers[5154]. It took 13 years and three major police inquiries for evidence to be released that may show RUC complicity in the murder of Finucane. Lies were told to the Stevens Inquiry (1989-1991) by police, e.g. about targeting of IRA men by loyalist murder gangs given police, security service and army assistance[5155]. Alan Simpson, one of the RUC's most senior investigators (no. 2 in Belfast CID) was called in to investigate the murder, but, as he recounts in his book 'Duplicity and Deception', he was warned not to probe too deeply by Wilfred Monahan, then the RUC's Assistant Chief Constable. The murder seems to have been state-sponsored: a member of the UDA admitted culpability.

Before a 2008 Panorama programme the families of the Omagh victims had no idea the security services had tape recordings of the bombers. Yet police have admitted they've given up pursuing a criminal case against the latter[5156].

John Stalker, the Assistant Chief Constable of the Greater Manchester force, has written in his book 'Stalker' how the RUC went to extraordinary lengths to obstruct an investigation into the conduct of its officers who had killed six men. He reveals how he was removed from the investigation at a critical juncture. Suspended on charges of impropriety back in Manchester, he was eventually reinstated[5157]. In 2007 the Northern Ireland Police Ombudsman was to re-examine the Stalker files, which were never published, despite supposedly being the definitive inquiry into the hot potato of whether the police secretly operated a 'shoot to kill' policy[5158]. The hostility Stalker encountered when he was investigating the RUC made him bloody-minded and determined to find the truth. A surveillance tape held the key to the enquiry, for it could prove or disprove the RUC's story that its officers had not shot one of the six men - there were three separate incidents over the space of a month - in cold blood. As Stalker got closer to getting his hands on the all-powerful tape, he was suspended after he made his fifth request for it to Sir John Hermon, the RUC's Chief Constable. Stalker was told it was destroyed, though a very well-placed journalist revealed to him a copy proved the warnings (alleged by the police) were never given, i.e. they did not say, "Come out, or we'll shoot". Stalker found there was no justification for the shootings, and, that the justification that had been put forward to the courts was false, and that, indeed, some post-dated records had been put into the system in order to justify the action that was eventually taken. "You know: false records... if coppers are going to decide who will live and who will die, you don't need courts".

A report by the Police Ombudsman of N. Ireland concluded that the RUC helped loyalist paramilitaries 'go on a murder spree'. Special Branch ensured they weren't brought to justice. Evidence was destroyed, weapons searches obstructed, and officers counselled the men during police interviews to avoid self-incrimination. The Ombudsman emphasised police resistance to her three-year inquiry[5159].

Files of murdered leading loyalist paramilitary Billy 'King Rat' Wright have been lost or destroyed, the Police Service of Northern Ireland being said to have delayed handing over material. It is claimed his killers were assisted by authorities such as the police. Thus the former RUC Chief Constable <u>Sir Hugh Annesley</u> allegedly said before the murder: 'It's just a question of who gets to the bastard first. Us, the IRA or the UVF'[5160].

In 1988 the Attorney General blocked the prosecution of RUC officers accused by the Stalker/Sampson inquiry of perverting the course of justice and obstruction of the police investigation[5161].

Detectives know the identities of four IRA terrorists who murdered six adults and three children in Claudy in 1972, but have not tried to arrest them. One of the IRA men was Catholic priest Fr. James Chesney, said a 2010 report by police ombudsman Al Hutchinson: a former RUC Special Branch officer said he was forbidden from arresting Chesney. The RUC 'colluded' with the Catholic Church and the N. Ireland Secretary to protect Chesney[5162].

Four Ulster policemen answering an emergency call died when their four-wheel drive Shogun smashed into a wall[5163].

Until 2007 (when the powers were being phased out) Ulster Police could question who people were, where they had been and where they were going: failure to cooperate could mean a criminal conviction and fine not exceeding £5,000[5164].

At its inception in 1922, about 20% of the RUC's personnel was R.C. By 1970 it had dropped to 11%. There was a feeling that Catholic policemen's chances of promotion were reduced[5165]. From April 2011 it was no longer necessary for the RUC to admit equal numbers of Catholic and Protestants to the force.

When Catholic mother Jean McConville was abducted by the IRA, the RUC neglected to even record the complaint, about which they were told twice: they persisted in refusing to accept she was missing, preferring to believe an anonymous tip that she had absconded with a British soldier. Even when her murdered body was found, the RUC failed to investigate her crime, and has since apologised for this[5166].

The most infamous Irish non-Troubles-related miscarriage of justice concerned the trial of Hay Gordon for the murder of Patricia Curran, daughter of Judge Lance Curran, a former Northern Ireland attorney-general. To placate public unease, inconsistencies were either ignored or brushed aside : despite the stabbings, there was no blood at the scene, despite rain her belongings were dry, and the family home was not searched until a week later (her "mystical" brother Desmond later became a priest in S. Africa, while others suspected her mother was the killer). During questioning police threatened to tell Gordon's god-fearing mother about his friendship with a local homosexual, so he signed a confession. His lawyers then ignored his attempt to retract it. The deference afforded the judge by the police, legal system and media was interpreted in many quarters as a closing of ranks within the establishment to protect a privileged family who harboured a murderer in their midst. Gordon, after enforced years in a mental hospital, was eventually exonerated by a dogged campaign[5167].

Michael McKevitt, the founder of the terrorist group behind the Omagh bomb atrocity, was likely to serve less than two years in jail (for Real IRA membership) in a deal designed to cover up M15's role in Ireland. The Republic's Dept. of Justice and the Garda

Siochana (Irish Police) are afraid a large-scale trial on directing acts of terrorism would expose M15's involvement in the state ("open up a can of worms"). "The authorities don't want a lot of dirt to come out about the events surrounding Omagh". The Omagh victims' families, frustrated at lack of progress by the police, raised £1 million to take civil action. "It might be the only chance we have to get the truth out": Chief Constable Flanagan was refusing to reveal information or documents. When Mr. Justice Weir acquitted the alleged Omagh bomber he heavily criticised the Police Service of N. Ireland (PSNI). Thus two PSNI officers concealed possible forensic evidence contamination, and there was a 'cavalier disregard' for the integrity of evidence: the police and scenes of crime officers were 'seemingly thoughtless and slapdash'. The Northern Ireland Police Ombudsman warned that the chance of convicting anyone for Omagh had been 'significantly reduced' by the old RUC's 'defective leadership, poor judgment and a lack of urgency'. A suspended Garda sergeant claimed in 2002 that crucial intelligence about the Omagh bombing (and earlier planned Real IRA attacks) was withheld from the RUC.

Confidence in Eire's police force was severely shaken by the Morris Tribunal's inquiry into a series of ostensibly unconnected incidents involving the Co. Donegal Police's allegations of rogue officers with close Provisional links helping to plant an IRA bomb, as well as fake Republican weapons caches to win promotion, not to mention the killing of a local farmer, for which an innocent family were framed.

Not only did the widespread use of 'supergrasses' in Northern Ireland (1981-1986) fail to secure convictions – their testimony was highly dubious – but they tarnished the reputation of the criminal justice system[5168].

The lives of scores of Ulster people were endangered as a stream of vehicles were allowed by police to pass close by an abandoned car (it was loaded with a 500lb bomb, and there had been a republican warning)[5169].

Two PSNI officers were fired for being drunk while armed.

In the case of the UDR Four, convicted of the murder in Armagh of a man they thought was an active IRA member, their allegations of miscarriage of justice revolved around three concerns. One of the convicted could point to oppressive police interrogation and conflicting identification evidence, while the police were shown to have tampered with the confessions by deleting requests to see solicitors and attaching false validations. Three of the Four were freed by the Court of Appeal in 1992 (the fourth had lied to the court and confirmed his original guilty admission)[5170].

Despite threats to her life, murdered Lurgan lawyer Rosemary Nelson was turned down twice for special RUC protection. There is a suspicion – always denied – that there was RUC collusion in making her a target: a public inquiry found a rogue member of the security services may have assisted the assassin(s), and that RUC officers verbally threatened and abused the lawyer, as well as assaulting her[5171].

The PSNI's crime detection rates have sunk so low officers are having to be drafted in from mainland forces (the rate has fallen from 42% to 16%, the lowest of any UK force). PSNI stands for 'Police Service, Nothing Investigated'. The best cops may be retiring early on the generous 'Patten's pay-offs'[5172].

Eight PSNI police ruined a young couple's wedding in Londonderry by stopping it to wrongly accuse them of being immigration scammers[5173].

CHAPTER XXVII

THE UNETHICAL POLICEMAN

The new College of Policing is drawing up a code of police ethics – not before time, some would say.

The police are no strangers to sharp practice, which, though not necessarily illegal, yet borders on the ethically unacceptable. Thus they may use surveillance in non-criminal investigations[5174], just as they employ antiterrorist legislation in civil cases.

Former City of London PC Neil Foreman – awarded the Queen's Medal for bravery in 1981 – spent £120,000 of his parents' retirement nestegg on a life of luxurious travel. Despite their claim that they gave him the money to invest for them he insisted it was a gift from his 'devious' father. A judge ordered him to pay it back[5175]. Former RUC officer John Lamberton, who stole over £400,000 from his ageing aunt and cheated his brother, was ordered to pay back £200,000. He got his aunt, who treated him like a son, to hand over her investments for him to manage: her son therefore never received his rightful inheritance. The Crown Office's Serious and Organised Crime Division said he pretended to be a loyal nephew, but he moved his aunt's share into his offshore account. Lamberton's 2005 sentence of seven years was reduced to five on appeal[5176].

Ads for RSS (Road Safety Support), an offshoot of ACPO, are using photos of celebrities breaking motoring laws. This may be unethical, if not illegal, as such pictures are supposed to only be available to prosecution and defence lawyers. This appears to breach ACPO's own guidelines.

A supergrass in prison for giving false evidence at a gangland murder trial was freed, thanks to Strathclyde Assistant Chief Constable Campbell Corrigan's plea to three Edinburgh Appeal Court judges, that failure to overturn the sentence could impede the fight against organised crime[5177].

Commander Bob Quick's wife didn't have an operating licence for the private-hire car business run from their home. The Met's former Assistant Commissioner had in his previous past as Chief Constable of Surrey helped produce a 36-page booklet setting out the rules affecting private hire car firms. The only firms allowed to operate (since 2008) without a licence are those only doing weddings and funerals, whereas the Quick business 'Aphrodite' offers a much wider range of services[5178].

The police chief involved in the Yorkshire Ripper case, the late Sir Andrew Sloan, was too short to join Strathclyde Police but managed to get into the West Riding force by standing on tiptoe while being measured. He became Chief Constable of Strathclyde in 1985[5179].

West Yorkshire Police took a convicted robber supergrass to a brothel, gave him cash and scheduled drugs, and told to take his pick of a dozen prostitutes. A WPC gave him regular sex. He was the main prosecution witness in a murder trial: the defendant was freed on appeal because of the prosecution misconduct. Despite the conspiracy to pervert the course of justice none of the many officers concerned ('some of very high rank') was prosecuted[5180].

Met community PC Stephen Holt was shown on Panorama (April, 2011) subletting his council house unethically for a profit (he has a chateau with winery near Bordeaux in France).

Tabloid journalist Melanie Phillips says 'the police have lost their way' and 'we need … restoration of our lost ethic of policing'[5181]. (See the Corruption section of The Criminal Policeman Chapter for other examples of amoral policing).

In 2012 Lothian and Borders Inspector Jillian Kerr became head of her force's licensing section, two years after she was disciplined in 2009 for falling asleep so deeply in a taxi that she couldn't be aroused – the driver took her to the nearest police station. In 2007 it was alleged she used a police pass to avoid parking charges in Edinburgh's centre.

The Deputy Chief Constable of Staffordshire, Adrian Lee, wants police to be able to opt out of duties they feel are immoral[5182]. Not before time.

Greater Manchester Police is recruiting apprentice cops on less than the minimum wage[5183].

An Open University study of police ethics using 520 officers from three anonymous forces found only about half would report a colleague for beating up a suspect who was trying to escape, even where they thought the case was serious. The study's author says there is still a 'blue wall of silence' in the police[5184].

Police have an ethical duty to uphold civil liberties, in particular the European Convention on Human Rights (ECHR) as well as UK Human Rights legislation. Yet the 'kettling' model of crowd management, so controversially used at G20, shows they have forgotten this. This tactic, launched during the 2001 May Day London protests, was applied willy-nilly at later protests, without the 'avenue of escape' for the innocent which was mandatory before that year. The courts have decreed kettling must only be used if appropriate, and must not compromise the innocent. The Met should ensure all officers policing protests should know their roles, which should not 'seriously' affect the tactical plan – this however has been kept secret in recent years!

Is it ethical for police to charge victims of crime for the return of their property? This happens with some forces, including Scottish, in the case of stolen cars.

Leveson and the Information Commissioner want police to conceal the identity of arrestees because it could breach their human rights. But is it ethical for police to deny the public this knowledge? Critics say this would turn Britain into a 'banana republic' in justice terms. The proposal for 'secret arrests' is being opposed by the Law Commission[5185].

Former SO10 undercover officer Christian Plowman claims his colleagues gave class A drugs to dealers for information, though he says they had to ensure the dealer consumed the drugs so he couldn't say the officers had criminally supplied them. But they were catching only the lowest in the drug hierarchy, e.g. crack addicts, not the bosses. When Plowman was a 'test purchase' officer he would buy scheduled drugs from junkies, who would then be charged (enticement/entrapment?), despite being forced to sell drugs by real criminals higher up the chain. The Met even set up a fake pawnshop (TJ's Trading Post) to lure poor people into criminal activity (e.g. trading ID documents)). Analogous unethical police behaviour is detailed in Appendix II.

The ethics of undercover policing and smearing of victims' families are dealt with elsewhere (The Secretive Policeman chapter and Appendix IV).

CHAPTER XXVIII

THE UNJUST POLICEMAN

CONTENTS

CHAPTER XXVIII

THE UNJUST POLICEMAN

Introduction

It is arguable, indeed likely, that the police-involved miscarriages of justice listed in Appendix 2 are just the tip of a very large iceberg. This chapter concentrates on cases where police incompetence or malice played a role. As there is a huge literature on miscarriage of justice, this chapter gives just a few of an indeterminate number of cases where the police were at least partly to blame for the injustice.

Like GPs the police are gatekeepers (to the criminal justice system), so their misdemeanours will affect everything that derives from them; indeed mistakes will become exaggerated and infiltrative. It is sometimes claimed that, because the British justice system is the best in the world, miscarriages are rare. This is not the case, and when they are identified mistakes are often not willingly corrected: the British system scores badly on both counts[5186].

Since the abolition of hanging in Britain at least 20 men have had their murder convictions quashed because the police had got the wrong man[5187]. Even before abolition innocent people have hanged, e.g. Edith Thomson in 1923 for her husband's murder by her lover, and Derek Bentley in 1953[5188].

The Met's controversial tactic of 'joint enterprise' (JE) in tackling problems such as knife crime involves charging and convicting members of gangs who might not even have been at the scenes of crimes, or only peripherally involved (e.g. standing nearby doing nothing). This 'blunt instrument', which was being investigated by MPs in 2011, was reportedly causing huge resentment against the police, who have admitted using JE more often. Critics are characterised by the acronym JENGBA (Joint Enterprise Not Guilty by Association)[5189].

Two Strathclyde Police community officers were fined for fabricating breach of the peace allegations against a law student: Neil Jones and Andrew MacRobert had been suspended on full pay for a year. The sheriff told them: 'The harm your conduct has done to the good name of the Strathclyde Police force is immeasurable'. Jones' counsel said he had been considered 'such a good role model' he was asked regularly to mentor young constables[5190].

The Court of Session has ruled (in the case of Kevin Ruddy, who fought for eight years for compensation for an alleged police assault) that Strathclyde Police have breached human rights law by failing to ensure complaints about them from the public are investigated independently[5191].

Some forces, e.g. North and South Yorkshire, are not enforcing new laws on child seats in cars[5192].

The Legal Background

When this author asked Keir Starmer ('Miscarriages of Justice – A review of Justice in Error', edited by Clive Walker and Keir Starmer) to comment on what proportion of miscarriages originated from police behaviour, he declined to say. But Michael Mansfield comments: 'the theme which runs through most miscarriages of justice is clear and constant. It is the failure of the police to conduct a proper investigation'[5193]. This applies to the re-investigations also carried out by the police - the Runciman Commission were given no powers by government to carry out their own re-investigations. 'The 1995 Act takes a trusting attitude to the police'[5194].

In 2007 the controversial low-copy number (LCN) DNA attracted such scathing criticism from the Omagh bomb case judge that UK forces suspended its use (it was used in the Madeleine McCann case, and was to be used in the Rachel Nickell case). The judge pointed out that there was no international consensus about its value[5195].

Police did not reveal to the psychiatrists examining Yorkshire Ripper Peter Sutcliffe that he wore a sexual 'killing kit' at the time of his arrest. This lack of a vital piece of evidence skewed the legal proceedings and almost led to a miscarriage of justice. Sutcliffe had been deliberately deceiving the doctors[5196].

In 13,000 cases, from 2006 to 2009, police failed to get paperwork to the CPS in time for court[5197].

The 2011 Green Paper on Justice and Security, if it becomes law, will give the power to ministers to make the courts more secretive, if they consider the subject (e.g. undercover policing) 'sensitive' (for this one can read embarrassing or inconvenient). If a citizen under this system loses his case, he'll never find out why. Even the 'Special Advocates' who do have access to the evidence heard in secret, will not communicate their knowledge to the protestant. The move would constitute a move away from natural justice[5198].

The law in Greater Manchester clubland in the 60s and 70s was different from the rest of the land – however serious the offence (whether violence or illegal drinking), the charge had to be avoided or at least reduced[5199].

Lying in Court

Wigan Special Constable Peter Lightfoot was given three years for brutally beating a war hero and lying five times under oath to cover his tracks[5200].

Eight men charged with mowing down three young men (killing them) walked free because the officer in charge of the investigation lied on oath[5201].

Four Scottish policemen lied to cover up for an undercover colleague who hurled an innocent shopper against a plate glass window.

St. Paul's Cathedral protesters have accused police of inflating crime figures at the camp ahead of a court hearing, saying the City of London Police's witness statements constitute a 'corruption of information'. Among the reported 'crimes' of protesters were a supposed hoax claim of a huge bomb in the church and a potato crisp being thrown by a woman, who was being probed on suspicion of 'common assault and battery'[5202].

A soldier arrested, kicked in the back and handcuffed by officers, was found guilty despite contrary CCTV evidence, only to have his conviction overturned by a judge who realised an officer had committed perjury[5203].

The IPCC

A 1987 study[5204] found 60% of the respondents were very dissatisfied with the IPCC's complaints process, with two-thirds of the 'dissatisfied' feeling there was a pro-police bias, while a 1991 survey[5205] revealed a 'dissatisfaction' rate of 74%. This public mistrust in the police investigating themselves is found in other countries. In nearly all cases the IPCC passively reads through the files prepared by the police, i.e. doesn't conduct its own probes.

Causes of Miscarriage

Following a series of miscarriages caused by flawed identification evidence in the 1970s, the Devlin Committee led to the Turnbull guidelines, which mean juries are told to exercise special caution when considering such evidence[5206]. In the USA it is suggested that about a half of wrongful convictions are due to misidentification by police and lay witnesses[5207].

As arrest and questioning are designed to elicit confessions from suspects it can be argued that police interrogation can never be truly reliable. If a confession, then, is intrinsically dubious the existence of supporting evidence (e.g. questionable scientific analysis) is no guarantee against wrongful conviction – witness the Birmingham Six[5208]. Police have been caught faking fingerprints.

Non-disclosure by the police in the Judith Ward, Guildford and Maguire cases nudged the courts towards demanding disclosure, but there was a furious backlash from the police, who said protection of witnesses and informants meant scores of cases were having to be dropped[5209].

Forensic experts say the only possible explanation for the anomalies in the Crippen case is that he was set up by detectives desperate for a conviction after missing out on Jack the Ripper (the detective in charge of Crippen, Chief Inspector Walter Dew, was in the Ripper squad).The police may have planted evidence and suppressed documents. The expert pathologist Spilsbury may have given flawed evidence in this and another six cases of possible miscarriages of justice[5210]: he committed suicide. New DNA evidence proves Dr. Crippen didn't murder his wife: the abdominal tissue used to convict him was that of a man[5211]. Police failed to reveal to the doctor's lawyers a letter purporting to be from Cora, his supposed victim[5212].

It is claimed Met police used 'primitive' methods to store forensic evidence in the Stephen Lawrence case, allowing cross-contamination. The Met's forensic lab has no system to separate victim and suspect items after they have been forensically examined[5213].

Sergeant John Docherty, of Fife Constabulary, has been accused of telling a colleague to falsely accuse a man of drink driving and of trying to stop an investigation by prosecutors[5214].

Sir Ian Blair became embroiled in an eavesdropping dispute amid accusations that a mole was secretly paid to inform on defendants' private legal discussions, so that appeals could be sabotaged[5215].

Six Met police officers, including Detective Chief Inspector <u>Dave McKelvey</u>, were investigated in 2007 about claims that evidence was buried in order to undermine a trial of alleged thieves[5216].

PACE

The expectation that PACE (the Police and Criminal Evidence Act, 1986) would address the problem of incompetent police investigations and reduce the numbers of serious miscarriages was not fulfilled, stymied by police resistance to and evasion of attempts to control their behaviour. The police can rely on 'consent' to sidestep legal regulations[5217]. By granting the police more powers PACE made inroads into the rights of suspects. An underlying assumption of PACE, that police are amenable to control by law, was wrong. The assumption too that PACE had largely solved the miscarriage problem contributed to the ineffectiveness of the Runciman Commission, set up after the release of the Birmingham Six, which case it didn't bother to analyse to find 'lessons to be learned'.

Even when officers feel they are working within PACE things can go wrong, e.g. in the Cardiff Three case a baker's dozen of policemen were accused (2009) of conspiracy to pervert the course of justice in regard to the 1988 murder of a Welsh prostitute. They allegedly set up the Cardiff Three: a neighbour of the victim and two other prostitutes were pressured by police to lie in court at the 1990 trial, by giving evidence against the three innocent men, whose conviction was quashed two years later. The three false witnesses were given 18 months for perjury, the judge commenting they had been 'seriously hounded, bullied, threatened, abused and manipulated by the police'. The CPS named three serving officers (PC <u>John Murray</u>, DS <u>Paul Stephen</u> and DC <u>Paul Jennings</u>), to be joined by retired officers (<u>Graham Mouncher</u>, <u>Richard Powell</u>, <u>Thomas Page</u>, <u>Michael Daniels</u>, <u>John Gillard</u>, <u>Peter Greenwood</u>, <u>John Seaford</u>, <u>Rachel O'Brien</u>, and <u>Stephen Hicks</u>) and <u>Wayne Pugh</u>, a former officer who is now a police staff member[5218]. The eight accused officers may sue for wrongful arrest, to the consternation of the Director of Public Prosecutions. They had denied conspiracy to pervert the course of justice[5219]. <u>Stephen Miller</u>'s 'confession' about the prostitute's (Lynette White) murder should have been excluded because it was obtained by an 'oppressive' 'travesty of an interview': the Lord Chief Justice was 'horrified' by the interrogation as revealed in the police interview tapes in this, the biggest miscarriage of justice trial, involving eight South Wales police officers, who framed these three men for the murder. Then Swansea Crown Court heard (January, 2012) that documents (four complaint files submitted to the IPCC) had not been destroyed after all, and had now been found[5220]. The police decided to 'mould, manipulate, influence and fabricate evidence' against five innocent men, the jury heard. The victim was stabbed 70 times by a security guard, who was jailed for life after admitting the murder[5221]. In another murder case, <u>Heron</u>, the defendant's 'confessions' were set aside as oppressive because detectives exaggerated the strength of the prosecution evidence, repeatedly told him he was guilty, asked offensive questions about his sex life, and suggested it was in his own interest to confess, despite his denying culpability 120 times.

The rights and welfare of suspects, for reasons such as the large volume of cases, are low on the police's list of priorities[5222]. The police continue to show remarkable complacency about the 'crisis in criminal justice'[5223].

The idea that fingerprinting and other body sampling should require judicial authorisation (as was the case prior to 1984) was strongly opposed by the police, who got their way in the Criminal Justice and Public Order Act 1994[5224].

Case Studies

Barry George, cleared of murdering Jill Dando by a retrial after two failed appeals, was refused compensation for his time (eight years) in jail, because he hadn't proved his innocence. Even when his original £1.4m claim was reduced to £250,000 (because he owed the state £40 a day for his bed and board inside), this too was rejected because the police had found no evidence pointing to a new suspect. The jurors who cleared him were not told of his earlier sex convictions or a 1983 incident when he was caught stalking Princess Diana behind Kensington Palace wearing combat gear, a rope and a knife[5225].

Former Fife Constabulary DCS Richard Munro, head of CID, framed two innocent men – Steven Johnston and Billy Allison – by suppressing witness statements in a 1996 murder case. Munro has been moved to an open prison after only 10 months into his five-year sentence. An inmate commented: 'The feeling's that he's getting special treatment because he was 'a policeman'[5226].

Armed police arrested Gloucester decorator Mile Bosnic – a political asylum refugee because as an Orthodox Christian he was persecuted by Serbs and Croatian Catholics – and imprisoned him for 12 days after mistaking him for a brutal war criminal. He was put before an extradition court in London: his identity card photo and fingerprints were wrongly attached to his Serb namesake's documents by Croatian investigators. The innocent Mr. Bosnic was eventually shown to be doing Yugoslav national service when he was supposed to be killing people. He was released from Wandsworth with no explanation[5227].

Warren Blackwell spent three years in jail (later increased to five without forensic evidence) after being falsely accused of rape, despite Northamptonshire police failing to disclose at the trial their knowledge that the accuser was 'unreliable', 'unstable' and 'attention –seeking'. She was a fantasist who had involved seven other blameless men (including her father) with the police. The victim was picked out of an identity parade. The IPCC criticised the police for taking over a year to give an apology and discipline the officers concerned, one of whom was meantime allowed to retire, with the other two merely receiving words of advice[5228]. When Blackwell applied for compensation, he was told he would be charged £7,000 for bed and breakfast. Why, he argued, was he being charged when other inmates (not getting compensation) weren't[5229]? Eventually the Criminal Cases Review Commission inquiry revealed the 'rape victim' was a serial liar: she was named in Parliament[5230].

The Brazilian cleaner Roselane Driza, who was finally cleared of stealing sex videos from one of the judiciary and blackmailing another (after 33 months in prison and an appeal), has issued a writ against Met Commissioner Sir Paul Stephenson, it is thought for malicious prosecution and possibly false arrest[5231].

A 'lost' police log of phone calls made on the night of the Bamber killings once more casts question marks over Jeremy Bamber's guilt. The Essex Police log was released in 2010 under FOIA: 'Daughter goes berserk' headed the log, which reads: 'Mr. Bamber, White House Farm, Tolleshunt D'Arcy. Daughter Sheila Bamber, aged 26 yrs, has got hold of one of my guns'. One interpretation makes the father's time of death incompatible with Bamber's guilt. However, the latter lost his final appeal to the CCRC in 2010[5232]. Campaigners for Bamber claim the scene of crime was doctored and Sheila Caffell's body was moved by police. The bullet fragments found in Sheila's neck became whole when presented at the murder trial, they say, proving he could not have faked her suicide. They claim police exchanged the bullet with one fired through a silencer to strengthen the prosecution case. Notes by a firearms officer which questioned the photographs of Sheila's body have also now been uncovered[5233]. The finding of a silencer at White House Farm led police to discount their first theory, that the psychotic sister Sheila Caffell shot her family dead. But there is now evidence that the gun didn't have a silencer: if confirmed there could have been a miscarriage of justice[5234]. Some of the world's best ballistics experts have revealed evidence directly pointing to Jeremy Bamber's innocence, 27 years after his conviction[5235].

A Scotland Yard team, headed by Chief Superintendent Martin Bridger, investigating corruption, arrested Cayman Island Justice Alexander Henderson unlawfully, giving rise to £749,000 legal expenses, with the judge also receiving £1 million compensation. A judicial review of the arrest conducted by Mr. Justice Creswell found that Bridger & Co had 'misled the courts', made 'deliberate misrepresentations' and that their behaviour was 'arbitrary and unfair', reflecting 'the gravest abuse'. As well as the fiasco over Justice Henderson, the only two people prosecuted over corruption were both acquitted. Bridger's 'Sunshine Squad' was led by police from its Directorate of Professional Standards (motto: 'Integrity cannot be compromised')[5236].

Martin Bridger

The notes of officer 'Owen' at the de Menezes inquest were altered the day prior to their submission as evidence to a Met Police solicitor. The IPCC's 2008 figures reveal public complaints over 'irregularity in relation to evidence/perjury' almost doubled in four years (493 in 2004 to 931 in 2008). The number of complaints made annually about 'corrupt practice' almost tripled over the same period (from 91 to 251)[5237].

In 1987 Winston Silcott, Engin Raghip and Mark Braithwaite were jailed for life for the murder of PC Blakelock. In 1991 the convictions were overturned by the Court of Appeal following doubts about the veracity of the police evidence (fabrication of confessions). In 1994 Silcott received £50,000 compensation from the Met. It is alleged that some police officers leaked information about Silcott after his release, feeding the continued press demonisation of him[5238]. He is on record as having been cleared of three murders – his conviction was overturned as 'unsafe' several years later on appeal because of the tainted police evidence[5239].

The decision of the Met's Bill Griffiths, Deputy Assistant Commissioner, to name John Cannan as the person responsible for Suzy Lamplugh's murder, without charging him, was unprecedented, overturning the presumption of innocence which is the sine qua non of justice[5240] in the UK (but not in some other countries).

The Criminal Cases Review Commission began to consider the case of <u>Glyn Razzell</u>, convicted of the murder of his mentally unstable wife, after he and his supporters compiled a dossier of 47 instances of alleged failings on the part of Wiltshire Police[5241]. The CCRC was also investigating the case of <u>Robert Kennedy</u>, who by 2007 had spent 17 years in prison: the DNA on cigarette butts, it was thought, could clear him. Devon and Cornwall Police were asked to reopen the inquiry in 2005[5242].

In 2007 it was reported that <u>Colin Stagg</u>, who spent a year in prison before he was cleared of murdering Rachel Nickell, would receive up to £250,000 compensation from the Home Office, with damages from Scotland Yard possibly reaching £1 million: the Crown Prosecution Service might also be forced to make a payment[5243]. For four years the Met refused to allow him to give a DNA sample, which would have eliminated him immediately in Rachel Nickell's murder[5244].

It is worth noting in the context of miscarriage of justice that no one has ever been convicted of a crime on DNA evidence alone. In 2009 Israeli scientists announced they had manufactured DNA, raising the spectre of use of 'fake' DNA by criminals[5245].

When <u>Kyle Fisher</u>'s mother's incarceration for his murder was revealed as a gross miscarriage of justice, it was shown that Cleveland Police never took statements from two specialist surgeons who had found the death was natural[5246].

The trial of a man accused by Tayside Police of putting an ex-partner's phone number on an internet sex ad was axed, because his confession was obtained without his lawyer being present. He claimed two officers threatened to remove his computer if he didn't confess, and that he had the right to a lawyer being present. Other cases have collapsed because of the UK Supreme Court's 'Cadder' ruling[5247].

<u>George Davis</u>, given 20 years in 1975 for armed robbery of the London Electricity Board, was freed the next year on the grounds that his conviction was unsafe. Because he had not been 'found innocent' he has fought for over 30 years to be cleared. The other three defendants were found innocent. The Criminal Cases Review Commission allowed a re-examination in 2011. The appeal centred on the reliability of D.C. <u>Brian Grove</u>, who identified Davis as one of the gang of thieves. The Court of Appeal heard that Grove was at the time in an unmarked police van picking up a freezer for D.I. <u>Brian Reynolds</u>, who later became Deputy Chief Constable of Thames Valley Police. Grove earlier was convinced <u>another</u> man was the culprit, but later identified Davis in an identity parade (he hadn't been asked to attend an earlier parade). Reynolds said that shortly before the 1975 trial Flying Squad officers pressurised him to conceal why Grove had not been detailed to attend the first parade: Reynolds in fact felt 'intimidated'[5248]. There was a huge 'George Davis is innocent' campaign by celebrities and others.

The police in the case of murdered Teresa de Simone refused to allow drug addict <u>Sean Hodgson</u> (<u>before</u> his trial) to retract his confession to a priest that he had murdered her. He claimed he was a pathological liar. Hodgson's blood group matched blood found at the crime scene. That was sufficient for the police, and over the next 27 years he staged hunger strikes in various jails, writing countless letters protesting his innocence (most were ignored, and a 1983 appeal failed). It proved very difficult to reopen his case because the original case files had gone missing. Forensic evidence finally proved Hodgson couldn't have been the killer, and it transpired that suicide David Luce, a teenage offender, had confessed to a female relative of his that he was the murderer, and his body exhumed to prove the confession was true[5249].

In the Joanna Yeates case her landlord Chris Jefferies was detained but then freed on bail protesting his innocence: as a result of being named by police he was the subject of such a media frenzy he had to leave home. Only after several weeks was he declared no longer a suspect. He is said to be suing Avon & Somerset police for wrongful arrest – his name and photo were widely circulated (to convince the public the police were being diligent?)[5250]. He says he had experienced 'a kind of rape', leaving him feeling 'violated'[5251].

In the Megrahi case, the Scottish Criminal Cases Review Commission pinpointed six grounds for believing a miscarriage of justice may have occurred: American citizen Abu Elias may have been the real Lockerbie bomber – he is the nephew of the terror group's leader, Ahmed Jibril[5252]. In 2007 a key piece of evidence (the crucial 'timer'), used to implicate Libya in the bombing, turned out to be a probable fake. An engineer apparently lied about the origin of the timer, and claims of shoddy investigative work have been levelled at the Scottish police and the FBI. The Scottish Criminal Cases Review Commission ruled in 2007 there was enough evidence to suggest a miscarriage of justice[5253]. It was a former Scottish member of ACPO – of assistant chief constable rank or higher – who gave Megrahi's lawyers the statement that key evidence in the Lockerbie trial was fake. He claimed the CIA planted the tiny fragment of circuit board which was pivotal in convicting the Libyan[5254]. The front page of 'Scotland on Sunday' (24.6.07) carried a special investigation article by Marcello Mega on the case, headlined 'Not Guilty'. Police surgeon Dr. David Fieldhouse claims a body vanished from Lockerbie as part of a cover-up, either of the identity of someone who should not have been on the plane, or of a CIA blunder that allowed the bomb past airport security[5255]. In 2012 a new book 'exonerated' Megrahi because of the failure of disclosure by the Scottish fiscal of prosecution evidence[5256].

In relation to the undercover cop/activists fiasco, the IPCC opened an inquiry into the alleged failure of Nottinghamshire Police to disclose secret tape recordings to the CPS, which risked a miscarriage of justice if a second trial had proceeded[5257].

A major Edinburgh drugs trial collapsed after a Lothian and Borders detective was accused of trying to identify a suspect in court. The officer was to be investigated by his force[5258].

The most senior Buckingham Palace courtier expressed deep concern in 2007 to PM Tony Blair's Chief of Staff Jonathan Powell about the Met's John Yates, (who was investigating the cash for honours scandal at the time). Powell was told that the Yates camp exaggerated the strength of the case against Burrell 'to get Prince William to give evidence against [him]', according to one source. Yates managed to persuade Prince Charles to consent to Burrell's prosecution on four counts of theft – he was later acquitted[5259]. (See the Yates section in The Murdoch Policeman chapter)

This 'case exaggeration' tendency applies to re-investigations (usually, if not nearly always, conducted by the police) as well as at the prosecution stage. Thus in the Birmingham Six case it took four re-investigations before the convictions were quashed, and it is arguable that it was the painstaking research and pressure by family and friends which trumped the police work[5260].

'Few people now doubt the fact that some police officers engage in very serious malpractice'. Though every year hundreds of people obtain substantial compensation for serious police misconduct, hardly ever is disciplinary action taken against the officers concerned. The judiciary insists bizarrely that neither the police nor the CPS owe a duty of care to those who suffer because of this incompetence[5261], but this has been refuted by the European Court of Human Rights. The police say that they don't have the duty of care imposed on professionals such as doctors, architects and dentists.

Confessions rendered unreliable by police pressure include the Cardiff Three, Guildford Four, Birmingham Six, Ward, Tottenham Three and the Treadaway cases. Non-disclosure of evidence by the police occurred in the cases of Guildford, Maguire, Darvell brothers and Ward. In the Birmingham Six case the defendants claimed their confessions had been beaten out of them, so that they pursued a claim against the police (and prison warders) for damages for assault. Four people convicted of planting bombs in Guildford and six convicted of the Birmingham bombing were released, on appeal, after 15 and 16 years in prison respectively[5262] (see Appendix II). Once it was discovered Surrey Police detectives had fabricated statements of the Guildford Four (particularly of Patrick Armstrong) and covered up evidence that could have shown their innocence, the convictions were quashed in 1989, immediately triggering a review of the Maguire Seven case[5263]. In the case of the Tottenham Three two officers were charged with perverting the course of justice, but were acquitted, and Silcott was not allowed to bring a civil action for conspiracy and malfeasance. In the Stefan Kiszko case a detective was charged with perverting justice, but the case was halted because of delay[5264]. Eight detectives fabricated the case – they persuaded witnesses to concoct stories – against the Cardiff Three, charged with killing the prostitute girlfriend of one of them, Stephen Miller[5265].

Despite a number of unsuccessful appeals, fresh doubts have arisen about the 1996 conviction for murder of 'contract killer' Kevin Lane, who has served over 18 years but should be released soon. During his trial special court orders prevented sensitive information reaching the public domain. DI Chris Spackman, who was instrumental in Lane's convicion, was jailed for corruption in 2003, but police knew about allegations that Spackman had been bent as long ago as 1994 (the year of the murder). Some of the critical public interest immunity certificates related to Spackman, so much information was never disclosed to Lane's defence.

Convictions of the Bridgewater Four rested largely on the confessions of one of them, Molloy, who retracted his statement, claiming he had been tricked by the West Midlands Serious Crime Squad: tests on the police documents revealed an imprint of a fake confession. The West Midlands officers' behaviour gave rise to 91 complaints about beatings, fabrications, etc[5266].

Two Stirlingshire brothers were falsely accused of murdering their sibling, and it took 18 months for a second murder team to bring the real culprit, a paedophile, to justice. Their father says: 'The main failing is that no one tells you anything. It's all hidden. There's probably a lot of things we should know but still don't. We were under horrendous pressure from police ... I was always brought up to believe the police ... when we complained they threatened me and my wife ...' He claims a hammer was planted by an officer who was not prosecuted, only reduced in rank. 'Forensics had already spent four days in the house when the hammer was discovered'[5267].

In the <u>Bakewell Tart</u> case there was a barely credible series of blunders and crucial omissions made by police, who, e.g., failed to test the alibi of a prime suspect, a prominent local businessman, and ignored the evidence of several witnesses. They also ignored alarming anomalies between <u>Stephen Downing</u>'s confession (at the age of 17) and the results of the post-mortem and forensic tests, and the court was never told that the victim had led a colourful life. In 1977 a man told Bakewell police that his uncle, who had provided the businessman's unchecked alibi, had recanted the story on his deathbed. His allegations were investigated by a Derbyshire D.C., who asked not to be named to protect him from recriminations. The officer has since come forward to tell the full story of his doubts about the safety of Downing's conviction. He says there was enough evidence to grant an appeal 24 years ago, but at the time he was prevented from carrying out a full investigation. He was told not to question the integrity of the force and the inquiry was dropped: during the inquiry a witness offered relevant vehicle registration numbers to a policeman, but he turned the information down. Downing, who had a reading age of 11, was never told by police that he was under arrest, was not informed of his right to access to a solicitor, and claims his confession was due to police pressure. When journalist Don Hale presented a dossier proving Downing's innocence to Derbyshire police they ignored him. But when he began to print his discoveries they began to fight back ferociously. They first threatened Hale with prosecution for obstructing the course of justice, then said they would sue him for defamation. Because he obviously had informants inside the force, CIB2 (the internal investigation department) investigated him for nine months in 1996, tapping his phones and intercepting his mail. The police put pressure on his employers, who in turn pressured him to stop publishing stories about Downing. Hale was threatened, abused and intimidated. The police, prison and judicial service, as well as the government, made life as difficult as possible. As the wrongly imprisoned have to pay for the privilege, Downing's compensation was at first debited with £160,000 boarding costs, but this was reduced to £85,000[5268].

The crucial witness who helped put <u>Michael Stone</u> behind bars for the murders of Lin and Megan Russell escaped prosecution for a series of alleged crimes immediately after he agreed to help detectives.

<u>Thomas Cochrane</u>, the Scottish model for Hornblower, became a radical MP who railed against corruption, so the authorities had the police frame him for fraud.

Scotland Yard pressed for murder charges to be brought over the death of Damilola Taylor because a secret bugging operation convinced them they were on the right track, but the relevant tapes and "Trojan horse" operation were not disclosed in court for "legal reasons".

40 years after <u>James Hanratty</u> was hanged for the A6 murder, Michael Mansfield QC alleged that substantial (24 instances) non-disclosure of evidence to the defence flawed the conviction. The senior police officer, Detective Superintendent <u>Robert Acott</u>, had fabricated evidence and misled the jury, he said.

In the case of <u>Michael Shirley</u>, wrongly convicted of killing a barmaid, the police suppressed evidence for many years (he spent 16 in prison)[5269].

A detective who investigated the death of <u>Stephen Lawrence</u> was involved in drug-dealing and theft, and behaved threateningly towards possibly important witnesses. Statements from a police supergrass were not passed to the family's lawyers. Detectives looking into allegations by Met DC <u>Neil Putnam</u>, the crooked detective's subordinate, wrote to the inquiry in 1998 about their concerns, but the Lawrence lawyers were never told. The final Macpherson report concluded that "(the) attitude of DS <u>John Davidson</u> and other officers is to be deplored". Putnam, a self-confessed corrupt copper and alcoholic wife-beater, was jailed for almost four years in 2000 after pleading guilty to 16 counts. He informed on the rest of the 'Groovy Gang', a hard-drinking bunch who specialised in seizing targeted loads of drugs and selling them off. Putnam shopped in particular <u>Davidson</u>, whom he claimed was in the pay of the father of Stephen Lawrence murder suspect David Norris, and that he and Davidson were into stolen watches as well as cocaine[5270].

<u>Stephen Armstrong</u>'s family and neighbours united behind him when he was jailed for trying to protect them from the teenage hooligans terrorising their Glasgow street. The neighbour had made 39 calls to police in four months[5271].

When young nurse <u>Elizabeth McCabe</u>'s body was found near Dundee in 1980 murder squad detectives convinced themselves that taxi driver <u>Vincent Simpson</u> had murdered her. He says: 'These police officers persecuted me and, even worse, they totally betrayed the McCabe family. Their fixation that I was the murderer meant that the case was not investigated properly and now it never will be'. When the case was reopened in 2007 a jury at Edinburgh's High Court found him not guilty[5272]. He was wrongly accused by Tayside Police as a result of low-copy DNA, a technique that has been heavily criticised. His things had been contaminated by being stored in a box with crime scene material, a well-known risk of police storage.

Retired Strathclyde detective <u>Alwyn Harries</u> was part of the team that saw <u>Stuart Gair</u> wrongly jailed for the 1989 murder of a 45-year-old man near a gay Glasgow pick-up. Gair was freed in 2006; Harries admitted in the appeal court he had removed the murder case papers from the police files and given them to his lawyer. Harries had also retained his police notebooks from 1989: he now works as a council warden. Justice campaigners aver that Gair's is one of the worst cases they have encountered[5273].

Tony Blair admitted his ID card initiative would enable police to trawl the records of millions of innocent people. Tory MPs predicted huge miscarriages of justice as a result[5274].

Following the guilty verdict in the Asbury murder trial at Glasgow High Court (1997), the conviction was later overturned because it was based on unreliable fingerprint evidence. Assistant Chief Constable James McKay uncovered 'cultural collusion' and 'manipulation of evidence' during the Asbury/McKie case. The infamous <u>Shirley McKie</u> fingerprint which placed her at the Marion Ross death scene <u>before</u> she attended as part of the investigating team – meant she was alternately stigmatised and wooed by fellow officers: chocolates, flowers and wine were used to try to sweeten her into a confession to perjury. Some of the nasty colleagues had worked closely with her father when he was in the police[5275]. Shirley was awarded £750,000 in damages against Strathclyde Police. Even after this, Strathclyde appointed two senior officers to rake over the case again when they received a dossier on the case from another former officer, <u>Les Brown</u>[5276]. A Sunday newspaper uncovered a secret police report that there had been 'criminality' and 'cover-up' in the way the case had been handled. Despite the police report the Lord Advocate Colin Boyd decided not to charge the fingerprint experts at the SCRO (Scottish Criminal Records Office) who got it wrong[5277]. But MSPs called (2007) for the Scottish Fingerprint Service to be put on probation for a few years, as a series of management defects had been revealed (e.g. a lack of common standards among the four Scottish fingerprint offices)[5278]. McKie has finally (14 years later) received an official apology from the Scottish Police Services Authority for the 'errors' and 'pain'. She had been tried for perjury[5279].

Wiltshire Sergeant <u>Mark Andrews</u>, whose conviction for allegedly dragging a woman across a cell floor was overturned, was able to return to the station where it happened[5280].

A BBC investigation by John Sweeney into the death of handicapped baby Kyle Fisher did not meet with cooperation from Cleveland Police: DS <u>Tony Hutchinson</u>, in charge of the inquiry, refused to answer Sweeney's questions. Thus the police failed to take statements from neurosurgical experts Professor Brian Avery and Sid Marks, who had examined the toddler a few months before he died. The BBC felt babysitter <u>Suzanne Holdsworth</u> – jailed for causing the death – was innocent, that the child died from natural causes, but she was disciplined for talking to the BBC[5281]. On June 19, 2011, an article, 'How Mary Poppins Was Jailed For Life For Child Murder She Didn't Commit' suggested the police did not investigate properly. In fact an IPCC investigation found such an allegation against the force to be unsubstantiated[5282]. But in June, 2011 the IPCC said that Cleveland Police should apologise to Suzanne Holdsworth for a terrible miscarriage of justice. She spent three years of a life sentence for a child murder she didn't commit. The police didn't properly consider the child's traumatic neurosurgical history before coming into Suzanne's care, nor the fact that the bannister – which the child's head had supposedly smashed against – was unmarked by any of the child's tissues[5283].

The trial of three men accused of armed robbery collapsed because police used 'dirty tricks' – two of the accused were put in adjoining cells, then their conversation was eavesdropped: what they said was to have been used against them[5284]. (See Appendix IV for even dirtier tricks).

<u>George McPhee</u>, cleared after serving 18 years for a murder he didn't commit, demanded a public inquiry into why a senior Northern Constabulary detective gave untrue evidence at his trial: DS <u>Andrew Lister</u> crucially said police scientists backed his evidence about footprints. This was false, the negative lab report never being shown to prosecution, defence or jury. The evidence of two other key prosecution witnesses was also condemned by the appeal judges[5285].

The sister of <u>Tom Bourke</u>, who by 2007 had spent 13 years in jail for a double murder, gathered 'evidence' from Manchester crime bosses as to who really shot two DOT (Department of Transport) garage inspectors. She claimed three 'witnesses' to the murders were recompensed by police to name Bourke, while another witness who said it wasn't Bourke told a detective, but the defence wasn't informed. She also claims a gun was planted in Tom's jail by a guard to persuade the jury he was trying to escape[5286]. The family obtained leave to appeal, but didn't.

The first investigation into the killing of PI <u>Daniel Morgan</u> is feared to have seen the killers shielded by corrupt officers. The 2011 attempt to convict the real killers collapsed after evidence from supergrasses was discredited[5287].

Former chief constable of Thames Valley Police, <u>Peter Neyroud</u>, said that the force's mantra in the 1980s was 'confinement brings confessions'. <u>Confessions were pre-prepared</u> for signing by the 'culprits'!

Defence lawyers have criticised the idea of mobile virtual courts – defendants face a judge by video link – because they are a 'short cut' to justice and can deny the right to a full and fair trial[5288].

IRA Commander Raymond McCartney and Eamonn MacDermott, convicted of murdering RUC officer Patrick McNulty in 1977 in Derry, were freed after it was suggested their confessions were obtained under duress. McCartney was also wrongly convicted of another murder a short time after, and spent 17 years in prison.

Tayside PC Stuart Johnstone threw an assault trial into jeopardy by having an affair with the accused's girlfriend – he gave evidence at the trial [5289].

A Scottish fatal accident inquiry was told that blunders by police and others meant that the nature of the victim's wounds – self or other-inflicted – couldn't be established. There was a failure to have the required two doctors perform the post-mortem, and there were no crime scene photos[5290].

During WWI Alice Wheeldon, a clothes dealer and socialist sympathiser, helped fugitive conscientious objectors. One got her husband to procure some curare (to poison some guard dogs) from the lab where he worked. The whole family were set up by Special Branch, accused of plotting to murder Lloyd George with a blowpipe while he golfed. Though the chief witness (who had asked for the poison) had disappeared, the couple and their daughter were sentenced to hard labour[5291].

The convictions of two brothers in Swansea in 1986 for the murder of a sex shop manageress were overturned in 1992: police notes and a confession had been redrafted at a later date, police witnesses who had identified the brothers were nine miles away at the time of the murder, while fingerprint evidence unfavourable to the prosecution was not disclosed and was even destroyed prior to the trial. John McGranaghan's conviction for rape on the basis of victim identification was quashed by forensic evidence not disclosed by the police.

The unreliability of an off-duty police witness (hypnotised to remember a car numberplate) meant Eddie Browning was acquitted of a motorist's murder after six years[5292].

Learning disabled Mark Cleary, convicted of murder in 1985, was pressured by police into making a statement he later retracted. In 1993 BBC TV's 'Trial and Error' alleged details suggested by the defendant were incorrect and the conviction was quashed.

Sussex Police trying to catch a burglar who smashed in the door of a house, arrested the black carpenter who repaired the damage. He was kept in a cell for an hour before the police admitted their mistake[5293].

In a landmark ruling of the High Court a teacher was found to have been falsely accused of assaulting a pupil, and decreed that West Midlands Police had arrested him unlawfully, awarding him damages. Only 5% of allegations about teachers lead to police action[5294].

Tough-guy actor Ray Winstone was imprisoned in Leeds for 72 hours because he was wrongly identified in an identi-fit picture on Crimewatch[5295].

In 2000 Scottish police had to apologise to gangster <u>Paul Ferris</u> for tampering with his criminal record (parole board members were wrongly informed he had an attempted murder conviction).

The Scottish Criminal Cases Review Commission received allegations (2007) that Scottish police plotted to mislead the Lockerbie inquiry, it is understood. It is claimed false evidence replaced evidence gathered at the scene that was lost or destroyed, so that Megrahi's investigation was "reverse-engineered" to provide evidence that matched a conclusion of guilt (e.g. a policeman allegedly showed a witness a picture of Megrahi shortly before his crucial identification of the Libyan at his trial).

Flasher <u>Raymond Gilmour</u>, who claimed to have confessed twice to strangling a 16-year-old girl because of police pressure, spent 21 years in jail before having his conviction overturned on appeal. Detective Superintendent James Brown believed his confession was a lie, and he was released, only to be made to confess to a new detective. Gilmour's confession contained several inaccuracies. During the hunt for the killer, police were shown evidence of a link between the crime and serial child killer Robert Black[5296].

In the case of the <u>UDR Four</u>, in respect of paramilitary activities (the murder of a man thought to belong to the IRA), they were convicted, but complained that there was police tampering with confessions – three of the four were freed on appeal.

In 2007 the £10m <u>Kieren Fallon</u> race-fix trial collapsed, the police having withheld crucial evidence – his lawyers called for an inquiry into the police evidence. The officer in charge of the case – acting DC <u>Mark Manning</u> – admitted he had been offered a job by the Horse Racing Regulatory Authority[5297].

The CPS are dropping tens of thousands of criminal cases annually because they are 'snowed under' – stopping trials 'in the public interest' still count towards government targets (in every case there was enough evidence to charge the criminal)[5298].

Merseyside Police incarcerated a mother of seven for 16 hours and hauled her before the courts for telling swearing ladettes in the street to be quiet, which resulted in a scuffle. She had been arrested for 'assault' but magistrates threw out the case[5299].

In 2008 police in Middlesbrough charged the mother of Britain's Got Talent favourite Dean Wilson with violent kidnap, despite her having an alibi. She had a miscarriage after her arrest. The CPS dropped all charges[5300].

A careworker was sacked because police had included an unfounded abuse allegation in his enhanced criminal record certificate (they have almost total discretion in what they include, e.g. non-conviction data)[5301].

Central Scotland Police removed a Wild West fan's replica guns (with solid barrels) – two 1860s-style Colts and a Winchester rifle – after a minor disturbance at his home which led to no further action. Replica guns are only illegal in Scotland in a public place. The police left the householder with his sword and dagger collection. Six weeks later his guns hadn't been returned[5302].

A couple were arrested, handcuffed and held for 10 hours by Cheshire Police on suspicion of murdering their toddler son, who had died of natural causes, having been misdiagnosed by paramedics[5303].

Police awarded an Asian student £20,000 in compensation for false arrest. He was suspected of terrorism after downloading part of an Al Qaeda protocol as part of his university research[5304].

Strathclyde Police threw an innocent man into Barlinnie Prison for three months for carrying a rose – they thought it looked like a knife[5305].

Armed Scottish police wearing baseball caps wrongly arrested a couple walking their dog over a blackmail plot, and threw them in jail for five days. Elizabeth Stewart says other prisoners treated her better than the police, seeming to accept she was telling the truth. The officers screamed at the top of their voices during the arrest. Husband Rab Stewart was on medication for a heart condition. During their long marriage this was the first time the couple had been apart. Their son and daughter were also taken to the police station to make statements and copy lines from a ransom note, but were not told their parents were in custody.

The shambles of the police inquiry into Neil and Christine Hamilton may have cost £1 million, having lasted 115 days. A secret internal police review details delays, management failures and 'poor decision-making' by detectives, and showed the pair had an incontrovertible alibi. There was no forensic evidence of sexual assault, and the complainant's story couldn't be corroborated. Lincolnshire Police warned the Met that the 'victim' had made false allegations before. DCI Chris Miller, who led the Hamilton inquiry, faced disciplinary action over another sex case where the investigation was 'grossly incompetent' (the £400,000 case was thrown out after four days).

A black Gloucestershire fireman won £15,000 compensation after being wrongly accused by police of selling drugs. He was handcuffed and forced to his knees in front of his son, yet when they realised he was innocent, they charged him with threatening behaviour. John James had to appear in court seven times over a year before the police's Professional Standards Department found in his favour.

The mother of a three-year-old sent home from hospital despite dying of pneumonia and septicaemia, was arrested on suspicion of murder by two West Midlands riot vans and 17 officers, within an hour of finding him dead in bed. Held for questioning overnight, she returned home to find forensics tents outside her door: she was not allowed to see her son until 11 days after his death[5306].

In 2010 a Dundee grandmother was jailed for five years for having a WWII heirloom gun in her home. Police looking for her son had found it under her mattress[5307].

A mother of five falsely accused of date-raping a rich businessman – she was cleared – says the police investigation was nightmarish. Six officers arrested her at home in front of her seven-year-old son. They ransacked her home, removed her phone, bedsheets and underwear and made her reveal what positions she used during intercourse. The 'victim' dropped the charge and refused to apologise, but was not even cautioned by police[5308].

A 19-year-old pregnant witness, who was too ill with morning sickness to attend a Scottish court, was arrested, incarcerated and handcuffed (the accused was out on bail). She had tried to contact the fiscal's office, but they weren't answering their phones[5309].

The circumstances of the murder of PC <u>Salt</u>, on a stakeout at an unlicensed Birmingham drinking club with PC <u>Berry</u>, were covered up by the latter: they were both drinking while they should have been engaged in surveillance (the media reported Berry's version for months: there was a suspect car and the officers had broken cover). The dereliction of duty was covered up by forced "confessions" by three black suspects, e.g. threats were made to plant drugs on family members. A 17-year-old girl was bullied into implicating the three blacks, one of whom confessed to theft from PC Salt to avoid the murder charge he was charged with anyway. When Mrs. Salt revealed nothing had been stolen, the "confessions" were destabilised, and one suspect said the police threat "we'll get you" meant at some point they would "stitch him up". The suspects' alibis were ignored, and there was no inquest. Disclosure rules were not followed - if they had been, one crucial statement would have exonerated the suspects. It took a year for murder charges to be dropped. The Crown Prosecution and West Midlands police refused to answer 'World in Action' journalists' questions or take part in their programme. As a tribute to PC Salt no mention was made at his funeral of his unprofessional behaviour or the cover-up, though these were well known to the top police brass attending. The case showed that even with audiotape recordings it was still possible for unscrupulous cops to extract false confessions.

A preservation order was placed on a terraced property after an Oxford professor bought the property. She developed polio so she replaced the heavy solid front door with a light plastic and glass one. Because she didn't obtain planning permission she faces jail (the council wouldn't accept her disability defence). This case was reported on 'Rough Justice', a 'Tonight' programme about questionable convictions broadcast in April 2006. Both the Home Office and ACPO refused to take part in the programme.

The presence of police can cause bias in forensic officers, with the innocent being imprisoned because experts misinterpret fingerprint data, according to research from Southampton University[5310].

For two years a 23-year-old black bar supervisor was wrongly accused of abuse and obstruction of a Thames Valley Police officer[5311].

Two former teachers in a care school were wrongly convicted of paedophilia after a trawl – asking those who had been in care if they had ever been molested – by Merseyside Police[5312].

Convicted fraudster <u>Lord Hanningfield</u> was suing Essex Police for unlawful arrest (inside his home – they didn't have a warrant), trespass and detention[5313].

The case of the <u>Gays</u>, accused of killing their foster child by salt poisoning, was one of the worst miscarriages of justice for infanticide since Sally Clark and Angela Cannings: police had insisted the couple had force-fed the child with salt as a punishment. It took a jury seven hours (in 2007) to clear them after the anguish of a second trial, which lasted six weeks, the whole process having taken four years. The parents accused the police of setting out to crucify them over the death[5314].

Paddy Hill spent 16 years in prison after a miscarriage of justice relating to the 1974 Birmingham pub bombings. He claims he suffered brutality at the hands of the police and prison authorities. In 1999 he founded the Miscarriage of Justice Organisation[5315].

David Carrington-Jones spent almost seven years of a ten-year term in prison for rape before a judge ruled his conviction unsafe – the 'victim' had a history of making false sexual allegations (e.g. against her brother, fiancée, stepfather, even one of her customers). The police knew this, but the jury was not told this. He was refused parole hearings because he denied his guilt[5316], compounding the injustice.

It is alleged that the case of convicted wife-killer Nat Fraser was a miscarriage of justice, that vital evidence was withheld by Grampian Police, and witnesses were never called or were intimidated. Fraser was released on bail pending his appeal[5317], a retrial being ordered in 2011.

The 'Babes in the Wood' investigation (a nine- and a ten-year-old girl found dead in 1986) was the largest in Sussex Police's history. Two decades later Phil Swan, the detective who arrested and quizzed the prime suspect, revealed that the jurors at the latter's trial were not allowed to hear crucial evidence, alleging a cover-up by senior Sussex officers. Blood found on one girl's clothing was never compared with the main suspect's, and key witnesses were 'mislaid' by the police. The suspect was not convicted, but was later, for attacking another young girl[5318].

Three appeal judges ruled there was a serious miscarriage of justice with regard to a 1995 murder in Dunfermline, and so overturned the convictions of two men who had spent a decade in prison. The police didn't furnish evidence to the jury that could have affected this decision – the detectives 'deliberately misled the Crown in a serious way'. The judge felt the police failed to follow several 'obvious' lines of inquiry: they rejected evidence from main witnesses, failing to pass it to either legal team. D.S. Richard Munro was branded a liar by the judges at the appeal – he resigned from the force in 2004 ahead of disciplinary action for corruption and fled the UK[5319]. Before he left the force, he was ironically working for HM Inspectorate of Constabulary. He allegedly threatened witnesses with jail, changed the testimony of witnesses, lied to his superiors, causing the deputy Chief Constable of Fife to lie to the Crown. In 2004, though facing a charge of having sex with a prostitute, he received a £100,000 payoff[5320].

Dr. Arthur Conan Doyle showed that horsehair found on George Hedalji's jacket (he was falsely convicted of disembowelling a pony and sentenced to seven years), had been planted by Staffordshire Police. Also it was the wrong jacket, the wounds couldn't have been made by George's razor, etc. Doyle also proved that Oscar Slater had been framed by Scottish police[5321].

Robert Brown always claimed he was the victim of a miscarriage of justice: he was freed in 2002 after 25 years in prison for murder. He insisted Greater Manchester Police had bullied and beaten him into signing a false confession. The Court of Appeal (who delivered an unsafe verdict) heard that one of the police investigators, Detective Chief Inspector Jack Butler, had been 'deeply corrupt', presiding over a 'culture of corruption' for six years at Platt Lane police station in Manchester. Because of Mr. Brown's refusal to admit guilt, he lost a decade's eligibility for parole[5322], another example of the compounding of an injustice.

One police blunder which helped to wrongly convict <u>Michael Stone</u> of the murder of Lin and Megan Russell was their grasping at a message from a doctor they regarded as a breakthrough. Psychiatrist Dr. Philip Sugarman responded to a 1997 Crimewatch reconstruction by opining that the photofit looked like Stone, one of his patients. An 'informal' briefing of newspapers by the police suggested the doctor had told them of Stone's 'nightmarish fantasies' which resembled the actual murders. The trouble was the doctor later categorically denied this, so one has to question why 'senior police sources' said differently. Then again, how likely is the police version that after over 30 of their interviews, in which Stone repeatedly protested his innocence, he would then 'confess' to nine other prisoners while on remand[5323]?

<u>Nick Freeman</u>, 'Mr Loophole', the rich lawyer who gets motorists off on technicalities, was arrested (2006) by six officers from Gwent Police for conspiracy to pervert the course of justice. Months later all accusations were dropped[5324].

<u>Barry George</u> was convicted (wrongly, as it turned out) of Jill Dando's murder on circumstantial evidence alone. Yet <u>Gary Mason</u>, in his Official History of the Met, justifies this use of evidence[5325].

By the end of 2011 1,030 Scottish court cases had been put on hold or abandoned because of the Supreme Court's Cadder ruling.

Penalty Notices for Disorder (PNDs) can be given officially for shoplifting (items up to a value of £200), vandalising (up to £500 in value), using threatening language, but in practice they are being handed out liberally for more serious crimes like fraud and assault. They are widely used for repeat offenders, even though this is contrary to guidelines: police gave one serial offender a shoplifting reprimand, a 'final' warning for shoplifting, a caution for police assault, another shoplifting caution, an on-the-spot fine and a third caution for the same offence. By now an habitual criminal, yet she had never appeared in court. The number of criminal cases which bypassed the court doubled in eight years[5326].

DPP head Keith Starmer refused (a) to say, in cases in which he was involved as a barrister, whether he knew police witnesses were undercover or (b) to examine the six or so cases annually to see if there were miscarriages of justice (where secret cops were involved)[5327]. Starmer has told how it was the police who destroyed evidence in the <u>Cardiff Three</u> case.

There have been calls to reinvestigate the cold case of the fatal Lanarkshire stabbing of <u>Surjit Singh Chhokar</u> in 1998 during a confrontation with white Scots men. The victim's family have criticised the police decision not to treat the crime as racist. After two inquiries into the police handling of the case, the Lord Advocate apologised for the 'incompetence, ignorance and institutional racism' in the police and prosecutors' behaviour. A parallel has been drawn with Stephen Lawrence[5328].

Nine officers have been told by regulation 14 notices they are under investigation over allegations of non-disclosure in a murder trial: the IPCC and the CCRC are involved. Other allegations are conspiracy to pervert the course of justice and misconduct in a public office. Senior officers include <u>Adrian Lee</u>, Chief Constable of Northamptonshire and ACPO's lead on the ethics of policing, as well as his Deputy Chief Constable <u>Suzette Davenport</u>. Others are <u>Jane Sawyers</u>, Assistant Staffordshire Chief Constable, and <u>Marcus Beale</u>, Assistant Chief Constable of West Midlands. They have not been suspended or arrested, unlike Cleveland's Chief Constable Sean Price, also subject to a separate IPCC investigation.

Some feel Hertfordshire Police's lie detector pilot using sex offenders is ill-conceived: it suggested 25 'low level' offenders were more dangerous to children than previously thought. (Devon and Cornwall Police previously used the technique on a one-off basis). It may not yet be reliable and valid enough – it is unclear whether the police have used appropriate control groups, and two of the experimental subjects reversed their testimony at later interview. Though polygraphic error is in the region of 10%, this can be much greater with some operators, despite digitalisation and photography supposedly increasing the equipment's reliability. Despite decades of use in the US in many states it is still not admissible in court[5329].

10 Rillington Place serial killer John Christie served at Harrow Road police station for four years. Wrongly executed learning-disabled Timothy Evans' last words on the gallows were: 'It was Christie that did it!' It seems obvious the Met would believe one of their own first (Christie was also an occupant of the murder house)[5330]. Ludovic Kennedy's book 'Ten Rillington Place' revealed that Christie was the true murderer[5331].

Years of partner abuse led to Lloyd Lothian finally stabbing her in the stomach (she nearly died), yet police initially accused her of stabbing herself and made her endure two days of hostile questioning. Because the trial judge fell ill a retrial was ordered, but the victim was too afraid and traumatised to give evidence again against the man who had been charged with attempted murder. So she was imprisoned while his sentence was reduced[5332].

Hundreds of shops attacked in the 2011 riots have been refused compensation because police say there weren't enough people involved to constitute a riot. The police have refused to pay out to some owners (under the Riot (Damages) Act) because there weren't '12 or more' rioters, e.g. a newsagent who closed early on police advice because about 100 troublemakers were running amok was refused compensation, as was a shoeshop whose owner says, 'Anyone who saw it would say it was a riot'. Shops in ex-minister Frank Dobson's Central London constituency were also turned down[5333].

Peter Hain has described how he was wrongly arrested and charged with robbing Barclays Bank – several squad cars and a 'black Maria' with a dozen police officers turned up unannounced at his home. Schoolboys had thought he resembled the thief and gave his car number to the police, though the oldest boy later ensured the truth emerged that it wasn't Hain. Fingerprints on the stolen money didn't match his, but the Sunday papers had a field day – bank staff read them prior to the identity parade, where only one staff member positively identified him. The South African apartheid security agency Boss seems to have set him up – their thief was hustled away to the Continent and then South Africa and was never caught (Boss had staked out Hain's home). MI5 seems also to have had a role in tipping off the Met he was the thief. The jury found him not guilty.

Ten police officers (from five or six squad cars) charged into the home of Bafta-nominated musician Simon Boswell, to arrest him on a false charge of domestic violence against his actress partner (he was found not guilty). On another occasion an aggressive policeman allegedly said to him: 'Are you the b......d what says she's got the menopause'. On another occasion the police illegally took his door keys from him and gave them to his partner. Until these experiences Boswell had always been a staunch supporter of the police – at one point he spent 22 hours in a cell at Islington Police Station; he was not allowed to call a friend or relative. He hoped to refer his many complaints to the IPCC. He was banned from his home while on police bail even though he hadn't been charged[5334].

Gail Sheridan, wife of Tommy Sheridan, jailed for perverting the course of justice (perjury), was subjected not only to sectarian hate mail but, she says, the heavy-handed way the police treated her. Though she was cleared of perjury, her solicitor has asked, via a whole tabloid page, certain answers from police: 'Why was a charge of theft of miniature whisky bottles put on a charge sheet for a High Court perjury trial (it was later dropped)? And why have neither the miniatures (nor her diaries) been returned? Why was her daughter's Christmas outfit seized from her home – what did this have to do with a warrant relating to perjury? Why did the raid officers choose to meet at Ibrox stadium before proceeding, and who told the media about the raid if it was so confidential? Who authorised release of police interview tapes (of Gail and Tommy) to the BBC: extracts were broadcast (23.12.10) in BBC Scotland's 'The Rise and Lies of Tommy Sheridan'? Detectives already knew Gail was RC (e.g. she used rosary beads at interview and they would know her religion from the raid on her house), so why was this religious questioning deemed essential? Why was she asked if she had been trained in IRA interrogation techniques? Was the prosecution's sudden abandonment of the entire case against Gail a tactic designed to pressure her husband? Who decided to place a gagging order on him following his release?' Gail has spoken at length how nine 'police stormtroopers' raided her house leaving her toddler daughter crying in the corner (she was getting ready for a Xmas party). The 2008 raid, during which her daughter's party dress and toy antlers were seized as 'evidence', lasted eight hours. The police dismantled Gabrielle's nappy bin and rummaged through her precious keepsakes box. <u>Five years</u> later the Crown promised to return 43 personal items, including Gail's intimate diaries.

The police often, if not usually, treat innocent householders no better than common criminals. When Salford resident <u>Peter Flanagan</u> stabbed one of a three-man intruder gang who was wielding a machete – he later died – the victim was arrested, incarcerated, and had to wait a month fearing he would be charged with murder (he had no criminal record). In 2010 builder <u>Omari Roberts</u> was prosecuted when a teenage burglar died in his home[5335].

A couple's life was torn apart when they were falsely arrested on the word of their wayward adopted daughter's 'feral friends'. The wife, a senior teacher, has been told her arrest will always show up on CRB checks, so her career has been ruined[5336].

The late lorry driver <u>Kevin Callan</u>'s conviction for murder was overturned in 1995. The victim was a four-year-old he was supposed to have shaken to death. He became an expert in child neuropathology by study in prison, and found other experts to confound the testimony of the doctors whose evidence was crucial in finding him guilty. The police found someone who claimed he had overheard Callan's admission of guilt in a police cell. The guerilla artist Banksy says: 'We are learning that the people we trust with our liberty cannot be trusted.' Callan had, with help, discredited the prosecution experts, one of whom had neglected to preserve part of the child's brain for further tests. Callan revealed all in his book 'Kevin Callan's Story'[5337].

Met (Battersea CID) DC <u>Stephanie Poorman</u> began a romance with <u>Andrew Markland</u>, a career armed robber, shortly before he was shot dead by police. She was arrested over claims she passed classified National Computer information to Markland's gang: her financial records and computer were seized. After threatening to sue for wrongful arrest (claiming double discrimination – she is black and female), Commissioner Ian Blair decided to reinstate her without even an internal disciplinary inquiry, sparking fury among the Flying

Squad who caught the gang: one officer said they had been kept completely in the dark over the matter[5338].

Up to a fifth of convicted criminals may have confessed to offences they didn't commit (e.g. Sean Hodgson spent 27 years in prison after such a confession). The police don't seem interested in researching the incidence and prevalence of false confessions in the hundred of thousands of police interviews each year. About 10% of 14-16-year-olds claim to have made a false confession to police, 'taking on a case' for a friend. US police are more likely to produce a false confession because they adopt a more guilt-presumptive, antagonistic approach[5339].

In the case of the killing of Scottish gangster Kevin Carroll by fellow gangsters in a busy supermarket car park, workmen found the guns involved, but when handed to police the latter forgot to ask for the container they were in. There is a claim too that the lead detective, Detective Superintendent Michael Orr (the son of former Chief Constable John Orr), pressured the forensics expert, Alison Colley, to spin her conclusions (about a miniscule amount of DNA found on the murder weapon) to support the prosecution case. He and Detective Inspector Callum Young were probed when they interviewed corrupt cop Derek McLeod at a Lothian and Borders police station (he was being held for leaking vital secret surveillance information on Carroll's movements which he passed to the killers – that officer also was storing 85 kilos of cannabis illegally, and was jailed). The corrupt officer was not mentioned till the end of the trial of the prime suspect, Ross Monaghan, which collapsed. The Scottish Police Service Authority was to investigate the handling of forensic evidence[5340].

Appeal Court judges released Sam Hallam on bail when they heard police had overlooked pictures on his mobile which proved he wasn't at the murder scene and exposed an 'eye' witness as unreliable. His conviction was then quashed as unsafe. Hallam had spent seven years in prison for a street murder which he denied carrying out with two others. The CCRC was instrumental in obtaining his freedom, as was a long campaign by the Hallam family backed by actor Ray Winstone[5341]. One police blunder was their failure to keep a 'policy book' recording their decisions and the reasons for them. The detective who later botched the 'Body In The Bag' case (2012) was the one in charge of Hallam's case. Superintendent Mick Broster and DI Chris Jones, his deputy, failed to follow national guidelines on selecting and recording evidence. Thames Valley Police's new investigation ruled that the Met probe was 'chaotic' and 'uncontrolled' ('quality control' was lacking in the case). Broster has reportedly been advertising his high-level security clearance (alongside his CV) as a selling point to potential employers on his LinkedIn website. In the Gareth Williams (Body in Bag case) case the Westminster coroner said Broster's faux pas had hampered the inquiry (she also questioned his impartiality). The Met says he is allowed to tout for business on a private website; citing his police credentials is presumably quite in order[5342]. Hallam claimed the identification evidence against him was so unreliable it should never have been presented to a jury by the Met, who should also have followed up leads which would have proved his innocence, as well as disclosed all relevant evidence to the defence, which they didn't. Broster reportedly failed to sign off over 800 control sheets which go with each document in the case, to show they have been read and assimilated. The rule that means a log should be kept of all documents which might have to be shown to the defence was broken[5343].

Teenager Adam Scott was wrongly labelled a rapist by police because of a DNA blunder. The testing company, LGC Forensics, had wrongly re-used equipment used for the victim. He was jailed for two months. The police have not apologised to Mr. Scott[5344].

The Court Martial Appeal Court has ruled that, in the case of a decorated para being pursued through the courts expensively, the Military Police had breached the rules of investigation[5345].

Cleveland Police traffic cop Sultan Alam was framed by bent colleagues for handling stolen goods after he claimed they were racist. He was cleared on appeal after nine months in jail. He is to receive £841,430 compensation. His fight for justice lasted 18 years[5346]. The Court of Appeal found serving officers deliberately suppressed crucial evidence, but though four were charged, the case collapsed and they were acquitted. Would ordinary members of the public have got off with it?

Three Muslims were deliberately mown down during the 2011 riots by a car, whose eight occupants were cleared, partly because the policeman in charge of the investigation lied on oath[5347].

Sussex Police Chief Constable Martin Richards was reported to the IPCC amid allegations of 'undue influence' in a police probe into a complaint of a sex attack, i.e. he was accused of interfering with his officers' investigations. Richards is chair of South East Region's ACPO and the regional lead for Serious and Organised Crime.

An Islington couple who were cleared twice of shaking their baby to death say the police made allegations without any real proof, but then acted on these allegations[5348].

From 2003 to 2007 the SCCRC, in response to Megrahi's application for a second appeal, reviewed the Lockerbie evidence. This review found the senior investigating officer of the Scottish police had recommended (to the US Department of Justice's Terrorist and Violent Crime Unit), after the first appeal, that Tony Gauci, the main prosecution witness, be paid $2m, with his brother $1m, under the Unit's Reward Programme. They received the payments: the British police even pressured that they should if possible be paid more. The SCCRC concluded that these financial incentives were 'capable of affecting the course of the evidence and the eventual outcome of the trial'[5349].

Though the IPCC's report on the shooting of Mark Duggan was due in September 2012, with only a month to go the IPCC hadn't interviewed any of the officers involved[5350] (the latter were later exonerated by the watchdog).

Police wrongly charged a white man, Mark Minick, with rape, even though the victim testified her attacker was black. Three officers told him they had watertight DNA evidence against him[5351].

Senior Cleveland civilian crime scene investigator Stephen Beattie was arrested (2012) on suspicion of perverting the course of justice as well as theft. 90 cases in which he was involved were being investigated, most relating to suspicious or sudden deaths over a ten year period: there may have been miscarriages of justice. An internal review by Cleveland Police pinpointed 120 problematic cases[5352].

Met DC Ryan Coleman-Farrow was jailed for 16 months for enabling a series of miscarriages of justice – 11 of 13 accused of rape and sexual assault walking free because he was lazy[5353].

It is suggested Scotland's new police supremo <u>Steve House</u>, who backs dispensing with corroboration in trials (vital to justice, many think), would not have got the job from Kenny MacAskill if he hadn't[5354].

It has been alleged that Hillsborough survivors were 'bullied' into changing their witness statements during prolonged and aggressive cross-examination by police officers. While this was happening the West Midlands' elite detectives were disbanded on suspicion of 'fitting up' armed robbers[5355].

Police CRB checks can include unsubstantiated abuse allegations which destroy careers and prevent work with vulnerable people. Seemingly the word of a person with disability can't be challenged, sometimes resulting in miscarriages of justice[5356].

When a celebrity portrait photographer offered to help a Muslim woman with her shopping, she was kicked, but <u>she</u> was charged with a 'racially aggravated assault'. Two Met officers believed the other person's story without hearing hers, she claimed[5357].

Several investigative blunders led to the collapse of the case against Soham detective <u>Brian Stevens</u>, who had become something of a national figure for his role supporting a victim's family: (1) the teenage girls' evidence was ignored; (2) others had access to his 'porn' computer, and because an IT expert made technical errors that meant he wasn't conclusively linked to the material; (3) BT wiped his phone records before the sloth-like police finally got round to requesting them; (4) Stevens' story was that his credit card details must have been stolen, yet he never reported the theft (the details were given to a child porn website)[5358].

<u>Barry White</u> was wrongly convicted of Rachel Manning's murder in 2002, but he received no compensation when the Court of Appeal overturned the conviction and the police repeated their usual mantra: 'We're not looking for anyone else'[5359].

CHAPTER XX1X

THE VICE POLICEMAN

If this chapter is read in conjunction with 'The Lustful Policeman' chapter, the word that may spring to the reader's mind is 'hypocrisy'.

Sex crimes unit detective <u>Ryan Coleman-Farrow</u> was given 16 months after being found guilty of 10 charges of misconduct in public office. He undermined a series of investigations by failing to interview suspects as well as sending crucial evidence for testing, allowing alleged rapists to go free[5360].

The law of unforeseen consequences comes into play as soon as society criminalises human weaknesses: drugs, pornography, screen violence are all subject to the vagaries of fashion at particular times. 'Vice' (which once included homosexuality) notoriously corrupted the law's enforcers, who were also often incompetent.

A classic case of a drugs squad copper who became addicted to the drugs (e.g. heroin, cocaine) she was policing, was that of international athlete West Midlands DC <u>Jane Aucott</u> (by 1986 she was the UK's top junior discus thrower). She joined a gang of thieves, who defrauded banks (she was identified despite wearing wigs), stole cars, handled stolen goods. Arrested in 2010 she went on the run and when caught admitted 13 fraud charges[5361]. Likewise police officers have been reported to use a Glasgow brothel in Newton Terrace (run by notorious Stephen Craig and Sarah Benkan) in a private capacity[5362]. Ex-vice squad Northumbria plain clothes officer <u>Julia Sturgeon</u>, a mother of two, became a vice girl in London, offering a string of services, including dressing up as a policewoman. She had become fed up with the force because she found her male colleagues were sexist bullies[5363]. The Met's Porn Squad was, according to the Lord Chief Justice, "involved in wholesale corruption". Police took bribes from pornography retailers when the law was stricter.

Corrupt vice squad officer <u>Ken Moody</u> organised sales of seized porn using unmarked cars, but sex boss Humphreys 'blew the gaff', revealing that Moody had corrupted <u>him</u>. Commander <u>Wally Virgo</u> was in overall charge of the corrupt cops – 600 CID left the force prematurely.

Police investigating people trafficking and the sex trade in two Leeds and Sheffield massage parlours failed to find any evidence to incarcerate the culprits, despite spending £4 million over three years. Incompetent police (e.g. PC <u>Paul Ferguson</u>) appearing for the prosecution forgot details of the case in court, and were accused by a judge of lying or making misleading statements. 250 police and 80 immigration officers raided the homes of suspected sex traffickers, 59 of whom were arrested. At trial the accused were acquitted because police had openly condoned the parlours, situated just hundreds of yards from police stations, even visiting them regularly to see they were keeping to the rules[5364]. Women's groups criticise the lack of police action against brothels known to be selling sex illegally using sex-trafficked victims. When pimp David Greenwood's Belle Air and Shangri-La were identified as brothels he ran and for which he was jailed, it transpired they had been known to police for years. One has closed but reopened under a new name[5365].

Despite a survey revealing at least 300 children in Scotland were being forced to sell sex, there have been no convictions for prostituting a child[5366].

Ian Shuttleworth, former Liverpool traffic cop, was arrested in Thailand in 2008 for allegedly trafficking women to the British sex slave trade. He took sexual advantage as well as charging his victims a fee before being sold on to brothels. He was running a P.I. business in Bangkok[5367].

Unlike drugs, trafficking is a low risk, high income trade. 'It's always the girl's fault in the eyes of the police'[5368].

In the decade to 2008 at least 89 UK sex workers were killed – half seemingly at the hands of clients – but in over a third the cases were unsolved, compared with 90% of national murders cleared up. 'The police don't really care much about the deaths of prostitutes, unless there is an obvious serial killer on the loose'[5369].

The methodology of ACPO's 2010 report (Project Acumen) into sex trafficking in England and Wales, showing only 2,600 victims, has been criticised by a senior police source as 'farcical, amateurish, even by police research standards'. They did not find a single trafficked woman from Africa, even though there was a shelter packed with such unfortunates. An African charity (Africa) agrees the police research is farcical. The Met (there may be at least 2,500 trafficked women in London alone) disbanded its dedicated trafficking team early in 2010 – instead of it doing the research for which the uniformed officers involved in closing nuisance brothels were commissioned. There may be a political motivation in downplaying the scale of the problem – the monies involved can be diverted by police managers to other purposes. South Wales Police D.C. Jennifer Coleman claimed in an employment tribunal bosses tried to 'conceal' the scale of sex trafficking because they wanted the resources channelled to meet crime detection targets instead[5370].The Human Trafficking Centre estimates that 80% of the sex workers in the 2,300 London brothels are foreign, i.e. 4,000 were trafficked: the accommodation units for trafficked victims are entirely peopled by Africans. ACPO refused to comment on their finding no African women[5371].

A huge kerb-crawling clampdown in Nottingham's Forest Road red light district featured WPCs dressed as hookers wearing minis, high heels and stockings: they netted 50 punters, who had to pay £200 each for rehab classes[5372, 5373] . A Lib Dem Holyrood candidate and vice-convenor of the social care and wellbeing committee had to step down after being snared in an undercover vice squad operation in Aberdeen's red light harbour district[5374]. Northern Constabulary had to apologise to a Scot they had arrested in connection with a serious sex crime: the Police Complaints Commissioner for Scotland upheld four of six complaints by the man[5375]. Male undercover detectives ('pretty policemen') used to importune cottagers in gents' toilets (while homosexuality was illegal, i.e. until 1967), with often disastrous effects on the punters' professional lives (Sir John Gielgud was a victim[5376]). Gay men convicted under the old cottaging laws have won the right for their criminal records to be expunged, despite being told they would remain on their records until they were 100 years old. Some have lost jobs without knowing, e.g. a 1959 buggery charge was responsible for this in the case of one man, who claims his 'confession' half a century before had been beaten out of him. Between 50,000 and 100,000 men were convicted of same-sex offences between 1885 and 2003[5377].

Central Scotland Police Drugs Squad and the MHRA found thousands of pounds worth of Viagra and other sex drugs (Spanish Fly, Horny Goat Weed, Stamina RX and Top

Gun) in a raid in rural Stirlingshire. The internet sex shop seems also to have been trading from a Strathclyde address[5378].

Lothian and Borders Police were secretly briefed in 2001 to turn a blind eye to rent boys plying their trade in the 'pink triangle' around Calton Hill and Broughton Street in central Edinburgh, as long as no other crimes were being committed. They are the first UK force to adopt the controversial 'softly-softly' approach (a punitive approach is followed in Leeds, Bradford and London). The force had introduced a similar 'toleration policy' for vice girls in about 1980[5379].

The West Yorkshire vice squad recorded the company car number of a 45-year-old mother of two on her way to drama rehearsals, resulting in a police letter addressed to her boss, whose company owned the car. The letter said they were investigating kerb crawling, and that the sighting of the Volvo estate would be 'kept on record'. The police failed to question her on the night in question, so failing to ascertain she was a lone woman. A man from her drama group had previously been stopped and put in a police van to explain what he was doing: police promised not to stop the drama members in future[5380].

The name of Scotland Yard's vice squad has been euphemised to 'Serious Crime Directorate 9: Human Exploitation and Organised Crime Command' (SCD9 for short). The Vice Squad began in 1932 as '8 Area Clubs and Vice Unit', and its officers were involved in the Profumo affair: after they charged osteopath Stephen Ward with living off immoral earnings he committed suicide[5381] (the gay Bletchley Park computer genius Alan Turing, who helped win the war, met the same fate after the vice squad became involved).

A prostitute claimed that Met D.S. <u>Graham Golder</u>, the subject of a Sunday newspaper exposé, had been accepting bribes from her for years, but he was eventually acquitted at trial, saying he was only <u>pretending</u> to be a 'bent copper'.

It is claimed that the attitude of Yorkshire Police helped the Yorkshire Ripper escape capture, despite being interviewed nine times: not only were they averse to investigating the deaths of sex workers but some officers falsified records. Murder was a risk prostitutes accepted, and similarly homophobic police culture may have delayed the arrests of Dennis Nilsen (a former policeman) and 'Gay Slayer' Colin Ireland.

The undisputed nightclub queen of twenties London was Kate Meyrick, who managed to put <u>Sergeant Goddard</u>, the plainclothes detective in charge of nightclub prosecutions, on the take. He had put in 26 years of service, was a veteran of 234 raids, and had been showered with commendations. Edward VII established Rosa Lewis's high-class brothel for MPs, the aristocracy, American millionaires, etc., but <u>it</u> somehow managed to escape the attention of the vice squad.

In 2001 the Met's obscene publications unit told the Saatchi Gallery in London to remove photos from its exhibition, 'I am a Camera', because they were indecent, and warned a London international fine publisher to remove from sale thousands of copies of Edward Booth-Clibborn's book of the same name. There were two unposed photos of a model's children on a family holiday – the pictures were supplied by their mother[5382].

Cynthia Payne's ('Madam Cyn''s) Streatham brothel was staked out for a long period in 1979 from a flat rented across the road by the Met (one client was identified as a Scotland Yard high-ranker). When it was raided by 40 policemen, the names and photos of 53 men and

13 women were taken. The police then spent over £100,000 for a sting: two vice squad officers – one pretending to be a transsexual – became clients, presenting Cynthia with flowers and chocolates in 1986. Despite 900 pages of police evidence she was exonerated and awarded costs, and the police were ridiculed by Press and Parliament. Another infamous prostitute case involved the Defence Minister Lord Jellicoe: the Lambton scandal led to a police crackdown which found in some girls' diaries '7.30 Earl Jellico', 'Earl Jellico with Mandy, 9pm'. Jellicoe confessed a single indiscretion to Edward Heath, who accepted his resignation. Too late was it revealed the 'Jellico' referred to by the girls was a Chelsea pub.

The 'vice squad' has taken on a new meaning in Vaslui (Romania), where the police chief has been pimping for his colleagues (he received seven years in jail)[5383]. Met PCSO Sean Griffin was sacked and jailed for nine months for laundering tens of thousands from a Hertfordshire brothel run by his wife, a prostitute[5384].

A recent film, the true crime thriller 'The Bank Job', shows two vice cops demanding bribes. Soon after the robbery there was a purge of corrupt Met officers.

The police in the UK have been instrumental in a patchy de facto decriminalisation of prostitution, with the numbers found guilty dropping in a decade by 90%, and vice squads disappearing[5385]. Who says the police aren't followers of fashion? Yet an independent MSP has criticised Stephen House's 2013 blitz on Edinburgh's 18 licensed sex saunas, reverting to the era before the managing of the sex industry replaced driving it underground with punitive action. Sauna supporters say they reduce street and underage and enslaved prostitution (i.e. the impact of criminal gangs is attenuated)[5386].

The Met has been accused of endangering sex workers by its targeting of brothels in London's Olympic boroughs as part of a clean-up before the 2012 games. 'Figures on the numbers of women trafficked into the UK have been exposed as false, yet are still used as an excuse to hound sex workers'. Critics of the police say they are mistaken in believing there are many trafficked women in brothels[5387].

Lancashire Police used a 15-year-old boy to go undercover with a 16-year-old friend at Blackpool lap-dance club Aphrodite's. The boys were allowed to buy beers and ogle the girls, so that the manager could be charged with underage offences[5388]. Police are using the 'test purchase' technique employed to ensnare drug pushers to expose prostitution. Thus PC Mark Wooldridge told a court of how £50 bought a 'hug of gratitude' from an 'escort' from Silk and Lace, one of Britain's biggest agencies[5389].

A photo from Elton John's art collection, possibly by cult US photographer Nan Golding, depicting a young child, is believed to have been seized by Northumbria porn police[5390]. Police once seized copies of Pasolini's 'Salo' under s.3 of the Obscene Publications Act.

A jury has acquitted an online pornographer running a mail-order business who was targeted by an undercover vice cop, who told Michael Peacock he wanted to buy videos of 'watersports' and other legal acts (in consensual sex), which appear on a CPS list of 'extreme porn' acts it thinks may be prosecuted under the 1959 Obscene Publications Act[5391].

Up till 1990 the Met would arrest gays kissing in public (two years in jail if convicted), on such pretexts as the behaviour was (a) outraging public decency, or (b) likely to cause a breach of the peace, or (c) likely to cause harassment, alarm or distress to members of the public (Public Order Act). Because the police had chosen to make the act of kissing political, indeed criminal, Peter Tatchell's Outrage group organised a mass kiss-in of 300 couples, which brought an immediate capitulation by the police, who promised that henceforth no one would be arrested just for kissing. It is surely deeply ironic that the once institutionally homophobic police (cottager entrapment, etc) would transmute in a generation into rabid homophiliacs who will arrest Christians exercising their right of free speech to denigrate homosexuality[5392]. Once traditionalists, the police now want to be in the vanguard of social change, whether or not that change is for the worse.

Mark Daniel

Met detective sergeant Mark Daniel was found guilty of kerb-crawling in Ipswich's red light district. He was followed by two Suffolk officers as he drove a vice girl to an industrial estate (he had picked her up in his unmarked police car). He was once a vice cop. He was appealing the verdict[5393].

A secret Blue Book was issued in the 1950s by the Home Secretary to all chief constables, consisting of 42 pages of supposedly obscene publications (e.g. it contained Moll Flanders, No Orchids for Miss Blandish (James Hadley Chase), Lady Chatterley's Lover, Henry Miller, as well as much pulp fiction). In 1954 the Met's furnace burned over 167,000 books and magazines[5394]. There was a precedent: during a 1937 'clean-up' in London, the Met visited West End bookstalls and ordered that 38,000 foreign magazines be destroyed[5395].

During WWI police kept the Rink cinema under constant surveillance because of the 'indecent behaviour' going on inside between 'amorous soldiers' and 'loose young women'[5396].

The Met's vice cops were accused of overkill in their approach to the banning of porn films in the late 20th Century, e.g. they tapped the phones of alleged pornographers.

Crooked West Yorkshire cop James Hughes was jailed for a year for stealing £3,840 during raids on vice dens. He also contacted escorts using the force computer[5397].

Greater Manchester Police DC Margaret Oliver resigned in disgust because, she says, the force allowed paedophiles to escape justice for up to eight years. Oliver alleges hundreds of cases were ignored or botched. Operation Augusta, which identified 208 suspects, was abandoned[5398]. Greater Manchester Chief Constable James Anderton ('God's Cop' 1975-1991) crusaded against the sex industry, and pronounced in 1986 that gays with AIDs were 'swirling in a cesspit of their own making'. His own daughter was lesbian[5399].

Prostitutes giving favours to beat officers for turning a blind eye in the Greater Manchester force area have been documented. Everyone up to the Superintendent allegedly had secret sex both on and off duty: there were more force cars working in the car parks at night than there were patrolling the streets. Drunk women drivers would also be pulled over for libidinal fraternisation[5400].

The ready acquiescence of British police officers in enforcing dubious social policies is also found in the immediate, overwhelming support they give to social workers engaged in wrenching children from their blameless parents, and can even be compared to the enthusiastic lead taken by German doctors in trailblazing the Holocaust. Did the vice squads do more harm than good? Certainly, if one considers their corruption potential for officers.

CHAPTER XXX

HOT OFF THE PRESS

The Arrogant Policeman

Met PC <u>Alex MacFarlane</u> directed a racist tirade against a black arrestee, saying, 'You will always be a n.....', and 'Don't hide behind your colour', as was proved by secret recordings. MacFarlane also told the suspect he must have had sex with his mother and would die within five years. [1]

The Big Brother Policeman

The 'targets culture' of <u>Police Scotland</u> may be destroying trust in the police (as that culture has in the NHS), e.g. it has been blamed for the increase in the number of stop-searches (186,463 in the first three months of the new force) – an inspector issued a memo to Glasgow divisions ordering officers to use overtime 'solely for the purpose of targeting stop searches'. According to frontline officers there has been a step-change from Key Performance Indicators (KPIs) which still allowed officers to use discretion (e.g. an old lady was put off driving forever because she was given a fixed-penalty for forgetting to wear her seat belt, instead of a reminder, which is no longer allowed). The Scottish Police Federation says there are areas where individual officers <u>have</u> been set individual targets (the source of these were not apparent, and some targets are quite arbitrary). Targets encourage 'gaming' by officers (e.g. 20 youths misbehaving as a group classed as 20 separate offences, or focussing on roads where catching speeders is easy). The targets pressure on division commanders, according to the rank and file, cascades down to officers on the beat. Theoretically there are no targets, but this is not how it is since <u>Sir Stephen House</u> became Scottish police supremo: in reality there are targets. [2]

Police Scotland's frontline officers say they are being made to perform illegal and 'unethical' searches when stopping drivers on very minor offences, as well as prescription carriers (e.g. methadone users) and off-sales customers leaving chemists and licensed premises, all to increase the percentage of positive stop-searches. In relation to the latter, 'nil returns' are unacceptable, with officers forced to chase minor key performance indicator offences at the expense of doing 'real police work'. Some police divisions' league tables pinpoint the officers with most stop-searches and those catching most speeders. One officer told the Scottish press '... over two decades I can say that the morale of the individual officers is at an all-time low'. Paradoxically police are missing their rape targets. [3]

The police are asking motorists to film bad drivers on cameras mounted on dashboards so the evidence can be used by police in court. Thousands of people have already fitted these 'dashcams'. [4]

Police Scotland has made 25,000 applications (via their assistant constables) to check communications 'metadata' (dates, times and duration of phone calls) in four years. Scottish police snooped on 1,000 phone calls, emails, texts and social media messages in one month, under R.I.P.A., in the autumn of 2012. [5]

It has been claimed that suppressing football fans' 'offensive' songs and the ramblings of online trolls destroys the ideal of free speech. Working class people are being imprisoned for speech crimes, an incredibly authoritarian development. [6]

Police Scotland was accused of setting a dangerous precedent - characteristic of a police state - by cancelling a sold-out music gig at the last minute. despite the promoters processing all the risk assessments required. It is believed to be a first such controversial decision for Police Scotland. A promoter successfully sued Manchester City Council in 2010 for a large sum over a cancelled concert. [7]

The Bogus Policeman

A Halloween reveller was charged with impersonating a police officer after trying to get into a Glasgow nightclub in a stolen female sergeant's uniform. [8]

Tom Winsor, HM Inspector of Constabulary for England and Wales, has never been a policeman yet has been wearing a police uniform on ceremonial occasions. Is this correct, but more to the point, is it legal? [9]

The Criminal Policeman

Child protection detective Gary Quigley was charged with trying to poison a colleague by replacing a Powerade drink with car screenwash (he wanted to teach a soft-drink thief a lesson). He denied administering a poisonous or noxious substance with intent, although in a police interview he had stated; 'I accept culpability for my actions. I am extremely sorry and deeply remorseful for what has happened.' [10]

Three armed Met DPG (Diplomatic Protection Group) officers guarding Downing Street have been arrested and a fourth interviewed but not arrested, in connection with allegations they exchanged hardcore porn ('of an extreme sexual nature') on their smartphones while on duty. The unit was also at the centre of 'Plebgate'. One of the arrestees (all of whose homes have been searched) was suspended, the other two put on restricted duties, as was the fourth man. Three DPG officers face a gross misconduct hearing regarding the leaking to the press of the Plebgate log; four others face Plebgate charges. The four arrests were only released by the Met when The Times inquired. [11]

Corruption

Seasoned 'Observer' columnist Henry Porter says, after compiling a 330-page file on cases involving police reported in the media, 'We must now consider ... that the police service in England and Wales is so infected by a culture of dishonesty, expediency and outright corruption that radical reform is now the only option'. Many of solicitor Iain Gould's clients don't bother with the IPCC's complaints procedure because they know they will fail at an early stage, so they go right away to civil law, when the police will settle 'without prejudice'.

11 members of the Scottish Police Credit Union defaulted on their loans in 2013, losing the lender £78,000, while in 2012 £65,000 was written off because of 20 bad debts. Tougher loan conditions are being introduced, but some officers feel this could make their colleagues vulnerable to corruption. [12]

CAVEAT CIVIS

The 2014 Ellison report tells how <u>Hogan-Howe's</u> 2012 review of corruption failed to disclose the fact that (1) almost all the corruption files (a 'lorry load' gathered over the decade since 1993 by Operation Othona) were secretly shredded over two days in 2003, or that (2) there were <u>surviving</u> records the Met failed to reveal. 41 boxes of Othona files (release of some of which have been restricted for 84 years) were crucially hidden from the 1998 Macpherson Inquiry. When Commander Roy Clark, anti-corruption head, was told his files had been shredded he was shocked, but fortunately his summary of the types of corruption he found escaped the grim reaper. The Ellison findings led to the Home Secretary ordering a public inquiry into undercover policing. [13]

'You heard what the commissioner said: "No more shredding of evidence" . . . ketchup?'

A court found (2013) David Hunt, the 'Long Fella', was a gangland boss involved in money laundering, fraud and 'extreme violence'. Witness intimidation and illegal drug imports also feature in the Hunt story. Thus in his unsuccessful lawsuit against The Sunday Times the latter's witness security guards failed to turn up, and another firm wouldn't accept the contract. Operation Tiberius (201) found Hunt's 'invulnerability' was facilitated by corrupt Met officers, who told the syndicate about its vehicles having police tracking devices on them, did checks for Hunt on the police computer, leaked information about a financial probe into him, as well as about a police enquiry into London gangs, including Hunt's. Tiberius names four detectives 'associated' with his gang, and Operation Blackjack, a covert inquiry, found evidence of a violent attack by Hunt, but the victim later withdrew his police statements. Moreover, three Met whistleblowers wrote a 54 page legal submission saying Hunt had used Met 'sleepers' to evade justice for three decades. [14]

If you underpay police officers ... the consequence is corruption.' Sir Hugh Orde. [15]

South Yorkshire PC Sarah Greaves pleaded guilty to offering to supply cocaine. [16]

Met DC Peter Cripps, the Old Bailey heard, leaked the imminent arrest of News of the World editor Andy Coulson to The Guardian, as well as other hacking - linked arrests, yet he wasn't charged, being allowed to quietly resign (with a sizeable pension?). Prosecuting him wouldn't have been 'in the public interest'. Yet DCI April Casburn got 18 months for complaining that officers were being seconded to hacking enquiries from more serious duties such as murder and anti-terrorism. In her case she communicated with a down-market red-top tabloid! [17]

Dundee PC David Fearn was charged with stalking his ex-partner over 20 months [using the CCTV at her hair salon (via a remote link), monitoring her emails, trying to access her mobile phone, loitering near her house, harassing her car with his while driving, menacing and swearing at her]. He was bailed to appear later at Dundee Sheriff Court and banned from two streets. [18]

Lothian and Borders PC Greig Anderson was paid a salary of £115,000 while suspended, after a conviction (2011) for neglect of duty following drugs seizure items(including cannabis and cocaine) found at his home and that of his girlfriend. [19]

An alleged police scam - claiming rewards from insurance companies where goods have been recovered and thieves convicted - has been revealed in 'Fifty Shades of Black 'n' Blue' by ex-cop Stephen Hayes, Thus one officer reportedly used Granada TV's make-up department to disguise himself when he went to collect the reward (wig, beard, false nose and black teeth). [20]

A traffic cop received a year's sentence for pocketing 'fines' from drivers. [21]

The Cruel Policeman

Lockerbie campaigner Dr. Jim Swire has told how he was threatened by a Scottish cop with arrest after viewing his daughter's body. The policeman said, 'What the f... are you doing here? You'd better sign this f...... form or you're going into a cell'. That was his introduction to Scottish policemen. [22]

Essex Police CID Officer Hannah Notley was jailed for not only failing to pass a rape file to the CPS, but also lying to superiors and the alleged rape victim that the CPS was not going to prosecute. Notley pled guilty to misconduct in public office (including naming of the CPS lawyer who had 'dropped' the case). [23]

For the first time Hillsborough fans have told (to BBC Newsnight) how they were intimidated by West Midlands Police, who investigated the disaster. Some officers treated them as anti-police, wasting police time, instead of victims, so their own trauma was aggravated. One 19-year-old was told by a policeman who didn't like his evidence: 'how can you give evidence like that?' 'Are you a left-wing agitator? Do you belong to the Socialist Workers Party?' Wearing a Mandela shirt was a red rag to the police bull! Another teenage fan had a home visit from two officers who sent his parents away while their son was questioned; the police 'stood around him oppressively', saying 'Just sign this', without letting him read the statement! One fan was told he hadn't been at the game! Another said the whole exercise was a cover-up of a cover-up. [24]

The beleaguered Police Federation has been accused of 'freezing out' its recently appointed director of communications Fiona McElroy, who, with a colleague who resigned in sympathy, are thought to have raised serious financial concerns about the organisation's accounting practices, such that the taxman argues that some expenses should be regarded as perks. An insider at the governing body, The Joint Central Committee, alleges a culture of heavy drinking at the federation hotel, as well as an excessively liberal expenses regime. There are also serious claims of the bullying of junior staff. McElroy says she suffered inappropriate behaviours and attitudes: her dismissal without due process contradicts the Federation's standards when their employers are mistreated by <u>others</u>. Six officers enjoy luxury surroundings at their Surrey based HQ in Leatherhead. [25]

<u>The Eccentric Policeman</u>

Police Scotland's boss Sir <u>Stephen House</u> has personally policed the motorway on a marked motocyle, regularly travelling the M8 on it. It is claimed he pulled over a car without back-up initially. Graeme Pearson, an ex-chief constable and now an MSP, together with a serving officer (who insisted on anonymity), have expressed concerns about their chief constable acting in this way. While Sir Stephen was in charge at Strathclyde, lower ranks reportedly were on alert for a lone cop on a motorcycle, and he is on record as asserting that the smoking ban had helped fuel murder rates. [26] Sir Stephen is also considering removing from his rank and file simple pleasures such as listening to music. [27]

Hertfordshire Police have told a cancer charity fundraiser to cover up a corpses and skeletons Halloween display in his garden.

In 17th Century England the bobby's predecessor, the constable, was used to arrest suspected witches (e.g. on a charge such as plotting to kill a man by witchcraft). Thus the Pendle 'witches' (about 20 individuals) were taken into custody by the constable, to await trial in cramped conditions at Lancaster Castle, with the possibility of capital punishment (by hanging) if found guilty of witchcraft (and if they had not succumbed to 'jail fever'). [28]

Police Scotland are turning out to dozens of reports of paranormal or alien activity: the Strathclyde force attended 57 ghostly incidents in three years from 2010. [29]

Nottinghamshire Police have been accused of trivialising rape after they distributed a bizarre poem about rape; ' Twas the Night Before Christmas' was adapted as 'The Nightmare Before Christmas!' and seemed to be aimed at children. [30]

The Central Motorway Group of the Midlands Police has acquired a £240,000 McLaren MP412C (a 207mph supercar), hoping it will break down barriers between police and motorists by encouraging conversation and relationships. [31]

Police Scotland CID officers say its logo now being placed on all 'unmarked' cars (as part of its' commitment to public visibility') defeats the point of working undercover and exposes them to ridicule, One force source says the branding is to avoid entrapment claims, but another source denied this. [32]

The police were rumoured to be using Ladybird books to teach car mechanics to officers.

Nottinghamshire Police plan to put ads on the sides of squad cars and on huge billboards outside police stations. [33]

Photographs of young police trainees letting their hair down at Ashford Police Training Centre in Kent, between 1973 and 2006 (when it closed), have recently been revealed by an ex-officer whistle blower, who was shocked by the mischievous and rule-breaking behaviour (e.g. theft of beer from the bar). Policemen wore Nazi regalia e.g. of a U boat commander and would black up or wear the uniform of a police sergeant (against the law?), while female recruits cavorted in suspenders, stockings and police blouses. These antics are accompanied (on a secret Facebook posting with a caption 'what happens at Ashford stays at Ashford') by sexist and homophobic jokes. One posting even suggests Ashford taught them to 'take suspects down an alley and sort 'em out!' An 'I survived Ashford Police Training Centre' association has over 2,000 officers and ex-officers as members [see also The Arrogant Policeman chapter]. [34]

The Familial Policeman

Tayside WPC Keri Murray's brother was jailed for threatening to kill her horse and stab her if she didn't pay his £3,000 drug debts. He also admitted assaulting a man to his severe injury in 2012. [35]

The Fictional Policeman

The nickname 'Plod' originated from Enid Blyton's children's books (the first, Little Noddy Goes To Toyland, dates from 1949). PC Plod cycled or plodded around his beat. The name only became common slang in the seventies. 'PC Plod' was the title of a 1971 play by The Scaffold which contained sketches and poems about the boys in blue. A single, WPC Hodges, was released under the name PC Plod by Gorman (of The Scaffold). Blyton's Plod is thought to be based on a rural beat PC where she often stayed. [36]

The Financial Policeman

Compensation

Gwent PC Mike Baillon, who smashed up an OAP's car was awarded £440,00 compensation (for loss of earnings and pension, and alleged bullying by fellow officers). He said he became a 'laughing stock' because of You Tube video footage showing him flying into a rage. Baillon hit the stroke victim's car's window 15 times with his baton, while a colleague kicked the windscreen. Amazingly, both officers were cleared of misconduct. [37]

Police have won age discrimination compensation claims worth millions after being forced to retire. In a test case five chief constables were found to have used police regulations improperly to rid themselves of ageing officers. [38]

Greedy

The Rubens, one of London's top hotels, is popular with senior police officers. [30]

While there will be significant numbers of Police Scotland civilian staff made redundant, over 100 senior officers are being promoted with large pay increases. [40]

The sale of 20 'surplus' Police Scotland properties in 2014 raised over £2m, with a further 12 buildings up for sale (all but one of Edinburgh's famous police boxes are to be let go). The drive to close police premises is claimed to be removing the public's choice to be able to report a crime locally or speak to an officer in person, without consultation. [41]

Police Scotland gave police chiefs an above inflation pay rise of £10,000 while making £4.2m cuts. Sir Stephen House is now (2014) on £208,000 p.a. [42]

Lord Chief Justice Thomas has warned the MET that they risk damaging their independence by acting on behalf of big business in a private lawsuit. The police were promised a 25% share of compensation Virgin Media hoped to recover from fraudsters in a private criminal prosecution. The police made sworn statements, a Sergeant Smith applying to magistrates for arrest warrants: the court wasn't told that Virgin would be the prosecutor. £8m was awarded to Virgin to be confiscated from the criminal profits, but the Met only received £4000 from the company. Such a private prosecution, which may need police support, may be quicker than the civil courts and may win larger sums. Such privatised policing surely means a two-tier justice system, possibly leading to officers being selective as to which crimes to investigate, the cash nexus biasing whole police teams. 'Creeping' privatisation may risk the poor being unable to afford justice the rich can, and may be another nail in the police coffin of trust. The Home Office and Mayor's office of policing refused to comment. [43]

Waste

Police in England and Wales are still, despite widespread cuts, spending public funds on art works: nearly £50,000 on artistic sandblasting (Hampshire), £51,000 on a steel and glass sculpture (Northumbria), £75,000 on a lighthouse sculpture (South Wales), £13,000 on portraits of ex-commissioners (the Met). [44]

Up to 200 Police Scotland officers have become desk-based to help their superiors devise cost-cutting reforms, such as taking other officers partly off the beat to assume the duties of 67 legal document staff who have been given voluntary redundancy. [45]

70 Scottish police stations whose counters are being closed to save money are being expensively refurbished. [46]

The Harmful Policeman

When columnist Peter Hitchens 'dared to criticise the police' in The Mail on Sunday, the response from many officers was 'coarse abuse'. [47]

Police Scotland's demand that sauna licences in Edinburgh should be conditional, on no 'items of a sexual nature' being allowed, would ban condoms, which are acknowledged to help prevent AIDS. Stephen House is now widening the police objections to gay saunas, raising accusations of homophobia and misogyny, despite allegations that the saunas have police clients. Police objections to two gay saunas were rejected by the licensing authority. The police's disastrous policy of closing injecting equipment suppliers in the 1980s led to the HIV Edinburgh epidemic. [48]

Ex-policeman Bill Bowles says of a Carnoustie PC who left his marked car in a disabled parking space outside a police station: 'It is very hypocritical of them to pull people up for things if the public see police officers doing exactly the same thing'. [49]

Plebgate Minister Mitchell's GP wife has spoken of black nurses in her practice who commented that the 'stitching up' of Plebgate was 'just like Bristol' (i.e. what happens to black citizens there).

Six Greater Manchester officers mistook a one-legged pensioner for a burglar when he tried to break into his home. They pinned him down such that his elbow was broken and his shoulder dislocated. He alleges he was thrown to the floor. The great-grandfather was awarded £45,000 compensation. [50]

Apart from foreign police helicopter crashes, there have been four UK incidents: 1990 – Eastwood Toll, Newton Mearns, Glasgow – when a sergeant died and two other officers along with the pilot, were injured; 1998 – border between Leicestershire and Northants – when a PC died; 2000 – a house in Cardiff, when no one was injured; 2002 – Muirkirk, Ayrshire – when 2 officers and the pilot were injured; 2013 – Clutha pub on the Clyde in central Glasgow – nine died, including two officers and the pilot, dozens injured. [51]

The IPCC was considering launching a Hillsborough-type inquiry into the 'Battle of Orgreave' (1984) after spending over a year investigating the infamous miners clash with police, who were accused of making up statements: the prosecution of all 95 miners charged by police collapsed. Lawsuits were brought against police for malicious prosecution, unlawful arrest and assault, with almost £0.5m compensation paid by South Yorkshire

Police to 39 miners (there was photographic evidence of miners beaten with truncheons). Two former senior officers (Simon Humphrey and Dai Davies) both chief superintendents, condemned the idea of a public inquiry. [52]

A Strathclyde Police probationer and graduate was told to resign after an anonymous call to Crimestoppers (allegedly by a colleague) smearing her as corrupt (in bed with gangsters). Three months later Chief Constable Campbell Corrigan said a mistake had been made and apologised to her personally, asking her to return with full pay (she could also choose where she could work). Superintendent Steven Reed has been suspended for a year - the Crown Office is deciding if he was involved, together with a female superintendent facing a wilful misconduct probe. In the latter's case it is claimed she failed to act on information relating to Reed and the victim', who was refused information as to what had been said about her. [53]

The Met has asked the Home Office for water cannons 'as a tactical measure' despite their 'limited usefulness' in riots. This ignores the negative worldwide image their use would represent in the heart of democracy. [54]

RTAs

PC Mark Williamson, who admitted dangerous driving (speeding through a red light and crashing into a police van), was given an absolute discharge at Inverness Sheriff Court. [55]

Aberdeenshire police driver <u>Allan Masson</u> was charged with dangerous driving after his police car allegedly caused serious injury to a pedestrian. [56]

Ex-officer <u>Andrew Caine</u> was fined £270 and given points after admitting careless driving. He lives near a school, drove his car at some of its pupils and their teacher on a pedestrian crossing. The teacher told Inverness Sheriff Court he had to shout 'You will kill the children'. [57]

Off-duty Edinburgh PC <u>Hamaad Khalid</u> killed a man in a hit and run, but has never been prosecuted, so the victim's widow is suing the (now resigned) policeman for £1.1m for damages. A charge of leaving the scene of an accident was dropped (would a member of the public have received such consideration?). Lothian and Borders admitted failing to breathalyse their officer, and a police report differed from a forensic postmortem on how the car struck the victim. [58]

A Durham Police driver escaped prosecution after showing off to a passenger he could drive at 140mph. Road safety charity Break said he should have been prosecuted. Instead his identity was kept secret and he was suspended from traffic duties while the case was referred to the IPCC. Would he have been charged (attracting a criminal conviction and driving ban) if he hadn't been a police officer? [59]

Scots police sergeant Tony Wallace threatened to make a man's day a 'living hell' because the man had photographed a serious car accident scene (the photos were later posted on You Tube). The officer was recorded saying: 'We'll nick you now and I will make your day a living hell because you'll be in that cell all day. What I'll probably do is I will ask for you to be remanded in custody and I will put you before the magistrate... You're lucky I didn't knock you out'. He seized the camera but returned it. [60]

Police Scotland officer <u>Michael Fullerton</u> was to stand trial accused of crashing his car (while on duty) to the injury of another motorist. He denied careless driving. [61]

The Historical Policeman

Debenhams department store, founded in 1813, established its own special Constabulary in 1899. [62]

The Incompetent Policeman

Sins of Commission

Police Scotland plans to close stations in some of the country's worst crime blackspots, e.g. the front-runner Anderston City Centre (though Anderston is narrowly beaten with respect to car crime by Govan, as part of Southside Central, which has Scotland's third highest crime rates). Anderston is worst for violence, drugs and vandalism, and second worst for burglary. [63]

In the Mark Duggan inquest Home Office pathologist Professor Derrick Pounder contradicted critical evidence from V53, the police shooter, on which of the two bullets killed Duggan in 2011 (triggering the worst English riots for many years). Pounder says Duggan's biceps was wounded first (the non-fatal shot), his chest <u>second</u> (the fatal shot); the marksman says it was the reverse of this. He also says the bullet couldn't have pursued the 46-degree trajectory inside the victim's body if he had been standing 'more or less upright', as V53 told the inquest. Again, military surgical expert Professor Jonathan Clasper, commissioned by the IPCC, said it was 'very unlikely' Duggan could have thrown the gun 7.3 metres after being shot, and Pounder confirmed this, which would again contradict the police assertions. [64]

Police gave out 200,000 cautions in England and Wales in 2012, of which 4,673 were repeats (some multiple). [65]

<u>The City of London Police</u> is paying £100,000 compensation to 11 'Space Hijackers' G20 protesters charged with impersonating officers: they were cleared. [66]

An HMIC report has revealed that <u>West Yorkshire Police</u> prioritise car crime and burglary over child sex crime. [67]

Despite Scottish police stations showing crime dropping to a 39-year low, in 2012 police officers were cited by the Crown Office and Procurator Fiscal Service to appear in court a record 41,410 times for <u>solemn proceedings</u> (i.e. trials of the most serious offences requiring a jury). [68]

Three North Yorkshire Police vans surrounded a minibus driven by a teacher taking her pupils on a school trip and accused her of stealing it (they were acting on a database report that should have been deleted). [69]

In the case of the Ding revenge murders (by the frustrated Chinese medicine practitioner) one of the victims had called 999, but the police were sent to the wrong address, only visiting the correct address two days after the murder. [70]   Police Scotland is trying to introduce an appointment system for 'minor' crimes, victims of some assaults, vandalism and thefts 'being fobbed off' with an arrangement to see an officer at a later date. The force is still pursuing the idea of makeshift offices in supermarkets while closing many police station counters. [71]

Child protection experts say new ACPO guidelines dealing with missing persons are putting vulnerable children at greater risk of abuse. The number of children listed as 'absent' will now not warrent an immediate police response, though 'absent' may miss children who are sexually compromised but go missing only for short periods.[72]

Blundering Scottish Crime and Drug Enforcement Agency officers caused illegal search of a suspect's car(they failed to give their uniformed colleagues the background information needed to make a lawful arrest). This means £215,000 of confiscated cash may have to be returned.[73]

Sins of Omission

Up to 1,000 killers have escaped justice in Scotland because police haven't tracked them down or prosecuted them. A second FOIA request by a tabloid has identified at least 750 homicides that are 'unresolved', though DS Alan Buchanan says: 'There is no current accurate record of all homicides committed in Scotland'. [74]

Police Scotland's Chief Constable Sir Stephen House has at last recognised the extent of 'back-filling' – beat officers being transferred to axed civilian staff jobs – when answering questions about an Audit Scotland report which revealed a lack of financial planning within the force. Despite cuts affecting front-line policing Police Scotland is spending £1,300 on things like Gaelic translations of official documents and the new force logo. [75]

Tom Winsor, HM chief Inspector of constabulary, is to make certain police forces (in England and Wales) are inspected about their 'honour crimes' failures. A 2009 ACPO research paper on 'honour- based violence' listed 14 such crimes - acid attacks, self harm suicides, child marriage, female genital mutilation (FGM), bride payments, blood feuds, murders, etc. The Karma Nirvanda charity gets many calls from officers who say they had received hardly any training in the subject. [76]

Chief constables are liable to dismissal if they miss targets, while front-line officers get bonuses if they keep crime figures down (e.g. rape victim recast as having 'mental' problems). [77]

Three police forces (South Wales, South Yorkshire and Bedfordshire) repeatedly ignored warnings from 2008 that rock star Ian Watkins was a dangerous paedophile. He wanted to kidnap children and had rape fantasies about them. By the time he was charged, six forces were inundated with tip-offs from girlfriends, fans and Crimestoppers informants. One ex-lover was warned by officers, who refused to probe her claims, that she could be charged with harassment. Watkins even attacked a baby the IPCC was investigating, particularly as to whether his celebrity status affected the police response. [78]

Rochdale MP Simon Danszuk said: 'Greater Manchester Police were discriminating against poor, white working-class girls- actively ignoring abuse going on'. The Chief Constable's attitude about the trafficked girls was 'defensive': he blamed the girls' 'lifestyle choices'. [79]

The Met were accused of giving celebrities special treatment by turning a blind eye to middle-class drug use following the decision not to prosecute Nigella Lawson (she confessed in court that she took cocaine, and two former assistants claimed she repeatedly used the drug). The Met said criminal proceedings could damage the criminal justice system and deter victims being 'candid' in the witness box. Police did not formally interview Nigella. [80]

A woman subjected to alleged sexual abuse by suspended Lib Dem MP Mike Hancock claims Hampshire Police failed to (1) take a formal written statement, (2) ask her to describe relevant parts of the MP's body, (3) ensure, when detectives called to take crucial video evidence, their camera equipment was working, (4) take her to a special suite where women alleging sex crimes are normally taken. The police reportedly lost a disc with evidence from the complainant's phone, but this was later found. She is taking legal action against the MP. [81]

Detective Superintendent <u>Steve Pilcher,</u> who led the Sian O'Callaghan murder, faced dismissal after being found guilty of gross misconduct. He failed to follow proper procedures by not taking killer Christopher Hillwell to a police station or cautioning him, after the killer told him of a second victim, Becky Edwards. The killer couldn't be tried for the second murder even though the body was found. [82]

Scotland's police watchdog found numerous failings in the police handling of a missing 37-year-old mental patient search, which ended with the discovery of the man's body in his Edinburgh home after a weekend visit to his mother, who raised 'significant concerns' six days before police forced entry to the vulnerable person's home. Professor John McNeill recommended changes to procedures and additional training at Scotland's E Division. [83]

The Insecure Policeman

The worst security breach at Buckingham Palace in three decades involved a man climbing over a 12ft fence, evading dozens of armed police to access a state room on the first floor (by apparently kicking a door down), only alerting the authorities by triggering a motion camera. A former head of the Met's royal protection squad says the breach showed terrorists could successfully enter the Palace. [84]

There have been 108 reported thefts (including from nuclear submarines) in five years at Scottish military bases, suggesting MOD police have questions to answer, but it took a FOIA request to learn this. [85]

A thief stole the keys of a marked Perth patrol car from the city's police station, leading dozens of officers on a dangerous high-speed chase for 20 miles.(e.g. he overtook two cars on a blind corner). [86]

The Lethal Policeman

Traffic officers seconded to convey critically ill people to hospital because of a lack of ambulances have faced internal affairs or IPCC probes when their passengers died. [87]

<u>Clive 'Taffy' Williams</u> was the Royal Military Police officer who led a hit 'ghost squad' – the Military Reaction Force (MRF) – accused of murdering IRA suspects. He was named by a police colleague in a Panorama exposé of the MRF. [88]

Manslaughter by proxy

Avon and Somerset Police have admitted they 'failed' to protect a disabled Bristol man, <u>Bijan Ebrahimi,</u> from being killed by a lynch mob who set him on fire because they wrongly thought he was a paedophile. He <u>had</u> been detained by police following false allegations that he had taken inappropriate photos of children. Other cases where police failed to act include: (1) <u>Clare Wood</u> was murdered in 2009 by George Appleton in Greater Manchester after meeting him on a social website. She had told police of her fears, but they failed to warn her that he had a history of partner violence. (2) <u>Julia Pemberton</u> and her son were stabbed multiple times in 2003 by her estranged husband Alan – Newbury police ignored his repeated threats to kill her. (3) A Derbyshire mother and son died from repeated stabbing by the child's mentally ill father Andrew Cairns, who committed suicide. The force's belief that the victims were at 'high risk of homicide' was not communicated to the mother. (4) Mark Chivers served 15 years in Germany for murdering his girlfriend, and went on to murder Maria Stubbings in 2008 after being in repeated contact with Essex Police. [89]

Derbyshire Police failings contributed to the death of Rachel Slack, murdered by her mentally ill ex-partner on police bail. [90]

Newly released (2014) files reveal the Met and Special Branch were told authoritatively that the 1984 Libyan Embassy protest was likely to be violent, but they allowed the demonstration to proceed, leading to WPC Yvonne Fletcher's death by gunshot. [91]

Custody deaths

Jake Michael died in custody while suffering a cocaine-induced 'excited delirium' – he was subdued by a pepper spray and up to 11 officers. [92]

Kingsley Burrell Brown, a black father of two with no mental illness background, died in 2011 after calling West Midlands Police for help. His son says his father was beaten up by police on his way to a mental hospital, and he was refused the right to see his family. Four officers were arrested over the death and the CPS has received the file from the IPCC. [93]

Shootings

An unidentified firearms Flying Squad (SC807) officer shot himself in the leg inside a Putney police building. A report has been sent to the IPCC. Each year police marksmen fire their guns oftener by mistake than when responding to actual threats. [94]

There have been 25 fatal shootings by police in a decade. Police trained to use firearms are advised to 'shoot to stop' (shooting at upper body). [95]

The Lustful Policeman

Heterosexual

Scotland Yard lawyers are arguing in court that sex can be used (i.e. may be 'necessary and proportionate') to advance the machinations of the Met's undercover officers, though in public the Met insisted it is not an authorised tactic. [96]

Grampian Police ex-chief superintendent Ian Paterson from Aberdeenshire was found guilty of groping several women and making inappropriate remarks. He was described by the depute fiscal as a sexual predator. [97] He was jailed for 18 months for sexual molestation. [98]

Scotland PC Gary Cryans was accused at Glasgow Sheriff Court of indecently assaulting four constables (one on several occasions in a public vehicle). [99]

P.C. Gavin Angus has denied charges of sexually assaulting two women at Grampian Police HQ and elsewhere. [100]

Paedophilia

Lanarkshire Special Constable <u>Barry Strang</u> was facing prison after being caught with indecent pictures of young boys: he had been volunteering with children at a leisure centre and swapping his porn images. He was placed on the sex offenders' register. [101]

'Depraved' ex-Lancashire Police sergeant <u>Jeffrey Lake</u> has been jailed for 18 years after being extradited from Australia, where he fled in 2002 to escape 20 charges of rape, indecency with a child and child cruelty (the victims were between four and 19 years old), committed in the 1960s and 1970s. His victims attempted suicide. [102]

Grampian Police sergeant Neil Shand was accused of taking (or allowing to be taken) indecent photos and of possessing child pornography images at his Aberchirder home over a two-year period. The suspended officer denied the charges and lodged special defences of alibi and incrimination. [103]

The Mentally Ill Policeman

Every member of the Armed Forces will be screened by the Forces In Mind Trust (a charity) using the structured mental health assessment to try to detect PTSD, depression and alcoholism. [104] The MOD's former head of psychology, Professor Janice Hacker Hughes, says army recruits should have mental health checks to reduce the chance of later PTSD (over 20% of troops quit with 'psychological wounds'). [105]

Devon and Cornwall PC <u>Gail Crocker</u> committed suicide with an overdose of tramadol and diphenhydramine. She had rowed with her husband over a text message to a police colleague she had dated, which she had by mistake sent to her husband. [106]

Following the PC <u>Keith Wallis</u> admission of lying in the Plebgate case, and Sir Bernard Hogan-Howe's resultant grovelling apology to Andrew Mitchell, it was revealed the Wallis defence is that he was psychologically disturbed at the time of concocting his story. This raises the question for the Met as to why a mentally unstable officer was allowed to work in the Diplomatic Protection Group, especially as his psychiatric history was 'ongoing'. [107]

After 9/11 scores of New York cops feigned mental illness to claim illegal disability benefits costing hundreds of millions of dollars. When UK officers take medical retirement they usually claim mental problems. [108]

Alcohol Problems

Renfrewshire PC <u>Fred Deakin</u>, an ex-soldier, was stopped while drink driving on the M8, but was banned for four years when he repeated the offence six months later - he nearly caused carnage while over thrice the limit. He was granted a medical discharge from the force. [109]

When PCSO <u>Andrew Seston</u> pulled over a driver he suspected of drink driving, they got into a argument, so back-up police were called - they found their <u>colleague</u> was twice over the limit. [110]

Suicide

Traffic cop <u>David Rathband</u> threatened to hang himself while estranged wife watched by putting his phone onto Facetime. He did hang himself at a later date. [111]

Neurosis (stress)

Eight of the 43 England and Wales forces refused to provide (under FOIA) stress related sickness rates: the other 35 have 787 officers signed off, with some of the smaller, largely rural areas having the some of the highest rates (the highest was Derbyshire). [112]

The PC Policeman

Chief Constable Alex Marshall, in charge of the College of Policing, wants the law changed to allow positive discrimination in favour of BEM officers. [113]

The Perverse Policeman

York officers arrested (and questioned for 45 minutes) a stag night dwarf stuntman dressed as a policeman, complete with handcuffs and baton, which were confiscated. The dwarf was attached to a pantomime horse. [114]

A grandmother with no criminal background who argued with the parent of children who kept sounding a car horn, was threatened by the mother, who had assault and affray convictions. Police arrested the grandmother, who had her legs bound together and placed in a 'spit hood' in front of jeering onlookers. Magistrates threw out the case against her. [115]

An Edinburgh jogger was stopped and quizzed by a Police Scotland officer armed with a pistol, CS spray and Taser, because his weighted exercise jacket was 'not normal', resembling a police flak jacket. The startled man, asked to provide his details on pain of being arrested for 'obstructing an officer in his duty', filmed the cop but was asked to turn off his camera because it infringed the officer's human rights. [116]

A gardener whose alarm went off in his premises tackled two burglars, one of whom suffered three broken limbs. The burglars received £75 fines, whereas the businessman was charged with GBH, which carries a maximum penalty of life, but at trial Andrew Woodhouse was cleared. [117]

Police Scotland reports that 80% of their stop-and-searches find nothing untoward [Scots are six times more liable to be stopped than people south of the border]. Negative results may well cause the innocent who are stopped to lose trust in and respect for the police. A quarter of 1.25m stops are unlawful. [118]

Though a nine-month toddler was wrapped up for winter, when a passer-by reported the mother, a nutritionist, for exposing a child to the cold, two officers were sent to question her. When she refused to give her name, one cop asked: 'So you don't want to cooperate?' [119]

Police in Rugeley, Staffs. arrested a shop owner who posted a couple of tasteless jokes about Nelson Mandela on the internet. He was questioned for eight hours, fingerprinted and DNA swab taken (as well as his computer). [120]

The Political Policeman

David Miranda, partner of journalist Glenn Greenwald who has, with the help of The Guardian, broken stories about the US National Security Agency, was detained by the Met for nine hours under terrorism powers, because he was thought to be promoting a 'political or ideological cause'. The director of Liberty said the police assessment represented a 'chilling' threat to democracy, while the Index on Censorship, which campaigns for free speech, said the police justification for holding Miranda was ' very dangerous' for investigative journalism. [121]

West Yorkshire Police and Fire Brigade Union pickets have confirmed that uniformed police (including a female officer) have been used to drive 'scab' fire engines to break firefighters' strike action. The picket lines include Leeds city centre fire station. Police have been used throughout the West Yorkshire strike. [122]

It has been claimed that the Police Scotland clampdown on Edinburgh saunas is an example of the unelected making the policy of the elected (council) unsustainable. The police are mounting legal challenges whenever the council withholds licences as well as when it grants them. [123]

A 1970s' South London Maoist sect which recruited female students from abroad was raided in 1978 by police (it had been under surveillance by the Met and MI5), with 14 arrested. It was claimed that the occupants of the Workers' Institute of Marxism-Leninism-Mao Tsedung Thought (whose leaders Balakrishnan and his wife Chanda were accused of white slavery three decades later) were assaulted and racially abused by some of the 200 officers (with dogs and riot shields): oppression by a fascist police state. The group inspired the classic TV comedy series 'Citizen Smith' [124]

Dozens of University of London students were arrested by the Met for protesting against university policy. Their bail conditions were draconian (e.g. the president of the Student Union was forbidden from protesting on any campus, and couldn't congregate with more than another three persons). As a result the NUS was organising (December 2013) a nationwide campus protest. [125]

The Secretive Policeman

A former child protection officer with the (now defunct) National Association of Young People In Care claims a Special Branch detective held a firearm to his head to halt his probing the notorious VIP paedophile ring based at the Elm Guest House in Barnes. He says he was pinned to a wall and choked, then warned to 'back away'. His colleagues (and even victims) were also 'routinely' threatened by Met officers acting 'like gangsters' when the scandal was revealed in 1990: he alleges '... Special Branch could do what they liked, they were a law unto themselves ... Victims who were actually abused at Elm House were also physically stopped from coming to speak to us at the NAYPIC office in north London.

I witnessed Special Branch officers manhandling them and turning them away with a warning to keep their mouths shut. It was blatant, it was open ... In the end we had to meet victims at a local community centre without the knowledge of the police ...'. The whistleblower also says he never found out who inflicted three bullet holes on his kitchen window. The guest house was raided by the vice squad in 1982, but allegations of paedophilia were never pursued. Belatedly Operation Fernbridge officers have now charged two men with sexual offences, and campaigner Bill Maloney says: 'These police cover-ups to protect the wealthy and the powerful need to stop now'. The Met refused to comment. [126]

'Out of the 'Plebgate' affair comes a thickening stench of falsehood and evasion, involving far more than a few individuals acting alone ... The self-inflicted damage done to the force is ... appalling'. [127]

Dyfed Powys Crime Commissioner Christopher Salmon says Plebgate 'appears uncomfortably close to a police conspiracy ... [their] culture is too closed, too defensive, too politicised and, in some cases, feral'. By autumn, 2013, the Greater Manchester Police review of how the Met handled Plebgate had not been released, though it was completed by mid-summer. Though Sir Bernard Hogan-Howe ordered the review to create 'more openness' he has refused to make it public. It has been established that it was Simon Chesterton, Deputy Chief Constable of West Mercia, who blocked disciplinary action against the three officers so controversially attacked by the IPCC. [128]

Surrey Police's interview with Savile was 'too informal' and 'lacked rigour', the police concerned being too sympathetic and failing to probe his answers. Transcripts of the interview had to be released under FOIA. [129] A retired Leeds policeman has said: 'There wasn't a copper in Leeds who didn't know Savile was a pervert ... The police were in the palm of his hand'. The officer, when he confronted Savile with an underage girl, was threatened by him: 'If you want to keep your job I suggest you get on your bike and f... off'. [130]

The police service has consistently refused to introduce personality tests for recruits. Yet even drivers on Edinburgh's new tram cars have to pass such tests to ensure they don't upset passengers: they don't want withdrawn introverts or boisterous extraverts, rather a bunch of ambiverts. [131]

PCs Simon Jones and Joanne Kelly were sacked for gross misconduct despite Merseyside Police insisting for four years they had done nothing wrong in respect of an innocent man being Tasered five times in their van. A third officer involved, Sergeant Charlie Tennant had already been fined over a separate matter. The victim said: 'I have never come across such brutality ...' He was subjected to an excruciating technique called a 'drive stun', where the barbs were driven into his body and discharged. One cop ripped the metal barbs out of his body, though this should only be done by a doctor. He was struck twice on the head and throttled by one officer's forearm. He was Tasered in the hand and handcuffed. The force tried to maintain the use of the Taser was 'necessary and proportionate'. CCTV footage contradicted the officers' denials, and the victim won compensation after suing them. [132]

The day three Police Federation officers were grilled about Plebgate by the Commons Home Affairs Select Committee (when the three still refused to apologise to Andrew Mitchell), BBC Newsnight tried unsuccessfully to get the police to comment on the momentous meeting: the Federation, ACPO, IPCC and the West Mercia and West Midlands forces were unable to provide a spokesperson (the Chief Constable of Warwickshire agreed to appear but called off at the last moment). The Warwickshire and West Mercia heads of professional standards for Chief Inspectors, Jerry Reakes-Williams, wanted the officers punished. The Committee chairman Keith Vaz told the three unapologetic Police Federation shop stewards that their evidence was 'most unsatisfactory', reminding them that it was an offence to lie to Parliament. [133]

A police insider whistleblower (and former child protection officer), who insisted on remaining anonymous, said he was warned by his superiors not to investigate suspected paedophiles belonging to the Establishment (e.g. a judge and a politician) – powerful people were plying children of both sexes with heroin before raping them. The whistleblower was told by a victim that a Cabinet Minister and the MP Stephen Milligan (who died in a bizarre way) attended her lingerie shop to have women's underwear fitted. Being warned to keep his mouth shut, it left him a broken man. 'Any system that patronises this behaviour is corrupt, rotten to the core'. [134]

The crucial evidence of the Nottingham Forest fans who were at Hillsborough may also have been doctored by West Midlands Police, according to the IPCC. [135]

The Met Commissioner is to demand in the Supreme Court the right to secret court hearings where the police try to force whistleblowers and journalists to reveal confidential information. This would constitute a massive assault on press freedom. [136] Hogan-Howe has also invited the IPCC to investigate apparently misleading statements he made about his actions at Hillsborough, when he was a South Yorkshire Police inspector (he seemingly never made, despite his senior role, any detailed statement about the disaster). [137]

The IPCC has directed Sussex Police to refer to them two detectives accused of persuading one of Jimmy Savile's alleged victims not to support a prosecution for his allegedly sexually assaulting her in a caravan. One officer is claimed to have told her the prosecution of a celebrity would be difficult, and he and the other officer wrongly told her there had to be corroboration. [138]

Police Scotland is refusing to identify 10 sex offenders on the run because of their 'right to privacy'. [139]

Audit Scotland (AS) claims crime statistics are being concealed and taxpayers aren't being given the 'full picture' of crime across Scotland. The issue is 'not so much about the accuracy of the information being reported, but more about the comprehensiveness and the clarity of it'. The Police Scotland merger is 'a shambles': AS found 'inconsistencies, assumptions, disagreements, distractions ...'. Campaigners have called the waste 'a shocking vanity project'. [140]

A charitable private school, Stanbridge Earls in Romsey, was being investigated by the Charity Commission for possible mismanagement – multiple complaints of sexual abuse incidents, knife fights, drug-taking – in the spring of 2013. Hampshire Police are assessing whether to take action against officers who conducted a previous investigation: allegations of perverting the course of justice may be referred to the IPCC. [141]

CPS officials accompanied by <u>City of London Police</u> visited a newsstand near the Old Bailey selling copies of Private Eye, about which the judge in the Rebekah Brooks phone-hacking trial had complained. The news-vendor refused to be browbeaten by the presence of police, keeping the controversial edition on sale. [142]

The Home Affairs Select Committee's stinging criticism of the Police Federation stewards (Inspector <u>MacKaill</u>, DS <u>Hinton</u> and Sergeant <u>Jones</u>) of the three forces (West Mercia, Warwickshire and West Midlands) concerned in the Plebgate affair, was compounded by the Committee's conclusion that the officers' 'stubborn and unashamed' refusal to apologise to Mitchell was 'incredible'. The Committee's chairman found Hinton 'mendacious'. [143] The Police Federation was established in 1990 with the understanding that the police wouldn't go on strike.

MSP Christine Grahame claims that police officers in Scotland are afraid to complain about targets in case it harms their careers – they tell her they are losing discretion in order to comply with numbers. [144] Thus Police Scotland has a fixed 'percentage target' for the number of stops and searches going forward (i.e. 'positive stops').

Organs from 12 female victims of Harold Shipman were secretly stored by Greater Manchester Police for 12 years, before being incinerated without the consent of relatives. [145]

Pervert DJ Michael Souter was jailed for 22 years for paedophile attacks on children in England over two decades. Alleged victim Jim Belcher claims there are dozens of secret Scottish victims, on the scale of Savile – Souter, he says, used his local celebrity status with Radio Clyde (he also was a volunteer Scout leader). Souter used these tactics to access his Norfolk victims. Belcher's complaint to Strathclyde Police in 2012 did not lead to any charges. [146]

The House of Commons Plebgate report heavily criticised the officers involved, accusing police of 'obstructing the truth': three chief constables of an 'absence of leadership', three Police Federation representatives of giving 'contradictory' evidence (Detective Sergeant <u>Stuart Hinton</u>, of Warwickshire Police, was 'mendacious'). It was 'extremely serious' that Assistant Chief Constable of West Midlands Police, <u>Gary Cann</u>, may have 'applied pressure to change the conclusions of the first investigation'. Sergeant <u>Jones</u> told the Select Committee he had never been subject to disciplinary proceedings by his force – action had in fact been taken on two of 13 complaints against him. A new inquiry has been started following the Commons report. [147]

Reporters and the public were barred from hearing evidence in Edinburgh Sheriff Court against policeman <u>Grant Mackay</u>, accused of lying to prosecutors (he is said to have given false information to obtain a drug search warrant). [148]

Three drugs cases were dropped at Dundee Sheriff Court after a sheriff refused to grant a witness anonymity order to 'test purchase' undercover cops because the case didn't involve high-level dealing or risk of real harm. [149]

A 2006 MOD survey found over 6,000 of 9,000 uk servicewomen experienced all sorts of sexism (from sexual assaults to abusive comments), but the MOD refuses to commission new research into the problem. Women Against Rape say for every victim coming forward there are at least six more too afraid to complain. Military police don't automatically investigate sexual assault complaints. An RMP (Royal Military Police) corporal, who had reported being raped by two RMP officers, committed suicide after the failure to bring charges against them. An RMP review into its inquiry into the death found nothing untoward. However because of pressure from the victim's family of 'rape-related bullying' and their tragic relatives' ostracism, there is to be a civilian police probe and a new inquest. [150]

Northumbria Police gave a confirmed criminal cautions on 50 occasions over 12 years, but refused to reveal his identity or anything about his offences. The force admits the punishments were used inappropriately! [151]

P.C George Park was jailed in 2010 for three attacks on his wife: he was freed after 10 months on remand (having been sentenced to 18 months). Sacked in 2011 the force kept quiet about his reinstatement 10 months later after an appeal. His full pay while on suspension amounted to £130,000. His social enquiry report described him as 'a potentially dangerous individual,' and his rehiring undermines Police Scotland's 'zero tolerance' campaign on domestic violence. He has boasted how lucrative the case has been for him. Interestingly, police don't realise that children are at increased risk in cases of spouse abuse. [152]

Leveson dismissed a classified 2006 police intelligence report revealing an apparently corrupt relationship between the News of the World and a very senior former officer. The existence of the suppressed document was first made public by The Independent, which commented on 'a secret campaign from inside the highest ranks of the force to oust former Met Commissioner Lord Blair!' The police claimed 'public interest immunity' over the report, preventing its inclusion in the Leveson conclusions. [153]

Sir David Normanton's report on the Police Federation says, what with its bullying (of Home Secretaries!), in-fighting, dysfunctional structure and lack of transparency, it's not fit for purpose, needing urgent reform. 30 branches refused Normanton's repeated requests for information about their secret bank accounts. The Federation holds reserves of £65m. 91% of the 120,000 officers aren't happy with the Federation. [154]

Between 2008 and 2012 almost 300 armed elite SO6 officers (diplomatic protection squad, guarding Downing street, royalty, visiting dignitaries, etc) were investigated over crimes or claims of misconduct, yet the Met made none of the cases public. It took an FOIA request from the Daily Mirror to reveal the situation. Despite the allegations of perjury, sexual misconduct, assault, "oppressive conduct or harassment', corrupt practice (54 of the most serious cases were proved), only four culprits were sacked, with three retiring to avoid disciplinary action. [155]

In 2013 Warwickshire Police refused to name a retired officer charged with stealing £113,000 from its HQ, but was forced to do so because of a national furore over the suspicion that police were trying to protect their own. Keith Bristow of that force is now in charge of the NCA (National Crime Agency), which has been heavily criticised for its throwing a blanket of secrecy over nearly all the 350 people it has arrested between October

2013 and March 2014. Bristow's predecessor at NCA's previous incarnation SOCA, former MI5 boss Sir Stephen Lander, boasted about his 'closed doors' (extreme secrecy). Now, despite calls from the PM, the Home Secretary and the college of policing for all police to be open about whom they arrest, the secret nighttime arrest without charge of top No. 10 aide Patrick Brook by Bristow's NCA (despite Bristow's pledge to be open and transparent) had to be discovered by a tabloid newspaper: the NCA still refused to reveal their arrestee's gender, or to confirm or deny its involvement in any 'on-going investigation', an unprecedented declaration. Why were explosive allegations made to the ultra-secretive NCA (about child porn) rather than the Met, which has a child abuse command? [156]

The Trustless Policeman

A caller (Mark Sikorski) to The Wright Stuff (8.11.13, Channel 5) said he was a serving police officer with 30 years' service who had lost his faith in the service. He instanced the changes in police recording methods, which were now 'all smoke and mirrors'.

Despite a marked rise in the number of drug users, Police Scotland are losing the war on drug-dealers as the seizure of Class A substance drops. 40% of Scots don't trust in the ability of the police to catch criminals. [157]

Builder Stephen Fletcher phoned the Wright Show (6.11.13) to report that police refused to return (after the allotted period) £18,000 he had found on a building site, because of its 'criminal origin'. The only evidence of the latter was the way the £20 notes were piled up! Another caller, Steven from Gloucestershire, handed in £350 he had found, but several months later the police told him they had no record of the deposition (he said they filled in forms when he handed the money in).

Two callers to a November edition of ITV's The Wright Stuff discussing the fallout from Plebgate expressed their disgust and distrust of the police. One, 'May' from Lincolnshire, an ex-Met cop, said there's always been a rotten minority of officers but it is now much more widespread. She attributed the deterioration to the 'soft justice' of the present day Department of Professional Standards, which is 'rotten to the core' and must be disbanded. Likewise, according to 'May', the IPCC, which is top-heavy with ex-cops, needs to be stripped of police members, not to mention the CPS – the 'Coppers Protection Society'. Between these three there is no retribution for police wrongdoing: Home Office guidelines – on police discipline – are not observed, 'slaps on the wrist' being the order of the day. Another caller, 'Joan' from West Midlands, a WPC for 18 years, told the programme she was deeply embarrassed and frustrated by how Plebgate had been managed.

Ex-Met Commissioner Iain Blair suggested in the early nineties a police code of ethics, but the Home Office turned it down. [158]

Former Met commissioner Lord Stevens says the public now regard the police as 'sadly deteriorated', with officers 'beating a retreat from the beat'. [159]

West Midlands Police offered (December 2013) £200 for information 'from friends or relatives' leading to the prosecution of a drink driver, but this seems to be quite unpopular with the public. One may surmise the move could be socially divisive and even be another nail in the coffin of trust in the police. [160]

According to a YouGuv survey (November, 2013) 26% of the public have lost faith in the lower ranks of the police since Plebgate, with double the percentage distrusting the top brass. Public trust in local police fell to 66% (from 71% in August), and 48% in senior police (from 50% in August). PC Keith Wallis was the only officer to be charged in relation to the scandal (with misconduct in a public office by 'falsely' claiming to have witnessed the incident).

Derek Penman, former Assistant Chief Constable of (now defunct) Central Scotland Police, was appointed to the role of Her Majesty's Inspector of Constabulary for Scotland, despite two unresolved complaints about his conduct, which seem to have effectively been dropped, without the complainants being told, by the Scottish Police Authority (SPA), of which Penman is now also in charge. When Police Scotland started, 17 'legacy' complaints were transferred to the SPA about Scotland's top police, with only four 'closed' (by early 2014): many of these investigations have been running for years, at huge cost. [161]

Chief constables have told Chief Inspector of Constabulary Tom Winsor that some UK communities will not involve the police at all: they receive 'close to zero" calls from some areas. [162]

Inspector Ken Mackaill, Sergeants Stuart Hinton and Christopher Jones have refused to be interviewed by the IPCC over the 'lies" in the Plebgate scandal, as they have challenged the new inquiry's legality, via a judicial review. The refusal has outraged MPs. The chairman of the Home Affairs Select Committee, Keith Vaz, said: 'They are undermining the apologies given by their chief constables and they risk further damaging the reputation of the police'. [163]

Scottish police officers are much more liable to be assaulted than in big English cities: 17,120 attacks in three years (i.e. a one-in-three chance of Scottish officers being attacked annually), compared with the Met's 31,000 officers, who suffer only 1,746 attacks a year, while Greater Manchester recorded an average of only 885 a year. Scotland's officers suffered 5,524 assaults in 2010, 6,041 in 2011, 5,555 in 2012: an average of 15 daily. [164]

In a submission to MPs the Committee on Standards in Public Life has warned that 'public trust in policing is declining'. [165]

In the aftermath of the lawful killing verdict on Mark Duggan Met boss Sir Bernard Hogan-Howe has admitted the police 'need to do more to build trust', and agreed for the first time to meet ex-cabinet minister Andrew Mitchell to apologise to him personally. [166]

The Vice Policeman

Private homes and hotels in central Edinburgh are being used by prostitutes in the wake of the Police Scotland crackdown on the capital's sex saunas. Vice, like drugs, tends to be driven underground and made more dangerous by heavy-handed police action. [167]

As in Edinburgh the Met have raided dozens of brothels and sex shops in Soho, following months of undercover surveillance. [168]

In Operation Demonfere, Soho brothel raids undercover Met vice squad officers were deployed as sellers of stolen mobile phones, etc. This surely smacks of entrapment. Media photographers were tipped off by the police, resulting in some women being horrified by their photos in the press. [169]

CAVEAT CIVIS

The erotic crime thrillers of the fifties and sixties by Hank Janson (a.k.a. Londoner Stephen Frances) were seized by puritanical police, who proceeded to destroy them (or were resold to 'porn merchants' by corrupt officers). Booksellers were prosecuted, the publisher and distributor fined and imprisoned for six months, all on police evidence. The police tracked Frances down in Spain, but he was acquitted of all charges. His work may have opened the door to other ' lascivious' titles like Fanny Hill and Lady Chatterley's Lover. [170]

References

[1] Greenwood, C. 'PC in dock for 'racially abusing' black suspect in riots'. Daily Mail. 16.10.12, p29.

[2] Adams, L. 'Police targets spark fears of massaged crime figures'. The Glasgow Herald. 18.11.13, p1,14.

[3] Adams,L. 'Police warn of 'illegal' searches in bid to meet new targets'. The Glasgow Herald. 1.1.14, p1,2.

[4] Littlejohn, R. Daily Mail. 7.1.14, p17.

[5] Jedrzejewski, N. 'Storm as police snoops keep tabs on thousands.' Daily Express. 27.1.14, p9.

[6] Watton, S. 'Snobs' Law: Criminalising 'football fans.'

[7] McKendry, G. 'Police stated claims after gig is called off'. Sunday Post 9.2.14, p12.

[8] Alexander, D. 'It's A Fair Cop'. Sunday Mail. 10.11.13, p38.

[9] O'Neill, S.'Police failing to stamp out 'honour crimes'. The Times. 31.1.14, p17.

[10] Chalk, N. Daily Express. 17.12.13, p26.

[11] Brown, D., Hamilton, F. 'No 10 police porn arrests.' The Times. 8.2.14, p1,3.

[12] Alexander, D. 'Bad debt cops on their toes.' Sunday Mail .22.12.13, p27.

[13] Rayment, T., Leppard, D. 'In the shredder: the Met's bid to wipe out corruption in its ranks'. The Sunday Times. 9.5.14, pp6,7.
Wright, S. 'Yard corruption probe files destroyed in 2 days'. Daily Mail. 19.3.14, p18.

[14] Leppard, D. 'Revealed: how currupt detectives shielded crime lord'. The Sunday Times 2.2.14, p1,14, 20.

[15] Macdonell, H. The Mail on Sunday. 19.1.14, p35.

[16] 'Officer pleads guilty to offering cocaine'. The Guardian. 15.11.13, p25.

[17] Littlejohn, R. 'It's one rule for those guardian angels...' Daily Mail. 28.1.14, p17.

[18] Beatson, J. 'Cop accused of stalking ex using CCTV at salon.' Daily Record. 11.1.14, p21.

[19] Crichton, T., Burns, J. Daily Record. 1.1.14, p8.

[20] Yates, C. Daily Record. 3.2.14, p14.

[21] Channel 5's 'The Wright Stuff'. 6.2.14.

[22] 'Thug cop ordeal of Pan Am dad Jim'. Sunday Mail. 17.11.13, p38.

[23] 'Jailed, WPC who falsely told woman her rape case had been dropped'. Daily Mail. 7.12,13, p53.

[24] BBC2 Newsnight. 3.2.14

[25] Leppard, D. 'Forced out over police bullies'. The Sunday Times. 9.2.14, p20.

[26] Brocklebank, J. 'House calls ... on driver breaking the speed limit'. Daily Mail. 21.10.13, p23.

[27] Macaskill, M. 'Police face the music over radio costs'. The Sunday Times. 13.10.13, p19.

[28] Potts, Thomas, Clerk to Lancaster Court. 'The Wonderfull Discoverie of Witches in the Countie of Lancaster'. 1612.

[29] Johnston, K. 'The thin BOO line'. The Mail on Sunday. 27.10.13, p39.

[30] Osborne, L. 'Fury as police trivialise sex attacks in Christmas poem'. Daily Mail. 14.12.13, p24.

[31] 'Long arm of the law? It's the heavy right foot.' Daily Mail. 11.1.14, p35.

[32] Watson, R. 'Undercover cars with police logo could be 'out of the Clouseau farce.''. Daily Express. 20.12.13, p9.

[33] Police Force wants to sell ads on squad cars'. Daily Mail. 25.1.14, p8.

[34] Greenwood, C. 'Police cadets in swastikas and suspenders!' Daily Mail. 7.2.14. p21

[35] 'Cop's Brother Jailed For Bid To Extort £3K'. Daily Record. 31.10.13, p29.

[36] Dodd, M. 'First Plod on the beat'. Daily Mail. 5.12.13, p78.

[37] Kitchner, B. '£440K for PC who smashed up OAP's car.' Daily Express. 6.2.14, p21.

[38] Barrett, D., Rudgard, O. The Sunday Telegraph. 9.12.14, p7

[39] Doughty, S., Brown, L. Daily Mail. 13.9.13, p13.

[40] Herbert, D. 'Top police cash in as force faces cuts'. Daily Express. 1.11.13, p2.

[41] Christison, G. '£3m police sell-off hits rural scots'. Sunday Express. 26.1.14, p15.

[42] Herbert, D. 'Top cops get £10,000 rise as service is cut'. Daily Express. 23.1.14, p10.

[43] Dodd, V. 'Met accused of acting on behalf of big business'. The Guardian.30.1.14, p1,2.

[44] Malone, C. 'Paintbrush with the law'. Sunday Mirror. 17.11.13, p29.

[45] Grant, G. 'From the beat to a desk'. Daily Mail. 7.11.13, p20.

[46] Howarth, M. 'Police spend £1 million on upgrading stations they closed to the public'. The Mail on Sunday. 19.1.14, p40.

[47] Hitchens, P. 'Our police: Guilty as charged'. The Mail on Sunday. 20.10.13, p31.

[48] Mathieson, J. 'Cops Lose War Of The Sex Saunas'. Daily Record. 24.10.13, p10.

[49] Beveridge, A. 'Boys In Blue Badge'. Daily Record. 1.11.13, p33.

[50] Brooks, T. '£45K for one-legged OAP 'thrown to floor' by police'. Daily Express. 29.11.13, p32.

[51] '10 times as many could have died'. Sunday Post. 1.12.13, p3.

[52] Wright, S., Fagge, N. '30 years on, police force inquiry over Battle of Orgreave'. Daily Mail. 30.1.14, p10.

[53] Findlay, R. 'I was devastated when they forced me out and astonished when they asked me back. I still don't know the truth of what was going on.' Sunday Mail. 2.2.14, p14.

[54] 'Police want water cannon despite 'limited use' in riots'. The Independent. 23.1.14.

[55] 'Mercy for crash cop'. Daily Express. 22.11.13, p36.

[56] Thomson, C. 'Cop on dangerous driving charge for hitting walker'. Daily Record. 12.12.13, p39.

[57] Love, D. 'Ex-cop drives car at kids and teacher'. Daily Record. 16.1.14, p20.

[58] Silvester, N. 'Widow suses cop for £1.1m after hit and run'. Sunday Mail. 26.1.14, p17.

[59] Jeeves, P. 'Let's see how fast it'll go... boast of 140mph police driver'. Daily Express. 25.1.14, p3.

[60] 'Bully On The Beat'. Daily Record. 8.1.14, p20.

[61] 'Cop faces crash trial'. Daily Record. 23.1.14, p12.

[62] Clinton, J. 'Mr Debenham and his fine store fit for a king.' Sunday Express. 29.12.13, p43.

[63] Johns, S. 'Focus: Scotland's Crime Hotspots'. The Mail on Sunday. 20.10.13, p15.

[64] Halliday, J. 'Duggan marksman 'got it wrong' over account of shooting'. The Guardian. 15.11.13, p9.

[65] The Wright Stuff. Channel 5. 14.11.13.

[66] Penrose, J. 'Police Pay £100K Over G20 Arrests'. Sunday Mirror. 15.9.13, p24.

[67] The Wright Stuff. Channel 5. 12.11.13.

[67] Blackstock, G. 'Police angry at the time wasted in court'. Sunday Post. 13.10.13, p38.

[69] Mini-busted!'. Daily Mail. 28.11.13, p39.

[70] STV News. 27.11.13.

71 Grant, G. 'Need the police? Then make an appointment'. Daily Mail. 14.1.14, p12.

72 Owen, J. 'New police tactics put you at risk'. The Independent. 22.12.13, p11

73 McKendry, G. 'Bungled police search causes case collapse'. Sunday Post.15.12.13, p8.

74 Grant, G. 'Getting away with murder'. Daily Mail. 2.11.13, p6.

75 Grant, G. 'How the 'poileas' blew £1,300 on a guide in Gaelic'. Daily Mail. 23.11.13, p29.

76 O'Neill, S. 'Police failing to stamp out 'honour crimes'. The Times. 31.1.14, p1,16,17.

77 Grant, G. 'House's red tape is taking PCs off the beat'. Daily Mail. 21.11.13, p10.

78 Eccles, L., Bentley, P. 'Why didn't police stop this monster?' Daily Mail. 19.12.13, p6.

79 Riches, C. 'Sex gang jailed in scandal of abuse of poor white girls'. Daily Express. 21.12.13, p20.

80 Greenwood, C. Daily Mail. 28.1.14, p13.

81 Murray, J. 'The police told me MP in sex assault claims was too powerful to take on'. Sunday Express. 26.1.14, p7.

82 Smith, R. 'Hero Cop Faces Sack'. Daily Mirror. 23.1.14.

83 'Report slams police search for patient'. Daily Record. 23.1.14, p27.

84 Sawer, P. 'Palace break-in: terrorist warning'. The Sunday Telegraph. 8.9.13, pp1,8.

85 Beatson, J. 'Nuclear Subs Are Targeted By Thieves'. Daily Record. 31.10.13, p36.

86 Currie, G. 'Man raided police HQ to steel £25K patrol car'. Daily Mail. 16.1.14, p36.

87 Boffey, D. 'Police cars forced to act as ambulances as A&E overflows'. The Observer. 20.10.13, p1,8.

88 Scott, M. 'Inside The Ghost Squad'. Sunday Mail. 1.12.13, p22.

89 Merrill, J. 'Police admit they 'failed to protect' disabled murder victim'. Daily Mail. 30.10.13, p21.

90 BBC1 News. 30.1.14.

91 'Tip-off could have saved WPC'. Daily Express.. 3.1.14,p17

92 Dowling, K., Gillespie, J. 'Burn The Paedo'. The Sunday Times. 3.11.13, p29.

93 Leppard, D. 'Deaths of black detainees – 'PM must say sorry''. The Sunday Times. 24.11.13, p10.

94 Collins, D. 'Flying Squad Officer Shoots Own Leg Holstering Weapon'. Daily Mirror. 25.1.14, p27.

95 BBC1 News. 9.1.14.

96 Woolf, M. 'Police defend sex as tactic'. The Sunday Times. 20.10.13, p3.

97 Thomson, C. 'Ex-senior cop guilty of groping 3 women'. The Sun. 15.10.13, p4.

98 Thomson, C. 'Ex-top cop sex pest jailed for 18 months'. Daily Express. 12.11.13, p7.

99 'PC fondled drunk cop'. Daily Express. 25.10.12, p30.

100 Thornton, P. 'Beast Cop's Child Abuse Pics Hoard'. The Sun. 4.11.13, p27.

101 Thomson, C. 'PC In Court On Sex Attack Charges'. Daily Record. 8.1.14, p6.

102 Riches, C. '18 years for child sex policeman aged 78'. Daily Express. 28.10.13, p34.

103 'Sergeant 'had vile images of children''. Daily Express. 21.11.13, p24.

104 Farmer, B. 'Forces to be tested for combat stress'. The Sunday Telegraph. 15.9.13, p8.

105 'Troops' stress fear'. Sunday Express. 3.11.13, p2.

106 Sheldrick, G. 'WPC's suicide over dating text she sent to husband by mistake'. Daily Express. 5.12.13, p39.

107 Wright, S., Shipman, T. 'Yard in crisis as PC confesses...' Daily Mail. 11.1.14, p8.

108 Chapman, J. '100 'Faked 9/11 health problems'. Daily Express. 9.1.14. p34.

109 Silvester, N. 'M8 cop caught drunk again'. Sunday Mail. 12.1.14, p6

110 'The Sun' reported on Matthew Wright Show, ITV. 9.1.14.

111 Jeeves, P. 'I will hang myself while you watch, blinded PC told wife'. Daily Express. 8.1.14, p16.

[112] Barrett, D., Rudgard, O. 'Hundreds of police signed off with stress on full pay'. The Sunday Telegraph. 9.2.14, p7.

[113] Boffey, D. 'Police recruiting chief: forces need positive discrimination.' The Observer. 19.1.14, p5

[114] Littlejohn, R. 'Send in the clowns … but mind how you go'. Daily Mail. 22.10.13, p17.

[115] Littlejohn, R. ''Smile, chummy, you've been framed'. Daily Mail. 25.10.13, p17.

[116] Watson, R. 'Jogger is quizzed by armed cop about vest'. Daily Express. 16.11.13, p33.

[117] 'In the dock, man who attacked the burglars' Daily Express. 23.1.14.

[118] 'Police respect at risk.' Leader. Daily Record. 18.1.14. p8.

[119] Brown, L. 'Police quiz mother because her baby looked cold.' Daily Mail. 16.1.14. p38.

[120] Littlejohn, R. Daily Mail. 10.12.13. p17.

[121] Doward, J. ' Met police detained Guardian journalist's partner for 'political causes.'' The Observer. 3.11.13. p 1,9.

[122] Lazenby, P. 'Police Officers Used To Break Firefighters' Strike'. Morning Star. 16.11.13, p1,12.

[123] Aitken, K. 'Who voted police into power?'. Daily Express. 14.11.13, p13.

[124] Harris, P. 'Leftist poison, Comrade Bala and Mrs. Busy Bee'. Daily Mail. 26.11.13, p9.

[125] Channel 4. 9.12.13.

[126] Fielding, J. 'Police gunman told me to ignore paedophiles'. Sunday Express. 20.10.13, p12.

[127] 'Police have to own up'. Leader. The Mail on Sunday. 20.10.13, p29.

[128] Beckford, M., Taher, A. 'Crime tsar savages 'feral' police force'. The Mail on Sunday. 20.10.13, p27.

[129] Daily Mail. 16.10.13, p6.

[130] Collins, D. 'Cop: Savile Was Above The Law'. Daily Record. 17.10.13, p6.

[131] Hartley, G. 'I Think, Therefore I Tram'. Daily Record. 6.7.13, p17.

[132] Greenwood, C., Narain, J. 'PCs sacked for Tasering innocent man 5 times in back of a police van'. Daily Mail. 22.10.13, p6.

[133] BBC Newsnight. 23.10.13.

[134] Fielding, J. 'Cover-up over VIPs who abuse children in care'. Sunday Express. 3.11.13, p12.

[135] Drake, M. 'Did Hillsborough cops doctor Forest fans' evidence too?'. Sunday Mirror. 3.11.13, p10.

[136] Rayment, S., Hookham, M. 'Met's secret court threat to press'. The Sunday Times. 10.11.13, p3.

[137] Conn, D. 'Met chief: 'I will welcome inquiry into statements on Hillsborough''. The Observer. 10.11.13, p9.

[138] 'Savile cops referred to watchdogs'. Daily Record. 8.11.13, p16.

[139] McLeod, K. '10 Sex Beasts On The Run'. Daily Record. 9.11.13, pp1,6.

[140] Clegg, D. 'House Cops It'. Daily Record. 14.11.13, p7.

[141] Griffiths, S., Henry, R. 'Lord of the Flies school ignored sex claims'. The Sunday Times. 31.3.13, p3.

[142] Cusick, J., Burrell, I. 'Jury warned against contempt of court as phone-hacking trial begins'. 30.10.13, p5.

[143] Stevenson, C. 'Mitchell police to face further investigation'. The Independent On Sunday. 3.11.13, p8.

[144] McLaughlin, M. Daily Record. 29.11.13, p10.

[145] Yates, S., White, S. 'Cops Torch Dr Death Victims' Body Parts'. Daily Record. 30.11.13, p33.

[146] Ferguson, J. 'Souter abused me too … face justice in Scotland'. Daily Record. 14.11.13, p17.

[147] Barrett, D. 'Plebgate police obstructed truth'. The Sunday Telegraph. 3.11.13, p6.

[148] 'Press barred in cop trial'. Daily Record. 21.11.13, p4.

[149] McGlone, P. 'Identity Crisis'. Daily Record. 23.11.13, p31.

[150] Townsend, M. 'Family hope for justice from fresh inquest into death of service woman.' The Observer. 2.2.14, p6.

[151] Greenwood, C. 'Career criminal who was let off with 50 cautions.' Daily Mail 30.12.13, p217.

[152] Mills, R. 'Police officer locked up for beating wife gets job back.' Daily Express. 31.12.13. p14.

[153] Harper, T. 'Leveson inquiry ignored Met's bombshell report'. The Independent on Sunday. 19.1.14. p6.

[154] Channel 4 News. 20.1.14.

[155] Pettifor, T. '440 Criminal Probes Into PM's Armed Cops'. Daily Record. 10.2.14, p22.

[156] Greenwood, C. 'Fury over crime unit that does everything in secret." Daily Mail. 5.3.14, P4.

[157] Grant, G. 'Drop in seizure of drugs 'shows police are losing the crime battle' '. Daily Record.

[158] Daily Mail. 6.11.13, p18.

[159] Barrett, D. 'Put bobbies back on the beat says ex-Yard chief'. The Sunday Telegraph. 24.11.13, p1,2.

[160] The Wright Stuff. ITV. 3.12.13.

[161] Picken, A. 'Police watchdog in complaints mystery'. Sunday Post. 9.2.14, p8.

[162] Hitchens, P. The Mail on Sunday. 26.1.14, p29.

[163] Oakeshott, I., Leppard, D. 'Plebgate police snub new inquiry'. The Sunday Times. 12.1.14, p2.

[164] Herbert, D. 'Figures reveal level of attacks on police'. Daily Express. 241.14, p10.

[165] Hope, C. 'Elected police chiefs should have ethics code, says watchdog'. The Daily Telegraph. 26.12.13, p18.

[166] Roycroft-Davis, C. 'Mark Duggan was a gangster not an innocent choirboy.' Daily Express. 10.1.14, p12.

[167] Alexander, D. Sunday Mail. 17.11.13, p8,9.

[168] Greenwood, C. '31 arrests as police blitz Soho brothels and clubs'. Daily Mail. 6.12.13, p35.

[169] Taylor, D., Townsend, M. 'This woman was killed working as a prostitute. Are the police to blame?' The Observer.19.1.14, p11.

[170] Dunne, C. 'The man who taught a generation about sex'. Daily Mail. 4.1.14, p38,40.

<u>CONCLUSION</u>

Has something gone wrong with the police? Well, the Coalition Government was establishing a Royal College of Policing by 2012 to improve the service's reputation and performance. It will set entry and promotion standards, and spells the end of the controversial ACPO. Ministers believe the College will improve leadership and efficiency, and concentrate on 'hard policing'[5401]. The idea of a Royal College for the police must surely derive from the caring professions (Royal Colleges of Physicians, GPs, nurses, etc.). So is policing to become a vocation rather than a job? A noble idea, but extremely difficult if nursing is anything to go by – many think nursing has become a job rather than the calling it once was[5402]. The new Royal College of Policing could do no better – to regain the public's trust – than start by pledging transparency (e.g. revealing all officers' Masonic links) and conducting overdue research (e.g. personality profiling of recruits or explaining why Ulster Police attract most complaints). Should the police become a 'force' again, and ditch the 'service' ethos which militates against confronting criminality?

There is certainly need for change. This book has summarised some of the evidence that British police officers are worth the watching. The evidence presented must be the tip of the iceberg, for if possible the police service tends to conceal its skeletons: cover-up is an automatic reflex. The 'sins' outlined certainly number more than the traditional seven. Some officers clearly are arrogant, incompetent, unjust, lustful, greedy, deadly, etc. Arguably they can, because they belong to a powerful institution, commit a wider variety of faux pas than members of the public, *and get away with them.* Much like doctors (see my 'Caveat Aeger' – Never Trust Your Doctor[5403]).

The problem is, how common is malfeasance? It would seem some police are persistent wrongdoers, others occasional, some never. Some one can presumably trust all of the time, some only at times and some never, but how does one know which category the officer one is confronting falls into?

The authors of 'The Fall of Scotland Yard'[5404], a Penguin Special, warn that 'the utmost vigilance is required if the old system is not to reassert itself'. Indeed, restoration of trust is surely the key. But are the police up to it?

Britons have become a nation of 'suspects', to whom policing is done, rather than with. At best, the police in the modern world are arguably a necessary evil.

CONCLUSION

Appendix 1

THE LONGCARE SCANDAL

Introduction

Care in the community may have worsened instead of improving the lot of the adult learning disabled (LD), as seen in the Longcare scandal – the LD are increasingly liable to be victims of serious crime.

The dismal performance of the Social Services departments of many councils in respect of Longcare at Stoke Poges (near Slough) has not deterred governments from retaining the social model of LD care. This, despite the LD continuing to be low on Social Services' list of priorities: the medical model of care remains anathema.

A quarter of all care homes are for the LD. Recent care scandals, such as Castlebeck's two Bristol homes (Winterbourne View and Rose Villa),[1] suggest that the politically-driven, expensive and experimental community care programme of the last few decades has not improved the lot of the vulnerable. Ann Craft, who was director of the National Association for the Protection from Sexual Abuse of Adults and Children with Learning Disabilities (their trailblazing book was 'It Could Never Happen Here'), believes abuse is widespread but undetected[2]. The present author has warned elsewhere of the dangers inherent in the community care of the LD[3,4].

The learning disabled Longcare residents at Stoke Place and Stoke Green (and their satellite flats in Slough) suffered the most appalling abuse at the hands of their proprietor, the bisexual paedophile psychiatric nurse Gordon Rowe (G.R.) and his acolytes. This 'cause infâme' was featured in the media (e.g. in a Panorama and BBC radio programmes as well as the press - the Slough Observer and The Independent), journalist John Pring's books 'Silent Victims'[5] and 'Longcare Survivors'[6], as well as social work literature.

The fact that G.R. cleverly employed close members of his own family in key positions – not only his wife and son but his brother, father, sister and brother-in-law – helps explain how he got away with his monstrous behaviour for so long. But his police connections no doubt helped enormously too, even though the police should have been the victims' frontline defenders.

Psychological Abuse

It is not an exaggeration to describe the Stoke Poges regime as a reign of terror. In five years (1988-1993) there were at least 140 allegations involving 51 residents. The larger home, Stoke Place, was essentially a 'correctional institution', where recalcitrant residents in other units were transferred for punishment. There were special 'punishment chairs', and the extensive gardens were also used for punishment (e.g. digging holes which then had to be filled in). Both staff and residents' quarters were bugged by management, and no-one (not even other 'informer' residents) could be trusted. Makaton – a standard communications system for the LD – was banned, to prevent staff bypassing G.R.'s surveillance. There was a deliberate policy to dismiss staff who became too friendly with clients, so that staff turnover was very high. Residents were also psychologically isolated by not being told of relatives' calls (or not allowed to phone them), and no parents' organisations or staff meetings were allowed on the premises. Miniature wooden coffins were used by the 'vicar' (he had bought an American pastor's qualification), one of G.R.'s henchmen who had married the latter's first wife, to instil in the residents the concept of fire drill. Toileting was only allowed at fixed times, with punishment (the latter often meant seclusion in the toilets) for the inevitable 'accidents', and if late for meals one had to go without. The boredom of confinement to bed for a week might be the consequence of refusing to work for nothing, and in fact there was very little recreation. Birthday presents or gift vouchers might be burned or possessions removed for infraction of the rules. Instead of his meal a resident who had accidentally torn his clothing had the latter dumped on his plate and told to eat it instead. An outside psychiatrist diagnosed one client with a generalised anxiety disorder due to the chronic stress of living in the home, while another consultant therapist concluded that the level of terror was 'enormous'. The barrister aunt of one resident mentioned 'nightmares and flashbacks'. Humiliation techniques included making males cross-dress (staff were also humiliated). Uniformed police officer friends of G.R. were brought in to give warnings to clients – an effective form of intimidation. G.R. loved to make fun of the residents, e.g. by giving them offensive nicknames, as well as staff behind their backs. The 'vicar' threatened potential whistleblowers with arrest or financial penalties, or they would receive threatening anonymous phone calls. One previously stable person became suicidal at Stoke Place, others became incontinent. Some were 'literally terrified' of becoming whistleblowers.

There was virtually no follow-up by sponsoring agencies (who had often lost the residents' records, so not even knowing they existed), even as long as 10 years after transfer, which must have made some clients feel even more abandoned. The further away a placement is made, the less follow-up there is by either authorities or families, probably because of the cost in time and money of long journeys. Visits by Buckinghamshire County Council (B.C.C.) social workers were few and far between: there were no key workers or advocates. The Council's inspectors – who did generally make the required number of visits – only started to detect irregularities after these had been repeatedly pointed out by complaining relatives, residents and professionals. The B.C.C. Inspectors' Report, as also the findings of an Independent Inquiry – June 1998, requested by the Parliamentary Under Secretary of State at the DH – were never made public, and B.C.C. even used public funds to try to cover up the scandal. Leaks to the media (the Slough Observer and The Independent) finally told the story which led to the closure of the homes, with rearguard threats from G.R.'s lawyers that they would sue. Even when nearly all the other residents had been found new homes, B.C.C. dragged its feet over the transfer of its own four clients ('to avoid a stampede'!). One bright ex-patient of a large hospital, where she was perfectly happy, suffered not only the nightmare of Longcare, but, when the latter closed, was shunted through five homes in five months (the first closed because it wasn't legally registered, in another she was sectioned because she retaliated against a carer who struck her).

<u>Physical Abuse</u>

Under G.R. punishments included being tied to furniture or trees for hours, cold baths or showers, kicking, slapping, punching, eating meals outside in inclement weather, being put outside in the most severe weather, force-feeding, food deprivation, made to eat raw potatoes, hosing down, soaked with buckets of water (e.g. for not eating), burned with cigarettes (leading in one case to dangerous chest wall abscesses), given ECT (allegedly), suspension by ankles out of top windows, hairpulling, dragging by the ears, legs whipped with wet towels, being left unwashed. Scratches, bruises and burns were excused as self-inflicted, even though they didn't appear de novo at home. Assaults were committed by G.R.'s son (at least three recorded against him) and wife, as well as other staff and G.R. himself. Residents were even ordered to fight with each other. Staff stopped reporting incontinence because of the harsh punishment which would ensue.

Sexual Abuse

LD clients have again a fourfold increased risk of being <u>sexually</u> abused[7]: this is actually commoner than physical abuse or neglect, with over 80% of day centre users experiencing sexual abuse. Interestingly an unpublished study by Hard and Plumb found over half the female victims were not believed, but all the men were. In 1969 G.R. drove a nine-year-old boy to a deserted spot, where he sexually assaulted the child. Contraceptive injections (probably Depo-Provera) were administered by Longcare's visiting GP: a pregnancy would lead to awkward questions. Bedroom doors were locked at night, except on the nights when G.R. was pimping (one resident successfully warded off intruders by acquiring a dog). 'Gordon's girls' (there were eight of them) were not only raped but coerced to watch themselves having sex with male residents on video, and forced bestiality was also filmed for watching (video copying gear was found by police). G.R. always talked about sex to the staff, ordering them to tell him of all instances of the residents' 'sexual activity', and attributed any complaints of sexual interference to the residents being over-sexed. He used sweets to obtain minor sexual favours (breast touching, kissing, etc) and indulged in mutual masturbation sessions with favourite males (e.g. four times a week with one man). The frequent complaint by the female residents of soreness between their legs, as well as anal scarring, bruising and bleeding in both sexes should have alerted the visiting doctor: obviously the appropriate physical examinations were not performed. G.R.'s wife, whom he may have abused as a child, would masturbate both sexes in the communal areas. Ironically, one of 'Gordon's girls' was raped by her careworker in her London home, whence she was transferred after G.R.'s demise. G.R. told one of the girls he was regularly raping that he would divorce Angela (his wife) and set up house with her. He had sex with another girl at a group home he controlled in Slough and in Stoke Place classrooms. The female Longcare resident who said she had ECT also had an abortion. Report books were censored (e.g. pages were missing or passages redacted with Tippex) and individual communication books were missing.

Financial Abuse

The Longcare residents were kept in a degree of privation (though they were dressed decently when on show) – poor bedding, no toilet rolls, one razor for eight, inadequate laundry facilities. When they had holiday breaks with relatives the latter noticed they were wearing other people's clothes. Decent clothes were kept in a locked room, and there was no rainwear (e.g. Wellingtons), even though livestock had to be tended in the grounds in all weathers. Residents were charged rentals for G.R.'s personal videos, and had to pay for their weekly fish and chips, which should have been free. Though supposedly ring-fenced, dowries that accompanied residents disappeared – discharging consultants at one S. W. Thames hospital were not told by management about the dowries – as did money from their personal accounts (e.g. for non-existent trips and night club tickets for staff), which were under the control of G.R.'s 'wife', who even committed benefit fraud in one case by claiming falsely a resident was funding his own placement. Police fraud officers said they could not make charges because of the extremely poor accounting records. The residents had to clean rooms, do gardening, landscaping and decorating (for G.R., his police buddies, etc.) without pay.

G.R.'s Personality

G.R. was a psychiatric nurse trained at Broadmoor Special Hospital (whence he returned on a sabbatical to learn the latest restraint techniques). While there he was reportedly in charge of the porn video collection, and was involved in a probe into the theft of a patient's gold rings. He subsequently trained as a social worker (his first attempt at the CQSW was abortive, reportedly being expelled for cheating in exams, and he may have had a sexual relationship with a client, but he was still allowed to join the social work profession), and worked as such in Brighton, where he was interviewed on camera by the BBC in 1973 and where he first met his second wife – aged 11 (there were rumours he had fathered several children with client women on the same housing estate). In due course, she was to join him at the Somerset home they managed for several years before blotting their copybook and setting up their own Longcare enterprise (they 'filched' four residents from the Somerset home). For a decade Rowe masqueraded as a 'pillar of the community', boasting about being a Freemason, with consequent close links with the police. He took the doctor covering his home for meals, and one of Rowe's family played golf with members of the GP practice. Longcare made G.R. rich – a Florida home and two others in Windsor, a Rolls-Royce, a sports car and Ferrari, a boat, furs, jewellery, etc. He was able to buy Stoke Green and the flats in Slough outright. Belatedly it was realised he started his paedophile career in the late sixties, and Somerset Police told B.C.C. of his sexual misbehaviour at this home for LD people in their jurisdiction in 1982, but this evidence was ignored when Buckinghamshire Council awarded his registration soon after. This would seem to be a remediable loophole in the system. Around this time warning letters from two London boroughs were also ignored. The B.C.C.'s Director of Registration at the time is said to have left to live in France after the scandal surfaced. G.R. even tried to browbeat a senior Berkshire council official into allowing him to expand in that county. As the authorities eventually closed in, G.R.'s sister described him as mentally ill. He locked himself in a bathroom for three days. Following a suicide attempt he received in-patient psychiatric treatment in Windsor and Reading, but he finally completed the act with carbon monoxide on the Devil's Highway near his alma mater (Broadmoor).

The Police

Three police investigations came to nothing, the last (Operation Skip) attempting to remove bias on the police's part by ensuring no officers took part who had socialised with G.R. (e.g. the latter provided minibuses for Slough police outings and free labour for at least one policeman's garden). One accuser was taken to Windsor Police Station under a pseudonym to ensure privacy. G.R. wore his Freemasonry on his sleeve, and it is well known that police seem to have shown favouritism to fellow Masons[8]. None of the third team of investigators belonged to the Brotherhood. But it was too late. One persistent difficulty was that of contacting the investigating officer (especially by the Council's Inspectorate): an interesting observation by that officer was that other forces were involved in similar investigations. Slough police officers used to visit Stoke Place Mansion, being told risqué jokes by G. R. in the reception area: there was a drinking den in the basement and the police would use Longcare's shooting gallery. The police helped with fundraisers at Stoke Place. When staff made complaints at Slough Police Station they were laughed out of the door. A social worker made a report to Amersham Police Station, which helped re-open the case. The B.C.C. Inspection Unit's final report (1994) didn't ask police to investigate further – it was press reports which in the same year prompted the Assistant Chief Constable of Thames Valley to launch Operation Skip (the previous officers had failed to use s. 127(2) of the

Mental Health Act (1983)), and three Longcare staff were successfully prosecuted as a result. Slough Police's Family Protection Unit was informed of the situation in 1992. Police costs of their investigation were almost £3m. Two officers were censured, a sergeant admonished and Thames Valley Police told to improve procedures by the P.C.C (Police Complaints Commission). It turned out that Officer A, who had misused the national computer on G.R.'s behalf, had been proposed for membership of G.R.'s Masonic lodge by G.R. himself in 1988. A detective chief inspector was admonished for warning residents about their alleged criminal behaviour, taking the time to visit them at Stoke Place, as well as using the police computer to do checks for G.R. The thing that most caused consternation among relatives was the police refusal to release documents crucial to their compensation claims unless the police were assured that there would be no proceedings against them. When the force was asked about Longcare in 2010, no one seemed to remember it!

The recent horrific case of 26 year-old Luton LD man Martin Gilbert[9], who was dismembered by his 'foster' family – it is uncertain whether his beheading occurred before or after death – who had been using him as a slave, involved, like Longcare, three botched police investigations (by separate forces in this case), shows the present community care system has to be overhauled, particularly in respect of the police service, who are often the front line professionals when things go wrong. One option would be to have a police officer co-opted onto the community safeguarding and multi-agency teams[10]. Safety concerns about Martin had been reported to the authorities on at least eight occasions. Steven Hoskin (Cornwall)[11] and Gemma Hayter (Warwickshire)[12] were likewise horribly murdered after chronic abuse, both victims of 'mate' crime – they supposed their killers were their friends. Steven was robbed, humiliated, treated like a slave, sexually abused, made to wear a dog collar and lead, forced to take an overdose of painkillers and fall from a railway viaduct. A serious case review of the Hoskin case found that every part of the Cornish adult protection system had failed him – there had been over 40 warnings and 'missed intervention opportunities' – and made 17 recommendations for improving safeguarding. Gemma's lifeless body was also found on a railway line after being stripped, strangled and knifed in the neck. Sunderland LD man Brent Martin was viciously murdered in 2001 for a £5 bet: he was partly stripped and chased through his town, being assaulted at four locations over several hours[13]. The IPCC found that 88 incidents of targeted harassment had been reported to the police before the death of David Askew in Tameside.

There have been serious allegations against former staff of Doncaster's Solar day centre for the LD – one client deliberately pricked with needles, pinned to a wall and struck around the head and threatened, another allegedly thrown from his wheelchair onto the floor[14]. As with Longcare, South Yorkshire Police failed to find enough evidence to press charges in the Solar case. Allegations from an earlier whistleblower (2003) about a facility in St. Catherine's Hospital near the Solar centre were apparently not handed to police.

After a decade's delay the government is finally setting up a confidential inquiry into the LD's 'premature and avoidable' deaths. The UK Disabled People's Council has submitted evidence (collected over just three years) of 68 violent deaths of disabled people and over 500 other potential disablism crimes. Voice UK said (2010) there have been real increases in horrific murders and very serious sexual assaults on the LD. Andrew Lee, a leader of the UK self-advocacy movement and member of the Human Rights Commission's disability committee, thinks things are 'getting worse'. One unintentional consequence of community care seems to be a rise in crimes against the LD – they are more visible and often end up in the most unsavoury areas.

APPENDIX I

The Equality and Human Rights Commission's report 'Promoting the Safety and Security of Disabled People' found serious under-reporting of incidents, and the disabled often being deemed 'unreliable witnesses'[15], by, for example, the police.

So what went wrong at Longcare? The problem was multifactorial:

(1)   Faulty vetting of personnel by B.C.C. at the initial registrations of Stoke Place (1983) and Stoke Green (1987) (as well as at re-registration when G.R. and his 'wife' stood down: the dubious managers allowed to carry on were G.R.'s son and the "vicar"): ignoring of Somerset Police and Brent Council and Hillingdon Council warnings (the police reported more than a dozen residents at The Old Rectory in Somerset had been sexually abused, but they couldn't prove it).

(2)   Faulty monitoring of residents' progress by B.C.C. inspectors, whose approach was 'instruction and persuasion' rather than 'intervention and enforcement'. They doubted the credibility of complainants. The Council had all the legal powers they needed, but didn't use them.

(3)   There was a perverse financial disincentive for the B.C.C. to investigate properly. The Council's legal advice was that its fiduciary duty to their taxpayers trumped their duty of care to the vulnerable. All the more reason for the police to fill the breach.

(4)   Both the GMC and the police failed to mount adequate investigations. Care Minister Paul Burstow's 'adult safeguarding boards' would not seem to have more teeth than the former council inspectorates.

The Longcare Inquiry report is still absent from the B.C.C website (a request for them to include it was refused). B.C.C. also admitted it needed to improve in 'learning the lessons' from serious case reviews and improve its liaisons with the police.

The politicians involved in ordering the Independent Inquiry did not ensure (a) its findings were made public, (b) it addressed the medical care of the residents, (c) the Freemasonry issue was probed - this wasn't addressed either by the Police Complaints Commission. Interestingly, Freemasonry was not considered by the Leveson Inquiry into phone hacking, despite a request by this author.

Nor did the Department of Health ensure that the B.C.C. Inspectorate Report was made public – only its leaking to the press triggered the commissioning of the Independent Inquiry. In the years that followed, B.C.C. seemed to wriggle at every turn to avoid acknowledging responsibility, with the legal battle dragged out.

[1] Verkaik, R. 'Nurse 'received sack threat' over her abuse alert'. The Mail on Sunday. 17.9.11, p40.

[2] Waterhouse, R. 'Sex abuse of handicapped put at 1400 cases'. The Independent.17.9.94, p4.

[3] Kinnell, H.G. Hard World Outside: Some Pitfalls to Avoid in the Community Care of the Mentally Handicapped. Lancet, Nov 24 1984, pp1202-1204.

[4] Kinnell, H. G. Community Care of People with Mental Handicaps: Room for Improvement. Mental Handicap Vol 15, December 1987, pp146-151.

[5] Pring, J. 'Silent Victims'. Gibson Square Books. 2003.

[6] Pring, J. 'Longcare Survivors'. 2009.

[7] Fenwick, A. 'Sexual abuse in adults with learning disabilities: a review of the literature'. BJLD. 22: pp53-56. 1994

[8] 'Inside The Brotherhood'. Granada TV (Castle Vision). 1989.

[9] Branagh, E. 'Investigations into killing of man kept as slave criticised'. The Independent. 8.7.11, p15.

[10] BBC News. 7.7.11.
[11] The Guardian. 14.9.10.
[12] Slater, R. 'Why was Gemma abandoned to be murdered for fun by a gang of savages who she thought were her friends?' The Mail on Sunday. 31.7.11, pp22,23.
[13] Quarmby, K. 'Getting Away With Murder'. August, 2008.
[14] Disability News Service. 15.9.10.
[15] Disability News Service. April, 2010.

APPENDIX I

Appendix II

A Police Pseudo-patient Sting*

An undercover police drugs team targeted a peripatetic medical slimming clinic in a hostelry's function room. The police admitted the targeting, no patient having complained about the doctor. The clinic was advertised regularly in the local press, and had been running for several months. The police officers (of both sexes) revealed their identity at the end of the clinic, and the doctor proffered identification and GMC registration, but, importantly, the police did not ask to see the patient drug records, and did not seem to want any further information. However, they had been listening in to the clinic, and later produced statements which the doctor claims distorted (in a derogatory fashion) his advice to patients.

However, another batch of undercover officers (this time all female) presented themselves as patients at a later clinic, this time armed with audiovisual monitoring devices, about which the doctor was not alerted. The ostensible reason for this second visit – again, the doctor's drug records were not requested – was later said to be for a 'test purchase', to see if the drugs were genuine and that the doctor was complying with the 1971 Misuse of Drugs Act. In fact, the CAS (centrally-acting appetite suppressants) capsules concerned were never tested, suggesting some hidden agenda – the doctor was referred to the GMC for disciplinary action. The police, in their submissions to the GMC, went into much clinical detail, which suggests that they had been medically briefed to look for any supposed faux pas. The audiovisual material formed the essence of the GMC case against the doctor.

It is illegal for the police to use surveillance techniques unless they suspect serious criminality. Thus in a recent case a Scottish drug boss was snared by a police sting (involving officers from the *Serious Crime* and Drug Enforcement Agency – my italics) after buying a bugged motorcar from another cocaine dealer.

In this case, the police knew the doctor running the clinic was qualified and registered and not committing any obvious criminal offence. At no time did the police find any evidence of criminality on the doctor's part, though they admitted trying, but they decided to compile a denigratory dossier for the doctor's regulatory body. The police had refused (under FOIA) access to information about the operation (which in the usual way was given a code name, in this case related to a well known eating disorder), which might have revealed who authorised the police to act as monitors of *clinical* rather than criminal behaviour.

The GMC toyed with the idea in 1997 of using pseudo-patients to root out incompetents and miscreants in general practice, but would not have used police officers – in any case, the idea was abandoned. An attempt in the US by Medicare criminal fraud investigators to use pseudo-patients to prosecute a psychiatrist – he was cleared – was heavily criticised by the American Psychiatric Association.

An account of a more recent political police sting – that of Mark Kennedy and his colleagues infiltrating the eco-protestors – is to be found in 'The Secretive Policeman' chapter.

An undercover officer charged with monitoring political campaigners tried to bribe a Cambridge activist to inform on Cambridge University students, as police have found it impossible to infiltrate their own officers into the university. The activist secretly filmed the officer. The police surveillance was also targeting UK Uncut, Unite Against Fascism, Cambridge Defend Education and environmentalists. The police wanted to know the names of protesting students, their leaders and vehicle details. The activist was also asked to trawl Facebook for the latest protest information, and attend students' planning meetings (to detect, for example, the names of the main speakers). He was asked to start locally monitoring groups in Cambridge, before going on to national campaigns, though the policeman wanted to know of any students going onto campaigns in other parts of the country.[1]

1. Evans, R., Khalili, M. 'Undercover police target students'. The Guardian. 15.11.13, pp1,2.

* Identifying details have been omitted for legal reasons.

Appendix III

Landmark Miscarriages of Justice

1953: Derek Bentley hanged for murder

1974: M62 bomber jailed for life

1974: Six charged over Birmingham pub bombs

1976: Guilty verdict for 'Maguire Seven'

1979: Bridgewater Paperboy's killers convicted
1997: 'Bridgewater Three' freed

1989: Guildford Four released after 15 years
1994: 'Guildford Four' man cleared of IRA murder

1991: Birmingham Six freed after 16 years

1991: Silcott not guilty of PC's murder
1999: Police award Silcott damages

2003: Solicitor cleared of killing sons

2003: Mother cleared of murdering babies

APPENDIX III

Appendix IV

POLICE DIRTY TRICKS

In the old days the dirty tricks brigades of the police tended to confine their stitching (or setting) up to the criminal fraternity, but getting away with this for so long perhaps emboldened them to try it on selected innocent targets when it suited them, e.g. to combat political activists or cover up police blunders, as in Hillsborough and, more recently, the Stephen Lawrence and de Menezes fiasco.

The osteopath Stephen Ward, a central figure in the Profumo scandal of the 1960s, committed suicide after being framed by the justice system; the establishment needed a scapegoat when the Secretary of State for War lied to the House of Commons. Ward had informed MI5 that his affair with Christine Keeler might constitute a security risk. The Met spent months digging up dirt against Ward, the police intimidating witnesses to give false evidence, as well as silencing those whose testimony favoured him. When, despite the best efforts of the 'end justifies the means' police, it looked like Ward might get off, unbelievably the Lord Chief Justice intervened to ensure he was found guilty, to the consternation of the legal profession at this unprecedented move. The two junior members of the four- strong police team (known then as 'the hunters') which fabricated the case against Ward (one of the seniors is deceased, the other's whereabouts in Australia unknown), have revealed exactly how his defence (that he was an MI5 recruiter) was compromised - MI5 have now admitted Ward was their spy.[1] So the police smearing that reared its ugly head in Hillsborough and Lawrence is nothing new.

Sir Norman Bettison, at the centre of the Hillsborough fan smearing scandal, has been referred to the IPCC amid claims of a national police conspiracy against the Stephen Lawrence family - there was concern Bettison tried to manipulate evidence from a key witness at the Macpherson Inquiry in 1998.[2] He had commissioned a six-page report into Bradford race relations worker Mohammed Amran prior to his testimony to the McPherson inquiry. The IPCC has declared there was no 'legitimate justification' for gathering this evidence, suggesting that Bettison might be guilty of 'the misuse of police information systems and unlawful processing of the witness's (sensitive) personal data'. In 2001 the West Yorkshire Police had compiled a much more extensive dossier on Amran – 167 pages – to try to have him removed from his post as a Commissioner with the Commission for Racial Equality.[3]

The Met has admitted[4] they surreptitiously recorded a meeting between Stephen Lawrence's friend Duwayne Brooks, witness to his murder, and the latter's lawyer. Documentary authorisation of the bugging in May, 2000 by assistant commissioner John Grieve has now surfaced. While admitting the smearing was 'hugely damaging' and 'really shaming' Grieve denies knowledge of it. Manchester's Special Branch asked (1998) for details of individuals likely to attend McPherson in the City, while South Yorkshire wanted monitoring of 'left-wing extremists' at events peripheral to the hearings.[5]

Amazingly, senior police officers have allegedly also strayed into smearing each other. A former Fraud investigator, now would-be police whistleblower, Peter Tickner, wanted to divulge to the Leveson Inquiry dirty tricks campaigns within Scotland Yard, e.g. leaking information to the media about rivals, to discredit them and promote themselves. Tickner was gagged by the Lord Justice after the Met's lawyers argued his evidence would be 'unfair' to senior people like <u>Sir Ian Blair</u> and <u>Sir Paul Stephenson</u>.[6] For the alleged smearing of Superintendent <u>Ray Mallon</u>, see page 67.

The recent revelations about the activities of the Special Demonstration Squad (SDS), about whose existence many senior officers were unaware, and into which <u>Sir Bernard Hogan-Howe</u> is refusing an independent inquiry, include the family led campaign for justice for Brian Douglas. The latter died in 1995 after being struck by a police baton, and the police whistle blower <u>Peter Francis</u> infiltrated the campaign surrounding the death, prior to his similar role in the Lawrence imbroglio. The SDS has morphed into the National Domestic Extremism Unit (their motto: 'By any means necessary'), whose database of nearly 9,000 extremists includes many political campaigners (EDL, BNP, animal rights, anti-capitalists, anti-war – the SDS was originally established to spy on Vietnam War demonstrators) with no criminal record. An 88-year-old campaigner who is on the database won a landmark case against the Met (March, 2013) at the court of Appeal, which ruled the Met had unlawfully kept details of his presence at over 55 protests.[7]

But the outrage at the Peter Francis (alias Peter Black) Stephen Lawrence admissions that he and his officers were subjected to 'huge and constant pressure' to 'hunt for disinformation' on the family and their friends, as well as preventing him revealing his role to the Macpherson Inquiry or the then Home Secretary Jack Straw, not to mention the use of dead children's identities) has led to the Met's handling of the case being described by a tabloid leader as plumbing 'depths of iniquity, hitherto unimagined'. The tabloid's commentator, Ruth Dudley Edwards, has described it as 'a sickening perversion of their work' for police chiefs to order officers to search for information not on the guilty, but on victims and the innocent. The Met is not only 'institutionally racist', as Macpherson pronounced, says Edwards, but also 'institutionally defensive'.[8]

The former Met commissioner who should have known about the Lawrence smear operation (Francis says yard bosses ordered it to try to suppress the Lawrence family campaign which might trigger public disorder) declares he didn't. <u>Condon</u> also denies personally rewarding 'the hairies' with bottles of whisky, which Francis alleges. MPs have backed Stephen's father's demand for a full independent inquiry.

Ex-SDS officer Francis (one of a four-man squad) admits using violence against a member of the public (who had made a racist remark) to help build his undercover identity, as well as against his police colleagues during a demo at a London bookshop. He has volunteered that his psyche contained 'a lot of suppressed rage' and aggression because of an adverse upbringing.[9] He posed as an anti-racist activist working for an organisation that fronted for left-wing Militant, and also monitored the various 'black justice' movements. He successfully sued the Met for psychological damage incurred in his work (settling out of court). He also revealed helping the shadowy Consulting Association compile a 'troublemaker' blacklist of union activists which was fed to 44 building firms so they could secretly exclude people from employment. GMB union chief Paul Kenny has called for a Leveson-style inquiry.[10]

Stephen Lawrence's family liaison officer recorded the identities of everyone calling at their home. The family always suspected police were gathering evidence on their visitors to discredit them, but had no concrete proof.[11]

For the attempted smearing of police shooting victim <u>Harry Stanley</u> see The Lethal Policeman chapter, p302.

The most recent instance of the toxic mixture of racism and smearing which has come to light is that of Janet Alder, a black paratrooper's sister, who fought for transparency about her brother Christopher's slow, agonising death in custody. Humberside Police have found that she and her family lawyer were illegally monitored by police at the time of the 2000 inquest (the verdict was unlawful killing). Janet's brother, CCTV showed, was face down, handcuffed, gasping for air, his trousers pulled down, as police joked around him. The force took a fortnight to inform his sister of his death, and she felt the police were monitoring her (stalked by plain clothes while shopping, mail going missing, attempts to obtain sensitive personal Social Services documents about her). A 2006 IPCC report dismissed the stalking claims. Unknown to the Alder family Christopher's body was secretly moved to Hull Royal Infirmary mortuary from the city's Northern Cemetery (an old woman was buried in his place). [12]

The Met's undercover officers infiltrated groups that tried to reveal corruption in the force, as well as those campaigning about deaths in custody ('black justice'). [13]

1.   Knightley, P., Kennedy, C. An Affair of State. Jonathan Cape.1987.
2.   Pettifor, T. 'Lawrence Smears Probe for Top Cop' Daily Record. 4.7.13, p4.
3.   Herbert, I. 'Anti-racism smear scandal: how low did the police stoop?' The Independent. 27.7.13, pp1,8.
4.   C4 News. 6.7.13
5.   Herbert, I. The Independent. 27.7.13, pp1,8.
6.   Verkaik, R. 'Did Leveson let the Met off the hook?' The Mail on Sunday 30.6.13. p14.
7.   Lewis, P. et al. 'Police unit monitors almost 9,000 'extremists'. The Guardian 26.6.13. pp 1, 8.
8.   Daily Mail letter. 'Exposing the depths of Stephen's betrayal'. 25.6.13, p14.
9.   Wright, S. et al. 'This Betrayal of my Family? Daily Mail. 25.6.13, pp 1, 4, 5.
10.   Ellis, M. 'Union chief in blacklist inquiry call'. Daily Mirror. 20.8.13, p19.
11.   Evans, R. , Lewis, P. 'Police spied on Lawrence family? The Guardian 24.6.13, pp 1, 8, 9, 26.
12.   Herbert, I. 'Anti-racism smear scandal: how low did the police stoop?' The Independent. 27.7.13, pp1,8.
13.   Evans, R., Lewis, P. 'Yard spied on critics of police corruption'. The Guardian. 25.6.13, p1.

APPENDIX IV

ALPHABETICAL NAME INDEX

Giamrasi, Mick	100
Giannesi, Mark	195
Gibbs (WPC)	417
Giff, Ricci	329
Gilbertson, David	93, 464
Gill, Davinder	84
Gill, Richard	338
Gillard, John	581
Gilmore, Daniel	260
Gilmour, Gordon	61
Gilmour, Raymond	591
Glanville, Mike	131
Glasse-Davies, Salvador	56
Glover, Andrew	177
Goddard, (Sergeant)	64, 68, 603
Godwin, Tim	15, 131, 133, 467
Golder, Graham	66, 603
Goldsmith, Alan	279
Goodman, Damon	172
Goodridge, Tony	339, 3347, 513
Goodwin, Alan	212
Goodwin, Andy	494
Goodwin, Jeanette	309
Gormley, Phil	465
Grace, Cherry	305
Graham, Caroline	336
Graham, Norma	187
Grainger, Anthony	303, 305
Gramphorn, Colin	409
Grange, Terry	80, 104, 329, 515
Grant, Linda	147
Gray, Keith	359
Gray, Les	26
Gray, Stuart	425, 445
Gray, Victor	47
Grayford, Darren	86
Graysonmark, Darren	70
Green, Anthony	193
Green, Steve	100, 254
Greenhorn, Stephen	172
Greenwood, Neil	185
Greenwood, Peter	581
Gregge, Leigh-Ann	325
Gregory, Julian	43
Greig, Paul	332, 339
Grieve, John	631 (App. IV)
Griffin, Sean	604
Griffiths, Bill	583

ALPHABETICAL NAME INDEX

BIBLIOGRAPHY

1. Bannon, J. Running With The Firm, My Double Life As An Undercover Hooligan. Ebury Press. 2013.

2. Blair, Sir Ian. Policing Controversy. Profile Books. 2009.

3. Bloggs, E.E. Diary of an On-Call Girl. Monday Books. 2007.

4. Blunkett, David. Rt. Hon. A People's Police Force – Police Accountability in the Modern Era. Home Office. 2009.

5. Brown, A. Watching The Detectives. Coronet Books. 1988.

6. Closing the Gap – A Review of the Fitness for Purpose of the Current Structure of Policing in England and Wales. HMIC. 13.9.05.

7. Copperfield, D. Wasting Police Time. Monday Books. 2006.

8. Cox, B., Shirley, J., Short M.. The Fall Of Scotland Yard. Penguin Books. 1977.

9. Emsley, C. The Great British Bobby. Quercus. London 2009.

10. Evans, R., Lewis, P. Undercover. Faber and Faber, 2013

11. Gadget, Inspector. Perverting the Course of Justice. Monday Books. 2008.

12. Gallacher, G. Gangsters, Killers And Me. Black & White Publishing. 2011.

13. Gilbertson, David. The Strange Death of Constable George Dixon. Why the Police Have Stopped Policing. Amazon Kindle. 2011 (November).

14. Hayes, Stephen. The Biggest Gang in Britain. Grosvenor House Publishing. 2013.

15. Hill, A. Miscarriages Of Justice. Blitz Editions (Bookmart Ltd). 1993.

16. Hitchens, P. A Brief History of Crime. Atlantic Books. 2003.

17. Hitchens, P. A Brief History of Crime – retitled The Abolition of Liberty: The Decline of Order and Justice in England. 2003.

18. Knight, S. The Brotherhood. Panther Books. London. 1985.

19. Knightley, P. , Kenedy, C. An Affair of State. Jonathan Cape. 1987

20. Kynaston, D. Austerity Britain. Bloomsbury. 2007.

21. Littlejohn, R. Littlejohn's Britain. Hutchinson (London) 2007.

22. Littlejohn, R. Littlejohn's House of Fun. Hutchinson (London) 2010.

23. Lock, J. The British Policewoman. Her Story. London. Robert Hale. 1979.

24.   Mason, G. The Official History of the Metropolitan Police. Carlton. 2004.

25.   Miller, J. Police Corruption in England and Wales. Home Office Online Report 11/03.

26.   Morrish, R. The Police and Crime Detection To-Day. Oxford University Press. 1959.

27.   Morton, J. Bent Coppers. Warner Books. 1994.

28.   Officer 'A'. The Crime Factory. Mainstream Publishing. 2012.

29.   Patrick, J. The Rest is Silence. Printed 1912. Amazon.co.uk, Ltd., Marston Gate.

30.   Policing For The People – Interim Report of the Police Reform Taskforce (2007). Conservative Party.

31.   Police Research Series. Research, Development and Statistics Directorate. Home Office.

32.   Ramsey, A. Girl in Blue. Macmillan. 2008.

33.   Reiner, Robert. 'Chief Constables'. 1991.

34.   Sergeant, H. The Public and The Police. Civitas. 2008.

35.   Tolley, H., Hodge, B. Tolley, C. The New Police Selection System. Kogan Page. 2007.

36.   Tomkinson, M. The Pornbrokers: The Rise of the Soho Sex Barons. Virgin Books. 1982

37.   Waldren, Michael, J. 'Armed Police: The Police Use of Firearms since 1945'.

38.   Wilson, D., Ashton, J., Sharp, D. What Everyone In Britain Should Know About the Police. Blackstone Press Ltd. 2001.

REFERENCES

[1] Sheridan, P. 'Secret shame of Hoover the hypocrite'. Daily Express. 20.1.12, p45.

[2] 'Revealed: J. Edgar's secret porn stash'. Sunday Express. 19.2.12, p43.

[3] Jenkins, S. 'It's not a Blair police state we need and fear, it's his state police'. The Sunday Times. 13.11.05.

[4] Daily Express Leader. 10.8.09.

[5] Leader. Daily Mail. 12.3.09, p4.

[6] Hyde, P. Daily Express. 11.8.09, p26.

[7] Sergeant, H. 'Inside Britain's Police Farce'. Daily Mail. 13.2.08, p36.

[8] Stephen Glover. Daily Mail. 17.3.09, p12.

[9] Taypayers Alliance. Daily Express. 26.3.07, p6.

[10] 'Police take rap over complaints'. Daily Record. 25.6.10, p32.

[11] Robson, D. 'From now on we will all be police'. Daily Express. 31.7.10, p14.

[12] Willey, J. 'Three-quarters of us think Britain is a dangerous place'. Daily Express. 4.4.07, p4.

[13] BBC1 News. 18.5.11.

[14] Hitchens, P. The Mail on Sunday. 19.8.07, p29.

[15] Littlejohn, R. 'Hacking? They can all go to hell in a handcart'. Daily Mail. 15.7.11, p17.

[16] Hitchens, P. The Mail on Sunday. 11.3.07. p29.

[17] The Independent On Sunday. 1.4.07, p7.

[18] Sergeant, H. 'Inside Britain's Police Farce'. Daily Mail. 11.2.08, pp26,27.

[19] Sergeant, H. 'Why Has the Public Lost Faith in the Police' in The Public & The Police. Civitas. 2008.

[20] Mason G. The Official History Of The Metropolitan Police. Carlton. 2004, p37.

[21] Liddle, R. Sunday Times 'Comment'. 2012.

[22] Littlejohn, R. Daily Mail. 9.7.12.

[23] Glover, S. Daily Mail. 14.9.12.

[24] Glover, S. 'Masters of Cover-up'. Daily Mail. 15.9.12, p16.

[25] Malone, Carole. Sunday Mirror. 23.12.12.

[26] Sunday Times. Leader. December 2012

[27] Hitchens, P. Daily Mail. 20.10.12.

[28] Forsyth, F. Daily Express. 2012.

[29] Hitchens, P. Mail on Sunday. 6.1.13.

[30] White, Roland. Sunday Times. Comment. 3.8.03.

[31] Cohey, N. The Observer.10.1.10.

[32] Pendlebury, R. 'Arrogance, lies and the downfall of a very PC police chief'. Daily Mail. 3.10.08, p4.

[33] Daily Mail. 3.10.08, p5.

[34] Hastings, M. 'Policing Controversy by Ian Blair'. Sunday Times Magazine. 31.10.09, p43.

[35] Wright, S. 'A £10,000 portrait of me? What a good idea says Sir Ian'. Daily Mail. 22.11.08, p47.

[36] 'Police chief backs off IRA story'. The Times. 31.3.07, p31.

[37] Wright, S. 'I am no celebrity, says new Met chief'. Daily Mail. 29.1.09, p20.

[38] Kay, R. Daily Mail. 4.2.09, p37.

[39] O'Hare, P. 'Police Are 'Arrogant and Out of Touch'. Daily Record. 30.11.07, p19.

[40] O'Hare, P. 'Why Did Police Refuse To Treat Kevin's Death As Murder?'. Daily Record. 18.1.13, p8.

[41] 'Shower-row police chief throws in the towel'. Daily Mail. 1.2.07, p31.

[42] Littlejohn, R. Daily Mail. 19.1.10, p17.

[43] Musson, C. 'We're Winning War Against Gangsters'. Daily Record. 20.1.10, p11.

[44] Dixon, C. '7/7 families' anger at MI5's 'arrogant' chiefs'. Daily Express. 7.5.11, p9.

[45] Smith, S. 'Rapist Cop Let Loose On Our Streets'. Sunday Mail. 5.10.08, p9.

[46] Daily Mail. 9.4.11, p50.

[47] Daily Mail. 9.4.11, p51.

[48] Emsley, C. 'The Great British Bobby'. Quercus. London, 2009, p244.

[49] Emsley, C. 'The Great British Bobby'. Quercus. London, 2009.

[50] Pilditch, D. 'WPC was 'arrogant' to bosses'. Daily Express. 7.8.09, p19.

[51] Little, A. Daily Express. 23.7.10, p15.

[52] Camber, R. 'Why middle-class drivers who speed are hypocrites ...'. Daily Mail. 10.8.10.

[53] Kay, R. 'Levy's Met guards in TV ruckus'. Daily Mail. 2.5.07, p37.

[54] Leader. Daily Mail. 28.3.11, p14.

[55] Emsley, C. 'The Great British Bobby'. Quercus. London, 2009 – Policing the Home Front.

[56] Campbell, B. 'The rape of human justice'. The Independent On Sunday. 28.1.07, p32.

[57] Murray, J. 'I was drunk, wearing a short skirt ...'. Daily Mail. 16.2.10, p14.

[58] Silvester, N. 'Probe as top cops clash over sex bias'. Sunday Mail. 21.9.08, p32.

[59] Campbell, B., Goodchild, S. 'Rapists escape justice 'because of police attitudes to women' '. The Independent On Sunday. 28.1.07, p2.

[60] Booth, S. 'Former Officer's Devastating Attack On Strathclyde Police'. Daily Record. 14.11.08, p13.

[61] Emsley, C. 'The Great British Bobby'. Quercus. London, 2009, p245.

[62] 'PC 'told to lose make-up' '. Daily Record. 21.9.10, p9.

[63] Gillett, K. 'Women Cop A Record'. Sunday Mail. 6.3.11, p40.

[64] Mason, G. The Official History Of The Metropolitan Police. Carlton. 2004, p21

[65] Gill, C. 'Macho tests 'hold women police back' '. Daily Mail. 27.12.07, p33.

[66] Bilton, M. 'NYPD Blues'. Sunday Times Magazine. 2.8.98, pp14-20

[67] http://www.bawp.org/.

[68] Helm, T. 'Four in 10 female police officers have considered quitting the force'. The Observer. 15.7.12, p7.

[69] Fairburn, R. 'Officers transferred over 'sexual and racist' emails'. Daily Mail. 1.3.13, p24.

[70] Kirker, A. 'Was Jean Scotland's first police woman?'. Sunday Post. 29.9.13, p34.

[71] Wright, S., Pendlebury, R. 'Ali Dizaei suspended'. Daily Mail. 19.9.08, p5.

[72] Kelly, T. 'Met policeman wanted to 'bring down the lazy blacks', tribunal is told'. Daily Mail. 3.3.09, p24.

[73] Mason, G. The Official History Of The Metropolitan Police. Carlton. 2004, p22.

[74] Grant, C. 'Call on every crime victim'. Daily Mail. 2.9.09, p12.

[75] Widdecombe, A. 'Matthews is bad but not 'pure evil''. Daily Express. 28.1.09, p13.

[76] 'Disabled Bay'. The People. 18.1.09, p23.

[77] Dowling, F. K. 'Ex-servicemen should get the jubilee medal'. The Sunday Telegraph. 4.12.11, p27.

[78] Caven, B. 'Party-pooping police 'ruin Christmas' '. Daily Mail. 14.12.12, p25,

[79] Hitchens, P. 'So you want to legalise cannabis?'. The Mail on Sunday. 16.12.12, p29.

[80] Wilkinson, P. 'What a joke'. Daily Express. 22.9.03, p15.

[81] Rees, A. 'Driver fined £60 – for admiring a pretty girl'. The Mail on Sunday. 8.7.12, p15.

[82] Colville, J. 'The Fringes of Power'.

[83] Levy, G. Wright, S. 'The Camp Commander'. Daily Mail. 21.2.02, p2.

[84] Petty, M. 'The traitor's tale'. Weekend. 30.11.02, pp6,8.

[85] Utton, T. 'The speed camera hypocrites (cont'd)'. Daily Mail. 16.6.03, p22.

[86] Hayes, S. 'The Biggest Gang In Britain'. 2013, p95.

[87] Dessau, B. Sunday Express. 2.10.11, p54.

[88] Mills, R. 'Police make a twit of it with online jibe at Tory'. Daily Express. 1.8.13, p4.

[89] Porter, H. 'It's the police who have a gun problem'. The Observer. 4.3.07, p33.

[90] Stewart, S. 'Cops Demand: Ban Old Firm'. Sunday Mail. 27.2.11, p5.

[91] Ranstorne, T. Special Report. Daily Mail. 21.3.09, p31.

[92] Slack, J. 'Police want power to tackle domestic bullies'. Daily Mail. 16.11.09, p5.

[93] Perry. A. 'Crime bosses and Nazi thugs 'will use new law to identify informants' '. Sunday Express. 26.12.04, p36.

[94] Chapman, J. 'Clegg pledges to expand freedom of information'. Daily Mail. 6.1.11, p8.

[95] Littlejohn, R. 'Smells Like A Red Herring'. Daily Mail. 17.7.09, p17.

[96] Booker, C. 'Britain's child snatchers are a scandal'. The Sunday Telegraph. 16.5.10, p29.

[97] Womack, S. 'Personal Finance'. The Mail on Sunday. 20.2.11, p79.

[98] 'KIDS' CIGS SNATCH'. Sunday Mail. 20.2.11, p39.

[99] Delaney, S. 'Framed'. The Sunday Telegraph, Seven. 17.8.08, p18.

[100] Brady, B. 'Councils and police rebuked for hi-tech snooping on public'. The Independent on Sunday. 17.7.11, p32.

[101] Pollard, S. 'Unintended consequences'. Daily Express. 3.3.11, p13.

[102] Hull, L. 'Storm over city's night-time curfew on ALL under-16s'. Daily Mail. 18.6.12, p25.

[103] Fairweather, F. 'Why the police now have to ask teenage muggers'. The Mail on Sunday. 18.5.08, p10.

[104] Camber, R. 'Police forced to get rid of all mugshots of innocents'. Daily Mail. 23.6.12.

[105] Whitehead, T., Barrett, D. 'Police use ant-terror law to seize data at will'. The Sunday Telegraph. 14.7.13, p10.

[106] Gallacher, S. 'Crooks may seek shelter in new ruling'. The Sunday Post. 12.10.08, p4.

[107] Macaskill, M. 'Stop and search powers reviewed' The Sunday Times, 7.7.13 p13.

[108] 'Police stop 'suspicious Barry George'. The Mail on Sunday. 24.8.08, p5.

[109] Parthen, A. 'Blair's new neighbours questioned at gunpoint'. The Mail on Sunday. 22.7.07, p23.

[110] Slack, J. 'Big Brother Marches On'. Daily Mail. 3.12.08, p1.

[111] Leppard, D. 'Police secretly snapping up to 14 drivers a day'. The Sunday Times. 4.4.10, p6.

REFERENCES

112 Slack, J. 'Stop And Search UK'. Daily Mail. 16.4.10, p8.

113 'Comedian's Police Payout'. Daily Mail. 21.4.10, p39..

114 'Police face legal threat over stop and search'. Daily Mail. 15.3.10, p31.

115 Woods, R. 'The Shooting Party's Over'. The Sunday Times Magazine. 7.3.10, p25.

116 Manning, S. 'How's my searching? Police hit wrong gang targets due to old intelligence'. The Independent on Sunday. 7.7.13, p26.

117 Herbert, D. 'Police stop and search checks double'. Daily Express. 3.8.13, p27.

118 Kampfer, J. The Sunday Times. 28.4.13, p25.

119 Slack, J. 'Civil liberties victory over stop and search'. Daily Mail. 9.7.10, p36.

120 Slack, J. 'Stop and search law illegal – but it stays'. Daily Mail. 2.7.10, p19.

121 Mellor, D. 'Why we must all stand up to these officious jobsworths'. Daily Mail. 6.8.10, p22.

122 Whitehead, T. 'Police to set up supermarket cells'. Daily Express. 29.8.08, p5.

123 ' 'Stops' by police up one-third in a year'. Daily Mail. 9.7.08, p13.

124 Dolan, A., Clark, L. 'Parents left in the dark as drugs police strip-search ten boys at a village school'. Daily Mail. 14.3.12, p7.

125 O'Hare, P. 'Laws Of The Game Driving Away Fans'. Daily Record. 22.6.13, p9.

126 Forsyth, F. 'It's time to stand up for the British'. Daily Express. 13.8.10, p13.

127 Forsyth, F. 'Put an end to breaches of our ancient rights'. Daily Express. 27.8.10, p13.

128 Brown, M. 'EU plan to let foreign police spy on Britons'. Daily Express. 17.7.10, p2.

129 'The Wright Stuff'. C5. 13.6.13.

130 Robertson, C. 'Pubs face backlash over new law'. The Sunday Post. 12.7.09, p4.

131 Fielding, J. 'Big Brother takes over the Olympics'. Sunday Express. 5.7.09, p15.

132 Cohen, N. 'The Censorship Olympics'. Daily Mail. 14.7.12, p16.

133 Leppard, D. 'Spy bugs may be deployed for 2012'. The Sunday Times. 7.6.09, p12.

134 Widdecombe, A. 'Wake up to Big Brother nightmare'. Daily Express. 28.12.05, p13.

135 Schofield, K. 'Speaker says raid cop broke the law'. Daily Record. 4.12.08, p4.

136 Allen, V. Camber, R. 'Police 'used Stasi tactics' arresting Sun news chiefs'. Daily Mail. 14.2.12, p10.

137 McBeth, J. 'Barra- Loads of Bargains'. Daily Mail. 2.3.13, pp44,45.

138 Armstrong, S. 'Nyman and his nemesis'. The Sunday Telegraph. 8.3.09, p19.

139 BBC1 News. 10.11.11.

140 Hickley, M. 'Soham police chief blasts the 'paranoia' over child protection'. Daily Mail. 16.9.09, p17.

141 Booth, L. 'Chatham chippie' law: when taking a photo is terrorism'. The Mail on Sunday. 6.12.09.

142 Moore, V. 'Why Taking A Photo Of Any Of These Sights Could Get You Arrested'. Daily Mail. 12.12.09, pp44-45.

143 'Police stop and search over a million suspects'. Daily Mail. 1.5.09 p2.

144 Grant, G. 'Big Brother fear as shop staff get 'bodycams' to film racists'. Daily Mail. 30.7.13, p21.

145 North, R. 'The Insolence of Office'. The Mail on Sunday. 9.1.11, p29.

146 Narain, J. 'Outcry as police ban Ku Klux Klan jibe at 'racist' soccer star'. Daily Mail. 13.2.12, p19.

147 Raab, D. 'Rest uneasy – the spooks will catch all the innocents'. The Sunday Times. 17.6.12, p23.

148 Littlejohn, R. Daily Mail. 26.3.13, p17.

149 Phillips, M. 'The Leveson lovers and a compromised Inquiry that's begun a chilling assault on free speech'. Daily Mail. 23.4.13, p14.

150 'Arrested at dawn and DNA tested for swearing once'. Daily Mail. 11.11.09, p32.

151 Booker, C. 'Britain's forced adoptions'. The Sunday Telegraph. 8.8.10, p6.

152 Booker, C. 'Who do these police serve?'. The Sunday Telegraph. 25.9.11, p37.

153 Slack, J. 'The end of Big Brother'. Daily Mail. 14.7.10, p8.

154 Widdecombe, A. Daily Express. 24.4.13, p13.

155 Baird, R. 'Big Brother is watching'. Daily Express. 24.1.02, p11.

156 Ronson, J. 'What Made This Man Destroy Everything He Loved?'. Daily Mail. 29.11.08, p65.

157 Slack, J., Doyle, J. 'Big Brother fear as drivers urged to spy on each other'. Daily Mail. 18.9.10, p23.

158 Millward, D. 'Police to get new device to trap drug drivers'. The Daily Telegraph. 6.8.10, p1.

159 Copping, J. 'Which one are you? How police pigeonhole the public'. The Sunday Telegraph. 12.12.10, p7.

160 Horne, M. 'Britain's secret war on the Scientologist 'mafia' '. The Mail on Sunday. 7.8.11, p32.

161 Braiden, G. 'Fears over police misuse of anti-sectarian powers'. The Herald. 28.2.13, pp1,14.

162 Bower, T. 'It's a truly terrifying paradox. In the name of freedom, Britain is becoming a police state'. Daily Mail. 5.2.08, p12.

163 Doward, J 'Police say sorry for 'spying' on audience at peace film show'. The Observer. 11.9.11, p17.

164 Slack, J. 'To catch a thief: Spend 13 hours filling in ten forms'. Daily Mail. 1.2.08, p31.

165 'Gadgets to check prints in the street'. Daily Express. 5.3.10, p31.

166 Harrison, I. 'Police search four-year-olds in the street'. The Sunday Post. 23.5.10, p10.

[167] Harrison, I. 'Police may access kids' fingerprints'. The Sunday Post. 7.10.07, p2.

[168] Leask, D. 'Crime-fighting tool too costly for Scots'. Scotland on Sunday. 9.5.10, p7.

[169] Lee, A. 'Rise Of Computer-Cop'. Daily Express. 20.8.11, p26.

[170] Goslett, M. 'Rapid rise of the citizen spies for hire'. The Sunday Times. 30.1.11, p9.

[171] Drury, I. 'Revealed, how RAF tried to 'cure' lesbian recruits'. Daily Mail. 16.4.11, p7.

[172] Smith, M. 'Secret probe into newsmen'. The Mail on Sunday. 8.2.04, p2.

[173] Emsley, C. 'The Great British Bobby'. Quercus. London. 2009.

[174] Rose, D. 'Anger as merger of 'spy cops' squads lumps protesters in with terrorists'. The Mail on Sunday. 23.1.11, p2.

[175] Lewis, J. 'Police keep secret files on 1900 protesters'. The Mail on Sunday. 23.5.10, p46.

[176] Doward, J. 'Home Office plans undercover police 'spies' in pubs'. The Observer. 7.10.07, p7.

[177] Slack, J. 'Jacqui's civilian snoopers given yet more power'. Daily Mail. 9.7.12, p18.

[178] Slack, J. '1,000 innocent victims of Big Brother Britain'. Daily Mail. 14.7.12, p10.

[179] Bates, D. 'Google's four requests a day to help the police'. Daily Mail. 19.6.12, p12.

[180] Littlejohn. 'So that's what they mean by the Flying Squad'. Daily Mail. 5.2.10, p19.

[181] McDermott, N. 'Police drones are grounded ... for breaking the law'. Daily Mail. 16.2.10, p24.

[182] Christian, N. 'War-zone drones to aid police in Britain'. Scotland on Sunday. 2009.

[183] Littlejohn, R. 'Spy planes should target terrorists, not tractor thieves'. Daily Mail. 2.2.10, p15.

[184] Blackstock. G. 'Police plans for spies in the skies'. The Sunday Post. 28.3.10, p2.

[185] Doyle, J. 'Big Brother society is bigger than ever'. Daily Mail. 12.11.10, p4.

[186] Giannangelli, M. 'Drivers face 'spy in the sky' checks on mobiles'. Sunday Express. 2.9.07, p33.

[187] Ward, P. 'Network of 'super' CCTV cameras to curb crime'. Daily Mail. 30.4.13, p31.

[188] Slack, J., Newling, D. 'Police order pubs to video all customers'. Daily Mail. 18.2.09, p15.

[189] 'Motorway cameras let police track all car trips'. The Mail on Sunday. 1.3.09, p37.

[190] Solomons, M. 'Camouflaged'. Sunday Mirror. 18.10.09, p15.

[191] Whitehead, T. 'CCTV being used to trap drivers rather than yobs'. Daily Express. 20.10.07, p17.

[192] '1 in 1,000 CCTVs cut crime'. Daily Express. 25.8.09, p9.

[193] Hall, M. 'CCTV cameras being used as cheap policing'. Daily Express. 18.12.09, p26.

[194] 'Cats-eyes to catch speeders'. Daily Express.

[195] Townsend, M. 'Call for 1000 more speed cameras to save lives'. The Observer. 21.8.05, pp1,2.

[196] 'Snap ... police van has got you'. Daily Express. 22.5.10.

[197] Salkeld, L. 'Scariest speed camera of all ...'. Daily Mail. 3.11.10, p13.

[198] Gray, c. 'Council recruits volunteers to spy on the neighbours'. Daily Express. 24.9.10, p27.

[199] Channel 4 News. 30.9.10.

[200] Massey, R. 'Parking fines quadruple in five years', 'Super-cameras will mean no hiding place for drivers'. Daily Mail. 29.12.07, p14.

[201] Dorman, N. 'Spy Car Is On Prowl'. The People. 22.8.10, p25.

[202] Williams, C. 'Police use anti-terror kit to chase parking fines'. The Sunday Times. 29.8.10, p11.

[203] 'Personal CCTV to protect NHS staff'. The Sunday Post. 4.7.10, p29.

[204] Salkeld, L. 'Deployed in secret, the satellite speed cameras'. Daily Mail. 20.4.10, p12.

[205] Camber, R. 'Police take 14m 'secret' photos of drivers every day'. Daily Mail. 5.4.10, p13.

[206] McLeod, K. 'Scotland's Spy Way network'. Daily Record. 27.8.11, p18.

[207] ' 'Sneaky' speed cam row'. Daily Record. 5.4.11, p6.

[208] Groves, J. 'Speed cameras 'do not cut accidents' '. Daily Mail. 24.8.11, p17.

[209] Brown, A. 'Taking Liberties'. Daily Record. 11.

[210] 'Cop-cams put neds in frame'. Daily Record. 25.1.12, p26.

[211] Reynolds, M. 'No hiding place as the police cut crime by tailing burglars'. Daily Express. 3.6.09, p17.

[212] 'Tory fury at police red tape'. Daily Express. 12.8.08, p10.

[213] McKinstry. L. 'How Labour's lies have diminished a once proud nation'. Daily Express. 19.2.09, p12.

[214] 'EU plans PC Spies'. News of the World. 4.1.09, p25.

[215] Leppard, D. 'Police to step up hacking of home PCs'. The Sunday Times. 4.1.09, p13.

[216] Bates, D., Stocks, J. 'Civil liberties chief targeted by police in Green leaks probe'. Daily Mail. 18.4.09, p2.

[217] 'Police can snoop on all of our emails'. The Mail on Sunday. 26.4.09, p6.

[218] Liddle, R. 'Terror warning! It's been raised from daft to perplexing'. The Sunday Times. 24.1.10, p19.

[219] Lewis, J. 'Phone firms net £9 million giving data to the police'. The Mail on Sunday. 14.12.08, p34.

[220] Newling, D. 'British police are bugging our calls'. Daily Mail. 20.9.07, p6.

[221] Townend, D. 'MI5 tapped the King's phones in Abdication'. Daily Express. 7.1.12, p26.

[222] Barrett, D. 'State can spy on your phone calls, texts and emails'. The Sunday Telegraph. 19.3.12. p12

[223] Doyle, J. 'Police storing the phone data of innocent people ... for life'. Daily Mail. 19.5.12, p14.

[224] Slack, J. 'Now foreign police forces can snoop on your emails'. Daily Mail. 4.7.12, p2.

REFERENCES

[225] Herbert, D. 'Scots targeted by email snoopers'. Daily Express. 5.8.13, p9.

[226] Asthana, A. 'US scientists crack 'anonymous' datasets'. The Observer. 24.1.10, p25.

[227] Willey, J. 'Complete fiasco has cost us £10m says hospital boss'. Daily Express. 14.2.09, p15.

[228] Brooks, H. 'No photos please'. The Sunday Times. 6.12.09, p22.

[229] Lewis, J. 'Outrage at secret probe into 47,00 innocent flyers'. The Mail On Sunday. 16.5.10, p32.

[230] McKinstry, L. 'How Labour's lies have diminished a once proud nation'. Daily Express. 19.2.09, p12.

[231] Breslin, J. P. 'Protesters slam police filming 'intimidation'. The Sunday Post. 29.8.10, p43.

[232] Slack, J. 'The few who knew his real ID'. Daily Mail. 5.3.10, p9.

[233] 'The Net Tightens'. The Sunday Times. 19.6.11, p22.

[234] Camber, R. 'Report a crime and end up on a secret database'. Daily Mail. 12.8.10, p10.

[235] Whelan, G. 'Scandal Of Big Brother Britain'. Daily Express. 1.3.11, pp1,4.

[236] Greenwood, C. 'One in four Britons put on new police database'. Daily Mail. 17.6.11, p22.

[237] Stewart, S. 'Prison Visitor Pics Plot Prompts Fury'. Sunday Mail. 3.7.11, p17.

[238] Boffey, D. 'Revealed: police link to blacklist of workers'. The Observer. 4.3.12, pp1,9.

[239] Green, D. 'DNA: Now it's the police's secret enemy'. The Mail on Sunday. 3.1.10, p30.

[240] Ford, R. 'Police will keep DNA if suspects acquitted'. The Times. 20.1.01, p4.

[241] Woolf, M. 'DNA database chaos with 500,000 false or misspelt entries'. The Independent on Sunday. 26.8.07, p22.

[242] Slack, J. 'DNA of a baby held on the national database'. Daily Mail. 10.3.09, p6.

[243] 'Cops kid DNA row'. The Sun. 29.4.12, p16.

[244] O'Grady, G. ' Fury over database with 1.1m. DNA samples from children' Daily Express. 28.2.09, p9.

[245] Hoyle, A. 'BBC personality made 40 false rape allegations'. The Mail on Sunday. 25.1.09, p9.

[246] Kampfner, J. 'You can't play the fame game with civil liberties'. Daily Mail. 22.8.09, p31.

[247] Hickley, M. 'Banish Big Brother'. Daily Mail. 6.2.09, p4.

[248] Slack, J. '250 innocent people added to police DNA files for every one removed'. Daily Mail. 15.1.10, p31.

[249] Slack, J. 'Hang on to unlawful DNA police chiefs told'. Daily Mail. 8.8.09, p19.

[250] Slack, J. 'The DNA snatchers'. Daily Mail. 24.11.09, p8.

[251] O'Flynn, P. 'Why Politicians Should Be Speaking UP For The DNA Database'. Daily Express. 2.1.10, p17.

[252] Daily Express. 19.1.11, p10.

[253] Lewis, J. 'Detectives trawl DNA database 60 times a year - hunting for criminals' relatives'. The Mail on Sunday. 28.2.10, p22.

[254] 'True Crime'. Sunday Telegraph Magazine. 21.3.10, p12.

[255] Doyle, J. 'EU police win access to our DNA bank'. Daily Mail. 14.3.12, p2.

[256] Robinson, W. 'Scottish Police DNA Database Snares The Innocent'. Scottish Daily Mail. 1.4.13, pp1,4.

[257] Camber, R. 'Another 165,000 on DNA database'. Daily Mail. 5.6.12, p27.

[258] Camber, R. 'We're innocent … but police are still keeping our DNA'. Daily Mail. 6.6.12, p24.

[259] Slack, J. 'Big Brother databases may ruin innocent lives, warns watchdog'. Daily Mail. 11.6.09, p13.

[260] 'Scores are branded criminals by mistake'. Daily Mail. 3.8.09.

[261] Slack, J. 'Millions of offences may be wiped from police computer'. Daily Mail. 23.6.09, p27.

[262] Ferrari, N. Sunday Express. 15.5.11, p23.

[263] Nelson, N. 'Barmy Rule Threatens Parents'. The People. 15.2.09, p31.

[264] Slack, J. '12,000 innocents are branded as criminals'. Daily Mail. 13.11.08, p14.

[265] Wright, S. 'Criminal record blunders brand innocents thugs and perverts'. Daily Mail. 14.4.10, p4.

[266] Ungoed-Thomas, J., Warren, G. 'Criminal records on sale for just £37'. The Sunday Times. 24.8.08, p7.

[267] 'Cop in snoop shame'. Daily Record. 22.7.09, p23.

[268] Kennedy, P. '300 cops snoop on Gerrard'. Sunday Mirror. 27.9.09, p33.

[269] Bowater, D. 'College gives files of climate change to police'. Daily Express. 16.4.10, p15.

[270] Whelan, A., Churcher, S. 'The Mail on Sunday. 1.8.10, p26.

[271] Hamilton, N. 'Going to hell in handcuffs'. Sunday Express. 7.12.08, p26.

[272] Findlay, R. 'What A Joke'. Sunday Mail. 22.11.09, p35.

[273] Musson, C. 'Fake Cops In Bank Heist'. Daily Record. 11.10.11, pp1,7.

[274] Aisley, J. 'Teen vigilante posed as policeman'. Daily Express. 18.10.09, p24.

[275] Wright, S. 'Bogus policeman even fooled his wife'. Daily Mail. 9.1.10, p34.

[276] 'Fake cop is an eejit'. Daily Record. 6.12.08, p23.

[277] Twomey, J. 'Untouchable' drug baron gets 18 years'. Daily Express. 7.8.08, p24.

[278] 'Stripper on fake cop car charge'. Daily Record. 28.5.09, p11.

[279] Dow, B. 'Stripper Copy Rage'. Daily Record. 17.1.09 p25.

[280] 'I'll strip to pay fake cop fine'. Daily Record. 17.7.09 p31.

[281] Scott, M. 'Stripper Cop's Baby Boom'. Sunday Mail. 19.8.12, pp1,7.

[282] 'What does it take to get a teacher fired?'. Daily Mail. 1.9.11, p10.

[283] 'Blue-light fever of a fake cop'. Sunday Mirror. 12.4.09, p21.

[284] Riches, C. 'Mum's terror as baby is stolen in car by fake PC'. Daily Express. 28.2.09 p11.

[285] Morgan. T. 'Taken into custody the scarecrow policeman'. Daily Express. 8.7.09, p29.

[286] Silvester, N. 'Shamed charity worker posed as cop'. Sunday Mail. 5.7.09, p27.

[287] Stute, M. 'Jailed conman who thought he was James Bond'. Daily Express. 1.11.08, p11.

[288] 'Two charged over death of accountant'. Daily Record. 1.12.08, p4.

[289] 'Bogus cops target OAPs'. Sunday Mail. 28.10.07, p33.

[290] 'Bogus cop is jailed'. Daily Record. 20.3.08, p27.

[291] 'Fake cops rob man, 94'. Daily Record. 2.4.08, p17.

[292] 'Raiders dress up as cops'. Sunday Mirror. 27.1.08, p33.

[293] 'Fake police in park theft'. Daily Record. 21.6.07, p27.

[294] Sanderson, D. 'Super Mario'. Big Brother. 15.6.08, p2.

[295] 'Bike 'cop' wanted to look the part'. Daily Record. 21.2.08, p17.

[296] Daily Express. 1.2.08, p31.

[297] MacKinnon, L. 'eBay Hero Is A Fake'. Daily Record. 25.7.07, pp1,4,5.

[298] Fagge, N. '£53 m. rubber-face gang'. Daily Express. 27.6.07, p10.

[299] 'Cop cons in phone fine scam'. Daily Record. 7.3.07, p12.

[300] O'Hare, P. 'Bogus Cops Pull Over Drivers For Drink Test'. Daily Record. 12.10.10, p19.

[301] Pilditch, D. 'Bogus PC with sirens on his fake patrol car'. Daily Express. 5.8.10, p30.

[302] 'Road fraud fake cops sentenced'. Daily Record. 9.3.07, p37.

[303] Leppard, D. 'Black bra, red stockings: is that a fair cop?' The Sunday Times. 27.09.09, p5

[304] 'Bogus cops get 5 years'. Sunday Mirror. 4.7.10, p28.

[305] 'Drug pair's 'cop' terror'. Sunday Mirror. 18.7.10, p28.

[306] '50 Years Ago'. Daily Express. 8.9.10, p10.

[307] Goslett, M. 'Met buys The Bill's kit to foil criminals'. The Sunday Times. 17.10.10, p11.

[308] '£20,000 bogus cop con'. Daily Record. 4.12.10, p10.

[309] Wright, S. '100-raid rampage of 'Crime Machine' freed early from prison'. Daily Mail. 15.2.07, p29.

[310] 'Bogus cops attack Brits'. Sunday Mirror. 5.12.10, p25.

[311] 'Fake cop mag scam'. Daily Record. 12.2.11, p27.

[312] 'Con cop on loose'. Sunday Mail. 12.2.12, p7.

[313] Chalk, N. 'Margaret's Rolls-Royce is sold'. Sunday Express. 19.6.11, p9.

[314] 'OAP loses £10K to bogus cops'. Daily Record. 5.8.11, p31.

[315] O'Neill, C. 'Bogus Cop Cons £40K From Gran'. Daily Record. 11.11.11, p20.

[316] Findlay, R. 'Bogus Cop's Terror Trail'. Sunday Mail. 10.3.13, p35.

[317] O'Hare, P. 'OAP Hit By Crime Gang Bank Hoax'. Daily Record. 6.12.11, p12.

[318] 'OAPs hit by con'. Daily Record. 8.3.12, p9.

[319] Littlejohn, R. 'Hounded by a bogus dog warden? You're barking'. Daily Mail. 10.2.12, p17.

[320] Mega, M. 'DNA expert's appliance of science called into question'. Scotland on Sunday. 18.5.08, p11.

[321] Camber, R. 'Thieves pose as policemen to prey on Olympic fans'. Daily Mail. 22.6.12, p27.

[322] Andrews, J. 'A 999 call and the credit card scam that cost one thousands'. Daily Mail. 18.12.12, p23.

[323] 'Man faces fake cop rap'. Daily Record. 21.12.12, p23.

[324] Beatson, J. 'Fake Cop Alert'. Daily Record. 5.1.13, p33.

[325] Gysin, C. 'The 'policeman' behind riot blog who turned out to be a conman'. Daily Mail. 14.7.12, p52.

[326] 'Joyrider on patrol'. Daily Mail. 17.9.02, p23.

[327] Bugler, T. Daily Express. 5.1.13, p27.

[328] Reynolds, M. 'Conman poses as police officer to fleece fiancees'. Daily Express. 31.1.13, p34.

[329] Chapman, J. 'Bogus police steal pup in house raid'. Daily Express. 6.2.13, p26.

[330] Beaston, J. 'Bogus cop accused women of offences'. Daily Express. 1.3.13, p36.

[331] 'Raiding is lost art'. The Sunday Post. 24.2.13, p45.

[332] Mills, R. 'Young mother terrorised by bogus car cop'. Daily Express. 28.3.13, p25.

[333] Bugles, T. 'Walter Pity'. Daily Record. 18.4.13, p32.

[334] Nick Hardwick. IPCC.

[335] Scougall, M. 'Painting the town BLOOD RED'. The Sunday Post. 21.4.13, p40.

[336] Lock J. 'The British Policewoman: Her Story', p94.

[337] Gallagher, P. 'Cops & Robbers & Thugs & Killers & Sex Offenders & Yobs & Urinaters & Fraudsters & Drink-Drivers & Child Abusers & Drug Barons & Wife-Batterers & Badger-Baiters'. The People. 28.9.08, p8.

[338] Chapman, J. 'On duty, 1,000 police found guilty of crimes'. Daily Mail. 11.3.09, p8.

[339] McLaughlin, M. '12-year-olds kept in police cells overnight'. Scotland on Sunday, 30.6.13.

[340] 'Met chief rooted out bent cops'. Daily Express. 9.10.10, p43.

REFERENCES

[341] Emsley, C. 'The Great British Bobby'. Quercus. London. 2009.

[342] Gladdis, K. 'Convict Coppers'. News Of The World. 28.10.07, p31.

[343] Greenwood, C. 'Almost 1,000 officers with convictions from drug dealing to perverting justice still in the police'. Daily Mail. 3.1.12, p10.

[344] Roberts, G. 'One in ten prisoners is a former soldier, new research reveals'. The Independent on Sunday. 15.7.12, p10.

[345] Allen, V. 'How criminal police officers are allowed to keep their jobs'. Daily Mail. 3.12.12, p12.

[346] Gilfeather, M. 'Saint George'. Sunday Mirror. 27.11.94, p31.

[347] Williams, D., Owen, J. 'Reminder to police: it is not good practice to doctor evidence'. The Independent On Sunday. 19.10.08, p49.

[348] Leader. 'Ignore the squeals, it's time for No. 10's dawn wake-up call'. The Mail on Sunday. 21.1.07, p33.

[349] O'Hare, P. 'It's Too Dear To Send Bent Cop To Jail'. Daily Record. 26.3.10, p27.

[350] 'Drunk cheat cop quits'. Sunday Mail. 298.3.10, p18.

[351] Thornton, P. 'Crooks Fight 'Dodgy' Cop Confessions'. Daily Record. 18.4.09, p15.

[352] Curran, J. 'Fit-up Coppers Quit Before They're Fired'. Daily Record. 12.2.09, p15.

[353] 'Policeman in the dock'. Daily Record. 13.11.10, p31.

[354] Hull, L. 'Officers 'bribed thief for false confessions' '. Daily Mail. 7.6.07, p41.

[355] 'Miscarriages of Justice – A review of Justice in Error'. edited by Clive Walker and Keir Starmer, p374.

[356] 'Corruption quiz for cop'. Sunday Mirror. 15.5.11, p10.

[357] The Official History Of The Metropolitan Police. Gary Mason. Carlton. 2004, p139.

[358] Newburn, T. 'Understanding and preventing police corruption: lessons from the literature'. Police Research series. Paper 110. Research Development and Statistics Directorate, Home Office.

[359] Leppard, D. 'Border officers 'in bribes for visas' racket'. The Sunday Times. 1.5.11, p11.

[360] Silvester, N. 'Speed Rap Cop: Gun Was Faulty'. Sunday Mail. 2.10.11, p10.

[361] Fallon, A. 'Ello 'ello, you're on a yellow line'. Daily Express. 4.4.09, p31.

[362] Dickson, B. 'Rogue warden breaks law again to book motorist'. Daily Record. 18.11.10, p32.

[363] 'Top 'Tec In Speed 'Fiddle' '. The Sun. 21.2.11, p14.

[364] 'Driving ban for cop who listed beer as interest'. Daily Record. 16.2.11, p10.

[365] McLean, M. 'Tsk, Tsk, Disc'. Daily Record. 3.8.13, p27.

[366] Alexander, S. 'Your Parking's Bang-Er Out Of Order, Officers', Daily Record. 26.4.12, p12.

[367] Riches, C. 'Fleeing PC outruns pursuing helicopter'. Daily Express. 2.4.10, p40.

[368] Officer 'A'. 'The Crime Factory'. Mainstream Publishing. 2012.

[369] 'Cop In Court'. Daily Record. 27.8.03, p19.

[370] 'Policeman who tried to trick the speed traps'. Daily Mail. 24.5.02, p23.

[371] Geddes, B. 'Sleuth stole lighter from cop shop'. Daily Record. 7.12.12, p41.

[372] 'Cop-lifting rap at mall'. News of the World. 26.7.09, p40.

[373] Dawar, A. 'Caught shoplifting, the PC on a stores patrol'. Daily Express. 9.11.09, p22.

[374] 'Shoplift PC saved from jail'. Daily Express. 2.12.09, p19.

[375] Hale, B. 'Facing ten years in jail, the Royal policeman who fleeced his friends'. Daily Mail. 18.7.09, p45.

[376] Gillard, M. 'Fraud At Heart Of The Palace'. The Sunday Times. 19.7.09, p10.

[377] McPherson, L. 'Let-off for shoplift rap cop'. Sunday Mail. 21.9.03, p10.

[378] Whelan, A. 'PC 'sold fake goods he seized from boot sales' '. The Mail on Sunday. 16.5.10, p36.

[379] Schlesinger. F. 'Police chief charge with make-up theft'. Daily Mail. 25.2.10, p33.

[380] 'Woman chief inspector is cleared of shoplifting'. Daily Mail. 12.11.10, p31.

[381] Syal, R. 'Card fraud probe targets 300 detectives'. The Observer. 14.6.09, p5.

[382] 'The Met's amnesty for its fiddling staff is a disgrace'. Daily Express. 10.8.09, p14.

[383] Townend, D. 'Secret amnesty for police over abusing credit cards'. Daily Express. 10.8.09, p8.

[384] Morgan, T. 'Jail for gambling PC who stole dead man's winnings'. Daily Express. 6.12.08, p46.

[385] Henderson, E. 'Benefits cheat PC jailed'. Sunday Express. 17.5.09, p19.

[386] Dickson, B. 'PC Fraud'. Daily Record. 8.5.09, p41.

[387] Mills, J. 'Police chiefs in M&S theft probe'. Daily Mail. 1.10.08, p43.

[388] Wright, S. '7/7 expenses fiddle'. Daily Mail. 13.5.09, p12.

[389] 'Cop 'stole sex lotion' '. Sunday Mail. 31.7.11, p32.

[390] C5 News. 4.8.11.

[391] Classic FM News. 4.8.11.

[392] 'Police Nicked'. Daily Record. 31.3.11, p28.

[393] Crooks, L. 'Cop Lifter'. Sunday Mail. 4.9.11, p16.

[394] Edge, S. 'Secret Suburban Life Of The Krays' Supergrass'. Daily Express. 13.2.08, p25.

[395] Utley, T. 'A heart-stopping call from the police, my sister's lost wallet and why you just can't trust anyone'. Daily Mail. 27.1.12, p14.

[396] 'Former cop in £68K fiddle'. Sunday Mail. 5.2.12, p38

[397] http://www.charitytimes.com/pages/et.features/may-june06.

[398] '9 months for police fund thief'. Daily Express. 26.11.11, p15.

[399] 'Cop Nabs £58K'. The Sun. 23.3.12, p34.

[400] 'Met theft pair guilty'. The Sun. 13.4.12, p19.

[401] Officer 'A'. 'The Crime Factory'. Mainstream Publishing. 2012.

[402] Chamberlain, A. '£10K Benefit Fraud … By Benefit Fraud Officer'. The Sun. 4.5.12, p43.

[403] Martin, A. 'Woman police chief is accused of stealing £30 of make-up from Asda'. Daily Mail. 15.9.12, p55.

[404] Blacklock, M. 'Former fraud squad officer 'stole £12,000' '. Daily Express. 4.9.02, p17.

[405] Sims, P., Camber, R. 'Police fear 90 cases may be tainted after crime scene officer is arrested'. Daily Mail. 29.8.12, p10.

[406] 'Cigs scam cops jailed'. The People. 1.7.12, p23.

[407] Thomas, C. 'By Day … Policeman on the beat. By Night … A serial burglar'. Sunday Mail. 23.3.03, p31.

[408] Loudon, A. 'MI5 spy on Al Qaeda mission is caught shoplifting'. Daily Mail .15.11.02, p4.

[409] Blacklock, M. 'Former fraud squad 'stole £12,000' '. Daily Express. 4.9.02, p17.

[410] Hayes, S. 'The Biggest Gang In Britain'. 2013, p53.

[411] 'Officer is charged with fraud'. Sunday Mail. 18.8.13, p12.

[412] Twomey, J. 'Crooked police chief jailed for false arrest'. Daily Express. 9.2.10, 9.

[413] Panton, L. 'Good Riddance To Swaggering Slug'. News of the World. 14.2.10, p17.

[414] Wright, S., Pendlebury, R. 'A Criminal In Uniform'. Daily Mail. 9.2.10, p12.

[415] Gallagher, I. The Mail on Sunday. 14.2.10, pp18,19.

[416] Gallagher, I. The Mail on Sunday. 14.2.10, p18.

[417] Wright, S., Pendlebury, R. 'Disgraced, jailed and now sacked … Dizaei faces ruin'. Daily Mail. 1.4.10, p35.

[418] Mahmood, M. 'Suspended Senior Met Officer Employed Bogus Asylum Seeker'. News of the World. 15.3.09, pp22-23.

[419] Wright, S. 'Dizaei of the Yard faces new trial for corruption'. Daily Mail. 22.5.09, p8.

[420] Dixon, C. 'Police chief suspended … after he is given job back'. Daily Express. 1.10.11, p8.

[421] Dixon, C. 'Shamed Yard chief can sue for racism'. Daily Express. 6.4.12, p18.

[422] Hughes, M. 'Root out corrupt officers, police told'. The Independent. 13.3.10, pp1,2.

[423] Hughes, M. 'Root out corrupt officers, police told'. The Independent. 13.2.10. p2.

[424] Barber, L. 'Members Only: The Life and Times of Paul Raymond'. Sunday Times Culture Magazine. 29.8.10.

[425] Ferguson, J., Yates, C. 'In the force we treated Scots like vermin …'. Daily Record. 10.6.13, pp10,11.

[426] Hayes, S. 'The Biggest Gang In Britain'. 2013, pp67-69.

[427] Rawstorne, T., Wright, S. 'Waterboarding and the Met'. Daily Mail. 4.7.09, pp28-29.

[428] Schlesinger, F. 'Police chief charged with make-up theft'. Daily Mail. 25.2.10, p33.

[429] Shipman, T. 'Lobbying curbs on way as peers hit by new sleaze scandal'. Daily Mail. 3.6.13, p10.

[430] 'Cops are warned over net crime trap'. Daily Record. 30.6.09, p25.

[431] Blackstock. G. 'Dozens of cops complain about other officers'. The Sunday Post. 17.5.09, p4.

[432] 'On This Day 25 Years Ago'. Daily Express. 5.12.09, p4.

[433] France, A. 'Cop Girl's 'Love For Criminal' '. The Sun. 18.5.12, p37

[434] Emsley, C. 'The Great British Bobby'. Quercus. London. 2009.

[435] Emsley, C. 'The Great British Bobby'. Quercus. London. 2009.

[436] Dorman, N. 'Policeman faces trial on brothel managing'. Sunday People. 21.4.13, p6.

[437] Seamark, M., Wright, S. 'Murderers'. Daily Mail. 27.7.06, p6.

[438] McLagan, G. 'The Bent Cop'. Panorama. 3.12.00.

[439] Slack, J. 'Cash-for-honours Chief takes over'. Daily Mail. 10.4.09, p6.

[440] Emsley, C. 'The Great British Bobby'. Quercus. London. 2009.

[441] Russell, A. 'Police sergeant with double life as a crime lord'. Daily Express. 6.11.10, p31.

[442] 'Times loses out in police corruption story libel appeal'. Press Gazette. 14.7.10.

[443] World In Action. Granada TV.

[444] Kelly, T. 'Met policeman wanted to 'bring down the lazy blacks', tribunal is told'. Daily Mail. 3.3.09, p24.

[445] 'Constable 'faked UK passport' '. Sunday People. 28.4.13, p18.

[446] Rose, D. ' 'Human bone' at centre of Jersey children's home inquiry is actually a piece of wood or coconut shell'. The Mail On Sunday. 18.5.08, p10.

[447] Hughes, M. 'Root out corrupt officers, police told'. The Independent. 13.2.10, pp1,2.

[448] 'US-style policing tactics deserve zero tolerance'. Leader. Daily Express. 22.6.00, p10.

[449] Oakeshott, I., Leppard, D. 'Ten Police Plotted Plebgate'. The Sunday Times. 24.3.13, pp1,2.

[450] Bartlett, D., Hennessy, P. 'Officer held in 'Plebgate' inquiry'. The Sunday Telegraph. 16.6.13, p1.

REFERENCES

451 Helm, T., Doward, J., Boffey, D. 'Senior Tory slams 'cancer' of corruption in UK police'. The Observer. 23.12.12, p1.

452 Leppard, D. 'Police insider blows whistle on Plebgate'. The Sunday Times. 13.10.13, pp1,2,3.

453 Murray, J. 'Who killed my brother?'. Sunday Express. 10.7.11, p11.

454 Campbell, D. 'Daniel Morgan was murdered, now it seems justice is dead, too'. The Observer. 13.3.11, p38.

455 'Detective hired by crook'. Daily Mail. 7.6.02, p23.

456 'Top cop in loan scam'. Daily Express. 9.10.03, p27.

457 Classic FM News. 14.3.11.

458 Tozer, J. '£6m drugs trial axed after juror talks to accused on Facebook'. Daily Mail. 23.4.11, p20.

459 BBC1. South Today. 26.7.10.

460 Jones. L. 'So how, exactly, was a spell in jail supposed to help my friend H?'. The Mail on Sunday. 4.7.10, p26.

461 Emsley, C. 'The Great British Bobby'. Quercus. London. 2009.

462 Newburn, T. 'Paper 110. Understanding and Preventing Police Corruption: Ch. 4. Corruption Control. Home Office. Research, Development and Statistics Directorate.

463 Ungoed-Thomas, J., Leppard, D. ' Cameron, Coulson and the crooked private detective'. The Sunday Times. 19.7.11, p18.

464 Twomey, J. 'The bent supercops'. Daily Express. 28.6.03, pp12,13

465 Penrose, J., Thompson, T. 'I had got away with the perfect crime … the cops couldn't prove it so they fitted me up'. Sunday Mirror. 28.7.13, p35.

466 Backstock, G. 'Bent copper almost cost Ronnie his life'. The Sunday Post. 12.8.07, p22.

467 Butler, J. 'Truth about race and muggers by liberal police chief'. Daily Mail. 11.10.02, p37.

468 Thurlbeck, N. 'Bent Copper For Hire'. News Of The World. 18.5.08, p23.

469 'Crooked drugs PC is jailed'. Daily Express. 13.3.10, p26.

470 Verkaik, R. 'Britain's FBI 'abandoned chasing crime Mr. Bigs because it's too difficult' '. The Mail on Sunday. 13.11.11, p15.

471 Townsend, M. 'Credit cards of 1400 officers are confiscated'. The Observer. 30.3.08, p18.

472 O'Grady, S. 'Bungling drug police force family into exile'. Sunday Express. 17.11.02, p28.

473 Pierce, A. 'Masters in fiddling'. Daily Mail. 5.3.12, p18.

474 Ungoed,-Thomas, J. 'Police 'nobbled' press inquiry into corruption'. The Sunday Times. 11.3.12, p16.

475 McEachran, J. 'Love Rat Scots Cop In Cayman Isle Probe'. Daily Record. 29.3.08, p17.

476 Wright, S. 'Dizaei set free and tagged after 2 weeks'. Daily Mail. 29.2.12, p13.

477 'We have corrupt officers'. Daily Record. 22.3.12, p19.

478 Officer 'A'. 'The Crime Factory'. Mainstream Publishing. 2012.

479 Officer 'A'. 'The Crime Factory'. Mainstream Publishing. 2012.

480 Greenwood, C. 'Yard corruption team 'took £20,000 bribes' '. Daily Mail. 23.5.12, p2.

481 'Jailed, Blunkett Bobby who hit hundreds of innocent people with fake fines'. Daily Mail. 17.7.12, p32.

482 BBC1 News. 23.5.12.

483 Transparency International. Channel 5's 'The Wright Stuff'. July, 2013.

484 Findlay, R. 'The Lyons King Exposed'. Sunday Mail. 24.6.12, p11.

485 Gallagher, I. 'Met Police accused of plot to hack phone of Foreign Minister'. The Mail on Sunday. 24.6.12, p1.

486 Greenwood, C. ' 'Shameful' police chief sacked over job inquiry'. Daily Mail. 6.10.12, p43.

487 Gillard, M. ' 'Phone hacking' security firm linked to Scotland Yard forced to hand over secret informants list'. The Mail on Sunday. 21.10.12, p23.

488 Lewis, J. 'On the police lothario's case'. The Sunday Telegraph. 2.12.12, p12.

489 Beckford, M. 'Scandal of 23,000 police with two jobs'. The Mail on Sunday. 30.12.12, p8.

490 Penrose, J. '760 Bad Cops In Britain's Biggest Force'. Sunday Mirror. 16.12.12, p24.

491 Steele, J. 'New breed of corrupt police ruin crime fight'. The Daily Telegraph. 17.6.02, p9.

492 Lavery, C. 'Bent Cops Probe'. Sunday Mail. 27.1.02, p3.

493 Tendler, S. 'Crooked detective jailed for 7 years'. The Times. 8.6.02, p7.

494 Tendler, S. 'Flying Squad corruption case collapses'. The Times. 28.6.03, p5.

495 Rees, A., Mudie, K. 'Elm Paed File Was Destroyed'. Sunday People. 24.2.13, p23.

496 'Disgraced Dizaei loses appeal over corruption'. Daily Mail. 15.2.13, p24.

497 Hayes, S. 'The Biggest Gang In Britain'. 2013, px.

498 Reynolds, M. 'In court, WPC who 'tipped off criminals' '. Daily Express. 15.5.13, p20

499 Littlejohn, R. 'So will M'lud Leveson now instigate phone-hacking lawyers? Don't hold your breath'. Daily Mail. 24.6.13, p7.

500 Dawar, A. '4,000 bent officers seized as crime by the police rockets'. Daily Express. 25.6.13, p15.

501 'PC assaulted wife when he ran out of bread to toast'. The Daily Telegraph. 23.12.11, p3.

502 McDonald, C. '3 Cops In The Same Court On Same Day'. Daily Record. 11.2.10, p9.

503 Findlay, R. 'Cop Charged Over Old Firm Loo Riot'. Sunday Mail. 20.5.12, p27.

504 Myers, R., McTague, T. 'Raid Cop Is Jailed For Knife Attack'. The People. 19.4.09, p8.

505 Jenkins, R. 'Video beating PC is jailed for two months'. The Times. 19.10.02, p7.

506 The Times. 19.10.02, p7.

507 Daily Mail. 13.5.02, p19.

508 Cross, I. 'Riot police who beat soccer fans escape rap'. The Mail on Sunday. 27.1.02, p43.

509 'Police in the dock'. Daily Record. 9.12.09, p2.

510 Findlay, R. Scott, M. 'Call this justice?'. Sunday Mail. 24.3.02, p30.

511 Penrose, J. 'Cop Sacked For Pest Texts to Ex'. Sunday Mirror. 12.6.11, p16.

512 Mulholland, J. 'Shamed PC sobs in the dock as he is convicted of two rapes'. Daily Mail. 28.2.13, p7.

513 Street-Porter, J. 'The plodding police work that has let Claudia down'. Daily Mail. 10.5.10, p49.

514 'Police girl 'in robbery''. Daily Express. 20.10.08, p15.

515 'DC charged for data breaches'. Reading Post. 25.8.10, p1.

516 Twomey, J. 'WPC on burglary charge'. Daily Express. 24.10.08, p27.

517 'Cop on data rap'. Daily Record. 21.3.09, p27.

518 'Police want to seize corrupt officer's assets'. The Sunday Post. 7.12.08, p4

519 'Snooper cop faces the sack'. Daily Record. 18.11.10, p41.

520 Mullen, kS. 'I'm a PC Hacker'. Sunday Mail. 24.10.10, p27.

521 Jedrzejewski, N. 'Crime file snoop cop dodges jail'. Daily Record. 27.4.13, p14.

522 'Bug cop sacked'. Daily Express. 7.12.10, p25.

523 'Jail term for tip-off WPC'. The People. 21.11.10, p18.

524 McPherson, L. 'Cop's War On Neighbours'. Sunday Mail. 24.2.08, p12.

525 'Cop was files spy for friend'. Daily Record. 2.9.03, p7.

526 Bayer, K. 'WPC Is Caged For Tipping Off Suspects'. Daily Record. 15.4.11, p19.

527 Stote, M. 'Face of deadly crime boss'. Daily Express. 3.8.07, p39.

528 'Gangsters' cop job bid'. Sunday Mirror. 5.8.07, p33.

529 Doward, J., Fellstrom, C. 'Monster gang baron who held police in his thrall'. The Observer. 5.8.07, pp8,9.

530 Alderson, A., Copping J. 'How police went to the dark side to regain control of city'. The Sunday Telegraph. 5.8.07, p10.

531 'Chief constable quits after woman complains over 'inappropriate emails' '. Daily Mail. 20.11.07, p21.

532 'Corrupt PC sold file to drug dealer'. Sunday Mirror. 8.8.10, p21.

533 Moncur, J. 'Rogue PC To Face Long Jail Time'. Daily Record. 13.5.08, p25.

534 'Officer charged'. Daily Record. 29.12.11, p21.

535 'Top cop on data charge'. Daily Record. 25.2.12, p32.

536 C4 News. 29.3.12.

537 'Cop faces hack rap'. Sunday Mail. 18.3.12, p12.

538 Silvester, N. 'The Killer, A Cop, His Lover And A Supergrass'. Sunday Mail. 8.4.12, p10.

539 Silvester, N. 'Rogue Cop 'Collected Debts For Murderer' '. Sunday Mail. 22.4.12, p40.

540 Findlay, R. 'Gangsters On The Beat'. Sunday Mail. 13.2.12, p2.

541 Lay, K. '263 cops beat rap on spying'. The People. 29.4.12, p19.

542 'Yard chief leak 'over Prescott' '. Daily Express. 8.1.13, p29

543 BBC1 News. 10.1.13.

544 'Reporter faces corruption case'. Daily Mail. 23.1.13, p24.

545 Kelly, T. 'PC admits he sold story about John Terry's shoplifter mother to The Sun'. Daily Mail. 9.3.13, p15.

546 BBC1 News. 26.2.13.

547 Martin, A. 'Top officer is held over 'unpaid tip to reporter' '. Daily Mail. 16.2.13, p18.

548 Brooke, C. 'Did police chief fiddle jobs drive?'. Daily Mail. 26.11.10, p45.

549 Brooke, C. 'Chief constable avoids sack over nepotism row'. Daily Mail. 11.5.11, p36.

550 BBC1 News. 9.5.11.

551 Blacklock, M., Twomey, J. 'Chief Constable and deputy are arrested in corruption probe'. Daily Express. 4.8.11, p15.

552 McKay, P. 'Why weren't the police this zealous with Savile?'. Daily Mail. 10.12.12, p17.

553 Hill, P. 'Cop leaks for worker blacklist to be probed'. Sunday People. 24.2.13, p22.

554 'Con Gets Cop's Job'. News of the World. 27.9.09, p46.

555 Stute, M. 'PC who lied about having cancer gets a year in jail'. Daily Express. 13.6.09, p41.

556 Taylor, D. 'Securishambles'. Sunday Mail. 14.6.09, p8.

557 Barrett, D. 'The 1800 suspended police who keep their pensions'. The Sunday Telegraph. 31.3.13, p13.

558 Penrose, J. 'Ex-cop held in probe on 'fake' bomb detectors'. Sunday Mirror. 24.1.10, p2.

559 Musson, C. 'Benefit Fraud Ex-Cop Serves One Day In Jail'. Daily Record. 18.6.09, p9.

[560] 'Conman is held'. Daily Express. 4.12.08, p17.

[561] 'On This Day 5 Years Ago'. Daily Express. 28.10.09, p2.

[562] Foggo, D. 'Shady past of the party bodyguards'. The Sunday Times. 25.20.09, p7.

[563] 'Policeman jailed over £1.43m fraud to fund high life'. Daily Mail. 23.11.09, p38.

[564] Petre, J. 'Police chief is suspended after probe into overseas property deals'. The Mail On Sunday. 12.12.10, p18.

[565] Tozer, J. '38 women, but police chief's job 'did not suffer' '. Daily Mail. 11.2.09, p34.

[566] Emsley, C. 'The Great British Bobby'. Quercus. London. 2009.

[567] The Argus. 9.6.10.

[568] The Argus. 26.8.10, p1.

[569] 'Detective helped lover in fraud'. The Times. 21.10.00, p8.

[570] 'Police chief punches air as cleared of all charges'. Newbury Weekly News. 3.2.11.p5.

[571] Harris, J. 'Cop Jailed For £500K RBS Sting'. Daily Record. 19.2.11, p29.

[572] Twomey, J. 'PC and wife jailed for £2m 'Reggie Perrin' death con'. Daily Express. 2.3.11, p27.

[573] Jeory, T. 'Fraud at police academy'. Sunday Express. 18.7.10, p35.

[574] 'Con Cop Dodges Prison'. Daily Record. 15.7.11, p31.

[575] Verkaik, R. 'The Metropolitan Masseurs' Force'. The Mail on Sunday. 18.9.11, p17.

[576] Fernandez, C. 'Facing jail, woman constable who lied about being mugged'. Daily Mail. 31.8.07, p13.

[577] 'Two sisters 'plotted £161m. tax scam' '. Daily Express. 8.11.11, p30.

[578] BBC News 11.11.11.

[579] '£6K crash fraud cop escapes a jail term'. Daily Record. 25.10.07, p33.

[580] Murray, J. 'Sikh police club faces curry quiz'. Sunday Express. 4.11.07, p45.

[581] Gill, C. '£2m fraud probe piles pressure on Met police chief'. Daily Mail. 12.11.07, p20.

[582] 'Ex-WPC's benefits con ... from Australia'. Daily Express. 21.3.12, p24.

[583] 'Cigs scam cops jailed'. The People. 1.7.12, p23.

[584] Jeeves, P. 'Jail for the PC who lied her daughter had cancer'. Daily Express. 31.7.12, p11.

[585] 'Jailed, Blunkett Bobby who hit hundreds of innocent people with fake fines'. Daily Mail. 17.7.12, p32.

[586] Gekoski, A. 'Cops And Robbers'. News of the World. 19.11.00, p40

[587] Twomey, J. 'Jailed, the detective who sold seized drugs back on to the streets'. Daily Express. 5.4.13, p13.

[588] 'Top barrister 'gave cocaine and heroin to husband' '. Daily Mail. 12.10.09, p25.

[589] 'Five police staff held in drug probe'. The Mail on Sunday. 14.6.09, p39.

[590] 'Police on drugs rap'. The People. 9.8.09, p6.

[591] North, N. 'Cocaine Cop's Fling With Criminal'. The People. 12.10.08, p27.

[592] Findlay, R. 'Hit' N' Run Feud'. Sunday Mail. 26.10.08, p36.

[593] Davidson, L. 'Drugs Squad Cops Facing Force Probe'. Daily Record. 8.10.08, p9.

[594] C3 News 29.11.09.

[595] Dow, I. 'Drugs Charge Cop In Court'. Daily Record. 7.10.08, p19.

[596] Davidson, L. Daily Record. 24.10.09.

[597] Twomey, J. 'Policewoman who bedded crook on run'. Daily Express. 5.6.13, p28.

[598] 'Cop Held In Coke Sting'. Sunday Mirror. 27.2.11, p7.

[599] BBC1 Local News. 17.4.09.

[600] Twomey, J. 'Ex-detective's £235M drug smuggling plot foiled when boat sank'. Daily Express. 25.2.10, p30.

[601] Johnson, W. 'Ex-cop Jailed For Drug Smuggling'. Daily Record. 19.3.10, p22.

[602] Penrose, J. 'Hero Cop Is Held Over Drug Deal'. Sunday Mirror. 4.9.11, p29.

[603] Gill, C. 'Ex-policeman is arrested over 1987 axe killing'. Daily Mail. 22.4.08, p16.

[604] 'Riots PC nailed for growing cannabis'. 24.3.12, p19.

[605] McLeod, K. '333 Scots cops have criminal records'. Daily Record. 5.7.12, p26.

[606] Milligan, J. 'Two Cops Accused Of Dealing Heroin'. Daily Record. 25.7.12, p9.

[607] 'Drug squad officers face probe quiz'. Daily Record. 29.11.12, p28.

[608] 'PC accused of stealing sex toys'. Daily Record. 29.12.12., p9.

[609] Pryer, N. 'Commander Paddick faces hypocrisy charge over 16-month cannabis ordeal of Brixton PC'. The Mail on Sunday. 31.3.02, p23.

[610] Tendler, S. 'Detective jailed over framed woman'. The Times. 16.12.00, p9.

[611] Wilde, J. 'Cops get boot from scandal-hit crime force'. Sunday People. 6.5.01, p28.

[612] Lavery, C. 'Cop Busted In Drugs Swoop'. Sunday Mail. 14.6.09, p15.

[613] White, S. 'Spot The Drug Addicts When They're Aged 2'. Daily Record. 14.3.11, p4.

[614] Hamilton, M., Griffiths, B. 'Struggling ex-soldiers resorting to crime'. Sunday Mirror. 6.3.11, p11.

[615] Officer 'A'. 'The Crime Factory'. Mainstream Publishing. 2012.

[616] McPherson, L. 'Special cop faces kidnap grilling'. Sunday Mail. 24.8.08, p23.

[617] Slack, J 'Cops and robbers'. Daily Mail. 15.11.08, p6.

[618] Knapp, M. 'Asylum police take law into own hands'. Sunday Express. 16.9.07, p6.

[619] Wright, S. ' 'Intruders' were Blunkett's Bobbies'. Daily Mail. 11.7.09, p12.

[620] Findlay, R. 'Securiwars Boss And Wife'. Sunday Mail. 15.6.03, p8.

[621] BBC1 News. 15.3.13.

[622] 'Cop facing vandal rap'. Daily Record. 12.7.13, p6.

[623] Emsley, C. 'The Great British Bobby'. Quercus. London, 2009, p165.

[624] Emsley, C. 'The Great British Bobby'. Quercus. London, 2009.

[625] Foster, J. 'So this is how we treat a family that cares for its own'. Daily Mail. 8.8.13, p41.

[626] Evans, M. '£½m. for PC bullied for being dyslexic'. Daily Express. 4.4.08, p15.

[627] Panton, L. 'I Took On Bully Cop … Now I Live In Fear'. News Of The World. 14.2.10, p16.

[628] O'Hare, P. 'Top Cop Bully Probe'. Daily Record. 13.3.10, pp1,2.

[629] 'Cops must show some humanity'. Sunday Mail. 14.3.10.

[630] Scott, M. 'Incompetent, Insensitive, Indefensible'. Sunday Mail. 14.3.10, p8.

[631] Johnston, J. 'You're Destroying Us'. Daily Mail. 5.6.08, p28.

[632] Thomson, C. '100mph Baby Dash Car Seized By Cops'. Daily Record. 14.12.10, 24.

[633] Mudie, K. 'Rape case teen 'in cops ordeal' '. Sunday People. 21.4.13, p11.

[634] Cohen, N. ' 'No' means 'no' to everyone expcept the British public'. The Observer. 20.12, p09, p35.

[635] Hobson, N. 'Policemen Behaving Badly'. Daily Mail. 24.4.06, p27.

[636] BBC1. 'Newsnight'. 24.2.11.

[637] Gilbertson, D. 'Why are police so rude? Because they are trained to be'. The Mail on Sunday. 27.2.11, p27.

[638] Channel 4's 4-Thought TV. 13.2.11.

[639] Broster, P. 'Police caution mum for leaving son, 14, to mind three-year-old brother'. Daily Express. 7.2.11, p7.

[640] Leake, C. 'Swearing rap for top police officer'. The Mail on Sunday. 13.2.11, p48.

[641] Briggs, B. 'Kirk admits part in persecuting Travellers'. Scotland on Sunday. 15.5.11, pp1,2.

[642] Daily Express. 5.9.11, p10.

[643] Christie, L 'Months of hell as our Down's son faced race attack charges'. Daily Record. 18.4.08, p7.

[644] Dolan, A. 'Parents held after death of daughter who spent 20 hours a day showering'. Daily Mail, 7.2.11, p5.

[645] Mega, M. 'Degrading, Obscene, Shameful'. Sunday Mail. 11.12.11, p10.

[646] 'Police pair are jailed for 'torture' of girl, 19'. Daily Express. 9.4.10, p15.

[647] Channel 4 Documentary on Alan Turing. November 2011.

[648] 'Video cops face probe'. Daily Record. 13.1.12, p13.

[649] Owen, J. 'Officer who posed as green activist has lost everything'. The Independent On Sunday. 13.11.11, p21.

[650] Herbert, D. 'Bullying cops forced girls to walk through pile of manure'. Daily Express. 26.7.13, p36.

[651] France, A. 'Big Fat Let-Off'. The Sun. 10.4.12, p6.

[652] Narain, J., Parveen, N. 'Did Police Have To Handcuff A Dementia Patient?'. Daily Mail. 5.7.12, p1.

[653] Littlejohn, R. ''Put your trousers on, Worzel … you're nicked'. Daily Mail. 16.11.12, p21.

[654] Petre, J. ' 'Harassed for being a Christian' – the policeman who objected to gay ribbons'. The Mail on Sunday. 20.7.08, pp46,47.

[655] 'Police in battle of balaclava'. Daily Express. 27.3.02, p6.

[656] Hitchens, P. 'You can't win with our helpless police'. The Mail on Sunday. 3.2.13, p27.

[657] Hayes, S. 'The Biggest Gang In Britain'. 2013, p175.

[658] BBC News. 20.6.13.

[659] Findlay, R. 'Councillor's cell ordeal'. Sunday Mail. 16.6.13, p19.

[660] Alexander, D. 'Cops In China Trained In Scotland'. Sunday Mail. 21.8.11, p2.

[661] 'Sherlock troubles Dartmoor'. The Sunday Post. 12.6.11, p47.

[662] Lee, A. 'Alien Cover-up'. Daily Express. 16.2.12, p29.

[663] Devine, A. 'Let Me Take Down Your Particulars'. Daily Record. 18.8.11, p11.

[664] 'For Fawkes' Sake'. The People. 19.8.07, p6.

[665] Smith, R. 'Police Inspectre'. Daily Record. p29.

[666] Bonnici, T. 'Shambles over Shambo'. Daily Express. 27.7.07, p14.

[667] Neill, S. 'Can This Blind Psychic See Into The Mind Of Murderers?'. Daily Mail. 14.8.07, p33.

[668] Penman, D. 'Is this proof we're all psychic?'. Daily Mail. 28.1.08, p29.

[669] Wright, S. 'Magic! Pagan PCs to get time off to mark Halloween'. Daily Mail. 17.7.09, p3.

[670] Flanagan, P. 'Pagan police win the right to time off for festivals'. Daily Express. 11.5.10, p8.

[671] Bennett, C. 'Baby P exposes our need to believe in the perfect parent'. Observer. 16.11.08, p33.

[672] Littlejohn, R. Daily Mail. 10.11.09, p17.

[673] Jarius, D. 'True spirit of the law'. Sunday Express. 2.11.08, p25.

[674] McGivern, M. 'Cop Circle'. Daily Record. 21.10.09, p27.

REFERENCES

675 McWhirter, F. 'May the (police) force be with you!'. The Mail on Sunday. 19.5.13, p9.

676 Walters, S. 'Revealed: Real reason that the 'Mad Mullah' police chief broke into his office'. The Mail on Sunday. 3.8.08, p15.

677 Hull, L. Daily Mail. 12.8.08, p23.

678 'Mad Mullah' police chief steps down'. Daily Mail. 2.5.09 p9.

679 Hickley, M. 'The Most Idiotic Police Chief In Britain'. Daily Mail. 2.1.08, pp 1, 4,5.

680 Leake, C. 'Police dump helmets for baseball caps'. The Mail on Sunday. 7.1.07, p15.

681 Hull, L. 'The baseball cap bobbies'. Daily Mail. 33.4.07, p55.

682 Broster, P. ' 'Pointless' scoring scheme for police'. Daily Express. 31.8.06, p2.

683 'Praying for justice'. Daily Record. 29.1.10, p11.

684 Maynard, G. 'Pray for us to catch more criminals plead the police'. Daily Express. 29.1.10, p29.

685 Holt, G. 'My prayers are foiling criminals says police chief'. Daily Express. 22.2.10, p5.

686 Fryer, J. '21st Century Exorcists'. Daily Mail. 20.11.10, p44.

687 Mikhailova, A. 'Scientologists enlist police to push anti-drugs drive in school'. The Sunday Times. 20.1.08, p7.

688 Rayner, G. 'Why did this top policeman agree to appear in a film for the Scientologists?'. Daily Mail. 12.5.07, p25.

689 Schlesinger, F. 'How four policemen in two 150mph patrol cars pursued Natalie Pinkham ... just for TV'. Daily Mail. 15.4.09, p27.

690 Brown, M. 'Police 'steal' from cars to shock drivers'. 26.8.09, p27.

691 Pilditch, D. 'Dressing down for police who let girls pose in their uniforms'. Daily Express. 15.12.09, p9.

692 Pilditch, D. 'Pupils sob as 'aliens' take their teacher'. Daily Express. 17.7.09, p24.

693 Moncur, J. 'Probe Into Patrol Car 'Taxi' For Party Cops'. Daily Record. 5.1.10, p19.

694 Jeeves, P. 'Not very PC: The Chief Constable's cheeky card'. Daily Express. 16.12.06, p36.

695 Rimmer, A. 'Walk half a mile? But we're in ACPO'. The Mail on Sunday. 4.6.10, p38.

696 Levy, A. 'Long Farm of the Law!'. Daily Mail. 3.9.10, p43.

697 Panther, L. 'Police Farce'. News Of The World. 21.9.08, p25.

698 Kirk, J. 'Overkill Bill'. The People. 20.5.07, p20.

699 Willey, J. 'Drivers with colds are a menace and should stay off the roads, say police'. Daily Express. 20.1.11, p19.

700 Nicol, M. 'The foul-mouthed traffic police caught on their own speed camera'. The Mail on Sunday. 12.8.07, p25.

701 Elliott, V. 'Police chief: Put all young drivers on Probation'. The Mail on Sunday. 4.12.11, p41.

702 Moult, J. 'Long leg of the law'. Daily Mail. 22.12.08, p23.

703 McGivern, M. 'Blink Before You Drive'. Daily Record. 1.12.09.

704 Pilditch, D. 'Police chief turns up at carnival ... as Bin Laden'. Daily Express. 11.9.08, p3.

705 Smyth, B. 'Cops could learn about sex slavery at Festival'. The Sunday Post. 22.8.10, p31.

706 Smyth, B. 'Police used hypnosis on Bible John witness'. The Sunday Post. 3.10.10. p14.

707 Sims, P. 'Police used Ray Mears in the hunt for fugitive Moat'. Daily Mail. 22.7.10, p11.

708 Platell, A. 'Fear's no joking matter'. Daily Mail. 10.1.10, p19.

709 'The sexist jibes faced by officer hunting Moat'. Daily Mail. 15.9.11, p26.

710 'Police plan to pay convicts for advice on fighting crime'. Daily Mail. 15.10. 08, p4.

711 Utley, T. 'If a Boy Scout pulls me over for speeding I'll throttle the snotty little blighter with his woggle'. Daily Mail. 21.1.11, p14.

712 'Not just any cops'. Daily Record. 28.5.11, p17.

713 Paul, D. 'Sketch violent crime police tell children'. Sunday Express. 17.7.11, p15.

714 Boztas, S. 'Meet the comic copper'. The Independent on Sunday. 9.8.09, p3.

715 'Sled cops feel the heat'. Daily Record. 15.1.10, p7.

716 Petre, J. 'Advertised in Police magazine: leg irons and neck collars 'ideal for dictators' '. The Mail on Sunday. 2.12.08, p45.

717 Goslett, M. 'Andrew 'ordered police guards to chase golf balls' in Palace garden'. The Mail on Sunday. 7.12.08, p19.

718 Dow, B. 'Cops grill expert on email rap'. Daily Record. 11.8.08, p11.

719 Greenhill, S., Gladdis, K. 'He was just normal and polite ...'. Daily Mail. 25.5.13, p7.

720 Gladdis, K. News of the World. 22.2.09, p25.

721 Levy. A. Daily Mail. 17.12.08, p19.

722 Findlay, R. 'It's not about the boss ... the whole thing was just a complete mess'. Sunday Mail. 7.12.08, p6.

723 Nelmes, A. 'My lot have murdered someone again. S... happens'. The People. 26.4.09, p9.

724 Brown, M. 'Thefts cut by long arm of the law'. Daily Express. 2.5.09, p27.

725 Westcott, S. 'Police sneak into homes ... to warn about burglaries'. Daily Express. 11.7.09, p27.

726 White, S. 'Turpin Unmasked'. Daily Record. 17.7.11, p41.

727 '40p silver bells that ring time on crime'. Daily Express. 16.7.09, p22.

728 Hitchens, P. 'Leave evil to the vicar, Mr. Plod'. The Mail on Sunday. 7.12.08, p29.

729 Wright, S. 'Curious case of the police chief and his swagger stick'. Daily Mail. 5.4.03, pp16-17.

730 Riches, C. 'Police Chief: Why we should treat children with guns as victims'. Daily Express. 18.4.07, p17.

731 Taylor, B. 'Sir Ian: Middle class look down on police'. Daily Mail. 17.11.05, p12.

732 Smith, M. 'Met chief's threat to go to court over Menezes report'. The Mail on Sunday. 28.1.07, p4.

733 Perry., A. 'Police radios blamed for PC's cancer death'. Sunday Express. 7.2.10, p4.

734 The People. 9.5.10, p5.

735 McKinstry, L. 'What's Wrong With Britain's Police Chiefs?'. Daily Mail. 7.12.07, p25.

736 Panton, L. 'Inn The Book'. News Of The World. 4.4.10, p29.

737 Arbuthnott, G. 'Revealed: Song lyrics used by two other siege officers'. The Mail on Sunday. 7.11.10, p10.

738 Maynard, G. 'Gay policeman and force call truce on earring'. Daily Express. 16.8.06, p15.

739 Phillips, M. 'Will we ever be told the truth about the death of Dr. David Kelly?'. Daily Mail. 24.7.06, p12.

740 'Blair in Soham apology'. Daily Record. 28.1.06, p6.

741 'Joke's On You, Sarge'. News Of The World. 23.9.07, p39.

742 Tendler, s. 'Police chief says prosecute my driver'. The Times. 27.1.01, p3.

743 Findlay, R. 'Who do you think you are kidding Mr Lumsden?'. Sunday Mail. 11.2.07, p35.

744 Elias, R. 'Cop Chief Blunders With Joke On Suicide Bombers'. 17.4.06, p9.

745 'Helmet-farce'. Daily Express. 16.5.08, p17.

746 Leask, D. 'All rookie cops face drugs tests'. Scotland on Sunday. 21.9.08, p9.

747 'Sex-change police want funding from taxpayers'. Daily Express. 15.8.09, p5.

748 'Smacking would help cut crime'. Daily Mail. 5.3.07, p37.

749 Gill, C. 'Chief Constables reject Smith's festive greeting'. Daily Mail. 22.12.07, p46.

750 Daily Express. 1.5.10, p23.

751 Littlejohn, R. Daily Mail. 31.5.13, p17.

752 Toksvig, S. 'How did South Yorkshire police end up with a 32b bra?'. Seven (Sunday Telegraph Magazine). 28.3.10, p7.

753 MacRae, R. 'Let's harpoon Nessie!'. Daily Mail. 27.4.10, p27.

754 Edwards, A. 'The Day The Music Died'. Daily Express. 12.4.10, p15.

755 Panton, L. 'Bizarre case of probe chief'. News Of The World. 14.9.08, p10.

756 Whitehead, T. 'Police 'fining children to meet targets' '. Daily Express. 6.2.08, p2.

757 Douglas, H. 'Helicopter stunt attacked'. Sunday Express. 6.12.09, p27.

758 MacDonald, S. 'It's Time To Buck Up Your Ideas'. Daily Record. 12.7.10, p26.

759 Alexander, S. 'Top Cop: Target Crooks Before They Are Born'. Daily Record. 11.6.10, p21.

760 Levy, A. 'Badger a burglar'. Daily Mail. 18.12.10, p49.

761 'Rebelling is admirable – ex Met chief'. The Mail on Sunday. 13.3.11, p24.

762 Emsley, C. 'The Great British Bobby'. Quercus. London. 2009.

763 Hitchens, P. The Mail on Sunday. 16.1.11, p31.

764 Penrose, J. 'PC 'Hung Up On 35,999 Callers' '. Sunday Mirror. 29.11.09, p15.

765 Littlejohn, R. 'Juliet Bravo is taking the proverbial!'. Daily Mail. 10.8.10, p17.

766 Tozer, J. 'Bobbies on the Tweet!'. Daily Mail. 15.10.10, p24.

767 Littlejohn, R. 'And now it's a crime to hate the Sex Pistols'. Daily Mail. 5.4.13, p17.

768 Templeton, S. 'Magnets slipped into undies ease the menopause'. The Sunday Times. 20.2.11, p7.

769 Emsley, C. 'The Great British Bobby'. Quercus. London. 2009.

770 'WPCs in a tight spot'. Daily Express. 13.5.11, p22.

771 'How hunt for escaped tiger became wild goose chase'. Daily Mail. 23.5.11, p39.

772 'The new police 'diversity' course starring Christina Aguilera'. The Mail on Sunday. 12.6.11, p47.

773 Camber R. 'Police guide to sandwich fillings and fluffy pillow'. Daily Mail. 30.5.11, p10.

774 O'Hare, P. 'Smoking Ban Is Murder'. Daily Record. 25.2.11, p31.

775 Littlejohn, R. Daily Mail. 5.7.11, p17.

776 'Fancy that! Expelled pupils get lessons in how to race pigeons'. Daily Mail. 14.6.11, p24.

777 BBC1 News. 14.6.11.

778 Littlejohn, R. Daily Mail. 24.7.07, p15.

779 Chittenden, M., Elliott, J. 'Britain's top cop is just a lost luvvie'. the Sunday Times. 13.2.05, p3.

780 Whitehead, T. 'Another daft gimmick by 'cool' police'. Daily Express. 16.8.07, p19.

781 'I'm a Particularly Cool Skateboard Officer'. Daily Mail. 16.8.07, p9.

782 Littlejohn, R. 'Skating towards a police state ...'. Daily Mail. 3.8.07, p17.

783 Brown, C. 'PC Knuckles and the art of sign language'. Daily Mail. 26.7.11, p16.

784 Reynolds, M 'Police play a trump card in the battle against crime'. Daily Express. 16.7.08, p27.

[785] Horne, M. 'Police tell men not to chat up women'. Scotland on Sunday. 13.5.07, p5.

[786] Ballinger, L. 'Police offer teenagers junk food for good behaviour'. Daily Mail. 25.7.08, p41.

[787] Russell, A. 'Police boss: we need to copy Argos'. Daily Express. 31.8.11, p22.

[788] Leapman, B. 'Police to consult the less discreet'. The Sunday Telegraph. 27.5.07, p6.

[789] The Official History Of The Metropolitan Police. Gary Mason. Carlton. 2004, pp 151, 152, 155.

[790] The Official History Of The Metropolitan Police. Gary Mason. Carlton. 2004, p85.

[791] 'Partygoers kept sweet'. Sunday Mirror. 4.12.11, p28.

[792] Morgan, T. 'Now burglars are afraid of the dark'. Daily Express. 26.11.11, p45.

[793] Jeeves, P. 'Police issue bum picture in bid to crack theft case'. Daily Express. 7.1.12, p29.

[794] Chorley, M. 'Change 'unsafe' law on assisted dying, says ex police chief'. The Independent on Sunday. 1.1.12, p8.

[795] 'Dear offenders … gotcha. Love, Santa'. Daily Record. 24.12.11, p8.

[796] Sky TV (BBC4) Documentary. 13.1.12.

[797] Moncur, J. 'Cops on patrol rock out at island gig'.

[798] Wright, S. ''Ere, Sarge, what rhymes with gender sensitivity?' Daily Mail. 18.2.12, p11.

[799] Carpenter, I. 'A Very Unholy Row'. Daily Express. 24.11.11, pp46,47.

[800] Wright, S. 'Pandering to a WPC killer'. Daily Mail. 10.3.12, p5.

[801] France, A. 'Sick Cop Mocks Hero Weston on Facebook'. The Sun. 26.3.12, p28.

[802] Narain, J. 'Joking with their guns, colleagues of officer shot in training'. Daily Mail. 29.3.12, p31.

[803] Eccles, L. 'Cotton wool Olympics'. Daily Mail. 21.4.12, p5.

[804] Officer 'A'. 'The Crime Factory'. Mainstream Publishing, 2012.

[805] Graham, G., Mackreath, H. 'Tweets on the beat slated for wasting police time'. The Sunday Times. 29.4.12, p9.

[806] Allen, V. 'Now Maddie police will probe leads from psychics'. Daily Mail. 4.5.12, p34.

[807] Slack, J. 'Feral youths should be in church care, says chief constable'. Daily Mail. 3.7.08, p22.

[808] Wright, S. 'The attractions of anarchy, by police chief behind soft stance on drugs'. Daily Mail. 20.2.02, p17.

[809] Herbert, D. ' 'Charging 50 for 999 calls' would halt the hoaxers'. Daily Express. 4.1.13, p13.

[810] 'Village People'. The Sunday Times Magazine. 1.8.99, p30.

[811] Hughes, L. 'Sir Walter Mitty Is Ex Policeman On Benefits'. Sunday Mail. 15.6.03, p28.

[812] Narain, J., Finney, S. '1mph over the limit!'. Daily Mail. 9.8.03, p15.

[813] Doyle, J. 'Professionals should be made to take drug tests says police chief'. Daily Mail. 30.1.13, p12.

[814] Clout, L. 'Now they want all our police to have a degree'. Daily Express. 20.11.09, p17.

[815] Wright, S. 'Police revolt over ban on Union Flag badge that backs troops'. Daily Mail. 29.7.09, p4.

[816] Littlejohn, R. Daily Mail. 8.12.09, p17.

[817] Hitchens, P. 'So it's MY fault if I'm mugged?'. The Mail on Sunday. 10.2.13, p29.

[818] Camber, R. 'Police saddled with a 93-page guide … on riding a bike!'. Daily Mail. 13.11.09, p8.

[819] Sims, P. 'Now police have a new tactic for dealing with a gang: Change the name of their streets!'. Daily Mail. 4.11.09, p25.

[820] Dawar, A. 'PC shops son for 'fraud' over £3,700 iPad'. Daily Express. 26.3.13.

[821] Garavelli, D. 'Missing the point!'. Scotland on Sunday. 9.8.09, p17.

[822] Littlejohn, R. 'Put your burqa on, luv, you're nicked'. Daily Mail. 7.8.09, p17.

[823] 'Public confidence plunges as the police lose the plot'. Leader. Daily Express. 15.8.09, p14.

[824] Alexander, D. 'It's not PC to look for love in your uniform'. Sunday Mail. 4.8.13, p7.

[825] Gallagher, I. 'Police say killers will go free in 'crazy' move to destroy all DNA samples after 6 months'. The Mail on Sunday. 5.5.13, p11.

[826] 'Girl 'too extreme for the SWP' '. Sunday Express. 12.12.10, p9.

[827] Twomey, J. 'Suicide dad shoots dead daughter, 4, and wounds wife'. Daily Express. 30.12.09, p5.

[828] Camber, R. 'Guilty of £40m gems heist, the policeman's son'. Daily Mail. 26.6.10, p41.

[829] Dixon, C. 'Shame of poppy-burner's father who served in Navy'. Daily Express. 14.3.11, p13.

[830] Joseph, C. 'Hero past of April killer's father: He was PC … and Moorgate crash rescuer'. The Mail on Sunday. 2.6.13, p17.

[831] Key, I. 'Woman police chief in probe over art sales'. Daily Express. 8.1.09, p30.

[832] 'Terror police in £100,000 rent fiddle'. Daily Mail. 23.1.10, p53.

[833] Riches, C. 'Police mum got rid of killing clues to help son'. Daily Express. 11.2.09, p29.

[834] Broster, P. 'Police mum held over model killing'. Daily Express. 13.11.08, p10.

[835] 'PC dad denies cover-up'. Daily Record. 13.6.08, p9.

[836] Dow, B. 'Masons Fitted Up My Son, Says Cop'. Daily Record. 27.6.08, p11.

[837] Chapman, J. 'WPC's sister tried to loot TV in riots'. Daily Express. 11.1.12, p21.

[838] Maris, S. 'Crash Cop's Wife Dodges Jail Over £11K ebay Fakes'. Daily Record. 19.12.08, p23.

[839] Blacklock, M. 'Police shoot dead suicidal crossbow dad'. Daily Express. 13.5.09, p11.

[840] Stretch, E. 'I warned murdered tots were in danger'. Daily Record. 29.1.10, pp1,7.

[841] 'PC's wife jailed for £25,000 bank con'. Daily Record. 30.3.10, p23.

[842] Personal communication.

[843] O'Hare, P. 'Why Wait 2 Yrs To Tell Us This Beast Is On Loose?' Daily Record. 11.3.08, p7.

[844] Musson, C. 'Cop Is Held In Cocaine Swoop'. Daily Record. 4.10.08, p5.

[845] Dow, I. 'Drugs Charge Cop In Court'. Daily Record. 7.10.08, p19.

[846] Watson, D. '43 Cops Done For Crimes In Just 2 Years'. Daily Record. 24.1.11. p4.

[847] Disley, J. 'Police chief candidate's son is benefit fraudster'. Daily Express. 30.10.12, p15.

[848] Moriarty, R., Veevers, L. 'Cregan 'Mum' Was A Cop In Same Force As Shot Officers'. The Sun. 23.9.12, p5.

[849] 'Arrest and Trial'. Channel 5. 22.6.01.

[850] Daily Record. 23.1.13, p11.

[851] Stevens, C. Daily Mail. 9.2.13, p46.

[852] Twomey, J. 'Jailed, the detective who sold seized drugs back on to the streets'. Daily Express. 5.4.13, p13.

[853] Chapman, J. 'Boy, 13, shoots dead his parents, gran and aunt … goes to school then kills himself'. Daily Express. 8.8.13, p13.

[854] McAnally, A. 'Jailed employee who stole as boss attended funerals'. Daily Mail. 13.8.13, p17.

[855] Tookey, C. Daily Mail. 11.6.13, p15.

[856] Emsley, C. 'The Great British Bobby'. Quercus. London. 2009.

[857] Emsley, C. 'The Great British Bobby'. Quercus. London. 2009, p154.

[858] Hitchens, P. 'The gendarmes on British streets'. The Mail on Sunday. 2.6.13, p29.

[859] Burke, N. 'Police should patrol our streets, not parade on TV'. Daily Express. 6.7.09, p13.

[860] Jarvis, D. 'We love Ashes star's old-school style, say police'. Sunday Express. 11.4.10, p35.

[861] Officer 'A'. 'The Crime Factory'. Mainstream Publishing. 2012.

[862] Hunter, A. 'Cops walk a fine line'. Daily Express. 11.6.10, p45.

[863] Galloway, G. 'Time People Realised Cops Aren't CSI …'. Daily Record. 12.7.10, p13.

[864] Emsley, C. 'The Great British Bobby'. Quercus. London. 2009, p2.

[865] Kynaston, D. 'Austerity Britain'. Bloomsbury. 2007, p360.

[866] Bray, C. 'The Man Who Has Spent His Career Trying to Escape Bond'. Daily Express. 23.8.10, p21.

[867] Edge, S. Daily Express. 28.5.10, p32.

[868] Smith, R. C. 'Britain blighted by rough justice'. Sunday Express. 6.7.08.

[869] 'The Great Soap Swap'. Daily Express. 19.4.11, p21.

[870] Ferguson, J. 'Acting Is My Life … I Couldn't Face Being Axed From My Role On The Bill'. Daily Record. 12.1.08, p25.

[871] Maynard, G. 'Shut it, Gene … good cop beats bad cop at getting a confession'. Daily Express. 3.2.11, p39.

[872] Brown, C. 'PC Knuckles and the art of sign language'. Daily Mail. 26.7.11, p16.

[873] Littlejohn, R. 'The National Office of Sex, Lies and Statistics'. Daily Mail. 30.9.11, p17.

[874] Fulton, R. 'Playing a racist, pervert copper could kill my career'. Daily Record. 27.12.11, pp24,25.

[875] Allardyce, J. 'Welsh attacks Indian film ban'. The Sunday Times. 28.7.13, p17.

[876] Macaskill, M. 'Filth writer calls for cleaner drugs'. The Sunday Times. 29.9.13, p13.

[877] English, P. 'Compston cops a top police part'. Daily Record. 18.8.2011, p5.

[878] Daily Express. 13.8.12, p10.

[879] Jefferies, M. 'Sir David's Chasin' 3m Lost Viewers'. Daily Record. 4.1.12, p11.

[880] 'Kirsty Cops A Family'. The Sun. 18.4.12, p3.

[881] Piers Morgan. ITV. 12.5.12.

[882] Lee, A. 'The Professionals'. Daily Express. 11.4.11, p28.

[883] Kolirin, L. 'Pink Panther's crazed police chief dies at 95'. Daily Express. 28.9.12, p26.

[884] Wright, S. 'Morse fans have more chance of solving crimes than my officers'. Daily Mail. 19.8.03, p31.

[885] Revour, P. 'Is Taggart about to be killed off?'. Daily Mail. 1.8.09, p7.

[886] Roberts, A. 'Kill the Bill'. Daily Mail. 31.10.03, p13.

[887] Dow, I. 'Cop who inspired Sean's Untouchable'. Daily Record. 6..9.08, p15.

[888] Wooding, D. 'Top Cop: Cuts Will Mean More Crime'. News of the World. 3.4.11, p41.

[889] 'Cops 'flout wage law'. The People. 5.9.10, p29.

[890] Speed, N. 'Council tax rise may have to double'. The Sunday Times. 28.9.03, p14.

[891] Lewis, J. 'Anti-terror cash spent on luxury police flats'. The Mail on Sunday. 21.2.10, p11.

[892] Basnett, G. 'Police, Camera Action'. News Of The World. 21.12.08, p11.

[893] Lewis, J. 'Road safety chiefs caught using police evidence shots of high-profile motorists to boost business'. The Mail on Sunday. 5.9.10, p17.

[894] Lewis, J., Clarke, L. 'Now 'Police Chiefs PLC' cashes in on speeders'. The Mail on Sunday. 22.2.09, p35.

[895] Lewis, J. 'Chief Constables PLC'. The Mail On Sunday. 15.2.09, p7.

896 Boyle, J. 'Patients shocked by phone cost scandal'. The Sunday Post. 8.5.11, p47.

897 Gunn, C. 'No stopping the SNP in drive to centralise police and fire service'. The Sunday Post. 11.9.11, p12.

898 Doyle, J. 'Police style powers may be handed to bouncers'. Daily Mail. 20.4.10, p30.

899 'The Big Cell Off'. Daily Record. 16.2.11, p6.

900 Barrett, D., Mendick, R. 'Need the police? Here is the Bill'. The Sunday Telegraph. 5.2.12, p8.

901 Caven, B. 'Personal injury claims net officers an annual £20m'. Daily Mail. 1.4.13, p10.

902 Mason, G. 'Cynicism is the real sickness in our police. How exploitation of welfare provisions is damaging the war on crime'. Daily Express. 6.12.01, p12.

903 'Shamed top cop's £250,000'. The Sun. 18.5.12, p22.

904 Blacklock, M. '£10,000 for PC who sued his own force'. Daily Express. 8.6.07, p31.

905 'PCs claim £2m for 'harassment'. Daily Express. 8.1.09, p15.

906 Murray, P. 'Pineapple Cop: I'm Not a Blackmailer'. Daily Record. 7.6.07, p27.

907 McIlwraith, G. 'WPC Pineapple Loses Big Chunk of Money'. Daily Record. 11.10.08, p9.

908 McKinstry, L. 'Why it's so vital to fight the scrabble for compensation'. Daily Express. 27.11.08, p12.

909 Wright, S. 'Met chief 'may lose his job' over £105,000 Olympics deal'. Daily Mail. 30.8.08, p12.

910 'Race-row Met officer rejects six-figure deal'. Daily Mail. 21.10.08, p11.

911 'Taxpayers foot bill for two Met chiefs at once'. Daily Mail. 27.11.08. p21.

912 Wright, S. 'Crisis at the Yard as top Asian officer sues for £1 million'. Daily Mail. 23.8.08, p21.

913 'Colour blind cops claim'. Daily Record. 19.1.11, p17.

914 Penrose, J. 'Dopey!'. Sunday Mirror. 14.4.13. p7.

915 'Policeman blinded by Moat sues his force for £1 million'. Daily Mail. 19.2.11, p20.

916 Green, N. 'Top cop told tragic Rathband to sue'. The Sunday Post. 4.3.12, p11.

917 'Dog cop sues force'. Daily Record. 5.8.10, p21.

918 Whitehead, T. 'Police paying millions for wrongful arrests'. Daily Express. 19.7.06, p19.

919 Moir, J. 'What kind of PC can't cope with being called Daisy?'. Daily Mail. 18.6.10, p37.

920 Verkaik, R. 'Woman inspector 'humiliated' by failing riot test wins up to £30K'. The Mail on Sunday. 12.6.11, p27.

921 'PC 'lied to get compensation' '. The Daily Telegraph. 14.6.11, p11.

922 Salkeld, L 'WPC's sick-leave show'. Daily Mail. 28.7.11, p27.

923 Martin, A. 'WPC's £400,000 For Hurting Her Back'. Daily Mail. 8.4.13, p19.

924 Greenwood, C. 'Black PC who used race card 14 times'. Daily Mail. 1.10.11, p48.

925 Stewart, S. 'Crash Cop's £300K Claim'. Sunday Mail. 4.9.11, p17.

926 'Disabled cop sues'. Daily Record. 1.9.11, p36.

927 Rafferty, S. 'English Cop's Race Bias Bid'. Daily Record. 30.1.06, p18.

928 Willey, J. 'What a police farce'. Daily Express. 15.8.06, p11.

929 Daily Express. 26.10.11, p10.

930 Constable, N. 'Police worker 'set to get £10K deal' in sex harassment case'. The Mail on Sunday. 23.10.11, p20.

931 Graham, C. 'I had to have sex with eco-warriors to keep my cover. Free love is part of that lifestyle'. The Mail on Sunday. 1.1.12, p17.

932 'Ten Cases That Make a Mockery Of British Justice'. Daily Mail. 12.1.12, p2.

933 Dixon, C. 'Former opera singer who claims police sacked her for cowardice'. Daily Express. 6.8.09, p7.

934 Hudson, C. 'Sex, fantasy and the police plot that blew apart the hunt for Rachel's killer'. Daily Mail. 3.7.00, pp34,35.

935 Lord Mackenzie. 'Greedy, out of touch and obsessed with political correctness … the grim truth about our police'. Daily Mail. 15.8.01, p10.

936 Camber, R. 'How police 'retire' with £100,000 – but return to the force the same day'. Daily Mail. 29.12.09, p19.

937 Sims, P. 'Canoe man tells police: Give me my £100 back or I will sue'. Daily Mail. 31.5.10, p13.

938 Silvester, N. 'Police Chief Wanted (no experience required)'. Sunday Mail. 26.7.09, p2.

939 McKendry, G. 'Singe Force Shambles'. The Sunday Post. 17.3.13, pp1,8,9.

940 Riches, C. 'Police chief told: Do the right thing and quit over Hillsborough disaster'. Daily Express. 14.9.12, p5.

941 'Fear of sirens' WPC wins payout'. Daily Express. 16.2.13, p11.

942 Graham, C. The Mail on Sunday. 25.11.12, p11.

943 Taylor, B. '£50,000 for WPC who refused to obey an order'. Daily Mail. 17.1.02, p29.

944 '£20K for 'cop' trip'. The Sun. 4.1.13, p15.

945 Taylor, B. '£270,000 for policewoman raped by a fellow officer'. Daily Mail. 4.8.03, p17.

946 'Court KO for stair fall cop'. Sunday Mail. 13.7.03, p19.

947 Bedford, M. 'Thief Sues Police For Refusing To Make Her a WPC'. The Mail on Sunday. 15.9.13, p29.

[948] Kirby, I. 'Cop On Blair Rich Project'. News of the World. 12.4.09, p38.

[949] 'Cashing In On Drivers'. Daily Mail. 3.3.09, p32.

[950] 'Cops and robbers'. Daily Mail. 28.5.09, p14.

[951] Verkaik, R. 'Ex-Met chief profits from £4m deal to train Libyan police … in Huddersfield'. The Mail on Sunday. 6.3.11, pp14,15.

[952] Leake, C. '£1000 a day … how Captain Beaujolais of the Met doubled his pay on Diana inquiry'. The Mail on Sunday. 23.12.07, p4.

[953] '17K for cop exes'. News of the World. 18.7.10, p8.

[954] Greenwood, C. 'Met chief with huge pension to work for firm advising police'. Daily Mail. 1.12.11, p41.

[955] Pooran, N. 'Police services boss paid £800K to consultants'. Daily Express. 14.3.13, p25.

[956] Kisiel, R. Daily Mail. 7.11.12, p18.

[957] Littlejon, R. 'A chopper to crack a nut'. Daily Mail. 28.9.10, p17.

[958] Levy, A. 'Police's £1,000 bill in helicopter search to catch … a shoplifter'. Daily Mail. 18.8.10.

[959] 'Cops In Luxury'. News of the World. 8.2.09, p33.

[960] Gill, C. Daily Mail. 11.9.10, p11.

[961] Silvester, N. 'House Pricey'. Sunday Mail. 25.10.09, p7.

[962] Narain, J. 'Anger over the Twitter patrol'. Daily Mail. 16.9.10, p2.

[963] Ferguson, J. '£26 m. Cop Car Hire'. Daily Record. 2.1.10, p31.

[964] Copping, J. 'The Bill: £800,000 for police music'. The Sunday Telegraph. 29.1.09, p5.

[965] O'Hare, P. 'College Cops Are Forced To Wash In Dark'. Daily Record. 4.5.09, p22.

[966] Collins, D. 'Jet Cops Huge Bill'. The People. 10.1.10, p20.

[967] Foggo, D., Cater, S. 'Yard's jet set runs up £12m air fare bill'. The Sunday Times. 23.08.09, p7.

[968] Wright, S. 'The Sunshine Squad'. Daily Mail. 23.5.09, p7.

[969] 'Police forces have spent £3m on tea and biscuits'. Daily Mail. 14.8.09, p11.

[970] Silvester, N. 'Heloo Heloo Heloo'. 6.9.09, p23.

[971] Clark, R. 'Criminal waste of public money just has to stop'. Daily Express. 9.9.09, p12.

[972] Kay, R. 'Daily Mail'. 1.9.10, p35

[973] Twomey, J. 'Police blow £1.5 million on giveaway gimmicks'. Daily Express. 3.9.10, p15.

[974] Littlejohn, R. 'NDPA Blue Cancelled Due To Lack of Interest'. Daily Mail. 13.8.10, p17.

[975] Reynolds, M. 'Joy for beat bobbies as minority police groups lose funding'. Daily Express. 23.3.11, p27.

[976] Basnett, G. News of the World. 21.9.08, p34.

[977] Hamilton, N. 'Tories must fight back'. Sunday Express. 26.10.08, p31.

[978] Lewis, J. 'Plebgate Probe cop Rap Over Freebies'. Sunday People. 9.6.13, p32

[979] McKinstry, L. 'We are betrayed by Labour's sick, so-called justice'. Daily Express. 25.1.10, p12.

[980] 'Fury over cop cash'. Sunday Mirror. 23.3.08, p29.

[981] Camber, R. 'The skiing squad'. Daily Mail. 6.2.10, p59.

[982] Groves, J. 'Police funds "wasted on red tape"'. Sunday Express. 23.12.07, p4.

[983] Goose, M. 'Police escort for injured Rooney was far too much'. Daily Express. 2.4.10, p34.

[984] Matthews, J. '£1,200 to chase a 53p fraud'. Daily Express. 10.12.10, p18.

[985] 'How police chiefs sailed through the queues'. Daily Mail. 23.4.10, p10.

[986] 'Cops in casuals'. News Of The World. 21.2.10, p28.

[987] Tozer, J. 'Bobbies on the Tweet'. Daily Mail. 15.10.10, p24.

[988] Slack, J., Doyle, J. 'Fury as police chief says cuts put children at risk'. Daily Mail. 25.2.11, p4.

[989] Narain, J. Daily Mail. 17.3.11, p31.

[990] Verkaik, R. 'IT firm handed £193m contract at Yard wined and dined staff. The Mail on Sunday. 18.8.11, p17.

[991] Herbert, N. 'We'll get rid of the paperwork and focus on public protection'. The Sunday Telegraph. 17.10.10, p2.

[992] Littlejohn, R. 'Mind How You Go Awards 2011'. Daily Mail. 1.3.11, p17.

[993] Riches, C. 'Hard-up police to seek tips'. Daily Express. 20.1.11, p35.

[994] Letts, Q. 'HOW police can drive down costs'. Daily Mail. 19.3.11, p34.

[995] O'Sullivan, K. 'Pander Cars'. Daily Record. 31.3.11, p9.

[996] Coyle, M. 'So if cops are about to axe 3,000 indians, why have they blown £2.2m on 109 luxury motors for all the chiefs?'. Sunday Mail. 7.10.12, p10.

[997] 'Police spend £11K on slogan'. Daily Express. 28.2.11.

[998] McFarlane, J. 'Police supercar cops a £20,000 crash repair bill'. Daily Express. 12.1.07, p41.

[999] Littlejohn, R. Daily Mail. 15.4.11, p17.

[1000] Littlejohn, R. Daily Mail. 9.2.10, p17.

[1001] Aitkin, J. 'The £65m Cop Shop'. Sunday Mail. 28.3.10, p10.

[1002] 'Cop swoop on man's pistol belt'. The People. 3.7.11, p29.

REFERENCES

[1003] '£500,000 bill for police to protect Blair at Iraq inquiry'. Daily Mail. 25.7.11, p24.

[1004] '£101K art at new police HQ blasted'. Sunday Mirror. 23.10.11.

[1005] McKinstry, L. 'Shameless quangocrats who jump from one state-funded gravy train onto another'. Daily Mail. 19.8.11, p14.

[1006] Buchanan, K. 'Scandal as millions are spent on town hall PRs'. Sunday Express. 25.7.10, p30.

[1007] Martin, D. 'Police foot £4.8m bill for union reps'. Daily Mail. 6.3.12, p27.

[1008] Welham, J. 'Seven officers are given £300K worth of cars ... at force cutting 2,000 jobs'. The Mail on Sunday. 8.7.12, p45.

[1009] Gunn, C. 'New single force will start with £100m of debt'. The Sunday Post. 16.12.12, p16.

[1010] Welham, J. The Mail on Sunday. 8.7.12, p45.

[1011] Hall, M. '£100,000 cost of takeaways for prisoners in police cells'. Daily Express. 28.7.08, p18.

[1012] Wright, S. 'Why life really must mean life, by head of police chiefs'. Daily Mail. 5.9.09, p12.

[1013] Clark, R. 'On-the-spot fines make a mockery of British justice'. Daily Express. 6.5.09, p12.

[1014] Ingham, J. '£1.5m refund for 24,000 drivers caught by illegal speed camera'. Daily Express. 19.9.11, p19.

[1015] Slack, J. 'How Labour milked £1bn in speeding fines from 17m drivers'. Daily Mail. 11.7.11, p10.

[1016] 'Police told: Fine more drivers'. Daily Mail. 28.9.06, p38.

[1017] 'Motorists squeezed again'. Daily Express. Leader. 15.6.12, p14.

[1018] Riches, C. 'Drivers fined for warning of speed trap'. Daily Express. 12.6.12, p28.

[1019] Emsley, C. 'The Great British Bobby'. Quercus. London. 2009.

[1020] Gill, C. 'Police chief used Yard's air miles to fund flights for family'. Daily Mail. 27.9.10, p28.

[1021] McKinstry. L. 'Ministers must not give in to public sector blackmail'. Daily Express. 13.9.10, p12.

[1022] BBC 'Horizon'. 15.9.10.

[1023] Whitehead, T. 'Police overtime to be slashed'. The Daily Telegraph. 24.7.10, p1.

[1024] Slack, J. 'Police will be ordered to cut overtime by £70 m'. Daily Mail. 2.12.09, p22.

[1025] Davis, M., Tominey C. 'The £80,000 bobbies'. Sunday Express. 27.6.10, p30.

[1026] Brown, M. ''and the PC raking in £100,000 wage'. Daily Express. 5.8.09, p7.

[1027] Whitelaw, T. 'Our £½ bn bill for police overtime'. Daily Express. 16.5.08, p17.

[1028] Macnab, S. 'Call for probe into overtime payments for football policing'. Scotland on Sunday. 20.2.11, p9.

[1029] O'Sullivan, K. 'Police Raking In £34 Million For Overtime'. Daily Record. 15.11.11, p4.

[1030] Dawar, A. 'Form-filling police put in £500m bill for overtime'. Daily Express. 27.4.09, p6.

[1031] Little, A. '50% increase in police overtime as bill hits £412m'. Daily Express. 10.2.10, p30.

[1032] Fagge, N. 'Fury over £50,000 rent-a-cop private security scheme'. Daily Express. 10.7.09, p25.

[1033] Doyle, J. 'Overtime costs for the police double to £1m a day'. Daily Mail. 7.3.11, p24.

[1034] Massey, R. 'The police who earn £500,000 overtime to man speed cameras'. Daily Mail. 13.7.05, p31.

[1035] Penrose, J. 'Cameron's Police Guards Double Pay With Overtime ... For Just Sitting At Home'. Sunday Mirror. 26.6.11, p8.

[1036] Leake, C. 'The thin blue phone line...'. The Mail on Sunday. 7.8.11, p45.

[1037] Gill, C. 'Police officers who sell lingerie just to make ends meet'. Daily Mail. 16.1.09, p39.

[1038] Holt, G. 'Alarm at huge rise in police with second job'. Daily Express. 14.6.10, p7.

[1039] Levin, A. 'MI5 man DID set up Mosley sting'. The Mail on Sunday. 3.8.08.

[1040] Pilditch, D. 'Police set up website to help them moonlight'. Daily Express. 15.8.08, p7.

[1041] 'Cop a load of my other job'. News Of The World. 4.4.10, p16.

[1042] Blacklock, M. 'Police take second jobs'. Daily Express. 12.8.08, p17.

[1043] Greaves, G. 'Crisis in the Police'. Daily Express. 15.5.00, p32.

[1044] Verkaik, R. 'The Metropolitan Masseurs' Force'. The Mail on Sunday. 18.9.11, p17.

[1045] Jeeves, P. '10% of PCs moonlight to boost their pay'. Daily Express. 28.1.11, p5.

[1046] 'Hard-up police take in ironing to boost wages'. Daily Express. 18.4.08, p8.

[1047] Craik, D. 'Belvoir pins hopes on boom in renting'. Daily Express. 9.1.12, p45.

[1048] Duffin, C., Mendick, R. 'Savile police chief under scrutiny'. The Sunday Telegraph. 19.5.13, p6.

[1049] McKinstry, L. Daily Mail. 9.1.13, p14.

[1050] Lavery, C. '£40K For Gay Bondage Cop'. Sunday Mail. 23.12.07, p26.

[1051] Verkaik, R., Whelan, A. '9,000 police officers have second jobs – from ski guides to Avon ladies'. The Mail on Sunday. 20.5.12, p43.

[1052] Verkaik, R. 'Now police get second jobs teaching follow officers to fire Tasers'. The Mail on Sunday. 27.5.12, p11.

[1053] Verkaik, R., Whelan, A. '9,000 police officers have second jobs – from ski guides to Avon ladies'. The Mail on Sunday. 20.5.12, p43.

[1054] Sunday Express Magazine. 1.11.92.

[1055] Wilson, D. et al. 'What Everyone In Britain Should Know About The Police'. Blackstone Press. 2001. P49.

[1056] Dawar, A. 'Plan to end 'jobs for life' for police officers'. Daily Express. 15.6.11, p15.

[1057] Daily Mail. 9.3.11, p13.

[1058] 'Police are wrong to ballot on strike action over pay'. Leader. Daily Express. 13.12.07, p12.

[1059] Hitchens, P. The Mail on Sunday. 25.5.08, p27.

[1060] O'Neill, S. 'The secret policeman's bonus scheme'. The Times. 24.1.09, p3.

[1061] McKay, P. 'For quite a few coppers more'. Daily Mail. 26.1.09, p17.

[1062] 'Cop Cash Storm'. Daily Record. 13.9.10, p2.

[1063] O'Neill, S. 'The secret policeman's bonus scheme'. The Times. 24.1.09, p3.

[1064] 'Cut bonuses says top cop'. The People. 25.1.09, p16.

[1065] 'Police receive £150m a year in bonuses just for doing their job'. Scotland on Sunday. 15.8.10, p6.

[1066] Disley, J. 'Plastic PCs cost £12k for 1 solved crime'. Daily Express. 14.9.10.

[1067] Slack, J. 'Police recruits to be paid less than trainee McDonald's manager'. Daily Mail. 16.1.13, p4.

[1068] Grant, G. 'Scots officers 'will be richest in Britain' '. Daily Mail. 18.4.13, p27.

[1069] '20,000 seek 60 police jobs'. Daily Express. 12.2.10, p23.

[1070] Taylor, B., Slack, J. 'Part-Time Police On Full-Time Salaries'. Daily Mail. 30.9.05, pp1,8.

[1071] Jeeves, P. 'Anger at £18m bonuses paid to police'. Daily Express. 12.11.09., p15.

[1072] 'PCs can earn more than their bosses with overtime'. Daily Mail. 18.8.09, p22.

[1073] Slack, J. 'Police to get up to £150 a day to stay at home'. Daily Mail. 1.8.09, p12.

[1074] Flanagan, P. 'Met chief gets £80,000 pension then walks into a £120,000 job'. Daily Express. 21.1.09, p19.

[1075] Turner, S. 'Our money should not go towards police bonuses'. Daily Express. 25.6.09, p39.

[1076] Lavery, C. 'Police Chiefs' £100K Bonus'. Sunday Mail. 16.8.09, p6.

[1077] Martin, D. '… And A PC Picking Up £100,000'. Daily Mail. 5.8.09, p16.

[1078] Martin, D. 'On the public payroll, 9,000 staff earning more than PM'. Daily Mail. 20.9.10, p12.

[1079] 'PCs on £70K to guard VIPs'. The Mail on Sunday. 10.4.11, p24

[1080] Crickmer, G. £157m police bonus for doing their job'. Daily Express. 4.8.08, p17.

[1081] Green, N. '£14m police bonuses for "difficult jobs" '. The Sunday Post. 2008, p12.

[1082] Wright, S. 'The police gravy train'. Daily Mail. 8.7.09, p12.

[1083] Schlesinger, Kisiel, R., Bates, D. 'The £70,000 secret perks for top police'. Daily Mail. 7.7.09, p6.

[1084] '£500 To Switch Cop Jobs'. News of the World. 1.6.08, p33.

[1085] Leapman, B. 'Police chiefs paid thousands in bonuses as "reward for failure" '. The Sunday Telegraph. 17.2.08, p14.

[1086] '£300 perks for police'. Daily Express. 30.11.10.

[1087] Littlejohn, R. Daily Mail. 13.3.12, p17.

[1088] Slack, J. 'Police threaten mass protests in battle over pay'. Daily Mail. 17.12.07, p25.

[1089] Phillips, J. 'Spartacus was a worker on strike'. The Sunday Post. 19.9.10, p35.

[1090] McKay, P. 'Lost Plot'. Daily Mail. 20.9.10, p17.

[1091] Delgado, M. The Mail on Sunday. 13.3.11, p15.

[1092] Ryan, R. 'Crime Commissioners blasted over staff costs'. The Sunday Post. 28.4.13, p28.

[1093] Slack, J. 'Now police threaten to march over squeeze on pay and perks'. Daily Mail. 9.3.11, pp12,13.

[1094] Crichton, T. 'Scandal of the Quango Bosses And The £10m Bonus Pot Of Gold'. Daily Record. 29.12.11, p9.

[1095] 'Cops give up £8m in bonuses'. Daily Record. 3.2.11, p6.

[1096] Slack, J., Doyle, J. '£5,000 Police Bonuses Are Axed'. Daily Mail. 3.3.11, pp1,4.

[1097] Whitehead, T., Reynolds, M. 'The beat with 25,000 police, but only when they want a pay rise'. Daily Express. 24.1.08, p3.

[1098] 'Cop probe row'. Daily Record. 4.2.11, p38.

[1099] Verkaik, R. 'Fury as MI6 'Dirty Dozen' get cutback busting pay-offs'. The Mail on Sunday. 30.1.11, p40.

[1100] 'Police agree three-year pay rise'. Daily Mail. 16.10.08, p7.

[1101] Doyle, J., Camber, R. 'Police jeer May as she stands firm on plans to reform pay'. Daily Mail. 19.5.11, p2.

[1102] Jeeves, P. 'I am NOT worth £213,000 a year says police chief'. Daily Express. 13.4.10, p15.

[1103] KcKinstry, L. 'This Excess Is Just The Tip Of The Iceberg'. Daily Mail. 2.6.10, p7.

[1104] 'Job 'not fair' cop'. News Of The World. 2.5.10, p52.

[1105] Panton, L. 'Cop Shop Hero On YouTube'. News Of The World'. 30.12.07, p33.

[1106] Wright, S. 'Met chief's deputy is forced to issue pledge of loyalty'. Daily Mail. 24.10.07, p8.

[1107] Leake, C. 'Yates of the Yard is still drawing £185,000 salary'. The Mail on Sunday. 11.9.11, p43.

[1108] 'Police to take pay row to High Court'. Daily Express. 5.2.08, p9.

[1109] Hobson, N. 'Policemen Behaving Badly'. Daily Mail. 24.4.06, pp26,27.

[1110] 'Police pay soars by £40 million'. Daily Record. 29.10.11, p7.

[1111] Doyle, J. '£40,000 police are in top 20% of all earners'. Daily Mail. 10.1.12, p10.

[1112] Chorley, M. 'Police 'stand-off' threatens to break Osborne's pay cap'. The Independent on Sunday. 8.1.12, p16.

[1113] Officer 'A'. 'The Crime Factory'. Mainstream Publishing. 2012.

[1114] Grant, G. 'Police paid £24m ... to do the dirty work'. Daily Mail. 2.10.12, p25.

[1115] Butler, E. 'No wonder We're All Scared Stiff'. Daily Mail. 15.4.09, p14.

[1116] Watson, D. 'Gun Cops Told: Get Fines For Littering'. Daily Record. 12.8.09, p6.

[1117] Roden, A. 'Top policeman's first legal fight is over his staff'. Daily Mail. 26.12.12, p6.

[1118] Sylvester, N. 'Too Many Chiefs Not Enough Jobs'. Sunday Mail. 30.12.12, p6.

[1119] Grant, G. 'Police chiefs keep money after losing the top job'. Daily Mail. 4.2.13, p36.

[1120] 'Row over force chief on £192,000'. Daily Express. 3.5.13, p1.

[1121] Emsley, C. 'The Great British Bobby'. Quercus. London. 2009.

[1122] Leake, C. '£2 m a day cost of police pensions'. The Mail on Sunday. 12.9.10, p44.

[1123] Harrison, I. 'Anger as shamed cop keeps police pension'. The Sunday Post. 15.11.09, p7.

[1124] Milland, G. 'Blunder boss'. Daily Express. 10.4.09, p4.

[1125] Leppard, D., Watts, R. 'Cop a load of this: senior police nab multi-million pension pots'. The Sunday Times. 20.9.09, p9.

[1126] Silvester, N. 'Love-split cop in battle for pension'. Sunday Mail. 4.3.07, p23.

[1127] Silvester, N. 'Police Pension Rush Arrested'. Sunday Mail. 20.5.07, p36.

[1128] Doward, J. 'Taxpayers in £481m police pension top-up'. The Observer. 22.11.09, p23.

[1129] Basnett, G. 'Cops' pension black hole costs You £1m a day'. News Of The World. 12.7.09, p24.

[1130] 'Retired staff outstrip serving firemen'. The Sunday Times. 26.10.08, p7.

[1131] 'Corrupt cop keeps pension'. The Sunday Post. 17.1.10, p5.

[1132] Smyth, S. 'Plan to end police damages attacked'. The Sunday Post. 31.8.08, p4.

[1133] Smyth, B. 'Ex-cops fury over pension bonanza snub'. The Sunday Post. 17.8.08, p2.

[1134] Twomey, J. 'Police chief Blair's £580K pay bonanza'. Daily Express. 20.6.09, p25.

[1135] Hamilton, N. Sunday Express. 30.1.08, p31.

[1136] Barrett, D. 'The 1800 suspended police who keep their pensions'. The Sunday Telegraph. 31.3.13, p13.

[1137] Watts, R. 'Golden pensions hit police forces'. The Sunday Times. 6.1.08, p2.

[1138] Moss, V. 'Axed Cops £200m Bill'. Sunday Mirror. 15.5.11, p4.

[1139] Murray, J. 'Top police chiefs face crunch on pensions'. Sunday Express. 22.8.10, p11.

[1140] Connett, D. 'Police force tries to stop corrupt officer getting his pension'. The Independent on Sunday. 16.5.10, p22.

[1141] Hall, M. 'Crackdown on town hall 'double dippers' '. Daily Express. 17.11.11, p29.

[1142] Burns, J. 'Sex-change cop pension rights fight'. Daily Record. 28.11.11, p11.

[1143] Bhatia, S., Owens, N., Hamilton, M. 'Bomb Is Smuggled Into Olympic Park'. Sunday Mirror. 8.1.12, p6.

[1144] Silvester, N. 'Hello, Hello, Hello'. Sunday Mail. 12.2.12, p9.

[1145] Hall, M. 'Police pensions bill now hits £2.5 billion'. Daily Express, 29.2.12, p2.

[1146] Infante, F. 'Pension Payout Police Handed £55K Jobs'. The Mail on Sunday. 6.1.13, pp1,2.

[1147] Johnson, K. 'Police merger costs £60m'. Daily Express. 28.1.13, p5.

[1148] '£300,000 payout for sacked cop'. Daily Record. 28.1.13, p20.

[1149] McKinstry. L. 'Ministers must not give in to public sector blackmail'. Daily Express. 13.9.10, p12.

[1150] Clegg, D. 'Police axe 1400 ... but boss's pal gets a job'. Daily Record. 28.1.13, p10.

[1151] Gladdis, K. 'Police Sickies Cost Us £110m'. News of the World. 9.3.08, p8.

[1152] Hickley, M. 'Collecting full pay, the police officers doing an hour a day'. Daily Mail. 17.6.08, p25.

[1153] '£800,000 cost of sick cops'. The People. 19.2.12, p29.

[1154] Doyle, J. 'Fat police are facing a pay cut'. Daily Mail. 16.3.12, p4.

[1155] Davis, M. 'Tennis ball perch on the MoD home front'. Sunday Express. 15.4.12, p32.

[1156] Henderson, E. 'PC who has been on sick for 10 years'. Daily Express. 19.11. 01, p21.

[1157] Swift, G. '£11bn scandal of sicknote Britain'. Daily Express. 27.8.03, p15.

[1158] Goodchild, S. 'Met to get free help for anxiety'. The Independent on Sunday. 20.5.01, p9.

[1159] The Official History Of the Metropolitan Police. Gary Mason. Carlton. 2004. p16.

[1160] Emsley, C. 'The Great British Bobby'. Quercus. London. 2009.

[1161] Callan, P. 'A Land Fit For Revolution'. Daily Express. 7.11.09, pp40-41.

[1162] Malnick, E. 'Your bill for the trade unions'. The Sunday Telegraph. 9.10.11, p4.

[1163] Black, N. 'Police work to rule will erode public support'. Daily Express. 15.8.08, p39.

[1164] Hickley, M. 'Crime fear over police work to rule threat'. Daily Mail. 14.8.08, p1,4.

[1165] Brown, M. 'Pensions War Will Cripple Britain'. Daily Express. 16.6.11, p1.

[1166] O'Hare, P. 'Cash Battle Cops Vote To Break Law'. Daily Record. 23.4.08.

[1167] Whitehead, T. 'Police lose court fight over blocked pay'. Daily Express. 11.6.08, p17.

[1168] Shipman, T., Peev, G. 'Firemen Strike On Bonfire Night'. 26.10.10, p1.

[1169] Whitehead, T. 'Britain faces first strike by police officers for a century'. Daily Express. 17.5.07, p11.

[1170] Greenwood, C., Collins, L. 'Police taken off the beat to prop up 999 centres'. Daily Mail. 1.7.11, p7.

[1171] BBC News. 30.8.11.

[1172] Shipman, T. 'Police 'work to rule' threat over pay cuts'. Daily Mail. 5.10.11, p17.

[1173] Slack, J., Wright, S. 'Blunkett's bobbies will get that police pay rise in full'. Daily Mail. 19.12.07, p7.

[1174] Hartley, S. '£8 million bill for the 300 police officers who don't even work'. Daily Express. 26.3.07, p6.

[1175] Leask, D. 'Policeman racks up four years' full-pay suspension'. Scotland on Sunday. 8.2.09, p10.

[1176] Musson, C. 'Suspension Scandal Cop Finally Quits'. Daily Record. 8.5.12, p13.

[1177] Whitehead, T. '£7.8m a year for police officers to do nothing'. Daily Express. 7.4.08, p16.

[1178] Camber, R. ''Broke' Dizaei is given legal aid for retrial'. Daily Mail. 8.10.11, p39.

[1179] Silvester, N. 'Cop Boss Is Paid £42,000 To Stay Home … .'. Sunday Mail. 3.2.08, p14.

[1180] Coyle, M. '170 Cops Net £5m Just To Sit At Home'. Daily Record. 13.7.12, pp8,9.

[1181] Coyle, M. '170 Cops Net £5m. Just To Sit At Home'. Daily Record. 13.7.12, p8.

[1182] Pendlebury, R., Wright, S. 'The day 'General' Dizaei met the Iranian president'. Daily Mail. 10.2.10, p21.

[1183] Sergeant, H. 'Inside Britain's Police Farce'. Daily Mail. 11.2.08, p26.

[1184] 'Open 'n' shut case'. News of the World. 19.6.11, p25.

[1185] Murphy, S. 'Scotland Yard pays £68,000 to move sign just 15 yards'. The Mail on Sunday. 21.4.13, p20.

[1186] Whitehead, T. 'Police paying millions for wrongful arrests'. Daily Express. 19.7.06, p19.

[1187] Narain, J. 'Chief Constable spends £30,000 of our money on her office shower'. Daily Mail. 20.10.06, p21.

[1188] Barrett, D. 'Forces splash out on 'flat-pack cops' costing £20,000'. The Sunday Telegraph. 1.2.09, p17.

[1189] Harrison, I. 'Police fuel foul-ups cost us £43,000'. The Sunday Post. 12.4.09, p12.

[1190] Silverman, R. 'Budget cut cops blow £100K on new shirts'. Sunday Mail. 4.7.10, p17.

[1191] Thornton, P. 'Tasers On Shun'. Daily Record. 18.5.09, p16.

[1192] Caplan, M. 'Ditch ads and give us more police on beat'. Daily Express. 25.1.10, p23.

[1193] Alexander, A. 'How to deal with the local drugs baron'. Daily Mail. 3.11.10, p16.

[1194] '22 pages to teach police how to email'. Daily Mail. 27.3.10, p58.

[1195] Smith, D. J. 'It's Official – There Was No Child Abuse In Jersey'. The Sunday Times Magazine. 10.5.09, p47.

[1196] Panton, L. 'Something evil had happened'. News Of The World. 16.11.08, p18.

[1197] Mills, R. 'Half a million pound bill for top cop probe'. Daily Express. 26.4.13, p10.

[1198] Fagge, N. 'Plastic police stop fighting crime … to pick up rubbish'. Daily Express. 17.8.09, p19.

[1199] 'Binge probe cost £80K'. Daily Express. 30.9.09, p15.

[1200] Hull, L. 'Look into my eyes: Police learning how to hypnotise'. Daily Mail. 18.12.09, p37.

[1201] Wilkes, D., Taylor, B. Daily Mail. 5.11.03, p23.

[1202] 'Police aid is on the cards'. Daily Express. 9.9.08, p25.

[1203] 'Police taking lessons in Urdu'. Daily Mail. 12.3.07, p20.

[1204] Bryce, T. 'Scots cops' translating costs soar'. The Sunday Post. 2.10.11, p37.

[1205] Dowling, K., Hookham, M. 'Interpreters cost taxpayer £180m'. The Sunday Times. 23.10.11, p7.

[1206] 'Speed cameras face the end of the road'. Daily Mail. 24.10.08, p10.

[1207] Morgan, T. '£35K 'wasted' on new police logo'. Daily Express. 28.10.08, p9.

[1208] 'PCs' red tape hell'. News Of The World. 17.2.08, p2.

[1209] Dolan, A. '100 Blunkett Bobbies hand out 15 fines in three years at a cost of £10m'. Daily Mail. 18.2.09, p31.

[1210] Holland, L. 'Thousands wasted on the case of three 'poisoned' £7 goldfish'. Daily Express. 23.1.10, p18.

[1211] Syal, R. 'Bungling Met lost £30 in Iceland'. The Observer. 5.4.09, p12.

[1212] Blackstock, G. 'Top cops up in arms over HQ waste claim'. The Sunday Post. 24.10.10, p8.

[1213] Aitken, M. 'Blundering Cops' £2m Compo Bill'. Sunday Mail. 20.9.09, p6.

[1214] Blackstock, G. 'Even police fall foul of capital's blue meanies'. The Sunday Post. 10.10.10, p8.

[1215] Osley, R. 'Six-year booze case ends with no charge … but £5m in costs'. The Independent On Sunday. 5.4.09, p18.

[1216] Gill, C. 'Patrol car has one flat tyre … so Yard replaces all of them'. Daily Mail. 26.11.10, p45.

[1217] Gill, C. 'Off their trolleys'. Daily Mail. 21.10.10, p38.

[1218] Slack J. 'More police doesn't mean less crime, claims ministers'. Daily Mail. 22.11.10, p4.

[1219] Gray, C. 'Now squatters have set up home … in a police station'. Daily Express. 7.10.10, p19.

[1220] 'Terror swoop? No, it's just to arrest a hoodie'. Daily Express. 30.3.07, p5.

[1221] Narain, J. 'Blimping useless'. Daily Mail. 12.11.10, p41.

[1222] 'Cop's call to cut red tape'. Sunday Mirror. 17.4.11, p32.

[1223] Kirby, I. 'Ello 'ello 'ello battery'. News of the World. 20.3.11, p30.

[1224] ITV News. 12.4.11.

[1225] Pilditch, D. 'New hope that Madeleine's alive'. Daily Express. 18.5.11, p11.

[1226] Murray, J. 'Yard: We Can Solve Maddie Mystery'. Sunday Express. 8.4.12, pp1,6.

[1227] Flanagan, P. '£2m cost of Met's Maddy case review'. Daily Express.

[1228] 'Police pay £1m for 'customer research' surveys'. The Mail on Sunday. 15.5.11, p40.

[1229] 'Big police presence stuns Old Firm pals'. Daily Record. 20.5.11, p19.

[1230] Barrett, D. 'Police buy young criminals theatre tickets for top shows'. The Sunday Telegraph. 22.5.11, p14.

[1231] Coates, J. 'Police splashing out millions on water'. Sunday Express. 19.6.11, p18.

[1232] Hooper, P. £1m cops' phone sets out of date'. Sunday People. 28.4.13, p21.

[1233] Daily Mail. 9.4.11, p51.

[1234] Hagger, A. 'Firm gets £4m for guarding police stations'. Daily Express. 22.6.10, p8.

[1235] Carlin, B. 'Whitehall farce as police probe chewing gum theft'. The Mail on Sunday. 5.6.11, p18.

[1236] Blackstock, G. 'Police flown from beach to witness box'. The Sunday Post. 25.4.10, p5.

[1237] 'Cops to protect 5 rare birds'. Daily Record. 9.7.11, p29.

[1238] Moodie, C. 'Jemima's pet detectives'. Daily Mail. 20.6.07, p3.

[1239] 'Police raid on peace activist cost £111,000'. Daily Mail. 14.7.07, p52.

[1240] Tozer, J. '£500,000 bill as fathers' rights duo are cleared'. Daily Mail. 4.10.07, p11.

[1241] 'Police send girl to bed'. Daily Mail. 20.8.07, p10

[1242] 'Your Money, Wasted'. Daily Mail. 11.5.06, p19.

[1243] Gladdis, K., Wright, S., Leigh, D. 'The Snorkelling Squad'. Daily Mail. 8.10.11, p6.

[1244] Lewis, J. 'Royals charge bodyguards rent'. The Mail on Sunday. 11.7.10, p22.

[1245] English, R. 'Six police see Kate gets to work on time'. Daily Mail. 5.1.07, p27.

[1246] English, R. 'Overstretched police assign eight officers (plus two minders) so Harry and Chelsy can go nightclubbing till 4AM in peace'. Daily Mail. 15.1.07, p21.

[1247] Hall, M. 'How civil servants waste your money by the billion'. Daily Express. 28.4.10 p17.

[1248] Little, A. 'From lingerie to beehives, the £6m police card spree'. Daily Express. 8.8.11, p15.

[1249] Booker, C. The Sunday Telegraph. 14.8.11, p27.

[1250] Hall, M. 'Taxpayers give £7m for unions to fight cutbacks'. Daily Express. 22.8.11, p30.

[1251] Dow, I. 'Old Bill Get A Big Bill For New Logo'. Daily Record. 21.2.08, p12.

[1252] Blackstock, G. 'Hardly a cheep from Tayside Twitter cops'. The Sunday Post. 1.9.11, p29.

[1253] Littlejohn, R. Daily Mail. 21.10.11, p17.

[1254] Duguid, K. 'Police take dim view of shady officers'. Scotland on Sunday. 16.10.11, p12.

[1255] Devine, A. 'The Bill'. Daily Record. 18.11.11, pp1,5.

[1256] Liddle, R. 'Simples – it's either undue lobbying or a waste of money'. The Sunday Times. 11.12.11, p27.

[1257] Kenny, J. 'Old style rotas would restore faith in police'. Daily Mail. 12.12.11, p47.

[1258] Camber, R. 'Ask a bobby for the time and he'll just phone the speaking clock'. Daily Mail. 19.1.12, p7.

[1259] Clark, R. 'Proof that police on the beat really do reduce crime'. Daily Express. 14.1.12, p18.

[1260] BBC News 15.2.12.

[1261] Blackstock, G. 'Calamity cops come a cropper'. The Sunday Post. 12.2.12, p35.

[1262] 'Cops pay £250K to crooks'. Daily Record. 2.9.11, p4.

[1263] Brown, M. 'Councils 'waste' £515m on CCTV in crime war'. Daily Express. 21.2.12, p24.

[1264] Littlejohn, R. Daily Mail. 27.3.12, p17.

[1265] BBC1 News. 10.4.12.

[1266] 'Police are so fuel-ish'. Daily Record. 21.4.12.

[1267] Blackstock, G. 'Police prangs costing taxpayers a fortune'. The Sunday Post. 22.4.12, p11.

[1268] 'Top cop buy blitz'. The Sun. 17.4.12, p25.

[1269] Doyle, J. 'Blunkett blasts bid to boost role of 'plastic PCs' '. Daily Mail. 14.4.12, p47.

[1270] BBC2 Newsnight. 16.4.12.

[1271] Silvester, N. 'Protection Row Police Chief Quits'. Sunday Mail. 15.4.12, p18.

[1272] Officer 'A'. 'The Crime Factory'. Mainstream Publishing. 2012.

[1273] 'Trial halted because policeman prefers to guard Olympic torch'. The Mail on Sunday. 29.4.12, p20.

[1274] Hill, P. Daily Express. 8.5.12, p14.

[1275] Doyle, J., Slack, J. 'The police boo-boys who cost us £6m a year'. Daily Mail. 18.5.12, p10.

[1276] Paddick, B. 'Unfit, scruffy, high-handed and corrupt: Britain's worst police need fixing'. The Mail on Sunday. 24.6.12, p27.

[1277] Slack, J. 'Police spend their time typing rather than fighting crime'. Daily Mail. 27.6.12, p17.

[1278] Grant, G. 'Police Scotland forced to scrap its 'illegal logo' '. Daily Mail. 22.2.13, p4.

[1279] 'Drury, P. 'What a waste!'. The Mail on Sunday. 3.3.13, p9.

[1280] Gales, D. 'We Cough Up For Cops To Quit Cigs'. Sunday Mirror. 20.9.09, p32.

[1281] Brown, M. 'You can't have a loo roll without a form, police told'. Daily Express. 11.12.09, p39.

[1282] Littlejohn, R. Daily Mail. 13.11.09, p17.

[1283] Evans, M. 'The fashion police'. Daily Express. 28.10.09, p11.

[1284] Pooran, N. 'Cop Boss Spends £800,000 On Being Told How To Behave'. Daily Record. 14.3.13, p30.

[1285] Herbert, D. 'Public faces £100K bill for an empty HQ'. Daily Express. 4.2.13, p10.

[1286] Beckford, M. 'Paranoid police have something to declare: a sandwich and orange juice'. The Mail on Sunday. 17.3.13, p8.

[1287] Dolan, a. 'Come to a party at our HQ, police say to travellers'. Daily Mail. 24.6.09, p13.

[1288] 'Police web cost storm'. The People. 17.1.10, p45.

[1289] Taher, A., Beckford, M. 'Met's astonishing £3.5 bn shopping list'. The Mail on Sunday. 25.11.12, pp18,19.

[1290] Murphy, S. '£250,000 bill to keep a police eye on the failings of private security'. Daily Mail. 12.12.12., p21.

[1291] 'Police are relying on specials'. Daily Record. 10.11.12, p2.

[1292] Musson, C. 'Fears As Cops Get Smartphones In Twitter Drive To Tackle Crime'. The Sun.28.10.12, pp10,11.

[1293] Beckford, M. 'Police 'fined' for locking up too many criminals'. The Mail on Sunday. 25.11.12, p48.

[1294] Doyle, J., Slack, J. 'The police boo-boys who cost us £6m a year'. Daily Mail. 18.5.12, p10.

[1295] Lavelle, C. 'Police fuel blunders cost £60K'. Daily Record. 14.5.12, p17.

[1296] Levy, A. Mail Online. 18.8.10.

[1297] Taylor, B. ' 'Wasteful' Met and its army of 64 race advisers'. Daily Mail. 16.2.02, p39.

[1298] Mills, R. 'Anger over police's road safety lessons'. Daily Express. 30.1.13, p8.

[1299] Hainey, R. 'The Bill Is £3m For Cops' Spin Doctors'. Sunday Mail. 8.6.08, p24.

[1300] Slack, J. 'A new tax on every household to pay for community policing'. Daily Mail. 27.5.08, p19.

[1301] Grant, G. 'New crisis for police as bill for computer revamp hits £45m'. Daily Mail. 21.6.13, p26.

[1302] Dawar, A. 'Police waste millions not bulk buying'. Daily Express. 17.9.13, p15.

[1303] Morkis, S., Andrews, K. 'The thin blue line'. The Courier. 8.10.13, p10.

[1304] Barrett, D. 'Number of police to fall as budgets tighten'. The Sunday Telegraph. 10.1.10, p14.

[1305] Kisiel, R. 'We can't help you, police tell man who found son's stolen car'. Daily Mail. 27.12.08, p47.

[1306] 'We can't afford to nab thief'. The Sun. 16.7.09, p27.

[1307] Cassidy, R. 'Overtime halted on drug probe'. Daily Record. 29.3.13, p9.

[1308] 'Madeleine police bill into £745K'. Daily Express. 4.8.09, p7.

[1309] McLeod, K. 'Cops' £35m Black Hole'. Daily Record. 3.8.09, p10.

[1310] O'Hare, P. 'Cops Are £60m In The Red'. Daily Record. 2.2.10, p6.

[1311] Salkeld, L. 'We can't afford to DNA test your skirt, police tell victim of sex attack'. Daily Mail. 21.10.09, p29.

[1312] Leake, C. 'New 'policing on the cheap' row as unpaid Specials join murder squad'. The Mail on Sunday. 9.8.09, p28.

[1313] Douglas, H. 'New 'vigilantes' a target for yobs'. Sunday Express. 2.11.08, p15.

[1314] Camber, R. 'Police spend just 13% of their time on the beat'. Daily Mail. 3.12.09, p30.

[1315] Twomey, J. 'Shopkeeper drives 'thief' to police after calling 999 in vain'. Daily Express. 5.11.08, p32.

[1316] Leask, D. 'Revealed: sorry state of Scots police stations'. Scotland on Sunday. 18.10.09, p8.

[1317] Littlejohn, R. 'Where were the police?'. Daily Mail. 3.10.08, p17.

[1318] 'Traffic police feel the heat'. Daily Express. 1.8.08, p26.

[1319] Slack, J. 'CPS 'letting criminals off lightly' to cut costs'. Daily Mail.

[1320] Doward, J. 'Police failing over internet paedophiles'. The Observer. 18.2.07, p17.

[1321] Riches, C. 'The 'too busy' Blue Line'. Daily Express. 10.4.06, p25.

[1322] Widdecombe, A. 'Police must look to their priorities'. Daily Express. 5.11.08, p13.

[1323] 'Polish police plan is just ridiculous'. Daily Express. 21.11.06, p7.

[1324] 'Police too busy chasing chickens to stop murder'. The Sunday Times. 10.12.06, pp1,2.

[1325] Brooks. T. 'The empty police car that failed to keep crooks away'. Daily Express. 22.9.06, p26.

[1326] 'Plastic police' face axe'. Daily Express. 23.10.10, p5.

[1327] O'Hare, P. 'Skint Blue Line'. Daily Record. 22.10.10, p4.

[1328] 'Police told not to plug in mobiles due to cuts'. The Mail on Sunday. 5.12.10, p37.

[1329] Ashworth, R. 'Police cars for sale on eBay'. Sunday Express. 3.7.11, p21.

[1330] Camber, R. 'It's a steal! Police sell ill-gotten gains on eBay'. Daily Mail. 28.9.09, p25.

[1331] Money Mail Special Investigation. Daily Mail. 8.6.11, p43.

[1332] Gosden, E. 'Police make millions by 'selling' accident details to breakdown firms'. The Daily Telegraph. 28.6.11, p9.

[1333] Slack, J., Massey, R. 'Victory for drivers as 'cash for crash' racket is outlawed'. Daily Mail. 9.9.11, p4.

[1334] 'Police told to get bus'. Daily Express. 16.10.10, p7.

[1335] 'Police are told to buy their own boots'. Daily Mail. 4.10.07, p21

[1336] Henderson, E. 'Claudia police 'lacking skills'. Sunday Express. 2.8.09, p46.

[1337] Wright, S. 'Top black officer warns of 'migrant crime surge'. Daily Mail. 28.1.08, p17.

[1338] Jones, G., Hyder, K. 'Tax Cuts For Good Citizens'. Sunday Express. 26.9.10, pp1,4.

[1339] 'Crime victim? Skype the cops'. Daily Mail. 10.8.13, p4.

[1340] Walters, S., Owen, G. 'Fears over flats for super-rich Russians … looking into No 10'. The Mail on Sunday. 13.11.11, p38.

[1341] Doyle, J., Greenwood, C. 'Calling police to report a crime? That's 15p please'. Daily Mail. 24.11.11, p7.

[1342] 'Old Bill is £4m'. News Of The World. 18.7.10, p8.

[1343] Gallagher, I. 'Police finance chief quits over hotel stay with blonde colleague'. The Mail on Sunday. 8.1.12, p10.

[1344] Paul, D. 'Police on patrol but villagers pay for the petrol'. Sunday Express. 27.4.08, p51

[1345] Jeeves, P. 'Police tell theft victim: Catch culprits yourself'. Daily Express. 15.10.11, p42.

[1346] 'Smartphones ' kept officers off the beat' '. Daily Mail. 27.1.12, p17.

[1347] Robson, C. 'The Mounties Get Their Ban'. Daily Record. 26.1.12, p35.

[1348] Kynaston, D. 'Austerity Britain'. Bloomsbury. 2007, p362.

[1349] McDonald, C. 'Wedding Stinger'. Daily Record. 10.11.11, p33.

[1350] Goslett, M. 'Police didn't have the money to catch burglars who beat me with a crowbar'. The Mail on Sunday. 18.5.08, p17.

[1351] Christie, K. 'Gay Cops Get Own £50,000 A Year Police Chief'. Daily Record. 12.7.08, p7.

[1352] Blackstock, G. 'Rebranded and disbanded'. The Sunday Post. 18.3.12, p42.

[1353] Twomey, J. '150 police for hacking … 27 for sex pests'. Daily Express. 30.3.12, p2.

[1354] Anderson, N. 'An Inspector Calls'. Daily Record. 27.3.12, p23.

[1355] Ross, N. 'You've Been Nicked'. Daily Mail. 8.7.04, p24.

[1356] Jeeves, P. 'Police browned off after bosses ban their sunbeds'. Daily Express. 6.4.12, p31.

[1357] Greenwood, C. 'Police station closed down? You'd better head to Tesco'. Daily Mail. 3.7.12, p10.

[1358] Greenwood, C., Fernandez, C., Salkeld, L. 'We can't patrol Twitter, insist police'. Daily Mail. 1.8.12, p5.

[1359] McWhirty, R. 'After four years off work on £175,000, car crash officer will retire on full pension'. The Mail on Sunday. 10.2.13, p35.

[1360] 'Police tangled in red tape as crime-solving bill jumps 60%'. Daily Mail. 9.11.09, p24.

[1361] Mills, R. 'Police fork out £13m. on doctors' fees'. Daily Express. 22.2.13, p9.

[1362] Phillips, M. 'I warned about these groups … but I was just laughed at'. Daily Mail. 8.6.11, p12.

[1363] Chancellor, A. 'Unfair Cop, Offisher!'. Daily Mail. 7.12.09, p15.

[1364] Gill, C. ' 'Christmas for criminals' as 40,000 police face the axe'. Daily Mail. 11.9.10, p11.

[1365] Wright, S. 'Police chief: Cuts could cause riots'. Daily Mail. 14.9.10, p2.

[1366] McDonald, C. 'Rape Cop Dodges Court Demo Fury'. Daily Record. 30.1.09, p23.

[1367] Wilson, D. et al. 'Everyone In Britain Should know About The Police'. Blackstone Press. 2001, P17.

[1368] Dinneen, S., Taylor, D. 'Wallet's Going On Here Then?'. Sunday Mail. 19.4.09, p37.

[1369] Leppard, D. 'Yard's anti-terror chief to be quizzed over credit-card expenses'. The Sunday Times. 10.5.09, p7.

[1370] Williamson, L. 'Royal policeman "fleeced his colleagues at the Palace" '. Daily Mail. 17.4.09, p9.

[1371] Gillard, M. 'Fraud At Heart Of The Palace'. The Sunday Times. 19.7.09, p11.

[1372] 'Royal police lose fortune in betting ring'. The Sunday Times. 6.7.08, p1.

[1373] 'Royal officers 'played poker on duty and dealt in porn' '. Daily Mail. 30.6.09, p31.

[1374] Twomey, J. 'Police officers sold guns handed in to be destroyed'. Daily Express. 12.1.10.

[1375] Munro, A. 'Hash Farm Found At Cop House'. Daily Record. 26.9.09, p29.

[1376] 'Inquiry over Yard chief to be headed by top policeman'. Daily Mail. 2.8.08, p12.

[1377] Gilligan, A. 'The PC, his victims' charity and the case of his missing money'. The Sunday Telegraph. 21.2.10, p9.

[1378] 'PC resigns over secret info leak'. The Sunday Post. 14.2.10, p4.

[1379] 'Cop "sold uniform" '. The Sun. 2.7.07, p15.

[1380] Boffey, D. 'Police security fears as official equipment gets touted on eBay'. The Mail on Sunday. 3.6.07, p37.

[1381] Rafferty, S., Silvester, N. 'Shopped'. Sunday Mail. 25.2.07, p23.

[1382] Sims, P. 'WPC's "secret life as a £100 an hour escort" '. Daily Mail. 9.12.08, p26.

[1383] 'Terror police chief's limo firm is banned from offering trips'. The Mail on Sunday. 25.1.09, p20.

[1384] Silvester, N. 'Cops and saucers'. Sunday Mail. 26.10.08, p18.

[1385] Leask, D. 'Right to buy to leave Hamish without home'. Scotland on Sunday. 19.7.09, p9.

[1386] Gill, C. 'Jail for the detective who spent £73,000 on his police credit card'. Daily Mail. 23.11.08, p24.

[1387] Summers, C. 'PC's greed led to blackmail plot'. BBC News. 18.12.08.

[1388] Leppard, D. 'Acting Met chief quizzed on audit'. The Sunday Times. 5.10.08, p3.

[1389] Leppard, D. 'Yard chief on spot over £3m contracts'. The Sunday Times. 3.8.08, p2.

[1390] Wright, S. 'Met Boss In New 'Cash For A Friend' Storm'. Daily Mail. 2.10.08, p1.

[1391] '£17K for cop exes'. News Of The World. 18.7.10, p8.

[1392] Phillips, R. 'Police net £33K from 0845 lines'. The Mail on Sunday. 29.3.09, p40.

[1393] Inside Out. BBC1. 4.2.09.

[1394] Barrie, J. 'Cops Flogged My Stolen Property'. Sunday Mail. 15.11.09, p27.

[1395] Dow, B. 'Cop Sacked For Flogging Off His Helmet On ebay'. Daily Record. 17.5.08, p21.

[1396] Hinsliff, G. 'Police face inquiry into media payouts'. The Observer. 12.7.09.

[1397] Silvester, N. 'SPL Chiefs Dodge The Bill'. Sunday Mail. 14.6.09, pp1,4.

[1398] 'Cop Fees Outrage'. News of the World. 27.4.08, p26.

[1399] 'As a middle class driver I must protest'. Daily Express. 20.8.10, p13.

[1400] Wooding, D. 'What A Lot We Copped'. 28.11.10, p45.

[1401] 'Probe into Met terror chief's 'work' air miles gift to family'. The Mail on Sunday. 5.12.10, p4.

[1402] Kember, B. 'Thousands of 'sicknote police' are still on full pay'. The Times. 4.12.10, p6.

[1403] 'The sick blue line'. The Sunday Times. 5.12.10, p31.

[1404] Whitehead, T. 'Police using civilians on murder inquiries'. Daily Express. 16.10.06, p6.

[1405] Wright, S. 'Blair's bodyguards 'bought a rocket launcher on expenses' '. Daily Mail. 4.12.10, p37.

[1406] Lewis, J. '5-Star Luxury Of The Blairs' Police Squad'. The Mail On Sunday. 4.7.10, p1.

[1407] O'Hare, P. 'Police chiefs try to slash cops 'wages' '. Daily Record. 11.11.10, p22.

[1408] Leppard, D. 'Quango buys assault rifles to 'use up budget' '. The Sunday Times. 6.2.11, p8.

[1409] Flyn, C., Ungoed-Thomas, J. 'You're hired!'. The Sunday Times. 7.8.11, p8.

[1410] McGee, S. 'Police sting taxpayer for lingerie and beehive'. The Sunday Times. 7.8.11, p9.

[1411] Delgado, M., Sandy, M. 'Police wives' firms paid £3.5m to type witness statements'. The Mail on Sunday. 12.12.10, p41.

[1412] Burns, J. 'Train Row Cop To Sue'. Daily Record. 29.11.10, p17.

[1413] Emsley, C. 'The Great British Bobby'. Quercus. London. 2009. p195.

[1414] Doward, J. 'Police boost funds from assets taken in raids on prostitutes'. The Observer. 25.4.10, p7.

[1415] Hastings, C. 'Out:450 staff at Raoul Moat force. In: A £50K 'steel ball in a hula hoop'. The Mail on Sunday. 6.2.11, p30.

[1416] Gillard, M. 'Top Yard officers 'untouchable' over expenses'. The Sunday Times. 9.12.07, p12.

[1417] Lewis, J. 'Police terror budget cut by millions after Ring of Steel blunder'. The Mail on Sunday. 28.2.10, p45.

[1418] Doyle, J. 'Police spend more time on holiday than at work'. Daily Mail. 20.7.10, p4.

[1419] Reynolds, M. 'Scandal of police retiring ... and still drawing £9m pay'. Daily Express. 9.7.10, p22.

[1420] 'Controversial police chief quits island job'. The Sunday Post. 25.7.10, p14.

[1421] Silvester, N. 'So What's Going On Here Then?'. Sunday Mail. 9.5.10, p4.

[1422] Lewis, J., Rimmer, A. 'As 28,000 police face axe, chiefs blow £500K on champagne gala'. The Mail on Sunday. 27.6.10, p35.

[1423] Harrison, I. 'Part-time cops 'should not be paid full wages' '. The Sunday Post. 13.6.10, p9.

[1424] Owens, N. 'Police For Hire'. Sunday Mirror. 9.5.10, p31.

[1425] Leigh, D., Kelly, J. 'Frying Squad'. Sunday Mirror. 9.10.11, p11.

[1426] Mendick, R. 'Police for sale: Virgin paid Met for help on fraud'. The Sunday Telegraph. 29.1.12, p10.

[1427] Doughty, S. '£400m police bill ... just for overtime'. Daily Mail. 14.5.10, p36.

[1428] 'Labour's legacy of waste on police'. Daily Express. 13.5.10, p17.

[1429] Murray, J. 'I lured 300 police investors boasts £35m 'mini Madoff' '. Sunday Express. 9.5.10, p16.

[1430] 'Police take 80 minutes to ask for a holiday'. Daily Mail. 30, 9.10, p47.

[1431] BBC1. Panorama. 14.3.11.

[1432] Gillard, M. 'Top Yard officers 'untouchable' over expenses'. Sunday Times. 9.12.07, p12.

[1433] Atkinson, D. 'Police recruiting City volunteers'. The Mail on Sunday. 13.3.11, p83.

[1434] Brooke, C. 'The Mc Coppers'. Daily Mail. 19.11.10, p27.

[1435] Lusher, A. 'The 170 fee for having your car stolen'. The Sunday Telegraph. 23.1.11, p15.

[1436] Musson, C. 'I'll Book 'Em And Hook 'Em'. Daily Record. 10.8.11, p9.

[1437] Ungoed-Thomas, J. 'Car-theft victims pay police £105 to investigate'. The Sunday Times. 15.4.07, p7.

[1438] Mathieson, J. 'Robbed ... But I Got Hit With £150 Charge'. Daily Record. 27.2.12, p21.

[1439] Gysin, C., English, R. 'PCs tried to sell Diana order of service on eBay'. Daily Mail. 5.9.07, p26.

[1440] Kay, A. 'Police refuse to protect Big Brother'. Sunday Express. 8.7.07, p21.

[1441] Lines, A. 'Police: Can we park our cars on your driveways?'. The Mail on Sunday. 17.6.07, p36.

[1442] Leader. Daily Mail. 'Just say no, officer'. 24.12.11, p14.

[1443] Greenwood, C. 'From Take That to Ascot ... police chief freebies are banned'. Daily Mail. 14.12.11, p7.

[1444] Jeeves, P. 'Disgraced gun racket PC wins a £40K payout'. Daily Express. 3.2.12, p22.

[1445] 'Police face MPs' fury on riot claims'. Sunday Mirror. 12.2.12, p8.

[1446] Millar, J. 'Cops argue over who foots riots wage bill'. The Sunday Post. 26.2.12, p6.

[1447] Musson, C. 'Drugs Cop's £115K To Stay Home'. Daily Record. 10.4.12, pp1,7.

[1448] Littlejohn, R. 'The cops watch the boys who watch the girls go by'. Daily Mail. 10.7.12, p17.

REFERENCES

[1449] McKim, C. 'Cops caught using patrol cars as cabs'. Daily Record. 4.6.12, p8.

[1450] 'Police anger after 'civilian' gets nod as watchdog'. Daily Mail. 9.6.12, p14.

[1451] Wright, S. '10,000 police climb on the Olympic gravy train'. Daily Mail. 29.5.12, p6.

[1452] Pooran, N. 'Police forces rake in corporate gifts'. Daily Mail. 14.3.13, p11.

[1453] Findlay, R. 'Bent Cop And The £1million Phoenix Swindle'. Sunday Mail. 2.6.02, p41.

[1454] Shaw, E. 'Dr Who dares … and wins in the battle of Tardis'. Daily Express. 23.10.02, p23.

[1455] Rayner, G. 'Burglars? But are you registered, Sir?'. Daily Mail. 13.6.03, p23.

[1456] Hayes, S. 'The Biggest Gang In Britain'. 2013, pp87,88.

[1457] Henderson, E. 'Police hacking into secret files'. Sunday Express. 31.7.11, p22.

[1458] Emsley, C. The Great British Bobby. pp150, 151.

[1459] Macfarlane, J. 'Police sergeant punched and kicked me too'. The Mail on Sunday. 12.9.10, p43.

[1460] 'Shove cop wins job'. Sunday Mail. 4.12.11, p35.

[1461] Booker, C. The Sunday Telegraph. 14.8.11, p27.

[1462] Gill, C. '£4,000 for teenager dumped in a bin by policeman'. Daily Mail. 31.8.07, p21.

[1463] Farrell, S. The Mail on Sunday. 12.12.10, p22.

[1464] BBC1 News. 24.8.11.

[1465] Townsend, M., Malik, S. 'Kettle tactics risk Hillsborough-style tragedy – doctor'. The Observer. 19.12.10, p20.

[1466] McIlwraith, G. 'A Disgrace To The Force'. Daily Record. 10.11.10, pp1,6.

[1467] 'PCs win appeal'. Daily Record. 2.7.11, p9.

[1468] McPherson, L. 'Domestic Abuse Cop's Threats To Kill Wife'. Sunday Mail. 29.11.09, p36.

[1469] Paterson, B. 'Shamed Ex-Cop Battered Lover In Street'. Daily Record. 28.10.10, p15.

[1470] 'The Crown Prosecution Service. The CPS incorporates RCPO'. http:/www.cps.gov.uk/news/press_releases/133_10/.

[1471] 'Cop faces assault rap'. Daily Record. 30.8.10, p10.

[1472] 'Car teen PC guilty'. The Sun. 10.3.12, p20.

[1473] 'Butt cop beats jail'. The Sun. 3.4.12, p22.

[1474] Blacklock, M. 'Thug PC caught on video faces jail'. Daily Express. 20.9.02, p20.

[1475] Chapman, J. Twomey, J. 'Police probe G20 brutality claims'. Daily Express. 16.4.09, p11.

[1476] Chapman, J. 'Baton-attack riot cop cleared of assault on G20 protest girl'. Daily Express. 1.4.10, 26.

[1477] Russell, J. 'Brutal police are Britain's untouchables'. The Sunday Times. 25.7.10, p23.

[1478] 'Detective on cop attack rap'. News Of The World. 18.4.10, p30.

[1479] 'Cop in dock on girlfriend assault rap'. Daily Record. 30.7.13, p22.

[1480] Temko, N., Watt, N. 'Blair aide's wife attacks police for 'Gestapo' tactics'. The Observer. 22.7.07, p1.

[1481] Bye, J. 'Taser: The Shocking Truth'. The Mail On Sunday Live Magazine Special Issue. 7.3.10, p22.

[1482] 'Taser cop is retrained'. Daily Record. 16.3.12, p30.

[1483] 'Police fire Taser as man has fit'. Daily Express. 14.4.10, p9.

[1484] Millbank, J., Farrell, S. 'Passenger tasered as police storm knife siege train'. The Mail on Sunday. 4.7.10, p19.

[1485] Leake, C. , Whelan, A. The Mail on Sunday. 18.7.10, p19.

[1486] Salkeld, L. 'Police Tasered driver in groin 'by accident' '. Daily Mail. 21.7.10, p20.

[1487] Paterson, B. 'Wife-Beating Cop Allowed To Walk Free'. Daily Record. 1.7.10, p28.

[1488] 'Armed cops in OAP raid'. Sunday Mirror. 11.4.10, p21.

[1489] Chapman, J. '£20K payout for driver, 73, after police smash up car'. Daily Express. 3.2.12, p14.

[1490] O'Hare, P. 'Ex-cop Neighbour Forced Us To Move'. Daily Record. 14.7.09, p29.

[1491] Mausey, K. 'My Fight For Justice By Hero Soldier Attacked by PC'. Sunday Mirror. 8.8.10, pp26,27.

[1492] 'Cop faces force rap'. Sunday Mail. 16.10.11, p37.

[1493] Paterson, B. 'Guess Who Got Done?'. Sunday Mail. 27.11.11, p23.

[1494] 'Officers fail to have case thrown out'. Daily Record, 21.12.11, p7.

[1495] McKelvie, G. 'Sticky Tape Assault Cop to Pay £1000'. Daily Record. 12.1.12, p32.

[1496] Emsley, C. 'The Great British Bobby'. p251.

[1497] Emsley, C. 'The Great British Bobby'.

[1498] Thompson v. Commissioner of Police for the Metropolis, Hsu v. Commissioner of Police for the Metropolis [1997]. All ER 762.

[1499] Booker, C. 'Girl,14, arrested by four police for 'assaulting' them'. The Sunday Telegraph. 23.10.11, p33.

[1500] Silvester, N. 'Cop in dock after police cell 'attack' '. Sunday Mail. 20.11.11, p36.

[1501] Greenwood, C. 'Road –rage PC who left an elderly driver to die'. Daily Mail. 20.3.12, p31.

[1502] 'Cop career now toast'. Daily Record. 16.3.12, p36.

[1503] 'Riot cop in punch quiz'. Sunday Mirror. 12.2.12, p20.

[1504] 'Axed cop to appeal'. Sunday Mail. 8.4.12, p22.

[1505] 'Sheriff is slated in 'attack' PC appeal'. Sunday Mail. 20.5.12, p19.

[1506] 'Baton rap cop for trial'. Daily Record. 7.7.12, p17.

[1507] Robertson, C. 'Wife Flees Cop Who Tried To Hack Off Her Head'. Daily Record. 25.5.12, pp1,4.

[1508] Moncur, J. 'Drugs Squad Cops On Assault Charge'. Daily Record. 23.5.12, p25.

[1509] C4 News. 11.5.12.

[1510] Richardson, A. 'Baton Cop Freed Over Assault Rap'. Daily Record. 1.3.13, p28.

[1511] 'Mercy for hammer rage cop'. Daily Record. 21.9.13, p4.

[1512] Moriarty, R. 'Cops Crash Car They Took Off 'Bad Driver' '. The Sun. 4.9.10, p31.

[1513] Penrose, J. 'Queen's Officers in 4x4 Flip'. Sunday Mirror. 2.10.11, p8.

[1514] Mills, J. 'Licensed to speed'. Daily Mail. 25.9.03, p35.

[1515] 'Cop car hits man after house raid'. Daily Record. 6.8.13, p28.

[1516] 'Cop admits speeding'. Daily Record. 19.7.13, p26.

[1517] Dixon, C. 'M-way death boy's beer warning'. Daily Express. 23.7.10, p15.

[1518] 'OAPs hurt in police crash'. Daily Record. 16.5.13, p33.

[1519] Broster, P., Jeeves, P. 'Britain's top traffic policeman faces a third speeding fine'. Daily Express. 31.10.07, p8.

[1520] Lewis. J. 'Chief Constables PLC'. The Mail on Sunday. 15.2.09, p7.

[1521] Key, I. 'Police roads chief lands speeding fine'. Daily Express. 29.12.06, p5.

[1522] 'Traffic cop on 120mph crash rap'. Daily Record. 15.9.11, p23.

[1523] Dickson, B. 'Breach Of The Piece'. Daily Record. 21.4.11, p31.

[1524] Dolan, A. 'MP's wife and son face jail after lying to beat drink drive charge'. Daily Mail. 15.12.10, p7.

[1525] 'Urine cop returns to court'. Daily Record. 28.4.11, p15.

[1526] 'Top cop faces 'cheat' probe'. The People. 22.6.08, p26.

[1527] Gilmartin, K. 'Battle To Save Cop's Leg After 3-Car Smash'. Daily Record. 4.11.10, p21.

[1528] Massey, R. 'Speed trap cameras 'raise fatal crash risk'. Daily Mail. 7.6.13, p11.

[1529] Aitken, M. 'Blundering Cops' £2m Compo Bill'. Sunday Mail. 20.9.09, p6.

[1530] 'PC faces court over crash on M8'. Sunday Mail. 10.10.10, p33.

[1531] Findlay, R. 'A Long Road To Justice'. Sunday Mail. 2.9.12, p35.

[1532] 'Ices van in cop chase'. The People. 17.10.10, p31.

[1533] 'Let-off' for crash cop'. The Sun. 28.10.12, p19.

[1534] Jeeves, P. 'Police sergeant drove with his lights flashing just because he was late'. Daily Express. 11.1.07, p33.

[1535] Flanagan, P. '£200K bill for crash-prone police'. Daily Express. 1.9.10, p31.

[1536] Mair. G. '4 Cops Hurt In Smash'. Daily Record. 17.6.09, p18.

[1537] Eliott, C. '79mph police chief: speed guns don't work'. Daily Mail. 20.8.10, p25.

[1538] Morgan, T. 'Police officer on trial over 'danger road block' crash'. Daily Express. 14.7.10, p28.

[1539] Moncur, J. 'Cop Chase Dad Who Drowned In Docks'. Daily Record. 19.3.10, p7.

[1540] 'Cop car in smash'. Daily Record. 16.7.10, p5.

[1541] Classic FM News. July, 2011.

[1542] 'Chase car rams cops'. The People. 6.11.11, p33.

[1543] 'Ton-up cop to face trial'. Daily Record. 29.10.11, p23.

[1544] 'Chase cops did 140mph to catch car'. Daily Record. 8.12.11, p5.

[1545] Robertson, D. 'Caught in the act'. Daily Mail. 23.6.07 p58.

[1546] Key, I. 'Cleared of speeding, the PC who raced to a Chinese takeaway'. Daily Express. 24.11.06, p7.

[1547] Daily Express. 18.5.10, p12.

[1548] 'Cop car in M8 crash'. Daily Record. 28.4.10, p19.

[1549] 'Police in cab crash'. The Sunday Post. 1.5.11, p19.

[1550] Blackstock. G. 'Police car crashes cost forces £1m a year'. The Sunday Post. 20.3.11, p7.

[1551] Taylor, D. 'Ambulance crash once every day'. Daily Record. 27.5.10.

[1552] 'Ambulance crashes up'. Daily Record. 1.9.11, p2.

[1553] 'Accident-prone police patrols'. Daily Mail. 31.1.12.

[1554] Mansfield, K. '999 Crash Bill Is £70K'. Daily Record. 26.4.10, p4.

[1555] Ingham, J. 'Police car smashes cost us £22,000 a day'. Daily Express. 30.11.09, p11.

[1556] Riches, C. 'Police have 238 crashes ... in their station car parks'. Daily Express. 5.2.11, p34.

[1557] 'Woman hit by police car'. The Sunday Post. 27.3.11, p2.

[1558] Narain, J. 'Police seize drink-driver's 156 mph supercar ... and this is how they left it'. Daily Mail. 1.6.11, p32.

[1559] MacGregor, V. 'Lying Car Crash Cop Dodges Jail'. Daily Record. 5.11.03, p23.

[1560] Nugent, H. 'The strange case of a policeman, a 2am car chase and an absent jury'. The Times. 10.2.07, p3.

[1561] '130mph cops get a let-off'. Daily Record. 2.11.07, p5.

[1562] '7 Hurt In Cop Car Crash'. Sunday Mail. 8.1.12, p23.

[1563] Jedrzejewski, N. 'Cop Hit 140mph'. Daily Record. 7.1.12, p9.

[1564] 'Cop denies dangerous driving rap'. Daily Record. 18.2.12, p9.

[1565] Moncur, J. 'Top woman cop probed over 'wrong side of road' car smash'. Daily Record. 11.2.12, p7.

[1566] Moncur, J. 'Police Chief Guilty of Horror Crash'. Daily Record. 2.5.13, p17.

[1567] Christie, K. 'Crash Probe Cop Retires At Only 49'. Daily Record. 25.4.12, p6.

[1568] Moncur, J. 'Police chief misses her court date'. Daily Record. 11.7.12, p11.

[1569] Kelso, D. 'Rugby Player Loses Both Legs'. Daily Record. 17.4.12, p17.

[1570] 'Bollards PC crash'. The Sun. 9.4.12, p15.

[1571] 'Cop car KO'd by bollards'. The Sun. 17.5.12, p19.

[1572] Burns, J. 'Cop Car Wrecked In Blizzard ...'. Daily Record. 27.1.12, p6.

[1573] http://www.the courier.co.uk/News/Dundee/article/22518

[1574] Camber, R. 'Police fear car chases will land them in court'. Daily Mail. 18.5.12, p17.

[1575] Camber, R. 'Police fear car chases will land them in court'. Daily Mail. 18.5.12, p17.

[1576] 'Cops in car fire terror'. Sunday Mirror. 22.7.12, p30.

[1577] 'Teen in cop car smash'. Sunday Mail. 15.7.12, p23.

[1578] 'Ton-up' cop to face trial'. Daily Record. 29.10.11, p23.

[1579] 'Drunk cop spared jail'. Daily Record. 14.7.12, p20.

[1580] 'A middle-class mother among the hoodies'. Daily Mail. 23.6.12, p16.

[1581] Riches, C. '48 police prangs ... in the car park'. Daily Express. 27.4.12, p23.

[1582] Hinds. D. 'Crown Fight Crash Let-Off For Top Cop'. Daily Record. 13.4.11, p17.

[1583] Selway, J. 'Risky game of cops and robbers'. Daily Express. 11.8.12, p19.

[1584] Jeeves, P. 'Boy 12, killed by car fleeing police'. Daily Express. 8.10.12, p19.

[1585] Silvester, N. 'Was hit and run cop on his phone?'. Sunday Mail. 7.10.12, p29.

[1586] 'PC sues girl of 13 she ran over for 'stress' that forced her to quit'. Daily Mail. 17.3.01, p19.

[1587] ' 'Ton-up' cop to face trial' '. Daily Record. 29.10.11, p23.

[1588] 'Officers injured as cop car crashes'. Daily Record. 7.12.12, p2.

[1589] 'Cops in car fire terror'. Sunday Mirror. 22.7.12, p30.

[1590] 'Teen in cop car smash'. Sunday Mail. 15.7.12, p23.

[1591] McQueen, C. 'Schoolgirl hurt in cop car crash'. Daily Record. 26.11.12, p17.

[1592] Wright, S. 'Police chief facing driving charge quits traffic role'. Daily Mail. 15.12,01, p35.

[1593] Pook, S. 'Video shows police 'assaulting injured suspect'. The Daily Telegraph. 10.12.01, p4.

[1594] Crawford, S. The Mirror. 18.4.01, p22.

[1595] Beatson, J. 'I heard my girl cry as cop's car hit us'. Daily Express. 13.2.13, p27.

[1596] Wilkie, S. 'Police driver cleared of injuring dad and girl, 7'. Daily Express. 14.6.13, p72.

[1597] Smith, S. 'Legal firm pull internet promo'. Sunday Mail. 24.2.13, p37.

[1598] Strachan, G. 'Police must learn lessons'. The Courier & Advertiser. 8.10.13, p3.

[1599] Murray, J. 'Proof SAS stormed de Menezes home'. Sunday Express. 9.9.07, p10.

[1600] 'PC shoots himself in the leg'. Daily Mail. 3.9.07, p33.

[1601] 'Police have shot more cows than criminals'. The Sunday Post. 30.5.10, p10.

[1602] Gilmartin, K. 'Gun Cops Scare The Living Daylights Out of Hugo And Ollie'. Daily Record. 11.8.10, p7.

[1603] 'Marksman suspended'. Daily Mail. 5.11.10, p39.

[1604] 'Royal officers 'played poker on duty and dealt in porn'. Daily Mail. 30.6.09, p31.

[1605] Camber, R., Wright, S. 'We need high powered weapons to take on the terrorists, say police'. Daily Mail. 15.4.10, p10.

[1606] Green, N. 'Shock rise in police Taser use'. The Sunday Post. 12.2.12, p10.

[1607] Brooke, C. 'Police taser a terrified Alzheimer's sufferer'. Daily Mail. 10.5.12, p5.

[1608] Littlejohn, R. 'When I said 'charge him' I didn't mean with 50,000 volts'. Daily Mail. 4.10.13, p17.

[1609] Gumm, C. 'Shock over a shotgun for a 10-year-old'. The Sunday Post. 19.12.10, p9.

[1610] Ferrari, N. 'Shock tactics will kill our love for the police'. Sunday Express. 21.10.12, p25.

[1611] Hitchens, P. The Mail on Sunday. 25.11.12, p31.

[1612] Harding, E. 'Bodybuilder died after 4 shots from police Taser in a minute'. Daily Mail. 22.1.13, p27.

[1613] Greenwood, C., Doyle, J. 'Three shot every day with Tasers'. Daily Mail. 24.9.12, p12.

[1614] Taylor, D. 'Gun Found Buried In Cop's Garden'. Daily Record. 6.8.13, p11.

[1615] Slack, J. 'Now serial criminals could be let off with caution after caution'. Daily Mail. 6.8.08, p26.

[1616] Cohen, T. 'Would you mind turning round while I Taser you?'. Daily Mail. 16.10.09, p43.

[1617] Ferguson, J. 'We were mocked by cops for being gay'. Daily Record. 30.5.13, p9.

[1618] 'Lesbian PC is guilty of campaign of terror against ex'. Daily Mail. 18.7.13, p9.

[1619] Ballinger, L. 'Girl of four attacked by police dog in the park'. Daily Mail. 7.4.10, p34.

[1620] The Sunday Telegraph. 13.3.11, p8.

[1621] Silvester, N. '400 Kerb-Crawlers Stopped In Cop Swoops On City Red Light Zones'. Sunday Mail. 14.10.07, p10.

[1622] Johnston, L. 'Police 'put us in more danger' '. Sunday Express. 17.12.06, p7.

[1623] Booker, C. 'Boy hides from social workers in the jungle'. The Sunday Telegraph. 17.10.10, p33.

[1624] Tozer, J. 'A case of unreasonable Force'. Daily Mail. 28.10.10, pp28,29.

[1625] McDonald. C. 'Dad Speaks Out After Slap Case Provokes National Debate'. Sunday Mail. 21.4.13, p13.

[1626] Kelly, T. 'Met policeman wanted to 'bring down the lazy blacks', tribunal is told'. Daily Mail. 3.3.09, p24.

[1627] Booth, S. 'Racism, sexism & sectarianism in the world's biggest gang'. Daily Record. 14.11.08, p13.

[1628] Wilkes, D. 'Top detective in £1m inquiry 'is victim of a witch hunt' '. Daily Mail. 7.4.03, p32.

[1629] Riches, C. 'Disgraced, the ex-CID chief caught spitting on his neighbours' cars'. Daily Express. 12.1.07, p15.

[1630] 'PCs 'had fight over van with new radio' '. Daily Express. 20.2.08, p31.

[1631] Petre, J. 'Now police wear the 'Fritz' helmet'. The Mail on Sunday. 11.7.10, p11.

[1632] Rao, N. 'Speed traps caused 28,000 crashes'. Daily Express. 6.8.10, p39.

[1633] Chapman, J. 'Terrifying PC who wrestled me to ground, by Tarrant's former wife'. Daily Express. 25.6.10, p19.

[1634] 'Police sirens silenced'. Sunday Express. 4.4.10, p23.

[1635] 'Police: Let us sedate suspects'. Sunday Express. 18.4.10, p21.

[1636] Donnelly, L. 'Officers tried to break into car for lost phone'. The Sunday Telegraph. 24.10.10, p12.

[1637] Pearson, A. 'Playing Russian Roulette with women's lives'. Daily Mail. 17.5.06, p13.

[1638] Barnett, A. 'Paedophile was set free to rape young children in their homes'. The Observer. 23.7.06, p7.

[1639] Goodchild, S. 'Police source for Forest Gate raid 'had IQ of 69' '.The Independent On Sunday. 18.6.06, p18.

[1640] Emsley, C. 'The Great British Bobby'. p163.

[1641] Emsley, C. 'The Great British Bobby'.

[1642] Dugan, E. 'Unlawfully deported'. The Independent on Sunday. 1.8.10, p7.

[1643] Tozer, J. 'The switch off that shows speed cameras don't stop accidents'. Daily Mail. 24.4.10, p14.

[1644] Camber, R. 'Why middle-class drivers who speed are hypocrites, by a chief constable'. Daily Mail. 10.8.10.

[1645] Lewis, J. 'Taser Gun Guards For Royals'. The Sunday Telegraph. 6.2.11, pp1,2.

[1646] Twomey, J. 'Menezes jury blame marksmen'. Daily Express. 13.12.08, p8.

[1647] 'Caught on Facebook, the very un-PC PCs'. Daily Mail. 28.3.11, p22.

[1648] Gall, C. 'Cop's Court Let-Off'. Daily Record. 14.4.11, p18.

[1649] 'Cop faces blade rap'. Daily Record. 14.4.11, p15.

[1650] 'G20 police crowd control tactics ruled to be unlawful'. Daily Mail. 15.4.11, p36.

[1651] 'Kettling' victory for the police'. Daily Express. 20.1.12, p39.

[1652] Townsend, M. 'Landlord to sue police for arrest in Jo Yeates case'. The Observer. 8.5.11, p18.

[1653] Tozer, J. 'Drunken soccer fan burning rival flag is policeman'. Daily Mail. 30.4.11, p63.

[1654] Akaki, S. Daily Mail. 15.6.11, p53.

[1655] Greenwood, C. 'Police dogs that died in baking car 'left for six hours' '. Daily Mail. 29.6.11, p29.

[1656] Carlin, T. 'Points for arrests in cop table'. The People. 22.4.07, p29.

[1657] Brooks, T. 'Police Chief is Tasered'. Daily Express. 7.9.07, p27.

[1658] O'Grady, S. 'Crime maps 'hit house prices' '. Daily Express. 13.7.11. p30.

[1659] Hastings, M. 'Corruption U.K.'. Daily Mail. 16.7.11, p98.

[1660] Gall, C. 'Curse Of Satan'. Daily Record. 4.4.11, p18.

[1661] Mansfield, K. 'We're The Boys In (Black And) Blue'. Daily Record. 1.8.11, p17.

[1662] Moncur, J. 'Dead girl's family ill-treated by cops'. Daily Record. 26.8.11, p18.

[1663] McDonald, C. 'I Was Attacked But They Charged'. Daily Record. 23.8.11, p24.

[1664] 'No action against Smiley officers'. The Sunday Post. 4.9.11, p19.

[1665] Paterson, B. 'You done me thong'. Sunday Mail. 6.4.08, p31.

[1666] Mann, K. 'Long and shameful history of disturbances'. The Sunday Post. 14.8.11, pp6,7.

[1667] Levy, A. 'Captain sues over treasures police didn't let him save'. Daily Mail. 1.8.07, p31.

[1668] Greenwood, C. 'But were officers too eager to fire their 50,000-volt Taser guns?'. Daily Mail. 20.10.11, p7.

[1669] Greenwood, C 'Jealous Blunkett Bobby faked hate campaign'. Daily Mail. 7.10.11, p5.

[1670] Channel 4 News. 1.11.11.

[1671] Brooks, T. 'Arrest 'hell' of party mother'. Daily Express. 8.12.11, p45.

[1672] Allardyce, J. 'Police test laser that 'blinds' rioters'. The Sunday Times. 11.12.11, p21.

[1673] 'Yobs Feel The Burn'. Daily Record. 23.1.12, p7.

[1674] 'PC on dog charge'. Daily Record. 28.2.12, p16.

[1675] C4 News. 14.3.12.

[1676] Chapman, J. 'Rioting killer thug planned to be PC'. Daily Express. 14.3.12, p27.

REFERENCES

[1677] Littlejohn, R. 'Scotland Yard Stasi and this sinister assault on freedom'. Daily Mail. 14.2.12, p17.

[1678] Hurley, K. 'How political correctness is ruining Britain's police'. Daily Mail. 15.2.12, p14.

[1679] 'He was assistant chief constable for just 14 months and has been suspended on full £150,000 salary for last year and a half'. Daily Record. 3.2.12, p32.

[1680] Report in Guardian. December, 2011.

[1681] ' 'Sgt Safe' banned'. The Sun. 4.3.12, p29.

[1682] 'Taser diplomacy for Kuwaiti official caught short on Blair's doorstep'. The Mail on Sunday. 22.4.12, p3.

[1683] Mathieson, J. 'Cop On Kidnap Charge'. Daily Record. 25.4.12, p25.

[1684] Love, D. 'Girls were bullied into 'dung walk'. Daily Express. 25.9.13, p23.

[1685] Kloster, U. 'Ex-policeman sues the Met over Al Qaeda camp claims'. Mail on Sunday. 13.5.12, p23.

[1686] BBC News. 12.4.12.

[1687] 'Drunken abuse PC is sacked'. Daily Mail. 16.7.12, p24.

[1688] Narain, J., Parveen, N. 'Did Police Have To Handcuff Dementia Patient?'. Daily Mail. 5.7.12, pp1,2.

[1689] Collins, D. 'Cops Taser dementia patient'. Daily Record. 11.5.12, p35.

[1690] Hill, P. Daily Express. 26.6.12, p14.

[1691] Camber, R. 'We all want to be armed with Tasers say police officers'. Daily Mail. 25.6.12, p13.

[1692] Greenwood, C. 'Police chiefs want the same assault rifles used by our soldiers'. Daily Mail. 2.7.12.

[1693] Bentley, P. 'Tasered twice, gran of 78 who snapped after a decade of caring for Alzheimer's husband'. Daily Mail. 22.5.12, p27.

[1694] Greenwood, C. 'Cricket star dies on rail track as he flees police'. Daily Mail. 19.6.12, p5.

[1695] 'Police assault claims on rise'. The Sunday Times. 11.11.07, p2.

[1696] Leask, D. 'Police told to cover up their tattoos'. Scotland on Sunday. 9.5.10, pp1,3.

[1697] Levin, A. 'At least half of all parents tried over shaken baby syndrome have been wrongly convicted'. The Mail on Sunday. 1.5.11, pp34,35.

[1698] Parker, A., Halls, A. 'Wedding Crushers'. The Sun. 12.4.12, p9.

[1699] Christie, K. 'Cop Chase Fan In Horror Fall'. Daily Record. 14.8.12, pp1,6.

[1700] Dolan, A. 'Fury as police posters suggest drunk women at fault in rape'. Daily Mail. 4.8.12, p48.

[1701] Bentley, P. Carey, T. 'Facebook troll 'is a policeman'. Daily Mail. 29.8.12, p7.

[1702] Levy, A. 'A young boy poses, deadly weapon in hand … it's the new police tactic in the war on Britain's growing gun culture'. Daily Mail. 15.8.08, p25.

[1703] Glover, M. ' 'Heavy handed' police chief suspended'. The Sunday Post. 16.9.12, p5.

[1704] Grant, C. 'Police 'left cases in tray marked Too Difficult' '. Daily Mail. 6.8.09, p19.

[1705] McGivern, M. 'Cops nicked me for crime I didn't commit then crushed my car'. Daily Record. 15.10.09, p9.

[1706] Johnston, L. 'Battered mother's children forced into adoption'. Sunday Express. 4.10. 09, p15.

[1707] Kerr, M. 'Cops Thought My Parsnips Were Pot'. Daily Record. 17.8.09, p7.

[1708] McKinistry, L. 'Honest citizens put in the dock as thugs go free'. Daily Express. 12.10.09.

[1709] Latchem, T. 'Cops' site knife sale'. The People. 3.8.08, p20.

[1710] Jenkins, S. 'Boris has wielded a cosh for real policing'. The Sunday Times.

[1711] Narain, J. 'Police who play burglar in the middle of the night'. Daily Mail. 12.2.10, p11.

[1712] 'Council steal kids' bonfire'. Sunday Mail. 2.11.08, p7.

[1713] Chapman, A., Lankston, C. 'Why did police not let her have counselling?'. The Mail on Sunday. 10.2.13.

[1714] 'Cannabis in our garden? It must have been a plant!'. Daily Mail. 6.12.08, p33.

[1715] Findlay, R. 'Top Cops Probed In Pipe Band Row'. Sunday Mail. 16.12.12, p23.

[1716] Reynolds, M. 'Police bosses tried to ruin my wedding claims WPC'. Daily Express. 9.11.12, p29.

[1717] Moncur, J. 'Cop college bully claim probe call'. Daily Record. 11.7.12, p11.

[1718] Smyth, B. ' 'Sweeney-style' cops not off the hook'. The Sunday Post. 31.3.13, p7.

[1719] Tozer, J., Parveen, N. 'Policeman loses his temper … and career'. Daily Mail. 11.10.12, p27.

[1720] Rayment, S. 'SAS chief sues police over arrest'. The Sunday Telegraph. 9.12.12, p12.

[1721] Wright, S., Greenwood, C. 'Former 'Blunkett bobby' is among six held in terror swoops'. Daily Mail. 6.7.12, pp4,5.

[1722] 'Police chief in sex case probe'. Daily Mail. 7.7.12, p34.

[1723] 'Baton rap cop for trial'. Daily Record. 7.7.12, p17.

[1724] Littlejohn, R. 'The cops watch the boys who watch the girls go by'. Daily Mail. 10.7.12, p17.

[1725] 'No surprise, says victim as officer gets job back'. The Mail on Sunday. 11.11.12, p42.

[1726] Findlay, R. 'Orr believes he has been hung out to dry over the Carroll fiasco and that his bosses must answer for'. Sunday Mail. 11.11.12, p4.

[1727] C4 News. 11.5.12.

[1728] Channel 4 News. 27.7.12.

[1729] Blackstock, G., Mann, K. 'Police accused of harassing dad'. The Sunday Post. 11.11.12, p41.

[1730] Malone, C. 'Why Plebgate is poisoning police'. Sunday Mirror. 23.12.12, p25.

[1731] Taylor, B. 'Classroom talks by police lead to more children trying out drugs'. Daily Mail. 4.4.03, p41.

[1732] Riddell, M. Daily Mail. 13.3.02, p19.

[1733] Lavery, C. 'Police Boot Out Hyacinth Bucket Boss'. Sunday Mail. 24.3.02, p43.

[1734] Smith, D. 'Police pranksters caught on camera'. Sunday Express. 13.5.01, p45.

[1735] Rantzen, E. 'Esther Blasts Savile Probe'. The Sunday Post. 6.1.13, pp1,6.

[1736] Baird, R. 'More police are found to cause offence'. Daily Express. 27.8.02, p2.

[1737] Graef, R. 'I've watched the police for 30 years and I still despair'. The Observer. 12.4.09, p29.

[1738] Disley, J. 'Hall hits at police 'pursuit' of stars after rape charge'. Daily Express. 24.1.13, p29.

[1739] Willey, J. 'Barmy campaign to warn police: Don't slip on leaves'. Daily Express. 30.10.09, p5.

[1740] Martin, A. 'Plebgate log 'could be a fake' '. Daily Mail. 4.2.13, p8.

[1741] 'Police New A New Breed of Leader'. The Sunday Times. 23.12.12, p20.

[1742] Owens, N., Cardy, P. 'Good cop … Kebad Cop'. Sunday Mirror. 30.12.12, p15.

[1743] 'Police criticised for 'newsagent drug-dealer' ad'. Daily Mail. 27.8.08, p25.

[1744] Owen, J. 'Hillsborough: Police chief sorry for 'insensitive' email'. The Independent. 24.2.13, p2.

[1745] McBeth, J. 'Buckfast in court bid over tagging'. Daily Mail. 23.2.13, p12.

[1746] Martin, A. 'Downing St. WPC held in 'Plebgate' investigation'. Daily Mail. 2.2.13, p12.

[1747] 'Police job ban on glazier'. Daily Express. 31.1. 09, p36.

[1748] Wilkie, S. 'Lidl wins fight over underage booze sting'. Daily Express. 6.4.13, p4.

[1749] Buckland, L. 'Parkinson's disease driver in 'drink' ban'. Scotland On Sunday. 14.4.13, p10.

[1750] Peachey, P. 'Police apologise for 'harassment' of forensic graduate'. The Independent. 20.7.13, p13.

[1751] Boffey, D. 'Police colluded in secret plan to blacklist 3,200 workers'. The Observer. 13.10.13, pp1,9.

[1752] Seamark, M. '£50,000 police payout for landlord held over murder'. Daily Mail. 17.9.13, p20.

[1753] Sandbrook, D. 'The long arm of the law'. Culture. The Sunday Times. 9.8.09, pp34,35.

[1754] Dunk, M. 'The Forgotten White Slaves'. Daily Express. 7.4.07, p45.

[1755] Edge, S. Daily Express. 17.10.08, p40.

[1756] Callan, P. 'Brothers Who Became Britain's First Bobbies'. Daily Express. 14.1.08, p31.

[1757] Millar, J. 'Tobacco baron who stubbed out crime in the Big Smoke'. The Sunday Post. 28.9.08, p25.

[1758] Edwards, A. 'Masters of Crime'. Daily Express. 29.8.11.

[1759] Judge, T. Daily Mail. 7.1.09, p51.

[1760] Emsley, C. 'The Great British Bobby'.

[1761] Emsley, C. 'The Great British Bobby'. Quercus. London. 2009.

[1762] Camber, R. '90 years of girls in blue'. Daily Mail. 25.11.09, pp36,37.

[1763] Emsley, C. 'The Great British Bobby'. Quercus. London. 2009.

[1764] Hanson, N. 'His Icelandic majesty'. The Sunday Times Magazine.

[1765] Emsley, C. 'The Great British Bobby'. Quercus. London. 2009. p129.

[1766] Brown, C. 'Our Fatal Attraction'. The Mail On Sunday. 16.1.11.

[1767] Womersley, T., Crawford, D. H. Bodysnatchers to Lifesavers: Three Centuries of Medicine in Edinburgh. Luath Press Ltd. 2010, pp72,75

[1768] Emsley, C. 'The Great British Bobby'. Quercus. London. 2009. p168.

[1769] 'When Met's top coppers were flying'. Daily Express. 11.3.11, p47.

[1770] Venning, A. 'The boy who stole Victoria's bloomers'. Daily Mail. 4.2.11, p43.

[1771] Daily Express. 12.3.10, p2.

[1772] Edge, S. 'Victorian Super Sleuth Of The Yard'. Daily Express. 17.10.11, p13.

[1773] Mason, G. The Official History Of The Metropolitan Police. Carlton. 2004, p16.

[1774] Mason, G. The Official History Of The Metropolitan Police. Carlton. 2004, p37.

[1775] Mason, G. The Official History Of The Metropolitan Police. Carlton. 2004, p23.

[1776] Daily Express. 25.8.11, p10.

[1777] Mason, G. The Official History Of The Metropolitan Police. Carlton. 2004, p30.

[1778] Mason, G. The Official History Of The Metropolitan Police. Carlton. 2004, p31.

[1779] Clinton, J. 'The Sufferings Of The Suffragettes'. Sunday Express. 5.2.12, p44.

[1780] Peter McKay. 'Moat's police hunters hardly merit our confidence'. Daily Mail. 12.7.10, p17.

[1781] Bianco, S. 'Still no justice from the Yard'. Sunday Express. 8.1.12, p37.

[1782] 'Confess, police tell boy aged six'. Daily Mail. 13.6.07, p5.

[1783] Devine, A., Musson, C., Mathieson, J. 'From The Red Light To The Websites'. Daily Record. 15.3.10, pp10,11.

[1784] Dolan, A. '£99,000 for the good citizen who police betrayed to drug-den thugs'. Daily Mail. 25.9.10, p17.

[1785] Reynolds, M. 'Police chief: Drivers must queue patiently after death crashes'. Daily Express. 5.4.07, p17.

[1786] 'Police rapped for closing M-way over pylon crash'. The Mail on Sunday. 18.10.09, p35.

[1787] Ino, P. H. 'Graduate' scheme is damaging the police'. Daily Mail. 26.1.06, p58.

[1788] Wright, S. Daily Mail. 31.5.13, p12.

[1789] BBC News. 11.10.10.

[1790] McCartney, B. 'Reunited'. Daily Record. 2.3.07, p7.

[1791] Moncur, J. 'No Charge'. Daily Record. 28.6.07, p4.

[1792] Rose, G. 'Stalking victim accused of wasting police time to sue for wrongful arrest'. Scotland on Sunday. 4.7.10, p10.

[1793] Gladdis, K., Greenwood, C. 'Why did MI5 let killer go to Kenya a second time?'. Daily Mail. 28.5.13, p8.

[1794] Daily Mail. 11.9.10, p57.

[1795] 'The cop cleared of being corrupt'. Daily Mail. 17.2.06, p19.

[1796] Roden, A. 'Jails chief who wants inmates to be released'. Daily Mail. 8.6.13, p43.

[1797] Flanagan, P. 'A snack attack lands police officers in a jam'. Daily Express. 11.10.06, p16.

[1798] Baylis. M. 'Official: pettiness rules'. Daily Express. 15.11.07, p55.

[1799] Clarke, N. 'How could they say I killed him?'. Daily Mail. 30.10.06, pp10,11.

[1800] Narain, J. 'The height of daftness'. Daily Mail. 26.10.06, p35.

[1801] Edge, S. 'The Bitter Butler's Back'. Daily Express. 15.5.07, p25.

[1802] Edward, R. D. Daily Mail. 17.2.07, p14.

[1803] 'Cops mix up ASBO twins'. Sunday Mail. 3.6.07, p19.

[1804] 'Police tags 'are advert to thieves'.'. Daily Express. 7.10.09, p28.

[1805] Barton, F., Waterhouse, R. 'The accusations couldn't have been more lurid'. Daily Mail. 15.10.05, pp38,39.

[1806] Reid, S. Daily Mail. 1.11.05, p26.

[1807] Kelly, T. 'So much for soft justice, Mr. Clarke'. Daily Mail. 5.8.10, p5.

[1808] 'Guide that tells police officers how to dress'. Daily Mail. 19.7.10, p3.

[1809] 'Bungling PCs locked in van'. Daily Express. 12.7.10, p22.

[1810] Silvester, N. 'Cop Boss: I Was Dead Wrong'. Sunday Mail. 11.7.10, p25.

[1811] Silvester, N. 'Single force is dangerous risk to take'. Sunday Mail. 31.3.13, p6.

[1812] 'Drugs raid on toddler'. The People. 11.7.10, p29.

[1813] Sergeant, H. 'Inside Britain's Police Farce'. Daily Mail. 11.2.08, p26.

[1814] Doyle, J. 'Shotgun licence given to child of ten by police'. Daily Mail. 8.7.10, p25.

[1815] 'Gun laws may be tightened'. Sunday Express. 19.12.10, p4.

[1816] Dawar, A. 'Anger as gun licence given to a child of 7'. Daily Express. 25.3.11, p10.

[1817] Hill, P. 'I introduced Atherton to guns … he wiped out my Mum, Sister & Aunt'. The People. 29.1.12, p16.

[1818] Mudie, K., Hill, P. 'I was mentally ill, fantasised about drive-by shootings, but was allowed to KEEP my shotguns'. The People, 22.1.12, p16.

[1819] Smith, J. 'In the face of narcissism, the police should stick to policing'. The Independent on Sunday. 11.7.10, p44.

[1820] 'On your bike … they're free if you are a crook'. Daily Express. 14.8.10, p4.

[1821] Wright, S. 'Freed terror suspects may sue police for false arrest'. Daily Mail. 20.9.10, p7.

[1822] Rumbold. 'Promoting incompetent police officers'. Pickled politics. http://www.pickledpolitics.com/archives/2598.

[1823] Derbyshire. D. 'Criminal profiling's never cracked a case'. Daily Mail. 14.9.10, p32.

[1824] 'Cops taser wrong man'. Sunday Mirror. 4.7.10, p8.

[1825] Lefort, R. '20mph limits fail to improve road safety'. The Sunday Telegraph. 3.10.10, p14.

[1826] Chorley, M. 'Police forced to release data on speed cameras'. The Independent on Sunday. 26.6.11, p22.

[1827] Brooke, C. 'Police to replace rape-case officers with civilian staff'. Daily Mail. 5.5.10, p24.

[1828] Goslett, M. 'Police have lost cardboard box carrying shot barrister's last message of love'. The Mail on Sunday. 5.10.08, p7.

[1829] Whitehead, T. 'Violent crime soars as police bungle figures'. Daily Express. 24.10.08.

[1830] Sergeant. H. 'Inside Britain's Police Farce'. Daily Mail. 11.2.08, p26.

[1831] 'Police web guide … to a porn site'. Daily Express. 9.8.08, p50.

[1832] Jones, D. 'Kids In Cop Raid Blunder'. The People. 14.9.08, p20.

[1833] Walters. S. 'Cops, wrong house! How police bungled MP 'Stake out' '. The Mail On Sunday. 15.2.09, p34.

[1834] 'Cops in bungled break-in'. Sunday Mirror. 28.12.08, p8.

[1835] Fairburn, R. 'Bungling Drug Cops Raid Gran'. Daily Record. 15.8.09, p27.

[1836] Flanagan, P. 'Too hot to handle'. Daily Express. 31.7.08, p22.

[1837] Henry, S. 'Police stage a drugs bust … on a widow's tomato plants'. Daily Mail. 27.11.08, p43.

[1838] Evans, D. 'Lethal Weapon'. News Of The World. 28.3.10, p21.

[1839] Bradbury, J. 'Long Arm Of The Snore!'. Daily Sport. 25.9.08, p7.

[1840] Thornton, P. 'Zzzz Cars'. Daily Record. 27.1.10, p25.

[1841] 'Street of shame of ticket cops'. Daily Record. 25.1.10, p17.

[1842] Smith, R. 'Police bungle cost me 9hr drive and speed fine'. Daily Record. 29.10.08, p28.

[1843] 'Police kept DNA samples in fridge with a takeaway'. Daily Mail. 4.8.09, p24.

[1844] Wright, S. 'Operation real face'. Daily Mail. 18.3.09, p7.

[1845] 'Parked car speed fine'. Sunday Mirror. 24.1.10, p36.

[1846] 'Cop cars lifted at station'. Sunday Mail. 3.8.08, p29.

[1847] Silvester, N. 'Detective reveals how cops lost the war on mobsters'. Sunday Mail. 18.9.11, pp4,5.

[1848] Barrett, D. 'Vanishing tricks and police crime figures'. The Sunday Telegraph. 6.12.09, p5.

[1849] Penrose, J. 'Cops 'sorry' after band gun blunder'. Sunday Mirror. 29.11.09, p19.

[1850] 'Cop blunder casts film stars as yobs'. Sunday Mail. 1.11.09, p8.

[1851] Camber, R. 'What happened to the polite force?'. Daily Mail. 24.9.09, p17.

[1852] 'I went to cover a match, and ended up in the middle of a nightmare'. The Sunday Post. 12.4.09, p26.

[1853] Bunyan, N. 'Detective lied over botched attempt to catch mass murderer'. The Daily Telegraph. 15.7.03, p4.

[1854] 'The police e-fit that would fit just about anybody'. The Mail on Sunday. 11.10.09, p20.

[1855] '£1.5m refund over illegal speed trap'. Daily Mail. 20.6.09, p19.

[1856] Brooke, C. 'Crash driver has to wait 5 hours for help'. Daily Mail. 7.11.08, p28.

[1857] C3 Tonight. 28.10.10.

[1858] Musson, C. 'Roller Brawl: Pair Go Free After Cops' Evidence Blunder'. Daily Record. 17.1.09, p29.

[1859] Jones, D. 'Nemesis For The Serial Killers'. Daily Mail. 26.1.08, p47.

[1860] 'Met chief apology'. Sunday Mail. 5.6.11, p23.

[1861] Osborne, P. 'Deported, without even an apology'. Daily Mail. 25.4.09, p29.

[1862] 'Noose gaffe police 'sorry' '. The People. 29.3.09, p20.

[1863] Ogilvy, G. 'Crown Told The Cops To Destroy My Diana Snap'. Sunday Mail. 14.1.07, p38.

[1864] C4 News. 15.9.11.

[1865] Watson, D. 'Cops 'Badly Trained' For Rangers Riot'. Daily Record. 10.9.08, p37.

[1866] Henderson, E. 'At last, police admit errors over Shipman'. Daily Express. 8.5.02, p25.

[1867] Pukas, A. 'I Was Ian Huntley's First Victim'. Daily Express. 10.3.06, p27.

[1868] Monair, J. 'Cops Lock Up Wrong Man For 4 Days'. Daily Record. 3.5.08, p29.

[1869] Dawar, R. 'Watchdog warned the police'. Daily Express. 7.6.10, p5.

[1870] Perry, A. 'Police website blunder'. Sunday Express. 27.6.10, p12.

[1871] Panton, D. 'Why won't politicians and police accept that white people can be victims of race crime?' The Mail on Sunday. 12.11.06, p62.

[1872] Hill, P. 'Mr Loophole Gets Monty Off 3rd Time'. Daily Record. 16.6.10, p19.

[1873] Slack, J. 'Girls of nine lured by the gang culture sweeping Britain'. Daily Mail. 23.6.10, p37.

[1874] Henry, R. 'Town's speed-camera ban puts brakes on accidents'. The Sunday Times. 3.10.10, p3.

[1875] Wright, S. Greenwood, C. '£4m bill to defend a serial killer'. Daily Mail. 25.6.11, p6.

[1876] Rudd, M. 'How Safe Is Your Street?'. The Sunday Times Focus. p18.

[1877] Lekhani, N. ' 'Shocking demise' of hospital threatens NHS reform'. The Independent on Sunday. 3.4.11, p28.

[1878] 'Ludicrous letter of the law'. Daily Mail. 19.4.07, p31.

[1879] Hudson, C. 'Sex, fantasy and the police plot that blew apart the hunt for Rachel's killer'. Daily Mail. 3.7.00, p34.

[1880] Littlejohn, R. 'It's the Jolly Boys Outing – directed by Quentin Tarantino'. Daily Mail. 1.4.11, p17.

[1881] Liddle, R. 'Next time, PC Plod, you use the stairs'. The Sunday Times. 3.4.11, p19.

[1882] Greenwood, C. Daily Mail. 5.7.11, p2.

[1883] Hitchens, P. 'Police who won't even defend our war dead'. The Mail on Sunday. 30.12.07, p29.

[1884] 'Pervert, freed in error is arrested'. Daily Express. 18.1.08, p9.

[1885] Evans, M. '7/7 bombings: Failings that let down the rescue teams'. Daily Express. 6.6.06, p9.

[1886] Willey, J. 'Police are injured by pounding computers instead of the beat'. Daily Express. 7.5.07, p8.

[1887] Levy, A. 'Why did police lock innocent woman in a cell for six hours?'. Daily Mail. 14.4.11, p11.

[1888] Dixon, C. 'My £372,000 payout … for not having a comb in cells'. Daily Express. 28.5.11, p5.

[1889] Slack, J. 'Police Your Own Streets'. Daily Mail. 12.2.08, p1.

[1890] Doyle, J., Greenwood, C. 'Bail chaos may open floodgate to claims'. Daily Mail. 1.7.11, p19.

[1891] Slack, J. 'Fines Please'. Daily Mail. 5.9.07, pp1,2.

[1892] Slack, J. '1.2m thieves and thugs dodge court with a spot fine'. Daily Mail. 24.12.11, p4.

[1893] Dolan, A., Faulkner, K. 'Cry rape slap on the wrist'. Daily Mail. 15.12.11, p31.

[1894] Doyle, J. 'The rioters let off with a slap on the wrist'. Daily Mail. 31.12.11, p4.

[1895] Doyle, J. '4,500 serial offenders are let off with caution'. Daily Mail. 24.2.12, p24.

[1896] McIlwraith, G. 'Inside Hologram Tam's £8m A Day Fake Factory'. Daily Record. 3.10.07, p4.

[1897] Silvester, N. 'Proper Charlies'. Sunday Mail. 12.8.07, pp1,9.

[1898] 'Cops ask rejects to be rookies'. Sunday Mirror. 5.8.07, p19.

[1899] Broster, P. 'Force hires more plastic policemen than real bobbies'. Daily Express. 20.9.07, p35.

[1900] '2,100 police leave as morale slumps'. Daily Express. 13.7.07, p9.

REFERENCES

[1901] Kirk, J. 'Crack gun cops in call centre jobs'. The People. 19.8.07, p17.

[1902] 'IPCC 'may have misled over death' '. Daily Record. 13.8.11, p6.

[1903] Camber, R. 'Bullet fired at officer 'belonged to police'. Daily Mail. 8.8.11, p6.

[1904] 'Biker cops a bad deal'. Daily Record. 29.7.11, p41.

[1905] Devine, A. 'Heartless'. Daily Record. 8.8.11, pp1,9.

[1906] Dawar, A. 'Police turn to Twitter as 21 stations face axe'. Daily Express. 24.8.11, p18.

[1907] Riches, C. '24-hour police stations close as cash cuts bite'. Daily Express. 28.9.11, p4.

[1908] Brooks, T. ' 'Call centre cops' tell raid victim: Phone us the details in two days'. Daily Express. 20.4.12, p27.

[1909] Sergeant, H. 'Inside Britain's Police Farce. The 999 Nightmare'. Daily Mail. 12.2.08, p29.

[1910] McCorkell, A. 'Police 'panicked' into arrest over hospital deaths'. The Independent On Sunday. 4.9.11, p16.

[1911] Wright, S. 'A Man Without Honour: Five Years of Blair Blunders'. Daily Mail. 2.11.07, p2.

[1912] 'WPCs in peril of shooting themselves'. Daily Express. 27.4.07, p7.

[1913] 'Are drug searches by the police too zealous?'. Daily Mail. 26.5.08, p57.

[1914] 'MP: Cut arrests of homeless', Sunday Mirror, 23.11.08, p20.

[1915] 'In court … beggar who was given 60p', Daily Express, 23.2.11, p22.

[1916] Jeeves, P. 'Bungling drugs squad swoop on guinea pig home'. Daily Express. 12.1.11, p29.

[1917] Littlejohn, R. Daily Mail, 14.1.11, p17.

[1918] Wilkes, D. 'Drugs factory? No, my insulation's gone to pot'. Daily Mail. 31.7.08, p33.

[1919] Narain, J. 'Sorry, wrong house'. Daily Mail. 18.4.08, p5.

[1920] Taylor, M. 'Harry Wins Damages Over Illegal Cop Raid'. Daily Record. 24.5.08, p33.

[1921] McLeod, K. 'The Mugs Squad'. Daily Record. 30.11.11, p25.

[1922] 'Tomtom Dums'. The Sun. 29.2.12, p29.

[1923] Wilks. A., Boffey, D. 'Maddy police's 2am raid on pensioner'. The Mail on Sunday. 3.6.07, p13.

[1924] Lavelle, C. '7009 complaints against police is three-year low'. Daily Record. 12.10.11, p20.

[1925] Greenwood, C. 'The spelling police'. Daily Mail. 15.10.11, p55.

[1926] Widdecombe, A. 'They went the extra mile to see the Pope'. Daily Express. 22.9.10, p13.

[1927] Pollard, S. 'Why do we allow career criminals to escape prison?'. Daily Express. 31.5.11, p12.

[1928] Littlejohn, R. 'If the Mad Mullah ran the Maddie inquiry …'. Daily Mail. 18.9.07, p17.

[1929] Blackstock, G. 'Is this the end of our local police stations?'. The Sunday Post. 13.11.11, p28.

[1930] Boffey, D., Townsend, M. 'Border chief to tell MPs: I acted on police advice'. The Observer. 13.11.11, p9.

[1931] Verkaik, R. 'Family 'Face of Asia' death plunge model: Detectives have betrayed us'. The Mail on Sunday. 4.12.11, pp14,15.

[1932] Camber, R. 'Police fury over LSE's bid to blame them for the summer riots'. Daily Mail. 6.12.11, p8.

[1933] Townsend, M. 'Revealed: how police lost control of summer riots in first crucial 48 hours'. The Observer. 4.12.11, p6.

[1934] Smith, D. J. 'Was It His Finger On The Trigger?'. The Sunday Times Magazine. 29.10.06, p33.

[1935] 'Cops alert is rubbish'. The People. 20.11.11, p30.

[1936] Hitchens, P. The Mail on Sunday. 20.11.11, p31.

[1937] 'Resolving cannabis'. Leader. Daily Mail. 4.4.08.

[1938] Taylor, B. 'Letting off drug users means we all get on better, says Yard'. Daily Mail. 11.1.07, p43.

[1939] Twomey, J. 'Jury shows secret police film of 'nervy' Lawrence suspect'. Daily Express. 22.11.11, p23.

[1940] Blanco, S. 'Still no justice from the Yard'. Sunday Express. 8.1.12, p37.

[1941] Daily Express. 11.1.12, p10.

[1942] Thomas, C. 'Guns Don't Work'. Sunday Mail. 4.12.11, p34.

[1943] Hull, L. 'Officers 'bribed thief for false confessions' '. Daily Mail. 7.6.07, p41.

[1944] Slack, J. '550,000 criminal DNA records are wrong'. Daily Mail. 27.2.08, p17.

[1945] Bungling police swoop on BBC man'. Daily Mail. 9.4.08, p9.

[1946] Wright, S. 'You don't know the law'. Daily Mail. 7.6.08, p8.

[1947] Sullivan, M. 'Spy-In-Bag Blunders'. The Sun. 31.3.12, p39.

[1948] 'That's a fair cop, officer'. Daily Express. 22.5.08, p27.

[1949] Crick, A. 'Wrong Harm Of The Paw'. The Sun. 2.4.12, p29.

[1950] Gilbertson, D. 'How the Olympics are draining YOUR streets of police (and why the looters can't wait for the Games to begin)'. The Mail on Sunday. 22.4.12, p29.

[1951] 'Cop's A Twit'. The Sun. 18.4.12, p26.

[1952] 'The £70m police smartphones fiasco'. Daily Mail. 30.5.12, p8.

[1953] Edge, S. 'I Put The Krays In Jail'. Daily Express. 26.5.12, p35.

[1954] 'Travellers invade sports field … with a little help from the boys in blue'. Daily Mail. 19.6.12, p13.

[1955] 'Cover-ups and mistakes' in hunt for Julie's killers. The Sunday Telegraph. 7.9.08, p7.

[1956] Mackenzie, K. 'We're on the case, Chloe …'. Daily Mail. 21.4.12, p21.

[1957] Littlejohn, R. Daily Mail. 29.5.12, p17.

[1958] 'May The Farce Be With You'. Daily Record. 28.11.12, p17.

[1959] McKinstry, L. Daily Express. 22.11.12, p14.

[1960] 'Barking Mad'. The Sunday Post. 24.2.13, p48.

[1961] Brennan, Z. 'No Wonder They Call Us Plods!'. Daily Mail. 13.9.08, p54.

[1962] BBC News. 26.2.13.

[1963] Grant, G. 'Predator used police phone to call schoolboys'. Daily Mail. 20.3.13, p19.

[1964] Barrett, D. 'The Thick Blue Line'. The Sunday Telegraph. 25.10.09, p19.

[1965] Grimston, J. 'Cautions banned for serious crimes'. The Sunday Times. 29.9.13, p2.

[1966] Blackley, M. '200,000 people a year use police desks facing axe'. The Mail on Sunday. 6.10.13, p42.

[1967] The Wright Stuff. Channel 5. 24.9.13.

[1968] 'Police kept DNA samples in fridge with a takeaway'. Daily Mail. 4.8.09, p24.

[1969] BBC News. 26.11.10.

[1970] Challand, C. 'I only hope to God this policeman is never put in charge of prisoners again'. The Mail On Sunday. 21.11.10, p45.

[1971] Flanagan, P. 'The police chief who commutes 1,000 miles to work'. Daily Express. 14.11.08, p42.

[1972] Mathieson, J. 'Officer Surfed Web As Teen Died In Cell'. Daily Record. 4.8.10, p5.

[1973] McGivern, M. 'Teenage Boy Dies In Police Custody'. Daily Record. 27.2.07, p11.

[1974] Sims, P. 'Dying man locked in cell for 25 hours because he looked drunk'. Daily Mail. 20.11.08, p43.

[1975] 'Man dies in cop cell'. Daily Record. 4.5.11, p14.

[1976] Review of the Crown Prosecution Service (Cmnd. 3960, Stationery Office, London. 1998).

[1977] 'I'm locked in cop shop'. Daily Record. 20.11.10, p17.

[1978] Leake, C. 'Barrister who was dragged from court in handcuffs wins £100K from the Met'. The Mail on Sunday. 10.10.10, p44.

[1979] Murray, P. 'Bobbyshambles'. Daily Record. 22.8.07, p9.

[1980] BBC Local News. 17.12.07.

[1981] BBC Local News. August, 2007.

[1982] Lakhani, N. 'Man paralysed after arrest demands a full public inquiry'. The Independent on Sunday. 31.1.10, p22.

[1983] Basnett, G. 'Couldn't Car Less'. News Of The World'. 15.11.09, p53.

[1984] Beckford, M. The Mail on Sunday. 28.10.12, p10.

[1985] Kenber, B. 'Police admit one in three crimes not investigated'. The Times. 30.7.11, pp1,10.

[1986] King, S. 'It's high time we sorted out law and order'. Sunday Express. 27.1.08, p26.

[1987] Hartley-Brewer, J. 'Locked into jail madness'. Sunday Express. 3.2.08, p29.

[1988] Dearsley, G. 'Sacked, the PC who couldn't pass muster'. Daily Express. 24.12.01, p26.

[1989] Robertson, D. 'Police watchdog in crisis as 100 lawyers quit over 'culture of incompetence' '. http://www.dailymail.co.uk/news/article-518504/Police-watchdog-crisis-100-lawyers-quit-culture-in.

[1990] 'Rise in cop complaints'. Daily Record. 4.10.10, p16.

[1991] Hitchens, P. The Mail on Sunday. 17.9.06, p31.

[1992] Temko, N. 'Police forces 'hobbled' by bad leadership'. The Observer. 30.10.05, p10.

[1993] Kite, M. 'Crime about to rise and swamp prisons, warns Blair team'. The Sunday Telegraph. 24.12.06, p4.

[1994] Scott, M. 'Annie Was Killed'. Sunday Mail. 1.9.02, p13.

[1995] Walker, K. 'How a quarter of bars and shops sell drinks to children'. Daily Mail. 27.12.06, p46.

[1996] Silvester, N. 'Highland Detectives Investigate Murder In Coatridge'. Sunday Mail. 2.6.13, p19.

[1997] Flanagan, P. 'PCs to let criminals off if shift is ending'. Daily Express. 20.2.10, p8.

[1998] Fielding, J. 'Thugs exploit a glaring error'. Sunday Express. 28.2.10, p32.

[1999] Chapman, J., Shipman, T. 'Daily Mail. 1.3.10, p9.

[2000] Sims, P. 'More police than ever, but only one in 58 is on the beat'. Daily Mail. 19.3.07, p28.

[2001] Harper, T., Leapman, B. 'Just one in 58 police is patrolling the streets'. The Sunday Telegraph. 18.3.07, pp1,2.

[2002] MacLeod, M. 'Police: we can't track Scots sex offenders'. Scotland on Sunday. 8.10.06, p1.

[2003] Perry, A. Revealed! The bullies of Deepcut'. Sunday Express. 10.11.02, p13.

[2004] Perry, A. 'Foreigner? No job? You can go free, police tell criminals'. Sunday Express. 7.1.07, p23.

[2005] Broster, P. 'The policeman who could have nailed Shipman'. Daily Express. 15.7.03, p9.

[2006] Sears, N., McIntyre, S., Wright, S. 'Soham detective: Third girl's porn claim 'ignored' '. Daily Mail. 22.8.03, p5.

[2007] Martin, A. Bains, I. 'Chances 'were missed to halt child sex gang' '. Daily Mail. 15.5.13, p27.

[2008] Trump, S., Nikkhah, R. 'Missing minutes and unanswered questions in case of fireball judge'. The Sunday Telegraph. 15.10.06, p17.

REFERENCES

[2009] Cunningham, T. Daily Mail. 4.11.06, p10.

[2010] Wright, S. 'Met chief attacked over Tube shooting'. Daily Mail. 19.1.07, p36.

[2011] Gardham, D. 'Police let bombers slip net'. The Daily Telegraph. 10.7.07, pp1,2.

[2012] Levy, A. 'Police 'too frightened' to enter travellers' site and recover stolen property'. Daily Mail. 28.9.11, p26.

[2013] Hickley, M. 'Violence soars, detection slumps'. Daily Mail. 16.6.08, p20.

[2014] 'Forensics fake gets five years'. Daily Record. 23.2.07, p39.

[2015] Doward, J. 'How police put their faith in the 'expert' witness who was a fraud'. The Observer. 23.3.08, p8.

[2016] Reynolds, M. 'Speed cameras 'fail to cut road deaths' '. Daily Express. 13.3.07, p8.

[2017] Wilkes, D. '£100,000 police search fails to find a turban-sized helmet'. Daily Mail. 16.6.08, p19.

[2018] Doyle, J. 'Police 'have lost the public's trust' '.Daily Mail. 24.9.10, p10.

[2019] 'Fury as 'pervert' remains on run'. Daily Express. 2.12.10, p39.

[2020] Harrison, I. 'Sex Offenders missing from 'wanted' website'. The Sunday Post. 21.11.10, p14.

[2021] Classic FM radio. 28.1.07.

[2022] Basnett, G. 'Cops lose hundreds of paedos'. News Of The World. 27.1.08, p32.

[2023] McNamara, P. 'Cops lose over 300 sex pervs'. News Of The World. 17.5.09, p16.

[2024] Bindel, J. 'Mothers of Prevention'. The Sunday Times Magazine. 30.9.07, pp24-33.

[2025] Gladdis, K. 'Brave Mum Nails Paedo'. News Of The World. 6.6.10, p41.

[2026] Levy, A. '3,000 danger men jump bail and are never tracked down'. Daily Mail. 28.12.06, p26.

[2027] Broster, P., Brooks, T. 'A load of old codswallop'. Daily Express. 27.1.07, p11.

[2028] Murray, J. 'QC fears clues to Jill's killer ignored'. Sunday Express. 1.8.10, p7.

[2029] Alexander, D. 'Drugs Swoop Filed Under Fiasco'. Sunday Mail. 21.11.10, p8.

[2030] Boyle, D. 'Cops Miss Blade In OAP's Back'. Daily Record. 12.10.10, p22.

[2031] Campbell, D. 'Men are hidden sufferers of domestic abuse'. The Observer. 5.9.10, p18.

[2032] Westcott, S. '999 operator sacked after blunders cost stab girl's life'. Daily Express. 23.10.10, p32.

[2033] McLaren, R. 'Police are letting the yobs get away with it'. The Sunday Post. 26.9.10, p16.

[2034] 'Louts on the loose'. The Sunday Times. 26.9.10, p25.

[2035] Greenhill, S. 'Don't Call Us For Help About Yobs Say Police'. Daily Mail. 26.9.09, p1.

[2036] 'Police accused of failures over antisocial behaviour'. BBC News at One. 11.3.10.

[2037] Classic FM. 23.9.10.

[2038] Clark, R. 'It's soft touch UK: Just occupy any house you fancy'. Daily Express. 24.9.10, p12.

[2039] Breslin, J. P. 'Chippy flouts gaming laws under cops' noses'. The Sunday Post .17.10.10, p12.

[2040] Freedman, N. Brighton News. The Argus. 9.6.10.

[2041] Staff, D. 'Myra's Last Secret'. Daily Mail. 21.2.07, p42.

[2042] 'Old Bill is £4m'. News of the World. 18.7.10, p8.

[2043] 'PCs miss body in dark cellar'. Daily Express. 11.10.08, p7.

[2044] Thornton, P. 'Kid Porn Pics Too Vile For The Cops'. Daily Record. 3.10.08, p23.

[2045] Hamilton, J. 'Bungling Cops Lose Sex Beast Cronin ... Again'. Daily Record. 29.8.09, p25.

[2046] Evans, M. 'Police: We can't chase motorbike thieves, they may hurt themselves'. Daily Express. 30.6.06, p9.

[2047] Palmer, A. 'Catch a thug – and make him even worse'. The Sunday Telegraph. 10.12.06, p24.

[2048] Hickley, M. 'Danger criminals left to their own devices'. Daily Mail. 8.9.06, p12.

[2049] Parkinson, D. 'The Police did nothing after young teacher was hit in face'. Daily Express. 27.9.06, p5.

[2050] Brooke, C. 'Crime victim held police hostage'. Daily Mail. 9.9.06, p44.

[2051] Bracchi, P. 'Squatters Inc.'. Daily Mail. 5.3.11, pp26,27.

[2052] Chittenden, M. 'Squatters lock mother-to-be out of home'. The Sunday Times. 4.9.11, p18.

[2053] Levy, A. 'My childhood home has been invaded by Moldovan squatters'. Daily Mail. 18.1.12, p21.

[2054] Morgan, T. '999 caller told: You told the burglars'. Daily Express. 14.9.11, p23.

[2055] Riches, C. 'Intruders batter family and police take a week to arrive'. Daily Express. 19.9.06, p11.

[2056] Mills, J. 'Police let my burglar go ... then gave him a lift home'. Daily Mail. 24.12.04.

[2057] Hall, M., Dixon, C. 'MP attacks police over Pope abuse'. Daily Express. 19.9.06, p8.

[2058] McKinstry, L. 'Just What Are The Police Prepared To Do These Days?'. Daily Express. 10.2.06, p10.

[2059] Poulter, S. 'Shops take on police role to tackle thieves'. Daily Mail. 7.12.10, p29.

[2060] Knowsley, J. 'We were left dying in our own blood even though a neighbour told police Horgan had fled'. The Mail On Sunday. 26.2.06, p12.

[2061] Fagge, N. 'Britain has the worst crime rate in all of Europe'. Daily Express. 6.2.07, p2.

[2062] Blackstock, G. 'We can't arrest and won't fine'. The Sunday Post. 31.10.10, p1.

[2063] Topham, L. 'Don't let my Dad out of jail until he reveals where he's hidden Mum's body'. Daily Mail. 9.7.10, p41.

[2064] Phillips, M. 'Yes, the terror threat is real. But we must stop and question this cynical stunt'. Daily Mail. 28.5.07, p12.

[2065] Hickley, M., Bennetto, J. 'One out of every five killers is an immigrant'. Daily Mail. 31.8.09, p18.

[2066] Doyle, J. 'Police cross-check just one in 7 foreign criminals' records'. Daily Mail. 7.12.11, p2.

[2067] Sims, P. 'Czech gets into Britain and attacks four women – and no one knew he was a murderer'. Daily Mail. 28.1.12, p7.

[2068] Shipman, T. 'Harman's unreliable statistics on rape scare off victims'. Daily Mail. 15.3.10, p12.

[2069] Twomey, J., Reynolds, M. 'How police fail to record nearly half of rape claims'. Daily Express. 22.9.09, p20.

[2070] The Catherine Deveney Investigation. Scotland on Sunday. 6.6.10, p8.

[2071] 'Call for advisers to help victims of rape'. Daily Express. 15.3.10, p22.

[2072] Doughty, S. 'Police incompetence blamed for lack of rape convictions'. Mail Online. http://www.dailymail.co.uk/news/article-432648.

[2073] Flanagan, P. 'Anger as rapists are let off with a caution'. Daily Express. 5.4.10, p15

[2074] 'Child Abuse Shock'. Daily Record. 22.3.10, p10.

[2075] Harrison, I. 'Underage sex ruling is 'recipe for disaster' '. The Sunday Post. 9.5.10, p12.

[2076] Doyle, J. 'Police failures 'allow foreign rapists to slip through the net' '. Daily Mail. 28.2.12, p19.

[2077] Carswell, C. 'Cops New Elite Squad To Fight The Sex Beasts'. Daily Record. 21.10.10, p14.

[2078] Hamilton, T. 'Anything you say may NOT be used against you …'. Daily Record. 27.10.10, p8.

[2079] Greaves, G. 'Crisis in the Police'. Daily Express. 15.5.00, p33.

[2080] Hickley, M. 'The speed trap cop-out'. Daily Mail.10.12.07, p9.

[2081] Chapman, J. '£100 fines for 'idiot' drivers'. Daily Mail. 11.5.11, p2.

[2082] Fielding, J. 'Who permitted Venables to live so near a school?'. Sunday Express. 25.7.10, p7.

[2083] Whitehead, T. 'Just one in ten police out on patrol'. The Daily Telegraph. 20.7.10, p1.

[2084] '15 raids next to cops' HQ'. Sunday Mirror. 4.7.10, p16.

[2085] Malone, C. 'Moat bunglers cop a drubbing'. News Of The World. 11.7.10, p23.

[2086] Collins, D., Armstrong, L. 'Betrayed By Blunders'. The People. 11.7.10, pp6,7

[2087] Leader. 'Lies, damned lies and statistics'. Daily Mail. 17.7.03, p12.

[2088] Camber, R. 'Police chief: We need mental health nurses as much as officers'. Daily Mail. 18.5.10, p31.

[2089] Widdecombe, A. 'Keep the hunt ban and take it seriously'. Daily Express. 24.3.10, p13.

[2090] 'The Fearless Coroner'. Daily Mail. 29.9.09, p5.

[2091] Kandohla, T. 'Yobs still terrorise community'. Sunday Express. 26.9.10, p13.

[2092] Herbert, D. 'Kids 5 And 2 Die In 'Arson' Horror!'. News Of The World. 25.4.10, p25.

[2093] Breslin, J. P. 'The hell of noisy neighbours – is anyone listening to the victims?'. The Sunday Post. 24.4.11, p20.

[2094] Breslin, J. P. 'Noisy neighbour complaints have reached an all-time high'. The Sunday Post. 17.4.11, p46.

[2095] Bonnici, T. 'Let off £200,000 bill … the lawyer brother who stood bail for killer policeman'. Daily Express. 19.2.08, p20.

[2096] Fitzpatrick, B. 'Force needs rethink'. Sunday Express. 6.6.10, p65.

[2097] Allen, F. 'I wish I'd shot raiders police made me let go says pub boss'. Daily Express. 8.3.10, p11.

[2098] Hull, L. 'My ID theft nightmare'. Daily Mail. 28.12.07, p25.

[2099] Boyle, J. 'Half of crash victims don't report to police'. The Sunday Post. 13.6.10, p8.

[2100] 'Test For Troubled Fraud Agency'. Daily Mail. 27.8.10, p7.

[2101] Disley, J. 'Police let motorbike thieves go because they had no helmets'. Daily Express. 17.8.10, p8.

[2102] Sims, P. 'Police refused to chase quad bike gang who stole kayak … because thieves had no helmet'. Daily Mail. 21.4.12, p27.

[2103] BBC News. 10.12.10.

[2104] Lee, S. 'The Villageantes'. Daily Express. 17.3.10, p26.

[2105] 'So that's where the police are…'. Daily Mail. 18.3.10, p19.

[2106] 'Babysitter raped girl'. Daily Express. 20.3.10, p4.

[2107] Rice, D. '129,000 only get warning'. The People. 14.3.10, p25.

[2108] 'Burglars only get cautions'. Daily Express. 15.3.10, p5.

[2109] Slack, J. 'Criminals let off by 'caution culture' '. Daily Mail. 18.8.10, p17.

[2110] Martin, D., Greenwood, C. '21,000 commit a new crime within a month of receiving a caution'. Daily Mail. 21.1.12, p22.

[2111] Classic FM News. 19.1.12.

[2112] Dawar, A. 'How recession has sent violent crimes souring by 11%'. Daily Express. 20.1.12, p2.

[2113] Mansey, K. 'Shamed: The police forces who let thugs caught with knives get away with a warning'. Sunday Mirror. 27.7.08, p25.

[2114] 'Service pledges by cops'. Daily Record. 2.9.10, p2.

REFERENCES

[2115] 'Island's police hol row'. Daily Record. 1.8.09, p35.

[2116] Bletchly, R. 'Criminal Negligence'. The People. 31.10.10, p20.

[2117] 'Police say sorry over blunder'. Daily Record. 7.7.09, p9.

[2118] Millbank, J. ' 'Reclaim our streets' police chief: I was forced into house move by drunken yobs'. The Mail on Sunday. 26.9.10, p13.

[2119] Young, F. 'Law Is A Samarass'. Sunday Mail. 19.9.10, p31.

[2120] Murray, J. 'We Lose Seven UK Terror Suspects'. Sunday Express. 12.9.10, pp1,4.

[2121] 'Trapped By Fear'. Daily Express. 28.5.10, p33.

[2122] Dorman, N. 'Baby Shock For Cop Annie'. The People. 3.10.10, p30.

[2123] Twomey, J. 'Errors that let stalker launch 20 sex attacks'. Daily Express. 29.6.10, p20.

[2124] 'Blunder Cops Free A Rapist'. News Of The World. 11.4.10, p36.

[2125] Hope, J., Macrae, F. 'Why fingerprints may not point to whodunnit'. Daily Mail. 23.3.07, p31.

[2126] Emsley, C. 'The Great British Bobby'. Quercus. 2009. p42.

[2127] Slack, J. 'Revealed … truth behind Brown's bogus statistics'. Daily Mail. 17.4.10, p8.

[2128] 'Cyclist case rap for cops'. Daily Record. 4.5.10, p18.

[2129] Jarvis, D. 'Police let killer flee – my son will never get justice'. Sunday Express. 3.12.12, p15

[2130] Dixon, C. 'Police Farce As Civilians Outstrip Officers'. Daily Express. 17.5.10, p1.

[2131] 'Roads risk as police are cut'. Daily Express. 24.5.10, p27.

[2132] Silvester, N. 'Police Chief Wanted'. Sunday Mail. 26.7.09, p2.

[2133] Cowing, E. '999 crews to lose 'health and safety' '. Scotland on Sunday. 20.6.10, p5.

[2134] Fagge, N. 'Stowaway clings to jet's landing gear on 97-minute flight'. Daily Express. 10.6.10, p17.

[2135] Garvey, J. 'Nursery worker had child porn videos'. Newbury Weekly News. 25.3.10, p1.

[2136] Silvester, N. 'Shambles'. Sunday Mail. 6.6.10, p10.

[2137] Knight, K. 'The father who risked his life to nail the drug dealer next door'. Daily Mail. 12.6.10, p55.

[2138] Doyle, J. 'Why were the police so slow to get on his trail?'. Daily Mail. 4.6.10, p8.

[2139] Wright, S. 'Delays in police and paramedic help were a disgrace say witnesses'. Daily Mail. 7.6.10, p9.

[2140] Mudie, K., Hill, P. 'I was mentally ill, fantasised about drive-by shootings, but was allowed to KEEP my shotguns'. The People. 22.1.12, pp16, 17.

[2141] 'Cops told to probe Lyons five years ago'. Sunday Mail. 4.4.10, p5.

[2142] Slack, J. 'One officer in 40 is free to answer 999 calls'. Daily Mail. 30.3.07, p10.

[2143] Hitchens, P. The Mail on Sunday. 16.11.08, p27.

[2144] Slack, J. 'The big policing idea: Put officers at crime hotspots!'. Daily Mail. 12.1.10, p21.

[2145] McCabe, G. 'Robber Jailed After 5 Years On The Run'. Daily Record. 17.9.09, p19.

[2146] Attwood, K. 'The smallest PC in British history'. Daily Express. 14.1.10, p10.

[2147] Ventura, S. 'Cab boss: Someone will die if police don't crack down on rogue drivers'. Daily Record. 6.3.06, p10.

[2148] Ungoed-Thomas, J., Leppard, D. 'Met boss offered to quit'. The Sunday Times. pp1,7,8,9.

[2149] Doward, J., Townsend, M. 'Police chief's murder probe study rejected'. The Observer. 5.2.06, p4.

[2150] Walker, D. 'Kebab Shop In Racist Storm'. Daily Record. 19.4.07, p17.

[2151] Hall, M. R. 'How grotesque to see MPs hide behind their ancient freedoms when they've spent the past 13 years trampling on ours'. Daily Mail. 9.2.10, p14.

[2152] Littlejohn, R. 'I'm On A Shout, Guv'. Daily Mail. 5.5.09, p17.

[2153] Blackburn, V. 'Too scared to go home alone from a cashpoint'. Daily Express. 7.5.09, p14.

[2154] 'Spot Fines For Theft Double'. Daily Mail. 20.12.08, p27.

[2155] Twomey, J. '£1bn-a-year is stolen as shoplifting booms'. Daily Express. 7.1.10, p27.

[2156] Syal, R. 'Police failings 'helped fraudster flee' '. The Observer. 30.11.08, p19.

[2157] Greenwood, C. 'The police recruits who can barely read or write'. Daily Mail. 14.9.11, p16.

[2158] Coles, B. 'The Queen's Toff Cop'. Daily Express. 10.1.09, pp34,35.

[2159] 'The Painful truth'. Daily Mail. 11.4.09, p14.

[2160] 'Hol holds up police probe'. The People. 30.11.08, p22.

[2161] Twomey, J. 'Fruitless search of terror suspects'. Daily Express. 29.10.10, p11.

[2162] Street-Porter, J. 'When WILL police learn to tackle anarchy in the UK?'. Daily Mail. 13.12.10, p47.

[2163] 'We'll cut crime in 15 years, say police'. Daily Express. 3.11.08, p22.

[2164] 'Blunder cops in payout'. News Of The World. 19.7.09, p25.

[2165] Brooks, T. 'Shambles as police are forced to tear up 2,115 speeding fines'. Daily Express. 25.6.09, p22.

[2166] 'Cops say sorry for wee mix-up'. News Of The World. 11.10.09, p34.

[2167] Love, D. 'Sergeant 'Botched' Criminal Probes'. Sunday Mail. 11.10.09, p25.

[2168] Twomey, J. 'Police lost vital evidence in Barrymore pool death'. Daily Express. 25.2.09, p19.

[2169] Hardman, R. 'Down in the woods, something stirred'. Daily Mail. 4.12.10, p43.

[2170] Tozer, J., Narain, J., Schlesinger, F. " 'Torture' Boys Had Just Been Grilled By Police". Daily Mail. 7.4.09, p1.

[2171] 'Police Deny Failings After Copycat Attack'. Daily Express. 23.1.10, p6.

[2172] Gall, C. 'Oliver's Army'. Daily Record. 31.3.09, p23.

[2173] Channel 4 News. 30.10.10.

[2174] Dow, B. 'Cops Make A Hash Of £800K Cannabis Case'. Daily Record. 24.3.09, p23.

[2175] Thornton, P. 'Weeding Out The Drug Labs'. The Sun. 11.8.13, p27.

[2176] Chapman, J. 'The serial offenders getting away with serial cautions'. Daily Mail. 23.12.09, p8.

[2177] Hackley, M. '118,000 violent thugs let off with a caution'. Daily Mail. 25.8.08, p29.

[2178] Jarvis, D. 'Police let 10 sex fiends a day off with a caution'. Sunday Express. 26.10.08, p12.

[2179] Doughty, S. '100 rapists are let off with a caution'. Daily Mail. 10.11.09, p10.

[2180] Brooke, C. 'Masked men caught <u>on</u> church roof stealing lead ... but that's not enough evidence, say police'. Daily Mail. 7.6.08, p44.

[2181] Hickley, M. Daily Mail. 20.12.08, p27.

[2182] Slack, J. 'Just 1 in 135 criminal cases ends in prison'. Daily Mail. 29.1.10, p36.

[2183] Martin, D. 'Send all violent criminals to court'. Daily Mail. 27.10.10, p8.

[2184] Edwards, R. 'Smarten up, new Yard chief tells scruffy officers'. The Daily Telegraph. 11.2.09, p6.

[2185] Hainey, R. 'Olympics Ban Scots Cops'. Sunday Mail. 15.2.09, p7.

[2186] Met 'had not trained for failed suicide bombings'. Daily Mail. 9.10, 08, p20.

[2187] 'The text detectives'. Daily Mail. 28.8.08, p35.

[2188] Pilditch, D. 'As police watch immigrants find new squat'. Daily Express. 15.1.10, p5.

[2189] Phillips, M. The Melanie Phillips Column. Daily Mail. 3.8.09, p12.

[2190] Slack, J. 'Police don't have time to visit 40% of crime victims'. Daily Mail. 23.10.08, p4.

[2191] Panther, L. 'Police Farce'. News Of The World. 21.9.08, p25.

[2192] Findlay, R. 'King Con Collared'. Sunday Mail. 22.2.09, p39.

[2193] Silvester, N. 'Blobbies on beat'. Sunday Mail. 7.9.08, p23.

[2194] Feltz, V. 'Weeble wobbly coppers'. Daily Express. 2.9.08, p13.

[2195] Greenwood, C. 'On the beat, the blobby bobbies'. Daily Mail. 30.9.11, p24.

[2196] 'Only 13 inept police fired in a decade'. Daily Mail. 5.9.08, p6.

[2197] Thornton, P. 'I told police they had the wrong man ... but no one would listen'. Sunday Mail. 14.9.08, p23.

[2198] Evans, A. 'I Told Cops Of Evil Brothers 15 Yrs Ago'. News Of The World. 5.10.08, p33.

[2199] Emsley, C. 'The Great British Bobby'.

[2200] David, D. 'The day I knew Bob Quick was flawed'. The Mail on Sunday. 12.4.09.

[2201] Silvester, N. 'Case Collapses After PC's Version of Tape Rejected'. Sunday Mail. 14.9.08, p9.

[2202] Salkeld, L., Slack. J. 'The 100 lost minutes'. Daily Mail. 27.7.06, p5.

[2203] Hobson, N. 'Policemen Behaving Badly'. Daily Mail. 24.4.06, p26.

[2204] Harris, P. 'This way to the cannabis room, this way for crack'. Daily Mail. 13.4.07, p10.

[2205] Kisiel, R., Greenhill, S. 'Nurse 'blinded in horror sex attack by her own son' '. Daily Mail. 15.11.10, p28.

[2206] Johnston, L. 'Sent home to die with broken arms and ribs'. Sunday Express. 27.6.10, p23.

[2207] Edge, S. 'Revealed: The True Identity Of Jack The Ripper'. Daily Express. 17.8.05, p29.

[2208] Milland, G. 'Why do police let these protesters wreak havoc?'. Daily Express. 21.4.09, p5.

[2209] 'Muslim arrests banned for Ramadan'. Daily Express. 23.10.06, p7.

[2210] Street-Porter, J 'The plodding police work that has let Claudia down'. Daily Mail. 10.5.10, p49.

[2211] O'Hare, P. 'Cops Lack Vital DNA Of Missing People'. Daily Record. 20.1.09, p25.

[2212] Davies, C. 'Nightmare of red tape and silence for parents of son missing in Africa'. The Daily Telegraph. 29.9.03, p4

[2213] Galloway, G. 'Old Firm's threats, lies and videotape'. Daily Record. 7.3.11, p13.

[2214] Murray, J. 'Deepcut probe botched, says police'. Sunday Express. 13.3.11, p25.

[2215] 'The thick blue line'. News of the World. 6.3.11, p35.

[2216] Tozer, J., McDermott, N., Brooke, C. 'Christmas dinner in house of death'. Daily Mail. 17.2.11, p5.

[2217] Hamilton, N. 'Stop this institutional idiocy'. Sunday Express. 30.11.08, p31.

[2218] Brooke, C. 'Report a crime at our police station? No, Sir, you have to phone it in'. Daily Mail. 28.4.10, p25.

[2219] Smith, D. 'Undercover PC exposes sex bias'. The Observer. 23.4.06, p15.

[2220] Coles, B., Riches, C. 'The Truth About Our Mean Streets'. Daily Express. 5.2.11, p23.

[2221] 'Street fury over crime hotspot tag'. Daily Express. 2.2.11, p9.

[2222] 'G20 protest police were badly trained, report finds'. Daily Mail. 8.7.09, p20.

[2223] Twomey, J. 'Police 'in chaos' on day of Tube shooting'. Daily Express. 10.10.08, p37.

[2224] Leake, C., Marunchak, A. 'Just William star targeted by stalker on Facebook'. The Mail on Sunday. 16.1.11, p3.

[2225] 'Police action is needed over grooming of girls'. The Sunday Times. 16.1.11, p23.

[2226] Bignell, P 'Cyclists 'left unprotected by police and courts' '. The Independent On Sunday. 9.1.11, p28.

[2227] 'Bobbies on the Tweet ...'. Daily Record. 17.1.11, p9.

[2228] Jennings, J. 'How cardboard PC has cut out crime'. Sunday Express. 17.10.10, p22.

[2229] 'Police won't tec on dull job'. News Of The World. 1.3.09, p23.

[2230] Hitchens, P. The Mail on Sunday. 13.2.11, p31.

[2231] Ricketts, M. 'Special service'. Daily Mail. 3.2.11, p73.

[2232] 'Assaulted mum told not to call officers'. Daily Express. 29.9.09, p5.

[2233] Rose, D. The Mail on Sunday. 18.5.08, p11.

[2234] Cashmore, P. Daily Mail. 20.1.11, pp50,51.

[2235] C4 News. 5.12.11.

[2236] Dixon, C. 'Police Afraid Of The Dark'. Daily Express. 28.1.11, pp1,5.

[2237] Mullen, S. 'Cop Misses Dope Farm In Her Flat'. Sunday Mail. 23.1.11, p23.

[2238] Lader, 'Police cell-off'. Daily Record. 16.2.11, p8.

[2239] Bostock, N. 'GPs lose police work to private firm'. GP News. 10.3.06, p18.

[2240] Riches, C. 'Your son's just been beaten up by yobs? Don't call 999, it's not serious enough'. Daily Express. 23.2.08, p31.

[2241] Townsend, M. The Observer. 6.2.11, p25.

[2242] Massey, R. 'As speed cameras are cut, road death toll falls'. Daily Mail. 5.2.11, p20.

[2243] BBC1. 29.10.10.

[2244] Dolan, A. 'Please don't let me die'. Daily Mail. 29.10.10, p21.

[2245] 'Left high and dry by police call'. Daily Express. 14.10.11, p14.

[2246] Littlejohn, R. 'Thin blue line of chickens'. Daily Mail. 9.10.09, p17.

[2247] Slack, J. 'Migrant Car Insurance Scam Exposed'. Daily Mail. 28.2.11, p18.

[2248] Phillips, M. ''We're regressing into a disorderly age and it looks to me as if the police aren't doing enough to halt the slide'. Daily Mail. 28.3.11, p14.

[2249] http://www.communitycare.co.uk/Articles/2004/10/14/46686/Criminal-Neglect.htm.

[2250] Littlejohn, R. 'Why decent folk deserve better from cops who let mobs run amok'. Daily Mail. 24.9.10, p17.

[2251] Hardy, F. 'It Took 30 Long Years To Prove I Was Raped'. Daily Mail. 2.4.11, p39.

[2252] Brooke, C. 'Storm as cry rape woman gets £80 fine'. Daily Mail. 25.3.11, p38.

[2253] Dawar, A. 'A victim of crime ... police chief robbed'. Daily Express. 23.4.11, p38.

[2254] Slack, J. 'A home is broken into every minute'. Daily Mail. 21.4.11, p19.

[2255] Greenwood, C. 'The invisible police'. Daily Mail. 30.3.11.

[2256] Dawar, A. 'Police fury at job cuts ... yet a third never go on frontline to fight crime'. Daily Express. 30.3.11, p2.

[2257] Acton, J. 'We'd be none the wiser if police patrolled in tutus'. Daily Express. 22.1.08, p45.

[2258] Stote, M. 'Where are the police, asks judge'. Daily Express. 20.2.08, p2.

[2259] Morgan, T. 'Night Stalker's 1000 Victims'. Daily Record. 25.3.11, pp10,11.

[2260] Bohdanowicz, K. 'I was the victim of a hammer attacker ... but what shocked me was police response to my ordeal'. Daily Express. 28.2.08.

[2261] Flanagan, P. 'Doctors warned of Baby P abuse'. Daily Express. 19.11.08, p27.

[2262] Moult, J., Ballinger, L. 'Yard accused of ignoring warnings over evil boyfriend'. Daily Mail. 18.11.08, p9.

[2263] Carpenter, J. 'My hell at the hands of a stalker'. Daily Express. 23.4.11, p35.

[2264] Owen, J., Brady, B. 'It wasn't revenge, I just wanted it to stop'. The Independent On Sunday. 5.2.12, p17.

[2265] Aitken, M. 'Put 999 Hoaxers in Dock'. Sunday Mail. 5.12.10, p20.

[2266] Malone, A. 'Wrecking Crew'. Daily Mail. 24.1.08, p33.

[2267] Milland, G. 'Fewer armed police as gun crime soars'. Daily Express. 26.12.07, p11.

[2268] Pring, J. 'Silent Victims'. Gibson Square Books. London N1 0RD, 2003. pp124-130.

[2269] Scougall, M. 'Senior cop report delayed again'. The Sunday Post. 8.5.11, p24.

[2270] Taher, A. 'Police pay Muslim with links to 7/7 leader to teach them how to fight terror'. The Mail on Sunday. 8.5.11, p18.

[2271] Derbyshire, D. 'How you can spot a criminal at the age of 3'. Daily Mail. 22.2.11, p20.

[2272] Green, N. 'Rapist cop case victims' anger at police force'. The Sunday Post. 27.2.11, p31.

[2273] Martin, A. 'How dithering emergency services made one blunder after another'. Daily Mail. 7.5.11, p15.

[2274] 'Police 'vandalism' special is wrecked'. Sunday Express. 12.6.11, p40.

[2275] 'Met Police chief slated in health and safety row'. The Sunday Post. 8.5.11, p2.

[2276] Cohen, T. 'Girl risks her life to save woman from hoodies – as police sit in their car and do nothing'. Daily Mail. 28.5.11, p11.

[2277] Phillips, L. 'Hurry up, PC Dawdle, they've gone and left the bank unlocked'. The Sunday Times. 12.6.11, p19.

[2278] Hull, L. 'Arrest me, pleads a burglar. We're too busy, the police reply'. Daily Mail. 5.2.08, p33.

[2279] Reynolds, M. 'Two plastic PCs hide from a yob aged 13 … and call 999 for help'. Daily Express. 1.2.08, p15.

[2280] Herbert, D. 'Flops 'n' robbers'. News Of The World. 15.5.11.

[2281] Wright, S., Bennetto, J. 'And They Call This Policing'. Daily Mail. 20.8.07, p9.

[2282] 'Plastic PCs' £1m fines'. Sunday Express. 3.4.11, p36.

[2283] Sawer, P. ' 'Trial destroyed Dowlers' privacy' says police chief'. The Sunday Telegraph. 26.6.11, p6.

[2284] Winter, S. 'How courts let the victim down'. Sunday Express. 26.6.11, p4.

[2285] Verkaik, R. 'Top officers at 'failed' crime agency walk away with £5m'. The Mail on Sunday. 26.6.11, p46.

[2286] Buchanan, K '200 sex fiends have vanished'. Sunday Express. 26.6.11, p12.

[2287] Crickmer, G. 'Mum: Arrest my girl for 'Skins' party that destroyed our house'. Daily Express. 13.4.07, p3.

[2288] Ballinger. L. 'Beaten up? Don't bother the police, just tell your MP'. Daily Mail. 22.8.07, p30

[2289] McAnally, A. 'If I Could Be Bothered, I'd Jail You'. Daily Record. 15.7.11, p31.

[2290] McAnally, A. 'Jail For The Laziest Cop In Scotland'. Daily Record. 26.8.11, p9.

[2291] Horne, B. 'Jailed Lazy Cop Is Free After 6 Days'. Daily Record. 1.9.11, p26.

[2292] Finlay, D. 'Lazy Cop Free After Serving 12 Days'. Daily Record. 11.11.11, p17.

[2293] Slack, J. 'Short arm of the law'. Daily Mail. 2.10.07, p26.

[2294] Wright, S. 'Babies On The Beat'. Daily Mail. 13.8.07, pp1,2.

[2295] Mason, G. 'How did Britain become Europe's crime capital?' Daily Express. 7.2.07, p12.

[2296] Widdecombe, A. 'A Community Support Policeman's Lot Is Not A Useful One'. Daily Express. 15.9.10, p13.

[2297] 'Just dopey!'. Daily Mail. 3.5.11, p33.

[2298] 'Plastic police are 'useless' '. Daily Express. 22.3.08 p28.

[2299] BRoster, P. 'Cycling ban on PCs in case they fall off'. Daily Express. 23.11.07, p14.

[2300] Salkeld, L. 'Mother begged for crazed son to be sectioned'. Daily Mail. 2.12.10, p35.

[2301] Paddick, B. 'The only code we used was '99' – it meant a WPC had just made the tea'. The Mail on Sunday. 2.3.08, pp2,3.

[2302] Daily Mail. 3.3.09, p17.

[2303] Currie, G. 'Runaway Prisoner At Home For 5 Months'. Daily Record. 9.10, 07, p15.

[2304] Smith, L. 'Puzzle of Holmes expert's death by garotte unsolved'. The Times. 24.4.04.

[2305] 'How bungling Yard let robber Biggs off hook'. Daily Express. 1.1.05, p5.

[2306] Stalker, J. 'The Met deserves a better boss than Mr. Bean of the Yard'. The Independent on Sunday. 5.8.07, p38.

[2307] 'Two policemen forgot about body in street'. Daily Express. 7.8.07, p9.

[2308] Riches, C. 'Climb a ladder? That's too high risk says council'. Daily Express. 8.8.07, p11.

[2309] McKinstry, L. 'Britain needs a moral revolution to beat the drunks, yobs and killers'. Daily Express. 17.8.07, p10.

[2310] Robson, D. 'This Culture of Complicity is poisoning society and betraying our brave citizens'. Daily Express. 18.8.07, p14.

[2311] Sanderson, D. 'Convict on run 14 years was staying at mum's'. News of the World. 7.10.07, p27.

[2312] Slack, J. Daily Mail. 21.8.07, p7.

[2313] Duffy, M. 'Deadly Spots … But No Cops'. Sunday Mirror. 26.8.07, p16.

[2314] Hitchens, P. The Mail on Sunday. 2.9.07, p29.

[2315] Rees, G. Daily Mail. 11.9.07, p29

[2316] Fagge, N. 'Police DNA bungle let sex attacker strike again'. Daily Express. 19.9.07, p25.

[2317] Foggo, D., Fellstrom, C. ' 'Gun city' police chief to lose job'. The Sunday Times. 23.9.07, p7.

[2318] Twomey, J. 'Dead woman found in her living room 3 weeks after police searched the house'. Daily Express. 21.9.07, p37.

[2319] Leapman, B. 'If you're drowning don't expect police to throw a life belt'. The Sunday Telegraph. 30.9.07, p8.

[2320] Brown, M. 'Police tell robbery victim: Handbag theft is not a crime'. Daily Express. 15.9.07, p27.

[2321] Gardham, D. 'Police let bombers slip net'. The Daily Telegraph. 10.7.07, p1.

[2322] Clark, R. 'There is no place for Sharia law in British society'. Daily Express. 29.7.11, p12.

[2323] Harper, T., Leapman, B. 'Jews far more likely to be victims of faith hatred than Muslims'. The Sunday Telegraph. 17.12.06, p10.

[2324] 'Cops row over dying man dash'. Daily Record. 28.7.11, p7.

[2325] Gilbertson, D. 'All week I've talked to old colleagues about why the Met got it so wrong. What they said shocked me to the core'. The Mail on Sunday. 14.8.11, p12.

[2326] Slack, J. 'How police abandoned the streets to riot mobs'. Daily Mail. 29.11.11.

[2327] 'Police Just Watched So We Thought, Why Not?'. Daily Record. 11.8.11, p6.

[2328] Camber, R. 'Surrender! Police let mob seize streets'. Daily Mail. 9.8.11, p2.

[2329] C4 News. 7.8.11.

[2330] BBC1 News. 12.8.11.

[2331] C4 News. 29.2.12.

[2332] Christian, N. ' 'No criminality' in police killing'. Scotland on Sunday. 4.8.13, p3.

[2333] C4 News. 19.8.11.

[2334] BBC1. Panorama. 15.8.11.

[2335] 'Police tactics to blame for spread of riots, say MPs'. Daily Mail. 19.12.11, p27.

[2336] Sheldrick, G. 'Half the country keeps a weapon under the bed'. Daily Express. 5.8.11, p34.

[2337] Hickley, M. 'Britain: Europe's Burglary Capital'. Daily Mail. 6.2.07, p1.

[2338] O'Grady, S. 'Police child-seat snub'. Daily Express. 16.2.07, p43.

[2339] Coates, J. 'Police fail to enforce new 20mph speed limit at schools'. Sunday Express. 25.9.11, p32.

[2340] 'The Spy In The Laptop'. Daily Mail. 16.8.11, p6.

[2341] Caroe, LO. 'Man, 75, driven to violence by taunting yobs'. Daily Express. 27.8.11, p45.

[2342] Sims. P. 'WPC was supervising 60 perverts ... one went on to kill a girl of 17'. Daily Mail. 25.8.11, p25.

[2343] Burns, J. 'Labour Back Call For Race Killing Probe'. Daily Record. 25.8.11, p10.

[2344] 'Cops snub car crash callouts'. Daily Record. 27.8.11, p10.

[2345] Littlejohn, R. 'Talk about adding insult to injury ...'. Daily Mail. 19.8.11, p17.

[2346] Eccles, L. 'Boy stabbed to death as police cleared their desks at axed station yards away'. Daily Mail. 19.8.11, p24.

[2347] Mathieson, J. 'Riot? Send us an email'. Daily Record. 18.8.11, p31.

[2348] Grant, C. 'Police in a muddle over eBay scam'. The Sunday Post. 7.1.07, p4.

[2349] Griffiths, S., Spencer, B. '£120,000 Cop Shop Robber'. Daily Record. 18.10.08, p1.

[2350] Knapp, M. 'Scandal of 10 officers for a town of 200,000'. Sunday Express. 11.3.07, p21.

[2351] Whitehead, T. 'Street attack every 12 seconds as crime soars under Labour'. Daily Express. 20.7.07, p9.

[2352] Hickley, M. '290 robberies a day as cash for crime runs out'. Daily Mail. 27.4.07, p4.

[2353] Whitehead, T. Daily Express. 27.4.07, p1.

[2354] Greenwood, C. 'Police forces where one one in four crimes is not investigated'. Daily Mail. 25.1.12, p18.

[2355] Utley, T. 'A midnight phone call from my son's mugger, and the case of the vanishing beat bobbies'. Daily Mail. 6.4.07, p14.

[2356] Slack, J. ' 'Three strikes' rule to tackle yob gangs'. Daily Mail. 30.1.12, p2.

[2357] Darbyshire, N. 'Glamorising Of An Evil Nobody'. Daily Mail. 5.9.11, p23.

[2358] Sky Crime programme.

[2359] Doyle, J. 'The 15,000 police who never make arrests'. Daily Mail. 5.9.11, p20.

[2360] Greenwood, C. 'Shaven-headed, starved and beaten, the 24 slaves rescued in police raid on traveller site'. Daily Mail. 12.9.11, p5.

[2361] Forensic 'crisis'. Daily Record. 5.2.10, 2.

[2362] 'Stop The Traffic'. Daily Record. 28.11.11, p4.

[2363] Dowling, K., Flyn, C. 'Hundreds of police stations to be closed to the public'. The Sunday Times. 2.10.11, p5.

[2364] 'Police give jewel thief 4-day start'. Sunday Mirror. 27.11.11, p23.

[2365] Taylor, D. 'Cops Delay Sex Beast Plea For Three Days'. Daily Record. 1.2.12, p23.

[2366] BBC1 News. 3.1.12.

[2367] Leader. Daily Mail. 15.6.13, p16.

[2368] Littlejohn, R. 'Don't drink that lager, Guv, it's not worth it'. Daily Mail. 6.1.12, p17.

[2369] Ross, P. 'Lord Watson calls for police to probe fox hunts'. Scotland on Sunday. 4.12.11, p11.

[2370] Levy, A. 'A record 171,000 drivers are fined for using mobiles'. Daily Mail. 30.12.11, p2.

[2371] Channel 4 News. 30.12.11.

[2372] Daily Express. 16.12.11, p14.

[2373] Faulkner, K. 'Elderly victims of domestic violence 'failed by the police''. Daily Mail. 26.12.11, p27.

[2374] 'Most stalkers avoid prison'. Daily Mail. 29.12.11, p20.

[2375] Musson, C. 'I went to the police about my £15,000 but they told me to get lost ...'. Daily Record. 20.1.12, p4.

[2376] Hookham, M. 'Iraq hero takes aim at PC Dolittle'. The Sunday Times. 29.1.12, p6.

[2377] 'Prisoner freed by gunman'. Daily Express. 26.1.12, p28.

[2378] Doyle, J. 'Ten per cent of all murders carried out by thugs on bail'. Daily Mail. 7.1.12, p4.

[2379] Watts, R. 'Revealed: Britain's crime hot spots'. The Sunday Telegraph. 26.2.12, p19.

[2380] Andrews, E. 'Police made me feel like a liar when I reported being raped'. Daily Mail. 2.3.12, p39.

[2381] 'Police tell students' murder suspect to wait in a queue'. Daily Express. 9.7.08, p5.

[2382] Pendlebury, R. Daily Mail. 4.6.07, pp32,33.

[2383] 'Come and spy for us, say police'. Daily Express. 25.7.08, p33.

[2384] Drury, I. 'MP escapes police probe over salary for his son'. Daily Mail. 21.3.08, p20.

[2385] Whitehead, T. '999 alert? Police will be with you in three hours'. Daily Express. 16.7.08, p9.

[2386] Almond, R. 'Shameful'. The Mail on Sunday. 13.4.08, pp1,8.

[2387] Sims, P. 'I caught a burglar but police were too busy to pick him up'. Daily Mail. 26.3.08, p25.

[2388] Sawer, P. 'Police had tip-off on the flat a week before they went in to find Shannon'. The Sunday Telegraph. 16.3.08, p4.

[2389] 'Police accused of missed chances to find her'. Daily Mail. 17.3.08, p7.

[2390] 'Driver lay dead in car for 3 days'. Daily Express. 6.6.08, p33.

[2391] 'Cop grovel to axe raid pair'. The People. 25.5.08, p23.

[2392] Slater, N. 'Apology For Nights In Jail'. Reading Evening Post. 22.5.08, pp1,5.

[2393] Warren, J. 'When 999 Really Was An Emergency'. Daily Express. 17.7.08, p35.

[2394] McGivern, M. 'Fraudsters Cost Every Scot £330'. Daily Record. 13.5.08, p12.

[2395] Groves, J. 'Taken in by the great CCTV con'. Sunday Express. 11.5.08, p22.

[2396] 'Why the party police are afraid of the dark'. Daily Mail. 9.5.08, p5.

[2397] Stewart, S. ' 'Gers No Room At The Inn For Fans – Hotels closing on UEFA night after cops say they can't cope with trouble'. Daily Record. 6.5.08, p17.

[2398] 'All forces need rape units, says police chief'. Daily Mail. 10.7.08, p10.

[2399] Doward, J. 'How police put their faith in the 'expert' witness who was a fraud'. The Observer. 23.3.08, p8.

[2400] Disley, J. 'Widow's grief as husband's body is found after 8 years'. Daily Express. 18.2.12, p4.

[2401] Hurley, K. 'How political correctness is ruining Britain's police'. Daily Mail. 15.2.12, p14.

[2402] Camber, R. 'Blunders that left thugs free to abduct royal aide'. Daily Mail. 13.2.12, p35.

[2403] Doyle, J. '850 Sex Offenders Have Gone On The Run'. Daily Mail. 5.3.12, p1,2.

[2404] Sales, D. 'Rathband let down by cops says bruv'. The Sun. 31.3.12, p7.

[2405] Littlejohn, R. Daily Mail. 27.3.12, p17.

[2406] Waugh Zone. 'Hoodwiinked. But I've got his number'. The Sunday Times. 4.12.11, p7.

[2407] Dugan, E. 'Domestic violence affects one million children in the UK'. The Independent on Sunday. 25.3.12, p6.

[2408] Harrison, I. 'Fury as police refuse victim support plea'. The Sunday Post. 25.3.12, p11.

[2409] Leach, B. 'Doctor barred after 20 years of sex abuse'. The Sunday Telegraph. 19.2.12, p16.

[2410] 'Scandal of UK doctors who are mutilating girls aged ten'. Daily Mail. 23.4.12, p25.

[2411] BBC Newsnight. 24.7.12.

[2412] Townsend, M. 'Watchdog seeks control of privatised police'. The Observer. 22.4.12, p16.

[2413] Harrison, I. 'Police are delaying child safety checks'. The Sunday Post. 22.4.12, p28.

[2414] Brooks, T. ' 'Call centre cops' tell raid victim: Phone us the details in two days'. Daily Express. 20.4.12, p27.

[2415] Dawar, A. 'Beat bobby cuts blamed as knife robberies soar'. Daily Express. 20.4.12, p15.

[2416] Mackenzie, K. 'A Cautionary Tale of Injustice'. Daily Mail. 14.4.12, p25.

[2417] Officer 'A'. 'The Crime Factory'. Mainstream Publishing. 2012.

[2418] Officer 'A'. 'The Crime Factory'. Mainstream Publishing. 2012.

[2419] Narain, J., Parveen, N. 'What They Did To Me Was Evil'. Daily Mail. 9.5.12, p6.

[2420] Ferrari, N. 'Failed by the real racists'. Sunday Express. 13.5.12, p29.

[2421] Scott, M. 'So Mr Chief Constable, Would You Like Us To Arrest Him Too?'. Sunday Mail. 6.5.12, p23.

[2422] FOI Standard Response Letter. IPCC. 12.4.12.

[2423] Salkeld, L. 'How vicar nabbed lead thief in five hours after police said it would take weeks to catch him'. Daily Mail. 23.5.12, p7.

[2424] 'Tell us why beast was free to kill'. Sunday Mail. 15.7.12, p16.

[2425] Ellicott, C. 'PC heard dying patient's cries for water'. Daily Mail. 10.7.12, p9.

[2426] 'Ward Off Crime'. The Sun. 24.4.12, p6.

[2427] Bamford, E. 'Long jail terms would slash 100,000 crimes'. Daily Express. 9.7.12, p15.

[2428] Penrose, J. 'Cops 'Too Busy' To Quiz Night Stalker Over Hundreds Of Other Crimes'. Sunday Mirror. 1.7.12, p37.

[2429] Gall, C. 'Arlene cop 'blew top' over rings'. Daily Record. 23.5.12, p9.

[2430] Coates, J. 'Fraud squad fails to raid a single suspect'. Sunday Express. 3.6.12, p22.

[2431] Mackenzie, K. 'We must halt this injustice'. Daily Mail. 26.5.12, p21.

[2432] Gardham, M. 'In a seat instead of pounding the beat'. Daily Record. 7.6.12.

[2433] BBC1 News. 15.5.12.

[2434] Newsnight. 20.6.12.

[2435] 'They even ignore armed robberies'. The Mail on Sunday. 15.6.2003. pp48,49.

[2436] Anonymous officer writing in to The Mail on Sunday, 2003.

[2437] Salkeld, L. 'Landslide victim's home burgled days after body is found'. Daily Mail. 24.7.12, p25.

REFERENCES

2438 Gilbride, P. 'Computer chaos as new police force is launched'. Daily Express. 1.4.13, p5.

2439 Jeeves, P. 'Yobs who can't speak English let off with fine'. Daily Express. 28.7.12, p15.

2440 Dawar, A. 'Let-off for metal thief who claimed: 'It's legal back home in Poland' '. Daily Express. 27.7.12, p7.

2441 Whitehead. T. 'Police chief attacked for sending officers to investigate all crimes'. Daily Express. 20.9.08, p7.

2442 Myers, R., Petre, J., Ellery, B. 'We DID search loft ... but missed Tia's body'. The Mail on Sunday. 12.8.12, p17.

2443 Channel 5 News. 22.3.13.

2444 Basnett, G. 'Paedo Postcode Lottery'. News Of The World'. 28.9.08, p27.

2445 Cahalan, P., Brady, B. 'Police go back over cases of FGM 'cutting' '. The Independent On Sunday. 7.4.13, p30.

2446 Clarke, R. 'The Whiplash Racket'. Daily Mail. 13.1.12, p15.

2447 O'Grady, s. 'Police child-seat snub'. Daily Express. 16.2.07, p43.

2448 Herbert, D. 'Want to report a crime to police? Come back later'. Daily Express. 1.3.13, p33.

2449 McKinstry, L. Daily Express. 24.9.09, p12.

2450 Milland, G. 'Police 'ignore violent crime to hit targets'!'. Daily Express. 23.10.09, p15.

2451 Coates, J., Davis, M. 'Make parents pay for crimes of very young'. Sunday Express. 17.6.12, p9.

2452 'Softly, softly for the police'. Daily Express. 4.11.09, p12.

2453 Grierson, J., Davis, M. 'Police Missed Chance To Nail Savile in 1964'. Daily Record. 12.3.13, p9.

2454 Bonnington, A. 'The truth on all these lies'. Daily Mail. 14.3.13, p14.

2455 Walters, S., Owen, G. '5,300 police aren't fit enough to walk the beat'. The Mail on Sunday. 17.2.13, p5.

2456 Hull, L. 'Facebook plea to her sister as she was raped'. Daily Mail. 14.2.13, p37.

2457 Kay, R. 'Police 'can't find' Camilla riot attackers'. Daily Mail. 8.3.13, p45.

2458 'Police escort sees Eugenie through her driving test'. Daily Mail. 30.1.09, p35.

2459 C5 News. 22.3.13.

2460 Wright, S. 'Officer in phone hacking probe is given CBE'. Daily Mail. 15.6.13, p7.

2461 Brocklebank, J., Jedrzejewski, N. 'Party girl thrown out of flat ... after 45 visits by police'. Daily Mail. 5.10.13, p12.

2462 Murray, J. 'How we let Jill's real killer get away'. Sunday Express. 2.7.06, p21.

2463 Slack, J. 'Police ignore callers who report a crime'. Daily Mail. 29.6.06, p19.

2464 Gallagher, I. The Mail on Sunday. 6.8.06, pp22,23.

2465 'Scandal of the car crash bandits'. The Mail on Sunday. 21.5.06, p15.

2466 Greenwood, C. 'Why did it take police a week to find her?'. Daily Mail. 14.5.13, p11.

2467 Lawrence, D. 'Fighting For Stephen'. Daily Mail. 12.6.06, p30.

2468 Smith, D. 'Undercover PC exposes sex bias'. The Observer. 23.4.06, p15.

2469 Rawstorne, T. Daily Mail. 11.11.06, pp44,45.

2470 Brooke, C. 'Police ignore school's 999 calls as raider brings terror'. Daily Mail. 7.10.06, p48.

2471 Boycott, R. 'Hitting Back'. Daily Mail. 2.2.07, p46.

2472 Martin Townsend. Sunday Express. 3.12.06, p34.

2473 McKinstry, L. 'Politicians are in denial about the menace we face'. Daily Express. 27.5.13, p12.

2474 Love, D. 'Cops took no action over child porn site'. Daily Record. 17.7.13, p4.

2475 Wilkes, D. 'Attacker goes free after police forgot all about his case'. Daily Mail. 6.11.06, p28.

2476 Reynolds, M. 'Police tell burglary victim: Sorry, you're not a priority'. Daily Express. 13.11.10, p7.

2477 Taylor, B. 'Burgled? Police won't turn up unless culprit is still in your house'. Daily Mail. 2.1.07, p21.

2478 Larkin, M. 'The Bank that likes to say: Help yourself'. Daily Express. 3.11.06, p9.

2479 Pilditch, D. 'NHS chief's dog is held to ransom for £2,000'. Daily Express. 3.11.06, p18.

2480 'Police snub 'impossible' child seat law'. Daily Mail. 12.2.07.

2481 'Mother does the police's job after her son is beaten up'. The Mail on Sunday. 28.1.07, p16.

2482 Calvert, J. 'Changing to success in Bradford, the city where everyone is a victim of bitterness'. Sunday Express. 15.7.01, pp10,11.

2483 Constable, N. 'Criminals? We're the shipwreck heroes'. Daily Express. 24.2.07, p21.

2484 Phillips, P. 'Yes, the terror threat is real'. Daily Mail. 28.5.07, p12.

2485 Barrett, D. 'Victims of crime find the police unhelpful'. The Sunday Telegraph. 24.10.10, p12.

2486 Dean, C. 'I was tormented like Fiona and no one ever helped'. Daily Express. 30.9.09, p12.

2487 Doyle, J. '113 offences, but burglar is let off with a caution'. Daily Mail 22.1.13, p22.

2488 'Police 'refuse to recover' stolen van from traveller site'. Daily Mail. 25.2.10, p37.

2489 Barnham, P. 'Solve It Yourself'. Daily Record. 25.5.07, p23.

2490 Brooke, C. 'Don't report thefts of under £20, police tell shopkeepers'. Daily Mail. 23.7.10, p25.

[2491] Hitchens, P. 'Where was the Robocop army when 'Mister' Moat was busy selling drugs?'. The Mail on Sunday. 11.7.10, p27.

[2492] Forsyth, F. 'Why was this thief allowed a spending spree?'. Daily Express. 25.6.10, p13.

[2493] Breen, P. The Mail On Sunday. 26.8.07, p27.

[2494] Collins, D. 'Cops In Tots Tragedy'. Daily Record. 14.11.08, p4.

[2495] Slack, J., Chapman, J. 'May: Time's up'. Daily Mail. 5.10.10, p8.

[2496] Jeeves, P. 'PC tells shopkeeper chasing yobs: Sorry I can't help, dial 999'. Daily Express. 6.4.10, p18.

[2497] Jeeves, P. 'Call 999, victim told at police HQ'. Daily Express. 28.4.10, p32.

[2498] Macfarlane, J., Craven, N. The Mail on Sunday. 13.6.10, p16.

[2499] Harvey, K. 'So Many Families So Many Women'. Sunday Mail. 6.6.10, p35.

[2500] Dolan, A. 'Mother knifed girl of 3 and dissolved her body in acid'. Daily Mail. 27.10.10, p41.

[2501] 'Cops smash cop-out row'. News Of The World. 28.3.10, p41.

[2502] Tozer, J. 'Been shot at? Don't walk in that park then, police tell a vicar's wife'. Daily Mail. 11.10.07, p44.

[2503] 'Pensioner who lost respect for politics'. Daily Mail. 9.4.07, p9.

[2504] Poulter, S. 'Credit card fraud victims are told: Don't bother police'. Daily Mail. 30.3.07, p6.

[2505] Wright, S. 'Huntley confesses'. Daily Mail. 23.4.07, p5.

[2506] Whitehead, T., Hartley, S. 'Only One In 40 Police Respond To Calls'. Daily Express. 30.3.07, pp1,5.

[2507] Porter, R. 'Betrayal of the Superwoman of Suburbia'. Daily Mail. 28.10.10, pp70,71.

[2508] McEachran, J. 'Policeman Who Turned A Blind Eye To Crime'. Daily Record. 31.3.07, p17.

[2509] Scott, M. 'Cops Ignored My Plea To Find Sons'. Sunday Mail. 7.12.08, p31.

[2510] Levy, A. 'Caught a thief? We are too busy to help'. Daily Mail. 5.11.08, p32.

[2511] Latchem, T. 'Burglar Off!'. News Of The World. 9.11.08, p31.

[2512] Roberts, K. 'Mockery of justice'. The Sunday Post. 25.9.11, p9.

[2513] 'Police ignored suicide mother'. Daily Express. 18.9.09, p10.

[2514] Fiona's mother is denied decent payout'. Sunday Express. 23.10.11, p34.

[2515] Doughty, s. 'Crimes against the disabled ignored by police and courts'. Daily Mail. 12.9.11, p16.

[2516] Malone, C. 'Sisters suffer Fiona's hell as cops sit back'. News Of The World. 10.1.10, p25.

[2517] Panton, L. 'Idiot Cop Left Me In Rape Hell'. News Of The World. 25.10.09, p78.

[2518] Dudley Edwards, R. 'Are we mad? Every organ of the state now seems intent on protecting those who would destroy us'. Daily Mail. 3.9.08, p12.

[2519] Hickley, M. 'Police may be told to ignore indecency in public places'. Daily Mail. 17.10.08, p36.

[2520] Slack, J., Kelly, T. 'How cannabis creates killers'. Daily Mail. 4.10.06, p20.

[2521] Sergeant, H. 'Inside Britain's Police Farce'. Daily Mail. 11.2.08, p26.

[2522] Andrews, E. 'Judge blames police for 'vigilante culture' '. Daily Mail. 27.5.09, p19.

[2523] Hyde, P. 'Police must make streets safe for our young people'. Daily Express. 9.9.08, p30.

[2524] Gill, C., Ballinger, L. 'Police blunders that left another serial rapist free to attack 20 more terrified women on their doorstep'. Daily Mail. 27.3.09, p20

[2525] Clements, J. 'Sorry We Left Sex Fiend On Loose'. Daily Record. 27.3.09, p12.

[2526] 'Police errors 'left football coach rapist free to attack'. Daily Mail. 5.6.09, p35.

[2527] Twomey, J. 'Blundering police fail to stop rapist's 4-year terror spree'. Daily Express. 27.3.09, p21.

[2528] Twomey, J. 'Error that left taxi rapist free to strike'. Daily Express. 14..3.09, p7.

[2529] Gill, C., Gysin, C. '500 victims'. Daily Mail. 14.3.09, pp1,4.

[2530] 'Facebook Cops Rap'. News Of The World. 18.10.09, p11.

[2531] Horne, B. 'Cop Search Finds Bail Jump Crook … AT Home'. Daily Record. 5.11.09, p24.

[2532] Morgan, T., Moyes, S. 'Cop from dud probe on Savile inquiry'. The Sun. 13.1.13, p18.

[2533] Brown, M. 'Sorry Sir, you can't report a crime, we're playing poker'. Daily Express. 25.2.09, p32.

[2534] Whitehead, T., Fagge, N. 'Outcry as more police shut shop'. Daily Express. 10.2.07, p7.

[2535] Duffill, G. 'Beaten up by a neighbour and police did … nothing'. The Sunday Times. 14.10.07, p7.

[2536] Coney, J. 'Victims lose out as police stop chasing card crooks'. Daily Mail. 1.7.09, p45.

[2537] Brown, M. 'I traced credit card fraudster … but the police did NOTHING'. Daily Express. 17.12.07, p33.

[2538] Slack, J. 'Don't expect us to attend every 999 call'. Daily Mail. 5.2.10, p37.

[2539] Tozer, J. 'Four-hour wait for police after rape threat'. Daily Mail. 13.8.09, p5.

[2540] Edge, S. 'How police chiefs have abandoned us to the nightmare of yob rule'. Daily Express. 3.5.05, p12.

[2541] Jeeves, P. 'Snubbed: Son's alert over the British Fritzl'. Daily Express. 20.12.08, p36.

[2542] Leake, C. 'Police 'ran away' from jeering Gaza demonstrators'. The Mail on Sunday. 1.2.09, p5.

[2543] Smith, A. 'Cops Left Kidnap Nurse Tied Up In Car Boot'. Daily Record. 29.1.09, pp1,5.

[2544] Little, A. 'Outcry As Police Let Off 4,256 Criminals'. Daily Express. 11.9.09, pp1,4.

[2545] Lakhani, N. 'Calls for inquiry as GMC 'runs out of time' in GP probe'. The Independent On Sunday. 23.8.09.

[2546] Whitehead, T. 'We are failing victims of rape says police boss'. Daily Express. 5.3.08, p15.

REFERENCES

[2547] 'Underage sex plea by cops'. Daily Record. 7.1.08, p2.

[2548] Currie, G. 'Mysterious case of the missing pigeon'. Daily Mail. 8.2.13, p9.

[2549] Littlejohn, R. 'Thank you for calling 999. Our business hours are 9-5'. Daily Mail. 7.3.08, p17.

[2550] Riches, C. 'Police drove by as couple seized yobs'. Daily Express. 7.3.08, p19.

[2551] Constable, N. 'How hunting ban is flouted'. Sunday Express. 23.12.07, p35.

[2552] Alexander, A. Daily Mail. 16.11.07, p18.

[2553] Slack, J. '60pc of serious offenders let off with a caution'. Daily Mail. 24.12.07, p10.

[2554] Dixon, C. 'Officer banned over dead dogs'. Daily Express. 13.10.11, p25.

[2555] Dawar, A. 'Foreign rapists missed by police'. Daily Express. 28.2.12, p4.

[2556] BBC1. 26.10.11.

[2557] Flanagan, P. 'Burgled tycoon's fury at police for CCTV 'bungle' '. Daily Express. 18.10.11.

[2558] Eccles, L. 'Force refuse to climb a 15ft ladder in case they get hurt'. Daily Mail. 14.10.11, p26.

[2559] Slack, J. 'More police doesn't mean less crime, claims minister'. Daily Mail. 22.11.10, p4.

[2560] Ferrari, N. Sunday Express. 17.10.10, p29

[2561] Garavellie, D. 'Touchline ban for bigotry'. Scotland on Sunday. 13.3.11, p19.

[2562] Archibald, B. 'Cops: Too Many Bigots To Jail'. Sunday Mail. 6.3.11, p10.

[2563] Paddick, B. 'Real reason police failed to stop the student riot'. The Mail on Sunday. 14.11.10, pp12,13.

[2564] Moss, V. 'Top Police Jobs Go As Cuts Bite'. Sunday Mirror. 3.4.11, p32.

[2565] Hull, M. 'Police chief's 'cut red tape' plea'. Daily Express. 13.9.07, p2.

[2566] Brooks, R. 'Nick Ross hits at policing methods'. The Sunday Times. 24.6.07, p21.

[2567] Booker, C. 'Police pick which laws must be obeyed'. The Sunday Telegraph. 6.11.11, p33.

[2568] 'New Law's Empty Threat Of Five Years Behind Bars'. Daily Mail. 31.10.11, p6.

[2569] Dugan, E., Bloodworth, J. 'Homophobia exacts a chilling price as hate crimes climb'. The Independent on Sunday. 23.10.11, p20.

[2570] Gardham, M. 'D.I.Y. Justice'. Daily Record. 2.11.11, p6.

[2571] Millar, J. 'Riots warning over huge fall in police numbers'. The Sunday Post. 13.11.11, p2.

[2572] Mason, G. The Official History Of The Metropolitan Police. Carlton. 2004, p66.

[2573] Ramdani, N. 'Police put the phone down on my complaint over Twitter racial abuse'. The Observer. 20.11.11, p36.

[2574] Hale, B. 'My nightmare, by the tycoon cleared of rape'. Daily Mail. 20.6.03, p5.

[2575] Brookes, T. 'Policeman left free to batter wife for 17 years'. Daily Express. 29.4.08, p29.

[2576] Corbin, J. 'Is this Britain's first white honour killing victim?'. Daily Mail. 17.3.12, p37.

[2577] Herbert, D. 'Child Porn Fiend Runs Website For Mums And Babies'. Sunday Mirror. 7.4.13, p25.

[2578] 'Cop Out'. Sunday Post. 25.9.11. p1.

[2579] Craven, N.. Myers, R. 'Brady victim family's fury over 'police bungling' as mother dies'. The Mail on Sunday. 19.8.12, pp1,6.

[2580] Mills, R. 'Police left a child sex-fiend free to rape boy'. Daily Express. 8.4.13, p24.

[2581] Hamilton, N. 'Flat-footed arrest is a police farce'. Sunday Express. 23.11.08, p31.

[2582] Widdecombe, A. 'Society Encourages Girls To Live Out Foolish Fantasies'. Daily Express. 26.9.12, p13.

[2583] 'Let-off for metal thief who claimed: It's legal back home in Poland'. Daily Express. 27.7.12, p7.

[2584] Bayliss, M. 'Killers Behind Bars'. Channel 5. 5.4.13, p51.

[2585] Tait, G. 'Cops Return 'Fraud' Tycoon's Seized Gear'. The Sun. 28.10.12, p19.

[2586] Doyle, J. 'Police rebuked for ignoring complaints'. Daily Mail. 24.10.12, p8.

[2587] Brown, A. 'Scots cop complaints on the up'. Daily Record. 8.10.12, p9.

[2588] Doyle, J. 'Police rebuked for ignoring complaints'. Daily Mail. 24.10.12, p8.

[2589] Mendick, R., Copping, J. 'Savile: the police blunders'. The Sunday Telegraph. 14.10.12, pp1,6.

[2590] Doward, J., Townsend, M., O'Neill, G. 'Seven police forces may face inquiry over Savile'. The Observer. 4.11.12, p18.

[2591] Townsend, M. 'Call a policeman? I wouldn't bother says a majority of the Met'. The Observer. 4.11.12, p23.

[2592] Whyte, S. 'Beat cop CS sprays himself'. Daily Record. 16.11.12, p13.

[2593] Dawar, A. 'Police 'failed' mum shot by her violent husband'. Daily Express. 29.11.12, p36.

[2594] Littlejohn, R. Daily Mail. 5.2.08, p15.

[2595] Grant, G. 'Yet another fine mess'. Daily Mail. 26.12.12, p11.

[2596] Daily Record. 10.8.12, p18.

[2597] Townsend, M. 'Police 'ignored' fears that Russian mob killed witness who fled to Britain'. The Observer. 2.12.12, p12.

[2598] Blackley, M. 'Record rise in police officers 'hiding the reality of backroom bobbies'. Daily Mail. 5.12.12, p10.

[2599] Mintowt-Czyz, L. 'Car thief is caught in the act but still not charged'. Daily Mail. 24.7.02, p31.

[2600] Gallagher, I. 'Sherbet dip boy, 11, thrown into cells for having a 'bag of drugs' '. The Mail on Sunday. 27.5.01, p15.

[2601] Daily Mail. 19.8.03, p31.

[2602] Tozer, J. 'PC shuns race attack case to go and watch motorbikes'. Daily Mail. 10.4.03, p26.

[2603] Brooke, C. '999 Storm'. Daily Mail. 18.8.03, pp1,2.

[2604] Rafferty, S. 'One CID Officer Polices Capital'. Sunday Mail. 27.4.03, p4.

[2605] Mason, G. 'Why you can never find a policeman when you need one'. Daily Express. 26.2.02, p17.

[2606] 'Police give up fight to catch the illegals'. Daily Mail. 23.5.03, p7.

[2607] 'Theft? Cop response in a week'. Daily Express. 24.5.03, p31.

[2608] Taylor, B. 'Speeding 'obsession' '. Daily Mail. 11.8.03, p19.

[2609] 'Speeding let-off over flaw in sign'. Daily Mail. 13.8.03, p10.

[2610] Taylor, B., Wright, S. Daily Mail. 6.3.02, p15.

[2611] Brooke, C. 'The Shaming of Justice'. Daily Mail. 23.1.03, pp1,2.

[2612] Greenhill, S. '£25m bill as judge kicks out drugs case after five years'. Daily Mail. 29.7.03, p8.

[2613] 'Why two dizzy cops rang 999'. Daily Express. 3.6.02, p31.

[2614] Smith, M. 'Now the police refuse to take action against hit-and-run motorists'. The Mail on Sunday. 5.5.02, p18.

[2615] C4 News. 8.1.13.

[2616] Hepburn, I. 'Shamed Anna cop in hiding'. The Sun. 15.1.01, p13.

[2617] Harrison, R. 'Great train bunglers'. Sunday Mirror. 6.1.13, pp34,35.

[2618] 'Could a US police chief cut crime in Britain?'. Daily Mail. 29.1.13, p51.

[2619] Edge, S. 'Hounded To Death By Neighbours From Hell'. Daily Express. 28.1.13, p21.

[2620] Palmer, A. 'Give criminals more time inside, and policemen less'. The Sunday Telegraph. 13.7.08, p25.

[2621] Doughty, S. 'Red tape that lets criminals go free'. Daily Mail. 1.8.08, p2.

[2622] 'Police missed 3 chances to stop paedophile DJ'. Daily Mail. 12.1.13, p9.

[2623] Buchanan, K. 'Four police forces join red-tape rebels'. Sunday Express. 1.6.08, p2.

[2624] Littlejohn, R. Daily Mail. 30.6.09, p17.

[2625] Chapman, J. 'Police Will Abandon The Beat'. Daily Express. 2.7.08, p1.

[2626] Ungoed-Thomas, J. et al. 'Police abandon 850,000 crime inquiries a year'. The Sunday Times. 5.5.13, pp1,4.

[2627] Philips, A. '18 Cops Investigated Fred's Bust Window'. Daily Record. 19.5.09, p2.

[2628] Nelson, N. 'Cops And Droppers'. The People. 18.1.09, p2.

[2629] Slack, J., Hickley, M. '500,000 violent criminals escaped justice last year'. Daily Mail. 1.9.09.

[2630] Silvester, N., Douglas, L. 'Case that shamed Scotland'. Sunday Mail. 2.6.13, p2.

[2631] Lyons, J. 'Cop-Out'. The News of the World. 27.2.11, p20.

[2632] 'A criminal statistic'. Leader. Daily Mail. 1.9.09, p12.

[2633] Harrison, I. 'New DNA breakthrough snubbed by Scots police'. The Sunday Post. 1.8.10, p13.

[2634] Jones, D. 'Nemesis For The Serial Killers'. Daily Mail. 26.1.08, p47.

[2635] Whitehead, T. 'Minor Crimes Shelved'. Daily Express. 15.10.08, p15.

[2636] Della-Ragione, J. 'I will bring these rapists to justice'. Daily Express. 3.11.11, p34.

[2637] Leach, B., Fagan, J. 'Police failing to investigate 1.5m crimes each year'. The Sunday Telegraph. 22.11.09, p6.

[2638] Slack, J. 'Police failing to clear up three out of four crimes'. Daily Mail. 16.7.10, p18.

[2639] Brown, M. '75% of most serious crimes never solved'. Daily Express. 22.10.10, p2.

[2640] Slack, J. 'Police Ignore 4 In 10 Crimes'. Daily Mail. 23.12.08, p1.

[2641] Beckett, R. 'Thugs will not fear tougher sentences when they'll never be convicted'. Daily Express. 9.1.03, p13.

[2642] 'Cop fridge full of DNA'. The People. 17.1.10, p19.

[2643] Riches, C. 'Solve every crime? No, we're not like The Bill says top police officer'. Daily Express. 22.9.10, p5.

[2644] Ungoed-Thomas, J., Prentice, H. 'Police 'screen out' half of crime'. The Sunday Times. 30.9.07, p20.

[2645] Lyons, J. 'Copper Bottom'. News Of The World. 30.12.07, p27.

[2646] Swik, J. 'Lockerbie verdict shouldn't have been reached'. The Sunday Post. 13.1.08, p41.

[2647] Brady, B. 'Families of murder victims deplore loss of 'cold case' unit'. The Independent On Sunday. 23.10.11, p28.

[2648] Littlejohn, R. 'Mind How You Go Awards 2011'. Daily Mail. 1.3.11, p17.

[2649] 'Cops are burgled'. News Of The World. 13.6.10, p43.

[2650] Crooks, L. 'Scooby's Boys Guard Cop Shop'. Sunday Mail. 20.3.11, p41.

[2651] Findlay, R. 'Gerbil Murder Leak Probe Cop Resigns'. Sunday Mail. 13.3.11, pp12,13.

[2652] Giannangell, M. 'Scandal of computers lost by MOD'. Sunday Express. 6.3.11, p12.

[2653] Burns, J. 'Secrets of Nike Nokia'. Daily Record. 18.5.09.

[2654] Duguid, E. 'Deadly weapons stolen from MoD'. The Sunday Post. 4.3.12, p35.

[2655] ' 'Tip' PC Cleared'. Daily Record. 18.11.10, p25.

[2656] Beatson, J. 'Cop worker spied on records'. Daily Record. 3.3.12, p29.

[2657] Bayer, K. 'Love-Triangle WPC: I Leaked Secret Cop Info To My Lover'. Daily Record. 5.2.11, p19.

[2658] Hackers 'graffiti' cop site'. Daily Record. 26.8.09, p27.

[2659] 'Police probes'. Daily Record. 10.9.11, p29.

[2660] Hamilton, T. 'Gail V Cops'. Daily Record. 20.1.11, p5.

[2661] McGiven, M. 'Cops Apologise Over Abuse Video Blunder'. Daily Record. 2.2.11, p5.

[2662] 'Thieves hit cop shop'. Daily Record. 6.4.11, p12.

[2663] Wright, S. 'Chauffeur who betrayed Queen gets a £30,000 job with police'. Daily Mail. 5.2.11, p59.

[2664] Wright, S. 'Security alert as police guard takes convict into the Palace'. Daily Mail. 8.8.09, p19.

[2665] Fairburn, R. 'Horror Police Files Put In Car Boot Sale'. Daily Record. 13.9.06, p9.

[2666] Whitehead, T. 'Police told: Use crooks to keep public informed'. Daily Express. 15.10.08, p15.

[2667] Flanagan, P. 'Police ask crooks for ... anti-burglary advice'. Daily Express. 24.7.09, p6.

[2668] 'Caught in cops' net'. Daily Record. 6.5.11, p34.

[2669] Taher, A. 'TV's pet detective quit police after helping his friend spy on ex-lover'. The Mail on Sunday. 10.4.11, p25.

[2670] Leake, C. 'Stolen: Top secret entry codes to 73 police stations'. The Mail on Sunday. 6.1.08, p17.

[2671] 'Cop Cuffs Nicked'. News Of The World. 9.5.10, p33.

[2672] Copping, J. 'Allo, allo ... what haven't we here?'. The Sunday Telegraph. 3.2.08, pp1,2.

[2673] 'Evenin' haul?'. Daily Record. 15.9.11, p23.

[2674] Taylor, D. 'Cops Freed Knifeman Before Sex Attack'. Sunday Mail. 28.5.06, p40.

[2675] Whitehead, T., Parkinson, D. 'Burglaries are not an emergency, say police'. Daily Express. 16.5.06, p4.

[2676] Wright, S. 'Thief has the bank details of 15,000 policemen'. Daily Mail. 22.11.06, p4.

[2677] Bugler, T. 'Walkie Talkie Properly'. Daily Record. 18.6.07, p22.

[2678] Hitchens, P. 'More Blitz spirit please ...'. The Mail on Sunday. 8.7.07, p29.

[2679] Hughes, D., Wright, S. 'PC Magoo's oversight'. Daily Mail. 6.12.04, p8.

[2680] Jeeves, P. 'Blunder by police frees sex menace'. Daily Express. 17.1.08, p39.

[2681] Chapman, J. Daily Express. 23.6.10, p41.

[2682] Hagger, A. 'Firm gets £4m for guarding police stations'. Daily Express. 22.6.10, p4.

[2683] McComb, R. 'From sat-navs to a patrol car, cheeky thieves plunder police'. Daily Express. 7.4.08, p20.

[2684] Ferguson, J. 'Cops Race To Fix £3m Crime Computer Glitch'. Daily Record. 15.9.09, p6.

[2685] 'Gord cops on camera'. Daily Record. 10.11.10, p25.

[2686] 'Why did police miss explosive?'. Daily Mail. 1.11.10, p5.

[2687] Gill, C. 'Just 225 police to hold back 50,0000'. Daily Mail. 11.11.10, p9.

[2688] 'Anger over G20 police bankers' braces joke'. The Mail on Sunday. 22.3.09, p13.

[2689] Parkinson, D. 'Day I was sent a police machine gun in the post'. Daily Express. 11.12.08, p17.

[2690] Chapman, J. 'I'm too scared to go shopping on my own admits police chief'. Daily Express. 15.1.10, p19.

[2691] Twomey, J, 'Police adviser on terror is on Interpol wanted list'. Daily Express. 16.12.08, p10.

[2692] Jarvis, D. 'Deepcut: Fury over police's Army briefings'. Sunday Express. 21.6.09, p23.

[2693] Slack, J. 'Why the terror raid fiasco could haunt ministers for years'. Daily Mail. 23.4.09, p21.

[2694] 'Cop cars' cover is blown'. Daily Record. 18.5.09, p19.

[2695] Coles, B. 'Our Private Police'. Daily Express. 21.11.09, p41.

[2696] Pragnell, C. 'Cops' Baby Blunder'. News Of The World. 20.12.09, p12.

[2697] 'Blair police guard loses gun'. Daily Express. 5.9.08, p18.

[2698] Silvester, N. 'Chiefs patrol Bebo bobbies'. Sunday Mail. 22.2.09, p30.

[2699] Baker, M. 'Blood Money Scum'. The People. 8.3.09, p8.

[2700] Bryce, T. 'Robbers outwit red-faced cops'. The Sunday Post. 26.4.09, p5.

[2701] 'Bell burglars hit bobbies'. The Sunday Post. 8.1.12, p4.

[2702] Alexander, D. 'Nicking In Nick'. Sunday Mail. 8.1.12, p23.

[2703] Penrose, J. '4 Laptops Swiped At Top Nick'. Sunday Mirror. 6.7.08, p18.

[2704] Panton, L. 'G20 cop vetting blunder'. News Of The World. 5.7.09, p23.

[2705] Macintyre, D. 'British justice didn't protect us from thugs'. Sunday Express. 7.11.10, p13.

[2706] McDonald, C. 'Keystone Cops'. Daily Record. 4.2.10, p7.

[2707] 'Cop file on train'. News Of The World. 2.8.09, p18.

[2708] Palmer, R. 'Bea's bodyguard left red-faced as her car is stolen'. Daily Express. 9.1.09, p36.

[2709] 'It's Key-stone Cops'. The People. 22.3.09, p23.

[2710] Hickley, M. 'Crime maps of the UK'. Daily Mail. 7.1.09, p12.

[2711] Silvester, N. 'Note Guilty'. Sunday Mail. 1.2.09, p33.

[2712] Young, F. 'Killer doc got job as police surgeon'. Sunday Mail. 14.11.10, p27.

[2713] Leppard, D. 'Terror suspect may have worked for police'. The Sunday Times. 10.10.10, p2.

[2714] Reynolds, M. 'Policewoman checked out secret files to find a lover'. Daily Express. 5.11.10, p30.

[2715] C4 News. 9.1.12.

[2716] 'Police clamped as they keep watch on Queen'. Daily Express. 28.5.11, p7.

[2717] 'Fraudster jailed for £500m con'. Daily Express. 9.5.11, p4.

[2718] Millar, J. 'Rising crimewave plagues Parliament'. The Sunday Post. 19.6.11, p4.

[2719] Fielding, J., Buchanan, K. 'Fears They Stole State Secrets'. Sunday Express. 18.3.12, pp1,5.

[2720] Moss, V. 'Three Miliband Break-Ins This Year'. Sunday Mirror. 25.3.12, p6.

[2721] Henderson, E. Sunday Express. 5.6.11, p21.

[2722] Lewis, J. 'Met catches 2000 officers accessing police database for own use'. The Sunday Telegraph. 21.8.11, p7.

[2723] Henderson, E. 'Police 'hacking into secret files' '. Sunday Express. 31.7.11, p22.

[2724] Scott, M. 'Ferris Cop In The Dock'. Sunday Mail. 12.6.11, pp1,9.

[2725] Myers, R. 'Eight resign over illegal searches of police files'. The Mail on Sunday. 15.1.12, p22.

[2726] Leppard, D. Oakeshott, I. 'Tories attack Met over 'disgusting' Plebgate leak'. The Sunday Times. 31.3.13, p1.

[2727] Collins, D. 'Police Losing It'. The People. 9.5.10, p27.

[2728] Gumm, C. 'Lost data reaches epidemic levels'. The Sunday Post. 29.8.10, p29

[2729] 'Cops: We lost £113K'. The Sun. 30.3.12, p29.

[2730] Camber, R., Bains, I., Fernandez, C. 'Cyber terrorist targeted CIA from Essex bungalow'. Daily Mail. 22.6.11, p5.

[2731] Kerr, J. 'Cops Hit By 'Cyber Attack' '. 19.6.11, p22.

[2732] Lewis, J. 'Hackers targeted police watchdog's sensitive emails'. The Sunday Telegraph. 7.8.11, p7.

[2733] Riches, C. 'Outcry over £500 bribes to stop police taking sickies'. Daily Express. 6.8.07, p15

[2734] Evans, D. 'That's Not Very PC, Constable'. News Of The World. 23.9.07, p41

[2735] 'Police woman gave details to car gang'. Daily Telegraph. 18.6.10.

[2736] Nugent, H. The Times. 10.2.07, p3.

[2737] 'Policeman On Paedo I.D. Charge'. Daily Record. 25.7.07 p10.

[2738] Millbank, J. 'Thieves steal vital police data from detective's home'. The Mail on Sunday. 28.8.11, p18.

[2739] 'Murdoch not the only victim of crime?'. The Sunday Telegraph. 4.9.11. p11.

[2740] Howarth, M. 'Rankin: Top Cop Helped Me Spy On Police'. Sunday Mail. 16.10.11, p40.

[2741] Slack, J. 'Illegal migrants cleared for security guard jobs'. Daily Mail. 12.11.07, p19.

[2742] BBC1 News. 8.2.12.

[2743] Scott, M. 'Shooting Down To The Shops'. Sunday Mail. 22.6.08, p8.

[2744] 'Cop held in drugs and cash swoop'. Sunday Mail. 12.2.12, p24.

[2745] Phillips, M. 'One lost top secret file is embarrassing. But two in a week?' Daily Mail. 16.6.08, p12.

[2746] Riches, C. 'Thieves net a £50,000 haul in from police'. Daily Express. 27.5.08, p17.

[2747] 'Airport security lapse before Queen's visit'. Daily Express. 14.3.08, p4.

[2748] Camber, R. 'Teenage hacker 'listens in on anti-terror unit officers' '. Daily Mail. 13.4.12, p2.

[2749] Littlejohn, R. Daily Mail. 5.2.08, p15.

[2750] Dolan, A., Eccles, L., Walker, K. 'Where have my parents gone?'. Daily Mail. 12.6.12, p9.

[2751] BBC1 News. 11.6.12.

[2752] Daily Express. 9.6.12, p10.

[2753] Dolan, A. 'How could a sex offender be allowed to mingle with royals on Jubilee barge?'. Daily Mail. 8.6.12, p30.

[2754] Faulkner, K., Harding, E. 'Moment an intruder shocked the inquiry'. Daily Mail. 29.5.12, p9.

[2755] Greenwood, C., Evans, R. 'Olympic Security Farce As Wembley Keys Lost'. Daily Mail. 30.7.12, pp1,2.

[2756] Bhatia, S., Owens, N., Hamilton, M. 'Bomb Is Smuggled Into Olympic Park'. Sunday Mirror. 8.1.12, p6.

[2757] Wright, S. 'Al Qaeda Fanatics Working In Police'. Daily Mail. 7.7.07, pp1,8.

[2758] Reynolds, M. 'Security officers were 'asleep at the wheel' '. Daily Express. 24.8.12, p3.

[2759] 'A police farce no one wants'. Leader. Sunday Mirror. 4.3.12, p14.

[2760] 'Look who's copped it'. Sunday Mirror. 30.12.12, p24.

[2761] Lea, M. 'Lax security 'lets criminals into UK' '. Daily Mail. 17.7.08, p19.

[2762] Shipman, T. 'Home Office turns into a hotbed of hi-tech theft'. Sunday Express. 27.1.02, p24.

[2763] Creasy, R. 'Police lost my car ... now I'm £172,000 out of pocket'. The Mail on Sunday. 14.7.02, p32.

[2764] Walker, A. 'Cop Shop Robbed'. Daily Record. 7.6.03, p29.

[2765] Leppard, D. 'Machinegun squads to keep Britain safe'. The Sunday Times. 31.10.10, p2.

[2766] Matheson, J. 'Hero cop praised after fire'. Daily Record. 5.3.13, p18.

[2767] Harris, P., Fagge, N. 'Abseil police save G8 activist from 60ft. fall'. Daily Mail. 12.6.13, p9

[2768] Pickard, M., Dixon, C. 'Police car 'fetching takeaway meal' kills mother on a stroll'. Daily Express. 26.8.08, p5.

[2769] 'Lethal pursuits'. The Sunday Times. 5.4.09, p12.

[2770] Narain, J. Daily Mail. 17.4.09, p35.

[2771] 'Police car chase death toll rises to 40 in a year'. Daily Mail. 17.7.09, p21.

[2772] 'On This Day'. Daily Express. 27.1.10, p2.

[2773] 'Driver killed by policeman on 104mph training run'. Daily Express. 17.9.08, p17.

[2774] BBC TV News. 7.10.08.

[2775] 'Teen badly hurt in cop chase crash'. Sunday Mirror. 25.9.11, p19.

[2776] Classic FM News. 2.10.11.

[2777] Narain, J. 'Boy killed in police chase after stealing his father's car'. Daily Mail. 17.4.09, p35.

[2778] Broster, P. ' Girl killed after getting a lift in police chase car'. Daily Express. 18.11.08, p20.

[2779] Groves, J. 'How police could call a halt to car chases'. Sunday Express. 8.2.09, p15.

[2780] Blacklock, M. '2 killed in police chase'. Daily Express. 28.8.09, p29.

[2781] Narain, J. 'Three die in police car chase horror'. Daily Mail. 17.11.08, p5.

[2782] Quigley, R. 'Jailed, the police worker whose 4x4 river crossing cost a teenager her life'. Daily Mail. 24.8.10, p31.

[2783] 'Couple killed by 'psychotic driver who thought his car had special powers like the Starship Enterprise'. Daily Mail. 25.8.10.

[2784] 'Prison for 94mph PC who killed schoolgirl'. Daily Mail. 2.5.09, p55.

[2785] Dawar, A., Brown, M. 'How speed cameras have cost up to 10,000 lives'. Daily Express. 13.5.09, p7.

[2786] Kelly, J. 'Pizza Row Boys Die As Cops Chase 'stolen' Car'. Sunday Mirror. 29.6.09, p28.

[2787] '999 crash death'. The Sunday Times. 21.6.09.

[2788] 'Crash rap for police van driver'. Daily Record. 20.6.09, p27.

[2789] 'Cop chase road crash'. Daily Record. 27.2.10, p6.

[2790] Schlesinger, F. 'How four policemen in two 150mph patrol cars pursued Natalie Pinkham … just for TV'. Daily Mail. 15.4.09, p27.

[2791] Hagger, A. 'Police chase killer is jailed for 8 years'. Daily Express. 4.6.10, p26.

[2792] 'Policeman ran over mum after using mobile'. Daily Mail. 3.5.10, p24.

[2793] Holland, L. 'Two killed in police car smash'. Sunday Express. 6.6.10, p36.

[2794] 'Man dies after motorway police chase'. Sunday Mail. 30.5.10, p19.

[2795] Classic FM News. 18.7.10.

[2796] 'Cop escaper dies'. Daily Record. 11.8.10, p11.

[2797] Twomey, J. '6 years for the ton-up PC who killed a mum'. Daily Express. 27.10.09, p17.

[2798] Dolan, A. 'Police worker caused crash that killed son and his best friend'. Daily Mail. 22.8.08, p27.

[2799] Maynard, G. 'A free taxi home for tired police'. Daily Express. 9.10.08, p30.

[2800] 'Freed, drunk police chief who killed four in crash'. Daily Mail. 16.12.09, p39.

[2801] Blacklock. M. 'Bride-to-be died after crash with 999 police driver'. Daily Express. 29.9.09, p18.

[2802] 'Ex-cop rap for wife kill'. Sunday Mirror. 10.1.10, p29.

[2803] BBC1 News. 16.3.11.

[2804] 'Killer cop keeps job'. Sunday Mirror. 26.6.11, p29.

[2805] O'Neill, Cordelia. 'Tribute to cops who died on duty'. Sunday Mail. 3.4.11, p10.

[2806] Delgado, M. 'Motorcyclist in death skid after spotting speed trap'. The Mail on Sunday. 10.4.11, p18.

[2807] Dolan, A. 'Girl, 17, dies after police chase driver over seat belt'. Daily Mail. 19.1.10, p25.

[2808] 'Sheriff in clear over 'Gestapo' cop jibe'. Daily Record. 16.6.11, p7.

[2809] Caroe, L. 'Road deaths fall to a record low as speed cameras turned off'. Daily Express. 1.7.11, p34.

[2810] Nugent, H. The Times. 10.2.07, p3.

[2811] McDonald, C. 'Hit And Done'. Daily Record. 21.10.11, p21.

[2812] 'Two Hit By Cop Car'. Daily Record. 15.11.11, p10.

[2813] Devine, A. 'Crash Cop On Drink Drive Rap'. Daily Record. 26.11.11, p33.

[2814] 'Sliced in half … so how did anyone get out alive?' Daily Mail. 9.1.12, p24.

[2815] 'Man is killed by police car'. Daily Record. 9.1.12, p22.

[2816] Burns, J. 'Cop Car Wrecked In Blizzard:… But Officers Get Out Alive'. Daily Record. 27.1.12, p6.

[2817] ' 'Killer' 999 car probe'. The Sun. 7.4.12, p6.

[2818] Stow, N. 'Fan Who Fled Cops Loses Fight For Life'. Daily Record. 15.8.12, p7.

[2819] 'Jury out on 999 death crash cop'. Daily Record. 31.10.12, p19.

[2820] Sergeant, H. 'A middle-class mother among the hardies'. Daily Mail. 23.6.12, p17.

[2821] Laville, S. 'Strikers free police'. The Daily Telegraph. 28.11.02, p4.

[2822] Daily Mail. 26.7.03, p23.

[2823] BBC1 News. 6.1.13.

2824 Dixon, C. 'Girl,13, is killed in police chase'. Daily Express. 8.1.13, p2.

2825 Hamilton, N. 'Police have lost the plot'. Sunday Express. 25.5.08, p29.

2826 Dawar, A. 'Let off ... police girl on phone in death crash'. Daily Express. 14.2.13, p29.

2827 Hills, M. 'Police girl on phone in death crash quits'. Daily Express. 18.2.13, p13.

2828 Riches, C. 'Man, 83, crushed to death by a runaway police van'. Daily Express. 3.6.13, p23.

2829 'WPC killed in 'stolen car' crash'. Sunday Express. 10.2.13, p9.

2830 Leader. 'Shooting rioters is not the answer'. Daily Mail. 21.12.11, p14.

2831 Leake, C., Delgodo, M., Arbuthnott, G. 'Police have shot dead 33 people since 1995'. The Mail on Sunday.
26.9.10, p25.

2832 Carpenter, J. 'Armed to the teeth'. Daily Express. 2.10.10, p36.

2833 'Hush money?'. Daily Mail leader. 1.8.05, p12.

2834 Leppard, D. 'Police call for dumdum bullets'. The Sunday Times. 22.8.10, p7.

2835 'Met gun teams get 'deadlier bullets' '. Daily Mail. 12.5.11, p34.

2836 Learder. 'Terror's friends among the police'. Daily Mail. 7.7.07, p14.

2837 Wright, S. Ellicott, C. 'Gun-wielding pensioner shot dead by police'. Daily Mail. 9.5.09, p29.

2838 Harrison, D., Johnston, T. 'Village in shock over 'lost soul' killed by police'. The Sunday Telegraph.
10.5.09, p10.

2839 Silvester, N. 'Gun Cops' victim 'Was Not Armed' '. Sunday Mail. 17.5.09, p7.

2840 Russell, A. 'PC playing a 'villain' shot dead in training'. Daily Express. 16.2.10, p34.

2841 'Widow's fury over shot PC'. Daily Express. 8.3.12, p31.

2842 Narain, J., Andrews, E. 'Policeman is killed in 'live bullet training blunder' '. Daily Mail. 10.6.08, p21.

2843 Camber, R. 'Was siege lawyer's gun even loaded?'. Daily Mail. 28.9.10, p13.

2844 Pilditch, D. 'No one will shoot you'. Daily Express. 23.9.10, p17.

2845 Pilditch, D. 'Siege lawyer begged police to see wife in gun stand-off'. Daily Express. 22.9.10.

2846 Camber, R. 'Siege coroner Lets return to common sense policing'. Daily Mail. 9.10.10, p16.

2847 Camber, R. 'The crucial flashpoints missed by siege chief'. Daily Mail. 7.10.10, p20.

2848 Twomey, J., Pilditch, D. 'Gun PC 'used song titles' in his evidence at inquest'. Daily Express. 3.11.10, p11.

2849 Gillard, M. 'Gun cams to film shootouts'. The Sunday Times. 6.11.11, p12.

2850 Findlay, R. 'Sickening'. Sunday Mail. 4.11.01, p15.

2851 Thompson, R. et al. 'Police knew Brazilian was 'not bomb risk' '. The Observer. 21.8.05, p1.

2852 Twomey, J. 'Police 'gave no warning before shooting dead de Menezes' '. Daily Express. 31.10.08, p13.

2853 Slack, J. 'He was no risk, says sister of barrister shot dead by police'. Daily Mail. 11.9.08, p21.

2854 Ballinger, L. 'Marksman's view of de Menezes shooting'. Daily Mail. 8.10.08, p4.

2855 Pilditch, D. 'How terror police fired 7 bullets into an innocent man'. Daily Express. 23.9.08, p10.

2856 Wiley, J. 'Gun Law'. News of The World. 8.2.09, p49.

2857 Andrews, E. 'Depressed loner shot dead by the police at cathedral 'was carrying replica gun' '. Daily Mail.
2.12.08, p29.

2858 Rose, D. 'The Memory Stick Killing'. The Mail on Sunday. 28.4.13, pp38,39.

2859 Leader. 'Police must hold their fire'. Daily Express. 18.7.01, p12.

2860 Greenhill, S. 'Whistleblower exposes a quango's cynical lie about child labour in an English onion field'.
Daily Mail. 25.6.11, p10.

2861 Giannangeli, M. 'Be ready to shoot to kill, Scotland Yard tells its marksmen'. Sunday Express. 24.4.11, p4.

2862 Greenwood, C. 'Police chiefs say: Rioting arsonists could be shot'. Daily Mail. 21.12.11.

2863 Catchpole, C. Sunday People. 31.3.13, p27.

2864 Winnett, R. 'SAS trainers denounce 'gung ho' armed police'. The Sunday Times. 18.9.05, p5.

2865 Gallagher, I., Farrell, S. 'We were beaten up ... it's carnage out there'. The Mail on Sunday. 7.8.11, p5.

2866 Little, A. 'Shot man's family to sue police'. Daily Express. 9.8.11, p7.

2867 Greenwood, C. 'Fiancée of 'gangster' whose death led to riots is let off drugs charge with caution'. Daily
Mail. 17.12.11, p22.

2868 Porter, H. 'It's the police who have a gun problem'. The Observer. 4.3.07, p33.

2869 'Crofter's rage at gun-toting nuclear police'. Daily Express. 11.7.13, p10.

2870 Camber, R. 'Demo police may get plastic bullets'. Daily Mail, 8.11.11, p2.

2871 Brooke, C., Tozer, J., Ellicott, C. 'Police gave killer his six guns back after he denied he was a suicide risk'.
Daily Mail. 4.1.12, p31.

2872 BBC1 News. 2.1.12.

2873 BBC 1 News. 2.1.12.

2874 Bonnici, T. 'Police probe over man who killed himself after attack with a Taser gun'. Daily Express.
21.1.08, p17.

2875 'Man cleared in drug trial fiasco is shot dead by police'. Daily Mail. 5.3.12, p25.

[2876] Rose, D. 'If you have a family member shot by police it feels like the cover-up starts from day one'. The Mail on Sunday. 1.4.12, p19.

[2877] Rose, D. 'Officer who shot suspect may face murder charge'. The Mail on Sunday. 8.4.12, p20.

[2878] McBeth, J. 'A Saviour Or A Torturer?'. Daily Mail. 27.4.13, p44.

[2879] Hayes, S. 'The Biggest Gang In Britain'. 2013, p34.

[2880] Townsend, M. 'Child killings reflect 'crisis in masculinity''. The Observer. 11.8.13, p12.

[2881] Chapman, J. 'Lies of policeman who left a drunk to die in the cold'. Daily Express. 6.10.10, p16.

[2882] 'Drugs dad choked by his heroin'. Daily Record. 22.11.11, p4.

[2883] 'Cop 'told no one in blaze car' '. Daily Record. 25.2.11, p5.

[2884] Sims, P. 'Police held us back from death blaze as pregnant mother begged for help'. Daily Mail. 30.3.09, p9.

[2885] Tozer, J. 'Driven to his grave by years of bullying'. Daily Mail. 8.12.11, p20.

[2886] Allen, V. 'Wild driver who killed 7 was reported a week ago'. Daily Mail. 10.3.08, p19.

[2887] BBC1 News.

[2888] Broster, P. 'How brave dad died to save me from gang'. Daily Express. 8.3.08, p37.

[2889] Tozer, J. 'Where were the police?'. Daily Mail. 6.3.08, p5.

[2890] BBC1 News. 4.3.13.

[2891] Widdecombe, A. 'Now even the police cite health and safety'. Daily Express. 1.4.09, p13.

[2892] Venning, A. 'A Very Suave Psycho Killer'. Daily Mail. 21.3.13, p15.

[2893] Camber, R., Sims, P. 'Moat's family pay for second post-mortem'. Daily Mail. 21.7.10, p8.

[2894] Jeeves, P. 'I saw my brother publicly executed on TV'. Daily Express. 12.7.10, p4.

[2895] Jones, D., Sims, P. 'Did police kill Moat?'. Daily Mail. 17.7.10, p11.

[2896] Brooke, C. 'We were like sitting ducks'. Daily Mail. 12.7.10, p4.

[2897] O'Hare, P. 'Tasers handed to cops'. Daily Record. 21.4.10, p19.

[2898] BBC News. 16.8.11.

[2899] ITV News. 7.9.11.

[2900] BBC News. 24.8.11.

[2901] Greenwood, C. 'Every police car 'could have a Taser'. Daily Mail. 23.11.11, p31.

[2902] Narain, J. 'Another man is dead after being shot by a police Taser'. Daily Mail, 25.8.11, p33.

[2903] 'Driver dies after being Tasered by police'. The Mail on Sunday. 20.1.13, p34.

[2904] Reid, S., Greenwood, C. 'Tasers on a blood-smeared street. And the question: Why weren't they enough to halt a knifeman who then had to be shot by police?' Daily Mail. 23.2.12, p13.

[2905] Greenwood, C. 'Did police shoot this man four times then Taser him?'. Daily Mail. 3.4.12.

[2906] Narain, J., Parveen, N. 'Shot dead by police Taser after argument in street'. Daily Mail. 12.7.13, p11.

[2907] Greenwood, C., Salkeld, L. 'Man burns to death in police Taser fireball'. Daily Mail. 27.4.13, p15.

[2908] Greenwood, C. 'Police chiefs want the same assault rifles used by our soldiers'. Daily Mail. 2.7.02.

[2909] Townend, D. 'Taser man engulfed by fireball'. Daily Express. 22.4.13, p5.

[2910] Brady, B. 'Catalogue of failings by police in abuse cases'. The Independent on Sunday. 11.8.13, p10.

[2911] 'Police rules that left man to die on motorway'. Daily Mail. 30.1.10, p35.

[2912] Brooks, T. 'Police freed man to kill ex-lover and their child'. Daily Express. 4.6.10, p23.

[2913] BBC News. 4.10.10.

[2914] Wright, S. 'Bungling Met refuses to compensate Rachael's son: Payouts and the Police'. Daily Mail. 9.10.10, p15.

[2915] Clark, R. 'Why should have-a-go heroes do the work of our law enforcers?'. Daily Express. 3.9.08, p12.

[2916] Widdecombe, A. 'True heroes always rip up the rule book'. Daily Express. 30.3.11, p13.

[2917] Greenhill, S. et al. 'Police 'called on killer mother before horror' '. Daily Mail. 17.4.13, p5.

[2918] Martin, A. 'Wife killed by her mentally ill husband had told police days earlier she feared for her life'. Daily Mail. 28.12.07, p19.

[2919] Doughty, S. 'How police and care staff failed the baby killed by his father'. Daily Mail. 1.3.08, p49.

[2920] Greenhill, S. 'The night police let strangling suspect go'. Daily Mail. 17.1.08, p10.

[2921] 'Police let strangler suspect go twice'. Daily Mail. 30.1.08, p20.

[2922] Tozer, J. 'A desperate plea for help from 'honour killing' girl'. Daily Mail. 10.1.08, p41.

[2923] Brady, B. 'Catalogue of failings by police in abuse cases'. The Independent on Sunday. 11.8.13, p10.

[2924] Scott, M. 'Cop Link To Dock Death'. Sunday Mail. 10.5.09, p7.

[2925] Alderson, A. 'Police files link officers to teacher's death'. The Sunday Telegraph. 25.4.10, p1.

[2926] Williams, D. 'Under fire, they waded in wielding truncheons'. Daily Mail. 28.4.10, p18.

[2927] Twomey, J. 'Killer PC who butchered wife goes free after just five years'. Daily Express. 30.12.09, p23.

[2928] Wright, S. 'The Met says sorry over Rachel Nickell blunders'. Daily Mail. 4.6.10, p13.

[2929] Bracchi, P., Shears, T. 'PC Predator'. Daily Mail. 14.7.07, p56.

[2930] Wright, S. 'Rachel Nickell Boyfriend Sues'. Daily Mail. 28.9.09, pp1,6.

[2931] Twomey, J. 'We could have saved Rachel admit police'. Daily Express. 19.12.08, pp4,5.

2932 Twomey, J. 'Murdered Rachel's partner to win £½m over police bungles'. Daily Express. 4.6.10, p19.

2933 Hardy, F. 'Failed by the police. Failed by Facebook. A family torn apart by the cunning of an online predator'. Daily Mail. 25.10.10, pp26-28.

2934 'Police payout to Pilkingtons'. Daily Mail. 10.3.12, p52.

2935 Greenhill, S. 'Police chief refuses to say sorry over hounded mum'. Daily Mail. 30.9.09, p6.

2936 Greenhill, S. 'Johnson attack on police over bullied mother and daughter'. Daily Mail. 28.9.09, p12.

2937 McGivern, M. 'Vigilante Killer: I've No Regrets'. Daily Record. 21.8.09, p37.

2938 Stute, M. '999 crews had tea as crash man lay dead'. Daily Express. 1.8.09, p15.

2939 Twomey, J. 'Yard left Potter actor's killer to roam streets'. Daily Express. 5.3.09, p17.

2940 Clements, J. 'Unmitigated Evil'. Daily Record. 5.6.09, p27.

2941 Chapman, J. 'Mum warned police of stalker … hours later she was dead'. Daily Express. 9.5.09, p9.

2942 Scott, M. 'If Police Had Done Their Job, Iain Would Be Alive And Paul Would Be Free'. Sunday Mail. 14.7.13, p29.

2943 Jeeves, P. 'Vicious thug given a final warning carried out ferocious murder'. Daily Express. 6.5.09, p5.

2944 Maynard, G. 'Police scorned 999 call of stab horror mother'. Daily Express. 23.1.10, p45.

2945 Tozer, J. 'I'm dying … my boyfriend stabbed me'. Daily Mail. 14.7.09, p5.

2946 Riches, C. 'Husband was left free to kill by prosecutors'. Daily Express. 7.3.09, p19.

2947 Blacklock, M. 'Ban speed cameras say road safety campaigners'. Daily Express. 9.8.08, p9.

2948 Wright, S. 'Severed hand victim twice called 999 after rows with husband'. Daily Mail. 20.11.09, p42.

2949 Levy, A. 'How did he slip through the net?'. Daily Mail. 15.12.09, p31.

2950 Dolan, A., Couzeus, G. 'Mother killed by ex-boyfriend was pregnant'. Daily Mail. 4.6.10, p41.

2951 Street-Porter, J. 'A 999 call is a call for help. Pity the police don't know'. The Independent on Sunday. 31.1.10, p21.

2952 Brooke, C., Kisiel, R. 'Father trying to calm gang of youths is killed by a brick.'. Daily Mail. 12.5.09, p5.

2953 Littlejohn, R. Daily Mail. 2.5.06, p15.

2954 White, S. 'How police failed my murdered son'. Daily Express. 25.8.06, p13.

2955 Narain, J. 'How police failed the family in arson horror'. Daily Mail. 5.4.07, p41.

2956 Brooks, T. 'Police totally failed murdered mother'. Daily Express. 19.12.09, p7.

2957 'The Countless Missed Chances To Save Alex'. Daily Mail. 3.2.11, p25.

2958 Dawar, A. 'Police 'let death threats dad kill his wife and son''. Daily Express. 25.11.08, p31.

2959 Twomey, J. 'Fury as psychotic killer walks free after 4 years'. Daily Express. 22.4.09, p27.

2960 Jarvis, D., Kanduhla, T. 'Police failed others over yob menace'. Sunday Express. 20.9.09, p12.

2961 Reynolds, M. 'Stab death blunders of police'. Daily Express. 27.7.10, p27.

2962 'Warning on child killings'. News Of The World. 6.6.10, p27.

2963 Wright, S., Cohen, T. 'Suicide woman's warning to police'. Daily Mail. 2.10.10, p15.

2964 Chapman, J., Twomey, J. 'Suicide pact woman was stalker victim'. 2.10.10, p4.

2965 Barton, F., Wright, S. 'Murdered girl's five cries for help'. Daily Mail. 12.6.07, p18.

2966 Mills, J. 'Rapist freed early from jail murdered his fiancée and her carer in stabbing frenzy'. Daily Mail. 15.6.07, p35.

2967 BBC1 News 16.11.10.

2968 Ellicott, C., Kisiel, R. ' 'Monster' murders his wife and two children before killing himself'. Daily Mail. 14.2.11, p5.

2969 Archibald, B. 'Police Chiefs Rapped Over 90 min Ned Siege. Ten 999 calls ignored'. Daily Record. 14.2.11, p23.

2970 C4 News. 21.3.10.

2971 Twomey, J. 'Stalker kills mum after police snub her pleas for help'. Daily Express. 4.3.11, p22.

2972 Dolan, A. 'Police duo ignored plea for help as mother was murdered'. Daily Mail. 11.3.11, p33.

2973 Kolirin, L. 'Reggae star Smiley dies in police raid'. Daily Express. 16.3.11.

2974 'Drug raid death man was dealer'. Sunday Mail. 8.5.11, p10.

2975 Camber, R., Fagge, N. 'Father 'killed his children then rang to tell ex-wife' '. Daily Mail. 15.2.11, p36.

2976 Kolirin, L. ' 'Abusive monster' killed partner and two children'. Daily Express. 14.2.11, p4.

2977 Gill, A. 'Police are the key to ending the deaths'. The Independent on Sunday. 10.2.08, p9.

2978 Stote, M. 'Police made errors over couple killed in revenge attack'. Daily Express. 23.2.08, p25.

2979 Jeeves, P. 'Police failed murdered mum who made 11 calls'. Daily Express. 19.10.11, p31.

2980 Rao, N. 'Body left in 2ft-deep pond for 30 minutes while police discuss health and safety'. Daily Express. 12.3.11, p39.

2981 Dixon, C. 'Strangled Red Cross girl 'told police she was being harassed' '. Daily Express. 30.5.11, p21.

2982 Chapman, J. 'Police ignored 999 plea over gun dad'. Daily Express. 8.6.11, p25.

2983 Riches, C. 'Fury over 'policemen' who weren't trained to save drowning boy'. Daily Express. 21.9.07, p17.

2984 'Murdered child was failed by 14 agencies'. Daily Mail. 24.6.11, p25.

[2985] Samuel, M. 'Our nasty little secret has been exposed at last'. Daily Mail. 12.8.11, p18.

[2986] France, A. The Mail on Sunday. 3.11.02, p44.

[2987] O'Hare, P. 'We Should Have Saved Them From Monster'. Daily Record. 12.11.11, pp1,4.

[2988] Street-Porter, J. 'Women must look after themselves, not rely on the law'. The Independent on Sunday. 30.10.11, p21.

[2989] Rowley, E. 'Police admit: We're failing stalker victims'. Daily Express. 28.9.09, p31.

[2990] The BBC. Panorama. 31.10.11.

[2991] Faulkner, K. 'Failed asylum seeker thrown out three times sneaks back to UK to murder his ex-lover'. Daily Mail. 4.11.11, p5.

[2992] Wark, P. 'Why Did Nobody Try To Stop My Brother From Killing His Family?'. The Sunday Telegraph. 27.11.11, p27.

[2993] Whitehead, T. 'Police: We let rapists go free'. Daily Express. 3.4.07, p8.

[2994] Harrison, I. 'Father's anger over police refusal to help'. The Sunday Post. 11.12.11, p7.

[2995] Koster, O. 'Harvey Nicks murderer was labelled a 'low risk' by WPC'. Daily Mail. 5.1.07, p33.

[2996] Toolis, K. 'How Can Any Father Kill His Child?'. Daily Mail. 4.1.10, p51.

[2997] Riches, C. '3 killed on 'oil slick' road the police said was safe'. Daily Express. 27.7.09, p11.

[2998] Riches, C. 'Killer's 'human rights' meant we could not stop him, claim police'. Daily Express. 7.10.09, p43.

[2999] Twomey, J., Giannangeli, M. 'Two detectives fired for bungles over father shot dead by a hoody'. Daily Express. 6.10.07, p12.

[3000] Street-Porter, J. 'When I was stalked, I got help. Where were the police for Arsema?' The Independent on Sunday. 8.6.08, p21.

[3001] Jeeves, P. 'Blunders that freed thug to kill his wife'. Daily Express. 14.5.08, p17.

[3002] Twomey, J. 'Murdered mother had begged police five times for help'. Daily Express. 31.10.12, p33.

[3003] Scott, M. 'They Left Him Free To Kill'. Sunday Mail. 15.7.12, p8.

[3004] Daily Express. 23.11.12, p14.

[3005] Pettifor, T. 'The Red Mist Cop'. Daily Record. 20.7.12, p7.

[3006] Camber, R. 'I could have shot him, says PC in G20 death'. Daily Mail. 4.7.12, p21.

[3007] Greenwood, C. 'Met apology and payout over G20 riots death'. Daily Mail. 6.8.13, p12.

[3008] Dolan, A. 'Everyone to blame but no one punished'. Daily Mail. 18.9.13, p17.

[3009] Dolan, A. 'Man knifed baby son and ex-lover to death 5 days after police set him free'. Daily Mail. 13.9.13, p29.

[3010] Emsley, C. 'The Great British Bobby'. Quercus. London. 2009.

[3011] C4 News. 23.5.09.

[3012] Lakhani, N. 'Family hit out at IPCC over death in custody'. The Independent on Sunday. 4.1.09, p12.

[3013] Channel 4 News and ITV News. 1.8.12.

[3014] Gill, C., Slack, J. 'Left to die by racist police'. Daily Mail. 28.3.06, p8.

[3015] 'Cops held over death'. Daily Record. 23.3.13, p28.

[3016] Observer. 9.1.00.

[3017] Channel 4 News. 2.7.13.

[3018] Currie, G. 'Cop Lied About Death In Cells'. Daily Record. 26.7.03, p27.

[3019] Channel 4 News. 7.10.13.

[3020] Channel 4. 9.10.13.

[3021] Tozer, J. 'PC is arrested over his police fiancée's death'. Daily Mail. 8.5.09, p29.

[3022] Evans, D. 'Kill Riddle Cop's Nights With Ex'. News of the World. 10.5.09, p22.

[3023] Tozer, J. 'PC killed fiancée with a hammer on eve of wedding'. Daily Mail. 24.11.09, p11.

[3024] Kolirin, L. "Wife was 'pushed off cliff' ". Daily Express. 14.4.10, p19.

[3025] Sales, D. '33 years for police veteran who threw his bride off a cliff'. Daily Express. 4.9.10.

[3026] Davidson, L. 'Murder Inc.'. Daily Record. 4.8.09, pp1,4.

[3027] Fraser, Donald M. 'The Book of Glasgow Murders'. pp127-133.

[3028] Jarvis, D. 'Nilsen's vile prison boast'. Sunday Express. 21.9.08, p31.

[3029] Leafe, D. 'The full stop that trapped a killer'. Daily Mail. 3.7.09, p28

[3030] Bonnici, T. 'Let off £200,000 bill ... the lawyer brother who stood bail for killer policeman'. Daily Express. 19.2.08, p20.

[3031] Martin, A. 'Husband 'killed by wife' who rang 1471 to trace his lover'. Daily Mail. 14.6.11, p13.

[3032] Rousewell, D. ' 'No divorce ... only way out is death'. Death By Daddy'. The People. 12.6.11, .

[3033] Worden, T. 'Jack the Ripper revealed as a Scotland Yard officer'. Daily Express. 6.8.11, p8.

[3034] Twomey, J. 'Ex-detective held after woman PC found dead'. Daily Express. 18.10.11, p15.

[3035] Meridian News. 30.4.12.

[3036] BBC1 News. 9.12.11.

3037 Dolan, A., Greenwood, C., Ellicott, C. 'Police inspector made 'cheating' wife watch as he launched his deadly attack on their children'. Daily Mail. 10.2.12, p11.

3038 Wilson, L. 'Return To The House of Horrors'. Daily Express. 19.8.10, p13.

3039 Chambers, S. 'Police Officer held 'after trying to kill lesbian lover'. Sunday Express. 9.4.00, p34.

3040 Fernandez, C., Stevens, J. 'Stabbed to death in her hair salon'. Daily Mail. 1.5.12, p5.

3041 McGivern, M. 'Police Beasts Plot to Beat The System'. Daily Record. 25.4.09, p15.

3042 'Met denial over sexual misconduct accusations'. The Sunday Post. 11.1.09, p3.

3043 Lee, A. 'How Did Hot Toddy Get Away With It For So Long?'. Daily Express. 29.11.08, p23.

3044 Hill, A. 'Your job is the key to a happy marriage'. The Observer. 6.12.09, p25.

3045 Lee, A. Daily Express. 29.11.08, p23.

3046 Baines, A., Acton M. 'Knickers Off'. News of the World. 29.3.09, p33.

3047 'Detective loses custody fight for beloved spaniel'. Daily Mail. 5.11.11, p59.

3048 Boffey, D. et al. 'Raoul Moat probe chief left wife for IPCC colleague'. The Mail on Sunday. 25.7.10, p19.

3049 Tozer, J. 'PC ignored 999 calls as he met lover for trysts'. Daily Mail. 3.7.10, p24.

3050 Murray, J. 'Did Claudia have a secret police lover?'. Sunday Express. 28.3.10, p49.

3051 Burns, J. 'No Cover-Up Over Inspector Undies'. Daily Record. 30.3.10, p25.

3052 Lavery, C. 'Inspector Probed Over Bust-up At Police Academy'. Sunday Mail. 2.8.09, p65.

3053 Goddard, D. 'Cheating Copper Nicks His Missus'. News Of The World. 26.10.03, p31.

3054 'Unfair Cop, Guv'. Sunday Mail. 7.11.10, p23.

3055 Archibald, B. 'Stalker Cop Pestered Me For Months'. Daily Record. 8.2.11, p21.

3056 Taylor, D. 'Love cheat cop's £600K romance'. Sunday Mail. 16.9.07, p19.

3057 Pendlebury, R., Wright, S. 'Police chief Tarique Ghaffur's first wife reveals the unedifying past of the man accusing the Met of bigotry'. Daily Mail. 5.7.08, pp12,13.

3058 Penrose, J. 'Top Cop Caught On Cam Kissing Woman'. Sunday Mirror. 7.11.10, p33.

3059 Lee, A. 'PC Casanova's double love life'. Daily Express. 5.12.01, p23.

3060 Silvester, N. 'Cheers I Moyra wins £½ m from top cop who walked out on her for best friend'. Sunday Mail. 10.6.07, p7.

3061 ' 'Bonking Bishop' loses unfair sacking claiming over 3 affairs'. Daily Express. 22.2.10, p9.

3062 Evans, D. ' 'Hot Toddy' HID Kinky Sex Kit'. News Of The World. 3.8.08 p25.

3063 Riches, C. 'Widow of cheating police chief says: I forgive him'. Daily Express. 11.2.09, p23.

3064 Bracchi, P., Craven, N. 'How many more lovers did he have?'. Daily Mail. 15.3.08, pp12,13.

3065 Bracchi, P., Craven, N. 'Last Secret Of A Ladies' (Police) Man'. Daily Mail. 5.4.08, p11.

3066 'Cop car sex sessions rap'. Daily Record. 26.1.08, p39.

3067 Borland, S. 'PC faces jail for his sex sessions on the late shift'. Daily Mail. 8.8.08, p33.

3068 Penrose, J. 'Married Cop Stalked His Shoplifter Lover'. Sunday Mirror. 12.10.08, p29.

3069 Gill, C. 'Police chief used Yard's air miles to fund flights for family'. Daily Mail. 27.9.10, p28.

3070 Kay, R. 'Yates of the Yard gets his woman'. Daily Mail. 23.1.12, p31.

3071 'Sarah cop in sex claims'. Sunday Mail. 8.3.09, p31.

3072 Levy, A. 'WPCs £2m claim over 'sex pest' colleagues'. Daily Mail. 8.1.09, p21.

3073 'Boozy Cop's Sick Pic Joke Shocks WPC'. News of the World. 26.4.09, p29.

3074 Greenhill, S., Wright, S., Gysin, C. 'Sunshine Squad'. Daily Mail. 24.10.09, p3.

3075 Bletchley, R. 'Cop jailed over vice girl fling'. The People. 13.9.09, p40.

3076 Gall, C. 'Dirty Ditty Cop Faces A New Sex Pest Probe'. Daily Record. 7.7.09, p9.

3077 'Photo rap cop freed'. Daily Record. 9.2.11, p17.

3078 Leake, C. 'Swearing rap for top police officer'. 13.2.11, p48.

3079 Perthen, A. 'Chief Constable Sara, her police lover and their banquets at Windsor Castle'. The Mail on Sunday. 6.2.11, p38

3080 Kolirin, L. 'Revealed ... bodyguard PC who had affair with Johnson's wife'. Daily Express. 31.1.11, p25.

3081 Camber, R. 'Bodyguard sacked for affair with MP's wife'. Daily Mail. 23.11.11, p27.

3082 'Love-cheat police chief cleared of fire attack'. Daily Express. 2.2.11, p17.

3083 Pickard, M. 'Swingers' club link to 'firebug police love rat' '. Daily Express. 24.1.11, p30.

3084 Alexander, D. 'Internal Affair'. Sunday Mail. 23.1.11, p8.

3085 'Police chief faces probe over 'bawdy' remarks'. The Mail on Sunday. 27.2.11, p40.

3086 Wright, S., Gysin, C. 'Police chief accused of making lewd remarks found hanged'. Daily Mail. 23.3.11, p5.

3087 Constable, N. 'Police worker 'set to get £10K deal' in sex harassment case.' The Mail on Sunday. 23.10.11, p20.

3088 Butler, A. 'The Filth!'. Sunday Mirror. 19.9.10, p15.

3089 'Cop used inside info for affairs'. Daily Record. 13.8.11, p9.

3090 Lewis, J. 'Police chief tipped for the Met who fathered child by mistress ran up £83,000 expenses'. The Mail on Sunday. 2.12.07, p5.

REFERENCES

3091 Jeeves, P. 'On-duty cop had sex in back of police van'. Daily Express. 13.4.12, p34.

3092 Jeeves, P. 'On-duty PC who had sex in police van faces prison'. Daily Express. 25.4.13, p23.

3093 Penrose, J. 'Cop Lays Down His Gun For Sex'. Sunday Mirror. 13.11.11, p20.

3094 Hull, L. 'PC who bedded 5 lovers while he worked'. Daily Mail. 20.1.12, p31.

3095 'Sex-mad PC wants job back'. Daily Express. 20.1.12, p39.

3096 Sims, P. 'Rathband, the 7/7 survivor and feud beyond the grave'. Daily Mail. 13.3.12, p31.

3097 'Police chief paid for affair on expenses'. Daily Express. 7.5.08, p17.

3098 Chapman, A., Lewis, T. 'Love-cheat police chief'. The Mail on Sunday. 5.10.03, p40.

3099 Brooks, R. 'PC was my first gay lover, says Paddick'. The Sunday Times. 18.11.07, p8.

3100 Levy, G., Wright, S. 'The Camp Commander'. Daily Mail. 21.2.02, p21.

3101 Officer 'A'. 'The Crime Factory'. Mainstream Publishing. 2012.

3102 Greenwood, C. 'Jailed elite gun PC who left post for trysts with secret lover'. Daily Mail. 19.3.13, p25.

3103 Thomson, C. 'Fake That'. Daily Record. 28.11.09, p39.

3104 Smith, S. 'Cop Quizzed After Wife Steals £90K'. Sunday Mail. 2.8.09, p22.

3105 'Cop wife caged for swindle'. Daily Record. 5.8.09, p9.

3106 Mathieson, J. 'Dirty Doctor Left My Life In Tatters'. Daily Record. 18.1.10, p27.

3107 Twomey, J. 'Disgraced ... swinger GP who had sex in surgery with a policeman's wife'. Daily Express. 7.1.10, p30.

3108 Twomey, J. 'Jail for the mum who cried rape because PC lover ignored her texts'. Daily Express. 12.6.10, p8.

3109 Atkinson, J., Evans, D. 'I love Lotto rapist'. News of the World. 5.10.08, p41.

3110 'Murdered PC: Husband arrested on drug offences'. The Mail on Sunday. 10.12.06, p23.

3111 Boyle, S., Boulton, J. 'Family At War'. The People. 26.4.09, pp20,21.

3112 Levy, A. 'Vandal granny from Neighbourhood Watch'. Daily Mail. 8.12.10, p21.

3113 Steward, S. 'Top cop and wife in clear over row'. Sunday Mail. 17.4.11, p15.

3114 McGivern, M. 'Battered WPC Gets Boot From The Force'. Daily Record. 13.6.11, p7.

3115 Beatson, J. 'Cop on trial after 'snog' with known criminal'. Daily Record. 11.1.12, p6.

3116 'Cop cleared on date with wanted man'. Daily Record. 9.2.12, p25.

3117 Long, C. 'Yes, but Bo Derek couldn't throw a javelin'. The Sunday Times. 11.12.11, p5.

3118 Davies, B. 'The Wife Who Won't Let Go'. Daily Mail. 31.3.12, pp12,13

3119 McDonald, C. '3 Cops In The Same Court On Same Day'. Daily Record. 11.2.10, p9.

3120 Caven, B. 'Policeman's sex assault on girl at Kirk outing to cinema'. Daily Mail. 5.4.13, p31.

3121 Married PC sent texts to teen'. Daily Record. 6.6.13, p29.

3122 Maynard, G. 'Jailed ... PC who let women off driving offences for sex'. Daily Express. 16.6.10, p37.

3123 Roberts, E. 'Copper Forced Woman Into Sex Act'. Daily Sport. 3.3.09, p7.

3124 Camber, R. 'Firearms WPC in sex jibes case wins £575,000'. Daily Mail. 15.6.10, p5.

3125 O'Hare, P. 'Sex Pest Officer Found Hanged'. Daily Record. 28.5.10, p45.

3126 Brown, A. 'Cop in court on rape and sex charges'. Daily Record. 28.5.13, p7.

3127 'Sex pest cop on perv list'. Daily Record. 2.4.10, p19.

3128 'Rapist cop bid for job at Tesco'. Daily Record. 25.7.09, p4.

3129 McGivern, M. 'Police Beasts Plot To Beat The System'. Daily Record. 25.4.09, p15.

3130 Macaskill, G. 'Wife Welcomes Rape Cop Home'. Sunday Mail. 3.8.08, p39.

3131 Findlay, R. 'Masonic Cover-up Claim On Rape Cop'. Sunday Mail. 10.6.01, p15.

3132 ' 'Sex bribe cop' held'. The People. 19.7.09, p25.

3133 Green, N. 'Rape cop's victims denied compensation'. The Sunday Post. 16.10.11, p8.

3134 'Policeman will face rape trial'. Daily Record. 1.6.13, p10.

3135 McCabe, G. 'Cop guilty of date site rape'. Daily Record. 25.9.13, p7.

3136 Salkeld, L. 'Cleared, gun PC caught in tryst with his trousers round his ankles'. Daily Mail. 3.8.13, p21.

3137 Salkeld, L. Daily Mail. 3.8.13, p21.

3138 'High-flying cop's sex rap case is dropped'. Sunday Mail. 31.8.03, p12.

3139 'Cop on rape rap'. Daily Record. 1.2.10, p7.

3140 Mathieson, J. 'Sex Pest Cop Keeps Pension'. Daily Record. 15.4.08, pp1,4,5.

3141 Ferguson, J. 'Cops' Boozy Romp Wrecks Wedding'. Daily Record. 28.8.09, p5.

3142 'Top cop quiz on 'groping' '. Sunday Mirror. 23.11.08, p29.

3143 Chapman, J. 'Detective 'in love triangle' attacked his police mistress'. Daily Express. 4.2.08, p7.

3144 Musson, C. 'Cop Up On Rape Charge'. Daily Record. 14.1.10, p25.

3145 Home, B. 'Sex abuse cop must stay in jail'. Daily Record. 15.6.07, p40.

3146 'Thug copper is forced to quit'. Daily Record. 2.7.11, p4.

3147 Roberts, L., Silvester, N. 'Officer Cleared Of Rape On 999 Call-Out'. Sunday Mail. 3.2.08, p7.

3148 Weldon, V. 'PC Horne Pinched My Bum'. Daily Record. 2.3.09, p27.

3149 Salkeld, L. 'PC accused of raping a handcuffed lap dancer'. Daily Mail. 15.1.09, p32.

3150 Archibald, B 'Besotted Sarge Is Cleared'. Daily Record. 17.3.11, p35.

3151 McIlwraith, G. 'Cop Accused Of Raping Woman As Bride Slept In Next Room'. Daily Record. 2.7.08, p7.

3152 Henderson, E. 'Police force hit by fresh sex scandal'. Sunday Express. 27.3.11, p30.

3153 Findlay, R. 'Sickening'. Sunday Mail. 4.11.01, p15.

3154 Munro, A. 'Speed Cop Is Sacked Over Sex Pest Claim'. Daily Record. 4.4.08, p33.

3155 Reynolds, M. 'How police 'sex pest' forced me to quit job'. Daily Express. 21.2.08, p30.

3156 Levy, A. 'The love-trap PC'. Daily Mail. 9.7.08, p25.

3157 'Sergeant Spanker'. Daily Mail. 30.4.08, p39.

3158 'The Troops Who Shame America'. Daily Mail. 13.1.12, p8.

3159 Scott, M. Sunday Mail. 1.4.12, p10.

3160 'Sex cop gets 2yrs'. The Sun. 9.5.12. p21.

3161 Pyle, M. 'Rapist Was A Police Support Officer'. Reading Post. 18.7.12, pp 1,4.

3162 Twomey, J. 'PC sacked for sexism'. Daily Express. 12.7.94, p15.

3163 'Police officer and former Mr. Gay UK charged with male rape.' http:www.dailymail.co.uk/news/article – 1287680.

3164 Dixon, C. 'Anguish of 'family man' PC outed as a gay sex predator'. Daily Express. 11.6.10, p36.

3165 Brooks, R. 'Sex finished Forster as a writer'. The Sunday Times. 6.6.10, p7.

3166 McDermott, N., Revoir, P. 'BBC host Digby is found dead in flat'. Daily Mail. 2.3.10, p13.

3167 Gloger, D. 'Sister has a son for her gay policeman brother'. Daily Express. 28.7.09, p20.

3168 Pyatt, J. 'Gay cop dads are already married to two other men'. Sun. 30.7.09, p13.

3169 'Top Cop at gay demo'. The People. 14.6.09, p21.

3170 Maynard, G. 'Gay policeman and force call truce on earring'. Daily Express. 16.8.06, p15.

3171 'Sleazy Cop Probe'. Sunday Mail. 17.8.08, p13.

3172 Findlay, R. 'Gay vice shame cop still on force'. Sunday Mail. 27.12.09, p7.

3173 Barrett, D. 'The 1,800 suspended police who keep their pensions'. The Sunday Telegraph. 31.3.13, p13.

3174 'Ex-SAS soldier 'killed gay love' '. Daily Express. 24.0.09, p8.

3175 'Gay PC cleared of rape charge'. Daily Express. 17.6.11, p19.

3176 McGivern, M. 'Lesbian Cop Wins £10K After Boss Calls Her 'Freak' '. Daily Record. 5.4.11, p21.

3177 Scott, D. 'Spurned lesbian lover terrorised her ex partner'. Daily Express. 11.6.13, p11.

3178 Emsley, C. 'The Great British Bobby'. Quercus. London. 2009. p185.

3179 Storrar, K. 'Lesbian Romp At The Old Cock Inn'. Daily Record. 16.2.07, p27.

3180 Daily Express. 19.10.10, p10.

3181 McDonald, C. 'Lesbian Redcap officer 'like a lovelorn teen' '. Daily Record. 3.3.11, p32.

3182 Dixon, C. 'The sex pest policewoman who stalked female tutor'. Daily Express. 5.11.11, p8.

3183 Bentley, P. 'The police woman who 'sexually assaulted 5 colleagues' '. Daily Mail. 10.5.12, p27.

3184 Stevens, J. 'Top crime writer's gay affair with 'smitten' police chief'. Daily Mail. 18.2.13, p11.

3185 Williams-Thomas, M. 'How Safe Is Your Daughter?'. Daily Mail. 22.9.09, p24.

3186 O'Hare, P. 'Cops Bust World's Biggest Paedo Ring'. Daily Record. 17.3.11, p16.

3187 Bayer, K. 'Cop Expert On Child Porn Rap'. Sunday Mail. 7.11.10, p7.

3188 Taylor, B. 'Fifty police among child porn suspects'. Daily Mail. 18.12.02, p13.

3189 Taylor, B. 'Police sergeant hoarded 25,000 child porn images'. Daily Mail. 13.8.03, p17.

3190 Lavery, C., McPherson, L. 'Haunted By Child Sex Fiend Sergeant'. Sunday Mail. 27.7.03, p25.

3191 Napier. A. 'Disgrace To The Uniform'. Gazette. 6.9.10, pp1,2.

3192 'Ex-cop denies abuse'. Daily Record. 8.4.09, p5.

3193 Riley, kW. 'You're Going To Have My Babies'. Daily Record. 18.5.10, p25.

3194 'Officer sex texted teen'. Sunday Mirror. 20.2.11, p27.

3195 'Cop on kid porn'. The People. 2.5.10, p25.

3196 'Top detective bailed on child sex charges'. Daily Express. 31.5.10, p10.

3197 Brooke, C. 'PC on paedophile squad 'groomed' a girl of 13 for sex'. Daily Mail. 22.6.07, p30

3198 Weldon, V. 'Ex-Cop: I'm No Satanic Sex Beast'. Daily Record. 9.6.09, p.18.

3199 Weldon, V,. 'Satan's Copper'. Daily Record. 11.6.09, p27.

3200 'Pervert cop's betrayal of kids'. Daily Record Leader. 5.6.08, p8.

3201 Bale, K. 'Child Unit Cop On Kiddie Porn Charges'. Daily Record. 17.1.08, pp1,7.

3202 Cook. F. 'I blame police sex ring ... '. The Mail on Sunday. 5.6.05, p41.

3203 Core, D. 'Wall of silence'. Daily Mail. 15.9.08, p57.

3204 Atkinson, J. 'Top Cop Dad Nicked Paedos Then Raped Me'. News of the World. 10.8.08, p29.

3205 'Ex-cop is jailed for 'worst' child porn'. Daily Record. 20.2.09, p24.

3206 Coles, J. 'Boast of kid-porn-cop killer'. Sun. 30.1.09, p31.

3207 Dawar, A. 'Ex-PC on child porn charges is stabbed to death'. Daily Express. 10.6.08, p17.

3208 'Abuse claims 'shock' '. Daily Record. 14.8.09, p41.

3209 'Cop on kid sex pic rap'. Sunday Mail. 20.9.09, p32.

3210 Brooks, T. 'PC jailed for attack on girl in patrol car'. Daily Express. 10.1.09, p50.

3211 'Kid Porn Cop Rap'. Daily Record. 23.3.11, p9.

3212 'Child porn cop jailed'. The People. 9.5.10, p23.

3213 'Raped By Fiend In Cop Car'. News of the World. 30.1.11, p33.

3214 Twomey, J. 'PC sacked over risqué texts to arrested girl, 14'. Daily Express. 1.6.11, p26.

3215 ' 'Abuse' cop found dead'. Sunday Mirror. 10.7.11, p38.

3216 McIlwraith, G. 'Babysitter cop Guilty of Raping Girls 36 Yrs Ago'. Daily Record. 2.7.11.

3217 Alexander, S. 'Sergeant had 54,000 child porn pictures'. Sunday Mirror. 12.6.11, p32.

3218 'Paedo cop had 4,000 vile images'. Sunday Mirror. 4.12.11, p31.

3219 BBCTV News. 29.11.10.

3220 Murray, J. 'This bungled trial is such a betrayal'. Daily Mail. 22.8.03, p12.

3221 'PC jailed over sexual relationship with girl'. The Times. 26.7.08, p15.

3222 'Sex call cop set for sack'. Daily Record. 23.12.11, p16.

3223 Beatson, J. 'You brought shame to your family and the force'. Daily Record. 31.1.12, p26.

3224 'Part-time PC raped girl of 15'. Daily Express. 28.1.12, p45.

3225 'Cop Texts To Girl'. The Sun. 29.2.12, p15.

3226 Newsnight. BBC2. 11.4.08.

3227 France, A. 'Paedo scourge is like a disease'. The Sun. 4.4.12, p7.

3228 '14 yrs for perv cop'. The Sun. 5.5.12, p28.

3229 Paterson, B. 'PC Pervert'. Sunday Mail. 27.5.12.

3230 Paterson, B. 'Paedo cop jailed for child porn'. Daily Record. 1.6.12, p23.

3231 'Shame of corporal jailed for child porn'. Daily Mail. 10.10.08, p22.

3232 Littlejohn, R. 'Remake the Sweeney? Don't do it Guv'nor!'. Daily Mail. 6.7.10, p17.

3233 Paditch, D. 'Sex-change police want funding from taxpayers'. Daily Express. 15.8.09, p5.

3234 Hull, L. 'Back on the beat, WPC show used to be a PC'. Daily Mail. 2.8.10, p27.

3235 Silvester, N. 'Sex change Ian swaps Paras for cops'. Sunday Mail. 3.5.09, p21.

3236 'Sailor Steve joins Met as policewoman'. Daily Express. 20.10.03, p4.

3237 Goslett, M. 'Capt Ian is WPC'. The Mail on Sunday. 3.5.09, p29.

3238 Gardham, M. 'I Want To Be First Sex Swap MSP'. Daily Record. 18.11.11, p7.

3239 Horbury, K. 'Sheer madness to pay out over infantile taunts'. Daily Express. 16.6.10, p30.

3240 'Royal officers' played poker on duty and dealt in porn'. Daily Mail. 30.6.09, p31.

3241 Camber, R. 'The thin very blue line'. Daily Mail. 2.1.10, p17

3242 Acton, M. 'From Bobby To Nobby'. News of the World. 17.2.08, p27.

3243 McTague, T. 'PC Kat's arresting new job'. The People. 8.3.09, p18.

3244 Latchem, T. 'Internet Porn Cops Are Fired'. News of the World. 16.11.08, p32.

3245 Smith, D. 'Undercover PC exposes sex bias'. The Observer. 23.4.06, p15.

3246 Camber, R. 'Banned on the beat, the VPPL (that is visible police panty line)'. Daily Mail. 20.8.10, p5.

3247 Rao, N. 'The panty inspectors ...'. Daily Express. 20.8.10, p26.

3248 'Pool cam perv cop is caged'. The Sun. 10.4.09, p23.

3249 'Rape cop victims in lawsuits'. News Of The World. 28.11.10, p23.

3250 'PC on sex charges'. Daily Express. 21.1.10, p5.

3251 McDonald, C. 'Cop Accused Of Sex Attacks On 19 Women'. Daily Record. 5.2.10, p33.

3252 Sims, P. 'Locked up: Rapist PC in five-year reign of fear'. Daily Mail. 25.11.10, p35.

3253 Green, N. 'Police start pay-outs for PC rapist's victims'. The Sunday Post. 15.4.12, p11.

3254 Emsley, C. 'The Great British Bobby'.

3255 Myers, R. 'Sleaze Shame Of Pope Guard'. The People. 21.11.10, p27.

3256 'WPC is one of evil inspector's 38 rape victims'. Sunday Mail. 14.9.08, pp1,14,15.

3257 Paterson, B. 'Sex Pest Party Cop Beats Jail'. Daily Record. 1.12.10, p25.

3258 Green, N. 'Northumbria Police hit by sex attack claim'. The Sunday Post. 5.12.10, p4.

3259 'Flash claim cop returns'. Sunday Mail. 28.11.10, p24.

3260 'Appeal win for text cop'. Daily Record. 14.10.10, p38.

3261 Willey, J. 'The police chief who had sex on duty with a stranger'. Daily Express. 14.8.07, p15.

3262 'Dogger cop betrays all policemen'. The People. 12.8.07, p37.

3263 Gregory, A., Lewis, P. 'Cop: This Will Dog Me For Rest Of My Life'. The People. 12.8.07, pp14,15.

3264 Camber, R., Russell, A. 'Rape squad policeman jailed over affair with a 'victim' '. Daily Mail. 6.8.11, p49.

3265 Chalk, N. 'Armed PC who had sex on duty cleared as gun was in reach'. Daily Express. 13.8.13, p18.

3266 Daily Express. 24.11.11, p14.

3267 Davidson, L. 'Police spies had secret children with activists'. Daily Mail. 21.1.12, p6.

3268 Archibald, B. 'Call-out cop took down my wife's particulars'. Sunday Mail. 26.2.12, p33.

3269 Hicks, B. ''Shocked mum slapped PC Starkie on the face'. The Sunday Post. 15.6.08, p17.

3270 Scott, M. 'Youth Work Cop On Indecency Rap'. Sunday Mail. 13.4.08, p14.

3271 'Sex rap ex-cop in court'. Daily Record. 10.5.08, p23.

3272 'PC drilled peephole to ogle woman in his police station'. Daily Mail. 20.12.07, p39.

3273 Silvester, N. 'Horsed out'. Sunday Mail. 24.2.08, p19.

3274 Hurley, K. 'How political correctness is ruining Britain's police'. Daily Mail. 15.2.12, p14.

3275 Sullivan, M. 'Inspector Coarse'. The Sun. 9.4.12, p23.

3276 Moncur, J. 'Top Cop's Lewd Text'. Daily Record. 12.7.12, pp1,4,5.

3277 Jones, Lesley-Ann. 'Is sordid world of swingers a taboo too far?'. Sunday Express. 8.6.08, p50.

3278 Wright, S. 'The Hi-de-Hi Olympics'. Daily Mail. 25.6.12, p31.

3279 Liddle, R. 'Keep your truncheon off the net, officer'. The Sunday Times. 16.12.12, p21.

3280 Gall, C. 'Assault rap ex-policeman quits charity'. Daily Record. 29.11.12, p29.

3281 McAnally, A. 'Wife Backs PC Cleared Of Sex Rape'. Daily Record. 31.10.12, p14.

3282 'Officer Faces Rap Raps'. Daily Record. 7.11.12.

3283 Byrne, P. 'Paedo MP: This'll kill my mum'. Daily Record. 30.11.12, p30.

3284 Townsend, M. 'Hillsborough police accused of sexually harassing survivor'. The Observer. 18.11.12, p12.

3285 Thornton, P. 'Creepy officer craved sex-swap romps with me'. The Sun. 11.11.12, pp8,9.

3286 Dawar, A. 'Punch-up as lover snares cheating PC at airport'. Daily Express. 4.12.12, p25.

3287 Pyle, M. 'Rapist Was A Police Support Officer'. Reading Post. 18.7.12, p1.

3288 Paterson, B. 'Paedo cop jailed for child porn'. Daily Record. 1.6.12, p23.

3289 Blacklock, M. 'How 'love-cheat' cop was caught in his police car by wife's private eye'. Daily Express. 28.9.02, p35.

3290 Chapman, A., Self, A. 'Was CPS clerk who gave the Soham cop an alibi really his secret lover?' The Mail on Sunday. 7.9.03, p9.

3291 'Porn trial for Soham police pair'. Daily Express. 4.1.03, p2.

3292 Marsh, G. 'PC Rigler 'made girl do sex act on patrol' '. Daily Express. 27.2.03, p16.

3293 Findlay, R. 'Booze theft inspector walks clear'. Sunday Mail. 26.1.03, p16.

3294 Stote, M. 'Panther PC faces jail for sex assaults'. Daily Express. 16.11.01, p24.

3295 Stote, M., Blacklock, M. 'Hello, hello, hello'. Daily Express. 4.9.03, p5.

3296 Marsh, G. 'Top cop in soup over dinner dance scandal'. Daily Express. 10.6.02, p16.

3297 Mitchell, A. 'Inspector Loverat's deceit'. Daily Express. 23.12.00, p20.

3298 McGivern, M. 'Cop Sex Assault With A Baton & Banana'. Daily Record. 11.5.01, p4.

3299 Grant, G. 'Police Call For 'Drink Ban On Wife-Beaters' '. Daily Mail. 6.2.13, p4.

3300 'Cop on wife assault charges'. Sunday Mail. 27.10.02, p15.

3301 Hayes, S. 'The Biggest Gang In Britain'. 2013, p37.

3302 Emsley, C. 'The Great British Bobby'. Quercus. London. 2009.

3303 'Inside The Brotherhood'. Granada TV (Castle Vision). 1989.

3304 Wight, D. 'Masons In The Palace'. News of the World. 23.11.08, p21.

3305 'Inside The Brotherhood'. Granada TV (Castle Vision). 1989.

3306 1.14 of the Independent Longcare Inquiry – First Term of Reference.

3307 Pring, J. 'Silent Victims'. p100.

3308 Dow, B. 'Masons Fitted Up My Son, Says Cop'. Daily Record. 27.6.08, p11.

3309 Moss, S. 'Secrets and ties'. The Guardian. G2. p2.

3310 Lewis. J. 'Police set up Masonic lodge'. The Sunday Telegraph. 21.8.11, p5.

3311 Williams, D. 'Row as jail prints freemasons' book'. Daily Mail. 1.12.00, p31.

3312 Officer 'A'. 'The Crime Factory'. Mainstream Publishing. 2012.

3313 'Police fake it to draw a pension'. Daily Express. 20.4.11, p17.

3314 Emsley, C. 'The Great British Bobby'. Quercus. London. 2009.

3315 Littlejohn, R. 'Don't drink that lager, Guv, it's not worth it'. Daily Mail. 6.1.12, p17.

3316 Davidson, L. 'Boozy Police Inspector Is Rapped For Dozing Off In A Taxi'. Daily Record. 22.12.09, p9.

3317 Weldon, V. ' Drunken Cops Clashed With Club Bouncers'. Daily Record. 20.8.08, p27.

3318 Beatson, J. 'Cursing Cop's Drunken Rant At Cup Match'. Daily Record. 23.5.08, p29.

3319 'Swift light ale cops in probe'. News of the World. 11.11.07, p44.

3320 Met plan to breath test its officers'. The Mail on Sunday. 29.7.07, p37.

3321 'Woman tells of life of abuse in 'lewd and crude' mounted police'. Daily Mail. 17.6.06, p44.

3322 Ogilvy, G. 'Stuporgrass'. Sunday Mail. 24.12.06, p31.

3323 'Nicked at the nick'. News of the World. 29.11.09, p34.

3324 Dunineen, S. 'Cop Binge Probe'. Sunday Mail. 10.6.07, p37.

3325 'Five boozed cops rapped'. The People. 30.11.08, p26.

REFERENCES

3326 'Drunken PC stole Met van'. Daily Express. 31.12.08, p31.

3327 'Police lawyer killed herself and daughter in drink-drive smash'. Daily Mail. 21.11.09, p13.

3328 'Binge cop forced to quit force'. Daily Record. 4.11.09, p27.

3329 Hamey, R. 'WPC Runs Down Her Love Rat Husband'. Sunday Mail. 16.3.08, p19.

3330 Hooper, P. 'Lying drink drive cop is sacked'. The People. 1.8.10, p33.

3331 'WPC sent to jail over drink-drive case lies'. Daily Mail. 25.1.06, p31.

3332 'A Short History of Policing'. pp18,19.

3333 Spencer, B. '118mph. But drunk ex-cop dodges dangerous driving charges'. Daily Record. 12.4.08, p25.

3334 'Breath test cop for chop'. Daily Record. 12.5.11, p7.

3335 Allen, P. 'Thin Blue Line'. Daily Record. 22.4.11, p43.

3336 Hitchens, P. 'The second-rate celebrity dopes'. The Mail on Sunday. 5.6.11, p29.

3337 Houston, B. 'Cop Is Caught Drink Driving While On Duty'. Daily Record. 25.7.07, p10.

3338 Little, A. ' 'Drunk' slur on police chief'. Daily Express. 16.8.07.

3339 Wright, S. 'Officer shops Met chief for being drunk in public'. Daily Mail. 16.8.07, p13.

3340 Camber, R. 'PC loitering within tent'. Daily Mail. 11.11.11, p29.

3341 Beatson, J. 'Cop Drank A Bucketful'. Daily Record. 3.11.07, p17.

3342 Giannangell, M. 'Help for heroes to beat alcoholism'. Sunday Express. 8.1.12, p32.

3343 Daily Express. 9.2.12, p10.

3344 Currie, G. 'Cop Was So Drunk He Couldn't Remember Driving'. Daily Record. 22.1.08, p23.

3345 'Drink rap PC'. Daily Record. 19.4.12, p7.

3346 Officer 'A'. 'The Crime Factory'.Mainstream Publishing. 2012.

3347 Officer 'A'. 'The Crime Factory'. Mainstream Publishing. 2012.

3348 Officer 'A'. 'The Crime Factory'. Mainstream Publishing. 2012.

3349 'PC twice the limit'. The Sun. 4.5.12, p37.

3350 Hardcastle, E. Daily Mail. 8.5.09, p19.

3351 'Drunk cop spared jail'. Daily Record. 14.7.12, p20

3352 'Drunken abuse PC is sacked'. Daily Mail. 16.7.12, p24.

3353 Beatson, J. 'Policeman in court on booze rap'. Daily Record. 26.4.13, p31.

3354 Brooke, C. 'Top traffic cop three times over the B-test limit'. Daily Mail. 21.8.03, p45.

3355 Daily Mail. 9.3.01, p23.

3356 'Ex top cop a drink-driver'. Sunday People. 24.2.13. p29.

3357 Hale, B. 'PC jumps under a train as mistress confronts his wife'. Daily Mail. 17.2.09, p29.

3358 Armstrong, L. 'Wife of 'Bullied' Police Boss who jumped 500ft to his death on first day back at work'. The People. 4.1.09, p16.

3359 Daily Express. 20.9.11, p10.

3360 Dawar, A. 'Robocop, scourge of drug traders, killed by heroin overdose'. Daily Express. 8.8.09, p47.

3361 Boffey, D. 'Snowdon tragedy of PC videoed hitting woman'. The Mail on Sunday. 20.7.08, p36.

3362 Flanagan, P. 'Taser guns chief kills himself after Moat shooting row'. Daily Express. 2.10.10, p25.

3363 Flanagan, P., Twomey, J. 'Camilla's gun guard shoots himself dead'. Daily Express. 11.3.08, p7.

3364 Cochlin, D. 'Camilla guard 'killed himself after wife left over his temper' '. The Mail on Sunday. 16.3.08, p59.

3365 Broster, B., Pilditch, D. 'Suicide police chief's threats to blonde lover'. Daily Express. 14.3.08, p5.

3366 Richardson, L. 'One of Life's Good Guys'. Daily Record. 15.3.08, p25.

3367 Ferguson, J. 'Inspector 'depressed' over job rap'. Daily Record. 4.6.08, p17.

3368 BBC1 News. 13.9.10.

3369 Pilditch, D. 'Inspector aimed to slaughter relatives'. Daily Express. 19.3.08, p10.

3370 'Tragic cop is found dead'. The People. 6.4.08, p21.

3371 'Beat cop commits suicide'. Sunday Mirror. 29.7.07, p37.

3372 Sims. P. 'Police chief who hanged himself over wife's affair'. Daily Mail. 7.2.07 p35.

3373 'PC's shotgun suicide'. Sunday Express. 1.5.11, p32.

3374 Dorman, N. 'Arrested Cop Dead'. Sunday People. 21.4.13, p20.

3375 'PC 'killed himself over job change' '. Daily Express. 27.9.08, p32.

3376 Kerbaj, R. 'Heroic PC dies without a penny for his injuries'. The Sunday Times. 21.7.13, p12.

3377 C4 News. 22.3.11.

3378 Kisiel, R. 'Hanged police chief had feared he was a pariah'. Daily Mail. 12.6.12, p29.

3379 Leader. Sunday Mirror. 30.1.11, p14.

3380 Chapman, J. 'Police chief 'so sad' over dogs that baked to death'. Daily Express. 29.6.11, p5.

3381 Evans, R., Geoghegan, J. 'Suicide pact of cliff car plunge couple'. Daily Mail. 20.8.11, p24.

3382 Brown, L., Sims, P., Stevens, J. 'Moat's final victim'. Daily Mail. 1.3.12, p9.

3383 'Police chief in corruption probe 'leapt to his death' '. Daily Express. 21.3.12, p26.

[3384] Maynard, G. 'Corporal, 30, hanged herself after working 80-your weeks'. Daily Express. 17.3.12, p7.

[3385] BBC1 News. April, 2012.

[3386] Officer 'A'. 'The Crime Factory'. Mainstream Publishing. 2012.

[3387] 'Officer in 'gun suicide' riddle'. Daily Mail. 15.5.12, p24.

[3388] Meridian Tonight. 30.7.12.

[3389] Grant, G., Infante, F. 'Officer's 'suicide' with his police gun'. Daily Mail. 6.11.12, pp1,5.

[3390] Williams, D., Wright, S. Daily Mail. 10.6.02, p25.

[3391] Twomey, J. 'Pregnant Special PC hanged herself in police uniform'. Daily Express. 6.2.13, p9.

[3392] ITV News. 3.3.13.

[3393] Beckford, M. 'Widow of suicide police chief will not go to court for 'speeding points swap' '. The Mail on Sunday. 10.3.13, p8.

[3394] Classic FM. 20.2.13.

[3395] Rayment, S. 'The rising price of combat trauma being paid by servicemen'. The Sunday Telegraph. 17.3.13, p2.

[3396] Camber, R. 'The feigning monarch'. Daily Mail. 28.7.06, p29.

[3397] Sapsted, D. 'WPC cleared of drunken attacks after 'drug plant' '. The Daily Telegraph. 26.4.2000, p15.

[3398] Davidson, L. ' 'Inspector Undies' 9-month Affair With Rookie WPC'. Daily Record. 1.4.11, p7.

[3399] Breezy, S. Daily Mail. 4.11.03, pp40,41.

[3400] Emsley, C. 'The Great British Bobby'. Quercus. London. 2009.

[3401] Hayes, S. 'The Biggest Gang In Britain'. 2013, p170.

[3402] Robertson, P. 'Cop wife choked by hubby, trial told'. Sunday Mail. 14.8.11, p22.

[3403] Silvester, N. 'Every cop to face drug test'. Sunday Mail. 13.4.08, p7.

[3404] Leask, D. 'All rookie cops face drugs tests'. Scotland on Sunday. 21.9.08, p9.

[3405] Robinson, B. 'Police failing to take drug tests'. The Sunday Post. 21.4.13, p43.

[3406] 'Drug romp cops free'. The People. 21.2.10, p33.

[3407] 'A Short History of Policing'. p149.

[3408] Salkeld, L. 'PC helped himself to confiscated cannabis 'to ease work trauma' '. Daily Mail. 5.7.08, p45.

[3409] 'Met plan to breath test its officers'. The Mail on Sunday. 29.7.07, p37.

[3410] Hamilton, J. 'On-duty Cop Accused Of Being High On Cocaine'. Sunday Mail. 16.4.06, p7.

[3411] 'All cops to get random drug tests'. Daily Record, 21.6.09, p37.

[3412] Lay, K. 'Rav's Roid Rage'. News of the World. 22.5.11, p14.

[3413] Saunders, L., Berry, J. 'Sack for the Paddick PC who smoked pot'. The Mail on Sunday. 2.6.02, p37.

[3414] 'Blair arrest PC on drug rap'. Daily Record. 19.1.01, p25.

[3415] Whitehead, T. 'Cost of police on long-term sick leave hits £90m a year'. Daily Express. 24.10.08, p9.

[3416] Silvester, N. 'The Sick Blue Line'. Sunday Mail. 24.8.08, p2.

[3417] MacLeod, M. 'Sicknote Scotland' costs £1bn a year'. Scotland on Sunday. 9.3.08, p11.

[3418] Ellas, R. 'Police to get 'peace rooms' '. Scotland on Sunday. 9.3.08, p11.

[3419] 'Cops on the sick'. Daily Record. 1.12.09, p4.

[3420] Kay, R. 'Archbishop's girl shares sweet tweets'. Daily Mail. 30.4.13, p33.

[3421] Chittenden, M. 'Easy, officer, reach for your stress card'. The Sunday Times. 3.8.08, p5.

[3422] 'Race-row WPC quite after 848 sick days'. Daily Mail. 29.4.11, p42.

[3423] Shields, T. 'The house that mends coppers'. The Independent on Sunday. 31.1.10, p28.

[3424] Stote, M. 'Handler may be let off for police dogs that baked to death in car'. Daily Express. 10.9.09, p9.

[3425] Evans, M. 'Taxpayers foot £10k massage bill for 999 staff'. Daily Express. 1.1.09, p20.

[3426] Young, J. Sunday Express. 19.10.03, p41.

[3427] Jones, G. '£32m bill for police stress'. Sunday Express. 19.9.10, p18.

[3428] Whitehead, T. 'Stressed-out police costing £1m a week'. Daily Express. 7.7.08, p15.

[3429] 'Stressed police get relaxation training'. Daily Mail. 27.8.10, p41.

[3430] Whitehead, T. 'Sicknote police cost £60m'. Daily Express. 18.1.06, p15.

[3431] Hickley, M. '1000 police are off work with stress every day'. Daily Mail. 20.2.07, p9.

[3432] McDonald, C. 'Cop Who's Afraid Of Sirens'. Daily Record. 19.11.11, pp1,5.

[3433] 'Stress fear for troops'. Sunday Express. 8.7.12, p14.

[3434] Marsh, G. 'Poor old cops to get stress checks'. Daily Express. 28.8.03, p4.

[3435] 'Concern over cops' sickness'. Daily Record. 26.2.13, p8.

[3436] Picken, A. 'Sick days soar in 'epidemic' of police stress'. The Mail on Sunday. 10.3.13, p4.

[3437] 'WPC took holiday in Barbados while on sick leave for stress'. Daily Mail. 16.9.13, p20.

[3438] DiVasto, P., Saxton, G. 'Munchausen's syndrome in law enforcement'. FBI Law Enforcement Bulletin. 61:11-14, 1992.

[3439] C4 News. 2.2.12.

[3440] Greenwood, C. 'Undercover police 'can't be banned from affairs' '. Daily Mail. 2.2.12, p5.

[3441] Gill, C. '26-year fight for justice by PC forced out as mentally ill'. Daily Mail. 20.10.08, p30.

[3442] Letts, Q. 'Courageous, Free Thinking, Principled. That's Why Kate Hoey is a very unusual MP'. Daily Mail. 30.4.08, p14.

[3443] Ferguson, J. 'Poison Pen Police Chief Ruined My Marriage'. Daily Record. 20.2.08, pp6,7.

[3444] ITV series: Born to Kill. 2013.

[3445] Hardcastle, E. Daily Mail. 7.12.07, p19.

[3446] Officer 'A'. 'The Crime Factory'. Mainstream Publishing. 2012.

[3447] 'Ex-cop's stitch-up'. The Sun. 29.4.12, p20.

[3448] 'Dyslexic cop sues bosses'. News of the World. 23.8.09, p16.

[3449] Sawer, P. 'Second chance' for staff who quit'. The Sunday Telegraph. 5.12.10, p5.

[3450] Jeeves, P. 'WPC on sick leave for 8 years 'hated force'. Daily Express. 12.10.10, p15.

[3451] McGivern, M. 'Police Chief Faces The Axe'. Daily Record. 11.8.10, pp1,5.

[3452] Booth, S. 'Racism, sexism and sectarianism in the world's biggest gang'. Daily Record. 14.11.08, p12.

[3453] Emsley, C. 'The Great British Bobby'. Quercus. London. 2009.

[3454] McKay, P. 'Justice for doggers?'. Daily Mail. 11.10.10, p17.

[3455] McNamara, P. 'Heroes' trauma hell'. News Of The World. 7.11.10, p10.

[3456] Caesar, E. 'From Hero To Zero'. The Sunday Times Magazine. 4.4.10, pp14-21

[3457] 'Stress fear fro troops'. Sunday Express. 8.7.12, p14.

[3458] Nicol, M. The Mail on Sunday. 8.7.12, p19.

[3459] Emsley, C. 'The Great British Bobby'. Quercus. London. 2009.

[3460] Daily Express. 8.3.11, p21.

[3461] Leonard, T., Gardner, D. 'Rampage Of Real Life Rambo'. Daily Mail. 9.2.13, pp20,21.

[3462] Harrison, I. 'Horror of huge rise in military self-harming'. The Sunday Post. 21.11.10, p41.

[3463] Perry, A. 'Revealed! The bullies of Deepcut'. Sunday Express. 10.11.02, p13.

[3464] Currie, G. 'Drink-Drive Cop Done 4 Times but Beats Jail'. Daily Record. 9.12.10, p23.

[3465] Boniface, S. 'Brit Soldier 'Killed Iraq Girl Aged 8 As She Played' '. Sunday Mirror. 24.10.10, p8.

[3466] Dorman, N. 'Navy sex shame'. The People. 26.9.10, p26.

[3467] The Lancet. 15.3.13.

[3468] Nelson, N. 'Army Booze Culture Rap'. Sunday People. 21.4.13, p30.

[3469] 'Psychotest for soldiers'. The People. 2.10.11, p4.

[3470] Chorley, M. 'All frontline soldiers 'to get psycho-screening …' '. The Independent On Sunday. 1.8.10, p28.

[3471] Stewart, S. 'Hidden Hell Of Our Boys'. Daily Record. 9.4.12, p1.

[3472] Latchem, T. 'Soldier Of Hate'. News Of The World. 24.1.10, p37.

[3473] Verkaik, R. 'Sex, violence and drugs land ex-servicemen behind bars'. 19.9.10, p4.

[3474] 'When 'hurt feelings' cost more than an arm and a leg'. Daily Mail. 28.11.08, p17.

[3475] Bates, D. 'The thrill-kill squad'. Daily Mail. 28.9.10, p26.

[3476] Evans, M. 'Navy academy 'hid' explosion of drugs use'. The Times. 19.12.12, p28.

[3477] Sanchez, R. 'Military records sharp rise in sex assaults'. The Daily Telegraph. 9.5.13, p17.

[3478] 'Shameful secrets of the GIs who preyed on women'. Daily Mail. 30.5.13, p33.

[3479] MacDonald, S. 'More soldiers are failing drug tests'. Daily Express. 11.12.12, p10.

[3480] Verkaik, R. 'British soldiers sexually abused us, claim Iraqis'. The Independent On Sunday. 15.11.09, p36.

[3481] 'Forces sex abuse men paid £1m'. Sunday Mail. 31.3.13, p28.

[3482] Graves, J. 'Deplorable, shocking, shameful'. Daily Mail. 9.9.11, p6.

[3483] Canalan, P. 'Mousa's lawyer warns of more army abuse cases'. The Independent On Sunday. 11.9.11, p23.

[3484] Little, A. 'Top police jobs for soldiers who have fought Taliban'. Daily Express. 25.7.11, p15.

[3485] Pickard, M. 'Brown: Did hackers target my phone too?'. Daily Express. 24.1.11, p2.

[3486] Doward, J. 'Scotland Yard tries to halt phone-hacking libel claim'. The Observer. 27.2.11, p3.

[3487] Greenwood, C. 'Collective Amnesia'. Daily Mail. 25.4.13, p4.

[3488] Barnes, E. 'Appeal of Irish Watchdog model'. Scotland on Sunday. 7.7.11, p3

[3489] Burrell, I. 'Officer who led hacking inquiry keeps Murdoch job'. The Independent. 9.7.11, p8.

[3490] Wright, S. 'Reporters 'paid police thousands' '. Daily Mail. 7.7.11. p6.

[3491] Classic FM News. 31.7.11.

[3492] C4 News. 23.9.11.

[3493] Martin, D. 'NoW paid former news chief £25,000 for Yard exclusives'. Daily Mail. 24.9.11, p6.

[3494] Little, A., Twomey, J. Daily Express. 21.7.07, p7.

[3495] Milland, G. 'I was leant on by No 10, says police chief in honours probe'. Daily Express. 24.10.07, p27.

[3496] Newsnight. 6.7.11.

[3497] Watt, N. 'Met chief 'almost paralysed' No 10 in Blair's last year'. The Observer. 10.10.10, p8.

[3498] Buckland, L. 'Former Met chief to overhaul Bahrain police service'. Scotland on Sunday. 4.12.11, p7.

[3499] Nicholl, K., Petre, J. 'Queen Invites Despot To Her Jubilee Lunch'. The Mail On Sunday. 8.4.12, pp1,5.

[3500] 'Profile. John Yates'. The Sunday Times. 28.10. 07, p19

[3501] Doyle, J. 'Minister slaps down anti-terror chief for 'alarming the public''. Daily Mail. 3.7.10, p32.

[3502] Channel 4 News. 4.9.10.

[3503] Mendick, R. 'Met officer treated journalists to champagne meals on expenses'. The Sunday Telegraph. 24.7.11, p12.

[3504] Hale, B. 'Officer Behind Failed Probe 'Feared Exposure' '. Daily Mail. 11.7.11, p9.

[3505] Leppard, D. 'Police chief cracks down on officers' credit cards'. The Sunday Times. 2.12.07, p12.

[3506] Camber, R. 'Brooks borrowed THAT horse after lunch with Ian Blair'. Daily Mail. 8.3.12, p20.

[3507] 'Yard chief who quit is cleared of misconduct'. Daily Mail. 113.12.07, p40.

[3508] Malone, C. 'A matter of lies & death'. Sunday Mirror. 5.8.07, p31.

[3509] Pendlebury, R. 'The police chief, text messages to a married blonde, and the truth about the Stockwell shooting fiasco'. Daily Mail. 10.12.07, p23.

[3510] Greenwood, C. 'Yard chiefs who quit over phone hacking 'are given £½m' '. Daily Mail. 7.1.12, p34.

[3511] McDermott, N., Camber, R. 'The Met chief and his 'back of an envelope' hacking probe'. Daily Mail. 6.3.12, p24.

[3512] Camber, R. 'Hacking scandal has prompted 30 inquiries'. Daily Mail. 12.10.11, p12.

[3513] Gilymount, S. 'Police knew MPs' phones were tapped'. Daily Express. 9.1.09, p8.

[3514] Shaw, A. 'Cop jailed for 2 years for tip-offs to The Sun'. Daily Mirror. 6.6.13, p19.

[3515] Hall, M. 'MPs to probe police in phone-hacking scandal'. Daily Express. 13.7.09, p17.

[3516] Hall, M. 'MPs demand police inquiry as News Group face fury over phone tap scandal'. Daily Express. 11.7.09, p6.

[3517] Ferguson, J. 'Hacking Victims Up 2000'. Daily Record. 4.11.11, p16.

[3518] C4 Dispatches. July 2011.

[3519] Camber, R. 'Met press chief and 'traded favours' '. Daily Mail. 14.3.12, p4.

[3520] Reynolds, M. 'Scotland Yard Slammed For Hiring Ex-Newspaper Chief'. Daily Express. 13.4.12, p7.

[3521] Camber, R. 'Shock arrest of another News of the World boss'. Daily Mail. 3.8.11, p8.

[3522] Flanagan, P. 'Brooks loaned police horse after lunch with Met chief'. Daily Express. 8.3.12, p23.

[3523] Gallagher, I. 'Was anti-terror boss who failed to nail the News of the World compromised by these pictures?'. The Mail on Sunday. 10.7.11, pp10,11.

[3524] C4 News. 12.8.11.

[3525] Dawar, A. 'Officer probed over Milly leak'. Daily Express. 13.8.11, p13.

[3526] 'Pressure mounts on NoW man'. Daily Express. 20.8.11, p4.

[3527] Greenwood, C. 'Police drop threat to use Secrets Act over Milly hacking leak'. Daily Mail. 21.9.11, p

[3528] Leigh, D. 'Met use Official Secrets Act to force hacking disclosure'. The Guardian. 17.9.11, pp1,10

[3529] Wright, S. 'Met demands Guardian's sources on hacking'. Daily Mail. 17.9.11, p7.

[3530] ITN News. 16.8.11.

[3531] Seamark. M. 'James Murdoch'misled MPs' over how much he really knew'. Daily Mail. 17.8.11, p7.

[3532] Hanning, J. 'Could Cameron's friend Brooks be the ultimate victim of phone hacking?'. The Independent On Sunday. 27.2.11, p29.

[3533] Rao, N. 'Sun editor may have broken the law'. Daily Express. 25.3.11, p4.

[3534] Pilditch, D. ' 'Press cash for police' probe'. Daily Express. 16.4.11. p5.

[3535] Hanning, J. 'Where exactly will it all end?'. The Independent on Sunday. 23.1.11, p16.

[3536] 'Prescott was right to take on police over phone hacking'. Daily Mail. 24.5.11, p28.

[3537] 'Murdoch: The Mogul Who Screwed the News'.Channel 4. 27.7.11.

[3538] BBC1 News. 14.3.11.

[3539] C4 News. 8.7.11.

[3540] BBC2 Newsnight. 7.7.11.

[3541] Crichton, T. 'MP slams 'immoral' deeds of newspaper'. Daily Record. 7.7.11, p4.

[3542] Sedmark, M. 'Coulson Named Over Police Payments'. Daily Mail. 6.7.11, p5.

[3543] Twomey, J. 'Jailed, policeman who spied on the rich and famous'. Daily Express. 12.10.07, p43.

[3544] McLeod, K. 'Hacking shame paper paid me to spy on Wills'. 9.11.11, p7.

[3545] ITV News. 4.11.11.

[3546] Verkaik, R. 'Media probe investigator quizzed over leak to paper'. The Mail on Sunday. 20.11.11, p25.

[3547] Wright, S. 'Blunders of police who insisted: The dad did it'. Daily Mail. 24.6.11, p6.

[3548] Greenwood, C. 'Were the police to blame for Milly's deleted voicemails?' Daily Mail. 12.12.11, p10.

[3549] Seamark, M. 'Police knew ten years ago that Milly's voicemail was hacked'. Daily Mail. 24.1.12, p8.

[3550] Hayman, A. 'We Put Our Best Cops On Case'. News Of The World. 12.7.09, p9.

[3551] Camber, R. 'Dangers of new rules on police and Press'. Daily Mail. 6.1.12, p4.

[3552] Daily Mail. 11.1.12, p12.

[3553] BBC TV News. 28.1.12.

REFERENCES

[3554] C4 News. 19.1.12.

[3555] Kelly, T., Seamark, M. 'The Sun 'created culture of illegal payments to police' '. Daily Mail. 28.2.12, p14.

[3556] Shaw, A. 'The Sun And A Network of Corruption'. Daily Record. 28.2.12, p8.

[3557] Seamark, M. 'How Rebekah Brooks got a 'gift' horse from the Met'. Daily Mail. 29.2.12, p20.

[3558] Hickman, M., Peachey, P. 'Senior police officer 'gave NI executive details of phone-hacking inquiry' '. The Independent. 25.2.12, pp1,4.

[3559] 'Labour 'blocked hacking probe' '. Daily Mail. 13.3.12, p30.

[3560] Leppard, D. 'Murdoch: The Sun will go on shining'. The Sunday Times. 12.2.12, p5.

[3561] Flanagan, P. 'Met chiefs 'filled their boots' with gifts'. Daily Express. 6.3.12, p15.

[3562] C4 News. 6.2.12.

[3563] Camber, R. 'I helped Met chiefs apply for the job, says ex-NOW executive'. Daily Mail. 3.4.12, p24.

[3564] Gallagher, I., Hall, A. 'Murdoch's Yard man and 'links to killer Noye' '. The Mail on Sunday. 1.4.12, p24.

[3565] Manning, S. 'The Scotland Yard officer in hot water over phone hacking'. The Independent on Sunday. 15.4.12, p6.

[3566] C4 News. 13.4.12.

[3567] Flanagan, P. 'New police probe into phone hacking scandal'. Daily Express. 27.1.11, p5.

[3568] Stevenson, C. 'Four Sun journalists held over payments to police'. The Independent on Sunday. 29.1.12, p7.

[3569] Classic FM. 21.12.11.

[3570] Channel 5 News. 27.3.13.

[3571] Owen, G. 'Murdoch driver: I told Jeremy Hunt about cash drops to Met police at Hyde Park tennis courts'. The Mail on Sunday. 13.5.12, pp8,9.

[3572] 'Police to face quiz on Milly'. Daily Express. 29.6.12, p27.

[3573] 'Top cop on leak rap'. Daily Record. 25.9.12, p5.

[3574] Littlejohn, R. 'Take you trousers off, she's from the Guardian'. Daily Mail. 22.3.13, p19.

[3575] Paddick, B. 'How DID we become a nation where police dread a 7am knock on the door ... simply for talking to a journalist?'. The Mail on Sunday. 10.3.13, p43.

[3576] Littlejohn, R. 'Without brave whistleblowers, Ali Dizaei would be running the Met police'. Daily Mail. 18.12.12, p17.

[3577] Slack, J. 'Day The Police Got Out of Jail'. Daily Mail. 30.11.12, p10.

[3578] Doyle, J. 'New busybody army'. Daily Mail. 27.9.11, p12.

[3579] 'Home Office in retreat on snooping'. Daily Mail. 18.6.02, p2.

[3580] Slack, J. 'Town halls are told to stop spying'. Daily Mail. 26.1.11, p4.

[3581] McKay, P. Daily Mail. 19.2.07, p17.

[3582] Dolan, A. 'Be prepared ... for Scouts as traffic police'. Daily Mail. 20.1.11, p11.

[3583] Reynolds, R. 'Edinburgh Parking Fines 'Are Illegal' '. Daily Record. 19.4.10, p10.

[3584] Boyle, J. 'Police-style powers may be handed to bouncers'. Daily Mail. 20.4.10, p30.

[3585] Rice, D. 'The hundreds of civilians who are operating speed cameras'. The Mail on Sunday. 22.10.06, p15.

[3586] 'Now health and safety police take an axe to apple trees'. Daily Mail. 13.9.10 p7.

[3587] Little, A. 'Scrap These Useless Laws'. Daily Express. 2.7.10, p25.

[3588] Hall, M. 'Tories promise to torch 'elf and safety' madness'. Daily Express. 20.9.10, p15.

[3589] 'Anti-crime stickers are banned ... as a fire hazard'. Daily Mail. 25.8.10.29.

[3590] Flintoff, J-P. 'Bin it, sir, or you'll taste Singapore-style justice'. The Sunday Times. 22.8.10, p7.

[3591] Wilkes, D. 'The £5,000 apple core'. Daily Mail. 31.1.08, p29.

[3592] Jeeves, P. 'Pipe smoker is fined £50 for dropping a matchstick'. Daily Express. 16.7.10, p19.

[3593] Littlejohn, R. Daily Mail. 3.9.10, p17.

[3594] Stote, M. 'A £75 litter fine ... for taking my son to feed the ducks'. Daily Express. 13.11.09, p19.

[3595] Dawar, A. ' 'Racist' gollies banned form Enid Blyton stall'. Daily Express. 24.9.11, p16.

[3596] Pilditch, D. 'Bin snoopers fined me £75 after finding address label'. Daily Express. 5.8.08, p18.

[3597] 'Beware the leaf police!'. Daily Mail. 3.9.10, p17.

[3598] 'Give us a break!'. Daily Mail. 29.7.10, p27.

[3599] Gray, R., Herrman, J. E. 'Bigger fines for overfilling a bin than shoplifting'. The Sunday Telegraph. 4.7.10, p5.

[3600] Dixon, C. 'Arrest and £1K fine ... for saving doomed goldfish'. Daily Express. 12.5.10, p30.

[3601] Delaney, S. 'Framed!'. The Sunday Telegraph, Seven. 17.8.08, pp18-21.

[3602] Slack, J. 'Police Your Own Streets'. Daily Mail. 12.2.08, p1.

[3603] Collins, D. 'It's Just A Wee Guy Who Needs To Be Noticed'. Daily Record. 9.4.11, p31.

[3604] Rudd, M. 'I'll only be here for a couple of minutes'. The Sunday Times Magazine. 21.11.10, p58.

[3605] 'Census 'police' seek 7m forms'. Daily Mail. 7.4.11, p30.

[3606] 'Shamed officer had hot currency'. Daily Record. 17.6.09, p9.

[3607] '£50 fine for litter takes the biscuit'. Daily Record. 29.8.11, p17.

[3608] Koster, O. Daily Mail. 25.8.08, p5.

[3609] MacDonald, S. '£50 Spot-Fines For Litterbug Children'. Daily Record. 12.10.11, p9.

[3610] Matthews, J. 'Tot given an Asbo threat for giggling'. Daily Express. 14.5.13, p25.

[3611] Groves, J. 'Big Brother bin searches double in a single year'. Daily Mail. 17.10.11, p4.

[3612] Dolan, A. 'My nightmare, by Fireman Sam creator branded a racist over quip to airport security'. Daily Mail. 27.2.12, p7.

[3613] Taylor, R. 'Police duties could be handed to private firms'. Daily Mail. 3.3.12, p11.

[3614] Russell, A. 'Now drivers filmed by wardens' badge?'. Daily Express. 19.3.12, p30.

[3615] Penrose, J. 'Private Bobbies On The Streets'. Sunday Mirror. 4.3.12, p6.

[3616] Massey, R. 'Rail ticket police 'act like cowboy clampers' '. Daily Mail. 22.5.12, p31.

[3617] 'Wardens nabbed'. Daily Express. 22.1.03, p9.

[3618] Langley, W. 'Pound away, but the foot soldiers won't give an inch'. The Sunday Telegraph. 12.10.08, p28.

[3619] Hitchens, P. 'Konk the Clown and the joke policeman'. The Mail on Sunday. 28.12.08, p27.

[3620] Gilbertson, D. 'The Strange Death of Constable George Dixon'. Kindle. Amazon. 2011.

[3621] Allen, V. 'Crackdown on 'idle' motorists'. Daily Mail. 29.5.13, p7.

[3622] Christison, G. 'Council spy scandal'. Sunday Express. 23.6.13, p6.

[3623] Daily Mail. 10.8.11, p13.

[3624] Twomey, J. 'Back to 'proper' policing as Met boss Blair finally quits'. Daily Express. 3.10.08, p5.

[3625] Townsend, M., Helm, T. 'Halve number of police forces, says spending tsar'. The Observer. 4.7.10, p4.

[3626] 'Army medals out, Gay Pride badges in, and theft blamed on badgers to cut crime rates'. Daily Mail. 9.4.11, p50.

[3627] Davidson, L. 'The Hidden Mongers'. Daily Record. 21.4.11, p8.

[3628] Mills, R. 'Accused of racism, man who wanted to keep out squatters'. Daily Express. 6.12.10, p9.

[3629] Biggs, P. 'Don't hand over public money to sex swap police'. Daily Express. 28.1.10, p56.

[3630] Littlejohn, R. 'They accuse Basil Brush and Prince Charles of hate crimes and let the real villains off Scot-free'. Daily Mail. 31.3.10, p30.

[3631] Littlejohn, R. Daily Mail. 17.7.09, p17.

[3632] Ferrari, N. Sunday Express. 11.7.10, p21.

[3633] 'Criminal Correctness'. Leader. Daily Express. 13.4.07, p10.

[3634] 'Held for racism … after singing Kung Fu Fighting in front of Chinese pair'. Daily Mail. 27.4.11, p3.

[3635] O'Flynn, P. 'The Notting Hill Carnival should be closed down'. Daily Express. 26.8.11, p13.

[3636] Littlejohn, R. 'Verily Plod moves in mysterious ways …'. Daily Mail. 25.1.08, p17.

[3637] Dixon, C. 'Mascot who is too white for our police'. Daily Express. 20.11.07, p22.

[3638] Whitehead, T. 'Terror Search Fiasco'. Daily Express. 5.7.07, pp1,5.

[3639] McKinstry, L. 'Just What Are The Police Prepared To Do These Days?'. Daily Express. 10.2.06, p10.

[3640] Johnston, J. 'I Was Hung Out To Dry'. Daily Mail. 2.7.05, pp12,13.

[3641] Littlejohn, R. 'Look for the Golly'. Daily Mail. 1.6.07, p17.

[3642] Wilkes, D. 'Police arrested my golliwog'. Daily Mail. 31.5.07, p9.

[3643] 'Shopped for gollies sale'. The People. 6.5.07, p26.

[3644] Chapman, J. 'Dropped, race-hate case over golliwog in window'. Daily Express. 25.10.11, p7.

[3645] Littlejohn, R. 'Demanding 'diversity' – with menaces'. Daily Mail. 15.9.06, p17.

[3646] Wright, S., Kelly, T. 'The race inquisition'. Daily Mail. 15.10.07, p7.

[3647] Harris, P., Taylor, B. Daily Mail. 19.5.04, p7.

[3648] Walker, N. 'Cops Probe Into Mackenzie Rant'. Daily Record. 15.10.07, p10.

[3649] 'Desperate C4 defend 'cash cow' '. Daily Express. 19.1.07, p9.

[3650] Ladyman, I., Lawton, M. 'Police probe allegations of West Ham race chants'. Daily Mail. 6.3.07, p84.

[3651] Wright, S. 'Met chief backs down on badge ban'. Daily Mail. 30.7.09, p13.

[3652] Tozer, J. 'It isn't a crime to call the Irish leprechauns'. Daily Mail. 31.10.08, p5.

[3653] 'Police learn Urdu at taxpayers' expense'. Daily Express. 12.3.07, p17.

[3654] Loudon, A. 'Policeman is carpeted for flying the flag'. Daily Mail. 23.12.02, p14.

[3655] Wright, S. 'Yard tells police to 'celebrate' travellers'. Daily Mail. 12.7.08, p37.

[3656] 'And from council killjoys, a ban on flags'. Daily Mail. 24.4.09, p29.

[3657] Clark, R. 'Electricians are worth more than diversity officers'. Daily Express. 12.1.10, p12.

[3658] Twomey, J. 'Unveiled, a new head scarf for police women to wear in mosques'. Daily Express. 28.7.09, p27.

[3659] Paul, D. 'Police 'Must Recruit Gypsies' '. Sunday Express. 12.7.09, pp1,4.

[3660] Wilkes, D., McDermott, N. 'Romanian squatters have stolen our home'. Daily Mail. 13.1.10, p21.

[3661] Dolan, A. 'After Officer Laptop, meet WPC Mouse'. Daily Mail. 16.1.10, p51.

[3662] Dawar, A. 'Outrage at curb on white men becoming PCs'. Daily Express. 23.5.09, p4.

[3663] Jeory, T. 'Race becomes a real issue again for police at the Yard'. Sunday Express. 12.5.13, p5.

REFERENCES

[3664] Barrett, D. 'How to arrest a witch, the official police guide'. The Sunday Telegraph. 31.10.10, p3.

[3665] Reynolds, M. 'Outcry over Home Office 'pandering' to Muslim police'. Daily Express. 13.3.10, p7.

[3666] Camber, R. 'PC brigade ban police from asking for Christian names'. Daily Mail. 19.3.10, p21.

[3667] Wilkie, S. 'Police needled by tattoo taboo'. Daily Express. 3.8.10, p28.

[3668] Keevins, H. 'We Will Snatch Hate Song Bigots'. Daily Record. 13.4.11, p1.

[3669] McLeod, K. 'I'll put yobs on Bigot Brother'. Daily Record. 18.6.11, p5.

[3670] Keevins, H. 'Cops Bigot Blitz'. Sunday Mail. 3.4.11, p7.

[3671] Townsend, M. 'Senior BNP election candidate arrested over Qur'an burning'. The Observer. 10.4.11, p8.

[3672] 'Losing Their Heads'. The People. 19.8.07, p6.

[3673] 'Non-PC cop quits'. News Of The World. 30.12.07, p13.

[3674] Daily Express. 20.10.03, p4.

[3675] Walters, S. 'Police attacked by TV watchdog over C4 mosque exposé'. The Mail on Sunday. 18.11.07, p11.

[3676] Evans, M. 'Bootees for sniffer dogs are just not necessary says imam'. Daily Express. 7.7.08, p7.

[3677] Widdecombe, A. 'If Basil Brush is racist then race law is an ass'. Daily Express. 19.3.08, p13.

[3678] Widdecombe, A. Daily Express. 4.6.08, p13.

[3679] Doughty, s. '7 out of 10 in the UK see themselves as Christian'. Daily Mail. 29.9.11, p28.

[3680] Whitehead, T. 'Police order: Take off your shoes before you raid a Muslim home'. Daily Express. 3.2.07, p7.

[3681] Phillips, M. 'It's time for our police to decide whose rights deserve protection'. Daily Mail. 6.2.06, p12.

[3682] Petre, J. ' 'Bonkers' police drop the word Christmas from poster to avoid upsetting other faiths'. The Mail on Sunday. 27.12, 09, p49.

[3683] Reynolds, M. 'Police give Muslims in cells compasses to pray towards Mecca'. Daily Express. 1.7.09, p10.

[3684] Ferguson, J. 'Hokey Cokey Could Land You In Pokey'. Daily Record. 22.12.08, p9.

[3685] Littlejohn, R. Daily Mail. 13.3.09, p17.

[3686] Dixon, C. 'Uproar as Islam cleric helps police on tactics'. Daily Express. 10.1.09, p4.

[3687] Gray, R. 'Easier to use for WPCs, the ladies' range of firearms'. The Sunday Telegraph. 4.3.07, p16.

[3688] Petre, J. ' 'Homosexuality is a sin' street preacher wins £7K from police'. The Mail on Sunday. 19.12.10, p45.

[3689] 'Are You Gay, Police Ask Neighbourhood Watch'. The Sunday Telegraph. 19.5.13, p4.

[3690] Archibald, B. 'Don't Tell The Cops About Underage Sex'. Daily Record. 4.12.10, p26.

[3691] Reynolds, M. 'Police told to protect outdoor sex fanatics'. Daily Express. 8.10.10, p27.

[3692] Johnston, J. 'You're Destroying Us'. Daily Mail. 5.6.08, p29.

[3693] 'Hallelujah'. Daily Mail. 29.9.06, p31.

[3694] Millar, A. 'Gay police get full-time coordinator to combat homophobia from fellow officers'. Scotland On Sunday. 11.6.06, p9.

[3695] Warner, G. 'Thugs On Our Streets And Not In Our Prisons'. Daily Mail. 8.6.13, p16.

[3696] Twomey, J. 'Police blow £1.5m on giveaway gimmicks'. Daily Express. 3.9.10, p15.

[3697] Littlejohn, R. Daily Mail. 9.9.08, p15.

[3698] 'Very PC Officers'. Daily Record. 19.3.10, p27.

[3699] Pierce, A. Daily Mail. 3.2.10, p14.

[3700] McKinstry, L. 'Labour Thought Police Making Us All Criminals'. Daily Express. 16.4.09, p12.

[3701] 'Police and nurses to be asked their sexuality'. Daily Mail. 13.1.11, p20.

[3702] Atkins, A. 'Free thinking takes a bow'. Sunday Express. 20.2.11, p37.

[3703] Owen, J. 'Father furious at police's reaction to son's email'. The Independent On Sunday. 1.4.07, p26.

[3704] Littlejohn, R. 'So that's what they mean by Blue Watch'. Daily Mail. 5.10.07, p17.

[3705] Chapman, J. '£2,000 victory for freedom of speech'. Daily Express. 16.1.08, p19.

[3706] Duguid, K. 'Breach Of The PC'. Daily Record. 24.9.11, p13.

[3707] Westcott, S. 'Pub where the drinkers don't mince their words'. Daily Express. 12.5.07, p19.

[3708] Whitehead, P. 'Police to quiz gay jibe pupils'. Daily Express. 29.12.06, p29.

[3709] Bright, M. 'Revealed: how the police encouraged lesbian love'. The Observer. 27.6.04, p9.

[3710] Littlejohn, R. 'New Labour's politically correct provisional wing'. Daily Mail. 17.1.06, p15.

[3711] Harris, P. 'The postcards so saucy they were seized by the obscenity squad'. Daily Mail. 29.9.11, p21.

[3712] Beaumont, R., Hodgson, N. 'Gay pornography verdict puts obscenity law's future in doubt'. The Observer. 8.1.12, p15.

[3713] Broster, P. 'Detective arrested ... for calling gay woman officer a 'dyke' '. Daily Express. 11.4.06, p9.

[3714] Day, E. 'My conviction in the biggest gay trial since Oscar Wilde changed Britain for ever'. The Mail on Sunday. 15.7.07, pp46-48.

[3715] Littlejohn, R. Daily Mail, 15.2.11, p17.

[3716] Barton, F. Daily Mail, 15.4.06, pp12,13

[3717] Hitchens, P. 'Police deciding when we can laugh?' The Mail on Sunday. 5.4.09, p27.

[3718] Reynolds, M. 'Grilled by police for 2 hours over a transsexual joke'. Daily Express. 31.3.09, p23.

[3719] Patell, A. 'Bully tactics'. Daily Mail. 12.12.09, p21.

[3720] Tozer, J. '350 police taken off beat for sex-swap awareness classes'. Daily Mail. 4.8.08, p27.

[3721] Petre, J. 'The police destroyed me for my Christian views on gay sex. How 'equal and diverse' is that?'. The Mail on Sunday. 7.12.08, p54.

[3722] Twomey, J. 'Wanted: Gay, lesbian and transgender gun guards for the Queen'. Daily Express. 22.9.09, p6.

[3723] Hitchens, P. 'Tearing down another safety net'. The Mail on Sunday. 21.6.09, p29.

[3724] Pilditch, D. 'And the gay rights banner above police station that caused a stir'. Daily Express. 4.2.09, p7.

[3725] 'Cops are tops for sex swaps'. Sunday Mail. 17.5.09, p11.

[3726] Littlejohn, R. 'The real cops neutered by transgender lobby'. Daily Mail. 18.8.09, p15.

[3727] Blackley, M. 'Police pledge to respect human rights (but not to catch criminals)'. The Mail on Sunday. 12.5.13, p6.

[3728] Channel 4. 9.8.10.

[3729] Slack, J. 'Ploddledygook: Attack on the police jargon mountain'. Daily Mail. 14.4.08, p25.

[3730] Hitchens, P. 'The Mail on Sunday. 26.9.10, p29.

[3731] Little, A. 'Police bogged down by a snowstorm of paperwork'. Daily Express. 2.7.10, p11.

[3732] 'Dial 999: police are killing the language'. The Sunday Times. 12.5.13, p19.

[3733] Evans, D. 'Once Upon A Crime'. News Of The World. 7.2.10, p37.

[3734] Palmer, R. 'Now police are told not to call tearaways yobs'. Daily Express. 2.10.06, p19.

[3735] Taylor, B. 'Censored'. Daily Mail. 15.5.02, p15.

[3736] Phillips, M. 'Now we know the truth: the police are not racist'. The Sunday Times. 24.9.00, p21.

[3737] 'Yard adopts 'polite' new riot tactics'. The Sunday Times. 27.2.11, p1.

[3738] 'PCs are too PC'. Leader. Daily Record. 17.10.11, p8.

[3739] Chapman, J. 'Police in line for award with a sentence of pure gibberish'. Daily Express. 3.7.09 p35.

[3740] O'Sullivan, K. 'Now police can't say Evenin'' All ... Its just not PC'. Daily Express. 26.10.09, p9.

[3741] Copping, J. 'Evenin' all. Sorry officer, but please don't say that any more'. The Sunday Telegraph. 25.10.09, p19.

[3742] Gill, C. 'PC force hiring officers 'who can't do the job' '. Daily Mail. 13.4.07, p9.

[3743] Gilbertson, D. 'Why 7/7 victims were left to bleed to death'. The Mail on Sunday. 24.10.10, p27.

[3744] Sanderson, E. 'Revealed: the form paralysing our police'. The Mail on Sunday. 31.10.10, pp46,47.

[3745] Lewis, J. 'Anger as elite police sent on 'treasure hunt' game'. The Mail on Sunday. 21.9.08, p22.

[3746] Riches, C. 'Yob's rooftop sieges banned ... in case he falls and sues police'. Daily Express. 21.4.10, p22.

[3747] Dowd, H. 'It's A Police Farce'. Daily Express. 27.9.08, p31.

[3748] Reynolds, M 'Q. Why can't a PCSO help children cross the road? A. It's against elf'n'safety'. Daily Express. 10.9.10, p5.

[3749] Reynolds, M. 'Earthquake Training For Police'. Daily Express. 10.9.10, pp1,5.

[3750] Bowater, D. 'Health & safety stops PC saving drowning man'. Daily Express. 25.5.10

[3751] Ellicott, C. 'Father hits out at safety rules that made fireman leave his son to drown in 3ft of water'. Daily Mail. 23.2.12, p5.

[3752] Widdecombe, A. 'When it is a good idea to break rules'. Daily Express. 13.4.11, p13.

[3753] 'Brakes on police cyclists'. Daily Express. 23.3.10, p22.

[3754] Copping, J. 'Lip balm, Jaffa Cakes and Gregory's Girl: the policeman's guide to riding a bike'. The Sunday Telegraph. 6.2.11, p7.

[3755] Hull, L. 'The police guide to riding a bike'. Daily Mail. 7.2.11, p22.

[3756] Littlejohn, R. 'Mind How You Go Awards 2011'. Daily Mail. 1.3.11, p17.

[3757] Gilbertson, D. 'Why 7/7 victims were left to bleed to death'. The Mail on Sunday. 24.10.10, p27.

[3758] Evans, M. 'Beat bobbies are banned over 'health and safety' '. Daily Express. 25.9.06, p10.

[3759] Reynolds, M. 'Safety fanatics tell pirates show: Lock up your cutlasses'. Daily Express. 18.1.08, p37.

[3760] Appleton, J. 'Trick or treaters will feel the full weight of the law'. Daily Express. 30.10.09, p10.

[3761] Hickley, M., Sears, N. 'You can't expect the police to be heroes'. Daily Mail. 8.10.09, p10.

[3762] Townsend, M. Sunday Express. 29.4.07, p34.

[3763] Delingpole, J. 'Put an end to this poisonous culture of human rights'. Daily Express. 28.1.10, p17.

[3764] Bugler, T. 'Dear Mr. Burglar'. Daily Record. 5.10.10, p7.

[3765] Archibald, B. 'A Ban Tattoo Far'. Daily Record. 3.8.10, p17.

[3766] Chapman, J. Daily Express. 31.7.13, p11.

[3767] Riches, C. 'Just for a change, police must suit their suspects'. Daily Express. 2.8.10, p15.

[3768] Dawar, a. 'Fury at courses for thugs'. Daily Express. 12.5.11, p4.

[3769] Brooke, C. Daily Mail. 12.5.11, p27.

[3770] Flanagan, P. 'Sorry Sir, is it all right if we set our police dog on you?'. Daily Express. 22.7.08, p10.

[3771] Whitehead, T. 'Be polite to yobs, police chief orders her officers'. Daily Express. 13.3.08, p37.

[3772] Levy, A. 'Watch out for these burglars'. Daily Mail. 6.3.07, p36.

[3773] Taylor, B. Daily Mail. 27.10.06, p37.

[3774] Littlejohn, R. 'Hell's teeth! Here's Sane Frankie Fraser'. Daily Mail. 25.5.07, p17.

[3775] Barton, F. 'Paper Tigers'. Daily Mail. 19.4.07, p26.

[3776] Walters, S. 'Boris: Thugs who swear at the police must be punished, not let off scot-free'. The Mail on Sunday. 2.10.11, p5.

[3777] Widdecombe, A. 'When the law sides with a truant of 13', Daily Express, 22.8.07, p13.

[3778] 'Police told to tone down naming and shaming of villains'. Daily Mail. 3.12.09, p22.

[3779] Schlesinger, F. 'Mark of madness'. Daily Mail. 26.9.09, p27.

[3780] Salkeld, L. 'Hope your cell was nice and comfy, sir'. Daily Mail. 14.8.09, p19.

[3781] 'Worried police veto Facebook hunt for rapist'. Daily Mail. 30.3.09, p2.

[3782] Doughty, S. 'Red tape that lets criminals go free'. Daily Mail. 1.8.08, p2.

[3783] Twomey, J. 'Red tape keeps bobbies off the beat'. Daily Express. 20.7.10, p27.

[3784] Doyle, J. 'Diktats that mean police help drunks home safely'. Daily Mail. 2.7.10, p4.

[3785] Ward, R. 'Red tape blues'. The Times. 12.3.11, p27.

[3786] Dawar, A. 'How police have to fill in 70 forms for just ONE burglary'. Daily Express. 3.11.10, p2.

[3787] Slack, J. 'A frightened force'. Daily Mail. 13.9.07, p8.

[3788] Barrett, D. 'PCs must fill in a 16-page form just to peep through a window'. The Sunday Telegraph. 17.10.10, p2.

[3789] Whitehead, T., Hall, M. ' 'Bureaucracy champ' to fight police red tape'. Daily Express. 17.7.08, p4.

[3790] Rider, C. 'The PC who is very PC ...'. Daily Express. 6.5.09, p19.

[3791] Faulkner, K. 'Police chief's scorn for the middle-class drivers who speed'. Daily Mail. 9.8.10, p8.

[3792] Littlejohn, R. 'Dixon of Dot Com'. Daily Mail. 18.2.11, p17.

[3793] Leapman, B. 'Police 'target forms, not criminality' '. The Sunday Telegraph. 8.7.07, p12.

[3794] Daily Express. 7.10.11, p14.

[3795] 75 Years Ago, Daily Express, 23.3.11, p10.

[3796] Brooks, T. 'Lathering for police with designer stubble'. Daily Express. 24.9.11, p26.

[3797] Hickley, M. 'Train police 'to use common sense' '. Daily Mail. 25.6.08, p19.

[3798] 'Futility of police diversity training'. Daily Mail. 1.10.07, p33.

[3799] 'Politeness for police'. Sunday Post. 11.8.13, p28.

[3800] McKinstry, L. 'Here is yet another casualty of oppressive political correctness'. Daily Express. 20.8.07, p12

[3801] Williams, M. 'The night I stood up to the thugs – and why I will never do it again'. Daily Mail. 20.8.07, p14.

[3802] Littlejohn, R. 'Anarchy In The UK!'. Daily Mail. 4.9.07, p15.

[3803] Groves, J. '...you pay for police to stage £2K party'. Sunday Express. 28.6.09, p13.

[3804] Maynard, G. 'Police swoop on shop boss to stop him telling jokes'. Daily Express. 19.12.08, p38.

[3805] Whitehead, T. 'Tories will let our police act as heroes again'. Daily Express. 15.5.08, p15.

[3806] Phillips, M. 'A woman dares to question gay adoption and the police move in ... George Orwell would be proud of them'. Daily Mail. 12.12.05, p14.

[3807] Bracchi, P. 'Victory for free speech'. Daily Mail. 10.10.09, pp22,23.

[3808] Littlejohn, R. Daily Mail. 13.11.09, p17.

[3809] Camber, R. 'I've been gagged'. Daily Mail. 19.12.08, p47.

[3810] Narain, J. 'Boy who threw sausage is cleared'. Daily Mail. 19.12.07, p24.

[3811] 'Wisdom from the bench'. Daily Express. 27.2.13, p11.

[3812] Slack, J. 'Target real criminals, police told'. Daily Mail. 2.2.08.

[3813] Paterson, B. 'Hate Mob Victim Is Cleared In Eight Minutes'. Sunday Mail. 5.12.10, p21.

[3814] Stote, M. 'Cops hold have-a-go hero trio'. Daily Express. 13.9.02, p25.

[3815] Doyles, J. 'Police 'have lost the public's trust' '. Daily Mail. 24.9.10 p11.

[3816] Littlejohn, R. 'Fireworks gunpowder, treason ... and Plod'. Daily Mail. 5.11.10, p17.

[3817] Murray, D. 'Don't 'Monitor' Him. Lock Him Up and Throw Away The Key'. Daily Mail. 6.6.13, p14.

[3818] Scott, M. 'Dad Arrested For Blowing Whistle On Abuse Suspect'. Sunday Mail. 6.10.02, p25.

[3819] Littlejohn, R. 'Proof no good deed ever goes unpunished'. Daily Mail. 3.5.13, p17.

[3820] McDonald, C. Daily Record. 28.2.08, p9.

[3821] Russell, J. 'He scolded a yob – and up facing prison for kidnap'. The Sunday Times. 7.11.10, p22.

[3822] 'Cops nab dad over bird food'. Sunday Mail. 28.9.08, p31.

[3823] Jedrzejewski, N. 'How beggar's toy gun broke firearms law'. Daily Mail. 30.4.13, p25.

[3824] Wyatt, P. Mail on Sunday Review. 12.9.10, p5.

[3825] Dolan, A. 'An OAP lies down to stop travellers invading park, guess who police move on'. Daily Mail. 12.8.10, p21.

[3826] 'I was arrested for catching burglars'. Daily Express. 13.3.10, p10.

[3827] 'Fury of mother arrested for refusing to give children their ball back'. Daily Mail. 10.7.10, p45.

[3828] Disley, J. 'Spared: Ex-soldier who snapped after years of yob torment'. Daily Express. 18.8.10, p6.

[3829] Bowater, D. 'Teachers leave boy of 5 stuck up a tree for 1 hour'. Daily Express. 25.3.10, p9.

[3830] Pilditch, D. 'Pair fined £80 ... for painting a garden fence'. Daily Express. 10.8.10, p27.

[3831] Hitchens, P. The Mail on Sunday. 14.4.13, p35.

[3832] Flanagan, P. 'Migrants stole our house while we were on holiday'. Daily Express. 26.5.10, p4.

[3833] Leader. 'Protect all homeowners'. Daily Express. 26.5.10, p12.

[3834] Brooke, C. Daily Mail. 28.4.10, p25.

[3835] Kisiel, R. 'Hop it! You could be a criminal'. Daily Mail. 10.5.13. p11.

[3836] Flanagan, P. 'In cells ... couple who stood up to 'hell neighbour'. Daily Express. 21.4.10, p17.

[3837] Kelly, T. 'Police ban a kickabout in the street'. Daily Mail. 22.9.10, p41.

[3838] McAulay, R. 'ASBO for playing kerbie'. Daily Record. 11.7.07, pp1,7.

[3839] Allen, V. 'Operation kickabout'. Daily Mail. 26.5.11, p9.

[3840] Leapman, B. 'Hopscotched: police swoop on children's street game'. The Sunday Telegraph. 8.4.07, p5.

[3841] Brooks, T. 'Fingerprinted and fined: Girl, 10, who crayoned on a wall'. Daily Express. 29.9.07, p29.

[3842] 'Six riot cops sent to nab Twix vandal'. Daily Record. 3.11.07, p27.

[3843] Tozer, J. 'The ketchup, an axe and a 'murder' prank to frighten away yobs that ended up in court'. Daily Mail. 4.2.11, p7.

[3844] Ross, C. 'Why should have-a-go heroes do the work of our law-enforcers?'. Daily Express. 3.9.08, p12.

[3845] 'Held for whacking a vandal'. Daily Record. 24.2.11, p5.

[3846] Pilditch, D. 'Gypsy threats woman dials 999 and police take her gun'. Daily Express. 27.4.11, p27.

[3847] Ferrari, N. 'Why you will never get a stab at self-defence'. Sunday Express. 26.6.11, p23.

[3848] Hagger, A. 'Killjoy PC swoops on 2 children for playing with toys'. Daily Express. 9.10.07, p27.

[3849] Narain, J. 'Assault with a sausage: How the law made a meal out of a boy's childish prank'. Daily Mail. 23.8.07, p25.

[3850] Richard & Judy. 'The police are taking the mickey ...'. Daily Express. 2.7.11, p20.

[3851] Widdecombe, A. 'If only our police would show a flash of common sense'. Daily Express. 29.8.07, p13.

[3852] Dolan, A. 'Topsy-turvy law'. Daily Mail. 26.9.07, p19.

[3853] McCartney, J. 'When there's no policeman ... there's too much uncertainty'. The Sunday Telegraph. 30.9.07, p25.

[3854] Frith Powell, H. 'Oh, Get A Grip!'. Daily Mail. 2.8.07, p51.

[3855] McGivern, M. 'Rib Sticklers'. Daily Record. 23.8.07, p12.

[3856] Blacklock, M. 'Barking ... teenager fined for growling at two Labradors'. Daily Express. 28.4.07, p20.

[3857] Littlejohn, R. 'A Toy Go-Kart? You're Nicked!'. Daily Mail. 1.5.07, p33.

[3858] Littlejohn, R. 'A Toy Go-Kart? You're Nicked!'. Daily Mail. 1.5.07, p33.

[3859] Sears. N. 'Photographing thugs 'is assault' '. Daily Mail. 21.7.08, p29.

[3860] Ferguson, J. 'The Police Keep Giving Me Stick'. Daily Record. 25.7.08, p33.

[3861] Gill, C. 'Don't be wet'. Daily Mail. 22.3.08, p21.

[3862] Broster, P. '18 Hours In Cell For Dropping An Apple Core'. Daily Express. 10.5.08, pp1,5.

[3863] Daily Express. 10.5.08.

[3864] McKinstry, L. 'Terrorists and thugs are left to rule in a justice system with no morals'. Daily Express. 26.6.08, p12.

[3865] Catchpole, C. 'The dim blue line'. The People. 11.9.11, p23.

[3866] Lusher, A. 'Back-to-front Britain looks after its yobs'. The Sunday Telegraph. 29.6.08, p20.

[3867] Reynolds, M. 'Man faces jail for chasing off yobs with lump of wood'. Daily Express. 9.7.08, p7.

[3868] Reynolds, M. 'Guilty, for trying to curb war memorial vandalism'. Daily Express. 11.7.08, p5.

[3869] Bonnici, R. 'Ex-Navy officer gets arrested after halting a grave ... for arming himself with a truncheon'. Daily Express. 14.6.08, p28.

[3870] Jeeves, P. 'Locked in a police cell, law-abiding pensioner who told yobs to behave'. Daily Express. 19.1.08, p7.

[3871] Pilditch, D. 'Police quiz for Wise after he tackles yobs'. Daily Express. 4.1.08, p25.

[3872] Madeley, R. 'Why they targeted Tarrant'. Daily Express. 19.5.07, p20.

[3873] Jeeves, P. 'Parkie who fired shots over vandals' heads is spared jail'. Daily Express. 16.9.11, p30.

[3874] Andrews, E. 'Charged with GBH, the boy, 12, who flicked paper at a classmate'. Daily Mail. 29.9.07, p13.

[3875] Martin, A. 'Swabbed for DNA, the man who tackled a litter lout'. Daily Mail. 20.10.07, p31.

[3876] Brooke, C. 'Police dawn raid on boy of 12 over school fight'. Daily Mail. 11.2.08, p36.

[3877] Reynolds, M. 'Facing arrest, the woman who dared to tackle yobs wrecking soldiers' graves'. Daily Express. 28.12.07, p33.

[3878] Riches, C. 'Dads make a citizen's arrest ... and get thrown in the cells'. Daily Express. 22.2.08, p15.

[3879] Widdecombe, A. Daily Express. 24.4.13, p13.

[3880] 'Arrested, the man who hit back at snowball yob'. Daily Mail. 15.2.07, p37.

[3881] Hull, L. 'Cowgirls face police firepower in stand-off at the Tesco corral'. Daily Mail. 19.5.07, p43.

[3882] Dolan, A. 'Girl, 11, gets police visit … over page on Facebook'. Daily Mail. 12.7.11, p25.

[3883] Coyle, M. 'Mum ends up in court for tackling her son's bullies'. Daily Express. 27.2.13, p9.

[3884] Littlejohn, R. Daily Mail. 8.1.13, p17.

[3885] Naumann, Z. '50 pc of drivers stopped by police'. Daily Mail. 8.5.02, p11.

[3886] Rodrick, V. 'Police made me walk home with my disabled son.' Daily Mail, 1.7.13. p24.

[3887] Gall, C. 'Facebook'. Daily Record. 9.1.13, pp1,4,5.

[3888] Lord Cardigan. The Mail on Sunday. 11.5.03, pp52, 53.

[3889] Hamilton, N. 'Police have lost the plot'. Sunday Express. 25.5.08, p29.

[3890] Hamilton, N. 'Police have lost the plot'. Sunday Express. 25.5.08, p29.

[3891] 'Arrest in peace'. Daily Mail. 5.9.03, p43.

[3892] Emsley, C. 'The Great British Bobby'. Quercus. London. 2009.

[3893] Greenwood, C. 'Six-point penalty for using mobile at wheel'. Daily Mail. 29.3.13, p7.

[3894] Rowley, E. 'Carrying a Swiss Army knife could land you in court'. Daily Express. 24.4.10, p8.

[3895] Stimpson, S. 'It's Osama Bin Ladder'. Daily Record. 4.12.10, p30.

[3896] McDonald, C. 'It's Poppycock!'. Daily Record. 11.11.10, p47.

[3897] Littlejohn, R. 'It's a case of 'Heads you're nicked, Tails you're nicked''. Daily Mail. 15.10.10, p17.

[3898] Littlejohn, R. Daily Mail. 9.2.10, p17.

[3899] Silvester, N. 'Tested Beyond Belief'. Sunday Mail. 22.8.10, p39.

[3900] Levy, A. 'Pensioner charged for driving after bag thief'. Daily Mail. 1.4.10, p22.

[3901] Dolan, A. 'A ticket? That's rubbish'. Daily Mail. 13.7.05, p25.

[3902] Littlejohn, R. 'Cowboy Coppers'. Daily Mail. 1.6.10, p17.

[3903] Jeeves, P. 'Police in riot van swoop on children in wheelchairs'. Daily Express. 24.9.10, p31.

[3904] Littlejohn, R. 'It's no wonder so many firms end up on the scrapheap'. Daily Mail. 8.4.11, p17.

[3905] Slack, J. 'No Escaping Big Brother'. Daily Mail. 2.8.07, pp1,2.

[3906] Fernandez, C. 'Ordeal goes on for ex-mayor aged 81 accused of attacking two PCs on his way home from Midnight Man'. Daily Mail. 29.8.07, p5.

[3907] Riches, C. 'Mr. Loophole's latest victory': Millionairess fleeing car yobs'. Daily Express. 18.9.07, p7.

[3908] 'Your Money, Wasted'. Daily Mail. 11.5.06, p19.

[3909] Sunday Express. 11.5.08, p19.

[3910] Khan, U., Gammell, C. 'Police held me for six hours over car park ticket row'. The Daily Telegraph. 20.5.08, p5.

[3911] Allen, V. 'Shopkeeper's traffic warden watch earns her a police warning'. Daily Mail. 29.5.08, p33.

[3912] Flanagan, P., Ingham, J. 'Police Told To Target Drivers'. Daily Express. 1.7.08, p9.

[3913] Hamilton, N. 'Don't ban drink, lock up louts'. Sunday Express. 6.1.08, p31.

[3914] Oliver, J. The Mail on Sunday. 4.2.07, p15.

[3915] Littlejohn, R. 'Are you being nicked? Fasten your seatbelt'. Daily Mail. 7.1.11, p17.

[3916] Heffer, S. 'Hunting, speed traps and the rise of pernicious laws that criminalise the law-abiding'. Daily Mail. 27.12.11, p14.

[3917] Sheldrick, G. 'Make way for the mobile gypsy palace'. Daily Express. 11.2.12, p8.

[3918] Taylor, R., Wilkes, D. 'Move your cars, police are taking a caravan to an illegal traveller site!' Daily Mail. 11.2.12, p27.

[3919] Geoghegan, J. 'Driver's rage at £60 fine for looking at a pretty girl in street'. Daily Express. 9.7.12, p25.

[3920] Dolan, A. 'One-way street to a cell for man who took snap of police'. Daily Mail. 20.8.08, p23.

[3921] Salkeld, L. 'Girl, 2, put on police file for hitting car with a stick'. Daily Mail. 16.10.09, p39.

[3922] Jeeves, P. 'Driver fined for playing his car radio too loudly'. Daily Express. 5.12.09, p36.

[3923] Slack, J. '48 criminals freed to rape and murder'. Daily Mail. 27.10.09, p4.

[3924] 'Police report pregnant woman to social services over half-decorated home'. Daily Mail. 10.11.09, p21.

[3925] Littlejohn, R. 'Mad Mullah's on his bike, but Taliban keeps trucking'. Daily Mail. 11.8.09, p17.

[3926] 'Police pull over driver for laughing'. Daily Record. 5.3.09, p6.

[3927] Pilditch, D. 'Police say mascot is a dangerous dog'. Daily Express. 6.8.09, p15.

[3928] Sears, N. 'Ingrid Tarrant was wrestled to the ground and thrown in a van after two-mile chase by a PC trying to give her a parking ticket'. Daily Mail. 17.7.09, p9.

[3929] Devine, A. 'Driver's Asbo For Detour In Royal Park'. Daily Record. 20.6.09, p19.

[3930] Masey, R. 'Speed causes only 3pc of crashes'. Daily Mail. 26.9.08, p10.

[3931] 'A crazy look at PC's world'. Daily Record. 28.1.10, p8.

[3932] Bonnici, T. 'Locked for taking chip shop PC's photo'. Daily Express. 20.8.08, p27.

[3933] 'Arrested over the colour of his MOT'. Daily Mail. 21.5.09, p43.

[3934] Doughty, S. 'Payout for Christian preacher held in cells'. Daily Mail. 10.12.10, p8.

3935 Petre, J. 'Christian preacher on hooligan charge after saying he believes that homosexuality is a sin'. The Mail on Sunday. 2.5.10, pp6,7.

3936 'Freedom of expression law: the revolt grows'. Daily Mail. 17.5.12, p10.

3937 Revior, R. 'Anger at police in 'race-hate' TV show inquiry'. Daily Mail. 20.11.07, p4.

3938 'Jailed for burning the Koran'. BBC News. 18.4.11.

3939 Dowd, H. 'Winston and the last witch-hunt'. Daily Express. 3.3.08, p24.

3940 Slater, R., Petre, J. 'Police tell café owner: Stop showing Bible DVDs – or we will have to arrest you'. The Mail on Sunday. 25.9.11, p9.

3941 Petre, J. 'Police say sorry to café owner threatened with arrest over Bible DVDs'. The Mail on Sunday. 9.10.11, p32.

3942 Littlejohn, R. 'Diversity? We've All Got A Cross To Bear'. Daily Mail. 22.9.09, p17.

3943 Jedrzejewski, N. 'A preach of the peace'. Daily Express. 21.9.13, p8.

3944 Widdecombe, A. 'Police with no sense of proportion'. Daily Express. 14.11.12, p13.

3945 Levy, A. 'Armed police squad raided my farm after I took potshot at fox and hit two intruders'. Daily Mail. 18.12.10, p20.

3946 Meads, A. 'Time to clarify laws over right to defend your home'. Daily Express. 12.1.10, p26.

3947 Reynolds, M. 'Outcry over the police who posed as burglars'. Daily Express. 30.3.10, p26.

3948 Dawar, A. 'Help! The police have broken in'. Daily Express. 24.6.11, p5.

3949 McKinstry, L. 'A little humiliation is just what most criminals deserve'. Daily Express. 17.2.11, p12.

3950 Narain, J. 'Homeowner arrested after the burglar he confronted falls 30ft'. Daily Mail. 9.8.07, p25.

3951 Leader. 'The law should have given more backing to this hero'. Daily Express. 6.1.12, p12.

3952 Glover, S. 'Why have our police lost their common sense?'. Daily Mail. 24.4.08, p14.

3953 Reynolds, M. 'Dad and son's disbelief at arrest for catching burglar'. Daily Express. 17.8.13, p9.

3954 Hill, P. Daily Express. 21.9.11, p16.

3955 Gallagher, I. 'The Mail on Sunday. 2.3.08, pp60,61.

3956 Flanagan, P. 'Hero Dad Guns Down Burglar'. Daily Express. 7.10.11, pp1,7.

3957 McCabe, G. 'Teenager Locked Up For Shooting Burglar'. Daily Record. 23.5.07, p6.

3958 Hitchens, P. 'Common sense, rotting in a police cell'. The Mail on Sunday. 4.3.07, p33.

3959 McKinstry, L. 'Just What Are The Police Prepared To Do These Days?'. Daily Express. 10.2.06, p10.

3960 Blacklock, M. 'DIY shopper arrested and fingerprinted … for 'stealing' his own plug'. Daily Express. 2.2.08, p13.

3961 Heffer, S. 'So what's gone wrong with Britain's police?'. Daily Mail. 22.1.04, p12.

3962 Bruxelles, Simon de. 'Shopkeeper fined £250 for hitting back against thieves'. The Times. 30.6.07, p25.

3963 Sims, P., Russell, A. Daily Mail. 18.6.11, p5.

3964 Widdecombe, A. 'Police must do more to merit real pay rise'. Daily Express. 2.1.08, p13.

3965 Owens, N., Willis, K. 'My Best Friend Used My ID To Steal £125,000 … and I was the one thrown in jail'. Sunday Mirror. 4.3.12, p19.

3966 'Threat to justice'. Leader. Daily Mail. 16.12.09, p14.

3967 Edge, S. 'Has justice been turned on its head?'. Daily Express. 16.12.09, p24.

3968 Evans, M. 'In the dock … builder who seized a burglar'. Daily Express. 25.3.09, p17.

3969 Greenwood, C. 'Farmer shot at thieves' van to save his mother's life. Now HE could face attempted murder trial'. Daily Mail. 15.9.12, p37.

3970 'Victim of burglary arrested'. Daily Express. 3.10.08, p21 or 31.10.08

3971 McIntosh, R. 'How could we let down these girls so badly?'. Sunday Mirror. 30.9.12, p33.

3972 Widdecombe, A. 'Criminally stupid way to respond'. Daily Express. 25.8.10, p13.

3973 Clark, R. 'Why single out the middle class for speeding?'. Daily Express. 10.8.10, p12.

3974 Daily Express. 9.7.10, p72.

3975 Hardman, R. 'Middle England's Last Stand'. Daily Mail. 15.5.10, pp12,13.

3976 Gall, C. 'Prankster's Racist Gnome Shame'. Daily Record. 3.4.07, p19.

3977 Littlejohn, R. 'Daily Mail. 13.4.12, p17.

3978 Dunbar, P. 'Betrayed by the PC police'. The Mail on Sunday. 8.7.12, pp34,35.

3979 Revoir, P. ' 'Racist' Basil has a brush with the law'. Daily Mail. 17.3.08, p37.

3980 Salkeld, L. ''Quizzed by police for trimming a hedge'. Daily Mail. 6.12.08, p37.

3981 Booker, C. 'Arrested and led away in handcuffs for fighting on the side of the red squirrel'. The Sunday Telegraph. 22.8.10, p27.

3982 Paterson, B. 'Move those mussels at your pearl'. Sunday Mail. 28.9.08, p23.

3983 Delgado, M. 'Arrested by the egg police – for selling this 100-year-old chest of drawers'. The Mail on Sunday. 14.3.10, p45.

3984 'Cops bid to save lizards'. Daily Record. 11.4.11, p27.

3985 Street-Porter, J. 'The plodding police work that has let Claudia down'. Daily Mail. 10.5.10, p49.

REFERENCES

[3986] Watson, D. 'That's not a corpse that's our boxer dog Mumbles'. Daily Record. 1.8.07, p21.

[3987] Iredale, W. 'Open up, it's the bee police: 266 laws let officials into your home'. The Sunday Times. 22.4.07, p4.

[3988] Widdecombe, A. 'Sign of our times to ban protestors'. Daily Express. 11.4.07, p13.

[3989] Mathieson, J. '8 cops cordon off the street just to collar little Matvi'. Daily Record. 20.6.07, p9.

[3990] McKinstry, L. 'The hounding of Jose shows how policing has gone to the dogs'. Daily Express. 18.5.07, p10.

[3991] Horsnell, M. 'He might be barking, but he's not breaking the law'. The Times. 28.4.07, p29.

[3992] Littlejohn, R. 'The Flying Squad are doing bird'. Daily Mail. 7.8.12, p17.

[3993] Sears, N. 'Clarkson and owl of derision'. Daily Mail. 26.5.12, p27.

[3994] Booker, C. 'Irish social workers are horrified by their ruthless English counterparts'. The Sunday Telegraph. 19.2.12, p33.

[3995] Booker, C. 'Kidnap – as sponsored by the state'. The Sunday Telegraph. 4.7.10, p31.

[3996] Booker, C. 'How can it be a crime to love your children?'. The Sunday Telegraph. 30.5.10, p29.

[3997] Booker, C. 'Police hunt on for Vicky though she is not a 'missing person' '. The Sunday Telegraph. 8.5.11, p29.

[3998] Levy, S. 'Ticked off, the mother who tackled a tantrum'. Daily Mail. 26.7.07, p21.

[3999] Taylor, R. 'Social workers tore me from my babies for a year'. Daily Mail. 15.12.12, p15.

[4000] Bentley, P., Camber, R. 'Generation of elderly turned into criminals'. 3.4.10, p6.

[4001] 'Stop police pettiness and collar the real criminals'. Leader. Daily Express. 18.10.03, p14.

[4002] Campbell, C. 'Kids driven to police station over 5p ticket'. The Sunday Post. 13.2.11, p47.

[4003] Levy, A. 'In court, girl who took food out of Tesco bins'. Daily Mail. 17.2.11, p39.

[4004] Kinchen, R. 'Parents risk jobs over home-alone children'. The Sunday Times. 6.2.11, p5.

[4005] Hamilton, N. 'Stop this institutional idiocy'. Sunday Express. 30.11.08, p31.

[4006] Ellicott, C. 'Driven mad by a faulty alarm …'. Daily Mail. 1.2.11, p5.

[4007] McKinstry, L. 'Police were quite right to reprimand daffodil pickers'. Daily Express. 17.3.11, p14.

[4008] Narain, J. 'The Snowball Squad'. Daily Mail. 16.1.13, p12.

[4009] Drury, P. 'All This For 5 Folk In A Flat'. Daily Record. 25.3.11, p17.

[4010] Littlejohn, R. Daily Mail. 25.3.11, p17.

[4011] Littlejohn, R. 'Fireworks case Mark is let off'. Daily Mail. 26.8.11, p17.

[4012] Littlejohn, R. 'The death of common sense and how our police are losing the plot'. Daily Mail. 28.4.11, p14.

[4013] Morgan, T. '£20,000 copter swoop on 47p 'thief' at a tip'. Daily Express. 6.4.11, p34.

[4014] Kelly, T. 'Mum-to-be faced arrest for fleeing stranded train'. Daily Mail. 11.6.11, p42.

[4015] Blackburn, V. 'Now it's a police farce on patrol'. Daily Express. 24.8.09, p14.

[4016] Clerkin, B. 'Targeted by police, the fringe terrorists with water pistols'. Daily Mail. 9.8.07, p5.

[4017] Booker, C. 'Full weight of the law comes down on metric martyr'. The Sunday Telegraph. 16.9.07, p18.

[4018] Scott, D. 'Police take down particulars of a stripogram PC'. Daily Express. 27.4.07, p24.

[4019] Levy, A. 'Police quiz boy … for throwing away his friend's bicycle dust cap'. Daily Mail. 22.7.11, p32.

[4020] 'Bar bans fork-bend magician'. Daily Express. 20.6.11, p11.

[4021] Gallacher, S. 'Police won't let Colin sell his old car'. Sunday Post. 13.2.11, p51.

[4022] Slack, J. 'Police Farce'. Daily Mail. 6.2.08, pp1,2.

[4023] Sears, N. 'Nailed!'. Daily Mail. 18.7.08, p7.

[4024] Hamilton, N. 'Our Carry On constables'. Sunday Express. 11.5.08, p27.

[4025] Slack, J. 'Police 'ignored child abusers to hit targets' '. Daily Mail. 12.11.07, p4.

[4026] O'Hare, P. 'Child of 2 Is Branded A Criminal'. Daily Record. 15.11.07, p17.

[4027] Hitchens, P. 'Our black-shirt bullies, all power and no law'. The Mail on Sunday. 9.10.05, p27.

[4028] Levy, A. 'Boris quizzed over his souvenir of Baghdad'. Daily Mail. 28.2.08, p41.

[4029] Hull, L. 'Arrested, DNA tested and locked up … just for paddling down a river'. Daily Mail. 27.6.08, p21.

[4030] 'Cop raid on ruins'. Sunday Mirror. 27.1.08, p30.

[4031] Beabey, K. 'Police 'arrest' scarecrow – for impersonating a traffic officer'. The Mail on Sunday. 2.4.07.

[4032] Hitchens, P. 'An enemy of the People's State'. The Mail on Sunday. 24.2.08, p27.

[4033] Forsyth, F. 'We are governed by mice, not men'. Daily Express. 17.2.12, p13.

[4034] Levy, A. 'Police call out helicopter and dog team … just to catch two boys who took plastic goalposts'. Daily Mail. 19.7.12, p13.

[4035] Hamilton, N. 'Save us from police farce'. Sunday Express. 12.4.09, p27.

[4036] Wynne-Jones, J. 'The gay march, a pensioner's letter of complaint and a visit from 'hate crime' police'. The Sunday Telegraph. 25.10.09, p13.

[4037] Brooks, T. 'Assault charge for widow who prodded thug'. Daily Express. 2.10.09, p11.

[4038] 'Accountability is central problem'. Leader. Daily Record. 3.10.13, p8.

[4039] Littlejohn, R. 'Sack the sniffer wardens – not soldiers or cops'. Daily Mail. 4.3.11, p17.

[4040] 'Police warn off sandwich seller at the school gates'. Daily Mail. 14.9.07, p41.

[4041] Milland, G. 'Cigs out … or bosses will call the police'. Daily Express. 28.4.07, p27.

[4042] Platell, A. 'Dishonouring the fallen'. Daily Mail. 6.10.07, p19.

[4043] Sergeant, H. 'Trying to catch the lift? You're nicked!'. Daily Mail. 11.2.08, p28.

[4044] 'Scooting to school? First pass the test'. Daily Mail. 30.4.13, p11.

[4045] Salkeld, L. 'Crackers! Police threat to cheese-making gran, 86 …'. Daily Mail. 24.5.13, p31.

[4046] 'Volts From The Blue'. The Sunday Times. 2011.

[4047] Dixon, C. 'Swoop on my toy gun calculators adds up to a waste of police time'. Daily Express. 27.1.12, p27.

[4048] Jeeves, P. 'Gun police in swoop on military games prop'. Daily Express. 10.2.12, p45.

[4049] Brooke, C. 'The 'weekend Nazi' his machine gun and a brush with the law'. Daily Mail. 10.2.12, p33.

[4050] Sunday Mirror. 30.9.12, p10.

[4051] Loudon, A. 'This vicar, frightened of being burgled again, was sent to jail yesterday for keeping a tiny antique gun in his bedroom. So, whatever happened to catching REAL criminals?'. Daily Mail. 26.6.02, p5.

[4052] Finlay, D. 'Grandad's WWI revolver lands man in court'. Daily Express. 1.2.12, p21.

[4053] Ferndale, N. 'The wrong target, again'. The Sunday Telegraph. 8.4.07, p25.

[4054] Littlejohn, R. Daily Mail. 29.5.12, p17.

[4055] Dixon, C. 'Rough justice for father who collared a yob'. Daily Express. 24.8.12, p11.

[4056] 'Police swoop on toy gun man'. Daily Express. 4.2.09, p53.

[4057] Stote, M. 'Toy guns trigger a police raid on fancy dress bash'. Daily Express. 11.2.09, p26.

[4058] Brown, M. 'Fury as perverts and violent yobs are let off'. Daily Express. 12.8.09, p17.

[4059] Henderson, E. 'Gamekeepers become prey'. Sunday Express. 13.12.09, p21.

[4060] Pooran, N. 'Police have taken away Braveheart's weapons (if not yet his freedom)'. Daily Mail. 15.3.13, p9.

[4061] 'Operation Overkill!'. Daily Mail. 14.2.13, p35.

[4062] Ferrari, N. 'Who'll cop to the £1 million gimmicks?'. Sunday Express. 5.9.10, p27.

[4063] Widdecombe, A. 'No closure over this bin issue'. Daily Express. 11.8.10 p13.

[4064] Morgan, T. 'Arrested and sacked … for helping himself to colleague's biscuits'. Daily Express. 23.3.10, p27.

[4065] Fagge, N. 'Outrage over police plan to give heroin junkies free needles'. Daily Express. 14.5.10, p23.

[4066] Sheldrick, G. '3 little girls get a police warning … for playing outside'. Daily Express. 16.8.13, p37.

[4067] Littlejohn, R. 'So unjust it makes you want to spit'. Daily Mail. 6.8.13, p17.

[4068] 'Call the cops! He wants to pay by cash'. The Sunday Post. 13.2.11, p27.

[4069] 'Starter pistol banned from historic fun run'. Daily Express. 28.5.11, p28.

[4070] Scott, M. 'You Muppets'. Sunday Mail. 29.4.07, p27.

[4071] 'Big police presence stuns Old Firm pals'. Daily Record. 20.5.11, p19.

[4072] 'Sex and the kitty'. The Sunday Times. 30.10.11, p29.

[4073] 'Plaque for war hero is seized'. Daily Express. 8.12.11, p14.

[4074] Jeeves, P. 'Ban on girl visiting her sister's grave in school uniform'. Daily Express. 26.11.11, p29.

[4075] Salkeld, L. 'Invaded by travellers, ignored by the police. Now this farmer is facing £20,000 fine'. Daily Mail. 6.5.11, p5.

[4076] McGivern, M. ' 'Big Man' Charged'. Daily Record. 22.12.11, p6.

[4077] Townend, D. 'Police raided our house after mistaking plant for cannabis'. Daily Express. 27.12.11, p25.

[4078] Salkeld, L. 'Accused of kidnap, son who took his mother out of care home for Christmas'. Daily Mail. 31.12.11, p38.

[4079] Brooke, C. 'Child porn nightmare'. Daily Mail. 7.3.12, p28.

[4080] Pyatt, J. 'Schlong Arm Of The Law'. The Sun. 4.3.12, p19.

[4081] 'Arrested … for not smiling'. Daily Express. 9.8.12, p3.

[4082] Roberts, A. 'I made a citizen's arrest and was NICKED'. Reading Post. 21.10.09, pp1,5.

[4083] Foster, E. 'Ball fan's red card for cops'. The Sun. 21.5.12, p11.

[4084] Rao, N. 'I'd do it again! Farmer sends travellers packing'. Daily Express. 15.6.12, p11.

[4085] Riches, C. 'Arrested … for being honest'. Daily Express. 2.4.09, p30.

[4086] Riches, C. 'The dad in court for ticking off a boy yob'. Daily Express. 17.3.09, p23.

[4087] Millbank, J. 'Businessman is arrested in front of wife and son … for 'anti-gypsy' email that he didn't even write'. The Mail on Sunday. 10.1.10, p7.

[4088] Wynne-Jones, J. 'Police follow woman home after threat to smack children'. The Sunday Telegraph. 8.11.09, p12.

[4089] Brooks, T. 'Locked up, father who slapped his daughter'. Daily Express. 14.8.08, p10.

[4090] 'Dad locked up in cell for smacking his son'. Daily Express. 18.11.08.

[4091] Pearson, A. 'Hate crime, a batty old lady and freedom'. Daily Mail. 28.10.09, p15.

[4092] 'Victory for father who tried to stop 'apple yobs' '. Daily Mail. 30.9.09, p18.

[4093] Littlejohn, R. 'Step away from the deep fat fryer'. Daily Mail. 21.4.09, p17.

[4094] Steele, J. 'Police 'are targeting middle England to raise tally of arrests' '. The Daily Telegraph. 15.5.07, p14.

[4095] Russell, J. 'All this power has gone to the fist of PC Thug'. The Sunday Times. 15.2.09, p21.

[4096] Daily Express. 11.1.10, p2.

[4097] Currie, L., Bayer, K. 'Father tries to protect family from drugs ... and is jailed'. Daily Mail. 17.2.09, p33.

[4098] Fagge, N. 'Seized by police ... the civic leader, 84, who's under siege from yobs'. Daily Express. 8.2.10, p7.

[4099] 'Nose-blow driver in the clear'. Daily Express. 27.2.10, p5.

[4100] Morgan, T. 'Fined for blowing my nose'. Daily Express. 29.1.10, p37.

[4101] Dorman, N. 'It's No Coke'. The People. 23.9.12, p24

[4102] Littlejohn, R. Daily Mail. 18.12.12, p17.

[4103] Devine, A. 'Gnome alone! Family say cops 'nicked' their garden ornaments'. Daily Record. 12.8.09, p27.

[4104] Morgan, T. 'I was seized by ten police officers, stripped and put in a cell ... for driving my car'. Daily Express. 2.10.08, p7.

[4105] Anderson, G. 'Battered By Police But I Was Thrown Into Jail'. Sunday Mirror. 9.8.09, p16.

[4106] Whyte, S. 'School disco police'. Daily Mail. 14.12.12, p3.

[4107] McLean, M. 'Nicked For Being A Good Samaritan'. Daily Record. 10.12.12, pp10,11.

[4108] 'Mind how you go, Sausage'. Daily Mail. 20.11.12, p17.

[4109] Hitchens, P. 'Farewell to a brave fighter for free speech'. The Mail on Sunday. 18.8. 02, p27.

[4110] Weathers, H. Daily Mail. 21.7.12, p46.

[4111] McLean, S. 'Having mad justice'. Daily Mail. 2.1.02, p15.

[4112] Sapsted, D. 'Landowner calls in police to halt rave – and is arrested'. The Daily Telegraph. 4.1.02, p6.

[4113] Hugill, B. 'Privacy is dead in a snoopers' society'. Daily Express. 1.8.03, p12.

[4114] Heffer, S. 'Glimmer Of Sanity'. Daily Mail. 21.4.01, p15.

[4115] Widdecombe, A. 'Esther speaks common sense on the police'. Daily Express. 9.1.13, p13.

[4116] McKinstry, L. 'Immigrants squat in your house and you're powerless?'. Daily Express. 14.1.10, p12.

[4117] 'Elected police chiefs are our best hope for justice'. Daily Express. 25.6.08, p12.

[4118] Evans, M. 'Give us proper police, not plastic say Britons'. Daily Express. 19.5.08, p15.

[4119] Sims, P. 'Arrested by eight police, handcuffed and thrown in a cell ... for confronting school bullies'. Daily Mail. 31.7.09, p5.

[4120] Walters, S. 'The Caviar Squad'. The Mail on Sunday. 28.9.08, p7.

[4121] Martin, D., Borland, S. 'The PC police trying to drive ice cream vans off our streets'. Daily Mail. 25.4.09, p9.

[4122] Morgan, T. 'Judge's anger at gardener accused of having a scythe'. Daily Express. 10.10.08, p39.

[4123] Brooke, C. 'My police ordeal over son's asthma death'. Daily Mail. 27.8.08, p25.

[4124] Morgan, T. 'Police kicked down my door ... and I have to pay a £100 bill'. Daily Express. 22.4.09 p16.

[4125] Dolan, A. Daily Mail. 23.4.09, p29.

[4126] Hickley, M. 'The new police crackdown? Street football'. Daily Mail. 1.1.09, p13.

[4127] Musson, C. 'Cops Bag Piper'. Daily Record. 20.12.08, p7.

[4128] Chapman, J. 'Thugs attack dad ... and HE gets arrested'. Daily Express. 21.5.09, p27.

[4129] Martin, A. '£5,000 farce over 'theft' of electricity worth just 0.003p'. Daily Mail. 19.8.09, p30.

[4130] Sunday Express. 18.11.07 p29.

[4131] Flanagan, P. 'How I was arrested for attempted murder of yob who beat up my lad'. Daily Express. 27.7.09, p5.

[4132] BBC Newsnight. 24.6.13.

[4133] Hutcheon, P. 'The end for 'licensed sex trade'?'. The Courier & Advertiser. 6.10.13, p4.

[4134] Littlejohn, R. Daily Mail. 28.6.13, p17.

[4135] Martin, A., Greenwood, C. 'Building bridges with the police – the Mitchell way!'. Daily Mail. 21.12.12, p25.

[4136] Crichton, T. 'Flaw & Order'. Daily Record. 1.4.13, p6.

[4137] Clegg, D. 'Police Chiefs In Turf War'. Daily Record. 28.11.12, p17.

[4138] Gilbride, P.. 'Police In Crisis As Top Staff Quit Jobs'. Daily Express. 13.6.13, pp 1,4.

[4139] Rowley, E. 'Greece in turmoil as cuts loom.' The Sunday Telegraph. 12.2.12, p33.

[4140] Emsley, C. 'The Great British Bobby'. Quercus. London. 2009.

[4141] Sergeant, H. 'Inside Britain's Police Farce'. Daily Mail. 11.2.08, p26.

[4142] Bennetto, J. 'Britain needs a more realistic approach to heroin addicts'. The Independent. 19.2.07, p2.

[4143] 'Scots cops' Africa beat'. Daily Record. 23.8.13, p21.

[4144] Jones, N. 'The Plimsoll Sensation'.

[4145] Murray, P. 'Plan to link Scots Police to military'. Sunday Express. 18.8.13, p2.

[4146] The Official History Of The Metropolitan Police. Gary Mason. Carlton. 2004, p28.

[4147] Payne, S. 'Police chief calls for end to role-play staff exams'. The Daily Telegraph. 18.8.03, p6.

[4148] Farrari, N. 'Cooper's cop review is an insult'. Sunday Express. 2.10.11, p31.

[4149] Townsend, M., Helm, T. 'Don't have nightmares ... the next chief of police might be Jordan'. The Observer. 11.12.11, p19.

[4150] Leppard, D. 'Top foreign police to be recruited as chief constables'. The Sunday Times. 20.1.13, p1.

[4151] Officer 'A'. 'The Crime Factory'. Mainstream Publishing. 2012.

[4152] McKinstry, L. 'Police have become a PC incompetent mess'. Daily Express. 24.9.09, p12.

[4153] Synon, M. E. 'March of the Euro Police'. The Mail on Sunday. 21.11.10, p43.

[4154] Jeory, T. 'Europe-wide 'FBI' set to battle organised crime'. Sunday Express. 29.8.10, p4.

[4155] Lewis, J. 'Chief forced to quit days before riots'. The Sunday Telegraph. 14.11.10, p12.

[4156] Daley, J. 'Inside every liberal lurks a secret policeman'. The Mail on Sunday. 25.9.05, p25.

[4157] Clegg, D. 'MSP calls for kettling cops probe'. Daily Record. 20.3.13, p25.

[4158] Emsley, C. 'The Great British Bobby'. Quercus. London. 2009.

[4159] Daily Express. 15.12.10, p10.

[4160] Daily Express. 5.3.12, p10.

[4161] Daily Express. 21.3.12, p10.

[4162] Daily Express. 4.10.11, p10.

[4163] BBC1 Panorama. 8.7.13.

[4164] Gilbride, P. 'Police face questions over Trump protests'. Daily Express. 15.5.13, p22.

[4165] Emsley, C. 'The Great British Bobby'. Quercus. London. 2009.

[4166] Brosten, P. '700 police in animal rights swoop'. Daily Express. 2.5.07, p17.

[4167] Daily Express. 18.11.10, p10.

[4168] Daily Express. 22.9.10, p10.

[4169] Doyle, J. 'Police try to ban far-right rally over fears of race riots'. Daily Mail. 19.8.10, p20.

[4170] SPF website.

[4171] Townsend, M., McVeigh, T. 'Police share anger of protesters over'. The Observer. 20.3.11, p16.

[4172] Silvester, N. Sunday Mail. 2.9.07, p2.

[4173] Willey, J. 'Burkha spoof carnival team sent home for being 'racist' '. Daily Express. 23.8.07, p39.

[4174] Massey, R. 'Police force lays down law to road-toll rebels'. Daily Mail. 16.2.07, p19.

[4175] Daily Express. 13.9.11, p10.

[4176] Reid, S. 'Death On The Rock'. Daily Mail. 21.7.07, p19.

[4177] Davidson, L. '20 Cops In 5AM Raid On School Protest'. Daily Record. 25.6.10, p37.

[4178] Findlay, R., Scott, M. 'Call this justice?'. Sunday Mail. 24.3.02, p30.

[4179] Wilson, C. 'Is 'Dame' Camilla now a step closer to becoming Queen?'. Daily Mail. 10.4.12, p13.

[4180] Walters, S., Owen, G. 'Tories order police to halt workfare demos'. The Mail on Sunday. 26.2.12, p17.

[4181] Ellery, B. 'Police: It is not our job to uphold respect'. The Mail on Sunday. 14.4.13, p20.

[4182] Woolf, M. 'Cuts to put mounted police out to grass'. The Sunday Times. 3.10.10, p10.

[4183] STRIKE – When Britain Went to War. June, 2011, C4. The Miners Strike (video) documentary.

[4184] Emsley, C. 'The Great British Bobby'. Quercus. London. 2009.

[4185] Clegg, D. 'Top Cop: Give Us Law To Crush Pickets'. Daily Record. 20.6.13, p8.

[4186] Harrison, I. 'Cops in double-standards row over protection bill'. The Sunday Post. 26.9.10, p11.

[4187] 100 Years Ago, Daily Express. 23.3.11, p10.

[4188] Daily Express. 30.6.11, p10.

[4189] Clark, N. 'Britain On The Brink'. Daily Express. 6.8.11, p42.

[4190] The Official History Of The Metropolitan Police. Gary Mason. Carlton. 2004, p19.

[4191] Sandbrook, D. 'Frenzy of Greed'. Daily Mail. 7.4.12, p16.

[4192] Tucker, R. 'Abundance of police when lorry protest hits road'. Daily Express. 28.5.08, p31.

[4193] Whitaker, A. 'Police goaded striking miners says ex-officer'. Scotland on Sunday. 23.12.12, p9.

[4194] BBC News. 22.10.12.

[4195] BBC 2 Documentary. 13.10.11.

[4196] Slack, J., Doyle, J. 'Fury as police chief says cuts put children at risk'. Daily Mail. 25.2.11, p4.

[4197] Doyle, J. 'Migrant arrests have doubled in just three years'. Daily Mail. 5.4.11, p20.

[4198] McKinstry, L. 'It's time to turn tables on greedy, self-serving elite'. Daily Express. 2.3.09.

[4199] Wright, S. 'Reid 'misled public over plan for police to hunt illegal immigrants'. Daily Mail. 23.12.06, p2.

[4200] Rose, G. 'Police chiefs backing single Scottish force'. Scotland on Sunday. 28, 11.10, p5.

[4201] Christison, G. 'Police State!'. Scottish Sunday Express. 31.3.13, pp1,2.

[4202] Silvester, N. 'The Single Line'. Sunday Mail. 22.8.10, p32.

[4203] Greenwood, C. 'New Met Chief: Let victims decide when the crime hunt ends'. Daily Mail.. 28.9.11, p2.

[4204] Copperfield, D. 'I left UK to be a proper copper'. The Sunday Telegraph. 25.7.10, p16.

[4205] McKinstry, L. 'Our police chiefs should be elected and held to account'. Daily Express. 24.5.10, p12.

[4206] McKeown, J. 'Be very afraid ...'. The Courier and Advertiser. 8.10.13, p23.

REFERENCES

[4207] Hitchens, P. 'I don't know if crooks fear Britain's new FBI – but it should terrify the rest of us'. The Mail on Sunday. 13.10.13, p29.

[4208] David, D. 'The day I knew Bob Quick was flawed'. The Mail on Sunday. 12.4.09, p19.

[4209] Shipman, T. 'Ministers lying about terror threat to justify draconian laws'. Daily Mail. 26.3.10, p8.

[4210] Delgado, M. 'Pensioners held on way to airport protest ...over 'inflammatory' T-shirts'. The Mail on Sunday. 15.6.08, p43.

[4211] 'Warning of police state by top cleric'. Daily Record. 5.2.07, p6.

[4212] 'The roughing-up of Walter aged 82'. Daily Mail. 29.9.05, p8.

[4213] Little, A. 'Labour's terror state'. Daily Express. 3.10.05, p6.

[4214] 'Terror plot' 'epidemic' warning'. Daily Mail. 10.1.0.07, p29.

[4215] Perry, A. 'How PM sparked fury of Sir John'. Sunday Express. 13.11.05, p9.

[4216] Collins, T. 'Deadly Cost Of Tying Police Hands'. Daily Mail. 11.3.09, p11.

[4217] Booth, L. 'Wake up and smell the pepper spray. These 3,609 new laws are to control us not protect us.' The Mail on Sunday. 19.4.09, p31.

[4218] Martin, S. 'Hauled out of his lessons in terror swoop ... schoolboy, 12, trying to save his youth club with demo in Cam's backyard'. Sunday Mirror. 12.12.10, p11.

[4219] Bracchi, P. 'Twitter and the bomb joke that's blown justice to bits'. Daily Mail. 16.11.10, p22.

[4220] Nicol, M. 'I only wanted to make fairy lights, says eBay man in terror raid'. The Mail on Sunday. 15.4.07, p51.

[4221] Alexander, A. 'The Thought Police have You in mind'. Daily Mail. 11.1.08, p18.

[4222] Butler, E. ' 'We' have all been made criminals' '. The Sunday Times. 1.3.09, p19.

[4223] Brown, W. 'Using anti-terror law to intimidate a journalist is a new low for UK'. Daily Record. 21.8.13, p8.

[4224] Littlejohn, R. 'Bonfire of insanity'. Daily Mail. 5.12.08, p17.

[4225] Booker, C. 'Another win for the child snatchers'. The Sunday Telegraph. 21.11.10, p37.

[4226] Booker, C. 'Why are the police providing the muscle for forced adoptions?'. The Sunday Telegraph. 26.9.10, p33.

[4227] Booker, C. 'Jail threat to mum for speaking to MP'. The Sunday Telegraph. 17.4.11.

[4228] Emsley, C. 'The Great British Bobby'. Quercus. London. 2009.

[4229] Leader. 'Join our crusade and put police back on the beat'. Sunday Express. 18.2.07, p26.

[4230] Silvester, N. 'Cop Chief's Show Of Force'. Sunday Mail. 17.10,10, pp1,4,5.

[4231] Watson, D. 'Police Cop 90% Rookie Fall'. Daily Record. 25.9.10, p10.

[4232] Gordon, I. 'Get police on patrol'. Sunday Express. 4.7.10, p67.

[4233] Hitchens, P. The Mail on Sunday. 4.7.10, p29.

[4234] McKinstry, L. 'The public sector must be brought under control now'. Daily Express. 21.7.10, p12.

[4235] Hughes, M. 'Root out corrupt officers, police told'. The Independent. 13.2.10, p1.

[4236] Slack, J. 'Labour's £5m police lie'. Daily Mail. 27.3.10, p45.

[4237] Gilbertson, D. 'Why are police so rude? Because they are trained to be'. The Mail on Sunday. 27.2.11, p27.

[4238] Sawer, P. '600 police stations lost already, now 40 more are under threat'. The Sunday Telegraph. 16.12.07, p6.

[4239] Sergeant, H. 'Inside Britain's Police Farce'. Daily Mail. 11.2.08, p26.

[4240] Oborne, P. 'A chip off the block'. Daily Mail. 6.10.06, p59.

[4241] Leppard, D. 'Public may get to set tasks for police'. The Sunday Times. 29.1.12, p6.

[4242] Greenwood, C. 'Burglary victims hit back as top policeman says: 'You're safer than ever at home'. Daily Mail. 3.10.12, p28.

[4243] Alexander, D. 'Victim Condemns Thug's Landmark Appeal'. Sunday Mail. 31.10.10, p14.

[4244] 'Rape cases review is vital'. Daily Record. 25.6.10, p8.

[4245] Thornton, P. 'Crooks Fight 'Dodgy' Cop Confessions'. Daily Record. 18.4.09, p15.

[4246] 'Jail cut if you confess'. Daily Express. 25.8.10, p15.

[4247] Ferrari, N. 'Hard truth about the riot wimps' soft option'. Sunday Express. 28.8.11, p3.

[4248] Connett, D. 'Bugging officer says he was part of 'police propaganda' operation'. The Independent on Sunday. 10.2.08, p21.

[4249] Hitchens, P. 'Professor Nutt, the cannabis propagandist in a scientist's white coat'. The Mail On Sunday. 21.11.10, p33.

[4250] Slack, J. 'Under-18s are given a licence to smoke dope'. Daily Mail. 22.1.07, p4.

[4251] Wright, S. 'Our folly over cannabis laws'. Daily Mail. 21.3.07, p16.

[4252] Townsend, M. 'Police chief issues call to decriminalise cannabis'. The Observer. 19.9.10, pp1,9.

[4253] BBC1 News. 27.6.11.

[4254] Hitchens, P. 'Clear out this nest of wriggling police chiefs'. The Mail on Sunday. 25.11.07, p33.

[4255] Churcher, S., Sheridan, P. 'How the Acid King confessed he DID set up Rolling Stones drug bust for MI5 and FBI'. The Mail on Sunday. 24.10,10, p36.

759

4256 Kinnell, H. G. 'The Great Diet Pill Conspiracy'. Athena Press. 2010.

4257 Doyle, J. 'Forget police targets, just fight crime, says Minister'. Daily Mail. 30.6.10, p13.

4258 Forsyth, J. 'Addicted to box ticking, the police chiefs who refuse to be set free'. The Mail on Sunday. 24.10.10, p39.

4259 Little, A. 'Police chief: 'We are not here just to catch crooks' '. Daily Express. 23.7.10, p15.

4260 Bowater, D. 'How red tape tied up police'. Daily Express. 30.4.10, p39.

4261 Walters, S. 'The Quangos In The Firing Line'. The Mail on Sunday. 23.5.10, p2.

4262 Morgan, D. 'Empire-building at fault for lack of cops on beat'. Daily Express. 18.5.10, p30.

4263 Sergeant, H. 'The Great Disconnect'. Daily Mail. 3.5.10, p30.

4264 Doughty, S. ' 'I'm ditching targets'. says police chief'. Daily Mail. 12.6.10, p57.

4265 Slack, J., Hickley, M. 'Craven police chiefs who became Clarke's puppets'. Daily Mail. 12.11.05, p5.

4266 'The police must be fit for purpose'. Leader. The Mail on Sunday. 17.2.13, p27.

4267 Owen, G. 'Mitchell blames Theresa May for forcing him out over 'Plebgate' '. The Mail on Sunday. 14.4.13, p6.

4268 Hall, M. 'Anti-terror chief's astonishing bid to smear the Tories'. Daily Express. 22.12.08, p10.

4269 Leppard, D., Walsh, G. 'Blair told police to silence letter pest'. The Sunday Times. 20.5.01, p4.

4270 Pearson, J. 'Sex, lies, Downing Street and the cover-up that left the Krays free to kill'. Daily Mail. 21.8.10, p45.

4271 Leppard, D. 'Met chief 'plotted to oust' race-row officer'. The Sunday Times. 29.6.08, p15.

4272 Fensome, J. 'Blunkett is trying to bring in a police state by the back door'. The Daily Telegraph. 4.7.02, p26.

4273 Little, A. 'Too much red tape is still keeping police off the beat'. Daily Express. 3.12.09, p8.

4274 Hellawell, K. 'The dangers we all face when police are too terrified to think for themselves'. The Mail on Sunday. 18.5.08, p27.

4275 Drill, S. 'At last, a police chief discards Labour targets'. Daily Express. 12.6.10, p24.

4276 'Top cop's body is found on mountain'. Daily Record. 12.3.08, p4.

4277 Gardham, M. 'Scottish National Police'. Daily Record. 24.9.10, p2.

4278 Pierce, A. 'Paddick's all set to carry on campaigning'. Daily Mail. 22.9.10, p13.

4279 Leader. 'Fawning to a tyrant'. Daily Mail. 19.9.11, p14.

4280 Wright, S. 'Met chief backs down on badge ban'. Daily Mail. 30.7.09, p13.

4281 'Gorbals is blamed over arrest of MP'. Daily Mail. 23.3.10, p28.

4282 Phillips, M. 'If the police won't tackle young thugs any more, then what ARE they for?'. Daily Mail. 28.9.09, p14.

4283 Murray, T. 'Does Blair really need 20 police to guard one home?'. Sunday Express. 18.7.10, pp22,23.

4284 McKinstry, L. 'The Government is losing the plot on law and order'. Daily Express. 26.7.10, p12.

4285 Heffer, S. Daily Mail. 22.1.04, p12.

4286 Silvester, N. 'Police Chief Wanted'. Sunday Mail. 26.7.09, p2.

4287 Townsend, M. 'NY police chief attacks coalition reform plans'. The Observer. 6.3.11, p10.

4288 Slack, J. 'Electing local chiefs is perverse, warns leading officer'. Daily Mail. 7.2.11, p10.

4289 Smith, B. 'There's nothing to fear if Scotland's eight police forces are cut back to one'. The Sunday Post. 16.1.11, p11.

4290 Smyth, B. 'Police chiefs condemn plans for 'superforce' '. The Sunday Post. 23.1.11, p19.

4291 Fairweather, E. '... I care about the victims of Jersey'. the Mail on Sunday. 19.4.09, pp8,9.

4292 Whitehead, T. 'Clarke 'conning the public' over new-look police'. Daily Express. 24.12.05, p2.

4293 Alberge, D. 'War veterans' mental suffering dramatised in film by ex-para'. The Observer. 20.3.11, p19.

4294 'A move that is desperate'. Daily Express. 25.7.11, p12.

4295 Woof, M., Leppard, D. 'Ministers want battle-hardened colonels to shake up police'. The Sunday Times. 20.7.11, p1

4296 Verkaik, R. 'Police fury at plan to bring in Army'. The Mail on Sunday. 14.8.11, p8.

4297 'Miscarriages of Justice – A review of Justice in Error'. edited by Clive Walker and Keir Starmer.

4298 Townsend, M. 'NY police chief attacks coalition reform plans'. The Observer. 6.3.11, p10.

4299 Doughty, S. 'Now we have more lawyers than police'. Daily Mail. 4.4.11, p13.

4300 Shannon, K. 'Scots Cops Are United ... Against One Force'. Daily Record. 21.4.11, p37.

4301 Bryce, T. 'Police chiefs attacked in single force furore'. The Sunday Post. 1.5.11, p17.

4302 Rose, G. 'Detectives to face 'value for money' tests'. Scotland on Sunday. 10.2.13, p6.

4303 Daily Express. 17.6.11, p10.

4304 Little, A., Pilditch, D. 'PM defends decision to reopen case on Madeleine'. Daily Express. 14.5.11, p9.

4305 BBC1 News. 7.7.11.

4306 Hills, J. 'Criminal waste of police time'. Sunday Express.

4307 Gill, C. 'Make legal drinking age 21, says embattled police chief'. Daily Mail.. 8.9.07, p25

4308 Osborne, P. 'The Triumph Of The Political Class'. Daily Mail. 4.9.07, p29.

[4309] Gardham, M. 'MacAskill To Unveil Single Police Force'. Daily Record. 15.8.11, p2.

[4310] Leader. 'Police shake-up can't be avoided'. Daily Record. 15.8.11, p8.

[4311] Shipman, T., Doyle, J. 'Police round on PM's 'supercop' '. Daily Mail. 15.8.11, p6.

[4312] Drury, I. 'I'd love to run the Met, says the cop who cleaned up New York'. Daily Mail. 8.8.11, p12.

[4313] Merrick, J. 'Police drop Prescott misconduct probe'. Daily Mail. 11.5.06, p19.

[4314] C4 News. 12.8.11.

[4315] Letts, Q. Daily Mail. 25.8.11, p14.

[4316] Hamilton, E. 'It Won't Be Hugh But It Could Be You'. Sunday Mail. 21.8.11, p31.

[4317] Leake, C., Taher, A. 'Candidate for top Yard job wears fake uniform with 'made-up' plastic badge'. The Mail on Sunday. 21.8.11, p17.

[4318] Forsyth, F. 'Hurry Up: You're Driving Me Mad!'. Daily Express. 26.8.11, p19.

[4319] Edwards, R. D. 'Time To Cut Out The Rot – Starting At The Top'. Daily Mail. 2.11.07, p13.

[4320] Coleman, B. 'Spare no pity for Sir Ian Blair, a most political policeman'. The Independent on Sunday. 4.11.07, p38.

[4321] Sergeant, H. 'Inside Britain's Police Farce'. Daily Mail. 13.2.08, p37.

[4322] Widdecombe, A. 'It's criminal to think we need fewer police'. Daily Express. 13.2.08, p13.

[4323] Broster, P. 'Chief of police in heroin law row'. Daily Express. 16.10, p07, p4.

[4324] Slack, J. 'Police force ratings 'overlook whites' '. Daily Mail. 100.10.07, p17.

[4325] Brogan, B. 'Anti-terror leaks are risking lives, says police chief'. Daily Mail. 26.4.07, p2.

[4326] Townsend, M., Doward, J. 'Lock terror suspects up indefinitely, say police'. The Observer. 15.7.07, p1.

[4327] Birrell, I. 'Secret Files: Labour Lied Over Gaddafi'. The Mail on Sunday. 4.9.11, p2.

[4328] 'Gaddafi's guests'. The Mail on Sunday. 4.9.11, p9.

[4329] Sears, N. 'How the Yard jumped to Libya's call over Saif 'assassination' threat'. Daily Mail. 5.9.11, p7.

[4330] Phillips, M. 'Cash for honours and why Labour is so desperate to defend Ian Blair'. Daily Mail. 12.11.07, p14.

[4331] 'Blair 'won extra cash for his local police force' '. The Mail on Sunday. 15.4.07, p26.

[4332] Loveday & Reid. 'Going Local'. 2003, p33.

[4333] Forsyth, R. 'Let's have justice in the open'. Daily Express. 9.9.11, p17.

[4334] Shipman, R., Wright, S. 'Sir Ian is accused of telling ministers: Blair is in the clear'. Daily Mail. 19.2.07, p6.

[4335] 'Peter Wright'. Daily Express. 22.10.11, p43.

[4336] Martin, D. 'May: All Hillsborough papers will be released'. Daily Mail. 18.10.1, p12.

[4337] Walton, S. 'Salmond: I'll order police to sabotage an early poll'. The Mail on Sunday. 15.1.12, p11.

[4338] McInnes, A. 'Does superforce spell end for real-life Hamish Macbeths?' Daily Record. 19.1.12, p8.

[4339] Officer 'A'. 'The Crime Factory'. Mainstream Publishing. 2012.

[4340] Whitehead, T. 'Police 'won't chase wanted criminals because jails are full' '. Daily Express. 28.5.08, p33.

[4341] Gallacher, S. 'The Way We Were'. The Sunday Post. 8.4.12, p47.

[4342] Reynolds, R. 'Scottish police officers call for right to enter premises without a warrant'. Scotland on Sunday. 15.4.12, p9.

[4343] Doward, J. 'Tobacco giant under fire over role in plain packaging lobby'. The Observer. 28.4.13, p18.

[4344] Doyle, J., Camber, R. 'Furious police call on May to quit over cuts'. Daily Mail. 17.5.12, p8.

[4345] Hitchens, P. 'Their dream is a 'British FBI' – the reality may be our own KGB'. The Mail on Sunday. 3.6.12, p27.

[4346] Littlejohn, R. 'This Was A Tragedy, Not Time For Plodspeak'. Daily Mail. 4.6.10, p17.

[4347] McKinstry, L. 'Just What Are The Police Prepared To Do These Days?'. Daily Express. 10.2.06, p10.

[4348] Edge, S. 'Leave Your Front Door Open! Is Ian Blair unhinged?'. Daily Express. 22.8.06, p12.

[4349] Hyde, P. 'Credit card amnesty just makes a nonsense of law'. Daily Express. 11.8.09, p26.

[4350] Barnes, E. 'At War On Crime'. Scotland on Sunday. 13.3.11, p14.

[4351] Online Forum, Scotland on Sunday. 13.3.11, p20.

[4352] Kellaway, R. 'Crime Street'. The People. 6.2.11, pp18,19.

[4353] Massey, R. '30% rise in traffic lights leaves drivers seeing red'. Daily Mail. 28.2.11, p23.

[4354] Sergeant, H. 'The Public & The Police'. p45

[4355] Graham, C. 'Police 'are at war with the CPS' '. The Mail on Sunday. 12.6.11, p2.

[4356] Little, A. 'Police shun uniforms to work'. Daily Express. 6.9.11, p7.

[4357] Glover, S. 'Whose Side Are These GAG-Happy Judges On?'. Daily Mail. 7.3.07, p6.

[4358] Channel 4 News. 23.1.12.

[4359] Watson, R., Hamilton, F. 'Plebgate police in dock for misleading No 10'. The Times. 19.12.12, pp1,7.

[4360] Brown, A. 'Arrested, convicted, sacked and blacklisted … yet like 500 other strikers Alex is innocent'. Daily Record. 12.12.12, p11.

[4361] Brown, M. 'Officers' anger as 'Plebgate' PC held'. Daily Express. 18.12.12, p4.

[4362] Jones, D. 'The ex-hippy who's made £100m carpeting Britain with wind turbines'. Daily Mail. 10.12.12, p33.

[4363] The Sunday Telegraph. 11.11.12, p27.

[4364] Beattie, J. 'Security Service Colluded Over Lawyer's Death'. Daily Record. 13.12.12, p33.

[4365] 'Protect the public from sex offenders'. Leader. Daily Mail. 17.11.12, p14.

[4366] Cohen, N. 'The Censorship Olympics'. Daily Mail. 14.7.12, p16.

[4367] Wootton, R. 'Zero tolerance on crime would clog up courts'. Daily Express. 1.11.12, p52.

[4368] Littlejohn, R. 'I'm not one to say I told you so, but…'. Daily Mail. 13.11.12, p17.

[4369] Twomey, J. 'Our best chance yet of finding Madeleine'. Daily Express. 25.4.12, p7.

[4370] Elias, R. 'Scottish 'FBI' demands end to red tape'. Scotland on Sunday. 6.4.08, p6.

[4371] Wilkie, S. 'Tax millions get splashed out on spin'. Daily Express. 31.12.12, p10.

[4372] Cohen, T. 'Anger over ex-police chief's call to boycott commission polls'. Daily Mail. 23.10.12, p12.

[4373] The Mail on Sunday. 27.4.08, p44.

[4374] Lewis, J. 'Concern as MOD 'private' police quiz thousands'. The Mail on Sunday. 27.4.08, p44.

[4375] Wright, S., Butler, J. 'Police chiefs' anger as American gets top job'. Daily Mail. 10.9.03, p8.

[4376] Hitchens, P. 'Boys in blue, but not ours'. The Mail on Sunday. 13.4.08, p29.

[4377] Wilson, G. 'Police condemn Blair's DPP over terrorism stance'. Daily Mail. 19.8.03, p2.

[4378] Glover, S. Daily Mail. 24.1.13, p17.

[4379] Hitchens, P. The Mail on Sunday. 9.8.09, p25.

[4380] Liddle, R. 'Look out, they want to nail the BNP – and our freedom of speech'. The Sunday Times. 12.11.06, p15.

[4381] Millar, J. 'Families Tribute To Heroes Of The General Strike'. Sunday Mail. 3.2.13, p15.

[4382] Blackstock, G. 'Another activist in cash for spies row'. The Sunday Post. 26.4.09, pp1,2.

[4383] 'Sir Ian was a stooge for Labour says Ghaffur'. Daily Mail. 8.12.08, p23.

[4384] Clark, R. 'How Labour broke its promise to be tough on crime'. Daily Express. 10.11.09, p12.

[4385] 'New row over 'politicised' police'. Daily Express. 7.5.08, p7.

[4386] Greenwood, C. 'McLibel leaflet 'written by undercover PC' '. Daily Mail. 22.6.13, p18.

[4387] Lawson, D. 'The Met had no chance against race-card Ali'. The Sunday Times. 14.2.10, p22.

[4388] Slack, J. 'Religion divides us more than race, say Britons'. Daily Mail. 20.1.09, p8.

[4389] 'Police are still guilty of racism, claim MPs'. Daily Mail. 22.7.09.

[4390] Brogan, B., Slack, J. 'Dangerous folly of institutional racism mantra, by equality chief'. Daily Mail. 19.1.09, p4.

[4391] Guardian. 25.2.99.

[4392] Emsley, C. 'The Great British Bobby'. Quercus. London. 2009.

[4393] Littlejohn. Daily Mail. 20.11.07, p17.

[4394] Alderson, A. 'Violent inner-city crime, the figures and a question of race'. The Sunday Telegraph. 27.6.10, p2.

[4395] BBC Documentary. 5.9.11.

[4396] Levy, A. 'Police in race row over 'Polish rioters' training'. Daily Mail. 31.5.10, p20.

[4397] Parsons, B. 'The police have a poor record in the fight against fascism'. The Observer. 21.3.10, p42.

[4398] Bracchi, P. Daily Mail. 3.7.10, p43.

[4399] Glover, S. ' 'Choc ice' jibes and lunacy of police trawling Twitter for so-called hate crime'. Daily Mail. 19.7.12, p17.

[4400] Musson, C. 'Kohli Brothers In Race Row Storm'. Daily Record. 18.9.08. p21.

[4401] Harrison, I. 'Police clueless on foreigners' crimes'. The Sunday Post. 6.6.10, p8.

[4402] Clapperton, S. Senior Psychologist. NPIA, Yew Tree Lane, Harrogate, HG2 9JZ.

[4403] Channel 5. The Wright Stuff. 20.7.13.

[4404] Knowsley, J. The Mail on Sunday. 21.9.03, p4.

[4405] 'Object and you'll run the risk of being called racist'. Daily Mail. 17.4.09, p11.

[4406] Slack, J. 'Today's police still as racist as Life On Mars'. Daily Mail 12.1.09, p12.

[4407] Wright, S., Pendlebury, R. 'Law firm in race row is closed by watchdog'. Daily Mail. 31.12.08, p19.

[4408] Booth, S. 'Racism, sexism & sectarianism in the world's biggest gang'. Daily Record. 14.11.08, p13.

[4409] Booth, S. 'Racism, sexism & sectarianism in the world's biggest gang'. Daily Record. 14.11.08, pp12,13.

[4410] 'Police in gun raid blunder'. Daily Record. 1.12.09, p24.

[4411] Jones, D. 'Did Obama lie about his birth to become President?'. Daily Mail. 28.11.09, p53.

[4412] 'Cop on race charge'. Daily Record. 19.9.08, p9.

[4413] Daly, M. 'The Secret Policeman goes back on the beat'. Sunday Mail. 5.10.08, p18.

[4414] Levy, A. 'Muslim PC sues after workmates 'laughed at his beard''. Daily Mail. 9.3.09, p27.

[4415] 'Sack for BNP police officer'. Sunday Express. 22.3.09, p13.

[4416] Chittenden, M., Grimston, J. 'Race Chief sparks revolt over police'. The Sunday Times. 5.4.09, p10.

[4417] Thomas, D. 'Cop Fury At Secret 999 Racist Test'. The People. 8.7.07, p32.

[4418] Phillips, M. Daily Mail. 28.5.07, p12.

[4419] Littlejohn, R. 'What, police feeling collars? Perish the thought'. Daily Mail. 20.7.07 p17.

[4420] 'Anarchy in the Met,' Leader, Daily Mail. 2.3.07, p14.

[4421] Revoir, P. 'Police 'too PC' on Asian vice gangs says top Muslim'. Daily Mail. 26.3.08, p39.

[4422] Courtenay-Smith, N. 'So How Can My Son Be A Racist?'. Daily Mail. 18.4.08, pp36,37.

[4423] 'Anti-Jewish crime 'high'.'. Daily Express. 16.5.08, p15.

[4424] Hellawell, K. 'The dangers we all face when police are too terrified to think for themselves'. The Mail on Sunday. 18.5.08, p27.

[4425] Evans, M. 'Police told me to hide 'racist' St. George flag'. Daily Express. 24.5.08, p13.

[4426] Dixon, C. 'You can't preach here: this is a Muslim area'. Daily Express. 2.6.08, p22.

[4427] Classic FM, 29.6.08.

[4428] Moncur, J. 'Police Apologise For Using Puppy In Advert'. Daily Record. 2.7.08, p27.

[4429] Williams, R., Barrett, D. 'Met Police trainer linked to 7/7 gang'. The Sunday Telegraph. 8.5.11, p10.

[4430] McKinstry, L. 'It's ludicrous to deny that there is a link between crime and immigration'. Daily Express. 17.4.08, p12.

[4431] Hickley, M., Slack, J. 'Migrant crime: 'We need cash!'. Daily Mail. 17.4.08, pp12,13.

[4432] Emsley, C. 'The Great British Bobby'. Quercus. London. 2009.

[4433] 'Top police 'ignorant' '. Daily Express. 21.8.06, p8.

[4434] Kilroy-Silk, R. 'Blunkett must face up to racist police bullies'. Sunday Express. 26.10.03, p25.

[4435] Archibald, B. 'Church To Prepare 'Hate Song' Dossier'. Daily Record. 26.3.11, p9.

[4436] Delgado, M. 'Minority officers are top in PCs' exam'. The Mail on Sunday. 6.1.08, p58.

[4437] Bentley, P. 'Wanted: Police interns, whites need not apply'. Daily Mail. 28.3.11, p19.

[4438] Dunbar, P. 'Coconut' hate crime investigation that shows NOBODY can escape Britain's Thought Police'. The Mail on Sunday. 12.6.11, pp42,43.

[4439] Hall, M. 'Uproar over lessons in Sharia law for all police'. Daily Express. 29.2.08, p37.

[4440] Alegiah, G. BBC documentary. 5.10.11.

[4441] Reynolds, M. 'Arrested for telling youths to go home', Daily Express, 25.7.08, p37.

[4442] Anthony, A. 'When did the police start collaring television?'. The Observer. 12.8.07, p27.

[4443] O'Hare, P. 'Police Learn Hate Songs'. Daily Record. 20.12.11, pp1,2.

[4444] 'Jailed over doc race jibe'. Sunday Mail. 8.5.11, p7.

[4445] Pettifor, T. Daily Record. 4.1.12, p8.

[4446] Channel 4 News. 3.1.12.

[4447] Wilkes, D. 'Stephen's legacy and why it must never be forgotten'. Daily Mail. 20.2.12, p12.

[4448] Wright, S. 'Anger of Stephen's brother as Met rejects racism claim' Daily Mail, 29.6.13. p12.

[4449] McLeod, K. 'Celtic and Rangers amateur pals slam police order to play match behind closed doors'. Daily Record. 6.3.12, p5.

[4450] Mackenzie, K. 'Wake-up call for the Met Commissioner'. Daily Mail. 7.4.12, p21.

[4451] Leppard, D. Sunday Times. 8.4.12, pp1,2.

[4452] Peachey, P. 'Police in crisis after flood of racism complaints'. The Independent. 6.4.12, pp1,2.

[4453] Townsend, M. 'Senior black officer calls for race watchdog to police Met'. The Observer. 8.4.12.

[4454] 'Tasered fireman in police race row'. The Sun. 20.4.12, p8.

[4455] Barrett, D. 'Racism claims hit second force'. The Sunday Telegraph. 8.4.12, p4.

[4456] Brady, B. 'Police 'in denial' over rise in racism complaints'. The Independent On Sunday. 6.5.12, p14.

[4457] Wells, T. 'Race Fear Cops Ban The Word 'Blacklist' '. The Sun. 7.5.12, p17.

[4458] 'Fear of racism impedes police'. Daily Mail. 6.8.12, p29.

[4459] Panther, L. 'Overblown'. The People,. 22.7.12, p32.

[4460] Brown, M. 'Hordes of illegals stroll free because our police fear being called racist'. Daily Express. 4.8.10, p2.

[4461] Townsend, M. 'Black people are 26 times more likely than whites to face stop-and-search'. The Observer. 17.10. 10, pp22-23.

[4462] Scotland on Sunday. 10.10.10, pp12-13.

[4463] Ryder, M. 'The police need to stop and think about stop and search'. The Observer. 3.5.09, p19.

[4464] Little, A. 'Police 'stop innocent white people so as not to look racist'. Daily Express. 18.6.09, p10.

[4465] Slack. J. 'Police search more whites just to balance the books'. Daily Mail. 18.6.09, p24.

[4466] Paddick, B. 'The police must have power to stop and search ethnic groups'. The Mail on Sunday. 17.10.10, p27.

[4467] 'Police forces 'are more racist than a decade ago'. Daily Mail. 24.2.09, p20.

[4468] McTague, T. 'Black Man Waylaid'. The People. 22.3.09, p26.

[4469] Greenhill, S. 'The MP's brother robbed at gunpoint then treated as if HE was the crook'. Daily Mail. 10.11.07, p52.

[4470] Wilkes, D. 'Are they joking?'. Daily Mail. 28.7.08, p25.

[4471] 'Have you nicked this car, police ask Bruno'. Daily Mail. 31.3.11, p32.

[4472] Paterson, P. 'Sorting riot from wrong'. Daily Mail. 11.4.06, p57.

[4473] Gill, C. 'Black people 'are 26 times more likely to be stopped' '. Daily Mail. 18.10.10, p19.

[4474] Doyle, J. '100,000 searches ... but not one arrest under terror laws'. Daily Mail. 29.10.10, p20.

[4475] Slack, J. 'How return of 'Sus' will let police target minorities'. Daily Mail. 16.10.10, p10.

[4476] Townsend, M. 'Race bias on drug arrest worse than US'. The Observer. 31.10.10, p20.

[4477] BBC1 News, 30.11.10.

[4478] Townsend, M. 'Police: stop more black suspects'. The Observer. 21.10,07, pp1,7.

[4479] Bishop, P. 'Brixton Riots, London, 1981'. The New Review, The Observer. 10.4.11, pp14-16.

[4480] Feltz, V. 'Police off-target'. Daily Express. 23.12.07, p11.

[4481] 'Anger at Muslim searches'. Daily Record. 2.11.07, p2.

[4482] BBC1 News. 3.1.12.

[4483] Townsend, M. 'Nineteen years after Lawrence murder, stop and search is poisoning race relations'. The Observer. 8.1.12, p5.

[4484] BBC1 News. 31.3.12. Also 'Met cop race rap'. The Sun. 1.4.12, p8.

[4485] Heffer, S. 'Stop this hysteria over race'. Daily Mail. 14.7.12, p47.

[4486] 'Met chiefs 'dismissed' racism alert'. Sunday Mirror. 8.4.12, p2.

[4487] Gill, C. 'White officers sue Met Police over race bias'. Daily Mail. 26.8.10, p38.

[4488] Wright, S. 'Now the white policeman who led the Dizaei inquiry is awarded £40,000 for HIS racial discrimination'. Daily Mail. 13.3.07, p36.

[4489] Foggo, D. 'Ku Klux' cop gets race equality job'. The Sunday Times. 17.12.06, p10.

[4490] Pilditch, D. 'More cash for detective who won £240,000 from the Met'. Daily Express. 19.9.08, p29.

[4491] McIntyre, S. '£20m bill for police race and sex claims'. Daily Mail. 9.11.01, p39.

[4492] Wright, S. 'Walking tall!'. Daily Mail. 22.5.10, p42.

[4493] Allen, V. 'I was sidelined by 'racist' Sir Ian, says Yard commander'. Daily Mail. 24.6.08, p32.

[4494] '£12,000 for Sikh PC told to remove his turban'. Daily Mail. 3.10.09, p28.

[4495] Townsend, M. 'Met officer fears for his life after race row death threats'. The Observer. 31.8.08, pp1,6.

[4496] Wright, S. 'Asian Met officer settles for a quarter of £2.1m race claim'. Daily Mail. 26.11.08, p6.

[4497] Gill, C., Grant, C. 'Muslim chef sues police for asking him to cook pork'. Daily Mail. 3.11.08, p5.

[4498] Hamilton, N. 'Kick out real Met racists'. Daily Express. 12.10,08, p31.

[4499] Hamilton, N. Sunday Express. 19.10.08, p3.

[4500] Wright, S. '£60,000 for Muslim hurt by police in terror raid'. Daily Mail. 19.3.09, p39.

[4501] Wright, S. 'Claiming damages, the Muslim removed from Blair guard duty'. Daily Mail. 2.5.08, p51.

[4502] Evans, M. 'Revealed: The Muslim PC banned from guarding Blair'. Daily Express. 9.11.06, p5.

[4503] Camber, R. 'Kate Middleton's new bodyguard was a sexist, racist bully claims WPC'. Daily Mail. 1.2.11, p20.

[4504] Gill, C. 'Six white police officers to sue the Met for racial discrimination'. Daily Mail online.

[4505] Jeeves, P. 'I missed out on top police job because I am white'. Daily Express. 20.2.07, p15.

[4506] Wright, S., Pendlebury, R. 'Race War Tearing The Yard To Pieces'. Daily Mail. 11.9.08, p1.

[4507] Flanagan, P. '200 police facing the sack for sending a 'racist' email'. Daily Express. 11.5.06, p33.

[4508] Phillips, M. 'When Will We British Learn To Stop Appeasing Terror?'. Daily Mail. 1.5.07, p9.

[4509] Hendry, T. 'Broadwater Farm hero: 'We have not learned any lessons' '. Sunday Express. 14.8.11, p8.

[4510] Barker. L. 'My son was discriminated against – for being white'. Daily Express. 18.4.07, p34.

[4511] Chapman, J. 'Outrage over the Muslim PC who snubbed her boss'. Daily Express. 22.1.07, p7.

[4512] Slack, J. 'Police snub whites'. Daily Mail. 27.9.06, p8.

[4513] Wright, S. 'PC in racism case lied that he was Met chief's nephew'. Daily Mail. 14.2.06, p36.

[4514] France, A. 'Stephen Lawrence? He deserved to die ... give the boys who killed him diplomatic immunity'. The Mail on Sunday. 19.10.03, p13.

[4515] Palmer, A. 'The obsessive pursuit of 'racism' hobbles the police'. Sunday Telegraph. 20.12.09, p30.

[4516] Dixon, C. 'Police officers wanted (whites need not apply)'. Daily Express. 24.5.06, p15.

[4517] 'Race quotas for the police under attack'. Daily Mail. 20.4.07, p28.

[4518] Slack, J. 'Police Race Quotas Axed'. Daily Mail. 21.2.09, pp1,4.

[4519] 'The cop cleared of being corrupt'. Daily Mail. 17.2.06, p19

[4520] Phillips, M. Daily Mail. 6.7.08, p27.

[4521] Wright, S. 'Al Qaeda Fanatics Working In Police'. Daily Mail. 7.7.07, pp,1,8.

[4522] Delgado, M. 'Police offering jobs to recruits who have failed anti-racism test'. The Mail on Sunday. 23.9.07, p59.

[4523] Reynolds, M. 'Police 'pick on white Britons' for hate crime'. Daily Express. 20.7.10, p23.

[4524] Townsend, M. 'Black police organisation must be scrapped, say white officers'. The Observer. 14.2.10, p25.

[4525] Whitehead, T. 'You're racist 'wrong MP' tells black officers'. Daily Express. 31.10.08, p10.

[4526] Ellicott, C. 'Muslim police in 'hatred' warning'. Daily Mail. 21.10, p2.

[4527] Wright, S. " 'Racism' in the force never held me back", Daily Mail. 11.10.08, p4.

[4528] Townsend, M. 'Black officers step up the pressure on new Met boss'. The Observer. 1.2.09, p19.

[4529] Marrin, M. 'A black police association – now that is racism in action'. The Sunday Times. 12.10.08, p16.

[4530] Harper, T. 'Met tried to 'take out' black officers'. The Sunday Telegraph. 25.2.07, p12.

[4531] Sawer, P. 'Black and Asian police line up race bias claims'. The Sunday Telegraph. 13.7.08, p2.

[4532] 'Crime fighters accused over actor's race role'. Daily Express. 5.7.08, p19.

[4533] 'Remove all veils'. Daily Mail. 17.10.06, p5.

[4534] Camber, R. 'Sikh policemen denied bulletproof turbans'. Daily Mail. 23.4.10, p21.

[4535] Hitchens, P. 'Racism: It must cut both ways Sir Trevor'. The Mail on Sunday. 16.9.07, p31.

[4536] HM's Inspectorate of Constabulary. 1999.

[4537] Roberts, L. 'Police pay C4 £100,000 over preachers libel'. Daily Mail. 15.5.08, p24.

[4538] Littlejohn, R. ' Plods, lies and videotape. Heads must surely roll'. Daily Mail. 16.5.08, p17.

[4539] ITV1. 'Muggers'. 8.6.11.

[4540] Emsley, C. 'The Great British Bobby'. Quercus. London. 2009.

[4541] Gill, C. 'Sacked at last, the PC who made monkey noises at a black suspect'. Daily Mail. 1.11.07, p27.

[4542] Pendlebury, R., Wright, S. 'Fall Of The Teflon Commander'. Daily Mail. 0.2.10, pp6,7.

[4543] Emsley, C. 'The Great British Bobby'. Quercus. London. 2009.

[4544] 'Taxi Rank Row Cop Sang IRA Slogans In Street'. Sunday Mail. 30.5.10, p42.

[4545] Mills, R. 'Police warning over Tartan Army T-shirt'. Daily Express. 24.2.10, p37.

[4546] Gall, C. 'Tease Shirts Row'. Daily Record. 24.2.10, p27.

[4547] Myers. R. 'PC Faces 'Racist' Jibe Quiz'. The People. 18.1.09, p10.

[4548] Liddle, R. 'No BNP in the force, please – but leftie thugs are welcome'. The Sunday Times Comment Section.

[4549] Leask, D., Azam, I. 'Police trainer probed over racism claim'. Scotland on Sunday. 3.1.10, p5.

[4550] Weldon, V. 'PC Bigot'. Sunday Mail. 7.12.08, p19.

[4551] Kelly, J. 'Met policeman wanted to 'bring down the lazy blacks', tribunal is told'. Daily Mail. 3.3.09, p24.

[4552] Wright, S. 'The Yard boss facing ruin over claims by woman from equality unit'. Daily Mail 23.10.10, p45.

[4553] Lee, A. 'Immigration Nightmare'. Daily Express. 16.6.07, p23.

[4554] Silvester, N. 'Cop's Race Probe'. Sunday Mail. 1.4.07, p11.

[4555] Andrews, E. 'White man who called three whites 'honky' is accused of race abuse'. Daily Mail. 3.7.08, p30.

[4556] Foggo, D. 'Police diversity officer keeps job after Nazi 'joke' '.

[4557] Widdecombe, A. 'Our police have lost their common sense'. Daily Express. 23.4.08, p13.

[4558] Kelly, T. 'Met policeman wanted to 'bring down the lazy blacks', tribunal is told'. Daily Mail. 3.3.09, p24.

[4559] Harper, T. 'Met chief is facing phone tap race row'. The Sunday Telegraph. 10.12.06, p2.

[4560] Greenwood, C., Sears, N., McDermott, N. 'Disgrace Of PC In Drunken Race Rant'. Daily Mail. 7.4.12, pp1,4.

[4561] 'Met PC will face charge of 'racist abuse' in riots'. Daily Mail. 18.4.12, p26.

[4562] Findlay, R. 'Cop Charged Over Old Firm Loo Riot'. Sunday Mail. 20.5.12, p27.

[4563] Taher, A. 'New UK border chief quizzed over links to holiday club called W.O.G.S.'. The Mail on Sunday. 3.6.12, p15.

[4564] 'Lead detective's racist and sexist past'. The Mail on Sunday. 23.6.13, p7.

[4565] Camber, R. 'Black men to blame for most violent city crime'. Daily Mail. 28.6.10, p26.

[4566] Drake, M., Gibson, M. 'Police chiefs won't say if they're on DNA database'. Sunday Express. 6.4.08, p48.

[4567] Doward, J. 'Police DNA files reveal 'racial bias'.'. The Observer. 9.8.09, p2.

[4568] Townsend, M. 'New figures reveal leap in police 'racial profiling' '. The Observer. 15.1.12, p18.

[4569] Heffer, S. 'Stop this hysteria over race'. Daily Mail. 14.7.12, p47.

[4570] Beckford, M. 'Met's black officers to get priority for top jobs'. The Mail on Sunday. 4.11.12, p24.

[4571] Maguire, M., Norris, C. 'The Conduct and Supervision of Criminal Investigations' (Royal Commission on Criminal Justice Research Study No. 5). HMSO. London. 1992, p41.

[4572] Findlay, R. 'Revealed. Cop Molehunt condemned'. Sunday Mail. 7.7.13, p13.

[4573] 'Fury at drink-driving cheat cop'. Daily Record. 15.8.09, p17.

[4574] Harding, E. 'Hundreds of police are sacked in secret'. Daily Mail. 9.5.11, p4.

[4575] Doyle, J. 'Child rapists taken off Sex Offenders' Register in secret'. Daily Mail. 7.5.13, p8.

[4576] Dean, C. 'I was tormented like Fiona and no one ever helped'. Daily Express. 30.9.09, p12.

[4577] Iversen, L. 'Speed, Ecstasy, Ritalin'. p145. OUP. 2008.

[4578] Paterson, B. 'I'm Delighted Cop Got Jail For Attacking Me'. Daily Record. 6.3.09, p21.

[4579] Groves, J. 'Arrested suspects MUST be named says ex-Met chief'. Daily Mail. 6.5.13, p10.

[4580] Findlay, R. 'Anger over 500 Unresolved Killings'. Sunday Mail. 19.5.13, p23.

[4581] Maynard, G. 'Gun and knife crime 'is being covered up'. Daily Express. 12.9.08, p6.

[4582] 'Ex-cop in fine let-off'. Sunday Mirror. 30.8.09, p25.

[4583] '£400,000 for skull case PC'. Daily Express. 14.11.08, p24.

[4584] 'Britain's FBI 'too secretive''. Sunday Express. 20.9.09, p32.

[4585] Greenwood, C. 'Official who kept incendiary dossier secret forced to quit'. Daily Mail. 2.8.13, p20.

[4586] Taher, A. et al. 'Revealed. 15 blue-chip firms linked to rogue private eyes ... and kept secret by police'. The Mail on Sunday. 25.8.13, p17.

[4587] Taher, A. et al. 'Private eye spied on 14-year-old girl brain-damaged in horror car crash'. The Mail on Sunday. 11.8.13, p22.

[4588] Findlay, R. 'Secret Police'. Sunday Mail. 4.10.09, p22.

[4589] Hitchens, P. The Mail on Sunday. 7.12.08, p29.

[4590] Streetwise Publications. 'Outcast ex-traffic cop goes into hiding after revealing speeding ticket loopholes'. Daily Express. 31.10.09, p65.

[4591] Sayed, V., Butler, A. 'Cops said we should keep quiet about attack on us'. Sunday Mirror. 1.11.09, p4.

[4592] Mills, D. 'Why speed cameras COST lives'. Daily Mail. 2.9.02, p10.

[4593] Mills, R, 'Inquiry to track Lockerbie bomb team a 'stitch-up''. Daily Express. 26.10.09, p16.

[4594] 'Lying in wait, the police van given a makeover to catch out speeders'. Daily Mail. 5.5.08, p17.

[4595] Jarvis, D. 'Foreigners are to blame for one in five of UK's murders'. Daily Express. 14.4.08, p8.

[4596] 'Cops fight info request'. Daily Record. 18.7.08, p27.

[4597] Hickley, M. 'Police have DNA of 1.5m young Britons'. Daily Mail. 10.3.08, p22.

[4598] Drake, M., Gibson, M. 'Police Chiefs won't say if they're on DNA database'. Sunday Express. 6.4.08, p48.

[4599] Reid, S. 'A Lethal Cover-up'. Daily Mail. 15.12.07, pp36,37.

[4600] Slack, J. 'Twice as many teenagers are carrying knives'. Daily Mail. 21.2.08, p42.

[4601] Bonnici, T. 'Let off £200,000 bill ... the lawyer brother who stood bail for killer policeman'. Daily Express. 19.2.08, p20.

[4602] Sanderson, E. Rimmer, B. 'As an immigration judge I already knew the frightening incompetence of the justice system: I thought the Old Bailey would run like a real court, I was wrong'. The Mail on Sunday. 29.7.07, p23.

[4603] McIlwraith, G. 'Detective under pressure to change story, court told'. Daily Record. 15.11.07, p19.

[4604] McIlwraith, G. Daily Record. 16.11.07, p15.

[4605] 'Dad's anger at learning of son's pond death ... four months too late'. Daily Express. 23.10.07, p30.

[4606] Henderson, E. 'Police must tell us how our boy died'. Sunday Express. 7.10.07, p15.

[4607] Leake, C. 'Police Plan Secret Strike On Pay'. The Mail on Sunday. 9.12.07, p1.

[4608] Hull, L. 'Police crack a 54-year-old murder. Then refuse to name killer to spare his family pain'. Daily Mail. 20.10.07, p25.

[4609] Chapman, J. 'Did the police stop Billie-Jo's sisters from telling the truth?' Daily Express. 3.7.04, p4.

[4610] Leake, C. 'SAS members stage revolt as 'PC Plod' joins their secret club'. The Mail on Sunday. 15.7.07, p52.

[4611] Twomey, J. 'Suicide of lawyer who lost it all'. Daily Express. 13.5.05, p23.

[4612] Hickley, M. 'Paedophiles slip thought the net to work with children'. Daily Mail. 7.7.07, p5.

[4613] Johnston, J. Daily Mail. 24.6.06, p39.

[4614] McGlore, J. 'Sins of the father'. Scotland on Sunday. 25.6.06, pp16-18.

[4615] Burns, J. 'No More Secrets'. Daily Record. 15.12.12, p6.

[4616] Milland, G. '20,0000 prisoners held in police cells over past year'. Daily Express. 16.5.07, p27.

[4617] Hitchens, P. The Mail on Sunday. 19.5.13, p29.

[4618] Emsley, C. 'The Great British Bobby'. Quercus. London. 2009.

[4619] Little, A. 'Sex-Swap PCs: Don't Take Our Particulars'. Daily Express. 2.7.10, p11.

[4620] Daily Record. 28.10.09, p29.

[4621] Adams, L. 'Shame of my bombing raids in the Blitz'. Daily Record. 3.5.05, p20.

[4622] Garavelli, D. 'Double trouble'. Scotland on Sunday. 16.1.11, p12.

[4623] Daily Express. 26.6.10, p12.

[4624] ITV News. 15.10.07.

[4625] McIver, B. 'Legal High Victim Died Under Arrest'. Daily Record. 5.7.13, p6.

[4626] Beckford, M. 'Now taxman cracks down on moonlighting police officers'. The Mail on Sunday. 18.8.13, p34.

[4627] Chapman, J. 'Police free to follow the evidence on phone hacking, insists Premier'. Daily Mail. 18.4.11, p10.

[4628] Silvester, N. 'Blunder Arrest'. Sunday Mail. 20.1.08, p29.

4629 Slack, J. 'A home is broken into every minute'. Daily Mail. 21.4.11, p19.

4630 Classic FM News. 24.5.11.

4631 'Cop probe under fire'. Daily Mirror. 21.8.13, p9.

4632 Jeeves, P. 'Ex-top cop is probed over 'help' for Savile'. Daily Express. 17.10.13, p27.

4633 Ellicott, C., Wright, S., Spencer, B. 'Savile's police crony 'fixed soft interview' '. Daily Mail. 17.10.13, p7.

4634 Dawar, A. 'Convicts on run can't be named to protect their human rights'. Daily Express. 12.1.11, p22.

4635 Doyle, J. 'Why 47 dangerous criminals on the run can't be named'. Daily Mail. 20.4.11.

4636 BBC South News. 21.11.02.

4637 Madeley, R. 'Why they targeted Tarrant'. Daily Express. 19.5.07, p20.

4638 Greenwood, C. 'Police chiefs 'failing to cut bureaucracy' '. Daily Mail. 5.7.11, p2.

4639 Reynolds, M. 'Deadly haul of weapons seized in the classroom'. Daily Express. 13.7.11, p19.

4640 Wooding, D. 'Speed Scameras'. News of the World. 26.6.11, p22.

4641 Dawar, A. 'Burglaries surge by 14% as police 'turn a blind eye' '. Daily Express. 15.7.11, p15.

4642 Derbyshire, D. 'How you can spot a criminal at the age of 3'. Daily Mail. 22.2.11, p20.

4643 Findlay, R. 'Masonic Cover-up Claim On Rape Cop'. Sunday Mail. 10.6.01, p15.

4644 Massey, R. 'Do speed cameras really help to cut road deaths toll?'. Daily Mail. 25.9.06, p18.

4645 Whitehead, T. 'How Labour massages the crime figures'. Daily Express. 26.6.07, p2.

4646 Sergeant, H. The Public & The Police. p74.

4647 Giannangeli, M. 'Stressed ex-troopers going to jail'. Sunday Express. 24.1.10, p20.

4648 'Misconduct police 'quit on the quiet' '. Daily Mail. 1.11.11, p13.

4649 Goslett, M. 'Rapid rise of the citizen spies for hire'. The Sunday Times.30.1.11, p9.

4650 BBC1 News 2.11.11.

4651 Slack, J., Camber, R. 'Police chiefs' body is stripped of power to run undercover units'. Daily Mail. 19.1.11, p6.

4652 Travis, A., Lewis, P., Wainwright, M. 'Minister orders clean-up of covert policing'. The Guardian. 19.1.11, pp1,2.

4653 Musson, C. 'Bodies are still hiding info'. Daily Record. 9.1.12, p6.

4654 McKun, C. 'Police refuse three-quarters of calls to identify paedophiles'. Scotland on Sunday. 8.4.12, p8.

4655 Stewart, S. 'Sex Fiends Off The Radar'. Daily Record. 25.7.12, pp1,4.

4656 Parker, N. 'MI6 Quizzed On Torture Of Libyans'. The Sun. 13.1.12, p29.

4657 Chapman, J. 'Secret justice and an abuse of power'. Daily Mail. 29.2.12, p4.

4658 Daily Mail Comment. 'We hear your fears over open justice loud and clear'. Daily Mail. 6.3.12, p6.

4659 Walters, S. 'How No. 10 misled MoS about Cameron and THAT police horse' – HORSEGATE. The Mail on Sunday. 4.3.12, p13.

4660 Camber, R. 'Law ties our hands on riot case say police'. Daily Mail. 30.3.12, p28.

4661 Duguid, E. 'Bitten on the beat'. The Sunday Post. 25.3.12, p47.

4662 Camber, R. 'Fury as police seek to hold riot death probe behind closed doors'. Daily Mail. 27.3.12, p28.

4663 Greenwood, C., Martin, A. 'Gun Cop Could Face Trial Over 'Execution' In Street'. Daily Mail. 6.7.13, p20.

4664 Musson, C. 'May The Force Be With You'. Daily Record. 6.4.12, p8.

4665 Slack, J. 'Let criminals see their police files says the EU'. Daily Mail. 23.4.12, p8.

4666 Officer 'A'. The Crime Factory. Mainstream Publishing. 2012.

4667 ITV News. 21.5.12.

4668 Evans, R. 'Secret files reveal covert network run by nuclear police'. The Guardian. 20.10.09.

4669 Jones, G. 'Secret court into police 'sex victims' '. Sunday Express. 7.10.12, p24.

4670 Musson, C. ' Police Speed Guns Fiasco'. Daily Record. 5.2.09, p18.

4671 O'Neill, S. 'The secret policeman's bonus scheme'. The Times. 24.1.09, p3.

4672 'Police chiefs must reveal their expenses'. Daily Mail. 30.3.10, p21.

4673 'This cult of secrecy will harm us all'. Leader. The Mail on Sunday. 21.4.13, p29.

4674 Harper, T. 'SOCA chief is accused of misleading MPs'. The Independent on Sunday. 7.7.13. pp8, 9.

4675 Gill, C. 'Police chief faces sack for failing to return child abuse images'. Daily Mail. 28.5.09, p22.

4676 Whiteside, P. 'Police hunting Soham killer 'were inept and indecisive' '. Daily Mail. 7.2.05, p19.

4677 Mair, G. 'Sneaky speed cops hide in shrubbery'. Daily Record. 16.4.09, p7.

4678 Thornton, P. 'Tasers On Shun'. Daily Record. 18.5.09, p16.

4679 Bugler, T. 'You Lied'. Sunday Mail. 17.2.02, p9.

4680 Armstrong, G., Hobbs, D. 'Tackled from behind'. in Giulianotti, R. et al. (eds), 'Football, Violence and Social Identity'. (Routledge, London, 1994). Stagg and Hall investigations. 'The Times'. 10.10.94.

4681 Munro, A. 'Cop apology doesn't change fact they've blood on their hands'. Daily Record. 20.12.07, p15.

4682 '£100K for cop to sit at home'. Daily Record. 29.7.11, p5.

4683 Jones, D. ''PC Liar' fired'. The People. 4.10.09, p18.

[4684] Ball, G. 'Shame, murder and lust: a perfect cover-up'. Sunday Express. 10.1.10, pp47-49.

[4685] 'Redcar row film to show at Parliament'. The Sunday Post. 26.4.09, p9.

[4686] McKay, P. Daily Mail. 22.4.13, p17.

[4687] Rayner, T., Tozer, J. 'Wanted For Crimes Against Common Sense'. Daily Mail. 6.1.07, p1.

[4688] Ford, R. 'Police reason for not issuing photos of the runaway killers is just nonsense'. The Times. 6.1.07, p9.

[4689] 'Cop boss is probed'. Sunday Mirror. 15.3.09, p28.

[4690] Findlay, R 'Masonic Cover-Up Claim On Rape Cop'. Sunday Mail. 10.6.01, p15.

[4691] McLeod, K. 'Lies Of Rapist Cop'. Daily Record. 14.11.08, pp1,9.

[4692] Cameron, L. 'Cops chiefs boost Lockerbie probe'. Daily Record. 25.1.12, p16.

[4693] Forsyth, F. 'Establishment still looks after its own'. Daily Express. 29.1.10, p13.

[4694] Cook, F. 'I blame police sex ring for conspiracy of silence over the Dunblane massacre'. The Mail on Sunday. 5.6.05, p41.

[4695] Kent. R. 'Cop Kid Quiz'. 25.11.07, p22.

[4696] 'Millionaire Huhne's Fight Over Legal Bill'. Daily Mail. 12.3.13, p4.

[4697] 'Civil liberties row over police 'anti-gay' files'. The Mail on Sunday. 7.1.07, p2.

[4698] Taylor, D. 'Sex Killer Quizzed In Hunt For 1970s Beast'. Sunday Mail. 24.5.09, p23.

[4699] Leader. 'Give us proper policemen'. Sunday Express. 7.10.07, p26.

[4700] Hodgson, J., Ahmed, K., Bright, M. 'Home Office 'tried to axe' BBC police race exposé'. The Observer. 26.10.03, p1.

[4701] Stote, M. 'Village sealed off for funeral of womanising police chief'. Daily Express. 22.3.08, p7.

[4702] 'Inquest into cop's death not personal'. The Sunday Post. 31.8.08, p4.

[4703] 'Fears over bid to hide identities of suspects'. Daily Mail. 15.4.13, p5.

[4704] Littlejohn, R. Daily Mail. 12.1.10, p17.

[4705] Whelan, A. ' 'Big Brother' police warn bird lover: You could be sued for filming parakeet cull'. The Mail on Sunday. 24.7.11, p23.

[4706] Leppard, D. 'One-third of police forces face axe'. The Sunday Times. 4.9.05, p12.

[4707] Cobain, I., Kennedy, d. 'Huntley police held secret Irish blacklist'. The Times. 20.12.03, p1.

[4708] Fairweather, E. The Mail on Sunday. 25.10.09, p38.

[4709] Silvester, N. 'Jersey Child Abuse Cop: Now They Want To Charge Me'. Sunday Mail. 18.1.09, p9.

[4710] Fairweather, E. 'I don't care what a few establishment cover-up merchants and their pet poodles say … I care about the victims of Jersey'. The Mail On Sunday. 19.4.09, pp8,9.

[4711] Martin, A. 'Jersey probe farce'. Daily Mail. 19.5.08, p13.

[4712] Fairweather, E. Special Report. The Mail on Sunday. 2.3.08, pp40,41.

[4713] Wilson, D., Ashton, J., Sharp, D. 'What Everyone in Britain Should Know About The Police'. Blackstone Press. Pp58,59,62,63,64,66.

[4714] 'Cam Off It'. Daily Record. 21.3.09, pp1,5.

[4715] 'Blogging blow as police 'spy' loses fight for anonymity'. Daily Mail. 17.6.09, p25.

[4716] Gossop, I. 'Defective records'. The Sunday Times. 26.10.08, p23.

[4717] Brooks, T. 'Held up by pistol raiders, the politician who was told: There's no gun crime here'. Daily Express. 12.1.08, p17.

[4718] 'Murder Cops Are 'So Slow''. News of the World. 31.12.06, p38.

[4719] Herbert, D. 'Police warned me paedo was after my son … but refused to reveal his name'. News Of The World. 4.7.10, p18.

[4720] Tozer, T. 'Police 'hid' abuse of 60 girls by Asian takeaway workers'. Daily Mail. 8.4.11, p25.

[4721] Drake, M. 'Law 'protects' perverts'. Sunday Express. 10.8.08, p5.

[4722] Kandohla, T. 'Mathe Cops In Paedos Bungle'. The People. 14.9.08, p15.

[4723] Gregory, A. 'Brit Police Watch And Listen From The Room Next Door. They even tell local cops what to ask'. The People. 9.9.07, p6.

[4724] 'Maddie files stay secret'. Daily Record. 4.1.10, p2.

[4725] Bentley, P. 'British police 'developed evidence' against McCanns'. Daily Mail. 14.12.10.

[4726] Gysin, C. 'Police tried to keep DNA test secret in Maddie case'. Daily Mail. 19.7.08, p5.

[4727] Brooke, C. 'Detectives led astray by sniffer dogs'. Daily Mail. 10.5.11, p11.

[4728] Hobson, N. 'Policeman Behaving Badly'. Daily Mail. 24.4.06, pp26,27.

[4729] 'The Fearless Coroner'. Daily Mail. 29.9.09, p5.

[4730] Hitchens, P. & Read – see 'Read the awful story of Fiona … then accuse me of 'moral panic'. The Mail on Sunday. 18.9.11, p31.

[4731] Devine, A. 'Cops keep the lid on 270 crimes'. Daily Record. 18.9.08, p22.

[4732] Stewart, S. 'Cops Pay £200K For Supergrass Secrets'. Daily Record. 14.5.09, p26.

[4733] 'Fears force has failed'. Sunday Mail. 30.11.08, p22.

REFERENCES

[4734] Pooran, N. 'Bird crime detective says guilty are let off'. Sunday Mail. 26.2.12, p5.

[4735] Murray, J. 'Tube death police stay anonymous at inquest'. Sunday Express. 21.9.08, p17.

[4736] 'Nothing went wrong, says de Menezes case officer'. Daily Mail. 2.10.08, p35.

[4737] Clements, J. 'Whitewash'. Daily Record. 13.12.08, p2.

[4738] 'Reminder to police: it is not good practice to doctor evidence'. The Independent on Sunday. 19.10.08, p49.

[4739] Waterhouse, K. 'Now it's one Blair after another'. Daily Mail. 25.8.05, p16.

[4740] Williams, D., Wright, S. 'Tragic trail of police blunders'. Daily Mail. 17.8.05, p5.

[4741] Wright, S. 'Yard chief 'trying to silence Paddick' '. Daily Mail. 16.8.08, p2.

[4742] Twomey, J. 'Officer cleared in Tube death'. Daily Express. 27.5.09, p4.

[4743] Stephenson, D. 'BBC drama will say de Menezes gun police lied'. Sunday Express. 28.12.08, p11.

[4744] Leake, C., Owen, G. 'Tube shooting inquiry chaos as chief resigns'. The Mail on Sunday. 2.4.06, p5.

[4745] Gill, C. 'Yard chief 'kept in dark on shooting for 24 hours' '. Daily Mail. 3.8.07, p8.

[4746] Murray, J. 'Was SAS responsible for killing de Menezes?'. Sunday Express. 7.9.07, p7.

[4747] Murray, J. 'Proof SAS stormed de Menezes home'. Sunday Express. 9.9.07, p10.

[4748] 'Bizarre conduct at a time of crisis'. Leader. Daily Mail. 1.10.05, p14.

[4749] Byrne, T. 'Taking account of shoot to kill'. The Sunday Times. 28.8.05, 18.

[4750] Panton, L. 'Furious cops gag chief backer'. News of the World. 11.11.07, p7.

[4751] 'Met chief slammed in report'. Daily Record. 9.11.07, p91.

[4752] 'De Menezes officer sues Met over 'cover-up' '. Daily Mail. 27.8.11, p51.

[4753] Twomey, J. 'Queen wins her right for VIP police squad'. Daily Express. 3.8.09, p15.

[4754] 'Cop in child sex abuse MP claim'. Daily Record. 26.3.13, p23.

[4755] McKay, P. 'Questions the police must face'. Daily Mail. 1.8.5, p15.

[4756] 'Police ordered to release 7/7 footage'. The Times. 4.4.09, p33.

[4757] Levy, A. 'Unlawfully killed'. Daily Mail. 5.5.04, p31.

[4758] Leppard, D., Winnett, R. 'Whitehall leak reveals plan to cover up terror death toll'. The Sunday Times. 3.10.04, p1.

[4759] 'No Justice'. Daily Record. 22.6.02, p11.

[4760] Hencke, D., Conrad, M. 'Paedo Cops Ignored Me'. Sunday People. 28.4.13, p2.

[4761] Walters, S. 'Baby P'. The Mail on Sunday. 15.3.09, p8.

[4762] Delgado, M., Powell, L. 'Officer in G20 death probe signs off sick'. The Mail on Sunday. 12.4.09, p37.

[4763] Robson, D. 'This wasn't any kind of fair cop'. Daily Express. 11.4.09, p16.

[4764] Twomey, J. 'Thousands of killers and rapists escape after DNA blunders'. Daily Express. 22.2.07, p19.

[4765] Callan, P. 'When childhood really was tough'. Daily Express. 15.2.07, p33.

[4766] Gillard, M. 'Accusations of Met cover-up put more heat on Ian Blair'. The Independent on Sunday. 31.8.08, p4.

[4767] Verkaik, R. 'Officers 'held back CCTV film of police race attack' '. The Mail On Sunday. 2.10.11, p22.

[4768] Drake, M. 'Why did police who shot lawyer hide their faces?' Sunday Express. 11.5.08, p14.

[4769] Gill, C. 'Did police marksmen collude on accounts of barrister's killing?' Daily Mail. 12.5.08, p25.

[4770] McKay, P. 'A loaded question'. Daily Mail. 12.5.08, p17.

[4771] Boffey, D. 'Barrister's shooting sparks Met probe into police who compare notes'. The Mail on Sunday. 19.10.08, p60.

[4772] Twomey, J. 'I'm sorry but I had to kill de Menezes'. Daily Express. 29.10.08, p9.

[4773] Reynolds, M. 'Why did police have to shoot my brother dead?'. Daily Express. 11.9.08, p22.

[4774] Shaw, H. 'If somebody dies, we MUST know why ...'. The Mail on Sunday. 25.10.09, p27.

[4775] BBC1 News. 12.3.13.

[4776] Palmer, R. 'Police chief is accused of helping to cover up the Diana 'murder' plot'. Daily Express. 18.1.08, p15.

[4777] Palmer, R. 'Diana's death fears ignored'. Daily Express. 16.1.08, p8.

[4778] 'Police boss 'linked to spies''. 18.12.07, p9.

[4779] Palmer, R. 'Diana guard accused of lies over her bugging fear'. Daily Express. 5.3.08, p11.

[4780] 'Scandal of the bailed murderers'. Daily Express. 15.9.09, p20.

[4781] Reynolds, M. 'Why was Diana's 'murder plot' note held back?' Daily Express. 18.9.09, p5.

[4782] Allen, K. 'Gagged'. The Independent on Sunday. 26.6.11, p25.

[4783] Dixon, C. Flanagan, P., Reynolds, M. 'Diana Police Face Arrest'. Daily Express. 22.7.11, pp1,4.

[4784] Reynolds, M. 'How plot to stop Diana and Dodi's love affair ended in tragic murder'. Daily Express. 29.3.10, p5.

[4785] Kilroy-Silk R. Sunday Express. 26.10.03, p25.

[4786] Flanagan, P. 'Police tried to make me change my evidence says key witness'. Daily Express. 6.12.06, pp1,5.

[4787] Palmer, R. 'Diana Death 'Cover-Up' by Police Chief'. Daily Express. 28.7.07, p1.

[4788] Koster, O. 'Lord Stevens demands an apology over Diana 'slurs''. Daily Mail. 15.2.08, p33.

[4789] Wright, S. '30 years on, will there be charges over Blair Peach?' Daily Mail. 19.12.09, p31.

[4790] 'MP 'abused boy in office' '. The Sunday Times. 2.12.12, p14.

[4791] Wright, S. 'Police pair arrested over Lawrence case 'cover-up''. Daily Mail. 19.12.09, p11.

[4792] Insight 'Police bugged Muslim MP'. The Sunday Times. 3.2.08, p1.

[4793] Thorpe, V. 'Row as heist film hints at royal scandal'. The Observer. 10.2.08, p21.

[4794] Littlejohn. Daily Mail. 4.3.08, p17.

[4795] Sabey, R. 'Four Brit Al-Qaeda Cops'. News of the World. 9.3.08, p 1,7.

[4796] Newsnight. BBC2. 28.5.08.

[4797] Gillard, M. 'Top Yard officers 'untouchable' over expenses'. The Sunday Times. 9.12.07, p12.

[4798] Roberts, G. 'Will Billy Reveal His Secrets From The Grave?' Daily Mail. 26.11.07, p31.

[4799] Wright, S., Pendlebury, R. 'Disgraced, jailed and now sacked … Dizaei faces ruin'. Daily Mail. 1.4.10, p35.

[4800] Wright, S. 'Paddick whitewash'. Daily Mail. 25.4.02, p19.

[4801] Taylor, B. 'Yard chief praises his Operation Bunglemen'. Daily Mail. 1.7.06, p137.

[4802] Wright, S. 'Telephone-tape police chief stays in his job for now'. Daily Mail. 14.3.06.

[4803] Rayment, T., Leake, J. '7-year snitch: 'Flash' the activist is a secret cop'. The Sunday Times. 19.12.10, p12.

[4804] BBC2. 17.4.09.

[4805] Boyley, M. 'Pressure grows on police chief'. Daily Mail. 19.8.05, p7.

[4806] Ballinger, L. 'MI5 and police will face the 7/7 inquest'. Daily Mail. 22.5.10, p43.

[4807] Shields, R. 'Met whistleblower forced out by officer he exposed'. The Independent On Sunday. 15.8.10, p16.

[4808] McKay, P. Daily Mail. 8.6.09, p17.

[4809] Chapman, J., Twomey, J. 'Police probe G20 brutality claims'. Daily Express. 16.4.09, p11.

[4810] Hartley-Brewer, J. Sunday Express. 25.7.10, p39.

[4811] Clements, J. 'Family of dad Ian hit out as prosecutor dumps G20 case'. Daily Record. 23.7.10, p4.

[4812] Anderson, P. 'Duke of Hazard'. Sunday Mirror. 21.3.10, p11.

[4813] Thomas, L., Gillard, M. 'After 12 years undercover, I was a broken biscuit'. The Independent On Sunday. 16.1.11, p22.

[4814] Malone, A. 'Sleeping with the enemy'. Daily Mail. 15.1.11, p27.

[4815] 'We need George Dixon, they give us James Bond'. The Mail on Sunday. 16.1.11, p29.

[4816] Graham, C. 'I Am In Fear For My Life'. The Mail on Sunday. 16.1.11, pp1,8.

[4817] Graham, C. 'Undercover Officers squandered millions'. The Mail on Sunday. 23.1.11, p44.

[4818] Camber, R. 'Activists are told by DPP to appeal over police sting'. Daily Mail. 19.4.11, p2.

[4819] Lewis, P., Evans, R., Davis R. 'Officer married activist he was sent to spy on'. The Guardian. 20.1.11, pp1,2.

[4820] Evans, R., Lewis, P. 'Police accused of letting covert officers lie in court'. The Guardian. 20.10.11, pp1, 12.

[4821] Wright, S. 'Corrupt police are blamed for £50m collapse of pub axeman murder case'. Daily Mail. 13.3.11, p51.

[4822] Townsend, M. 'Kennedy case brings calls for full inquiry into the role of undercover police'. The Observer. 16.1.11, p3.

[4823] Pukas, A. 'Hypocrisy of the police fatheads'. Sunday Express. 5.1.03, p43.

[4824] Doyle, J. 'Crime fell as riots raged, say the police'. Daily Mail. 6.10.11, p27.

[4825] Wright, S. 'Now Sir Ian is accused over 'muddled' crime figures'. Daily Mail. 5.11.07, p2.

[4826] Barrett, D. 'Battle for the Ripper secrets'. The Sunday Telegraph. 15.5.11, p15.

[4827] 'Mystifying pursuit of secrecy in 'cash for honours' probe'. Leader. The Mail on Sunday. 4.3.07, p31.

[4828] Forsyth, F. 'Men behaving badly just aren't a novelty'. Daily Express. 3.6.11, p13.

[4829] Brady, B., Dugan, E., Dutta, K. 'Police ignored warnings over violent protest'. The Independent on Sunday. 21.8.11, p8.

[4830] Barrett, D., Hennessy, T. 'When thin blue line snapped'. The Sunday Telegraph. 14.8.11, p6.

[4831] Maynard, G. '£111,000 cost of police raid on war protester'. Daily Express. 14.7.07, p35.

[4832] Liddle, R. 'We can't deal with young, black crime by hiding its name'. The Sunday Times. 11.9.11.

[4833] Camber, R. '999 call-handler sacked for ignoring urgent calls'. Daily Mail. 26.10.11, p12.

[4834] Fernandaz, C. 'G20 death case officer to face a public grilling'. Daily Mail. 5.5.11, p8.

[4835] Delgado, M. 'Did this man's change of mind thwart case against G20 officer?'. The Mail on Sunday. 22.8.10, p24.

[4836] Gill, C. et al. 'G20 tragedy: The damning new film?'. Daily Mail. 9.4.09, p11.

[4837] Emsley, C. 'The Great British Bobby'. Quercus. London. 2009, p161.

[4838] Channel 4 News. 29.11.10.

[4839] Daily Mirror. 7.8.13.

[4840] Rampling, R. 'Where is the justice for my murdered son Troy?'. Sunday Express. 23.9.07, p49.

[4841] Greenwood, C. 'Hackers hack into Yard's hacking probe'. Daily Mail. 4.2.12, p10.

[4842] Littlejohn, R. 'No need to send in the heavy mob at dawn'. Daily Mail. 31.1.12, p17.

[4843] Camber, R. 'We let down the victims in NOW scandal, says Yard'. Daily Mail. 8.2.12, p4.

[4844] Walters, S., Carlin, B. 'MP 'Head Butted Me On The Nose' '. The Mail on Sunday. 26.2.12, p6.

[4845] Inside Out. 19.2.12. BBC1.

[4846] Milmo, C. 'Secrecy over rubber bullets' 'potential use' '. 'i on Saturday'. (The Independent). 17.3.12, p4.

[4847] Glover, S. 'Secret courts, the cover-up of a Mafia-style shooting, and a worryingly unaccountable police force'. Daily Mail. 29.3.12, p17.

[4848] Bracchi, P. 'Why Moscow's Brotherhood of Murder has its sights on London'. Daily Mail. 31.3.12, p28.

[4849] Wells, T. 'Cop BNP Shame'. The Sun. 7.4.12, p15.

[4850] Wright, S. 'Theresa May offers to meet Mrs. Lawrence over 'corrupt police' claims'. Daily Mail. 25.4.12, p33.

[4851] 'Lawrence murder: Watchdog in probe'. Daily Express. 12.5.12, p13.

[4852] Jones, G. 'Shamed police row'. Sunday Express. 5.8.12, p26.

[4853] Verkaik, R. 'Yard investigates transvestite smear against spy Gareth'. The Mail on Sunday. 6.5.12, p22.

[4854] Littlejohn, R. 'Call The Midwife'. Daily Mail. 25.9.12, p17.

[4855] Birrell, I. 'Why does no one ever take the blame?'. Daily Mail. 13.2.13, p14.

[4856] C4 News. 10.6.13.

[4857] McGivern, M. 'If our children are in danger we deserve to be told the truth'. Daily Record. 19.3.13, pp1,5.

[4858] O'Neill. 'Top police protected celebrity suspects'. The Times. 20.3.13, pp1,6.

[4859] Levy, A. 'Hallelujah! Police finally admit all crime victims should be visited at home by an officer'. Daily Mail. 11.12.08, p24.

[4860] Evans, R., Lewis, P. 'Their son was killed by racists. So why did the police spy on them?'. The Guardian. 24.6.13.

[4861] Kelly, L. 'Big Brother cop is a flop in my book'. The Sunday Post. 16.6.13, p21.

[4862] Harper, T. 'Met supergrass scandal'. The Independent. 26.6.13, p1.

[4863] Wak, J. 'The words that might have saved Omagh'. The Sunday Telegraph. News Review. 14.9.08, p17.

[4864] Bowcott, O. 'Northern Ireland ombudsman questions powers of MI5'. The Guardian. 20.7.07, p14.

[4865] Glennie, A. 'MI5 and Special Branch 'covered up Cyril Smith's abuse of boys' '. Daily Mail. 12.9.13, p30.

[4866] Palmer, R. Moriarty, R. 'Huge cost to protect Martin's freedom'. Daily Express. 30.7.03, p8.

[4867] Levy, A. 'Cover-up' fury as police deny getting 999 call about break-in'. Daily Mail. 2.9.06, p45.

[4868] Rogers, L. 'Toxic Chemicals A Secret Cold War Experiment. And An Explosion Of Lethal Cancers Baffling Doctors'. Daily Mail. 30.12.06, p18.

[4869] Twomey, J. 'It's not a crime to vandalise a car, say police'. Daily Express. 6.5.08, p7.

[4870] Scott, M. 'Police chief blocks death probe'. Sunday Mail. 24.2.08, p14.

[4871] Smith, S. 'I should have pushed for inquiry into riddle of our Willie's death'. Daily Record. 11.9.06, p19.

[4872] Scott, M. 'Family slam cover-up after police close Kevin's case'. Sunday Mail. 6.4.03, p31.

[4873] Green, N. 'Crime cover-up'. Daily Mail. 12.1.10, p57.

[4874] Green, N. 'Police slammed over lack of crime details'. The Sunday Post. 1.5.11, p4.

[4875] Green, N. 'MPs criticise cops over crime disclosure rates'. The Sunday Post. 22.5.11, p10.

[4876] Alexander, D. 'Did Blundering Cops Kill Moat?'. Sunday Mail. 11.7.10, p2.

[4877] Green, N. 'North cops will reveal cost of Moat manhunt'. The Sunday Post. 6.2.11, p4.

[4878] Green, N. 'Shocking drugs toll in pubs'. The Sunday Post. 23.5.10, pp1,3.

[4879] Green, N. 'Rape cop's force in scandal 'cover-up'. The Sunday Post. 16.1.11, pp1,4.

[4880] Kilroy-Silk, R. 'Blunkett must face up to racist police bullies'. Sunday Express. 26.10.03, p25.

[4881] Dolan, A. 'Judge's fury over speeding police chief let off by PC'. Daily Mail. 10.12.10, p37.

[4882] Dixon, C. 'Beat bobby: Why we are failing on crime'. Daily Express. 3.7.06, p15.

[4883] C4 News. 20.7.11.

[4884] 'Let-off on cop boob'. The Sun. 5.4.12, p12.

[4885] Harrison, I., Blackstock, G. 'Rapists and perverts taken off sex list'. The Sunday Post. 9.6.13, p4.

[4886] Grant, G. 'Police secrecy row over 'true scale' of unsolved murders'. Daily Mail. 14.5.13, p19.

[4887] 'Labour in bid to end cop secrecy'. Sunday Mail. 25.8.13, p8.

[4888] Findlay, R. 'So Who Did Call The Cops To Hunt a Mole?'. Sunday Mail. 14.7.13, p19.

[4889] 'Police need to be more open'. Leader. The Courier. 8.10.13, p24.

[4890] '£1.2m police cash goes to informants'. Daily Record. 8.10.13, p21.

[4891] Rose, G. 'Police data on attacks 'give false picture' '. Scotland on Sunday. 6.10.13, p7.

[4892] Clark, R. '17 suicides in one town but a police chief says the media is to blame'. Daily Express. 21.2.08, p11.

[4893] Drury, I., Slack, J. 'Mother fears a cover-up over blunders in paedophile case'. Daily Mail. 28.7.06, p25.

[4894] Mausey, K. 'Hillsborough Cover-Up Scandal: Woman PC Tells How She Was Forced To Hide The Truth'. Sunday Mirror. 26.4.09, p19.

[4895] 'Secret files on disaster out early'. Daily Express. 20.4.09, p5.

[4896] Bird, S. 'Did the Tories cover up the truth about Hillsborough?'. Daily Mail. 27.8.11, p27.

[4897] Little, A. 'Hillsborough secrets to be released'. Daily Express. 27.7.11, p5.

[4898] Slack, J., Tozer, J., Walker, K. 'Disgraceful lies, slurs and cover-up'. Daily Mail. 13.9.12, pp4,5.

[4899] C4 News. 13.9.2012.

[4900] Thornton, L. 'This Vile Cover-up'. Daily Record. 13.9.12, pp4,5.

[4901] C4 News. 13.9.12.

[4902] Tozer, J., Brooke, C., Slack, J. 'Now Put Police Liars In The Dock'. Daily Mail. 14.9.12, pp1,6,7.

[4903] Diaz, A. 'Hillsborough police video tamper claim'. The Courier & Advertiser. 8.10.13, p13.

[4904] Traynor, L. 'What should we do with Hillsborough family fund?'. Daily Mirror. 20.8.13, p11.

[4905] Jeeves, P. 'New justice is a joke says veteran bobby'. Daily Express. 11.2.11, p19.

[4906] Doyle, J. 'Police 'turned blind eye to sex grooming gangs' '. Daily Mail. 25.9.12, p25.

[4907] Lavery, C. 'Shellsuit Bobby'. Sunday Mail. 10.5.09, p29.

[4908] Findlay, R., Scott, M. 'Call this justice?' Sunday Mail. 24.3.02, p30.

[4909] McIlwraith, G. 'A Disgrace To The Force'. Daily Record. 10.11.10, p6.

[4910] Wheldon, V. 'Gay Cop 'Lied To Protect Lover Accused Of Theft' '. Daily Record. 18.11.10, p25.

[4911] Booth, S. 'Racism, sexism and sectarianism in the world's biggest gang'. Daily Record. 14.11.08, p13.

[4912] Scott, M. 'Bible John Was A Cop'. Sunday Mail. 29.8.13, pp 14,15.

[4913] Boyle, J. 'Half of crash victims don't report to police'. The Sunday Post. 2010.

[4914] Thomas, C. 'Parents Fight For Truth On Tragic Sam'. Sunday Mail. 16.5.10, p18.

[4915] Rose, G. 'Police have no suspects after 'terror plot' blast'. Scotland on Sunday. 16.1.11, p10.

[4916] O'Hare, T. 'Cops told to reveal pervert numbers'. Daily Record. 20.7.11, p12.

[4917] O'Hare, P. 'Cop 'stole £175,000 evidence' '. Daily Record. 31.1.12, p27.

[4918] Aitken, M. 'It took police two years to tell us this sex offender is missing ... yesterday they had to admit there are at least 26 others'. Sunday Mail. 16.3.08, p2.

[4919] 'Cops hunt scar-faced patient'. Sunday Mail. 1.4.12, p6.

[4920] Scott, M. 'Being told cop would not be in the dock for raping me was devastating ... but I can't give up and I won't give up'. Sunday Mail. 1.4.12, p10.

[4921] O'Hare, P. 'Ex Top Cop Got £25K Police Guard For Aunt'. Daily Record. 5.4.12, p5.

[4922] Findlay, R., Cassidy, R. 'Probe call over cop's clan links'. Sunday Mail. 5.8.12, p25.

[4923] Silvester, N. 'Probe Cop Sent Home'. Sunday Mail. 24.2.13, p23.

[4924] Jarvis, D. 'New doubts over deaths at Deepcut'. Sunday Express. 29.8.10, p30.

[4925] Jarvis, D. 'Riddle of axed Deepcut talks'. Sunday Express. 31.5.09, p35.

[4926] Leader. 'Deepcut report rage'. Sunday Express. 4.9.05, p40.

[4927] 'Deepcut probe hit over 'lies' by police'. Sunday Express. 7.9.03, p14.

[4928] Flanagan, P. 'Police chiefs 'snub' Deepcut parents'. Daily Express. 9.9.03, p15.

[4929] Noxson, M. 'Deepcut: Proof soldiers could not have killed themselves'. The Mail on Sunday. 3.8.03, pp14,15.

[4930] Owen, J. 'Deepcut families call for inquiry after review criticises police'. The Independent on Sunday. 13.3.11, p26.

[4931] 'Top copy in sleaze allegation'. Sunday Mirror. 22.6.08, p11.

[4932] Greenwood, C. 'Collective Amnesia'. Daily Mail. 25.4.13, p4.

[4933] Findlay, R. 'Police, Camera, Silence'. Sunday Mail. 22.7.07, p23.

[4934] Stewart, S. 'Cop In The Dock'. Sunday Mail. 16.5.10, p23.

[4935] Reid, D. 'Was Dr. Kelly Murdered?' Daily Mail. 6.3.04, p20.

[4936] Churcher, S. 'David's right hand was so weak he couldn't cut steak. So he could never have used it to kill himself'. The Mail on Sunday. 31.8.08, p13.

[4937] Baker, N. 'Travesty of the Truth'. Daily Mail. 23.10.07, p28.

[4938] Malone, S. 'Why I'm certain my friend Dr Kelly was murdered'. Daily Mail. 10.7.10, p9.

[4939] Goslett, M. 'Kelly investigation was 'inadequate' '. Daily Mail. 13.8.10, p2.

[4940] Goslett, M. 'Kelly death fingerprints riddle grows'. Daily Mail. 27.1.11, p19.

[4941] Goslett, M. 'David Kelly's mobile phone logs ignored by detectives'. Daily Mail. 7.1.11, p30.

[4942] Goslett, M. 'Fingerprint riddle leads to new call for Kelly inquest'. Daily Mail. 2.3.11, p20.

[4943] 'Doubts over Dr. Kelly that won't go away'. Leader. Daily Mail. 14.5.11, p16.

[4944] Goslett, M. 'Riddle of helicopter that landed at scene of Dr. Kelly's death'. Daily Mail. 14.5.11. p11.

[4945] 'Police force 'hacked website of Kelly group' '. The Mail on Sunday. 11.3.12, p40.

[4946] Green, N. 'Police farce'. Daily Mail. 28.10.08, p56.

[4947] Bracchi, P. 'The True Cost of Immigration'. Daily Mail. 2.11.07, p39.

[4948] Wright, S., Martin, A., Parveen, N. 'Girls in care aged 11 are 'bought and sold' for sex'. Daily Mail. 23.3.12, p4.

[4949] Daily Record. 27.1.12, p5.

[4950] Kisiel, R. 'Police lie that delayed hunt for rail death girl'. Daily Mail. 30.3.09, p34.

[4951] Silvester, N. 'Police hero accused of lies to beat motor rap'. Sunday Mail. 30.11.08, p38.

[4952] Cavendish, C. 'The arrested must be named …'. The Sunday Times. 5.5.13, p13.

[4953] Emsley, C. 'The Great British Bobby'. p 81. Quercus. London. 2009.

[4954] Camber, R. 'Police secretly kept organs of murder victims for decades'. Daily Mail. 28.7.11, p31.

[4955] Lollrun, L. 'MOD laptop with details of 600,000 recruits is stolen'. Daily Express. 19.1.08, p2

[4956] Brown, J., Morris, N. 'IPCC slams former top cop Bettison', The Independent. 29.3.13, pp1,4.

[4957] Gallagher, I., Rimmer, A. ''Orwellian' police in bid to silence ex-boyfriend stalked by youngest magistrate'. The Mail on Sunday. 8.6.08.

[4958] Pettifor, T. 'Savile: Cops Will Fix It'. Daily Record. 12.1.13, p6.

[4959] Brook, C. 'Report that clears police on Savile is a bag of lies'. Daily Mail. 11.5.13, p36.

[4960] Twomey, J. 'Bungling police let Savile go in 1964'. Daily Express. 12.3.13, p2.

[4961] Leppard, D. 'Home Secretary slaps gag on MI5's 7/7 'failures'. The Sunday Times. 16.1.11, p6.

[4962] 'Exposure: Forced To Marry'. STV. 9.10.13.

[4963] Gysin, C., Rees, A. 'Why didn't police tell me of my husband's bigamy'. Daily Mail. 26.11.07, p7.

[4964] Martin, A. 'Sergeant gets 6 months for assault on woman'. Daily Mail. 8.9.10, p33.

[4965] Constable, N. 'Police worker 'set to get £10K deal' in sex harassment case'. The Mail On Sunday. 23.10.11, p20.

[4966] Leppard, D. 'Border Force chief 'botched' sex case'. The Sunday Times. 25.3.12, p4.

[4967] 'Race fix' case cop accused of lying'. Daily Record. 14.11.07, p24.

[4968] Bilton, M. 'The Ripper's Secrets'. The Sunday Times News Review. 19.1.03, pp1,2.

[4969] Gallagher, P., Townsend, M. 'Hillsborough lawyer calls for permanent 'truth commission' to prevent cover-ups'. The Observer. 16.9.12, p6.

[4970] Crooks, L. 'That terrible day was unbearable … what came after was unforgiveable'. Sunday Mail. 16.9.12, p5.

[4971] Riches, C. 'Families a step closer to justice for Hillsborough'. Daily Express. 20.12.12, p15.

[4972] Peev, G. '1,444 officers face Hillsborough probe'. Daily Mail. 23.10.12, p35.

[4973] Littlejohn. 'So who did let Savile loose in the wards?' Daily Mail. 21.12.12, p17.

[4974] Wilkie, S. 'Outside force probes Scots drugs squad'. Daily Express. 29.11.12, p8.

[4975] 'Inquiry over pervert MPs'. Daily Record. 15.12.12,p6.

[4976] Greenwood, G. 'Met 'bid to cover up' their love-trap spies'. Daily Mail. 20.11.12, p8.

[4977] McKay, P. 'So why did No 10 throw Mitchell to the lions?'. Daily Mail. 24.12.12, p17.

[4978] 'Yard man faces data leak retrial'. Daily Mail. 21.12.12, p47.

[4979] Merrick, J., Brady, B. 'The cold revenge of Andrew Mitchell'. The Independent. 23.12.12, p21.

[4980] Mitchell, A. 'It's An Unfair Cop'. The Sunday Times. 23.12.12, pp1,2,3.

[4981] Groves, J. 'Police 'in 11th-hour Plebgate cover-up'. Daily Mail. 17.10.13, p6.

[4982] Hastings, M. 'Many officers do a wonderful job: But I fear the police are in danger of losing the public's trust'. Daily Mail. 17.10.13, p14.

[4983] Doward, J. 'Runaway children at greater risk through police and council failings, report warns'. The Observer. 23.12.12, p8.

[4984] Fifield, N., Penrose, J. 'Let-off For 1800 Sex Offenders'. Sunday Mirror. 4.1.12, p25.

[4985] 'Lawrence murder: Watchdog in probe'. Daily Express. 12.5.12, p13.

[4986] Kloster, U. 'Ex-policeman sues the Met over Al Qaeda camp claims'. Mail on Sunday. 13.5.12, p23.

[4987] Camber, R. 'Anguish of families over body parts police kept for decades'. Daily Mail. 22.5.12, p8.

[4988] Levin, A. 'My MI5 husband DID set up Max Mosley'. Mail Online. 3.8.08.

[4989] 'Hillsborough disaster smear MP dies at 83'. Daily Express. 31.12.12, p27.

[4990] Wright, S. 'The non-PC guide to policing'. Daily Mail. 1.1.10, p21.

[4991] Slack, J. 'Cab drivers forced to spy on customers'. Daily Mail. 26.7.12, p9.

[4992] Slack, J. 'Jacqui's civilian snoopers given yet more power'. Daily Mail. 9.7.12, p18.

[4993] Levy, A. 'How police plan to cut crime: They won't count vandalism'. Daily Mail. 6.5.08, p11.

[4994] Laville, S. 'Firemen told: Your emergency help isn't welcome'. The Daily Telegraph. 28.11.02, p4.

[4995] Hind, S., Whyte, S. 'Cops Probed Over Phone Films Fury'. Daily Record. 5.1.13, p2.

[4996] Findlay, R. 'Top Cop Mugged'. Sunday Mail. 11.5.03, p11.

[4997] Johnson, R. 'PCs plod into action at last'. The Mail on Sunday. 6.1.13, p31.

[4998] Hitchens, P. 'Crime statistics – a job for the Fraud Squad'. The Mail on Sunday. 6.1.13, p29.

[4999] Clarke, M. 'Scandal of Secret Crimewave'. Daily Mail. 26.3.02, p28.

[5000] Kay, R. 'Charles seeks revenge over Diana guard's revelations'. Daily Mail. 20.8.12, p12.

[5001] 'Top cop still suspended'. The Sunday Post. 6.1.13, p43.

[5002] ' 'Rude' cop is axed'. Daily Record. 11.7.03, p35.

5003 Stokes, P. 'Zero tolerance police chief forced out in misconduct row'. The Daily Telegraph. 12.2.02, p6.

5004 Foggo, D., Fellstrom, C. 'Revealed: how the Home Office hides the true level of crime'. The Sunday Telegraph. 17.4.05, p10.

5005 Doyle, J. 'Police are accused of exaggerating falls in crime to meet targets'. Daily Mail. 25.1.13, p19.

5006 Gill, C. 'Watchdog 'Too Close To Police' '.Daily Mail. 10.4.09, p26.

5007 Knight, K. 'The Teenage Sex Slaves'. Daily Mail. 27.3.08, p61.

5008 Martin, A. 'Police spies stole the identities of 80 dead babies'. Daily Mail. 4.2.13, p6.

5009 Leake, C. 'Race row policeman's new £90K job 'buried' '. The Mail on Sunday. 16.3.08, p52.

5010 Slack, J. 'Don't talk about crime, police are told. It might frighten the public'. Daily Mail. 8.1.10, p19.

5011 Barratt, D., Mendick, R. 'Did Jimmy Fix His Interrogation?'. The Sunday Telegraph. 13.1.13, p16.

5012 Martin, A. 'Secret arrests' fears as police chiefs seek ban on naming crime suspects'. Daily Mail. 8.4.13, p12.

5013 Daily Express Leader. 30.5.08, p12.

5014 Gilbertson, D. 'The Strange Death of Constable George Dixon. Why the Police Have Stopped Policing'. Amazon Kindle. 2011 (November).

5015 Townsend, M. 'Johnson set for grilling as police scandals mount'. The Observer. 7.7.13, p16.

5016 MacRae, F. 'Genes which mean you're destined to be a Yes man'. Daily Mail. 20.4.11, p31.

5017 Hanning, J., Brady, B. 'Police inquiry into phone-hacking keeps on growing'. The Independent on Sunday. 30.1.11, p17.

5018 Fitzgerald et al. Public Policing Preferences. 2002:41.

5019 Copperfield, D. 'Confessions of a very un-PC PC'. Daily Mail. 14.10.06, p48.

5020 Hitchens, P. The Mail on Sunday. 19.9.10, p31.

5021 Derbyshire, D. 'How to get the measure of a shifty man ... check out the width of his face'. Daily Mail. 6.7.11, p30.

5022 Grant, G. 'Police have lost trust of the public, warns head of new authority'. Daily Mail. 26.2.13, p19.

5023 Randall, D. 'The man who was trying to get home'. The Independent on Sunday. Newsweek. 12.4.09, pp47,48.

5024 Furedi, F. 'Working mums are now seen as suspect'. Daily Express. 29.9.09, p14.

5025 Burke, N. 'Police should patrol our streets not parade on TV'. Daily Express. 6.7.09, p13.

5026 Camber, R. 'Police too scared to speak to Press says ex-Met boss'. Daily Mail. 7.3.12, p18.

5027 26.10.10: BBC News.

5028 McCrum, R. 'From Harry Potter to Facebook radicals: how Britain's schoolkids turned angry'. The Observer. 28.11.10, p33.

5029 Emsley, C. 'The Great British Bobby'. Quercus. London. 2009.

5030 'Labour Red Tape 'Hampers Police' '. Daily Express. 29.4.10, p15.

5031 Little, A. 'The invisible blue line'. Daily Express. 2.4.07, p22.

5032 Hughes, T. Daily Express. 9.8.13, p11.

5033 Whitehead, T. 'Cost of police on long-term sick leave hits £90m a year'. Daily Express. 24.10.08, p9.

5034 Harrison, I. 'Calls for action over assaults on police by youths'. The Sunday Post. 26.7.09, p12.

5035 Gunn, C. 'Shock figures reveal vandalism of emergency services' property'. The Sunday Post. 12.9.10, p8.

5036 Yarranton, L. '56 cops hit in Belfast riot night'. Sunday People. 11.8.13, p4.

5037 Burn, G. 'The Sunday Times. 20.11.11, p29.

5038 Sandbrook, D. 'The Year Shame Died'. Daily Mail. 30.12.11, p15.

5039 Alexander, S. 'One in three police officers assaulted'. Daily Mail. 21.6.13, p9.

5040 ITV1 News. 8.6.11.

5041 Sergeant, H. 'Inside Britain's Police Farce'. Daily Mail. 11.2.08, p26.

5042 Doyle, J. 'Police have lost the public's trust'. Daily Mail. 24.9.10, pp10,11.

5043 Doyle, J. 'Police 'have lost the public's trust' '. Daily Mail. 24.9.10, p10.

5044 Poulter, S. 'In Google we trust (just as much as we do in God)'. Daily Mail. 30.4.13, p21.

5045 'OK, now cop this!'. News Of The World. 18.7.10, p25.

5046 Parcell, S. 'It's sick to admire a murderer'. Sunday Express. 18.7.10.

5047 Smith, D. 'Every party should carry a government health warning'. You Gov poll commissioned by The Sunday Times Magazine. 3.5.09, p25.

5048 Sergeant, H. 'The Public & The Police'. Pp 56,65.

5049 Whitehead, T. 'Rise of Robocop and how we lost faith in justice'. Daily Express. 2.9.08, p4.

5050 Nelson, N. '300,000 angered by police'. The People. 21.12.08, p27.

5051 'Police panned'. Daily Record. 20.1.10, p2.

5052 Peev, G. 'After 13 years of Labour, public mood shifts right'. Daily Mail. 13.12.10, p4.

5053 Platell, A. Daily Mail. 27.6.09, p19.

5054 Whitehead, T. 'Fears as civilians take jobs of police'. Daily Express. 23.5.08, p4.

REFERENCES

[5055] McKinstry, L. 'So will bonfire of the quangos just be a damp squib?'. Daily Express. 15.10.10, p12.

[5056] Gilbertson, D. 'Why are police so rude? Because they are trained to be'. The Mail on Sunday. 27.2.11, p27.

[5057] Walker, C. 'Miscarriages of justice: An inside job?' Annual Lecture of the Centre for Criminology and Criminal Justice. University of Hull. May, 2001.

[5058] Twomey, J. 'Rise of the rude bobby'. Daily Express. 15.11.07, p19.

[5059] Slack, J. 'It's the rude blue line'. Daily Mail. 24.2.11, p13.

[5060] Reynolds, M. 'Police, help: My hamster has got out of its cage'. Daily Express. 4.7.09, p27.

[5061] Emsley, C. 'The Great British Bobby'. Quercus. London. 2009, p212.

[5062] Jarvis, D., Spurr, H. 'Score Points If You Injure Police'. Sunday Express. 14.11.10, p1.

[5063] O'Brien, J. 'Pig Ignorant'. Daily Record. 19.8.09, p25.

[5064] Fagge, N. 'McCanns make fresh plea after court ordeal'. Daily Express. 11.2.10, p15.

[5065] Bentley, P. 'British police 'developed evidence' against McCanns'. Daily Mail. 14.12.10, p12.

[5066] BBC2 Newsnight. 10.5.13.

[5067] McBeth, J. 'Mystery after secret file on ex-police chief goes missing'. Daily Mail. 11.5.13, p24.

[5068] Hardman, R. 'Long Distance Deception?'. Daily Mail. 2.4.07, p31.

[5069] Davidson, L. 'Cop Too Lazy To Fight Crime Is Spared Jail'. Daily Record. 27.4.07, p35.

[5070] Stopes, H. 'Police 'paid' to seek football banning orders'. The Independent On Sunday. 18.8.13, p10.

[5071] Pilditch, D. 'No one will shoot you'. Daily Express. 23.9.10, p17.

[5072] Paul, D. 'Moat Cop 'ignored' '. Sunday Mirror. 25.9.11, p8.

[5073] McKinstry, L. 'Failed hunt ban has left class warriors chasing their tails'. Daily Express. 27.12.06, p12.

[5074] Love, D. Daily Record. 17.8.13, p11.

[5075] Reynolds, T. 'Respect the police? Only when they do their job!'. Daily Mail. 30.4.13, p57.

[5076] Mackie, A. 'Pensioned-off police officers back on books'. Daily Mail. 11.5.13, p52.

[5077] Whitehead, T. 'Police using civilians on murder inquiries'. Daily Express. 16.10.06, p6.

[5078] Hitchens, P. The Mail on Sunday. 12.5.13, p27.

[5079] Sheldrick, G. 'Don't nick swearing yobs' PCs told'. Daily Express. 27.6.11, p2.

[5080] Giannangeli, M. 'Police snub for Poppy Day'. Sunday Express. 18.8.13, p28.

[5081] Hitchens, P. 'What Has Really Gone Wrong With Our Police'. The Mail on Sunday. 16.3.03, pp49-52.

[5082] Murray, J. 'A dangerous desire'. Sunday Express. 11.8.13, p27.

[5083] Slack, J. 'Rise of the 'walk on by' society as decent people fear the police'. Daily Mail. 19.6.08, p8.

[5084] Mason, G. 'Police 'super forces' will fail to fight the crimes that blight everyday life'. Daily Express. 21.12.05, p12.

[5085] Leader. 'Chilling threat to the public's right to know'. Daily Mail. 6.1.12, p14.

[5086] Curne, G. 'Doh!pe'. Sunday Mail. 22.1.12, p27.

[5087] 'Grill applicants for police'. Daily Record. Sunday Express. 29.1.12, p36.

[5088] Flyn, C. 'G4S staff to help solve murders'. The Sunday Times. 14.4.13, p2.

[5089] Slack, J. 'Our 'arrest-shy' police'. Daily Mail. 17.6.08, p19.

[5090] Jeeves, P. 'Superbike PCs nicked in speeding crackdown'. Daily Express. 15.9.12, p44.

[5091] Mair, G. 'Sneaky speed cops hide in shrubbery'. Daily Record. 16.4.09, p7.

[5092] Boffey, D., McClenaghan, M. 'Police take longer for 999 calls as spending cuts bite'. The Observer, 14.7.13, p4.

[5093] 'Cop road searches soaring'. Sunday Mail. 29.9.13, p6.

[5094] Christian. G. 'Top lawyer blasts police 'persecution' of motorists'. Sunday Express. 6.10.13, p22.

[5095] Mills, R. 'Police tracking down just one in four housebreakers'. Daily Express. 9.9.13, p11.

[5096] Greenwood, C. 'Only One In 15 Online Child Porn Suspects Is Arrested'. Scottish Daily Mail. 10.6.13, p1.

[5097] Silvester, N. 'Investigation Reveals How Cops Keep Crimes Secret'. Sunday Mail. 18.8.13, p12.

[5098] Silvester, N. 'Investigation Reveals How Cops Keep Crimes Secret'. Sunday Mail. 18.8.13, p13.

[5099] Groves, J. et al. 'May demands an apology over 'lies' of senior police in Plebgate scandal'. Daily Mail. 16.10.13, p12.

[5100] Daily Mail. 18.2.08, p8.

[5101] Carlin, B. 'Met chief in the dock over 'trick crime figures'. The Mail on Sunday. 2.3.08, p4.

[5102] Grant, G. 'Police fiddled figures, admits new force chief'. Daily Mail. 27.2.13, p27.

[5103] Kirby, I. 'Cops told: Don't use the C-word'. News of the World. 17.1.10, p36.

[5104] Edwards, T. 'Christina police shambles'. Daily Express. 16.3.13, p10.

[5105] 'Casual cops not trusted'. The People. 28.3.10, p10.

[5106] 'We don't like cops in caps'. Sunday Mirror. 28.3.10, p31.

[5107] 'Tasers will cause fear, warns Met'. Daily Mail. 25.11.08, p30.

[5108] Paddick. B. 'How can the public feel safe if the police look so scared?'. The Mail on Sunday. 11.7.10, p25.

[5109] Wright, S. 'Civil war at the Yard'. Daily Mail. 29.8.08, p9.

[5110] 'Police chief is forced to say sorry'. Daily Mail. 14.6.07 , p19.

[5111] McGivern, M. 'Police Beasts Plot To Beat The System'. Daily Record. 25.4.09, p15.

[5112] Hicks, B. 'Rapist's victims are still living in fear'. The Sunday Post. 24.8.08, p8.

[5113] Blackburn, V. 'Bent cop deserves only sheer contempt'. Daily Express. 17.6.10, p16.

[5114] Butler, A. 'The Filth'. Sunday Mirror. 19.9.10, p15.

[5115] McCabe, G. 'QC Findlay: Was Lennon Bomb Plot A Cop Set-up?'. Daily Record. 1.3.12, p23.

[5116] 'Murdoch knew cops were paid'. Daily Record. 4.7.13, p27.

[5117] Channel 5. The Wright Stuff. 9.7.13.

[5118] 'Cop's 'Dodge' '. The People. 22.7.12, p26.

[5119] Lay, K. '263 cops beat rap on spying'. The People. 29.4.12, p19.

[5120] Pollard, C. '7 journos in corrupt cop quiz 8 yrs ago'. The Sun. 10.5.12, p9.

[5121] Moore, S. 'My £1 run-in with the Met's Oyster card squad... and what it tells us about the way we police our 'free' country'. The Mail on Sunday. 12.4.09, p29.

[5122] Perry, G. NHS Outreach, London. BBC2 Newsweek. 27.5.10.

[5123] 'Police, terrorism and Britain's lost liberties'. Daily Mail. 16.4.10, p14.

[5124] Waterhouse, K. 'Why we are losing that mutual trust'. Daily Mail. 16.4.09, p18.

[5125] Benfield, R. 'Louts on the loose'. The Sunday Times. 26.9.10, p25.

[5126] 'G20: Top officer's concern'. Daily Express. 22.4.09, p19.

[5127] 'Public lose patience with police'. Daily Mail. 3.9.10, p32.

[5128] Moore, S. '1,433 deaths, no convictions'. The Mail on Sunday. 22.7.12, p31.

[5129] Doughty, S. 'Police have let us down, say three in four Britons'. Daily Mail. 24.6.09, p12.

[5130] Clark, R. 'He's free but what an outrage that he was prosecuted'. Daily Express. 22.1.10, p12.

[5131] Whitehead, T. 'Speedcams have to be axed warns police chief'. Daily Express. 12.9.08, p2.

[5132] Graef, R. Daily Mail. 17.1.11, p11.

[5133] Millbank, J. 'Victims get power to sue police if they fail to tackle yobs'. The Mail on Sunday. 30.1.11, p2.

[5134] West, R. 'Ill-mannered response will forfeit the public's respect'. Daily Express. 20.5.11, p35

[5135] Harrison, A. 'Yates of the Yard says sorry'. Sunday Express. 10.7.11, p8.

[5136] Kynaston, D. Austerity Britain. Bloomsbury. 2007, p364.

[5137] Hickley, M. 'Let's have a few more BOTB'. Daily Mail. 23.5.09 p37.

[5138] Burrell, I. 'Philandering policemen, secret courts and this insidious threat to our faith in justice'. Daily Mail. 20.11.12, p14.

[5139] Findlay, R. 'Cops say hoods' seized cars looked like a car showroom . But they had just borrowed them from a car showroom'. Sunday Mail. 4.11.12, p19.

[5140] Findlay, R. 'Car Stunt Cops Did Not Make a Penny'. Sunday Mail. 30.12.12, p37.

[5141] 'Why a trip to the dentist is more fun than the gym'. The Mail on Sunday. 19.8.12, p42.

[5142] Ferrari, N. 'Shock tactics will kill our love for the police'. Sunday Express. 21.10.12, p25.

[5143] Coyle, M. 'Facebook trolls target police page'. Daily Record. 26.9.12, p27.

[5144] 'Don't tell cops how our Kevin died ... we don't trust them now'. Daily Record. 26.9.12, p27.

[5145] McLeod, K. '333 Scots cops have criminal records'. Daily Record. 5.7.12, p26.

[5146] Thornton, P. 'Fury At Convicted Cops Still On Beat'. The Sun. 25.8.13, p16.

[5147] Lord Mackenzie. Daily Mail. 16.8.01, p10.

[5148] Blackley, M. 'Police face daily fight against mindless vandalism ... and that's just on their cars'. Daily Mail. 3.1.13, p19.

[5149] 'Shots fired in flags protest'. The Mail on Sunday. 6.1.13, p7.

[5150] McDonalds, C., McLean, M. 'Facecrooks'. Daily Record. 10.1.13, p7.

[5151] 'Labour's Crime Bill is a fraud'. The Sunday Telegraph. 22.11.09, p25.

[5152] 'Public don't trust police'. Daily Record. 18.1.13, p12.

[5153] Twomey, J. '2,000 officers investigated over multiple complaints'. Daily Express. 3.9.10, p15.

[5154] Williams, D. Daily Mail. 14.9.04, p6.

[5155] Murray, J. 'Britain was behind IRA lawyer's murder'. Sunday Express. 4.4.10, p35.

[5156] Robertson, C.. 'Omagh families' threat to force Blair into court'. The Sunday Post. 21.9.08, p10.

[5157] Stalker, J. 'Stalker'. Harrap. London. 1988.

[5158] Bowcott, O. 'Shoot to kill inquiry to be reopened'. The Guardian. 20.7.07. p1.

[5159] Chapman, J. 'RUC 'let informers go on murder spree' '. Daily Mail. 23.1.07, p17.

[5160] Erwin, A. 'Murder probe hears of 'deliberate' action'. Daily Record. 31.5.07, p12.

[5161] HC Debs. Vol. 126, col.21, 25 Jan, 1988.

[5162] Murray, J. 'Police told me names of killers'. Sunday Express. 29.8.10, p13.

[5163] Pickard, M. 'Four policemen killed in smash'. Daily Express. 24.11.08, p25.

[5164] Phillips, M. 'Yes, the terror threat is real. But we must stop and question this cynical stunt'. Daily Mail. 28.5.07, p12.

[5165] Emsley, C. The Great British Bobby. Quercus. London. 2009, p258.

[5166] Foreman, A. 'Sinn Fein should never be able to escape Jean McConville's ghost'. The Observer. 5.12.10, p42.

[5167] O'Hagan, S. 'Dreaming blue murder'. The Observer Review. 8.7.01, p6.

[5168] 'Miscarriages of Justice – A review of Justice in Error'. edited by Clive Walker and Keir Starmer, p6.

[5169] McKittrick, D. 'Police treated massive bomb as abandoned vehicle'. The Independent on Sunday. 10.4.11, p28.

[5170] 'Miscarriages of Justice – A review of Justice in Error'. edited by Clive Walker and Keir Starmer, p48.

[5171] Chapman, J. 'RUC 'did not collude' in Ulster lawyer's murder'. Daily Express. 24.5.11.

[5172] Sharrock, D. 'Wanted: 90 detectives to help flagging force'. The Times. 29.9.07, p30.

[5173] McGivern, M. 'Bride And Prejudice'. Daily Record. 23.7.11, p21.

[5174] Kinnell, H. G. The Great Diet Pill Conspiracy. Athena Press. London. 2010. Ch. 10, pp206-7 - see Appendix I of this publication.

[5175] Fielding J., McKay, J. 'Bully father gave me £120K as a gift'. Sunday Express. 10.1.10, p23.

[5176] O'Hare, P. '£420,000 scam cop stole from brother and aunt'. Daily Record. 4.2.12, p4.

[5177] McIlwraith, G. 'Supergrass Set Free After Top Cop's Plea'. Daily Record. 28.8.10, p15.

[5178] Delgado, M. 'Terror chief car hire firm is not licensed'. The Mail on Sunday. 28.12.08, p23.

[5179] Daily Express. 21.11.09, p43.

[5180] Jeeves, P. 'Supergrass taken to brothel by police and told: Take your pick'. Daily Express. 22.7.11, p27.

[5181] Phillips, M. 'The police have lost their way but the answer isn't to let them be run by meddlers like Prescott'. Daily Mail. 30.1.12, p14.

[5182] Whitehead, T. 'Let PCs duck jobs they find unethical'. Daily Express. 18.4.08, p8.

[5183] 'Cops on £10K pay'. The Sun. 11.11.12, p16.

[5184] Doyle, J. 'Only half of police would report a colleague'. Daily Mail. 15.1.13, p19.

[5185] 'Fears over bid to hide identities of suspects'. Daily Mail. 15.4.13, p5.

[5186] 'Miscarriages of Justice – A review of Justice in Error'. Edited by Clive Walker and Keir Starmer.

[5187] Forsyth, F. 'Saddam's death was fine by me'. Daily Express. 12.1.07, p11.

[5188] Atkins, A. 'Questions of life and death'. Sunday Express. 29.9.11, p39.

[5189] BBC1 News. 1.11.11.

[5190] Curran, J. 'Lying Police Officers Are Facing The Sack'. Daily Record. 8.5.08, p25.

[5191] Grant, G. 'Man's rights breached over police complaint'. Daily Mail. 4.9.13, p6.

[5192] 'Police child-seat snub'. Daily Express. 16.2.07, p43.

[5193] Mansfield M. 'Presumed Guilty'. Heinemann. London. 1993, p184.

[5194] Malet, D. 'The new regime for the correction of miscarriages of justice' (1995) 159 Justice of the Peace, 716, at p736.

[5195] Henderson, M. 'Judge's concerns over the smallest of clues'. The Times. 22.12.07, p4.

[5196] Bilton, M. 'Pulling the wool over their eyes'. The Sunday Times. 26.1.03, p10.

[5197] Jarvis, D., Jeory, T. 'The Death Of Justice'. Sunday Express. 29.11.09, pp1,2.

[5198] Rose, D. 'Secret Justice'. The Mail on Sunday. 8.1.12, p27.

[5199] Hayes, S. 'The Biggest Gang In Britain'. 2013, p197.

[5200] Mansey, K. 'I'm so glad lying cop has been jailed ... my two-year hell is over'. Sunday Mirror. 5.9.10, p22.

[5201] Platell, A. 'Dignity of a wronged father'. Daily Mail. 21.7.12, p21.

[5202] Townsend, M. 'St Paul's camp accuses police of inflating crime figures'. The Observer. 18.12.11, p16.

[5203] Hayes, S. 'The Biggest Gang In Britain'. 2013, p46.

[5204] Brown, D. The Police Complaints Procedure: A Survey of Complainants' Views. (HORS93, HMSO. London. 1987).

[5205] Maguire, M., Corbett, C. 'A Study Of The Police Complaints System'. (HMSO. London. 1991).

[5206] 'Miscarriages of Justice – A review of Justice in Error'. Edited by Clive Walker and Keir Starmer, p194.

[5207] 'Miscarriages of Justice – A review of Justice in Error'. Edited by Clive Walker and Keir Starmer, p53.

[5208] 'Miscarriages of Justice – A review of Justice in Error'. Edited by Clive Walker and Keir Starmer, p192.

[5209] Police Service 'Submission'. para 2.3.2, p133; Rozenberg, J. 'The Search for Justice'. (Hodder & Stoughton. London. 1994), p341; Pollard, C. 'A case for disclosure'. Criminal Law Review 42.

[5210] Graef, R. 'Desperate police 'framed' Crippen for wife's murder'. The Sunday Times. 29.6.08, p13.

[5211] Thompson, P. 'CSI proves Crippen innocent'. Sunday Express. 16.1.11, p30.

[5212] Palmer, R. 'Innocent Crippen should be given a pardon by Queen.' Daily Express. 1.1.09, p31.

[5213] McDermott, N., Kisiel, R., Harris, P. 'Lawrence: The 'clues' they didn't find for 14 years'. Daily Mail. 25.11.11, p30.

[5214] 'Cop faces drink drive plot charge'. Daily Record. 29.5.09, p38.

[5215] Gillard, M. 'Met chief's secret squad 'used illegal informant''. The Independent On Sunday. 15.6.08, p28.

[5216] Penrose, J. 'Cops hid gang trial evidence'. Sunday Mirror. 4.11.07, p33.

[5217] 'Miscarriages of Justice – A review of Justice in Error'. Edited by Clive Walker and Keir Starmer, pp 65,66,70.

[5218] Gill, C. '13 police are accused of framing vice murder trio.' Daily Mail. 4.3.09, p26.

[5219] Twomey, J. '£10m police corruption case collapses'. Daily Express. 2.12.11, p5.

[5220] BBC News Bulletins. January. 2012.

[5221] Twomey, J. '8 police 'framed three for call girl murder' '. Daily Express. 7.7.11, p15.

[5222] Maguire, M., Norris, C. 'Police investigations: practice and malpractice'. 1994, 21, Journal of Law & Society, 72, pp10 and 62.

[5223] 'Miscarriages of Justice – A review of Justice in Error'. Edited by Clive Walker and Keir Starmer, p82.

[5224] 'Miscarriages of Justice – A review of Justice in Error'. Edited by Clive Walker and Keir Starmer.

[5225] Panton, L. 'Prove you didn't kill TV Jill'. News Of The World. 18.4.10, p15.

[5226] Coyle, M. 'Crook Cop Moved To Cushy Jail'. Sunday Mail. 9.6.13, p44.

[5227] Constable, N. 'Decorator thrown into jail – because he has same name as a Balkan war criminal'. The Mail On Sunday. 18.4.10, p34.

[5228] Camber, R. 'Police knew that woman in cry-rape case was 'unreliable' '. Daily Mail. 18.6.10, p41.

[5229] Greenhill, S. 'Wrongly charged!'. Daily Mail. 28.5.07, p5.

[5230] Greenhill, S. 'Named, woman whose false rape claim sent a dad to jail for 3 years'. 20.10.06, p7.

[5231] Kay, R. " 'Chilli Hot Stuff' to sue police". Daily Mail. 22.6.10, p39.

[5232] Edge, S. 'Could New Evidence Free Jeremy Bamber?'. Daily Express. 6.8.10, p25.

[5233] Douglas, H. 'Do these pictures prove Bamber is innocent?'. Sunday Express. 29.8.10, p35.

[5234] Riches, C. ' 'No silencer' evidence may clear Bamber of murders'. Daily Express. 6.2.12, p15.

[5235] Allison, E., Townsend, M. 'Gun experts cast doubt on Bamber verdict'. The Observer. 5.2.12, p10.

[5236] Wright, S. 'It Aint' Half Hot, Sarge'. Daily Mail. 17.10, 09, pp10,11.

[5237] Williams, D., Owen, J. 'Reminder to police: it is not good practice to doctor evidence'. The Independent On Sunday. 19.10.08, p49.

[5238] Craig, O. 'They butchered Keith Blakelock'. The Sunday Telegraph. 3.10, 04, p10.

[5239] Levy, G. 'Canonised by the Left he could enter the record books as the only man cleared of three different murders. So as Winston Silcott is exposed as a shoplifter why have his apologists gone so quiet …'. Daily Mail. 7.4.07, p56.

[5240] 'Policing Casablanca-style'. Leader, The Daily Telegraph. 7.11.02, p29.

[5241] Weathers, H. Daily Mail. 22.2.07, pp66,67.

[5242] Bennetto, J. 'DNA on cigarette may clear man jailed for 17 years for gay killing'. The Independent. 27.1.07, p17.

[5243] Wright, S. 'Colin Stagg is awarded £250,000'. Daily Mail. 10.1.07, p13.

[5244] Johnson, J. I'd never had a girlfriend until I was jailed for Rachel's murder'. Daily Mail. 30.11.07, p15.

[5245] Laurie, G. The Sunday Post. 28.11.10, p35.

[5246] Sweeney, J. Daily Mail. 27.12.08, p38.

[5247] Moncur, J. 'Cop Gaffe Ends Sex Ad Ex Trial'. Daily Record. 27.1.11, p27.

[5248] Wilkes, D. 'Evidence in George Davis case 'covered up' '. Daily Mail. 24.2.11, p26.

[5249] Lee, A. 'We feel sorry for the way a fantasist and the police let our precious daughter's killer go free'. Daily Express. 19.9.09, p41.

[5250] Flanagan, P. 'Landlord 'is still a suspect'. say police'. Daily Express. 21.1.11, p37.

[5251] Murray, J. 'Jo landlord: I felt like I'd been raped'. Sunday Express. 9.10.11, p7.

[5252] Lambie, D. 'Lockerbie's last secret'. Sunday Express. 1.7.07, p33.

[5253] Smith, A. D. 'Vital Lockerbie evidence 'was tampered with' '. The Observer. 2.9.07, p37.

[5254] Mega, M. 'Police chief – Lockerbie evidence was faked'. Scotland on Sunday. 28.8.05, p1.

[5255] Lambie, D. 'The Lockerbie 'cover-up' '. Sunday Express. 9.4.06, p32.

[5256] ITV News. 27.2.12.

[5257] Rayment, T., Henry, R. 'Revealed: The Hidden Family Of Undercover Cop'. The Sunday Times. 16.1.11, p18.

[5258] Silvester, N. 'Cop Fingered'. Sunday Mail. 13.2.11, p19.

[5259] Watt, N. 'Palace told Blair aide: beware of honours probe chief'. The Observer. 29.4.07, pp1,2.

[5260] 'Miscarriages of Justice – A review of Justice in Error'. Edited by Clive Walker and Keir Starmer, p238.

[5261] 'Miscarriages of Justice – A review of Justice in Error'. Edited by Clive Walker and Keir Starmer, pp374, 375.

[5262] Emsley, C. The Great British Bobby. p260, Quercus. London. 2009.

[5263] 'Miscarriages of Justice – A review of Justice in Error'. Edited by Clive Walker and Keir Starmer, p46.

[5264] 'Miscarriages of Justice – A review of Justice in Error'. Edited by Clive Walker and Keir Starmer, pp 47, 50.

[5265] ITV. 7.9.11.

5266 'Miscarriages of Justice – A review of Justice in Error'. Edited by Clive Walker and Keir Starmer, p49.

5267 Findlay, R., Scott, M. 'Cops Probe Cops'. Sunday Mail. 24.3.02, p30.

5268 Leake, C. ' 'Bakewell Tart' accused pays £85,000 jail costs'. The Mail on Sunday. 22.10.06, p13.

5269 BBC 1 News. 3.7.03

5270 Daily Mail. 27.7.06, p6.

5271 Macaskill, G. 'Free Our Hero Dad'. Sunday Mail. 17.2.08, pp4,5.

5272 McCartney, B. 'Police have persecuted me and betrayed McCabe family'. Daily Record. 15.12.07, p8.

5273 Findlay, R. 'Bungled murder case cop is warden'. Sunday Mail. 18.11.07, p35.

5274 Hosein, G. 'Database Britain'. The Mail on Sunday. 4.3.07, p31.

5275 Jones, D. 'A Travesty Of Justice'. Daily Mail. 26.4.07, p42.

5276 Smyth, B. 'Ex-cop sparks new McKie investigation'. The Sunday Post. 18.2.07, p2.

5277 Barnes, E. 'Salmond fights for full inquiry into McKie fingerprint scandal'. Scotland on Sunday. 30.9.07, p11.

5278 King, D. 'Fingerprint Service 'On Probation' '. Daily Record. 16.2.07, p4.

5279 Bussey, K. 'Forensic Blunder apology'. Daily Record. 15.12.11, p28.

5280 'Cop cleared of attack is back at job'. Sunday Mirror. 14.4.13, p29.

5281 Sweeney, J. Daily Mail. 6.12.07, pp74,75.

5282 The Mail on Sunday. 21.08.11, p32.

5283 Levin, A. The Mail on Sunday. 19.6.11, p45.

5284 Leader. 'Victim let down'. Daily Record. 20.5.06, p6.

5285 McIlwraith, G. 'Cleared'. Daily Record. 7.12.05, p6.

5286 Paul, D. ' 'Miss Marple' to free brother framed for a double murder'. Sunday Express. 14.10.07, p38.

5287 Wright, S. 'Corrupt police are blamed for £50m collapse of pub axeman murder case'. Daily Mail. 12.3.11, p51.

5288 Leppard, D. 'Mobile justice at the Olympic Games'. The Sunday Times. 27.3.11, p13.

5289 Currie, G. 'Cop accused of affair with trial victim'. Sunday Mail. 15.5.11, p7.

5290 Mega, M. 'Revealed. 3 Lethal Errors'. Sunday Mail. 29.5.11, p16.

5291 Lewis, P. 'The Courage NOT To Go To War'. Daily Mail. 20.5.11, p56.

5292 'Miscarriages of Justice – A review of Justice in Error'. Edited by Clive Walker and Keir Starmer, p51.

5293 'Cops in bloody blunder'. Daily Record. 8.6.11, p25.

5294 Loveys, K. 'Teacher wins £1,000 over 'pupil assault'. Daily Mail. 31.3.11, p33.

5295 Pukas, A. 'Ray Winstone'. Daily Express. 23.11.06, p28.

5296 Home, B. 'Cleared Of Sex Killing After 21 Years In Jail'. Daily Record. 31.8.07, p19.

5297 Twomey, J. '£10m farce as Fallon race-fix trial collapses'. Daily Express. 8.12.07, p25.

5298 Harper, T. 'Thugs go free as CPS drops 25,000 cases'. The Mail on Sunday. 6.1.08, p40.

5299 Hull. L. ' 'I was thrown in a cell and accused of assault … just for standing up to foul-mouthed girls'. Daily Mail. 25.3.08, p29.

5300 Baker, M. 'My Kidnap Nightmare'. The People. 25.5.08, p8.

5301 Leach, B. 'The care worker who can't get a job because of a crime he didn't commit'. The Sunday Telegraph. 29.6.08, p6.

5302 McLeod, K. 'Sick Shooter'. Daily Record. 25.3.08, p19.

5303 Brooks, T. 'Agony of parents held for murder of their son after playground fall'. Daily Express. 21.6.08, p17.

5304 Classic FM News. 15.9.11.

5305 McDonald, C. '3 Months In Jail For Carrying A Rose'. Daily Record. 28.8.10, pp1,5.

5306 Elliot, C. 'How could police accuse me of murder after I found my boy dead?'. Daily Mail. 9.7.11, p29.

5307 McIlwraith, G. 'Bang Out Of Order'. Daily Record. 29.6.11, p9.

5308 Dunbar, P., Creasy, R. 'How could I, a 5ft woman, have possibly raped a strapping 6ft businessman?'. The Mail on Sunday. 9.9.07, p48.

5309 'Court blunder must never happen again'. Daily Record. 17.5.08, p8.

5310 'Fingerprints 'not foolproof' '. Daily Express. 23.3.07, p33.

5311 Marcetau, F. 'Cleared Of Abusing PC'. Reading Post. 25.4.07, pp1, 10.

5312 'Distressing injustice of police trawls'. Daily Express. 22.3.03, p15.

5313 'Fraud Lord's battle over 'unlawful arrest'. Daily Mail. 25.10.11, p17.

5314 Wilkes, D., Gysin, C. 'Police set out to crucify us, say couple cleared over salt killing'. Daily Mail. 3.3.07, pp6,7.

5315 Bright, M., Hill, A. 'Birmingham Six man wins £1m payout'. The Observer. 9.6.02, p9.

5316 Gysin, C., Clerkin, B. 'After six years in jail for double rape, man is cleared'. Daily Mail. 17.10.07, p30.

5317 'Police must be held to account'. Daily Record Leader. 13.5.06, p8.

5318 Fairweather, E. 'I can't stay silent any more'. The Mail on Sunday. 10.12.06, p63.

5319 McIlwraith, G. 'Stitched Up'. Daily Record. 18.3.06, p9.

5320 McGivern, M. 'Bent Cop Tracked Down By TV Sleuths'. Daily Record. 24.3.08, p9.

5321 'Arthur Conan Doyle For The Defence'. BBC4.

5322 Pook, S. 'Victim of corrupt police freed after 25 years in jail'. The Daily Telegraph. 14.11.02, p16.

5323 Goodwin, J. 'I Still Think He's Innocent'. Daily Mail. 6.10.01, pp20-21.

5324 Day, E. 'Meet the Loopholes'. The Mail on Sunday. 20.5.07, p50.

5325 Mason, G. The Official History Of The Metropolitan Police. Carlton. 2004, p76.

5326 Clark, R. 'Lord Chief Justice is spot on about on-the-spot fines!'. Daily Express. 9.7.11, p12.

5327 Newsnight. 6.12.11.

5328 Rose, G., Peterkin, T. 'Call to re-open case of murdered waiter'. Scotland on Sunday. 8.1.12, p4.

5329 Hamilton, F., Devlin, H. 'Suspects to face police lie detector for first time'. The Times. 31.12.11, pp1, 8.

5330 Kynaston, D. 'Austerity Britain'. Bloomsbury. 2007, p359.

5331 Howard, A. 'An invitation to corruption?' The Sunday Times Magazine.

5332 'End this cruel punishment of the victims'. Leader. Sunday Mirror. 22.1.12.

5333 Hayward, S. 'Riot-hit Shops Refused Compo ... Because There Were Too Few Looters'. Sunday Mirror. 22.1.12, p18.

5334 Boswell, S. 'Suddenly 10 police charged through the door looking for a maniac. They met me in my pyjamas'. The Mail on Sunday. 22.1.12, pp22-24.

5335 Pollard, S. 'Time for the law to stop treating heroes as villains'. Daily Express. 7.1.12, p18.

5336 Jeory, T. 'The social workers lied about our girl's sex abuse'. Sunday Express. 4.3.12, p7.

5337 http://www.innocent.org.uk/cases/kevincallan/index.html.

5338 Drake, M. 'Police lover of shot gangster back at work'. Sunday Express. 6.1.08, p15.

5339 Campbell, D., Townsend, M. 'Police warned about danger of false confessions'. The Observer. 9.10.11, p14.

5340 'Cops and Crown on trial now'. Leader. Sunday Mail. 6.5.12, p16.

5341 Greenwood, C. 'Freed, the innocent man jailed for murder'. Daily Mail. 17.5.12, p24.

5342 Rose, D. Special Report. The Mail on Sunday. 20.5.12, pp14,15,16.

5343 Reynolds, M. 'I want my life back says man wrongly jailed for seven years'. Daily Express. 18.5.12, p30.

5344 Sullivan, M. 'Locked Up For Rape After DNA Blunder'. The Sun. 17.5.12, p19.

5345 Clarke, N., Drury, I. 'Fury Of A Hero Betrayed'. Daily Mail. 28.4.12, p9.

5346 '£850K for 'fit-up' PC'. The Sun. 17.4.12, p7.

5347 Platell, A. Daily Mail. 21.7.12, p21.

5348 Ellicott, C., Reid, S. 'Agony of the couple wrongly accused TWICE of shaking four-month-old son to death'. Daily Mail. 20.4.12, p5.

5349 Ashton, J. 'I can prove the 'Lockerbie bomber was INNOCENT' '. Daily Mail. 22.5.12, p15.

5350 Channel 4 News. 3.8.12.

5351 Martin, A. 'My nightmare, by white man charged in hunt for black rapist'. Daily Mail. 9.2.08, p29.

5352 Sims, P., Camber, R. 'Police fear 90 cases may be tainted after crime scene officer is arrested'. Daily Mail. 29.8.12, p10.

5353 Twomey, J. 'Rape case sabotage DC jailed'. Daily Express. 30.10.12, p19.

5354 Hickey. 'Evidence of why police job came Steve's way'. Daily Express. 24.12.12, p13.

5355 Townsend, M. 'Hillsborough survivors: police bullied us to change evidence'. The Observer. 4.11.12, p20.

5356 Courtenay-Smith, N. 'Presumed Guilty'. Daily Mail. 27.8.08, p34.

5357 Dunbar, P. 'Betrayed by the PC police'. The Mail on Sunday. 8.7.12, p35.

5358 'Police bungling becomes a habit'. Leader. Daily Mail. 21.8.03, p12.

5359 BBC1 News. 4.9.13.

5360 Bracchi, P. 'Corrupt Or Just A Scapegoat'. Daily Mail. 9.2.13, p41.

5361 Brooke, C. 'The discus champion who threw it all away'. Daily Mail. 8.3.12, p37.

5362 Brown, A. 'My Life With the Sex Traffickers'. Daily Record. 6.10.11.

5363 Duffy, M., Penrose, J. 'From Vice Cop To Vice Girl'. Sunday Mirror. 12.8.07, p25

5364 Paul, D. 'Judge blasts failed sex trade probe'. Sunday Express. 1.4.07, p47.

5365 Townsend, M. 'Kidnap, beating, rape: my story of sex slavery in the UK'. The Observer. 6.2.11, p25.

5366 Harrison, I. 'Charities demand action against child sex trade'. The Sunday Post. 14.2.10, p9.

5367 'Ex-police officer held over Thai 'sex slaves' '. Daily Mail. 22.5.08, p24.

5368 Goodchild, S., Burling, K. 'Sex traffic'. The Independent On Sunday. 25.2.07, pp8,9.

5369 Moreton, C. 'The tragedy of the cases still unsolved'. The Independent On Sunday. 24.2.08, p32.

5370 Wright, S. 'I'm not bothered about stopping people trafficking – just burglary'. Daily Mail. 12.2.11, p55.

5371 Smith, J., Dugan, E. 'Police report into brothels dismissed as 'amateurish' '. The Independent On Sunday. 15.8.10, p3.

5372 'Cops' sin blue line'. News Of The World. 22.7.07 p31.

5373 'Dad asked undercover PC to have sex with his son, 14'. Daily Express. 16.5.09, p40.

[5374] Gall, C. 'Lib Dem in vice arrest'. Daily Record. 23.2.11, pp1,7.

[5375] 'Cops Are Rapped'. Daily Record. 26.4.10, p11.

[5376] Warren, J. 'Gielgud's Secret Shame'. Daily Express. 19.5.11, p36.

[5377] Brady, B. 'At last, the stigma of 50 years is removed'. The Independent On Sunday. 30.1.11, p26.

[5378] Bugler, T. 'Cops Grab Sex Pills In Country Cottage Raid'. Sunday Mail. 20.5.07, p18.

[5379] Lironi, B. 'Police in secret pact on rent boys'. Sunday Mail. 12.8.01, p42.

[5380] Brooke, C. 'Mother accused of kerb crawling on way to drama class'. Daily Mail. 7.1.11, p24.

[5381] Barrett, D. 'Vice squad gets a PC makeover'. The Sunday Telegraph. 24.10.10, p7.

[5382] Pook, S. 'Gallery defiant on naked child photos'. The Daily Telegraph. 12.3.01, p6.

[5383] 'Vice squad boss jailed'. Daily Record. 17.5.11, p12.

[5384] 'Vice cash cop jailed'. The People. 20.3.11, p26.

[5385] Ramesh, R. 'The sex trade: still in a very British muddle'. The Observer. 2.1.11, p31.

[5386] Findlay, R. 'Margo Slams Police Chief's Sauna Blitz'. Sunday Mail. 9.6.13, p12.

[5387] Doward, J. 'Sex workers 'put at risk' by Olympics crackdown'. The Observer. 10.4.11, p19.

[5388] 'Boy of 15 is sex club bait'. The People. 22.4.07, p29.

[5389] Howe, M. 'Cop's Undie Cover Sting'. Daily Record. 5.10.07, p24.

[5390] Brooke, C. 'Child-porn police 'seize picture from Elton art collection' '. Daily Mail. 26.9.07, p35.

[5391] Beaumont, P., Hodgson, N. 'Gay pornography verdict puts obscenity law's future in doubt'. The Observer. 8.1.12, p15.

[5392] Jo Brand on Kissing. ITV. February, 2012.

[5393] Riches, C. 'I was looking for a burger says kerb crawling policeman'. Daily Express. 13.9.07, p17.

[5394] Sky TV. McGill's saucy postcards.

[5395] Daily Express. 6.2.12, p10.

[5396] Norman, B. 'When Silence is Golden'. Daily Mail. 23.2.12, p22.

[5397] 'Cop's raid shame'. Daily Record. 26.5.12, p12.

[5398] Smith, D. J. 'Police 'abandoned' child sex victims'. The Sunday Times. 14.4.13, p4.

[5399] Hayes, S. 'The Biggest Gang In Britain'. 2013, p109.

[5400] Hayes, S. 'The Biggest Gang In Britain'. 2013, pp77, 82, 85.

[5401] Leppard, D. 'Royal college of policing to rebuild forces' image'. The Sunday Times. 23.10.11, p19.

[5402] Kinnell, H.G. Killer Carers. 2007. London. Athena Press.

[5403] Kinnell, H. G. Caveat Aeger – Never Trust Your Doctor. Bonacia. 2012.

[5404] Cox, B., Shirley, J., Short M.. The Fall Of Scotland Yard. Penguin Books. 1977.